CISSP®

Certified Information Systems Security Professional

Study Guide

Sixth Edition

CISSP®
Certified Information Systems Security Professional
Study Guide
Sixth Edition

James M. Stewart

Mike Chapple

Darril Gibson

WILEY

John Wiley & Sons, Inc.

Senior Acquisitions Editor: Jeff Kellum
Development Editor: Stef Jones
Technical Editors: David Seidl and Debbie Dahlin
Production Editor: Dassi Zeidel
Copy Editors: Judy Flynn and Liz Welch
Editorial Manager: Pete Gaughan
Production Manager: Tim Tate
Vice President and Executive Group Publisher: Richard Swadley
Vice President and Publisher: Neil Edde
Media Project Manager 1: Laura Moss-Hollister
Media Associate Producer: Josh Frank
Media Quality Assurance: Marilyn Hummel
Book Designer: Judy Fung
Proofreader: Josh Chase, Word One New York
Indexer: Ted Laux
Project Coordinator, Cover: Katherine Crocker
Cover Designer: Ryan Sneed

Copyright © 2012 by John Wiley & Sons, Inc., Indianapolis, Indiana

Published simultaneously in Canada

ISBN: 978-1-118-31417-3
ISBN: 978-1-118-46389-5 (ebk.)
ISBN: 978-1-118-33210-8 (ebk.)
ISBN: 978-1-118-33539-0 (ebk.)

For general information on our other products and services or to obtain technical support, please contact our Customer Care Department within the U.S. at (877) 762-2974, outside the U.S. at (317) 572-3993 or fax (317) 572-4002.

Wiley publishes in a variety of print and electronic formats and by print-on-demand. Some material included with standard print versions of this book may not be included in e-books or in print-on-demand. If this book refers to media such as a CD or DVD that is not included in the version you purchased, you may download this material at http://booksupport.wiley.com. For more information about Wiley products, visit www.wiley.com.

Library of Congress Control Number: 2012940018

10 9 8 7 6 5 4 3

Dear Reader,

Thank you for choosing *CISSP: Certified Information Systems Security Professional Study Guide, Sixth Edition*. This book is part of a family of premium-quality Sybex books, all of which are written by outstanding authors who combine practical experience with a gift for teaching.

Sybex was founded in 1976. More than 30 years later, we're still committed to producing consistently exceptional books. With each of our titles, we're working hard to set a new standard for the industry. From the paper we print on, to the authors we work with, our goal is to bring you the best books available.

I hope you see all that reflected in these pages. I'd be very interested to hear your comments and get your feedback on how we're doing. Feel free to let me know what you think about this or any other Sybex book by sending me an email at nedde@wiley.com. If you think you've found a technical error in this book, please visit http://sybex.custhelp.com. Customer feedback is critical to our efforts at Sybex.

Best regards,

Neil Edde
Vice President and Publisher
Sybex, an Imprint of Wiley

Acknowledgments

I'd like to express my thanks to Sybex for continuing to support this project. Thanks to Mike Chapple for continuing to contribute to this project. Thanks to Darril Gibson for stepping up and taking over several chapters. Ed, we missed your input and perspective. Thanks also to all my CISSP course students who have provided their insight and input to improve my training courseware and ultimately this tome. Extra thanks to the sixth edition developmental editor, Stef Jones, and technical editor, David Seidl, who performed amazing feats in guiding us to improve this book.

To my wonderful wife, Cathy: Our life together is getting more complicated and more wonderful every day. To my son, Xzavier Slayde, and daughter, Remington Annaliese: May you grow to be more than we could imagine; you've already outshined all our expectations. To my parents, Dave and Sue: Thanks for your love and consistent support. To Mark: No matter how much time has passed or how little we see each other, I have been and always will be your friend. And finally, as always, to Elvis—the world could use a little "Hunka Hunka Burnin' Love!"

—James Michael Stewart

Special thanks go to the information security team at the University of Notre Dame who provided hours of interesting conversation and debate on security issues that inspired and informed much of the material in this book.

I would like to thank the team at Wiley who provided invaluable assistance throughout the book development process. I also owe a debt of gratitude to my literary agent, Carole Jelen of Waterside Productions. My coauthors, James Michael Stewart and Darril Gibson, were great collaborators. It would be remiss not to also thank Ed Tittel, our coauthor on the first five editions of this book, who was unable to participate in this revision. David Seidl, who joined the team as our technical editor, provided valuable insight as we brought this edition to press.

I'd also like to thank the many people who participated in the production of this book but whom I never had the chance to meet: the graphics team, the production staff, and all of those involved in bringing this book to press.

—Mike Chapple

Thanks to Ed Tittel for thinking of me when his schedule was too full to take on the update of this book. No one can fill Ed's shoes, but I am grateful for the opportunity to contribute to this book in his place. Thanks to James Michael Stewart and Mike Chapple for the work they've done with this book in the past, and especially in this edition. I'm also grateful to Jeff Kellum at Wiley for inviting me into the project and to Carole Jelen, my agent at Waterside Productions, for getting all the pieces to fit together. Last, thanks to all the editing, graphics, and production work done by the team at Wiley.

—Darril Gibson

About the Authors

James Michael Stewart, CISSP, has been writing and training for more than 18 years, with a current focus on security. He has been teaching CISSP training courses since 2002, not to mention other courses on Windows security and ethical hacking/penetration testing. He is the author of several books and courseware sets on security certification, Microsoft topics, and network administration. More information about Michael can be found at his website: www.impactonline.com.

Mike Chapple, CISSP, PhD, is an IT professional with the University of Notre Dame. In the past, he was chief information officer of Brand Institute and an information security researcher with the National Security Agency and the U.S. Air Force. His primary areas of expertise include network intrusion detection and access controls. Mike is a frequent contributor to TechTarget's SearchSecurity site and the author of several information security titles, including *The GSEC Prep Guide* from Wiley and *Information Security Illuminated* from Jones and Bartlett Publishers.

Darril Gibson, CISSP, is the CEO of Security Consulting and Training, LLC, and has authored or coauthored 25 books and served as the technical editor on many others. He has been a Microsoft Certified Trainer (MCT) since 1999 and holds a multitude of certifications. He regularly teaches classes on security and Microsoft topics as a traveling trainer and as an adjunct professor at ECPI University. Darril regularly blogs at blogs. GetCertifiedGetAhead.com.

CISSP: Certified Information Systems Security Professional Study Guide, 6th Edition

CISSP Common Body of Knowledge

KEY AREA OF KNOWLEDGE	CHAPTER

1. ACCESS CONTROL

A. Control access by applying the following concepts/methodology/techniques   **1, 2**
   A.1 Policies
   A.2 Types of controls (preventative, detective, corrective, etc.)
   A.3 Techniques (e.g., non-discretionary, discretionary and mandatory)
   A.4 Identification and Authentication
   A.5 Decentralized/distributed access control techniques
   A.6 Authorization mechanisms
   A.7 Logging and monitoring

B. Understand access control attacks   **2**
   B.1 Threat modeling
   B.2 Asset valuation
   B.3 Vulnerability analysis
   B.4 Access aggregation

C. Assess effectiveness of access controls   **2**
   C.1 User entitlement
   C.2 Access review & audit

D. Identity and access provisioning lifecycle (e.g., provisioning, review, revocation)   **1**

2. TELECOMMUNICATIONS AND NETWORK SECURITY

A. Understand secure network architecture and design (e.g., IP & non-IP protocols, segmentation)
   A.1 OSI and TCP/IP models
   A.2 IP networking
   A.3 Implications of multi-layer protocols

B. Securing network components   **3**
   B.1 Hardware (e.g., modems, switches, routers, wireless access points)
   B.2 Transmission media (e.g., wired, wireless, fiber)
   B.3 Network access control devices (e.g., firewalls, proxies)
   B.4 End-point security

Sybex®
An Imprint of
WILEY

KEY AREA OF KNOWLEDGE	CHAPTER

C. Establish secure communication channels (e.g., VPN, TLS/SSL, VLAN)   4
   C.1 Voice (e.g., POTS, PBX, VoIP)
   C.2 Multimedia collaboration (e.g., remote meeting technology, instant messaging)
   C.3 Remote access (e.g., screen scraper, virtual application/desktop, telecommuting); Data communications

D. Understand network attacks (e.g., DDoS, spoofing)   4

3. INFORMATION SECURITY GOVERNANCE & RISK MANAGEMENT

A. Understand and align security function to goals, mission, and objectives of the organization   5

B. Understand and apply security governance   5
   B.1 Organizational processes (e.g., acquisitions, divestitures, governance committees)
   B.2 Security roles and responsibilities
   B.3 Legislative and regulatory compliance
   B.4 Privacy requirements compliance
   B.5 Control frameworks
   B.6 Due care
   B.7 Due diligence

C. Understand and apply concepts of confidentiality, availability, and integrity   5

D. Develop and implement security policy   5
   D.1 Security policies
   D.2 Standards/baselines
   D.3 Procedures
   D.4 Guidelines
   D.5 Documentation

E. Manage the information life cycle (e.g., classification, categorization, and ownership)   5

F. Manage third-party governance (e.g., on-site assessment, document exchange and review, process/policy review)   6

G. Understand and apply risk management concepts   6
   G.1 Identify threats and vulnerabilities
   G.2 Risk assessment/analysis (qualitative, quantitative, hybrid)
   G.3 Risk assignment/acceptance
   G.4 Countermeasure selection
   G.5 Tangible and intangible asset valuation

Sybex®
An Imprint of

WILEY

KEY AREA OF KNOWLEDGE	CHAPTER

H. Manage personnel security — 6
   H.1 Employment candidate screening (e.g., reference checks, education verification)
   H.2 Employment agreements and policies
   H.3 Employee termination processes
   H.4 Vendor, consultant and contractor controls

I. Develop and manage security education, training, and awareness — 6

J. Manage the Security Function — 6
   J.1 Budget
   J.2 Metrics
   J.3 Resources
   J.4 Develop and implement information security strategies
   J.5 Assess the completeness and effectiveness of the security program

4. SOFTWARE DEVELOPMENT SECURITY

A. Understand and apply security in the software development life cycle — 7
   A.1 Development Life Cycle
   A.2 Maturity models
   A.3 Operation and maintenance
   A.4 Change management

B. Understand the environment and security controls — 7, 8
   B.1 Security of the software environment
   B.2 Security issues of programming languages
   B.3 Security issues in source code (e.g., buffer overflow, escalation of privilege, backdoor)
   B.4 Configuration management

C. Assess the effectiveness of software security — 7

5. CRYPTOGRAPHY

A. Understand the application and use of cryptography — 9
   A.1 Data at rest (e.g., Hard Drive)
   A.2 Data in transit (e.g., On the wire)

B. Understand the cryptographic life cycle (e.g., cryptographic limitations, algorithm/protocol governance) — 9

Sybex®
An Imprint of
WILEY

KEY AREA OF KNOWLEDGE	CHAPTER

C. Understand encryption concepts   9, 10
- C.1 Foundational concepts
- C.2 Symmetric cryptography
- C.3 Asymmetric cryptography
- C.4 Hybrid cryptography
- C.5 Message digests
- C.6 Hashing

D. Understand key management process   9, 10
- D.1 Creation/distribution
- D.2 Storage/destruction
- D.3 Recovery
- D.4 Key escrow

E. Understand digital signatures   10

F. Understand non-repudiation   9, 10

G. Understand methods of cryptanalytic attacks   10
- G.1 Chosen plain-text
- G.2 Social engineering for key discovery
- G.3 Brute Force (e.g., rainbow tables, specialized/scalable architecture)
- G.4 Cipher-text only
- G.5 Known plaintext
- G.6 Frequency analysis
- G.7 Chosen cipher-text
- G.8 Implementation attacks

H. Use cryptography to maintain network security   10

I. Use cryptography to maintain application security   10

J. Understand Public Key Infrastructure (PKI)   10

K. Understand certificate related issues   10

L. Understand information hiding alternatives (e.g., steganography, watermarking)   10

6. SECURITY ARCHITECTURE & DESIGN

A. Understand the fundamental concepts of security models (e.g., Confidentiality; Integrity; and Multi-level Models   11

Sybex®
An Imprint of
WILEY

KEY AREA OF KNOWLEDGE	CHAPTER

B. Understand the components of information systems security evaluation models   11
    B.1 Product evaluation models (e.g., common criteria)
    B.2 Industry and international security implementation guidelines
      (e.g., PCI-DSS, ISO)

C. Understand security capabilities of information systems (e.g., memory   11
  protection; virtualization, trusted platform module)

D. Understand the vulnerabilities of security architectures   12
    D.1 System (e.g., covert channels; states attacks; emanations)
    D.2 Technology and process integration (e.g., single point of failure, service
      oriented architecture)

E. Understand software and system vulnerabilities and threats   7, 8, 12
    E.1 Web-based (e.g., XML, SAML, OWASP)
    E.2 Client-based (e.g., applets)
    E.3 Server-based (e.g., data flow control)
    E.4 Database security (e.g., inference, aggregation, data mining, warehousing)
    E.5 Distributed systems (e.g., cloud computing, grid computing, peer to peer)

F. Understand countermeasure principles (e.g., defense in depth)   12

7. SECURITY OPERATIONS

A. Understand security operations concepts   13
    A.1 Need-to-know/least privilege
    A.2 Separation of duties and responsibilities
    A.3 Monitor special privileges (e.g., operators, administrators)
    A.4. Job rotation
    A.5 Marking, handling, storing, and destroying of sensitive information
      and media
    A.6 Record retention

B. Employ resource protection   13
    B.1 Media management
    B.2 Asset management (e.g., equipment life cycle, software licensing)

C. Manage incident response   14
    C.1 Detection
    C.2 Response
    C.3 Reporting
    C.4 Recovery
    C.5 Remediation and review (e.g., root cause analysis)

Sybex®
An Imprint of
WILEY

KEY AREA OF KNOWLEDGE	CHAPTER
D. Implement preventative measures against attacks (e.g., malicious code, zero-day exploit, denial of service)	8, 14
E. Implement and support patch and vulnerability management	8, 13
F. Understand change and configuration management (e.g., versioning, baselining)	13
G. Understand system resilience and fault tolerance requirements	14

8. BUSINESS CONTINUITY & DISASTER RECOVERY

A. Understand business continuity requirements	15
A.1 Develop and document project scope and plan	
B. Conduct business impact analysis	15
B.1 Identify and prioritize critical business functions	
B.2 Determine maximum tolerable downtime and other criteria	
B.3 Assess exposure to outages (e.g., local, regional, global); Define recovery objectives	
C. Develop a recovery strategy	16
C.1 Implement a backup storage strategy (e.g., offsite storage, electronic vaulting, tape rotation)	
C.2 Recovery site strategies	
D. Understand disaster recovery process	16
D.1 Response	
D.2 Personnel	
D.3 Communications	
D.4 Assessment	
D.5 Restoration	
D.6 Provide training	
E. Exercise, assess and maintain the plan (e.g., version control, distribution)	15, 16

9. LEGAL, REGULATIONS, INVESTIGATIONS, AND COMPLIANCE

A. Understand legal issues that pertain to information security internationally	17, 18
A.1 Computer crime	
A.2 Licensing and intellectual property (e.g., copyright, trademark)	
A.3 Import/Export	
A.4 Trans-border data flow	
A.5 Privacy	
B. Understand professional ethics	18
B.1 (ISC)[2] Code of Professional Ethics	
B.2 Support organization's code of ethics	

Sybex®
An Imprint of
WILEY

KEY AREA OF KNOWLEDGE	CHAPTER
C. Understand and support investigations	18
C.1 Policy, roles and responsibilities (e.g., rules of engagement, authorization, scope)	
C.2 Incident handling and response	
C.3 Evidence collection and handling (e.g., chain of custody, interviewing)	
C.4 Reporting and documenting	
D. Understand forensic procedures	18
D.1 Media analysis	
D.2 Network analysis	
D.3 Software analysis	
D.4 Hardware/embedded device analysis	
E. Understand compliance requirements and procedures	17
E.1 Regulatory environment	
E.2 Audits	
E.3 Reporting	
F. Ensure security in contractual agreements and procurement processes (e.g., cloud computing, outsourcing, vendor governance)	17

10. PHYSICAL (ENVIRONMENTAL) SECURITY

A. Understand site and facility design considerations	19
B. Support the implementation and operation of perimeter security (e.g., physical access control and monitoring, audit trails/access logs)	19
C. Support the implementation and operation of internal security (e.g., escort requirements/visitor control, keys and locks)	19
D. Support the implementation and operation of operations or facility security (e.g., technology convergence)	19
D.1 Communications and server rooms	
D.2 Restricted and work area security	
D.3 Data center security	
D.4 Utilities and Heating, Ventilation and Air Conditioning (HVAC) considerations	
D.5 Water issues (e.g., leakage, flooding)	
D.6 Fire prevention, detection and suppression	
E. Support the protection and securing of equipment	19
F. Understand personnel privacy and safety (e.g., duress, travel, monitoring)	19

The (ISC)[2] BOK is subject to change at any time without prior notice and at (ISC)[2]'s sole discretion. Please visit (ISC)[2]'s website (www.isc2.org) for the most up-to-date information.

Contents at a Glance

Introduction   *xxxv*

Assessment Test   *xliv*

Chapter 1   Access Control   1

Chapter 2   Access Control Attacks and Monitoring   47

Chapter 3   Secure Network Architecture and Securing
                Network Components   87

Chapter 4   Secure Communications and Network Attacks   151

Chapter 5   Security Governance Concepts, Principles, and Policies   205

Chapter 6   Risk and Personnel Management   239

Chapter 7   Software Development Security   275

Chapter 8   Malicious Code and Application Attacks   327

Chapter 9   Cryptography and Symmetric Key Algorithms   361

Chapter 10 PKI and Cryptographic Applications   403

Chapter 11 Principles of Security Models, Design, and Capabilities   437

Chapter 12 Security Architecture Vulnerabilities,
                Threats, and Countermeasures   477

Chapter 13 Security Operations   531

Chapter 14 Incident Management   571

Chapter 15 Business Continuity Planning   617

Chapter 16 Disaster Recovery Planning   643

Chapter 17 Laws, Regulations, and Compliance   681

Chapter 18 Incidents and Ethics   713

Chapter 19 Physical Security Requirements   745

Appendices

Appendix A   Answers to Review Questions   781

Appendix B   Answers to Written Labs   815

Appendix C   About the Additional Study Tools   829

Index   *833*

Contents

Introduction   *xxxv*

Assessment Test   *xliv*

Chapter   1   Access Control   **1**

Access Control Overview   2
    Users, Owners, and Custodians   3
    The CIA Triad   3
    Policies   4
    Compare Permissions, Rights, and Privileges   4
    Types of Access Control   5
    Defense in Depth   7
    Access Control Elements   8
Identification and Authentication Techniques   11
    Passwords   12
    Smart Cards and Tokens   14
    Biometrics   17
    Multifactor Authentication   20
Access Control Techniques   21
    Security Operations Principles   21
    Discretionary Access Controls   22
    Nondiscretionary Access Controls   22
    Mandatory Access Controls   24
    Role-Based Access Control   25
    Centralized versus Decentralized Access Control   26
    Single Sign-On   27
    AAA Protocols   31
Authorization Mechanisms   33
Identity and Access Provisioning Life Cycle   35
    Provisioning   35
    Account Review   36
    Account Revocation   37
Summary   38
Exam Essentials   39
Written Lab   41
Review Questions   42

Chapter   2   Access Control Attacks and Monitoring   **47**

Understanding Access Control Attacks   48
    Introduction to Risk Elements   49

Asset Valuation	49
Threat Modeling	50
Vulnerability Analysis	53
Common Access Control Attacks	53
Preventing Access Control Attacks	62
Logging and Monitoring	64
Assessing Effectiveness of Access Controls	73
Handling Audit Reports	77
Summary	79
Exam Essentials	80
Written Lab	82
Review Questions	83

Chapter 3   Secure Network Architecture and Securing Network Components   87

OSI Model	88
History of the OSI Model	89
OSI Functionality	89
Encapsulation/Deencapsulation	90
OSI Layers	92
TCP/IP Model	99
TCP/IP Protocol Suite Overview	100
Secure Network Components	113
Network Access Control	114
Firewalls	115
Endpoint Security	119
Other Network Devices	119
Cabling, Wireless, Topology, and Communications Technology	123
Network Cabling	123
Wireless Communications and Security	128
Network Topologies	137
LAN Technologies	140
Summary	144
Exam Essentials	145
Written Lab	146
Review Questions	147

Chapter 4   Secure Communications and Network Attacks   151

Network and Protocol Security Mechanisms	152
Secure Communications Protocols	153
Authentication Protocols	154

Virtual Private Network	155
Tunneling	155
How VPNs Work	157
Common VPN Protocols	157
Virtual LAN	159
Remote Access Security Management	160
Plan Remote Access Security	163
Dial-Up Protocols	164
Centralized Remote Authentication Services	165
Network Address Translation	165
Private IP Addresses	167
Stateful NAT	168
Static and Dynamic NAT	168
Automatic Private IP Addressing	169
Switching Technologies	170
Circuit Switching	170
Packet Switching	171
Virtual Circuits	172
WAN Technologies	172
WAN Connection Technologies	174
Dial-Up Encapsulation Protocols	178
Virtualization	178
Miscellaneous Security Control Characteristics	179
Transparency	179
Verify Integrity	180
Transmission Mechanisms	181
Manage Email Security	181
Email Security Goals	181
Understand Email Security Issues	183
Email Security Solutions	183
Secure Voice Communications	186
Social Engineering	186
Fraud and Abuse	187
Phreaking	189
Security Boundaries	190
Network Attacks and Countermeasures	190
DoS and DDoS	191
Eavesdropping	192
Impersonation/Masquerading	193
Replay Attacks	193
Modification Attacks	193
Address Resolution Protocol Spoofing	194
DNS Poisoning, Spoofing, and Hijacking	194
Hyperlink Spoofing	195

	Summary	196
	Exam Essentials	197
	Written Lab	200
	Review Questions	201
Chapter 5	**Security Governance Concepts, Principles, and Policies**	**205**
	Security Management Planning	206
	Security Governance	208
	Security Roles and Responsibilities	209
	Protection Mechanisms	210
	Layering	210
	Abstraction	211
	Data Hiding	211
	Encryption	211
	Privacy Requirements Compliance	212
	Control Frameworks: Planning to Plan	213
	Security Management Concepts and Principles	214
	Confidentiality	214
	Integrity	215
	Availability	217
	Other Security Concepts	218
	Develop and Implement Security Policy	221
	Security Policies	221
	Security Standards, Baselines, and Guidelines	222
	Security Procedures	223
	Change Control/Management	224
	Data Classification	225
	Summary	229
	Exam Essentials	230
	Written Lab	233
	Review Questions	234
Chapter 6	**Risk and Personnel Management**	**239**
	Manage Third-Party Governance	240
	Risk Management	241
	Risk Terminology	242
	Risk Assessment Methodologies	245
	Quantitative Risk Analysis	248
	Qualitative Risk Analysis	253
	Handle Risk	255

Manage Personnel Security   257
   Screening and Background Checks   259
   Employment Agreements   259
   Vendor, Consultant, and Contractor Controls   261
   Employee Termination   261
Develop and Manage Security Education, Training,
  and Awareness   263
Manage the Security Function   264
Summary   265
Exam Essentials   266
Written Lab   269
Review Questions   270

Chapter   7   Software Development Security   275

Application Issues   276
   Local/Nondistributed Computing   276
   Distributed Computing   278
Databases and Data Warehousing   282
   Database Management System Architecture   282
   Database Transactions   286
   Security for Multilevel Databases   287
   ODBC   289
   Aggregation   290
   Data Mining   291
Data/Information Storage   293
   Types of Storage   293
   Storage Threats   294
Knowledge-Based Systems   294
   Expert Systems   295
   Neural Networks   296
   Decision Support Systems   297
   Security Applications   297
Systems Development Controls   297
   Software Development   297
   Systems Development Life Cycle   303
   Life Cycle Models   306
   Gantt Charts and PERT   312
   Change and Configuration Management   313
   Software Testing   314
   Security Control Architecture   316
   Service-Level Agreements   318
Summary   319
Exam Essentials   319

Written Lab	321
Review Questions	322

Chapter 8   Malicious Code and Application Attacks   327

Malicious Code	328
Sources of Malicious Code	328
Viruses	329
Logic Bombs	335
Trojan Horses	335
Worms	336
Spyware and Adware	339
Active Content	339
Countermeasures	339
Password Attacks	341
Password Guessing	341
Dictionary Attacks	342
Social Engineering	343
Countermeasures	344
Application Attacks	344
Buffer Overflows	344
Time-of-Check-to-Time-of-Use	345
Back Doors	346
Escalation of Privilege and Rootkits	346
Web Application Security	346
Cross-Site Scripting (XSS)	347
SQL Injection	348
Reconnaissance Attacks	350
IP Probes	351
Port Scans	351
Vulnerability Scans	351
Dumpster Diving	352
Masquerading Attacks	352
IP Spoofing	352
Session Hijacking	353
Summary	353
Exam Essentials	354
Written Lab	355
Review Questions	356

Chapter 9   Cryptography and Symmetric Key Algorithms   361

Historical Milestones in Cryptography	362
Caesar Cipher	362
American Civil War	363
Ultra vs. Enigma	364

Cryptographic Basics   364
    Goals of Cryptography   364
    Cryptography Concepts   366
    Cryptographic Mathematics   368
    Ciphers   374
Modern Cryptography   380
    Cryptographic Keys   381
    Symmetric Key Algorithms   382
    Asymmetric Key Algorithms   383
    Hashing Algorithms   386
Symmetric Cryptography   386
    Data Encryption Standard   387
    Triple DES   389
    International Data Encryption Algorithm   390
    Blowfish   390
    Skipjack   390
    Advanced Encryption Standard   391
    Symmetric Key Management   393
Cryptographic Life Cycle   395
Summary   396
Exam Essentials   396
Written Lab   398
Review Questions   399

Chapter   10   **PKI and Cryptographic Applications**   **403**

Asymmetric Cryptography   405
    Public and Private Keys   405
    RSA   406
    El Gamal   408
    Elliptic Curve   408
Hash Functions   409
    SHA   410
    MD2   411
    MD4   411
    MD5   412
Digital Signatures   413
    HMAC   414
    Digital Signature Standard   415
Public Key Infrastructure   415
    Certificates   415
    Certificate Authorities   416
    Certificate Generation and Destruction   417

Asymmetric Key Management	419
Applied Cryptography	420
Portable Devices	420
Electronic Mail	421
Web Applications	422
Networking	425
Cryptographic Attacks	428
Summary	430
Exam Essentials	431
Written Lab	432
Review Questions	433

Chapter 11   Principles of Security Models, Design, and Capabilities   437

Understand the Fundamental Concepts of Security Models	438
Trusted Computing Base	440
State Machine Model	441
Information Flow Model	441
Noninterference Model	442
Take-Grant Model	443
Access Control Matrix	443
Bell-LaPadula Model	444
Biba Model	446
Clark-Wilson Model	448
Brewer and Nash Model (aka Chinese Wall)	449
Goguen-Meseguer Model	449
Sutherland Model	450
Graham-Denning Model	450
Objects and Subjects	450
Closed and Open Systems	451
Techniques for Ensuring Confidentiality, Integrity, and Availability	452
Controls	453
Trust and Assurance	454
Understand the Components of Information Systems Security Evaluation Models	454
Rainbow Series	455
ITSEC Classes and Required Assurance and Functionality	460
Common Criteria	461
Industry and International Security Implementation Guidelines	465
Certification and Accreditation	466

Understand Security Capabilities
    Of Information Systems   469
Summary   470
Exam Essentials   470
Written Lab   472
Review Questions   473

**Chapter   12   Security Architecture Vulnerabilities,
                 Threats, and Countermeasures   477**

Computer Architecture   478
    Hardware   479
    Input/Output Structures   499
    Firmware   500
Avoiding Single Points of Failure   501
    Redundant Servers   501
    Failover Solutions   502
    RAID   502
Distributed Architecture   504
    Cloud Computing   508
Security Protection Mechanisms   510
    Technical Mechanisms   511
    Security Policy and Computer Architecture   513
    Policy Mechanisms   514
Common Flaws and Security Issues   515
    Covert Channels   515
    Attacks Based on Design or Coding
       Flaws and Security Issues   516
    Programming   520
    Timing, State Changes, and Communication
       Disconnects   520
    Technology and Process Integration   521
    Electromagnetic Radiation   521
Summary   522
Exam Essentials   522
Written Lab   525
Review Questions   526

Chapter   13   Security Operations   531

Security Operations Concepts   532
    Need to Know and Least Privilege   532
    Separation of Duties and Responsibilities   534
    Job Rotation   538

Mandatory Vacations   538
Monitor Special Privileges   538
Managing Sensitive Information   539
Resource Protection   546
Media Management   546
Asset Management   549
Patch and Vulnerability Management   551
Patch Management   551
Vulnerability Management   552
Common Vulnerabilities and Exposures   555
Change and Configuration Management   555
Configuration Management   556
Change Management   559
Security Audits and Reviews   561
Summary   562
Exam Essentials   563
Written Lab   565
Review Questions   566

Chapter 14   Incident Management   571

Managing Incident Response   572
Defining an Incident   572
Incident Response Steps   573
Implement Preventive Measures Against Attacks   578
Basic Preventive Measures   579
Malicious Code   580
Zero-Day-Exploit   582
Denial-of-Service Attacks   583
Miscellaneous Attacks   588
Intrusion Detection and Prevention   590
Penetration Testing   598
Warning Banners   602
Understand System Resilience and Fault
   Tolerance   603
Protecting Hard Drives   603
Protecting Servers   605
Protecting Power Sources   606
Trusted Recovery   606
Summary   608
Exam Essentials   609
Written Lab   611
Review Questions   612

Chapter   15   Business Continuity Planning   617

Planning for Business Continuity   618
Project Scope and Planning   619
    Business Organization Analysis   620
    BCP Team Selection   620
    Resource Requirements   622
    Legal and Regulatory Requirements   624
Business Impact Assessment   625
    Identify Priorities   626
    Risk Identification   626
    Likelihood Assessment   627
    Impact Assessment   628
    Resource Prioritization   629
Continuity Planning   630
    Strategy Development   630
    Provisions and Processes   631
    Plan Approval   633
    Plan Implementation   633
    Training and Education   633
BCP Documentation   634
    Continuity Planning Goals   634
    Statement of Importance   634
    Statement of Priorities   635
    Statement of Organizational Responsibility   635
    Statement of Urgency and Timing   635
    Risk Assessment   635
    Risk Acceptance/Mitigation   636
    Vital Records Program   636
    Emergency-Response Guidelines   636
    Maintenance   636
    Testing and Exercises   637
Summary   637
Exam Essentials   637
Written Lab   638
Review Questions   639

Chapter   16   Disaster Recovery Planning   643

The Nature of Disaster   644
    Natural Disasters   645
    Man-Made Disasters   649
Recovery Strategy   654
    Business Unit and Functional Priorities   655
    Crisis Management   656

Emergency Communications   656
Work Group Recovery   656
Alternate Processing Sites   657
Mutual Assistance Agreements   661
Database Recovery   662
Recovery Plan Development   663
Emergency Response   664
Personnel and Communications   664
Assessment   665
Backups and Offsite Storage   666
Software Escrow Arrangements   669
External Communications   670
Utilities   670
Logistics and Supplies   670
Recovery vs. Restoration   670
Training and Documentation   671
Testing and Maintenance   672
Checklist Test   672
Structured Walk-Through   673
Simulation Test   673
Parallel Test   673
Full-Interruption Test   673
Maintenance   674
Summary   674
Exam Essentials   675
Written Lab   675
Review Questions   676

Chapter   17   Laws, Regulations, and Compliance   681

Categories of Laws   682
Criminal Law   682
Civil Law   684
Administrative Law   684
Laws   685
Computer Crime   685
Intellectual Property   689
Licensing   695
Import/Export   696
Privacy   697
Compliance   703
Contracting and Procurement   704
Summary   705
Exam Essentials   706

Written Lab   707
Review Questions   708

Chapter   18   Incidents and Ethics   713

Investigations   714
    Evidence   714
    Investigation Process   719
Major Categories of Computer Crime   721
    Military and Intelligence Attacks   721
    Business Attacks   722
    Financial Attacks   722
    Terrorist Attacks   723
    Grudge Attacks   723
    Thrill Attacks   725
Incident Handling   725
    Common Types of Incidents   726
    Response Teams   728
    Incident Response Process   730
    Interviewing Individuals   733
    Incident Data Integrity and Retention   733
    Reporting Incidents   734
Ethics   735
    (ISC)² Code of Ethics   735
    Ethics and the Internet   736
Summary   737
Exam Essentials   738
Written Lab   740
Review Questions   741

Chapter   19   Physical Security Requirements   745

Site and Facility Design Considerations   746
    Secure Facility Plan   746
    Physical Security Controls   747
    Site Selection   749
    Visibility   749
    Accessibility and Perimeter Security   750
    Natural Disasters   750
    Facility Design   750
    Work Areas and Internal Security   751
    Server Rooms and Data Center Security   751
    Visitors   752
Forms of Physical Access Controls   753
    Fences, Gates, Turnstiles, and Mantraps   753

Lighting   755
Security Guards and Dogs   755
Keys and Combination Locks   756
Badges   757
Motion Detectors   757
Intrusion Alarms   758
Secondary Verification Mechanisms   759
Technical Controls   760
Smart Cards   760
Proximity Readers   760
Access Abuses   761
Intrusion Detection Systems   761
Emanation Security   762
Environment and Life Safety   763
Personnel Privacy and Safety   763
Power and Electricity   764
Noise   765
Temperature, Humidity, and Static   766
Water   766
Fire Prevention, Detection, and Suppression   767
Equipment Failure   772
Privacy Responsibilities and Legal Requirements   772
Protection of Privacy   772
Regulatory Requirements   773
Summary   773
Exam Essentials   774
Written Lab   776
Review Questions   777

Appendix   A   **Answers to Review Questions**   **781**

Appendix   B   **Answers to Written Labs**   **815**

Appendix   C   **About the Additional Study Tools**   **829**

Index   *833*

Introduction

The *CISSP: Certified Information Systems Security Professional Study Guide, Sixth Edition,* offers you a solid foundation for the Certified Information Systems Security Professional (CISSP) exam. By purchasing this book, you've shown a willingness to learn and a desire to develop the skills you need to achieve this certification. This introduction provides you with a basic overview of this book and the CISSP exam.

This book is designed for readers and students who want to study for the CISSP certification exam. If your goal is to become a certified security professional, then the CISSP certification and this study guide are for you. The purpose of this book is to adequately prepare you to take the CISSP exam.

Before you dive into this book, you need to have accomplished a few tasks on your own. You need to have a general understanding of IT and of security. You should have the necessary five years of experience (or four years if you have a college degree) in one of the 10 domains covered by the CISSP exam. If you are qualified to take the CISSP exam according to (ISC)^2, then you are sufficiently prepared to use this book to study for it. For more information on (ISC)^2, see the next section.

(ISC)^2

The CISSP exam is governed by the International Information Systems Security Certification Consortium (ISC)^2 organization. (ISC)^2 is a global not-for-profit organization. It has four primary mission goals:

- Maintain the Common Body of Knowledge (CBK) for the field of information systems security.
- Provide certification for information systems security professionals and practitioners.
- Conduct certification training and administer the certification exams.
- Oversee the ongoing accreditation of qualified certification candidates through continued education.

The (ISC)^2 is operated by a board of directors elected from the ranks of its certified practitioners. You can obtain more information about (ISC)^2 from its website at www.isc2.org.

CISSP and SSCP

(ISC)^2 supports and provides two primary certifications: CISSP and SSCP. These certifications are designed to verify the knowledge and skills of IT security professionals across all industries. The Certified Information Systems Security Professional credential is for security professionals responsible for designing and maintaining security infrastructure within an organization. The Systems Security Certified Practitioner (SSCP) is a credential for security professionals responsible for implementing or operating a security infrastructure in an organization.

The CISSP certification covers material from the 10 CBK domains:

- Access Control
- Telecommunications and Network Security
- Information Security Governance and Risk Management
- Software Development Security
- Cryptography
- Security Architecture and Design
- Security Operations
- Business Continuity and Disaster Recovery Planning
- Legal, Regulations, Investigations and Compliance
- Physical (Environmental) Security

The SSCP certification covers material from seven CBK domains:

- Access Controls
- Cryptography
- Malicious Code and Activity
- Monitoring and Analysis
- Networks and Communications
- Risk, Response, and Recovery
- Security Operations and Administration

The content for the CISSP and SSCP domains overlap significantly, but the focus is different for each set of domains. The CISSP focuses on theory and design, whereas the SSCP focuses more on implementation and best practices. This book focuses only on the domains for the CISSP exam.

Prequalifications

(ISC)^2 has defined the qualification requirements you must meet to become a CISSP. First, you must be a practicing security professional with at least five years' experience or with four years' experience and a recent IT or IS degree. Professional experience is defined as security work performed for salary or commission within one or more of the 10 CBK domains.

Second, you must agree to adhere to a formal code of ethics. The CISSP Code of Ethics is a set of guidelines the (ISC)^2 wants all CISSP candidates to follow to maintain professionalism in the field of information systems security. You can find it in the Information section on the (ISC)^2 website at www.isc2.org.

(ISC)^2 also offers an entry program known as an Associate of (ISC)^2. This program allows someone without any or enough experience to qualify as a CISSP to take the CISSP exam anyway and then obtain experience afterward. Associates are granted six years to obtain five years' of security experience. Only after providing proof of such experience, usually by means of endorsement and a resume, can the individual be awarded CISSP certification.

To sign up, visit the (ISC)[2] website, and follow the instructions listed there for registering to take the CISSP exam. You'll provide your contact information, payment details, and security-related professional experience. You'll also select one of the available time and location settings for the exam. Once (ISC)[2] approves your application to take the exam, you'll receive a confirmation email with all the details you'll need to find the testing center and take the exam. By the way, be sure to print out a copy of your confirmation letter with your assigned candidate ID number because this is the third form of proof required to enter the testing location (the first two forms are a picture ID and something with your signature on it).

Overview of the CISSP Exam

The CISSP exam consists of 250 questions, and you have 6 hours to complete it. The exam is still administered using a paper booklet and answer sheet. This means you'll be using a pencil to fill in answer bubbles.

However, (ISC)[2] just announced a new partnership with Pearson Vue. This partnership will allow the CISSP exam, and other (ISC)[2] certification exams, to be taken at a Pearson Vue CBT (computer based testing) facility starting June 1, 2012. This change in testing venues will be implemented worldwide. For more details on this development, please visit www.isc2.org.

The CISSP exam focuses on security from a 30,000-foot view; it deals more with theory and concept than implementation and procedure. It is very broad but not very deep. To successfully complete this exam, you'll need to be familiar with every domain in the CBK but not necessarily be a master of each domain.

You'll need to register for the exam through the (ISC)[2] website at www.isc2.org.

(ISC)[2] has traditionally administered the exam under its own direct guidance and control. In most cases, the exams were held in large conference rooms at hotels. Existing CISSP holders were recruited to serve as proctors or administrators for these exams. However, with the upcoming change to offering CISSP as a computer-based test (CBT), the location-based test offerings may be eliminated or reduced (especially in areas where Pearson Vue locations are widely accessible). Once you are ready to schedule your exam, please check with (ISC)[2] to see if you have the option of a CBT or a paper-based, location-based exam.

If you take a paper-based, location-based exam, be sure to arrive at the testing center around 8 a.m., and keep in mind that absolutely no one will be admitted into the exam after 8:30 a.m. Once all test takers are signed in and seated, the exam proctors will pass out the testing materials and read a few pages of instructions. This may take 30 minutes or more. Once that process is finished, the 6 hour window for taking the test will begin.

CISSP Exam Question Types

Every question on the CISSP exam is a four-option, multiple-choice question with a single correct answer. Some are straightforward, such as asking you to select a definition. Some are a bit more involved, asking you to select the appropriate concept or best practice. And some questions present you with a scenario or situation and ask you to select the best response. Here's an example:

1. What is the most important goal and top priority of a security solution?

   A. Preventing disclosure

   B. Maintaining integrity

   C. Maintaining human safety

   D. Sustaining availability

You must select the one correct or best answer and mark it on your answer sheet. In some cases, the correct answer will be very obvious to you. In other cases, several answers may seem correct. In these instances, you must choose the best answer for the question asked. Watch for general, specific, universal, superset, and subset answer selections. In other cases, none of the answers will seem correct. In these instances, you'll need to select the least incorrect answer.

 By the way, the correct answer for this sample question is C. Maintaining human safety is always your first priority.

Advice on Taking the Exam

The CISSP exam consists of two key elements. First, you need to know the material from the 10 CBK domains. Second, you must have good test-taking skills. With 6 hours to complete a 250-question exam, you have just less than 90 seconds for each question. Thus, it is important to work quickly, without rushing but also without wasting time.

One key factor to remember is that guessing is better than not answering a question. If you don't answer a question, you will not get any credit. But if you guess, you have at least a 25 percent chance of improving your score. Wrong answers are not counted against you. So, near the end of the sixth hour, be sure an answer is selected for every line on the answer sheet.

You can write on the test booklet, but nothing written on it will count for or against your score. Use the booklet to make notes and keep track of your progress. We recommend circling your selected answer in the question booklet before you mark it on your answer sheet.

To maximize your test-taking activities, here are some general guidelines:

- Answer easy questions first.

- Skip harder questions, and return to them later. Consider creating a column on the front cover of your testing booklet to keep track of skipped questions.

- Eliminate wrong answers before selecting the correct one.
- Watch for double negatives.
- Be sure you understand what the question is asking.

Manage your time. You should try to complete about 50 questions per hour. This will leave you with about an hour to focus on skipped questions and double-check your work. Be very careful to mark your answers by the correct question number on the answer sheet.

If you're attending a paper-based, location-based test, be sure to bring food and drink to the test site. You will not be allowed to leave to obtain sustenance. Your food and drink will be stored against one wall of the testing room. You can eat and drink at any time, but only against that wall. Be sure to bring any medications or other essential items, but leave all things electronic at home or in your car. Wear a watch, but make sure it is not a programmable one. Bring pencils, a manual pencil sharpener, and an eraser. We also recommend bringing foam ear plugs, wearing comfortable clothes, and taking a light jacket with you (some testing locations are a bit chilly).

If you take your exam at a Pearson Vue center, you may be prohibited from using your own paper and pen/pencil because they usually provide a dry erase board and marker. Pearson Vue testing centers usually have a no food or drink policy, but with a potentially 6-hour exam, new accommodations will be required. Please be sure to contact your testing location and inquire about the procedures and limitations for food and drink.

If English is not your first language, you can register for one of several other language versions of the exam. Or, if you choose to use the English version of the exam, a translation dictionary is allowed. You must be able to prove that you need such a dictionary; this is usually accomplished with your birth certificate or your passport.

Occasionally, small changes are made to the exam or exam objectives. When that happens, Sybex will post updates to its website. Visit www.sybex.com/go/cissp6e before you sit for the exam to make sure you have the latest information.

Study and Exam Preparation Tips

We recommend planning for a month or so of nightly intensive study for the CISSP exam. Here are some suggestions to maximize your learning time; you can modify them as necessary based on your own learning habits:

- Take one or two evenings to read each chapter in this book and work through its review material.
- Answer all the review questions and take the practice exams provided in the book and on the test engine. Complete the written labs from each chapter, and use the review questions for each chapter to help guide you to topics for which more study or time spent working through key concepts and strategies might be beneficial.

- Review the (ISC)²'s study guide from www.isc2.org.
- Use the flashcards included with the study tools to reinforce your understanding of concepts.

We recommend spending about half of your study time reading and reviewing concepts and the other half taking practice exams. Students have reported that the more time they spent taking practice exams, the better they retained test topics. You might also consider visiting resources such as www.cccure.org, www.cissp.com, and other CISSP-focused websites.

Completing the Certification Process

Once you have been informed that you successfully passed the CISSP certification, there is one final step before you are actually awarded the CISSP certification. That final step is known as *endorsement*. Basically, this involves getting someone who is a CISSP, or other (ISC)² certification holder, in good standing and familiar with your work history to submit an endorsement form on your behalf. The endorsement form is accessible through the email notifying you of your achievement in passing the exam. The endorser must review your resume, ensure that you have sufficient experience in the 10 CISSP domains, and then submit the signed form to (ISC)² via fax or post mail. You must have submitted the endorsement files to (ISC)² within 90 days after receiving the confirmation-of-passing email. Once (ISC)² receives your endorsement form, the certification process will be completed and you will be sent a welcome packet via USPS.

If you happen to fail the exam, you may take the exam a second time as soon as you can find another open slot in a testing location. However, you will need to pay full price for your second attempt. In the unlikely case you need to test a third time, (ISC)² requires that you wait six months.

Post-CISSP Concentrations

(ISC)² has added three concentrations to its certification lineup. These concentrations are offered only to CISSP certificate holders. The (ISC)² has taken the concepts introduced on the CISSP exam and focused on specific areas, namely, architecture, management, and engineering. These three concentrations are as follows:

Information Systems Security Architecture Professional (ISSAP)   Aimed at those who specialize in information security architecture. Key domains covered here include access control systems and methodology; cryptography; physical security integration; requirements analysis and security standards, guidelines, and criteria; technology-related aspects of business continuity planning and disaster recovery planning; and telecommunications and network security. This is a credential for those who design security systems or infrastructure or for those who audit and analyze such structures.

Information Systems Security Management Professional (ISSMP)   Aimed at those who focus on management of information security policies, practices, principles, and procedures. Key domains covered here include enterprise security management practices; enterprise-wide system development security; law, investigations, forensics, and ethics; oversight for operations security compliance; and understanding business continuity planning, disaster recovery planning, and continuity of operations planning. This is a credential for professionals who are responsible for security infrastructures, particularly where mandated compliance comes into the picture.

Information Systems Security Engineering Professional (ISSEP)   Aimed at those who focus on the design and engineering of secure hardware and software information systems, components, or applications. Key domains covered include certification and accreditation, systems security engineering, technical management, and US government information assurance rules and regulations. Most ISSEPs work for the US government or for a government contractor that manages government security clearances.

For more details about these concentration exams and certifications, please see the (ISC)^2 website at www.isc2.org.

Notes on This Book's Organization

This book is designed to cover each of the 10 CISSP Common Body of Knowledge domains in sufficient depth to provide you with a clear understanding of the material. The main body of this book comprises 19 chapters. The first 9 domains are each covered by 2 chapters, and the final domain, Physical (Environmental) Security, is covered in Chapter 19. The domain/chapter breakdown is as follows:

Chapters 1 and 2   Access Control

Chapters 3 and 4   Telecommunications and Network Security

Chapters 5 and 6   Information Security Governance and Risk Management

Chapters 7 and 8   Software Development Security

Chapters 9 and 10   Cryptography

Chapters 11 and 12   Security Architecture and Design

Chapters 13 and 14   Security Operations

Chapters 15 and 16   Business Continuity and Disaster Recovery Planning

Chapters 17 and 18   Legal, Regulations, Investigations, and Compliance

Chapter 19   Physical (Environmental) Security

Each chapter includes elements to help you focus your studies and test your knowledge, detailed in the following sections.

The Elements of This Study Guide

You'll see many recurring elements as you read through this study guide. Here are descriptions of some of those elements:

Summaries   The summary is a brief review of the chapter to sum up what was covered.

Exam Essentials   The Exam Essentials highlight topics that could appear on the exam in some form. While we obviously do not know exactly what will be included in a particular exam, this section reinforces significant concepts that are key to understanding the Common Body of Knowledge (CBK) area and the test specs for the CISSP exam.

Chapter review questions   Each chapter includes practice questions that have been designed to measure your knowledge of key ideas that were discussed in the chapter. After you finish each chapter, answer the questions; if some of your answers are incorrect, it's an indication that you need to spend some more time studying the corresponding topics. The answers to the practice questions can be found at the end of each chapter.

Written labs   Each chapter includes written labs that synthesize various concepts and topics that appear in the chapter. These raise questions that are designed to help you put together various pieces you've encountered individually in the chapter and assemble them to propose or describe potential security strategies or solutions.

Real World Scenarios   As you work through each chapter, you'll find descriptions of typical and plausible workplace situations where an understanding of the security strategies and approaches relevant to the chapter content could play a role in fixing problems or in fending off potential difficulties. This gives readers a chance to see how specific security policies, guidelines, or practices should or may be applied to the workplace.

What's Included With the Additional Study Tools

Readers of this book can get access to a number of additional study tools. We worked really hard to provide some essential tools to help you with your certification process. All of the following gear should be loaded on your workstation when studying for the test.

 Readers can get access to the following tools by visiting www.sybex .com/go/cissp6e.

The Sybex Test Preparation Software

The test preparation software, made by experts at Sybex, prepares you for the CISSP exam. In this test engine, you will find all the review and assessment questions from the book plus additional bonus practice exams that are included with the study tools. You can take the assessment test, test yourself by chapter, take the practice exams, or take a randomly generated exam comprising all the questions.

Electronic Flashcards

Sybex's electronic flashcards include hundreds of questions designed to challenge you further for the CISSP exam. Between the review questions, practice exams, and flashcards, you'll have more than enough practice for the exam!

Glossary of Terms in PDF

Sybex offers a robust glossary of terms in PDF format. This comprehensive glossary includes all of the key terms you should understand for the CISSP, in a searchable format.

Bonus Practice Exams

Sybex includes bonus practice exams, each comprising questions meant to survey your understanding of key elements in the CISSP CBK. This book has three bonus exams, each comprised of 250 full-length questions.

How to Use This Book's Study Tools

This book has a number of features designed to guide your study efforts for the CISSP certification exam. It assists you by listing at the beginning of each chapter the CISSP body of knowledge domain topics covered in the chapter and by ensuring that each topic is fully discussed within the chapter. The review questions at the end of each chapter and the practice exams are designed to test your retention of the material you've read to make sure you are aware of areas in which you should spend additional study time. Here are some suggestions for using this book and study tools (found at www.sybex.com/go/cissp6e):

- Take the assessment test before you start reading the material. This will give you an idea of the areas in which you need to spend additional study time as well as those areas in which you may just need a brief refresher.

- Answer the review questions after you've read each chapter; if you answer any incorrectly, go back to the chapter and review the topic, or utilize one of the additional resources if you need more information.

- Download the flashcards to your mobile device, and review them when you have a few minutes during the day.

- Take every opportunity to test yourself. In addition to the assessment test and review questions, there are bonus practice exams included with the additional study tools. Take these exams without referring to the chapters and see how well you've done—go back and review any topics you've missed until you fully understand and can apply the concepts.

Finally, find a study partner if possible. Studying for, and taking, the exam with someone else will make the process more enjoyable, and you'll have someone to help you understand topics that are difficult for you. You'll also be able to reinforce your own knowledge by helping your study partner in areas where they are weak.

Assessment Test

1. Which of the following types of access control seeks to discover evidence of unwanted, unauthorized, or illicit behavior or activity?

    A. Preventive

    B. Deterrent

    C. Detective

    D. Corrective

2. Define and detail the aspects of password selection that distinguish good password choices from ultimately poor password choices.

    A. Difficult to guess or unpredictable

    B. Meet minimum length requirements

    C. Meet specific complexity requirements

    D. All of the above

3. Which of the following is most likely to detect DoS attacks?

    A. Host-based IDS

    B. Network-based IDS

    C. Vulnerability scanner

    D. Penetration testing

4. Which of the following is considered a denial of service attack?

    A. Pretending to be a technical manager over the phone and asking a receptionist to change their password

    B. While surfing the Web, sending to a web server a malformed URL that causes the system to consume 100 percent of the CPU

    C. Intercepting network traffic by copying the packets as they pass through a specific subnet

    D. Sending message packets to a recipient who did not request them simply to be annoying

5. At which layer of the OSI model does a router operate?

    A. Network layer

    B. Layer 1

    C. Transport layer

    D. Layer 5

6. Which type of firewall automatically adjusts its filtering rules based on the content of the traffic of existing sessions?

    A. Static packet filtering

    B. Application-level gateway

    C. Stateful inspection

    D. Dynamic packet filtering

7. A VPN can be established over which of the following?

   A. Wireless LAN connection

   B. Remote access dial-up connection

   C. WAN link

   D. All of the above

8. Email is the most common delivery vehicle for which of the following?

   A. Viruses

   B. Worms

   C. Trojan horse

   D. All of the above

9. The CIA Triad comprises what elements?

   A. Contiguousness, interoperable, arranged

   B. Authentication, authorization, accountability

   C. Capable, available, integral

   D. Availability, confidentiality, integrity

10. Which of the following is not a required component in the support of accountability?

   A. Auditing

   B. Privacy

   C. Authentication

   D. Authorization

11. Which of the following is not a defense against collusion?

   A. Separation of duties

   B. Restricted job responsibilities

   C. Group user accounts

   D. Job rotation

12. A data custodian is responsible for securing resources after _____ has assigned the resource a security label.

   A. Senior management

   B. Data owner

   C. Auditor

   D. Security staff

13. In what phase of the Capability Maturity Model for Software (SW-CMM) are quantitative measures utilized to gain a detailed understanding of the software development process?

   A. Repeatable

   B. Defined

   C. Managed

   D. Optimizing

14. Which one of the following is a layer of the ring protection scheme that is not normally implemented in practice?

   A. Layer 0

   B. Layer 1

   C. Layer 3

   D. Layer 4

15. What is the last phase of the TCP/IP three-way handshake sequence?

   A. SYN packet

   B. ACK packet

   C. NAK packet

   D. SYN/ACK packet

16. Which one of the following vulnerabilities would best be countered by adequate parameter checking?

   A. Time-of-check-to-time-of-use

   B. Buffer overflow

   C. SYN flood

   D. Distributed denial of service

17. What is the value of the logical operation shown here?

   X: 0 1 1 0 1 0

   Y: 0 0 1 1 0 1

   _____

   X ∨ Y: ?

   A. 0 1 1 1 1 1

   B. 0 1 1 0 1 0

   C. 0 0 1 0 0 0

   D. 0 0 1 1 0 1

18. In what type of cipher are the letters of the plain-text message rearranged to form the cipher text?

   A. Substitution cipher

   B. Block cipher

   C. Transposition cipher

   D. One-time pad

19. What is the length of a message digest produced by the MD5 algorithm?

   A. 64 bits

   B. 128 bits

   C. 256 bits

   D. 384 bits

20. If Renee receives a digitally signed message from Mike, what key does she use to verify that the message truly came from Mike?

   A. Renee's public key

   B. Renee's private key

   C. Mike's public key

   D. Mike's private key

21. Which of the following is not a composition theory related to security models?

   A. Cascading

   B. Feedback

   C. Iterative

   D. Hookup

22. The collection of components in the TCB that work together to implement reference monitor functions is called the _____.

   A. Security perimeter

   B. Security kernel

   C. Access matrix

   D. Constrained interface

23. Which of the following statements is true?

   A. The less complex a system, the more vulnerabilities it has.

   B. The more complex a system, the less assurance it provides.

   C. The less complex a system, the less trust it provides.

   D. The more complex a system, the less attack surface it generates.

24. Ring 0, from the design architecture security mechanism known as protection rings, can also be referred to as all but which of the following?

   A. Privileged mode

   B. Supervisory mode

   C. System mode

   D. User mode

25. Audit trails, logs, CCTV, intrusion detection systems, antivirus software, penetration testing, password crackers, performance monitoring, and cyclic redundancy checks (CRCs) are examples of what?

   A. Directive controls

   B. Preventive controls

   C. Detective controls

   D. Corrective controls

26. System architecture, system integrity, covert channel analysis, trusted facility management, and trusted recovery are elements of what security criteria?

   A. Quality assurance

   B. Operational assurance

   C. Life cycle assurance

   D. Quantity assurance

27. Which of the following is a procedure designed to test and perhaps bypass a system's security controls?

   A. Logging usage data

   B. War dialing

   C. Penetration testing

   D. Deploying secured desktop workstations

28. Auditing is a required factor to sustain and enforce what?

   A. Accountability

   B. Confidentiality

   C. Accessibility

   D. Redundancy

29. What is the formula used to compute the ALE?

   A. ALE = AV * EF * ARO

   B. ALE = ARO * EF

   C. ALE = AV * ARO

   D. ALE = EF * ARO

30. What is the first step of the business impact assessment process?

   A. Identification of priorities

   B. Likelihood assessment

   C. Risk identification

   D. Resource prioritization

31. Which of the following represent natural events that can pose a threat or risk to an organization?

   A. Earthquake

   B. Flood

   C. Tornado

   D. All of the above

32. What kind of recovery facility enables an organization to resume operations as quickly as possible, if not immediately, upon failure of the primary facility?

A. Hot site

B. Warm site

C. Cold site

D. All of the above

33. What form of intellectual property is used to protect words, slogans, and logos?

A. Patent

B. Copyright

C. Trademark

D. Trade secret

34. What type of evidence refers to written documents that are brought into court to prove a fact?

A. Best evidence

B. Payroll evidence

C. Documentary evidence

D. Testimonial evidence

35. Why are military and intelligence attacks among the most serious computer crimes?

A. The use of information obtained can have far-reaching detrimental strategic effects on national interests in an enemy's hands.

B. Military information is stored on secure machines, so a successful attack can be embarrassing.

C. The long-term political use of classified information can impact a country's leadership.

D. The military and intelligence agencies have ensured that the laws protecting their information are the most severe.

36. What type of detected incident allows the most time for an investigation?

A. Compromise

B. Denial of service

C. Malicious code

D. Scanning

37. If you want to restrict access into or out of a facility, which would you choose?

A. Gate

B. Turnstile

C. Fence

D. Mantrap

38. What is the point of a secondary verification system?

    A. To verify the identity of a user

    B. To verify the activities of a user

    C. To verify the completeness of a system

    D. To verify the correctness of a system

Answers to Assessment Test

1. C. Detective access controls are used to discover (and document) unwanted or unauthorized activity. For more information, please see Chapter 1.

2. D. Strong password choices are difficult to guess, unpredictable, and of specified minimum lengths to ensure that password entries cannot be computationally determined. They may be randomly generated and utilize all the alphabetic, numeric, and punctuation characters; they should never be written down or shared; they should not be stored in publicly accessible or generally readable locations; and they shouldn't be transmitted in the clear. For more information, please see Chapter 1.

3. B. Network-based IDSs are usually able to detect the initiation of an attack or the ongoing attempts to perpetrate an attack (including denial of service, or DoS). They are, however, unable to provide information about whether an attack was successful or which specific systems, user accounts, files, or applications were affected. Host-based IDSs have some difficulty with detecting and tracking down DoS attacks. Vulnerability scanners don't detect DoS attacks; they test for possible vulnerabilities. Penetration testing may cause a DoS or test for DoS vulnerabilities, but it is not a detection tool. For more information, please see Chapter 2.

4. B. Not all instances of DoS are the result of a malicious attack. Errors in coding OSs, services, and applications have resulted in DoS conditions. Some examples of this include a process failing to release control of the CPU or a service consuming system resources out of proportion to the service requests it is handling. Social engineering and sniffing are typically not considered DoS attacks. For more information, please see Chapter 2.

5. A. Network hardware devices, including routers, function at layer 3, the Network layer. For more information, please see Chapter 3.

6. D. Dynamic packet-filtering firewalls enable the real-time modification of the filtering rules based on traffic content. For more information, please see Chapter 3.

7. D. A VPN link can be established over any other network communication connection. This could be a typical LAN cable connection, a wireless LAN connection, a remote access dial-up connection, a WAN link, or even an Internet connection used by a client for access to the office LAN. For more information, please see Chapter 4.

8. D. Email is the most common delivery mechanism for viruses, worms, Trojan horses, documents with destructive macros, and other malicious code. For more information, please see Chapter 4.

9. D. The components of the CIA Triad are confidentiality, availability, and integrity. For more information, please see Chapter 5.

10. B. Privacy is not necessary to provide accountability. For more information, please see Chapter 5.

11. C. Group user accounts allow for multiple people to log in under a single user account. This allows collusion because it prevents individual accountability. For more information, please see Chapter 6.

12. B. The data owner must first assign a security label to a resource before the data custodian can secure the resource appropriately. For more information, please see Chapter 6.

13. C. The Managed phase of the SW-CMM involves the use of quantitative development metrics. The Software Engineering Institute (SEI) defines the key process areas for this level as Quantitative Process Management and Software Quality Management. For more information, please see Chapter 7.

14. B. Layers 1 and 2 contain device drivers but are not normally implemented in practice. Layer 0 always contains the security kernel. Layer 3 contains user applications. Layer 4 does not exist. For more information, please see Chapter 7.

15. B. The SYN packet is first sent from the initiating host to the destination host. The destination host then responds with a SYN/ACK packet. The initiating host sends an ACK packet, and the connection is then established. For more information, please see Chapter 8.

16. B. Parameter checking is used to prevent the possibility of buffer overflow attacks. For more information, please see Chapter 8.

17. A. The ∨ OR symbol represents the OR function, which is true when one or both of the input bits are true. For more information, please see Chapter 9.

18. C. Transposition ciphers use an encryption algorithm to rearrange the letters of the plaintext message to form a ciphertext message. For more information, please see Chapter 9.

19. B. The MD5 algorithm produces a 128-bit message digest for any input. For more information, please see Chapter 10.

20. C. Any recipient can use Mike's public key to verify the authenticity of the digital signature. For more information, please see Chapter 10.

21. C. Iterative is not one of the composition theories related to security models. Cascading, feedback, and hookup are the three composition theories. For more information, please see Chapter 11.

22. B. The collection of components in the TCB that work together to implement reference monitor functions is called the security kernel. For more information, please see Chapter 11.

23. B. The more complex a system, the less assurance it provides. More complexity means more areas for vulnerabilities to exist and more areas that must be secured against threats. More vulnerabilities and more threats mean that the subsequent security provided by the system is less trustworthy. For more information, please see Chapter 12.

24. D. Ring 0 has direct access to the most resources, thus user mode is not an appropriate label because user mode requires restrictions to limit access to resources. For more information, please see Chapter 12.

25. C. Examples of detective controls are audit trails, logs, CCTV, intrusion detection systems, antivirus software, penetration testing, password crackers, performance monitoring, and CRCs. For more information, please see Chapter 13.

26. B. Assurance is the degree of confidence you can place in the satisfaction of security needs of a computer, network, solution, and so on. Operational assurance focuses on the basic features and architecture of a system that lend themselves to supporting security. For more information, please see Chapter 13.

27. C. Penetration testing is the attempt to bypass security controls to test overall system security. For more information, please see Chapter 14.

28. A. Auditing is a required factor to sustain and enforce accountability. For more information, please see Chapter 14.

29. A. The annualized loss expectancy (ALE) is computed as the product of the asset value (AV) times the exposure factor (EF) times the annualized rate of occurrence (ARO). This is the longer form of the formula ALE = SLE * ARO. The other formulas displayed here do not accurately reflect this calculation. For more information, please see Chapter 15.

30. A. Identification of priorities is the first step of the business impact assessment process. For more information, please see Chapter 15.

31. D. Natural events that can threaten organizations include earthquakes, floods, hurricanes, tornados, wildfires, and other acts of nature as well. Thus options A, B, and C are correct because they are natural and not man made. For more information, please see Chapter 16.

32. A. Hot sites provide backup facilities maintained in constant working order and fully capable of taking over business operations. Warm sites consist of preconfigured hardware and software to run the business, neither of which possesses the vital business information. Cold sites are simply facilities designed with power and environmental support systems but no configured hardware, software, or services. Disaster recovery services can facilitate and implement any of these sites on behalf of a company. For more information, please see Chapter 16.

33. C. Trademarks are used to protect the words, slogans, and logos that represent a company and its products or services. For more information, please see Chapter 17.

34. C. Written documents brought into court to prove the facts of a case are referred to as documentary evidence. For more information, please see Chapter 17.

35. A. The purpose of a military and intelligence attack is to acquire classified information. The detrimental effect of using such information could be nearly unlimited in the hands of an enemy. Attacks of this type are launched by very sophisticated attackers. It is often very difficult to ascertain what documents were successfully obtained. So when a breach of this type occurs, you sometimes cannot know the full extent of the damage. For more information, please see Chapter 18.

36. D. Scanning incidents are generally reconnaissance attacks. The real damage to a system comes in the subsequent attacks, so you may have some time to react if you detect the scanning attack early. For more information, please see Chapter 18.

37. B. A turnstile is a form of gate that prevents more than one person from gaining entry at a time and often restricts movement to one direction. It is used to gain entry but not exit, or vice versa. For more information, please see Chapter 19.

38. D. Secondary verification mechanisms are set in place to establish a means of verifying the correctness of detection systems and sensors. This often means combining several types of sensors or systems (CCTV, heat and motion sensors, and so on) to provide a more complete picture of detected events. For more information, please see Chapter 19.

Chapter

1

Access Control

THE CISSP EXAM TOPICS COVERED IN THIS CHAPTER INCLUDE:

1. **Access Control**

    A. Control access by applying the following concepts/methodology/techniques:

    A.1 Policies

    A.2 Types of controls (preventive, detective, corrective, etc.)

    A.3 Techniques (e.g., nondiscretionary, discretionary, and mandatory)

    A.4 Identification and authentication

    A.5 Decentralized/distributed access control techniques

    A.6 Authorization mechanisms

    D. Identity and access provisioning lifecycle (e.g., provisioning, review, revocation)

The Access Control domain in the Common Body of Knowledge (CBK) for the CISSP certification exam deals with topics and issues related to granting and revoking the right to access data or perform an action on a system. Generally, an *access control* is any hardware, software, or organizational administrative policy or procedure that performs the following tasks:

- Identifies users or other subjects attempting to access resources.
- Determines whether the access is authorized.
- Grants or restricts access.
- Monitors and records access attempts.
- In this chapter and in Chapter 2, "Access Control Attacks and Monitoring," we discuss the Access Control domain. Be sure to read and study the materials from both chapters to ensure complete coverage of the essential material for this domain of the CISSP certification exam objectives.

Access Control Overview

Controlling access to resources is one of the central themes of security. Access control addresses more than just which users can access which files or services. It is about the relationships between *entities* (that is, subjects and objects). The transfer of information from an object to a subject is called *access*, which makes it important to understand the definition of both subject and object.

Subject   A *subject* is an active *entity* that accesses a passive object to receive information from, or data about, an object. Subjects can be users, programs, processes, computers, or anything else that can access a resource. When authorized, subjects can modify objects.

Object   An *object* is a passive entity that provides information to active subjects. Some examples of objects include files, databases, computers, programs, processes, printers, and storage media.

You can often simplify these access control topics by substituting the word *user* for *subject* and the word *file* for *object*. For example, instead of *a subject accesses an object*, you can think of it as *a user accesses a file*. However, it's also important to remember that subjects comprise more than users and objects comprise more than just files.

You may have noticed that some examples, such as programs and computers, are listed as both subjects and objects. This is because the roles of subject and object can switch back and forth. In many cases, when two entities interact, they perform different functions. Sometimes they may be requesting information and other times providing information. The key difference is that the subject is always the active entity that receives information about, or data from, the passive object. The object is always the passive entity that provides or hosts the information or data.

For example, consider a common web application that provides dynamic web pages to users. Users query the web application to retrieve a web page, so the application starts as an object. The application then switches to a subject role as it queries the user's computer to retrieve a cookie and then queries a database to retrieve information about the user based on the cookie. Finally, the application switches back to an object as it sends back the dynamic web page.

Access control is not limited to logical and technical applications. It also applies to physical security and can involve controlling access to entire complexes, entire buildings, or even individual rooms.

Users, Owners, and Custodians

When discussing access to objects, three subject labels are used: user, owner, and custodian.

User   A *user* is any subject who accesses objects on a system to perform some action or accomplish a work task.

Owner   An *owner*, or information owner, is the person who has final organizational responsibility for classifying and labeling objects and protecting and storing data. The owner may be liable for negligence if they fail to perform due diligence in establishing and enforcing security policies to protect and sustain sensitive data.

Custodian   A *custodian* is a subject who has been assigned or delegated the day-to-day responsibility of properly storing and protecting objects.

A user is any end user on the system. The owner is typically the CEO, president, or department head. The custodian is typically the Information Technology (IT) staff or the system security administrator.

The CIA Triad

One of the primary reasons that access control mechanisms are implemented is to prevent losses. There are three categories of IT loss: loss of *confidentiality*, loss of *availability*, and loss of *integrity*. Protecting against these losses is so integral to IT security that they are frequently referred to the *CIA Triad* (or sometimes the AIC Triad or Security Triad).

Chapter 5, "Security Governance Concepts, Principles, and Policies," explores losses in greater depth.

Confidentiality   Access controls help ensure that only authorized subjects can access objects. When unauthorized entities are able to access systems or data, it results in a loss of confidentiality.

Integrity   Integrity ensures that data or system configurations are not modified without authorization. If unauthorized or unwanted changes to objects occur, or go undetected, this is known as loss of integrity.

Availability   Authorized requests for objects must be granted to subjects within a reasonable amount of time. In other words, systems and data should be available to users and other subjects when they are needed. If the systems are not operational, or the data is not accessible, this is a loss of availability.

Policies

A *security policy* is a document that defines the security requirements for an organization. It identifies assets that need protection and the extent to which security solutions should go to protect them. Some organizations create a security policy as a single document and other organizations create multiple security policies with each one focused on a separate area. (Security policies are explored in greater depth in Chapter 5.)

Policies are an important element of access control because they help personnel within the organization understand what security requirements are important. The security policy is created or approved by senior leadership, and it provides a broad overview of an organization's security needs but usually does not go into details about how to fulfill the needs. For example, it may state the need to implement and enforce separation of duties and least privilege principles but not state how to do so. Professionals within the organization use the security policies as a guide to implement security requirements. Standards are also created from security policies.

Compare Permissions, Rights, and Privileges

When studying access control topics, you'll often come across the terms *permissions*, *rights*, and *privileges*. These are sometimes used interchangeably, but they don't always mean the same thing.

Permissions   In general, permissions refer to the access granted for an object and determine what you can do with it. If you have read permission for a file, you'll be able to open it and read it. Users may be granted permissions to create, read, edit, or delete a file on a file server. Similarly, users can be granted access rights to a file, so in this context, access rights and permissions are synonymous. For example, you may be granted read and execute permissions for an application file, which gives you the right to run the application. Additionally, you may be granted data rights within a database, allowing you to retrieve or update information in the database.

Rights   A right also refers to the ability to take an action on an object. For example, a user might have the right to modify the system time on a computer or the right to restore backed-up data. This is a subtle distinction and not always stressed, but the right to take action on a system is rarely referred to as a permission.

Privileges   Combined, rights and permissions are commonly referred to as *privileges*. For example, an administrator for a computer will have full privileges, granting the administrator full rights and permissions on the computer. The administrator will be able to perform any actions and access any data on the computer.

Types of Access Control

The term *access control* refers to a broad range of controls that perform such tasks as ensuring that only authorized users can log on and preventing unauthorized users from gaining access to resources. Controls mitigate a wide variety of information security risks.

The three primary access control types are preventive, detective, and corrective.

Whenever possible you want to *prevent* any type of security problem or incident. Of course, this isn't always possible and unwanted events occur. When they do, you want to *detect* the event as soon as possible. And once you detect the event, you want to *correct* it.

There are also four other access control types, commonly known as deterrent, recovery, directive, and compensation access controls.

As you read through the controls in the following sections, you'll notice that some are listed as an example in more than one access control type. For example, a *fence* (or perimeter-defining device) placed around a building can be a preventive control (physically barring someone from gaining access to a building compound) and/or a deterrent control (discouraging someone from trying to gain access).

Preventive access control   A *preventive access control* (sometimes called a preventative access control in CISSP materials) is deployed to thwart or stop unwanted or unauthorized activity from occurring. Examples of preventive access controls include fences, locks, biometrics, mantraps, lighting, alarm systems, separation of duties, job rotation, data classification, penetration testing, access control methods, encryption, auditing, presence of security cameras or closed circuit television (CCTV), smart cards, callback procedures, security policies, security awareness training, antivirus software, firewalls, and intrusion prevention systems.

Detective access control   A *detective access control* is deployed to discover or detect unwanted or unauthorized activity. Detective controls operate after the fact and can discover the activity only after it has occurred. Examples of detective access controls include security guards, motion detectors, recording and reviewing of events captured by security cameras or CCTV, job rotation, mandatory vacations, audit trails, honeypots or honeynets, intrusion detection systems, violation reports, supervision and reviews of users, and incident investigations.

Corrective access control   A *corrective access control* modifies the environment to return systems to normal after an unwanted or unauthorized activity has occurred. They attempt to correct any problems that occurred as a result of a security incident. Corrective controls can be simple, such as terminating malicious activity or rebooting a system.

They also include antivirus solutions that can remove or quarantine a virus, backup and restore plans to ensure that lost data can be restored, and active intrusion detection systems that can modify the environment to stop an attack in progress.

Chapter 14, "Incident Management" covers intrusion detection systems and intrusion prevention systems in more depth.

Deterrent access control A *deterrent access control* is deployed to discourage violation of security policies. Deterrent and preventive controls are similar, but deterrent controls often depend on individuals deciding not to take an unwanted action. In contrast, a preventive control actually blocks the action. Some examples include policies, security awareness training, locks, fences, security badges, guards, mantraps, and security cameras.

Recovery access control A *recovery access control* is deployed to repair or restore resources, functions, and capabilities after a violation of security policies. Recovery controls are an extension of corrective controls but have more advanced or complex abilities. Examples of recovery access controls include backups and restores, fault-tolerant drive systems, system imaging, server clustering, antivirus software, and database or virtual machine shadowing.

Directive access control A *directive access control* is deployed to direct, confine, or control the actions of subjects to force or encourage compliance with security policies. Examples of directive access controls include security policy requirements or criteria, posted notifications, escape route exit signs, monitoring, supervision, and procedures.

Compensation access control A *compensation access control* is deployed to provide various options to other existing controls to aid in enforcement and support of security policies. They can be any controls used in addition to, or in place of, another control. For example, an organizational policy may dictate that all personally identifiable information (PII) must be encrypted. A review discovers that a preventive control is encrypting all PII data within databases, but PII transferred over the network is sent in cleartext. A compensation control would be added to protect the data in transit.

The terms *types* and *categories* are sometimes used interchangeably when grouping controls. For example, the CISSP Candidate Information Bulletin (CIB) lists "types of controls" as "preventive, detective, corrective," but many other sources identify these as *categories* of controls instead of *types*. Similarly, other sources identify administrative, technical, and physical controls as access control *types* instead of *categories*. For the exam, it isn't important to know if a control grouping is a type or category, but you should be able to differentiate between the meanings of the different controls.

Access controls are also categorized by how they are implemented. Controls can be implemented administratively, logically/technically, or physically. Any of the access control types mentioned previously can include any of these types of implementation.

Administrative controls   *Administrative access controls* are the policies and procedures defined by an organization's security policy and other regulations or requirements. They are sometimes referred to as management controls. These controls focus on personnel and business practices. Examples of administrative access controls include policies, procedures, hiring practices, background checks, data classifications and labeling, security awareness and training efforts, vacation history, reports and reviews, work supervision, personnel controls, and testing.

Logical/technical controls   *Logical access controls* (also known as *technical access controls*) are the hardware or software mechanisms used to manage access and to provide protection for resources and systems. As the name implies, they use technology. Examples of logical or technical access controls include authentication methods (such as usernames, passwords, smart cards, and biometrics), encryption, constrained interfaces, access control lists, protocols, firewalls, routers, intrusion detection systems, and clipping levels.

Physical controls   *Physical access controls* are items you can physically touch. They include physical mechanisms deployed to prevent, monitor, or detect direct contact with systems or areas within a facility. Examples of physical access controls include guards, fences, motion detectors, locked doors, sealed windows, lights, cable protection, laptop locks, badges, swipe cards, guard dogs, video cameras, mantraps, and alarms.

When preparing for the CISSP exam, you should be able to easily identify the type of any control. For example, you should recognize that a firewall is a preventive control because it can prevent attacks by blocking traffic, while an intrusion detection system (IDS) is a detective control because it can detect attacks in progress or after they've occurred. You should also be able to identify both as logical/technical controls.

Defense in Depth

Access controls are implemented using a *defense-in-depth strategy*, in which multiple layers or levels of access controls are deployed to provide layered security. As an example, consider Figure 1.1. It shows two servers and two disks to represent assets owned by an organization that need to be protected. Intruders or attackers need to overcome multiple layers of defense to reach these protected assets.

FIGURE 1.1 Defense in depth with layered security

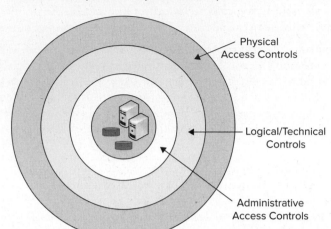

Controls are implemented using multiple methods. You can't depend on technology alone to provide security; you must also use physical access controls and administrative access controls. For example, if a server has strong authentication but is stored on an unguarded desk, a thief can easily steal it and take his time hacking into the system. Similarly, users may have strong passwords, but social engineers may trick them into giving up their password if they haven't been adequately trained.

This concept of defense in depth highlights several important points:

- An organization's security policy, one of the administrative access controls, provides the first or innermost layer of defense for assets.

- Personnel are a key focus for access controls. Only with proper training and education can they implement, comply with, and support security elements defined in your security policy.

- A combination of administrative, technical, and physical access controls provides a much stronger defense. Using only administrative, only technical, or only physical controls results in weaknesses that attackers can discover and exploit.

Access Control Elements

The different security elements that come together to support access control are grouped into four types: identification, authentication, authorization, and accountability. This list provides a short introduction:

Identification A subject claims an identity. For example, users claim identities based on usernames.

Authentication   A subject proves a claimed identity. For example, users can prove usernames are theirs by providing a password with the username.

Authorization   Subjects are granted access to objects based on proven identities. For example, a user can be granted access to files based on the user's proven identity.

Accountability   Users and other subjects can be held accountable for their actions when auditing is implemented. Auditing tracks subjects and records when they access objects, creating an audit trail in one or more audit logs. For example, auditing can record when a user reads, modifies, or deletes a file. Auditing provides accountability.

All four of these elements are needed in an effective access control system. Subjects must be uniquely identified and authenticated before authentication and accountability can occur. When subjects are identified and authenticated, and their actions are recorded in audit logs, they can be held accountable for their actions.

Identification

Identification is the process by which a subject professes an identity and accountability is initiated. For example, a user provides a username, a logon ID, or a smart card to represent an identification process. Similarly, an application can provide a process ID number as identification. Once a subject has identified itself, the claimed identity becomes accountable for any further actions undertaken by that subject. IT systems track activity by identities, not by subjects themselves. A computer doesn't know one human from another, but it does know that your user account is different from all other user accounts.

Authentication

Authentication is the process of verifying or testing that a claimed identity is valid. Authentication requires that a subject provide additional information that must correspond exactly to the professed identity. An authentication system checks the professed identity and the authentication against a database. If the database includes the identity and the correct authentication is included, the subject is authenticated.

The three basic methods of authentication are also known as types or factors. They are introduced here and expanded in the section "Identification and Authentication Techniques" later in this chapter.

Type 1   A Type 1 authentication factor is *something you know*. It is any string of characters you have memorized and can reproduce on a keyboard when prompted. Examples include a password, personal identification number (PIN), passphrase, or mother's maiden name.

Type 2   A Type 2 authentication factor is *something you have*. It is a physical device that you must have in your possession at the time of authentication. Examples include a *token device*, *smart card*, *memory card*, or USB drive.

> The main difference between a memory card and a smart card is that a memory card is used only to store information while a smart card has the ability to process data. For example, a memory card can hold information to authenticate a user, while a smart card includes a microprocessor in addition to a certificate that can be used for authentication, to encrypt data, to digitally sign email, and more.

Type 3 A Type 3 authentication factor is *something you are* or *something you do*. It is a physical characteristic of a person identified with different types of biometrics. Examples in the "something you are" category include fingerprints, voice prints, retina patterns, iris patterns, face shapes, palm topology, and hand geometry. Examples in the "something you do" category include signature and keystroke dynamics, also known as behavioral biometrics.

These types are progressively stronger when implemented correctly, with Type 1 being the weakest and Type 3 being the strongest. In other words, passwords (Type 1) are the weakest, and a fingerprint (Type 3) is stronger than a password—but even Type 3 authentication factors can be breached. For example, an attacker may be able to create a duplicate fingerprint on a gummi bear candy and fool a fingerprint reader.

Somewhere You Are

These three basic factors ("something you know," "something you have," and "something you are") are the most common elements in authentication systems. However, a factor known as *somewhere you are* is sometimes used. It can identify a subject's location based on a specific computer, a phone number identified by caller ID, or a country identified by an IP address. Controlling access by physical location forces a subject to be present in a specific location. For example, remote access users may be authorized to dial in from home. Caller ID and callback techniques are used to verify that the user is actually calling from home. "Somewhere you are" is sometimes considered part of Type 2, "something you have."

This factor isn't reliable on its own because any type of address information can be spoofed by a dedicated attacker. However, it can be effective when used in combination with other factors.

Authorization

Authorization indicates who is trusted to perform specific operations. If the action is allowed, the subject is authorized; if disallowed, the subject is not authorized. Here's a simple example: If a user attempts to open a file, the authorization mechanism checks to ensure that the user has at least read permission on the file.

It's important to realize that just because users or other entities can authenticate to a system, that doesn't mean they are given access to anything and everything. Instead, subjects are authorized access to specific objects based on their proven identity. The process of authorization ensures that the requested activity or object access is possible based on the privileges assigned to the subject.

Identification and authentication are "all-or-nothing" aspects of access control. Either a user's credentials prove a professed identity, or they don't. In contrast, authorization occupies a wide range of variations. For example, a user may be able to read a file but not delete it or print a document but not alter the print queue.

Accountability

Accountability, which is done via auditing, logging, and monitoring, ensures that subjects can be held accountable for their actions. Auditing is the process of tracking and recording subject activities within logs. Logs typically record who took an action, when and where the action was taken, and what the action was. One or more logs create an *audit trail* that can be used to reconstruct events and to verify whether a security policy or authorization was violated. When contents of audit trails are reviewed, people associated with the accounts can be held accountable for their actions. (Logging and monitoring is covered in more depth in Chapter 2.)

There's a subtle but important point to stress about accountability. Accountability relies on effective identification and authentication, but it does not require effective authorization. In other words, if users are adequately identified and authenticated, accountability mechanisms such as audit logs can track their activity, even when they access resources they shouldn't.

Identification and Authentication Techniques

Identification is a fairly straightforward concept. A subject must provide an identity to a system to start the authentication, authorization, and accountability processes. Providing an identity might entail typing a username, swiping a smart card, waving a token device, speaking a phrase, or positioning your face, hand, or finger for a camera or scanning device. Without an identity, a system has no way to correlate an authentication factor with the subject.

Authentication verifies the identity of the subject by comparing one or more factors against a database of valid identities, such as user accounts. The authentication information used to verify an identity is considered private information. The ability of the subject and system to maintain the secrecy of the authentication information for identities directly reflects the level of security of that system.

Identification and authentication always occur together as a single two-step process. Providing an identity is the first step, and providing the authentication information is the second step. Without both, a subject cannot gain access to a system.

Each authentication technique or factor has unique benefits and drawbacks. Thus, it is important to evaluate each mechanism in light of the environment in which it will be deployed to determine viability.

Passwords

The most common authentication technique is the use of a *password* (a string of characters entered by a user) with Type 1 authentication (something you know), but this is also considered the weakest form of protection. Passwords are poor security mechanisms for several reasons:

- Users often choose passwords that are easy to remember and therefore easy to guess or crack.

- Randomly generated passwords are hard to remember; thus, many users write them down.

- Passwords are easily shared, written down, and forgotten.

- Passwords can be stolen through many means, including observation, recording and playback, and security database theft.

- Passwords are sometimes transmitted in cleartext or with easily broken encryption protocols.

- Password databases are sometimes stored in publicly accessible online locations.

- Weak passwords can be discovered quickly in brute-force attacks.

Password Encryption

Passwords are rarely stored in plain text. Instead, a system will create a hash of a password using a hashing algorithm such as Message Digest 5 (MD5) or Secure Hash Algorithm 1 (SHA-1). The hash is a number and the algorithm will always create the same number if the password is the same. When a user enters the password for authentication, it is hashed and compared to the stored password's hash. If they are the same, the user is authenticated.

Password Selection

Passwords can be effective if selected intelligently and managed properly. A *password policy* can be part of the organization's written policy that dictates the requirements for passwords. Many systems also include technical password policies that enforce the *password restriction* requirements. Password policies can, for example, ensure that users change their passwords regularly (a maximum age setting might specify that users must change their password every 45 days). The following list includes some other password policy settings:

Password length   The length is the number of characters in the password. End user passwords should be at least eight characters long, and many organizations require privileged account passwords to be at least 15 characters long. This specifically overcomes a weakness in how passwords are stored in some Windows systems.

Password complexity   The complexity of a password refers to how many character types it includes. An eight-character password using uppercase characters, lowercase characters, symbols, and numbers is much stronger than an eight-character password using only numbers.

Password history   Many users get into the habit of switching between two passwords. A password history remembers a certain number of previous passwords (perhaps six) and prevents users from reusing a password in the history. This is often combined with a minimum password age setting, preventing users from changing a password repeatedly until they can set the password back to the original one. Minimum password age is often set to one day.

However, even with strong software-enforced password restrictions, it remains possible to create passwords that may be easily guessed or cracked. Users don't always understand the need for strong passwords, or even how to create them. An organization's security policy will usually stress the need for strong passwords and define the contents of a strong password. If end users create their own passwords, suggestions like the following can help them create strong ones:

- Do not use any part of your name, logon name, email address, employee number, Social Security number, phone number, extension, or other identifying name or code.

- Do not use dictionary words (including words in foreign dictionaries), slang, or industry acronyms.

- Do use nonstandard capitalization and spelling.

- Do switch letters and replace letters with numbers.

In some environments, initial passwords for user accounts are generated automatically. Often the generated password is a form of a composition password, which is constructed from two or more unrelated words joined together with a number or symbol in between. Composition passwords are easy for computers to generate, but they should not be used for extended periods of time because they are vulnerable to password-guessing attacks. If the algorithm for computer-generated passwords is discovered, all passwords created by the system are in jeopardy of being compromised.

Password Phrases

A password mechanism that is more effective than a basic password is a *passphrase*. A passphrase is a string of characters similar to a password but it has unique meaning to the user. Passphrases are often basic sentences modified to simplify memorization. Here's an example: "I passed the CISSP exam" can be converted to the following passphrase: "IP@$$edTheCISSPEx@m." Using a passphrase has several benefits. It is difficult to crack a passphrase using a brute-force tool, and it encourages the use of a lengthy string with numerous characters, but it is still easy to remember.

Cognitive Passwords

Another interesting password mechanism is the *cognitive password*. A cognitive password is usually a series of questions about facts or predefined responses that only the subject should know. For example, three to five questions such as these might be asked of the subject:

- What is your birth date?
- What is your mother's maiden name?
- What is the name of your division manager?
- What was your score on your last evaluation exam?
- Who was your favorite player in the 1984 World Series?

If all questions are answered correctly, the subject is authenticated. The most effective cognitive password systems ask a different set of questions each time. The primary limitation for cognitive password systems is that each question must be answered at the time of user enrollment (in other words, user account creation) and answered again during the logon process, which increases the time to complete that process.

Cognitive passwords are often employed to assist with password management using self-service password reset systems or assisted password reset systems. For example, if users forget their original password, they can ask for help. The password management system can then challenge the user with one or more of these cognitive password questions presumably known only by the user. If the user answers correctly, the user is either provided with the original password or granted the ability to change the password.

One of the flaws associated with cognitive passwords is that the information is often easily available via the Internet. For example, an attacker broke into Sarah Palin's personal Yahoo! email account when she was a vice presidential candidate in 2008. He accessed biographical information about her that he found on the Internet and was able to answer questions posed by Yahoo!'s account recovery process.

Smart Cards and Tokens

Smart cards and tokens (or smart tokens) are both examples of a Type 2, or "something you have," factor of authentication. They are rarely used by themselves but are commonly combined with another factor of authentication, providing multifactor authentication.

Smart Cards

A *smart card* is a credit-card-sized ID or badge and has an integrated circuit chip embedded in it. Smart cards contain information about the authorized bearer that can be used for identification and/or authentication purposes. Most current smart cards include a microprocessor and one or more certificates. The certificates are used for asymmetric cryptography such as encryption and digitally signing email. (Asymmetric cryptography topics are covered in more depth in Chapter 10, "PKI and Cryptographic Applications.") Smart cards are tamper resistant and provide users with an easy way to carry and use complex encryption keys.

Users insert the card into a smart card reader when authenticating. It's common to require users to also enter a PIN or password as a second factor of authentication with the smart card.

Note that smart cards can provide both identification and authentication. Because users could share or swap smart cards, they aren't effective identification methods by themselves. Another authentication factor must be used. Smart cards are almost always used with PINs as a secondary factor to improve their security value.

Personnel within the US government use either *common access cards (CACs)* or *Personal Identity Verification (PIV) cards*. CACs and PIV cards are smart cards that include pictures and other identifying information about the owner. Users wear them as a badge while walking around and insert them into card readers at their computer when logging on. Chapter 19, "Physical Security Requirements," has more information on smart cards.

Tokens

A token, or *token device*, is a password-generating device that users can carry with them. A common token used today includes an LCD that displays a number that is used as a password and changes at a fixed time interval, such as every 60 seconds. This number is derived from several elements, including a unique token device identifier, a built-in clock, and a cryptographic key that is different for each specific token. An authentication server stores the details of the token, so at any moment, the server knows what number is displayed in the LCD of the user's token device.

The token device is rarely used by itself, but it is used with another method of authentication. For example, a user could use the token to log onto a company website. The authentication page might include text boxes for the user to enter a username, password or PIN, and the number displayed in the token. As with any method of multifactor authentication, this is stronger than using a single factor of authentication. If the token device is lost or stolen, it can't be used by itself.

However, token systems do have failings. If the battery dies or the device breaks, the user won't be able to gain access. Additionally, users may be tempted to write their access code or PIN on the device, severely compromising its effectiveness. If it is lost, anyone who finds it can try to use it. Users should also understand that the device identifies them, so they should not loan the token and PIN to anyone else, including co-workers.

The two most common types of tokens are synchronous and asynchronous dynamic password tokens, but static tokens are also used. Synchronous and asynchronous tokens work as one-time password generators. They include a unique identifier similar to a serial number, which is mapped to the user's account.

One-Time Password Generators

One-time passwords are dynamic passwords that change every time they are used. They can be effective for security purposes, but most people find it difficult to remember passwords that change so frequently. One-time password generators are token devices that create passwords, making one-time passwords reasonable to deploy. They are usually used with a PIN. With token-device-based authentication systems, an environment can benefit from the strength of one-time passwords without relying on users to be able to memorize complex passwords.

Synchronous dynamic password tokens   The LCD token described earlier is a *synchronous dynamic password token.* It generates passwords at fixed time intervals, such as every 60 seconds. Time interval tokens must have their clocks synchronized to an authentication server. To authenticate, the user enters the password shown on the LCD along with a PIN or passphrase as a second factor of authentication. The generated password provides identification, and the PIN/passphrase provides authentication.

Asynchronous dynamic password tokens   An *asynchronous dynamic password token* does not use a clock; it generates passwords based on an occurrence of some event. These tokens often generate a password after the user enters a PIN into the token device. The authentication process commonly includes a challenge and a response in which a server sends the user a PIN and the user enters the PIN to create the password. These tokens have a unique seed (or random number) embedded along with a unique identifier for the device. The authentication server also knows the seed and identifier that is assigned to any user.

For example, a user would first submit a username and password to a web page. After validating the user's credentials, the authentication system uses the token's identifier and seed to create a challenge number and sends it back to the user. The challenge number changes each time a user authenticates, so it is often called a nonce (short for "number used once"). The challenge number will only produce the correct one-time password on the device belonging to that user.

The user enters the challenge number into the token and the token creates a password. The user then enters the password into the website to complete the authentication process.

Static tokens   A *static token* can be a swipe card, a smart card, a floppy disk, a USB dongle, or even something as simple as a key for a physical lock. Static tokens often require an additional factor to provide authentication, such as a password or biometric factor.

Many static token devices host a *cryptographic key* such as a *private key*, *digital signature*, or encrypted *logon credentials*. Some disk encryption schemes, such as Microsoft's BitLocker, support the use of a USB startup key. As long as the USB thumb drive with the startup key is inserted into the system when it starts, BitLocker will read the key and unlock the drive.

Biometrics

Another common authentication and identification technique is the use of *biometrics*. *Biometric factors* fall into the Type 3, "something you are," authentication category.

Biometric factors can be used as an identifying or authentication technique, or both. Using a biometric factor instead of a username or account ID as an identification factor requires a one-to-many search of the offered biometric pattern against a stored database of enrolled and authorized patterns. Capturing a single image of a person and searching a database of many people looking for a match is an example of a one-to-many search. As an identification technique, biometric factors are used in physical access controls.

Using a biometric factor as an authentication technique requires a one-to-one match of the offered biometric pattern against a stored pattern for the offered subject identity. In other words, the user claims an identity, and the biometric factor is checked to see if the person matches the claimed identity. As an authentication technique, biometric factors are used in logical access controls.

Biometric characteristics are often defined as either physiological or behavioral. Physiological biometric methods include fingerprints, face scans, retina scans, iris scans, palm scans (also known as palm topography or palm geography), hand geometry, and voice patterns. Behavioral biometric methods include signature dynamics and keystroke patterns (keystroke dynamics). These are sometimes referred to as "something you do" authentication.

Fingerprints   Fingerprints are the visible patterns on the fingers and thumbs of people. They are unique to an individual and have been used for decades in physical security for identification. Fingerprint readers are now commonly used on laptop computers and USB flash drives as a method of identification and authentication.

Face scans   *Face scans* utilize the geometric patterns of faces for detection and recognition. If you've ever watched the TV show *Las Vegas*, you've probably seen how they can take a picture of a person and then match the characteristics of the face against a database. This allows them to quickly identify a person. Similarly, face scans are used to identify and authenticate people before accessing secure spaces such as a secure vault.

Retina scans   *Retina scans* focus on the pattern of blood vessels at the back of the eye. They are the most accurate form of biometric authentication and are able to differentiate between identical twins. However, they are the least acceptable biometric scanning means because retina scans can reveal medical conditions, such as high blood pressure and pregnancy. Older retinal scans blew a puff of air into the user's eye, but newer ones typically use an infrared light instead.

Iris scans   Focusing on the colored area around the pupil, *iris scans* are the second most accurate form of biometric authentication. Iris scans are often recognized as having a longer useful authentication life span than other biometric factors because the iris remains relatively unchanged throughout a person's life (barring eye damage or illness). Iris scans are considered more acceptable by general users than retina scans because they don't reveal personal medical information. Some scanners can be fooled with a high-quality image in place of a person's eye. Additionally, accuracy can be affected by changes in lighting.

Palm scans   *Palm scans*, sometimes called palm topography or palm geography, scan the palm of the hand for identification. They use near-infrared light to measure vein patterns in the palm, which are as unique as fingerprints. Individuals don't need to touch the scanner but instead place their palm over a scanner. For example, Boca Ciega High School in Gulfport, Florida, replaced fingerprint scanners with palm scanners to identify students in their lunch lines, and some hospitals are also starting to use palm scanners. Some palm scanners include the fingers and measure the layout of ridges, creases, and grooves, as a full hand scan.

Hand geometry   Hand geometry recognizes the physical dimensions of the hand. This includes the width and length of the palm and fingers. It captures a silhouette of the hand, but not the details of fingerprints or vein patterns. Hand geometry is rarely used by itself since it is difficult to uniquely identify an individual using this method.

Heart/pulse patterns   Measuring the user's pulse or heartbeat ensures that a real person is providing the biometric factor. It is often employed as a secondary biometric to support another type of authentication. Some researchers theorize that heartbeats are unique between individuals and claim it is possible to use electrocardiography for authentication. However, a reliable method has not been created or fully tested.

Voice pattern recognition   This type of biometric authentication relies on the characteristics of a person's speaking voice, known as a voiceprint. The user speaks a specific phrase, which is recorded by the authentication system. To authenticate, they repeat the same phrase and it is compared to the original. *Voice pattern recognition* is sometimes used as an additional authentication mechanism but rarely used by itself.

> Speech recognition is commonly confused with voice pattern recognition, but they are different. Speech recognition software, such as dictation software, extracts communications from sound. In other words, voice pattern recognition differentiates between one voice and another for identification or authentication, while speech recognition differentiates between words within any person's voice.

Signature dynamics   This recognizes how a subject writes a string of characters. *Signature dynamics* examine both how a subject performs the act of writing and features in a written sample. The success of signature dynamics relies upon pen pressure, stroke pattern, stroke length, and the points in time when the pen is lifted from the writing surface. The speed at which the written sample is created is usually not an important factor.

Keystroke patterns   *Keystroke patterns* (also known as *keystroke dynamics*) measure how a subject uses a keyboard by analyzing flight time and dwell time. *Flight time* is how long it takes between key presses, and *dwell time* is how long a key is pressed. Using keystroke patterns is inexpensive, nonintrusive, and often transparent to the user (for both use and enrollment). Unfortunately, keystroke patterns are subject to wild variances. Simple changes in user behavior greatly affect this biometric factor, such as using only one hand, being cold, standing rather than sitting, changing keyboards, or sustaining an injury to the hand or a finger.

The use of biometrics promises universally unique identification for every person on the planet. Unfortunately, biometric technology has yet to live up to this promise. For biometric factors to be useful, they must be extremely sensitive.

Biometric Factor Error Ratings

The most important aspect of a biometric device is its accuracy. To use biometrics for identification, a biometric device must be able to detect minute differences in information, such as variations in the blood vessels in a person's retina or tones and timbres in their voice. Because most people are basically similar, biometric methods often result in false negative and false positive authentications. Biometric devices are rated for performance by examining the different types of errors they produce.

Type 1 error   A Type 1 error occurs when a valid subject is not authenticated. This is also known as a false negative authentication. For example, Dawn could use her fingerprint to authenticate herself, but the system incorrectly rejects her valid fingerprint. The ratio of Type 1 errors to valid authentications is known as the *false rejection rate (FRR)*.

Type 2 error   A Type 2 error occurs when an invalid subject is authenticated. This is also known as a false positive authentication. The ratio of Type 2 errors to valid authentications is called the *false acceptance rate (FAR)*. For example, hacker Joe doesn't have an account but he uses his fingerprint to authenticate and the system recognizes him.

Most biometric devices have a sensitivity adjustment. When a biometric device is too sensitive, Type 1 errors (false negatives) are more common. When a biometric device is not sensitive enough, Type 2 errors (false positives) are more common.

You can compare the overall quality of biometric devices with the *crossover error rate (CER)*, also known as the equal error rate (ERR). Figure 1.2 shows the FRR and FAR percentages when a device is set to different sensitivity levels. The point where the FRR and FAR percentages are equal is the CER, and the CER is used as a standard assessment value to compare the accuracy of different biometric devices. Devices with lower CERs are more accurate than devices with higher CERs.

FIGURE 1.2   Graph of FRR and FAR errors indicating the CER point

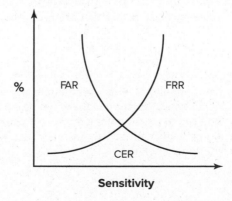

It's not necessary, and often not desirable, to operate a device with the sensitivity set at the CER level. For example, an organization may use a facial recognition system to allow or deny access to a secure area because they want to ensure that unauthorized individuals are never granted access. In this case, the organization would set the sensitivity very high so there is very little chance of a Type 2 error (false acceptance). This may result in more false rejections, but a false rejection is more acceptable than a possible false acceptance.

Biometric Registration

Biometric devices can be ineffective or unacceptable due to factors known as enrollment time, throughput rate, and acceptance. For a biometric device to work as an identification or authentication mechanism, a process called *enrollment* (or registration) must take place, during which a subject's biometric factor must be sampled and stored in the device's database. The stored sample of a biometric factor is called a *reference profile* (also known as a *reference template*).

The time required to scan and store a biometric factor depends on which physical or performance characteristic is measured. The longer it takes to enroll using a biometric mechanism, the less willingly the user community accepts the inconvenience. In general, enrollment times over 2 minutes are unacceptable. If you use a biometric characteristic that changes over time, such as a person's voice tones, facial hair, or signature pattern, reenrollment must occur at regular intervals, adding inconvenience.

The *throughput rate* is the amount of time the system requires to scan a subject and approve or deny access. The more complex or detailed a biometric characteristic, the longer processing takes. Subjects typically accept a throughput rate of about 6 seconds or faster.

Multifactor Authentication

Multifactor authentication is any authentication using two or more factors. *Two-factor authentication* requires two different factors to provide authentication. For example, when using a debit card at the grocery store, you must usually swipe the card ("something you have") and enter a PIN ("something you know") to complete the transaction. Similarly, smart cards almost always require users to insert their card into a reader and also enter a PIN. As a general rule, the more types of factors that are used, the more secure is the resultant authentication.

Multifactor authentication must use multiple *types* of factor, such as the "something you know" factor and the "something you have" factor. For example, requiring users to enter a password and a PIN is not multifactor authentication because both methods are from a single authentication factor ("something you know").

When two authentication methods of the same factor are used together, the strength of the authentication is no greater than it would be if just one method were used because the same attack that could steal or obtain one could also obtain the other. For example, using two passwords together is no more secure than using a single password because a password-cracking attempt could discover both in a single successful attack or the user might write both passwords on the same piece of paper.

In contrast, when two or more different factors are employed, two or more different methods of attack must succeed to collect all relevant authentication elements. For example, if a token, a password, and a biometric factor are all used for authentication, then a physical theft, a password crack, and a biometric duplication attack must all succeed simultaneously to allow an intruder to gain entry into the system.

Access Control Techniques

Once a subject has been identified and authenticated, it must be authorized to access resources or perform actions based on its proven identity. Systems provide authorization to subjects through the use of access controls that manage the type and extent of access granted to subjects for different objects.

There are several categories for access control techniques and the CISSP CIB specifically mentions three: discretionary, nondiscretionary, and mandatory. The following sections introduce some basic security operations principles used by these techniques and describe common access control techniques.

Security Operations Principles

This section provides a short explanation of some common security operations concepts. These are important to understand when reviewing the different access control techniques.

Need to know   This principle ensures that subjects are granted access only to what they need to know for their work tasks and job functions. Subjects may have clearance to access classified or restricted data but are not granted authorization to the data unless they actually need it to perform a job.

Least privilege   This principle ensures that subjects are granted only the privileges they need to perform their work tasks and job functions. This is sometimes lumped together with need to know. The only difference is that least privilege will also include rights to take action on a system.

Separation of duties and responsibilities   This principle ensures that sensitive functions are split into tasks performed by two or more employees. It helps to prevent fraud and errors by creating a system of checks and balances.

Chapter 13, "Security Operations," covers security operations principles in more depth.

Discretionary Access Controls

A system that employs *discretionary access controls (DACs)* allows the owner or creator of an object to control and define subject access to that object. All objects have owners, and access control is based on the discretion or decision of the owner.
For example, if a user creates a new spreadsheet file, that user is the owner of the file. As the owner, the user can modify the permissions of the file to grant or deny access to other users.

DAC is also referred to as identity-based access control because access is granted to subjects based on their identity. The identity is typically based on a user's account, but it can also be based on their membership in a group.

A DAC model is implemented using access control lists (ACLs) on objects. Each ACL defines the types of access granted or denied to subjects. It does not offer a centrally controlled management system because owners can alter the ACLs on their objects at will. Access to objects is easy to change, especially when compared to the static nature of mandatory access controls.

Within a DAC environment, users' privileges can easily be suspended while they are on vacation, resumed when they return, or terminated when they leave an organization.

Here are some distinguishing points about DAC: Every object has an owner, and owners have full control over their objects. Permissions are maintained in an ACL, and owners can easily change permissions. This makes the model very flexible.

Nondiscretionary Access Controls

The major difference between discretionary and *nondiscretionary access controls* is in how they are controlled and managed. Administrators centrally administer nondiscretionary access controls and can make changes that affect the entire environment. In contrast, with discretionary access controls, owners can make their own changes, and their changes don't affect other parts of the environment.

In a non-DAC model, access does not focus on user identity. Instead, a static set of rules governing the whole environment is used to manage access. Non-DAC systems are centrally controlled and easier to manage (although less flexible). Rule-based access controls and lattice-based access controls are both considered nondiscretionary.

Rule-based Access Controls

Rule-based access controls are used in a rule-based system. A set of rules, restrictions, or filters determines what can and cannot occur on the system, such as granting a subject access to an object or granting the ability to perform an action.

We utilize acronyms throughout this book to conserve space and to make terms easier to memorize. On the exam, you will be tested with all terms and acronyms spelled out, so there will be no confusion between a rule-based access control (RBAC) system and a role-based access control (RBAC) system. Study each system and its defining characteristics carefully, but you don't need to memorize the acronyms.

In general, rule-based access control systems are more appropriate for environments that experience frequent changes to data permissions, such as changes to the security domain or the labels for objects. Rule-based systems can implement sweeping changes just by changing centralized rules without having to manipulate or "touch" every subject and/or object in the environment. However, in most cases, once rules are established, they remain fairly static and unchanged throughout the life of the environment.

A common example of a rule-based access control system is a firewall. A firewall is governed by a set of rules or filters defined by the administrator. The firewall examines all the traffic going through it and allows only traffic that meets a specific rule. Firewalls often include a final rule denying all other traffic. In other words, if traffic didn't meet the condition of any previous rule, then the final rule ensures that the traffic is blocked. This final rule is sometimes explicitly stated, but an ACL can also include an implicit deny rule.

Lattice-Based Access Controls

Many nondiscretionary access controls can be labeled as *lattice-based access controls*. Lattice-based access controls were originally developed to address information flow, which primarily concerns itself with confidentiality. Lattice-based access controls define upper and lower bounds of access for every relationship between a subject and an object. These boundaries usually follow military or corporate security label levels (although they can also be arbitrary).

A subject with the lattice permissions shown in Figure 1.3 can access resources up to Private and down to Sensitive but cannot access resources labeled Confidential/Proprietary or Public. Subjects under lattice-based access controls acquire a least upper bound and a greatest lower bound of access to labeled objects based on their assigned lattice positions. A common example of a lattice-based access control is a mandatory access control.

FIGURE 1.3   A representation of the boundaries provided by lattice-based access controls

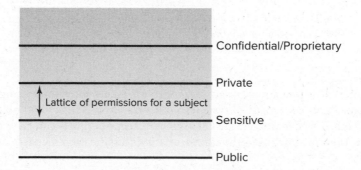

Mandatory Access Controls

A *mandatory access control* (MAC) system relies upon the use of classification labels. Each classification label represents a security *domain*, or a realm of security. A security domain is a collection of subjects and objects that share a common security policy. For example, a security domain could have the label Secret, and all objects with the Secret label would be protected in the same manner. Similarly, the requirement for subjects to gain the Secret label is the same for all subjects.

Mandatory access controls are often considered to be nondiscretionary controls because they are lattice based. However, the CISSP CIB lists them separately, so we have covered them separately in this chapter.

Subjects are labeled by their level of clearance, which is a form of privilege. Objects are labeled by their level of classification or sensitivity. For example, the military uses the labels of top secret, secret, confidential, sensitive but unclassified (SBU), and unclassified to classify its data. Businesses in the private sector often use labels such as confidential (or proprietary), private, sensitive, and public. Chapter 5 discusses data classification topics in more depth.

Once the labels are identified and assigned to subjects and objects, the system determines access based on the labels. In a MAC system, subjects are able to access objects that have the same or a lower level of classification. For example, someone with a secret clearance and secret label is approved to access any data marked as secret or lower.

An expansion of this access control method is known as *need to know*. Subjects with specific clearance levels are granted access to resources only if their work tasks require such access. In other words, someone with a secret clearance and a secret label is not automatically authorized to access all secret data. If they don't have a need to know the information, they are denied access, even if they have sufficient clearance.

Mandatory access control is prohibitive rather than permissive, and it uses an implicit deny philosophy. If access is not specifically granted, it is forbidden. It is generally recognized as being more secure than DAC, but it isn't as flexible or scalable.

A distinguishing factor between MAC and rule-based access controls is that MAC controls have labels while the nondiscretionary rule-based access controls do not use labels.

Using security labels in mandatory access controls presents some interesting problems. First, for a mandatory access control system to function, every subject and object must have a security label. Depending on the environment, security labels can refer to sensitivity, value to the organization, need for confidentiality, classification, department, project, and so on. A large environment with multiple classifications, subjects, and objects becomes increasingly difficult to manage.

Security classifications indicate a hierarchy of sensitivity. For example, if you consider the military security labels of top secret, secret, confidential, sensitive but unclassified (SBU), and unclassified, the top secret label includes the most sensitive data and unclassified is the least sensitive. Because of this hierarchy, it's logical that if someone is cleared for top secret data, they would also be cleared for secret and less-sensitive data. However, classifications don't have to include lower levels. It is possible to use MAC labels so that a clearance for a higher-level label does not include clearance for a lower-level label.

A distinguishing point about the MAC model is that every object and every subject has a label. These labels are predefined and the system makes a determination of access based on them.

Additionally, it's possible to segment or compartmentalize labels within each level. For example, instead of a single top secret label, objects can be further identified with labels for multiple compartments within a level. The top secret level could have compartments called CISSP Student, CISSP Associate, and CISSP Professional with matching labels. Subjects will be authorized access to only the specific compartment based on their labels.

Classifications within a MAC model use one of the following three types of environment:

Hierarchical environment   A *hierarchical environment* relates various classification labels in an ordered structure from low security to medium security to high security. Each level or classification label in the structure is related. Clearance in one level grants the subject access to objects in that level as well as to all objects in all lower levels but prohibits access to all objects in higher levels.

Compartmentalized environment   In a *compartmentalized environment*, there is no relationship between one security domain and another. Each domain represents a separate isolated compartment. To gain access to an object, the subject must have specific clearance for its security domain.

Hybrid environment   A *hybrid environment* combines both hierarchical and compartmentalized concepts so that each hierarchical level may contain numerous subdivisions that are isolated from the rest of the security domain. A subject must have the correct clearance and also the need to know for a specific compartment to gain access to the compartmentalized object. A hybrid MAC environment provides more granular control over access but becomes increasingly difficult to manage as it grows.

Role-Based Access Control

Systems that employ role-based or task-based access controls define a subject's ability to access an object based on the subject's role or assigned tasks. Roles are commonly identified by job descriptions or work functions. If a subject occupies a management position, it will have greater access to resources than a subject who is in a temporary job. Role-based access controls are useful in dynamic environments with frequent personnel changes because access depends on a role rather than on subject identity.

Role-based access control (RBAC) is often implemented using groups. For example, a bank may have tellers, loan officers, and managers. Administrators can create groups named Tellers, Loan Officers, and Managers and assign privileges to the groups based on their needs. Any user account placed into one of the groups automatically has the privileges granted to that group. Additionally, as soon as a user is removed from a group, they no longer have the privileges assigned to the group. This helps enforce the principle of least privilege.

> RBAC is sometimes called a discretionary model, and other times it's called a nondiscretionary model. While people can get into spirited debates over which it is, the category it falls into isn't important for the CISSP exam. It is important to know that access is based on the subject's job, role, or assigned tasks.

It's easy to confuse DAC and RBAC because they can both use groups, but they differ in their deployment and use.

DAC and RBAC are similar in that groups can be used in both and they serve as containers to organize users into manageable units.

However, in a strict RBAC system, users have only the privileges granted by assignment to a role—privileges are not assigned to users directly. Furthermore, access is not determined by owner discretion, as it is in DAC. Access is derived from the inherent responsibilities of an assigned role based on the job description and not on the user's identity. Two different users with the same assigned role will have the same access and privileges.

Another method related to RBAC is called *task-based access control (TBAC)*. TBAC is basically the same as RBAC, but instead of being assigned a single role, each user is assigned an array of tasks. These items all relate to assigned work tasks for the person associated with a user account. Under TBAC, the focus is on controlling access by assigned tasks rather than by user identity.

> A distinguishing point about the role-based access control model is that access is granted based on membership in a role. Roles can be created based on jobs or tasks, and privileges can be assigned to the role.

Centralized versus Decentralized Access Control

Access control techniques generally fall into one of two categories: centralized and decentralized/distributed.

- *Centralized access control* implies that all authorization verification is performed by a single entity within a system.
- *Decentralized access control* (also known as *distributed access control*) implies that various entities located throughout a system perform authorization verification.

Centralized and decentralized access control methodologies offer the same benefits and drawbacks found in any centralized or decentralized system. A small team or individual can manage centralized access control. Administrative overhead is lower because all changes are made in a single location and a single change affects the entire system. Decentralized access control often requires several teams or multiple individuals. Administrative overhead is higher because changes must be implemented across numerous locations. Maintaining consistency across a system becomes more difficult as the number of access control points increases. Changes made to any individual access control point need to be repeated at every access point.

Within a single organization, a centralized access control system is often used. For example, a *directory service* is a centralized database of objects that includes information about resources available to a network along with information about subjects such as users and computers. You can think of it as a telephone directory for network services and assets. Users, clients, and processes consult the directory service to learn where a desired system or resource resides. Subjects must authenticate to the directory service before performing queries and lookup activities. Even after authentication, the directory service will reveal only certain information to a subject, based on that subject's assigned privileges.

 Directory services are often based on the Lightweight Directory Access Protocol (LDAP). Microsoft's Active Directory and Novell's NetWare Directory Services (NDS), now known as eDirectory, are well-known directory services.

Multiple domains and trusts are commonly used in decentralized access control systems. As mentioned previously, a security domain is a collection of subjects and objects that share a common security policy, and individual domains can operate separately from other domains. *Trusts* are established between the domains to create a security bridge and allow users from one domain to access resources in another. Trusts can be one way only, or they can be two way.

Both centralized and decentralized access control systems can be used to support single sign-on capabilities.

Single Sign-On

Single sign-on (SSO) is a centralized access control technique that allows a subject to be authenticated only once on a system and to access multiple resources without repeated authentication prompts. For example, users can authenticate once on a network and then access resources throughout the network without being required to authenticate again.

SSO is very convenient for users, but it also increases security. When users have to remember multiple usernames and passwords, they often resort to writing them down, ultimately weakening security. Users are less likely to write down a single password. SSO also eases administration by reducing the number of accounts required for a subject.

The primary disadvantage to SSO is that once an account is compromised, an attacker gains unrestricted access to all of the authorized resources. However, most SSO systems include methods to protect user credentials.

The following sections discuss several common SSO mechanisms.

Kerberos

Ticket authentication is a mechanism that employs a third-party entity to prove identification and provide authentication. The most common and well-known ticket system is *Kerberos.*

The Kerberos name is borrowed from Greek mythology. A three-headed dog named Kerberos guards the gates to the underworld. The dog faces inward, preventing escape rather than denying entrance.

Kerberos provides a single sign-on solution for users and also provides protection for logon credentials. The current version, Kerberos 5, relies upon symmetric-key cryptography (also known as secret-key cryptography) using the Advanced Encryption Standard (AES) symmetric encryption protocol. Kerberos provides confidentiality and integrity for authentication traffic using end-to-end security and helps prevent against eavesdropping and replay attacks. It uses several different elements that are important to understand:

Key distribution center (KDC)   The KDC is the trusted third party that provides authentication services. Kerberos uses symmetric-key cryptography to authenticate clients to servers. All clients and servers are registered with the KDC, and it maintains the secret keys for all network members.

Kerberos authentication server (KAS)   The authentication server hosts the functions of the KDC: a ticket-granting service (TGS), and an authentication service (AS). The *authentication service* verifies or rejects the authenticity and timeliness of tickets. This server is often called the KDC.

Ticket-granting ticket (TGT)   A TGT provides proof that a subject has authenticated through a KDC and is authorized to request tickets to access other objects. A TGT is encrypted and includes a symmetric key, an expiration time, and the user's IP address. Subjects present the TGT when requesting tickets to access objects.

Ticket   A ticket is an encrypted message that provides proof that a subject is authorized to access an object. It is sometimes called a service ticket (ST). Subjects request tickets to access objects, and if they have authenticated and are authorized (based on having a TGT), they are given a ticket. Kerberos tickets have specific lifetimes and usage parameters. Once a ticket expires, a client must request a renewal or a new ticket to continue communications with any server.

Kerberos requires a database of accounts, which is often contained in a directory service. It uses an exchange of tickets between clients, network servers, and the KDC to prove identity and provide authentication. This allows a client to request resources from the server with both the client and server having assurances of the identity of the other. These encrypted tickets also ensure that logon credentials, session keys, and authentication messages are never transmitted in cleartext.

The Kerberos logon process is as follows:

1. The user types a username and password into the client.
2. The client encrypts the credentials with AES for transmission to the KDC.
3. The KDC verifies the user credentials against a database of known credentials.
4. The KDC generates an encrypted time-stamped TGT.
5. The TGT is encrypted with AES before transmission to the client.
6. The client installs the TGT for use until it expires.

When a client wants to access an object, such as a resource, hosted on the network, it must request a ticket through the Kerberos server. The following steps are involved in this process:

1. The client sends its TGT back to the KDC with a request for access to the resource.
2. The KDC verifies that the TGT is valid and checks its access control matrix to verify that the user has sufficient privileges to access the requested resource.
3. The KDC generates a service ticket and sends it to the client.
4. The client sends the ticket to the server or service hosting the resource.
5. The server or service hosting the resource verifies the validity of the ticket with the KDC.
6. Once identity and authorization is verified, Kerberos activity is complete. The server or service host then opens a session with the client and begins communications or data transmission.

Kerberos is a versatile authentication mechanism that works over local LANs, remote access, and client-server resource requests. However, Kerberos presents a single point of failure—the KDC. If the KDC is compromised, the secret key for every system on the network is also compromised. Also, if a KDC goes offline, no subject authentication can occur.

Kerberos also has strict time requirements, and the default configuration requires that all systems be time-synchronized within five minutes of each other. If a system is not synchronized or the time is changed, a previously issued TGT will no longer be valid and the system will not be able to receive any new tickets. In effect, the client will be denied access to any protected network resources.

Federated Identity Management and SSO

SSO has been common on internal networks for quite a while, but not on the Internet. However, with the explosion of cloud-based applications, an SSO solution has been needed for users accessing resources over the Internet. Federated identity management is often used as a form of decentralized or distributed access control to support this need.

Identity management is the management of user identities and their credentials. Federated identity management extends this beyond a single organization. Multiple organizations can join a federation, or group, where they agree on a method to share identities between them. Users in each organization can log on once in their own organization and their credentials are matched with a federated identity. They can then use this federated identity to access resources in any other organization within the group.

A federation can be composed of multiple unrelated networks within a single university campus, multiple college and university campuses, multiple organizations sharing resources, or any other group that can agree on a common federated identity management system. User credentials within an organization are matched with a federated identity.

Many corporate online training websites use federated SSO systems. When the organization coordinates with the online training company for employee access, they also coordinate the details needed for federated access. These are managed behind the scenes and are usually transparent to users. Users simply access the training website using a web browser and they are automatically authenticated without any further action. Based on their identities, they are then given access to appropriate training courses.

A challenge with multiple companies communicating together is finding a common language. They often have different operating systems, but they still need to share a common language. Federated identity systems often use the Service Provisioning Markup Language (SPML). As background, here's a short description of some markup languages.

Hypertext Markup Language (HTML)   Commonly used to display static web pages. HTML was derived from the Standard Generalized Markup Language (SGML) and the Generalized Markup Language (GML). HTML describes how data is displayed using tags to manipulate the size and color of the text. For example, the following H1 tag causes the heading to be displayed as a level one heading: `<H1>I Passed The CISSP</H1>`.

Extensible Markup Language (XML)   XML goes beyond just describing how the data is displayed and describes the data. XML can include tags to describe data as anything desired. For example, the following tag identifies the data as the results of taking an exam: `<CISSPExamResults>Passed</CISSPExamResults>`.

Databases from multiple vendors can import and export data to and from an XML format, which means that XML is a common language used to exchange information. Many specific schemas have been created so that companies know exactly what tags are being used for specific purposes.

Security Assertion Markup Language (SAML)   Security Assertion Markup Language is an XML-based language that is commonly used to exchange authentication and authorization (AA) information between federated organizations. It is often used to provide SSO capabilities for browser access.

Service Provisioning Markup Language (SPML)   SPML is a newer framework based on XML but specifically designed for exchanging user information for federated identity single sign-on purposes. It is based on the Directory Service Markup Language (DSML), which can display LDAP-based directory service information in an XML format.

Extensible Access Control Markup Language (XACML)   XACML is used to define access control policies within an XML format, and it commonly implements role-based access controls. It helps provide assurances to all members in a federation that they are granting the same level of access to different roles.

Other Examples of Single Sign-On

Although Kerberos may be the most widely recognized and deployed form of single sign-on, it is not the only one of its kind. In this section, we summarize other SSO mechanisms you may encounter.

Scripted access or *logon scripts* establish communication links by providing an automated process by which logon credentials are transmitted to resource hosts at the start of a logon session. Scripted access can often simulate SSO even though the environment still requires a unique authentication process to connect to each server or resource. Scripts can be used to implement SSO in environments where true SSO technologies are not available. Scripts and batch files should be stored in a protected area because they usually contain access credentials.

The *Secure European System for Applications in a Multivendor Environment (SESAME)* is a ticket-based authentication system developed to address weaknesses in Kerberos. However, it did not compensate for all the problems with Kerberos. Eventually, later Kerberos versions and various vendor implementations resolved the initial problems with Kerberos, bypassing SESAME. In the professional security world, SESAME is no longer considered a viable product.

KryptoKnight is a ticket-based authentication system developed by IBM. It is similar to Kerberos but uses peer-to-peer authentication instead of a third party. It was incorporated into the NetSP product. Like SESAME, KryptoKnight and NetSP never took off and are no longer widely used.

AAA Protocols

Several protocols are designed to provide authentication, authorization, and accounting and are sometimes referred to as AAA protocols. These are commonly used with remote access systems such as virtual private networks (VPNs) and other types of network access servers to provide centralized access control. They prevent internal LAN authentication systems and other servers from being attacked remotely. When a separate system is used for remote access, only the remote access users are affected if this system is successfully attacked. In other words, the attacker won't have access to internal accounts. The AAA protocols are also commonly used for mobile IP, which provides access to mobile users with smart phones.

These AAA protocols use the access control elements of identification, authentication, authorization, and accountability as described in "Access Control Elements," earlier in this chapter. They ensure that users have valid credentials to authenticate and verify that the user is authorized to connect to the remote access server based on the user's proven identity. Additionally, the accounting element can track the user's network resource usage and can be used for billing purposes. Some common AAA protocols are RADIUS, TACACS+, and Diameter.

RADIUS

Remote Authentication Dial-in User Service (RADIUS) centralizes authentication for remote dial-up connections. It is typically used when an organization has more than one remote access server. A user can connect to any remote access server, which then passes on the user's credentials to the RADIUS server to verify authentication and authorization and to track accounting. In this context, the remote access server is the RADIUS client and a RADIUS server will provide AAA services for multiple remote access servers.

Many Internet service providers (ISPs) use RADIUS for authentication. Users can access the ISP from anywhere and the ISP server then forwards the user's connection request to the RADIUS server. Organizations can also use RADIUS; it is often implemented with callback security for an extra layer of protection. Users call in, and after authentication, the RADIUS server terminates the connection and initiates a call back to the user's predefined phone number. If a user's authentication credentials are compromised, the callback security prevents an attacker from using them.

RADIUS uses the User Datagram Protocol (UDP) and encrypts only the exchange of the password. It doesn't encrypt the entire session, but additional protocols can be used to encrypt the data session. The current version is defined in RFC 2865.

TACACS+

Terminal Access Controller Access-Control System (TACACS) was introduced as an alternative to RADIUS. Cisco later introduced extended TACACS (XTACACS) as a proprietary protocol. However, TACACS and XTACACS are not commonly used today. TACACS Plus (TACACS+) was later created as an open publicly documented protocol, and it is the most commonly used of the three.

TACACS+ provides several improvements over the earlier versions and over RADIUS. It separates authentication, authorization, and accounting into separate processes, which can actually be hosted on three separate servers if desired. The other versions combine two or three of these processes. Additionally, TACACS+ encrypts all of the authentication information, not just the password as RADIUS does. TACACS and XTACACS used UDP port 49, while TACACS+ uses Transmission Control Protocol (TCP) port 49, providing a higher level of reliability for the packet transmissions.

Diameter

Building on the success of RADIUS and TACACS+, an enhanced version of RADIUS named Diameter was developed. It supports a wide range of protocols, including traditional IP, Mobile IP, and Voice over IP (VoIP). Because it supports extra commands, it is becoming popular in situations where roaming support is desirable, such as with wireless devices and smart phones.

Diameter uses TCP port 3868 or Stream Control Transmission Protocol (SCTP) port 3868, providing better reliability than UDP used by RADIUS. It also supports Internet Protocol Security (IPsec) and Transport Layer Security (TLS) for encryption.

> In geometry, the radius of a circle is the distance from the center to an edge, and the diameter is twice the radius going from edge to edge through the circle. The Diameter name implies that Diameter is twice as good as RADIUS. While that may not be exactly true, it is an improvement over RADIUS and helps to reinforce that Diameter came later and is an improvement.

Authorization Mechanisms

There are many different types of authorization mechanisms, or methods used to control who can access specific objects. This section provides a brief introduction to some common mechanisms.

Implicit Deny   A basic principle of access control is implicit deny. Most authorization mechanisms use it. The implicit deny principle ensures that access to an object is denied unless access has been explicitly granted to a subject. For example, if Jeff is granted Full Control to a file but no one else is granted access, Jeff is the only user that has access. All other users are denied access.

ACLs on firewalls use this principle. Explicit rules identify traffic that is allowed, and all other traffic is blocked. The last rule in the ACL is a "deny all" rule that specifically blocks all traffic that hasn't been previously allowed. This last rule can be explicitly stated as "deny all" to deny all traffic in or out for any traffic that hasn't been allowed. However, on many firewalls the deny rule is implicit and does not need to be explicitly stated. Configuration settings within the firewall can apply the rule even if it isn't in the ACL.

Access control matrix   An access control matrix is a table that includes subjects, objects, and assigned privileges. When a subject attempts an action, the system evaluates the access control matrix to determine if the subject is authorized.

For example, an access control matrix can include a group of files as the objects and a group of users as the subjects. It will show the exact permissions authorized by each user for each file. Note that this covers much more than a single ACL. In this example, each file within the matrix has a separate ACL that lists the authorized users and their assigned permissions.

Capability tables are another way that an access control matrix can be implemented. They are different from ACLs in that a capability table is created for each subject, such as for each role. For example, a capability table created for the accounting role will include a list of all objects that the accounting role can access and will also include the specific privileges assigned to the accounting role for these objects. In contrast, ACLs are assigned to objects. An ACL for a file would list all the users and/or groups that are authorized access to the file and the specific access granted to each.

> The difference between an ACL and a capability table within an access control matrix is based on the focus or perspective. ACLs are assigned to each *object* and identify access granted to subjects. Capability tables are created for each *subject,* and they identify the objects that the subject can access.

Access control matrices are described in more detail in Chapter 11, "Principles of Security Models, Design, and Capabilities."

Constrained interface   A constrained or restricted interface is implemented within an application to restrict what users can do or see based on their privileges. Users with full privileges have access to all the capabilities of the application. Users with restricted privileges have limited access.

Applications constrain the interface using different methods. A common method is to hide the capability if the user doesn't have permissions to use it. Commands might be available to administrators via a menu or by right-clicking an item, but if a regular user doesn't have permissions, the command does not appear. Other times, the command is shown but is dimmed or disabled. The regular user can see it but will not be able to use it.

Content- or context-dependent control   Some authentication mechanisms control access based on the content of an object or the context of the activity taken by a subject.

Content-dependent access controls restrict access to data based on the content within an object. Database views are commonly used as content-dependent controls. Chapter 7, "Software Development Security," discusses database views in more depth, but in short, a view is a virtual table. It retrieves a limited data set from one or more tables and restricts what users can see. For example, database tables could include customer names, email addresses, phone numbers, and credit card data. A view might show only certain information within these tables, such as only names and email addresses. Users are granted access to content via the view but cannot access the data in the underlying tables.

Context-dependent access controls require specific activity before access is granted. For example, transactions are commonly completed using context-dependent controls. Here's a simple example: Users can't view a web page used to provide credit card information until they begin a purchase transaction. The user's activities are controlled through a specific group of web pages with previous pages setting up the context for future pages.

Date and time controls are also considered context dependent. For example, it's possible to restrict access to computers and applications based on the current day and/or time. If a user tries to access the resource outside the allowed time, they are denied access.

Identity and Access Provisioning Life Cycle

The *identity and access provisioning life cycle* refers to the creation, management, and deletion of accounts. Although these activities may seem mundane, they are essential to a system's access control capabilities. Without properly defined and maintained user accounts, a system is unable to establish accurate identity, perform authentication, provide authorization, or track accountability. As mentioned previously, identification occurs when a subject claims an identity. This identity is most commonly a user account, but it also includes computer accounts and service accounts.

Access control administration is the collection of tasks and duties involved in managing accounts, access, and accountability during the life of the account. These tasks are contained within three main responsibilities of the identity and access provisioning life cycle:

- Provisioning
- Review
- Revocation

Provisioning

An initial step in identity management is the creation of new accounts and provisioning them with appropriate privileges. Creating new user accounts is usually a simple process, but the process must be protected and secured via organizational security policy procedures. User accounts should not be created at an administrator's whim or in response to random requests. Rather, proper provisioning ensures that a specific procedure is followed.

The initial creation of a new user account is often called an *enrollment*. The enrollment process creates a new identity and establishes the factors the system needs to perform authentication. It is critical that the enrollment process be completed fully and accurately. It is also critical that the identity of the individual being enrolled be proved through whatever means your organization deems necessary and sufficient. Photo ID, birth certificate, background check, credit check, security clearance verification, FBI database search, and even calling references are all valid forms of verifying a person's identity before enrolling them in any secured system.

Many organizations have automated provisioning systems. For example, once a person is hired, the HR department completes initial identification and in-processing steps and then forwards a request to the IT department to create an account. Users within the IT department enter information such as the employee's name and their assigned department via an application. The application then creates the account using predefined rules. Automated provisioning systems ensure that accounts are created consistently, such as always creating usernames the same way and treating duplicate usernames consistently. If the policy dictates that usernames are created from first and last names, then the application will create a username as `suziejones` for a user named Suzie Jones. If a second employee is hired with the same name, then the second username might be `suziejones2`.

If the organization is using groups (or roles), the application can automatically add the new user account to the appropriate groups based on the user's department or job responsibilities. The groups will already have appropriate privileges assigned, so this step provisions the account with appropriate privileges.

As part of the hiring process, new employees should be trained on organization security policies and procedures. Before hiring is complete, employees are typically required to review and sign an agreement committing to uphold the organization's security standards. This often includes an acceptable usage policy. Chapter 5 covers the importance of developing and managing a security education, training, and awareness program to ensure that employees are aware of the organization's policies and procedures.

Throughout the life of a user account, ongoing maintenance is required. Organizations with fairly static organizational hierarchies and low employee turnover or promotion will conduct significantly less account administration than an organization with a flexible or dynamic organizational hierarchy and high employee turnover and promotion rates. Most account maintenance deals with altering rights and privileges. Procedures similar to those used when creating new accounts should be established to govern how access is changed throughout the life of a user account. Unauthorized increases or decreases in an account's access capabilities can cause serious security repercussions.

Account Review

Accounts should be reviewed periodically to ensure that security policies are being enforced. This includes ensuring that inactive accounts are disabled and employees do not have excessive privileges.

Many administrators use scripts to periodically check for inactive accounts. For example, if an account has not been logged into in the past 30 days, the script can disable and isolate the account. Similarly, scripts can be used to ensure that membership in privileged administrator groups is limited to specific users. When other users are added to these groups, the script can automatically remove them.

Account review is often formalized in auditing procedures. Chapter 2 covers assessing the effectiveness of access control, including the ability to assess user entitlement and perform access reviews and audits.

Excessive Privilege and Creeping Privileges

It's important to guard against two problems related to access control: excessive privilege and creeping privileges. *Excessive privilege* occurs when users have more privileges than their assigned work tasks dictate. If a user account is discovered to have excessive privileges, the unnecessary privileges should be immediately revoked. *Creeping privileges* involve a user account accumulating privileges over time as job roles and assigned tasks change. This can occur because new tasks are added to a user's job and additional privileges are added but no privileges are ever removed, even if the user no longer needs them. Creeping privileges result in excessive privilege.

Both of these situations violate the basic security principle of least privilege, and account reviews are effective at discovering these problems.

Account Revocation

When employees leave an organization for any reason, their user accounts should be disabled as soon as possible. Additionally, if an employee takes a leave of absence, their account should be disabled to prevent access while they are gone. Whenever possible, this task should be automated and tied into the HR department. For example, if an employee is terminated, the account should be disabled during the exit interview.

If a terminated employee retains access to a user account after the exit interview, the risk for sabotage is very high. Even if the employee doesn't take malicious action, someone else may be able to use the account if they discover the password. The activity will be logged in the name of the terminated employee instead of the person actually taking the action. When it's determined that the account is no longer needed, it should be deleted. Deletion of the account is normally done within 30 days after an account is disabled, but it can vary depending on the needs of the organization.

Many systems have the ability to automatically set specific expiration dates for any account. These can be set for temporary or short-term employees when the accounts are created. This maintains a degree of control without requiring ongoing administrative oversight.

 Real World Scenario

Dangers of Failing to Revoke Account Access

Fannie Mae learned firsthand of the dangers of not immediately revoking account access after firing an employee. At about 2 p.m. on October 24, 2008, a UNIX engineer at Fannie Mae was fired. He turned in his badge at 4:45 but he retained administrative access until about 10:00 p.m. that day.

He used his account after being fired to grant himself remote access to Fannie Mae's servers and at some point inserted malicious code in a legitimate script that ran daily at 9 a.m. The full content of his malicious code was set to run on January 31, 2009, as a logic bomb and would have destroyed data on 4,000 Fannie Mae servers. Many experts believe it would have taken Fannie Mae as long as a week to restore functionality if the code ran successfully.

Another engineer discovered the malicious code about a week after the fired employee inserted it so it didn't cause any damage. However, the incident could have been avoided completely by revoking the employee's access immediately.

Summary

The first domain of the CISSP CBK is Access Control. It covers the management, administration, and implementation aspects of granting or restricting subject access to objects. Subjects are active entities (such as users), and objects are passive entities (such as files). Access controls are central to establishing a secure system. They protect against security incidents, which can result in the loss of confidentially, integrity, and/or availability of resources.

Users, owners, and custodians are three specific types of subjects. A user accesses objects such as files on a system. The owner is ultimately responsible for classifying, labeling, and protecting objects. A custodian is delegated day-to-day responsibilities for properly storing and protecting objects.

Three primary types of access controls are preventive, detective, and corrective. Preventive access controls attempt to prevent incidents before they can occur. Detective access controls attempt to detect incidents after they've occurred, and corrective access controls attempt to correct problems caused by incidents once they've been detected.

Controls are implemented as administrative, logical, and physical. Administrative controls are also known as management controls and include policies and procedures. Logical controls are also known as technical controls and are implemented through technology. Physical controls use physical means to protect objects.

Key access control elements include identification, authentication, authorization, and accountability. Subjects claim an identity, which is proved with authentication. The three factors of authentication are "something you know" (such as passwords or PINs), "something you have" (such as smart cards or tokens), and "something you are" (identified with biometrics). Multifactor authentication uses more than one authentication factor, and it is stronger than using any single authentication factor. Once subjects are authenticated, authorization mechanisms control their access and audit trails log their activities so that they can be held accountable for their actions.

There are various models for access control or authorization. These include discretionary, nondiscretionary, mandatory, and role-based access controls. With discretionary access controls, all objects have an owner, and the owner has full control over the object. Nondiscretionary controls are centrally controlled by an administrator. Mandatory access controls require all objects to have labels, and the access is based on subjects having a matching label. Role-based access controls use roles, and these roles are granted appropriate privileges based on jobs or tasks. Subjects are placed into roles and they inherit the privileges assigned to the roles.

Single sign-on allows users to authenticate once and access any resources in a network without authenticating again. Kerberos is a popular single sign-on authentication protocol using ticket authentication for identification and authentication. Kerberos uses a database of subjects, symmetric cryptography, and time synchronization of systems to issue tickets.

Federated identity management is a single sign-on solution that can extend beyond a single organization. Multiple organizations create or join a federation and agree on a method to share identities between the organizations. Users can authenticate within their organization and access resources in other organizations without authenticating again.

AAA protocols provide authentication, authorization, and accounting. Popular AAA protocols are RADIUS, TACACS+, and Diameter.

The identity and access provisioning life cycle includes the processes to create, manage, and delete accounts used by subjects. Provisioning includes the initial steps of creating the accounts and ensuring that they are granted appropriate access to objects. As users' jobs change, they often require changes to the initial access, and provisioning includes modifying access while also ensuring that the principle of least privilege is followed. When accounts are no longer needed, they should be disabled as soon as possible and then deleted.

Exam Essentials

Know the difference between subjects and objects and know common subject labels.   You'll find that CISSP questions and security documentation commonly use the terms *subject* and *object*, so it's important to know the difference between them. Subjects are active entities (such as users) that access passive objects (such as files). A user is a subject who accesses objects in the course of performing some action or accomplishing a work task. The owner is the subject responsible for classifying and labeling objects and for protecting and storing data on any system. A custodian has day-to-day responsibilities for protecting and storing objects.

Know the various types of access control.   You should be able to identify the type of any given access control. Access controls may be preventive (to stop unwanted or unauthorized activity from occurring), detective (to discover unwanted or unauthorized activity), or corrective (to restore systems to normal after an unwanted or unauthorized activity has occurred). Other access controls are deterrent (to discourage violation of security policy), recovery (to repair or restore resources, functions and capabilities after a violation of security policy has occurred), directive (to direct, confine, or control the action of subjects to force or encourage compliance with security policy), or compensation (to provide various options to other existing controls to aid in enforcement and support of security policy). Additionally, controls are implemented as administrative (policies or procedures to implement and enforce overall access control), logical/technical (hardware or software mechanisms used to manage access to resources and systems and to provide protection for those resources and systems), and physical (physical barriers deployed to prevent direct contact with systems or areas within a facility).

Understand the difference between identification, authentication, and authorization.   Access controls depend on effective identification, authentication, and authorization, so it's important to understand the differences among them. Subjects claim an identity, and identification can be as simple as a username for a user. Subjects prove their identity by providing authentication credentials such as the matching password for a username. Subjects are then granted authorization to objects based on their proven identity.

Understand the details of the three authentication factors.   The three factors of authentication are something you know (such as a password or PIN), something you have (such as a smart card or token), and something you are (based on biometrics). Multifactor authentication includes two or more authentication factors, and using it is more secure than using a single authentication factor. Passwords are the weakest form of authentication, but password policies help increase their security by enforcing complexity and history requirements. Smart cards include microprocessors and cryptographic certificates, and tokens create one-time passwords. Biometric methods identify users based on characteristics such as fingerprints. The accuracy of a biometric method is identified by the crossover error rate, where Type 1 errors (false rejection rate) are equal to Type 2 errors (false acceptance rate).

Know details about each of the access control techniques.   There are several categories of access control techniques commonly tested on the CISSP exam, including discretionary, nondiscretionary, mandatory, and role-based access controls. With discretionary controls, all objects have owners and the owners can modify permissions. Nondiscretionary controls are centrally managed, such as rules on a firewall. Mandatory access controls use labels for subjects and objects, and matching labels are required for access. Role-based access controls use task-based roles and users gain privileges when their accounts are placed within a role.

Identify common authorization mechanisms.   Authorization ensures that the requested activity or object access is possible given the privileges assigned to the authenticated identity. Common authorization mechanisms include implicit deny, access control matrices, access control lists, constrained interfaces, and content- or context-dependent controls.

Understand single sign-on.   Single sign-on (SSO) is a mechanism that allows a subject to be authenticated once on a system and be able to access multiple objects without authenticating again. It is commonly used within and between organizations, so it's an important mechanism to understand. Kerberos is the most common SSO method used within organizations, and it uses symmetric cryptography and tickets to prove identification and provide authentication. When multiple organizations want to use a common SSO system, they often use a federated identity management system, where the federation, or group of organizations, agrees on a common method of authentication. Service Provisioning Markup Language (SPML) is commonly used to share federated identity information. Other SSO methods are scripted access, SESAME and KryptoKnight.

Understand the purpose of AAA protocols. Several protocols provide centralized authentication, authorization, and accounting services and are commonly used for remote access. RADIUS uses UDP and encrypts the password only. TACACS+ uses TCP and encrypts the entire session. Diameter is based on RADIUS and improves many of the weaknesses of RADIUS, but Diameter is not compatible with RADIUS. Diameter is becoming more popular with mobile IP systems such as smart phones.

Understand the identity and access provisioning life cycle. The identity and access provisioning life cycle refers to the creation, management, and deletion of accounts. Provisioning accounts ensures that they have appropriate privileges based on task requirements. Periodic reviews ensure that accounts don't have excessive privileges and thus violate the principle of least privilege. Revocation includes disabling accounts as soon as possible when they are not needed, such as when an employee leaves the company, and deleting them when it's determined they are no longer needed.

Written Lab

1. Name at least seven access control types.
2. Describe the three primary authentication factor types.
3. Name the method that allows users to log on once and access resources in multiple organizations without authenticating again.
4. Identify the three primary elements within the identity and access provisioning life cycle.

Review Questions

1. Which of the following is true related to a subject?
   A. A subject is always a user account.
   B. The subject is always the entity that provides or hosts the information or data.
   C. The subject is always the entity that receives information about or data from the object.
   D. A single entity can never change roles between subject and object.

2. Which of the following is considered a primary goal of access control?
   A. Preserve confidentiality, integrity, and availability of systems.
   B. Ensure that only valid objects can authenticate on a system.
   C. Prevent unauthorized access to subjects.
   D. Ensure that all subjects are authenticated.

3. Which of the following types of access control uses fences, security policies, security awareness training, and antivirus software to stop an unwanted or unauthorized activity from occurring?
   A. Preventive
   B. Detective
   C. Corrective
   D. Authoritative

4. What type of access controls are hardware or software mechanisms used to manage access to resources and systems and to provide protection for those resources and systems?
   A. Administrative
   B. Logical/technical
   C. Physical
   D. Preventive

5. All of the following are needed for system accountability except for one. Which one is not needed?
   A. Identification
   B. Authentication
   C. Auditing
   D. Authorization

6. Which of the following is an example of a Type 2 authentication factor?

   A. "Something you have," such as a smart card, ATM card, token device, and memory card

   B. "Something you are," such as fingerprints, voice print, retina pattern, iris pattern, face shape, palm topology, and hand geometry

   C. "Something you do," such as typing a passphrase, or signing your name

   D. "Something you know," such as a password, personal identification number (PIN), lock combination, passphrase, mother's maiden name, and favorite color

7. Users are given a device that generates one-time passwords every 60 seconds. A server hosted within the organization knows what this password is at any given time. What type of device is this?

   A. Synchronous token

   B. Asynchronous token

   C. Smart card

   D. Common access card

8. What can be used as an authentication factor that is a behavioral or physiological characteristic unique to a subject?

   A. Account ID

   B. Biometric factor

   C. Token

   D. PIV

9. What does the crossover error rate (CER) for a biometric device indicate?

   A. It indicates that the sensitivity is tuned too high.

   B. It indicates that the sensitivity is tuned too low.

   C. It indicates the point where false rejection rate and the false acceptance rate are equal.

   D. It indicates that the biometric device is not properly configured.

10. A biometric system has falsely rejected a valid user, indicating that the user is not recognized. What type of error is this?

    A. Type 1 error

    B. Type 2 error

    C. Crossover error rate

    D. Equal error rate

11. A large table includes multiple subjects and objects. It identifies the specific access each subject has to different objects. What is this table called?

    A. Access control list

    B. Access control matrix

    C. Federation

    D. Creeping privilege

12. What is an access control list (ACL) based on?

    A. An object

    B. A subject

    C. A role

    D. An account

13. What type of access controls rely upon the use of labels?

    A. Discretionary

    B. Nondiscretionary

    C. Mandatory

    D. Role based

14. An organization has created an access control policy that grants specific privileges to accountants. What type of access control is this?

    A. Discretionary

    B. Mandatory

    C. Rule based

    D. Role based

15. Which of the following is not used to support single sign-on?

    A. Kerberos

    B. Federated identity management system

    C. TACACS+

    D. SPML

16. Which of the following is the best choice to support federated identity management systems?

    A. Kerberos

    B. Hypertext Markup Language (HTML)

    C. Extensible Markup Language (XML)

    D. Service Provisioning Markup Language (SPML)

17. Which of the following authentication, authorization, and accounting (AAA) protocols is based on RADIUS and supports Mobile IP and Voice over IP?

    A. Distributed access control

    B. Diameter

    C. TACACS+

    D. TACACS

Refer the following scenario when answering questions 18 through 20:

An administrator has been working within an organization for over 10 years. He has moved between different IT divisions within the company and has retained privileges from each of the jobs that he's had during his tenure. Recently, he has been admonished for making unauthorized changes to systems. He once again made an unauthorized change and this change resulted in an unexpected outage. Management decided to terminate his employment at the company. He was allowed to come back to work the following day to clean out his desk and belongings, and during this time he installed a malicious script that was scheduled to run as a logic bomb on the first day of the following month. The script will change administrator passwords, delete files, and shut down over 100 servers in the data center.

18. Which of the following basic principles was violated while the administrator was employed?

    A. Implicit deny

    B. Loss of availability

    C. Defensive privileges

    D. Least privilege

19. Which of the following concepts was not adequately addressed for the identity and access provisioning life cycle?

    A. Provisioning

    B. Separation of duties

    C. Revocation

    D. Authentication methods

20. What could have discovered problems with this user's account while he was employed?

    A. Policy requiring strong authentication

    B. Multifactor authentication

    C. Logging

    D. Account review

Chapter

2

Access Control Attacks and Monitoring

THE CISSP EXAM TOPICS COVERED IN THIS CHAPTER INCLUDE:

1. Access Control

  A. Control access by applying the following concepts/ methodology/techniques:

    A.7 Logging and monitoring

  B. Understand access control attacks

    B.1 Threat modeling

    B.2 Asset valuation

    B.3 Vulnerability analysis

    B.4 Access aggregation

  C. Assess effectiveness of access controls

    C.1 User entitlement

    C.2 Access review & audit

Chapter 1, "Access Control," presented several important topics related to the Access Control domain of the Common Body of Knowledge (CBK) for the CISSP certification exam. This chapter builds on those topics and includes key information on logging and monitoring, access control attacks, and assessing the effectiveness of access controls. Be sure to read and study the materials from each of these chapters to ensure complete coverage of the essential material for the CISSP certification exam.

Understanding Access Control Attacks

As discussed in Chapter 1, one of the goals of access control is to prevent unauthorized access to objects. This includes access into any information system, including networks, services, communications links, computers, and unauthorized access to data. In addition to controlling access, IT security methods seek to prevent unauthorized alteration and disclosure and to provide consistent availability, which is one of the categories of the CIA Triad (confidentiality, integrity, and availability) covered in Chapter 1.

Security professionals need to be aware of common attack methods so that they can take proactive steps to prevent attacks, recognize them when they occur, and respond appropriately. The following sections provide an introduction to risk elements and cover some common access control attacks. You'll also read about other types of attacks in future chapters.

Crackers, Hackers, and Attackers

Crackers are malicious users intent on waging an attack against a person or system. Crackers may be motivated by greed, power, or recognition. Their actions can result in stolen property (data, ideas, and so on), disabled systems, compromised security, negative public opinion, loss of market share, reduced profitability, and lost productivity.

A term commonly confused with crackers is *hackers*. Hackers are technology enthusiasts with no malicious intent. Many authors and the media use the term *hacker* when they are actually discussing issues relating to crackers. To avoid confusion, we use the term *attacker* for malicious intruders throughout this book. An attack is any attempt to exploit the vulnerability of a system.

Introduction to Risk Elements

A *risk* is the possibility or likelihood that a threat will exploit a vulnerability resulting in a loss such as harm to an asset. (Chapter 6, "Risk and Personnel Management," covers risk and risk management in more depth.) A *threat* is a potential occurrence that can be caused by anything or anyone and can result in an undesirable outcome. Natural occurrences such as floods or earthquakes, accidental acts by an employee, or intentional attacks can all be threats to an organization. A *vulnerability* is any type of weakness. The weakness can be due to, for example, a flaw, a limitation, or the absence of a security control.

Risk management attempts to reduce or eliminate vulnerabilities or reduce the impact of potential threats by implementing controls or countermeasures. It is not possible, or desirable, to eliminate risk. Instead, an organization focuses on reducing the risks that can cause the most harm to their organization. With this in mind, key steps in risk management are as follows:

- Identifying assets
- Identifying threats
- Identifying vulnerabilities

Asset Valuation

Asset valuation refers to identifying the actual value of assets so that they can be prioritized. Risk management focuses on assets with the highest value and identifies controls to mitigate risks to these assets.

The value of an asset is more than just the purchase price. For example, a web server that is generating 10 thousand dollars a day in sales is much more valuable than just the cost of the hardware and software. If this server failed, it would result in the loss of revenue from direct sales and also loss of customer goodwill.

> Customer goodwill is one of many intangible aspects of the value of an asset.

Knowing the asset value also helps with cost benefit analysis, which seeks to determine the cost effectiveness of different types of security controls. For example, if an asset is valued at hundreds of thousands of dollars, an effective security control that costs one hundred dollars is justified. Then again, spending hundreds of dollars to protect against the theft of a 10 dollar mouse is not a justifiable expense. Instead, an organization will often accept risks associated with low-value assets.

In the context of access control attacks, it's important to evaluate the value of data. For example, if a database of customer information is compromised, what is the potential loss to the company? This isn't always easy to quantify, but recent attacks on Sony provide some perspective. (See the sidebar "Data Breaches at Sony.")

Real World Scenario

Data Breaches at Sony

Sony suffered multiple data breaches throughout 2011, an occurrence that severely tarnished its image.

A massive data breach in April 2011 resulted in attackers stealing data from 77 million Sony PlayStation customer accounts. In May 2011, 24.5 million Sony Online Entertainment accounts were compromised. In June 2011, an attack on Sony Pictures compromised over one million user accounts, and the attackers bragged that they used a single SQL injection attack to retrieve data. (For more on injection attacks, see Chapter 8, "Malicious Code and Application Attacks.") In October 2011, when Sony locked almost 100 thousand PlayStation accounts, it said the credentials were stolen from other sites and sent email messages to users encouraging them to "choose unique, hard-to-guess passwords"—implying the problem was the customers' fault. Ironically, Sony may have been correct because many users have a single password they use for multiple online accounts. But coming after the recent spate of attacks, its advice was met with skepticism.

Losses from the April 2011 Sony PlayStation breach are estimated at 171 million dollars, but losses from the other attacks haven't been publicized. Additionally, intangible losses aren't publicly available. It's highly likely that many gamers have chosen to quit using the PlayStation and/or purchase another competing product. Were these losses preventable? Many security professionals say yes. At the Black Hat conference in 2011, Sony was nominated for "Most Epic Fail" for these attacks and also for laying off numerous information security personnel months before the first cyber-attack.

It's possible that Sony simply didn't recognize the value of the data in its databases. However, after the attacks, it has quantifiable data it can use to measure the costs of the loss. Effective asset valuation is able to determine the value of the data before such massive losses.

Threat Modeling

After identifying and prioritizing assets, an organization attempts to identify any possible threats to the valuable systems. *Threat modeling* refers to the process of identifying, understanding, and categorizing potential threats. A goal is to identify a potential list of threats to these systems and to analyze the threats.

Attackers aren't the only type of threat. A threat can be something natural, such as a flood or earthquake, or it could be accidental, such as a user accidentally deleting a file. However, when considering access control, threats are primarily unauthorized individuals (commonly attackers) attempting unauthorized access to resources.

Threat modeling isn't meant to be a single event. Instead it's common for an organization to begin threat modeling early in the design process of a system and continue throughout its lifecycle. For example, Microsoft uses a Security Development Lifecycle process to consider and implement security at each stage of a product's development. This supports the motto of "Secure by Design, Secure by Default, Secure in Deployment and Communication" (also known as SD3+C). It has two goals in mind with this process:

- To reduce the number of security-related design and coding defects
- To reduce the severity of any remaining defects

In other words, it attempts to reduce vulnerabilities and reduce the impact of any vulnerabilities that remain. The overall result is reduced risk.

Threat Modeling Approaches

There's an almost infinite possibility of threats, so it's important to use a structured approach to accurately identify relevant threats. For example, some organizations use one or more of the following three approaches:

Focused on assets This method uses asset valuation results and attempts to identify threats to the valuable assets. For example, a specific asset can be evaluated to determine if it is susceptible to an attack. If the asset hosts data, access controls can be evaluated to identify threats that can bypass authentication or authorization mechanisms.

Focused on attackers Some organizations are able to identify potential attackers and can identify the threats they represent based on the attacker's goals. For example, a government is often able to identify potential attackers and recognize what the attackers want to achieve. They can then use this knowledge to identify and protect their relevant assets. A challenge with this approach is that new attackers can appear that weren't previously considered a threat.

Focused on software If an organization develops software, it can consider potential threats against the software. While organizations didn't commonly develop their own software years ago, it's common to do so today. Specifically, most organizations have a web presence, and many create their own web pages. Fancy web pages drive more traffic, but they also require more sophisticated programming and present additional threats. Chapter 8 covers application attacks and web application security.

If the threat is identified as an attacker (as opposed to a natural threat), threat modeling attempts to identify what the attacker may be trying to accomplish. Some attackers may want to disable a system, while other attackers may want to steal data. Once such threats are identified, they are categorized based on their goals or motivations. Additionally, it's common to pair threats with vulnerabilities to identify threats that can exploit vulnerabilities and represent significant risks to the organization. An ultimate goal of threat modeling is to prioritize the potential threats against an organization's valuable assets.

Advanced Persistent Threat

Any threat model should take into account the existence of known threats, and a relatively new threat is known as an *Advanced Persistent Threat (APT)*. It refers to a group of attackers who are working together and are highly motivated, skilled, and patient. They have advanced knowledge and a wide variety of skills to detect and exploit vulnerabilities. They are persistent and are focused on exploiting one or more specific targets rather than just any target of opportunity. APTs are often funded by a government, but they can also be funded by others, such as a group of organized criminals.

It used to be that to keep your network safe, you only needed to be more secure than other networks. The attackers would go after the easy targets and avoid the secure networks. You might remember the old line "How fast do you need to run when you're being chased by a grizzly bear?" Answer: "Only a little faster than the slowest person in your group." However, if you're carrying a jar of honey that the bear wants, he may ignore the others and go after only you. This is what an APT does. It goes after specific targets based on what it wants to exploit from those targets. Here are a few attacks that have been attributed to APTs:

Google   Google released details of a highly sophisticated attack against it and several other companies that occurred in December 2009. It said the attack originated from China and resulted in the theft of intellectual property. The attack also targeted Gmail accounts of Chinese human rights activists. Google discovered that accounts for other advocates of human rights in China were routinely accessed by third parties, indicating that credentials for these accounts had been compromised.

US Department of Defense   An attack in 2008 began after an infected USB flash drive was inserted into a computer. The malware spread to highly classified networks and for 14 months periodically sent out packets of information over the Internet. It has been called the worst breach of US military computers in history. Operation Buckshot Yankee finally eradicated the malware in 2009.

The French government   A successful spear phishing attack allowed attackers to remotely control over 150 computers in the French Ministry of Economy. They retrieved documents for over three months ending in March 2011. Spear phishing is described later in this chapter.

RSA   Socially engineered emails were used to exploit a zero-day vulnerability in Adobe Flash in March 2011. Attackers were able to steal information related to RSA's SecurID token devices. They then used this information to target contractors such as Lockheed Martin and L-3 Communications.

Stuxnet   Stuxnet was a worm that exploited several zero-day vulnerabilities and was reported to have caused a significant amount of damage to Iranian nuclear facilities. Due to the sophistication of Stuxnet, many security professionals believe that it was created by an APT targeting Iran. (For more about Stuxnet, see Chapter 8.)

The important point to remember about APTs is that they can target any company, not just governments.

Vulnerability Analysis

After identifying valuable assets and potential threats, an organization will perform *vulnerability analysis*. In other words, it attempts to discover weaknesses in these systems against potential threats. In the context of access control, vulnerability analysis attempts to identify the strengths and weaknesses of the different access control mechanisms and the potential of a threat to exploit a weakness.

Vulnerability analysis is an ongoing process and can include both technical and administrative steps. In larger organizations, specific individuals may be doing vulnerability analysis as a full-time job. They regularly perform vulnerability scans, looking for a wide variety of vulnerabilities, and report the results. In smaller organizations, a network administrator may run vulnerability scans on a periodic basis, such as once a week or once a month.

A risk analysis will often include a vulnerability analysis by evaluating systems against known threats and vulnerabilities.

Chapter 8 covers vulnerability scanners and Chapter 14, "Incident Management," covers penetration tests. Vulnerability scanners are technical tools used to analyze vulnerabilities, while penetration tests can include both technical and nontechnical means to analyze vulnerabilities and an attacker's ability to exploit them.

Common Access Control Attacks

Access control attacks attempt to bypass or circumvent access control methods. As mentioned in Chapter 1, access control starts with identification and authorization and access control attacks often try to steal user credentials. After attackers have stolen a user's credentials, they can launch an online *impersonation attack* by logging in as the user and accessing the user's resources. In other cases, an access control attack can bypass authentication mechanisms and just steal the data as was mentioned in the Sony examples earlier in this chapter.

Multiple attacks are covered throughout this book. The following sections cover some common attacks directly related to access control.

Access Aggregation Attacks

Access aggregation refers to collecting multiple pieces of nonsensitive information and combining (i.e., aggregating) them to learn sensitive information. In other words, a person or group may be able to collect multiple facts about a system and then use these facts to launch an attack.

Reconnaissance attacks (covered in Chapter 8) are access aggregation attacks that combine multiple tools to identify multiple elements of a system, such as IP addresses, open ports, running services, operating systems, and more. Aggregation attacks are also employed against databases. Chapter 7, "Software Development Security," covers aggregation and inference attacks that indirectly allow unauthorized individuals access to data using aggregation and inference techniques.

Combining defense-in-depth, need-to-know, separation of duties, and least privilege principles helps prevent access aggregation attacks.

Password Attacks

As mentioned in Chapter 1, passwords are the weakest form of authentication. If an attacker is successful in a password attack, the attacker can gain access to the account and access resources authorized to the account. If a root or administrator password is ever compromised, the attacker can access any other account and its resources. If administrator passwords are compromised in a high-security environment, the security of the environment can never be fully trusted again. The attacker could have created other accounts or back doors to access the system at a later date. Instead of accepting the risk, an organization may choose to rebuild the entire system from scratch.

A *strong password* helps prevent password attacks and includes at least eight characters with a combination of at least three of the four character types (uppercase, lowercase, numbers, and special characters). As password crackers get better, some people believe that strong passwords must be at least 15 characters, though it's difficult to get regular users to buy into this. While security professionals usually know what makes a strong password, many users do not, and it is not uncommon for users to use short passwords with only a single character type. For example, attackers published account information they stole from one of the Sony attacks mentioned previously. Analysis showed that the top 10 passwords were seinfeld, password, winner, 123456, purple, sweeps, contest, princess, maggie, and 9452. These passwords can easily be cracked using one of the common password attacks.

The following sections describe common password attacks using dictionary, brute-force, rainbow table, and sniffing methods. Some of these attacks are possible against online accounts. However, it's more common for an attacker to steal an account database and then crack the passwords offline.

Chapter 8 expands on password attack topics in the context of application attacks.

Dictionary Attacks

A *dictionary attack* is an attempt to discover passwords by using every possible password in a predefined database or list of common or expected passwords. In other words, an attacker starts with a database of words commonly found in a dictionary. Dictionary attack databases also include character combinations that aren't normally found in a dictionary but are commonly used as passwords. For example, you will probably see the list of passwords found in the published Sony accounts database in many password cracking dictionaries.

Additionally, dictionary attacks often scan for one-upped-constructed passwords. A *one-upped-constructed password* is a password in which a single character differs from its original form. For example, password1 is one-upped from password, as are Password, 1password, and passXword. This approach is often used to generate rainbow tables (discussed later in this chapter).

Some people think that using a foreign word as a password will beat dictionary attacks. However, password cracking dictionaries can, and often do, include foreign words.

Brute-Force Attacks

A *brute-force attack* is an attempt to discover passwords for user accounts by systematically attempting all possible combinations of letters, numbers, and symbols. Attackers don't typically type these in manually but instead have programs that can programmatically try all the combinations. A *hybrid attack* attempts a dictionary attack and then performs a type of brute-force attack with one-upped-constructed passwords.

The longer and more complex a password is, the more costly and time consuming a brute-force attack becomes. As the number of possibilities increases, the cost of performing an exhaustive attack goes up. In other words, the longer the password and the more character types it includes, the more secure it is against brute-force attacks.

Passwords and usernames are stored in an account database file on secured systems. However, instead of being stored as plain text, passwords are commonly hashed and only their hash values are retained. When a user authenticates, the system will hash the password provided by the user and send the hash to the authenticating system. The authenticating system then compares this hash to the stored hash This provides several levels of protection. Passwords aren't sent across a network in cleartext and passwords aren't stored in cleartext.

Chapter 10, "PKI and Cryptographic Applications," covers hash functions in more depth, but in short, a hash function creates a fixed-length message digest from a password, message, or file. For example, Message Digest 5 (MD5) uses a 128-bit message digest commonly displayed as a 32-character hexadecimal number. The hash created by the hash function will always be the same when calculated on identical data.

However, password attacker tools often look for passwords with the same hash value as an entry stored in the account database file. With this type of password attack, the attacker doesn't need to discover the actual password but instead only needs to discover another password that results in the same hash.

For example, the password IPASSED may have a stored hash value of 1A5C7G hexadecimal (though the actual hash would be much longer). A brute-force password tool would guess a password, calculate the hash, and compare it against the stored hash value. This is also known as comparative analysis. When a hash value match occurs, it indicates that the guessed password is very likely the original password. In this case, the tool is said to have cracked the password.

If two separate passwords create the same hash, it is called a collision. Ideally, collisions aren't possible, but some hashing functions (such as MD5) are not collision free. This allows an attacker to create a different password that results in the same hash as a hashed password stored in the account database file.

A *birthday attack* focuses on finding collisions. It is so named based on a statistical phenomenon known as the birthday paradox. The birthday paradox states that if there are 23 people in a room, there is a 50 percent chance that any two of them will have the same birthday. Omitting February 29th, there are only 365 possible days, but the point is that you do not need 366 people in the room to get a match.

This is similar to finding any two passwords with the same hash. If a hashing function could only create 365 different hashes, then an attacker with a sample of only 23 hashes has a 50 percent chance of discovering two passwords that will create the same hash. Hashing algorithms can create many more than 365 different hashes, but the point is that the birthday attack method doesn't need all possible hashes to see a match.

From another perspective, imagine that you are one of the people in the room and you want to find someone else with the same birthday as you. In this example, you'll need 253 people in the room to reach the same 50 percent probability of finding someone else with the same birthday. Even though you need more people in the room, the point is that you don't need 366 people in the room to find a match.

Similarly, it is possible for some tools to come up with another password that creates the same hash of a given hash. For example, if you know that the hash of the administrator account password is 1A5C7G, some tools can identify a password that will create the same hash of 1A5C7G. It isn't necessarily the same password, but if can create the same hash, it is just as effective as the original password.

Birthday attacks are mitigated by using hashing algorithms with a sufficient number of bits to make collisions computationally infeasible. There was a time when MD5 (using 128 bits) was considered to be collision free. However, computing power continues to improve, and MD5 is no longer considered safe against collisions. SHA-2 (short for Secure Hash Algorithm version 2) can use as many as 512 bits and is considered safer against birthday attacks and collisions—at least for now. Computing power continues to improve, so at some point larger hashes will be needed. With the speed of modern computers and the ability to employ distributed computing, brute-force attacks prove successful even against strong passwords. With enough time, any password can be discovered using a brute-force attack.

The actual time it takes to discover passwords depends upon the algorithm used to encrypt them and the power of the computer. Many attackers are using graphics processing units (GPUs) in brute-force attacks. Blogger Vijay Devakumar ran some tests using an older CPU-based password cracker named Cain & Abel against a newer GPU-based tool named ighashgpu. He reported that it took Cain & Abel up to 1 hour and 30 minutes to crack a six-character password but ighashgpu took less than 4 seconds to crack the same password.

Rainbow Table Attacks

When attempting to find passwords by guessing them, hashing them, and then comparing them, it takes a long time to perform the hash functions. However, this time can be reduced with a *rainbow table*. Rainbow tables are large databases of precomputed hashes for guessed passwords. In other words, passwords are guessed (using either brute-force or dictionary methods) and then each guessed password is hashed. These guessed passwords and their hash values are stored in a rainbow table.

A password cracker can then compare every hash in the rainbow table against the hash in a stolen database file. A traditional password cracking tool must guess the password and hash it before it can compare the hashes. However, when the rainbow table is used, the password cracker doesn't spend any time guessing passwords and calculating hashes. It simply compares the hashes until it finds a match. This can significantly reduce the time it takes to crack a password.

A wide variety of different rainbow tables are available for free download. Rainbow tables that have hashes for 14-character passwords using the 4 character types are approximately 7.5 GB in size. While these take some time to download, attackers are willing to wait. A passphrase using 15 characters or more will beat most rainbow tables.

Many systems commonly *salt* passwords to reduce the effectiveness of rainbow table attacks. Additional random bits are added to the password before hashing it, which increases its complexity. Cryptographic methods are used to add the additional bits, making it significantly more difficult for an attacker to use rainbow tables against salted passwords. However, given enough time, salted passwords can still be beaten using a brute-force attack.

Sniffer Attacks

Sniffing is a form of traffic monitoring using a sniffer, which is also called a packet analyzer or protocol analyzer. A sniffer is a software application that can capture traffic going over the network. Sniffers are commonly used by network administrators to analyze network traffic and troubleshoot problems.

Of course, attackers can also use sniffers. A *sniffer attack* (also called a snooping attack or eavesdropping attack) occurs when an attacker uses a sniffer to capture information transmitted over a network. Any data sent over a network in cleartext, including passwords, can be captured and read by the program.

Wireshark is a popular protocol analyzer available as a free download. Figure 2.1 shows that Wireshark has captured the contents of a file that was opened on a file server and transferred over the network.

FIGURE 2.1:   Wireshark capture

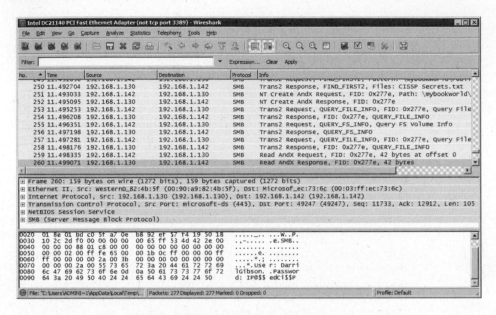

In the top pane, packet 260 is selected. The contents of this packet appear in the bottom pane. It includes the text `User: DarrilGibson Password: IP@$$edCi$$P`. If you look at the first packet in the top pane (packet number 250), you can see that the file being opened is named `CISSP Secrets.txt`.

To prevent successful sniffing attacks, the following methods can be used:

▪ Sensitive data (including passwords) sent over a network should be encrypted. Encrypted data cannot be read with a sniffer. You can use, for example, Kerberos to encrypt tickets to prevent sniffing attacks.

▪ One-time passwords can prevent the success of sniffing attacks; because a one-time password isn't reused, it isn't valuable to the attack in which it's captured.

▪ Controlling physical access to routers and switches can prevent attackers from installing sniffers on the network devices.

▪ Intrusion detection systems can monitor the network for sniffing signatures to detect when a sniffer is capturing data.

Spoofing Attacks

Spoofing (also known as masquerading) is pretending to be something or someone else. There is a wide variety of spoofing attacks. A spoofing attack involves, for example, using someone else's credentials to enter a building or access an IT system. Some applications spoof legitimate logon screens. One attack brought up a logon screen that looked exactly like the operating system logon screen. When the user entered credentials, the credentials were captured and the attacker was able to use them later. Some phishing attacks (described later in this section) mimic this with bogus websites.

In an IP spoofing attack, attackers replace a valid source IP address with a false one to either hide their identity or to impersonate a trusted system. Other types of spoofing are used in access control attacks, including email spoofing and phone number spoofing.

Email spoofing   Spammers commonly spoof the email address in the From field to make an email appear to come from another source. This is often done in phishing attacks to trick users into thinking the email is coming from a legitimate source. The Reply To field can be a different email address and is usually not displayed until a user actually replies.

Phone number spoofing   Caller ID services allow users to identify the phone number of any caller. Phone number spoofing allows a caller to replace this number with another one, which is a common technique on Voice over Internet Protocol (VoIP) systems.

Chapter 8 covers masquerading attacks, including IP spoofing and session hijacking.

Social Engineering Attacks

Sometimes, the easiest way to get someone's password is to ask for it, and this is a common method used by social engineers. *Social engineering* occurs when an attacker attempts to gain the trust of someone by using deceit, such as false flattery or impersonation, or by using conniving behavior. The attacker attempts to trick someone into revealing information they wouldn't normally reveal or performing an action they wouldn't normally perform. Often the goal of the social engineer is to gain access to the IT infrastructure or the physical facility.

For example, a skilled social engineer can convince an uneducated help desk employee that they are associated with upper management and working remotely but have forgotten their password. If fooled, the employee may reset the password and provide the attacker with the new password. Other times, regular users are tricked into revealing their own password, providing the attacker with access to their account. Educating employees on common social engineer tactics reduces their effectiveness.

Social engineering attacks can happen over the phone, in person, and via email. In person, malicious individuals often impersonate repair technicians to gain physical access. If they gain access to the network infrastructure, they can then install a sniffer to capture sensitive data. Verifying visitor identities before providing access can mitigate these types of impersonation attacks.

Sometimes a social engineer just tries to look over the shoulder of an individual to read information on the computer screen or watch the keyboard as they type. This is commonly called *shoulder surfing*. Screen filters can restrict the view of an attacker. Additionally, password masking (displaying an alternate character such as an asterisk instead of the actual characters of the password) is often used to mitigate shoulder surfing.

Phishing is a form of social engineering using email. The associated risks can commonly be avoided by following some simple rules:

- Be suspicious of unexpected email messages
- Never open unexpected email attachments.
- Never share sensitive information via email.

There are phishing attacks and then several variations, including spear phishing, whaling, and vishing:

Phishing

Phishing is a form of social engineering that attempts to trick users into giving up sensitive information, opening an attachment, or clicking a link. It often tries to obtain personally identifiable information such as usernames, passwords, or credit card details by masquerading as a legitimate company. Attackers send phishing emails indiscriminately, without knowing who will get them but in the hope that some users will be fooled. They commonly inform the user of a bogus problem and say that if the user doesn't take action, the user's account will be locked. For example, the email may state that suspicious activity has been noted on the account and unless the user verifies username and password information, the account will be locked.

Simple phishing attacks inform users of the problem and ask the recipient to respond in an email with their username, password, and other details. The From email address is often spoofed to look legitimate, but the Reply To email address is an account controlled by the attacker. More sophisticated attacks include a link to a bogus website that looks legitimate. For example, if the phishing email describes a problem with a PayPal account, the bogus website looks like the PayPal website. If the user enters credentials, the website captures them and passes them to the attacker.

Other times, the goal of sending phishing email is to install malware on user systems. The message may include an infected file as an attachment and encourage the user to open it. The email could include a link to a website that installs a malicious drive-by download without the user's knowledge.

 A drive-by download is a type of malware that installs itself without the user's knowledge when the user visits a website. Drive-by downloads take advantage of vulnerabilities in browsers or plug-ins.

Some malicious websites try to trick the user into downloading and installing the software. For example, rogue antivirus software (sometimes called rogueware) has become popular with attackers, and phishing is sometimes used to drive users to sites hosting rogueware. The website may claim to offer free antivirus software, but the software is actually malicious. Phishing is often accomplished via email, but other means can be used, such as instant messaging and VoIP.

Spear phishing

Spear phishing is a form of phishing targeted to a specific group of users. It may appear to originate from a colleague or co-worker within the organization or from an external source.

For example, attackers exploited a zero-day vulnerability in Adobe PDF files that allowed malicious code to be embedded within the file. If a user opened the PDF file, malware would infect the user's system. The attackers named the PDF file FY12 ... Contract Guide and stated in the email that it provided updated information on the contract award process. They sent the email to targeted email addresses at well-known government contractors such as Lockheed Martin. If any contractors opened the file, it would have infected their systems and allowed attackers remote access to the contractor's computer.

Whaling

Whaling is a variant of phishing that targets senior or high-level executives such as CEOs and presidents. A well-known whaling attack targeted about 20,000 senior corporate executives in 2008. The email identified each recipient by name and stated they were being subpoenaed to appear before a grand jury. It included a link to get more information on the subpoena, and if the executive clicked, it indicated that they needed to install a browser add-on to read the file. Executives that approved the installation of the add-on actually installed malicious software that logged their keystrokes, capturing log-in credentials for different websites they visited. It also gave the attacker remote access to the infected system to read the data.

Vishing

Vishing is a variant of phishing that uses the phone system or VoIP. A common attack uses an automated call to the user explaining a problem with a credit card account. The user is encouraged to verify or validate information such as the credit card number, expiration date, and security code on the back of the card. Vishing attacks commonly spoof the caller ID number to impersonate a valid bank or financial institution.

Smart Card Attacks

Smart cards provide better authentication than passwords, especially when they're combined with another factor of authentication such as a personal identification number (PIN). However, smart cards are also susceptible to attacks. A *side-channel attack* is a passive, noninvasive attack intended to observe the operation of a device. When the attack is successful, the attacker is able to learn valuable information contained within the card, such as an encryption key.

A smart card includes a microprocessor, but it doesn't have internal power. Instead, power is provided when the card is inserted into, or placed near, the card reader. A *proximity reader* works with cards that are placed near it. The reader has an electromagnetic coil that excites electronics on the card. This provides enough power for the smart card to transmit data to the reader.

Side-channel attacks analyze the information sent to the reader. Sometimes they are able to measure the power consumption of a chip, using a power monitoring attack or differential power analysis attack, to extract information. In a timing attack, they are able to monitor the processing timings to gain information based on how much time different computations require. Fault analysis attacks attempt to cause faults, such as by providing too little power to the card, to glean valuable information.

Denial of Service Attacks

A *denial of service (DoS)* attack prevents a system from processing or responding to legitimate traffic or requests for resources. When the system fails, all legitimate access to the system is blocked, disrupted, or slowed. As a simple example, if a server is not protected with physical security, an attacker can unplug it, removing it from service.

DoS attacks often occur over a network, including over the Internet. Buffer overflow attacks (covered in Chapter 8) are common attacks against unpatched systems. A DoS attack comes from a single source. A distributed denial of service (DDoS) attack has the same result as a DoS attack, but it comes from multiple sources. The classic example of DDoS attack is from zombies in a botnet. Chapter 4, "Secure Communications and Network Attacks," mentions DoS and DDoS in the context of network attacks, and Chapter 14 presents information on both DoS and DDoS attacks and methods to prevent them.

Preventing Access Control Attacks

Protecting against access control attacks requires numerous security precautions and rigid adherence to a strong security policy. The following list identifies many security precautions, but it's important to realize that this isn't a comprehensive list of all proactive preventative steps an organization can take. You'll find additional controls that help prevent attacks covered throughout this book.

Control physical access to systems.   An old saying related to security is that if an attacker has unrestricted physical access to a computer, the attacker owns it. If an attacker can gain physical access to an authentication server, they can often steal the password file in a very short time. Once a password file is stolen, the attacker can crack the passwords offline. All passwords should be considered compromised, but the problem can be prevented by controlling physical access.

Control electronic access to password files.   Tightly control and monitor electronic access to password files. End users and those who are not account administrators have no need to access the password database file for daily work tasks. Any unauthorized access to password database files should be investigated immediately.

Encrypt password files.   Encrypt password files with the strongest encryption available for your operating system. One-way encryption (hashing) is commonly used for passwords instead of storing them in plain text. Maintain rigid control over all media containing a copy of the password database file, such as backup tapes or repair disks. Passwords should also be encrypted when transmitted over the network.

Create a strong password policy.   A password policy can programmatically enforce the use of strong passwords and ensure that users regularly change their passwords. The stronger and longer a password, the longer it will take for it to be discovered in an attack. However, with enough time, all passwords can be discovered via brute-force methods. Thus, changing passwords regularly is required to maintain security. More secure or sensitive environments require passwords to be changed more frequently. Use separate password policies for privileged accounts such as administrator accounts to ensure that they have stronger passwords and that the passwords are changed more frequently.

Use password masking.   Ensure that applications never display passwords in cleartext on any screen. Instead, mask the display of the password by displaying an alternate character such as an asterisk (*). This reduces shoulder surfing attempts, but users should be aware that an attacker may be able to watch the keystrokes to discover the password.

Deploy multifactor authentication.   Deploy multifactor authentication, such as using biometrics or token devices. If passwords are not the only means used to protect the security of a network, their compromise will not automatically result in a system breach.

Use account lockout controls.   Account lockout controls help prevent online password attacks. They lock an account after the incorrect password is entered a predefined number of times. It's common to allow a user to incorrectly enter the password as many as five times before the account is locked out. For systems and services that don't support account lockout controls, such as most FTP servers, employ extensive logging and an intrusion detection system to look for password attacks.

Account lockout controls help prevent an attacker from guessing a password in an online account. However, this does not prevent an attacker from using a password cracking tool against a stolen database file.

Use last logon notification.   Many systems display a message including the time, date, and location (such as the computer name or IP address) of the last successful logon. If users pay attention to this message, they might notice if their account has been accessed by someone else. For example, if the last time a user logged on was the previous Friday but a message indicates that the account was accessed on Saturday, it's apparent the account has been breached. Users who suspect that their account is under attack or has been compromised can report this to a system administrator.

Educate users about security.   Properly train users about the necessity of maintaining security and the use of strong passwords. Inform users that passwords should never be shared or written down; the only possible exception is that long, complex passwords for the most sensitive accounts, such as administrator or root accounts, can be written down and stored in a vault or safety deposit box. Offer tips to users on how to create strong passwords and how to prevent shoulder surfing. Inform users of the risk of using the same password for different accounts. For example, a user that uses the same password for banking accounts and a gaming account can have all their accounts compromised after a successful attack on a single system. Additionally, inform users about social engineering tactics.

Audit access controls. Regular reviews and audits of access control processes help assess the effectiveness of access controls. For example, auditing can track logon success and failure of any account. An intrusion detection system can monitor these logs and easily identify logon prompt attacks and notify administrators.

Actively manage accounts. When an employee leaves an organization or takes a leave of absence, the account should be disabled as soon as possible. Inactive accounts should be deleted when it is determined they are no longer needed. Regular user entitlement and access reviews can discover excessive or creeping privileges.

Use vulnerability scanners. Vulnerability scanners can detect access control vulnerabilities and, when run regularly, help an organization mitigate these vulnerabilities. Many vulnerability scanners include password cracking tools that will detect weak passwords in addition to tools that can verify that systems are kept up-to-date with patches.

Future chapters cover many different types of controls to protect against attacks. For example, Chapter 13, "Security Operations," covers patch management to keep systems up-to-date and change management to prevent unwanted changes. Chapter 14 covers intrusion detection and prevention systems that can detect access control attacks and take steps to block them.

Logging and Monitoring

Logging records information and monitoring reviews it. Combined, logging and monitoring allow an organization to track, record, and review activity, providing overall accountability. This helps an organization detect undesirable events that can negatively affect confidentiality, integrity, or availability of systems. It is also useful in reconstructing activity after an event has occurred to identify what happened and sometimes to prosecute responsible personnel.

Logging Techniques

Logging is the process of recording information about events to a log file or database. Logging captures events, changes, messages, and other data that describe activities that occurred on a system. Logs will commonly record details such as what happened, when it happened, where it happened, who did it, and sometimes how it happened. When you need to find information about an incident that occurred in the recent past, logs are a good place to start.

As an example, Figure 2.2 shows Event Viewer on a Microsoft server with a log entry selected and expanded. This log entry shows that a user named Marcus deleted a file named CISSP Study Notes.rtf originally located in a folder named C:\CISSP Study Notes on a server named SQL1. Marcus deleted the file at 2:32 p.m. on January 2, 2012.

FIGURE 2.2:   Viewing a log entry

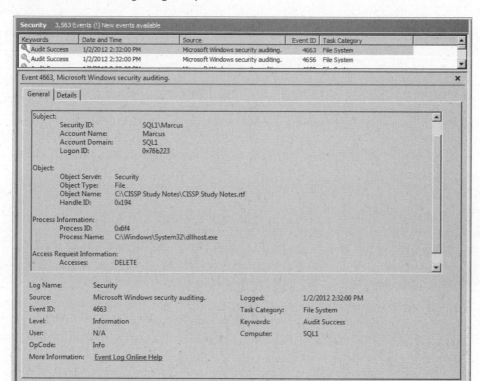

As long as the identification and authentication processes are secure, this is enough to hold Marcus accountable for deleting the file. On the other hand, if the organization doesn't use secure authentication processes and it's easy for someone to impersonate users, Marcus may be wrongly accused. This reinforces the requirement for secure identification and authentication practices as a prerequisite for accountability.

 Logs are often referred to as audit logs, and logging is often called audit logging. However, it's important to realize that auditing (described later in this chapter) is more than just logging. Logging records events while auditing examines or inspects an environment for compliance.

Common Log Types

There are many different types of logs. The following is a short list of common logs that are often available within an IT environment.

Security logs   Security logs record access to resources such as files, folders, printers, and so on. For example, they can record when a user accessed, modified, or deleted a file, as shown in Figure 2.2. Many systems automatically record access to some key system files but require an administrator to enable auditing on other resources before access is logged.

System logs   System logs record system events such as when a system was started or stopped or when services were stopped or started. If attackers are able to shut down a system and reboot it with a CD or USB flash drive, they can steal data from the system without any record of the data access. Similarly, if attackers are able to stop a service that is monitoring the system, they may be able to access the system without their actions being recorded.

Application logs   These logs record information for specific applications. Application developers choose what to record in the application logs. For example, a database developer can choose to record when specific data objects are accessed.

Firewall logs   Firewall logs can record all activity that has been passed by the firewall and/or all activity that has been blocked. These logs commonly log key packet information such as source and destination IP addresses and source and destination ports.

Proxy logs   Proxy servers are used to improve Internet access performance for users and can control what websites users visit. Proxy logs include the ability to record details such as what sites specific users visit and how much time they spend on these sites. They can also record when users attempt to visit known prohibited sites.

Change logs   Change logs record change requests, approvals, and actual changes to a system as a part of an overall change management process. Change management is covered in more depth in Chapter 13.

Logging is usually a native feature in an operating system, for most applications and services. Thus, configuring a system to record information about specific types of events is fairly straightforward. When configuring logging, it is important to ensure that any activity from privileged accounts such as administrator or root user accounts is always logged. This helps prevent attacks from a malicious insider and will document activity that can be used for prosecution if necessary.

Protecting Log Data

Databases and log files must be protected against unauthorized access and unauthorized modification. They contain valuable information that is useful to an organization and can be damaging if accessed or modified by attackers. If the files can be modified, malicious users can attempt to rewrite history, effectively nullifying the value of the data. The files may no longer include accurate information and may not be admissible as evidence to prosecute attackers.

It's common to store copies of log file data on a central system to protect it. Even if an attack modifies or corrupts the original files, a copy is still available. Log files should be protected with permissions to limit their access and archived copies should be set to read-only to prevent modification.

Log file data is backed up and retained based on the needs of the organization. Some government organizations are required to keep data forever, but most organizations can dispose of the data at some point. When the data is no longer needed, it should be destroyed using acceptable methods. Chapter 13 talks more about data retention and data destruction practices that apply to any types of data, including audit trail data.

If logs are transmitted across a network from a monitoring agent to a central server, they should be encrypted.

Log data is commonly referred to as audit data. According to the National Institute of Standards and Technology (NIST) in its document *Minimum Security Requirements for Federal Information and Information Systems (FIPS 200)*, audit data recording must comply with the following requirements:

- Create, protect, and retain information system audit records to the extent needed to enable the monitoring, analysis, investigation, and reporting of unlawful, unauthorized, or inappropriate information system activity.

- Ensure that the actions of individual information system users can be uniquely traced to those users so they can be held accountable for their actions.

 NIST documents are very useful to review when preparing for the CISSP exam to give you a broader idea of different security concepts. They are freely available and you can access them at http://csrc.nist.gov. You can download the FIPS 200 document here: http://csrc.nist.gov/publications/fips/fips200/FIPS-200-final-march.pdf.

Monitoring Techniques

Monitoring is the process of manually or programmatically reviewing information logs looking for something specific. Monitoring is necessary to detect malicious actions by subjects as well as attempted intrusions and system failures. It can help reconstruct events, provide evidence for prosecution, and produce problem reports for analysis. *Log analysis* is a detailed and systematic form of monitoring in which the logged information is analyzed for trends and patterns as well as abnormal, unauthorized, illegal, and policy-violating activities. Log analysis isn't necessarily in response to an incident but is performed periodically to detect potential issues.

In manual log analysis, administrators simply open the log files and look for relevant data. This can be very tedious and time consuming, even when using tools to search through the files looking for specific events or ID codes. In many cases, when sufficient logging and auditing are enabled to monitor a system or network, it produces so much information that important details can get lost in the sheer volume of data.

Many tools are available that can automate the process. For example, intrusion detection systems (covered in Chapter 14) can actively monitor multiple logs and detect malicious intrusions in real time. An intrusion detection system can help detect and track attacks from external attackers and record access to resources. Operations management software is available from multiple vendors to actively monitor the security, health, and performance of systems throughout the network. This software looks for suspicious or abnormal activities that can indicate problems such as an attack or unauthorized access.

Many organizations use a centralized application to automate monitoring of systems on a network. There are several terms used to describe these tools, including Security Information and Event Management (SIEM), Security Event Management (SEM), and Security Information Management (SIM). These tools provide real-time analysis of events occurring on systems throughout an organization. They include agents installed on the remote systems that monitor for specific events known as alarm triggers. When the trigger occurs, the agents report the event back to the central monitoring software.

For example, a SIEM can be configured to monitor a group of email servers. Each time an event is logged on any of the servers, a SIEM agent examines the event to determine if it is an item of interest. If it is, the SIEM agent forwards the event to a central SIEM server, and depending on the event, it may raise an alarm for an administrator. If the send queue of an email server starts backing up, for example, a SIEM application can detect the issue and raise an alert to administrators before the problem is serious.

Most SIEMs are configurable, allowing personnel within the organization to specify what items are of interest and should be forwarded. SIEMs have agents that can be installed on just about any type of server or network device. In some cases they are used to monitor network flows for traffic and trend analysis. The tools can also collect all the logs from target systems and use data-mining techniques to retrieve relevant data. All entries from all the relevant logs are periodically sent to the central monitoring computer, which analyzes the data and can report the results using different methods.

Some monitoring tools are also used for inventory and status purposes. For example, tools can query all the available systems and document details. They can identify the names of the computers, IP addresses, operating system, installed patches and updates, and installed software. They can then create reports of any system based on the needs of the organization. For example, they can identify how many systems are active, identify systems with missing patches, or flag systems that have unauthorized software installed.

Illegal software monitoring watches for attempted or successful installations of unapproved software, use of unauthorized software, or unauthorized use of approved software. This can reduce the risk of a virus or Trojan horse being installed or of software circumventing existing security controls.

Audit Trails

Audit trails are records created when information about events and occurrences is stored in one or more databases or log files. Audit trails provide a record of system activity and are used to reconstruct an event, to extract information about an incident, to prove or disprove culpability, and much more. Audit trails allow events to be examined or traced in forward or reverse order. This flexibility helps when tracking down problems, coding errors, performance issues, attacks, intrusions, security breaches, and other policy violations.

Audit trails provide a comprehensive record of system activity and can help detect a wide variety of security violations, software flaws, and performance problems.

Using audit trails is a passive form of detective security control. Their use serves as a deterrent in the same manner that closed circuit television (CCTV) or security guards do. If attackers know they are being watched and their activities are being recorded, they are less likely to engage in illegal, unauthorized, or malicious activity—at least in theory (in reality, some criminals are too careless or clueless for this to apply consistently). Audit trails are also essential as evidence in the prosecution of criminals. They can often be used to produce a before-and-after picture of the state of resources, systems, and assets. This in turn helps to determine whether a change or alteration is the result of an action by a user, an action by the OS or software, or caused by some other source, such as hardware failure.

Sampling

Sampling, or *data extraction*, is the process of extracting specific elements from a large collection of data to construct a meaningful representation or summary of the whole. In other words, sampling is a form of data reduction that allows someone to glean valuable information by looking at only a small sample of data in an audit trail.

Statistical sampling uses precise mathematical functions to extract meaningful information from a very large volume of data. This is similar to the science used by pollsters to learn the opinions of large populations without actually interviewing everyone in the population. There is always a risk that sampled data is not an accurate representation of the whole body of data, and statistical sampling can identify the actual margin of error.

Clipping Levels

Clipping is a form of nonstatistical sampling. It selects only events that exceed a *clipping level*, which is a predefined cutoff point for the event. For example, some failed logon attempts are common in any system. Instead of raising an alarm for every single failed logon attempt, a clipping level can be set to raise an alarm only if it detects five failed logon attempts within a 30-minute period. Many account lockout controls use a similar clipping level. They don't lock the account after a single failed logon. Instead, they are configured to count the failed logons and lock the account when the predefined threshold is reached.

Clipping levels are widely used in the process of auditing events to establish a baseline of system or user activity that is considered routine activity. If this baseline is exceeded, an alarm is triggered to signal abnormal events. This works especially well when there are too many people with unrestricted access and for serious intrusion patterns.

Additionally, clipping levels are often associated with a form of mainframe auditing known as violation analysis. In violation analysis, an older form of auditing, the environment is monitored for error occurrences. The baseline for errors is expected and known, and this level of expected, known errors defines the clipping level. Any errors that exceed the clipping level threshold trigger a violation and details about such events are recorded into a violation record for later analysis.

In general, nonstatistical sampling can be described as discretionary sampling or sampling at the auditor's discretion. It doesn't offer an accurate representation of the whole body of data and will ignore events that don't reach the clipping level threshold. However, it is effective when used to focus on specific events. Additionally, nonstatistical sampling is less expensive and easier to implement than statistical sampling.

Both statistical and nonstatistical sampling are accepted as valid mechanisms to create summaries or overviews of large bodies of audit data. However, statistical sampling is more reliable and mathematically defensible.

Other Monitoring Tools

While logs are the primary tools used with auditing, there are some additional tools used within organizations that are worth mentioning. For example, a CCTV can be configured to automatically record events onto tape for later review. Security personnel can also watch for unwanted, unauthorized, or illegal activities in real time. This system can work alone or in conjunction with security guards, who themselves can be monitored by the CCTV and held accountable for any illegal or unethical activity. Other tools include keystroke monitoring, traffic analysis and trend analysis monitoring, and network data loss prevention devices.

Keystroke monitoring   *Keystroke monitoring* is the act of recording the keystrokes a user performs on a physical keyboard. The monitoring is commonly done via technical means such as a hardware device or a software program. However, a video recorder can perform visual monitoring. In most cases, keystroke monitoring is used by attackers for malicious purposes. However, in extreme circumstances and highly restricted environments, keystroke monitoring is employed legitimately by an organization as a means to audit and analyze the activity of its users. It can be extremely useful to track the keystroke-by-keystroke activities of physical intruders to learn about the kinds of attacks and methods used to infiltrate a system.

Companies can and do utilize keystroke monitoring in some situations. However, in almost all cases, they are required to inform employees of the monitoring.

Keystroke monitoring is often compared to wiretapping. There is some debate about whether keystroke monitoring should be restricted and controlled in the same manner as telephone wiretaps. Because there is no legal precedent as yet, many organizations that employ keystroke monitoring notify both authorized and unauthorized users of such monitoring through employment agreements, security policies, and warning banners at sign-on or login areas. The software or hardware devices used to perform keystroke monitoring can be described as keystroke loggers, popularly known as keyloggers.

Traffic analysis and trend analysis   *Traffic analysis* and *trend analysis* are forms of monitoring that examine the flow of packets rather than actual packet contents. This is sometimes referred to as network flow monitoring. It can be used to infer a lot of information, such as primary and backup communication routes, sources of encrypted traffic, location of primary servers, amount of traffic supported by the network, typical direction of traffic flow, frequency of communications, and much more.

These techniques can sometimes reveal questionable traffic patterns, such as when an employee mass-emails a resume to dozens of employers on any given day or when an unscrupulous insider forwards internal information to unauthorized parties via an email attachment. Such events leave behind distinct signatures that can often be detected through traffic or trend analysis.

Network data loss prevention   Some network data loss protection devices can monitor and analyze traffic leaving an organization to look for suspicious data. For example, if an organization has been working on a highly sensitive project named *CISSP Secrets*, it can use a data loss protection device to scan every packet leaving the organization for the phrase CISSP Secrets. These devices can also scan for specific patterns. For example, a Social Security number is commonly expressed with numbers separated by dashes like this: 123-45-6789. The devices can detect when traffic includes these patterns, suggesting that a document includes such data.

The Role of Monitoring

Monitoring provides several benefits for an organization, including increasing accountability, helping with investigations, and basic troubleshooting. The following sections describe these benefits in more depth.

Monitoring and Accountability

Monitoring is a necessary function to ensure that subjects are held accountable for their actions and activities. Accountability is maintained for individual subjects through the use of audit trails after they have been identified and authenticated. When activities and events are recorded while users are online, the users can be held accountable for their actions. This directly promotes positive user behavior and compliance with the organization's security policy. Users who are aware that their IT activities are being recorded are less likely to try to circumvent security controls or to perform unauthorized or restricted activities.

Once a security policy violation or a breach occurs, the source of that violation should be determined. If it is possible to identify the individuals responsible, they should be held accountable based on the organization's security policy. Severe cases can result in terminating employment for employees or prosecution for external attackers.

Real World Scenario

Monitoring Activity

Accountability is absolutely necessary at every level of business, from the frontline infantry to the high-level commanders overseeing daily operations. If you don't monitor the actions and activities of users and their applications on a given system, you aren't able to hold them accountable for mistakes or misdeeds they commit.

As an example, consider Duane, a quality assurance supervisor for the data entry department at an oil-drilling data mining company. During his daily routine, he sees many highly sensitive documents that include the kind of valuable information that can earn a heavy tip or bribe from interested parties. He also corrects the kind of mistakes that could cause serious backlash from his company's clientele because sometimes a minor clerical error can cause serious issues for a client's entire project.

Whenever Duane touches or transfers such information on his workstation, his actions leave an electronic trail of evidence that his supervisor, Nicole, can examine in the event that Duane's actions should come under scrutiny. She can observe where he obtained or placed pieces of sensitive information, when he accessed and modified such information, and just about anything else related to the handling and processing of the data as it flows in from the source and out to the client.

This accountability provides protection to the company should Duane misuse this information. It also provides Duane with protection against anyone falsely accusing him of misusing the data he handles.

Monitoring and accountability practices are often required by legislation such as the Sarbanes-Oxley Act of 2002, Health Insurance Portability and Accountability Act (HIPAA), and European Union (EU) privacy laws for many organizations.

Monitoring and Investigations

Audit trails give investigators the ability to reconstruct events long after they have occurred. They can record access abuses, privilege violations, attempted intrusions, and many different types of attacks.

When a security violation is detected, the conditions and system state leading up to the event, during the event, and after the event can be reconstructed through a close examination of the audit trail. This process is largely facilitated and validated through the use of accurate time stamps, which must remain consistent throughout the network environment.

Many organizations synchronize one computer's time with an external time source and use this system to synchronize the time on all other systems.

Systems should have their time synchronized against a centralized or trusted public time server. This ensures that all audit logs are in sync and can provide accurate information on the time of events.

Monitoring and Problem Identification

Audit trails offer details about recorded events that are useful for administrators. They can record system failures, OS bugs, and software errors in addition to malicious attacks. Some log files can even capture the contents of memory when an application or system crashes. This information can help pinpoint the cause of the event and eliminate it as a possible attack. For example, if a system keeps crashing due to faulty memory, crash dump files can help diagnose the problem.

Using log files for this purpose is often labeled as problem identification. Once a problem is identified, problem resolution involves little more than following up on the disclosed information.

Assessing Effectiveness of Access Controls

Chapter 1 discussed identification, authentication, and authorization in depth. A goal is to ensure that subjects are uniquely identified and that they can access only objects they are authorized to access. Policies that require strong authentication and restrict access to resources based on core principles of need to know and least privilege are often in place. However, just because the policies are in place doesn't mean they are followed. Many times an organization will want to assess the effectiveness of these access controls by *auditing* the environment.

Auditing is a methodical examination or review of an environment to ensure compliance with regulations and to detect abnormalities, unauthorized occurrences, or outright crimes. It is used to verify that the security mechanisms deployed in an environment are providing adequate security for the environment. The audit process is designed to ensure that the requirements dictated by the security policy or other regulations are followed and that no significant holes or weaknesses exist in deployed security solutions.

Auditors are responsible for reviewing and verifying that processes and procedures are in place to properly implement the security policy or other regulations. They also verify that these processes and procedures are being followed and are adequate to meet the organization's requirements. In other words, they perform the auditing.

Auditing and Auditing

The term *auditing* has two different distinct meanings within the context of IT security, so it's important to recognize the differences.

- First, *auditing* refers to *the use of audit logs and monitoring tools to track activity*. For example, audit logs can record when any user accesses a file and document exactly what the user did with the file and when.

- Second, *auditing* also refers to an inspection or evaluation. Specifically, an audit is an *inspection or evaluation of a specific processes or results to determine whether an organization is following specific rules or guidelines*.

These rules may be from the organization's security policy or a result of external laws and regulations. For example, a security policy may dictate that inactive accounts should be disabled as soon as an employee is terminated. An audit can check for inactive accounts and even verify the exact time accounts were disabled and match this to the time of a terminated employee's exit interview. Inspection audits can be done internally or by an external auditor, and they will often use the logs created from auditing and monitoring as part of the evaluation process.

Inspection Audits

Secure IT environments rely heavily on auditing as a detective security control to discover vulnerabilities. Two important audits within the context of access control are access review audits and user entitlement audits.

The frequency of a security audit or security review is based on risk. An organization evaluates vulnerabilities and threats against its valuable assets to determine the level of risk. This helps the organization determine if the expense of an audit is warranted and how frequently an audit is needed. It's important to clearly define and adhere to the frequency of audit reviews.

 Audits cost time and money, so the frequency of an audit is based on the associated risk. For example, user entitlement audits to examine privileged accounts would be performed much more often than user entitlement audits of nonprivileged accounts because compromised privileged accounts represent a higher risk to the organization.

As with many other aspects of deploying and maintaining security, security audits are often viewed as key elements of due care. If senior management fails to enforce compliance with regular periodic security reviews, then they will be held accountable and liable for any asset losses that occur because of security breaches or policy violations. When audits aren't performed, it can result in the perception that management is not exercising due care.

Access Review Audits

Many organizations perform periodic access reviews and audits to ensure that object access and account management practices support the security policy. These audits check that users do not have excessive privileges and that accounts are managed appropriately. They ensure that processes and procedures are in place, being followed, and working as expected.

For example, highly valuable data should be restricted to only the users who need it. An access review audit will verify that data has been classified and that data classifications are clear to the users. Additionally, it will ensure that the requirements to be granted access to data are clearly understood by anyone who has the authority to grant access. If a help desk professional can grant access to highly classified data, the help desk professional needs to know what makes a user eligible for the access.

When examining account management practices, an access review audit will ensure that that accounts are disabled and deleted in accordance with best practices and security policies. For example, inactive accounts should be disabled as soon as an employee is terminated. A typical termination procedure policy often includes the following elements: At least one witness is present during the exit interview, account access is disabled during the interview, employee identification badges and other physical credentials such as smart cards are collected, and the employee is escorted off the premises immediately after the interview. The access review will verify that a policy exists and then check to see if it is being followed. When terminated employees have continued access to the network after an exit interview, they can easily cause damage.

Audits usually focus on policies rather than implementation. For example, a review of user account management typically does not address whether some specific password conforms to stated company password policy. That issue is addressed by enrollment tools, password policies, and periodic penetration testing or ethical hacking.

User Entitlement Audits

User entitlement refers to the privileges granted to users. Users need rights and permissions (privileges) to perform their job, but they only need a limited number of privileges. In the context of user entitlement, the principle of least privilege ensures that users have only the privileges they need to perform their job and no more. (Chapter 1 briefly mentioned the principle of least privilege, which is expanded in Chapter 13.)

While access controls attempt to enforce the principle of least privilege, there are times when users are granted excessive privileges. User entitlement reviews can discover when users do have excessive privileges or violate security policies related to user entitlement.

Audits of Privileged Groups

Many organizations use groups as part of a role-based access control model. It's important to limit the membership of those groups. It's also important to make sure group members are using their high-privilege accounts only when absolutely necessary. Audits can help determine if these policies are being followed.

High-Level Administrator Groups

Many operating systems have privileged groups such as an Administrators group. The Administrators group is typically granted full privileges on a system, and when a user account is placed in the Administrators group, the user also has full privileges. With this in mind, a user entitlement review will often review membership in any privileged groups, including the different administrator groups.

Some groups have such high privileges that even in organizations with tens of thousands of users, their membership is limited to a very few people. For example, Microsoft domains include a group known as the Enterprise Admins group. Users in this group can do anything on any domain within a Microsoft forest (group of related domains). This group has so much power that membership is often restricted to only two or three high-level administrators. Monitoring and auditing membership in this group can uncover unauthorized individuals who have been added.

It is possible to use automated methods to monitor membership in privileged accounts so that attempts to add unauthorized users automatically fail. However, audit logs will also record this action, and an entitlement review can check for these events. The audit trail can then be examined to determine who attempted to add the unauthorized account.

An organization can also create additional groups with elevated privileges. For example, the organization may create an IT Admins group for some users in the IT department. They would grant this group privileges based on the needs of its users and place the user accounts in the IT department into the group. Needless to say, only users from the IT department should be in the group. A user entitlement audit can verify that users in other departments are not in the group. This is one way to detect creeping privileges.

A user entitlement audit can also detect whether processes are in place and when processes are not followed to remove privileges when they are no longer needed, such as when a user is transferred to a different department.

Dual Administrator Accounts

Many organizations require administrators to maintain two accounts. One account is used for regular day-to-day use and the second account has additional privileges and is used for administrative work. This is often done to reduce the risk associated with this privileged account.

For example, if a system is infected while a user is logged on, the malware can often assume the privileges of the user. If the user is logged on with a privileged account, the malware starts with these elevated privileges. However, if an administrator uses the administrator account only 10 percent of the time to perform administrative actions, this reduces the potential risk of an infection occurring at the same time the administrator is logged on with an administrator account.

Auditing can verify that administrators are using the privileged account appropriately. For example, an organization may estimate that administrators will need to use a privileged account only about 10 percent of the time during a typical day and should use their regular account the rest of the time. An analysis of logs can show whether this is an accurate estimate and whether administrators are following the rule. If the administrator account is constantly used but the regular user account is rarely accessed, an audit can flag this obvious violation of policy.

Similarly, the administrator account requires a stronger password. A policy may state that regular passwords must be at least 8 characters long but that administrators are required to maintain passwords more than 15 characters long. Password cracking tools can attempt to discover the passwords of administrator accounts to verify that administrators are using stronger passwords.

Handling Audit Reports

The actual formats used by an organization to produce reports from audit trails will vary greatly. However, those reports should all address a few basic or central concepts:

- The purpose of the audit
- The scope of the audit
- The results discovered or revealed by the audit

In addition to these basic concepts, audit reports often include many details specific to the environment, such as time, date, and which systems were audited. They can also include a wide range of content that focuses on problems, events, and conditions; standards, criteria, and baselines; causes, reasons, impact, and effect; or recommended solutions and safeguards.

Audit reports should have a structure or design that is clear, concise, and objective. It is common for an auditor to include opinions or recommendations for response to the content of a report, but its actual findings should be based on fact and evidence from audit trails.

Protecting Audit Results

Audit reports include sensitive information and should be assigned a classification label and handled appropriately. Only those people with sufficient privilege should have access to audit reports. This includes high-level executives and security personnel involved in the creation of the report or responsible for the correction of discovered items.

An audit report may also be prepared with limited data for other personnel. This modified report provides only the details relevant to the target audience. For example, senior management does not need to know all the minute details of an audit report. Therefore, the audit report for senior management is much more concise and offers more of an overview or summary of findings. An audit report for a security administrator responsible for correction of the problems should be very detailed and include all available information on the events it covers.

On the other hand, the fact that an audit is being performed is often very public. This lets personnel know that senior management is actively taking steps to maintain security.

Distributing Audit Reports

Once an audit report is completed, it should be submitted to its assigned recipients (as defined in security policy documentation) and a signed confirmation of receipt should be filed. When an audit report contains information about serious security violations or performance issues, that report should be escalated to higher levels of management for review, notification, and assignment of a response.

Using External Auditors

Many organizations choose to conduct independent audits by hiring external security auditors. External audits are required by some laws and regulations. External audits provide a level of objectivity that an internal audit cannot provide and bring a fresh, outside perspective to internal policies, practices, and procedures.

 Many organizations also hire external security experts to perform penetration testing against their system as a form of testing. (For more about penetration testing, see Chapter 14.)

An external auditor is given access to the company's security policy and the authorization to inspect every aspect of the IT and physical environment. Thus, the auditor must be a trusted entity. The goal of the audit activity is to obtain a final report that details findings and suggests countermeasures when appropriate.

An external audit can take a considerable amount of time to complete—weeks or months, in some cases. During the course of the audit, the auditor may issue interim reports. An *interim report* is a written or verbal report given to the organization about any observed security weaknesses or policy/procedure mismatches that demand immediate attention. Interim reports are issued whenever a problem or issue is too important to wait until a final audit report is issued.

Once the auditors complete their investigations, an exit conference is held. During that conference, the auditors present and discuss their findings and discuss resolution issues with the affected parties. However, only after the exit conference is over and the auditors have left the premises do they write and submit their final audit report to the organization. This allows the final audit report to remain unaffected by office politics and coercion.

After the final audit report is received, internal auditors should determine whether the recommendations in the report should be acted upon. It is the responsibility of senior management to select which recommendations to follow and to delegate their implementation to the security team.

Summary

It's important to understand basic risk elements when evaluating the potential loss from the multiple types of access control attacks that exist. Risk is the possibility or likelihood that a threat can exploit a vulnerability, resulting in a loss. Asset valuation identifies the value of assets, threat modeling identifies potential threats, and vulnerability analysis identifies vulnerabilities.

Common access control attacks attempt to circumvent authentication mechanisms. Access aggregation is the act of collecting and aggregating nonsensitive information in an attempt to infer sensitive information. Passwords are a common authentication mechanism, and several different types of attacks attempt to crack passwords. Password attacks include dictionary attacks, brute-force attacks, rainbow table attacks, and sniffer attacks. Side-channel attacks are passive attacks against smart cards. Social engineering techniques are often used in an attempt to get passwords and other data.

Logging and monitoring provide overall accountability when combined with effective identification and authentication practices. Logging involves recording events in logs and database files. Security logs, system logs, application logs, firewall logs, proxy logs, and change management logs are all common log files. Log files include valuable data and should be protected to ensure that they aren't modified, deleted, or corrupted. If they are not protected, attackers will often try to modify or delete them, and they will not be admissible as evidence to prosecute an attacker.

Monitoring involves reviewing logs in real time and also later as part of an audit. Audit trails are the records created by recording information about events and occurrences into one or more databases or log files, and they can be used to reconstruct events, extract information about incidents, and prove or disprove culpability. Audit trails provide a passive form of detective security control and serve as a deterrent in the same manner as CCTV or security guards do. In addition, they can be essential as evidence in the prosecution of criminals. Logs can be quite large, so different methods are used to analyze them or reduce their size. Sampling is a statistical method used to analyze logs, and using clipping levels is a nonstatistical method involving predefined thresholds for items of interest.

The effectiveness of access controls can be assessed using different types of audits and reviews. Auditing is a methodical examination or review of an environment to ensure compliance with regulations and to detect abnormalities, unauthorized occurrences, or outright crimes. Access review audits ensure that object access and account management practices support an organization's security policy. User entitlement audits ensure that the principle of least privilege is followed.

Audit reports document the results of an audit. These reports should be protected and distribution should be limited to only specific people in an organization. Senior management and security professionals have a need to access the results of security audits, but if attackers have access to audit reports, they can use the information to identify vulnerabilities they can exploit.

Exam Essentials

Understand basic risk elements.   Risk is the possibility or likelihood that a threat can exploit a vulnerability and cause damage to assets. Asset valuation identifies the value of assets, threat modeling identifies threats against these assets, and vulnerability analysis identifies weaknesses in an organization's valuable assets. Access aggregation is a type of attack that combines, or aggregates, nonsensitive information to learn sensitive information and is used in reconnaissance attacks.

Know how brute-force and dictionary attacks work.   Brute-force and dictionary attacks are carried out against a stolen password database file or the logon prompt of a system. They are designed to discover passwords. In brute-force attacks, all possible combinations of keyboard characters are used, whereas a predefined list of possible passwords is used in a dictionary attack. Online brute-force attacks are mitigated with account lockout controls.

Understand the need for strong passwords.   Strong passwords make password cracking utilities less successful. Strong passwords include multiple character types and are not words contained in a dictionary. Password policies ensure that users create strong policies. Passwords should be encrypted when stored and encrypted when sent over a network. Authentication can be strengthened by using an additional factor beyond just passwords.

Understand spoofing attacks.   Spoofing is pretending to be something or someone else, and it is used in many types of attacks, including access control attacks. Attackers often try to obtain the credentials of users so that they can spoof the user's identity. Spoofing attacks include email spoofing, phone number spoofing, and IP spoofing. Many phishing attacks use spoofing methods.

Understand sniffer attacks.   A sniffer attack (or snooping attack) is any activity that results in a malicious user obtaining information about a network or traffic on that network. A sniffer is a packet-capturing program that dumps the contents of packets traveling over the network medium into a file. Data sent over a network in cleartext can be captured and read by an attacker.

Understand social engineering.   A social engineering attack is an attempt by an attacker to convince an employee to provide information (such as a password) or perform an action they wouldn't normally perform, resulting in a security compromise. Often the goal of social engineering is to gain access to the IT infrastructure or the physical facility. User education is an effective tool to prevent the effectiveness of social engineering attacks.

Understand phishing.   Phishing attacks are commonly used to try to trick users into giving up personal information, including user account names and passwords. Spear phishing targets specific groups of users, and whaling targets high-level executives. Vishing uses VoIP technologies.

Know the types of log files.   Log data is recorded in databases and different types of log files. Common log files include security logs, system logs, application logs, firewall logs, proxy logs, and change management log. Log files should be protected by centrally storing them and using permissions to restrict access; archived logs should be set to read-only to prevent modifications.

Understand monitoring and uses of monitoring tools.   Monitoring is a form of auditing that focuses on active review of log file data. Monitoring is used to hold subjects accountable for their actions and to detect abnormal or malicious activities. It is also used to monitor system performance. Monitoring tools such as IDSs or SIEMs automate monitoring and provide real-time analysis of events.

Understand how accountability is maintained.   Accountability is maintained for individual subjects through the use of auditing. Activities of users and events caused by the actions of users while online can be recorded so users can be held accountable for their actions. This directly promotes good user behavior and compliance with the organization's security policy.

Understand audit trails.   Audit trails are the records created by recording information about events and occurrences into one or more databases or log files. They are used to reconstruct an event, to extract information about an incident, and to prove or disprove culpability. Using audit trails is a passive form of detective security control, and audit trails are essential evidence in the prosecution of criminals.

Understand sampling.   Sampling, or data extraction, is the process of extracting elements from a large body of data to construct a meaningful representation or summary of the whole. Statistical sampling uses precise mathematical functions to extract meaningful information from a large volume of data. Clipping is a form of nonstatistical sampling that only records events that exceed a threshold.

Understand auditing and the need for frequent security audits.   Auditing is a methodical examination or review of an environment to ensure compliance with regulations and to detect abnormalities, unauthorized occurrences, or outright crimes. Secure IT environments rely heavily on auditing. Overall, auditing serves as a primary type of detective control used within a secure environment. The frequency of an IT infrastructure security audit or security review is based on risk. An organization determines whether sufficient risk exists to warrant the expense and interruption of a security audit; degree of risk also affects how often an audit is performed. It is important to clearly define and adhere to the frequency of audit reviews.

Understand that auditing is an aspect of due care.   Security audits and effectiveness reviews are key elements in displaying due care. Senior management must enforce compliance with regular periodic security reviews or they will likely be held accountable and liable for any asset losses that occur.

Understand the need to control access to audit reports.   Audit reports typically address common concepts: the purpose of the audit, the scope of the audit, and the results discovered or revealed by the audit. They often include other details specific to the environment and can include sensitive information such as problems, standards, causes, and recommendations. Audit reports that include sensitive information should be assigned a classification label and handled appropriately. Only people with sufficient privilege should have access to them. An audit report can be prepared in various versions for different target audiences to include only the details needed by a specific audience. For example, senior security administrators might have a report with all the relevant details, while a report for executives would provide only high-level information.

Understand access review and user entitlement audits.   An access review audit ensures that object access and account management practices support the security policy. User entitlement audits ensure that the principle of least privilege is followed and often focus on privileged accounts.

Written Lab

1. List three elements to identify when evaluating access control attacks.

2. Name at least three types of attacks used to discover passwords.

3. Describe the relationship between auditing and audit trails.

4. What should an organization do to verify that accounts are managed properly?

Review Questions

1. When an organization is attempting to identify risks, what should they identify first?

   A. Assets

   B. Threats

   C. Vulnerabilities

   D. Public attacks

2. What would an organization do to identify weaknesses?

   A. Asset valuation

   B. Threat modeling

   C. Vulnerability analysis

   D. Access review

3. Which of the following is not a valid measure to take to improve protection against brute-force and dictionary attacks?

   A. Enforce strong passwords through a security policy.

   B. Maintain strict control over physical access.

   C. Require all users to log in remotely.

   D. Use two-factor authentication.

4. What type of attack can detect passwords sent across a network in cleartext?

   A. Spoofing attack

   B. Spamming attack

   C. Sniffing attack

   D. Side-channel attack

5. Which of the following can help mitigate the success of an online brute-force attack?

   A. Rainbow table

   B. Account lockout

   C. Salting passwords

   D. Encryption of password

6. What is an attack that attempts to detect flaws in smart cards?

   A. Whaling

   B. Side-channel attack

   C. Brute-force

   D. Rainbow table attack

7. What type of attack uses email and attempts to trick high-level executives?

    A. Phishing

    B. Spear phishing

    C. Whaling

    D. Vishing

8. What provides data for recreating the history of an event, intrusion, or system failure?

    A. Security policies

    B. Log files

    C. Audit reports

    D. Business continuity planning

9. What can be used to reduce the amount of logged or audited data using nonstatistical methods?

    A. Clipping levels

    B. Sampling

    C. Log analysis

    D. Alarm triggers

10. Which of the following focuses more on the patterns and trends of data than on the actual content?

    A. Keystroke monitoring

    B. Traffic analysis

    C. Event logging

    D. Security auditing

11. What is used to keep subjects accountable for their actions while they are authenticated to a system?

    A. Authentication

    B. Monitoring

    C. Account lockout

    D. User entitlement reviews

12. Audit trails are considered to be what type of security control?

    A. Administrative

    B. Passive detective

    C. Corrective

    D. Physical

13. The absence of which of the following can result in the perception that due care is not being maintained?

   A. Periodic security audits

   B. Deployment of all available controls

   C. Performance reviews

   D. Audit reports for shareholders

14. Which of the following options is a methodical examination or review of an environment to ensure compliance with regulations and to detect abnormalities, unauthorized occurrences, or outright crimes?

   A. Penetration testing

   B. Auditing

   C. Risk analysis

   D. Entrapment

15. When performing access review audits, which type of account is the most important to audit?

   A. None is more important. They are all equal.

   B. Regular user accounts

   C. Auditor accounts

   D. Privileged accounts

16. What would detect when a user has more privileges than necessary?

   A. Account management

   B. User entitlement audit

   C. Logging

   D. Reporting

17. Why should access to audit reports be controlled and restricted?

   A. They contain copies of confidential data stored on the network.

   B. They contain information about the vulnerabilities of the system.

   C. They are useful only to upper management.

   D. They include the details about the configuration of security controls.

Refer to the following scenario when answering questions 18 through 20:

An organization has recently suffered a series of security breaches that have significantly damaged its reputation. Several successful attacks have stolen customer database files accessible via one of the company's web servers. Additionally, an employee had access to secret data from previous job assignments. This employee made copies of the data and sold it to competitors. The organization has hired a security consultant to help them reduce their risk from future attacks.

18. What would the consultant use to identify potential attackers?

    A. Asset valuation

    B. Threat modeling

    C. Vulnerability analysis

    D. Access review and audit

19. What would need to be completed to ensure that the consultant has the correct focus?

    A. Asset valuation

    B. Threat modeling

    C. Vulnerability analysis

    D. Creation of audit trails

20. What could have prevented the employee from stealing and selling the secret data?

    A. Asset valuation

    B. Threat modeling

    C. Vulnerability analysis

    D. User entitlement review

Chapter 3

Secure Network Architecture and Securing Network Components

THE CISSP EXAM TOPICS COVERED IN THIS CHAPTER INCLUDE:

2. **Telecommunications and Network Security**

   A. Understand secure network architecture and design (e.g., IP and non-IP protocols, segmentation):

      A.1 OSI and TCP/IP models

      A.2 IP networking

      A.3 Implications of multi-layer protocols

   B. Securing network components:

      B.1 Hardware (e.g., modems, switches, routers, wireless access points)

      B.2 Transmission media (e.g., wired, wireless, fiber)

      B.3 Network access control devices (e.g., firewalls, proxies)

      B.4 Endpoint security

Computers and networks emerge from the integration of communication devices, storage devices, processing devices, security devices, input devices, output devices, operating systems, software, services, data, and people. The CISSP CBK states that a thorough knowledge of these hardware and software components is an essential element of being able to implement and maintain security. This chapter discusses the OSI model as a guiding principle in networking, cabling, wireless connectivity, TCP/IP and related protocols, networking devices, and firewalls.

The Telecommunications and Network Security domain for the CISSP certification exam deals with topics related to network components (i.e., network devices and protocols); specifically, how they function and how they are relevant to security. This domain is discussed in this chapter and in Chapter 4, "Secure Communications and Network Attacks." Be sure to read and study the materials in both chapters to ensure complete coverage of the essential material for the CISSP certification exam.

OSI Model

Communications between computers over networks are made possible by protocols. A *protocol* is a set of rules and restrictions that define how data is transmitted over a network medium (e.g., twisted-pair cable, wireless transmission). In the early days of network development, many companies had their own proprietary protocols, which meant interaction between computers of different vendors was often difficult, if not impossible. In an effort to eliminate this problem, the International Organization for Standardization (ISO) developed the Open Systems Interconnection (OSI) Reference Model for protocols in the early 1980s. Specifically, ISO 7498 defines the OSI Reference Model (more commonly called the OSI model). Understanding the OSI model and how it relates to network design, deployment, and security is essential in preparing for the CISSP exam.

In order to properly establish secure data communications, it is important to fully understand all of the technologies involved in computer communications. From hardware and software to protocols and encryption and beyond, there are lots of details to know, standards to understand, and procedures to follow. Additionally, the basis of secure network architecture and design is a thorough knowledge of the OSI and TCP/IP models as well as IP networking in general.

History of the OSI Model

The OSI model wasn't the first or only attempt to streamline networking protocols or establish a common communications standard. In fact, the most widely used protocol today, TCP/IP (which is based upon the DARPA model, also known now as the *TCP/IP model*) was developed in the early 1970s. The OSI model was not developed until the late 1970s.

The OSI protocol was developed to establish a common communication structure or standard for all computer systems. The actual OSI protocol was never widely adopted, but the theory behind the OSI protocol, the OSI model, was readily accepted. The OSI model serves as an abstract framework, or theoretical model, for how protocols should function in an ideal world on ideal hardware. Thus, the OSI model has become a common reference point against which all protocols can be compared and contrasted.

OSI Functionality

The *OSI model* divides networking tasks into seven distinct layers. Each layer is responsible for performing specific tasks or operations for the ultimate goal of supporting data exchange (in other words, network communication) between two computers. The layers are always numbered from bottom to top (see Figure 3.1). They are referred to by either their name or their layer number. For example, *layer 3* is also known as the *Network layer*. The layers are ordered specifically to indicate how information flows through the various levels of communication. Each layer communicates directly with the layer above it as well as the layer below it, plus the peer layer on a communication partner system.

FIGURE 3.1   Representation of the OSI model

Application	7
Presentation	6
Session	5
Transport	4
Network	3
Data Link	2
Physical	1

The OSI model is an open network architecture guide for network product vendors. This standard, or guide, provides a common foundation for the development of new protocols, networking services, and even hardware devices. By working from the OSI model, vendors are able to ensure that their products will integrate with products from other companies and be supported by a wide range of operating systems. If all vendors developed their own networking framework, interoperability between products from different vendors would be next to impossible.

The real benefit of the OSI model is its expression of how networking actually functions. In the most basic sense, network communications occur over a physical connection (whether that physical connection is electrons over copper, photons over fiber, or radio signals through the air). Physical devices establish channels through which electronic signals can pass from one computer to another. These physical device channels are only one type of the seven logical communication types defined by the OSI model. Each layer of the OSI model communicates via a logical channel with its peer layer on another computer. This enables protocols based on the OSI model to support a type of authentication by being able to identify the remote communication entity as well as authenticate the source of the received data.

Encapsulation/Deencapsulation

Protocols based on the OSI model employ a mechanism called *encapsulation*. Encapsulation is the addition of a header, and possibly a footer, to the data received by each layer from the layer above before it's handed off the data to the layer below. As the message is encapsulated at each layer, the previous layer's header and payload combine to become the payload of the current layer. Encapsulation occurs as the data moves down through the OSI model layers from Application to Physical. The inverse action occurring as data moves up through the OSI model layers from Physical to Application is known as *deencapsulation*. The encapsulation/deencapsulation process is as follows:

1. The Application layer creates a message.

2. The Application layer passes the message to the Presentation layer.

3. The Presentation layer encapsulates the message by adding information to it. Information is usually added only at the beginning of the message (called a *header*); however, some layers also add material at the end of the message (called a *footer*), as shown in Figure 3.2.

FIGURE 3.2 Representation of OSI model encapsulation

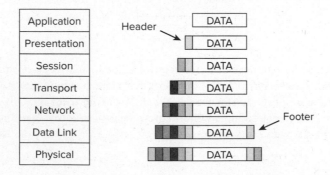

4. The process of passing the message down and adding layer-specific information continues until the message reaches the Physical layer.

5. At the Physical layer, the message is converted into electrical impulses that represent bits and is transmitted over the physical connection.

6. The receiving computer captures the bits from the physical connection and recreates the message in the Physical layer.

7. The Physical layer converts the message from bits into a Data Link frame and sends the message up to the Data Link layer.

8. The Data Link layer strips its information and sends the message up to the Network layer.

9. This process of deencapsulation is performed until the message reaches the Application layer.

10. When the message reaches the Application layer, the data in the message is sent to the intended software recipient.

The information removed by each layer contains instructions, checksums, and so on that can be understood only by the peer layer that originally added or created the information (see Figure 3.3). This information is what creates the logical channel that enables peer layers on different computers to communicate.

FIGURE 3.3 Representation of the OSI model peer layer logical channels

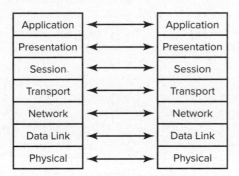

The message sent into the protocol stack at the Application layer (layer 7) is called the *data stream*. It retains the label of data stream until it reaches the Transport layer (layer 4), where it is called a *segment* (TCP protocols) or a *datagram* (UDP protocols). In the Network layer (layer 3), it is called a *packet*. In the Data Link layer (layer 2), it is called a *frame*. In the Physical layer (layer 1), the data has been converted into bits for transmission over the physical connection medium. Figure 3.4 shows how each layer changes the data through this process.

FIGURE 3.4   OSI model data names

Application	Data stream
Presentation	Data stream
Session	Data stream
Transport	Segment (TCP)/Datagram (UDP)
Network	Packet
Data Link	Frame
Physical	Bits

OSI Layers

Understanding the functions and responsibilities of each layer of the OSI model will help you understand how network communications function, how attacks can be perpetrated against network communications, and how security can be implemented to protect network communications. We discuss each layer, starting with the bottom layer, in the following sections.

> For more information on the TCP/IP stack, search for *TCP/IP* on Wikipedia (http://en.wikipedia.org).

 Real World Scenario

Remember the OSI

Although it can be argued that the OSI has little practical use and that most technical workers don't use the OSI on a regular basis, you can rest assured that the OSI model and its related concepts are firmly positioned within the CISSP exam. To make the most of the OSI, you must first be able to remember the names of the seven layers in their proper order. One common method of memorizing them is to create a mnemonic from the initial letters of the layer names so they are easier to remember. One of our favorites is Please Do Not Teach Surly People Acronyms. Do take note that this memorization mnemonic works from the Physical layer up to the Application layer. A mnemonic working from the Application layer down is All Presidents Since Truman Never Did Pot. There are many other OSI memorization schemes out there; just be sure you know whether they are top-down or bottom-up.

Physical Layer

The *Physical layer (layer 1)* accepts the frame from the Data Link layer and converts the frame into bits for transmission over the physical connection medium. The Physical layer is also responsible for receiving bits from the physical connection medium and converting them into a frame to be used by the Data Link layer.

The Physical layer contains the device drivers that tell the protocol how to employ the hardware for the transmission and reception of bits. Located within the Physical layer are electrical specifications, protocols, and interface standards such as the following:

- EIA/TIA-232 and EIA/TIA-449

- X.21

- High-Speed Serial Interface (HSSI)

- Synchronous Optical Network (SONET)

- V.24 and V.35

Through the device drivers and these standards, the Physical layer controls throughput rates, handles synchronization, manages line noise and medium access, and determines whether to use digital or analog signals or light pulses to transmit or receive data over the physical hardware interface.

Network hardware devices that function at layer 1, the Physical layer, are network interface cards (NICs), hubs, repeaters, concentrators, and amplifiers. These devices perform hardware-based signal operations, such as sending a signal from one connection port out on all other ports (a hub) or amplifying the signal to support greater transmission distances (a repeater).

Data Link Layer

The *Data Link layer (layer 2)* is responsible for formatting the packet from the Network layer into the proper format for transmission. The proper format is determined by the hardware and the technology of the network. There are numerous possibilities, such as Ethernet (IEEE 802.3), Token Ring (IEEE 802.5), asynchronous transfer mode (ATM), Fiber Distributed Data Interface (FDDI), and Copper DDI (CDDI). Within the Data Link layer resides the technology-specific protocols that convert the packet into a properly formatted frame. Once the frame is formatted, it is sent to the Physical layer for transmission.

The following list includes some of the protocols found within the Data Link layer:

- Serial Line Internet Protocol (SLIP)

- Point-to-Point Protocol (PPP)

- Address Resolution Protocol (ARP)

- Reverse Address Resolution Protocol (RARP)

- Layer 2 Forwarding (L2F)

- Layer 2 Tunneling Protocol (L2TP)

- Point-to-Point Tunneling Protocol (PPTP)

- Integrated Services Digital Network (ISDN)

Part of the processing performed on the data within the Data Link layer includes adding the hardware source and destination addresses to the frame. The hardware address is the Media Access Control (MAC) address, which is a 6-byte (48-bit) binary address written in hexadecimal notation (for example, 00-13-02-1F-58-F5). The first 3 bytes (24 bits) of the address denote the vendor or manufacturer of the physical network interface. This is known as the Organizationally Unique Identifier (OUI). OUIs are registered with IEEE, who controls their issuance. The OUI can be used to discover the manufacturer of a NIC through the IEEE website at `http://standards.ieee.org/regauth/oui/index.shtml`. The last 3 bytes (24 bits) represent a unique number assigned to that interface by the manufacturer. No two devices can have the same MAC address.

EUI-48 to EUI-64

The MAC address has been 48 bits for decades. A similar addressing method is the EUI-48. EUI stands for Extended Unique Identifier. The original 48-bit MAC addressing scheme for IEEE 802 was adopted from the original Xerox Ethernet addressing method. MAC addresses typically are used to identify network hardware, while EUI is used to identity other types of hardware as well as software.

The IEEE has decided that *MAC-48* is an obsolete term and should be deprecated in favor of *EUI-48*.

There is also a move to convert from EUI-48 to EUI-64. This is preparation for future world-wide adoption of IPv6 as well as the exponential growth of the number of networking devices and network software packages, all of which need a unique identifier.

A MAC-48 or EUI-48 address can be represented by an EUI-64. In the case of MAC-48, two additional octets of FF:FF are added between the OUI (first 3 bytes) and the unique NIC specification (last 3 bytes)—for example, ccccccFFFFeeeeee. In the case of EUI-48, the two additional octets are FF:FE—for example, ccccccFFFEeeeeee.

Among the protocols at the Data Link layer (layer 2) of the OSI model, the two you should be familiar with are Address Resolution Protocol (ARP) and Reverse Address Resolution Protocol (RARP). ARP is used to resolve IP addresses into MAC addresses. Traffic on a network segment (for example, cables across a hub) is directed from its source system to its destination system using MAC addresses. RARP is used to resolve MAC addresses into IP addresses.

The Data Link layer contains two sublayers: the Logical Link Control (LLC) sublayer and the MAC sublayer. Details about these sublayers are not critical for the CISSP exam.

Network hardware devices that function at layer 2, the Data Link layer, are switches and bridges. These devices support MAC-based traffic routing. Switches receive a frame on one port and send it out another port based on the destination MAC address. MAC address destinations are used to determine whether a frame is transferred over the bridge from one network to another.

Network Layer

The *Network layer (layer 3)* is responsible for adding routing and addressing information to the data. The Network layer accepts the segment from the Transport layer and adds information to it to create a packet. The packet includes the source and destination IP addresses.

The routing protocols are located at this layer and include the following:

- Internet Control Message Protocol (ICMP)
- Routing Information Protocol (RIP)
- Open Shortest Path First (OSPF)
- Border Gateway Protocol (BGP)
- Internet Group Management Protocol (IGMP)
- Internet Protocol (IP)
- Internet Protocol Security (IPSec)
- Internetwork Packet Exchange (IPX)
- Network Address Translation (NAT)
- Simple Key Management for Internet Protocols (SKIP)

The Network layer is responsible for providing routing or delivery information, but it is not responsible for verifying guaranteed delivery (that is the responsibility of the Transport layer). The Network layer also manages error detection and node data traffic (in other words, traffic control).

Non-IP Protocols

Non-IP protocols are protocols that serve as an alternative to IP at the OSI Network layer (3). In the past, non-IP protocols were widely used. However, with the dominance and success of TCP/IP, non-IP protocols have become the purview of special-purpose networks. The three most recognized non-IP protocols are IPX, AppleTalk, and NetBEUI. Internetwork Packet Exchange (IPX) is part of the IPX/SPX protocol suite commonly used (although not strictly required) on Novell NetWare networks in the 1990s. AppleTalk is a suite of protocols developed by Apple for networking of Macintosh systems, originally released in 1984. Support for AppleTalk was removed from the Apple operating system as of the release of Mac OS X v10.6 in 2009. Both IPX and AppleTalk can be used as IP alternatives in a dead-zone network implementation using IP-to-alternate-protocol gateways (a dead zone is a network segment using an alternative Network layer protocol instead of IP). NetBIOS Extended User Interface (NetBEUI, aka NetBIOS Frame protocol, or NBF) is most widely known as a Microsoft protocol developed in 1985 to support file and printer sharing. Microsoft has enabled support of NetBEUI on modern networks by devising NetBIOS over TCP/IP (NBT). This in turn supports the Windows sharing protocol of Server Message Block (SMB) which is also known as Common Internet File System (CIFS). NetBEUI is no longer supported as a lower-layer protocol; only its SMB and CIFS variants are still in use.

A potential security risk exists when non-IP protocols are in use in a private network. Because non-IP protocols are rare, most firewalls are unable to perform packet header, address, or payload content filtering on those protocols. Thus, when it comes to non-IP protocols, a firewall typically must either block all or allow. If your organization is dependent on a service that operates over only a non-IP protocol, then you may have to live with the risk of passing all non-IP protocols through your firewall. This is mostly a concern within a private network when non-IP protocols traverse between network segments. However, non-IP protocols can be encapsulated in IP to be communicated across the Internet. In an encapsulation situation, IP firewalls are rarely able to perform content filtering on such encapsulation and thus security has to be set to an allow all or deny all configuration.

Routers and bridge routers (brouters) are among the network hardware devices that function at layer 3. *Routers* determine the best logical path for the transmission of packets based on speed, hops, preference, and so on. Routers use the destination IP address to guide the transmission of packets. A *brouter*, working primarily in layer 3 but in layer 2 when necessary, is a device that attempts to route first, but if that fails, it defaults to bridging.

Routing Protocols

There are two broad categories of routing protocols: distance vector and link state. *Distance vector* routing protocols maintain a list of destination networks along with metrics of direction and distance as measured in hops (in other words, the number of routers to cross to reach the destination). *Link state* routing protocols maintain a topography map of all connected networks and use this map to determine the shortest path to the destination. Common examples of distance vector routing protocols are RIP, Interior Gateway Routing Protocol (IGRP), and BGP, while a common example of a link state routing protocol is OSPF.

Transport Layer

The *Transport layer (layer 4)* is responsible for managing the integrity of a connection and controlling the session. It accepts a PDU (variably spelled out as Protocol Data Unit, Packet Data Unit, or Payload Data Unit—i.e., a container of information or data passed between network layers) from the Session layer and converts it into a segment. The Transport layer controls how devices on the network are addressed or referenced, establishes communication connections between nodes (also known as *devices*), and defines the rules of a session. Session rules specify how much data each segment can contain, how to verify the integrity of data transmitted, and how to determine whether data has been lost. Session rules are established through a handshaking process. (Please see the section "Transport Layer Protocols" later in this chapter for the discussion of the SYN/ACK three-way handshake of TCP.)

The Transport layer establishes a logical connection between two devices and provides end-to-end transport services to ensure data delivery. This layer includes mechanisms for segmentation, sequencing, error checking, controlling the flow of data, error correction, multiplexing, and network service optimization. The following protocols operate within the Transport layer:

- Transmission Control Protocol (TCP)
- User Datagram Protocol (UDP)
- Sequenced Packet Exchange (SPX)
- Secure Sockets Layer (SSL)
- Transport Layer Security (TLS)

Session Layer

The *Session layer (layer 5)* is responsible for establishing, maintaining, and terminating communication sessions between two computers. It manages dialogue discipline or dialogue control (simplex, half-duplex, full-duplex), establishes checkpoints for grouping and recovery, and retransmits PDUs that have failed or been lost since the last verified checkpoint. The following protocols operate within the Session layer:

- Network File System (NFS)
- Structured Query Language (SQL)
- Remote Procedure Call (RPC)

Communication sessions can operate in one of three different discipline or control modes:

Simplex   One-way direction communication

Half-duplex   Two-way communication, but only one direction can send data at a time

Full-duplex   Two-way communication, in which data can be sent in both directions simultaneously

Presentation Layer

The *Presentation layer (layer 6)* is responsible for transforming data received from the Application layer into a format that any system following the OSI model can understand. It imposes common or standardized structure and formatting rules onto the data. The Presentation layer is also responsible for encryption and compression. Thus, it acts as an interface between the network and applications. This layer is what allows various applications to interact over a network, and it does so by ensuring that the data formats are supported by both systems. Most file or data formats operate within this layer. This includes formats for images, video, sound, documents, email, web pages, control sessions, and so on. The following list includes some of the format standards that exist within the Presentation layer:

- American Standard Code for Information Interchange (ASCII)
- Extended Binary-Coded Decimal Interchange Mode (EBCDICM)
- Tagged Image File Format (TIFF)
- Joint Photographic Experts Group (JPEG)
- Moving Picture Experts Group (MPEG)
- Musical Instrument Digital Interface (MIDI)

 Real World Scenario

So Many Protocols, So Many Layers

With seven layers and more than 50 protocols, it may seem daunting to remember the layer in which each protocol resides. One way to learn this is to create flash cards. On the front of each card, write the name of the protocol; then on the back, write the layer name. After shuffling the cards, put the card for each protocol in a pile representing its supposed layer. Once you have placed all the protocols, check your work by viewing the backs of the cards. Repeat this process until you are able to place each one correctly.

Application Layer

The *Application layer (layer 7)* is responsible for interfacing user applications, network services, or the operating system with the protocol stack. It allows applications to communicate with the protocol stack. The Application layer determines whether a remote communication partner is available and accessible. It also ensures that sufficient resources are available to support the requested communications.

The application is not located within this layer; rather, the protocols and services required to transmit files, exchange messages, connect to remote terminals, and so on are found here. Numerous application-specific protocols are found within this layer, such as the following:

- Hypertext Transfer Protocol (HTTP)
- File Transfer Protocol (FTP)
- Line Print Daemon (LPD)
- Simple Mail Transfer Protocol (SMTP)
- Telnet
- Trivial File Transfer Protocol (TFTP)
- Electronic Data Interchange (EDI)
- Post Office Protocol version 3 (POP3)
- Internet Message Access Protocol (IMAP)
- Simple Network Management Protocol (SNMP)
- Network News Transport Protocol (NNTP)
- Secure Remote Procedure Call (S-RPC)
- Secure Electronic Transaction (SET)

There is a network device (or service) that works at the Application layer, namely, the gateway. However, an Application layer gateway is a specific type of component. It serves as a protocol translation tool. For example, an IP-to-IPX gateway takes inbound communications from TCP/IP and translates them over to IPX/SPX for outbound transmission. Application layer firewalls also operate at this layer. Other networking devices or filtering software may observe or modify traffic at this layer.

TCP/IP Model

The TCP/IP model (also called the DARPA or the DOD model) consists of only four layers, as opposed to the OSI Reference Model's seven. The four layers of the TCP/IP model are Application, Transport (also known as Host-to-Host), Internet (sometimes Internetworking), and Link (although Network Interface and sometimes Network Access are used). Figure 3.5 shows how they compare to the seven layers of the OSI model. The TCP/IP protocol suite was developed before the OSI Reference Model was created. The designers of the OSI Reference Model took care to ensure that the TCP/IP protocol suite fit their model because of its established deployment in networking.

FIGURE 3.5   Comparing the OSI model with the TCP/IP model

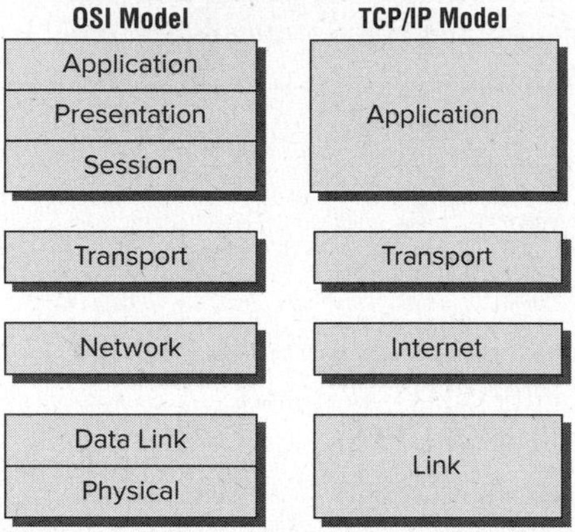

OSI Model

| Application |
| Presentation |
| Session |

| Transport |

| Network |

| Data Link |
| Physical |

TCP/IP Model

| Application |

| Transport |

| Internet |

| Link |

The TCP/IP model's Application layer corresponds to layers 5, 6, and 7 of the OSI model. The TCP/IP model's Transport layer corresponds to layer 4 from the OSI model. The TCP/IP model's Internet layer corresponds to layer 3 from the OSI model. The TCP/IP model's Link layer corresponds to layers 1 and 2 from the OSI model.

It has become common practice (through confusion, misunderstanding, and probably laziness) to also call the TCP/IP model layers by their OSI model layer equivalent names. The TCP/IP model's Application layer is already using a name borrowed from the OSI, so that one is a snap. The TCP/IP model's Host-to-Host layer is sometimes called the Transport layer (the OSI model's fourth layer). The TCP/IP model's Internet layer is sometimes called the Network layer (the OSI model's third layer). And the TCP/IP model's Link layer is sometimes called the Data Link or the Network Access layer (the OSI model's second layer).

Since the TCP/IP model layer names and the OSI model layer names can be used interchangeably, it is important to know which model is being addressed in various contexts. Unless informed otherwise, always assume that the OSI model provides the basis for discussion because it's the most widely used network reference model.

TCP/IP Protocol Suite Overview

The most widely used protocol suite is TCP/IP, but it is not just a single protocol; rather, it is a protocol stack comprising dozens of individual protocols (see Figure 3.6). TCP/IP is a platform-independent protocol based on open standards. However, this is both a benefit and a drawback. TCP/IP can be found in just about every available operating system, but it consumes a significant amount of resources and is relatively easy to hack into because it was designed for ease of use rather than for security.

FIGURE 3.6   The four layers of TCP/IP and its component protocols

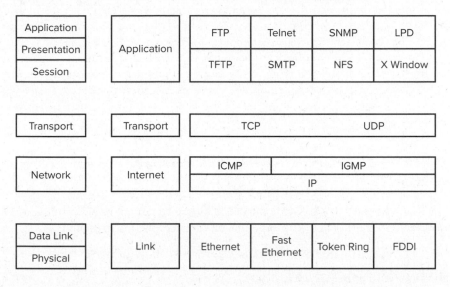

TCP/IP can be secured using VPN links between systems. VPN links are encrypted to add privacy, confidentiality, and authentication and to maintain data integrity. Protocols used to establish VPNs are Point-to-Point Tunneling Protocol (PPTP), Layer 2 Tunneling Protocol (L2TP), and Internet Protocol Security (IPSec). Another method to provide protocol-level security is to employ TCP wrappers. A *TCP wrapper* is an application that can serve as a basic firewall by restricting access to ports and resources based on user IDs or system IDs. Using TCP wrappers is a form of port-based access control.

Transport Layer Protocols

The two primary Transport layer protocols of TCP/IP are TCP and UDP. TCP is a connection-oriented protocol, whereas UDP is a connectionless protocol. When a communication connection is established between two systems, it is done using ports. TCP and UDP each have 65,536 ports. Since port numbers are 16-digit binary numbers, the total number of ports is 2^{16}, or 65,536, numbered from 0 through 65,535. A port (also called a *socket*) is little more than an address number that both ends of the communication link agree to use when transferring data. Ports allow a single IP address to be able to support multiple simultaneous communications, each using a different port number.

The first 1,024 of these ports (0–1,023) are called the *well-known ports* or the *service ports*. This is because they have standardized assignments as to the services they support. For example, port 80 is the standard port for web (HTTP) traffic, port 23 is the standard port for Telnet, and port 25 is the standard port for SMTP. You can find a list of ports worth knowing for the exam in the section "Common Application Layer Protocols" later in this chapter.

Ports 1024 to 49151 are known as the registered software ports. These are ports that have one or more networking software products specifically registered with the International Assigned Numbers Authority (IANA, www.iana.org) in order to provide a standardized port numbering system for clients attempting to connect to their products.

Ports 49152 to 65535 are known as the random, dynamic, or ephemeral ports because they are often used randomly and temporarily by clients as a source port. These random ports are also used by several networking services when negotiating a data transfer pipeline between client and server outside the initial service or registered ports, such as performed by common FTP.

Port Numbers

The IANA recommends that ports 49152 to 65535 be used as dynamic and/or private ports. However, not all OSs abide by this, such as, for example, the following:

- Berkeley Software Distribution (BSD) uses ports 1024 through 4999.

- Many Linux kernels use 32768 to 61000.

- Microsoft, up to and including Windows Server 2003, uses the range 1025 to 5000.

- Windows Vista, Windows 7, and Windows Server 2008 use the IANA range.

- FreeBSD, since version 4.6, has used the IANA suggested port range.

Transmission Control Protocol (TCP) operates at layer 4 (the Transport layer) of the OSI model. It supports full-duplex communications, is connection oriented, and employs reliable sessions. TCP is connection oriented because it employs a handshake process between two systems to establish a communication session. Upon completion of this handshake process, a communication session that can support data transmission between the client and server is established. The three-way handshake process is as follows:

1. The client sends a SYN (synchronize) flagged packet to the server.

2. The server responds with a SYN/ACK (synchronize and acknowledge) flagged packet back to the client.

3. The client responds with an ACK (acknowledge) flagged packet back to the server.

When a communication session is complete, there are two methods to disconnect the TCP session. First, and most common, is the use of FIN (finish) flagged packets instead of SYN flagged packets. Each side of a conversation will transmit a FIN flagged packet once all of its data is transmitted, triggering the opposing side to confirm with an ACK flagged packet. Thus, it takes four packets to gracefully tear down a TCP session. Second is the use of a RST (reset) flagged packet, which causes an immediate and abrupt session termination. (Please see the discussion of the TCP header flag later in this section.)

The segments of a TCP transmission are tagged with a sequence number. This allows the receiver to rebuild the original communication by reordering received segments back into their proper arrangement in spite of the order in which they were received. Data communicated through a TCP session is periodically verified with an acknowledgement. The acknowledgement is sent by the receiver back to the sender by setting the TCP header's acknowledgement sequence value to the last sequence number received from the sender within the transmission window. The number of packets transmitted before an acknowledge packet is sent is known as the *transmission window*. Data flow is controlled through a mechanism called *sliding windows*. TCP is able to use different sizes of windows (in other words, a different number of transmitted packets) before sending an acknowledgment. Larger windows allow for faster data transmission, but they should be used only on reliable connections where lost or corrupted data is minimal. Smaller windows should be used when the communication connection is unreliable. TCP should be employed when the delivery of data is required. Sliding windows allow this size to vary dynamically because the reliability of the TCP session changes while in use. In the event that all packets of a transmission window were not received, no acknowledgement is sent. After a timeout period, the sender will re-send the entire transmission window set of packets again.

The TCP header is relatively complex when compared to its sister protocol UDP. A TCP header is 20 to 60 bytes long. This header is divided into several sections, or fields, as detailed in Table 3.1.

TABLE 3.1 TCP header construction
(ordered from beginning of header to end)

Size in Bits	Field
16	Source port
16	Destination port
32	Sequence number
4	Data offset
4	Reserved for future use
8	Flags (see Table 3.2)
16	Window size
16	Checksum
16	Urgent pointer
Variable	Various options; must be a multiple of 32 bits

All of these fields have unique parameters and requirements, most of which are beyond the scope of the CISSP exam. However, you should be familiar with the details of the flags field. The flags field can contain a designation of one or more flags, or control bits. These flags indicate the function of the TCP packet and request that the recipient respond in a specific manner. The flag field is 8 bits long. Each of the bit positions represents a single flag, or control setting. Each position can be set on with a value of 1 or off with a value of 0. There are some conditions in which multiple flags can be enabled at once (in other words, the second packet in the TCP three-way handshake when both the SYN and ACK flags are set). Table 3.2 details the flag control bits.

TABLE 3.2   The TCP header flag field values

Flag Bit Designator	Name	Description
CWR	Congestion Window Reduced	Used to manage transmission over congested links; see RFC 3168
ECE	ECN-Echo (Explicit Congestion Notification)	Used to manage transmission over congested links; see RFC 3168
URG	Urgent	Indicates urgent data
ACK	Acknowledgement	Acknowledges synchronization or shutdown request
PSH	Push	Indicates need to push data immediately to application
RST	Reset	Causes immediate disconnect of TCP session
SYN	Synchronization	Requests synchronization with new sequencing numbers
FIN	Finish	Requests graceful shutdown of TCP session

An additional important tidbit is that the IP header protocol field value for TCP is 6 (0x06). The protocol field value is the label or flag found in the header of every IP packet that tells the receiving system what type of packet it is. The IP header's protocol field indicates the identity of the next encapsulated protocol (in other words, the protocol contained in the payload from the current protocol layer, such as ICMP or IGMP, or the next layer up, such as TCP or UDP). Think of it as like the label on a mystery-meat package wrapped in butcher paper you pull out of the freezer. Without the label, you would have to open it and inspect it to figure out what it was. But with the label, you can search or filter quickly to find items of interest. For a list of other protocol field values, please visit `www.iana.org/assignments/protocol-numbers`.

Unskilled Attackers Pester Real Security Folk

It might be a good idea to memorize at least the last six of the eight TCP header flags in their correct order. The first two flags (CWR and ECE) are rarely used today and thus are generally ignored/overlooked. However, the last six (URG, ACK, PHS, RST, SYN, and FIN) are still in common widespread use.

Keep in mind that these eight flags are eight binary positions (i.e., a byte) that can be presented in either hex or binary format. For example, 0x12 is the hex presentation of the byte 00010010. This specific byte layout indicates that the fourth and seventh flags are enabled. With the flag layout (using one letter per flag and leaving out CWR and ECE and replacing them with XX), XXUAPRSF is 000A00S0, or the SYN/ACK flag set.

You can memorize this flag order using the phrase "Unskilled Attackers Pester Real Security Folk," in which the first letter of each word corresponds to the first letter of the flags in positions 3 through 8.

 ### Real World Scenario

Protocol Discovery

Hundreds of protocols are in use on a typical TCP/IP network at any given moment. Using a sniffer, you can discover what protocols are in use on your current network. Before using a sniffer, though, make sure you have the proper permission or authorization. Without approval, using a sniffer can be considered a security violation because it enables you to eavesdrop on unprotected network communications. If you can't obtain permission at work, try this on your home network instead. Download and install a sniffer, such as Wireshark. Then use the sniffer to monitor the activity on your network. Discover just how many protocols (in other words, subprotocols of TCP/IP) are in use on your network.

Another step in using a sniffer is to analyze the contents of captured packets. Pick out a few different protocol packets and inspect their headers. Look for TCP, ICMP, ARP, and UDP packets. Compare the contents of their headers. Try to locate any special flags or field codes used by the protocols. You'll likely discover that there is a lot more going on within a protocol than you ever imagined.

User Datagram Protocol (UDP) also operates at layer 4 (the Transport layer) of the OSI model. It is a connectionless "best-effort" communications protocol. It offers no error detection or correction, does not use sequencing, does not use flow control mechanisms, does not use a preestablished session, and is considered unreliable. UDP has very low overhead and thus can transmit data quickly. However, UDP should be used only when the delivery of data is not essential. UDP is often employed by real-time or streaming communications for audio and/or video. The IP header protocol field value for UDP is 17 (0x11).

As mentioned earlier, the UDP header is relatively simple in comparison with the TCP header. A UDP header is 8 bytes (64 bits) long. This header is divided into four sections, or fields (each 16 bits long):

- Source port
- Destination port
- Message length
- Checksum

Network Layer Protocols and IP Networking Basics

Another important protocol in the TCP/IP protocol suite operates at the Network layer of the OSI model, namely, Internet Protocol (IP). IP provides route addressing for data packets. It is this route addressing that is the foundation of global Internet communications because it provides a means of identity and prescribes transmission paths. Similar to UDP, IP is connectionless and is an unreliable datagram service. IP does not offer guarantees that packets will be delivered or that packets will be delivered in the correct order, and it does not guarantee that packets will be delivered only once. Thus, you must employ TCP on IP to gain reliable and controlled communication sessions.

IPv4 vs. IPv6

IPv4 is the version of Internet Protocol that is most widely used around the world. However, a version known as IPv6 is primed to take over and improve network addressing and routing. IPv4 uses a 32-bit addressing scheme, while IPv6 uses 128 bits for addressing. IPv6 offers many new features that are not available in IPv4. Some of IPv6's new features are scoped addresses, autoconfiguration, and Quality of Service (QoS) priority values. Scoped addresses give administrators the ability to group and then block or allow access to network services, such as file servers or printing. Autoconfiguration removes the need for both DHCP and NAT. QoS priority values allow for traffic management based on prioritized content.

IPv6 is supported by most operating systems released since 2000, either natively or via an add-in. However, IPv6 has been slowly adopted. Most of the IPv6 networks are currently located in private networks such as those in large corporations, research laboratories, and universities.

IP classes

Basic knowledge of IP addressing and IP classes is a must for any security professional. If you are rusty on addressing, subnetting, classes, and other related topics, take the time to refresh yourself. Table 3.3 and Table 3.4 provide a quick overview of the key details of classes and default subnets. A full Class A subnet supports 16,777,214 hosts; a full class B subnet supports 65,534 hosts; and a full Class C subnet supports 254 hosts. Class D is used for multicasting, while Class E is reserved for future use.

TABLE 3.3 IP classes

Class	First Binary Digits	Decimal Range of First Octet
A	0	1–126
B	10	128–191
C	110	192–223
D	1110	224–239
E	1111	240–255

TABLE 3.4 IP classes' default subnet masks

Class	Default Subnet Mask	CIDR Equivalent
A	255.0.0.0	/8
B	255.255.0.0	/16
C	255.255.255.0	/24

Note that the entire Class A network of 127 was set aside for the loopback address, although only a single address is actually needed for that purpose.

Another option for subnetting is to use Classless Inter-Domain Routing (CIDR) notation. CIDR uses mask bits rather than a full dotted-decimal notation subnet mask. Thus, instead of 255.255.0.0, a CIDR is added to the IP address after a slash, as in 172.16.1.1/16, for example. One significant benefit of CIDR over traditional subnet-masking techniques is the ability to combine multiple noncontiguous sets of addresses into a single subnet. For example, it is possible to combine several Class C subnets into a single larger subnet grouping. If CIDR piques your interest, see the CIDR article on Wikipedia or visit the IETF's RFC for CIDR at http://tools.ietf.org/html/rfc4632.

ICMP and IGMP are other protocols in the Network layer of the OSI model:

ICMP   Internet Control Message Protocol (ICMP) is used to determine the health of a network or a specific link. ICMP is utilized by `ping`, `traceroute`, `pathping`, and other network management tools. The `ping` utility employs ICMP echo packets and bounces them off remote systems. Thus, you can use `ping` to determine whether the remote system is online, whether the remote system is responding promptly, whether the intermediary systems are supporting communications, and the level of performance efficiency at which the intermediary systems are communicating. The `ping` utility includes a redirect function that allows the echo responses to be sent to a different destination than the system of origin.

Unfortunately, the features of ICMP are often exploited in various forms of bandwidth-based denial of service attacks, such as Ping of Death, Smurf, and Ping Floods. Ping of Death sends a malformed ping larger than 65,535 bytes (larger than the maximum IPv4 packet size) to a computer to attempt to crash it. Smurf attacks generate enormous amounts of traffic on a target network by spoofing broadcast pings, and ping floods are a basic DoS attack relying on consuming all of the bandwidth that a target has available.

You should be aware of several important details regarding ICMP. First, the IP header protocol field value for ICMP is 1 (0x01). Second, the type field in the ICMP header defines the type or purpose of the message contained within the ICMP payload. There are more than 40 defined types, but only 7 are commonly used (see Table 3.5). You can find a complete list of the ICMP type field values at www.iana.org/assignments/icmp-parameters. It may be worth noting that many of the types listed may also support codes. A code is simply an additional data parameter offering more detail about the function or purpose of the ICMP message payload.

TABLE 3.5   Common ICMP type field values

Type	Function
0	Echo reply
3	Destination unreachable
5	Redirect
8	Echo request
9	Router advertisement
10	Router solicitation
11	Time exceeded

IGMP   Internet Group Management Protocol (IGMP) allows systems to support multicasting. Multicasting is the transmission of data to multiple specific recipients. (RFC 1112 discusses the requirements to perform IGMP multicasting.) IGMP is used by IP hosts to register their dynamic multicast group membership. It is also used by connected routers to discover these groups. Through the use of IGMP multicasting, a server can initially transmit a single data signal for the entire group rather than a separate initial data signal for each intended recipient. With IGMP, the single initial signal is multiplied at the router if divergent pathways exist to the intended recipients. The IP header protocol field value for IGMP is 2 (0x02).

ARP and Reverse ARP   Address Resolution Protocol (ARP) and Reverse Address Resolution Protocol (RARP) are essential to the interoperability of logical and physical addressing schemes. ARP is used to resolve IP addresses (32-bit binary number for logical addressing) into Media Access Control (MAC) addresses (48-bit binary number for physical addressing)—or EUI-48 or even EUI-64. Traffic on a network segment (for example, cables across a hub) is directed from its source system to its destination system using MAC addresses. RARP is used to resolve MAC addresses into IP addresses.

Both ARP and RARP function using caching and broadcasting. The first step in resolving an IP address into a MAC address, or vice versa, is to check the local ARP cache. If the needed information is already present in the ARP cache, it is used. This activity is sometimes abused using a technique called *ARP cache poisoning*, where an attacker inserts bogus information into the ARP cache. If the ARP cache does not contain the necessary information, an ARP request in the form of a broadcast is transmitted. If the owner of the queried address is in the local subnet, it can respond with the necessary information. If not, the system will default to using its default gateway to transmit its communications. Then, the default gateway (in other words, a router) will need to perform its own ARP or RARP process.

Common Application Layer Protocols

In the Application layer of the TCP/IP model (which includes the Session, Presentation, and Application layers of the OSI model) reside numerous application- or service-specific protocols. A basic knowledge of these protocols and their relevant service ports is important for the CISSP exam:

Telnet, TCP port 23   This is a terminal emulation network application that supports remote connectivity for executing commands and running applications but that does not support transfer of files.

File Transfer Protocol (FTP), TCP ports 20 and 21   This is a network application that supports an exchange of files that requires anonymous or specific authentication.

Trivial File Transfer Protocol (TFTP), UDP port 69   This is a network application that supports an exchange of files that does not require authentication.

Simple Mail Transfer Protocol (SMTP), TCP port 25   This is a protocol used to transmit email messages from a client to an email server and from one email server to another.

Post Office Protocol (POP3), TCP port 110   This is a protocol used to pull email messages from an inbox on an email server down to an email client.

Internet Message Access Protocol (IMAP), TCP port 143   This is a protocol used to pull email messages from an inbox on an email server down to an email client. IMAP is more secure than POP3 and offers the ability to pull headers down from the email server as well as to delete messages directly off the email server without having to download to the local client first.

Dynamic Host Configuration Protocol (DHCP), UDP ports 67 and 68   DHCP uses port 67 for server point-to-point response and port 68 for client request broadcasts. It is used to assign TCP/IP configuration settings to systems upon bootup. DHCP enables centralized control of network addressing.

Hypertext Transport Protocol (HTTP), TCP port 80   This is the protocol used to transmit web page elements from a web server to web browsers.

Secure Sockets Layer (SSL), TCP port 443 (for HTTP encryption)   This is a VPN-like security protocol that operates at the Transport layer. SSL was originally designed to support secured web communications (HTTPS) but is capable of securing any Application layer protocol communications.

Line Print Daemon (LPD), TCP port 515   This is a network service that is used to spool print jobs and to send print jobs to printers.

X Window, TCP ports 6000–6063   This is a GUI API for command-line operating systems.

Bootstrap Protocol (BootP)/Dynamic Host Configuration Protocol (DHCP), UDP ports 67 and 68   This is a protocol used to connect diskless workstations to a network through autoassignment of IP configuration and download of basic OS elements. BootP is the forerunner to Dynamic Host Configuration Protocol (DHCP).

Network File System (NFS), TCP port 2049   This is a network service used to support file sharing between dissimilar systems.

Simple Network Management Protocol (SNMP), UDP port 161 (UDP port 162 for trap messages)   This is a network service used to collect network health and status information by polling monitoring devices from a central monitoring station.

Implications of Multilayer Protocols

As you can see from the previous sections, TCP/IP as a protocol suite comprises dozens of individual protocols spread across the various protocol stack layers. TCP/IP is therefore a multilayer protocol. TCP/IP derives several benefits from its multilayer design, specifically in relation to its mechanism of encapsulation. For example, when communicating between a web server and a web browser over a typical network connection, the HTTP protocol is encapsulated in TCP, which in turn is encapsulated in IP, which is in turn encapsulated in Ethernet. This could be presented as follows:

```
[ Ethernet [ IP [ TCP [ HTTP ] ] ] ]
```

However, this is not the extent of TCP/IP's encapsulation support. It is also possible to add additional layers of encapsulation. For example, adding SSL/TLS encryption to the communication would insert a new encapsulation between HTTP and TCP:

```
[ Ethernet [ IP [ TCP [ SSL [ HTTP ] ] ] ] ]
```

This in turn could be further encapsulated with a Network layer encryption such as IPSec:

```
[ Ethernet [ IPSec [ IP [ TCP [ SSL [ HTTP ] ] ] ] ] ]
```

However, encapsulation is not always implemented for benign purposes. There are numerous covert channel communication mechanisms that use encapsulation to hide or isolate an unauthorized protocol inside another authorized one. For example, if a network blocks the use of FTP but allows HTTP, then tools such as HTTP Tunnel can be used to bypass this restriction. This could result in an encapsulation structure such as this:

```
[ Ethernet [ IP [ TCP [ HTTP [ FTP ] ] ] ] ]
```

Normally, HTTP carries its own web-related payload, but with the HTTP Tunnel tool, the standard payload is replaced with an alternative protocol. This false encapsulation can even occur lower in the protocol stack. For example, the ICMP protocol is typically used for network health testing and not for general communication. However, with utilities such as Loki, ICMP is transformed into a tunnel protocol to support TCP communications. The encapsulation structure of Loki is as follows:

```
[ Ethernet [ IP [ ICMP [ TCP [ HTTP ] ] ] ] ]
```

Another area of concern caused by unbounded encapsulation support is the ability to jump between VLANs. This attack, known as VLAN hopping, is performed by creating a double encapsulated IEEE 802.1Q VLAN tag:

```
[ Ethernet [ VLAN1 [ VLAN2 [ IP [ TCP [ HTTP ] ] ] ] ] ]
```

With this double encapsulation, the first encountered switch will strip away the first VLAN tag, and then the next switch will be fooled by the interior VLAN tag and move the traffic into the other VLAN.

Multilayer protocols provide the following benefits:

- A wide range of protocols can be used at higher layers.
- Encryption can be incorporated at various layers.
- Flexibility and resiliency in complex network structures is supported.

There are a few drawbacks of multilayer protocols:

- Covert channels are allowed.
- Filters can be bypassed.
- Logically imposed network segment boundaries can be overstepped.

TCP/IP Vulnerabilities

TCP/IP's vulnerabilities are numerous. Improperly implemented TCP/IP stacks in various operating systems are vulnerable to buffer overflows, SYN flood attacks, various DoS attacks, fragment attacks, oversized packet attacks, spoofing attacks, man-in-the-middle attacks, hijack attacks, and coding error attacks.

TCP/IP (as well as most protocols) is also subject to passive attacks via monitoring or sniffing. *Network monitoring* is the act of monitoring traffic patterns to obtain information about a network. *Packet sniffing* is the act of capturing packets from the network in hopes of extracting useful information from the packet contents. Effective packet sniffers can extract usernames, passwords, email addresses, encryption keys, credit card numbers, IP addresses, system names, and so on.

Packet sniffing and other attacks are discussed in more detail in Chapter 4.

Domain Name Resolution

Addressing and naming are important components that make network communications possible. Without addressing schemes, networked computers would not be able to distinguish one computer from another or specify the destination of a communication. Likewise, without naming schemes, humans would have to remember and rely upon numbering systems to identify computers. It is much easier to remember Google.com than 64.233.187.99. Thus, most naming schemes were enacted for human use rather than computer use.

It is reasonably important to grasp the basic ideas of addressing and numbering as used on TCP/IP-based networks. There are three different layers to be aware of. They're presented in reverse order here because the third layer is the most basic:

- The third, or bottom, layer is the MAC address. The MAC address, or hardware address, is a "permanent" physical address.

- The second, or middle, layer is the IP address. The IP address is a "temporary" logical address assigned over or onto the MAC address.

- The top layer is the domain name. The domain name or computer name is a "temporary" human-friendly convention assigned over or onto the IP address.

"Permanent" and "Temporary" Addresses

The reason these two adjectives are within quotation marks is that they are not completely accurate. MAC addresses are designed to be permanent physical addresses. However, some NICs support MAC address changes, and most modern operating systems (including Windows and Linux) do as well. When the NIC supports the change, the change occurs on the hardware. When the OS supports the change, the change is only in memory, but it looks like a hardware change to all other network entities.

An IP address is temporary because it is a logical address and could be changed at any time, either by DHCP or by an administrator. However, there are instances where systems are statically assigned an IP address. Likewise, computer names or DNS names might appear permanent, but they are logical and thus able to be modified by an administrator.

This system of naming and addressing grants each networking component the information it needs while making its use of that information as simple as possible. Humans get human-friendly domain names, networking protocols get router-friendly IP addresses, and the network interfaces get physical addresses. However, all three of these schemes must be linked together to allow interoperability. Thus, the Domain Name System (DNS) and the ARP/RARP system were developed. DNS resolves a human-friendly domain name into its IP address equivalent. Then, ARP resolves the IP address into its MAC address equivalent. Both of these resolutions also have an inverse, namely, DNS reverse lookups and RARP (see "ARP and Reverse ARP" earlier in this chapter).

Further Reading on DNS

For an excellent primer to advanced discussion on DNS, its operation, known issues, and the Dan Kaminski vulnerability, please visit "An Illustrated Guide to the Kaminsky DNS Vulnerability":

`http://unixwiz.net/techtips/iguide-kaminsky-dns-vuln.html`

For a look into the future of DNS, specifically the defense against the Kaminski vulnerability, visit `www.dnssec.net`.

Secure Network Components

The Internet is host to countless information services and numerous applications, including the Web, email, FTP, Telnet, newsgroups, chat, and so on. The Internet is also home to malicious people whose primary goal is to locate your computer and extract valuable data from it, use it to launch further attacks, or damage it in some way. You should be familiar with the Internet and able to readily identify its benefits and drawbacks from your own online experiences. Because of the success and global use of the Internet, many of its technologies were adapted or integrated into the private business network. This created two new forms of network segments: intranets and extranets.

An *intranet* is a private network that is designed to host the same information services found on the Internet. Networks that rely upon external servers (in other words, ones positioned on the public Internet) to provide information services internally are not considered intranets. Intranets provide users with access to the Web, email, and other services on internal servers that are not accessible to anyone outside the private network.

An *extranet* is a cross between the Internet and an intranet. An extranet is a section of an organization's network that has been sectioned off so that it acts as an intranet for the private network but also serves information to the public Internet. An extranet is often reserved for use by specific partners or customers. It is rarely on a public network. An extranet for public consumption is typically labeled a demilitarized zone (DMZ) or perimeter network.

Networks are not typically configured as one single large collection of systems. Usually networks are segmented or subdivided into smaller organizational units. These smaller units, grouping, segments, or subnetworks (i.e., subnets) can be used to improve various aspects of the network:

Boosting performance   Network segmentation can improve performance through an organizational scheme in which systems that often communicate are located in the same segment while systems that rarely or never communicate are located in other segments.

Reducing communication problems   Network segmentation often reduces congestion and contains communication problems, such as broadcast storms, to individual subsections of the network.

Providing security   Network segmentation can also improve security by isolating traffic and user access to those segments where they are authorized.

Segments can be created by using switch-based VLANs, routers, or firewalls, individually or in combination. A private LAN or intranet, a DMZ, and an extranet are all types of network segments.

When you're designing a secure network (whether a private network, an intranet, or an extranet), you must evaluate numerous networking devices. Not all of these components are necessary for a secure network, but they are all common network devices that may have an impact on network security.

Network Access Control

Network Access Control (NAC) is a concept of controlling access to an environment through strict adherence to and implementation of security policy. The goals of NAC are as follows:

- Prevent/reduce zero-day attacks

- Enforce security policy throughout the network

- Use identities to perform access control

The goals of NAC can be achieved through the use of strong detailed security policies that define all aspects of security control, filtering, prevention, detection, and response for every device from client to server and for every internal or external communication. NAC acts as an automated detection and response system that can react in real time to stop threats as they occur and before they cause damage or a breach.

Originally, 802.1X (which provides port-based NAC) was thought to embody NAC, but most supporters believe that 802.1X is only a simple form of NAC or just one component in a complete NAC solution.

NAC can be implemented with a preadmission philosophy or a postadmission philosophy, or aspects of both:

The preadmission philosophy requires a system to meet all current security requirements (such as patch application and antivirus updates) before it is allowed to communicate with the network.

The postadmission philosophy allows and denies access based on user activity, which is based on a predefined authorization matrix.

Other issues around NAC include client/system agent versus overall network monitoring (agent-less); out-of-band versus in-band monitoring; and resolving any remediation, quarantine, or captive portal strategies. These and other NAC concerns must be considered and evaluated prior to implementation.

Firewalls

Firewalls are essential tools in managing and controlling network traffic. A *firewall* is a network device used to filter traffic. It is typically deployed between a private network and a link to the Internet, but it can be deployed between departments within an organization. Without firewalls, it would not be possible to prevent malicious traffic from the Internet from entering into your private network. Firewalls filter traffic based on a defined set of rules, also called *filters* or *access control lists*. They are basically a set of instructions that are used to distinguish authorized traffic from unauthorized and/or malicious traffic. Only authorized traffic is allowed to cross the security barrier provided by the firewall.

Firewalls are useful for blocking or filtering traffic. They are most effective against unrequested traffic and attempts to connect from outside the private network and can also be used for blocking known malicious data, messages, or packets based on content, application, protocol, port, or source address. They are capable of hiding the structure and addressing scheme of a private network from the public. Most firewalls offer extensive logging, auditing, and monitoring capabilities as well as alarms and basic intrusion detection system (IDS) functions.

Firewalls are typically unable to block viruses or malicious code (i.e., firewalls do not typically scan traffic as an antivirus scanner would) transmitted through otherwise authorized communication channels, prevent unauthorized but accidental or intended disclosure of information by users, prevent attacks by malicious users already behind the firewall, or protect data after it passes out of or into the private network. However, you can add these features through special add-in modules or companion products, such as antivirus scanners and IDS tools. There are firewall appliances that are preconfigured to perform all (or most) of these "add-on" functions natively.

In addition to logging network traffic activity, firewalls should log several other events as well:

- A reboot of the firewall
- Proxies or dependencies being unable to or not starting
- Proxies or other important services crashing or restarting
- Changes to the firewall configuration file
- A configuration or system error while the firewall is running

Firewalls are only one part of an overall security solution. With a firewall, many of the security mechanisms are concentrated in one place, and thus a firewall can be a single point of failure. Firewall failure is most commonly caused by human error and misconfiguration. Firewalls provide protection only against traffic that crosses the firewall from one subnet to another. They offer no protection against traffic within a subnet (in other words, behind the firewall).

There are four basic types of firewalls: static packet-filtering firewalls, application-level gateway firewalls, circuit-level gateway firewalls, and stateful inspection firewalls. There are also ways to create hybrid or complex gateway firewalls by combining two or more of these firewall types into a single firewall solution. In most cases, having a multilevel firewall provides greater control over filtering traffic. Regardless, we'll cover the various firewall types and discuss firewall deployment architectures as well.

Static packet-filtering firewalls   A *static packet-filtering firewall* filters traffic by examining data from a message header. Usually, the rules are concerned with source, destination, and port addresses. Using static filtering, a firewall is unable to provide user authentication or to tell whether a packet originated from inside or outside the private network, and it is easily fooled with spoofed packets. Static packet-filtering firewalls are known as first-generation firewalls; they operate at layer 3 (the Network layer) of the OSI model. They can also be called *screening routers* or *common routers*.

Application-level gateway firewalls   An *application-level gateway firewall* is also called a *proxy* firewall. A proxy is a mechanism that copies packets from one network into another; the copy process also changes the source and destination addresses to protect the identity of the internal or private network. An application-level gateway firewall filters traffic based on the Internet service (in other words, the application) used to transmit or receive the data. Each type of application must have its own unique proxy server. Thus, an application-level gateway firewall comprises numerous individual proxy servers. This type of firewall negatively affects network performance because each packet must be examined and processed as it passes through the firewall. Application-level gateways are known as second-generation firewalls, and they operate at the Application layer (layer 7) of the OSI model.

Circuit-level gateway firewalls   *Circuit-level gateway firewalls* are used to establish communication sessions between trusted partners. They operate at the Session layer (layer 5) of the OSI model. SOCKS (from *sockets*, as in TCP/IP ports) is a common implementation of a circuit-level gateway firewall. Circuit-level gateway firewalls, also known as *circuit proxies*, manage communications based on the circuit, not the content of traffic. They permit or deny forwarding decisions based solely on the endpoint designations of the communication circuit (in other words, the source and destination addresses and service port numbers). Circuit-level gateway firewalls are considered second-generation firewalls because they represent a modification of the application-level gateway firewall concept.

Stateful inspection firewalls   *Stateful inspection firewalls* (also known as *dynamic packet filtering firewalls*) evaluate the state or the context of network traffic. By examining source and destination addresses, application usage, source of origin, and relationship between current packets and the previous packets of the same session, stateful inspection firewalls are able to grant a broader range of access for authorized users and activities and actively watch for and block unauthorized users and activities. Stateful inspection firewalls generally operate more efficiently than application-level gateway firewalls. They are known as third-generation firewalls, and they operate at the Network and Transport layers (layers 3 and 4) of the OSI model.

Multihomed Firewalls

Some firewall systems have more than one interface. For instance, a multihomed firewall must have at least two interfaces to filter traffic (they're also known as *dual-homed* firewalls). All multihomed firewalls should have IP forwarding disabled to force the filtering rules to control all traffic rather than allowing a software-supported shortcut between one interface and another. A bastion host or a screened host is just a firewall system logically positioned between a private network and an untrusted network. Usually, the bastion host is located behind the router that connects the private network to the untrusted network. All inbound traffic is routed to the bastion host, which in turn acts as a proxy for all the trusted systems within the private network. It is responsible for filtering traffic coming into the private network as well as for protecting the identity of the internal client.

The word *bastion* comes from medieval castle architecture. A bastion guardhouse was positioned in front of the main entrance to serve as a first layer of protection. Using this term to describe a firewall indicates that the firewall is acting as a sacrificial host that will receive all inbound attacks.

A screened subnet is similar to the screened host (in other words, the bastion host) in concept, except a subnet is placed between two routers and the bastion host(s) is located within that subnet. All inbound traffic is directed to the bastion host, and only traffic proxied by the bastion host can pass through the second router into the private network. This creates a subnet where some external visitors are allowed to communicate with resources offered by the network. This is the concept of a DMZ, which is a network area (usually a subnet) that is designed to be accessed by outside visitors but that is still isolated from the private network of the organization. The DMZ is often the host of public web, email, file, and other resource servers.

Firewall Deployment Architectures

There are three commonly recognized firewall deployment architectures: single tier, two tier, and three tier (also known as *multitier*).

As you can see in Figure 3.7, a single-tier deployment places the private network behind a firewall, which is then connected through a router to the Internet (or some other untrusted network). Single-tier deployments are useful against generic attacks only. This architecture offers only minimal protection.

FIGURE 3.7 Three firewall deployment architecture

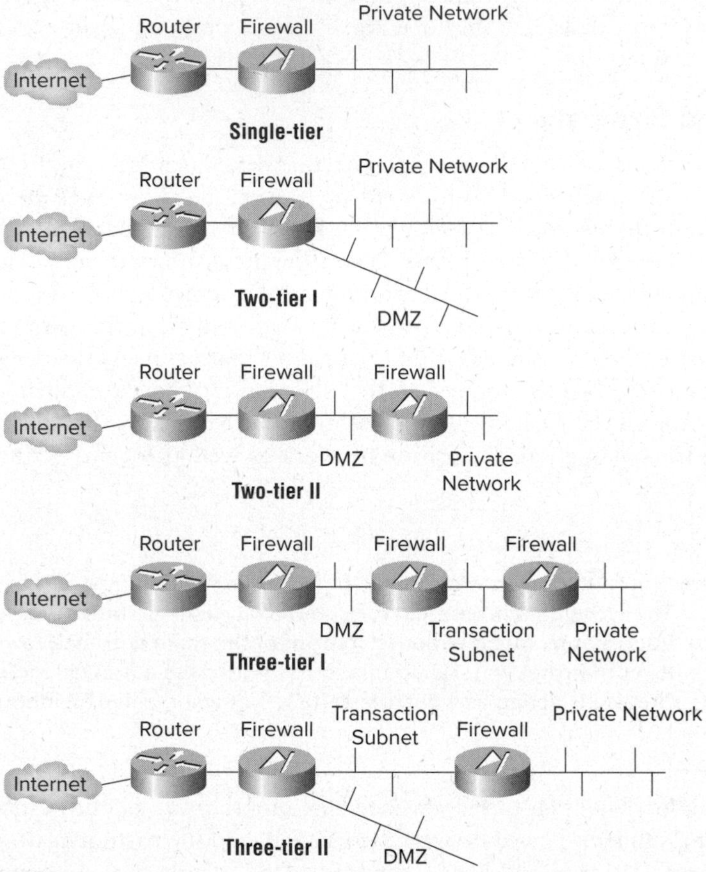

A two-tier deployment architecture may be one of two different designs. One uses a firewall with three or more interfaces. The other uses two firewalls in a series. This allows for a DMZ or a publicly accessible extranet. In the first design, the DMZ is located off one of the interfaces of the primary firewall, while in the second design the DMZ is located between the two serial firewalls. The DMZ is used to host information server systems to which external users should have access. The firewall routes traffic to the DMZ or the trusted network according to its strict filtering rules. This architecture introduces a moderate level of routing and filtering complexity.

A three-tier deployment architecture is the deployment of multiple subnets between the private network and the Internet separated by firewalls. Each subsequent firewall has more stringent filtering rules to restrict traffic to only trusted sources. The outermost subnet is usually a DMZ. A middle subnet can serve as a transaction subnet where systems needed to support complex web applications in the DMZ reside. The third, or backend, subnet can support the private network. This architecture is the most secure; however, it is also the most complex to design, implement, and manage.

Endpoint Security

Endpoint security is the concept that each individual device must maintain local security whether or not its network or telecommunications channels also provide or offer security. Sometimes this is expressed as "the end device is responsible for its own security." However, a clearer perspective is that any weakness in a network, whether on the border, on a server, or on a client, presents a risk to all elements within the organization.

Traditional security has depended upon the network border sentries, such as appliance firewalls, proxies, centralized virus scanners, and even IDS/IPS/IDP solutions, to provide security for all of the interior nodes of a network. This is no longer considered best business practice because threats exist from within as well as without. A network is only as secure as its weakest element.

Lack of internal security is even more problematic when remote access services, including dial-up, wireless, and VPN, might allow an external entity (authorized or not) to gain access to the private network without having to go through the border security gauntlet.

Endpoint security should therefore be viewed as an aspect of the effort to provide sufficient security on each individual host. Every system should have an appropriate combination of a local host firewall, antimalware scanners, authentication, authorization, auditing, spam filters, and IDS/IPS services.

Other Network Devices

You'll use numerous hardware devices when constructing a network. Strong familiarity with the hardware components of networks can assist you in designing an IT infrastructure that avoids single points of failure and provides strong support for availability.

Collisions vs. Broadcasts

A collision occurs when two systems transmit data at the same time onto a connection medium that supports only a single transmission path. A broadcast occurs when a single system transmits data to all possible recipients. Generally, collisions are always something to avoid and prevent, while broadcasts have useful purposes from time to time. The management of collisions and broadcasts introduces a new term known as *domains*.

A *collision domain* is a group of networked systems that could cause a collision if any two (or more) of the systems in that group transmitted simultaneously. Any system outside the collision domain cannot cause a collision with any member of that collision domain.

> A *broadcast domain* is a group of networked systems in which all other members receive a broadcast signal when one of the members of the group transmits it. Any system outside a broadcast domain would not receive a broadcast from that broadcast domain.
>
> As you design and deploy a network, you should consider how collision domains and broadcast domains will be managed. Collision domains are divided by using any layer 2 or higher device, and broadcast domains are divided by using any layer 3 or higher device. When a domain is divided, it means that systems on opposite sides of the deployed device are members of different domains.

These are some of the hardware devices in a network:

Repeaters, concentrators, and amplifiers   Repeaters, concentrators, and amplifiers are used to strengthen the communication signal over a cable segment as well as connect network segments that use the same protocol. These devices can be used to extend the maximum length of a specific cable type by deploying one or more repeaters along a lengthy cable run. Repeaters, concentrators, and amplifiers operate at OSI layer 1. Systems on either side of a repeater, concentrator, or amplifier are part of the same collision domain and broadcast domain.

Hubs   Hubs are used to connect multiple systems in a star topology and connect network segments that use the same protocol. They repeat inbound traffic over all outbound ports. This ensures that the traffic will reach its intended host. A hub is a multiport repeater. Hubs operate at OSI layer 1. Systems on either side of a hub are part of the same collision and broadcast domains. Most organizations have a no-hub security policy to limit or reduce the risk of sniffing attacks.

Modems   A traditional land-line modem (modulator-demodulator) is a communications device that covers or modulates between an analog carrier signal and digital information in order to support computer communications of public switched telephone network (PSTN) lines. From about 1960 until the mid-1990s, modems were a common means of WAN communications. Modems have generally been replaced by digital broadband technologies including ISDN, cable modems, DSL modems, 802.11 wireless, and various forms of wireless modems.

 The term *modem* is used incorrectly on any device that does not actually perform modulation. Most modern devices labeled as modems (cable, DSL, ISDN, wireless, etc.) are routers, not modems.

Bridges   A bridge is used to connect two networks together—even networks of different topologies, cabling types, and speeds—in order to connect network segments that use the same protocol. A bridge forwards traffic from one network to another. Bridges that connect networks using different transmission speeds may have a buffer to store packets until they can be forwarded to the slower network. This is known as a *store-and-forward* device. Bridges operate at OSI layer 2. Systems on either side of a bridge are part of the same broadcast domain but are in different collision domains.

Switches Rather than using a hub, you might consider using a switch, or intelligent hub. Switches know the addresses of the systems connected on each outbound port. Instead of repeating traffic on every outbound port, a switch repeats traffic only out of the port on which the destination is known to exist. Switches offer greater efficiency for traffic delivery, create separate collision domains, and improve the overall throughput of data. Switches can also create separate broadcast domains when used to create VLANs. In such configurations, broadcasts are allowed within a single VLAN but not allowed to cross unhindered from one VLAN to another. Switches operate primarily at OSI layer 2. When switches have additional features, such as routing, they can operate at OSI layer 3 as well (such as when routing between VLANs). Systems on either side of a switch operating at layer 2 are part of the same broadcast domain but are in different collision domains. Systems on either side of a switch operating at layer 3 are part of different broadcast domains and different collision domains. Switches are used to connect network segments that use the same protocol.

Routers Routers are used to control traffic flow on networks and are often used to connect similar networks and control traffic flow between the two. They can function using statically defined routing tables, or they can employ a dynamic routing system. There are numerous dynamic routing protocols, such as RIP, OSPF, and BGP. Routers operate at OSI layer 3. Systems on either side of a router are part of different broadcast domains and different collision domains. Routers are used to connect network segments that use the same protocol.

Brouter Brouters are combination devices comprising a router and a bridge. A brouter attempts to route first, but if that fails, it defaults to bridging. Thus, a brouter operates primarily at layer 3 but can operate at layer 2 when necessary. Systems on either side of a brouter operating at layer 3 are part of different broadcast domains and different collision domains. Systems on either side of a brouter operating at layer 2 are part of the same broadcast domain but are in different collision domains. Brouters are used to connect network segments that use the same protocol.

Gateways A gateway connects networks that are using different network protocols. A gateway is responsible for transferring traffic from one network to another by transforming the format of that traffic into a form compatible with the protocol or transport method used by each network. Gateways, also known as *protocol translators*, can be stand-alone hardware devices or a software service (for example, an IP-to-IPX gateway). Systems on either side of a gateway are part of different broadcast domains and different collision domains. Gateways are used to connect network segments that use different protocols. There are many types of gateways, including data, mail, application, secure, and Internet. Gateways typically operate at OSI layer 7.

Proxies A proxy is a form of gateway that does not translate across protocols. Instead, proxies serve as mediators, filters, caching servers, and even NAT/PAT servers for a network. A proxy performs a function or requests a service on behalf of another system and connects network segments that use the same protocol. Proxies are most often used in the context of providing clients on a private network with Internet access while protecting the identity of the clients. A proxy accepts requests from clients, alters the source address of the requester, maintains a mapping of requests to clients, and sends the altered request packets out. This mechanism is commonly known as Network Address Translation (NAT). Once a reply is received, the proxy server determines which client it is destined for by reviewing its mappings and then sends the packets on to the client. Systems on either side of a proxy are part of different broadcast domains and different collision domains.

Network Infrastructure Inventory

If you can gain approval from your organization, perform a general survey or inventory of the significant components that make up your network. See how many different network devices you can locate within your network. Also, do you notice any patterns of device deployment, such as devices always deployed in parallel or in series? Is the exterior of a device usually sufficient to indicate its function, or must you look up its model number?

LAN extender   A LAN extender is a remote access, multilayer switch used to connect distant networks over WAN links. This is a strange beast of a device in that it creates WANs but marketers of this device steer clear of the term *WAN* and use only *LAN* and *extended LAN*. The idea behind this device was to make the terminology easier to understand and thus make the product easier to sell than a normal WAN device with complex concepts and terms tied to it. Ultimately, it was the same product as a WAN switch or WAN router. (We agree with the Golgafrinchans, a race of aliens from Douglas Adams's *The Hitchhikers Guide to the Galaxy* series, who believed the marketing people should be shipped out with the lawyers and phone sanitizers on the first spaceship to the far end of the universe.)

While managing network security with filtering devices such as firewalls and proxies is important, we must not overlook the need for endpoint security. Endpoints are the ends of a network communication link. One end is often at a server where a resource resides, and the other end is often a client making a request to use a network resource. Even with secured communication protocols, it is still possible for abuse, misuse, oversight, or malicious action to occur across the network because it originated at an endpoint. All aspects of security from one end to the other, often called *end-to-end security*, must be addressed. Any unsecured point will be discovered eventually and abused.

Cabling, Wireless, Topology, and Communications Technology

Establishing security on a network involves more than just managing the operating system and software. You must also address physical issues, including cabling, wireless, topology, and communications technology.

LANs vs. WANs

There are two basic types of networks: LANs and WANs. A *local area network (LAN)* is a network typically spanning a single floor or building. This is commonly a limited geographical area. *Wide area network (WAN)* is the term usually assigned to the long-distance connections between geographically remote networks.

WAN connections and communication links can include private circuit technologies and packet-switching technologies. Common private circuit technologies include dedicated or leased lines and PPP, SLIP, ISDN, and DSL connections. Packet-switching technologies include X.25, Frame Relay, asynchronous transfer mode (ATM), Synchronous Data Link Control (SDLC), and High-Level Data Link Control (HDLC). Packet-switching technologies use virtual circuits instead of dedicated physical circuits. A virtual circuit is created only when needed, which makes for efficient use of the transmission medium and is extremely cost-effective. (We discuss the WAN technologies in Chapter 4.)

Network Cabling

The type of connectivity media employed in a network is important to the network's design, layout, and capabilities. Without the right cabling or transmission media, a network may not be able to span your entire enterprise, or it may not support the necessary traffic volume. In fact, the most common causes of network failure (in other words, violations of availability) are caused by cable failures or misconfigurations. It is important for you to understand that different types of network devices and technologies are used with different types of cabling. Each cable type has unique useful lengths, throughput rates, and connectivity requirements.

Coaxial Cable

Coaxial cable, also called *coax*, was a popular networking cable type used throughout the 1970s and 1980s. In the early 1990s, its use quickly declined because of the popularity and capabilities of twisted-pair wiring (explained in more detail later). Coaxial cable has a center core of copper wire surrounded by a layer of insulation, which is in turn surrounded by a conductive braided shielding and encased in a final insulation sheath.

The center copper core and the braided shielding layer act as two independent conductors, thus allowing two-way communications over a coaxial cable. The design of coaxial cable makes it fairly resistant to electromagnetic interference (EMI) and makes it able to support high bandwidths (in comparison to other technologies of the time period), and it offers longer usable lengths than twisted-pair. It ultimately failed to retain its place as the popular networking cable technology because of twisted-pair's much lower cost and ease of installation. Coaxial cable requires the use of segment terminators, whereas twisted-pair cabling does not. Coaxial cable is bulkier and has a larger minimum arc radius than twisted-pair. (The arc radius is the maximum distance the cable can be bent before damaging the internal conductors.) Additionally, with the widespread deployment of switched networks, the issues of cable distance became moot because of the implementation of hierarchical wiring patterns.

There are two main types of coaxial cable: thinnet and thicknet. *Thinnet*, also known as 10Base2, was commonly used to connect systems to backbone trunks of thicknet cabling. Thinnet can span distances of 185 meters and provide throughput up to 10 Mbps. *Thicknet*, also known as 10Base5, can span 500 meters and provide throughput up to 10 Mbps (Megabits per second).

The most common problems with coax cable are as follows:

- Bending the coax cable past its maximum arc radius and thus breaking the center conductor

- Deploying the coax cable in a length greater than its maximum recommended length (which is 185 meters for 10Base2 or 500 meters for 10Base5)

- Not properly terminating the ends of the coax cable with a 50 ohm resistor

Baseband and Broadband Cables

The naming convention used to label most network cable technologies follows the syntax *XXyyyyZZ*. *XX* represents the maximum speed the cable type offers, such as 10 Mbps for a 10Base2 cable. The next series of letters, *yyyy*, represents the baseband or broadband aspect of the cable, such as baseband for a 10Base2 cable. Baseband cables can transmit only a single signal at a time, and broadband cables can transmit multiple signals simultaneously. Most networking cables are baseband cables. However, when used in specific configurations, coaxial cable can be used as a broadband connection, such as with cable modems. *ZZ* either represents the maximum distance the cable can be used or acts as shorthand to represent the technology of the cable, such as the approximately 200 meters for 10Base2 cable (actually 185 meters, but it's rounded up to 200) or T or TX for twisted-pair in 10Base-T or 100Base-TX. (Note that 100Base-TX is implemented using two Cat 5 UTP or STP cables—one issued for receiving, the other for transmitting.)

Table 3.6 shows the important characteristics for the most common network cabling types.

TABLE 3.6 Important characteristics for common network cabling types

Type	Max Speed	Distance	Difficulty of Installation	Susceptibility to EMI	Cost
10Base2	10 Mbps	185 meters	Medium	Medium	Medium
10Base5	10 Mbps	500 meters	High	Low	High
10Base-T (UTP)	10 Mbps	100 meters	Low	High	Very low
STP	155 Mbps	100 meters	Medium	Medium	High
100Base-T/100Base-TX	100 Mbps	100 meters	Low	High	Low
1000Base-T	1 Gbps	100 meters	Low	High	Medium
Fiber-optic	2+ Gbps	2+ kilometers	Very high	None	Very high

Twisted-Pair

Twisted-pair cabling is extremely thin and flexible compared to coaxial cable. It consists of four pairs of wires that are twisted around each other and then sheathed in a PVC insulator. If there is a metal foil wrapper around the wires underneath the external sheath, the wire is known as *shielded twisted-pair (STP)*. The foil provides additional protection from external EMI. Twisted-pair cabling without the foil is known as *unshielded twisted-pair (UTP)*. UTP is most often used to refer to 10Base-T, 100Base-T, or 1000Base-T, which are now considered out-dated references.

The wires that make up UTP and STP are small, thin copper wires that are twisted in pairs. The twisting of the wires provides protection from external radio frequencies and electric and magnetic interference and reduces crosstalk between pairs. Crosstalk occurs when data transmitted over one set of wires is picked up by another set of wires due to radiating electromagnetic fields produced by the electrical current. Each wire pair within the cable is twisted at a different rate (in other words, twists per inch); thus, the signals traveling over one pair of wires cannot cross over onto another pair of wires (at least within the same cable). The tighter the twist (the more twists per inch), the more resistant the cable is to internal and external interference and crosstalk, and thus the capacity for throughput (that is, higher bandwidth) is greater.

There are several classes of UTP cabling. The various categories are created through the use of tighter twists of the wire pairs, variations in the quality of the conductor, and variations in the quality of the external shielding. Table 3.7 shows the original UTP categories.

TABLE 3.7   UTP categories

UTP Category	Throughput	Notes
Cat 1	Voice only	Not suitable for networks, but usable by modems
Cat 2	4 Mbps	Not suitable for most networks; often employed for host-to-terminal connections on mainframes
Cat 3	10 Mbps	Primarily used in 10Base-T Ethernet networks (offers only 4 Mpbs when used on Token Ring networks) and as telephone cables
Cat 4	16 Mbps	Primarily used in Token Ring networks
Cat 5	100 Mbps	Used in 100Base-TX, FDDI, and ATM networks
Cat 6	1,000 Mbps	Used in high-speed networks
Cat 7	10 Gbps	Used on 10 gigabit-speed networks

Cat 5e is an enhanced version of Cat 5 designed to protect against far-end crosstalk. In 2001, the TIA/EIA-568-B no longer recognized the original Cat 5 specification. Now, the Cat 5e standard is rated for use by 100Base-T and even 1000Base-T deployments.

The following problems are the most common with twisted-pair cabling:

- Using the wrong category of twisted-pair cable for high-throughput networking
- Deploying a twisted-pair cable longer than its maximum recommended length (in other words, 100 meters)
- Using UTP in environments with significant interference

Conductors

The distance limitations of conductor-based network cabling stem from the resistance of the metal used as a conductor. Copper, the most popular conductor, is one of the best and least expensive room-temperature conductors available. However, it is still resistant to the flow of electrons. This resistance results in a degradation of signal strength and quality over the length of the cable.

Plenum cable is a type of cabling sheathed with a special material that does not release toxic fumes when burned, as does traditional PVC coated wiring. Often plenum-grade cable must be used to comply with building codes, especially if the building has enclosed spaces that could trap gases.

The maximum length defined for each cable type indicates the point at which the level of degradation could begin to interfere with the efficient transmission of data. This degradation of the signal is known as *attenuation*. It is often possible to use a cable segment that is longer than the cable is rated for, but the number of errors and retransmissions will be increased over that cable segment, ultimately resulting in poor network performance. Attenuation is more pronounced as the speed of the transmission increases. It is recommended that you use shorter cable lengths as the speed of the transmission increases.

Long cable lengths can often be supplemented through the use of repeaters or concentrators. A repeater is a signal amplification device, much like the amplifier for your car or home stereo. The repeater boosts the signal strength of an incoming data stream and rebroadcasts it through its second port. A concentrator does the same thing except it has more than two ports. However, using more than four repeaters (or hubs) in a row is discouraged (see the sidebar "5-4-3 Rule").

5-4-3 Rule

The 5-4-3 rule is used whenever Ethernet or other IEEE 802.3 shared-access networks are deployed in a tree topology (in other words, a central trunk with various splitting branches). This rule defines the number of repeaters/concentrators and segments that can be used in a network design. The rule states that between any two nodes (a node can be any type of processing entity, such as a server, client, or router), there can be a maximum of five segments connected by four repeaters/concentrators, and it states that only three of those five segments can be populated (in other words, have additional or other user, server, or networking device connections).

The 5-4-3 rule does not apply to switched networks or the use of bridges or routers.

An alternative to conductor-based network cabling is fiber-optic cable. Fiber-optic cables transmit pulses of light rather than electricity. This gives fiber-optic cable the advantage of being extremely fast and nearly impervious to tapping and interference. However, it is difficult to install and expensive; thus, the security and performance it offers come at a steep price.

Wireless Communications and Security

Wireless communications is a quickly expanding field of technologies for networking, connectivity, communication, and data exchange. There are literally thousands of protocols, standards, and techniques that can be labeled as wireless. These include cell phones, Bluetooth, cordless phones, and wireless networking. As wireless technologies continue to proliferate, your organization's security efforts must go beyond locking down its local network. Security should be an end-to-end solution that addresses all forms, methods, and techniques of communication.

General Wireless Concepts

Wireless communications employ radio waves to transmit signals over a distance. There is a finite amount of radio wave spectrum; thus, its use must be managed properly to allow multiple simultaneous uses with little to no interference. The radio spectrum is measured or differentiated using *frequency*. Frequency is a measurement of the number of wave oscillations within a specific time and identified using the unit Hertz (Hz), or oscillations per second. Radio waves have a frequency between 3 Hz and 300 GHz. Different ranges of frequencies have been designated for specific uses, such as AM and FM radio, VHF and UHF television, and so on. Currently, the 900 MHz, 2.4 GHz, and 5 GHz frequencies are the most commonly used in wireless products because of their unlicensed categorization. However, to manage the simultaneous use of the limited radio frequencies, several spectrum-use techniques were developed. This included spread spectrum, FHSS, DSSS, and OFDM.

Most devices operate within a small subsection of frequencies rather than all available frequencies. This is because of frequency-use regulations (in other words, the FCC in the United States), power consumption, and the expectation of interference.

Spread spectrum means that communication occurs over multiples frequencies at the same time. Thus, a message is broken into pieces, and each piece is sent at the same time but using a different frequency. Effectively this is a parallel communication rather than a serial communication.

Frequency Hopping Spread Spectrum (FHSS) was an early implementation of the spread spectrum concept. However, instead of sending data in a parallel fashion, it transmits data in a series while constantly changing the frequency in use. The entire range of available frequencies is employed, but only one frequency at a time is used. As the sender changes from one frequency to the next, the receiver has to follow the same hopping pattern to pick up the signal. FHSS was designed to help minimize interference by not using only a single frequency that could be affected. Instead, by constantly shifting frequencies, it minimizes interference.

Direct Sequence Spread Spectrum (DSSS) employs all the available frequencies simultaneously in parallel. This provides a higher rate of data throughput than FHSS. DSSS also uses a special encoding mechanism known as *chipping code* to allow a receiver to reconstruct data even if parts of the signal were distorted because of interference. This occurs in much the same way that the parity of RAID-5 allows the data on a missing drive to be re-created.

Orthogonal Frequency-Division Multiplexing (OFDM) is yet another variation on frequency use. OFDM employs a digital multicarrier modulation scheme that allows for a more tightly compacted transmission. The modulated signals are perpendicular (orthogonal) and thus do not cause interference with each other. Ultimately, OFDM requires a smaller frequency set (aka channel bands) but can offer greater data throughput.

Cell Phones

Cell phone wireless communications consist of using a portable device over a specific set of radio wave frequencies to interact with the cell phone carrier's network and either other cell phone devices or the Internet. The technologies used by cell phone providers are numerous and are often confusing. One point of confusion is the use of terms like *2G* and *3G*. These do not refer to technologies specifically but instead to the generation of cell phone technology. Thus, 1G is the first generation (mostly analog), 2G is the second (mostly digital, as are 3G and 4G), and so forth. There are even discussions of 2.5G when systems integrate second- and third-generation technologies. Table 3.8 attempts to clarify some of these confusing issues (this is only a partial listing of the technologies).

TABLE 3.8   Some wireless telephone technologies

Technology	Generation
NMT	1G
AMPS	1G
TACS	1G
GSM	2G
iDEN	2G
TDMA	2G
CDMA	2G
PDC	2G
HSCSD	2.5G

TABLE 3.8 Some wireless telephone technologies
(Continued)

Technology	Generation
GPRS	2.5G
W-CDMA	3G
TD-CDMA	3G
UWC	3G
EDGE	3G
DECT	3G
UMTS	3G
HSPDA	3.5G
WiMax – IEEE 802.16	4G
XOHM (Brand name of WiMax)	4G
Mobile Broadband – IEEE 801.20	4G
LTE (Long Term Evolution)	4G

Some of the technologies listed in this table are labeled and marketed as 4G, while not actually meeting the technical requirements to be classified as 4G. The International Telecommunications Union-Radio communications sector (ITU-R) defined the requirements for 4G in 2008, but in 2010 acquiesced that carriers can call their non-compliant technologies 4G as long as they lead to future compliant services.

There are a few key issues to keep in mind with regard to cell phone wireless transmissions. First, not all cell phone traffic is voice; often cell phone systems are used to transmit text and even computer data. Second, communications over a cell phone provider's network, whether voice, text, or data, are not necessarily secure. Third, with specific wireless-sniffing equipment, your cell phone transmissions can be intercepted. In fact, your provider's towers can be simulated to conduct man-in-the-middle attacks. Fourth, using your cell phone connectivity to access the Internet or your office network provides attackers with yet another potential avenue of attack, access, and compromise. Many of these devices can potentially act as bridges, creating unsecured access into your network.

One important cell phone technology to discuss is Wireless Application Protocol (WAP). WAP is not a standard; instead, it is a functioning industry-driven protocol stack. Via WAP-capable devices, users can communicate with the company network by connecting from their cell phone or PDA through the cell phone carrier network over the Internet and through a gateway into the company network. WAP is a suite of protocols working together. One of these protocols is Wireless Transport Layer Security (WTLS), which provides security connectivity services similar to those of SSL or TLS.

WAP vs. WAP

Wireless Application Protocol is often confused with wireless networking (802.11) because the same acronym (WAP) is used for both. WAP stands for wireless access point when used in relation to 802.11. Keep in mind the difference between them:

- With Wireless Application Protocol, portable devices use a cell phone carrier's network to establish communication links with the Internet

- With wireless networking, an organization deploys its own wireless access points to allow its wireless clients to connect to its local network.

One very important security issue to recognize with WAP or with any security service provided by a telco is that you are unlikely to obtain true end-to-end protection from a communications service provider. The US law known as the Communications Assistance for Law Enforcement Act (CALEA) mandates that all telcos, regardless of the technologies involved, must make it possible to wiretap voice and data communications when a search warrant is presented. Thus, a telco cannot provide customers with end-to-end encryption. At some point along the communication path, the data must be returned to clear form before being resecured for the remainder of the journey to its destination. WAP complies with the CALEA restriction as follows: A secure link is established between the mobile device and the telco's main server using WAP/WTLS. The data is converted into its clear form before being reencapsulated in SSL, TLS, IPSec, and so on for its continued transmission to its intended destination. Knowing this, use telco services appropriately, and whenever possible, feed pre-encrypted data into the telco link rather than clear form data.

WAP 1.0 was implemented in 1999, mostly on European mobile phones. WAP 2.0 was released in 2002. Today, few phones still use WAP; the mechanisms used to support TCP/IP communications between mobile phones and the Internet are based on 3G and 4G technologies (including GSM, EDGE, HPDSA, and LTE).

Bluetooth (802.15)

Bluetooth, or IEEE 802.15, personal area networks (PANs) are another area of wireless security concern. Headsets for cell phones, mice, keyboards, GPS devices, and many other interface devices and peripherals are connected via Bluetooth. Many of these connections are set up using a technique known as *pairing*, where the primary device scans the 2.4 GHz radio frequencies for available devices, and then, once a device is discovered, a four-digit PIN is used to "authorize" the pairing. This process does reduce the number of accidental pairings; however, a four-digit PIN is not secure (not to mention that the default PIN is often 0000). In addition, there are attacks against Bluetooth-enabled devices. One technique, known as *bluejacking*, allows an attacker to transmit SMS-like messages to your device. *Bluesnarfing* allows hackers to connect with your Bluetooth devices without your knowledge and extract information from them. This form of attack can offer attackers access to your contact lists, your data, and even your conversations. *Bluebugging* is an attack that grants hackers remote control over the feature and functions of a Bluetooth device. This could include the ability to turn on the microphone to use the phone as an audio bug. Fortunately, Bluetooth typically has a limited range of 30 feet, but some devices can function from more than 100 meters away. Bluetooth devices sometimes employ encryption, but it is not dynamic and can usually be cracked with modest effort. Use Bluetooth for those activities that are not sensitive or confidential. Whenever possible, change the default PINs on your devices. Do not leave your devices in discovery mode, and always turn off Bluetooth when it's not in active use.

Cordless Phones

Cordless phones represent an often-overlooked security issue. Cordless phones are designed to use any one of the unlicensed frequencies, in other words, 900 MHz, 2.4 GHz, or 5 GHz. These three unlicensed frequency ranges are employed by many different types of devices, from cordless phones and baby monitors to Bluetooth and wireless networking devices. The issue that is often overlooked is that someone could easily eavesdrop on a conversation on a cordless phone since its signal is rarely encrypted. With a frequency scanner, anyone can listen in on your conversations.

Wireless Networking (802.11)

Wireless networking is a popular method of connecting systems for communications because of the ease of deployment and relatively low cost. Historically, wireless networking has been fairly insecure, mainly because of a lack of knowledge by end users and organizations as well as insecure default configurations set by device manufacturers.

Wireless networking is primarily based on the IEEE 802.11 standard. It uses two primary components: an access point and host interfaces. The access point or wireless access point is the radio signal hub for the wireless network. The wireless access point supports associations with host devices with wireless interfaces (wireless NICs). The wireless access point performs a proxy function of converting the radio signal transmissions into cable-based transmissions in order to support communications between the wireless clients and the wired network and often ultimately the Internet.

There are two primary types of wireless network deployments: ad hoc and infrastructure. An *ad hoc network* (also called a *peer-to-peer network)* links wireless clients directly without the use of a wireless access point. *Infrastructure mode* is any wireless network configuration using a wireless access point to connect wireless clients. Within the infrastructure mode concept are several variations, including stand-alone, wired extension, enterprise extended, and bridge. A *stand-alone mode* infrastructure occurs when there is a wireless access point connecting wireless clients to each other but not to any wired resources. The wireless access point serves as a wireless hub exclusively. A *wired extension mode* infrastructure occurs when the wireless access point acts as a connection point to link the wireless clients to the wired network. An *enterprise extended mode* infrastructure occurs when multiple wireless access points (WAPs—see the sidebar "WAP vs. WAP" for disambiguation between the two terms using the same acronym) are used to connect a large physical area to the same wired network. Each wireless access point will use the same extended service set identifier (ESSID) so clients can roam the area while maintaining network connectivity, even while their wireless NICs change associations from one wireless access point to another. A *bridge mode* infrastructure occurs when a wireless connection is used to link two wired networks. This often uses dedicated wireless bridges and is useful when wired bridges are inconvenient, such as when linking networks between floors or buildings.

The term SSID (which stands for service set identifier) is typically used to indicate the name of a wireless network. Technically there are two related identifiers: extended service set identifier (ESSID) and basic service set identifier (BSSID). An ESSID is the name of a wireless network when a wireless base station or WAP is used (i.e., infrastructure mode). A BSSID is the MAC address of the base station hosting the ESSID in order to differentiate multiple base stations supporting a single extended wireless network. In ad-hoc or peer-to-peer mode, the value for the BSSID is randomly generated.

 Real World Scenario

Wireless Channels

There are many topics within wireless networking that we are not addressing because of space limitations and because they're not covered on the exam. For instance, you may want to learn more about wireless channels. Within the assigned frequency of the wireless signal are subdivisions known as *channels*. Think of channels as lanes on the same highway. In the United States there are 11 channels, in Europe there are 13, and in Japan there are 14. The differences stem from local laws regarding frequency management (think international versions of the United States's FCC). Wireless communications take place between a client and access point over a single channel. However, when two or more access points are relatively close to each other physically, signals on one channel can interfere with signals on another channel. One way to prevent this problem is to set the channels of physically close access points as differently as possible to minimize channel overlap interference. For example, if a building has four access points arranged in a line along the length of the building, the channel settings could be 1, 11, 1, and 11. However, if the building is square and an access point is in each corner, the channel settings may need to be 1, 4, 8, and 11. Think of the signal within a single channel as like a wide-load truck in a lane on the highway. The wide-load truck is using part of each lane to either side of it, thus making passing the truck in those lanes dangerous. Likewise, wireless signals in adjacent channels will interfere with each other.

Wireless networks are assigned a service set identifier (SSID) to differentiate one wireless network from another. If multiple base stations or wireless access points are involved in the same wireless network, an extended station set identifier (ESSID) is defined. The SSID is similar to the name of a workgroup. If a wireless client knows the SSID, they can configure their wireless NIC to communicate with the associated WAP. Knowledge of the SSID does not always grant entry, though, because the WAP can use numerous security features to block unwanted access. SSIDs are defined by default by vendors, and because these default SSIDs are well known, standard security practice dictates that the SSID should be changed to something unique before deployment. The SSID is broadcast by the WAP via a special transmission called a *beacon frame*. This allows any wireless NIC within range to see the wireless network and make connecting as simple as possible. This default broadcasting of the SSID should be disabled to keep the wireless network secret. However, attackers can still discover the SSID with a wireless sniffer because the SSID must still be used in transmissions between wireless clients and the WAP. Thus, disabling SSID broadcasting is not a true mechanism of security. Instead, use WPA2-Enterprise as a reliable authentication and encryption solution rather than trying to hide the existence of the wireless network.

The IEEE 802.11 standard defines two methods that wireless clients can use to authenticate to WAPs before normal network communications can occur across the wireless link. These two methods are open system authentication (OSA) and shared key authentication (SKA).

> *Open system authentication (OSA)* means there is no real authentication required. As long as a radio signal can be transmitted between the client and WAP, communications are allowed. It is also the case that wireless networks using OSA typically transmit everything in cleartext, thus providing no secrecy or security.

Shared key authentication (SKA) means that a challenge handshake authentication must take place before network communications can occur.

The 802.11 standard defines one optional technique for encryption known as *Wired Equivalent Privacy* (WEP). WEP encryption employs Rivest Cipher 4 (RC4), a symmetric stream cipher (see Chapter 9, "Cryptography and Symmetric Key Algorithms," for more on encryption in general). WEP is considered insufficient for security because of several deficiencies in its design and implementation. WEP uses static keys, weak initialization vectors, and does not maintain true packet integrity. Because of these factors, attackers have developed techniques to crack WEP in less than a minute. Therefore, WEP should be used only when no other more secure option is available. Fortunately, WEP was replaced with more robust forms of encryption.

An interim solution to WEP was WiFi Protected Access (WPA). Using the RC4-based cryptosystem known as TKIP, it was available as a firmware update to early WEP radios. While it was more complex than WEP, WPA could still be compromised. WPA encryption is often combined with PSK static passphrases. Unfortunately, the repeated use of a single static passphrase is the downfall of any PSK or SKA system. An attacker can simply run a brute-force guessing attack against a WPA network to discover the base passphrase. If the passphrase is 14 characters or more, this is usually a time-prohibitive proposition, but not an impossible one. Especially with knowledge of the passphrase, the dynamic keys of TKIP become crackable with a variety of techniques.

The final solution to WEP is WPA2, an encryption scheme known as the Counter Mode with Cipher Block Chaining Message Authentication Code Protocol (CCMP), which uses the Advanced Encryption Standard (AES) encryption scheme (see Chapter 9). Both WPA and WPA2 support the enterprise authentication known as 802.1X/EAP, a standard port-based network access control that ensures clients cannot communicate with a resource until proper authentication has taken place. Effectively, 802.1X is a hand-off system that allows the wireless network to leverage the existing network infrastructure's authentication services. Through the use of 802.1X, other techniques and solutions such as RADIUS, TACACS, certificates, smart cards, token devices, and biometrics can be integrated into wireless networks providing techniques for both mutual and multi-factor authentication. Not all EAP are secure. For example, EAP-MD5 and a pre-release EAP known as LEAP are also crackable. However, to date, no real-world attack has compromised the encryption of a properly configured WPA2-enterprise wireless network.

Even though wireless networks are often inexpensive to initially deploy, some organizations have decided that the long-term cost to maintain and secure wireless is much higher than the cost of a wired network. If a wireless network is present, you can take several steps to improve its security. (These are in order of consideration and application/installation. Additionally, this order does not imply which step offers more security. For example, using WPA-2 is a real security feature as opposed to SSID broadcast disabling.) Here are the steps:

1. Change the default administrator password.
2. Disable the SSID broadcast.

3. Change the SSID to something unique.

4. Enable MAC filtering if the pool of wireless clients is relatively small (usually less than 20) and static.

5. Consider using static IP addresses, or configure DHCP with reservations (applicable only for small deployments).

6. Turn on the highest form of authentication and encryption supported: WEP, WPA, or WPA-2 (802.11i).

7. Treat wireless as remote access, and manage access using 802.1X.

8. Treat wireless as external access, and separate the WAP from the wired network using a firewall.

9. Treat wireless as an entry point for attackers, and monitor all WAP-to-wired-network communications with an IDS.

10. Require all transmissions between wireless clients and WAPs to be encrypted; in other words, require a VPN link.

Often, adding layers of data encryption (WPA2 and IPSec VPN) and other forms of filtering to a wireless link can reduce the effective throughput as much as 80 percent. In addition, greater distances from the base station and the presence of interference will reduce the effective throughput even further.

Wireless Attacks

Even with wireless security present, wireless attacks can still occur. There is an ever-increasing variety of attacks against networks, and many of these work against both wired and wireless environments. A few focus on wireless networks alone. For example, there is a collection of techniques, commonly called *wardriving*, to discover that a wireless network is present. This activity involves using a wireless interface or a wireless detector to locate wireless network signals. Once an attacker knows there is a wireless network present, they can use sniffers to gather wireless packets for investigation. With the right tools, an attacker can discover hidden SSIDs, active IP addresses, valid MAC addresses, and even the authentication mechanism in use by the wireless clients. From there, attackers can grab dedicated cracking tools to attempt to break into the connection or attempt to conduct man-in-the-middle attacks. The older and weaker your protections, the faster and more successful such attacks are likely to be.

Four main 802.11 wireless network amendments define unique frequencies and speeds of transmission (among many other technical details). Table 3.9 lists several of these along with their speed and frequency. The *b*, *g*, and *n* amendments all use the same frequency; thus, they maintain backward compatibility.

TABLE 3.9   802.11 wireless networking amendments

Amendment	Speed	Frequency
802.11a	54 Mbps	5 GHz
802.11b	11 Mbps	2.4 GHz
802.11g	54 Mbps	2.4 GHz
802.11n	600 Mbps	2.4 GHz or 5 GHz

Two final items to note in the realm of wireless networking are WiMax (802.16) and Mobile Broadband (802.20). These standards are designed to support broadband access over a metropolitan area, in other words, citywide wireless network connectivity. For more information on this topic, please visit Wikipedia or the IEEE standards page (http://standards.ieee.org/about/get/) and follow its external links.

Network Topologies

The physical layout and organization of computers and networking devices is known as the *network topology*. The *logical topology* is the grouping of networked systems into trusted collectives. The physical topology is not always the same as the logical topology. There are four basic topologies of the physical layout of a network: ring, bus, star, and mesh.

Ring topology   A ring topology connects each system as points on a circle (see Figure 3.8). The connection medium acts as a unidirectional transmission loop. Only one system can transmit data at a time. Traffic management is performed by a token. A token is a digital hall pass that travels around the ring until a system grabs it. A system in possession of the token can transmit data. Data and the token are transmitted to a specific destination. As the data travels around the loop, each system checks to see whether it is the intended recipient of the data. If not, it passes the token on. If so, it reads the data. Once the data is received, the token is released and returns to traveling around the loop until another system grabs it. If any one segment of the loop is broken, all communication around the loop ceases. Some implementations of ring topologies employ a fault tolerance mechanism, such as dual loops running in opposite directions, to prevent single points of failure.

FIGURE 3.8   A ring topology

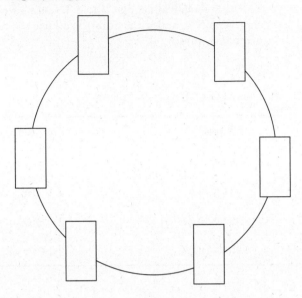

Bus topology   A bus topology connects each system to a trunk or backbone cable. All systems on the bus can transmit data simultaneously, which can result in collisions. A collision occurs when two systems transmit data at the same time; the signals interfere with each other. To avoid this, the systems employ a collision avoidance mechanism that basically "listens" for any other currently occurring traffic. If traffic is heard, the system waits a few moments and listens again. If no traffic is heard, the system transmits its data. When data is transmitted on a bus topology, all systems on the network hear the data. If the data is not addressed to a specific system, that system just ignores the data. The benefit of a bus topology is that if a single segment fails, communications on all other segments continue uninterrupted. However, the central trunk line remains a single point of failure.

There are two types of bus topologies: linear and tree. A linear bus topology employs a single trunk line with all systems directly connected to it. A tree topology employs a single trunk line with branches that can support multiple systems. Figure 3.9 illustrates both types. The primary reason a bus is rarely if ever used today is that it must be terminated at both ends and any disconnection can take down the entire network.

Star topology   A star topology employs a centralized connection device. This device can be a simple hub or switch. Each system is connected to the central hub by a dedicated segment (see Figure 3.10). If any one segment fails, the other segments can continue to function. However, the central hub is a single point of failure. Generally, the star topology uses less cabling than other topologies and makes the identification of damaged cables easier.

FIGURE 3.9   A linear bus topology and a tree bus topology

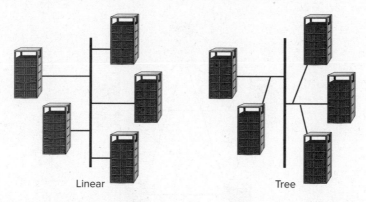

Linear   Tree

FIGURE 3.10   A star topology

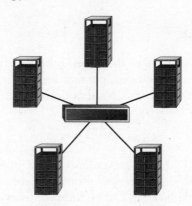

A logical bus and a logical ring can be implemented as a physical star. Ethernet is a bus-based technology. It can be deployed as a physical star, but the hub or switch device is actually a logical bus connection device. Likewise, Token Ring is a ring-based technology. It can be deployed as a physical star using a multistation access unit (MAU). An MAU allows for the cable segments to be deployed as a star while internally the device makes logical ring connections.

Mesh topology   A mesh topology connects systems to other systems using numerous paths (see Figure 3.11). A full mesh topology connects each system to all other systems on the network. A partial mesh topology connects many systems to many other systems. Mesh topologies provide redundant connections to systems, allowing multiple segment failures without seriously affecting connectivity.

FIGURE 3.11   A mesh topology

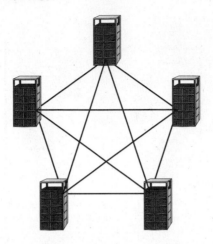

LAN Technologies

There are three main types of LAN technologies: Ethernet, Token Ring, and FDDI. There are a handful of other LAN technologies, but they are not as widely used. Only the main three are addressed on the CISSP exam. Most of the differences between LAN technologies exist at and below the Data Link layer.

Ethernet

Ethernet is a shared-media LAN technology (also known as a *broadcast technology*). That means it allows numerous devices to communicate over the same medium but requires that the devices take turns communicating and perform collision detection and avoidance. Ethernet employs broadcast and collision domains. A *broadcast domain* is a physical grouping of systems in which all the systems in the group receive a broadcast sent by a single system in the group. A *broadcast* is a message transmitted to a specific address that indicates that all systems are the intended recipients.

A *collision domain* consists of groupings of systems within which a data collision occurs if two systems transmit simultaneously. A data collision takes place when two transmitted messages attempt to use the network medium at the same time. It causes one or both of the messages to be corrupted.

Ethernet can support full-duplex communications (in other words, full two-way) and usually employs twisted-pair cabling. (Coaxial cabling was originally used.) Ethernet is most often deployed on star or bus topologies. Ethernet is based on the IEEE 802.3 standard. Individual units of Ethernet data are called *frames*. Fast Ethernet supports 100 Mbps throughput. Gigabit Ethernet supports 1,000 Mbps (1 Gbps) throughput. 10 Gigabit Ethernet support 10,000 Mbps (10 Gbps) throughput.

Token Ring

Token Ring employs a token-passing mechanism to control which systems can transmit data over the network medium. The token travels in a logical loop among all members of the LAN. Token Ring can be employed on ring or star network topologies. It is rarely used today because of its performance limitations, higher cost compared to Ethernet, and increased difficulty in deployment and management.

Token Ring can be deployed as a physical star using a multistation access unit (MAU). A MAU allows for the cable segments to be deployed as a star while internally the device makes logical ring connections.

Fiber Distributed Data Interface (FDDI)

Fiber Distributed Data Interface (FDDI) is a high-speed token-passing technology that employs two rings with traffic flowing in opposite directions. FDDI is often used as a backbone for large enterprise networks. Its dual-ring design allows for self-healing by removing the failed segment from the loop and creating a single loop out of the remaining inner and outer ring portions. FDDI is expensive but was often used in campus environments before Fast Ethernet and Gigabit Ethernet were developed. A less-expensive, distance-limited, and slower version known as Copper Distributed Data Interface (CDDI) uses twisted-pair cables. CDDI is also more vulnerable to interference and eavesdropping.

Subtechnologies

Most networks comprise numerous technologies rather than a single technology. For example, Ethernet is not just a single technology but a superset of subtechnologies that support its common and expected activity and behavior. Ethernet includes the technologies of digital communications, synchronous communications, and baseband communications, and it supports broadcast, multicast, and unicast communications and Carrier-Sense Multiple Access with Collision Detection (CSMA/CD). Many of the LAN technologies, such as Ethernet, Token Ring, and FDDI, may include many of the subtechnologies described in the following sections.

Analog and Digital

One subtechnology common to many forms of network communications is the mechanism used to actually transmit signals over a physical medium, such as a cable. There are two types: analog and digital.

Analog communications occur with a continuous signal that varies in frequency, amplitude, phase, voltage, and so on. The variances in the continuous signal produce a wave shape (as opposed to the square shape of a digital signal). The actual communication occurs by variances in the constant signal.

Digital communications occur through the use of a discontinuous electrical signal and a state change or on-off pulses.

Digital signals are more reliable than analog signals over long distances or when interference is present. This is because of a digital signal's definitive information storage method employing direct current voltage where voltage on represents a value of 1 and voltage off represents a value of 0. These on-off pulses create a stream of binary data. Analog signals become altered and corrupted because of attenuation over long distances and interference. Since an analog signal can have an infinite number of variations used for signal encoding as opposed to digital's two states, unwanted alterations to the signal make extraction of the data more difficult as the degradation increases.

Synchronous and Asynchronous

Some communications are synchronized with some sort of clock or timing activity. Communications are either synchronous or asynchronous.

Synchronous communications rely upon a timing or clocking mechanism based upon either an independent clock or a time stamp embedded in the data stream. Synchronous communications are typically able to support very high rates of data transfer.

Asynchronous communications rely upon a stop and start delimiter bit to manage the transmission of data. Because of the use of delimiter bits and the stop and start nature of its transmission, asynchronous communication is best suited for smaller amounts of data. Public switched telephone network (PSTN) modems are good examples of asynchronous communication devices.

Baseband and Broadband

How many communications can occur simultaneously over a cable segment depends on whether you use baseband technology or broadband technology.

Baseband technology can support only a single communication channel. It uses a direct current applied to the cable. A current that is at a higher level represents the binary signal of 1, and a current that is at a lower level represents the binary signal of 0. Baseband is a form of digital signal. Ethernet is a baseband technology.

Broadband technology can support multiple simultaneous signals. Broadband uses frequency modulation to support numerous channels, each supporting a distinct communication session. Broadband is suitable for high throughput rates, especially when several channels are multiplexed. Broadband is a form of analog signal. Cable television and cable modems, ISDN, DSL, T1, and T3 are examples of broadband technologies.

Broadcast, Multicast, and Unicast

Broadcast, multicast, and unicast technologies determine how many destinations a single transmission can reach.

Broadcast technology supports communications to all possible recipients.

Multicast technology supports communications to multiple specific recipients.

Unicast technology supports only a single communication to a specific recipient.

LAN Media Access

There are at least five LAN media access technologies that are used to avoid or prevent transmission collisions. These technologies define how multiple systems all within the same collision domain are to communicate. Some of these technologies actively prevent collisions, while others respond to collisions.

Carrier-Sense Multiple Access (CSMA)   This is the LAN media access technology that performs communications using the following steps:

1. The host listens to the LAN media to determine whether it is in use.

2. If the LAN media is not being used, the host transmits its communication.

3. The host waits for an acknowledgment.

4. If no acknowledgment is received after a time-out period, the host starts over at step 1.

CSMA does not directly address collisions. If a collision occurs, the communication would not have been successful, and thus an acknowledgment would not be received. This causes the sending system to retransmit the data and reperform the CSMA process.

Carrier-Sense Multiple Access with Collision Avoidance (CSMA/CA)   This is the LAN media access technology that performs communications using the following steps:

1. The host has two connections to the LAN media: inbound and outbound. The host listens on the inbound connection to determine whether the LAN media is in use.

2. If the LAN media is not being used, the host requests permission to transmit.

3. If permission is not granted after a time-out period, the host starts over at step 1.

4. If permission is granted, the host transmits its communication over the outbound connection.

5. The host waits for an acknowledgment.

6. If no acknowledgment is received after a time-out period, the host starts over at step 1.

AppleTalk and 802.11 wireless networking are examples of networks that employ CSMA/CA technologies. CSMA/CA attempts to avoid collisions by granting only a single permission to communicate at any given time. This system requires designation of a master or primary system, which responds to the requests and grants permission to send data transmissions.

Carrier-Sense Multiple Access with Collision Detection (CSMA/CD)   This is the LAN media access technology that performs communications using the following steps:

1. The host listens to the LAN media to determine whether it is in use.

2. If the LAN media is not being used, the host transmits its communication.

3. While transmitting, the host listens for collisions (in other words, two or more hosts transmitting simultaneously).

4. If a collision is detected, the host transmits a jam signal.

5. If a jam signal is received, all hosts stop transmitting. Each host waits a random period of time and then starts over at step 1.

Ethernet networks employ the CSMA/CD technology. CSMA/CD responds to collisions by having each member of the collision domain wait for a short but random period of time before starting the process over. Unfortunately, allowing collisions to occur and then responding or reacting to collisions causes delays in transmissions as well as a required repetition of transmissions. This results in about 40 percent loss in potential throughput.

Token passing   This is the LAN media access technology that performs communications using a digital token. Possession of the token allows a host to transmit data. Once its transmission is complete, it releases the token to the next system. Token passing is used by Token Ring networks, such as FDDI. Token Ring prevents collisions since only the system possessing the token is allowed to transmit data.

Polling   This is the LAN media access technology that performs communications using a master-slave configuration. One system is labeled as the primary system. All other systems are labeled as secondary. The primary system polls or inquires of each secondary system in turn whether they have a need to transmit data. If a secondary system indicates a need, it is granted permission to transmit. Once its transmission is complete, the primary system moves on to poll the next secondary system. Synchronous Data Link Control (SDLC) uses polling.

Polling addresses collisions by attempting to prevent them from using a permission system. Polling is an inverse of the CSMA/CA method. Both use masters and slaves (or primary and secondary), but while CSMA/CA allows the slaves to request permissions, polling has the master offer permission. Polling can be configured to grant one (or more) system priority over other systems. For example, if the standard polling pattern was 1, 2, 3, 4, then to give system 1 priority, the polling pattern could be changed to 1, 2, 1, 3, 1, 4.

Summary

The tasks of designing, deploying, and maintaining security on a network require intimate knowledge of the technologies involved in networking. This includes protocols, services, communication mechanisms, topologies, cabling, and networking devices.

    The OSI model is a standard against which all protocols are evaluated. Understanding how the OSI model is used and how it applies to real-world protocols can help system designers and system administrators improve security. The TCP/IP model is derived directly from the protocol and roughly maps to the OSI model.

Most networks employ TCP/IP as the primary protocol. However, there are numerous subprotocols, supporting protocols, services, and security mechanisms that can be found in a TCP/IP network. A basic understanding of these various entities can help you when designing and deploying a secure network.

In addition to routers, hubs, switches, repeaters, gateways, and proxies, firewalls are an important part of a network's security. There are four primary types of firewalls: static packet filtering, application-level gateway, circuit-level gateway, and stateful inspection.

There is a wide range of hardware components that can be used to construct a network, not the least of which is the cabling used to tie all the devices together. Understanding the strengths and weaknesses of each cabling type is part of designing a secure network.

Wireless communications occur in many forms, including cell phone, Bluetooth (802.15), and networking (802.11). Wireless communication is more vulnerable to interference, eavesdropping, denial of service, and man-in-the-middle attacks.

There are three common LAN technologies: Ethernet, Token Ring, and FDDI. Each can be used to deploy a secure network. There are also several common network topologies: ring, bus, star, and mesh.

Exam Essentials

Know the OSI model layers and which protocols are found in each. The seven layers and the protocols supported by each of the layers of the OSI model are as follows:

> *Application*: HTTP, FTP, LPD, SMTP, Telnet, TFTP, EDI, POP3, IMAP, SNMP, NNTP, S-RPC, and SET
>
> *Presentation*: Encryption protocols and format types, such as ASCII, EBCDICM, TIFF, JPEG, MPEG, and MIDI
>
> *Session*: NFS, SQL, and RPC
>
> *Transport*: SPX, SSL, TLS, TCP, and UDP
>
> *Network*: ICMP, RIP, OSPF, BGP, IGMP, IP, IPSec, IPX, NAT, and SKIP
>
> *Data Link*: SLIP, PPP, ARP, RARP, L2F, L2TP, PPTP, FDDI, ISDN
>
> *Physical*: EIA/TIA-232, EIA/TIA-449, X.21, HSSI, SONET, V.24, and V.35

Have a thorough knowledge of TCP/IP. Know the difference between TCP and UDP; be familiar with the four TCP/IP layers (Application, Transport, Internet, and Link) and how they correspond to the OSI model. In addition, understand the usage of the well-known ports, and be familiar with the subprotocols.

Know the different cabling types and their lengths and maximum throughput rates. This includes STP, 10Base-T (UTP), 10Base2 (thinnet), 10Base5 (thicknet), 100Base-T, 1000Base-T, and fiber-optic. You should also be familiar with UTP categories 1 through 7.

Be familiar with the common LAN technologies.   These are Ethernet, Token Ring, and FDDI. Also be familiar with analog versus digital communications; synchronous vs. asynchronous communications; baseband vs. broadband communications; broadcast, multicast, and unicast communications; CSMA, CSMA/CA, and CSMA/CD; token passing; and polling.

Understand secure network architecture and design   Network security should take into account IP and non-IP protocols, network access control, using security services and devices, managing multilayer protocols, and implementing endpoint security.

Understand the various types and purposes of network segmentation   Network segmentation can be used to manage traffic, improve performance, and enforce security. Examples of network segments or subnetworks include intranet, extranet, and DMZ.

Understand the different wireless technologies.   Cell phones, Bluetooth (802.15), and wireless networking (802.11) are all called wireless technologies, even though they are all different. Be aware of their differences, strengths, and weaknesses. Understand the basics of securing 802.11 networking.

Know the standard network topologies.   These are ring, bus, star, and mesh.

Know the common network devices.   Common network devices are firewalls, routers, hubs, bridges, modems, repeaters, switches, gateways, and proxies.

Understand the different types of firewalls.   There are four basic types of firewalls: static packet filtering, application-level gateway, circuit-level gateway, and stateful inspection.

Know the protocol services used to connect to LAN and WAN communication technologies.   These are Frame Relay, SMDS, X.25, ATM, HSSI, SDLC, HDLC, and ISDN.

Written Lab

1. Name the layers of the OSI model and their numbers from top to bottom.

2. Name three problems with cabling and the methods to counteract those issues.

3. What are the various technologies employed by wireless devices to maximize their use of the available radio frequencies?

4. Discuss methods used to secure 802.11 wireless networking.

5. Name the LAN shared media access technologies and examples of their use, if known.

Review Questions

1.   What is layer 4 of the OSI model?

     A.   Presentation

     B.   Network

     C.   Data Link

     D.   Transport

2.   What is encapsulation?

     A.   Changing the source and destination addresses of a packet

     B.   Adding a header and footer to data as it moves down the OSI stack

     C.   Verifying a person's identity

     D.   Protecting evidence until it has been properly collected

3.   Which OSI model layer manages communications in simplex, half-duplex, and full-duplex modes?

     A.   Application

     B.   Session

     C.   Transport

     D.   Physical

4.   Which of the following is the least resistant to EMI?

     A.   Thinnet

     B.   10Base-T UTP

     C.   10Base5

     D.   Coaxial cable

5.   Which of the following is not an example of network segmentation?

     A.   Intranet

     B.   DMZ

     C.   Extranet

     D.   VPN

6.   Which of the following is not considered a non-IP protocol?

     A.   IPX

     B.   UDP

     C.   AppleTalk

     D.   NetBEUI

7. If you are the victim of a bluejacking attack, what was compromised?

   A. Your car

   B. Your switch

   C. Your cell phone

   D. Your web cookies

8. Which networking technology is based on the IEEE 802.3 standard?

   A. Ethernet

   B. Token Ring

   C. FDDI

   D. HDLC

9. What is a TCP wrapper?

   A. An encapsulation protocol used by switches

   B. An application that can serve as a basic firewall by restricting access based on user IDs or system IDs

   C. A security protocol used to protect TCP/IP traffic over WAN links

   D. A mechanism to tunnel TCP/IP through non-IP networks

10. What is both a benefit and a potentially harmful implication of multilayer protocols?

   A. Throughput

   B. Encapsulation

   C. Hash integrity checking

   D. Logical addressing

11. By examining the source and destination addresses, the application usage, the source of origin, and the relationship between current packets with the previous packets of the same session, _____ firewalls are able to grant a broader range of access for authorized users and activities and actively watch for and block unauthorized users and activities.

   A. Static packet-filtering

   B. Application-level gateway

   C. Stateful inspection

   D. Circuit-level gateway

12. _____ firewalls are known as third-generation firewalls.

   A. Application-level gateway

   B. Stateful inspection

   C. Circuit-level gateway

   D. Static packet-filtering

13. Which of the following is not true regarding firewalls?

   A. They are able to log traffic information.

   B. They are able to block viruses.

   C. They are able to issue alarms based on suspected attacks.

   D. They are unable to prevent internal attacks.

14. Which of the following is not a routing protocol?

   A. OSPF

   B. BGP

   C. RPC

   D. RIP

15. A _____ is an intelligent hub because it knows the addresses of the systems connected on each outbound port. Instead of repeating traffic on every outbound port, it repeats traffic only out of the port on which the destination is known to exist.

   A. Repeater

   B. Switch

   C. Bridge

   D. Router

16. Which of the following is not a technology specifically associated with 802.11 wireless networking?

   A. WAP

   B. WPA

   C. WEP

   D. 802.11i

17. Which wireless frequency access method offers the greatest throughput with the least interference?

   A. FHSS

   B. DSSS

   C. OFDM

   D. OSPF

18. What security concept encourages administrators to install firewalls, malware scanners, and an IDS on every host?

   A. Endpoint security

   B. Network access control (NAC)

   C. VLAN

   D. RADIUS

19. What function does the RARP protocol perform?

   A. It is a routing protocol.

   B. It converts IP addresses into MAC addresses.

   C. It resolves physical addresses into logical addresses.

   D. It manages multiplex streaming.

20. What form of infrastructure mode wireless networking deployment supports large physical environments through the use of a single SSID but numerous access points?

   A. Stand-alone

   B. Wired extension

   C. Enterprise extension

   D. Bridge

Chapter

4

Secure Communications and Network Attacks

THE CISSP EXAM TOPICS COVERED IN THIS CHAPTER INCLUDE:

2. Telecommunications and Network Security

C. Establish secure communication channels (e.g., VPN, TLS/SSL, VLAN):

C.1 Voice (e.g., POTS, PBX, VoIP)

C.2 Multimedia collaboration (e.g., remote meeting technology, instant messaging)

C.3 Remote access (e.g., screen scraper, virtual application/desktop, telecommuting)

C.4 Data communications

D. Understand network attacks (e.g., DDoS, spoofing)

Data residing in a static form on a storage device is fairly simple to secure. As long as physical access control is maintained and reasonable logical access controls are implemented, stored files remain confidential, retain their integrity, and are available to authorized users. However, once data is used by an application or transferred over a network connection, the process of securing it becomes much more difficult.

Communications security covers a wide range of issues related to the transportation of electronic information from one place to another. That transportation may be between systems on opposite sides of the planet or between systems on the same business network. Once it is involved in any means of transportation, data becomes vulnerable to a plethora of threats to its confidentiality, integrity, and availability. Fortunately, many of these threats can be reduced or eliminated with the appropriate countermeasures.

Communications security is designed to detect, prevent, and even correct data transportation errors (that is, it provides integrity protection). This is done to sustain the security of networks while supporting the need to exchange and share data. This chapter covers the many forms of communications security, vulnerabilities, and countermeasures.

The Telecommunications and Network Security domain for the CISSP certification exam deals with topics of communications security and vulnerability countermeasures. This domain is discussed in this chapter and in the preceding chapter (Chapter 3, "Secure Network Architecture and Securing Network Components"). Be sure to read and study the materials in both chapters to ensure complete coverage of the essential material for the CISSP certification exam.

Network and Protocol Security Mechanisms

TCP/IP is the primary protocol suite used on most networks and on the Internet. It is a robust protocol suite, but it has numerous security deficiencies. In an effort to improve the security of TCP/IP, many subprotocols, mechanisms, or applications have been developed to protect the confidentiality, integrity, and availability of transmitted data. It is important to remember that even with the foundational protocol suite of TCP/IP, there are literally hundreds, if not thousands, of individual protocols, mechanisms, and applications in use across the Internet. Some of them are designed to provide security services. Some protect integrity, others protect confidentiality, and others provide authentication and access control. In the next sections, we'll discuss some of the more common network and protocol security mechanisms.

Secure Communications Protocols

Protocols that provide security services for application-specific communication channels are called *secure communication protocols*. The following list includes some of the options available:

Simple Key Management for Internet Protocol (SKIP)   This is an encryption tool used to protect sessionless datagram protocols. SKIP was designed to integrate with IPSec; it functions at layer 3. It is able to encrypt any subprotocol of the TCP/IP suite. SKIP was replaced by Internet Key Exchange (IKE) in 1998.

Software IP Encryption (swIPe)   This is another layer 3 security protocol for IP. It provides authentication, integrity, and confidentiality using an encapsulation protocol.

Secure Remote Procedure Call (S-RPC)   This is an authentication service and is simply a means to prevent unauthorized execution of code on remote systems.

Secure Sockets Layer (SSL)   This is an encryption protocol developed by Netscape to protect the communications between a web server and a web browser. SSL can be used to secure web, email, FTP, or even Telnet traffic. It is a session-oriented protocol that provides confidentiality and integrity. SSL is deployed using a 40-bit key or a 128-bit key. SSL is superseded by Transport Layer Security (TLS).

Transport Layer Security (TLS)   TLS functions in the same general manner as SSL, but it uses stronger authentication and encryption protocols.

SSL and TLS both have the following features:

- Support secure client-server communications across an insecure network while preventing tampering, spoofing, and eavesdropping.
- Support one-way authentication.
- Support two-way authentication using digital certificates.
- Often implemented as the initial payload of a TCP package, allowing it to encapsulate all higher-layer protocol payloads.
- Can be implemented at lower layers, such as layer 3 (the Network layer) to operate as a VPN. This implementation is known as OpenVPN.

In addition, TLS can be used to encrypt UDP and Session Initiation Protocol (SIP) connections. (SIP is a protocol associated with VoIP.)

Secure Electronic Transaction (SET)   This is a security protocol for the transmission of transactions over the Internet. SET is based on Rivest, Shamir, and Adelman (RSA) encryption and Data Encryption Standard (DES). It has the support of major credit card companies, such as Visa and MasterCard. However, SET has not been widely accepted by the Internet in general; instead, SSL/TLS encrypted sessions are the preferred mechanism for secure e-commerce.

These five secure communication protocols (SKIP, SWIPE, S-RPC, SSL/TLS, and SET) are just a few examples of options available. Keep in mind that there are many other secure protocols, such as IPSec.

Authentication Protocols

After a connection is initially established between a remote system and a server or a network, the first activity that should take place is to verify the identity of the remote user. This activity is known as *authentication*. There are several authentication protocols that control how the logon credentials are exchanged and whether those credentials are encrypted during transport:

Challenge Handshake Authentication Protocol (CHAP)   This is one of the authentication protocols used over PPP links. CHAP encrypts usernames and passwords. It performs authentication using a challenge-response dialogue that cannot be replayed. CHAP also periodically reauthenticates the remote system throughout an established communication session to verify persistent identity of the remote client. This activity is transparent to the user.

Password Authentication Protocol (PAP)   This is a standardized authentication protocol for PPP. PAP transmits usernames and passwords in the clear. It offers no form of encryption; it simply provides a means to transport the logon credentials from the client to the authentication server.

Extensible Authentication Protocol (EAP)   This is a framework for authentication instead of an actual protocol. EAP allows customized authentication security solutions, such as supporting smart cards, tokens, and biometrics. (See the sidebar "EAP, PEAP, and LEAP" for information about other protocols based on EAP.)

These three authentication protocols were initially used over dial-up PPP connections. Today, these and many other, newer authentication protocols and concepts are in use over a wide number of distance connection technologies, including broadband and virtual private networks (VPNs).

EAP, PEAP, and LEAP

Protected Extensible Authentication Protocol (PEAP) encapsulates EAP in a TLS tunnel. PEAP is preferred to EAP because EAP assumes that the channel is already protected but PEAP imposes its own security. PEAP is used for securing communications over 802.11 wireless connections. PEAP can be employed by WiFi Protected Access (WPA) and WPA-2 connections.

PEAP is also preferred over Cisco's proprietary EAP known as Lightweight Extensible Authentication Protocol (LEAP). LEAP was Cisco's initial response to insecure WEP. LEAP supported frequent reauthentication and changing of WEP keys (whereas WEP used single authentication and a static key). However, LEAP is crackable using a variety of tools and techniques, including the exploit tool asLEAP.

Virtual Private Network

A *virtual private network (VPN)* is a communication tunnel that provides point-to-point transmission of both authentication and data traffic over an intermediary untrusted network. Most VPNs use encryption to protect the encapsulated traffic, but encryption is not necessary for the connection to be considered a VPN.

VPNs are most commonly associated with establishing secure communication paths through the Internet between two distant networks. However, they can exist anywhere, including within private networks or between end-user systems connected to an ISP. The VPN can link two networks or two individual systems. They can link clients, servers, routers, firewalls, and switches. VPNs are also helpful in providing security for legacy applications that rely upon risky or vulnerable communication protocols or methodologies, especially when communication is across a network.

VPNs can provide confidentiality and integrity over insecure or untrusted intermediary networks. They do not provide or guarantee availability.

Tunneling

Before you can truly understand VPNs, you must first understand tunneling. Tunneling is the network communications process that protects the contents of protocol packets by encapsulating them in packets of another protocol. The encapsulation is what creates the logical illusion of a communications tunnel over the untrusted intermediary network. This virtual path exists between the encapsulation and the deencapsulation entities located at the ends of the communication.

In fact, sending a snail mail letter to your grandmother involves the use of a tunneling system. You create the personal letter (the primary content protocol packet) and place it in an envelope (the tunneling protocol). The envelope is delivered through the postal service (the untrusted intermediary network) to its intended recipient.

You can use tunneling in many situations, such as when you're bypassing firewalls, gateways, proxies, or other traffic control devices. The bypass is achieved by encapsulating the restricted content inside packets that are authorized for transmission. The tunneling process prevents the traffic control devices from blocking or dropping the communication because such devices don't know what the packets actually contain.

Tunneling is often used to enable communications between otherwise disconnected systems. If two systems are separated by a lack of network connectivity, a communication link can be established by a modem dial-up link or other remote access or wide area network (WAN) networking service. The actual LAN traffic is encapsulated in whatever communication protocol is used by the temporary connection, such as Point-to-Point Protocol (PPP) in the case of modem dial-up. If two networks are connected by a network employing a different protocol, the protocol of the separated networks can often be encapsulated within the intermediary network's protocol to provide a communication pathway.

Regardless of the actual situation, tunneling protects the contents of the inner protocol and traffic packets by encasing, or wrapping, it in an authorized protocol used by the intermediary network or connection. Tunneling can be used if the primary protocol is not routable and to keep the total number of protocols supported on the network to a minimum.

 Real World Scenario

The Proliferation of Tunneling

Tunneling is such a common activity within communication systems that many of us use tunneling on a regular basis without even recognizing it. For example, every time you access a website using a secured SSL or TLS connection, you are using tunneling. Your plain-text web communications are being tunneled within an SSL or TLS session. Also, if you use Internet telephone or VoIP systems, your voice communication is being tunneled inside a VoIP protocol.

How many other instances of tunneling can you pinpoint that you encounter on a weekly basis?

If the act of encapsulating a protocol involves encryption, tunneling can provide a means to transport sensitive data across untrusted intermediary networks without fear of losing confidentiality and integrity.

Tunneling is not without its problems. It is generally an inefficient means of communicating because most protocols include their own error detection, error handling, acknowledgment, and session management features, so using more than one protocol at a time compounds the overhead required to communicate a single message. Furthermore, tunneling creates either larger packets or additional packets that in turn consume additional network bandwidth. Tunneling can quickly saturate a network if sufficient bandwidth is not available. In addition, tunneling is a point-to-point communication mechanism and is not designed to handle broadcast traffic. Tunneling also makes it difficult, if not impossible, to monitor the content of the traffic in some circumstances, creating issues for security practitioners.

How VPNs Work

A VPN link can be established over any other network communication connection. This could be a typical LAN cable connection, a wireless LAN connection, a remote access dial-up connection, a WAN link, or even a client using an Internet connection for access to an office LAN. A VPN link acts just like a typical direct LAN cable connection; the only possible difference would be speed based on the intermediary network and on the connection types between the client system and the server system. Over a VPN link, a client can perform the same activities and access the same resources as if they were directly connected via a LAN cable.

VPNs can connect two individual systems or two entire networks. The only difference is that the transmitted data is protected only while it is within the VPN tunnel. Remote access servers or firewalls on the network's border act as the start points and endpoints for VPNs. Thus, traffic is unprotected within the source LAN, protected between the border VPN servers, and then unprotected again once it reaches the destination LAN.

VPN links through the Internet for connecting to distant networks are often inexpensive alternatives to direct links or leased lines. The cost of two high-speed Internet links to local ISPs to support a VPN is often significantly less than the cost of any other connection means available.

Common VPN Protocols

VPNs can be implemented using software or hardware solutions. In either case, there are four common VPN protocols: PPTP, L2F, L2TP, and IPSec. PPTP, L2F, and L2TP operate at the Data Link layer (layer 2) of the OSI model. PPTP and IPSec are limited for use on IP networks, whereas L2F and L2TP can be used to encapsulate any LAN protocol.

 SSL can also be used as a VPN protocol, not just as a session encryption tool operating on top of TCP. The CISSP exam does not seem to include SSL VPN content at this time.

Point-to-Point Tunneling Protocol

Point-to-Point Tunneling Protocol (PPTP) is an encapsulation protocol developed from the dial-up protocol Point-to-Point Protocol (PPP). It operates at the Data Link layer (layer 2) of the OSI model and is used on IP networks. PPTP creates a point-to-point tunnel between two systems and encapsulates PPP packets. It offers protection for authentication traffic through the same authentication protocols supported by PPP:

- Microsoft Challenge Handshake Authentication Protocol (MS-CHAP)
- Challenge Handshake Authentication Protocol (CHAP)
- Password Authentication Protocol (PAP)
- Extensible Authentication Protocol (EAP)
- Shiva Password Authentication Protocol (SPAP)

 The CISSP exam focuses on the RFC 2637 version of PPTP, not the Microsoft implementation, which was customized using proprietary modifications to support data encryption using Microsoft Point-to-Point Encryption (MPPE).

The initial tunnel negotiation process used by PPTP is not encrypted. Thus, the session establishment packets that include the IP address of the sender and receiver—and can include usernames and hashed passwords—could be intercepted by a third party. PPTP is used on VPNs, but it is often replaced by the L2TP, which can use IPSec to provide traffic encryption for VPNs.

PPTP does not support TACACS+ and RADIUS.

Layer 2 Forwarding Protocol and Layer 2 Tunneling Protocol

Cisco developed its own VPN protocol called Layer 2 Forwarding (L2F), which is a mutual authentication tunneling mechanism. However, L2F does not offer encryption. L2F was not widely deployed and was soon replaced by L2TP. As their names suggest, both operate at Layer 2. Both can encapsulate any LAN protocol.

Layer 2 Tunneling Protocol (L2TP) was derived by combining elements from both PPTP and L2F. L2TP creates a point-to-point tunnel between communication endpoints. It lacks a built-in encryption scheme, but it typically relies upon IPSec as its security mechanism. L2TP also supports TACACS+ and RADIUS. IPSec is commonly used as a security mechanism for L2TP.

IP Security Protocol

The most commonly used VPN protocol is now IPSec. IP Security (IPSec) is both a standalone VPN protocol and the security mechanism for L2TP, and it can be used only for IP traffic. IPSec works only on IP networks and provides for secured authentication as well as encrypted data transmission. IPSec has two primary components, or functions:

Authentication Header (AH)   AH provides authentication, integrity, and nonrepudiation.

Encapsulating Security Payload (ESP)   ESP provides encryption to protect the confidentiality of transmitted data, but it can also perform limited authentication. It operates at the Network layer (layer 3) and can be used in transport mode or tunnel mode. In transport mode, the IP packet data is encrypted but the header of the packet is not. In tunnel mode, the entire IP packet is encrypted and a new header is added to the packet to govern transmission through the tunnel.

Table 4.1 illustrates the main characteristics of VPN protocols.

TABLE 4.1   VPN characteristics

VPN Protocol	Native Authentication Protection	Native Data Encryption	Protocols Supported	Dial-Up Links Supported	Number of Simultaneous Connections
PPTP	Yes	No	IP only	Yes	Single point to point
L2F	Yes	No	IP only	Yes	Single point to point
L2TP	Yes	No (can use IPSec)	Any	Yes	Single point to point
IPSec	Yes	Yes	IP only	No	Multiple

A VPN device is a network add-on device used to create VPN tunnels separately from server or client OSs. The use of the VPN devices is transparent to networked systems.

Virtual LAN

A virtual LAN (VLAN) is used for hardware-imposed network segmentation. VLANs are used to logically segment a network without altering its physical topology.

VLANs are created by switches. By default, all ports on a switch are part of VLAN #1. But as the switch administrator changes the VLAN assignment on a port-by-port basis, various ports can be grouped together and be distinct from other VLAN port designations. Thus, multiple logical network segments can be created on the same physical network.

Communication between ports within the same VLAN occurs without hindrance. Communication between VLANs can be denied or enabled using a routing function. Routing can be provided by an external router or by the internal software of the switch (suggested by the term *multilayer switch*).

VLAN management is the use of VLANs to control traffic for security or perfor-mance reasons. VLANs perform several traffic management functions, some of which are security-related:

- Control and restrict broadcast traffic. Block broadcasts between subnets and VLANs.

- Isolate traffic between network segments. By default, different VLANs do not have a route for communication with each other. You can also allow communication between VLANs but specify a deny filter between certain VLANs (or certain members of a VLAN).

- Reduce a network's vulnerability to sniffers.

- Protect against broadcast storms (floods of unwanted broadcast network traffic).

VLANs work like subnets, but keep in mind that they are not actual sub-nets. VLANs are created by switches. Subnets are created by IP address and subnet mask assignments.

VLAN Management for Security

Any network segment that does not need to communicate with another to accomplish a work task/function should not be able to do so. Use VLANs to allow what is necessary, but block/deny anything not necessary. Remember, "deny by default; allow by exception" is not just a guideline for firewall rules, but for security in general.

Remote Access Security Management

Telecommuting, or working remotely, has become a common feature of business computing. Telecommuting usually requires remote access, the ability of a distant client to establish a communication session with a network. Remote access can take the following forms (among others):

- Using a modem to dial up directly to a remote access server

- Connecting to a network over the Internet through a VPN

- Connecting to a terminal server system through a thin-client connection

The first two examples use fully capable clients. They establish connections just as if they were directly connected to the LAN. In the last example, all computing activities occur on the terminal server system rather than on the distant client.

Telecommuting also usually involves telephone communications. Telephony is the collection of methods by which telephone services are provided to an organization or the mechanisms by which an organization uses telephone services for either voice and/or data communications. Traditionally, telephony included plain old telephone service (POTS)—also called public switched telephone network (PSTN)—combined with modems. However, private branch exchange (PBX), VoIP, and VPNs are commonly used for telephone communications as well.

POTS and PSTN refer to traditional land-line telephone connections. POTS/PSTN connections were the only or primary remote network links for many businesses until high-speed, cost-effective, and ubiquitous access methods were available. POTS/PSTN also waned in use for home-user Internet connectivity once broadband and wireless services became more widely available. POTS/PSTN connections are sometimes still used as a backup option for remote connections when broadband solutions fail, as rural Internet and remote connections, and as standard voice lines when ISDN or VoIP are unavailable or not cost effective.

When remote access capabilities are deployed in any environment, security must be considered and implemented to provide protection for your private network against remote access complications:

- Remote access users should be stringently authenticated before being granted access.

- Only those users who specifically need remote access for their assigned work tasks should be granted permission to establish remote connections.

- All remote communications should be protected from interception and eavesdropping. This usually requires an encryption solution that provides strong protection for the authentication traffic as well as all data transmission.

It is important to establish secure communication channels before initiating the transmission of sensitive, valuable, or personal information. Remote access can pose several potential security concerns if not protected and monitored sufficiently:

- If anyone with a remote connection can attempt to breach the security of your organization, the benefits of physical security are reduced.

- Telecommuters might use insecure or less-secure remote systems to access sensitive data and thus expose it to greater risk of loss, compromise, or disclosure.

- Remote systems might be exposed to malicious code and could be used as a carrier to bring malware into the private LAN.

- Remote systems might be less physically secure and thus be at risk of being used by unauthorized entities or stolen.

- Remote systems might be more difficult to troubleshoot, especially if the issues revolve around remote connection.

- Remote systems might not be as easy to upgrade or patch due to their potential infrequent connections or slow throughput links.

Remote access security in general is important, but you should also focus on the specifics of the various work tasks that require secured communications. This can include Voice over IP (VoIP), multimedia collaboration, and instant messaging.

Voice over Internet Protocol (VoIP)   VoIP is a technology that encapsulates audio into IP packets to support telephone calls over TCP/IP network connections. VoIP has become a popular and inexpensive telephony solution for companies and individuals worldwide.

It is important to keep security in mind when selecting a VoIP solution to ensure that it provides the privacy and security you expect. Some VoIP systems are essentially plain-form communications that are easily intercepted and eavesdropped; others are highly encrypted, and any attempt to interfere or wiretap is deterred and thwarted.

VoIP is not without its problems. Hackers can wage a wide range of potential attacks against a VoIP solution:

- Caller ID can be falsified easily using any number of VoIP tools, so hackers can perform vishing (VoIP phishing) or Spam over Internet Telephony (SPIT) attacks.

- The call manager systems and the VoIP phones themselves might be vulnerable to host OS attacks and DoS attacks. If a device's or software's host OS or firmware has vulnerabilities, hacker exploits are often not far off.

- Hackers might be able to perform man-in-the-middle (MitM) attacks by spoofing call managers or endpoint connection negotiations and/or responses.

- Depending on the deployment, there are also risks associated with deploying VoIP phones off the same switches as desktop and server systems. This could allow for 802.1X authentication falsification as well as VLAN and VoIP hopping (i.e., jumping across authenticated channels).

Multimedia collaboration   Multimedia collaboration is the use of various multimedia-supporting communication solutions to enhance distance collaboration (people working on a project together remotely). Often, collaboration allows workers to work simultaneously as well as across different time frames. Collaboration can also be used for tracking changes and including multimedia functions. Collaboration can incorporate email, chat, VoIP, videoconferencing, use of a whiteboard, online document editing, real-time file exchange, versioning control, and other tools. It is often a feature of advanced forms of remote meeting technology.

Remote meeting technology is used for any product, hardware, or software that allows for interaction between remote parties. These technologies and solutions are known by many other terms: digital collaboration, virtual meetings, video conferencing, software or application collaboration, shared whiteboard services, virtual training solutions, and so on. Any service that enables people to communicate, exchange data, collaborate on materials/data/documents, and otherwise perform work tasks together can be considered a remote meeting technology service.

No matter what form of multimedia collaboration is implemented, the attendant security implications must be evaluated. Does the service use strong authentication techniques? Does the communication occur across an open protocol or an encrypted tunnel? Does the solution allow for true deletion of content? Are activities of users audited and logged? Multimedia collaboration and other forms of remote meeting technology can improve the work environment and allow for input from a wider range of diverse workers across the globe, but this is only a benefit if the security of the communications solution can be ensured.

Instant messaging   *Instant messaging (IM)* is a mechanism that allows for real-time text-based chat between two users located anywhere on the Internet. Some IM utilities allow for file transfer, multimedia, voice and videoconferencing, and more. Some forms of IM are based on a peer-to-peer service while others use a centralized controlling server. Peer-to-peer-based IM is easy for end users to deploy and use, but it's difficult to manage from a corporate perspective because it's generally insecure. It has numerous vulnerabilities: It's susceptible to packet sniffing, it lacks true native security capabilities, and it provides no protection for privacy.

Many forms of instant messaging lack common security features, such as encryption or user privacy. Many IM clients are susceptible to malicious code deposit or infection through their file transfer capabilities. Also, IM users are often subject to numerous forms of social-engineering attacks, such as impersonation or convincing a victim to reveal information that should remain confidential (such as passwords).

Plan Remote Access Security

When outlining your remote access security management strategy, be sure to address the following issues:

Remote connectivity technology   Each type of connection has its own unique security issues. Fully examine every aspect of your connection options. This can include modems, DSL, ISDN, wireless networking, and cable modems.

Transmission protection   There are several forms of encrypted protocols, encrypted connection systems, and encrypted network services or applications. Use the appropriate combination of secured services for your remote connectivity needs. This can include VPNs, SSL, TLS, Secure Shell (SSH), IPSec, and L2TP.

Authentication protection   In addition to protecting data traffic, you must ensure that all logon credentials are properly secured. This requires the use of an authentication protocol and may mandate the use of a centralized remote access authentication system. This can include Password Authentication Protocol (PAP), Challenge Handshake Authentication Protocol (CHAP), Extensible Authentication Protocol (EAP; or its extensions, PEAP or LEAP), Remote Authentication Dial-In User Service (RADIUS), and Terminal Access Controller Access Control System (TACACS).

Remote user assistance   Remote access users may periodically require technical assistance. You must have a means established to provide this as efficiently as possible. This can include, for example, addressing software and hardware issues and user training issues. If an organization is unable to provide a reasonable solution for remote user technical support, it could result in loss of productivity, compromise of the remote system, or an overall breach of organizational security.

If it is difficult or impossible to maintain a similar level of security on a remote system as is maintained in the private LAN, remote access should be reconsidered in light of the security risks it represents.

The ability to use remote access or establish a remote connection should be tightly controlled. You can control and restrict the use of remote connectivity by means of filters, rules, or access controls based on user identity, workstation identity, protocol, application, content, and time of day.

To restrict remote access only to authorized users, you can use callback and caller ID. Callback is a mechanism that disconnects a remote user upon initial contact and then immediately attempts to reconnect to them using a predefined phone number (in other words, the number defined in the user account's security database). Callback does have a user-defined mode. However, this mode is not used for security; it is used to reverse toll charges to the company rather than charging the remote client. Caller ID verification can be used for the same purpose as callback—by potentially verifying the physical location (via phone number) of the authorized user.

It should be a standard element in your security policy that no unauthorized modems be present on any system connected to the private network. You may need to further specify this policy by indicating that those with portable systems must either remove their modems before connecting to the network or boot with a hardware profile that disables the modem's device driver.

Dial-Up Protocols

When a remote connection link is established, a protocol must be used to govern how the link is actually created and to establish a common communication foundation over which other protocols can work. It is important to select protocols that support security whenever possible. At a minimum, a means to secure authentication is needed, but adding the option for data encryption is also preferred. The two primary examples of dial-up protocols, PPP and SLIP, provide link governance, not only for true dial-up links, but also for some VPN links:

Point-to-Point Protocol (PPP)   This is a full-duplex protocol used for transmitting TCP/IP packets over various non-LAN connections, such as modems, ISDN, VPNs, Frame Relay, and so on. PPP is widely supported and is the transport protocol of choice for dial-up Internet connections. PPP authentication is protected through the use of various protocols, such as CHAP and PAP. PPP is a replacement for SLIP and can support any LAN protocol, not just TCP/IP.

Serial Line Internet Protocol (SLIP)   This is an older technology developed to support TCP/IP communications over asynchronous serial connections, such as serial cables or modem dial-up. SLIP is rarely used but is still supported on many systems. It can support only IP, requires static IP addresses, offers no error detection or correction, and does not support compression.

 One of the many proprietary dial-up protocols is Microcom Networking Protocol (MNP). MNP was found on Microcom modems in the 1990s. It supports its own form of error control called Echoplex.

Centralized Remote Authentication Services

As remote access becomes a key element in an organization's business functions, it is often important to add layers of security between remote clients and the private network. Centralized remote authentication services, such as RADIUS and TACACS, provide this extra layer of protection. These mechanisms provide a separation of the authentication and authorization processes for remote clients from that performed for LAN or local clients. The separation is important for security because if the RADIUS or TACACS servers are ever compromised, then only remote connectivity is affected, not the rest of the network.

Remote Authentication Dial-In User Service (RADIUS)   This is used to centralize the authentication of remote dial-up connections. A network that employs a RADIUS server is configured so the remote access server passes dial-up user logon credentials to the RADIUS server for authentication. This process is similar to the process used by domain clients sending logon credentials to a domain controller for authentication.

Terminal Access Controller Access-Control System (TACACS)   This is an alternative to RADIUS. TACACS is available in three versions: original TACACS, Extended TACACS (XTACACS), and TACACS+. TACACS integrates the authentication and authorization processes. XTACACS keeps the authentication, authorization, and accounting processes separate. TACACS+ improves XTACACS by adding two-factor authentication.

Network Address Translation

The goals of hiding the identity of internal clients, masking the design of your private network, and keeping public IP address leasing costs to a minimum are all made simple to achieve through the use of Network Address Translation (NAT). NAT is a mechanism for converting the internal IP addresses found in packet headers into public IP addresses for transmission over the Internet.

NAT was developed to allow private networks to use any IP address set without causing collisions or conflicts with public Internet hosts with the same IP addresses. In effect,

NAT translates the IP addresses of your internal clients to leased addresses outside your environment.

NAT offers numerous benefits, including the following:

▪ You can connect an entire network to the Internet using only a single (or just a few) leased public IP addresses.

▪ You can use the private IP addresses defined in RFC 1918 in a private network and still be able to communicate with the Internet.

▪ NAT hides the IP addressing scheme and network topography from the Internet.

▪ NAT restricts connections so that only traffic stemming from connections originating from the internal protected network are allowed back into the network from the Internet. Thus, most intrusion attacks are automatically repelled.

 Real World Scenario

Are You Using NAT?

Most networks, whether at an office or at home, employ NAT. There are at least three ways to tell whether you are working within a NATed network:

1. Check your client's IP address. If it is one of the RFC 1918 addresses and you are still able to interact with the Internet, then you are on a NATed network.

2. Check the configuration of your proxy, router, firewall, modem, or gateway device to see whether NAT is configured. (This action requires authority and access to the networking device.)

3. If your client's IP address is not an RFC 1918 address, then compare your address to what the Internet thinks your address is. You can do this by visiting any of the IP-checking websites; a popular one is http://whatismyipaddress.com. If your client's IP address and the address that What Is My IP Address claims is your address are different, then you are working from a NATed network.

 Frequently, security professionals refer to NAT when they really mean PAT. By definition, NAT maps one internal IP address to one external IP address. However, Port Address Translation (PAT) maps one internal IP address to an external IP address and port number combination. Thus, PAT can theoretically support 65,536 (2^{32}) simultaneous communications from internal clients over a single external leased IP address. So with NAT, you must lease as many public IP addresses as you want to have for simultaneous communications, while with PAT you can lease fewer IP addresses and obtain a reasonable 100:1 ratio of internal clients to external leased IP addresses.

NAT is part of a number of hardware devices and software products, including firewalls, routers, gateways, and proxies. It can be used only on IP networks and operates at the Network layer (layer 3).

Private IP Addresses

The use of NAT has proliferated recently because of the increased scarcity of public IP addresses and security concerns. With only roughly 4 billion addresses (2^{32}) available in IPv4, the world has simply deployed more devices using IP than there are unique IP addresses available. Fortunately, the early designers of the Internet and the TCP/IP protocol had good foresight and put aside a few blocks of addresses for private, unrestricted use. These IP addresses, commonly called the *private IP addresses*, are defined in RFC 1918. They are as follows:

- 10.0.0.0–10.255.255.255 (a full Class A range)
- 172.16.0.0–172.31.255.255 (16 Class B ranges)
- 192.168.0.0–192.168.255.255 (256 Class C ranges)

 Real World Scenario

Can't NAT Again!

On several occasions we've needed to re-NAT an already NATed network. This might occur in the following situations:

- You need to make an isolated subnet within a NATed network and attempt to do so by connecting a router to host your new subnet to the single port offered by the existing network.

- You have a DSL or cable modem that offers only a single connection but you have multiple computers or want to add wireless to your environment.

By connecting a NAT proxy router or a wireless access point, you are usually attempting to re-NAT what was NATed to you initially. One configuration setting that can either make or break this setup is the IP address range in use. It is not possible to re-NAT the same subnet. For example, if your existing network is offering 192.168.1.x addresses, then you cannot use that same address range in your new NATed subnet. So, change the configuration of your new router/WAP to perform NAT on a slightly different address range, such as 192.168.5.x, so you won't have the conflict. This seems obvious, but it is quite frustrating to troubleshoot the unwanted result without this insight.

All routers and traffic-directing devices are configured by default not to forward traffic to or from these IP addresses. In other words, the private IP addresses are not routed by default. Thus, they cannot be directly used to communicate over the Internet. However, they can be easily used on private networks where routers are not employed or where slight modifications to router configurations are made. Using private IP addresses in conjunction with NAT greatly reduces the cost of connecting to the Internet by allowing fewer public IP addresses to be leased from an ISP.

> Attempting to use these private IP addresses directly on the Internet is futile because all publicly accessible routers will drop data packets containing a source or destination IP address from these RFC 1918 ranges.

Stateful NAT

NAT operates by maintaining a mapping between requests made by internal clients, a client's internal IP address, and the IP address of the Internet service contacted. When a request packet is received by NAT from a client, it changes the source address in the packet from the client's to the NAT server's. This change is recorded in the NAT mapping database along with the destination address. Once a reply is received from the Internet server, NAT matches the reply's source address to an address stored in its mapping database and then uses the linked client address to redirect the response packet to its intended destination. This process is known as *stateful NAT* because it maintains information about the communication sessions between clients and external systems.

NAT can operate on a one-to-one basis with only a single internal client able to communicate over one of its leased public IP addresses at a time. This type of configuration can result in a bottleneck if more clients attempt Internet access than there are public IP addresses. For example, if there are only five leased public IP addresses, the sixth client must wait until an address is released before its communications can be transmitted over the Internet. Other forms of NAT employ multiplexing techniques in which port numbers are used to allow the traffic from multiple internal clients to be managed on a single leased public IP address. Technically, this multiplexing form of NAT is known as Port Address Translation (PAT) or Overloaded NAT, but it seems that the industry still uses the term NAT to refer to this newer version.

Static and Dynamic NAT

You can use NAT in two modes: static and dynamic.

Static NAT   Use static mode NAT when a specific internal client's IP address is assigned a permanent mapping to a specific external public IP address. This allows for external entities to communicate with systems inside your network even if you are using RFC 1918 IP addresses.

Dynamic NAT   Use dynamic mode NAT to grant multiple internal clients access to a few leased public IP addresses. Thus, a large internal network can still access the Internet without having to lease a large block of public IP addresses. This keeps public IP address usage abuse to a minimum and helps keep Internet access costs to a minimum.

In a dynamic mode NAT implementation, the NAT system maintains a database of mappings so that all response traffic from Internet services are properly routed to the original internal requesting client. Often NAT is combined with a proxy server or proxy firewall to provide additional Internet access and content-caching features.

NAT is not directly compatible with IPSec because it modifies packet headers, which IPSec relies upon to prevent security violations. However, there are versions of NAT proxies designed to support IPSec over NAT. Specifically, NAT-Traversal (RFC 3947) was designed to support IPSec VPNs through the use of UDP encapsulation of IKE. IP Security (IPSec) is a standards-based mechanism for providing encryption for point-to-point TCP/IP traffic.

Automatic Private IP Addressing

Automatic Private IP Addressing (APIPA), aka Link-Local address assignment (defined in RFC 3927), assigns an IP address to a system in the event of a DHCP assignment failure. APIPA is primarily a feature of Windows. APIPA assigns each failed DHCP client with an IP address from the range of 169.254.0.1 to 169.254.255.254 along with the default Class B subnet mask of 255.255.0.0. This allows the system to communicate with other APIPA-configured clients within the same broadcast domain but not with any system across a router or with a correctly assigned IP address.

Don't confuse APIPA with the private IP address ranges, defined in RFC 1918.

APIPA is not usually directly concerned with security. However, it is still an important issue to understand. If you notice that a system is assigned an APIPA address instead of a valid network address, that indicates a problem. It could be as mundane as a bad cable or power failure on the DHCP server, but it could also be a symptom of a malicious attack on the DHCP server. You might be asked to decipher issues in a scenario where IP addresses are presented. You should be able to discern whether an address is a public address, an RFC 1918 private address, an APIPA address, or a loopback address.

Converting IP Address Numbers

IP addresses and subnet masks are actual binary numbers, and through their use in binary, all the functions of routing and traffic management occur. Therefore, it is a good idea to know how to convert between decimal, binary, and even hexadecimal. Also, don't forget how to convert from a dotted-decimal notation IP address (such as 172.16.1.1) to its binary equivalent (that is, 10101100000100000000000100000001). And it is probably not a bad idea to be able to convert the 32-bit binary number to a single decimal number (that is, 2886729985). Knowledge of number conversions comes in handy when attempting to identify obfuscated addresses. If you are rusty in this skill area, take advantage of online conversion primers, such as at the following location:

www.learn-programming.za.net/articles_decbinhexoct.html

Real World Scenario

The Loopback Address

Another IP address range that you should be careful not to confuse with the private IP address ranges defined in RFC 1918 is the loopback address. The loopback address is purely a software entity. It is an IP address used to create a software interface that connects to itself via the TCP/IP protocol. The loopback address allows for the testing of local network settings in spite of missing, damaged, or nonfunctional network hardware and related device drivers. Technically, the entire 127.x.x.x network is reserved for loopback use. However, only the 127.0.0.1 address is widely used.

Windows XP SP2 (and possibly other OS updates) restricted the client to use only 127.0.0.1 as the loopback address. This caused several applications that used other addresses in the upper ranges of the 127.x.x.x network services to fail. In restricting client use to only 127.0.0.1, Microsoft has attempted to open up a wasted Class A address. Even if this tactic is successful for Microsoft, it will affect only Windows systems.

Switching Technologies

When two systems (individual computers or LANs) are connected over multiple intermediary networks, the task of transmitting data packets from one to the other is a complex process. To simplify this task, switching technologies were developed. The first switching technology was circuit switching.

Circuit Switching

Circuit switching was originally developed to manage telephone calls over the public switched telephone network. In circuit switching, a dedicated physical pathway is created between the two communicating parties. Once a call is established, the links between the two parties remain the same throughout the conversation. This provides for fixed or known transmission times, a uniform level of quality, and little or no loss of signal or communication interruptions. Circuit-switching systems employ permanent, physical connections. However, the term *permanent* applies only to each communication session. The path is permanent throughout a single conversation. Once the path is disconnected, if the two parties communicate again, a different path may be assembled. During a single conversation, the same physical or electronic path is used throughout the communication and is used only for that one communication. Circuit switching grants exclusive use of a communication path to the current communication partners. Only after a session has been closed can a pathway be reused by another communication.

🌐 **Real World Scenario**

Real-World Circuit Switching

There is very little real-world circuit switching in the modern world (or at least in the past 10 to 15 years or so). Packet switching, discussed next, has become ubiquitous for data and voice transmissions. Decades ago we could often point to the plain old telephone service (POTS)—also called public switched telephone network (PSTN)—as a prime example of circuit switching, but with the advent of digital switching and VoIP systems, those days are long gone. That's not to say that circuit switching is nonexistent in today's world; it is just not being used for data transmission. Instead, you can still find circuit switching in rail yards, irrigation systems, and even electrical distribution systems.

Packet Switching

Eventually, as computer communications increased as opposed to voice communications, a new form of switching was developed. Packet switching occurs when the message or communication is broken up into small segments (usually fixed-length packets, depending on the protocols and technologies employed) and sent across the intermediary networks to the destination. Each segment of data has its own header that contains source and destination information. The header is read by each intermediary system and is used to route each packet to its intended destination. Each channel or communication path is reserved for use only while a packet is actually being transmitted over it. As soon as the packet is sent, the channel is made available for other communications.

Packet switching does not enforce exclusivity of communication pathways. It can be seen as a logical transmission technology because addressing logic dictates how communications traverse intermediary networks between communication partners. Table 4.2 compares circuit switching to packet switching.

TABLE 4.2 Circuit switching vs. packet switching

Circuit Switching	Packet Switching
Constant traffic	Bursty traffic
Fixed known delays	Variable delays
Connection oriented	Connectionless
Sensitive to connection loss	Sensitive to data loss
Used primarily for voice	Used for any type of traffic

In relation to security, there are a few potential issues to consider. A packet-switching system places data from different sources on the same physical connection. This could lend itself to disclosure, corruption, or eavesdropping. Proper connection management, traffic isolation, and usually encryption are needed to protect against shared physical pathway concerns. A benefit of packet-switching networks is that they are not as dependent on specific physical connections as circuit switching is. Thus, when or if a physical pathway is damaged or goes offline, an alternate path can be used to continue the data/packet delivery. A circuit-switching network is often interrupted by physical path violations.

Virtual Circuits

A virtual circuit (also called a communication path) is a logical pathway or circuit created over a packet-switched network between two specific endpoints. Within packet-switching systems are two types of virtual circuits:

- Permanent virtual circuits (PVCs)
- Switched virtual circuits (SVCs)

A PVC is like a dedicated leased line; the logical circuit always exists and is waiting for the customer to send data. A PVC is a predefined virtual circuit that is always available. The virtual circuit may be closed down when not in use, but it can be instantly reopened whenever needed. An SVC is more like a dial-up connection because a virtual circuit has to be created using the best paths currently available before it can be used and then disassembled after the transmission is complete. In either type of virtual circuit, when a data packet enters point A of a virtual circuit connection, that packet is sent directly to point B or the other end of the virtual circuit. However, the actual path of one packet may be different from the path of another packet from the same transmission. In other words, multiple paths may exist between point A and point B as the ends of the virtual circuit, but any packet entering at point A will end up at point B.

A PVC is like a two-way radio or walkie-talkie. Whenever communication is needed, you press the button and start talking; the radio reopens the predefined frequency automatically (that is, the virtual circuit). An SVC is more like a shortwave or ham radio. You must tune the transmitter and receiver to a new frequency every time you want to communicate with someone.

WAN Technologies

Wide area network (WAN) links are used to connect distant networks, nodes, or individual devices together. This can improve communications and efficiency, but it can also place data at risk. Proper connection management and transmission encryption is needed to ensure a secure connection, especially over public network links. WAN links and long-distance connection technologies can be divided into two primary categories:

A *dedicated line* (also called a leased line or point-to-point link) is one that is indefinably and continually reserved for use by a specific customer (see Table 4.3). A dedicated line is always on and waiting for traffic to be transmitted over it. The link between the customer's LAN and the dedicated WAN link is always open and established. A dedicated line connects two specific endpoints and only those two endpoints.

TABLE 4.3 Examples of dedicated lines

Technology	Connection Type	Speed
Digital Signal Level 0 (DS-0)	Partial T1	64 Kbps up to 1.544 Mbps
Digital Signal Level 1 (DS-1)	T1	1.544 Mbps
Digital Signal Level 3 (DS-3)	T3	44.736 Mbps
European digital transmission format 1	EI	2.108 Mbps
European digital transmission format 3	E3	34.368 Mbps
Cable modem or cable routers		10+ Mbps

A *nondedicated line* is one that requires a connection to be established before data transmission can occur. A nondedicated line can be used to connect with any remote system that uses the same type of nondedicated line.

Achieving Fault Tolerance with Carrier Network Connections

To obtain fault tolerance with leased lines or with connections to carrier networks (that is, Frame Relay, ATM, SONET, SMDS, X.25, and so on), you must deploy two redundant connections. For even greater redundancy, you should purchase the connections from two different telcos or service providers. However, when you're using two different service providers, be sure they don't connect to the same regional backbone or share any major pipeline. The physical location of multiple communication lines leading from your building is also of concern because a single disaster or human error (e.g., a misguided back-hoe) could cause multiple lines to fail at once. If you cannot afford to deploy an exact duplicate of your primary leased line, consider a nondedicated DSL, ISDN, or cable modem connection. These less-expensive options may still provide partial availability in the event of a primary leased line failure.

Standard modems, DSL, and ISDN are examples of nondedicated lines. Digital subscriber line (DSL) is a technology that exploits the upgraded telephone network to grant consumers speeds from 144 Kbps to 6 Mbps (or more). There are numerous formats of DSL, such as ADSL, xDSL, CDSL, HDSL, SDSL, RASDSL, IDSL, and VDSL. Each format varies as to the specific downstream and upstream bandwidth provided.

For the exam, just worry about the general idea of DSL instead of trying to memorize all the details about the various DSL subformats.

The maximum distance a DSL line can be from a central office (that is, a specific type of distribution node of the telephone network) is approximately 1,000 meters.

Integrated Services Digital Network (ISDN) is a fully digital telephone network that supports both voice and high-speed data communications. There are two standard classes, or formats, of ISDN service:

Basic Rate Interface (BRI) offers customers a connection with two B channels and one D channel. The B channels support a throughput of 64 Kbps and are used for data transmission. The D channel is used for call establishment, management, and teardown and has a bandwidth of 16 Kbps. Even though the D channel was not designed to support data transmissions, a BRI ISDN is said to offer consumers 144 Kbps of total throughput.

Primary Rate Interface (PRI) offers consumers a connection with multiple 64 Kbps B channels (2 to 23 of them) and a single 64 Kbps D channel. Thus, a PRI can be deployed with as little as 192 Kbps and up to 1.544 Mbps. However, remember that those numbers are bandwidth, not throughput, because they include the D channel, which cannot be used for actual data transmission (at least not in most normal commercial implementations).

When considering connection options, don't forget about satellite connections. Satellite connections may offer high-speed solutions even in locales that are inaccessible by cable-based, radio-wave-based, and line-of-sight-based communications. Satellites are usually considered insecure because of their large surface footprint: Communications over a satellite can be intercepted by anyone. But if you have strong encryption, satellite communications can be reasonably secured. Just think of satellite radio. As long as you have a receiver, you can get the signal anywhere. But without a paid service plan, you can't gain access to the audio content.

WAN Connection Technologies

Numerous WAN connection technologies are available to companies that need communication services between multiple locations and even external partners. These WAN technologies vary greatly in cost and throughput. However, most share the common feature of being transparent to the connected LANs or systems. A WAN switch, specialized router, or border connection device provides all the interfacing needed between the network carrier service and a company's LAN. The border connection device is called the *channel service unit/data service unit (CSU/DSU)*. These devices convert LAN signals into the format used by the WAN carrier network and vice versa. The CSU/DSU contains data terminal equipment/data circuit-terminating equipment (DTE/DCE), which provides the actual connection point for the LAN's router (the DTE) and the WAN carrier network's switch (the DCE). The CSU/DSU acts as a translator, a store-and-forward device, and a link conditioner. A WAN switch is simply a specialized version of a LAN switch that is constructed with a built-in CSU/DSU for a specific type of carrier network. There are many types of carrier networks, or WAN connection technologies, such as X.25, Frame Relay, ATM, and SMDS.

 Real World Scenario

Remote Access and Telecommuting Techniques

As previously discussed, telecommuting is performing work at a remote location (i.e., other than the primary office). In fact, there is a good chance that you perform some form of telecommuting as part of your current job. Telecommuting clients use many remote access techniques to establish connectivity to the central office LAN. There are four main types of remote access techniques:

Service specific   Service-specific remote access gives users the ability to remotely connect to and manipulate or interact with a single service, such as email.

Remote control   Remote control remote access grants a remote user the ability to fully control another system that is physically distant from them. The monitor and keyboard act as if they are directly connected to the remote system.

Screen scraper/scraping   This term can be used in two different circumstances. First, it is sometimes used to refer to remote control, remote access, or remote desktop services. These services are also called virtual applications or virtual desktops. The idea is that the screen on the target machine is scraped and shown to the remote operator. Since remote access to resources presents additional risks of disclosure or compromise during the distance transmission, it is important to employ encrypted screen scraper solutions.

Second, screen scraping is a technology that can allow an automated tool to interact with a human interface. For example, some stand-alone data-gathering tools use search engines in their operation. However, most search engines must be used through their normal Web interface. For example, Google requires that all searches be performed through a Google Web search form field. (In the past, Google offered an API that enabled products to interact with the backend directly. However, Google terminated this practice to support the integration of advertisements with search results.) Screen scraping technology can interact with the human-friendly designed Web front end to the search engine, then parse the web page results to extract just the relevant information. Site Digger from Foundstone/MacAfee is a great example of this type of product.

Remote node operation   Remote node operation is just another name for dial-up connectivity. A remote system connects to a remote access server. That server provides the remote client with network services and possible Internet access.

X.25 WAN Connections

X.25 is an older packet-switching technology that was widely used in Europe. It uses permanent virtual circuits to establish specific point-to-point connections between two systems or networks. It is the predecessor to Frame Relay and operates in much the same fashion. However, X.25 use is declining because of its lower performance and throughput rates when compared to Frame Relay or ATM.

Frame Relay Connections

Like X.25, Frame Relay is a packet-switching technology that also uses PVCs (see the earlier discussion of virtual circuits). However, unlike X.25, Frame Relay supports multiple PVCs over a single WAN carrier service connection. Frame Relay is a layer 2 connection mechanism that uses packet-switching technology to establish virtual circuits between communication endpoints. Unlike dedicated or leased lines, for which cost is based primarily on the distance between endpoints, Frame Relay's cost is primarily based on the amount of data transferred. The Frame Relay network is a shared medium across which virtual circuits are created to provide point-to-point communications. All virtual circuits are independent of and invisible to each other.

A key concept related to Frame Relay is the Committed Information Rate (CIR). The CIR is the guaranteed minimum bandwidth a service provider grants to its customers. It is usually significantly less than the actual maximum capability of the provider network. Each customer may have a different CIR established and defined in their contract. The service network provider may allow customers to exceed their CIR over short intervals when additional bandwidth is available. This is known as *bandwidth on demand*. (Although at first this might sound like an outstanding benefit, the reality is that the customer is charged a premium rate for the extra consumed bandwidth.) Frame Relay operates at layer 2 (the Data Link layer) of the OSI model as a connection-oriented packet-switching transmission technology.

Frame Relay requires the use of DTE/DCE at each connection point. The customer owns the DTE, which acts like a router or a switch and provides the customer's network with access to the Frame Relay network. The Frame Relay service provider owns the DCE, which performs the actual transmission of data over the Frame Relay as well as establishing and maintaining the virtual circuit for the customer.

ATM

Asynchronous transfer mode (ATM) is a cell-switching WAN communication technology, as opposed to a packet-switching technology like Frame Relay. It fragments communications into fixed-length 53-byte cells. The use of fixed-length cells allows ATM to be very efficient and offer high throughputs. ATM can use either PVCs or SVCs. As with Frame Relay providers, ATM providers can guarantee a minimum bandwidth and a specific level of quality to their leased services. Customers can often consume additional bandwidth as needed when available on the service network for an additional pay-as-you-go fee. ATM is a connection-oriented packet-switching technology.

SMDS

Switched Multimegabit Data Service (SMDS) is a connectionless packet-switching technology. Often, SMDS is used to connect multiple LANs to form a metropolitan area network (MAN) or a WAN. SMDS was often a preferred connection mechanism for linking remote LANs that communicate infrequently. SMDS supports high-speed bursty traffic and bandwidth on demand. It fragments data into small transmission cells. SMDS can be considered a forerunner to ATM because of the similar technologies used.

Specialized Protocols

Some WAN connection technologies require additional specialized protocols to support various types of specialized systems or devices. Three of these protocols are SDLC, HDLC, and HSSI:

Synchronous Data Link Control (SDLC)   Synchronous Data Link Control (SDLC) is used on permanent physical connections of dedicated leased lines to provide connectivity for mainframes, such as IBM Systems Network Architecture (SNA) systems. SDLC uses polling, operates at OSI layer 2 (the Data Link layer), and is a bit-oriented synchronous protocol.

High-Level Data Link Control (HDLC)   High-Level Data Link Control (HDLC) is a refined version of SDLC designed specifically for serial synchronous connections. HDLC supports full-duplex communications and supports both point-to-point and multipoint connections. HDLC, like SDLC, uses polling and operates at OSI layer 2 (the Data Link layer). HDLC offers flow control and includes error detection and correction.

High Speed Serial Interface (HSSI)   High Speed Serial Interface (HSSI) is a DTE/DCE interface standard that defines how multiplexors and routers connect to high-speed network carrier services such as ATM or Frame Relay. A multiplexor is a device that transmits multiple communications or signals over a single cable or virtual circuit. HSSI defines the electrical and physical characteristics of the interfaces or connection points and thus operates at OSI layer 1 (the Physical layer).

Dial-Up Encapsulation Protocols

The Point-to-Point Protocol (PPP) is an encapsulation protocol designed to support the transmission of IP traffic over dial-up or point-to-point links. PPP allows for multivendor interoperability of WAN devices supporting serial links. All dial-up and most point-to-point connections are serial in nature (as opposed to parallel). PPP includes a wide range of communication services, including the assignment and management of IP addresses, management of synchronous communications, standardized encapsulation, multiplexing, link configuration, link quality testing, error detection, and feature or option negotiation (such as compression).

PPP was originally designed to support CHAP and PAP for authentication. However, recent versions of PPP also support MS-CHAP, EAP, and SPAP. PPP can also be used to support Internetwork Packet Exchange (IPX) and DECnet protocols. PPP is an Internet standard documented in RFC 1661. It replaced the Serial Line Internet Protocol (SLIP). SLIP offered no authentication, supported only half-duplex communications, had no error detection capabilities, and required manual link establishment and teardown.

Virtualization

Virtualization technology is used to host one or more operating systems within the memory of a single host computer. This mechanism allows virtually any OS to operate on any hardware. It also allows multiple operating systems to work simultaneously on the same hardware. Common examples include VMWare, Microsoft's Virtual PC, Microsoft Virtual Server, Hyper-V with Windows Server 2008, VirtualBox, and Apple's Bootcamp.

Virtualized servers and services are indistinguishable from traditional servers and services from a user's perspective.

Virtualization has several benefits, such as being able to launch individual instances of servers or services as needed, real-time scalability, and being able to run the exact OS version needed for the needed application. Additionally, recovery from damaged, crashed, or corrupted virtual systems is often quick: Simply replace the virtual system's main hard drive file with a clean backup version, and then relaunch it.

In relation to security, virtualization offers several benefits. It is often easier and faster to make backups of entire virtual systems than the equivalent native hardware installed system. Plus, when there is an error or problem, the virtual system can be replaced by a backup in minutes. Malicious code compromise or infection of virtual systems rarely affects the host OS. This allows for safe testing and experimentation.

Virtualization is used for a wide variety of new architectures and system design solutions. Cloud computing is ultimately a form of virtualization (See Chapter 12, "Security Architecture Vulnerabilities, Threats, and Countermeasures," for more on cloud computing). Locally (or at least within an organization's private infrastructure), virtualization can be used to host servers, client operating systems, limited user interfaces (i.e., virtual desktops), applications, and more.

A virtual application is a software product deployed in such a way that it is fooled into believing it is interacting with a full host OS. A virtual (or virtualized) application has been packaged or encapsulated to make it portable and able to operate without the full installation of its original host OS. A virtual application has enough of the original host OS included in its encapsulation bubble (technically called a virtual machine, or VM) that it operates/functions as if it was traditionally installed. Some forms of virtual applications are used as portable apps (short for applications) on USB drives. Other virtual applications are designed to be executed on alternate host OS platforms—for example, running a Windows application within a Linux OS.

The term *virtual desktop* refers to at least three different types of technology:

- A remote access tool that grants the user access to a distant computer system by allowing remote viewing and control of the distant desktop's display, keyboard, mouse, and so on.

- An extension of the virtual application concept encapsulating multiple applications and some form of "desktop" or shell for portability or cross-OS operation. This technology offers some of the features/benefits/applications of one platform to users of another without the need for multiple computers, dual-booting, or virtualizing an entire OS platform.

- An extended or expanded desktop larger than the display being used allows the user to employ multiple application layouts, switching between them using keystrokes or mouse movements.

See Chapter 11, "Principles of Security Models, Design, and Capabilities," and 12 for more information on virtualization as part of Security Architecture and Design.

Miscellaneous Security Control Characteristics

When you're selecting or deploying security controls for network communications, you need to evaluate numerous characteristics in light of your circumstances, capabilities, and security policy. We discuss these issues in the following sections.

Transparency

Just as the name implies, *transparency* is the characteristic of a service, security control, or access mechanism that ensures that it is unseen by users. Transparency is often a desirable feature for security controls. The more transparent a security mechanism is, the less likely a user will be able to circumvent it or even be aware that it exists. With transparency, there is a lack of direct evidence that a feature, service, or restriction exists, and its impact on performance is minimal.

In some cases, transparency may need to function more as a configurable feature than as a permanent aspect of operation, such as when an administrator is troubleshooting, evaluating, or tuning a system's configurations.

Verify Integrity

To verify the integrity of a transmission, you can use a checksum called a *hash total*. A hash function is performed on a message or a packet before it is sent over the communication pathway. The hash total obtained is added to the end of the message and is called the *message digest*. Once the message is received, the hash function is performed by the destination system, and the result is compared to the original hash total. If the two hash totals match, then there is a high level of certainty that the message has not been altered or corrupted during transmission. Hash totals are similar to cyclic redundancy checks (CRCs) in that they both act as integrity tools. In most secure transaction systems, hash functions are used to guarantee communication integrity.

 Real World Scenario

Checking the Hash

Checking the hash value of files is always a good idea. This simple task can prevent the use of corrupted files and prevent the accidental acceptance of maligned data. Several intrusion detection systems (IDSs) and system integrity verification tools use hashing as a means to check that files did not change over time. This is done by creating a hash for every file on a drive, storing those hashes in a database, and then periodically recalculating hashes for files and checking the new hash against the historical one. If there is ever any difference in the hashes, then you should investigate the file.

Another common use of hashes is to verify downloads. Many trusted Internet download sites provide MD5 and SHA hash totals for the files they offer. You can take advantage of these hashes in at least two ways. First, you can use a download manager that automatically checks the hashes for you upon download completion. Second, you can obtain a hashing tool, such as md5sum or sha1sum, to generate your own hash values. Then manually compare your generated value from the downloaded file against the claimed hash value from the download site. This mechanism ensures that the file you ultimately have on your system matches to the last bit the file from the download site.

Record sequence checking is similar to a hash total check; however, instead of verifying content integrity, it verifies packet or message sequence integrity. Many communications services employ record sequence checking to verify that no portions of a message were lost and that all elements of the message are in their proper order.

Transmission Mechanisms

Transmission logging is a form of auditing focused on communications. Transmission logging records the particulars about source, destination, time stamps, identification codes, transmission status, number of packets, size of message, and so on. These pieces of information may be useful in troubleshooting problems and tracking down unauthorized communications or used against a system as a means to extract data about how it functions.

Transmission error correction is a capability built into connection- or session-oriented protocols and services. If it is determined that a message, in whole or in part, was corrupted, altered, or lost, a request can be made for the source to resend all or part of the message. Retransmission controls determine whether all or part of a message is retransmitted in the event that a transmission error correction system discovers a problem with a communication. Retransmission controls can also determine whether multiple copies of a hash total or CRC value are sent and whether multiple data paths or communication channels are employed.

Manage Email Security

Email is one of the most widely and commonly used Internet services. The email infrastructure employed on the Internet primarily consists of email servers using Simple Mail Transfer Protocol (SMTP) to accept messages from clients, transport those messages to other servers, and deposit them into a user's server-based inbox. In addition to email servers, the infrastructure includes email clients. Clients retrieve email from their server-based inboxes using Post Office Protocol version 3 (POP3) or Internet Message Access Protocol (IMAP). Clients communicate with email servers using SMTP. Many Internet-compatible email systems rely upon the X.400 standard for addressing and message handling.

Sendmail is the most common SMTP server for UNIX systems, Exchange is the most common SMTP server for Microsoft systems, and GroupWise is (or at least was) the most common SMTP server for Novell systems. In addition to these three popular products, numerous alternatives exist, but they all share the same basic functionality and compliance with Internet email standards.

If you deploy an SMTP server, it is imperative that you properly configure authentication for both inbound and outbound mail. SMTP is designed to be a mail relay system. This means it relays mail from sender to intended recipient. However, you want to avoid turning your SMTP server into an *open relay* (also known as an *open relay agent* or *relay agent*), which is an STMP server that does not authenticate senders before accepting and relaying mail. Open relays are prime targets for spammers because they allow spammers to send out floods of emails by piggybacking on an insecure email infrastructure.

Email Security Goals

For email, the basic mechanism in use on the Internet offers the efficient delivery of messages but lacks controls to provide for confidentiality, integrity, or even availability.

In other words, basic email is not secure. However, you can add security to email in many ways. Adding security to email may satisfy one or more of the following objectives:

- Provide for nonrepudiation
- Restrict access to messages to their intended recipients (i.e., privacy and confidentiality)
- Maintain the integrity of messages
- Authenticate and verify the source of messages
- Verify the delivery of messages
- Classify sensitive content within or attached to messages

As with any aspect of IT security, email security begins in a security policy approved by upper management. Within the security policy, you must address several issues:

- Acceptable use policies for email
- Access control
- Privacy
- Email management
- Email backup and retention policies

Acceptable use policies define what activities can and cannot be performed over an organization's email infrastructure. It is often stipulated that professional, business-oriented email and a limited amount of personal email can be sent and received. Specific restrictions are usually placed on performing personal business (that is, work for another organization, including self-employment) and sending or receiving illegal, immoral, or offensive communications as well as on engaging in any other activities that would have a detrimental effect on productivity, profitability, or public relations.

Access control over email should be maintained so that users have access only to their specific inbox and email archive databases. An extension of this rule implies that no other user, authorized or not, can gain access to an individual's email. Access control should provide for both legitimate access and some level of privacy, at least from other employees and unauthorized intruders.

The mechanisms and processes used to implement, maintain, and administer email for an organization should be clarified. End users may not need to know the specifics of email management, but they do need to know whether email is considered private communication. Email has recently been the focus of numerous court cases in which archived messages were used as evidence—often to the chagrin of the author or recipient of those messages. If email is to be retained (that is, backed up and stored in archives for future use), users need to be made aware of this. If email is to be reviewed for violations by an auditor, users need to be informed of this as well. Some companies have elected to retain only the last three months of email archives before they are destroyed, whereas others have opted to retain email for years. Depending upon your country and industry, there are often regulations that dictate retention policies.

Understand Email Security Issues

The first step in deploying email security is to recognize the vulnerabilities specific to email. The protocols used to support email do not employ encryption. Thus, all messages are transmitted in the form in which they are submitted to the email server, which is often plain text. This makes interception and eavesdropping easy. However, the lack of native encryption is one of the least important security issues related to email.

Email is the most common delivery mechanism for viruses, worms, Trojan horses, documents with destructive macros, and other malicious code. The proliferation of support for various scripting languages, autodownload capabilities, and autoexecute features has transformed hyperlinks within the content of email and attachments into a serious threat to every system.

Email offers little in the way of source verification. Spoofing the source address of email is a simple process for even a novice attacker. Email headers can be modified at their source or at any point during transit. Furthermore, it is also possible to deliver email directly to a user's inbox on an email server by directly connecting to the email server's SMTP port. And speaking of in-transit modification, there are no native integrity checks to ensure that a message was not altered between its source and destination.

In addition, email itself can be used as an attack mechanism. When sufficient numbers of messages are directed to a single user's inbox or through a specific STMP server, a denial of service (DoS) attack can result. This attack is often called *mail-bombing* and is simply a DoS performed by inundating a system with messages. The DoS can be the result of storage capacity consumption or processing capability utilization. Either way, the result is the same: Legitimate messages cannot be delivered.

Like email flooding and malicious code attachments, unwanted email can be considered an attack. Sending unwanted, inappropriate, or irrelevant messages is called *spamming*. Spamming is often little more than a nuisance, but it does waste system resources both locally and over the Internet. It is often difficult to stop spam because the source of the messages is usually spoofed.

Email Security Solutions

Imposing security on email is possible, but the efforts should be in tune with the value and confidentiality of the messages being exchanged. You can use several protocols, services, and solutions to add security to email without requiring a complete overhaul of the entire Internet-based SMTP infrastructure. These include S/MIME, MOSS, PEM, and PGP. We'll discuss S/MIME further in Chapter 10, "PKI and Cryptographic Applications."

Secure Multipurpose Internet Mail Extensions (S/MIME)   Secure Multipurpose Internet Mail Extensions (S/MIME) offers authentication and confidentiality to email through public key encryption and digital signatures. Authentication is provided through X.509 digital certificates. Privacy is provided through the use of Public Key Cryptography Standard (PKCS) encryption. Two types of messages can be formed using S/MIME: signed messages and secured enveloped messages. A signed message provides integrity, sender authentication, and nonrepudiation. An enveloped message provides integrity, sender authentication, and confidentiality.

MIME Object Security Services (MOSS)   MIME Object Security Services (MOSS) can provide authentication, confidentiality, integrity, and nonrepudiation for email messages. MOSS employs Message Digest 2 (MD2) and MD5 algorithms; Rivest, Shamir, and Adelman (RSA) public key; and Data Encryption Standard (DES) to provide authentication and encryption services.

Privacy Enhanced Mail (PEM)   Privacy Enhanced Mail (PEM) is an email encryption mechanism that provides authentication, integrity, confidentiality, and nonrepudiation. PEM uses RSA, DES, and X.509.

Pretty Good Privacy (PGP) Pretty Good Privacy (PGP)   is a public-private key system that uses a variety of encryption algorithms to encrypt files and email messages. The first version of PGP used RSA, the second version, International Data Encryption Algorithm (IDEA), but later versions offered a spectrum of algorithm options. PGP is not a standard but rather an independently developed product that has wide Internet grassroots support.

 Real World Scenario

Free PGP Solution

PGP started off as a free product for all to use, but it has since splintered into various divergent products. PGP is a commercial product, while OpenPGP is a developing standard that GnuPG is compliant with and that was independently developed by the Free Software Foundation. If you have not used PGP before, we recommend downloading the appropriate GnuPG version for your preferred email platform. This secure solution is sure to improve your email privacy and integrity. You can learn more about GnuPG at http://gnupg.org. You can learn more about PGP by visiting its pages on *Wikipedia*.

By using these and other security mechanisms for email and communication transmissions, you can reduce or eliminate many of the security vulnerabilities of email. Digital signatures can help eliminate impersonation. The encryption of messages reduces eavesdropping. And the use of email filters keep spamming and mail-bombing to a minimum.

Blocking attachments at the email gateway system on your network can ease the threats from malicious attachments. You can have a 100 percent no-attachments policy or block only attachments that are known or suspected to be malicious, such as attachments with extensions that are used for executable and scripting files. If attachments are an essential part of your email communications, you'll need to train your users and use antivirus tools for protection. Training users to avoid contact with suspicious or unexpected attachments greatly reduces the risk of malicious code transference via email. Antivirus software is generally effective against known viruses, but it offers little protection against new or unknown viruses.

 Real World Scenario

Fax Security

Fax communications are waning in popularity because of the widespread use of email. Electronic documents are easily exchanged as attachments to email. Printed documents are just as easy to scan and email as they are to fax. However, you must still address faxing in your overall security plan. Most modems give users the ability to connect to a remote computer system and send and receive faxes. Many operating systems include built-in fax capabilities, and there are numerous fax products for computer systems. Faxes sent from a computer's fax/modem can be received by another computer or by a regular fax machine.

Even with declining use, faxes still represent a communications path that is vulnerable to attack. Like any other telephone communication, faxes can be intercepted and are susceptible to eavesdropping. If an entire fax transmission is recorded, it can be played back by another fax machine to extract the transmitted documents.

Some of the mechanisms that can be deployed to improve the security of faxes are fax encryptors, link encryption, activity logs, and exception reports. A fax encryptor gives a fax machine the capability to use an encryption protocol to scramble the outgoing fax signal. The use of an encryptor requires that the receiving fax machine support the same encryption protocol so it can decrypt the documents. Link encryption is the use of an encrypted communication path, like a VPN link or a secured telephone link, to transmit the fax. Activity logs and exception reports can be used to detect anomalies in fax activity that could be symptoms of attack.

In addition to the security of a fax transmission, it is important to consider the security of a received fax. Faxes that are automatically printed may sit in the out tray for a long period of time, therefore making them subject to viewing by unintended recipients. Studies have shown that adding banners of CONFIDENTIAL, PRIVATE, and so on spur the curiosity of passersby. So, disable automatic printing. Also, avoid using faxes employing ribbons or duplication cartridges that retain images of the printed faxes. Consider integrating your fax system with your network so you can email faxes to intended recipients instead of printing them to paper.

Secure Voice Communications

The vulnerability of voice communication is tangentially related to IT system security. However, as voice communication solutions move on to the network by employing digital devices and VoIP, securing voice communications becomes an increasingly important issue. When voice communications occur over the IT infrastructure, it is important to implement mechanisms to provide for authentication and integrity. Confidentiality should be maintained by employing an encryption service or protocol to protect the voice communications while in transit.

Normal private branch exchange (PBX) or POTS/PSTN voice communications are vulnerable to interception, eavesdropping, tapping, and other exploitations. Often, physical security is required to maintain control over voice communications within the confines of your organization's physical locations. Security of voice communications outside your organization is typically the responsibility of the phone company from which you lease services. If voice communication vulnerabilities are an important issue for sustaining your security policy, you should deploy an encrypted communication mechanism and use it exclusively.

Social Engineering

Malicious individuals can exploit voice communications through a technique known as *social engineering*. Social engineering is a means by which an unknown, untrusted, or at least unauthorized person gains the trust of someone inside of your organization. Adept individuals can convince employees that they are associated with upper management, technical support, the help desk, and so on. Once convinced, the victim is often encouraged to make a change to their user account on the system, such as resetting their password. Other attacks include instructing the victim to open specific email attachments, launch an application, or connect to a specific URL. Whatever the actual activity is, it is usually directed toward opening a back door that the attacker can use to gain network access.

The people within an organization make it vulnerable to social engineering attacks. With just a little information or a few facts, it is often possible to get a victim to disclose confidential information or engage in irresponsible activity. Social engineering attacks exploit human characteristics such as a basic trust in others, a desire to provide assistance, or a propensity to show off. Overlooking discrepancies, being distracted, following orders, assuming others know more than they actually do, wanting to help others, and fearing reprimands can also lead to attacks. Attackers are often able to bypass extensive physical and logical security controls because the victim opens an access pathway from the inside, effectively punching a hole in the secured perimeter.

Real World Scenario

The Fascinating World of Social Engineering

Social engineering is a fascinating subject. It is the means to break into the perfectly technically secured environment. Social engineering is the art of using an organization's own people against it. Although not necessary for the CISSP exam, there are lots of excellent resources, examples, and discussions of social engineering that can increase your awareness of this security problem. Some are also highly entertaining. We suggest doing some searching on the term *social engineering* to discover books and online videos. You'll find the reading informative and the video examples addicting.

The only way to protect against social engineering attacks is to teach users how to respond and interact with any form of communications, whether voice-only, face to face, IM, chat, or email. Here are some guidelines:

- Always err on the side of caution whenever voice communications seem odd, out of place, or unexpected.

- Always request proof of identity. This can be a driver's license number, Social Security number, employee ID number, customer number, or a case or reference number, any of which can be easily verified. It could also take the form of having a person in the office that would recognize the caller's voice take the call. For example, if the caller claims to be a department manager, you could confirm their identity by asking their administrative assistant to take the call.

- Require callback authorizations on all voice-only requests for network alterations or activities.

- Classify information (usernames, passwords, IP addresses, manager names, dial-in numbers, and so on), and clearly indicate which information can be discussed or even confirmed using voice communications.

- If privileged information is requested over the phone by an individual who should know that giving out that particular information over the phone is against the company's security policy, ask why the information is needed and verify their identity again. This incident should also be reported to the security administrator.

- Never give out or change passwords via voice-only communications.

- When disposing of office documentation (according to policy and regulation compliance) always use a secure disposal or destruction process, especially for any paperwork or media that contains information about the IT infrastructure or its security mechanisms.

Fraud and Abuse

Another voice communication threat is PBX fraud and abuse. Many PBX systems can be exploited by malicious individuals to avoid toll charges and hide their identity. Malicious attackers known as *phreakers* abuse phone systems in much the same way that attackers abuse computer networks. Phreakers may be able to gain unauthorized access to personal voice mailboxes, redirect messages, block access, and redirect inbound and outbound calls.

Countermeasures to PBX fraud and abuse include many of the same precautions you would employ to protect a typical computer network: logical or technical controls, administrative controls, and physical controls. Here are several key points to keep in mind when designing a PBX security solution:

- Consider replacing remote access or long-distance calling through the PBX with a credit card or calling card system.

- Restrict dial-in and dial-out features to authorized individuals who require such functionality for their work tasks.

- For your dial-in modems, use unpublished phone numbers that are outside the prefix block range of your voice numbers.

- Block or disable any unassigned access codes or accounts.

- Define an acceptable use policy and train users on how to properly use the system.

- Log and audit all activities on the PBX and review the audit trails for security and use violations.

- Disable maintenance modems (i.e., remote access modems used by the vendor to remotely manage, update, and tune a deployed product) and accounts.

- Change all default configurations, especially passwords and capabilities related to administrative or privileged features.

- Block remote calling (that is, allowing a remote caller to dial in to your PBX and then dial out again, thus directing all toll charges to the PBX host).

- Deploy Direct Inward System Access (DISA) technologies to reduce PBX fraud by external parties. (But be sure to configure it properly; see the sidebar "DISA: A Disease and the Cure.")

- Keep the system current with vendor/service provider updates.

Additionally, maintaining physical access control to all PBX connection centers, phone portals, and wiring closets prevents direct intrusion from onsite attackers.

 Real World Scenario

DISA: A Disease and the Cure

An often-touted "security" improvement to PBX systems is Direct Inward System Access (DISA). This system is designed to help manage external access and external control of a PBX by assigning access codes to users. Although great in concept, this system is being compromised and abused by phreakers. Once an outside phreaker learns the PBX access codes, they can often fully control and abuse the company's telephone network. This can include using the PBX to make long-distance calls that are charged to your company's telephone account rather than the phreaker's phone.

DISA, like any other security feature, must be properly installed, configured, and monitored in order to obtain the desired security improvement. Simply having DISA is not sufficient. Be sure to disable all features that are not required by the organization, craft user codes/passwords that are complex and difficult to guess, and then turn on auditing to keep watch on PBX activities.

Phreaking

As mentioned earlier, *phreaking* is a specific type of attack directed toward the telephone system. Phreakers use various types of technology to circumvent the telephone system to make free long-distance calls, to alter the function of telephone service, to steal specialized services, and even to cause service disruptions. Some phreaker tools are actual devices, whereas others are just particular ways of using a regular telephone. No matter what the tool or technology actually is, phreaker tools are referred to as colored boxes (black box, red box, and so on). Over the years, many box technologies have been developed and widely used by phreakers, but only a few of them work against today's telephone systems based on packet switching. Here are a few of the phreaker tools you need to recognize for the exam:

- *Black boxes* are used to manipulate line voltages to steal long-distance services. They are often just custom-built circuit boards with a battery and wire clips.
- *Red boxes* are used to simulate tones of coins being deposited into a pay phone. They are usually just small tape recorders.
- *Blue boxes* are used to simulate 2600 Hz tones to interact directly with telephone network trunk systems (that is, backbones). This could be a whistle, a tape recorder, or a digital tone generator.
- *White boxes* are used to control the phone system. A white box is a dual-tone multifrequency (DTMF) generator (that is, a keypad). It can be a custom-built device or one of the pieces of equipment that most telephone repair personnel use.

As you probably know, cell phone security is a growing concern. Captured electronic serial numbers (ESNs) and mobile identification numbers (MINs) can be burned into blank phones to create clones (even subscriber identity modules—SIMs—can be duplicated). When a clone is used, the charges are billed to the original owner's cell phone account. Furthermore, conversations and data transmission can be intercepted using radio frequency scanners. Also, anyone in the immediate vicinity can overhear at least one side of the conversation. So, don't talk about confidential, private, or sensitive topics in public places.

Security Boundaries

A *security boundary* is the line of intersection between any two areas, subnets, or environments that have different security requirements or needs. A security boundary exists between a high-security area and a low-security one, such as between a LAN and the Internet. It is important to recognize the security boundaries both on your network and in the physical world. Once you identify a security boundary, you need to deploy mechanisms to control the flow of information across those boundaries.

Divisions between security areas can take many forms. For example, objects may have different classifications. Each classification defines what functions can be performed by which subjects on which objects. The distinction between classifications is a security boundary.

Security boundaries also exist between the physical environment and the logical environment. To provide logical security, you must provide security mechanisms that are different from those used to provide physical security. Both must be present to provide a complete security structure, and both must be addressed in a security policy. However, they are different and must be assessed as separate elements of a security solution.

Security boundaries, such as a perimeter between a protected area and an unprotected one, should always be clearly defined. It's important to state in a security policy the point at which control ends or begins and to identify that point in both the physical and logical environments. Logical security boundaries are the points where electronic communications interface with devices or services for which your organization is legally responsible. In most cases, that interface is clearly marked, and unauthorized subjects are informed that they do not have access and that attempts to gain access will result in prosecution.

The security perimeter in the physical environment is often a reflection of the security perimeter of the logical environment. In most cases, the area over which the organization is legally responsible determines the reach of a security policy in the physical realm. This can be the walls of an office, the walls of a building, or the fence around a campus. In secured environments, warning signs are posted indicating that unauthorized access is prohibited and attempts to gain access will be thwarted and result in prosecution.

When transforming a security policy into actual controls, you must consider each environment and security boundary separately. Simply deduce what available security mechanisms would provide the most reasonable, cost-effective, and efficient solution for a specific environment and situation. However, all security mechanisms must be weighed against the value of the objects they are to protect. Deploying countermeasures that cost more than the value of the protected objects is unwarranted.

Network Attacks and Countermeasures

Communication systems are vulnerable to attacks in much the same way any other aspect of the IT infrastructure is vulnerable. Understanding the threats and possible countermeasures is an important part of securing an environment. Any activity or condition that can cause harm to data, resources, or personnel must be addressed and mitigated if possible.

Keep in mind that harm includes more than just destruction or damage; it also includes disclosure, access delay, denial of access, fraud, resource waste, resource abuse, and loss. Common threats against communication system security include denial of service, eavesdropping, impersonation, replay, and modification.

DoS and DDoS

A *denial of service (DoS) attack* is a resource consumption attack that has the primary goal of preventing legitimate activity on a victimized system. A DoS attack renders the target unable to respond to legitimate traffic.

There are two basic forms of denial of service:

- Attacks exploiting a vulnerability in hardware or software. This exploitation of a weakness, error, or standard feature of software intends to cause a system to hang, freeze, consume all system resources, and so on. The end result is that the victimized computer is unable to process any legitimate tasks.

- Attacks that flood the victim's communication pipeline with garbage network traffic. These attacks are sometimes called traffic generation or flooding attacks. The end result is that the victimized computer is unable to send or receive legitimate network communications.

In either case, the victim has been denied the ability to perform normal operations (services).

DoS isn't a single attack but rather an entire class of attacks. Some attacks exploit flaws in operating system software, whereas others focus on installed applications, services, or protocols. Some attacks exploit specific protocols, including Internet Protocol (IP), Transmission Control Protocol (TCP), Internet Control Message Protocol (ICMP), and User Datagram Protocol (UDP).

DoS attacks typically occur between one attacker and one victim. However, they aren't always that simple. Most DoS attacks employ some form of intermediary system (usually an unwilling and unknowing participant) to hide the attacker from the victim. For example, if an attacker sends attack packets directly to a victim, it's possible for the victim to discover who the attacker is. This is made more difficult, although not impossible, through the use of spoofing (described in more detail elsewhere in this chapter).

Many DoS attacks begin by compromising or infiltrating one or more intermediary systems that then serve as launch points or attack platforms. These intermediary systems are commonly referred to as secondary victims. The attacker installs remote-control tools, often called *bots*, *zombies*, or *agents*, onto these systems. Then, at an appointed time or in response to a launch command from the attacker, the DoS attack is conducted against the victim. The victim may be able to discover zombied systems that are causing the DoS attack but probably won't be able to track down the actual attacker. Attacks involving zombied systems are known as distributed denial-of-service (DDoS) attacks. Deployments of numerous bots or zombies across numerous unsuspecting secondary victims have become known as *botnets*.

Here are some countermeasures and safeguards against these attacks:

- Adding firewalls, routers, and intrusion detection systems (IDSs) that detect DoS traffic and automatically block the port or filter out packets based on the source or destination address
- Disabling echo replies on external systems
- Disabling broadcast features on border systems
- Blocking spoofed packets from entering or leaving your network
- Keeping all systems patched with the most current security updates from vendors

For further discussion of DoS and DDoS, see Chapter 14, "Incident Management."

Eavesdropping

As the name suggests, *eavesdropping* is simply listening to communication traffic for the purpose of duplicating it. The duplication can take the form of recording data to a storage device or using an extraction program that dynamically attempts to extract the original content from the traffic stream. Once a copy of traffic content is in the hands of a attacker, they can often extract many forms of confidential information, such as usernames, passwords, process procedures, data, and so on.

Eavesdropping usually requires physical access to the IT infrastructure to connect a physical recording device to an open port or cable splice or to install a software-recording tool onto the system. Eavesdropping is often facilitated by the use of a network traffic capture or monitoring program or a protocol analyzer system (often called a *sniffer*). Eavesdropping devices and software are usually difficult to detect because they are used in passive attacks. When eavesdropping or wiretapping is transformed into altering or injecting communications, the attack is considered an active attack.

 Real World Scenario

You Too Can Eavesdrop on Networks

Eavesdropping on networks is the act of collecting packets from the communication medium. As a valid network client, you are limited to seeing just the traffic designated for your system. However, with the right tool (and authorization from your organization!), you can see all the data that passes your network interface. Sniffers such as Wireshark and NetWitness and dedicated eavesdropping tools such as T-sight and Paros can show you what is going on over the network. Some tools will display only the raw network packets, while others will reassemble the original data and display it for you in real time on your screen. We encourage you to experiment with a few eavesdropping tools (only on networks where you have the proper approval) so you can see firsthand what can be gleaned from network communications.

You can combat eavesdropping by maintaining physical access security to prevent unauthorized personnel from accessing your IT infrastructure. As for protecting communications that occur outside your network or for protecting against internal attackers, using encryption (such as IPSec or SSH) and one-time authentication methods (that is, one-time pads or token devices) on communication traffic will greatly reduce the effectiveness and timeliness of eavesdropping.

The common threat of eavesdropping is one of the primary motivations to maintain reliable communications security. While data is in transit, it is often easier to intercept than when it is in storage. Furthermore, the lines of communication may lie outside your organization's control. Thus, reliable means to secure data while in transit outside your internal infrastructure is of utmost importance. Some of the common network health and communication reliability evaluation and management tools, such as sniffers, can be used for nefarious purposes and thus require stringent controls and oversight to prevent abuse.

Impersonation/Masquerading

Impersonation, or *masquerading*, is the act of pretending to be someone or something you are not to gain unauthorized access to a system. This usually implies that authentication credentials have been stolen or falsified in order to satisfy (i.e., successfully bypass) authentication mechanisms. This is different from spoofing, where an entity puts forth a false identity but without any proof (such as falsely using an IP address, MAC addresses, email address, system name, domain name, etc.). Impersonation is often possible through the capture of usernames and passwords or of session setup procedures for network services.

Some solutions to prevent impersonation are using one-time pads and token authentication systems, using Kerberos, and using encryption to increase the difficulty of extracting authentication credentials from network traffic.

Replay Attacks

Replay attacks are an offshoot of impersonation attacks and are made possible through capturing network traffic via eavesdropping. Replay attacks attempt to reestablish a communication session by replaying captured traffic against a system. You can prevent them by using one-time authentication mechanisms and sequenced session identification.

Modification Attacks

In *modification* attacks, captured packets are altered and then played against a system. Modified packets are designed to bypass the restrictions of improved authentication mechanisms and session sequencing. Countermeasures to modification replay attacks include using digital signature verifications and packet checksum verification.

Address Resolution Protocol Spoofing

The Address Resolution Protocol (ARP) is a subprotocol of the TCP/IP protocol suite and operates at the Network layer (layer 3). ARP is used to discover the MAC address of a system by polling using its IP address. ARP functions by broadcasting a request packet with the target IP address. The system with that IP address (or some other system that already has an ARP mapping for it) will reply with the associated MAC address. The discovered IP-to-MAC mapping is stored in the ARP cache and is used to direct packets.

If you find the idea of misdirecting traffic through the abuse of the ARP system interesting, then consider experimenting with attacking tools that perform this function. Some of the well-known tools for performing ARP spoofing attacks include Ettercap, Cain & Abel, and arpspoof. Using these tools in combination with a network sniffer (so you can watch the results) will give you great insight into this form of network attack. However, as always, perform these activities only on networks where you have proper approval; otherwise, your attacker activities could land you in legal trouble.

ARP mappings can be attacked through spoofing. Spoofing provides false MAC addresses for requested IP-addressed systems to redirect traffic to alternate destinations. ARP attacks are often an element in man-in-the-middle attacks. Such attacks involve an intruder's system spoofing its MAC address against the destination's IP address into the source's ARP cache. All packets received from the source system are inspected and then forwarded to the actual intended destination system. You can take measures to fight ARP attacks, such as defining static ARP mappings for critical systems, monitoring ARP caches for MAC-to-IP-address mappings, or using an IDS to detect anomalies in system traffic and changes in ARP traffic.

DNS Poisoning, Spoofing, and Hijacking

DNS poisoning and *DNS spoofing* are also known as resolution attacks. DNS poisoning occurs when an attacker alters the domain-name-to-IP-address mappings in a DNS system to redirect traffic to a rogue system or to simply perform a denial of service against a system. DNS spoofing occurs when an attacker sends false replies to a requesting system, beating the real reply from the valid DNS server. This is also technically an exploitation of race conditions. Protections against false DNS results caused by poisoning and spoofing include allowing only authorized changes to DNS, restricting zone transfers, and logging all privileged DNS activity.

In 2008, a fairly significant vulnerability was discovered and disclosed to the world by Dan Kaminsky. The vulnerability lies in the method by which local or caching DNS servers obtain information from root servers regarding the identity of the authoritative servers for a particular domain. By sending falsified replies to a caching DNS server for nonexistent subdomains, an attacker can hijack the entire domain's resolution details. For an excellent detailed explanation on how DNS works and how this vulnerability threatens the current DNS infrastructure, visit "An Illustrated Guide to the Kaminsky DNS Vulnerability" located at

`http://unixwiz.net/techtips/iguide-kaminsky-dns-vuln.html`

The only real solution to this DNS hijacking vulnerability is to upgrade DNS to Domain Name System Security Extensions (DNSSEC). For details, please visit `dnssec.net`.

Hyperlink Spoofing

Yet another related attack is *hyperlink spoofing*, which is similar to DNS spoofing in that it is used to redirect traffic to a rogue or imposter system or to simply divert traffic away from its intended destination. Hyperlink spoofing can take the form of DNS spoofing or can simply be an alteration of the hyperlink URLs in the HTML code of documents sent to clients. Hyperlink spoofing attacks are usually successful because most users do not verify the domain name in a URL via DNS; rather, they assume that the hyperlink is valid and just click it.

 Real World Scenario

Going Phishing?

Hyperlink spoofing is not limited to just DNS attacks. In fact, any attack that attempts to misdirect legitimate users to malicious websites through the abuse of URLs or hyperlinks could be considered hyperlink spoofing. Spoofing is falsifying information, which includes falsifying the relationship between a URL and its trusted and original destination.

Phishing is another attack that commonly involves hyperlink spoofing. The term means fishing for information. Phishing attacks can take many forms, including the use of false URLs.

Be wary of any URL or hyperlink in an email, PDF file, or productivity document. If you want to visit a site offered as such, go to your web browser and manually type in the address, use your own preexisting URL bookmark, or use a trusted search engine to find the site. These methods do involve more work on your part, but it will establish a pattern of safe behaviors that will serve you well. There are too many attackers in the world to be casual or lazy about following proffered links and URLs.

An attack related to phishing is *pretexting*, which is the practice of obtaining your personal information under false pretenses. Pretexting is often used to obtain personal identity details that are then sold to others who actually perform the abuse of your credit and reputation.

Protections against hyperlink spoofing include the same precautions used against DNS spoofing as well as keeping your system patched and using the Internet with caution.

Summary

Remote access security management requires security system designers to address the hardware and software components of the implementation along with policy issues, work task issues, and encryption issues. This includes deployment of secure communication protocols. Secure authentication for both local and remote connections is an important foundational element of overall security.

Maintaining control over communication pathways is essential to supporting confidentiality, integrity, and availability for network, voice, and other forms of communication. Numerous attacks are focused on intercepting, blocking, or otherwise interfering with the transfer of data from one location to another. Fortunately, there are also reasonable countermeasures to reduce or even eliminate many of these threats.

Tunneling, or encapsulation, is a means by which messages in one protocol can be transported over another network or communications system using a second protocol. Tunneling can be combined with encryption to provide security for the transmitted message. VPNs are based on encrypted tunneling.

A VLAN is a hardware-imposed network segmentation created by switches. VLANs are used to logically segment a network without altering its physical topology. VLANs are used for traffic management.

Telecommuting, or remote connectivity, has become a common feature of business computing. When remote access capabilities are deployed in any environment, security must be considered and implemented to provide protection for your private network against remote access complications. Remote access users should be stringently authenticated before being granted access; this can include the use of RADIUS or TACACS. Remote access services include Voice over IP (VoIP), multimedia collaboration, and instant messaging.

NAT is used to hide the internal structure of a private network as well as to enable multiple internal clients to gain Internet access through a few public IP addresses. NAT is often a native feature of border security devices, such as firewalls, routers, gateways, and proxies.

In circuit switching, a dedicated physical pathway is created between the two communicating parties. Packet switching occurs when the message or communication is broken up into small segments (usually fixed-length packets, depending on the protocols and technologies employed) and sent across the intermediary networks to the destination. Within packet-switching systems are two types of communication: paths and virtual circuits. A virtual circuit is a logical pathway or circuit created over a packet-switched network between two specific endpoints. There are two types of virtual circuits: permanent virtual circuits (PVCs) and switched virtual circuits (SVCs).

WAN links, or long-distance connection technologies, can be divided into two primary categories: dedicated and nondedicated lines. A dedicated line connects two specific endpoints and only those two endpoints. A nondedicated line is one that requires a connection to be established before data transmission can occur. A nondedicated line can be used to connect with any remote system that uses the same type of nondedicated line. WAN connection technologies include X.25, Frame Relay, ATM, SMDS, SDLC, HDLC, and HSSI.

When selecting or deploying security controls for network communications, you need to evaluate numerous characteristics in light of your circumstances, capabilities, and security policy. Security controls should be transparent to users. Hash totals and CRC checks can be used to verify message integrity. Record sequences are used to ensure sequence integrity of a transmission. Transmission logging helps detect communication abuses.

Virtualization technology is used to host one or more operating systems within the memory of a single host computer. This mechanism allows virtually any OS to operate on any hardware. It also allows multiple operating systems to work simultaneously on the same hardware. Virtualization offers several benefits, such as being able to launch individual instances of servers or services as needed, real-time scalability, and being able to run the exact OS version needed for the needed application.

Internet-based email is insecure unless you take steps to secure it. To secure email, you should provide for nonrepudiation, restrict access to authorized users, make sure integrity is maintained, authenticate the message source, verify delivery, and even classify sensitive content. These issues must be addressed in a security policy before they can be implemented in a solution. They often take the form of acceptable use policies, access controls, privacy declarations, email management procedures, and backup and retention policies.

Email is a common delivery mechanism for malicious code. Filtering attachments, using antivirus software, and educating users are effective countermeasures against that kind of attack. Email spamming or flooding is a form of denial of service that can be deterred through filters and IDSs. Email security can be improved using S/MIME, MOSS, PEM, and PGP.

Fax and voice security can be improved by using encryption to protect the transmission of documents and prevent eavesdropping. Training users effectively is a useful countermeasure against social engineering attacks.

A security boundary can be the division between one secured area and another secured area, or it can be the division between a secured area and an unsecured area. Both must be addressed in a security policy.

Communication systems are vulnerable to many attacks, including distributed denial of service (DDoS), eavesdropping, impersonation, replay, modification, spoofing, and ARP and DNS attacks. Fortunately, effective countermeasures exist for each of these. PBX fraud and abuse and phone phreaking are problems that must also be addressed.

Exam Essentials

Understand the issues around remote access security management. Remote access security management requires that security system designers address the hardware and software components of an implementation along with issues related to policy, work tasks, and encryption.

Be familiar with the various protocols and mechanisms that may be used on LANs and WANs for data communications. These are SKIP, SWIPE, SSL, SET, PPP, SLIP, CHAP, PAP, EAP, and S-RPC. This can also include VPN, TLS/SSL, and VLAN.

Know what tunneling is.   Tunneling is the encapsulation of a protocol-deliverable message within a second protocol. The second protocol often performs encryption to protect the message contents.

Understand VPNs.   VPNs are based on encrypted tunneling. They can offer authentication and data protection as a point-to-point solution. Common VPN protocols are PPTP, L2F, L2TP, and IPSec.

Be able to explain NAT.   NAT protects the addressing scheme of a private network, allows the use of the private IP addresses, and enables multiple internal clients to obtain Internet access through a few public IP addresses. NAT is supported by many security border devices, such as firewalls, routers, gateways, and proxies.

Understand the difference between packet switching and circuit switching.   In circuit switching, a dedicated physical pathway is created between the two communicating parties. Packet switching occurs when the message or communication is broken up into small segments and sent across the intermediary networks to the destination. Within packet-switching systems are two types of communication paths, or virtual circuits: permanent virtual circuits (PVCs) and switched virtual circuits (SVCs).

Understand the difference between dedicated and nondedicated links.   A dedicated line is always on and is reserved for a specific customer. Examples of dedicated lines include T1, T3, E1, E3, and cable modems. A nondedicated line requires a connection to be established before data transmission can occur. It can be used to connect with any remote system that uses the same type of nondedicated line. Standard modems, DSL, and ISDN are examples of nondedicated lines.

Know various issues related to remote access security.   Be familiar with remote access, dial-up connections, screen scrapers, virtual applications/desktops, and general telecommuting security concerns.

Know the various types of WAN technologies.   Know that most WAN technologies require a channel service unit/data service unit (CSU/DSU), sometimes called a WAN switch. There are many types of carrier networks and WAN connection technologies, such as X.25, Frame Relay, ATM, and SMDS. Some WAN connection technologies require additional specialized protocols to support various types of specialized systems or devices. Three of these protocols are SDLC, HDLC, and HSSI.

Understand the differences between PPP and SLIP.   The Point-to-Point Protocol (PPP) is an encapsulation protocol designed to support the transmission of IP traffic over dial-up or point-to-point links. PPP includes a wide range of communication services, including assignment and management of IP addresses, management of synchronous communications, standardized encapsulation, multiplexing, link configuration, link quality testing, error detection, and feature or option negotiation (such as compression). PPP was originally designed to support CHAP and PAP for authentication. However, recent versions of PPP also support MS-CHAP, EAP, and SPAP. PPP replaced Serial Line Internet Protocol (SLIP). SLIP offered no authentication, supported only half-duplex communications, had no error detection capabilities, and required manual link establishment and teardown.

Understand common characteristics of security controls.   Security controls should be transparent to users. Hash totals and CRC checks can be used to verify message integrity. Record sequences are used to ensure sequence integrity of a transmission. Transmission logging helps detect communication abuses.

Understand how email security works.   Internet email is based on SMTP, POP3, and IMAP. It is inherently insecure. It can be secured, but the methods used must be addressed in a security policy. Email security solutions include using S/MIME, MOSS, PEM, or PGP.

Know how fax security works.   Fax security is primarily based on using encrypted transmissions or encrypted communication lines to protect the faxed materials. The primary goal is to prevent interception. Activity logs and exception reports can be used to detect anomalies in fax activity that could be symptoms of attack.

Know the threats associated with PBX systems and the countermeasures to PBX fraud.   Countermeasures to PBX fraud and abuse include many of the same precautions you would employ to protect a typical computer network: logical or technical controls, administrative controls, and physical controls.

Understand the security issues related to VoIP.   VoIP is at risk for Caller ID spoofing, vishing, SPIT, call manager software/firmware attacks, phone hardware attacks, DoS, MitM, spoofing, and switch hopping.

Recognize what a phreaker is.   Phreaking is a specific type of attack in which various types of technology are used to circumvent the telephone system to make free long-distance calls, to alter the function of telephone service, to steal specialized services, or even to cause service disruptions. Common tools of phreakers include black, red, blue, and white boxes.

Understand voice communications security.   Voice communications are vulnerable to many attacks, especially as voice communications become an important part of network services. You can obtain confidentiality by using encrypted communications. Countermeasures must be deployed to protect against interception, eavesdropping, tapping, and other types of exploitation. Be familiar with voice communication topics, such as POTS, PSTN, PBX, and VoIP.

Be able to explain what social engineering is.   Social engineering is a means by which an unknown person gains the trust of someone inside your organization by convincing employees that they are, for example, associated with upper management, technical support, or the help desk. The victim is often encouraged to make a change to their user account on the system, such as reset their password, so the attacker can use it to gain access to the network. The primary countermeasure for this sort of attack is user training.

Explain the concept of security boundaries.   A security boundary can be the division between one secured area and another secured area. It can also be the division between a secured area and an unsecured area. Both must be addressed in a security policy.

Understand the various network attacks and countermeasures associated with communications security.   Communication systems are vulnerable to many attacks, including distributed denial of service (DDoS), eavesdropping, impersonation, replay, modification, spoofing, and ARP and DNS attacks. Be able to know effective countermeasures for each.

Written Lab

1. Describe the differences between transport mode and tunnel mode of IPSec.
2. Discuss the benefits of NAT.
3. What are the main differences between circuit switching and packet switching?
4. What are some security issues with email and options for safeguarding against them?

Review Questions

1. _____ is a layer 2 connection mechanism that uses packet-switching technology to establish virtual circuits between the communication endpoints.

    A. ISDN

    B. Frame Relay

    C. SMDS

    D. ATM

2. Tunnel connections can be established over all except for which of the following?

    A. WAN links

    B. LAN pathways

    C. Dial-up connections

    D. Stand-alone systems

3. _____ is a standards-based mechanism for providing encryption for point-to-point TCP/IP traffic.

    A. UDP

    B. IDEA

    C. IPSec

    D. SDLC

4. Which of the following IP addresses is not a private IP address as defined by RFC 1918?

    A. 10.0.0.18

    B. 169.254.1.119

    C. 172.31.8.204

    D. 192.168.6.43

5. Which of the following cannot be linked over a VPN?

    A. Two distant Internet-connected LANs

    B. Two systems on the same LAN

    C. A system connected to the Internet and a LAN connected to the Internet

    D. Two systems without an intermediary network connection

6. What is needed to allow an external client to initiate a communication session with an internal system if the network uses a NAT proxy?

    A. IPSec tunnel

    B. Static mode NAT

    C. Static private IP address

    D. Reverse DNS

7. Which of the following VPN protocols do not offer native data encryption? (Choose all that apply.)

- **A.** L2F
- **B.** L2TP
- **C.** IPSec
- **D.** PPTP

8. At which OSI model layer does the IPSec protocol function?

- **A.** Data Link
- **B.** Transport
- **C.** Session
- **D.** Network

9. Which of the following is not defined in RFC 1918 as one of the private IP address ranges that are not routed on the Internet?

- **A.** 169.172.0.0–169.191.255.255
- **B.** 192.168.0.0–192.168.255.255
- **C.** 10.0.0.0–10.255.255.255
- **D.** 172.16.0.0–172.31.255.255

10. Which of the following is not a benefit of NAT?

- **A.** Hiding the internal IP addressing scheme
- **B.** Sharing a few public Internet addresses with a large number of internal clients
- **C.** Using the private IP addresses from RFC 1918 on an internal network
- **D.** Filtering network traffic to prevent brute-force attacks

11. A significant benefit of a security control is when it goes unnoticed by users. What is this called?

- **A.** Invisibility
- **B.** Transparency
- **C.** Diversion
- **D.** Hiding in plain sight

12. When you're designing a security system for Internet-delivered email, which of the following is least important?

- **A.** Nonrepudiation
- **B.** Availability
- **C.** Message integrity
- **D.** Access restriction

13. Which of the following is typically not an element that must be discussed with end users in regard to email retention policies?

A. Privacy

B. Auditor review

C. Length of retainer

D. Backup method

14. What is it called when email itself is used as an attack mechanism?

A. Masquerading

B. Mail-bombing

C. Spoofing

D. Smurf attack

15. Why is spam so difficult to stop?

A. Filters are ineffective at blocking inbound messages.

B. The source address is usually spoofed.

C. It is an attack requiring little expertise.

D. Spam can cause denial-of-service attacks.

16. Which of the following is a type of connection that can be described as a logical circuit that always exists and is waiting for the customer to send data?

A. ISDN

B. PVC

C. VPN

D. SVC

17. In addition to maintaining an updated system and controlling physical access, which of the following is the most effective countermeasure against PBX fraud and abuse?

A. Encrypting communications

B. Changing default passwords

C. Using transmission logs

D. Taping and archiving all conversations

18. Which of the following can be used to bypass even the best physical and logical security mechanisms to gain access to a system?

A. Brute-force attacks

B. Denial of service

C. Social engineering

D. Port scanning

19. Which of the following is *not* a denial-of-service attack?

    A. Exploiting a flaw in a program to consume 100 percent of the CPU

    B. Sending malformed packets to a system, causing it to freeze

    C. Performing a brute-force attack against a known user account

    D. Sending thousands of emails to a single address

20. What authentication protocol offers no encryption or protection for logon credentials?

    A. PAP

    B. CHAP

    C. SSL

    D. RADIUS

Chapter 5

Security Governance Concepts, Principles, and Policies

THE CISSP EXAM TOPICS COVERED IN THIS CHAPTER INCLUDE:

3. Information Security Governance and Risk Management

- A. Understand and align security function to goals, mission, and objectives of the organization.

- B. Understand and apply security governance

  - B.1 Organizational processes (e.g., acquisitions, divestitures, governance committees)

  - B.2 Security roles and responsibilities

  - B.3 Legislative and regulatory compliance

  - B.4 Privacy requirements compliance

  - B.5 Control frameworks

  - B.6 Due care

  - B.7 Due diligence

- C. Understand and apply concepts of confidentiality, integrity, and availability.

- D. Develop and implement security policy

  - D.1 Security policies

  - D.2 Standards/baselines

  - D.3 Procedures

  - D.4 Guidelines

  - D.5 Documentation

- E. Manage the information life cycle (e.g., classification, categorization, and ownership)

The Information Security Governance and Risk Management domain of the Common Body of Knowledge (CBK) for the CISSP certification exam deals with the common and foundational elements of security solutions. These include elements essential to the design, implementation, and administration of security mechanisms.

This domain is discussed in this chapter and in Chapter 6, "Risk and Personnel Management." Be sure to read and study the materials from both chapters to ensure complete coverage of the essential material for the CISSP certification exam.

Security Management Planning

Security management planning ensures proper creation, implementation, and enforcement of a security policy. The most effective way to tackle security management planning is to use a top-down approach. Upper, or senior, management is responsible for initiating and defining policies for the organization. Security policies provide direction for all levels of the organization's hierarchy. It is the responsibility of middle management to flesh out the security policy into standards, baselines, guidelines, and procedures. The operational managers or security professionals must then implement the configurations prescribed in the security management documentation. Finally, the end users must comply with all the security policies of the organization.

The opposite of the top-down approach is the bottom-up approach. In a bottom-up approach environment, the IT staff makes security decisions directly without input from senior management. The bottom-up approach is rarely utilized in organizations and is considered problematic in the IT industry.

Security management is a responsibility of upper management, not of the IT staff, and is considered a business operations issue rather than an IT administration issue. The team or department responsible for security within an organization should be autonomous. The information security (InfoSec) team should be led by a designated chief security officer (CSO) who must report directly to senior management. Placing the autonomy of the CSO and the CSO's team outside the typical hierarchical structure in an organization can improve security management across the entire organization. It also helps to avoid cross-department and internal political issues.

Elements of security management planning include defining security roles; prescribing how security will be managed, who will be responsible for security, and how security will be tested for effectiveness; developing security policies; performing risk analysis; and requiring security education for employees. These efforts are guided through the development of management plans.

The best security plan is useless without one key factor: approval by senior management. Without senior management's approval of and commitment to the security policy, the policy will not succeed. It is the responsibility of the policy development team to educate senior management sufficiently so it understands the risks, liabilities, and exposures that remain even after security measures prescribed in the policy are deployed. Developing and implementing a security policy is evidence of due care and due diligence on the part of senior management. If a company does not practice due care and due diligence, managers can be held liable for negligence and held accountable for both asset and financial losses.

A security management planning team should develop three types of plans:

Strategic plan   A strategic plan is a long-term plan that is fairly stable. It defines the organization's security purpose. It also helps to understand security function and align it to goals, mission, and objectives of the organization. It's useful for about five years if it is maintained and updated annually. The strategic plan also serves as the planning horizon. Long-term goals and visions for the future are discussed in a strategic plan. A strategic plan should include a risk assessment.

Tactical plan   The tactical plan is a midterm plan developed to provide more details on accomplishing the goals set forth in the strategic plan. A tactical plan is typically useful for about a year and often prescribes and schedules the tasks necessary to accomplish organizational goals. Some examples of tactical plans include project plans, acquisition plans, hiring plans, budget plans, maintenance plans, support plans, and system development plans.

Operational plan   An operational plan is a short-term, highly detailed plan based on the strategic and tactical plans. It is valid or useful only for a short time. Operational plans must be updated often (such as monthly or quarterly) to retain compliance with tactical plans. Operational plans spell out how to accomplish the various goals of the organization. They include resource allotments, budgetary requirements, staffing assignments, scheduling, and step-by-step or implementation procedures. Operational plans include details on how the implementation processes are in compliance with the organization's security policy. Examples of operational plans include training plans, system deployment plans, and product design plans.

Security is a continuous process. Thus, the activity of security management planning may have a definitive initiation point, but its tasks and work are never fully accomplished or complete. Effective security plans focus attention on specific and achievable objectives, anticipate change and potential problems, and serve as a basis for decision making for the entire organization. Security documentation should be concrete, well defined, and clearly stated. For a security plan to be effective, it must be developed, maintained, and actually used.

Security Governance

Security governance is the collection of practices related to supporting, defining, and directing the security efforts of an organization. Security governance is closely related to and often intertwined with corporate and IT governance. The goals of these three governance agendas are often the same or interrelated. For example, a common goal of organizational governance is to ensure that the organization will continue to exist and will grow or expand over time. Thus, the common goal of governance is to maintain business processes while striving toward growth and resiliency.

Some aspects of governance are imposed on organizations due to legislative and regulatory compliance needs, while others are imposed by industry guidelines or license requirements. All forms of governance, including security governance, must be assessed and verified from time to time. Various requirements for auditing and validation may be present due to government regulations or industry best practices. Governance compliance issues often vary from industry to industry and from country to country. As many organizations expand and adapt to deal with a global market, governance issues become more complex. This is especially problematic when laws in different countries differ or in fact conflict. The organization as a whole should be given the direction, guidance, and tools to provide sufficient oversight and management to address threats and risks with a focus on eliminating downtime and keeping potential loss or damage to a minimum.

As you can tell, the definitions of security governance are often rather stilted and high level. Ultimately, security governance is the implementation of a security solution and a management method that are tightly interconnected. Security governance directly oversees and gets involved in all levels of security. Security is not and should not be treated as an IT issue only. Instead, security affects every aspect of an organization. It is no longer just something the IT staff can handle on their own. Security is a business operations issue. Security is an organizational process, not just something the IT geeks do behind the scenes. Using the term *security governance* is an attempt to emphasize this point by indicating that security needs to be managed and governed throughout the organization, not just in the IT department.

Security governance needs to address every aspect of an organization. This includes acquisitions, divestitures, and governance committees. Acquisitions and mergers place an organization at an increased level of risk. Such risks include inappropriate information disclosure, data loss, downtime, or failure to achieve sufficient return on investment (ROI). In addition to all the typical business and financial aspects of mergers and acquisitions, a healthy dose of security oversight and increased scrutiny is often essential to reduce the likelihood of losses during such a period of transformation. Similarly, a divestiture or any form of asset or employee reduction is another time period of increased risk and thus increased need for focused security governance. Often, security governance is managed by a governance committee or at least a board of directors. This is the group of influential knowledge experts whose primary task is to oversee and guide the actions of security and operations for an organization.

Security Roles and Responsibilities

A security role is the part an individual plays in the overall scheme of security implementation and administration within an organization. Security roles are not necessarily prescribed in job descriptions because they are not always distinct or static. Familiarity with security roles will help in establishing a communications and support structure within an organization. This structure will enable the deployment and enforcement of the security policy. The following six roles are presented in the logical order in which they appear in a secured environment:

Senior manager   The organizational owner (senior manager) role is assigned to the person who is ultimately responsible for the security maintained by an organization and who should be most concerned about the protection of its assets. The senior manager must sign off on all policy issues. In fact, all activities must be approved by and signed off on by the senior manager before they can be carried out. There is no effective security policy if the senior manager does not authorize and support it. The senior manager's endorsement of the security policy indicates the accepted ownership of the implemented security within the organization. The senior manager is the person who will be held liable for the overall success or failure of a security solution and is responsible for exercising due care and due diligence in establishing security for an organization.

Even though senior managers are ultimately responsible for security, they rarely implement security solutions. In most cases, that responsibility is delegated to security professionals within the organization.

Security professional   The security professional, information security (InfoSec) officer or computer incident response team (CIRT) role is assigned to a trained and experienced network, systems, and security engineer who is responsible for following the directives mandated by senior management. The security professional has the functional responsibility for security, including writing the security policy and implementing it. The role of security professional can be labeled as an IS/IT function role. The security professional role is often filled by a team that is responsible for designing and implementing security solutions based on the approved security policy. Security professionals are not decision makers; they are implementers. All decisions must be left to the senior manager.

Data owner   The data owner role is assigned to the person who is responsible for classifying information for placement and protection within the security solution. The data owner is typically a high-level manager who is ultimately responsible for data protection. However, the data owner usually delegates the responsibility of the actual data management tasks to a data custodian.

Data custodian   The data custodian role is assigned to the user who is responsible for the tasks of implementing the prescribed protection defined by the security policy and senior management. The data custodian performs all activities necessary to provide adequate protection for the CIA Triad (confidentiality, integrity, and availability) of data and to fulfill the requirements and responsibilities delegated from upper management. These activities can include performing and testing backups, validating data integrity, deploying security solutions, and managing data storage based on classification.

User   The user (end user or operator) role is assigned to any person who has access to the secured system. A user's access is tied to their work tasks and is limited so they have only enough access to perform the tasks necessary for their job position (the principle of least privilege). Users are responsible for understanding and upholding the security policy of an organization by following prescribed operational procedures and operating within defined security parameters.

Auditor   An auditor is responsible for reviewing and verifying that the security policy is properly implemented and the derived security solutions are adequate. The auditor role may be assigned to a security professional or a trained user. The auditor produces compliance and effectiveness reports that are reviewed by the senior manager. Issues discovered through these reports are transformed into new directives assigned by the senior manager to security professionals or data custodians. However, the auditor is listed as the last or final role because the auditor needs a source of activity (that is, users or operators working in an environment) to audit or monitor.

All of these roles serve an important function within a secured environment. They are useful for identifying liability and responsibility as well as for identifying the hierarchical management and delegation scheme.

Protection Mechanisms

Another aspect of security solution concepts and principles is the element of protection mechanisms. These are common characteristics of security controls. Not all security controls must have them, but many controls offer their protection for confidentiality, integrity, and availability through the use of these mechanisms. These mechanisms include using multiple layers or levels of access, employing abstraction, hiding data, and using encryption.

Layering

Layering, also known as *defense in depth*, is simply the use of multiple controls in a series. No one control can protect against all possible threats. Using a multilayered solution allows for numerous, different controls to guard against whatever threats come to pass. When security solutions are designed in layers, most threats are eliminated, mitigated, or thwarted.

Using layers in a series rather than in parallel is important. Performing security restrictions in a series means to perform one after the other in a linear fashion. Only through a series configuration will each attack be scanned, evaluated, or mitigated by every security control. In a series configuration, failure of a single security control does not render the entire solution ineffective. If security controls were implemented in parallel, a threat could pass through a single checkpoint that did not address its particular malicious activity.

Serial configurations are very narrow but very deep, whereas parallel configurations are very wide but very shallow. Parallel systems are useful in distributed computing applications, but parallelism is not often a useful concept in the realm of security.

Think of physical entrances to buildings. A parallel configuration is used for shopping malls. There are many doors in many locations around the entire perimeter of the mall. A series configuration would most likely be used in a bank or an airport. A single entrance is provided, and that entrance is actually several gateways or checkpoints that must be passed in sequential order to gain entry into active areas of the building.

Layering also includes the concept that networks comprise numerous separate entities, each with its own unique security controls and vulnerabilities. In an effective security solution, there is a synergy between all networked systems that creates a single security front. Using separate security systems creates a layered security solution.

Abstraction

Abstraction is used for efficiency. Similar elements are put into groups, classes, or roles that are assigned security controls, restrictions, or permissions as a collective. Thus, the concept of abstraction is used when classifying objects or assigning roles to subjects. The concept of abstraction also includes the definition of object and subject types or of objects themselves (that is, a data structure used to define a template for a class of entities). Abstraction is used to define what types of data an object can contain, what types of functions can be performed on or by that object, and what capabilities that object has. Abstraction simplifies security by enabling you to assign security controls to a group of objects collected by type or function.

Data Hiding

Data hiding is exactly what it sounds like: preventing data from being discovered or accessed by a subject by positioning the data in a logical storage compartment that is not accessible or seen by the subject. Forms of data hiding include keeping a database from being accessed by unauthorized visitors and restricting a subject at a lower classification level from accessing data at a higher classification level. Preventing an application from accessing hardware directly is also a form of data hiding. Data hiding is often a key element in security controls as well as in programming.

Encryption

Encryption is the art and science of hiding the meaning or intent of a communication from unintended recipients. Encryption can take many forms and be applied to every type of electronic communication, including text, audio, and video files as well as applications themselves. Encryption is an important element in security controls, especially in regard to the transmission of data between systems. There are various strengths of encryption, each of which is designed and/or appropriate for a specific use or purpose. Encryption is discussed at length in Chapter 9, "Cryptography and Symmetric Key Algorithms," and Chapter 10, "PKI and Cryptographic Applications."

Privacy Requirements Compliance

Privacy can be a difficult entity to define. The term is used frequently in numerous contexts without much quantification or qualification. Here are some partial definitions of privacy:

- Active prevention of unauthorized access to information that is personally identifiable (that is, data points that can be linked directly to a person or organization)

- Freedom from unauthorized access to information deemed personal or confidential

- Freedom from being observed, monitored, or examined without consent or knowledge

A concept that comes up frequently in discussions of privacy is *personally identifiable information (PII)*. PII is any data item that can be easily and/or obviously traced back to the person of origin or concern.

When addressing privacy in the realm of IT, there is usually a balancing act between individual rights and the rights or activities of an organization. Some claim that individuals have the right to control whether information can be collected about them and what can be done with it. Others claim that any activity performed in public view—such as most activities performed over the Internet or activities performed on company equipment—can be monitored without knowledge of or permission from the individuals being watched and that the information gathered from such monitoring can be used for whatever purposes an organization deems appropriate or desirable.

Protecting individuals from unwanted observation, direct marketing, and disclosure of private, personal, or confidential details is usually considered a worthy effort. However, some organizations profess that demographic studies, information gleaning, and focused marketing improve business models, reduce advertising waste, and save money for all parties.

There are many legislative and regulatory compliance issues in regard to privacy. Many US regulations—such as the Health Insurance Portability and Accountability Act (HIPAA), the Sarbanes-Oxley Act of 2002 (SOX), and the Gramm-Leach-Bliley Act—as well as the EU's Directive 95/46/EC (aka the Data Protection Directive) and the contractual requirement Payment Card Industry Data Security Standard (PCI DSS) include privacy requirements. It is important to understand all government regulations that your organization is required to adhere to and ensure compliance, especially in the areas of privacy protection.

Whatever your personal or organizational stance is on the issue of online privacy, it must be addressed in an organizational security policy. Privacy is an issue not just for external visitors to your online offerings but also for your customers, employees, suppliers, and contractors. If you gather any type of information about any person or company, you must address privacy.

In most cases, especially when privacy is being violated or restricted, the individuals and companies must be informed; otherwise, you may face legal ramifications. Privacy issues must also be addressed when allowing or restricting personal use of email, retaining email, recording phone conversations, gathering information about surfing or spending habits, and so on.

Control Frameworks: Planning to Plan

Crafting a security stance for an organization often involves a lot more than just writing down a few lofty ideals. In most cases, a significant amount of planning goes into developing a solid security policy. Many Dilbert fans may recognize the seemingly absurd concept of holding a meeting to plan a meeting for a future meeting. But it turns out that planning for security must start with planning to plan, then move into planning for standards and compliance, and finally move into the actual plan development and design. Skipping any of these "planning to plan" steps can derail an organization's security solution before it even gets started.

One of the first and most important security planning steps is to consider the overall control framework or structure of the security solution desired by the organization. You can choose from several options in regard to security concept infrastructure; however, the one covered on the CISSP exam is Control Objectives for Information and Related Technology (COBIT). COBIT is a documented set of best IT security practices crafted by the Information Systems Audit and Control Association (ISACA). It prescribes goals and requirements for security controls and encourages the mapping of IT security ideals to business objectives. COBIT 5 is based on five key principles for governance and management of enterprise IT: Principle 1: Meeting Stakeholder Needs, Principle 2: Covering the Enterprise End-to-End, Principle 3: Applying a Single, Integrated Framework, Principle 4: Enabling a Holistic Approach, and Principle 5: Separating Governance From Management. COBIT is used not only to plan the IT security of an organization but also as a guideline for auditors.

Fortunately, COBIT is only modestly referenced on the exam, so further details are not necessary. However, if you have interest in this concept, please visit the ISACA website (www.isaca.org), or if you want a general overview, read the COBIT entry on *Wikipedia*.

There are many other standards and guidelines for IT security. A few of these are Open Source Security Testing Methodology Manual (OSSTMM), ISO/IEC 27002 (which replaced ISO 17799), and the Information Technology Infrastructure Library (ITIL) (see www.itlibrary.org for more information).

Why is planning to plan security so important? One reason is the requirement for due care and due diligence. *Due care* is using reasonable care to protect the interests of an organization. *Due diligence* is practicing the activities that maintain the due care effort. For example, due care is developing a formalized security structure containing a security policy, standards, baselines, guidelines, and procedures. Due diligence is the continued application of this security structure onto the IT infrastructure of an organization. Operational security is the ongoing maintenance of continued due care and due diligence by all responsible parties within an organization.

In today's business environment, prudence is mandatory. Showing due care and due diligence is the only way to disprove negligence in an occurrence of loss. Senior management must show due care and due diligence to reduce their culpability and liability when a loss occurs.

Security Management Concepts and Principles

Security management concepts and principles are inherent elements in a security policy and solution deployment. They define the basic parameters needed for a secure environment. They also define the goals and objectives that both policy designers and system implementers must achieve to create a secure solution. It is important for real-world security professionals, as well as CISSP exam students, to understand these items thoroughly.

The primary goals and objectives of security are contained within the *CIA Triad*, which is the name given to the three primary security principles:

- Confidentiality
- Integrity
- Availability

Security controls are typically evaluated on how well they address these core information security tenets. Overall, a complete security solution should adequately address each of these tenets. Vulnerabilities and risks are also evaluated based on the threat they pose against one or more of the CIA Triad principles. Thus, it is a good idea to be familiar with these principles and use them as guidelines for judging all things related to security.

These three principles are considered the most important within the realm of security. However important each specific principle is to a specific organization depends on the organization's security goals and requirements and on the extent to which the organization's security might be threatened.

Confidentiality

The first principle of the CIA Triad is *confidentiality*. If a security mechanism offers confidentiality, it offers a high level of assurance that data, objects, or resources are restricted from unauthorized subjects. If a threat exists against confidentiality, unauthorized disclosure could take place.

In general, for confidentiality to be maintained on a network, data must be protected from unauthorized access, use, or disclosure while in storage, in process, and in transit. Unique and specific security controls are required for each of these states of data, resources, and objects to maintain confidentiality.

Numerous attacks focus on the violation of confidentiality. These include capturing network traffic and stealing password files as well as social engineering, port scanning, shoulder surfing, eavesdropping, sniffing, and so on.

Violations of confidentiality are not limited to directed intentional attacks. Many instances of unauthorized disclosure of sensitive or confidential information are the result of human error, oversight, or ineptitude. Events that lead to confidentiality breaches include failing to properly encrypt a transmission, failing to fully authenticate a remote system before transferring data, leaving open otherwise secured access points, accessing malicious code that opens a back door, or even walking away from an access terminal while data is displayed on the monitor. Confidentiality violations can result from the actions of an end user or a system administrator. They can also occur because of an oversight in a security policy or a misconfigured security control.

Numerous countermeasures can help ensure confidentiality against possible threats. These include encryption, network traffic padding, strict access control, rigorous authentication procedures, data classification, and extensive personnel training.

Confidentiality and integrity depend on each other. Without object integrity, confidentiality cannot be maintained. Other concepts, conditions, and aspects of confidentiality include sensitivity, discretion, criticality, concealment, secrecy, privacy, seclusion, and isolation.

Integrity

The second principle of the CIA Triad is *integrity*. For integrity to be maintained, objects must retain their veracity and be intentionally modified by only authorized subjects. If a security mechanism offers integrity, it offers a high level of assurance that the data, objects, and resources are unaltered from their original protected state. Alterations should not occur while the object is in storage, in transit, or in process. Thus, maintaining integrity means the object itself is not altered and the operating system and programming entities that manage and manipulate the object are not compromised.

Integrity can be examined from three perspectives:

- Preventing unauthorized subjects from making modifications

- Preventing authorized subjects from making unauthorized modifications, such as mistakes

- Maintaining the internal and external consistency of objects so that their data is a correct and true reflection of the real world and any relationship with any child, peer, or parent object is valid, consistent, and verifiable

For integrity to be maintained on a system, controls must be in place to restrict access to data, objects, and resources. Additionally, activity logging should be employed to ensure that only authorized users are able to access their respective resources. Maintaining and validating object integrity across storage, transport, and processing requires numerous variations of controls and oversight.

Numerous attacks focus on the violation of integrity. These include viruses, logic bombs, unauthorized access, errors in coding and applications, malicious modification, intentional replacement, and system back doors.

As with confidentiality, integrity violations are not limited to intentional attacks. Human error, oversight, or ineptitude accounts for many instances of unauthorized alteration of sensitive information. Events that lead to integrity breaches include accidentally deleting files; entering invalid data; altering configurations, including errors in commands, codes, and scripts; introducing a virus; and executing malicious code such as a Trojan horse. Integrity violations can occur because of the actions of any user, including administrators. They can also occur because of an oversight in a security policy or a misconfigured security control.

Numerous countermeasures can ensure integrity against possible threats. These include strict access control, rigorous authentication procedures, intrusion detection systems, object/data encryption, hash total verifications (see Chapter 9), interface restrictions, input/function checks, and extensive personnel training.

Integrity is dependent upon confidentiality. Without confidentiality, integrity cannot be maintained. Other concepts, conditions, and aspects of integrity include accuracy, truthfulness, authenticity, validity, nonrepudiation, accountability, responsibility, completeness, and comprehensiveness.

 Real World Scenario

CIA Priority

Every organization has unique security requirements. On the CISSP exam, most security concepts are discussed in general terms, but in the real world, general concepts and best practices don't get the job done. The management team and security team must work together to prioritize an organization's security needs. This includes establishing a budget and spending plan, allocating expertise and hours, and focusing the IT and security staff efforts. One key aspect of this effort is to prioritize the security requirements of the organization. Knowing which tenet or asset is more important than another guides the creation of a security stance and ultimately the deployment of a security solution. Often, getting started in establishing priorities is a challenge. A possible solution to this challenge is to start with prioritizing the three primary security tenets of confidentiality, integrity, and availability. Defining which of these elements is most important to the organization is essential in crafting a sufficient security solution. This establishes a pattern that can be replicated from concept through design, architecture, deployment, and finally, maintenance.

Do you know the priority your organization places on each of the components of the CIA Triad? If not, find out.

An interesting generalization of this concept of CIA prioritization is that in many cases military and government organizations tend to prioritize confidentiality above integrity and availability, while private companies tend to prioritize availability above confidentiality and integrity. Although such prioritization focuses efforts on one aspect of security over another, it does not imply that the second or third prioritized items are ignored or improperly addressed.

Availability

The third principle of the CIA Triad is *availability*, which means authorized subjects are granted timely and uninterrupted access to objects. If a security mechanism offers availability, it offers a high level of assurance that the data, objects, and resources are accessible to authorized subjects. Availability includes efficient uninterrupted access to objects and prevention of denial of service (DoS) attacks. Availability also implies that the supporting infrastructure—including network services, communications, and access control mechanisms—is functional and allows authorized users to gain authorized access.

For availability to be maintained on a system, controls must be in place to ensure authorized access and an acceptable level of performance, to quickly handle interruptions, to provide for redundancy, to maintain reliable backups, and to prevent data loss or destruction.

There are numerous threats to availability. These include device failure, software errors, and environmental issues (heat, static, flooding, power loss, and so on). There are also some forms of attacks that focus on the violation of availability, including denial of service attacks, object destruction, and communication interruptions.

As with confidentiality and integrity, violations of availability are not limited to intentional attacks. Many instances of unauthorized alteration of sensitive information are caused by human error, oversight, or ineptitude. Some events that lead to availability breaches include accidentally deleting files, overutilizing a hardware or software component, underallocating resources, and mislabeling or incorrectly classifying objects. Availability violations can occur because of the actions of any user, including administrators. They can also occur because of an oversight in a security policy or a misconfigured security control.

Numerous countermeasures can ensure availability against possible threats. These include designing intermediary delivery systems properly, using access controls effectively, monitoring performance and network traffic, using firewalls and routers to prevent DoS attacks, implementing redundancy for critical systems, and maintaining and testing backup systems. Most security policies, as well as business continuity planning (BCP), focus on the use of fault tolerance features at the various levels of access/storage/security (i.e., disk, server, site) with the goal of eliminating single points of failure to maintain availability of critical systems.

Availability depends upon both integrity and confidentiality. Without integrity and confidentiality, availability cannot be maintained. Other concepts, conditions, and aspects of availability include usability, accessibility, and timeliness.

Other Security Concepts

In addition to the CIA Triad, you need to consider a plethora of other security-related concepts and principles when designing a security policy and deploying a security solution. The following sections discuss identification, authentication, authorization, auditing, accountability, and nonrepudiation.

Identification

Identification is the process by which a subject professes an identity and accountability is initiated. A subject must provide an identity to a system to start the process of authentication, authorization, and accountability. Providing an identity can involve typing in a username; swiping a smart card; waving a proximity device; speaking a phrase; or positioning your face, hand, or finger for a camera or scanning device. Providing a process ID number also represents the identification process. Without an identity, a system has no way to correlate an authentication factor with the subject.

Once a subject has been identified (that is, once the subject's identity has been recognized and verified), the identity is accountable for any further actions by that subject. IT systems track activity by identities, not by the subjects themselves. A computer doesn't know one human from another, but it does know that your user account is different from all other user accounts. A subject's identity is typically labeled as, or considered to be, public information. However, simply claiming an identity does not imply access or authority. The identity must be proven or verified before access to controlled resources is allowed. That process is authentication.

Authentication

The process of verifying or testing that the claimed identity is valid is *authentication*. Authentication requires from the subject additional information that must exactly correspond to the identity indicated. The most common form of authentication is using a password (this includes the password variations of PINs and passphrases). Authentication verifies the identity of the subject by comparing one or more factors against the database of valid identities (that is, user accounts). The authentication factor used to verify identity is typically labeled as, or considered to be, private information. The capability of the subject and system to maintain the secrecy of the authentication factors for identities directly reflects the level of security of that system. If the process of illegitimately obtaining and using the authentication factor of a target user is relatively easy, then the authentication system is insecure. If that process is relatively difficult, then the authentication system is reasonably secure.

Identification and authentication are always used together as a single two-step process. Providing an identity is the first step, and providing the authentication factor(s) is the second step. Without both, a subject cannot gain access to a system—neither element alone is useful in terms of security.

A subject can provide several types of authentication (for example, something you know, something you have, and so on). Each authentication technique or factor has its unique benefits and drawbacks. Thus, it is important to evaluate each mechanism in light of the environment in which it will be deployed to determine viability. (We discussed authentication at length in Chapter 1, "Access Control.")

Authorization

Once a subject is authenticated, access must be authorized. The process of *authorization* ensures that the requested activity or access to an object is possible given the rights and privileges assigned to the authenticated identity. In most cases, the system evaluates an access control matrix that compares the subject, the object, and the intended activity. If the specific action is allowed, the subject is authorized. If the specific action is not allowed, the subject is not authorized.

Keep in mind that just because a subject has been identified and authenticated does not mean they have been authorized to perform any function or access all resources within the controlled environment. It is possible for a subject to be logged onto a network (that is, identified and authenticated) but to be blocked from accessing a file or printing to a printer (that is, by not being authorized to perform that activity). Most network users are authorized to perform only a limited number of activities on a specific collection of resources. Identification and authentication are all-or-nothing aspects of access control. Authorization has a wide range of variations between all or nothing for each object within the environment. A user may be able to read a file but not delete it, print a document but not alter the print queue, or log on to a system but not access any resources. Authorization is usually defined using one of the concepts of access control, such as DAC, MAC, or RBAC (see Chapter 1).

Auditing

Auditing, or monitoring, is the programmatic means by which a subject's actions are tracked and recorded for the purpose of holding the subject accountable for their actions while authenticated on a system. It is also the process by which unauthorized or abnormal activities are detected on a system. Auditing is recording activities of a subject and its objects as well as recording the activities of core system functions that maintain the operating environment and the security mechanisms. The audit trails created by recording system events to logs can be used to evaluate the health and performance of a system. System crashes may indicate faulty programs, corrupt drivers, or intrusion attempts. The event logs leading up to a crash can often be used to discover the reason a system failed. Log files provide an audit trail for recreating the history of an event, intrusion, or system failure. Auditing is needed to detect malicious actions by subjects, attempted intrusions, and system failures and to reconstruct events, provide evidence for prosecution, and produce problem reports and analysis. Auditing is usually a native feature of operating systems and most applications and services. Thus, configuring the system to record information about specific types of events is fairly straightforward.

Accountability

An organization's security policy can be properly enforced only if *accountability* is maintained. In other words, you can maintain security only if subjects are held accountable for their actions. Effective accountability relies upon the capability to prove a subject's identity and track their activities. Accountability is established by linking a human to the activities of an online identity through the security services and mechanisms of auditing, authorization, authentication, and identification. Thus, human accountability is ultimately dependent on the strength of the authentication process. Without a strong authentication process, there is doubt that the human associated with a specific user account was the actual entity controlling that user account when the undesired action took place.

To have viable accountability, you must be able to support your security in a court of law. If you are unable to legally support your security efforts, then you will be unlikely to be able to hold a human accountable for actions linked to a user account. With only a password as authentication, there is significant room for doubt. Passwords are the least secure form of authentication, with dozens of different methods available to compromise them. However, using multifactor authentication, such as a password, smart card, and fingerprint scan in combination, there is very little possibility that any other human could have compromised the authentication process in order to impersonate the human responsible for the user account.

Legally Defensible Security

The point of security is to keep bad things from happening while supporting the occurrence of good things. When bad things do happen, organizations often desire assistance from law enforcement and the legal system for compensation. To obtain legal restitution, you must demonstrate that a crime was committed, that the suspect committed that crime, and that you took reasonable efforts to prevent the crime. This means your organization's security needs to be legally defensible. If you are unable to convince a court that your log files are accurate and that no other person other than the subject could have committed the crime, you will not obtain restitution. Ultimately, this requires a complete security solution that has unbreachable authentication techniques, solid authorization mechanisms, and impeccable auditing systems. Additionally, you must show that the organization complied with all applicable laws and regulations, that proper warnings and notifications were posted, that both logical and physical security were not otherwise compromised, and that there are no other possible reasonable interpretations of the electronic evidence.

Nonrepudiation

Nonrepudiation ensures that the subject of an activity or event cannot deny that the event occurred. Nonrepudiation prevents a subject from claiming not to have sent a message, not to have performed an action, or not to have been the cause of an event. It is made possible through identification, authentication, authorization, accountability, and auditing. Nonrepudiation can be established using digital certificates, session identifiers, transaction logs, and numerous other transactional and access control mechanisms. If nonrepudiation is not built into a system and properly enforced, you will not be able to verify that a specific entity performed a certain action. Nonrepudiation is an essential part of accountability. A suspect cannot be held accountable if they can repudiate the claim against them.

Develop and Implement Security Policy

For most organizations, maintaining security is an essential part of ongoing business. If their security were seriously compromised, many organizations would fail. To reduce the likelihood of a security failure, the process of implementing security has been somewhat formalized. This formalization has greatly reduced the chaos and complexity of designing and implementing security solutions for IT infrastructures. The formalization of security solutions involves a hierarchical organization of documentation. Each level focuses on a specific type or category of information and issues.

Security Policies

The top tier of the formalization is known as a *security policy*. A security policy is a document that defines the scope of security needed by the organization and discusses the assets that need protection and the extent to which security solutions should go to provide the necessary protection. The security policy is an overview or generalization of an organization's security needs. It defines the main security objectives and outlines the security framework of an organization. It also identifies the major functional areas of data processing and clarifies and defines all relevant terminology. It should clearly define why security is important and what assets are valuable. It is a strategic plan for implementing security. It should broadly outline the security goals and practices that should be employed to protect the organization's vital interests. The document discusses the importance of security to every aspect of daily business operation and the importance of the support of the senior staff for the implementation of security. The security policy is used to assign responsibilities, define roles, specify audit requirements, outline enforcement processes, indicate compliance requirements, and define acceptable risk levels. This document is often used as the proof that senior management has exercised due care in protecting itself against intrusion, attack, and disaster. Security policies are compulsory.

Many organizations employ several types of security policies to define or outline their overall security strategy. An organizational security policy focuses on issues relevant to every aspect of an organization. An issue-specific security policy focuses on a specific network service, department, function, or other aspect that is distinct from the organization as a whole. A system-specific security policy focuses on individual systems or types of systems and prescribes approved hardware and software, outlines methods for locking down a system, and even mandates firewall or other specific security controls.

In addition to these focused types of security policies, there are three overall categories of security policies: regulatory, advisory, and informative. A *regulatory policy* is required whenever industry or legal standards are applicable to your organization. This policy discusses the regulations that must be followed and outlines the procedures that should be used to elicit compliance. An *advisory policy* discusses behaviors and activities that are acceptable and defines consequences of violations. It explains senior management's desires for security and compliance within an organization. Most policies are advisory. An *informative policy* is designed to provide information or knowledge about a specific subject, such as company goals, mission statements, or how the organization interacts with partners and customers. An informative policy provides support, research, or background information relevant to the specific elements of the overall policy.

From the security policies flow many other documents or subelements necessary for a complete security solution. Policies are broad overviews, whereas standards, baselines, guidelines, and procedures include more specific, detailed information on the actual security solution. Standards are the next level below security policies.

Security Policies and Individuals

As a rule of thumb, security policies (as well as standards, guidelines, and procedures) should not address specific individuals. Instead of assigning tasks and responsibilities to a person, the policy should define tasks and responsibilities to fit a role. That role is a function of administrative control or personnel management. Thus, a security policy does not define who is to do what but rather defines what must be done by the various roles within the security infrastructure. Then these defined security roles are assigned to individuals as a job description or an assigned work task.

Acceptable Use Policy

An *acceptable use policy* is a commonly produced document that exists as part of the overall security documentation infrastructure. The acceptable use policy is specifically designed to assign security roles within the organization as well as ensure the responsibilities tied to those roles. This policy defines a level of acceptable performance and expectation of behavior and activity. Failure to comply with the policy may result in job action warnings, penalties, or termination.

Security Standards, Baselines, and Guidelines

Once the main security policies are set, then the remaining security documentation can be crafted under the guidance of those policies. Standards define compulsory requirements for the homogenous use of hardware, software, technology, and security controls. They provide a course of action by which technology and procedures are uniformly implemented throughout an organization. Standards are tactical documents that define steps or methods to accomplish the goals and overall direction defined by security policies.

At the next level are baselines. A baseline defines a minimum level of security that every system throughout the organization must meet. All systems not complying with the baseline should be taken out of production until they can be brought up to the baseline. The baseline establishes a common foundational secure state upon which all additional and more stringent security measures can be built. Baselines are usually system specific and often refer to an industry or government standard, like the Trusted Computer System Evaluation Criteria (TCSEC) or Information Technology Security Evaluation and Criteria (ITSEC). For example, most military organizations require that all systems support the TCSEC C2 security level at a minimum.

Guidelines are the next element of the formalized security policy structure. A guideline offers recommendations on how standards and baselines are implemented and serves as an operational guide for both security professionals and users. Guidelines are flexible so they can be customized for each unique system or condition and can be used in the creation of new procedures. They state which security mechanisms should be deployed instead of prescribing a specific product or control and detailing configuration settings. They outline methodologies, include suggested actions, and are not compulsory.

Security Procedures

Procedures are the final element of the formalized security policy structure. A procedure is a detailed, step-by-step how-to document that describes the exact actions necessary to implement a specific security mechanism, control, or solution. A procedure could discuss the entire system deployment operation or focus on a single product or aspect, such as deploying a firewall or updating virus definitions. In most cases, procedures are system and software specific. They must be updated as the hardware and software of a system evolve. The purpose of a procedure is to ensure the integrity of business processes. If everything is accomplished by following a detailed procedure, then all activities should be in compliance with policies, standards, and guidelines. Procedures help ensure standardization of security across all systems.

All too often, policies, standards, baselines, guidelines, and procedures are developed only as an afterthought at the urging of a consultant or auditor. If these documents are not used and updated, the administration of a secured environment will be unable to use them as guides. And without the planning, design, structure, and oversight provided by these documents, no environment will remain secure or represent proper diligent due care.

It is also common practice to develop a single document containing aspects of all these elements. This should be avoided. Each of these structures must exist as a separate entity because each performs a different specialized function. At the top of the formalization security policy documentation structure there are fewer documents because they contain general broad discussions of overview and goals. There are more documents further down the formalization structure (in other words, guidelines and procedures) because they contain details specific to a limited number of systems, networks, divisions, and areas.

Keeping these documents as separate entities provides several benefits:

- Not all users need to know the security standards, baselines, guidelines, and procedures for all security classification levels.

- When changes occur, it is easier to update and redistribute only the affected material rather than updating a monolithic policy and redistributing it throughout the organization.

Crafting the totality of security policy and all supporting documentation can be a daunting task. Many organizations struggle just to define the foundational parameters of their security, much less detail every single aspect of their day-to-day activities. However, in theory, a detailed and complete security policy supports real-world security in a directed, efficient, and specific manner. Once the security policy documentation is reasonably complete, it can be used to guide decisions, train new users, respond to problems, and predict trends for future expansion. A security policy should not be an afterthought but a key part of establishing an organization.

Change Control/Management

Another important aspect of security management is the control or management of change. Change in a secure environment can introduce loopholes, overlaps, missing objects, and oversights that can lead to new vulnerabilities. The only way to maintain security in the face of change is to systematically manage change. This usually involves extensive planning, testing, logging, auditing, and monitoring of activities related to security controls and mechanisms. The records of changes to an environment are then used to identify agents of change, whether those agents are objects, subjects, programs, communication pathways, or even the network itself.

The goal of change management is to ensure that any change does not lead to reduced or compromised security. Change management is also responsible for making it possible to roll back any change to a previous secured state. Change management can be implemented on any system despite the level of security. It is a requirement for systems complying with the Information Technology Security Evaluation and Criteria (ITSEC) classifications of B2, B3, and A1. Ultimately, change management improves the security of an environment by protecting implemented security from unintentional, tangential, or affected diminishments. Although an important goal of change management is to prevent unwanted reductions in security, its primary purpose is to make all changes subject to detailed documentation and auditing and thus able to be reviewed and scrutinized by management.

Change management should be used to oversee alterations to every aspect of a system, including hardware configuration and OS and application software. Change management should be included in design, development, testing, evaluation, implementation, distribution, evolution, growth, ongoing operation, and modification. It requires a detailed inventory of every component and configuration. It also requires the collection and maintenance of complete documentation for every system component, from hardware to software and from configuration settings to security features.

The change control process of configuration or change management has several goals or requirements:

- Implement changes in a monitored and orderly manner. Changes are always controlled.

- A formalized testing process is included to verify that a change produces expected results.

- All changes can be reversed.

- Users are informed of changes before they occur to prevent loss of productivity.

- The effects of changes are systematically analyzed.

- The negative impact of changes on capabilities, functionality, and performance is minimized.

One example of a change management process is a *parallel run*, which is a type of new system deployment testing where the new system and the old system are run in parallel. Each major or significant user process is performed on each system simultaneously to ensure that the new system supports all required business functionality that the old system supported or provided.

Data Classification

Data classification, or categorization, is the primary means by which data is protected based on its need for secrecy, sensitivity, or confidentiality. It is inefficient to treat all data the same way when designing and implementing a security system because some data items need more security than others. Securing everything at a low security level means sensitive data is easily accessible. Securing everything at a high security level is too expensive and restricts access to unclassified, noncritical data. Data classification is used to determine how much effort, money, and resources are allocated to protect the data and control access to it. Data classification, or categorization, is the process of organizing items, objects, subjects, and so on into groups, categories, or collections with similarities. These similarities could include value, cost, sensitivity, risk, vulnerability, power, privilege, possible levels of loss or damage, or need to know.

The primary objective of data classification schemes is to formalize and stratify the process of securing data based on assigned labels of importance and sensitivity. Data classification is used to provide security mechanisms for storing, processing, and transferring data. It also addresses how data is removed from a system and destroyed.

The following are benefits of using a data classification scheme:

- It demonstrates an organization's commitment to protecting valuable resources and assets.

- It assists in identifying those assets that are most critical or valuable to the organization.

- It lends credence to the selection of protection mechanisms.

- It is often required for regulatory compliance or legal restrictions.

- It helps to define access levels, types of authorized uses, and parameters for declassification and/or destruction of resources that are no longer valuable.

The criteria by which data is classified vary based on the organization performing the classification. However, you can glean numerous generalities from common or standardized classification systems:

- Usefulness of the data

- Timeliness of the data

- Value or cost of the data

- Maturity or age of the data

- Lifetime of the data (or when it expires)

- Association with personnel

- Data disclosure damage assessment (that is, how the disclosure of the data would affect the organization)

- Data modification damage assessment (that is, how the modification of the data would affect the organization)

- National security implications of the data

- Authorized access to the data (that is, who has access to the data)

- Restriction from the data (that is, who is restricted from the data)

- Maintenance and monitoring of the data (that is, who should maintain and monitor the data)

- Storage of the data

Using whatever criteria is appropriate for the organization, data is evaluated, and an appropriate data classification label is assigned to it. In some cases, the label is added to the data object. In other cases, labeling occurs automatically when the data is placed into a storage mechanism or behind a security protection mechanism.

To implement a classification scheme, you must perform seven major steps, or phases:

1. Identify the custodian, and define their responsibilities.

2. Specify the evaluation criteria of how the information will be classified and labeled.

3. Classify and label each resource. (The owner conducts this step, but a supervisor should review it.)

4. Document any exceptions to the classification policy that are discovered, and integrate them into the evaluation criteria.

5. Select the security controls that will be applied to each classification level to provide the necessary level of protection.

6. Specify the procedures for declassifying resources and the procedures for transferring custody of a resource to an external entity.

7. Create an enterprise-wide awareness program to instruct all personnel about the classification system.

Declassification is often overlooked when designing a classification system and documenting the usage procedures. Declassification is required once an asset no longer warrants or needs the protection of its currently assigned classification or sensitivity level. In other words, if the asset were new, it would be assigned a lower sensitivity label than it currently is assigned. When assets fail to be declassified as needed, security resources are wasted, and the value and protection of the higher sensitivity levels is degraded.

The two common classification schemes are government/military classification and commercial business/private sector classification. There are five levels of government/military classification (listed here from highest to lowest):

Top secret   The highest level of classification. The unauthorized disclosure of top secret data will have drastic effects and cause grave damage to national security.

Secret   Used for data of a restricted nature. The unauthorized disclosure of data classified as secret will have significant effects and cause critical damage to national security.

Confidential   Used for data of a private, sensitive, proprietary, or highly valuable nature. The unauthorized disclosure of data classified as confidential will have noticeable effects and cause serious damage to national security. This classification is used for all data between secret and sensitive but unclassified classifications.

Sensitive but unclassified   Used for data of a sensitive or private nature. The disclosure of this data would not cause significant damage.

Unclassified   The lowest level of classification. This is used for data that is neither sensitive nor classified. The disclosure of unclassified data does not compromise confidentiality or cause any noticeable damage.

> An easy way to remember the names of the five levels of the government or military classification scheme in least secure to most secure order is with a memorization acronym: U.S. Can Stop Terrorism. Notice that the five uppercase letters represent the five named classification levels, from least secure on the left to most secure on the right (or from bottom to top in the preceding list of items).

Items labeled as confidential, secret, and top secret are collectively known as *classified*. Often, revealing the actual classification of data to unauthorized individuals is a violation of that data. Thus, the term *classified* is generally used to refer to any data that is ranked above the sensitive but unclassified level. All classified data is exempt from the Freedom of Information Act as well as many other laws and regulations. The US military classification scheme is most concerned with the sensitivity of data and focuses on the protection of confidentiality (that is, the prevention of disclosure). You can roughly define each level or label of classification by the level of damage that would be caused in the event of a confidentiality violation. Data from the top secret level would cause grave damage to national security, while data from the unclassified level would not cause any serious damage to national or localized security.

Commercial business/private sector classification systems can vary widely because they typically do not have to adhere to a standard or regulation. The CISSP exam focuses on four common or possible business classification levels (listed highest to lowest):

Confidential   The highest level of classification. This is used for data that is extremely sensitive and for internal use only. A significant negative impact could occur for a company if confidential data is disclosed. Sometimes the label *proprietary* is substituted for *confidential*. Sometimes proprietary data is considered a specific form of confidential information. If proprietary data is disclosed, it can have drastic effects on the competitive edge of an organization.

Private   Used for data that is of a private or personal nature and intended for internal use only. A significant negative impact could occur for the company or individuals if private data is disclosed.

 Confidential and private data in a commercial business/private sector classification scheme both require roughly the same level of security protection. The real difference between the two labels is that confidential data is company data while private data is data related to individuals, such as medical data.

Sensitive   Used for data that is more classified than public data. A negative impact could occur for the company if sensitive data is disclosed.

Public   The lowest level of classification. This is used for all data that does not fit in one of the higher classifications. Its disclosure does not have a serious negative impact on the organization.

Another consideration related to data classification or categorization is ownership. *Ownership* is the formal assignment of responsibility to an individual or group. Ownership can be made clear and distinct within an operating system where files or other types of objects can be assigned an owner. Often, an owner has full capabilities and privileges over the object they own. The ability to take ownership is often granted to the most powerful accounts in an operating system, such as the administrator in Windows or root in UNIX or Linux. In most cases, the subject that creates a new object is by default the owner of that object. In some environments, the security policy mandates that when new objects are created, a formal change of ownership from end users to an administrator or management user is necessary. In this situation, the admin account can simply take ownership of the new objects.

Ownership of objects outside of formal IT structures is often not as obvious. A company document can define owners for the facility, business tasks, processes, assets, and so on. However, such documentation does not always "enforce" this ownership in the real world. The ownership of a file object is enforced by the operating system and file system, while ownership of a physical object, intangible asset, or organizational concept (such as the research department or a development project) is defined only on paper and can be more easily undermined. Additional security governance must be implemented to provide enforcement of ownership in the physical world.

Summary

Security governance, management concepts, and principles are inherent elements in a security policy and in solution deployment. They define the basic parameters needed for a secure environment. They also define the goals and objectives that both policy designers and system implementers must achieve in order to create a secure solution.

The primary goals and objectives of security are contained within the CIA Triad: confidentiality, integrity, and availability. These three principles are considered the most important within the realm of security. Their importance to an organization depends on the organization's security goals and requirements and on how much of a threat to security exists in its environment.

The first principle from the CIA Triad is confidentiality, the principle that objects are not disclosed to unauthorized subjects. Security mechanisms that offer confidentiality offer a high level of assurance that data, objects, or resources are not exposed to unauthorized subjects. If a threat exists against confidentiality, there is the possibility that unauthorized disclosure could take place.

The second principle from the CIA Triad is integrity, the principle that objects retain their veracity and are intentionally modified by only authorized subjects. Security mechanisms that offer integrity offer a high level of assurance that the data, objects, and resources are unaltered from their original protected state. This includes alterations occurring while the object is in storage, in transit, or in process. Maintaining integrity means the object itself is not altered and the operating system and programming entities that manage and manipulate the object are not compromised.

The third principle from the CIA Triad is availability, the principle that authorized subjects are granted timely and uninterrupted access to objects. Security mechanisms that offer availability offer a high level of assurance that the data, objects, and resources are accessible to authorized subjects. Availability includes efficient uninterrupted access to objects and prevention of denial of service attacks. It also implies that the supporting infrastructure is functional and allows authorized users to gain authorized access.

Other security-related concepts, principles, and tenets that should be considered and addressed when designing a security policy and deploying a security solution are privacy, identification, authentication, authorization, accountability, nonrepudiation, and auditing.

Other aspects of security solution concepts and principles are the elements of protection mechanisms: layering, abstraction, data hiding, and encryption. These are common characteristics of security controls, and although not all security controls must have them, many controls use these mechanisms to protect confidentiality, integrity, and availability.

Security roles determine who is responsible for the security of an organization's assets. Those assigned the senior management role are ultimately responsible and liable for any asset loss, and they are the ones who define security policy. Security professionals are responsible for implementing security policy, and users are responsible for complying with the security policy. The person assigned the data owner role is responsible for classifying information, and a data custodian is responsible for maintaining the secure environment and backing up data. An auditor is responsible for making sure a secure environment is properly protecting assets.

A formalized security policy structure consists of policies, standards, baselines, guidelines, and procedures. These individual documents are essential elements to the design and implementation of security in any environment.

The control or management of change is an important aspect of security management practices. When a secure environment is changed, loopholes, overlaps, missing objects, and oversights can lead to new vulnerabilities. You can, however, maintain security by systematically managing change. This typically involves extensive logging, auditing, and monitoring of activities related to security controls and security mechanisms. The resulting data is then used to identify agents of change, whether objects, subjects, programs, communication pathways, or even the network itself.

Data classification is the primary means by which data is protected based on its secrecy, sensitivity, or confidentiality. Because some data items need more security than others, it is inefficient to treat all data the same when designing and implementing a security system. If everything is secured at a low security level, sensitive data is easily accessible, but securing everything at a high security level is too expensive and restricts access to unclassified, noncritical data. Data classification is used to determine how much effort, money, and resources are allocated to protect the data and control access to it.

An important aspect of security management planning is the proper implementation of a security policy. To be effective, the approach to security management must be a top-down approach. The responsibility of initiating and defining a security policy lies with upper or senior management. Security policies provide direction for the lower levels of the organization's hierarchy. Middle management is responsible for fleshing out the security policy into standards, baselines, guidelines, and procedures. It is the responsibility of the operational managers or security professionals to implement the configurations prescribed in the security management documentation. Finally, the end users' responsibility is to comply with all security policies of the organization.

Security management planning includes defining security roles, developing security policies, performing risk analysis, and requiring security education for employees. These responsibilities are guided by the developments of management plans. The security management team should develop strategic, tactical, and operational plans.

Exam Essentials

Understand the CIA Triad elements of confidentiality, integrity, and availability.   Confidentiality is the principle that objects are not disclosed to unauthorized subjects. Integrity is the principle that objects retain their veracity and are intentionally modified by only authorized subjects. Availability is the principle that authorized subjects are granted timely and uninterrupted access to objects. Know why these are important, the mechanisms that support them, the attacks that focus on each, and the effective countermeasures.

Know how privacy fits into the realm of IT security.   Know the multiple meanings/definitions of privacy, why it is important to protect, and the issues surrounding it, especially in a work environment.

Be able to explain how identification works.   Identification is the process by which a subject professes an identity and accountability is initiated. A subject must provide an identity to a system to start the process of authentication, authorization, and accountability.

Understand the process of authentication.   The process of verifying or testing that a claimed identity is valid is authentication. Authentication requires information from the subject that must exactly correspond to the identity indicated.

Know how authorization fits into a security plan.   Once a subject is authenticated, its access must be authorized. The process of authorization ensures that the requested activity or object access is possible given the rights and privileges assigned to the authenticated identity.

Understand security governance.   Security governance is the collection of practices related to supporting, defining, and directing the security efforts of an organization.

Be able to explain the auditing process.   Auditing, or monitoring, is the programmatic means by which subjects are held accountable for their actions while authenticated on a system. Auditing is also the process by which unauthorized or abnormal activities are detected on a system. Auditing is needed to detect malicious actions by subjects, attempted intrusions, and system failures and to reconstruct events, provide evidence for prosecution, and produce problem reports and analysis.

Understand the importance of accountability.   An organization's security policy can be properly enforced only if accountability is maintained. In other words, security can be maintained only if subjects are held accountable for their actions. Effective accountability relies upon the capability to prove a subject's identity and track their activities.

Be able to explain nonrepudiation.   Nonrepudiation ensures that the subject of an activity or event cannot deny that the event occurred. It prevents a subject from claiming not to have sent a message, not to have performed an action, or not to have been the cause of an event.

Understand security management planning.   Security management is based on three types of plans: strategic, tactical, and operational. A strategic plan is a long-term plan that is fairly stable. It defines the organization's goals, mission, and objectives. The tactical plan is a midterm plan developed to provide more details on accomplishing the goals set forth in the strategic plan. Operational plans are short-term and highly detailed plans based on the strategic and tactical plans.

Know the elements of a formalized security policy structure.   To create a comprehensive security plan, you need the following items in place: security policy, standards, baselines, guidelines, and procedures. Such documentation clearly states security requirements and creates due diligence on the part of the responsible parties.

Understand key security roles.   The primary security roles are senior manager, organizational owner, upper management, security professional, user, data owner, data custodian, and auditor. By creating a security role hierarchy, you limit risk overall.

Know how to implement security awareness training.   Before actual training can take place, awareness of security as a recognized entity must be created for users. Once this is accomplished, training, or teaching employees to perform their work tasks and to comply with the security policy, can begin. All new employees require some level of training so they will be able to comply with all standards, guidelines, and procedures mandated by the security policy. Education is a more detailed endeavor in which students/users learn much more than they actually need to know to perform their work tasks. Education is most often associated with users pursuing certification or seeking job promotion.

Know how layering simplifies security.   Layering is simply the use of multiple controls in series. Using a multilayered solution allows for numerous controls to guard against threats.

Be able to explain the concept of abstraction.   Abstraction is used to collect similar elements into groups, classes, or roles that are assigned security controls, restrictions, or permissions as a collective. It adds efficiency to carrying out a security plan.

Understand data hiding.   Data hiding is exactly what it sounds like: preventing data from being discovered or accessed by a subject. It is often a key element in security controls as well as in programming.

Understand the need for encryption.   Encryption is the art and science of hiding the meaning or intent of a communication from unintended recipients. It can take many forms and be applied to every type of electronic communication, including text, audio, and video files, as well as programs themselves. Encryption is an important element in security controls, especially in regard to the transmission of data between systems.

Be able to explain the concepts of change control and change management.   Change in a secure environment can introduce loopholes, overlaps, missing objects, and oversights that can lead to new vulnerabilities. The only way to maintain security in the face of change is to systematically manage change.

Know why and how data is classified.   Data is classified to simplify the process of assigning security controls to groups of objects rather than to individual objects. The two common classification schemes are government/military and commercial business/private sector. Know the five levels of government/military classification and the four levels of commercial business/private sector classification.

Understand the importance of declassification.   Declassification is required once an asset no longer warrants the protection of its currently assigned classification or sensitivity level.

Know the basics of COBIT.   Control Objectives for Information and Related Technology (COBIT) is a security concept infrastructure used to organize the complex security solutions of companies.

Written Lab

1. Discuss and describe the CIA Triad.

2. What are the requirements to hold a person accountable for the actions of their user account?

3. Describe the benefits of change control management.

4. What are the seven major steps or phases in the implementation of a classification scheme?

5. Name the six primary security roles as defined by ISC2 for CISSP.

6. What are the four components of a complete organizational security policy and their basic purpose?

Review Questions

1. Which of the following contains the primary goals and objectives of security?
   A. A network's border perimeter
   B. The CIA Triad
   C. A stand-alone system
   D. The Internet

2. Vulnerabilities and risks are evaluated based on their threats against which of the following?
   A. One or more of the CIA Triad principles
   B. Data usefulness
   C. Due care
   D. Extent of liability

3. Which of the following is a principle of the CIA Triad that means authorized subjects are granted timely and uninterrupted access to objects?
   A. Identification
   B. Availability
   C. Encryption
   D. Layering

4. Which of the following is *not* considered a violation of confidentiality?
   A. Stealing passwords
   B. Eavesdropping
   C. Hardware destruction
   D. Social engineering

5. Which of the following is not true?
   A. Violations of confidentiality include human error.
   B. Violations of confidentiality include management oversight.
   C. Violations of confidentiality are limited to direct intentional attacks.
   D. Violations of confidentiality can occur when a transmission is not properly encrypted.

6. Confidentiality is dependent upon which of the following?
   A. Accountability
   B. Availability
   C. Nonrepudiation
   D. Integrity

7. If a security mechanism offers availability, then it offers a high level of assurance that authorized subjects can _____ the data, objects, and resources.

   A. Control

   B. Audit

   C. Access

   D. Repudiate

8. Which of the following describes the freedom from being observed, monitored, or examined without consent or knowledge?

   A. Integrity

   B. Privacy

   C. Authentication

   D. Accountability

9. All but which of the following items require awareness for all individuals affected?

   A. Restricting personal email

   B. Recording phone conversations

   C. Gathering information about surfing habits

   D. The backup mechanism used to retain email messages

10. What element of data categorization management can override all other forms of access control?

    A. Classification

    B. Physical access

    C. Custodian responsibilities

    D. Taking ownership

11. What ensures that the subject of an activity or event cannot deny that the event occurred?

    A. CIA Triad

    B. Abstraction

    C. Nonrepudiation

    D. Hash totals

12. Which of the following is the most important and distinctive concept in relation to layered security?

    A. Multiple

    B. Series

    C. Parallel

    D. Filter

13. Which of the following is *not* considered an example of data hiding?

   A. Preventing an authorized reader of an object from deleting that object

   B. Keeping a database from being accessed by unauthorized visitors

   C. Restricting a subject at a lower classification level from accessing data at a higher classification level

   D. Preventing an application from accessing hardware directly

14. What is the primary goal of change management?

   A. Maintaining documentation

   B. Keeping users informed of changes

   C. Allowing rollback of failed changes

   D. Preventing security compromises

15. What is the primary objective of data classification schemes?

   A. To control access to objects for authorized subjects

   B. To formalize and stratify the process of securing data based on assigned labels of importance and sensitivity

   C. To establish a transaction trail for auditing accountability

   D. To manipulate access controls to provide for the most efficient means to grant or restrict functionality

16. Which of the following is typically *not* a characteristic considered when classifying data?

   A. Value

   B. Size of object

   C. Useful lifetime

   D. National security implications

17. What are the two common data classification schemes?

   A. Military and private sector

   B. Personal and government

   C. Private sector and unrestricted sector

   D. Classified and unclassified

18. Which of the following is the lowest military data classification for classified data?

   A. Sensitive

   B. Secret

   C. Sensitive but unclassified

   D. Private

19. Which commercial business/private sector data classification is used to control information about individuals within an organization?

A. Confidential

B. Private

C. Sensitive

D. Proprietary

20. Data classifications are used to focus security controls over all but which of the following?

A. Storage

B. Processing

C. Layering

D. Transfer

Chapter

6

Risk and Personnel Management

THE CISSP EXAM TOPICS COVERED IN THIS CHAPTER INCLUDE:

3. Information Security Governance and Risk Management

- F. Manage third-party governance (e.g., on-site assessment, document exchange and review, process/policy review)
- G. Understand and apply risk management concepts
  - G.1 Identify threats and vulnerabilities
  - G.2 Risk assessment/analysis (qualitative, quantitative, hybrid)
  - G.3 Risk assignment/acceptance
  - G.4 Countermeasure selection
  - G.5 Tangible and intangible asset valuation
- H. Manage personnel security
  - H.1 Employment candidate screening (e.g., reference checks, education verification)
  - H.2 Employment agreements and policies
  - H.3 Employee termination processes
  - H.4 Vendor, consultant, and contractor controls
- I. Develop and manage security education, training, and awareness.
- J. Manage the security function
  - J.1 Budget
  - J.2 Metrics
  - J.3 Resources
  - J.4 Develop and implement information security strategies
  - J.5 Assess the completeness and effectiveness of the security program

The Information Security Governance and Risk Management domain of the Common Body of Knowledge (CBK) for the CISSP certification exam deals with hiring practices, formalizing security structure, risk management, awareness training, and management planning.

This domain is discussed in this chapter and in the preceding chapter (Chapter 5, "Security Governance Concepts, Principles, and Policies"). Be sure to read and study the materials in both chapters to ensure complete coverage of the essential material for the CISSP certification exam.

Because of the complexity and importance of hardware and software controls, security management for employees is often overlooked in overall security planning. This chapter explores the human side of security, from establishing secure hiring practices and job descriptions to developing an employee infrastructure. Additionally, we look at how employee training, management, and termination practices are considered an integral part of creating a secure environment. Finally, we examine how to assess and manage security risks.

Manage Third-Party Governance

Security governance is the collection of practices related to supporting, defining, and directing the security efforts of an organization. Security governance is closely related to and often intertwined with corporate and IT governance. The goals of these three governance agendas often interrelate or are the same. For example, a common goal of organizational governance is to ensure that the organization will continue to exist and will grow or expand over time. Thus, the goal of all three forms of governance is to maintain business processes while striving toward growth and resiliency.

Third-party governance is the system of oversight that may be mandated by law, regulation, industry standards, or licensing requirements. The actual method of governance may vary but it generally involves an outside investigator or auditor. These auditors might be designated by a governing body or might be consultants hired by the target organization.

Another aspect of third-party governance is the application of security oversight on third parties that your organization relies upon. Many organizations choose to outsource various aspects of their business operations. Outsourced operations can include security guards, maintenance, technical support, and accounting services. These parties need to stay in compliance with the primary organization's security stance. Otherwise, they present additional risks and vulnerabilities to the primary organization.

Third-party governance focuses on verifying compliance with stated security objectives, requirements, regulations, and contractual obligations. On-site assessments can provide first-hand exposure to the security mechanisms employed at a location. Those performing on-site assessment or audits need to follow auditing protocols (such as COBIT) and have a specific checklist of requirements to investigate.

In the auditing and assessment process, both the target and the governing body should participate in full and open document exchange and review. An organization needs to know the full details of all requirements it must comply with. The organization should submit security policy and self-assessment reports back to the governing body. This open document exchange ensures that all parties involved are in agreement about all the issues of concern. It reduces the chances of unknown requirements or unrealistic expectations. Document exchange does not end with the transmission of paperwork or electronic files. Instead, it leads into the process of documentation review.

Documentation review is the process of reading the exchanged materials and verifying them against standards and expectations. The documentation review is typically performed before any on-site inspection takes place. If the exchanged documentation is sufficient and meets expectations (or at least requirements), then an on-site review will be able to focus on compliance with the stated documentation. However, if the documentation is incomplete, inaccurate, or otherwise insufficient, the on-site review is postponed until the documentation can be updated and corrected. This step is important because if the documentation is not in compliance, chances are the location will not be in compliance either.

In many situations, especially related to government or military agencies or contractors, failing to provide sufficient documentation to meet requirements of third-party governance can result in a loss of or a voiding of authorization to operate (ATO). Complete and sufficient documentation can often maintain existing ATO or provide a temporary ATO (TATO). However, once an ATO is lost or revoked, a complete documentation review and on-site review showing full compliance is usually necessary to reestablish the ATO.

A portion of the documentation review is the logical and practical investigation of the business processes and organizational policies. This review ensures that the stated and implemented business tasks, systems, and methodologies are practical, efficient, and cost effective and most of all (at least in relation to security governance) that they support the goal of security through the reduction of vulnerabilities and the avoidance, reduction, or mitigation of risk. Risk management, risk assessment, and addressing risk are all methods and techniques involved in performing process/policy review.

Risk Management

Security is aimed at preventing loss or disclosure of data while sustaining authorized access. The possibility that something could happen to damage, destroy, or disclose data or other resources is known as *risk*. Understanding risk management concepts is not only important for the CISSP exam, it's also essential to the establishment of a sufficient security stance, proper security governance, and legal proof of due care and due diligence.

Managing risk is therefore an element of sustaining a secure environment. Risk management is a detailed process of identifying factors that could damage or disclose data, evaluating those factors in light of data value and countermeasure cost, and implementing cost-effective solutions for mitigating or reducing risk. The overall process of risk management is used to develop and implement information security strategies. The goal of these strategies is to reduce risk and to support the mission of the organization.

The primary goal of risk management is to reduce risk to an acceptable level. What that level actually is depends upon the organization, the value of its assets, the size of its budget, and many other factors. What is deemed acceptable risk to one organization may be an unreasonably high level of risk to another. It is impossible to design and deploy a totally risk-free environment; however, significant risk reduction is possible, often with little effort.

Risks to an IT infrastructure are not all computer based. In fact, many risks come from noncomputer sources. It is important to consider all possible risks when performing risk evaluation for an organization. Failing to properly evaluate and respond to all forms of risk will leave a company vulnerable. Keep in mind that IT security, commonly referred to as logical or technical security, can provide protection only against logical or technical attacks. To protect IT against physical attacks, physical protections must be erected.

The process by which the goals of risk management are achieved is known as *risk analysis*. It includes examining an environment for risks, evaluating each threat event as to its likelihood of occurring and the cost of the damage it would cause if it did occur, assessing the cost of various countermeasures for each risk, and creating a cost/benefit report for safeguards to present to upper management. In addition to these risk-focused activities, risk management also requires evaluation, assessment, and the assignment of value for all assets within the organization. Without proper asset valuations, it is not possible to prioritize and compare risks with possible losses.

Risk Terminology

Risk management employs a vast terminology that must be clearly understood, especially for the CISSP exam. This section defines and discusses all the important risk-related terminology:

Asset   An asset is anything within an environment that should be protected. It is anything used in a business process or task. It can be a computer file, a network service, a system resource, a process, a program, a product, an IT infrastructure, a database, a hardware device, furniture, product recipes/formulas, personnel, software, facilities, and so on. If an organization places any value on an item under its control and deems that item important enough to protect, it is labeled an asset for the purposes of risk management and analysis. The loss or disclosure of an asset could result in an overall security compromise, loss of productivity, reduction in profits, additional expenditures, discontinuation of the organization, and numerous intangible consequences.

Asset valuation   Asset valuation is a dollar value assigned to an asset based on actual cost and nonmonetary expenses. These can include costs to develop, maintain, administer, advertise, support, repair, and replace an asset; they can also include more elusive values, such as public confidence, industry support, productivity enhancement, knowledge equity, and ownership benefits. Asset valuation is discussed in detail later in this chapter.

Threats   Any potential occurrence that may cause an undesirable or unwanted outcome for an organization or for a specific asset is a threat. Threats are any action or inaction that could cause damage, destruction, alteration, loss, or disclosure of assets or that could block access to or prevent maintenance of assets. Threats can be large or small and result in large or small consequences. They can be intentional or accidental. They can originate from people, organizations, hardware, networks, structures, or nature. Threat agents intentionally exploit vulnerabilities. Threat agents are usually people, but they could also be programs, hardware, or systems. Threat events are accidental and intentional exploitations of vulnerabilities. They can also be natural or manmade. Threat events include fire, earthquake, flood, system failure, human error (due to a lack of training or ignorance), and power outage.

Vulnerability   The weakness in an asset or the absence or the weakness of a safeguard or countermeasure is a vulnerability.

In other words, a vulnerability is a flaw, loophole, oversight, error, limitation, frailty, or susceptibility in the IT infrastructure or any other aspect of an organization. If a vulnerability is exploited, loss or damage to assets can occur.

Exposure   Exposure is being susceptible to asset loss because of a threat; there is the possibility that a vulnerability can or will be exploited by a threat agent or event. Exposure doesn't mean that a realized threat (an event that results in loss) is actually occurring (the exposure to a realized threat is called *experienced exposure*). It just means that if there is a vulnerability and a threat that can exploit it, there is the possibility that a threat event, or potential exposure, can occur.

Risk   Risk is the possibility or likelihood that a threat will exploit a vulnerability to cause harm to an asset. It is an assessment of probability, possibility, or chance. The more likely it is that a threat event will occur, the greater the risk. Every instance of exposure is a risk. When written as a formula, risk can be defined as follows:

```
risk = threat * vulnerability
```

Thus, reducing either the threat agent or the vulnerability directly results in a reduction in risk.

When a risk is realized, a threat agent or a threat event has taken advantage of a vulnerability and caused harm to or disclosure of one or more assets. The whole purpose of security is to prevent risks from becoming realized by removing vulnerabilities and blocking threat agents and threat events from jeopardizing assets. As a risk management tool, security is the implementation of safeguards.

Safeguards A *safeguard*, or *countermeasure*, is anything that removes or reduces a vulnerability or protects against one or more specific threats. A safeguard can be installing a software patch, making a configuration change, hiring security guards, altering the infrastructure, modifying processes, improving the security policy, training personnel more effectively, electrifying a perimeter fence, installing lights, and so on. It is any action or product that reduces risk through the elimination or lessening of a threat or a vulnerability anywhere within an organization. Safeguards are the only means by which risk is mitigated or removed. It is important to remember that a safeguard, security control, or countermeasure need not involve the purchase of a new product; reconfiguring existing elements or even removing elements from the infrastructure are also valid safeguards.

Attack An attack is the exploitation of a vulnerability by a threat agent. In other words, an attack is any intentional attempt to exploit a vulnerability of an organization's security infrastructure to cause damage, loss, or disclosure of assets. An attack can also be viewed as any violation or failure to adhere to an organization's security policy.

Breach A breach is the occurrence of a security mechanism being bypassed or thwarted by a threat agent. When a breach is combined with an attack, a penetration, or intrusion, can result. A penetration is the condition in which a threat agent has gained access to an organization's infrastructure through the circumvention of security controls and is able to directly imperil assets.

The elements asset, threat, vulnerability, exposure, risk, and safeguard are related, as shown in Figure 6.1. Threats exploit vulnerabilities, which results in exposure. Exposure is risk, and risk is mitigated by safeguards. Safeguards protect assets that are endangered by threats.

FIGURE 6.1 The elements of risk

Risk Assessment Methodologies

Risk management/analysis is primarily an exercise for upper management. It is their responsibility to initiate and support risk analysis and assessment by defining the scope and purpose of the endeavor. The actual processes of performing risk analysis are often delegated to security professionals or an evaluation team. However, all risk assessments, results, decisions, and outcomes must be understood and approved by upper management as an element in providing prudent due care.

All IT systems have risk. There is no way to eliminate 100 percent of all risks. Instead, upper management must decide which risks are acceptable and which are not. Determining which risks are acceptable requires detailed and complex asset and risk assessments.

Risk Analysis

Risk analysis is performed to provide upper management with the details necessary to decide which risks should be mitigated, which should be transferred, and which should be accepted. The result is a cost/benefit comparison between the expected cost of asset loss and the cost of deploying safeguards against threats and vulnerabilities. Risk analysis identifies risks, quantifies the impact of threats, and aids in budgeting for security. It helps integrate the needs and objectives of the security policy with the organization's business goals and intentions. The risk analysis/risk assessment is a "point in time" metric. Threats and vulnerabilities constantly change, and the risk assessment needs to be redone periodically.

The first step in risk analysis is to appraise the value of an organization's assets. If an asset has no value, then there is no need to provide protection for it. A primary goal of risk analysis is to ensure that only cost-effective safeguards are deployed. It makes no sense to spend $100,000 protecting an asset that is worth only $1,000. The value of an asset directly affects and guides the level of safeguards and security deployed to protect it. As a rule, the annual costs of safeguards should not exceed the expected annual cost of asset loss.

Asset Valuation

When the cost of an asset is evaluated, there are many aspects to consider. The goal of *asset valuation* is to assign to an asset a specific dollar value that encompasses tangible costs as well as intangible ones. Determining an exact value is often difficult if not impossible, but nevertheless, a specific value must be established. (Note that the discussion of qualitative versus quantitative risk analysis in the next section may clarify this issue.) Improperly assigning value to assets can result in failing to properly protect an asset or implementing financially infeasible safeguards. The following list includes some of the tangible and intangible issues that contribute to the valuation of assets:

- Purchase cost
- Development cost
- Administrative or management cost
- Maintenance or upkeep cost

- Cost in acquiring asset
- Cost to protect or sustain asset
- Value to owners and users
- Value to competitors
- Intellectual property or equity value
- Market valuation (sustainable price)
- Replacement cost
- Productivity enhancement or degradation
- Operational costs of asset presence and loss
- Liability of asset loss
- Usefulness

Assigning or determining the value of assets to an organization can fulfill numerous requirements. It serves as the foundation for performing a cost/benefit analysis of asset protection through safeguard deployment. It serves as a means for selecting or evaluating safeguards and countermeasures. It provides values for insurance purposes and establishes an overall net worth or net value for the organization. It helps senior management understand exactly what is at risk within the organization. Understanding the value of assets also helps to prevent negligence of due care and encourages compliance with legal requirements, industry regulations, and internal security policies.

After asset valuation, threats must be identified and examined. This involves creating an exhaustive list of all possible threats for the organization and its IT infrastructure. The list should include threat agents as well as threat events. It is important to keep in mind that threats can come from anywhere. Threats to IT are not limited to IT sources. When compiling a list of threats, be sure to consider the following:

- Viruses
- Cascade errors (a series of escalating errors) and dependency faults (caused by relying on events or items that don't exist)
- Criminal activities by authorized users
- Movement (vibrations, jarring, etc.)
- Intentional attacks
- Reorganization
- Authorized user illness or epidemics
- Hackers
- User errors
- Natural disasters (earthquakes, floods, fire, volcanoes, hurricanes, tornadoes, tsunamis, and so on)

- Physical damage (crushing, projectiles, cable severing, and so on)
- Misuse of data, resources, or services
- Changes or compromises to data classification or security policies
- Government, political, or military intrusions or restrictions
- Processing errors, buffer overflows
- Personnel privilege abuse
- Temperature extremes
- Energy anomalies (static, EM pulses, radio frequencies [RFs], power loss, power surges, and so on)
- Loss of data
- Information warfare
- Bankruptcy or alteration/interruption of business activity
- Coding/programming errors
- Intruders (physical and logical)
- Environmental factors (presence of gases, liquids, organisms, and so on)
- Equipment failure
- Physical theft
- Social engineering

In most cases, a team rather than a single individual should perform risk assessment and analysis. Also, the team members should be from various departments within the organization. It is not usually a requirement that all team members be security professionals or even network/system administrators. The diversity of the team based on the demographics of the organization will help to exhaustively identify and address all possible threats and risks.

The Consultant Cavalry

Risk assessment is a highly involved, detailed, complex, and lengthy process. Often risk analysis cannot be properly handled by existing employees because of the size, scope, or liability of the risk; thus, many organizations bring in risk management consultants to perform this work. This provides a high level of expertise, does not bog down employees, and can be a more reliable measurement of real-world risk. But even risk management consultants do not perform risk assessment and analysis on paper only; they typically employ complex and expensive risk assessment software. This software streamlines the overall task, provides more reliable results, and produces standardized reports that are acceptable to insurance companies, boards of directors, and so on.

Once you develop a list of threats, you must individually evaluate each threat and its related risk. There are two risk assessment methodologies: quantitative and qualitative. *Quantitative risk analysis* assigns real dollar figures to the loss of an asset. *Qualitative risk analysis* assigns subjective and intangible values to the loss of an asset. Both methods are necessary for a complete risk analysis.

Quantitative Risk Analysis

The quantitative method results in concrete probability percentages. That means the end result is a report that has dollar figures for levels of risk, potential loss, cost of countermeasures, and value of safeguards. This report is usually fairly easy to understand, especially for anyone with knowledge of spreadsheets and budget reports. Think of quantitative analysis as the act of assigning a quantity to risk; in other words, placing a dollar figure on each asset and threat. However, a purely quantitative analysis is not sufficient; not all elements and aspects of the analysis can be quantified because some are qualitative, subjective, or intangible.

The process of quantitative risk analysis starts with asset valuation and threat identification. Next, you estimate the potential and frequency of each risk. This information is then used to calculate various cost functions that are used to evaluate safeguards.

The six major steps or phases in quantitative risk analysis are as follows:

1. Inventory assets, and assign a value (asset value, or AV).

2. Research each asset, and produce a list of all possible threats of each individual asset. For each listed threat, calculate the exposure factor (EF) and single loss expectancy (SLE).

3. Perform a threat analysis to calculate the likelihood of each threat being realized within a single year, that is, the annualized rate of occurrence (ARO).

4. Derive the overall loss potential per threat by calculating the annualized loss expectancy (ALE).

5. Research countermeasures for each threat, and then calculate the changes to ARO and ALE based on an applied countermeasure.

6. Perform a cost/benefit analysis of each countermeasure for each threat for each asset. Select the most appropriate response to each threat.

Cost Functions

The cost functions associated with quantitative risk analysis include exposure factor, single loss expectancy, annualized rate of occurrence, and annualized loss expectancy:

Exposure factor   The *exposure factor (EF)* represents the percentage of loss that an organization would experience if a specific asset were violated by a realized risk. The EF can also be called the *loss potential*. In most cases, a realized risk does not result in the total loss of an asset. The EF simply indicates the expected overall asset value loss because of a single realized risk. The EF is usually small for assets that are easily replaceable, such as hardware. It can be very large for assets that are irreplaceable or proprietary, such as product designs or a database of customers. The EF is expressed as a percentage.

Single loss expectancy   The EF is needed to calculate the SLE. The *single loss expectancy (SLE)* is the cost associated with a single realized risk against a specific asset. It indicates the exact amount of loss an organization would experience if an asset were harmed by a specific threat occurring.

The SLE is calculated using the following formula:

SLE = asset value (AV) * exposure factor (EF)

or more simply:

SLE = AV * EF

The SLE is expressed in a dollar value. For example, if an asset is valued at $200,000 and it has an EF of 45 percent for a specific threat, then the SLE of the threat for that asset is $90,000.

Annualized rate of occurrence   The *annualized rate of occurrence (ARO)* is the expected frequency with which a specific threat or risk will occur (that is, become realized) within a single year. The ARO can range from a value of 0.0 (zero), indicating that the threat or risk will never be realized, to a very large number, indicating that the threat or risk occurs often. Calculating the ARO can be complicated. It can be derived from historical records, statistical analysis, or guesswork. ARO calculation is also known as *probability determination*. The ARO for some threats or risks is calculated by multiplying the likelihood of a single occurrence by the number of users who could initiate the threat. For example, the ARO of an earthquake in Tulsa may be .00001, whereas the ARO of an email virus in an office in Tulsa may be 10,000,000.

Annualized loss expectancy   The *annualized loss expectancy (ALE)* is the possible yearly cost of all instances of a specific realized threat against a specific asset.

The ALE is calculated using the following formula:

ALE = single loss expectancy (SLE) * annualized rate of occurrence (ARO)

Or more simply:

ALE = SLE * ARO

For example, if the SLE of an asset is $90,000 and the ARO for a specific threat (such as total power loss) is .5, then the ALE is $45,000. On the other hand, if the ARO for a specific threat (such as compromised user account) were 15, then the ALE would be $1,350,000.

Threat/Risk Calculations

The task of calculating EF, SLE, ARO, and ALE for every asset and every threat/risk is a daunting one. Fortunately, quantitative risk assessment software tools can simplify and automate much of this process. These tools produce an asset inventory with valuations and then, using predefined AROs along with some customizing options (that is, industry, geography, IT components, and so on), produce risk analysis reports. The following calculations are often involved.

Calculating annualized loss expectancy with a safeguard   In addition to determining the annual cost of the safeguard, you must calculate the ALE for the asset if the safeguard is implemented. This requires a new EF and ARO specific to the safeguard. In most cases, the EF to an asset remains the same even with an applied safeguard. (Recall that the EF is the amount of loss incurred if the risk becomes realized.) In other words, if the safeguard fails, how much damage does the asset receive? Think about it this way: If you have on body armor but the body armor fails to prevent a bullet from piercing your heart, you are still experiencing the same damage that would have occurred without the body armor. Thus, if the safeguard fails, the loss on the asset is usually the same as when there is no safeguard. However, some safeguards *do* reduce the resultant damage even when they fail to fully stop an attack. For example, body armor will absorb a significant amount of energy from a bullet and thus the bullet will cause less damage to the body.

Even if the EF remains the same, a safeguard changes the ARO. In fact, the whole point of a safeguard is to reduce the ARO. In other words, a safeguard should reduce the number of times an attack is successful in causing damage to an asset. The best of all possible safeguards would reduce the ARO to zero. Although there are some perfect safeguards, most are not. Thus, many safeguards have an applied ARO that is smaller (you hope much smaller) than the nonsafeguarded ARO, but it is not often zero. With the new ARO (and possible new EF), a new ALE with the application of a safeguard is computed.

With the pre-safeguard ALE and the post-safeguard ALE calculated, there is yet one more value needed to perform a cost/benefit analysis. This additional value is the annual cost of the safeguard.

Calculating safeguard costs   For each specific risk, you must evaluate one or more safeguards, or countermeasures, on a cost/benefit basis. To perform this evaluation, you must first compile a list of safeguards for each threat. Then you assign each safeguard a deployment value. In fact, you must measure the deployment value or the cost of the safeguard against the value of the protected asset. The value of the protected asset therefore determines the maximum expenditures for protection mechanisms. Security should be cost effective, and thus it is not prudent to spend more (in terms of cash or resources) protecting an asset than its value to the organization. If the cost of the countermeasure is greater than the value of the asset (that is, the cost of the risk), then you should accept the risk.

Numerous factors are involved in calculating the value of a countermeasure:

- Cost of purchase, development, and licensing
- Cost of implementation and customization

- Cost of annual operation, maintenance, administration, and so on
- Cost of annual repairs and upgrades
- Productivity improvement or loss
- Changes to environment
- Cost of testing and evaluation

Once you know the potential cost of a safeguard, it is then possible to evaluate the benefit of that safeguard if applied to an infrastructure. As mentioned earlier, the annual costs of safeguards should not exceed the expected annual cost of asset loss.

Calculating Safeguard Cost/Benefit   One of the final computations in this process is the cost/benefit calculation to determine whether a safeguard actually improves security without costing too much. To make the determination of whether the safeguard is financially equitable, use the following formula:

ALE before safeguard – ALE after implementing the safeguard – annual cost of safeguard (ACS) = value of the safeguard to the company

If the result is negative, the safeguard is not a financially responsible choice. If the result is positive, then that value is the annual savings your organization may reap by deploying the safeguard because the rate of occurrence is not a guarantee of occurrence.

The annual savings or loss from a safeguard should not be the only consideration when evaluating safeguards. You should also consider the issues of legal responsibility and prudent due care. In some cases, it makes more sense to lose money in the deployment of a safeguard than to risk legal liability in the event of an asset disclosure or loss.

In review, to perform the cost/benefit analysis of a safeguard, you must calculate the following three elements:

- The pre-countermeasure ALE for an asset-and-threat pairing
- The post-countermeasure ALE for an asset-and-threat pairing
- The ACS

With those elements, you can finally obtain a value for the cost/benefit formula for this specific safeguard against a specific risk against a specific asset:

(pre-countermeasure ALE – post-countermeasure ALE) – ACS

Or, even more simply:

(ALE1 – ALE2) – ACS

The countermeasure with the greatest resulting value from this cost/benefit formula makes the most economic sense to deploy against the specific asset-and-threat pairing.

Table 6.1 illustrates the various formulas associated with quantitative risk analysis.

TABLE 6.1   Quantitative risk analysis formulas

Concept	Formula
Exposure factor (EF)	%
Single loss expectancy (SLE)	SLE = AV * EF
Annualized rate of occurrence (ARO)	# / year
Annualized loss expectancy (ALE)	ALE = SLE * ARO or ALE = AV * EF * ARO
Annual cost of the safeguard (ACS)	$ / year
Value or benefit of a safeguard	(ALE1 – ALE2) – ACS

Yikes, So Much Math!

Yes, quantitative risk analysis involves a lot of math. Math questions on the exam are likely to involve basic multiplication. Most likely, you will be asked definition, application, and concept synthesis questions on the CISSP exam. This means you need to know the definition of the equations/formulas and values, what they mean, why they are important, and how they are used to benefit an organization. The concepts you must know are AV, EF, SLE, ARO, ALE, and the cost/benefit formula.

It is important to realize that with all the calculations used in the quantitative risk assessment process, the end values are used for prioritization and selection. The values themselves do not truly reflect real-world loss or costs due to security breaches. This should be obvious because of the level of guesswork, statistical analysis, and probability predictions required in the process.

Once you have calculated a cost/benefit for each safeguard for each risk that affects each asset, you must then sort these values. In most cases, the cost/benefit with the highest value is the best safeguard to implement for that specific risk against a specific asset. But as all things in the real world, this is only one part of the decision-making process. Although very important and often the primary guiding factor, it is not the sole element of data. Other items include actual cost, security budget, compatibility with existing systems, skill/knowledge base of IT staff, and availability of product as well as political issues, partnerships, market trends, fads, marketing, contracts, and favoritism. As part of senior management or even the IT staff, is it your responsibility to either obtain or use all available data and information to make the best security decision for your organization.

Most organizations have a limited and all-to-finite budget to work with. Thus, obtaining the best security for the cost is an essential part of security management. To effectively manage the security function, you must assess the budget, the benefit and performance metrics, and the necessary resources of each security control. Only after a thorough evaluation can you determine which controls are essential and beneficial not only to security, but also your bottom line.

Qualitative Risk Analysis

Qualitative risk analysis is more scenario based than it is calculator based. Rather than assigning exact dollar figures to possible losses, you rank threats on a scale to evaluate their risks, costs, and effects. Since a purely quantitative risk assessment is not possible, balancing the results of a quantitative analysis is essential. The method of combining quantitative and qualitative analysis into a final assessment of organizational risk is known as hybrid assessment or hybrid analysis. The process of performing qualitative risk analysis involves judgment, intuition, and experience. You can use many techniques to perform qualitative risk analysis:

- Brainstorming
- Delphi technique
- Storyboarding
- Focus groups
- Surveys
- Questionnaires
- Checklists
- One-on-one meetings
- Interviews

Determining which mechanism to employ is based on the culture of the organization and the types of risks and assets involved. It is common for several methods to be employed simultaneously and their results compared and contrasted in the final risk analysis report to upper management.

Scenarios

The basic process for all these mechanisms involves the creation of scenarios. A *scenario* is a written description of a single major threat. The description focuses on how a threat would be instigated and what effects its occurrence could have on the organization, the IT infrastructure, and specific assets. Generally, the scenarios are limited to one page of text to keep them manageable. For each scenario, one or more safeguards are described that would completely or partially protect against the major threat discussed in the scenario. The analysis participants then assign to the scenario a threat level, a loss potential, and the advantages of each safeguard. These assignments can be grossly simple—such as High, Medium, and Low or a basic number scale of 1 to 10—or they can be detailed essay responses. The responses from all participants are then compiled into a single report that is presented to upper management. For examples of reference ratings and levels, please see Table 3-6 and Table 3-7 in NIST SP 800-30:

http://csrc.nist.gov/publications/nistpubs/800-30/sp800-30.pdf

The usefulness and validity of a qualitative risk analysis improves as the number and diversity of the participants in the evaluation increases. Whenever possible, include one or more people from each level of the organizational hierarchy, from upper management to end user. It is also important to include a cross section from each major department, division, office, or branch.

Delphi Technique

The *Delphi technique* is probably the only mechanism on the previous list that is not immediately recognizable and understood. The Delphi technique is simply an anonymous feedback-and-response process used to enable a group to reach an anonymous consensus. Its primary purpose is to elicit honest and uninfluenced responses from all participants. The participants are usually gathered into a single meeting room. To each request for feedback, each participant writes down their response on paper anonymously. The results are compiled and presented to the group for evaluation. The process is repeated until a consensus is reached.

Both the quantitative and qualitative risk analysis mechanisms offer useful results. However, each technique involves a unique method of evaluating the same set of assets and risks. Prudent due care requires that both methods be employed. Table 6.2 describes the benefits and disadvantages of these two systems.

TABLE 6.2   Comparison of quantitative and qualitative risk analysis

Characteristic	Qualitative	Quantitative
Employs complex functions	No	Yes
Uses cost/benefit analysis	No	Yes
Results in specific values	No	Yes
Requires guesswork	Yes	No
Supports automation	No	Yes
Involves a high volume of information	No	Yes
Is objective	No	Yes
Uses opinions	Yes	No
Requires significant time and effort	No	Yes
Offers useful and meaningful results	Yes	Yes

Handle Risk

The results of risk analysis are many:

- Complete and detailed valuation of all assets

- An exhaustive list of all threats and risks, rate of occurrence, and extent of loss if realized

- A list of threat-specific safeguards and countermeasures that identifies their effectiveness and ALE

- A cost/benefit analysis of each safeguard

This information is essential for management to make educated, intelligent decisions about safeguard implementation and security policy alterations.

Once the risk analysis is complete, management must address each specific risk. There are four possible responses to risk:

- Reduce or mitigate

- Assign or transfer

- Accept

- Reject or ignore

You need to know the following information about the four responses:

Risk mitigation   Reducing risk, or risk mitigation, is the implementation of safeguards and countermeasures to eliminate vulnerabilities or block threats. Picking the most cost-effective or beneficial countermeasure is part of risk management, but it is not an element of risk assessment. In fact, countermeasure selection is a post-risk-assessment or -risk-analysis activity. Another potential variation of risk mitigation is risk avoidance. The risk is avoided by eliminating the risk cause. A simple example is removing the FTP protocol from a server to avoid FTP attacks, and a larger example is to move to an inland location to avoid the risks from hurricanes.

Risk assignment   Assigning risk or transferring risk is the placement of the cost of loss a risk represents onto another entity or organization. Purchasing insurance and outsourcing are common forms of assigning or transferring risk.

Risk acceptance   Accepting risk, or acceptance of risk, is the valuation by management of the cost/benefit analysis of possible safeguards and the determination that the cost of the countermeasure greatly outweighs the possible cost of loss due to a risk. It also means that management has agreed to accept the consequences and the loss if the risk is realized. In most cases, accepting risk requires a clearly written statement that indicates why a safeguard was not implemented, who is responsible for the decision, and who will be responsible for the loss if the risk is realized, usually in the form of a sign-off letter. An organization's decision to accept risk is based on its risk tolerance. Risk tolerance is the ability of an organization to absorb the losses associated with realized risks.

Risk rejection   A final but unacceptable possible response to risk is to reject or ignore risk. Denying that a risk exists or hoping that it will never be realized are not valid or prudent due-care responses to risk.

Once countermeasures are implemented, the risk that remains is known as *residual risk*. Residual risk comprises threats to specific assets against which upper management chooses not to implement a safeguard. In other words, residual risk is the risk that management has chosen to accept rather than mitigate. In most cases, the presence of residual risk indicates that the cost/benefit analysis showed that the available safeguards were not cost-effective deterrents.

Total risk is the amount of risk an organization would face if no safeguards were implemented. A formula for total risk is as follows:

threats * vulnerabilities * asset value = total risk

(Note that the * here does not imply multiplication, but a combination function; this is not a true mathematical formula.) The difference between total risk and residual risk is known as the *controls gap*. The controls gap is the amount of risk that is reduced by implementing safeguards. A formula for residual risk is as follows:

total risk − controls gap = residual risk

As with risk management in general, handling risk is not a one-time process. Instead, security must be continually maintained and reaffirmed. In fact, repeating the risk assessment and analysis process is a mechanism to assess the completeness and effectiveness of the security program over time. Additionally, it helps locate deficiencies and areas where change has occurred. Because security changes over time, reassessing on a periodic basis is essential to maintaining reasonable security.

Selecting a countermeasure within the realm of risk management relies heavily on the cost/benefit analysis results. However, you should consider several other factors:

- The cost of the countermeasure should be less than the value of the asset.

- The cost of the countermeasure should be less than the benefit of the countermeasure.

- The result of the applied countermeasure should make the cost of an attack greater for the perpetrator than the derived benefit from an attack.

- The countermeasure should provide a solution to a real and identified problem. (Don't install countermeasures just because they are available, are advertised, or sound cool.)

- The benefit of the countermeasure should not be dependent upon its secrecy. This means that "security through obscurity" is not a viable countermeasure and that any viable countermeasure can withstand public disclosure and scrutiny.

- The benefit of the countermeasure should be testable and verifiable.

- The countermeasure should provide consistent and uniform protection across all users, systems, protocols, and so on.

- The countermeasure should have few or no dependencies to reduce cascade failures.

- The countermeasure should require minimal human intervention after initial deployment and configuration.

- The countermeasure should be tamperproof.

- The countermeasure should have overrides accessible to privileged operators only.

- The countermeasure should provide fail-safe and/or fail-secure options.

Manage Personnel Security

Humans are the weakest element in any security solution. No matter what physical or logical controls are deployed, humans can discover ways to avoid them, circumvent or subvert them, or disable them. Thus, it is important to take into account the humanity of your users when designing and deploying security solutions for your environment. To understand and apply security governance, you must address the weakest link in your security chain—namely, people.

Issues, problems, and compromises related to humans occur at all stages of a security solution development. This is because humans are involved throughout the development, deployment, and ongoing administration of any solution. Therefore, you must evaluate the effect users, designers, programmers, developers, managers, and implementers have on the process.

Hiring new staff typically involves several distinct steps: creating a job description, setting a classification for the job, screening employment candidates, and hiring and training the one best suited for the job. Without a job description, there is no consensus on what type of individual should be hired. Thus, crafting job descriptions is the first step in defining security needs related to personnel and being able to seek out new hires. Personnel should be added to an organization because there is a need for their specific skills and experience. Any job description for any position within an organization should address relevant security issues. You must consider items such as whether the position requires the handling of sensitive material or access to classified information. In effect, the job description defines the roles to which an employee needs to be assigned to perform their work tasks. The job description should define the type and extent of access the position requires on the secured network. Once these issues have been resolved, assigning a security classification to the job description is fairly standard.

The Importance of Job Descriptions

Job descriptions are important to the design and support of a security solution. However, many organizations either have overlooked this or have allowed job descriptions to become stale and out-of-sync with reality. Try to track down your job description. Do you even have one? If so, when was it last updated? Does it accurately reflect your job? Does it describe the type of security access you need to perform the prescribed job responsibilities?

Important elements in constructing job descriptions that are in line with organizational processes include separation of duties, job responsibilities, and job rotation.

Separation of duties   Separation of duties is the security concept in which critical, significant, and sensitive work tasks are divided among several individual administrators or high-level operators. This prevents any one person from having the ability to undermine or subvert vital security mechanisms. Think of separation of duties as the application of the principle of least privilege to administrators. Separation of duties is also a protection against *collusion*, which is the occurrence of negative activity undertaken by two or more people, often for the purposes of fraud, theft, or espionage.

Job responsibilities   Job responsibilities are the specific work tasks an employee is required to perform on a regular basis. Depending on their responsibilities, employees require access to various objects, resources, and services. On a secured network, users must be granted access privileges for those elements related to their work tasks. To maintain the greatest security, access should be assigned according to the principle of least privilege. The principle of least privilege states that in a secured environment, users should be granted the minimum amount of access necessary for them to complete their required work tasks or job responsibilities. True application of this principle requires low-level granular access control over all resources and functions.

Job rotation   Job rotation, or rotating employees among numerous job positions, is simply a means by which an organization improves its overall security. Job rotation serves two functions. First, it provides a type of knowledge redundancy. When multiple employees are all capable of performing the work tasks required by several job positions, the organization is less likely to experience serious downtime or loss in productivity if an illness or other incident keeps one or more employees out of work for an extended period of time.

Second, moving personnel around reduces the risk of fraud, data modification, theft, sabotage, and misuse of information. The longer a person works in a specific position, the more likely they are to be assigned additional work tasks and thus expand their privileges and access. As a person becomes increasingly familiar with their work tasks, they may abuse their privileges for personal gain or malice. If misuse or abuse is committed by one employee, it will be easier to detect by another employee who knows the job position and work responsibilities. Therefore, job rotation also provides a form of peer auditing and protects against collusion. Job rotation is also known as cross-training.

When multiple people work together to perpetrate a crime, it's called collusion. Employing the principles of separation of duties, restricted job responsibilities, and job rotation reduces the likelihood that a co-worker will be willing to collaborate on an illegal or abusive scheme because of the higher risk of detection. Collusion and other privilege abuses can be reduced through strict monitoring of special privileges, such as those of an administrator, backup operator, user manager, and others.

Job descriptions are not used exclusively for the hiring process; they should be maintained throughout the life of the organization. Only through detailed job descriptions can a comparison be made between what a person should be responsible for and what they actually are responsible for. It is a managerial task to ensure that job descriptions overlap as little as possible and that one worker's responsibilities do not drift or encroach on those of another. Likewise, managers should audit privilege assignments to ensure that workers do not obtain access that is not strictly required for them to accomplish their work tasks.

Screening and Background Checks

Employment candidate screening for a specific position is based on the sensitivity and classification defined by the job description. The sensitivity and classification of a specific position is dependent upon the level of harm that could be caused by accidental or intentional violations of security by a person in the position. Thus, the thoroughness of the screening process should reflect the security of the position to be filled.

Employment candidate screening, background checks, and security clearance validation are essential elements in proving that a candidate is adequate, qualified, and trustworthy for a secured position. Background checks include obtaining a candidate's work and educational history; reference checks; education verification; interviewing colleagues, neighbors, and friends; checking police and government records for arrests or illegal activities; verifying identity through fingerprints, driver's license, and birth certificate; and holding a personal interview. This process could also include a polygraph test, drug testing, and personality testing/evaluation.

Performing online background checks and reviewing the social networking accounts of applicants has become standard practice for many organizations. If a potential employee has posted inappropriate materials to their photo sharing site, social networking biographies, or public instant messaging services, then they are not as attractive a candidate as those who did not. Our actions in the public eye become permanent when they are recorded in text, photo, or video and then posted online. A general picture of a person's attitude, intelligence, loyalty, common sense, diligence, honesty, respect, consistency, and adherence to social norms and/or corporate culture can be gleaned quickly by viewing a person's online identity.

Employment Agreements

When a new employee is hired, they should sign an employment agreement. Such a document outlines the rules and restrictions of the organization, the security policy, the acceptable use and activities policies, details of the job description, violations and consequences, and the length of time the position is to be filled by the employee. These items might be separate documents. In such a case, the employment agreement is used to verify that the employment candidate has read and understood the associated documentation for their prospective job position.

In addition to employment agreements, there may be other security-related documentation that must be addressed. One common document is a *nondisclosure agreement (NDA)*. An NDA is used to protect the confidential information within an organization from being disclosed by a former employee. When a person signs an NDA, they agree not to disclose any information that is defined as confidential to anyone outside the organization. Violations of an NDA are often met with strict penalties.

⊕ **Real World Scenario**

NCA: The NDA's Evil Twin

The NDA has a common companion contract known as the *noncompete agreement (NCA)*. The noncompete agreement attempts to prevent an employee with special knowledge of secrets from one organization from working in a competing organization in order to prevent that second organization from benefiting from the worker's special knowledge of secrets. NCAs are also used to prevent workers from jumping from one company to another competing company just because of salary increases or other incentives. Often NCAs have a time limit, such as six months, one year, or even three years. The goal is to allow the original company to maintain its competitive edge by keeping its human resources working for its benefit rather than against it.

Many companies require new hires to sign NCAs. However, fully enforcing an NCA in court is often a difficult battle. The court recognizes the need for a worker to be able to work using the skills and knowledge they have in order to provide for themselves and their families. If the NCA would prevent a person from earning a reasonable income, the courts often invalidate the NCA or prevent its consequences from being realized.

Even if an NCA is not always enforceable in court, however, that does not mean it doesn't have benefits to the original company, such as the following:

- The threat of a lawsuit because of NCA violations is often sufficient incentive to prevent a worker from violating the terms of secrecy when they seek employment with a new company.

- If a worker does violate the terms of the NCA, then even without specifically defined consequences being levied by court restrictions, the time and effort, not to mention the cost, of battling the issue in court is a deterrent.

Did you sign an NCA when you were hired? If so, do you know the terms and the potential consequences if you break that NCA?

Throughout the employment lifetime of personnel, managers should regularly audit the job descriptions, work tasks, privileges, and so on for every staff member. It is common for work tasks and privileges to drift over time. This can cause some tasks to be overlooked and others to be performed multiple times. Drifting can also result in security violations. Regularly reviewing the boundaries of each job description in relation to what is actually occurring aids in keeping security violations to a minimum.

A key part of this review process is enforcing mandatory vacations. In many secured environments, mandatory vacations of one to two weeks are used to audit and verify the work tasks and privileges of employees. The vacation removes the employee from the work environment and places a different worker in their position, which makes it easier to detect abuse, fraud, or negligence on the part of the original employee.

Vendor, Consultant, and Contractor Controls

Vendor, consultant, and contractor controls are used to define the levels of performance, expectation, compensation, and consequences for entities, persons, or organizations that are external to the primary organization. Often these controls are defined in a document or policy known as a service-level agreement (SLA).

Using SLAs is an increasingly popular way to ensure that organizations providing services to internal and/or external customers maintain an appropriate level of service agreed upon by both the service provider and the vendor. It's a wise move to put SLAs in place for any data circuits, applications, information processing systems, databases, or other critical components that are vital to your organization's continued viability. The following issues are commonly addressed in SLAs:

- System uptime (as a percentage of overall operating time)
- Maximum consecutive downtime (in seconds/minutes/and so on)
- Peak load
- Average load
- Responsibility for diagnostics
- Failover time (if redundancy is in place)

SLAs also commonly include financial and other contractual remedies that kick in if the agreement is not maintained. For example, if a critical circuit is down for more than 15 minutes, the service provider might agree to waive all charges on that circuit for one week.

SLAs and vendor, consultant, and contractor controls are an important part of risk reduction and risk avoidance. By clearly defining the expectations and penalties for external parties, everyone involved knows what is expected of them and what the consequences are in the event of a failure to meet those expectations. While it may be very cost effective to use outside providers for a variety of business functions or services, it does increase potential risk by expanding the potential attack surface and range of vulnerabilities. SLAs should include a focus on protecting and improving security in addition to ensuring quality and timely services at a reasonable price.

Employee Termination

When an employee must be terminated, numerous issues must be addressed. An employee termination process or procedure policy is essential to maintaining a secure environment when a disgruntled employee must be removed from the organization. The reactions of terminated employees can range from calm, understanding acceptance to violent, destructive rage. A sensible procedure for handling terminations must be designed and implemented to reduce incidents.

The termination of an employee should be handled in a private and respectful manner. However, this does not mean that precautions should not be taken. Terminations should take place with at least one witness, preferably a higher-level manager and/or a security guard. Once the employee has been informed of their release, they should be escorted off the premises and not allowed to return to their work area without an escort for any reason. Before the employee is released, all organization-specific identification, access, or security badges as well as cards, keys, and access tokens should be collected. Generally, the best time to terminate an employee is at the end of their shift midweek. A early to midweek termination provides the ex-employee with time to file for unemployment and/or start looking for new employment before the weekend. Also, end-of-shift terminations allow the worker to leave with other employees in a more natural departure, thus reducing stress.

When possible, an exit interview should be performed. However, this typically depends upon the mental state of the employee upon release and numerous other factors. If an exit interview is unfeasible immediately upon termination, it should be conducted as soon as possible. The primary purpose of the exit interview is to review the liabilities and restrictions placed on the former employee based on the employment agreement, nondisclosure agreement, and any other security-related documentation.

The following list includes some other issues that should be handled as soon as possible:

- Make sure the employee returns any organizational equipment or supplies from their vehicle or home.

- Remove or disable the employee's network user account.

- Notify human resources to issue a final paycheck, pay any unused vacation time, and terminate benefit coverage.

- Arrange for a member of the security department to accompany the released employee while they gather their personal belongings from the work area.

- Inform all security personnel and anyone else who watches or monitors any entrance point to ensure that the ex-employee does not attempt to reenter the building without an escort.

In most cases, you should disable or remove an employee's system access at the same time or just before they are notified of being terminated. This is especially true if that employee is capable of accessing confidential data or has the expertise or access to alter or damage data or services. Failing to restrict released employees' activities can leave your organization open to a wide range of vulnerabilities, including theft and destruction of both physical property and logical data.

 Real World Scenario

Firing: Not Just a Pink Slip Anymore

Firing an employee has become a complex process. Gone are the days of firing merely by placing a pink slip in an employee's mail slot. In most IT-centric organizations, termination can create a situation in which the employee could cause harm, putting the organization at risk. That's why you need a well-designed exit interview process.

However, just having the process isn't enough. It has to be followed correctly every time. Unfortunately, this doesn't always happen. You might have heard of some fiasco caused by a botched termination procedure. Common examples include performing any of the following before the employee is officially informed of their termination (thus giving the employee prior warning of their termination):

- The IT department requesting the return of a notebook

- Disabling a network account

- Blocking a person's PIN or smart card for building entrance

- Revoking a parking pass

- Distributing a company reorganization chart

- Positioning a new employee in the cubicle

- Allowing layoff information to be leaked to the media

It should go without saying that in order for the exit interview and safe termination processes to function properly, they must be implemented in the correct order and at the correct time (that is, at the start of the exit interview), as in the following example:

- Inform the person that they are relieved of their job.

- Request the return of all access badges, keys, and company equipment.

- Disable the person's electronic access to all aspects of the organization.

- Remind the person about the NDA obligations.

- Escort the person off the premises.

Develop and Manage Security Education, Training, and Awareness

The successful implementation of a security solution requires changes in user behavior. These changes primarily consist of alterations in normal work activities to comply with the standards, guidelines, and procedures mandated by the security policy. Behavior modification involves some level of learning on the part of the user. To develop and manage security education, training, and awareness, all relevant items of knowledge transference must be clearly identified and programs of presentation, exposure, synergy, and implementation crafted.

A prerequisite to actual security training is *awareness*. The goal of creating awareness is to bring security into the forefront and make it a recognized entity for users. Awareness establishes a common baseline or foundation of security understanding across the entire organization and focuses on key or basic topics and issues related to security that all employees must understand and comprehend. Awareness is not exclusively created through a classroom type of exercise but also through the work environment. Many tools can be used to create awareness, such as posters, notices, newsletter articles, screen savers, T-shirts, rally speeches by managers, announcements, presentations, mouse pads, office supplies, and memos as well as the traditional instructor-led training courses.

Awareness establishes a minimum standard common denominator or foundation of security understanding. All personnel should be fully aware of their security responsibilities and liabilities. They should be trained to know what to do and what not to do.

The issues that users need to be aware of include avoiding waste, fraud, and unauthorized activities. All members of an organization, from senior management to temporary interns, need the same level of awareness. The awareness program in an organization should be tied in with its security policy, incident-handling plan, and disaster recovery procedures. For an awareness-building program to be effective, it must be fresh, creative, and updated often. The awareness program should also be tied to an understanding of how the corporate culture will affect and impact security for individuals as well as the organization as a whole. If employees do not see enforcement of security policies and standards, especially at the awareness level, then they may not feel obligated to abide by them.

Training is teaching employees to perform their work tasks and to comply with the security policy. Training is typically hosted by an organization and is targeted to groups of employees with similar job functions. All new employees require some level of training so they will be able to comply with all standards, guidelines, and procedures mandated by the security policy. New users need to know how to use the IT infrastructure, where data is stored, and how and why resources are classified. Many organizations choose to train new employees before they are granted access to the network, whereas others will grant new users limited access until their training in their specific job position is complete. Training is an ongoing activity that must be sustained throughout the lifetime of the organization for every employee. It is considered an administrative security control.

Awareness and training are often provided in-house. That means these teaching tools are created and deployed by and within the organization itself. However, the next level of knowledge distribution is usually obtained from an external third-party source.

Education is a more detailed endeavor in which students/users learn much more than they actually need to know to perform their work tasks. Education is most often associated with users pursuing certification or seeking job promotion. It is typically a requirement for personnel seeking security professional positions. A security professional requires extensive knowledge of security and the local environment for the entire organization and not just their specific work tasks.

Manage the Security Function

To manage the security function, an organization must implement proper and sufficient security governance. The act of performing a risk assessment to drive the security policy is the clearest and most direct example of management of the security function.

Security must be cost effective. Organizations do not have infinite budgets and thus must allocate their funds appropriately. Additionally, an organizational budget includes a percentage of monies dedicated to security just as most other business tasks and processes require capital, not to mention payments to employees, insurance, retirement, and so on. Security should be sufficient to withstand typical or standard threats to the organization but not when such security is more expensive than the assets being protected. As discussed in "Risk Management" earlier in this chapter, a countermeasure that is more costly than the value of the asset itself is not usually an effective solution.

Security must be measurable. Measurable security means that the various aspects of the security mechanisms actually function, provide a clear benefit, and have one or more metrics that can be recorded and analyzed. Similar to performance metrics, security metrics are measurements of performance, function, operation, action, and so on as related to the operation of a security feature. When a countermeasure or safeguard is implemented, security metrics should show a reduction in unwanted occurrences or an increase in the detection of attempts. Otherwise, the security mechanism is not providing the expected benefit. The act of measuring and evaluating security metrics is the practice of assessing the completeness and effectiveness of the security program. This should also include measuring it against common security guidelines and tracking the success of its controls. Tracking and assessing security metrics are part of effective security governance. However, it is worth noting that choosing incorrect security metrics can cause significant problems, such as choosing to monitor or measure something the security staff has little control over or that is based on external drivers.

Resources will be consumed both by the security mechanisms themselves and by the security governance processes. Obviously, security mechanisms should consume as few resources as possible and impact the productivity or throughput of a system at as low a level as feasible. However, every hardware and software countermeasure as well as every policy and procedure users must follow will consume resources. Being aware of and evaluating resource consumption before and after countermeasure selection, deployment, and tuning is an important part of security governance and managing the security function.

Managing the security function includes the development and implementation of information security strategies. This task is mostly addressed in this chapter in the section "Risk Management" and in Chapter 5 in the section "Develop and Implement Security Policy." However, this topic is not limited to these sections and chapters. Most of the content of the CISSP exam, and hence this book, addresses the various aspects of development and implementation of information security strategies.

Summary

Third-party governance is a system of oversight that is sometimes mandated by law, regulation, industry standards, or licensing requirements. The actual method of governance can vary, but it generally involves an outside investigator or auditor. Auditors might be designated by a governing body, or they might be consultants hired by the target organization.

The process of identifying, evaluating, and preventing or reducing risks is known as risk management. The primary goal of risk management is to reduce risk to an acceptable level. Determining this level depends upon the organization, the value of its assets, and the size of its budget. Although it is impossible to design and deploy a completely risk-free environment, it is possible to significantly reduce risk with little effort. Risk analysis is the process by which risk management is achieved and includes analyzing an environment for risks, evaluating each risk as to its likelihood of occurring and the cost of the resulting damage, assessing the cost of various countermeasures for each risk, and creating a cost/benefit report for safeguards to present to upper management.

When planning a security solution, it's important to consider how humans are the weakest element. Regardless of the physical or logical controls deployed, humans can discover ways to avoid them, circumvent or subvert them, or disable them. Thus, it is important to take users into account when designing and deploying security solutions for your environment. The aspects of secure hiring practices, roles, policies, standards, guidelines, procedures, risk management, awareness training, and management planning all contribute to protecting assets. The use of these security structures provides some protection from the threat humans present against your security solutions.

Secure hiring practices require detailed job descriptions. Job descriptions are used as a guide for selecting candidates and properly evaluating them for a position. Maintaining security through job descriptions includes the use of separation of duties, job responsibilities, and job rotation.

A termination policy is needed to protect an organization and its existing employees. The termination procedure should include witnesses, return of company property, disabling network access, an exit interview, and an escort from the property.

For a security solution to be successfully implemented, user behavior must change. Such changes primarily consist of alterations in normal work activities to comply with the standards, guidelines, and procedures mandated by the security policy. Behavior modification involves some level of learning on the part of the user. There are three commonly recognized learning levels: awareness, training, and education.

Exam Essentials

Be able to discuss third-party governance of security.   Third-party governance is the system of oversight that may be mandated by law, regulation, industry standards, or licensing requirements.

Be able to define overall risk management.   The process of identifying factors that could damage or disclose data, evaluating those factors in light of data value and countermeasure cost, and implementing cost-effective solutions for mitigating or reducing risk is known as risk management. By performing risk management, you lay the foundation for reducing risk overall.

Understand risk analysis and the key elements involved.   Risk analysis is the process by which upper management is provided with details to make decisions about which risks are to be mitigated, which should be transferred, and which should be accepted. To fully evaluate risks and subsequently take the proper precautions, you must analyze the following: assets, asset valuation, threats, vulnerability, exposure, risk, realized risk, safeguards, countermeasures, attacks, and breaches.

Know how to evaluate threats.   Threats can originate from numerous sources, including IT, humans, and nature. Threat assessment should be performed as a team effort to provide the widest range of perspectives. By fully evaluating risks from all angles, you reduce your system's vulnerability.

Understand quantitative risk analysis.   Quantitative risk analysis focuses on hard values and percentages. A complete quantitative analysis is not possible because of intangible aspects of risk. The process involves asset valuation and threat identification and then determining a threat's potential frequency and the resulting damage; the result is a cost/benefit analysis of safeguards.

Be able to explain the concept of an exposure factor (EF).   An exposure factor is an element of quantitative risk analysis that represents the percentage of loss that an organization would experience if a specific asset were violated by a realized risk. By calculating exposure factors, you are able to implement a sound risk management policy.

Know what single loss expectancy (SLE) is and how to calculate it.   SLE is an element of quantitative risk analysis that represents the cost associated with a single realized risk against a specific asset. The formula is SLE = asset value (AV) * exposure factor (EF).

Understand annualized rate of occurrence (ARO).   ARO is an element of quantitative risk analysis that represents the expected frequency with which a specific threat or risk will occur (in other words, become realized) within a single year. Understanding AROs further enables you to calculate the risk and take proper precautions.

Know what annualized loss expectancy (ALE) is and how to calculate it.   ALE is an element of quantitative risk analysis that represents the possible yearly cost of all instances of a specific realized threat against a specific asset. The formula is ALE = single loss expectancy (SLE) * annualized rate of occurrence (ARO).

Know the formula for safeguard evaluation.   In addition to determining the annual cost of a safeguard, you must calculate the ALE for the asset if the safeguard is implemented. Use the formula: ALE before safeguard − ALE after implementing the safeguard − annual cost of safeguard = value of the safeguard to the company, or (ALE1 − ALE2) − ACS.

Understand qualitative risk analysis.   Qualitative risk analysis is based more on scenarios than calculations. Exact dollar figures are not assigned to possible losses; instead, threats are ranked on a scale to evaluate their risks, costs, and effects. Such an analysis assists those responsible in creating proper risk management policies.

Understand the Delphi technique.   The Delphi technique is simply an anonymous feedback-and-response process used to arrive at a consensus. Such a consensus gives the responsible parties the opportunity to properly evaluate risks and implement solutions.

Know the options for handling risk.   Reducing risk, or risk mitigation, is the implementation of safeguards and countermeasures. Assigning risk or transferring a risk places the cost of loss a risk represents onto another entity or organization. Purchasing insurance is one form of assigning or transferring risk. Accepting risk means the management has evaluated the cost/benefit analysis of possible safeguards and has determined that the cost of the countermeasure greatly outweighs the possible cost of loss due to a risk. It also means that management has agreed to accept the consequences and the loss if the risk is realized.

Be able to explain total risk, residual risk, and controls gap.   Total risk is the amount of risk an organization would face if no safeguards were implemented. To calculate total risk, use this formula: threats * vulnerabilities * asset value = total risk. Residual risk is the risk that management has chosen to accept rather than mitigate. The difference between total risk and residual risk is the controls gap, which is the amount of risk that is reduced by implementing safeguards. To calculate residual risk, use the following formula: total risk − controls gap = residual risk.

Understand the security implications of hiring new employees.   To properly plan for security, you must have standards in place for job descriptions, job classification, work tasks, job responsibilities, preventing collusion, candidate screening, background checks, security clearances, employment agreements, and nondisclosure agreements. By deploying such mechanisms, you ensure that new hires are aware of the required security standards, thus protecting your organization's assets.

Be able to explain separation of duties.   Separation of duties is the security concept of dividing critical, significant, sensitive work tasks among several individuals. By separating duties in this manner, you ensure that no one person can compromise system security.

Understand the principle of least privilege.   The principle of least privilege states that in a secured environment, users should be granted the minimum amount of access necessary for them to complete their required work tasks or job responsibilities. By limiting user access only to those items that they need to complete their work tasks, you limit the vulnerability of sensitive information.

Know why job rotation and mandatory vacations are necessary.   Job rotation serves two functions. It provides a type of knowledge redundancy, and moving personnel around reduces the risk of fraud, data modification, theft, sabotage, and misuse of information. Mandatory vacations of one to two weeks are used to audit and verify the work tasks and privileges of employees. This often results in easy detection of abuse, fraud, or negligence.

Understand vendor, consultant, and contractor controls.   Vendor, consultant, and contractor controls are used to define the levels of performance, expectation, compensation, and consequences for entities, persons, or organizations that are external to the primary organization. Often these controls are defined in a document or policy known as an service-level agreement (SLA).

Be able to explain proper termination policies. A termination policy defines the procedure for terminating employees. It should include items such as always having a witness, disabling the employee's network access, and performing an exit interview. A termination policy should also include escorting the terminated employee off the premises and requiring the return of security tokens and badges and company property.

Know how to implement security awareness training and education. Before actual training can take place, awareness of security as a recognized entity must be created for users. Once this is accomplished, training, or teaching employees to perform their work tasks and to comply with the security policy, can begin. All new employees require some level of training so they will be able to comply with all standards, guidelines, and procedures mandated by the security policy. Education is a more detailed endeavor in which students/users learn much more than they actually need to know to perform their work tasks. Education is most often associated with users pursuing certification or seeking job promotion.

Understand how to manage the security function. To manage the security function, an organization must implement proper and sufficient security governance. The act of performing a risk assessment to drive the security policy is the clearest and most direct example of management of the security function. This also relates to budget, metrics, resources, information security strategies, and assessing the completeness and effectiveness of the security program.

Written Lab

1. Name six different administrative controls used to secure personnel.

2. What are the basic formulas used in quantitative risk assessment?

3. Describe the process or technique used to reach an anonymous consensus during a qualitative risk assessment?

4. Discuss the need to perform a balanced risk assessment. What are the techniques that can be used and why is this necessary?

Review Questions

1. Which of the following is the weakest element in any security solution?

   A. Software products

   B. Internet connections

   C. Security policies

   D. Humans

2. When seeking to hire new employees, what is the first step?

   A. Create a job description.

   B. Set position classification.

   C. Screen candidates.

   D. Request resumes.

3. Which of the following is a primary purpose of an exit interview?

   A. To return the exiting employee's personal belongings

   B. To review the nondisclosure agreement

   C. To evaluate the exiting employee's performance

   D. To cancel the exiting employee's network access accounts

4. When an employee is to be terminated, which of the following should be done?

   A. Inform the employee a few hours before they are officially terminated.

   B. Disable the employee's network access just as they are informed of the termination.

   C. Send out a broadcast email informing everyone that a specific employee is to be terminated.

   D. Wait until you and the employee are the only people remaining in the building before announcing the termination.

5. If an organization contracts with outside entities to provide key business functions or services, such as account or technical support, what is the process called that is used to ensure that these entities support sufficient security?

   A. Asset identification

   B. Third-party governance

   C. Exit interview

   D. Qualitative analysis

6. A portion of the _____ is the logical and practical investigation of business processes and organizational policies. This process/policy review ensures that the stated and implemented business tasks, systems, and methodologies are practical, efficient, cost-effective, but most of all (at least in relation to security governance) that they support security through the reduction of vulnerabilities and the avoidance, reduction, or mitigation of risk.

    A. Hybrid assessment

    B. Risk aversion process

    C. Countermeasure selection

    D. Documentation review

7. Which of the following statements is *not* true?

    A. IT security can provide protection only against logical or technical attacks.

    B. The process by which the goals of risk management are achieved is known as risk analysis.

    C. Risks to an IT infrastructure are all computer based.

    D. An asset is anything used in a business process or task.

8. Which of the following is *not* an element of the risk analysis process?

    A. Analyzing an environment for risks

    B. Creating a cost/benefit report for safeguards to present to upper management

    C. Selecting appropriate safeguards and implementing them

    D. Evaluating each threat event as to its likelihood of occurring and cost of the resulting damage

9. Which of the following would generally *not* be considered an asset in a risk analysis?

    A. A development process

    B. An IT infrastructure

    C. A proprietary system resource

    D. Users' personal files

10. Which of the following represents accidental or intentional exploitations of vulnerabilities?

    A. Threat events

    B. Risks

    C. Threat agents

    D. Breaches

11. When a safeguard or a countermeasure is not present or is not sufficient, what remains?

    A. Vulnerability

    B. Exposure

    C. Risk

    D. Penetration

12. Which of the following is not a valid definition for risk?

  A. An assessment of probability, possibility, or chance

  B. Anything that removes a vulnerability or protects against one or more specific threats

  C. Risk = threat * vulnerability

  D. Every instance of exposure

13. When evaluating safeguards, what is the rule that should be followed in most cases?

  A. The expected annual cost of asset loss should not exceed the annual costs of safeguards.

  B. The annual costs of safeguards should equal the value of the asset.

  C. The annual costs of safeguards should not exceed the expected annual cost of asset loss.

  D. The annual costs of safeguards should not exceed 10 percent of the security budget.

14. How is single loss expectancy (SLE) calculated?

  A. Threat + vulnerability

  B. Asset value ($) * exposure factor

  C. Annualized rate of occurrence * vulnerability

  D. Annualized rate of occurrence * asset value * exposure factor

15. How is the value of a safeguard to a company calculated?

  A. ALE before safeguard − ALE after implementing the safeguard − annual cost of safeguard

  B. ALE before safeguard * ARO of safeguard

  C. ALE after implementing safeguard + annual cost of safeguard − controls gap

  D. Total risk − controls gap

16. What security control is directly focused on preventing collusion?

  A. Principle of least privilege

  B. Job descriptions

  C. Separation of duties

  D. Qualitative risk analysis

17. What process or event is typically hosted by an organization and is targeted to groups of employees with similar job functions?

  A. Education

  B. Awareness

  C. Training

  D. Termination

18. Which of the following is not specifically or directly related to managing the security function of an organization?

   A. Worker job satisfaction

   B. Metrics

   C. Information security strategies

   D. Budget

19. While performing a risk analysis, you identify a threat of fire and a vulnerability because there are no fire extinguishers. Based on this information, which of the following is a possible risk?

   A. Virus infection

   B. Damage to equipment

   C. System malfunction

   D. Unauthorized access to confidential information

20. You've performed a basic quantitative risk analysis on a specific threat/vulnerability/risk relation. You select a possible countermeasure. When performing the calculations again, which of the following factors will change?

   A. Exposure factor

   B. Single loss expectancy

   C. Asset value

   D. Annualized rate of occurrence

Chapter 7

Software Development Security

**THE CISSP EXAM TOPICS COVERED
IN THIS CHAPTER INCLUDE:**

4. Software Development Security

   A. Understand and apply security in the software development life cycle

      A.1 Development life cycle

      A.2 Maturity models

      A.3 Operation and maintenance

      A.4 Change management

   B. Understand the environment and security controls

      B.1 Security of the software environment

      B.2 Security issues of programming languages

      B.4 Configuration management

   C. Assess the effectiveness of software security

6. Security Architecture and Design

   E. Understand software and system vulnerabilities and threats

      E.3 Database security (e.g., inference, aggregation, data mining, warehousing)

All too often, security administrators are unaware of system vulnerabilities caused by applications with security flaws (either intentional or unintentional). Security professionals often have a background in system administration and don't have an in-depth understanding of the application development process and therefore of application security. This can be a critical oversight. As you will learn in Chapter 18, "Incidents and Ethics," organization insiders (in other words, employees, contractors, and trusted visitors) are the most likely people to commit computer crimes. Security administrators must be aware of all threats to ensure that adequate checks and balances exist to protect against a malicious insider or application vulnerability.

In this chapter, we examine some of the common threats that applications pose to both traditional and distributed computing environments. Next, we explore how to protect data. Finally, we take a look at some of the systems development controls that can help ensure the accuracy, reliability, and integrity of internal application development processes.

Application Issues

As technology marches on, application environments are becoming much more complex than they were in the days of isolated mainframes running precompiled code. To understand the application environment and security controls, you need to evaluate the variety of different situations that software will encounter. Organizations are now faced with challenges that arise from connecting their systems to networks of all shapes and sizes (from the office LAN to the global Internet) as well as from distributed computing environments. These challenges come in the form of malicious code, denial of service attacks, application attacks, and other security risks. In the following sections, we'll take a brief look at a few of these issues.

Local/Nondistributed Computing

In a traditional, nondistributed computing environment, individual computer systems store and execute programs to perform functions for the local user. These functions range from word processing and spreadsheets on the local system to networked applications that provide access to remote resources, such as websites, file servers and electronic mail.

It is important to understand that nondistributed systems can certainly be networked and utilize network applications. The key characteristic of a nondistributed system is that all user-executed code is stored on the single machine (or on a file system accessible to that machine, such as a file server on the machine's LAN) and executed using processors on that machine.

The threats that local/nondistributed computing environments face are some of the more common malicious code objects that you are most likely already familiar with, at least in passing. The following sections contain brief descriptions of those objects from an application security standpoint. We cover them in greater detail in Chapter 8, "Malicious Code and Application Attacks."

Viruses

Viruses are the oldest form of malicious code objects that still pose a risk to computers today. Once they are in a system, they attach themselves to legitimate operating system and user files and applications and usually perform some sort of undesirable action, ranging from the somewhat innocuous display of an annoying message on the screen to the more malicious destruction of the entire local file system.

Before the advent of networked computing, viruses spread from system to system through infected media. For example, suppose a user's hard drive is infected with a virus. That user might then format a floppy disk and inadvertently transfer the virus to it along with some data files. When the user inserts the disk into another system and reads the data, that system would also become infected with the virus. The virus might then get spread to several other users, who go on to share it with even more users in an exponential fashion.

 Macro viruses were among the most insidious viruses out there. They're extremely easy to write and take advantage of some of the advanced features of modern productivity applications to significantly broaden their reach. For this reason, office applications today are set by default to disable the use of macros that haven't been digitally signed by a trusted author.

In this day and age, almost every computer has at least an indirect connection to the Internet. This greatly increases the number of mechanisms that can transport viruses from system to system and expands the potential magnitude of these infections to epidemic proportions. After all, an email macro virus that can automatically propagate itself to every contact in your address book can inflict far more widespread damage than a boot sector virus that requires the sharing of physical storage media to transmit infection. The majority of viruses today are designed to create large botnets. While they historically were designed to cause damage to the infected machine, and many still do this today, most viruses lie hidden as zombies or clones waiting for direction from the botnet controllers. These topics are covered in more detail in Chapter 8.

Trojan Horses

During the Trojan War, the Greek military used a wooden horse filled with soldiers to gain access to the fortified city of Troy. The Trojans fell prey to this deception because they believed the horse to be a generous gift and were unaware of its insidious cargo. Modern computer users face a similar threat from today's electronic version of the Trojan horse. A *Trojan horse* is a malicious code object that appears to be a benevolent program—such as a game or simple utility. When a user executes the application, it performs the "cover" functions, as advertised; however, electronic Trojan horses also carry a secret payload. While the computer user is using the cover program, the Trojan horse performs some sort of malicious action—such as opening a security hole in the system for hackers to exploit, tampering with data, or installing keystroke-monitoring software.

Logic Bombs

Logic bombs are malicious code objects that lie dormant until events occur that satisfy one or more logical conditions. At that time, they spring into action, delivering their malicious payload to unsuspecting computer users. They are often planted by disgruntled employees or other individuals who want to harm an organization but for one reason or another want to delay the malicious activity for a period. Many simple logic bombs operate based solely upon the system date or time. For example, an employee who was terminated might set a logic bomb to destroy critical business data on the first anniversary of their termination. Other logic bombs operate using more complex criteria. For example, a programmer who fears termination might plant a logic bomb that alters payroll information after the programmer's account is locked out of the system.

Worms

Worms are an interesting type of malicious code that greatly resemble viruses, with one major distinction. Like viruses, worms spread from system to system bearing some type of malicious payload. However, whereas viruses require some type of user action to propagate, worms are self-replicating. They remain resident in memory and exploit one or more networking vulnerabilities to spread from system to system under their own power. Obviously, this allows for much greater propagation and can result in a denial of service attack against entire networks. Indeed, the famous Internet Worm launched by Robert Tappan Morris in November 1988 (we present the technical details of this worm in Chapter 8) crippled the entire Internet for several days.

Distributed Computing

The previous sections discussed how the advent of networked computing facilitated the rapid spread of malicious code objects between computing systems. The following sections examine how distributed computing (an offshoot of networked computing) introduces a variety of new malicious code threats that information system security practitioners must understand and protect their systems against.

Essentially, distributed computing allows a single user to harness the computing power of one or more remote systems to achieve a single goal. A common example of this is the client-server interaction that takes place when a user requests a dynamic web page, such as starting a retail checkout process. The client uses a web browser (such as Microsoft Internet Explorer, Mozilla Firefox, or Google Chrome) to request the page from a remote server. The remote server's web hosting software then receives and processes the request. In the case of a static web page, the web server fulfills the request by retrieving an HTML file from the local file system and transmitting it to the remote client. However, this would not work for a shopping cart process because the remote server would not be able to pregenerate a file with the contents desired by the end user. That's where dynamic pages come into play. The server must generate custom content tailored to the needs of the individual user (such as the contents of a shopping cart). The web user is causing remote server(s) to perform actions on their behalf.

Another great example of distributed computing is the SETI@home project conducted by Search for Extraterrestrial Intelligence (SETI). The researchers conducting the SETI project have massive amounts of data to process searching for signs of life in outer space. It is simply not feasible for them to purchase enough computing power to handle it all, so they turned to the Internet to find users willing to donate the unused power on their home and business computers to participate in the effort. Whenever participating computers go idle, the research system sends them a small part of the problem to compute. The answers are sent back to the main system and reassembled. Thus, solving the main problem (Is there intelligent life in space?) is distributed among thousands of computers around the world.

Agents

Agents (also known as *bots*) are intelligent code objects that perform actions on behalf of a user. Agents typically take initial instructions from the user and then carry on their activity in an unattended manner for a predetermined period of time, until certain conditions are met, or for an indefinite period.

The most common type of intelligent agent in use today is the *web bot*. These agents continuously crawl a variety of websites retrieving and processing data on behalf of the user. For example, a user interested in finding a low airfare between two cities might use an intelligent agent to scour a variety of airline and travel websites and continuously check fare prices. Whenever the agent detects a fare lower than previous fares, it might send the user an email message, text message, or other notification of the cheaper travel opportunity. More adventurous bot programmers might even provide the agent with credit card information and instruct it to actually order a ticket when the fare reaches a certain level.

 Real World Scenario

Stop Orders as User Agents

If you invest in the stock market, you're probably familiar with another type of user agent: stop orders. These allow investors to place predefined orders instructing their broker (or, more realistically, their broker's computer system) to make trades on the investor's behalf when certain conditions occur.

Stop orders can be used to limit an investor's loss on a stock. Suppose you buy shares of Acme Corporation at $30 and wish to ensure that you don't lose more than 50 percent of your initial investment. You might place a stop loss order at $15, which instructs your broker to sell your stock at the current market price if the share price ever falls below $15.

Similarly, you can use stop orders to lock in profits. In the previous example, the investor might target a 20 percent profit by placing a stop order to execute whenever the stock price exceeds $36.

The popularity of online auctions has created another market for intelligent agents: auction *sniping*. Agents using this strategy log into an auction website seconds before an auction closes to place a last-minute bid on behalf of a buyer. Buyers use sniping in an attempt to ward off last-minute bidding wars.

Although agents can be useful computing objects, they also introduce a variety of new security concerns that must be addressed. For example, what if a hacker programs an agent to continuously probe a network for security holes and report vulnerable systems in real time? How about a malicious individual who uses a number of agents to flood a website with bogus requests, thereby mounting a denial of service attack against that site? Or perhaps a commercially available agent accepts credit card information from a user and then transmits it to a hacker at the same time that it places a legitimate purchase.

Applets

Recall that agents are code objects sent from a user's system to query and process data stored on remote systems. *Applets* perform the opposite function; these code objects are sent from a server to a client to perform some action. In fact, applets are actually self-contained miniature programs that execute independently of the server that sent them.

Imagine a web server that offers a variety of financial tools to web users. One of these tools might be a mortgage calculator that processes a user's financial information and provides a monthly mortgage payment based upon the loan's principal and term and the borrower's credit information. Instead of processing this data and returning the results to the client system, the remote web server might send to the local system an applet that enables it to perform those calculations itself. This provides a number of benefits to both the remote server and the end user:

- The processing burden is shifted to the client, freeing up resources on the web server to process requests from more users.

- The client is able to produce data using local resources rather than waiting for a response from the remote server. In many cases, this results in a quicker response to changes in the input data.

- In a properly programmed applet, the web server does not receive any data provided to the applet as input, therefore maintaining the security and privacy of the user's financial data.

However, just as with agents, applets introduce a number of security concerns. They allow a remote system to send code to the local system for execution. Security administrators must take steps to ensure that code sent to systems on their network is safe and properly screened for malicious activity. Also, unless the code is analyzed line by line, the end user can never be certain that the applet doesn't contain a Trojan horse component. For example, the mortgage calculator might indeed transmit sensitive financial information to the web server without the end user's knowledge or consent.

Two common applet types are Java applets and ActiveX controls.

Java applets   Java is a platform-independent programming language developed by Sun Microsystems (which was acquired in 2010 by Oracle Corporation). Most programming languages use compilers that produce applications custom-tailored to run under a specific operating system. This requires the use of multiple compilers to produce different versions of a single application for each platform it must support. Java overcomes this limitation by inserting the Java Virtual Machine (JVM) into the picture. Each system that runs Java code downloads the version of the JVM supported by its operating system. The JVM then takes the Java code and translates it into a format executable by that specific system. The great benefit of this arrangement is that code can be shared among operating systems without modification. Java applets are simply short Java programs transmitted over the Internet to perform operations on a remote system.

Security was of paramount concern during the design of the Java platform, and the Java development team created the "sandbox" concept to place privilege restrictions on Java code. The sandbox isolates Java code objects from the rest of the operating system and enforces strict rules about the resources those objects can access. For example, the sandbox would prohibit a Java applet from retrieving information from areas of memory not specifically allocated to it, preventing the applet from stealing that information.

ActiveX controls   ActiveX controls are Microsoft's answer to Java applets. They operate in a similar fashion, but they can be implemented using a variety of languages, including Visual Basic, C, and C++ as well as Java.

There are two key distinctions between Java applets and ActiveX controls. First, ActiveX controls use proprietary Microsoft technology and, therefore, can execute only on systems running Microsoft browsers. Second, ActiveX controls are not subject to the sandbox restrictions placed on Java applets. They have full access to the Windows operating environment and can perform a number of privileged actions. Therefore, you must take special precautions when deciding which ActiveX controls to download and execute. Some security administrators have taken the somewhat harsh position of prohibiting the download of any ActiveX content from all but a select handful of trusted sites.

Databases and Data Warehousing

Almost every modern organization maintains some sort of database that contains information critical to operations—be it customer contact information, order-tracking data, human resource and benefits information, or sensitive trade secrets. It's likely that many of these databases contain personal information that users hold secret, such as credit card usage activity, travel habits, grocery store purchases, and telephone records. Because of the growing reliance on database systems, information security professionals must ensure that adequate security controls exist to protect them against unauthorized access, tampering, or destruction of data.

In the following sections, we'll discuss database management system (DBMS) architecture, including the various types of DBMSs and their features. Then we'll discuss database security considerations, including polyinstantiation, ODBC, aggregation, inference, and data mining.

Database Management System Architecture

Although there are a variety of database management system (DBMS) architectures available today, the vast majority of contemporary systems implement a technology known as relational database management systems (RDBMSs). For this reason, the following sections focus primarily on relational databases. However, first we'll discuss two other important DBMS architectures: hierarchical and distributed.

Hierarchical and Distributed Databases

A hierarchical data model combines records and fields that are related in a logical tree structure. This results in a one-to-many data model, where each node may have zero, one, or many children but only one parent. An example of a hierarchical data model appears in Figure 7.1.

FIGURE 7.1   Hierarchical data model

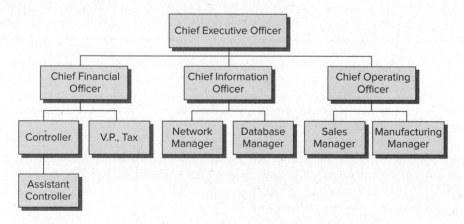

The hierarchical model in Figure 7.1 is a corporate organization chart. Notice that the one-to-many data model holds true in this example. Each employee has only one manager (the *one* in *one-to-many*), but each manager may have one or more (the *many*) employees. Other examples of hierarchical data models include the NCAA March Madness bracket system and the hierarchical distribution of Domain Name System (DNS) records used on the Internet. Hierarchical databases store data in this type of hierarchical fashion and are useful for specialized applications that fit the model. For example, biologists might use a hierarchical database to store data on specimens according to the kingdom/phylum/class/order/family/genus/species hierarchical model used in that field.

The distributed data model has data stored in more than one database, but those databases are logically connected. The user perceives the database as a single entity, even though it comprises numerous parts interconnected over a network. Each field can have numerous children as well as numerous parents. Thus, the data mapping relationship for distributed databases is many-to-many.

Relational Databases

A relational database consists of flat two-dimensional tables made up of rows and columns. In fact, each table looks very similar to a spreadsheet file. The row and column structure provides for one-to-one data mapping relationships. The main building block of the relational database is the table (also known as a *relation*). Each table contains a set of related records. For example, a sales database might contain the following tables:

- Customers table that contains contact information for all the organization's clients
- Sales Reps table that contains identity information on the organization's sales force
- Orders table that contains records of orders placed by each customer

---

Object-Oriented Programming and Databases

Object-relational databases combine relational databases with the power of object-oriented programming. True object-oriented databases (OODBs) benefit from ease of code reuse, ease of troubleshooting analysis, and reduced overall maintenance. OODBs are also better suited than other types of databases for supporting complex applications involving multimedia, CAD, video, graphics, and expert systems.

Each table contains a number of attributes, or *fields*. Each attribute corresponds to a column in the table. For example, the Customers table might contain columns for company name, address, city, state, zip code, and telephone number. Each customer would have its own record, or *tuple*, represented by a row in the table. The number of rows in the relation is referred to as *cardinality*, and the number of columns is the *degree*. The *domain* of an attribute is the set of allowable values that the attribute can take. Figure 7.2 shows an example of a Customers table from a relational database.

FIGURE 7.2 Customers table from a relational database

Company ID	Company Name	Address	City	State	ZIP Code	Telephone	Sales Rep
1	Acme Widgets	234 Main Street	Columbia	MD	21046	(301) 555-1212	14
2	Abrams Consulting	1024 Sample Street	Miami	FL	33131	(305) 555-1995	14
3	Dome Widgets	913 Sorin Street	South Bend	IN	46556	(574) 555-5863	26

In this example, the table has a cardinality of three (corresponding to the three rows in the table) and a degree of eight (corresponding to the eight columns). It's common for the cardinality of a table to change during the course of normal business, such as when a sales rep adds new customers. The degree of a table normally does not change frequently and usually requires database administrator intervention.

> To remember the concept of cardinality, think of a deck of cards on a desk, with each card (the first four letters of *cardinality*) being a row. To remember the concept of degree, think of a wall thermometer as a column (in other words, the temperature in degrees as measured on a thermometer).

Relationships between the tables are defined to identify related records. In this example, a relationship exists between the Customers table and the Sales Reps table because each customer is assigned a sales representative and each sales representative is assigned to one or more customers. This relationship is reflected by the Sales Rep field/column in the Customer table, shown in Figure 7.2. The values in this column refer to a Sales Rep ID field contained in the Sales Rep table (not shown). Additionally, a relationship would probably exist between the Customers table and the Orders table because each order must be associated with a customer and each customer is associated with one or more product orders. The Orders table (not shown) would likely contain a Customer field that contained one of the Customer ID values shown in Figure 7.2.

Records are identified using a variety of keys. Quite simply, *keys* are a subset of the fields of a table and are used to uniquely identify records. They are also used to join tables when you wish to cross-reference information. You should be familiar with three types of keys:

Candidate keys A *candidate key* is a subset of attributes that can be used to uniquely identify any record in a table. No two records in the same table will ever contain the same values for all attributes composing a candidate key. Each table may have one or more candidate keys, which are chosen from column headings.

Primary keys A *primary key* is selected from the set of candidate keys for a table to be used to uniquely identify the records in a table. Each table has only one primary key, selected by the database designer from the set of candidate keys. The RDBMS enforces the uniqueness of primary keys by disallowing the insertion of multiple records with the same primary key. In the Customers table shown in Figure 7.2, the Customer ID would likely be the primary key.

Foreign keys   A *foreign key* is used to enforce relationships between two tables, also known as *referential integrity*. Referential integrity ensures that if one table contains a foreign key, it corresponds to a still-existing primary key in the other table in the relationship. It makes certain that no record/tuple/row contains a reference to a primary key of a nonexistent record/tuple/row. In the example described earlier, the Sales Rep field shown in Figure 7.2 is a foreign key referencing the primary key of the Sales Reps table.

All relational databases use a standard language, Structured Query Language (SQL), to provide users with a consistent interface for the storage, retrieval, and modification of data and for administrative control of the DBMS. Each DBMS vendor implements a slightly different version of SQL (like Microsoft's Transact-SQL and Oracle's PL/SQL), but all support a core feature set. SQL's primary security feature is its granularity of authorization. This means that SQL allows you to set permissions at a very fine level of detail. You can limit user access by table, row, column, or even an individual cell in some cases.

Database Normalization

Database developers strive to create well-organized and efficient databases. To assist with this effort, they've defined several levels of database organization known as *normal forms*. The process of bringing a database table into compliance with normal forms is known as *normalization*.

Although a number of normal forms exist, the three most common are first normal form (1NF), second normal form (2NF), and third normal form (3NF). Each of these forms adds requirements to reduce redundancy in the tables, eliminating misplaced data and performing a number of other housekeeping tasks. The normal forms are cumulative; in other words, to be in 2NF, a table must first be 1NF compliant. Before making a table 3NF compliant, it must first be in 2NF.

The details of normalizing a database table are beyond the scope of the CISSP exam, but several web resources can help you understand the requirements of the normal forms in greater detail. For example, refer to the article "Database Normalization":

`http://databases.about.com/od/specificproducts/a/normalization.htm`

SQL provides the complete functionality necessary for administrators, developers, and end users to interact with the database. In fact, the graphical database interfaces popular today merely wrap some extra bells and whistles around a standard SQL interface to the DBMS. SQL itself is divided into two distinct components: the Data Definition Language (DDL), which allows for the creation and modification of the database's structure (known as the *schema*), and the Data Manipulation Language (DML), which allows users to interact with the data contained within that schema.

Database Transactions

Relational databases support the explicit and implicit use of transactions to ensure data integrity. Each transaction is a discrete set of SQL instructions that will either succeed or fail as a group. It's not possible for one part of a transaction to succeed while another part fails. Consider the example of a transfer between two accounts at a bank. You might use the following SQL code to first add $250 to account 1001 and then subtract $250 from account 2002:

```
BEGIN TRANSACTION

UPDATE accounts
SET balance = balance + 250
WHERE account_number = 1001;

UPDATE accounts
SET balance = balance - 250
WHERE account_number = 2002

END TRANSACTION
```

Imagine a case where these two statements were not executed as part of a transaction but were instead executed separately. If the database failed during the moment between completion of the first transaction and completion of the second transaction, $250 would have been added to account 1001, but there would be no corresponding deduction from account 2002. The $250 would have appeared out of thin air! Flipping the order of the two statements wouldn't help—this would cause $250 to disappear into thin air if interrupted! This simple example underscores the importance of transaction-oriented processing.

When a transaction successfully finishes, it is said to be committed to the database and cannot be undone. Transaction committing may be explicit, using SQL's COMMIT command, or it can be implicit if the end of the transaction is successfully reached. If a transaction must be aborted, it can be rolled back explicitly using the ROLLBACK command or implicitly if there is a hardware or software failure. When a transaction is rolled back, the database restores itself to the condition it was in before the transaction began.

All database transactions have four required characteristics: atomicity, consistency, isolation, and durability. Together, these attributes are known as the *ACID model*, which is a critical concept in the development of database management systems. Let's take a brief look at each of these requirements:

Atomicity   Database transactions must be atomic—that is, they must be an "all-or-nothing" affair. If any part of the transaction fails, the entire transaction must be rolled back as if it never occurred.

Consistency   All transactions must begin operating in an environment that is consistent with all of the database's rules (for example, all records have a unique primary key).

When the transaction is complete, the database must again be consistent with the rules, regardless of whether those rules were violated during the processing of the transaction itself. No other transaction should ever be able to utilize any inconsistent data that might be generated during the execution of another transaction.

Isolation The isolation principle requires that transactions operate separately from each other. If a database receives two SQL transactions that modify the same data, one transaction must be completed in its entirety before the other transaction is allowed to modify the same data. This prevents one transaction from working with invalid data generated as an intermediate step by another transaction.

Durability Database transactions must be durable. That is, once they are committed to the database, they must be preserved. Databases ensure durability through the use of backup mechanisms, such as transaction logs.

In the following sections, we'll discuss a variety of specific security issues of concern to database developers and administrators.

Security for Multilevel Databases

As you learned in Chapter 5, "Security Governance Concepts, Principles, and Policies," many organizations use data classification schemes to enforce access control restrictions based upon the security labels assigned to data objects and individual users. When mandated by an organization's security policy, this classification concept must also be extended to the organization's databases.

Multilevel security databases contain information at a number of different classification levels. They must verify the labels assigned to users and, in response to user requests, provide only information that's appropriate. However, this concept becomes somewhat more complicated when considering security for a database.

When multilevel security is required, it's essential that administrators and developers strive to keep data with different security requirements separate. Mixing data with different classification levels and/or need-to-know requirements is known as *database contamination* and is a significant security challenge. Often, administrators will deploy a trusted front end to add multilevel security to a legacy or insecure DBMS.

 Real World Scenario

Restricting Access with Views

Another way to implement multilevel security in a database is through the use of database views. Views are simply SQL statements that present data to the user as if the views were tables themselves. Views may be used to collate data from multiple tables, aggregate individual records, or restrict a user's access to a limited subset of database attributes and/or records.

Views are stored in the database as SQL commands rather than as tables of data. This dramatically reduces the space requirements of the database and allows views to violate the rules of normalization that apply to tables. However, retrieving data from a complex view can take significantly longer than retrieving it from a table because the DBMS may need to perform calculations to determine the value of certain attributes for each record.

Because views are so flexible, many database administrators use them as a security tool—allowing users to interact only with limited views rather than with the raw tables of data underlying them.

Concurrency

Concurrency, or edit control, is a preventative security mechanism that endeavors to make certain that the information stored in the database is always correct or at least has its integrity and availability protected. This feature can be employed on a single level or multilevel database. Concurrency uses a "lock" feature to allow one user to make changes but deny other users access to view or make changes to data elements at the same time. Then, after the changes have been made, an "unlock" feature restores the ability of other users to access the data they need. In some instances, administrators will use concurrency with auditing mechanisms to track document and/or field changes. When this recorded data is reviewed, concurrency becomes a detective control.

Other Security Mechanisms

Administrators can deploy several other security mechanisms when using a DBMS. These features are relatively easy to implement and are common in the industry. The mechanisms related to semantic integrity, for instance, are common security features of a DBMS. Semantic integrity ensures that user actions don't violate any structural rules. It also checks that all stored data types are within valid domain ranges, ensures that only logical values exist, and confirms that the system complies with any and all uniqueness constraints.

Administrators may employ time and date stamps to maintain data integrity and availability. Time and date stamps often appear in distributed database systems. When a time stamp is placed on all change transactions and those changes are distributed or replicated to the other database members, all changes are applied to all members, but they are implemented in correct chronological order.

Another common security feature of a DBMS is that objects can be controlled granularly within the database; this can also improve security control. Content-dependent access control is an example of granular object control. Content-dependent access control is based on the contents or payload of the object being accessed. Because decisions must be made on an object-by-object basis, content-dependent control increases processing overhead. Another form of granular control is *cell suppression*. Cell suppression is the concept of hiding individual database fields or cells or imposing more security restrictions on them.

Context-dependent access control is often discussed alongside content-dependent access control because of the similarity of the terms. Context-dependent access control evaluates the big picture to make access control decisions. The key factor in context-dependent access control is how each object or packet or field relates to the overall activity or communication. Any single element may look innocuous by itself, but in a larger context that element may be revealed to be benign or malign.

Administrators might employ database partitioning to subvert aggregation and inference vulnerabilities, which are discussed in the section "Aggregation" later in this chapter. Database partitioning is the process of splitting a single database into multiple parts, each with a unique and distinct security level or type of content.

Polyinstantiation occurs when two or more rows in the same relational database table appear to have identical primary key elements but contain different data for use at differing classification levels. It is often used as a defense against some types of inference attacks (see the sidebar "Inference" later in this chapter).

Consider a database table containing the location of various naval ships on patrol. Normally, this database contains the exact position of each ship stored at the secret classification level. However, one particular ship, the USS *UpToNoGood*, is on an undercover mission to a top-secret location. Military commanders do not want anyone to know that the ship deviated from its normal patrol. If the database administrators simply change the classification of the *UpToNoGood*'s location to top secret, a user with a secret clearance would know that something unusual was going on when they couldn't query the location of the ship. However, if polyinstantiation is used, two records could be inserted into the table. The first one, classified at the top-secret level, would reflect the true location of the ship and be available only to users with the appropriate top secret security clearance. The second record, classified at the secret level, would indicate that the ship was on routine patrol and would be returned to users with a secret clearance.

Finally, administrators can insert false or misleading data into a DBMS in order to redirect or thwart information confidentiality attacks. This is a concept known as noise and perturbation. You must be extremely careful when using this technique to ensure that noise inserted into the database does not affect business operations.

ODBC

Open Database Connectivity (ODBC) is a database feature that allows applications to communicate with different types of databases without having to be directly programmed for interaction with each type. ODBC acts as a proxy between applications and backend database drivers, giving application programmers greater freedom in creating solutions without having to worry about the backend database system. Figure 7.3 illustrates the relationship between ODBC and a backend database system.

FIGURE 7.3   ODBC as the interface between applications and a backend
database system

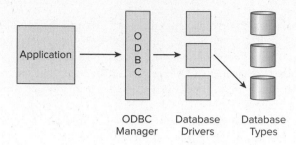

Application → ODBC

ODBC
Manager

Database
Drivers

Database
Types

Aggregation

SQL provides a number of functions that combine records from one or more tables to produce potentially useful information. This process is called *aggregation*. Aggregation is not
without its security vulnerabilities. Aggregation attacks are used to collect numerous low-
level security items or low-value items and combine them to create something of a higher
security level or value. Some of the functions, known as the *aggregate functions*, are listed
here:

COUNT( )   Returns the number of records that meet specified criteria

MIN( )   Returns the record with the smallest value for the specified attribute or combination of attributes

MAX( )   Returns the record with the largest value for the specified attribute or combination of attributes

SUM( )   Returns the summation of the values of the specified attribute or combination of
attributes across all affected records

AVG( )   Returns the average value of the specified attribute or combination of attributes
across all affected records

These functions, although extremely useful, also pose a risk to the security of information in a database. For example, suppose a low-level military records clerk is responsible for
updating records of personnel and equipment as they are transferred from base to base. As
part of his duties, this clerk may be granted the database permissions necessary to query
and update personnel tables.

The military might not consider an individual transfer request (in other words, Sergeant
Jones is being moved from Base X to Base Y) to be classified information. The records
clerk has access to that information because he needs it to process Sergeant Jones's transfer.
However, with access to aggregate functions, the records clerk might be able to count the
number of troops assigned to each military base around the world. These force levels are
often closely guarded military secrets, but the low-ranking records clerk could deduce them
by using aggregate functions across a large number of unclassified records.

Inference

The database security issues posed by inference attacks are very similar to those posed by the threat of data aggregation. As with aggregation, inference attacks involve combining several pieces of nonsensitive information to gain access to information that should be classified at a higher level. However, inference makes use of the human mind's deductive capacity rather than the raw mathematical ability of modern database platforms.

A commonly cited example of an inference attack is that of the accounting clerk at a large corporation who is allowed to retrieve the total amount the company spends on salaries for use in a top-level report but is not allowed to access the salaries of individual employees. The accounting clerk often has to prepare those reports with effective dates in the past and so is allowed to access the total salary amounts for any day in the past year. Say, for example, that this clerk must also know the hiring and termination dates of various employees and has access to this information. This opens the door for an inference attack. If an employee was the only person hired on a specific date, the accounting clerk can now retrieve the total salary amount on that date and the day before and deduce the salary of that particular employee—sensitive information that the user would not be permitted to access directly.

As with aggregation, the best defense against inference attacks is to maintain constant vigilance over the permissions granted to individual users. Furthermore, intentional blurring of data may be used to prevent the inference of sensitive information. For example, if the accounting clerk were able to retrieve only salary information rounded to the nearest million, they would probably not be able to gain any useful information about individual employees. Finally, you can use database partitioning (discussed earlier in this chapter) to help subvert these attacks.

For this reason, it's especially important for database security administrators to strictly control access to aggregate functions and adequately assess the potential information they may reveal to unauthorized individuals.

Data Mining

Many organizations use large databases, known as *data warehouses*, to store large amounts of information from a variety of databases for use with specialized analysis techniques. These data warehouses often contain detailed historical information not normally stored in production databases because of storage limitations or data security concerns.

A *data dictionary* is commonly used for storing critical information about data, including usage, type, sources, relationships, and formats. DBMS software reads the data dictionary to determine access rights for users attempting to access data.

Data mining techniques allow analysts to comb through data warehouses and look for potential correlated information. For example, an analyst might discover that the demand for lightbulbs always increases in the winter months and then use this information when planning pricing and promotion strategies. Data mining techniques result in the development of data models that can be used to predict future activity.

The activity of data mining produces metadata. Metadata is data about data or information about data. Metadata is not exclusively the result of data mining operations; other functions or services can produce metadata as well. Think of metadata from a data mining operation as a concentration of data. It can also be a superset, a subset, or a representation of a larger data set. Metadata can be the important, significant, relevant, abnormal, or aberrant elements from a data set.

One common security example of metadata is that of a security incident report. An incident report is the metadata extracted from a data warehouse of audit logs through the use of a security auditing data mining tool. In most cases, metadata is of a greater value or sensitivity (due to disclosure) than the bulk of data in the warehouse. Thus, metadata is stored in a more secure container known as the *data mart.*

You may also hear data mining referred to as Knowledge Discovery in Databases (KDD). It is closely related to the fields of machine learning and artificial intelligence.

Data warehouses and data mining are significant to security professionals for two reasons. First, as previously mentioned, data warehouses contain large amounts of potentially sensitive information vulnerable to aggregation and inference attacks, and security practitioners must ensure that adequate access controls and other security measures are in place to safeguard this data. Second, data mining can actually be used as a security tool when it's used to develop baselines for statistical anomaly–based intrusion detection systems (see Chapter 14, "Incident Management," for more information on the various types and functionality of intrusion detection systems).

 Real World Scenario

Data Mining for Anomaly Detection

With several colleagues, Mike Chapple, one of this book's authors, published a paper titled "Authentication Anomaly Detection" that explored the usefulness of data mining techniques to examine authentication logs from a virtual private network (VPN). In the study, they used *expectation maximization (EM)* clustering, a data mining technique, to develop models of normal user behavior based upon a user's affiliation with the organization, the distance between the data center and their physical location, the day of the week, the hour of the day, and other attributes.

After developing the models through data mining, the researchers applied the models to future activity and identified user connection attempts that didn't look "normal," as defined by the model. Using this approach, they identified several unauthorized uses of the VPN.

Data/Information Storage

Database management systems have helped harness the power of data and gain some modicum of control over who can access it and the actions they can perform on it. However, security professionals must keep in mind that DBMS security covers access to information through only the traditional "front-door" channels. Data is also processed through a computer's storage resources—both memory and physical media. Precautions must be in place to ensure that these basic resources are protected against security vulnerabilities as well. After all, you would never incur a lot of time and expense to secure the front door of your home and then leave the back door wide open, would you?

Types of Storage

Modern computing systems use several types of storage to maintain system and user data. The systems strike a balance between the various storage types to satisfy an organization's computing requirements. There are several common storage types:

Primary (or "real") memory consists of the main memory resources directly available to a system's CPU. Primary memory normally consists of volatile random access memory (RAM) and is usually the most high-performance storage resource available to a system.

Secondary storage consists of more inexpensive, nonvolatile storage resources available to a system for long-term use. Typical secondary storage resources include magnetic and optical media, such as tapes, disks, hard drives, flash drives, and CD/DVD storage.

Virtual memory allows a system to simulate additional primary memory resources through the use of secondary storage. For example, a system low on expensive RAM might make a portion of the hard disk available for direct CPU addressing.

Virtual storage allows a system to simulate secondary storage resources through the use of primary storage. The most common example of virtual storage is the RAM disk that presents itself to the operating system as a secondary storage device but is actually implemented in volatile RAM. This provides an extremely fast file system for use in various applications but provides no recovery capability.

Random access storage allows the operating system to request contents from any point within the media. RAM and hard drives are examples of random access storage resources.

Sequential access storage requires scanning through the entire media from the beginning to reach a specific address. A magnetic tape is a common example of a sequential access storage resource.

Volatile storage loses its contents when power is removed from the resource. RAM is the most common type of volatile storage resource.

Nonvolatile storage does not depend upon the presence of power to maintain its contents. Magnetic/optical media and nonvolatile RAM (NVRAM) are typical examples of nonvolatile storage resources.

Storage Threats

Information security professionals should be aware of two main threats posed against data storage systems. First, the threat of illegitimate access to storage resources exists no matter what type of storage is in use. If administrators do not implement adequate file system access controls, an intruder might stumble across sensitive data simply by browsing the file system. In more sensitive environments, administrators should also protect against attacks that involve bypassing operating system controls and directly accessing the physical storage media to retrieve data. This is best accomplished through the use of an encrypted file system, which is accessible only through the primary operating system. Furthermore, systems that operate in a multilevel security environment should provide adequate controls to ensure that shared memory and storage resources are set up with fail-safe controls so that data from one classification level is not readable at a lower classification level.

Covert channel attacks pose the second primary threat against data storage resources. Covert storage channels allow the transmission of sensitive data between classification levels through the direct or indirect manipulation of shared storage media. This may be as simple as writing sensitive data to an inadvertently shared portion of memory or physical storage. More complex covert storage channels might be used to manipulate the amount of free space available on a disk or the size of a file to covertly convey information between security levels. For more information on covert channel analysis, see Chapter 12, "Security Architecture Vulnerabilities, Threats, and Countermeasures."

Knowledge-Based Systems

Since the advent of computing, engineers and scientists have worked toward developing systems capable of performing routine actions that would bore a human and consume a significant amount of time. The majority of the achievements in this area focused on relieving the burden of computationally intensive tasks. However, researchers have also made giant strides toward developing systems that have an "artificial intelligence" that can simulate (to some extent) the purely human power of reasoning.

The following sections examine two types of knowledge-based artificial intelligence systems: expert systems and neural networks. We'll also take a look at their potential applications to computer security problems.

Expert Systems

Expert systems seek to embody the accumulated knowledge of experts on a particular subject and apply it in a consistent fashion to future decisions. Several studies have shown that expert systems, when properly developed and implemented, often make better decisions than some of their human counterparts when faced with routine decisions.

Every expert system has two main components: the knowledge base and the inference engine.

The knowledge base contains the rules known by an expert system. The knowledge base seeks to codify the knowledge of human experts in a series of "if/then" statements. Let's consider a simple expert system designed to help homeowners decide whether they should evacuate an area when a hurricane threatens. The knowledge base might contain the following statements (these statements are for example only):

- If the hurricane is a Category 4 storm or higher, then flood waters normally reach a height of 20 feet above sea level.
- If the hurricane has winds in excess of 120 miles per hour (mph), then wood-frame structures will be destroyed.
- If it is late in the hurricane season, then hurricanes tend to get stronger as they approach the coast.

In an actual expert system, the knowledge base would contain hundreds or thousands of assertions such as those just listed.

The second major component of an expert system—the inference engine—analyzes information in the knowledge base to arrive at the appropriate decision. The expert system user employs some sort of user interface to provide the inference engine with details about the current situation, and the inference engine uses a combination of logical reasoning and fuzzy logic techniques to draw a conclusion based upon past experience. Continuing with the hurricane example, a user might inform the expert system that a Category 4 hurricane is approaching the coast with wind speeds averaging 140 mph. The inference engine would then analyze information in the knowledge base and make an evacuation recommendation based upon that past knowledge.

Expert systems are not infallible—they're only as good as the data in the knowledge base and the decision-making algorithms implemented in the inference engine. However, they have one major advantage in stressful situations—their decisions do not involve judgment clouded by emotion. Expert systems can play an important role in analyzing emergency events, stock trading, and other scenarios in which emotional investment sometimes gets in the way of a logical decision. For this reason, many lending institutions now utilize expert systems to make credit decisions instead of relying upon loan officers who might say to themselves, "Well, Jim hasn't paid his bills on time, but he seems like a perfectly nice guy."

Fuzzy Logic

As previously mentioned, inference engines commonly use a technique known as *fuzzy logic*. This technique is designed to more closely approximate human thought patterns than the rigid mathematics of set theory or algebraic approaches that utilize "black-and-white" categorizations of data. Fuzzy logic replaces them with blurred boundaries, allowing the algorithm to think in the "shades of gray" that dominate human thought. Fuzzy logic as used by an expert system has four steps or phases: fuzzification, inference, composition, and defuzzification.

For example, consider the task of determining whether a website is undergoing a denial of service attack. Traditional mathematical techniques may create basic rules, such as "If we have more than 1,000 connections per second, we are under attack." Fuzzy logic, on the other hand, might define a blurred boundary, saying that 1,000 connections per second represents an 80 percent chance of an attack, while 10,000 connections per second represents a 95 percent chance and 100 connections per second represents a 5 percent chance. The interpretation of these probabilities is left to the analyst.

Neural Networks

In neural networks, chains of computational units are used in an attempt to imitate the biological reasoning process of the human mind. In an expert system, a series of rules is stored in a knowledge base, whereas in a neural network, a long chain of computational decisions that feed into each other and eventually sum to produce the desired output is set up.

Keep in mind that no neural network designed to date comes close to having the reasoning power of the human mind. Nevertheless, neural networks show great potential to advance the artificial intelligence field beyond its current state. Benefits of neural networks include linearity, input-output mapping, and adaptivity. These benefits are evident in the implementations of neural networks for voice recognition, face recognition, weather prediction, and the exploration of models of thinking and consciousness.

Typical neural networks involve many layers of summation, each of which requires weighting information to reflect the relative importance of the calculation in the overall decision-making process. The weights must be custom-tailored for each type of decision the neural network is expected to make. This is accomplished through the use of a training period during which the network is provided with inputs for which the proper decision is known. The algorithm then works backward from these decisions to determine the proper weights for each node in the computational chain. This activity is performed using what is known as the *Delta rule* or *learning rule*. Through the use of the Delta rule, neural networks are able to learn from experience.

Decision Support Systems

A *decision support system (DSS)* is a knowledge-based application that analyzes business data and presents it in such a way as to make business decisions easier for users. It is considered more of an informational application than an operational application. Often a DSS is employed by knowledge workers (such as help desk or customer support personnel) and by sales services (such as phone operators). This type of application may present information in a graphical manner to link concepts and content and guide the script of the operator. Often a DSS is backed by an expert system controlling a database.

Security Applications

Both expert systems and neural networks have great applications in the field of computer security. One of the major advantages offered by these systems is their capability to rapidly make consistent decisions. One of the major problems in computer security is the inability of system administrators to consistently and thoroughly analyze massive amounts of log and audit trail data to look for anomalies. It seems like a match made in heaven!

One successful application of this technology to the computer security arena is the Next-Generation Intrusion Detection Expert System (NIDES) developed by Phillip Porras and his team at the Information and Computing Sciences System Design Laboratory of SRI International. This system provides an inference engine and knowledge base that draws information from a variety of audit logs across a network and provides notification to security administrators when the activity of an individual user varies from the user's standard usage profile.

Systems Development Controls

Many organizations use custom-developed hardware and software systems to achieve flexible operational goals. As you will learn in Chapter 8 and Chapter 12, these custom solutions can present great security vulnerabilities as a result of malicious and/or careless developers who create trap doors, buffer overflow vulnerabilities, or other weaknesses that can leave a system open to exploitation by malicious individuals.

To protect against these vulnerabilities, it's vital to introduce security concerns into the entire systems development life cycle. An organized, methodical process helps ensure that solutions meet functional requirements as well as security guidelines. The following sections explore the spectrum of systems development activities with an eye toward security concerns that should be foremost on the mind of any information security professional engaged in solutions development.

Software Development

Security should be a consideration at every stage of a system's development, including the software development process. Programmers should strive to build security into every application they develop, with greater levels of security provided to critical applications and those that process sensitive information. It's extremely important to consider the security implications of a software development project from the early stages because it's much easier to build security into a system than it is to add security onto an existing system.

Assurance

To ensure that the security control mechanisms built into a new application properly implement the security policy throughout the life cycle of the system, administrators use *assurance procedures*. Assurance procedures are simply formalized processes by which trust is built into the life cycle of a system. The Trusted Computer System Evaluation Criteria (TCSEC) Orange Book refers to this process as *life cycle assurance*.

Avoiding System Failure

No matter how advanced your development team, your systems will likely fail at some point in time. You should plan for this type of failure when you put the software and hardware controls in place, ensuring that the system will respond appropriately. You can employ many methods to avoid failure, including using limit checks and creating fail-safe or fail-open procedures. Let's talk about these in more detail.

Limit checks   Environmental controls and hardware devices cannot prevent problems created by poor program coding. It is important to have proper software development and coding practices to ensure that security is a priority during product development. Using limit checks is a technique for managing data types, data formats, and data length when accepting input from a user or another application. Limit checks ensure that data does not fall outside the range of allowable values. For example, when creating a database that contains the age of individuals, a limit check might restrict the possible values so that they must be greater than 0 and less than 130. Depending on the application, you may also need to include sequence checks to ensure that data input is properly ordered. Limit checks are a form of input validation—checking to ensure that user input meets the requirements of the application.

In most organizations, security professionals come from a system administration background and don't have professional experience in software development. If your background doesn't include this type of experience, don't let that stop you from learning about it and educating your organization's developers on the importance of secure coding.

Fail-secure and fail-open   In spite of the best efforts of programmers, product designers, and project managers, developed applications will be used in unexpected ways. Some of these conditions will cause failures. Since failures are unpredictable, programmers should design into their code a general sense of how to respond to and handle failures.

There are two basic choices when planning for system failure, fail-secure (also called fail-safe) or fail-open:

- The *fail-secure failure state* puts the system into a high level of security (and possibly even disables it entirely) until an administrator can diagnose the problem and restore the system to normal operation.
- The *fail-open state* allows users to bypass failed security controls, erring on the side of permissiveness.

In the vast majority of environments, fail-secure is the appropriate failure state because it prevents unauthorized access to information and resources.

Software should revert to a fail-secure condition. This may mean closing just the application or possibly stopping the operation of the entire host system. An example of such failure response is seen in the Windows OS with the appearance of the infamous Blue Screen of Death (BSOD), indicating the occurrence of a STOP error. A STOP error occurs when an undesirable activity occurs in spite of the OS's efforts to prevent it. This could include an application gaining direct access to hardware, an attempt to bypass a security access check, or one process interfering with the memory space of another. Once one of these conditions occurs, the environment is no longer trustworthy. So, rather than continuing to support an unreliable and insecure operating environment, the OS initiates a STOP error as its fail-secure response.

Once a fail-secure operation occurs, the programmer should consider the activities that occur afterward. The options are to remain in a fail-secure state or to automatically reboot the system. The former option requires an administrator to manually reboot the system and oversee the process. This action can be enforced by using a boot password. The latter option does not require human intervention for the system to restore itself to a functioning state, but it has its own unique issues. For example, it must restrict the system to reboot into a nonprivileged state. In other words, the system should not reboot and perform an automatic logon; instead, it should prompt the user for authorized access credentials.

WARNING   In limited circumstances, it may be appropriate to implement a fail-open failure state. This is sometimes appropriate for lower-layer components of a multilayered security system. Fail-open systems should be used with extreme caution. Before deploying a system using this failure mode, clearly validate the business requirement for this move. If it is justified, ensure that adequate alternative controls are in place to protect the organization's resources should the system fail. It's extremely rare that you'd want all your security controls to utilize a fail-open approach.

Even when security is properly designed and embedded in software, that security is often disabled in order to support easier installation. Thus, it is common for the IT administrator to have the responsibility of turning on and configuring security to match the needs of their specific environment. Maintaining security is often a trade-off with user-friendliness and functionality, as you can see from Figure 7.4. Additionally, as you add or increase security, you will also increase costs, increase administrative overhead, and reduce productivity/throughput.

FIGURE 7.4   Security vs. user-friendliness vs. functionality

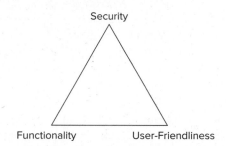

Programming Languages

As you probably know, software developers use programming languages to develop software code. You might not know that several types of languages can be used simultaneously by the same system. This section takes a brief look at the different types of programming languages and the security implications of each.

Computers understand binary code. They speak a language of 1s and 0s, and that's it! The instructions that a computer follows consist of a long series of binary digits in a language known as *machine language*. Each CPU chipset has its own machine language, and it's virtually impossible for a human being to decipher anything but the simplest machine language code without the assistance of specialized software. Assembly language is a higher-level alternative that uses mnemonics to represent the basic instruction set of a CPU but still requires hardware-specific knowledge of a relatively obscure language. It also requires a large amount of tedious programming; a task as simple as adding two numbers together could take five or six lines of assembly code!

Programmers don't want to write their code in either machine language or assembly language. They prefer to use high-level languages, such as C++, Java, and Visual Basic. These languages allow programmers to write instructions that better approximate human communication, decrease the length of time needed to craft an application, possibly decrease the number of programmers needed on a project, and also allow some portability between different operating systems and hardware platforms. Once programmers are ready to execute their programs, two options are available to them: compilation and interpretation.

Some languages (such as C++, Java, and FORTRAN) are compiled languages. When using a compiled language, the programmer uses a tool known as a *compiler* to convert the higher-level language into an executable file designed for use on a specific operating system. This executable is then distributed to end users who may use it as they see fit. Generally speaking, it's not possible to view or modify the software instructions in an executable file.

Other languages (such as JavaScript and VBScript) are interpreted languages. When these languages are used, the programmer distributes the source code, which contains instructions in the higher-level language. End users then use an interpreter to execute that source code on their system. They're able to view the original instructions written by the programmer.

Each approach has security advantages and disadvantages. Compiled code is generally less prone to manipulation by a third party. However, it's also easier for a malicious (or unskilled) programmer to embed back doors and other security flaws in the code and escape detection because the original instructions can't be viewed by the end user. Interpreted code, however, is less prone to the insertion of malicious code by the original programmer because the end user may view the code and check it for accuracy. On the other hand, everyone who touches the software has the ability to modify the programmer's original instructions and possibly embed malicious code in the interpreted software. You'll learn more about the exploits attackers use to undermine software in the section "Application Attacks" in Chapter 8.

Generations of Languages

For the CISSP exam, you should also be familiar with the programming language generations, which are defined as follows:

- *First-generation languages (1GL)* include all machine languages.

- *Second-generation languages (2GL)* include all assembly languages.

- *Third-generation languages (3GL)* include all compiled languages.

- *Fourth-generation languages (4GL)* attempt to approximate natural languages and include SQL, which is used by databases.

- *Fifth-generation languages (5GL)* allow programmers to create code using visual interfaces.

Object-Oriented Programming

Many modern programming languages, such as C++, Java, and the .NET languages, support the concept of object-oriented programming (OOP). Older programming styles, such as functional programming, focused on the flow of the program itself and attempted to model the desired behavior as a series of steps. Object-oriented programming focuses on the objects involved in an interaction. You can think of it as a group of objects that can be requested to perform certain operations or exhibit certain behaviors. Objects work together to provide a system's functionality or capabilities. OOP has the potential to be more reliable and able to reduce the propagation of program change errors. As a type of programming method, it is better suited to modeling or mimicking the real world. For example, a banking program might have three object classes that correspond to accounts, account holders, and employees, respectively. When a new account is added to the system, a new instance, or copy, of the appropriate object is created to contain the details of that account.

Each object in the OOP model has methods that correspond to specific actions that can be taken on the object. For example, the account object can have methods to add funds, deduct funds, close the account, and transfer ownership.

Objects can also be subclasses of other objects and inherit methods from their parent class. For example, the account object may have subclasses that correspond to specific types of accounts, such as savings, checking, mortgages, and auto loans. The subclasses can use all the methods of the parent class and have additional class-specific methods. For example, the checking object might have a method called `write_check()`, whereas the other subclasses do not.

From a security point of view, object-oriented programming provides a black-box approach to abstraction. Users need to know the details of an object's interface (generally the inputs, outputs, and actions that correspond to each of the object's methods) but don't necessarily need to know the inner workings of the object to use it effectively. To provide the desired characteristics of object-oriented systems, the objects are encapsulated (self-contained), and they can be accessed only through specific messages (in other words, input). Objects can also exhibit the substitution property, which allows different objects providing compatible operations to be substituted for each other.

Here is a list of common object-oriented programming terms you might come across in your work:

Message   A message is a communication to or input of an object.

Method   A method is internal code that defines the actions an object performs in response to a message.

Behavior   The results or output exhibited by an object is a behavior. Behaviors are the results of a message being processed through a method.

Class   A collection of the common methods from a set of objects that defines the behavior of those objects is a class.

Instance   Objects are instances of or examples of classes that contain their methods.

Inheritance   Inheritance occurs when methods from a class (parent or superclass) are inherited by another subclass (child).

Delegation   Delegation is the forwarding of a request by an object to another object or delegate. An object delegates if it does not have a method to handle the message.

Polymorphism   A polymorphism is the characteristic of an object that allows it to respond with different behaviors to the same message or method because of changes in external conditions.

Cohesiveness   Cohesion describes the strength of the relationship between the purposes of the methods within the same class.

Coupling   Coupling is the level of interaction between objects. Lower coupling means less interaction. Lower coupling provides better software design because objects are more independent. Lower coupling is easier to troubleshoot and update. Objects that have low cohesion require lots of assistance from other objects to perform tasks and have high coupling.

Systems Development Life Cycle

Security is most effective if it is planned and managed throughout the life cycle of a system or application. Administrators employ project management to keep a development project on target and moving toward the goal of a completed product. Often project management is structured using life cycle models to direct the development process. Using formalized life cycle models helps ensure good coding practices and the embedding of security in every stage of product development.

All systems development processes should have several activities in common. Although they may not necessarily share the same names, these core activities are essential to the development of sound, secure systems:

- Conceptual definition

- Functional requirements determination

- Control specifications development

- Design review

- Code review walk-through

- System test review

- Maintenance and change management

The section "Life Cycle Models" later in this chapter examines two life cycle models and shows how these activities are applied in real-world software engineering environments.

It's important to note at this point that the terminology used in systems development life cycles varies from model to model and from publication to publication. Don't spend too much time worrying about the exact terms used in this book or any of the other literature you may come across. When taking the CISSP examination, it's much more important that you have an understanding of how the process works and of the fundamental principles underlying the development of secure systems.

Conceptual Definition

The conceptual definition phase of systems development involves creating the basic concept statement for a system. It's a simple statement agreed upon by all interested stakeholders (the developers, customers, and management) that states the purpose of the project as well as the general system requirements. The conceptual definition is a very high-level statement of purpose and should not be longer than one or two paragraphs. If you were reading a detailed summary of the project, you might expect to see the concept statement as an abstract or introduction that enables an outsider to gain a top-level understanding of the project in a short period of time.

It's very helpful to refer to the concept statement at all phases of the systems development process. Often, the intricate details of the development process tend to obscure the overarching goal of the project. Simply reading the concept statement periodically can assist in refocusing a team of developers.

Functional Requirements Determination

Once all stakeholders have agreed upon the concept statement, it's time for the development team to sit down and begin the functional requirements process. In this phase, specific system functionalities are listed, and developers begin to think about how the parts of the system should interoperate to meet the functional requirements. The deliverable from this phase of development is a functional requirements document that lists the specific system requirements.

As with the concept statement, it's important to ensure that all stakeholders agree on the functional requirements document before work progresses to the next level. When it's finally completed, the document shouldn't be simply placed on a shelf to gather dust—the entire development team should constantly refer to this document during all phases to ensure that the project is on track. In the final stages of testing and evaluation, the project managers should use this document as a checklist to ensure that all functional requirements are met.

Control Specifications Development

Security-conscious organizations also ensure that adequate security controls are designed into every system from the earliest stages of development. It's often very useful to have a control specifications development phase in your life cycle model. This phase takes place soon after the development of functional requirements and often continues as the design and design review phases progress.

During the development of control specifications, it's important to analyze the system from a number of security perspectives. First, adequate access controls must be designed into every system to ensure that only authorized users are allowed to access the system and that they are not permitted to exceed their level of authorization. Second, the system must maintain the confidentiality of vital data through the use of appropriate encryption and data protection technologies. Next, the system should provide both an audit trail to enforce individual accountability and a detective mechanism for illegitimate activity. Finally, depending upon the criticality of the system, availability and fault-tolerance issues should be addressed as corrective actions.

Keep in mind that designing security into a system is not a one-time process and it must be done proactively. All too often, systems are designed without security planning, and then developers attempt to retrofit the system with appropriate security mechanisms. Unfortunately, these mechanisms are an afterthought and do not fully integrate with the system's design, which leaves gaping security vulnerabilities. Also, the security requirements should be revisited each time a significant change is made to the design specification. If a major component of the system changes, it's very likely that the security requirements will change as well.

Design Review

Once the functional and control specifications are complete, let the system designers do their thing! In this often-lengthy process, the designers determine exactly how the various parts of the system will interoperate and how the modular system structure will be laid out. Also, during this phase, the design management team commonly sets specific tasks for various teams and lays out initial timelines for the completion of coding milestones.

After the design team completes the formal design documents, a review meeting with the stakeholders should be held to ensure that everyone is in agreement that the process is still on track for the successful development of a system with the desired functionality.

Code Review Walk-Through

Once the stakeholders have given the software design their blessing, it's time for the software developers to start writing code. Project managers should schedule several code review walk-though meetings at various milestones throughout the coding process. These technical meetings usually involve only development personnel who sit down with a copy of the code for a specific module and walk through it, looking for problems in logical flow or other design/security flaws. The meetings play an instrumental role in ensuring that the code produced by the various development teams performs according to specification.

System Test Review

After many code reviews and a lot of long nights, there will come a point at which a developer puts in that final semicolon and declares the system complete. As any seasoned software engineer knows, the system is never complete. Now it's time to begin the system test review phase. Initially, most organizations perform the initial system tests using development personnel to seek out any obvious errors. Once this phase is complete, a series of beta test deployments takes place to ensure that customers agree that the system meets all functional requirements and performs according to the original specification. As with any critical development process, it's important that you maintain a copy of the written system test plan and test results for future review.

Maintenance and Change Management

Once a system is operational, a variety of maintenance tasks are necessary to ensure continued operation in the face of changing operational, data processing, storage, and environmental requirements. It's essential that you have a skilled support team in place to handle any routine or unexpected maintenance. It's also important that any changes to the code be handled through a formalized change management process, as described in Chapter 5.

Life Cycle Models

One of the major complaints you'll hear from practitioners of the more established engineering disciplines (such as civil, mechanical, and electrical engineering) is that software engineering is not an engineering discipline at all. In fact, they contend, it's simply a combination of chaotic processes that somehow manage to scrape out workable solutions from time to time. Indeed, some of the "software engineering" that takes place in today's development environments is nothing but bootstrap coding held together by "duct tape and chicken wire."

However, the adoption of more formalized life cycle management processes is seen in mainstream software engineering as the industry matures. After all, it's hardly fair to compare the processes of an age-old discipline such as civil engineering to those of an industry that's barely a few decades old. In the 1970s and 1980s, pioneers like Winston Royce and Barry Boehm proposed several software development life cycle (SDLC) models to help guide the practice toward formalized processes. In 1991, the Software Engineering Institute introduced the Capability Maturity Model, which described the process organizations undertake as they move toward incorporating solid engineering principles into their software development processes. In the following sections, we'll take a look at the work produced by these studies. Having a management model in place should improve the resultant products. However, if the SDLC methodology is inadequate, the project may fail to meet business and user needs. Thus, it is important to verify that the SDLC model is properly implemented and is appropriate for your environment. Furthermore, one of the initial steps of implementing an SDLC should include management approval.

Waterfall Model

Originally developed by Winston Royce in 1970, the waterfall model seeks to view the systems development life cycle as a series of iterative activities. As shown in Figure 7.5, the traditional waterfall model has seven stages of development. As each stage is completed, the project moves into the next phase. As illustrated by the backward arrows, the modern waterfall model does allow development to return to the previous phase to correct defects discovered during the subsequent phase. This is often known as the *feedback loop characteristic* of the waterfall model.

FIGURE 7.5 The waterfall life cycle model

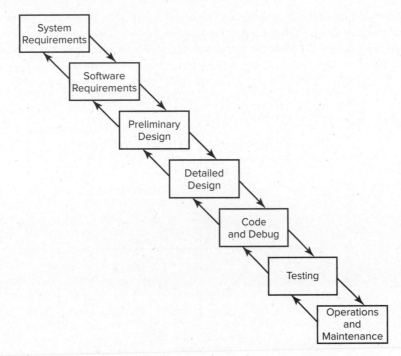

The waterfall model was one of the first comprehensive attempts to model the software development process while taking into account the necessity of returning to previous phases to correct system faults. However, one of the major criticisms of this model is that it allows the developers to step back only one phase in the process. It does not make provisions for the discovery of errors at a later phase in the development cycle.

The waterfall model was improved by adding validation and verification steps to each phase. Verification evaluates the product against specifications, while validation evaluates how well the product satisfies real-world requirements. The improved model was labeled the *modified* waterfall model. However, it did not gain widespread use before the spiral model dominated the project management scene.

Spiral Model

In 1988, Barry Boehm of TRW proposed an alternative life cycle model that allows for multiple iterations of a waterfall-style process. Figure 7.6 illustrates this model. Because the spiral model encapsulates a number of iterations of another model (the waterfall model), it is known as a *metamodel*, or a "model of models."

FIGURE 7.6   The spiral life cycle model

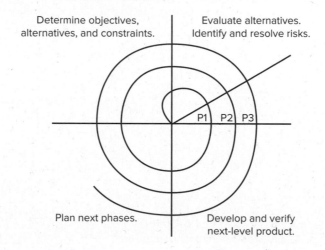

Determine objectives, alternatives, and constraints.

Evaluate alternatives. Identify and resolve risks.

P1 P2 P3

Plan next phases.

Develop and verify next-level product.

Notice that each "loop" of the spiral results in the development of a new system prototype (represented by P1, P2, and P3 in the illustration). Theoretically, system developers would apply the entire waterfall process to the development of each prototype, thereby incrementally working toward a mature system that incorporates all the functional requirements in a fully validated fashion. Boehm's spiral model provides a solution to the major criticism of the waterfall model—it allows developers to return to the planning stages as changing technical demands and customer requirements necessitate the evolution of a system.

Agile Software Development

More recently, the agile model of software development has gained popularity within the software engineering community. Beginning in the mid-1990s, developers began to embrace approaches to software development that eschewed the rigid models of the past in favor of approaches that placed an emphasis on the needs of the customer and on quickly developing new functionality that meets those needs in an iterative fashion.

Seventeen pioneers of the agile development approach got together in 2001 and produced a document titled *Manifesto for Agile Software Development* (http://agilemanifesto.org) that states the core philosophy of the agile approach:

We are uncovering better ways of developing software by doing it and helping others do it. Through this work we have come to value:

Individuals and interactions over processes and tools

Working software over comprehensive documentation

Customer collaboration over contract negotiation

Responding to change over following a plan

That is, while there is value in the items on the right, we value the items on the left more.

The *Agile Manifesto* also defines 12 principles that underlie the philosophy, which are available here:

```
http://agilemanifesto.org/principles.html
```

The 12 principles, as stated in the Agile Manifesto, are as follows:

- Our highest priority is to satisfy the customer through early and continuous delivery of valuable software.
- Welcome changing requirements, even late in development. Agile processes harness change for the customer's competitive advantage.
- Deliver working software frequently, from a couple of weeks to a couple of months, with a preference to the shorter timescale.
- Business people and developers must work together daily throughout the project.
- Build projects around motivated individuals. Give them the environment and support they need, and trust them to get the job done.
- The most efficient and effective method of conveying information to and within a development team is face-to-face conversation.
- Working software is the primary measure of progress.
- Agile processes promote sustainable development. The sponsors, developers, and users should be able to maintain a constant pace indefinitely.
- Continuous attention to technical excellence and good design enhances agility.
- Simplicity—the art of maximizing the amount of work not done—is essential.
- The best architectures, requirements, and designs emerge from self-organizing teams.
- At regular intervals, the team reflects on how to become more effective, then tunes and adjusts its behavior accordingly.

The agile development approach is quickly gaining momentum in the software community and has many variants, including Scrum, Agile Unified Process (AUP), the Dynamic Systems Development Model (DSDM), and Extreme Programming (XP).

Software Capability Maturity Model

The Software Engineering Institute (SEI) at Carnegie Mellon University introduced the Capability Maturity Model for Software, also known as the Software Capability Maturity Model (abbreviated as SW-CMM, CMM, or SCMM), which contends that all organizations engaged in software development move through a variety of maturity phases in sequential fashion. The SW-CMM describes the principles and practices underlying software process maturity. It is intended to help software organizations improve the maturity and quality of their software processes by implementing an evolutionary path from ad hoc, chaotic processes to mature, disciplined software processes. The idea behind the SW-CMM is that the quality of software depends on the quality of its development process.

The stages of the SW-CMM are as follows:

Level 1: Initial   In this phase, you'll often find hard-working people charging ahead in a disorganized fashion. There is usually little or no defined software development process.

Level 2: Repeatable   In this phase, basic life cycle management processes are introduced. Reuse of code in an organized fashion begins to enter the picture, and repeatable results are expected from similar projects. SEI defines the key process areas for this level as Requirements Management, Software Project Planning, Software Project Tracking and Oversight, Software Subcontract Management, Software Quality Assurance, and Software Configuration Management.

Level 3: Defined   In this phase, software developers operate according to a set of formal, documented software development processes. All development projects take place within the constraints of the new standardized management model. SEI defines the key process areas for this level as Organization Process Focus, Organization Process Definition, Training Program, Integrated Software Management, Software Product Engineering, Intergroup Coordination, and Peer Reviews.

Level 4: Managed   In this phase, management of the software process proceeds to the next level. Quantitative measures are utilized to gain a detailed understanding of the development process. SEI defines the key process areas for this level as Quantitative Process Management and Software Quality Management.

Level 5: Optimizing   In the optimized organization, a process of continuous improvement occurs. Sophisticated software development processes are in place that ensure that feedback from one phase reaches to the previous phase to improve future results. SEI defines the key process areas for this level as Defect Prevention, Technology Change Management, and Process Change Management. For more information on the Capability Maturity Model for Software, visit the Software Engineering Institute's website at www.sei.cmu.edu.

IDEAL Model

The Software Engineering Institute also developed the IDEAL model for software development, which implements many of the SW-CMM attributes. The IDEAL model has five phases:

I: Initiating   In the initiating phase of the IDEAL model, the business reasons behind the change are outlined, support is built for the initiative, and the appropriate infrastructure is put in place.

D: Diagnosing   During the diagnosing phase, engineers analyze the current state of the organization and make general recommendations for change.

E: Establishing   In the establishing phase, the organization takes the general recommendations from the diagnosing phase and develops a specific plan of action that helps achieve those changes.

A: Acting   In the acting phase, it's time to stop "talking the talk" and "walk the walk." The organization develops solutions and then tests, refines, and implements them.

L: Learning   As with any quality improvement process, the organization must continuously analyze its efforts to determine whether it has achieved the desired goals and, when necessary, propose new actions to put the organization back on course.

The IDEAL model is illustrated in Figure 7.7.

FIGURE 7.7   The IDEAL model

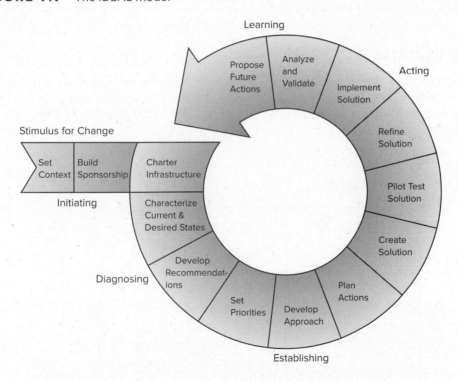

Special permission to reproduce "IDEAL Model," ©2004 by Carnegie Mellon University, is granted by the Carnegie Mellon Software Engineering Institute.

SW-CMM and IDEAL Model Memorization

To help you remember the initial letters of each of the 10 level names of the SW-CMM and IDEAL models (II DR ED AM LO), imagine yourself sitting on the couch in a psychiatrist's office saying, "I...I, Dr. Ed, am lo(w)." If you can remember that phrase, then you can extract the 10 initial letters of the level names. If you write the letters out into two columns, you can reconstruct the level names in order of the two systems. The left column is the IDEAL model, and the right represents the levels of the SW-CMM.

Initiating	Initiating
Diagnosing	Repeatable
Establishing	Defined
Acting	Managed
Learning	Optimized

Gantt Charts and PERT

A Gantt chart is a type of bar chart that shows the interrelationships over time between projects and schedules. It provides a graphical illustration of a schedule that helps to plan, coordinate, and track specific tasks in a project. Figure 7.8 shows an example of a Gantt chart.

FIGURE 7.8   Gantt chart

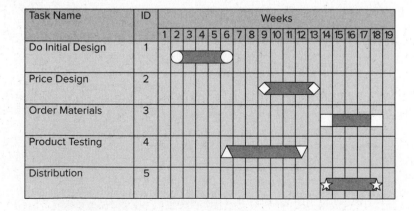

Program Evaluation Review Technique (PERT) is a project-scheduling tool used to judge the size of a software product in development and calculate the standard deviation (SD) for risk assessment. PERT relates the estimated lowest possible size, the most likely size, and the highest possible size of each component. PERT is used to direct improvements to project management and software coding in order to produce more efficient software. As the capabilities of programming and management improve, the actual produced size of software should be smaller.

Change and Configuration Management

Once software has been released into a production environment, users will inevitably request the addition of new features, correction of bugs, and other modifications to the code. Just as the organization developed a regimented process for developing software, they must also put a procedure in place to manage changes in an organized fashion.

 Real World Scenario

Change Management as a Security Tool

Change management (also known as control management) plays an important role when monitoring systems in the controlled environment of a data center. One of the authors recently worked with an organization that used change management as an essential component of its efforts to detect unauthorized changes to computing systems.

In Chapter 8, you'll learn how tools for monitoring file integrity, such as Tripwire, allow you to monitor a system for changes. This organization used Tripwire to monitor hundreds of production servers. However, the organization quickly found itself overwhelmed by file modification alerts resulting from normal activity. The author worked with them to tune the Tripwire-monitoring policies and integrate them with the organization's change management process. Now all Tripwire alerts go to a centralized monitoring center where administrators correlate them with approved changes. System administrators receive an alert only if the security team identifies a change that does not appear to correlate with an approved change request.

This approach greatly reduced the time spent by administrators reviewing file integrity reports and improved the usefulness of the tool to security administrators.

The change management process has three basic components:

Request control The request control process provides an organized framework within which users can request modifications, managers can conduct cost/benefit analysis, and developers can prioritize tasks.

Change control The change control process is used by developers to recreate the situation encountered by the user and analyze the appropriate changes to remedy the situation. It also provides an organized framework within which multiple developers can create and test a solution prior to rolling it out into a production environment. Change control includes conforming to quality control restrictions, developing tools for update or change deployment, properly documenting any coded changes, and restricting the effects of new code to minimize diminishment of security.

Release control Once the changes are finalized, they must be approved for release through the release control procedure. An essential step of the release control process is to double-check and ensure that any code inserted as a programming aid during the change process (such as debugging code and/or back doors) is removed before releasing the new software to production. Release control should also include acceptance testing to ensure that any alterations to end user work tasks are understood and functional.

In addition to the change management process, security administrators should be aware of the importance of configuration management. This process is used to control the version(s) of software used throughout an organization and formally track and control changes to the software configuration. It has four main components:

Configuration identification During the configuration identification process, administrators document the configuration of covered software products throughout the organization.

Configuration control The configuration control process ensures that changes to software versions are made in accordance with the change control and configuration management policies. Updates can be made only from authorized distributions in accordance with those policies.

Configuration status accounting Formalized procedures are used to keep track of all authorized changes that take place.

Configuration audit A periodic configuration audit should be conducted to ensure that the actual production environment is consistent with the accounting records and that no unauthorized configuration changes have taken place.

Together, change and configuration management techniques form an important part of the software engineer's arsenal and protect the organization from development-related security issues.

Software Testing

As part of the development process, your organization should thoroughly test any software before distributing it internally (or releasing it to market). The best time to address testing is as the modules are designed. In other words, the mechanisms you use to test a product and the data sets you use to explore that product should be designed in parallel with the product itself. Your programming team should develop special test suites of data that exercise all paths of the software to the fullest extent possible and know the correct resulting outputs beforehand. This extensive test suite process is known as a *reasonableness check*.

Furthermore, while conducting stress tests, you should check how the product handles normal and valid input data, incorrect types, out-of-range values, and other bounds and/or conditions. Live workloads provide the best stress testing possible. However, you should not use live or actual field data for testing, especially in the early development stages, since a flaw or error could result in the violation of integrity or confidentiality of the test data.

When testing software, you should apply the same rules of separation of duties that you do for other aspects of your organization. In other words, you should assign the testing of your software to someone other than the programmer(s) who developed the code to avoid a conflict of interest and assure a more successful finished product. When a third party tests your software, you have a greater likelihood of receiving an objective and nonbiased examination. The third-party test allows for a broader and more thorough test and prevents the bias and inclinations of the programmers from affecting the results of the test.

You can utilize three testing methods or ideologies for software testing:

White-box testing   White-box testing examines the internal logical structures of a program and steps through the code line by line, analyzing the program for potential errors.

Black-box testing   Black-box testing examines the program from a user perspective by providing a wide variety of input scenarios and inspecting the output. Black-box testers do not have access to the internal code. Final acceptance testing that occurs prior to system delivery is a common example of black-box testing.

Gray-box testing   Gray-box testing combines the two approaches and is a popular approach to software validation. In this approach, testers approach the software from a user perspective, analyzing inputs and outputs. They also have access to the source code and use it to help design their tests. They do not, however, analyze the inner workings of the program during their testing.

In addition to assessing the quality of software, programmers and security professionals should also carefully assess the security of their software to ensure that it meets the organization's security requirements. This is especially critical for web applications that are exposed to the public. There are two categories of testing used specifically to evaluate application security:

Static testing   Static testing evaluates the security of software without running it by analyzing either the source code or the compiled application. Static analysis usually involves the use of automated tools designed to detect common software flaws, such as buffer overflows. In mature development environments, application developers are given access to static analysis tools and use them throughout the design/build/test process.

Dynamic testing   Dynamic testing evaluates the security of software in a runtime environment and is often the only option for organizations deploying applications written by someone else. In those cases, testers often do not have access to the underlying source code. One common example of dynamic software testing is the use of web application scanning tools to detect the presence of cross-site scripting, SQL injection, or other flaws in web applications. Dynamic tests on a production environment should always be carefully coordinated to avoid an unintended interruption of service.

Proper software test implementation is a key element in the project development process. Many of the common mistakes and oversights often found in commercial and in-house software can be eliminated. Keep the test plan and results as part of the system's permanent documentation.

Security Control Architecture

All secure systems implement some sort of security control architecture. At the hardware and operating system levels, controls should ensure enforcement of basic security principles. The following sections examine several basic control principles that should be enforced in a secure computing environment.

Process Isolation

Process isolation is one of the fundamental security procedures put into place during system design. Process isolation mechanisms (whether part of the operating system or part of the hardware itself) ensure that each process has its own isolated memory space for storage of data and the actual executing application code itself. This guarantees that processes cannot access each other's reserved memory areas and protects against confidentiality violations or intentional/unintentional modification of data by an unauthorized process. *Hardware segmentation* is a technique that implements process isolation at the hardware level by enforcing memory access constraints.

Protection Rings

The ring-oriented protection scheme provides for several modes of system operation, thereby facilitating secure operation by restricting processes to running in the appropriate security ring. Figure 7.9 shows the four-layer ring protection scheme supported by Intel microprocessors.

In this scheme, each of the rings has a separate and distinct function:

FIGURE 7.9   Ring protection scheme

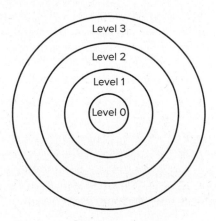

Level 0 represents the ring where the operating system itself resides. This ring contains the security kernel—the core set of operating system services that handles all user/application requests for access to system resources. The kernel also implements the reference monitor, an operating system component that validates all user requests for access to resources against an access control scheme. Processes running at Level 0 are often said to be running in supervisory mode, also called *privileged mode.* Level 0 processes have full control of all system resources, so it's essential to ensure that they are fully verified and validated before implementation.

Levels 1 and 2 contain device drivers and other operating system services that provide higher-level interfaces to system resources. However, in practice, most operating systems do not implement either one of these layers.

Level 3 represents the security layer where user applications and processes reside. This layer is commonly referred to as *user mode*, or *protected mode*, and applications running here are not permitted direct access to system resources. In fact, when an application running in protected mode attempts to access an unauthorized resource, a General Protection Fault (GPF) error occurs.

 The security kernel and reference monitor are extremely important computer security topics that must be understood by any information security practitioner. These topics commonly appear on the CISSP exam.

The reference monitor component (present at Level 0) is an extremely important element of any operating system offering multilevel secure services. This concept was first formally described in the Department of Defense Trusted Computer System Evaluation Criteria (commonly referred to as the Orange Book because of the color of its cover). The DoD set forth the following three requirements for an operational reference monitor:

- It must be tamperproof.
- It must always be invoked when a program or user requests access to resources.
- It must be small enough to be subject to analysis and tests, the completeness of which can be assured.

Abstraction

Abstraction is a valuable tool drawn from the object-oriented software development model that can be extrapolated to apply to the design of all types of information systems. In effect, abstraction states that a thorough understanding of a system's operational details is not often necessary to perform day-to-day activities. For example, a system developer might need to know that a certain procedure, when invoked, writes information to disk, but it's not necessary for the developer to understand the underlying principles that enable the data to be written to disk or the exact format that the disk procedures use to store and retrieve data. The process of developing increasingly sophisticated objects that draw upon the abstracted methods of lower-level objects is known as *encapsulation*. The deliberate concealment of lower levels of functionality from higher-level processes is known as *data hiding* or *information hiding*.

Security Modes

In a secure environment, information systems are configured to process information in one of four security modes. These modes are set out by the Department of Defense in CSC-STD-003-85 (the "light yellow book") as follows:

- Systems running in *compartmented security mode* may process two or more types of compartmented information. All system users must have an appropriate clearance to access all information processed by the system but do not necessarily have a need to know all of the information in the system. Compartments are subcategories or compartments within the different classification levels, and extreme care is taken to preserve the information within the different compartments. The system may be classified at the secret level but contain five different compartments, all classified secret. If a user has the need to know about only two of the five different compartments to do their job, that user can access the system but can access only the two compartments.

- Systems running in *dedicated security mode* are authorized to process only a specific classification level at a time, and all system users must have clearance and a need to know that information.

- Systems running in *multilevel security mode* are authorized to process information at more than one level of security even when all system users do not have appropriate clearances or a need to know for all information processed by the system.

- Systems running in *system-high security mode* are authorized to process only information that all system users are cleared to read and have a valid need to know. These systems are not trusted to maintain separation between security levels, and all information processed by these systems must be handled as if it were classified at the same level as the most highly classified information processed by the system.

Service-Level Agreements

Using service-level agreements (SLAs) is an increasingly popular way to ensure that organizations providing services to internal and/or external customers maintain an appropriate level of service agreed upon by both the service provider and the vendor. It's a wise move to put SLAs in place for any data circuits, applications, information processing systems, databases, or other critical components that are vital to your organization's continued viability. The following issues are commonly addressed in SLAs:

- System uptime (as a percentage of overall operating time)
- Maximum consecutive downtime (in seconds/minutes/and so on)
- Peak load

- Average load
- Responsibility for diagnostics
- Failover time (if redundancy is in place)

Service-level agreements also often commonly include financial and other contractual remedies that kick in if the agreement is not maintained. For example, if a critical circuit is down for more than 15 minutes, the service provider might agree to waive all charges on that circuit for one week.

Summary

Data is the most valuable resource many organizations possess. Therefore, it's critical that information security practitioners understand the necessity of safeguarding the data itself and the systems and applications that assist in the processing of that data. Protections against malicious code, database vulnerabilities, and system/application development flaws must be implemented in every technology-aware organization.

Malicious code objects pose a threat to the computing resources of organizations. In the nondistributed environment, such threats include viruses, logic bombs, Trojan horses, and worms.

By this point, you no doubt recognize the importance of placing adequate access controls and audit trails on these valuable information resources. Database security is a rapidly growing field; if databases play a major role in your security duties, take the time to sit down with database administrators, courses, and textbooks and learn the underlying theory. It's a valuable investment.

Finally, there are various controls that can be put into place during the system and application development process to ensure that the end product of these processes is compatible with operation in a secure environment. Such controls include process isolation, hardware segmentation, abstraction, and contractual arrangements, such as service level agreements (SLA). Security should always be introduced in the early planning phases of any development project and continually monitored throughout the design, development, deployment, and maintenance phases of production.

Exam Essentials

Understand common threats to applications. Describe the functioning of viruses, worms, Trojan horses, and logic bombs. Understand the impact each type of threat may have on a system and the methods they use to propagate. Know the basic functioning of agents and the impact they may have on computer/network security. Understand the functionality behind Java applets and ActiveX controls and be able to determine the appropriate security controls for a given computing environment.

Explain the basic architecture of a relational database management system (RDBMS).   Know the structure of relational databases. Be able to explain the function of tables (relations), rows (records/tuples), and columns (fields/attributes). Know how relationships are defined between tables and the roles of various types of keys. Describe the database security threats posed by aggregation and inference.

Know the various types of storage.   Explain the differences between primary memory and virtual memory, secondary storage and virtual storage, random access storage and sequential access storage, and volatile storage and nonvolatile storage.

Explain how expert systems and neural networks function.   Expert systems consist of two main components: a knowledge base that contains a series of "if/then" rules and an inference engine that uses that information to draw conclusions about other data. Neural networks simulate the functioning of the human mind to a limited extent by arranging a series of layered calculations to solve problems. Neural networks require extensive training on a particular problem before they are able to offer solutions.

Understand the models of systems development.   Know that the waterfall model describes a sequential development process that results in the development of a finished product. Developers may step back only one phase in the process if errors are discovered. The spiral model uses several iterations of the waterfall model to produce a number of fully specified and tested prototypes. Agile development models place an emphasis on the needs of the customer and quickly developing new functionality that meets those needs in an iterative fashion.

Describe software development maturity models.   Know that maturity models help software organizations improve the maturity and quality of their software processes by implementing an evolutionary path from ad hoc, chaotic processes to mature, disciplined software processes. Describe the SW-CMM and IDEAL models.

Understand the importance of change and configuration management.   Know the three basic components of change control—request control, change control, and release control—and how they contribute to security. Explain how configuration management controls the versions of software used in an organization.

Explain the ring protection scheme.   Understand the four rings of the ring protection scheme and the activities that typically occur within each ring. Know that most operating systems only implement Level 0 (privileged or supervisory mode) and Level 3 (protected or user mode).

Describe the function of the security kernel and reference monitor.   The security kernel is the core set of operating system services that handles user requests for access to system resources. The reference monitor is a portion of the security kernel that validates user requests against the system's access control mechanisms.

Understand the importance of testing.   Software testing should be designed as part of the development process. Testing should be used as a management tool to improve the design, development, and production processes.

Understand the four security modes approved by the Department of Defense. Know the differences between compartmented security mode, dedicated security mode, multilevel security mode, and system-high security mode. Understand the different types of classified information that can be processed in each mode and the types of users that can access each system.

Written Lab

1. How does a worm travel from system to system?

2. Describe three benefits of using applets instead of server-side code for web applications.

3. What are the three requirements for an operational reference monitor in a secure computing system?

4. What operating systems are capable of processing ActiveX controls posted on a website?

5. What type of key is selected by the database developer to uniquely identify data within a relational database table?

6. What database security technique appears to permit the insertion of multiple rows sharing the same uniquely identifying information?

7. Explain the difference between static and dynamic analysis of application code.

8. How far backward does the waterfall model allow developers to travel when a development flaw is discovered?

Review Questions

1. Which one of the following malicious code objects might be inserted in an application by a disgruntled software developer with the purpose of destroying system data after the developer's account has been deleted (presumably following their termination)?

    A. Virus

    B. Worm

    C. Trojan horse

    D. Logic bomb

2. What term is used to describe code objects that act on behalf of a user and operate in an unattended manner?

    A. Agent

    B. Worm

    C. Applet

    D. Browser

3. What portion of the change management process allows developers to prioritize tasks?

    A. Release control

    B. Configuration control

    C. Request control

    D. Change audit

4. Which of the following characteristics can be used to differentiate worms from viruses?

    A. Worms infect a system by overwriting data on storage devices.

    B. Worms always spread from system to system without user intervention.

    C. Worms always carry a malicious payload that impacts infected systems.

    D. All of the above.

5. What programming language(s) can be used to develop ActiveX controls for use on an Internet site?

    A. Visual Basic

    B. C

    C. Java

    D. All of the above

6. What form of access control is concerned primarily with the data stored by a field?

    A. Content-dependent

    B. Context-dependent

    C. Semantic integrity mechanisms

    D. Perturbation

7. Which one of the following key types is used to enforce referential integrity between database tables?

    A. Candidate key

    B. Primary key

    C. Foreign key

    D. Super key

8. Richard believes that a database user is misusing his privileges to gain information about the company's overall business trends by issuing queries that combine data from a large number of records. What process is the database user taking advantage of?

    A. Inference

    B. Contamination

    C. Polyinstantiation

    D. Aggregation

9. What database technique can be used to prevent unauthorized users from determining classified information by noticing the absence of information normally available to them?

    A. Inference

    B. Manipulation

    C. Polyinstantiation

    D. Aggregation

10. Which one of the following terms cannot be used to describe the main RAM of a typical computer system?

    A. Volatile

    B. Sequential access

    C. Real memory

    D. Primary memory

11. What type of information is used to form the basis of an expert system's decision-making process?

  A. A series of weighted layered computations

  B. Combined input from a number of human experts, weighted according to past performance

  C. A series of "if/then" rules codified in a knowledge base

  D. A biological decision-making process that simulates the reasoning process used by the human mind

12. Which one of the following intrusion detection systems makes use of an expert system to detect anomalous user activity?

  A. PIX

  B. ID10T

  C. AAFID

  D. NIDES

13. Which of the following acts as a proxy between two different systems to support interaction and simplify the work of programmers?

  A. SDLC

  B. ODBC

  C. DSS

  D. Abstraction

14. In what type of software testing does the tester have access to the underlying source code?

  A. Static testing

  B. Dynamic testing

  C. Cross-site scripting testing

  D. Black box testing

15. In systems utilizing a ring protection scheme, at what level does the security kernel reside?

  A. Level 0

  B. Level 1

  C. Level 2

  D. Level 3

16. Which database security risk occurs when data from a higher classification level is mixed with data from a lower classification level?

  A. Aggregation

  B. Inference

  C. Contamination

  D. Polyinstantiation

17. What database security technology involves creating two or more rows with seemingly identical primary keys that contain different data for users with different security clearances?

    A. Polyinstantiation

    B. Cell suppression

    C. Aggregation

    D. Views

18. Which one of the following is not part of the change management process?

    A. Request control

    B. Release control

    C. Configuration audit

    D. Change control

19. What transaction management principle ensures that two transactions do not interfere with each other as they operate on the same data?

    A. Atomicity

    B. Consistency

    C. Isolation

    D. Durability

20. Tom built a database table consisting of the names, telephone numbers, and customer IDs for his business. The table contains information on 30 customers. What is the degree of this table?

    A. Two

    B. Three

    C. Thirty

    D. Undefined

Chapter

8

Malicious Code and Application Attacks

THE CISSP EXAM TOPICS COVERED IN THIS CHAPTER INCLUDE:

4. Software Development Security

- B. Understand the environment and security controls

    - B.1 Security of the software environment

    - B.2 Security issues of programming languages

    - B.3 Security issues in source code (e.g., buffer overflow, escalation of privilege, backdoor)

6. Security Architecture & Design

- E. Understand software and system vulnerabilities and threats

    - E.2 Client-based (e.g., applets)

In previous chapters, you learned about many general security principles and the policy and procedure mechanisms that help security practitioners develop adequate protection against malicious individuals. This chapter takes an in-depth look at some of the specific threats faced on a daily basis by administrators in the field.

This material is not only critical for the CISSP exam, it's also some of the most basic information a computer security professional must understand to effectively practice their trade. We'll begin this chapter by looking at the risks posed by malicious code objects— viruses, worms, logic bombs, and Trojan horses. We'll then take a look at some of the other security exploits used by someone attempting to gain unauthorized access to a system or to prevent legitimate users from gaining such access.

Malicious Code

Malicious code objects include a broad range of programmed computer security threats that exploit various network, operating system, software, and physical security vulnerabilities to spread malicious payloads to computer systems. Some malicious code objects, such as computer viruses and Trojan horses, depend upon irresponsible computer use by humans in order to spread from system to system with any success. Other objects, such as worms, spread rapidly among vulnerable systems under their own power.

All information security practitioners must be familiar with the risks posed by the various types of malicious code objects so they can develop adequate countermeasures to protect the systems under their care as well as implement appropriate responses if their systems are compromised.

Sources of Malicious Code

Where does malicious code come from? In the early days of computer security, malicious code writers were extremely skilled (albeit misguided) software developers who took pride in carefully crafting innovative malicious code techniques. Indeed, they actually served a somewhat useful function by exposing security holes in popular software packages and operating systems, raising the security awareness of the computing community. For an example of this type of code writer, see the sidebar "RTM and the Internet Worm" later in this chapter.

Modern times have given rise to the *script kiddie*—the malicious individual who doesn't understand the technology behind security vulnerabilities but downloads ready-to-use software (or scripts) from the Internet and uses them to launch attacks against remote systems. This trend gave birth to a new breed of virus creation software that allows anyone with a minimal level of technical expertise to create a virus and unleash it upon the Internet. This is reflected in the large number of viruses documented by antivirus experts to date. The amateur malicious code developers are usually just experimenting with a new tool they downloaded or attempting to cause problems for one or two enemies. Unfortunately, the malware sometimes spread rapidly and creates problems for Internet users in general.

In addition, the tools used by script kiddies are freely available to those with more sinister criminal intent. Indeed, many in law enforcement believe that international organized crime syndicates may now play a role in malware proliferation. These criminals, located in countries with weak law enforcement mechanisms, use malware to steal the money and identities of people from around the world, especially residents of the United States. In fact, the Zeus Trojan horse is widely believed to be the product of a Eastern European organized crime ring seeking to infect as many systems as possible to log keystrokes and harvest online banking passwords. The Zeus outbreak began in 2007 and continues today. This is just one example of an emerging trend in malware development.

Viruses

The computer virus is perhaps the earliest form of malicious code to plague security administrators. Indeed, viruses are so prevalent nowadays that major outbreaks receive attention from the mass media and provoke mild hysteria among average computer users. According to Symantec, one of the major antivirus software vendors, there were over 286 million strains of malicious code roaming the global network in 2010. Hundreds of thousands of variations of these viruses strike unsuspecting computer users each day. Many carry malicious payloads that cause damage ranging in scope from displaying a profane message on the screen all the way to causing complete destruction of all data stored on the local hard drive.

As with biological viruses, computer viruses have two main functions—propagation and destruction. Miscreants who create viruses carefully design code to implement these functions in new and innovative methods that they hope escape detection and bypass increasingly sophisticated antivirus technology. It's fair to say that an arms race has developed between virus writers and antivirus technicians, each hoping to develop technology one step ahead of the other. The propagation function defines how the virus will spread from system to system, infecting each machine it leaves in its wake. A virus's payload delivers the destructive power by implementing whatever malicious activity the virus writer had in mind. This could be anything that negatively impacts the confidentiality, integrity, or availability of systems or data.

Virus Propagation Techniques

By definition, a virus must contain technology that enables it to spread from system to system, aided by unsuspecting computer users seeking to share data by exchanging disks, sharing networked resources, sending electronic mail, or using some other means. Once they've "touched" a new system, they use one of several propagation techniques to infect the new victim and expand their reach. In this section, we'll look at four common propagation techniques: master boot record infection, file infection, macro infection, and service injection.

Master boot record viruses   The *master boot record (MBR) virus* is one of the earliest known forms of virus infection. These viruses attack the MBR—the portion of bootable media (such as a hard disk, USB drive, or CD/DVD) that the computer uses to load the operating system during the boot process. Because the MBR is extremely small (usually 512 bytes), it can't contain all the code required to implement the virus's propagation and destructive functions. To bypass this space limitation, MBR viruses store the majority of their code on another portion of the storage media. When the system reads the infected MBR, the virus instructs it to read and execute the code stored in this alternate location, thereby loading the entire virus into memory and potentially triggering the delivery of the virus's payload.

The Boot Sector and the Master Boot Record

You'll often see the terms *boot sector* and *master boot record* used interchangeably to describe the portion of a storage device used to load the operating system and the types of viruses that attack that process. This is not technically correct. The MBR is a single disk sector, normally the first sector of the media that is read in the initial stages of the boot process. The MBR determines which media partition contains the operating system and then directs the system to read that partition's boot sector to load the operating system.

Viruses can attack both the MBR and the boot sector, with substantially similar results. MBR viruses act by redirecting the system to an infected boot sector, which loads the virus into memory before loading the operating system from the legitimate boot sector. Boot sector viruses actually infect the legitimate boot sector and are loaded into memory during the operating system load process.

Most MBR viruses are spread between systems through the use of infected media inadvertently shared between users. If the infected media is in the drive during the boot process, the target system reads the infected MBR, and the virus loads into memory, infects the MBR on the target system's hard drive, and spreads its infection to yet another machine.

File infector viruses   Many viruses infect different types of executable files and trigger when the operating system attempts to execute them. For Windows-based systems, the names of these files end with .exe and .com extensions. The propagation routines of *file infector viruses* may slightly alter the code of an executable program, thereby implanting the technology the virus needs to replicate and damage the system. In some cases, the virus might actually replace the entire file with an infected version. Standard file infector viruses that do not use cloaking techniques such as stealth or encryption (see the section "Virus Technologies" later in this chapter) are often easily detected by comparing file characteristics (such as size and modification date) before and after infection or by comparing hash values. The section "Antivirus Mechanisms" provides technical details of these techniques.

A variation of the file infector virus is the *companion virus*. These viruses are self-contained executable files that escape detection by using a filename similar to, but slightly different from, a legitimate operating system file. They rely on the default filename extensions that Windows-based operating systems append to commands when executing program files (.com, .exe, and .bat, in that order). For example, if you had a program on your hard disk named game.exe, a companion virus might use the name game.com. If you then open a Command tool and simply type **GAME**, the operating system would execute the virus file, game.com, instead of the file you actually intended to execute, game.exe. This is a very good reason to avoid shortcuts and fully specify the name of the file you want to execute.

Macro viruses   Many common software applications implement some sort of scripting functionality to assist with the automation of repetitive tasks. These functionalities often use simple, yet powerful, programming languages such as Visual Basic for Applications (VBA). Although macros do indeed offer great productivity-enhancing opportunities to computer users, they also expose systems to yet another avenue of infection—macro viruses.

Macro viruses first appeared on the scene in the mid-1990s, utilizing crude technologies to infect documents created in the popular Microsoft Word environment. Although they were relatively unsophisticated, these viruses spread rapidly because the antivirus community didn't anticipate them, and therefore, antivirus applications didn't provide any defense against them. Macro viruses quickly became more and more commonplace, and vendors rushed to modify their antivirus platforms to scan application documents for malicious macros. In 1999, the Melissa virus spread through the use of a Word document that exploited a security vulnerability in Microsoft Outlook to replicate. The infamous I Love You virus quickly followed on its heels, exploiting similar vulnerabilities in early 2000.

WARNING   Macro viruses proliferate because of the ease of writing code in the scripting languages (such as VBA) utilized by modern productivity applications.

After a rash of macro viruses in the late part of the twentieth century, productivity software developers made important changes to the macro development environment, restricting the ability of untrusted macros to run without explicit user permission. A drastic reduction in the prevalence of macro viruses was the result.

Service injection viruses   Recent outbreaks of malicious code use yet another technique to infect systems and escape detection—injecting themselves into trusted runtime processes of the operating system, such as svchost.exe, winlogin.exe and explorer.exe. By successfully compromising these trusted processes, the malicious code is able to bypass detection by any antivirus software running on the host. One of the best techniques to protect systems against service injection is to ensure that all software allowing the viewing of web content (browsers, media players, helper applications) receive current security patches.

Platforms Vulnerable to Viruses

Just as most macro viruses infect systems running the popular Microsoft Office suite of applications, most computer viruses are designed to disrupt activity on systems running versions of the world's most popular operating system—Microsoft Windows. It's estimated that less than 1 percent of the viruses "in the wild" today are designed to impact other operating systems, such as UNIX and Mac OS.

The main reason for this is that there is no single UNIX operating system. Rather, there is a series of many similar operating systems that implement the same functions in a similar fashion and that are independently designed by a large number of developers. Large-scale corporate efforts compete with the myriad of freely available versions of the Linux operating system developed by the public at large. The sheer number of UNIX versions and the fact that they are developed on entirely different kernels (the core code of an operating system) make it difficult to write a virus that would impact a large portion of UNIX systems.

That said, Macintosh and UNIX users should not fail to be vigilant. Although only a few viruses pose a risk to their systems, one of those viruses could affect their systems at any moment. Anyone responsible for the security of a computer system should implement adequate antivirus mechanisms to ensure the continued safety of their resources.

Antivirus Mechanisms

Almost every desktop computer in service today runs some sort of antivirus software package. Popular desktop titles include McAfee VirusScan and Norton AntiVirus, but a plethora of other products on the market offer protection for anything from a single system to an entire enterprise; other packages are designed to protect against specific common types of virus invasion vectors, such as inbound email.

The vast majority of these packages utilize a method known as *signature-based detection* to identify potential virus infections on a system. Essentially, an antivirus package maintains an extremely large database that contains the telltale characteristics of all known viruses. Depending upon the antivirus package and configuration settings, it scans storage media periodically, checking for any files that contain data matching those criteria. If any are detected, the antivirus package takes one of the following actions:

- If the software can eradicate the virus, it disinfects the affected files and restores the machine to a safe condition.

- If the software recognizes the virus but doesn't know how to disinfect the files, it may quarantine the files until the user or an administrator can examine them manually.

- If security settings/policies do not provide for quarantine or the files exceed a predefined danger threshold, the antivirus package may delete the infected files in an attempt to preserve system integrity.

When using a signature-based antivirus package, it's essential to remember that the package is only as effective as the virus definition file upon which it's based. If you don't frequently update your virus definitions (usually requiring an annual subscription fee), your antivirus software will not be able to detect newly created viruses. With thousands of viruses appearing on the Internet each year, an outdated definition file will quickly render your defenses ineffective.

Many antivirus packages also use heuristic-based mechanisms to detect potential malware infections. These methods analyze the behavior of software, looking for the telltale signs of virus activity, such as attempts to elevate privilege level, cover their electronic tracks, and alter unrelated or operating system files.

Most of the modern antivirus software products are able to detect and remove a wide variety of types of malicious code and then clean the system. In other words, antivirus solutions are rarely limited to just viruses. These tools are often able to provide protection against worms, Trojan horses, logic bombs, rootkits, spyware, and various other forms of email- or web-borne code. In the event that you suspect new malicious code is sweeping the Internet, your best course of action is to contact your antivirus software vendor to inquire about your state of protection against the new threat. Don't wait until the next scheduled or automated signature dictionary update. Furthermore, never accept the word of any third party about protection status offered by an antivirus solution. Always contact the vendor directly. Most responsible antivirus vendors will send alerts to their customers as soon as new, substantial threats are identified, so be sure to register for such notifications as well.

Other security packages, such as the popular Tripwire data integrity assurance package, also provide a secondary antivirus functionality. Tripwire is designed to alert administrators of unauthorized file modifications. It's often used to detect web server defacements and similar attacks, but it also may provide some warning of virus infections if critical system executable files, such as command.com, are modified unexpectedly. These systems work by maintaining a database of hash values for all files stored on the system (see Chapter 9, "Cryptography and Symmetric Key Algorithms," for a full discussion of the hash functions used to create these values). These archived hash values are then compared to current computed values to detect any files that were modified between the two periods. At the most basic level, a hash is a number used to summarize the contents of a file. As long as the file stays the same, the hash will stay the same. If the file is modified, even slightly, the hash will change dramatically, indicating that the file has been modified. Unless the action seems explainable, such as happening after the installation of new software, application of an operating system patch, or similar change, sudden changes in executable files may be a sign of malware infection.

Virus Technologies

As virus detection and eradication technology rises to meet new threats programmed by malicious developers, new kinds of viruses designed to defeat those systems emerge. This section examines four specific types of viruses that use sneaky techniques in an attempt to escape detection—multipartite viruses, stealth viruses, polymorphic viruses, and encrypted viruses.

Multipartite viruses   *Multipartite viruses* use more than one propagation technique in an attempt to penetrate systems that defend against only one method or the other. For example, the Marzia virus discovered in 1993 infects critical COM and EXE files, most notably the command.com system file, by adding 2,048 bytes of malicious code to each file. This characteristic qualifies it as a file infector virus. In addition, two hours after it infects a system, it writes malicious code to the system's master boot record, qualifying it as a boot sector virus.

Stealth viruses   *Stealth viruses* hide themselves by actually tampering with the operating system to fool antivirus packages into thinking that everything is functioning normally. For example, a stealth boot sector virus might overwrite the system's master boot record with malicious code but then also modify the operating system's file access functionality to cover its tracks. When the antivirus package requests a copy of the MBR, the modified operating system code provides it with exactly what the antivirus package expects to see—a clean version of the MBR free of any virus signatures. However, when the system boots, it reads the infected MBR and loads the virus into memory.

Polymorphic viruses   *Polymorphic viruses* actually modify their own code as they travel from system to system. The virus's propagation and destruction techniques remain the same, but the signature of the virus is somewhat different each time it infects a new system. It is the hope of polymorphic virus creators that this constantly changing signature will render signature-based antivirus packages useless. However, antivirus vendors have "cracked the code" of many polymorphism techniques, so current versions of antivirus software are able to detect known polymorphic viruses. However, it tends to take vendors longer to generate the necessary signature files to stop a polymorphic virus in its tracks, which means the virus can run free on the Internet for a longer time.

Encrypted viruses   *Encrypted viruses* use cryptographic techniques, such as those described in Chapter 9, to avoid detection. In their outward appearance, they are actually quite similar to polymorphic viruses—each infected system has a virus with a different signature. However, they do not generate these modified signatures by changing their code; instead, they alter the way they are stored on the disk. Encrypted viruses use a very short segment of code, known as the *virus decryption routine*, which contains the cryptographic information necessary to load and decrypt the main virus code stored elsewhere on the disk. Each infection utilizes a different cryptographic key, causing the main code to appear completely different on each system. However, the virus decryption routines often contain telltale signatures that render them vulnerable to updated antivirus software packages.

Hoaxes

No discussion of viruses is complete without mentioning the nuisance and wasted resources caused by virus *hoaxes*. Almost every email user has, at one time or another, received a message forwarded by a friend or relative that warns of the latest virus threat roaming the Internet. Invariably, this purported "virus" is the most destructive virus ever unleashed, and no antivirus package is able to detect and/or eradicate it. One famous example of such a hoax is the Good Times virus warning that first surfaced on the Internet in 1994 and still circulates today.

For more information on this topic, the renowned virus hoax expert Rob Rosenberger maintains a website that contains a comprehensive repository of virus hoaxes. You can find it at www.vmyths.com.

Logic Bombs

As you learned in Chapter 7, "Software Development Security," *logic bombs* are malicious code objects that infect a system and lie dormant until they are triggered by the occurrence of one or more conditions such as time, program launch, website logon, and so on. The vast majority of logic bombs are programmed into custom-built applications by software developers seeking to ensure that their work is destroyed if they unexpectedly leave the company. Chapter 7 provided several examples of this type of logic bomb.

Like all malicious code objects, logic bombs come in many shapes and sizes. Indeed, many viruses and Trojan horses contain a logic bomb component. The famous Michelangelo virus caused a media frenzy when it was discovered in 1991 because of the logic bomb trigger it contained. The virus infected a system's master boot record through the sharing of infected floppy disks and then hid itself until March 6—the birthday of the famous Italian artist Michelangelo Buonarroti. On that date, it sprung into action, reformatting the hard drives of infected systems and destroying all the data they contained.

Trojan Horses

System administrators constantly warn computer users not to download and install software from the Internet unless they are absolutely sure it comes from a trusted source. In fact, many companies strictly prohibit the installation of any software not prescreened by the IT department. These policies serve to minimize the risk that an organization's network will be compromised by a *Trojan horse*—a software program that appears benevolent but carries a malicious, behind-the-scenes payload that has the potential to wreak havoc on a system or network.

Trojans differ very widely in functionality. Some will destroy all the data stored on a system in an attempt to cause a large amount of damage in as short a time frame as possible. Some are fairly innocuous. For example, a series of Trojans appeared on the Internet in mid-2002 that claimed to provide PC users with the ability to run games designed for the Microsoft Xbox gaming system on their computers. When users ran the program, it simply didn't work. However, it also inserted a value into the Windows Registry that caused a specific web page to open each time the computer booted. The Trojan creators hoped to cash in on the advertising revenue generated by the large number of page views their website received from the Xbox Trojan horses. Unfortunately for them, antivirus experts quickly discovered their true intentions, and the website was shut down.

One category of Trojan that has recently made a significant impact on the security community is rogue antivirus software. This software tricks the user into installing it by claiming to be an antivirus package, often under the guise of a pop-up ad that mimics the look and feel of a security warning. Once the user installs the software, it either steals personal information or prompts the user for payment to "update" the rogue antivirus. The "update" simply disables the Trojan!

 Real World Scenario

Botnets

A few years ago, one of the authors of this book visited an organization that suspected it had a security problem, but the organization didn't have the expertise to diagnose or resolve the issue. The major symptom was network slowness. A few basic tests found that none of the systems on the company's network ran basic antivirus software, and some of them were infected with a Trojan horse.

Why did this cause network slowness? Well, the Trojan horse made all the infected systems members of a *botnet*, a collection of computers (sometimes thousands or even millions!) across the Internet under the control of an attacker known as the *botmaster*.

The botmaster of this particular botnet used the systems on their network as part of a denial of service attack against a website that he didn't like for one reason or another. He instructed all the systems in his botnet to retrieve the same web page, over and over again, in hopes that the website would fail under the heavy load. With close to 30 infected systems on the organization's network, the botnet's attack was consuming almost all its bandwidth!

The solution was simple: Antivirus software was installed on the systems and it removed the Trojan horse. Network speeds returned to normal quickly.

Worms

Worms pose a significant risk to network security. They contain the same destructive potential as other malicious code objects with an added twist—they propagate themselves without requiring any human intervention.

The Internet Worm was the first major computer security incident to occur on the Internet. Since that time, hundreds of new worms (with thousands of variant strains) have unleashed their destructive power on the Internet. The following sections examine some specific worms.

Code Red Worm

The Code Red worm received a good deal of media attention in the summer of 2001 when it rapidly spread among web servers running unpatched versions of Microsoft's Internet Information Server (IIS). Code Red performed three malicious actions on the systems it penetrated:

- It randomly selected hundreds of IP addresses and then probed those addresses to see whether they were used by hosts running a vulnerable version of IIS. Any systems it found were quickly compromised. This greatly magnified Code Red's reach because each host it infected sought many new targets.

- It defaced HTML pages on the local web server, replacing normal content with the following text:

```
Welcome to http://www.worm.com!
Hacked By Chinese!
```

- It planted a logic bomb that would initiate a denial of service attack against the IP address 198.137.240.91, which at that time belonged to the web server hosting the White House's home page. Quick-thinking government web administrators changed the White House's IP address before the attack actually began.

The destructive power of Internet Worm, Code Red, and their many variants poses an extreme risk to the modern Internet. System administrators simply must ensure that they apply appropriate security patches to their Internet-connected systems as software vendors release them. As a case in point, a security fix for an IIS vulnerability exploited by Code Red was available from Microsoft for more than a month before the worm attacked the Internet. Had security administrators applied it promptly, Code Red would have been a miserable failure.

RTM and the Internet Worm

In November 1988, a young computer science student named Robert Tappan Morris brought the fledgling Internet to its knees with a few lines of computer code. He released a malicious worm he claimed to have created as an experiment onto the Internet. It spread quickly and crashed a large number of systems.

This worm spread by exploiting four specific security holes in the Unix operating system.

Sendmail debug mode   Then-current versions of the popular sendmail software package used to route electronic mail messages across the Internet contained a security vulnerability. This vulnerability allowed the worm to spread itself by sending a specially crafted email message that contained the worm's code to the sendmail program on a remote system. When the remote system processed the message, it became infected.

Password attack   The worm also used a dictionary attack to attempt to gain access to remote systems by utilizing the username and password of a valid system user (see "Dictionary Attacks" later in this chapter).

Finger vulnerability   Finger, a popular Internet utility, allowed users to determine who was logged on to a remote system. Then-current versions of the finger software contained a buffer-overflow vulnerability that allowed the worm to spread (see "Buffer Overflows" later in this chapter). The finger program has since been removed from most Internet-connected systems.

Trust relationships   After the worm infected a system, it analyzed any existing trust relationships with other systems on the network and attempted to spread itself to those systems through the trusted path.

This multipronged approach made Internet Worm extremely dangerous. Fortunately, the (then-small) computer security community quickly put together a crack team of investigators who disarmed the worm and patched the affected systems. Their efforts were facilitated by several inefficient routines in the worm's code that limited the rate of its spread.

Because of the lack of experience among law enforcement authorities and the court system in dealing with computer crimes along with a lack of relevant laws, Morris received only a slap on the wrist for his transgression. He was sentenced to three years' probation, 400 hours of community service, and a $10,000 fine under the Computer Fraud and Abuse Act of 1986. Ironically, Morris's father, Robert Morris, was serving as the director of the National Security Agency's National Computer Security Center (NCSC) at the time of the incident.

Stuxnet

In mid-2010, a worm named Stuxnet surfaced on the Internet. This highly sophisticated worm uses a variety of advanced techniques to spread, including multiple previously undocumented vulnerabilities. Stuxnet used the following propagation techniques:

- Searching for unprotected administrative shares of systems on the local network
- Exploiting zero-day vulnerabilities in the Windows Server service and Windows Print Spooler service
- Connecting to systems using a default database password
- Spreading by the use of shared infected USB drives

While Stuxnet spread from system to system with impunity, it was actually searching for a very specific type of system—one using a controller manufactured by Siemens and allegedly used in the production of material for nuclear weapons. When it found such a system, it executed a series of actions designed to destroy centrifuges attached to the Siemens controller.

Stuxnet appeared to begin its spread in the Middle East, specifically on systems located in Iran. It is alleged to have been designed by Western nations with the intent of disrupting an Iranian nuclear weapons program. According to a story in the *New York Times*, a facility in Israel contained equipment used to test the worm. The story stated, "Israel has spun nuclear centrifuges nearly identical to Iran's" and went on to say that "the operations there, as well as related efforts in the United States, are...clues that the virus was designed as an American-Israeli project to sabotage the Iranian program."

If these allegations are true, Stuxnet marks two major evolutions in the world of malicious code: the use of a worm to cause major physical damage to a facility and the use of malicious code in warfare between nations.

Spyware and Adware

Two other types of unwanted software interfere with the way you normally use your computer. *Spyware* monitors your actions and transmits important details to a remote system that spies on your activity. For example, spyware might wait for you to log into a banking website and then transmit your username and password to the creator of the spyware. Alternatively, it might wait for you to enter your credit card number on an e-commerce site and transmit it to a fraudster to resell on the black market.

Adware, while quite similar to spyware in form, has a different purpose. It uses a variety of techniques to display advertisements on infected computers. The simplest forms of adware display pop-up ads on your screen while you surf the Web. More nefarious versions may monitor your shopping behavior and redirect you to competitor websites.

Active Content

The increasing demand of web users for dynamic content on the sites they visit has created a dilemma for web administrators. Delivering dynamic content requires the use of web applications that can place an enormous computational burden on the server, and the increased demand for them requires a commitment of a large number of resources.

In an effort to solve this problem, software developers created the concept of *active content*, web programs that are downloaded to users' own computers for execution rather than consuming server-side resources. These programs, utilizing technologies such as Java applets and ActiveX controls, greatly reduce the load on the server and client waiting time. Most web browsers allow users to choose to have the active content automatically downloaded, installed, and executed from trusted sites. Additionally, developers have the ability to digitally sign active content to identify the author, and users can configure their browsers to run only signed content from trusted sources, reducing the risk of running active content.

Unfortunately, this technology can pose a major threat to client systems. Unsuspecting users may download active content from an untrusted source and allow it to execute on their systems, creating a significant security vulnerability. This vulnerability led to the creation of a whole new type of malicious code—the *hostile applet*. Like other forms of malware, hostile applets have a variety of intentions, from causing a denial of service attack that merely consumes system resources to more insidious goals, such as theft of data.

Countermeasures

The primary means of defense against malicious code is the use of antivirus-filtering software. These packages are primarily signature-based systems, designed to detect known viruses running on a system. It's wise to consider implementing antivirus filters in at least three key areas, described here:

Client systems   Every workstation on a network should have updated antivirus software searching the local file system for malicious code.

Server systems   Servers should have similar protections. This is even more critical than protecting client systems because a single virus on a common server could quickly spread throughout an entire network.

Content filters   The majority of viruses today are exchanged over email. It's a wise move to implement content filtering on your network that scans inbound and outbound electronic mail and web traffic for signs of malicious code.

With current antivirus software, removal is often possible within hours after new malicious code is discovered. *Removal* removes the malicious code but does not repair the damage caused by it. Cleaning capabilities are usually made available within a few days after new malicious code is discovered. *Cleaning* not only removes the code, it also repairs any damage it causes.

Remember, most antivirus filters are signature based. Therefore, they're only as good as the most recent update to their virus definition files. It's critical that you update these files frequently, especially when a new piece of high-profile malicious code appears on the Internet.

Signature-based filters rely upon the descriptions of known viruses provided by software developers. Therefore, there is a period of time between when any given virus first appears "in the wild" and when updated filters are made available. This problem has two solutions that are commonly used today:

- Integrity checking software, such as Tripwire (an open source version is available at www.tripwire.org), scans your file system for unexpected modifications and reports to you periodically.

- Access controls limit the ability of malicious code to damage your data and spread on your network. They should be strictly maintained and enforced.

Three additional techniques can specifically prevent systems from being infected by malicious code embedded in active content:

- Java's sandbox provides applets with an isolated environment in which they can run safely without gaining access to critical system resources.

- ActiveX control signing utilizes a system of digital signatures to ensure that the code originates from a trusted source. It is up to the end user to determine whether the authenticated source should be trusted.

- Whitelisting applications at the operating system level requires administrators to specify approved applications. The operating system uses this list to allow only known good applications to run.

For an in-depth explanation of digital signature technology, see Chapter 10, "PKI and Cryptographic Applications."

Many forms of malicious code take advantage of zero-day vulnerabilities, security flaws discovered by hackers that have not been thoroughly addressed by the security community. There are two main reasons systems are affected by these vulnerabilities:

- The necessary delay between the discovery of a new type of malicious code and the issuance of patches and antivirus updates

- Slowness in applying updates on the part of system administrators

The existence of zero-day vulnerabilities makes it critical that you have a strong patch management program in your organization that ensures the prompt application of critical security updates. Additionally, you may wish to use a vulnerability scanner to scan your systems on a regular basis for known security issues.

Password Attacks

One of the simplest techniques attackers use to gain illegitimate access to a system is to learn the username and password of an authorized system user. Once they've gained access as a regular user, they have a foothold into the system. At that point, they can use other techniques, including automated rootkit packages, to gain increased levels of access to the system (see the section "Escalation of Privilege and Rootkits" later in this chapter). They may also use the compromised system as a jumping-off point for attacks on other, more attractive targets on the same network.

The following sections examine three methods attackers use to learn the passwords of legitimate users and access a system: password-guessing attacks, dictionary attacks, and social-engineering attacks. Many of these attacks rely upon weak password storage mechanisms. For example, many UNIX operating systems store encrypted versions of a user's password in the /etc/passwd file.

Password Guessing

In the most basic type of password attack, attackers simply attempt to guess a user's password. No matter how much security education users receive, they often use extremely weak passwords. If attackers are able to obtain a list of authorized system users, they can often quickly figure out the correct usernames. (On most networks, usernames consist of the first initial of the user's first name followed by a portion of their last name.) With this information, they can begin making some educated guesses about the user's password. The most commonly used password is some form of the user's last name, first name, or username. For example, the user mchapple might use the weak password elppahcm because it's easy to remember. Unfortunately, it's also easy to guess.

If that attempt fails, attackers turn to widely available lists of the most common passwords on the Internet. Some of these are shown in the sidebar "Most Common Passwords."

Most Common Passwords

Attackers often use the Internet to distribute lists of commonly used passwords based on data gathered during system compromises. Many of these are no great surprise. Here are just a very few of the 815 passwords contained in an attacker list retrieved from the Internet:

Password	computer	work
Secret	football	office
sex	hello	online
money	morning	terminal
love	ibm	internet

Along with these common words, the password list contained more than 300 first names, 70 percent of which were female names.

Finally, a little knowledge about a person can provide extremely good clues about their password. Many people use the name of a spouse, child, family pet, relative, or favorite entertainer. Common passwords also include birthdays, anniversaries, Social Security numbers, phone numbers, and (believe it or not!) ATM PINs.

Dictionary Attacks

As mentioned previously, many UNIX systems store encrypted versions of user passwords in an /etc/passwd file accessible to all system users. To provide some level of security, the file doesn't contain the actual user passwords; it contains an encrypted value obtained from a one-way encryption function (see Chapter 9 for a discussion of encryption functions). When a user attempts to log on to the system, access verification routines use the same encryption function to encrypt the password entered by the user and then compare it with the encrypted version of the actual password stored in the /etc/passwd file. If the values match, the user is allowed access.

Password attackers use automated tools like the Crack program to run automated dictionary attacks that exploit a simple vulnerability in this mechanism. They take a large dictionary file that contains thousands of words and then run the encryption function against all those words to obtain their encrypted equivalents. Crack then searches the password file for any encrypted values for which there is a match in the encrypted dictionary. When a match is found, it reports the username and password (in plain text), and the attacker gains access to the system.

Password Crackers

Crack is just one password cracking program. There are many others available on the Internet that use a variety of attack techniques. These include Cain & Abel, John the Ripper, L0phtcrack, Pwdump, and RainbowCrack. Each tool specializes in different operating systems and password types. Password crackers are discussed in more detail in Chapter 2, "Access Control Attacks and Monitoring."

It sounds like simple security mechanisms and education would prevent users from using passwords that are easily guessed by Crack, but the tool is surprisingly effective at compromising live systems. As new versions of Crack are released, more advanced features are introduced to defeat common techniques used by users to defeat password complexity rules. Some of these are included in the following list:

- Rearranging the letters of a dictionary word
- Appending a number to a dictionary word
- Replacing each occurrence of the letter O in a dictionary word with the number 0 (or the letter l with the number 1)
- Combining two dictionary words in some form

Social Engineering

Social engineering is one of the most effective tools attackers use to gain access to a system. In its most basic form, a social-engineering attack consists of simply calling the user and asking for their password, posing as a technical support representative or other authority figure who needs the information immediately. Fortunately, most contemporary computer users are aware of these scams, and the effectiveness of directly asking a user for a password is somewhat diminished today. Instead, these attacks rely upon phishing emails that prompt users to log in to a fake site using their actual username and password, which are then captured by the attacker and used to log into the actual site. Phishing attacks often target financial services websites, where user credentials can be used to quickly transfer cash. In addition to tricking users into giving up their passwords, phishing attacks are often used to get users to install malware or provide other sensitive personal information.

Although users are becoming more savvy, social engineering still poses a significant threat to the security of passwords (and networks in general). Attackers can often obtain sensitive personal information by "chatting up" computer users, office gossips, and administrative personnel. This information can provide excellent ammunition when mounting a password-guessing attack. Furthermore, attackers can sometimes obtain sensitive network topography or configuration data that is useful when planning other types of electronic attacks against an organization.

Countermeasures

The cornerstone of any security program is education. Security personnel should continually remind users of the importance of choosing a secure password and keeping it secret. Users should receive training when they first enter an organization, and they should receive periodic refresher training, even if it's just an email from the administrator reminding them of the threats.

Provide users with the knowledge they need to create secure passwords. Tell them about the techniques attackers use when guessing passwords, and give them advice on how to create a strong password. One of the most effective techniques is to use a mnemonic device such as thinking of an easy-to-remember sentence and creating a password out of the first letter of each word. For example, "My son Richard likes to eat four pies" would become MsRlte4p—an extremely strong password. You may also wish to consider providing users with a secure tool that allows for the storage of these strong passwords. Password Safe and LastPass are two commonly used examples. These tools allow users to create unique, strong passwords for each service they use without the burden of memorizing them all.

One of the most common mistakes made by overzealous security administrators is to create a series of strong passwords and then assign them to users (who are then prevented from changing their password). At first glance, this seems to be a sound security policy. However, the first thing a user will do when they receive a password like 1mf0A8flt is write it down on a sticky note and put it under their computer keyboard. Whoops! Security just went out the window (or under the keyboard)!

If your network includes UNIX operating systems that implement the /etc/passwd file, consider using some other access verification mechanism to increase security. One popular technique available in many versions of UNIX and Linux is the use of a shadow password file, /etc/shadow. This file contains the true encrypted passwords of each user, but it is not accessible to anyone but the administrator. The publicly accessible /etc/passwd file then simply contains a list of usernames without the data necessary to mount a dictionary attack.

Application Attacks

In Chapter 7, you learned about the importance of utilizing solid software engineering processes when developing operating systems and applications. In the following sections, you'll take a brief look at some of the specific techniques attackers use to exploit vulnerabilities left behind by sloppy coding practices.

Buffer Overflows

Buffer overflow vulnerabilities exist when a developer does not properly validate user input to ensure that it is of an appropriate size. Input that is too large can "overflow" a data structure to affect other data stored in the computer's memory. For example, if a web form has a field that ties to a backend variable that allows 10 characters but the form processor does not verify the length of the input, the operating system may try to simply write data past the end of the memory space reserved for that variable, potentially corrupting other data stored in memory. In the worst case, that data can be used to overwrite system commands, allowing an attacker to exploit the buffer overflow vulnerability to execute arbitrary commands on the server.

When creating software, developers must pay special attention to variables that allow user input. Many programming languages do not enforce size limits on variables intrinsically—they rely on the programmer to perform this bounds checking in the code. This is an inherent vulnerability because many programmers feel parameter checking is an unnecessary burden that slows down the development process. As a security practitioner, it's your responsibility to ensure that developers in your organization are aware of the risks posed by buffer overflow vulnerabilities and that they take appropriate measures to protect their code against this type of attack.

Anytime a program variable allows user input, the programmer should take steps to ensure that each of the following conditions is met:

- The user can't enter a value longer than the size of any buffer that will hold it (for example, a 10-letter word into a 5-letter string variable).

- The user can't enter an invalid value for the variable types that will hold it (for example, a letter into a numeric variable).

- The user can't enter a value that will cause the program to operate outside of its specified parameters (for example, answer a "yes" or "no" question with "maybe").

Failure to perform simple checks to make sure these conditions are met can result in a buffer overflow vulnerability that may cause the system to crash or even allow the user to execute shell commands and gain access to the system. Buffer overflow vulnerabilities are especially prevalent in code developed rapidly for the Web using CGI or other languages that allow unskilled programmers to quickly create interactive web pages. Most buffer overflow vulnerabilities are mitigated with patches provided by software and operating system vendors, magnifying the importance of keeping systems and software up-to-date.

Time-of-Check-to-Time-of-Use

The *time-of-check-to-time-of-use (TOCTTOU or TOC/TOU)* issue is a timing vulnerability that occurs when a program checks access permissions too far in advance of a resource request. For example, if an operating system builds a comprehensive list of access permissions for a user upon logon and then consults that list throughout the logon session, a TOCTTOU vulnerability exists. If the system administrator revokes a particular permission, that restriction would not be applied to the user until the next time they log on. If the user is logged on when the access revocation takes place, they will have access to the resource indefinitely. The user simply needs to leave the session open for days, and the new restrictions will never be applied.

Back Doors

Back doors are undocumented command sequences that allow individuals with knowledge of the back door to bypass normal access restrictions. They are often used during the development and debugging process to speed up the workflow and avoid forcing developers to continuously authenticate to the system. Occasionally, developers leave these back doors in the system after it reaches a production state, either by accident or so they can "take a peek" at their system when it is processing sensitive data to which they should not have access. In addition to back doors planted by developers, many types of malicious code create back doors on infected systems that allow the developers of the malicious code to remotely access infected systems.

No matter how they arise on a system, the undocumented nature of back doors makes them a significant threat to the security of any system that contains them. Individuals with knowledge of the back door may use it to access the system and retrieve confidential information, monitor user activity, or engage in other nefarious acts.

Escalation of Privilege and Rootkits

Once attackers gain a foothold on a system, they often quickly move on to a second objective—expanding their access from the normal user account they may have compromised to more comprehensive, administrative access. They do this by engaging in *escalation of privilege attacks*.

One of the most common ways that attackers wage escalation of privilege attacks is through the use of *rootkits*. Rootkits are freely available on the Internet and exploit known vulnerabilities in various operating systems. Attackers often obtain access to a standard system user account through the use of a password attack or social engineering and then use a rootkit to increase their access to the root (or administrator) level. This increase in access from standard to administrative privileges is known as an escalation of privilege attack.

Administrators can take one simple precaution to protect their systems against escalation of privilege attacks, and it's nothing new. Administrators must keep themselves informed about new security patches released for operating systems used in their environment and apply these corrective measures consistently. This straightforward step will fortify a network against almost all rootkit attacks as well as a large number of other potential vulnerabilities.

Web Application Security

The Web allows you to purchase airline tickets, check your email, pay your bills, and purchase stocks all from the comfort of your living room. Almost every business today operates a website, and many allow you to conduct sensitive transactions through that site.

Along with the convenience benefits of web applications comes a series of new vulnerabilities that may expose web-enabled organizations to security risks. In the next several sections, we'll cover two common web application attacks. Additional detail on web application security can be found in Chapter 12, "Security Architecture Vulnerabilities, Threats, and Countermeasures."

Cross-Site Scripting (XSS)

Cross-site scripting (XSS) attacks occur when web applications contain some type of *reflected input*. For example, consider a simple web application that contains a single text box asking a user to enter their name. When the user clicks Submit, the web application loads a new page that says, "Hello, *name*."

Under normal circumstances, this web application functions as designed. However, a malicious individual could take advantage of this web application to trick an unsuspecting third party. As you may know, you can embed scripts in web pages by using the HTML tags <SCRIPT> and </SCRIPT>. Suppose that, instead of entering *Mike* in the Name field, you enter the following text:

```
Mike<SCRIPT>alert('hello')</SCRIPT>
```

When the web application "reflects" this input in the form of a web page, your browser processes it as it would any other web page: It displays the text portions of the web page and executes the script portions. In this case, the script simply opens a pop-up window that says "hello" in it. However, you could be more malicious and include a more sophisticated script that asks the user to provide a password and transmits it to a malicious third party.

At this point, you're probably asking yourself how anyone would fall victim to this type of attack. After all, you're not going to attack yourself by embedding scripts in the input that you provide to a web application that performs reflection. The key to this attack is that it's possible to embed form input in a link. A malicious individual could create a web page with a link titled "Check your account at First Bank" and encode form input in the link. When the user visits the link, the web page appears to be an authentic First Bank website (because it is!) with the proper address in the toolbar and a valid SSL certificate. However, the website would then execute the script included in the input by the malicious user, which appears to be part of the valid web page.

What's the answer to cross-site scripting? When you create web applications that allow any type of user input, you must be sure to perform *input validation*. At the most basic level, you should never allow a user to include the <SCRIPT> tag in a reflected input field. However, this doesn't solve the problem completely; there are many clever alternatives available to an industrious web application attacker. The best solution is to determine the type of input that you *will* allow and then validate the input to ensure that it matches that pattern. For example, if you have a text box that allows users to enter their age, you should accept only one to three digits as input. Your application should reject any other input as invalid.

SQL Injection

SQL injection attacks are even riskier than XSS attacks from an organization's perspective. As with XSS attacks, SQL injection attacks use unexpected input to a web application. However, instead of using this input to attempt to fool a user, SQL injection attacks use it to gain unauthorized access to an underlying database.

Dynamic Web Applications

In the early days of the Web, all web pages were *static*, or unchanging. Webmasters created web pages containing information and placed them on a web server, where users could retrieve them using their web browsers. The Web quickly outgrew this model because users wanted the ability to access customized information based upon their individual needs. For example, visitors to a bank website aren't interested only in static pages containing information about the bank's locations, hours, and services. They also want to retrieve *dynamic* content containing information about their personal accounts. Obviously, the webmaster can't possibly create pages on the web server for each individual user with that user's personal account information. At a large bank, that would require maintaining millions of pages with up-to-the-minute information. That's where dynamic web applications come into play.

Web applications take advantage of a database to create content on demand when the user makes a request. In the banking example, the user logs into the web application, providing an account number and password. The web application then retrieves current account information from the bank's database and uses it to instantly create a web page containing the user's current account information. If that user returns an hour later, the web server would repeat the process, obtaining updated account information from the database. Figure 8.1 illustrates this model.

FIGURE 8.1 Typical database-driven website architecture

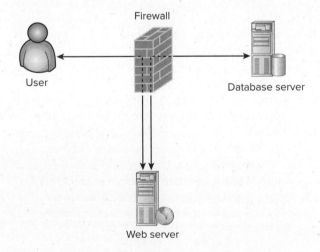

What does this mean to you as a security professional? Web applications add complexity to our traditional security model. As shown in Figure 8.1, the web server, as a publicly accessible server, belongs in a separate network zone from other servers, commonly referred to as a demilitarized zone (DMZ). The database server, on the other hand, is not meant for public access, so it belongs on the internal network. The web application needs access to the database, so the firewall administrator must create a rule allowing access from the web server to the database server. This rule creates a potential path for Internet users to gain access to the database server. (For more on firewalls and DMZs, see Chapter 3, "Secure Network Architecture and Securing Network Components.") If the web application functions properly, it will allow only authorized requests to the database. However, if there is a flaw in the web application, it may allow individuals to tamper with the database in an unexpected and unauthorized fashion through the use of SQL injection attacks.

SQL Injection Attacks

SQL injection attacks allow a malicious individual to directly perform SQL transactions against the underlying database, in violation of the isolation model shown in Figure 8.1.

For more on databases and SQL, see Chapter 7.

In the example used earlier, a bank customer might enter an account number to gain access to a dynamic web application that retrieves current account details. The web application must use a SQL query to obtain that information, perhaps of the following form, where *<number>* is the account number provided by the user on the web form:

```
SELECT *
FROM transactions
WHERE account_number = '<number>'
```

There's one more important fact you need to know: Databases will process multiple SQL statements at the same time, provided that you end each one with a semicolon.

If the web application doesn't perform proper input validation, the user may be able to insert their own SQL code into the statement executed by the web server. For example, if the user's account number is 145249, they could enter the following:

```
145249'; DELETE * FROM transactions WHERE 'a' = 'a
```

The web application would then obediently plug this in to the *<number>* field in the earlier SQL statement, resulting in the following:

```
SELECT *
FROM transactions
WHERE account_number ='145249'; DELETE * FROM transactions WHERE 'a' = 'a'
```

Reformatting that command slightly, you get the following:

```
SELECT *
FROM transactions
WHERE account_number ='145249';
DELETE *
FROM transactions
WHERE 'a' = 'a'
```

This is a valid SQL transaction containing two statements. The first one retrieves the requested information from the database. The second statement deletes all the records stored in the database. Whoops!

Protecting against SQL Injection

You can use three techniques to protect your web applications against SQL injection attacks:

Perform input validation   As described earlier in this chapter when talking about cross-site scripting, input validation allows you to limit the types of data a user provides in a form. In the case of the SQL injection example we provided in the previous section, removing the single quote characters (') from the input would prevent the successful use of this attack. This is the most effective means of preventing SQL injection attacks.

Limit account privileges   The database account used by the web server should have the smallest set of privileges possible. If the web application needs only to retrieve data, it should have that ability only. In the example, the DELETE command would fail if the account had SELECT privileges only.

Use stored procedures   Developers of web applications should leverage database stored procedures to limit the application's ability to execute arbitrary code. With stored procedures, the SQL statement resides on the database server and may be modified only by database administrators. Web applications calling the stored procedure may pass parameters to it but may not alter the underlying structure of the SQL statement.

Reconnaissance Attacks

As with any attacking force, attackers require solid intelligence to effectively focus their efforts against the targets most likely to yield the best results. To assist with this targeting, attacker-tool developers have created a number of automated tools that perform network reconnaissance. In the following sections, we'll cover three of those automated techniques—IP probes, port scans, and vulnerability scans—and then explain how these techniques can be supplemented by the more physically intensive dumpster-diving technique.

IP Probes

IP probes (also called *IP sweeps* or *ping sweeps*) are often the first type of network reconnaissance carried out against a targeted network. With this technique, automated tools simply attempt to ping each address in a range. Systems that respond to the ping request are logged for further analysis. Addresses that do not produce a response are assumed to be unused and are ignored.

The Nmap tool is one of the most common tools used to perform both IP probes and port scans. It's available for free download from www.nmap.org.

IP probes are extremely prevalent on the Internet today. Indeed, if you configure a system with a public IP address and connect it to the Internet, you'll probably receive at least one IP probe within hours of booting up. The widespread use of this technique makes a strong case for disabling ping functionality, at least for users external to a network.

Port Scans

After an attacker performs an IP probe, they are left with a list of active systems on a given network. The next task is to select one or more systems to target with additional attacks. Often, attackers have a type of target in mind; web servers, file servers, and other servers supporting critical operations are prime targets.

To narrow down their search, attackers use *port scan* software to probe all the active systems on a network and determine what public services are running on each machine. For example, if the attacker wants to target a web server, they might run a port scan to locate any systems with a service running on port 80, the default port for HTTP services.

Vulnerability Scans

The third technique is the *vulnerability scan*. Once the attacker determines a specific system to target, they need to discover a specific vulnerability in that system that can be exploited to gain the desired access permissions. A variety of tools available on the Internet assist with this task. Two of the more popular ones are the Nessus and Saint vulnerability scanners. These packages contain a database of known vulnerabilities and probe targeted systems to locate security flaws. They then produce very attractive reports that detail every vulnerability detected. From that point, it's simply a matter of locating a script that exploits a specific vulnerability and launching an attack against the victim.

It's important to note that vulnerability scanners are highly automated tools. They can be used to launch an attack against a specific system, but it's just as likely that an attacker would use a series of IP probes, port scans, and vulnerability scans to narrow down a list of potential victims. However, chances are an intruder will run a vulnerability scanner against an entire network to probe for any weakness that could be exploited.

Once again, simply updating operating systems to the most recent security patch level can repair almost every weakness reported by a vulnerability scanner. Furthermore, wise system administrators learn to think like the enemy—they download and run these vulnerability scanners against their own networks (with the permission of upper management) to see what security holes might be pointed out to a potential attacker. This allows them to quickly focus their resources on fortifying the weakest points on their networks.

Dumpster Diving

Every organization generates trash—often significant amounts on a daily basis. Have you ever taken the time to sort through your trash to see the sensitivity of the materials that hit the recycle bin? Give it a try—the results may frighten you. When you're analyzing the work papers thrown away each day, look at them from an attacker's perspective. What type of intelligence could you glean from them that might help you launch an attack? Is there sensitive data about network configurations or installed software versions? A list of employees' birthdays from a particular department that might be used in a social-engineering attack? A policy manual that contains detailed procedures on the creation of new accounts? Discarded floppy disks or other storage media?

Don't underestimate the value of even trivial corporate documents to a social engineer. Kevin Mitnick, a famous social engineer, once admitted to using company newsletters as a key component of his attacks. He skipped right to the section containing a listing of new hires, recognizing that these individuals were perfect victims, all too eager to please someone calling from the "top floor" requesting sensitive information.

Dumpster diving is one of the oldest attacker tools in the book, and it's still used today. The best defense against these attacks is quite simple—make them more difficult. Purchase shredders for key departments, and encourage employees to use them. Keep the trash locked up in a secure area until the garbage collectors arrive. A little common sense goes a long way in this area.

Masquerading Attacks

One of the easiest ways to gain access to resources you're not otherwise entitled to use is to impersonate someone who does have the appropriate access permissions. In the offline world, teenagers often borrow the driver's license of an older sibling to purchase alcohol, and the same type of thing happens in the computer security world. Attackers borrow the identities of legitimate users and systems to gain the trust of third parties. In the following sections, we'll take a look at two common masquerading attacks—IP spoofing and session hijacking.

IP Spoofing

In an *IP spoofing attack*, the malicious individual simply reconfigures their system so that it has the IP address of a trusted system and then attempts to gain access to other external resources. This is surprisingly effective on many networks that don't have adequate filters installed to prevent this type of traffic from occurring. System administrators should configure filters at the perimeter of each network to ensure that packets meet at least the following criteria:

- Packets with internal source IP addresses don't enter the network from the outside.
- Packets with external source IP addresses don't exit the network from the inside.
- Packets with private IP addresses don't pass through the router in either direction (unless specifically allowed as part of an intranet configuration).

These three simple filtering rules can eliminate the vast majority of IP spoofing attacks and greatly enhance the security of a network.

Session Hijacking

Session hijacking attacks occur when a malicious individual intercepts part of the communication between an authorized user and a resource and then uses a hijacking technique to take over the session and assume the identity of the authorized user. The following list includes some common techniques:

- Capturing details of the authentication between a client and server and using those details to assume the client's identity
- Tricking the client into thinking the attacker's system is the server, acting as the middleman as the client sets up a legitimate connection with the server, and then disconnecting the client
- Accessing a web application using the cookie data of a user who did not properly close the connection

All of these techniques can have disastrous results for the end user and must be addressed with both administrative controls (such as antireplay authentication techniques) and application controls (such as expiring cookies within a reasonable period of time).

Summary

Applications developers have a lot to worry about! As hackers become more sophisticated in their tools and techniques, the application layer is increasingly becoming the focus of their attacks due to its complexity and multiple points of vulnerability.

Malicious code, including viruses, worms, Trojan horses, and logic bombs, exploits vulnerabilities in applications and operating systems or uses social engineering to infect systems and gain access to their resources and confidential information.

Applications themselves also may contain a number of vulnerabilities. Buffer overflow attacks exploit code that lacks proper input validation to affect the contents of a system's memory. Back doors provide former developers and malicious code authors with the ability to bypass normal security mechanisms. Rootkits provide attackers with an easy way to conduct escalation of privilege attacks.

Many applications are moving to the Web, creating a new level of exposure and vulnerability. Cross-site scripting attacks allow hackers to trick users into providing sensitive information to unsecure sites. SQL injection attacks allow the bypassing of application controls to directly access and manipulate the underlying database.

Reconnaissance tools provide attackers with automated tools they can use to identify vulnerable systems that may be attacked at a later date. IP probes, port scans, and vulnerability scans are all automated ways to detect weak points in an organization's security controls. Masquerading attacks use stealth techniques to allow the impersonation of users and systems.

Exam Essentials

Understand the propagation techniques used by viruses.   Viruses use four main propagation techniques—file infection, service injection, boot sector infection, and macro infection—to penetrate systems and spread their malicious payloads. You need to understand these techniques to effectively protect systems on your network from malicious code.

Know how antivirus software packages detect known viruses.   Most antivirus programs use signature-based detection algorithms to look for telltale patterns of known viruses. This makes it essential to periodically update virus definition files in order to maintain protection against newly authored viruses as they emerge.

Explain the techniques that attackers use to compromise password security.   Passwords are the most common access control mechanism in use today and it is essential that you understand how to protect against attackers who seek to undermine their security. Know how password crackers, dictionary attacks, and social engineering can be used to defeat password security.

Be familiar with the various types of application attacks attackers use to exploit poorly written software.   Application attacks are one of the greatest threats to modern computing. Attackers exploit buffer overflows, trap doors, time-of-check-to-time-of-use vulnerabilities, and rootkits to gain illegitimate access to a system. Security professionals must have a clear understanding of each of these attacks and associated countermeasures.

Understand common web application vulnerabilities and countermeasures.   As many applications move to the Web, developers and security professionals must understand the new types of attacks that exist in this environment and how to protect against them. The two most common examples are cross-site scripting (XSS) and SQL injection attacks.

Know the network reconnaissance techniques used by attackers preparing to attack a network.   Before launching an attack, attackers use IP sweeps to search out active hosts on a network. These hosts are then subjected to port scans and other vulnerability probes to locate weak spots that might be attacked in an attempt to compromise the network. You should understand these attacks to help protect your network against them, limiting the amount of information attackers may glean.

Written Lab

1. What is the major difference between a virus and a worm?
2. Explain the four propagation methods used by Robert Tappan Morris's Internet Worm.
3. What are the actions an antivirus software package might take when it discovers an infected file?
4. Explain how a data integrity assurance package like Tripwire provides some secondary virus detection capabilities.

Review Questions

1. What is the most commonly used technique to protect against virus attacks?
   - **A.** Signature detection
   - **B.** Heuristic detection
   - **C.** Data integrity assurance
   - **D.** Automated reconstruction

2. You are the security administrator for an e-commerce company and are placing a new web server into production. What network zone should you use?
   - **A.** Internet
   - **B.** DMZ
   - **C.** Intranet
   - **D.** Sandbox

3. Which one of the following types of attacks relies upon the difference between the timing of two events?
   - **A.** Smurf
   - **B.** TOCTTOU
   - **C.** Land
   - **D.** Fraggle

4. Which of the following techniques requires that administrators identify appropriate applications for an environment?
   - **A.** Sandboxing
   - **B.** Control signing
   - **C.** Integrity monitoring
   - **D.** Whitelisting

5. What advanced virus technique modifies the malicious code of a virus on each system it infects?
   - **A.** Polymorphism
   - **B.** Stealth
   - **C.** Encryption
   - **D.** Multipartitism

6. Which one of the following tools provides a solution to the problem of users forgetting complex passwords?

    A. LastPass

    B. Crack

    C. Shadow password files

    D. Tripwire

7. What type of application vulnerability most directly allows an attacker to modify the contents of a system's memory?

    A. Rootkit

    B. Back door

    C. TOC/TOU

    D. Buffer overflow

8. Which one of the following passwords is least likely to be compromised during a dictionary attack?

    A. mike

    B. elppa

    C. dayorange

    D. fsasoalg

9. What file is instrumental in preventing dictionary attacks against UNIX systems?

    A. /etc/passwd

    B. /etc/shadow

    C. /etc/security

    D. /etc/pwlog

10. What character should always be treated carefully when encountered as user input on a web form?

    A. !

    B. &

    C. *

    D. '

11. What database technology, if implemented for web forms, can limit the potential for SQL injection attacks?

    A. Triggers

    B. Stored procedures

    C. Column encryption

    D. Concurrency control

12. What type of reconnaissance attack provides attackers with useful information about the services running on a system?

    A. Session hijacking

    B. Port scan

    C. Dumpster diving

    D. IP sweep

13. What condition is necessary on a web page for it to be used in a cross-site scripting attack?

    A. Reflected input

    B. Database-driven content

    C. .NET technology

    D. CGI scripts

14. What type of virus utilizes more than one propagation technique to maximize the number of penetrated systems?

    A. Stealth virus

    B. Companion virus

    C. Polymorphic virus

    D. Multipartite virus

15. What is the most effective defense against cross-site scripting attacks?

    A. Limiting account privileges

    B. Input validation

    C. User authentication

    D. Encryption

16. What worm was the first to cause major physical damage to a facility?

    A. Stuxnet

    B. Code Red

    C. Melissa

    D. rtm

17. Ben's system was infected by malicious code that modified the operating system to allow the malicious code author to gain access to his files. What type of exploit did this attacker engage in?

    A. Escalation of privilege

    B. Back door

    C. Rootkit

    D. Buffer overflow

18. What technology does the Java language use to minimize the threat posed by applets?

   A. Confidentiality

   B. Encryption

   C. Stealth

   D. Sandbox

19. What HTML tag is often used as part of a cross-site scripting (XSS) attack?

   A. <H1>

   B. <HEAD>

   C. <XSS>

   D. <SCRIPT>

20. When designing firewall rules to prevent IP spoofing, which of the following principles should you follow?

   A. Packets with internal source IP addresses don't enter the network from the outside.

   B. Packets with internal source IP addresses don't exit the network from the inside.

   C. Packets with public IP addresses don't pass through the router in either direction.

   D. Packets with external source IP addresses don't enter the network from the outside.

Chapter
9

Cryptography and Symmetric Key Algorithms

THE CISSP EXAM TOPICS COVERED IN THIS CHAPTER INCLUDE:

5. Cryptography

    A. Understand the application and use of cryptography

        A.1 Data at rest (e.g., hard drive)

        A.2 Data in transit (e.g., on the wire)

    B. Understand the cryptographic life cycle (e.g., cryptographic limitations, algorithm/protocol governance)

    C. Understand encryption concepts

        C.1 Foundational concepts

        C.2 Symmetric cryptography

        C.3 Asymmetric cryptography

        C.5 Message digests

        C.6 Hashing

    D. Understand key management processes

        D.1 Creation/distribution

        D.2 Storage/destruction

        D.3 Recovery

        D.4 Key escrow

    F. Understand non-repudiation

Cryptography provides added levels of security to data during processing, storage, and communications. Over the years, mathematicians and computer scientists have developed a series of increasingly complex algorithms designed to ensure confidentiality, integrity, authentication, and nonrepudiation. While cryptographers spent time developing strong encryption algorithms, hackers and governments alike devoted significant resources to undermining them. This led to an "arms race" in cryptography and resulted in the development of the extremely sophisticated algorithms in use today. This chapter looks at the history of cryptography, the basics of cryptographic communications, and the fundamental principles of private key cryptosystems. The next chapter continues the discussion of cryptography by examining public key cryptosystems and the various techniques attackers use to defeat cryptography.

Historical Milestones in Cryptography

Since the beginning of mankind, human beings have devised various systems of written communication, ranging from ancient hieroglyphics written on cave walls to flash storage devices stuffed with encyclopedias full of information in modern English. As long as mankind has been communicating, we've used secretive means to hide the true meaning of those communications from the uninitiated. Ancient societies used a complex system of secret symbols to represent safe places to stay during times of war. Modern civilizations use a variety of codes and ciphers to facilitate private communication between individuals and groups. In the following sections, you'll look at the evolution of modern cryptography and several famous attempts to covertly intercept and decipher encrypted communications.

Caesar Cipher

One of the earliest known cipher systems was used by Julius Caesar to communicate with Cicero in Rome while he was conquering Europe. Caesar knew that there were several risks when sending messages—one of the messengers might be an enemy spy or might be ambushed while en route to the deployed forces. For that reason, Caesar developed a cryptographic system now known as the *Caesar cipher*. The system is extremely simple. To encrypt a message, you simply shift each letter of the alphabet three places to the right. For example, A would become D, and B would become E. If you reach the end of the alphabet during this process, you simply wrap around to the beginning so that X becomes A, Y becomes B, and Z becomes C. For this reason, the Caesar cipher also became known as the ROT3 (or Rotate 3) cipher. The Caesar cipher is a substitution cipher that is monoalphabetic; it's also known as a C3 cipher.

While the Caesar cipher uses a shift of 3, the more general shift cipher uses the same algorithm to shift any number of characters desired by the user. For example, the ROT12 cipher would turn an *A* into an *M*, a *B* into an *N*, and so on.

Here's an example of the Caesar cipher in action. The first line contains the original sentence, and the second line shows what the sentence looks like when it is encrypted using the Caesar cipher:

```
THE DIE HAS BEEN CAST
WKH GLH KDV EHHQ FDVW
```

To decrypt the message, you simply shift each letter three places to the left.

Although the Caesar cipher is easy to use, it's also easy to crack. It's vulnerable to a type of attack known as frequency analysis. As you may know, the most common letters in the English language are *E, T, A, O, N, R, I, S,* and *H*. An attacker seeking to break a Caesar-style cipher merely needs to find the most common letters in the encrypted text and experiment with substitutions of these common letters to help determine the pattern.

American Civil War

Between the time of Caesar and the early years of the United States, scientists and mathematicians made significant advances beyond the early ciphers used by ancient civilizations. During the American Civil War, Union and Confederate troops both used relatively advanced cryptographic systems to secretly communicate along the front lines because each side was tapping into the telegraph lines to spy on the other side. These systems used complex combinations of word substitutions and transposition (see the section "Ciphers," later in this chapter, for more details) to attempt to defeat enemy decryption efforts. Another system used widely during the Civil War was a series of flag signals developed by army doctor Albert Myer.

Photos of many of the items discussed in this chapter are available online at www.nsa.gov/about/cryptologic_heritage/museum.

Ultra vs. Enigma

Americans weren't the only ones who expended significant resources in the pursuit of superior code-making machines. Prior to World War II, the German military-industrial complex adapted a commercial code machine nicknamed Enigma for government use. This machine used a series of three to six rotors to implement an extremely complicated substitution cipher. The only possible way to decrypt the message with contemporary technology was to use a similar machine with the same rotor settings used by the transmitting device. The Germans recognized the importance of safeguarding these devices and made it extremely difficult for the Allies to acquire one.

The Allied forces began a top-secret effort known by the code name Ultra to attack the Enigma codes. Eventually, their efforts paid off when the Polish military successfully reconstructed an Enigma prototype and shared their findings with British and American cryptology experts. The Allies successfully broke the Enigma code in 1940, and historians credit this triumph as playing a significant role in the eventual defeat of the Axis powers.

The Japanese used a similar machine, known as the Japanese Purple Machine, during World War II. A significant American attack on this cryptosystem resulted in breaking the Japanese code prior to the end of the war. The Americans were aided by the fact that Japanese communicators used very formal message formats that resulted in a large amount of similar text in multiple messages, easing the cryptanalytic effort.

Cryptographic Basics

The study of any science must begin with a discussion of some of the fundamental principles upon which it is built. The following sections lay this foundation with a review of the goals of cryptography, an overview of the basic concepts of cryptographic technology, and a look at the major mathematical principles utilized by cryptographic systems.

Goals of Cryptography

Security practitioners utilize cryptographic systems to meet four fundamental goals: confidentiality, integrity, authentication, and nonrepudiation. Achieving each of these goals requires the satisfaction of a number of design requirements, and not all cryptosystems are intended to achieve all four goals. In the following sections, we'll examine each goal in detail and give a brief description of the technical requirements necessary to achieve it.

Confidentiality

Confidentiality ensures that data remains private while at rest, such as when stored on a disk, or in transit, such as during transmission between two or more parties. This is perhaps the most widely cited goal of cryptosystems—the preservation of secrecy for stored information or for communications between individuals and groups. Two main types of cryptosystems enforce confidentiality. Symmetric key cryptosystems use a shared secret key available to all users of the cryptosystem. Asymmetric cryptosystems utilize individual combinations of public and private keys for each user of the system. Both of these concepts are explored in the section "Modern Cryptography" later in this chapter.

The concept of protecting data at rest and data in transit is often covered on the CISSP exam. You should also know that data in transit is also commonly called data "on the wire," referring to the network cables that carry data communications.

When developing a cryptographic system for the purpose of providing confidentiality, you must think about two different types of data:

Data at rest, or stored data, is that which resides in a permanent location awaiting access. Examples of data at rest include data stored on hard drives, backup tapes, USB devices, and other storage media.

Data in motion, or data "on the wire," is data being transmitted across a network between two systems. Data in motion might be traveling on a corporate network, a wireless network, or the public Internet.

Both data in motion and data at rest pose different types of confidentiality risks that cryptography can protect against. For example, data in motion may be susceptible to eavesdropping attacks, while data at rest is more susceptible to the theft of physical devices.

Integrity

Integrity ensures that data is not altered without authorization. If integrity mechanisms are in place, the recipient of a message can be certain that the message received is identical to the message that was sent. Similarly, integrity checks can ensure that stored data was not altered between the time it was created and the time it was accessed. Integrity controls protect against all forms of alteration: intentional alteration by a third party attempting to insert false information and unintentional alteration by faults in the transmission process.

Message integrity is enforced through the use of encrypted message digests, known as digital signatures created upon transmission of a message. The recipient of the message simply verifies that the message's digital signature is valid, ensuring that the message was not altered in transit. Integrity can be enforced by both public and secret key cryptosystems. This concept is discussed in detail in the section "Digital Signatures" in Chapter 10. The use of cryptographic hash functions to protect file integrity is discussed in Chapter 8, "Malicious Code and Application Attacks."

Authentication

Authentication verifies the claimed identity of system users and is a major function of cryptosystems. For example, suppose that Bob wants to establish a communications session with Alice and they are both participants in a shared secret communications system. Alice might use a challenge-response authentication technique to ensure that Bob is who he claims to be.

Figure 9.1 shows how this challenge-response protocol might work in action. In this example, the shared-secret code used by Alice and Bob is quite simple—the letters of each word are simply reversed. Bob first contacts Alice and identifies himself. Alice then sends a challenge message to Bob, asking him to encrypt a short message using the secret code known only to Alice and Bob. Bob replies with the encrypted message. After Alice verifies that the encrypted message is correct, she trusts that Bob himself is truly on the other end of the connection.

FIGURE 9.1 Challenge-response authentication protocol

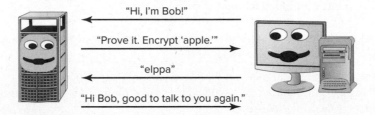

"Hi, I'm Bob!"

"Prove it. Encrypt 'apple.'"

"elppa"

"Hi Bob, good to talk to you again."

Nonrepudiation

Nonrepudiation provides assurance to the recipient that the message was actually originated by the sender and not someone masquerading as the sender. It also prevents the sender from claiming that they never sent the message in the first place (also known as *repudiating* the message). Secret key, or symmetric key, cryptosystems (such as simple substitution ciphers) do not provide this guarantee of nonrepudiation. If Jim and Bob participate in a secret key communication system, they can both produce the same encrypted message using their shared secret key. Nonrepudiation is offered only by public key, or asymmetric, cryptosystems, a topic discussed in greater detail in Chapter 10.

Cryptography Concepts

As with any science, you must be familiar with certain terminology before studying cryptography. Let's take a look at a few of the key terms used to describe codes and ciphers. Before a message is put into a coded form, it is known as a *plaintext* message and is represented by the letter P when encryption functions are described. The sender of a message uses a cryptographic algorithm to *encrypt* the plaintext message and produce a *ciphertext* message, represented by the letter C. This message is transmitted by some physical or electronic means to the recipient. The recipient then uses a predetermined algorithm to decrypt the ciphertext message and retrieve the plaintext version. (For an illustration of this process, see Figure 9.3 later in this chapter.)

All cryptographic algorithms rely upon *keys* to maintain their security. For the most part, a key is nothing more than a number. It's usually a very large binary number, but a number nonetheless. Every algorithm has a specific *key space*. The key space is the range of values that are valid for use as a key for a specific algorithm. A key space is defined by its *bit size*. Bit size is nothing more than the number of binary bits (0s and 1s) in the key. The key space is the range between the key that has all 0s and the key that has all 1s. Or to state it another way, the key space is the range of numbers from 0 to 2^n, where n is the bit size of the key. So, a 128-bit key can have a value from 0 to 2^{128} (which is roughly 3.40282367 * 10^{38}, a very big number!). It is absolutely critical to protect the security of secret keys. In fact, all of the security you gain from cryptography rests on your ability to keep the keys used private.

The Kerchoff Principle

All cryptography relies upon algorithms. An *algorithm* is a set of rules, usually mathematical, that dictates how enciphering and deciphering processes are to take place. Most cryptographers follow the Kerchoff principle, a concept that makes algorithms known and public, allowing anyone to examine and test them. Specifically, the *Kerchoff principle* (also known as Kerchoff's assumption) is that a cryptographic system should be secure even if everything about the system, except the key, is public knowledge. The principle can be summed up as "The enemy knows the system."

A large number of cryptographers adhere to this principle, but not all agree. In fact, some believe that better overall security can be maintained by keeping both the algorithm and the key private. Kerchoff's adherents retort that the opposite approach includes the dubious practice of "security through obscurity" and believe that public exposure produces more activity and exposes more weaknesses more readily, leading to the abandonment of insufficiently strong algorithms and quicker adoption of suitable ones.

As you'll learn in this chapter and the next, different types of algorithms require different types of keys. In private key (or secret key) cryptosystems, all participants use a single shared key. In public key cryptosystems, each participant has their own pair of keys. Cryptographic keys are sometimes referred to as *cryptovariables*.

The art of creating and implementing secret codes and ciphers is known as *cryptography*. This practice is paralleled by the art of *cryptanalysis*—the study of methods to defeat codes and ciphers. Together, cryptography and cryptanalysis are commonly referred to as *cryptology*. Specific implementations of a code or cipher in hardware and software are known as *cryptosystems*. Federal Information Processing Standard (FIPS) 140–2, "Security Requirements for Cryptographic Modules," defines the hardware and software requirements for cryptographic modules that the federal government uses.

> Be sure to understand the meanings of the terms in this section before continuing your study of this chapter and the following chapter. They are essential to understanding the technical details of the cryptographic algorithms presented in the following sections.

Cryptographic Mathematics

Cryptography is no different from most computer science disciplines in that it finds its foundations in the science of mathematics. To fully understand cryptography, you must first understand the basics of binary mathematics and the logical operations used to manipulate binary values. The following sections present a brief look at some of the most fundamental concepts with which you should be familiar.

Boolean Mathematics

Boolean mathematics defines the rules used for the bits and bytes that form the nervous system of any computer. You're most likely familiar with the decimal system. It is a base 10 system in which an integer from 0 to 9 is used in each place and each place value is a multiple of 10. It's likely that our reliance upon the decimal system has biological origins—human beings have 10 fingers that can be used to count.

> Boolean math can be very confusing at first, but it's worth the investment of time to learn how logical functions work. You need to understand these concepts to truly understand the inner workings of cryptographic algorithms.

Similarly, the computer's reliance upon the boolean system has electrical origins. In an electrical circuit, there are only two possible states—on (representing the presence of electrical current) and off (representing the absence of electrical current). All computation performed by an electrical device must be expressed in these terms, giving rise to the use of boolean computation in modern electronics. In general, computer scientists refer to the on condition as a *true* value and the off condition as a *false* value.

Logical Operations

The boolean mathematics of cryptography utilizes a variety of logical functions to manipulate data. We'll take a brief look at several of these operations.

AND

The AND operation (represented by the $\wedge$ symbol) checks to see whether two values are both true. The truth table that follows illustrates all four possible outputs for the AND function. Remember, the AND function takes only two variables as input. In boolean math, there are only two possible values for each of these variables, leading to four possible inputs to the AND function. It's this finite number of possibilities that makes it extremely easy for computers to implement logical functions in hardware. Notice in the following truth table that only one combination of inputs (where both inputs are true) produces an output value of true:

X	Y	X $\wedge$ Y
0	0	0
0	1	0
1	0	0
1	1	1

Logical operations are often performed on entire boolean words rather than single values. Take a look at the following example:

```
X:   0 1 1 0 1 1 0 0
Y:   1 0 1 0 0 1 1 1
```
```
X ∧ Y:   0 0 1 0 0 1 0 0
```

Notice that the AND function is computed by comparing the values of X and Y in each column. The output value is true only in columns where both X and Y are true.

OR

The OR operation (represented by the $\vee$ symbol) checks to see whether at least one of the input values is true. Refer to the following truth table for all possible values of the OR function. Notice that the only time the OR function returns a false value is when both of the input values are false:

X	Y	X $\vee$ Y
0	0	0
0	1	1
1	0	1
1	1	1

We'll use the same example we used in the previous section to show you what the output would be if X and Y were fed into the OR function rather than the AND function:

```
X:    0 1 1 0 1 1 0 0
Y:    1 0 1 0 0 1 1 1

X ∨ Y:  1 1 1 0 1 1 1 1
```

NOT

The NOT operation (represented by the ~ or ! symbol) simply reverses the value of an input variable. This function operates on only one variable at a time. Here's the truth table for the NOT function:

X	~X
0	1
1	0

In this example, you take the value of X from the previous examples and run the NOT function against it:

```
X:    0 1 1 0 1 1 0 0

~X:   1 0 0 1 0 0 1 1
```

Exclusive OR

The final logical function you'll examine in this chapter is perhaps the most important and most commonly used in cryptographic applications—the exclusive OR (XOR) function. It's referred to in mathematical literature as the XOR function and is commonly represented by the ⊕ symbol. The XOR function returns a true value when only one of the input values is true. If both values are false or both values are true, the output of the XOR function is false. Here is the truth table for the XOR operation:

X	Y	X ⊕ Y
0	0	0
0	1	1
1	0	1
1	1	0

The following operation shows the X and Y values when they are used as input to the XOR function:

```
X:   0 1 1 0 1 1 0 0
Y:   1 0 1 0 0 1 1 1
```
_____

```
X ⊕ Y:   1 1 0 0 1 0 1 1
```

Modulo Function

The *modulo* function is extremely important in the field of cryptography. Think back to the early days when you first learned division. At that time, you weren't familiar with decimal numbers and compensated by showing a remainder value each time you performed a division operation. Computers don't naturally understand the decimal system either, and these remainder values play a critical role when computers perform many mathematical functions. The modulo function is, quite simply, the remainder value left over after a division operation is performed.

 The modulo function is just as important to cryptography as the logical operations are. Be sure you're familiar with its functionality and can perform simple modular math.

The modulo function is usually represented in equations by the abbreviation *mod*, although it's also sometimes represented by the % operator. Here are several inputs and outputs for the modulo function:

```
 8 mod 6 = 2
 6 mod 8 = 6
10 mod 3 = 1
10 mod 2 = 0
32 mod 8 = 0
```

We'll revisit this function in Chapter 10 when we explore the RSA public key encryption algorithm (named after Rivest, Shamir, and Adleman, its inventors).

One-Way Functions

A *one-way function* is a mathematical operation that easily produces output values for each possible combination of inputs but makes it impossible to retrieve the input values. Public key cryptosystems are all based upon some sort of one-way function. In practice, however, it's never been proven that any specific known function is truly one way. Cryptographers rely upon functions that they suspect may be one way, but it's theoretically possible that they might be broken by future cryptanalysts.

Here's an example. Imagine you have a function that multiplies three numbers together. If you restrict the input values to single-digit numbers, it's a relatively straightforward matter to reverse-engineer this function and determine the possible input values by looking at the numerical output. For example, the output value 15 was created by using the input values 1, 3, and 5. However, suppose you restrict the input values to five-digit prime numbers. It's still quite simple to obtain an output value by using a computer or a good calculator, but reverse-engineering is not quite so simple. Can you figure out what three prime numbers were used to obtain the output value 10,718,488,075,259? Not so simple, eh? (As it turns out, the number is the product of the prime numbers 17,093; 22,441; and 27,943.) There are actually 8,363 five-digit prime numbers, so this problem might be attacked using a computer and a brute-force algorithm, but there's no easy way to figure it out in your head, that's for sure!

Nonce

Cryptography often gains strength by adding randomness to the encryption process. One method by which this is accomplished is through the use of a nonce. A *nonce* is a random number that acts as a placeholder variable in mathematical functions. When the function is executed, the nonce is replaced with a random number generated at the moment of processing for one-time use. The nonce must be a unique number each time it is used. One of the more recognizable examples of a nonce is an initialization vector (IV), a random bit string that is the same length as the block size and is XORed with the message. IVs are used to create unique ciphertext every time the same message is encrypted using the same key.

Zero-Knowledge Proof

One of the benefits of cryptography is found in the mechanism to prove your knowledge of a fact to a third party without revealing the fact itself to that third party. This is often done with passwords and other secret authenticators.

The classic example of a *zero-knowledge proof* involves two individuals: Peggy and Victor. Peggy knows the password to a secret door located inside a circular cave, as shown in Figure 9.2. Victor would like to buy the password from Peggy, but he wants Peggy to prove that she knows the password before paying her for it. Peggy doesn't want to tell Victor the password for fear that he won't pay later. The zero-knowledge proof can solve their dilemma.

FIGURE 9.2   The magic door (illustration by Dake)

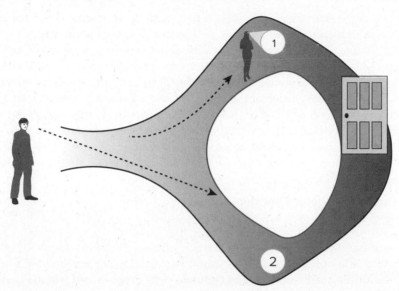

Victor can stand at the entrance to the cave and watch Peggy depart down the path. Peggy then reaches the door and opens it using the password. She then passes through the door and returns via path 2. Victor saw her leave down path 1 and return via path 2, proving that she must know the correct password to open the door.

Split Knowledge

When the information or privilege required to perform an operation is divided among multiple users, no single person has sufficient privileges to compromise the security of an environment. This separation of duties and two-person control contained in a single solution is called *split knowledge*. Split knowledge is mentioned in Chapter 13, "Security Operations," but it makes most sense as it relates to cryptography.

The best example of split knowledge is seen in the concept of *key escrow*. Using key escrow, cryptographic keys, digital signatures, and even digital certificates can be stored or backed up in a special database called the *key escrow database*. In the event a user loses or damages their key, that key can be extracted from the backup. However, if only a single key escrow recovery agent exists, there is opportunity for fraud and abuse of this privilege. *M of N Control* requires that a minimum number of agents (M) out of the total number of agents (N) work together to perform high-security tasks. So, implementing three of eight controls would require three people out of the eight with the assigned work task of key escrow recovery agent to work together to pull a single key out of the key escrow database (thereby also illustrating that M is always less than or equal to N).

Work Function

You can measure the strength of a cryptography system by measuring the effort in terms of cost and/or time using a *work function* or work factor. Usually the time and effort required to perform a complete brute-force attack against an encryption system is what the work function represents. The security and protection offered by a cryptosystem is directly proportional to the value of the work function/factor. The size of the work function should be matched against the relative value of the protected asset. The work function need be only slightly greater than the time value of that asset. In other words, all security, including cryptography, should be cost effective and cost efficient. Spend no more effort to protect an asset than it warrants, but be sure to provide sufficient protection. Thus, if information loses its value over time, the work function needs to be only large enough to ensure protection until the value of the data is gone.

Ciphers

Cipher systems have long been used by individuals and governments interested in preserving the confidentiality of their communications. In the following sections, we'll cover the definition of a cipher and explore several common cipher types that form the basis of modern ciphers. It's important to remember that these concepts seem somewhat basic, but when used in combination, they can be formidable opponents and cause cryptanalysts many hours of frustration.

Codes vs. Ciphers

People often use the words *code* and *cipher* interchangeably, but technically, they aren't interchangeable. There are important distinctions between the two concepts. *Codes*, which are cryptographic systems of symbols that represent words or phrases, are sometime secret, but they are not necessarily meant to provide confidentiality. A common example of a code is the "10 system" of communications used by law enforcement agencies. Under this system, the sentence "I received your communication and understand the contents" is represented by the code phrase "10-4." This code is commonly known by the public, but it does provide for ease of communication. Some codes are secret. They may convey confidential information using a secret codebook where the meaning of the code is known only to the sender and recipient. For example, a spy might transmit the sentence "The eagle has landed" to report the arrival of an enemy aircraft.

Ciphers, on the other hand, are always meant to hide the true meaning of a message. They use a variety of techniques to alter and/or rearrange the characters or bits of a message to achieve confidentiality. Ciphers convert messages from plain text to ciphertext on a bit basis (that is, a single digit of a binary code), character basis (that is, a single character of an ASCII message), or block basis (this is, a fixed-length segment of a message, usually expressed in number of bits). The following sections cover several common ciphers in use today.

An easy way to keep the difference between codes and ciphers straight is to remember that codes work on words and phrases whereas ciphers work on individual characters and bits.

Transposition Ciphers

Transposition ciphers use an encryption algorithm to rearrange the letters of a plaintext message, forming the ciphertext message. The decryption algorithm simply reverses the encryption transformation to retrieve the original message.

In the challenge-response protocol example in Figure 9.1, earlier in this chapter, a simple transposition cipher was used to reverse the letters of the message so that *apple* became *elppa*. Transposition ciphers can be much more complicated than this. For example, you can use a keyword to perform a *columnar transposition*. In the following example, we're attempting to encrypt the message "The fighters will strike the enemy bases at noon" using the secret key *attacker*. Our first step is to take the letters of the keyword and number them in alphabetical order. The first appearance of the letter *A* receives the value 1; the second appearance is numbered 2. The next letter in sequence, C, is numbered 3, and so on. This results in the following sequence:

```
A T T A C K E R
1 7 8 2 3 5 4 6
```

Next, the letters of the message are written in order underneath the letters of the keyword:

```
A T T A C K E R
1 7 8 2 3 5 4 6
T H E F I G H T
E R S W I L L S
T R I K E T H E
E N E M Y B A S
E S A T N O O N
```

Finally, the sender enciphers the message by reading down each column; the order in which the columns are read corresponds to the numbers assigned in the first step. This produces the following ciphertext:

```
T E T E E F W K M T I I E Y N H L H A O G L T B O T S E S N H R R N S E S I E A
```

On the other end, the recipient reconstructs the eight-column matrix using the ciphertext and the same keyword and then simply reads the plaintext message across the rows.

Substitution Ciphers

Substitution ciphers use the encryption algorithm to replace each character or bit of the plaintext message with a different character. The Caesar cipher discussed in the beginning of this chapter is a good example of a substitution cipher. Now that you've learned a little bit about cryptographic math, we'll take another look at the Caesar cipher. Recall that we simply shifted each letter three places to the right in the message to generate the ciphertext. However, we ran into a problem when we got to the end of the alphabet and ran out of letters. We solved this by wrapping around to the beginning of the alphabet so that the plaintext character Z became the ciphertext character C.

You can express the ROT3 cipher in mathematical terms by converting each letter to its decimal equivalent (where A is 0 and Z is 25). You can then add three to each plaintext letter to determine the ciphertext. You account for the wrap-around by using the modulo function discussed in the section "Cryptographic Mathematics." The final encryption function for the Caesar cipher is then this:

```
C = (P + 3) mod 26
```

The corresponding decryption function is as follows:

```
P = (C - 3) mod 26
```

As with transposition ciphers, there are many substitution ciphers that are more sophisticated than the examples provided in this chapter. Polyalphabetic substitution ciphers use multiple alphabets in the same message to hinder decryption efforts. One of the most notable examples of a polyalphabetic substitution cipher system is the Vigenere cipher. The Vigenere cipher uses a single encryption/decryption chart as shown here:

```
A B C D E F G H I J K L M N O P Q R S T U V W X Y Z
A B C D E F G H I J K L M N O P Q R S T U V W X Y Z
B C D E F G H I J K L M N O P Q R S T U V W X Y Z A
C D E F G H I J K L M N O P Q R S T U V W X Y Z A B
D E F G H I J K L M N O P Q R S T U V W X Y Z A B C
E F G H I J K L M N O P Q R S T U V W X Y Z A B C D
F G H I J K L M N O P Q R S T U V W X Y Z A B C D E
G H I J K L M N O P Q R S T U V W X Y Z A B C D E F
H I J K L M N O P Q R S T U V W X Y Z A B C D E F G
I J K L M N O P Q R S T U V W X Y Z A B C D E F G H
J K L M N O P Q R S T U V W X Y Z A B C D E F G H I
K L M N O P Q R S T U V W X Y Z A B C D E F G H I J
L M N O P Q R S T U V W X Y Z A B C D E F G H I J K
M N O P Q R S T U V W X Y Z A B C D E F G H I J K L
N O P Q R S T U V W X Y Z A B C D E F G H I J K L M
O P Q R S T U V W X Y Z A B C D E F G H I J K L M N
P Q R S T U V W X Y Z A B C D E F G H I J K L M N O
Q R S T U V W X Y Z A B C D E F G H I J K L M N O P
R S T U V W X Y Z A B C D E F G H I J K L M N O P Q
S T U V W X Y Z A B C D E F G H I J K L M N O P Q R
```

```
T U V W X Y Z A B C D E F G H I J K L M N O P Q R S
U V W X Y Z A B C D E F G H I J K L M N O P Q R S T
V W X Y Z A B C D E F G H I J K L M N O P Q R S T U
W X Y Z A B C D E F G H I J K L M N O P Q R S T U V
X Y Z A B C D E F G H I J K L M N O P Q R S T U V W
Y Z A B C D E F G H I J K L M N O P Q R S T U V W X
Z A B C D E F G H I J K L M N O P Q R S T U V W X Y
```

Notice that the chart is simply the alphabet written repeatedly (26 times) under the master heading, shifting by one letter each time. You need a key to use the Vigenere system. For example, the key could be *secret*. Then, you would perform the following encryption process:

1. Write out the plain text.

2. Underneath, write out the encryption key, repeating the key as many times as needed to establish a line of text that is the same length as the plain text.

3. Convert each letter position from plain text to ciphertext.

   a. Locate the column headed by the first plaintext character (*a*).

   b. Next, locate the row headed by the first character of the key (*s*).

   c. Finally, locate where these two items intersect, and write down the letter that appears there (*s*). This is the ciphertext for that letter position.

4. Repeat steps 1 through 3 for each letter in the plaintext version.

Plain text:	a t t a c k a t d a w n
Key:	s e c r e t s e c r e t
Ciphertext:	s x v r g d s x f r a g

While polyalphabetic substitution protects against direct frequency analysis, it is vulnerable to a second-order form of frequency analysis called *period analysis*, which is an examination of frequency based upon the repeated use of the key.

One-Time Pads

A *one-time pad* is an extremely powerful type of substitution cipher. One-time pads use a different substitution alphabet for each letter of the plaintext message. They can be represented by the following encryption function, where K is the encryption key used to encrypt the plaintext letter P into the ciphertext letter C:

$$C = (P + K) \bmod 26$$

Usually, one-time pads are written as a very long series of numbers to be plugged into the function.

One-time pads are also known as *Vernam ciphers*, after the name of their inventor, Gilbert Sandford Vernam of AT&T.

The great advantage of one-time pads is that, when used properly, they are an unbreakable encryption scheme. There is no repeating pattern of alphabetic substitution, rendering cryptanalytic efforts useless. However, several requirements must be met to ensure the integrity of the algorithm:

- The one-time pad must be randomly generated. Using a phrase or a passage from a book would introduce the possibility that cryptanalysts could break the code.

- The one-time pad must be physically protected against disclosure. If the enemy has a copy of the pad, they can easily decrypt the enciphered messages.

You may be thinking at this point that the Caesar cipher, Vigenere cipher, and one-time pad sound very similar. They are! The only difference is the key length. The Caesar shift cipher uses a key of length one, the Vigenere cipher uses a longer key (usually a word or sentence), and the one-time pad uses a key that is as long as the message itself.

- Each one-time pad must be used only once. If pads are reused, cryptanalysts can compare similarities in multiple messages encrypted with the same pad and possibly determine the key values used.

- The key must be at least as long as the message to be encrypted. This is because each character of the key is used to encode only one character of the message.

These one-time pad security requirements are essential knowledge for any network security professional. All too often, people attempt to implement a one-time pad cryptosystem but fail to meet one or more of these fundamental requirements. Read on for an example of how an entire Soviet code system was broken because of carelessness in this area.

If any one of these requirements is not met, the impenetrable nature of the one-time pad instantly breaks down. In fact, one of the major intelligence successes of the United States resulted when cryptanalysts broke a top-secret Soviet cryptosystem that relied upon the use of one-time pads. In this project, code-named VENONA, a pattern in the way the Soviets generated the key values used in their pads was discovered. The existence of this pattern violated the first requirement of a one-time pad cryptosystem: The keys must be randomly generated without the use of any recurring pattern. The entire VENONA project was recently declassified and is publicly available on the National Security Agency website at

```
www.nsa.gov/about/_files/cryptologic_heritage/publications/coldwar/venona_
story.pdf
```

One-time pads have been used throughout history to protect extremely sensitive communications. The major obstacle to their widespread use is the difficulty of generating, distributing, and safeguarding the lengthy keys required. One-time pads can realistically be used only for short messages, because of key lengths.

Running Key Ciphers

Many cryptographic vulnerabilities surround the limited length of the cryptographic key. As you learned in the previous section, one-time pads avoid these vulnerabilities by using a key that is at least as long as the message. However, one-time pads are awkward to implement because they require the physical exchange of pads.

One common solution to this dilemma is the use of a *running key cipher* (also known as a *book cipher*). In this cipher, the encryption key is as long as the message itself and is often chosen from a common book. For example, the sender and recipient might agree in advance to use the text of a chapter from *Moby Dick*, beginning with the third paragraph, as the key. They would both simply use as many consecutive characters as necessary to perform the encryption and decryption operations.

Let's look at an example. Suppose you wanted to encrypt the message "Richard will deliver the secret package to Matthew at the bus station tomorrow" using the key just described. This message is 66 characters in length, so you'd use the first 66 characters of the running key: "With much interest I sat watching him. Savage though he was, and hideously marred." Any algorithm could then be used to encrypt the plaintext message using this key. Let's look at the example of modulo 26 addition, which converts each letter to a decimal equivalent, then adds the plain text to the key, and then performs a modulo 26 operation to yield the ciphertext. If you assign the letter *A* the value 0 and the letter *Z* the value 25, you have the following encryption operation for the first two words of the ciphertext:

Plain text	R	I	C	H	A	R	D	W	I	L	L
Key	W	I	T	H	M	U	C	H	I	N	T
Numeric plain text	17	8	2	7	0	17	3	22	8	11	11
Numeric key	22	8	19	7	12	20	2	7	8	13	19
Numeric ciphertext	13	16	21	14	12	11	5	3	16	24	4
Ciphertext	N	Q	V	O	M	L	F	D	Q	Y	E

When the recipient receives the ciphertext, they use the same key and then subtract the key from the ciphertext, perform a modulo 26 operation, and then convert the resulting plain text back to alphabetic characters.

Block Ciphers

Block ciphers operate on "chunks," or blocks, of a message and apply the encryption algorithm to an entire message block at the same time. The transposition ciphers are examples of block ciphers. The simple algorithm used in the challenge-response algorithm takes an entire word and reverses its letters. The more complicated columnar transposition cipher works on an entire message (or a piece of a message) and encrypts it using the transposition algorithm and a secret keyword. Most modern encryption algorithms implement some type of block cipher.

Stream Ciphers

Stream ciphers operate on one character or bit of a message (or data stream) at a time. The Caesar cipher is an example of a stream cipher. The one-time pad is also a stream cipher because the algorithm operates on each letter of the plaintext message independently. Stream ciphers can also function as a type of block cipher. In such operations there is a buffer that fills up to real-time data that is then encrypted as a block and transmitted to the recipient.

Confusion and Diffusion

Cryptographic algorithms rely upon two basic operations to obscure plaintext messages—confusion and diffusion. *Confusion* occurs when the relationship between the plain text and the key is so complicated that an attacker can't merely continue altering the plain text and analyzing the resulting ciphertext to determine the key. *Diffusion* occurs when a change in the plain text results in multiple changes spread throughout the ciphertext. Consider, for example, a cryptographic algorithm that first performs a complex substitution and then uses transposition to rearrange the characters of the substituted ciphertext. In this example, the substitution introduces confusion and the transposition introduces diffusion.

Modern Cryptography

Modern cryptosystems utilize computationally complex algorithms and long cryptographic keys to meet the cryptographic goals of confidentiality, integrity, authentication, and non-repudiation. The following sections cover the roles cryptographic keys play in the world of data security and examine three types of algorithms commonly used today: symmetric encryption algorithms, asymmetric encryption algorithms, and hashing algorithms.

Cryptographic Keys

In the early days of cryptography, one of the predominant principles was "security through obscurity." Some cryptographers thought the best way to keep an encryption algorithm secure was to hide the details of the algorithm from outsiders. Old cryptosystems required communicating parties to keep the algorithm used to encrypt and decrypt messages secret from third parties. Any disclosure of the algorithm could lead to compromise of the entire system by an adversary.

Modern cryptosystems do not rely upon the secrecy of their algorithms. In fact, the algorithms for most cryptographic systems are widely available for public review in the accompanying literature and on the Internet. Opening algorithms to public scrutiny actually improves their security. Widespread analysis of algorithms by the computer security community allows practitioners to discover and correct potential security vulnerabilities and ensure that the algorithms they use to protect their communications are as secure as possible.

Instead of relying upon secret algorithms, modern cryptosystems rely upon the secrecy of one or more cryptographic keys used to personalize the algorithm for specific users or groups of users. Recall from the discussion of transposition ciphers that a keyword is used with the columnar transposition to guide the encryption and decryption efforts. The algorithm used to perform columnar transposition is well known—you just read the details of it in this book! However, columnar transposition can be used to securely communicate between parties as long as a keyword is chosen that would not be guessed by an outsider. As long as the security of this keyword is maintained, it doesn't matter that third parties know the details of the algorithm.

Although the public nature of the algorithm does not compromise the security of columnar transposition, the method does possess several inherent weaknesses that make it vulnerable to cryptanalysis. It is therefore an inadequate technology for use in modern secure communication.

In the discussion of one-time pads earlier in this chapter, you learned that the main strength of the one-time pad algorithm is derived from the fact that it uses an extremely long key. In fact, for that algorithm, the key is at least as long as the message itself. Most modern cryptosystems do not use keys quite that long, but the length of the key is still an extremely important factor in determining the strength of the cryptosystem and the likelihood that the encryption will not be compromised through cryptanalytic techniques.

The rapid increase in computing power allows you to use increasingly long keys in your cryptographic efforts. However, this same computing power is also in the hands of cryptanalysts attempting to defeat the algorithms you use. Therefore, it's essential that you outpace adversaries by using sufficiently long keys that will defeat contemporary cryptanalysis efforts. Additionally, if you want to improve the chance that your data will remain safe from cryptanalysis some time into the future, you must strive to use keys that will outpace the projected increase in cryptanalytic capability during the entire time period the data must be kept safe.

Several decades ago, when the Data Encryption Standard was created, a 56-bit key was considered sufficient to maintain the security of any data. However, there is now widespread agreement that the 56-bit DES algorithm is no longer secure because of advances in cryptanalysis techniques and supercomputing power. Modern cryptographic systems use at least a 128-bit key to protect data against prying eyes. Remember, the length of the key directly relates to the work function of the cryptosystem: the longer the key, the harder it is to break the cryptosystem.

Symmetric Key Algorithms

Symmetric key algorithms rely upon a "shared secret" encryption key that is distributed to all members who participate in the communications. This key is used by all parties to both encrypt and decrypt messages, so the sender and the receiver both possess a copy of the shared key. The sender encrypts with the shared secret key and the receiver decrypts with it. When large-sized keys are used, symmetric encryption is very difficult to break. It is primarily employed to perform bulk encryption and provides only for the security service of confidentiality. Symmetric key cryptography can also be called *secret key cryptography* and *private key cryptography*. Figure 9.3 illustrates the symmetric key encryption and decryption processes.

FIGURE 9.3   Symmetric key cryptography

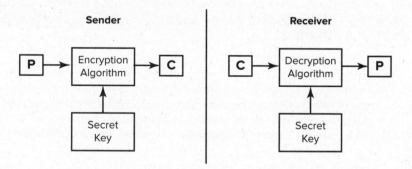

The use of the term *private key* can be tricky because it is part of three different terms that have two different meanings. The term *private key* by itself always means the private key from the key pair of public key cryptography (aka asymmetric). However, both *private key cryptography* and *shared private key* refer to symmetric cryptography. The meaning of the word *private* is stretched to refer to two people sharing a secret that they keep confidential. (The true meaning of *private* is that only a single person has a secret that's kept confidential.) Be sure to keep these confusing terms straight in your studies.

Symmetric key cryptography has several weaknesses:

Key distribution is a major problem.   Parties must have a secure method of exchanging the secret key before establishing communications with a symmetric key protocol. If a secure electronic channel is not available, an offline key distribution method must often be used (that is, out-of-band exchange).

Symmetric key cryptography does not implement nonrepudiation.   Because any communicating party can encrypt and decrypt messages with the shared secret key, there is no way to prove where a given message originated.

The algorithm is not scalable.   It is extremely difficult for large groups to communicate using symmetric key cryptography. Secure private communication between individuals in the group could be achieved only if each possible combination of users shared a private key.

Keys must be regenerated often.   Each time a participant leaves the group, all keys known by that participant must be discarded.

The major strength of symmetric key cryptography is the great speed at which it can operate. Symmetric key encryption is very fast, often 1,000 to 10,000 times faster than asymmetric algorithms. By nature of the mathematics involved, symmetric key cryptography also naturally lends itself to hardware implementations, creating the opportunity for even higher-speed operations.

The section "Symmetric Cryptography" later in this chapter provides a detailed look at the major secret key algorithms in use today.

Asymmetric Key Algorithms

Asymmetric key algorithms, also known as *public key algorithms*, provide a solution to the weaknesses of symmetric key encryption. In these systems, each user has two keys: a public key, which is shared with all users, and a private key, which is kept secret and known only to the user. But here's a twist: opposite and related keys must be used in tandem to encrypt and decrypt. In other words, if the public key encrypts a message, then only the corresponding private key can decrypt it, and vice versa.

Figure 9.4 shows the algorithm used to encrypt and decrypt messages in a public key cryptosystem. Consider this example: If Alice wants to send a message to Bob using public key cryptography, she creates the message and then encrypts it using Bob's public key. The only possible way to decrypt this ciphertext is to use Bob's private key, and the only user with access to that key is Bob. Therefore, Alice can't even decrypt the message herself after she encrypts it. If Bob wants to send a reply to Alice, he simply encrypts the message using Alice's public key, and then Alice reads the message by decrypting it with her private key.

FIGURE 9.4   Asymmetric key cryptography

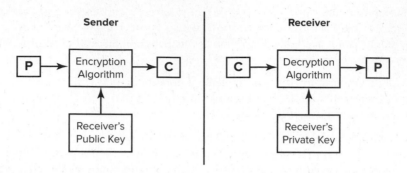

Real World Scenario

Key Requirements

In a class one of the authors of this book taught recently, a student wanted to see an illustration of the scalability issue associated with symmetric encryption algorithms. The fact that symmetric cryptosystems require each pair of potential communicators to have a shared private key makes the algorithm nonscalable. The total number of keys required to completely connect n parties using symmetric cryptography is given by the following formula:

$$\text{Number of Keys} = \frac{n*(n-1)}{2}$$

Now, this might not sound so bad (and it's not for small systems), but consider the following figures. Obviously, the larger the population, the less likely a symmetric cryptosystem will be suitable to meet its needs.

Number of Participants	Number of Symmetric Keys Required	Number of Asymmetric Keys Required
2	1	4
3	3	6
4	6	8
5	10	10
10	45	20
100	4,950	200
1,000	499,500	2,000
10,000	49,995,000	20,000

Asymmetric key algorithms also provide support for digital signature technology. Basically, if Bob wants to assure other users that a message with his name on it was actually sent by him, he first creates a message digest by using a hashing algorithm (you'll find more on hashing algorithms in the next section). Bob then encrypts that digest using his private key. Any user who wants to verify the signature simply decrypts the message digest using Bob's public key and then verifies that the decrypted message digest is accurate. Chapter 10 explains this process in greater detail.

The following is a list of the major strengths of asymmetric key cryptography:

The addition of new users requires the generation of only one public-private key pair. This same key pair is used to communicate with all users of the asymmetric cryptosystem. This makes the algorithm extremely scalable.

Users can be removed far more easily from asymmetric systems. Asymmetric cryptosystems provide a key revocation mechanism that allows a key to be canceled, effectively removing a user from the system.

Key regeneration is required only when a user's private key is compromised. If a user leaves the community, the system administrator simply needs to invalidate that user's keys. No other keys are compromised and therefore key regeneration is not required for any other user.

Asymmetric key encryption can provide integrity, authentication, and nonrepudiation. If a user does not share their private key with other individuals, a message signed by that user can be shown to be accurate and from a specific source and cannot be later repudiated.

Key distribution is a simple process. Users who want to participate in the system simply make their public key available to anyone with whom they want to communicate. There is no method by which the private key can be derived from the public key.

No preexisting communication link needs to exist. Two individuals can begin communicating securely from the moment they start communicating. Asymmetric cryptography does not require a preexisting relationship to provide a secure mechanism for data exchange.

The major weakness of public key cryptography is its slow speed of operation. For this reason, many applications that require the secure transmission of large amounts of data use public key cryptography to establish a connection and then exchange a symmetric secret key. The remainder of the session then uses symmetric cryptography. Table 9.1 compares the symmetric and asymmetric cryptography systems. Close examination of this table reveals that a weakness in one system is matched by a strength in the other.

TABLE 9.1 Comparison of symmetric and asymmetric cryptography systems

Symmetric	Asymmetric
Single shared key	Key pair sets
Out-of-band exchange	In-band exchange
Not scalable	Scalable
Fast	Slow
Bulk encryption	Small blocks of data, digital signatures, digital envelopes, digital certificates
Confidentiality	Confidentiality, integrity, authenticity, nonrepudiation

  Chapter 10 provides technical details on modern public key encryption algorithms and some of their applications.

Hashing Algorithms

In the previous section, you learned that public key cryptosystems can provide digital signature capability when used in conjunction with a message digest. Message digests are summaries of a message's content (not unlike a file checksum) produced by a hashing algorithm. It's extremely difficult, if not impossible, to derive a message from an ideal hash function, and it's very unlikely that two messages will produce the same hash value.

The following are some of the more common hashing algorithms in use today:

- Message Digest 2 (MD2)
- Message Digest 5 (MD5)
- Secure Hash Algorithm (SHA-0, SHA-1, and SHA-2)
- Hashed Message Authentication Code (HMAC)

Chapter 10 provides details on these contemporary hashing algorithms and explains how they are used to provide digital signature capability, which helps meet the cryptographic goals of integrity and nonrepudiation.

Symmetric Cryptography

You've learned the basic concepts underlying symmetric key cryptography, asymmetric key cryptography, and hashing functions. In the following sections, we'll take an in-depth look at several common symmetric cryptosystems: the Data Encryption Standard (DES), Triple

DES (3DES), International Data Encryption Algorithm (IDEA), Blowfish, Skipjack, and the Advanced Encryption Standard (AES).

Data Encryption Standard

The US government published the Data Encryption Standard in 1977 as a proposed standard cryptosystem for all government communications. Indeed, many government entities continue to use DES for cryptographic applications today, even though it was superseded by the Advanced Encryption Standard in December 2001. DES is a 64-bit block cipher that has five modes of operation: Electronic Codebook (ECB) mode, Cipher Block Chaining (CBC) mode, Cipher Feedback (CFB) mode, Output Feedback (OFB) mode, and Counter (CTR) mode. These modes are explained in the following sections. All of the DES modes operate on 64 bits of plain text at a time to generate 64-bit blocks of ciphertext. The key used by DES is 56 bits long.

DES utilizes a long series of exclusive OR (XOR) operations to generate the ciphertext. This process is repeated 16 times for each encryption/decryption operation. Each repetition is commonly referred to as a *round* of encryption, explaining the statement that DES performs 16 rounds of encryption.

As mentioned, DES uses a 56-bit key to drive the encryption and decryption process. However, you may read in some literature that DES uses a 64-bit key. This is not an inconsistency—there's a perfectly logical explanation. The DES specification calls for a 64-bit key. However, of those 64 bits, only 56 actually contain keying information. The remaining 8 bits are supposed to contain parity information to ensure that the other 56 bits are accurate. In practice, however, those parity bits are rarely used. You should commit the 56-bit figure to memory.

Electronic Codebook Mode

Electronic Codebook (ECB) mode is the simplest mode to understand and the least secure. Each time the algorithm processes a 64-bit block, it simply encrypts the block using the chosen secret key. This means that if the algorithm encounters the same block multiple times, it will produce the same encrypted block. If an enemy were eavesdropping on the communications, they could simply build a "code book" of all the possible encrypted values. After a sufficient number of blocks were gathered, cryptanalytic techniques could be used to decipher some of the blocks and break the encryption scheme.

This vulnerability makes it impractical to use ECB mode on all but the shortest transmissions. In everyday use, ECB is used only for exchanging small amounts of data, such as keys and parameters used to initiate other DES modes as well as the cells in a database.

Cipher Block Chaining Mode

In Cipher Block Chaining (CBC) mode, each block of unencrypted text is XORed with the block of ciphertext immediately preceding it before it is encrypted using the DES algorithm. The decryption process simply decrypts the ciphertext and reverses the XOR operation. CBC implements an IV and XORs it with the first block of the message, producing a unique output every time the operation is performed. The IV must be sent to the recipient, perhaps by tacking the IV onto the front of the completed ciphertext in plain form or by protecting it with ECB mode encryption using the same key used for the message. One important consideration when using CBC mode is that errors propagate—if one block is corrupted during transmission, it becomes impossible to decrypt that block and the next block as well.

Cipher Feedback Mode

Cipher Feedback (CFB) mode is the streaming cipher version of CBC. In other words, CFB operates against data produced in real time. However, instead of breaking a message into blocks, it uses memory buffers of the same block size. As the buffer becomes full, it is encrypted and then sent to the recipient(s). Then the system waits for the next buffer to be filled as the new data is generated before it is in turn encrypted and then transmitted. Other than the change from preexisting data to real-time data, CFB operates in the same fashion as CBC. It uses an IV and it uses chaining.

Output Feedback Mode

In Output Feedback (OFB) mode, DES operates in almost the same fashion as it does in CFB mode. However, instead of XORing an encrypted version of the previous block of ciphertext, DES XORs the plain text with a seed value. For the first encrypted block, an initialization vector is used to create the seed value. Future seed values are derived by running the DES algorithm on the previous seed value. The major advantages of OFB mode are that there is no chaining function and transmission errors do not propagate to affect the decryption of future blocks.

Counter Mode

DES that is run in Counter (CTR) mode uses a stream cipher similar to that used in CFB and OFB modes. However, instead of creating the seed value for each encryption/decryption operation from the results of the previous seed values, it uses a simple counter that increments for each operation. As with OFB mode, errors do not propagate in CTR mode.

CTR mode allows you to break an encryption or decryption operation into multiple independent steps. This makes CTR mode well suited for use in parallel computing.

Triple DES

As mentioned in previous sections, the Data Encryption Standard's 56-bit key is no longer considered adequate in the face of modern cryptanalytic techniques and supercomputing power. However, an adapted version of DES, Triple DES (3DES), uses the same algorithm to produce a more secure encryption.

There are four versions of 3DES. The first simply encrypts the plain text three times, using three different keys: K_1, K_2, and K_3. It is known as DES-EEE3 mode (the Es indicate that there are three encryption operations, whereas the numeral 3 indicates that three different keys are used). DES-EEE3 can be expressed using the following notation, where $E(K,P)$ represents the encryption of plaintext P with key K:

$E(K_1, E(K_2, E(K_3, P)))$

DES-EEE3 has an effective key length of 168 bits.

The second variant (DES-EDE3) also uses three keys but replaces the second encryption operation with a decryption operation:

$E(K_1, D(K_2, E(K_3, P)))$

The third version of 3DES (DES-EEE2) uses only two keys, K_1 and K_2, as follows:

$E(K_1, E(K_2, E(K_1, P)))$

The fourth variant of 3DES (DES-EDE2) also uses two keys but uses a decryption operation in the middle:

$E(K_1, D(K_2, E(K_1, P)))$

Both the third and fourth variants have an effective key length of 112 bits.

> Technically, there is a fifth variant of 3DES, DES-EDE1, which uses only one cryptographic key. However, it results in the same algorithm as standard DES, which is unacceptably weak for most applications. It is provided only for backward-compatibility purposes.

These four variants of 3DES were developed over the years because several cryptologists put forth theories that one variant was more secure than the others. However, the current belief is that all modes are equally secure.

> Take some time to understand the variants of 3DES. Sit down with a pencil and paper and be sure you understand the way each variant uses two or three keys to achieve stronger encryption.

This discussion raises an obvious question—what happened to Double DES (2DES)? You'll read in Chapter 10 that Double DES was tried but quickly abandoned when it was proven that an attack existed that rendered it no more secure than standard DES.

International Data Encryption Algorithm

The International Data Encryption Algorithm (IDEA) block cipher was developed in response to complaints about the insufficient key length of the DES algorithm. Like DES, IDEA operates on 64-bit blocks of plain text/ciphertext. However, it begins its operation with a 128-bit key. This key is broken up in a series of operations into 52 16-bit subkeys. The subkeys then act on the input text using a combination of XOR and modulus operations to produce the encrypted/decrypted version of the input message. IDEA is capable of operating in the same five modes utilized by DES: ECB, CBC, CFB, OFB, and CTR.

All of this material on key length block size and the number of rounds of encryption may seem dreadfully boring; however, it's important material, so be sure to brush up on it while preparing for the exam.

The IDEA algorithm is patented by its Swiss developers. However, they have granted an unlimited license to anyone who wants to use IDEA for noncommercial purposes. One popular implementation of IDEA is found in Phil Zimmerman's popular Pretty Good Privacy (PGP) secure email package. Chapter 10 covers PGP in further detail.

Blowfish

Bruce Schneier's Blowfish block cipher is another alternative to DES and IDEA. Like its predecessors, Blowfish operates on 64-bit blocks of text. However, it extends IDEA's key strength even further by allowing the use of variable-length keys ranging from a relatively insecure 32 bits to an extremely strong 448 bits. Obviously, the longer keys will result in a corresponding increase in encryption/decryption time. However, time trials have established Blowfish as a much faster algorithm than both IDEA and DES. Also, Mr. Schneier released Blowfish for public use with no license required. Blowfish encryption is built into a number of commercial software products and operating systems. There are also a number of Blowfish libraries available for software developers.

Skipjack

The Skipjack algorithm was approved for use by the US government in Federal Information Processing Standard (FIPS) 185, the Escrowed Encryption Standard (EES). Like many block ciphers, Skipjack operates on 64-bit blocks of text. It uses an 80-bit key and supports the same four modes of operation supported by DES. Skipjack was quickly embraced by the US government and provides the cryptographic routines supporting the Clipper and Capstone encryption chips.

However, Skipjack has an added twist—it supports the escrow of encryption keys. Two government agencies, the National Institute of Standards and Technology (NIST) and the Department of the Treasury, hold a portion of the information required to reconstruct a Skipjack key. When law enforcement authorities obtain legal authorization, they contact the two agencies, obtain the pieces of the key, and are able to decrypt communications between the affected parties.

Skipjack and the Clipper chip were not embraced by the cryptographic community at large because of its mistrust of the escrow procedures in place within the US government.

Rivest Cipher 5 (RC5)

Rivest Cipher 5, or RC5, is a symmetric algorithm patented by Rivest, Shamir, and Adleman (RSA) Data Security, the people who developed the RSA asymmetric algorithm. RC5 is a block cipher of variable block sizes (32, 64, or 128 bits) that uses key sizes between 0 (zero) length and 2,040 bits.

Advanced Encryption Standard

In October 2000, the National Institute of Standards and Technology (NIST) announced that the Rijndael (pronounced "rhine-doll") block cipher had been chosen as the replacement for DES. In November 2001, NIST released FIPS 197, which mandated the use of AES/Rijndael for the encryption of all sensitive but unclassified data by the US government.

The AES cipher allows the use of three key strengths: 128 bits, 192 bits, and 256 bits. AES only allows the processing of 128-bit blocks, but Rijndael exceeded this specification, allowing cryptographers to use a block size equal to the key length. The number of encryption rounds depends upon the key length chosen:

- 128-bit keys require 10 rounds of encryption.
- 192-bit keys require 12 rounds of encryption.
- 256-bit keys require 14 rounds of encryption.

Twofish

The Twofish algorithm developed by Bruce Schneier (also the creator of Blowfish) was another one of the AES finalists. Like Rijndael, Twofish is a block cipher. It operates on 128-bit blocks of data and is capable of using cryptographic keys up to 256 bits in length.

Twofish utilizes two techniques not found in other algorithms:

Prewhitening involves XORing the plain text with a separate subkey before the first round of encryption.

Postwhitening uses a similar operation after the 16th round of encryption.

AES is just one of the many symmetric encryption algorithms you need to be familiar with. Table 9.2 lists several common and well-known symmetric encryption algorithms along with their block size and key size.

TABLE 9.2   Symmetric memorization chart

Name	Block Size	Key Size
Advanced Encryption Standard (AES)	128	128, 192, 256
Rijndael	Variable	128, 192, 256
Blowfish (often used in SSH)	Variable	1–448
Data Encryption Standard (DES)	64	56
IDEA (used in PGP)	64	128
Rivest Cipher 2 (RC2)	64	128
Rivest Cipher 4 (RC4)	Streaming	128
Rivest Cipher 5 (RC5)	32, 64, 128	0–2,040
Skipjack	64	80
Triple DES (3DES)	64	112 or 168
Twofish	128	1–256

Symmetric Key Management

Because cryptographic keys contain information essential to the security of the cryptosystem, it is incumbent upon cryptosystem users and administrators to take extraordinary measures to protect the security of the keying material. These security measures are collectively known as key management practices. They include safeguards surrounding the creation, distribution, storage, destruction, recovery and escrow of secret keys.

Creation and Distribution of Symmetric Keys

As previously mentioned, one of the major problems underlying symmetric encryption algorithms is the secure distribution of the secret keys required to operate the algorithms. The three main methods used to exchange secret keys securely are offline distribution, public key encryption, and the Diffie-Hellman key exchange algorithm.

Offline distribution   The most technically simple method involves the physical exchange of key material. One party provides the other party with a sheet of paper or piece of storage media containing the secret key. In many hardware encryption devices, this key material comes in the form of an electronic device that resembles an actual key that is inserted into the encryption device. However, every offline key distribution method has its own inherent flaws. If keying material is sent through the mail, it might be intercepted. Telephones can be wiretapped. Papers containing keys might be inadvertently thrown in the trash or lost.

Public key encryption   Many communicators want to obtain the speed benefits of secret key encryption without the hassles of key distribution. For this reason, many people use public key encryption to set up an initial communications link. Once the link is successfully established and the parties are satisfied as to each other's identity, they exchange a secret key over the secure public key link. They then switch communications from the public key algorithm to the secret key algorithm and enjoy the increased processing speed. In general, secret key encryption is thousands of times faster than public key encryption.

Diffie-Hellman   In some cases, neither public key encryption nor offline distribution is sufficient. Two parties might need to communicate with each other, but they have no physical means to exchange key material, and there is no public key infrastructure in place to facilitate the exchange of secret keys. In situations like this, key exchange algorithms like the Diffie-Hellman algorithm prove to be extremely useful mechanisms.

   Secure RPC (S-RPC) employs Diffie-Hellman for key exchange.

About the Diffie-Hellman Algorithm

The Diffie-Hellman algorithm represented a major advance in the state of cryptographic science when it was released in 1976. It's still in use today. The algorithm works as follows:

1. The communicating parties (we'll call them Richard and Sue) agree on two large numbers: p (which is a prime number) and g (which is an integer) such that $1 < g < p$.

2. Richard chooses a random large integer r and performs the following calculation:

$$R = g^r \bmod p$$

3. Sue chooses a random large integer s and performs the following calculation:

$$S = g^s \bmod p$$

4. Richard sends R to Sue and Sue sends S to Richard.

5. Richard then performs the following calculation:

$$K = S^r \bmod p$$

6. Sue then performs the following calculation:

$$K = R^s \bmod p$$

At this point, Richard and Sue both have the same value, K, and can use this for secret key communication between the two parties.

Storage and Destruction of Symmetric Keys

Another major challenge with the use of symmetric key cryptography is that all of the keys used in the cryptosystem must be kept secure. This includes following best practices surrounding the storage of encryption keys:

- Never store an encryption key on the same system where encrypted data resides. This just makes it easier for the attacker!

- For sensitive keys, consider providing two different individuals with half of the key. They then must collaborate to re-create the entire key. This is known as the principle of *split knowledge* (discussed earlier in this chapter).

When a user with knowledge of a secret key leaves the organization or is no longer permitted access to material protected with that key, the keys must be changed and all encrypted materials must be reencrypted with the new keys. The difficulty of destroying a key to remove a user from a symmetric cryptosystem is one of the main reasons organizations turn to asymmetric algorithms, as discussed in Chapter 10.

Key Escrow and Recovery

Cryptography is a powerful tool. Like most tools, it can be used for a number of beneficent purposes, but it can also be used with malicious intent. To gain a handle on the explosive growth of cryptographic technologies, governments around the world have floated ideas to implement key escrow systems. These systems allow the government, under limited circumstances such as a court order, to obtain the cryptographic key used for a particular communication from a central storage facility.

There are two major approaches to key escrow that have been proposed over the past decade:

Fair cryptosystems   In this escrow approach, the secret keys used in a communication are divided into two or more pieces, each of which is given to an independent third party. Each of these pieces is useless on its own but may be recombined to obtain the secret key. When the government obtains legal authority to access a particular key, it provides evidence of the court order to each of the third parties and then reassembles the secret key.

Escrowed encryption standard   This escrow approach provides the government with a technological means to decrypt ciphertext. This standard is the basis behind the Skipjack algorithm discussed earlier in this chapter.

It's highly unlikely that government regulators will ever overcome the legal and privacy hurdles necessary to implement key escrow on a widespread basis. The technology is certainly available, but the general public will likely never accept the potential government intrusiveness it facilitates.

Cryptographic Life Cycle

With the exception of the one-time pad, all cryptographic systems have a limited life span. Moore's law, a commonly cited trend in the advancement of computing power, states that the processing capabilities of a state-of-the-art microprocessor will double approximately every two years. This means that, eventually, processors will reach the amount of strength required to simply guess the encryption keys used for a communication.

Security professionals must keep this cryptographic life cycle in mind when selecting an encryption algorithm and have appropriate governance controls in place to ensure that the algorithms, protocols, and key lengths selected are sufficient to preserve the integrity of a cryptosystem for however long it is necessary to keep the information it is protecting secret. Security professionals can use the following algorithm and protocol governance controls:

- Specifying the cryptographic algorithms (e.g., AES, 3DES, RSA) acceptable for use in an organization

- Identifying the acceptable key lengths for use with each algorithm based upon the sensitivity of information transmitted

- Enumerating the secure transaction protocols (e.g., SSL, TLS) that may be used

For example, if you're designing a cryptographic system to protect the security of business plans that you expect to execute next week, you don't need to worry about the theoretical risk that a processor capable of decrypting them might be developed a decade from now. On the other hand, if you're protecting the confidentiality of information that could be used to construct a nuclear bomb, it's virtually certain that you'll still want that information to remain secret 10 years in the future!

Summary

Cryptographers and cryptanalysts are in a never-ending race to develop more secure cryptosystems and advanced cryptanalytic techniques designed to circumvent those systems.

Cryptography dates back as early as Caesar and has been an ongoing topic for study for many years. In this chapter, you learned some of the fundamental concepts underlying the field of cryptography, gained a basic understanding of the terminology used by cryptographers, and looked at some historical codes and ciphers used in the early days of cryptography.

This chapter also examined the similarities and differences between symmetric key cryptography (where communicating parties use the same key) and asymmetric key cryptography (where each communicator has a pair of public and private keys).

We then analyzed some of the symmetric algorithms currently available and their strengths and weaknesses. We wrapped up the chapter by taking a look at the cryptographic life cycle and the role of algorithm/protocol governance in enterprise security.

The next chapter expands this discussion to cover contemporary public key cryptographic algorithms. Additionally, some of the common cryptanalytic techniques used to defeat both types of cryptosystems will be explored.

Exam Essentials

Understand the role that confidentiality, integrity, and nonrepudiation play in cryptosystems.   Confidentiality is one of the major goals of cryptography. It protects the secrecy of data while it is both at rest and in transit. Integrity provides the recipient of a message with the assurance that data was not altered (intentionally or unintentionally) between the time it was created and the time it was accessed. Nonrepudiation provides undeniable proof that the sender of a message actually authored it. It prevents the sender from subsequently denying that they sent the original message.

Know how cryptosystems can be used to achieve authentication goals.   Authentication provides assurances as to the identity of a user. One possible scheme that uses authentication is the challenge-response protocol, in which the remote user is asked to encrypt a message using a key known only to the communicating parties. Authentication can be achieved with both symmetric and asymmetric cryptosystems.

Be familiar with the basic terminology of cryptography.   When a sender wants to transmit a private message to a recipient, the sender takes the plaintext (unencrypted) message and encrypts it using an algorithm and a key. This produces a ciphertext message that is transmitted to the recipient. The recipient then uses a similar algorithm and key to decrypt the ciphertext and re-create the original plaintext message for viewing.

Understand the difference between a code and a cipher and explain the basic types of ciphers.   Codes are cryptographic systems of symbols that operate on words or phrases and are sometimes secret but don't always provide confidentiality. Ciphers, however, are always meant to hide the true meaning of a message. Know how the following types of ciphers work: transposition ciphers, substitution ciphers (including one-time pads), stream ciphers, and block ciphers.

Know the requirements for successful use of a one-time pad.   For a one-time pad to be successful, the key must be generated randomly without any known pattern. The key must be at least as long as the message to be encrypted. The pads must be protected against physical disclosure, and each pad must be used only one time and then discarded.

Understand the concept of zero-knowledge proof.   Zero-knowledge proof is a communication concept. A specific type of information is exchanged but no real data is transferred, as with digital signatures and digital certificates.

Understand split knowledge.   Split knowledge means that the information or privilege required to perform an operation is divided among multiple users. This ensures that no single person has sufficient privileges to compromise the security of the environment. M of N Control is an example of split knowledge.

Understand work function (work factor).   Work function, or work factor, is a way to measure the strength of a cryptography system by measuring the effort in terms of cost and/or time to decrypt messages. Usually the time and effort required to perform a complete brute-force attack against an encryption system is what a work function rating represents. The security and protection offered by a cryptosystem is directly proportional to the value of its work function/factor.

Understand the importance of key security.   Cryptographic keys provide the necessary element of secrecy to a cryptosystem. Modern cryptosystems utilize keys that are at least 128 bits long to provide adequate security. It's generally agreed that the 56-bit key of the Data Encryption Standard (DES) is no longer sufficiently long enough to provide security.

Know the differences between symmetric and asymmetric cryptosystems.   Symmetric key cryptosystems (or secret key cryptosystems) rely upon the use of a shared secret key. They are much faster than asymmetric algorithms, but they lack support for scalability, easy key distribution, and nonrepudiation. Asymmetric cryptosystems use public-private key pairs for communication between parties but operate much more slowly than symmetric algorithms.

Be able to explain the basic operational modes of the Data Encryption Standard (DES) and Triple DES (3DES).   The Data Encryption Standard operates in four modes: Electronic

Codebook (ECB) mode, Cipher Block Chaining (CBC) mode, Cipher Feedback (CFB) mode, and Output Feedback (OFB) mode. ECB mode is considered the least secure and is used only for short messages. 3DES uses three iterations of DES with two or three different keys to increase the effective key strength to 112 or 168 bits, respectively.

Know the Advanced Encryption Standard (AES).   The Advanced Encryption Standard (AES) utilizes the Rijndael algorithm and is the US government standard for the secure exchange of sensitive but unclassified data. AES uses key lengths of 128, 192, and 256 bits and a fixed block size of 128 bits to achieve a much higher level of security than that provided by the older DES algorithm.

Written Lab

1. What is the major hurdle preventing the widespread adoption of one-time pad cryptosystems to ensure data confidentiality?

2. Encrypt the message "I will pass the CISSP exam and become certified next month" using columnar transposition with the keyword SECURE.

3. Decrypt the message "F R Q J U D W X O D W L R Q V B R X J R W L W" using the Caesar ROT3 substitution cipher.

Review Questions

1. How many possible keys exist in a 4-bit key space?

   A. 4

   B. 8

   C. 16

   D. 128

2. John recently received an electronic mail message from Bill. What cryptographic goal would need to be met to convince John that Bill was actually the sender of the message?

   A. Nonrepudiation

   B. Confidentiality

   C. Availability

   D. Integrity

3. What is the length of the cryptographic key used in the Data Encryption Standard (DES) cryptosystem?

   A. 56 bits

   B. 128 bits

   C. 192 bits

   D. 256 bits

4. What type of cipher relies upon changing the location of characters within a message to achieve confidentiality?

   A. Stream cipher

   B. Transposition cipher

   C. Block cipher

   D. Substitution cipher

5. Which one of the following is not a possible key length for the Advanced Encryption Standard Rijndael cipher?

   A. 56 bits

   B. 128 bits

   C. 192 bits

   D. 256 bits

6. Which one of the following cannot be achieved by a secret key cryptosystem?

   A. Nonrepudiation

   B. Confidentiality

   C. AvailabilityD.

   D. Key distribution

7. When correctly implemented, what is the only cryptosystem known to be unbreakable?

   A. Transposition cipher

   B. Substitution cipher

   C. Advanced Encryption Standard

   D. One-time pad

8. What is the output value of the mathematical function **16 mod 3**?

   A. 0

   B. 1

   C. 3

   D. 5

9. In the 1940s, a team of cryptanalysts from the United States successfully broke a Soviet code based upon a one-time pad in a project known as VENONA. What rule did the Soviets break that caused this failure?

   A. Key values must be random.

   B. Key values must be the same length as the message.

   C. Key values must be used only once.

   D. Key values must be protected from physical disclosure.

10. Which one of the following cipher types operates on large pieces of a message rather than individual characters or bits of a message?

    A. Stream cipher

    B. Caesar cipher

    C. Block cipher

    D. ROT3 cipher

11. What is the minimum number of cryptographic keys required for secure two-way communications in symmetric key cryptography?

    A. One

    B. Two

    C. Three

    D. Four

12. Dave is developing a key escrow system that requires multiple people to retrieve a key but does not depend upon every participant being present. What type of technique is he using?

    A. Split knowledge

    B. M of N Control

    C. Work function

    D. Zero-knowledge proof

13. Which one of the following Data Encryption Standard (DES) operating modes can be used for large messages with the assurance that an error early in the encryption/decryption process won't spoil results throughout the communication?

    A. Cipher Block Chaining (CBC)

    B. Electronic Codebook (ECB)

    C. Cipher Feedback (CFB)

    D. Output Feedback (OFB)

14. Many cryptographic algorithms rely upon the difficulty of factoring the product of large prime numbers. What characteristic of this problem are they relying upon?

    A. It contains diffusion.

    B. It contains confusion.

    C. It is a one-way function.

    D. It complies with Kerchoff's principle.

15. How many keys are required to fully implement a symmetric algorithm with 10 participants?

    A. 10

    B. 20

    C. 45

    D. 100

16. What block size is used by the Advanced Encryption Standard?

    A. 32 bits

    B. 64 bits

    C. 128 bits

    D. Variable

17. What kind of attack makes the Caesar cipher virtually unusable?

    A. Meet-in-the-middle attack

    B. Escrow attack

    C. Frequency analysis attack

    D. Transposition attack

18. What type of cryptosystem commonly makes use of a passage from a well-known book for the encryption key?

   A. Vernam cipher

   B. Running key cipher

   C. Skipjack cipher

   D. Twofish cipher

19. Which AES finalist makes use of prewhitening and postwhitening techniques?

   A. Rijndael

   B. Twofish

   C. Blowfish

   D. Skipjack

20. How many encryption keys are required to fully implement an asymmetric algorithm with 10 participants?

   A. 10

   B. 20

   C. 45

   D. 100

Chapter

10

PKI and Cryptographic Applications

THE CISSP EXAM TOPICS COVERED IN THIS CHAPTER INCLUDE:

5. Cryptography

- C. Understand encryption concepts
    - C.3 Asymmetric cryptography
    - C.4 Hybrid cryptography
    - C.5 Message digests
    - C.6 Hashing
- D. Understand key management processes
    - D.1 Creation/distribution
    - D.2 Storage/destruction
    - D.3 Recovery
    - D.4 Key escrow
- E. Understand digital signatures
- F. Understand non-repudiation
- G. Understand methods of cryptanalytic attacks
    - G.2 Social engineering for key discovery
    - G.3 Brute force (e.g., rainbow tables, specialized/scalable architecture)
    - G.4 Cipher-text only
    - G.5 Known plaintext
    - G.6 Frequency analysis
    - G.7 Chosen cipher-text
    - G.8 Implementation attacks

H. Use cryptography to maintain network security

I. Use cryptography to maintain application security

J. Understand Public Key Infrastructure (PKI)

K. Understand certificate related issues

L. Understand information hiding alternatives (e.g., steganography, watermarking)

In Chapter 9, "Cryptography and Symmetric Key Algorithms," we introduced basic cryptography concepts and explored a variety of private key cryptosystems. These symmetric cryptosystems offer fast, secure communication but introduce the substantial challenge of key exchange between previously unrelated parties. This chapter explores the world of asymmetric (or public key) cryptography and the public key infrastructure (PKI) that supports worldwide secure communication between parties that don't necessarily know each other prior to the communication. We'll also explore several practical applications of cryptography: securing electronic mail, web communications, electronic commerce, and networking. The chapter concludes with an examination of a variety of attacks malicious individuals might use to compromise weak cryptosystems.

Asymmetric Cryptography

The section "Modern Cryptography" in Chapter 9 introduced the basic principles behind both private (symmetric) and public (asymmetric) key cryptography. You learned that symmetric key cryptosystems require both communicating parties to have the same shared secret key, creating the problem of secure key distribution. You also learned that asymmetric cryptosystems avoid this hurdle by using pairs of public and private keys to facilitate secure communication without the overhead of complex key distribution systems. The security of these systems relies upon the difficulty of reversing a one-way function.

In the following sections, we'll explore the concepts of public key cryptography in greater detail and look at three of the more common public key cryptosystems in use today: RSA, El Gamal, and the elliptic curve cryptosystem.

Public and Private Keys

Recall from Chapter 9 that *public key cryptosystems* rely on pairs of keys assigned to each user of the cryptosystem. Every user maintains both a public key and a private key. As the names imply, public key cryptosystem users make their public keys freely available to anyone with whom they want to communicate. The mere possession of the public key by third parties does not introduce any weaknesses into the cryptosystem. The private key, on the other hand, is reserved for the sole use of the individual who owns the keys. It is never shared with any other cryptosystem user.

Normal communication between public key cryptosystem users is quite straightforward. Figure 10.1 shows the general process.

FIGURE 10.1 Asymmetric key cryptography

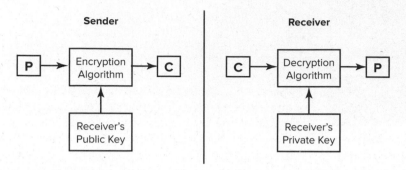

Notice that the process does not require the sharing of private keys. The sender encrypts the plain-text message (P) with the recipient's public key to create the ciphertext message (C). When the recipient opens the ciphertext message, they decrypt it using their private key to recreate the original plain-text message. Once the sender encrypts the message with the recipient's public key, no user (including the sender) can decrypt that message without knowing the recipient's private key (the second half of the public-private key pair used to generate the message). This is the beauty of public key cryptography—public keys can be freely shared using unsecured communications and then used to create secure communications channels between users previously unknown to each other.

You also learned in the previous chapter that public key cryptography entails a higher degree of computational complexity. Keys used within public key systems must be longer than those used in private key systems to produce cryptosystems of equivalent strengths.

RSA

The most famous public key cryptosystem is named after its creators. In 1977, Ronald Rivest, Adi Shamir, and Leonard Adleman proposed the *RSA public key algorithm* that remains a worldwide standard today. They patented their algorithm and formed a commercial venture known as RSA Security to develop mainstream implementations of their security technology. Today, the RSA algorithm forms the security backbone of a large number of well-known security infrastructures produced by companies like Microsoft, Nokia, and Cisco.

The RSA algorithm depends upon the computational difficulty inherent in factoring large prime numbers. Each user of the cryptosystem generates a pair of public and private keys using the algorithm described in the following steps:

1. Choose two large prime numbers (approximately 200 digits each), labeled p and q.

2. Compute the product of those two numbers: $n = p * q$.

3. Select a number, e, that satisfies the following two requirements:

    a. e is less than n.

    b. e and $(n-1)(q-1)$ are relatively prime—that is, the two numbers have no common factors other than 1.

4. Find a number, d, such that $(ed - 1) \bmod (p - 1)(q - 1) = 0$.

5. Distribute e and n as the public key to all cryptosystem users. Keep d secret as the private key.

If Alice wants to send an encrypted message to Bob, she generates the ciphertext (C) from the plain text (P) using the following formula (where e is Bob's public key and n is the product of p and q created during the key generation process):

$$C = P^e \bmod n$$

When Bob receives the message, he performs the following calculation to retrieve the plain-text message:

$$P = C^d \bmod n$$

Merkle-Hellman Knapsack

Another early asymmetric algorithm, the Merkle-Hellman Knapsack algorithm, was developed the year after RSA was publicized. Like RSA, it's based upon the difficulty of performing factoring operations, but it relies upon a component of set theory known as *super-increasing sets* rather than on large prime numbers. Merkle-Hellman was proven ineffective when it was broken in 1984.

Importance of Key Length

The length of the cryptographic key is perhaps the most important security parameter that can be set at the discretion of the security administrator. It's important to understand the capabilities of your encryption algorithm and choose a key length that provides an appropriate level of protection. This judgment can be made by weighing the difficulty of defeating a given key length (measured in the amount of processing time required to defeat the cryptosystem) against the importance of the data.

Generally speaking, the more critical your data, the stronger the key you use to protect it should be. Timeliness of the data is also an important consideration. You must take into account the rapid growth of computing power—the famous Moore's law suggests that computing power doubles approximately every 18 months. If it takes current computers one year of processing time to break your code, it will take only three months if the attempt is made with contemporary technology three years down the road. If you expect that your data will still be sensitive at that time, you should choose a much longer cryptographic key that will remain secure well into the future.

The strengths of various key lengths also vary greatly according to the cryptosystem you're using. The key lengths shown in the following table for three asymmetric cryptosystems all provide equal protection:

Cryptosystem	Key Length
RSA	1,088 bits
DSA	1,024 bits
Elliptic curve	160 bits

El Gamal

In Chapter 9, you learned how the Diffie-Hellman algorithm uses large integers and modular arithmetic to facilitate the secure exchange of secret keys over insecure communications channels. In 1985, Dr. T. El Gamal published an article describing how the mathematical principles behind the Diffie-Hellman key exchange algorithm could be extended to support an entire public key cryptosystem used for encrypting and decrypting messages.

At the time of its release, one of the major advantages of El Gamal over the RSA algorithm was that it was released into the public domain. Dr. El Gamal did not obtain a patent on his extension of Diffie-Hellman, and it is freely available for use, unlike the then-patented RSA technology. (RSA released its algorithm into the public domain in 2000.)

However, El Gamal also has a major disadvantage—the algorithm doubles the length of any message it encrypts. This presents a major hardship when encrypting long messages or data that will be transmitted over a narrow bandwidth communications circuit.

Elliptic Curve

Also in 1985, two mathematicians, Neal Koblitz from the University of Washington and Victor Miller from International Business Machines (IBM), independently proposed the application of *elliptic curve cryptography* theory to develop secure cryptographic systems.

The mathematical concepts behind elliptic curve cryptography are quite complex and well beyond the scope of this book. However, you should be generally familiar with the elliptic curve algorithm and its potential applications when preparing for the CISSP exam. If you are interested in learning the detailed mathematics behind elliptic curve cryptosystems, an excellent tutorial exists at www.certicom.com/index.php/ecc-tutorial.

Any elliptic curve can be defined by the following equation:

$$y^2 = x^3 + ax + b$$

In this equation, x, y, a, and b are all real numbers. Each elliptic curve has a corresponding *elliptic curve group* made up of the points on the elliptic curve along with the point O, located at infinity. Two points within the same elliptic curve group (P and Q) can be added together with an elliptic curve addition algorithm. This operation is expressed, quite simply, as follows:

$$P + Q$$

This problem can be extended to involve multiplication by assuming that Q is a multiple of P, meaning the following:

$$Q = xP$$

Computer scientists and mathematicians believe that it is extremely hard to find x, even if P and Q are already known. This difficult problem, known as the elliptic curve discrete logarithm problem, forms the basis of elliptic curve cryptography. It is widely believed that this problem is harder to solve than both the prime factorization problem that the RSA cryptosystem is based upon and the standard discrete logarithm problem utilized by Diffie-Hellman and El Gamal. This is illustrated by the data shown in the table in the sidebar "Importance of Key Length," which noted that a 1,088-bit RSA key is cryptographically equivalent to a 160-bit elliptic curve cryptosystem key.

Hash Functions

Later in this chapter, you'll learn how cryptosystems implement digital signatures to provide proof that a message originated from a particular user of the cryptosystem and to ensure that the message was not modified while in transit between the two parties. Before you can completely understand that concept, we must first explain the concept of *hash functions*. We will explore the basics of hash functions and look at several common hash functions used in modern digital signature algorithms.

Hash functions have a very simple purpose—they take a potentially long message and generate a unique output value derived from the content of the message. This value is commonly referred to as the *message digest*. Message digests can be generated by the sender of a message and transmitted to the recipient along with the full message for two reasons. First, the recipient can use the same hash function to recompute the message digest from the full message. They can then compare the computed message digest to the transmitted one to ensure that the message sent by the originator is the same one received by the recipient. If the message digests do not match, that means the message was somehow modified while in transit. Second, the message digest can be used to implement a digital signature algorithm. This concept is covered in "Digital Signatures" later in this chapter.

The term *message digest* is used interchangeably with a wide variety of synonyms, including *hash, hash value, hash total, CRC, fingerprint, check-sum*, and *digital ID*.

In most cases, a message digest is 128 bits or larger. However, a single-digit value can be used to perform the function of parity, a low-level or single-digit checksum value used to provide a single individual point of verification. In most cases, the longer the message digest, the more reliable its verification of integrity.

According to RSA Security, there are five basic requirements for a cryptographic hash function:

- The input can be of any length.

- The output has a fixed length.

- The hash function is relatively easy to compute for any input.

- The hash function is one-way (meaning that it is extremely hard to determine the input when provided with the output). One-way functions and their usefulness in cryptography are described in Chapter 9.

- The hash function is collision free (meaning that it is extremely hard to find two messages that produce the same hash value).

In the following sections, we'll look at four common hashing algorithms: SHA, MD2, MD4, and MD5. HMAC is also discussed later in this chapter.

There are numerous hashing algorithms not addressed in this exam. But in addition to SHA, MD2, MD4, MD5, and HMAC, you should recognize HAVAL. Hash of Variable Length (HAVAL) is a modification of MD5. HAVAL uses 1,024-bit blocks and produces hash values of 128, 160, 192, 224, and 256 bits.

SHA

The Secure Hash Algorithm (SHA) and its successors, SHA-1 and SHA-2, are government standard hash functions developed by the National Institute of Standards and Technology (NIST) and are specified in an official government publication—the Secure Hash Standard (SHS), also known as Federal Information Processing Standard (FIPS) 180.

SHA-1 takes an input of virtually any length (in reality, there is an upper bound of approximately 2,097,152 terabytes on the algorithm) and produces a 160-bit message digest. The SHA-1 algorithm processes a message in 512-bit blocks. Therefore, if the message length is not a multiple of 512, the SHA algorithm pads the message with additional data until the length reaches the next highest multiple of 512.

Recent cryptanalytic attacks demonstrated that there are weaknesses in the SHA-1 algorithm. This led to the creation of SHA-2, which has four variants:

- SHA-256 produces a 256-bit message digest using a 512-bit block size.

- SHA-224 uses a truncated version of the SHA-256 hash to produce a 224-bit message digest using a 512-bit block size.

- SHA-512 produces a 512-bit message digest using a 1,024-bit block size.

- SHA-384 uses a truncated version of the SHA-512 hash to produce a 384-bit digest using a 1,024-bit block size.

Although it might seem trivial, you should take the time to memorize the size of the message digests produced by each one of the hash algorithms described in this chapter.

The cryptographic community generally considers the SHA-2 algorithms secure, but they theoretically suffer from the same weakness as the SHA-1 algorithm. In 2007, the federal government announced a multi-year competition to create SHA-3. As of the time of this writing, five finalists remained in the SHA-3 competition and NIST was expected to announce a winner in the second quarter of 2012.

MD2

The Message Digest 2 (MD2) hash algorithm was developed by Ronald Rivest (the same Rivest of Rivest, Shamir, and Adleman fame) in 1989 to provide a secure hash function for 8-bit processors. MD2 pads the message so that its length is a multiple of 16 bytes. It then computes a 16-byte checksum and appends it to the end of the message. A 128-bit message digest is then generated by using the entire original message along with the appended checksum.

Cryptanalytic attacks exist against the MD2 algorithm. Specifically, Nathalie Rogier and Pascal Chauvaud discovered that if the checksum is not appended to the message before digest computation, collisions may occur. Frederic Mueller later proved that MD2 is not a one-way function. Therefore, it should no longer be used.

MD4

In 1990, Rivest enhanced his message digest algorithm to support 32-bit processors and increase the level of security. This enhanced algorithm is known as MD4. It first pads the message to ensure that the message length is 64 bits smaller than a multiple of 512 bits. For example, a 16-bit message would be padded with 432 additional bits of data to make it 448 bits, which is 64 bits smaller than a 512-bit message.

The MD4 algorithm then processes 512-bit blocks of the message in three rounds of computation. The final output is a 128-bit message digest.

> The MD2, MD4, and MD5 algorithms are no longer accepted as suitable hashing functions. However, the details of the algorithms may still appear on the CISSP exam.

Several mathematicians have published papers documenting flaws in the full version of MD4 as well as improperly implemented versions of MD4. In particular, Hans Dobbertin published a paper in 1996 outlining how a modern PC could be used to find collisions for MD4 message digests in less than one minute. For this reason, MD4 is no longer considered to be a secure hashing algorithm, and its use should be avoided if at all possible.

MD5

In 1991, Rivest released the next version of his message digest algorithm, which he called MD5. It also processes 512-bit blocks of the message, but it uses four distinct rounds of computation to produce a digest of the same length as the MD2 and MD4 algorithms (128 bits). MD5 has the same padding requirements as MD4—the message length must be 64 bits less than a multiple of 512 bits.

MD5 implements additional security features that reduce the speed of message digest production significantly. Unfortunately, recent cryptanalytic attacks demonstrated that the MD5 protocol is subject to collisions, preventing its use for ensuring message integrity. Specifically, Arjen Lenstra and others demonstrated in 2005 that it is possible to create two digital certificates from different public keys that have the same MD5 hash.

Table 10.1 lists well-known hashing algorithms and their resultant hash value lengths in bits. Earmark this page for memorization.

TABLE 10.1 Hash algorithm memorization chart

Name	Hash Value Length
Hash of Variable Length (HAVAL)—an MD5 variant	128, 160, 192, 224, and 256 bits
Hash Message Authenticating Code (HMAC)	Variable
Message Digest 2 (MD2)	128
Message Digest 4 (MD4)	128
Message Digest 5 (MD5)	128
Secure Hash Algorithm (SHA-1)	160
SHA-224	224
SHA-256	256
SHA-384	384
SHA-512	512

Digital Signatures

Once you have chosen a cryptographically sound hashing algorithm, you can use it to implement a *digital signature* system. Digital signature infrastructures have two distinct goals:

- Digitally signed messages assure the recipient that the message truly came from the claimed sender. They enforce nonrepudiation (that is, they preclude the sender from later claiming that the message is a forgery).

- Digitally signed messages assure the recipient that the message was not altered while in transit between the sender and recipient. This protects against both malicious modification (a third party altering the meaning of the message) and unintentional modification (because of faults in the communications process, such as electrical interference).

Digital signature algorithms rely upon a combination of the two major concepts already covered in this chapter—public key cryptography and hashing functions.

If Alice wants to digitally sign a message she's sending to Bob, she performs the following actions:

1. Alice generates a message digest of the original plain-text message using one of the cryptographically sound hashing algorithms, such as SHA-512.

2. Alice then encrypts only the message digest using her private key. This encrypted message digest is the digital signature.

3. Alice appends the signed message digest to the plain-text message.

4. Alice transmits the appended message to Bob.

When Bob receives the digitally signed message, he reverses the procedure, as follows:

1. Bob decrypts the digital signature using Alice's public key.

2. Bob uses the same hashing function to create a message digest of the full plain-text message received from Alice.

3. Bob then compares the decrypted message digest he received from Alice with the message digest he computed himself. If the two digests match, he can be assured that the message he received was sent by Alice. If they do not match, either the message was not sent by Alice or the message was modified while in transit.

 Digital signatures are used for more than just messages. Software vendors often use digital signature technology to authenticate code distributions that you download from the Internet, such as applets and software patches.

Note that the digital signature process does not provide any privacy in and of itself. It only ensures that the cryptographic goals of integrity, authentication, and nonrepudiation are met. However, if Alice wanted to ensure the privacy of her message to Bob, she could add a step to the message creation process. After appending the signed message digest to the plain-text message, Alice could encrypt the entire message with Bob's public key. When Bob received the message, he would decrypt it with his own private key before following the steps just outlined.

HMAC

The Hashed Message Authentication Code (HMAC) algorithm implements a partial digital signature—it guarantees the integrity of a message during transmission, but it does not provide for nonrepudiation.

 Real World Scenario

Which Key Should I Use?

If you're new to public key cryptography, selecting the correct key for various applications can be quite confusing. Encryption, decryption, message signing, and signature verification all use the same algorithm with different key inputs. Here are a few simple rules to help keep these concepts straight in your mind when preparing for the CISSP exam:

- If you want to encrypt a message, use the recipient's public key.

- If you want to decrypt a message sent to you, use your private key.

- If you want to digitally sign a message you are sending to someone else, use your private key.

- If you want to verify the signature on a message sent by someone else, use the sender's public key.

These four rules are the core principles of public key cryptography and digital signatures. If you understand each of them, you're off to a great start!

HMAC can be combined with any standard message digest generation algorithm, such as SHA-2, by using a shared secret key. Therefore, only communicating parties who know the key can generate or verify the digital signature. If the recipient decrypts the message digest but cannot successfully compare it to a message digest generated from the plain-text message, that means the message was altered in transit.

Because HMAC relies on a shared secret key, it does not provide any nonrepudiation functionality (as previously mentioned). However, it operates in a more efficient manner than the digital signature standard described in the following section and may be suitable for applications in which symmetric key cryptography is appropriate. In short, it represents a halfway point between unencrypted use of a message digest algorithm and computationally expensive digital signature algorithms based upon public key cryptography.

Digital Signature Standard

The National Institute of Standards and Technology specifies the digital signature algorithms acceptable for federal government use in Federal Information Processing Standard (FIPS) 186-3, also known as the Digital Signature Standard (DSS). This document specifies that all federally approved digital signature algorithms must use the SHA-1 or SHA-2 hashing functions.

DSS also specifies the encryption algorithms that can be used to support a digital signature infrastructure. There are three currently approved standard encryption algorithms:

- The Digital Signature Algorithm (DSA) as specified in FIPS 186-3
- The Rivest, Shamir, Adleman (RSA) algorithm as specified in ANSI X9.31
- The Elliptic Curve DSA (ECDSA) as specified in ANSI X9.62

Two other digital signature algorithms you should recognize, at least by name, are Schnorr's signature algorithm and Nyberg-Rueppel's signature algorithm.

Public Key Infrastructure

The major strength of public key encryption is its ability to facilitate communication between parties previously unknown to each other. This is made possible by the *public key infrastructure (PKI)* hierarchy of trust relationships. These trusts permit combining asymmetric cryptography with symmetric cryptography along with hashing and digital certificates, giving us hybrid cryptography. In the following sections, you'll learn the basic components of the public key infrastructure and the cryptographic concepts that make global secure communications possible. You'll learn the composition of a digital certificate, the role of certificate authorities, and the process used to generate and destroy certificates.

Certificates

Digital *certificates* provide communicating parties with the assurance that the people they are communicating with truly are who they claim to be. Digital certificates are essentially endorsed copies of an individual's public key. When users verify that a certificate was signed by a trusted CA, they know that the public key is legitimate.

Digital certificates contain specific identifying information, and their construction is governed by an international standard—X.509. Certificates that conform to X.509 contain the following data:

- Version of X.509 to which the certificate conforms

- Serial number (from the certificate creator)

- Signature algorithm identifier (specifies the technique used by the certificate authority to digitally sign the contents of the certificate)

- Issuer name (identification of the certificate authority that issued the certificate)

- Validity period (specifies the dates and times—a starting date and time and an ending date and time—during which the certificate is valid)

- Subject's name (contains the distinguished name, or DN, of the entity that owns the public key contained in the certificate)

- Subject's public key (the meat of the certificate—the actual public key the certificate owner used to set up secure communications)

The current version of X.509 (version 3) supports certificate extensions—customized variables containing data inserted into the certificate by the certificate authority to support tracking of certificates or various applications.

> If you're interested in building your own X.509 certificates or just want to explore the inner workings of the public key infrastructure, you can purchase the complete official X.509 standard from the International Telecommunications Union (ITU). It's part of the Open Systems Interconnection (OSI) series of communication standards and can be purchased electronically on the ITU website at www.itu.int.

X.509 has not been officially accepted as a standard, and implementations can vary from vendor to vendor. However, both Microsoft and Mozilla have adopted X.509 as their de facto standard for Secure Sockets Layer (SSL) communication between their web clients and servers. SSL is covered in greater detail in the section "Applied Cryptography" later in this chapter.

Certificate Authorities

Certificate authorities (CAs) are the glue that binds the public key infrastructure together. These neutral organizations offer notarization services for digital certificates. To obtain a digital certificate from a reputable CA, you must prove your identify to the satisfaction of the CA. The following list includes the major CAs:

- VeriSign

- Thawte

- Geotrust
- Comodo Limited
- Starfield Technologies
- GoDaddy
- DigiCert
- Network Solutions, LLC
- Entrust

Nothing is preventing any organization from simply setting up shop as a CA. However, the certificates issued by a CA are only as good as the trust placed in the CA that issued them. This is an important item to consider when receiving a digital certificate from a third party. If you don't recognize and trust the name of the CA that issued the certificate, you shouldn't place any trust in the certificate at all. PKI relies upon a hierarchy of trust relationships. If you configure your browser to trust a CA, it will automatically trust all of the digital certificates issued by that CA. Browser developers preconfigure browsers to trust the major CAs to avoid placing this burden on users.

Registration authorities (RAs) assist CAs with the burden of verifying users' identities prior to issuing digital certificates. They do not directly issue certificates themselves, but they play an important role in the certification process, allowing CAs to remotely validate user identities.

 Real World Scenario

Certificate Path Validation

You may have heard of *certificate path validation (CPV)* in your studies of certificate authorities. CPV means that each certificate in a certificate path from the original start or root of trust down to the server or client in question is valid and legitimate. CPV can be important if you need to verify that every link between "trusted" endpoints remains current, valid, and trustworthy. This issue arises from time to time when intermediary systems' certificates expire or are replaced; this can break the chain of trust or the verification path. By forcing a reverification of all stages of trust, you can reestablish all trust links and prove that the assumed trust remains assured.

Certificate Generation and Destruction

The technical concepts behind the public key infrastructure are relatively simple. In the following sections, we'll cover the processes used by certificate authorities to create, validate, and revoke client certificates.

Enrollment

When you want to obtain a digital certificate, you must first prove your identity to the CA in some manner; this process is called *enrollment*. As mentioned in the previous section, this sometimes involves physically appearing before an agent of the certification authority with the appropriate identification documents. Some certificate authorities provide other means of verification, including the use of credit report data and identity verification by trusted community leaders.

Once you've satisfied the certificate authority regarding your identity, you provide them with your public key. The CA next creates an X.509 digital certificate containing your identifying information and a copy of your public key. The CA then digitally signs the certificate using the CA's private key and provides you with a copy of your signed digital certificate. You may then safely distribute this certificate to anyone with whom you want to communicate securely.

Verification

When you receive a digital certificate from someone with whom you want to communicate, you *verify* the certificate by checking the CA's digital signature using the CA's public key. Next, you must check and ensure that the certificate was not published on a *certificate revocation list (CRL)*. At this point, you may assume that the public key listed in the certificate is authentic, provided that it satisfies the following requirements:

- The digital signature of the CA is authentic.
- You trust the CA.
- The certificate is not listed on a CRL.
- The certificate actually contains the data you are trusting.

The last point is a subtle but extremely important item. Before you trust an identifying piece of information about someone, be sure that it is actually contained within the certificate. If a certificate contains the email address (`billjones@foo.com`) but not the individual's name, you can be certain only that the public key contained therein is associated with that email address. The CA is not making any assertions about the actual identity of the `billjones@foo.com` email account. However, if the certificate contains the name Bill Jones along with an address and telephone number, the CA is vouching for that information as well.

Digital certificate verification algorithms are built in to a number of popular web browsing and email clients, so you won't often need to get involved in the particulars of the process. However, it's important to have a solid understanding of the technical details taking place behind the scenes to make appropriate security judgments for your organization. It's also the reason that, when purchasing a certificate, you choose a CA that is widely trusted. If a CA is not included in, or is later pulled from, the list of CAs trusted by a major browser, it will greatly limit the usefulness of your certificate.

Revocation

Occasionally, a certificate authority needs to *revoke* a certificate. This might occur for one of the following reasons:

- The certificate was compromised (for example, the certificate owner accidentally gave away the private key).

- The certificate was erroneously issued (for example, the CA mistakenly issued a certificate without proper verification).

- The details of the certificate changed (for example, the subject's name changed).

- The security association changed (for example, the subject is no longer employed by the organization sponsoring the certificate).

 Revocation request grace period is the maximum response time within which a CA will perform any requested revocation. This is defined in the *certificate practice statement (CPS)*. The CPS states the practices a CA employs when issuing or managing certificates.

You can use two techniques to verify the authenticity of certificates and identify revoked certificates:

Certificate revocation lists   Certificate revocation lists (CRLs) are maintained by the various certification authorities and contain the serial numbers of certificates that have been issued by a CA and have been revoked along with the date and time the revocation went into effect. The major disadvantage to certificate revocation lists is that they must be downloaded and cross-referenced periodically, introducing a period of latency between the time a certificate is revoked and the time end users are notified of the revocation. However, CRLs remain the most common method of checking certificate status in use today.

Online Certificate Status Protocol (OCSP)   This protocol eliminates the latency inherent in the use of certificate revocation lists by providing a means for real-time certificate verification. When a client receives a certificate, it sends an OCSP request to the CA's OCSP server. The server then responds with a status of valid, invalid, or unknown.

Asymmetric Key Management

When working within the public key infrastructure, it's important that you comply with several best practice requirements to maintain the security of your communications.

First, choose your encryption system wisely. As you learned earlier, "security through obscurity" is not an appropriate approach. Choose an encryption system with an algorithm in the public domain that has been thoroughly vetted by industry experts. Be wary of systems that use a "black-box" approach and maintain that the secrecy of their algorithm is critical to the integrity of the cryptosystem.

You must also select your keys in an appropriate manner. Use a key length that balances your security requirements with performance considerations. Also, ensure that your key is truly random. Any patterns within the key increase the likelihood that an attacker will be able to break your encryption and degrade the security of your cryptosystem.

When using public key encryption, keep your private key secret! Do not, under any circumstances, allow anyone else to gain access to your private key. Remember, allowing someone access even once permanently compromises all communications that take place (past, present, or future) using that key and allows the third party to successfully impersonate you.

Retire keys when they've served a useful life. Many organizations have mandatory key rotation requirements to protect against undetected key compromise. If you don't have a formal policy that you must follow, select an appropriate interval based upon the frequency with which you use your key. You might want to change your key pair every few months, if practical.

Back up your key! If you lose the file containing your private key because of data corruption, disaster, or other circumstances, you'll certainly want to have a backup available. You may want to either create your own backup or use a key escrow service that maintains the backup for you. In either case, ensure that the backup is handled in a secure manner. After all, it's just as important as your primary key file!

Applied Cryptography

Up to this point, you've learned a great deal about the foundations of cryptography, the inner workings of various cryptographic algorithms, and the use of the public key infrastructure to distribute identity credentials using digital certificates. You should now feel comfortable with the basics of cryptography and prepared to move on to higher-level applications of this technology to solve everyday communications problems. In the following sections, we'll examine the use of cryptography to secure data at rest, such as that stored on portable devices, as well as data in transit, using techniques that include secure electronic mail, encrypted web communications, and networking.

Portable Devices

The now ubiquitous nature of notebook computers, netbooks, smartphones, and tablets brings new risks to the world of computing. Those devices often contain highly sensitive information that, if lost or stolen, could cause serious harm to an organization and its customers, employees, and affiliates. For this reason, many organizations turn to encryption to protect the data on these devices in the event they are misplaced.

Current versions of popular operating systems now include disk encryption capabilities that make it easy to apply and manage encryption on portable devices. For example,

Microsoft Windows includes the BitLocker and Encrypting File System (EFS) technologies, Mac OS X includes FileVault encryption, and the TrueCrypt open-source package allows the encryption of disks on Linux, Windows, and Mac systems. There is also a wide variety of commercial tools available that provide added features and management capability. The major differentiators between these tools are how they protect keys stored in memory, whether they provide full disk or volume-only encryption, and whether they integrate with hardware-based Trusted Platform Modules (TPMs) to provide added security. Any effort to select encryption software should include an analysis of how well the alternatives compete on these characteristics.

Don't forget about smartphones when developing your portable device encryption policy. Most major smartphone and tablet platforms include enterprise-level functionality that supports encryption of data stored on the phone.

Electronic Mail

We have mentioned several times that security should be cost effective. When it comes to electronic mail, simplicity is the most cost-effective option, but sometimes cryptography functions provide specific security services that you can't avoid using. Since ensuring security is also cost effective, here are some simple rules about encrypting email:

- If you need confidentiality when sending an email message, then encrypt the message.
- If your message must maintain integrity, then you must hash the message.
- If your message needs authentication, integrity and/or nonrepudiation, then you should digitally sign the message.
- If your message requires confidentiality, integrity, authentication, and nonrepudiation, then you should encrypt and digitally sign the message.

It is always the responsibility of the sender to put proper mechanisms in place to ensure that the security (that is, confidentiality, integrity, authenticity, and nonrepudiation) of a message or transmission is maintained.

One of the most in-demand applications of cryptography is encrypting and signing electronic mail messages. Until recently, encrypted email required the use of complex, awkward software that in turn required manual intervention and complicated key exchange procedures. An increased emphasis on security in recent years resulted in the implementation of strong encryption technology in mainstream electronic mail packages. Next, we'll look at some of the secure electronic mail standards in widespread use today.

Pretty Good Privacy

Phil Zimmerman's Pretty Good Privacy (PGP) secure email system appeared on the computer security scene in 1991. It combines the CA hierarchy described earlier in this chapter with the "web of trust" concept—that is, you must become trusted by one or more PGP users to begin using the system. You then accept their judgment regarding the validity of additional users and, by extension, trust a multilevel "web" of users descending from your initial trust judgments. PGP initially encountered a number of hurdles to widespread use. The most difficult obstruction was the US government export regulations, which treated encryption technology as munitions and prohibited the distribution of strong encryption technology outside the United States. Fortunately, this restriction has since been repealed, and PGP may be freely distributed to most countries.

PGP is available in two versions. The commercial version uses RSA for key exchange, IDEA for encryption/decryption, and MD5 for message digest production. The freeware version (based upon the extremely similar OpenPGP standard) uses Diffie-Hellman key exchange, the Carlisle Adams/Stafford Tavares (CAST) 128-bit encryption/decryption algorithm, and the SHA-1 hashing function.

S/MIME

The Secure Multipurpose Internet Mail Extensions (S/MIME) protocol has emerged as a *de facto* standard for encrypted electronic mail. S/MIME utilizes the RSA encryption algorithm and has received the backing of major industry players, including RSA Security. S/MIME has already been incorporated in a large number of commercial products, including these:

- Microsoft Outlook and Outlook Express
- Mozilla Thunderbird
- Mac OS X Mail

S/MIME relies upon the use of X.509 certificates for exchanging cryptographic keys. The public keys contained in these certificates are used for digital signatures and for the exchange of symmetric keys used for longer communications sessions. RSA is the only public key cryptographic protocol supported by S/MIME. The protocol supports the AES and 3DES symmetric encryption algorithms.

Despite strong industry support for the S/MIME standard, technical limitations have prevented its widespread adoption. While major desktop mail applications support S/MIME email, mainstream web-based email systems do not support it out of the box (the use of browser extensions is required).

Web Applications

Although secure electronic mail is still in its early days, secure web browsing has achieved widespread acceptance. This is mainly because of the strong movement toward electronic commerce and the desire of both e-commerce vendors and consumers to securely exchange financial information (such as credit card information) over the Web. We'll look at the two technologies that are responsible for the small lock icon within web browsers—Secure Sockets Layer (SSL) and Transport Layer Security (TLS).

Secure Sockets Layer (SSL) was developed by Netscape to provide client/server encryption for web traffic. Hypertext Transfer Protocol over Secure Sockets Layer (HTTPS) uses port 443 to negotiate encrypted communications sessions between web servers and browser clients. Although SSL originated as a standard for Netscape browsers, Microsoft also adopted it as a security standard for its popular Internet Explorer browser. The incorporation of SSL into both of these products made it the de facto Internet standard.

SSL relies upon the exchange of server digital certificates to negotiate RSA encryption/decryption parameters between the browser and the web server. SSL's goal is to create secure communications channels that remain open for an entire web browsing session.

SSL relies upon a combination of symmetric and asymmetric cryptography. The following steps are involved:

1. When a user accesses a website, the browser retrieves the web server's certificate and extracts the server's public key from it.

2. The browser then creates a random symmetric key, uses the server's public key to encrypt it, and then sends the encrypted symmetric key to the server.

3. The server then decrypts the symmetric key using its own private key, and the two systems exchange all future messages using the symmetric encryption key.

This approach allows SSL to leverage the advanced functionality of asymmetric cryptography while encrypting and decrypting the vast majority of the data exchanged using the faster symmetric algorithm.

In 1999, security engineers proposed Transport Layer Security (TLS) as a replacement for the SSL standard, which was at the time in its third version. As with SSL, TLS uses TCP port 443. Based upon SSL technology, TLS incorporated many security enhancements and was eventually adopted as a replacement for SSL in most applications. Early versions of TLS supported downgrading communications to SSL v3.0 when both parties did not support TLS. However, in 2011, TLS v1.2 dropped this backward compatibility.

Even though TLS has been in existence for more than a decade, many people still mistakenly call it SSL. For this reason, TLS has gained the nickname SSL 3.1.

Steganography and Watermarking

Steganography is the art of using cryptographic techniques to embed secret messages within another message. Steganographic algorithms work by making alterations to the least significant bits of the many bits that make up image files. The changes are so minor that there is no appreciable effect on the viewed image. This technique allows communicating parties to hide messages in plain sight—for example, they might embed a secret message within an illustration on an otherwise innocent web page.

Steganographers often embed their secret messages within images or WAV files because these files are often so large that the secret message would easily be missed by even the most observant inspector. Steganography techniques are often used for illegal or questionable activities, such as espionage and child pornography. However, they can also be used for legitimate purposes. Adding digital watermarks to documents to protect intellectual property is accomplished by means of steganography. The hidden information is known only to the file's creator. If someone later creates an unauthorized copy of the content, the watermark can be used to detect the copy and (if uniquely watermarked files are provided to each original recipient) trace the offending copy back to the source.

Steganography is an extremely simple technology to use, with free tools openly available on the Internet. Figure 10.2 shows the entire interface of one such tool, iSteg. It simply requires that you specify a text file containing your secret message and an image file that you wish to use to hide the message. Figure 10.3 shows an example of a picture with an embedded secret message; the message is impossible to detect with the human eye.

FIGURE 10.2 Steganography tool

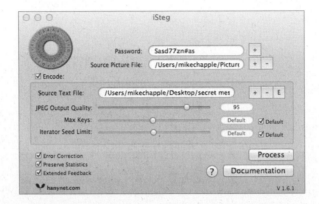

FIGURE 10.3 Image with embedded message

Networking

The final application of cryptography we'll explore in this chapter is the use of cryptographic algorithms to provide secure networking services. In the following sections, we'll take a brief look at two methods used to secure communications circuits. We'll also look at IPSec and ISAKMP as well as some of the security issues surrounding wireless networking.

Circuit Encryption

Security administrators use two types of encryption techniques to protect data traveling over networks—link encryption and end-to-end encryption:

- *Link encryption* protects entire communications circuits by creating a secure tunnel between two points using either a hardware solution or a software solution that encrypts all traffic entering one end of the tunnel and decrypts all traffic entering the other end of the tunnel. For example, a company with two offices connected via a data circuit might use link encryption to protect against attackers monitoring at a point in between the two offices.

- *End-to-end encryption* protects communications between two parties (for example, a client and a server) and is performed independently of link encryption. An example of end-to-end encryption would be the use of TLS to protect communications between a user and a web server. This protects against an intruder who might be monitoring traffic on the secure side of an encrypted link or traffic sent over an unencrypted link.

The critical difference between link and end-to-end encryption is that in link encryption, all the data, including the header, trailer, address, and routing data, is also encrypted. Therefore, each packet has to be decrypted at each hop so it can be properly routed to the next hop and then reencrypted before it can be sent along its way, which slows the routing. End-to-end encryption does not encrypt the header, trailer, address, and routing data, so it moves faster from point to point but is more susceptible to sniffers and eavesdroppers.

When encryption happens at the higher OSI layers, it is usually end-to-end encryption, and if encryption is done at the lower layers of the OSI model, it is usually link encryption.

Secure Shell (SSH) is a good example of an end-to-end encryption technique. This suite of programs provides encrypted alternatives to common Internet applications such as FTP, Telnet, and rlogin. There are actually two versions of SSH. SSH1 (which is now considered insecure) supports the DES, 3DES, IDEA, and Blowfish algorithms. SSH2 drops support for DES and IDEA but adds support for several other algorithms.

IPSec

Various security architectures are in use today, each one designed to address security issues in different environments. One such architecture that supports secure communications is the Internet Protocol Security (IPSec) standard. IPSec is a standard architecture set forth by the Internet Engineering Task Force (IETF) for setting up a secure channel to exchange information between two entities. The two entities could be two systems, two routers, two gateways, or any combination of entities. Although generally used to connect two networks, IPSec can be used to connect individual computers, such as a server and a workstation or a pair of workstations (sender and receiver, perhaps). IPSec does not dictate all implementation details but is an open, modular framework that allows many manufacturers and software developers to develop IPSec solutions that work well with products from other vendors.

IPSec uses public key cryptography to provide encryption, access control, nonrepudiation, and message authentication, all using IP-based protocols. The primary use of IPSec is for virtual private networks (VPNs), so IPSec can operate in either transport or tunnel mode. IPSec is commonly paired with the Layer 2 Tunneling Protocol (L2TP) as L2TP/IPSec.

The IP Security (IPSec) protocol provides a complete infrastructure for secured network communications. IPSec has gained widespread acceptance and is now offered in a number of commercial operating systems out of the box. IPSec relies upon security associations, and there are two main components:

- The Authentication Header (AH) provides assurances of message integrity and nonrepudiation. AH also provides authentication and access control and prevents replay attacks.

- The Encapsulating Security Payload (ESP) provides confidentiality and integrity of packet contents. It provides encryption and limited authentication and prevents replay attacks.

> ESP also provides some limited authentication, but not to the degree of the AH. Though ESP is sometimes used without AH, it's rare to see AH used without ESP.

IPSec provides for two discrete modes of operation. When IPSec is used in *transport mode*, only the packet payload is encrypted. This mode is designed for peer-to-peer communication. When it's used in *tunnel mode*, the entire packet, including the header, is encrypted. This mode is designed for gateway-to-gateway communication.

> IPSec is an extremely important concept in modern computer security. Be certain that you're familiar with the component protocols and modes of IPSec operation.

At runtime, you set up an IPSec session by creating a *security association (SA)*. The SA represents the communication session and records any configuration and status information about the connection. The SA represents a simplex connection. If you want a two-way channel, you need two SAs, one for each direction. Also, if you want to support a bidirectional channel using both AH and ESP, you will need to set up four SAs.

Some of IPSec's greatest strengths come from being able to filter or manage communications on a per-SA basis so that clients or gateways between which security associations exist can be rigorously managed in terms of what kinds of protocols or services can use an IPSec connection. Also, without a valid security association defined, pairs of users or gateways cannot establish IPSec links.

Further details of the IPSec algorithm are provided in Chapter 3, "Secure Network Architecture and Securing Network Components."

ISAKMP

The Internet Security Association and Key Management Protocol (ISAKMP) provides background security support services for IPSec by negotiating, establishing, modifying, and deleting security associations. As you learned in the previous section, IPSec relies upon a system of security associations (SAs). These SAs are managed through the use of ISAKMP. There are four basic requirements for ISAKMP, as set forth in Internet RFC 2408:

- Authenticate communicating peers.
- Create and manage security associations.
- Provide key generation mechanisms.
- Protect against threats (for example, replay and denial of service attacks).

Wireless Networking

The widespread rapid adoption of wireless networks poses a tremendous security risk. Many traditional networks do not implement encryption for routine communications between hosts on the local network and rely upon the assumption that it would be too difficult for an attacker to gain physical access to the network wire inside a secure location to eavesdrop on the network. However, wireless networks transmit data through the air, leaving them extremely vulnerable to interception. There are two main types of wireless security:

Wired Equivalent Privacy Wired Equivalent Privacy (WEP) provides 64-, and 128-bit encryption options to protect communications within the wireless LAN. WEP is described in IEEE 802.11 as an optional component of the wireless networking standard.

WARNING Cryptanalysis has conclusively demonstrated that significant flaws exist in the WEP algorithm, making it possible to completely undermine the security of a WEP-protected network within seconds. You should never use WEP encryption to protect a wireless network. In fact, the use of WEP encryption on a store network was the root cause behind the TJX security breach that was widely publicized in 2007. Again, you should *never* use WEP encryption on a wireless network.

WiFi Protected Access WiFi Protected Access (WPA) improves upon WEP encryption by implementing the Temporal Key Integrity Protocol (TKIP), eliminating the cryptographic weaknesses that undermined WEP. A further improvement to the technique, dubbed WPA2, adds AES cryptography. WPA2 provides secure algorithms appropriate for use on modern wireless networks.

> Remember that WPA does not provide an end-to-end security solution. It encrypts traffic only between a mobile computer and the nearest wireless access point. Once the traffic hits the wired network, it's in the clear again.

Another commonly used wireless security standard, IEEE 802.1x, provides a flexible framework for authentication and key management in wired and wireless networks. To use 802.1x, the client runs a piece of software known as the *supplicant*. The supplicant communicates with the authentication server. After successful authentication, the network switch or wireless access point allows the client to access the network. WPA was designed to interact with 802.1x authentication servers.

Cryptographic Attacks

As with any security mechanism, malicious individuals have found a number of attacks to defeat cryptosystems. It's important that you, as a security administrator, understand the threats posed by various cryptographic attacks to minimize the risks posed to your systems:

Analytic attack   This is an algebraic manipulation that attempts to reduce the complexity of the algorithm. Analytic attacks focus on the logic of the algorithm itself.

Implementation attack   This is a type of attack that exploits weaknesses in the implementation of a cryptography system. It focuses on exploiting the software code, not just errors and flaws but the methodology employed to program the encryption system.

Statistical attack   A statistical attack exploits statistical weaknesses in a cryptosystem, such as floating-point errors and inability to produce truly random numbers. Statistical attacks attempt to find a vulnerability in the hardware or operating system hosting the cryptography application.

Brute force   Brute-force attacks are quite straightforward. Such an attack attempts every possible valid combination for a key or password. They involve using massive amounts of processing power to methodically guess the key used to secure cryptographic communications. For a nonflawed protocol, the average amount of time required to discover the key through a brute-force attack is directly proportional to the length of the key. A brute-force attack will always be successful given enough time. Every additional bit of key length doubles the time to perform a brute-force attack because the number of potential keys doubles.

There are two modifications that attackers can make to enhance the effectiveness of a brute-force attack:

- Rainbow tables provide precomputed values for cryptographic hashes. These are commonly used for cracking passwords stored on a system in hashed form.

- Specialized, scalable computing hardware designed specifically for the conduct of brute-force attacks may greatly increase the efficiency of this approach.

Frequency analysis and the ciphertext only attack   In many cases, the only information you have at your disposal is the encrypted ciphertext message, a scenario known as the *ciphertext only attack*. In this case, one technique that proves helpful against simple ciphers is frequency analysis—counting the number of times each letter appears in the ciphertext. Using your knowledge that the letters *E, T, O, A, I,* and *N* are the most common in the English language, you can then test several hypotheses:

- If these letters are also the most common in the ciphertext, the cipher was likely a transposition cipher, which rearranged the characters of the plain text without altering them.

- If other letters are the most common in the ciphertext, the cipher is probably some form of substitution cipher that replaced the plain-text characters.

This is a simple overview of frequency analysis, and many sophisticated variations on this technique can be used against polyalphabetic ciphers and other sophisticated cryptosystems.

Known plain text   In the known plain-text attack, the attacker has a copy of the encrypted message along with the plain-text message used to generate the ciphertext (the copy). This knowledge greatly assists the attacker in breaking weaker codes. For example, imagine the ease with which you could break the Caesar cipher described in Chapter 9 if you had both a plain-text copy and a ciphertext copy of the same message.

Chosen ciphertext   In a chosen ciphertext attack, the attacker has the ability to decrypt chosen portions of the ciphertext message and use the decrypted portion of the message to discover the key.

Chosen plain text   In a chosen plain-text attack, the attacker has the ability to encrypt plain-text messages of their choosing and can then analyze the ciphertext output of the encryption algorithm.

Meet in the middle   Attackers might use a meet-in-the-middle attack to defeat encryption algorithms that use two rounds of encryption. This attack is the reason that Double DES (2DES) was quickly discarded as a viable enhancement to the DES encryption (it was replaced by Triple DES, or 3DES). In the meet-in-the-middle attack, the attacker uses a known plain-text message. The plain text is then encrypted using every possible key (k1), while the equivalent ciphertext is decrypted using all possible keys (k2). When a match is found, the corresponding pair (k1, k2) represents both portions of the double encryption. This type of attack generally takes only double the time necessary to break a single round of encryption (or 2^n rather than the anticipated $2^n * 2^n$), offering minimal added protection.

Man in the middle   In the man-in-the-middle attack, a malicious individual sits between two communicating parties and intercepts all communications (including the setup of the cryptographic session). The attacker responds to the originator's initialization requests and sets up a secure session with the originator. The attacker then establishes a second secure session with the intended recipient using a different key and posing as the originator. The attacker can then "sit in the middle" of the communication and read all traffic as it passes between the two parties.

> Be careful not to confuse the meet-in-the-middle attack with the man-in-the-middle attack. They may have similar names, but they are quite different!

Birthday   The birthday attack, also known as a *collision attack* or *reverse hash matching* (see the discussion of brute-force and dictionary attacks in Chapter 2, "Access Control Attacks and Monitoring"), seeks to find flaws in the one-to-one nature of hashing functions. In this attack, the malicious individual seeks to substitute in a digitally signed communication a different message that produces the same message digest, thereby maintaining the validity of the original digital signature.

> Don't forget that social engineering techniques can also be used in cryptanalysis. If you're able to obtain a decryption key by simply asking the sender for it, that's much easier than attempting to crack the cryptosystem!

Replay   The replay attack is used against cryptographic algorithms that don't incorporate temporal protections. In this attack, the malicious individual intercepts an encrypted message between two parties (often a request for authentication) and then later "replays" the captured message to open a new session. This attack can be defeated by incorporating a time stamp and expiration period into each message.

Summary

Asymmetric key cryptography, or public key encryption, provides an extremely flexible infrastructure, facilitating simple, secure communication between parties that do not necessarily know each other prior to initiating the communication. It also provides the framework for the digital signing of messages to ensure nonrepudiation and message integrity. This chapter explored public key encryption, which provides a scalable cryptographic architecture for use by large numbers of users. We also described some popular cryptographic algorithms, such as link encryption and end-to-end encryption. Finally, we introduced you to the public key infrastructure, which uses certificate authorities (CAs) to generate digital certificates containing the public keys of system users and digital signatures, which rely upon a combination of public key cryptography and hashing functions.

We also looked at some of the common applications of cryptographic technology in solving everyday problems. You learned how cryptography can be used to secure electronic mail (using PGP and S/MIME), web communications (using SSL and TLS), and both peer-to-peer and gateway-to-gateway networking (using IPSec and ISAKMP) as well as wireless communications (using WPA and WPA2).

Finally, we covered some of the more common attacks used by malicious individuals attempting to interfere with or intercept encrypted communications between two parties. Such attacks include birthday, cryptanalytic, replay, brute-force, known plain-text, chosen plain-text, chosen ciphertext, meet-in-the-middle, man-in-the-middle, and birthday attacks. It's important for you to understand these attacks in order to provide adequate security against them.

Exam Essentials

Understand the key types used in asymmetric cryptography.   Public keys are freely shared among communicating parties, whereas private keys are kept secret. To encrypt a message, use the recipient's public key. To decrypt a message, use your own private key. To sign a message, use your own private key. To validate a signature, use the sender's public key.

Be familiar with the three major public key cryptosystems.   RSA is the most famous public key cryptosystem; it was developed by Rivest, Shamir, and Adleman in 1977. It depends upon the difficulty of factoring the product of prime numbers. El Gamal is an extension of the Diffie-Hellman key exchange algorithm that depends upon modular arithmetic. The elliptic curve algorithm depends upon the elliptic curve discrete logarithm problem and provides more security than other algorithms when both are used with keys of the same length.

Know the fundamental requirements of a hash function.   Good hash functions have five requirements. They must allow input of any length, provide fixed-length output, make it relatively easy to compute the hash function for any input, provide one-way functionality, and be collision free.

Be familiar with the major hashing algorithms.   The successors to the Secure Hash Algorithm (SHA), SHA-1 and SHA-2, make up the government standard message digest function. SHA-1 produces a 160-bit message digest while SHA-2 supports variable lengths, ranging up to 512 bits.

Understand how digital signatures are generated and verified.   To digitally sign a message, first use a hashing function to generate a message digest. Then encrypt the digest with your private key. To verify the digital signature on a message, decrypt the signature with the sender's public key and then compare the message digest to one you generate yourself. If they match, the message is authentic.

Know the components of the Digital Signature Standard (DSS).   The Digital Signature Standard uses the SHA-1 message digest function along with one of three encryption algorithms: the Digital Signature Algorithm (DSA); the Rivest, Shamir, Adleman (RSA) algorithm; or the Elliptic Curve DSA (ECDSA) algorithm.

Understand the public key infrastructure (PKI).   In the public key infrastructure, certificate authorities (CAs) generate digital certificates containing the public keys of system users. Users then distribute these certificates to people with whom they want to communicate. Certificate recipients verify a certificate using the CA's public key.

Know the common applications of cryptography to secure electronic mail.   The emerging standard for encrypted messages is the S/MIME protocol. Another popular email security tool is Phil Zimmerman's Pretty Good Privacy (PGP).

Know the common applications of cryptography to secure web activity.   The de facto standard for secure web traffic is the use of HTTP over Transport Layer Security (TLS) or the older Secure Sockets Layer (SSL). Most web browsers support both standards.

Know the common applications of cryptography to secure networking.   The IPSec protocol standard provides a common framework for encrypting network traffic and is built in to a number of common operating systems. In IPSec transport mode, packet contents are encrypted for peer-to-peer communication. In tunnel mode, the entire packet, including header information, is encrypted for gateway-to-gateway communications.

Describe IPSec.   IPSec is a security architecture framework that supports secure communication over IP. IPSec establishes a secure channel in either transport mode or tunnel mode. It can be used to establish direct communication between computers or to set up a VPN between networks. IPSec uses two protocols: Authentication Header (AH) and Encapsulating Security Payload (ESP).

Explain common cryptographic attacks.   Brute-force attacks are attempts to randomly find the correct cryptographic key. Known plain-text, chosen ciphertext, and chosen plaintext attacks require the attacker to have some extra information in addition to the ciphertext. The meet-in-the-middle attack exploits protocols that use two rounds of encryption. The man-in-the-middle attack fools both parties into communicating with the attacker instead of directly with each other. The birthday attack is an attempt to find collisions in hash functions. The replay attack is an attempt to reuse authentication requests.

Written Lab

1. Explain the process Bob should use if he wants to send a confidential message to Alice using asymmetric cryptography.

2. Explain the process Alice would use to decrypt the message Bob sent in question 1.

3. Explain the process Bob should use to digitally sign a message to Alice.

4. Explain the process Alice should use to verify the digital signature on the message from Bob in question 3.

Review Questions

1. In the RSA public key cryptosystem, which one of the following numbers will always be largest?

   A. e

   B. n

   C. p

   D. q

2. Which cryptographic algorithm forms the basis of the El Gamal cryptosystem?

   A. RSA

   B. Diffie-Hellman

   C. 3DES

   D. IDEA

3. If Richard wants to send an encrypted message to Sue using a public key cryptosystem, which key does he use to encrypt the message?

   A. Richard's public key

   B. Richard's private key

   C. Sue's public key

   D. Sue's private key

4. If a 2,048-bit plain-text message were encrypted with the El Gamal public key cryptosystem, how long would the resulting ciphertext message be?

   A. 1,024 bits

   B. 2,048 bits

   C. 4,096 bits

   D. 8,192 bits

5. Acme Widgets currently uses a 1,024-bit RSA encryption standard companywide. The company plans to convert from RSA to an elliptic curve cryptosystem. If it wants to maintain the same cryptographic strength, what ECC key length should it use?

   A. 160 bits

   B. 512 bits

   C. 1,024 bits

   D. 2,048 bits

6. John wants to produce a message digest of a 2,048-byte message he plans to send to Mary. If he uses the SHA-1 hashing algorithm, what size will the message digest for this particular message be?

   A. 160 bits

   B. 512 bits

   C. 1,024 bits

   D. 2,048 bits

7. Which one of the following technologies is considered flawed and should no longer be used?

   A. SHA-2

   B. PGP

   C. WEP

   D. TLS

8. What encryption technique does WPA use to protect wireless communications?

   A. TKIP

   B. DES

   C. 3DES

   D. AES

9. Richard received an encrypted message sent to him from Sue. Which key should he use to decrypt the message?

   A. Richard's public key

   B. Richard's private key

   C. Sue's public key

   D. Sue's private key

10. Richard wants to digitally sign a message he's sending to Sue so that Sue can be sure the message came from him without modification while in transit. Which key should he use to encrypt the message digest?

    A. Richard's public key

    B. Richard's private key

    C. Sue's public key

    D. Sue's private key

11. Which one of the following algorithms is not supported by the Digital Signature Standard?

    A. Digital Signature Algorithm

    B. RSA

    C. El Gamal DSA

    D. Elliptic Curve DSA

12. Which International Telecommunications Union (ITU) standard governs the creation and endorsement of digital certificates for secure electronic communication?

   A. X.500

   B. X.509

   C. X.900

   D. X.905

13. What cryptosystem provides the encryption/decryption technology for the commercial version of Phil Zimmerman's Pretty Good Privacy secure email system?

   A. ROT13

   B. IDEA

   C. ECC

   D. El Gamal

14. What TCP/IP communications port is utilized by Transport Layer Security traffic?

   A. 80

   B. 220

   C. 443

   D. 559

15. What type of cryptographic attack rendered Double DES (2DES) no more effective than standard DES encryption?

   A. Birthday attack

   B. Chosen ciphertext attack

   C. Meet-in-the-middle attack

   D. Man-in-the-middle attack

16. Which of the following tools can be used to improve the effectiveness of a brute-force password cracking attack?

   A. Rainbow tables

   B. Hierarchical screening

   C. TKIP

   D. Random enhancement

17. Which of the following links would be protected by WPA encryption?

   A. Firewall to firewall

   B. Router to firewall

   C. Client to wireless access point

   D. Wireless access point to router

18. What is the major disadvantage of using certificate revocation lists?

    A. Key management

    B. Latency

    C. Record keeping

    D. Vulnerability to brute force attacks

19. Which one of the following encryption algorithms is now considered insecure?

    A. El Gamal

    B. RSA

    C. Skipjack

    D. Merkle-Hellman Knapsack

20. What does IPSec define?

    A. All possible security classifications for a specific configuration

    B. A framework for setting up a secure communication channel

    C. The valid transition states in the Biba model

    D. TCSEC security categories

Chapter
11

Principles of Security Models, Design, and Capabilities

THE CISSP EXAM TOPICS COVERED IN THIS CHAPTER INCLUDE:

6. **Security Architecture and Design**

   A. Understand the fundamental concepts of security models (e.g., Confidentiality, Integrity, and Multi-Level Models)

   B. Understand the components of information systems security evaluation models

      B.1 Product evaluation models (e.g., common criteria)

      B.2 Industry and international security implementation guidelines (e.g., PCI-DSS, ISO)

   C. Understand security capabilities of information systems (e.g., memory protection, virtualization, trusted platform module)

Understanding the philosophy behind security solutions helps to limit your search for the best controls for specific security needs. In this chapter, we discuss security models, including state machine, Bell-LaPadula, Biba, Clark-Wilson, Take-Grant, and Brewer and Nash. This chapter also describes Common Criteria and other methods governments and corporations use to evaluate information systems from a security perspective, with particular emphasis on US Department of Defense and international security evaluation criteria. Finally, we discuss commonly encountered design flaws and other issues that can make information systems susceptible to attack.

The process of determining how secure a system is can be difficult and time-consuming. In this chapter, we describe the process of evaluating a computer system's level of security. We begin by introducing and explaining basic concepts and terminology used to describe information system security concepts and talk about secure computing, secure perimeters, security and access monitors, and kernel code. We turn to security models to explain how access and security controls can be implemented. We also briefly explain how system security may be categorized as either open or closed; describe a set of standard security techniques used to ensure confidentiality, integrity, and availability of data; discuss security controls; and introduce a standard suite of secure networking protocols.

Understand the Fundamental Concepts of Security Models

In information security, models provide a way to formalize security policies. Such models can be abstract or intuitive (some are decidedly mathematical), but all are intended to provide an explicit set of rules that a computer can follow to implement the fundamental security concepts, processes, and procedures that make up a security policy. These models offer a way to deepen your understanding of how a computer operating system should be designed and developed to support a specific security policy.

A security model provides a way for designers to map abstract statements into a security policy that prescribes the algorithms and data structures necessary to build hardware and software. Thus, a security model gives software designers something against which to measure their design and implementation. That model, of course, must support each part of the security policy. In this way, developers can be sure their security implementation supports the security policy.

Tokens, Capabilities, and Labels

Several different methods are used to describe the necessary security attributes for an object. A security *token* is a separate object that is associated with a resource and describes its security attributes. This token can communicate security information about an object prior to requesting access to the actual object. In other implementations, various lists are used to store security information about multiple objects. A *capabilities list* maintains a row of security attributes for each controlled object. Although not as flexible as the token approach, capabilities lists generally offer quicker lookups when a subject requests access to an object. A third common type of attribute storage is called a *security label*, which is generally a permanent part of the object to which it's attached. Once a security label is set, it usually cannot be altered. This permanence provides another safeguard against tampering that neither tokens nor capabilities lists provide.

You'll explore several security models in the following sections; all of them can shed light on how security enters into computer architectures and operating system design:

- Trusted computing base
- State machine model
- Information flow model
- Noninterference model
- Take-Grant model
- Access control matrix
- Bell-LaPadula model
- Biba model
- Clark-Wilson model
- Brewer and Nash model (also known as Chinese Wall)
- Goguen-Meseguer model
- Sutherland model
- Graham-Denning model

Although no system can be totally secure, it is possible to design and build reasonably secure systems. In fact, if a secured system complies with a specific set of security criteria, it can be said to exhibit a level of trust. Therefore, trust can be built into a system and then evaluated, certified, and accredited. But before we can discuss each security model, we have to establish a foundation upon which most security models are built. This foundation is the TCB.

Trusted Computing Base

An old US Department of Defense standard known colloquially as the Orange Book (DoD Standard 5200.28, covered in more detail later in this chapter in the section "Rainbow Series") describes a *trusted computing base (TCB)* as a combination of hardware, software, and controls that work together to form a trusted base to enforce your security policy. The TCB is a subset of a complete information system. It should be as small as possible so that a detailed analysis can reasonably ensure that the system meets design specifications and requirements. The TCB is the only portion of that system that can be trusted to adhere to and enforce the security policy. It is not necessary that every component of a system be trusted. But anytime you consider a system from a security standpoint, your evaluation should include all trusted components that define that system's TCB.

In general, TCB components in a system are responsible for controlling access to the system. The TCB must provide methods to access resources both inside and outside the TCB itself. TCB components commonly restrict the activities of components outside the TCB. It is the responsibility of TCB components to ensure that a system behaves properly in all cases and that it adheres to the security policy under all circumstances.

Security Perimeter

The *security perimeter* of your system is an imaginary boundary that separates the TCB from the rest of the system. For the TCB to communicate with the rest of the system, it must create secure channels, also called *trusted paths*. A trusted path is a channel established with strict standards to allow necessary communication to occur without exposing the TCB to security vulnerabilities. A trusted path also protects system users (sometimes known as *subjects*) from compromise as a result of a TCB interchange. As you learn more about formal security guidelines and evaluation criteria later in this chapter, you'll also learn that trusted paths are required in systems that seek to deliver high levels of security to their users. According to the TCSEC guidelines described in "Understand the Components of Information Systems Security Evaluation Models" later in this chapter, trusted paths are required in B2 and higher systems.

Reference Monitors and Kernels

When the time comes to implement a secure system, it's essential to develop some part of the TCB to enforce access controls on system assets and resources (sometimes known as *objects*). The part of the TCB that validates access to every resource prior to granting access requests is called the *reference monitor*. The reference monitor stands between every subject and object, verifying that a requesting subject's credentials meet the object's access requirements before any requests are allowed to proceed. If such access requirements aren't met, access requests are turned down. The reference monitor may be a conceptual part of the TCB; it doesn't need to be an actual, stand-alone, or independent working system component.

The collection of components in the TCB that work together to implement reference monitor functions is called the *security kernel*. The reference monitor is a concept or theory that is put into practice via the implementation of a security kernel in software and hardware. The purpose of the security kernel is to launch appropriate components to enforce reference monitor functionality and resist all known attacks. The security kernel uses a trusted path to communicate with subjects. It also mediates all resource access requests, granting only those requests that match the appropriate access rules in use for a system.

The reference monitor requires descriptive information about each resource that it protects. Such information normally includes its classification and designation. When a subject requests access to an object, the reference monitor consults the object's descriptive information to discern whether access should be granted or denied (see the sidebar "Tokens, Capabilities, and Labels" for more information on how this works).

State Machine Model

The *state machine model* describes a system that is always secure no matter what state it is in. It's based on the computer science definition of a finite state machine (FSM). An FSM combines an external input with an internal machine state to model all kinds of complex systems, including parsers, decoders, and interpreters. Given an input and a state, an FSM transitions to another state and may create an output. Mathematically, the next state is a function of the current state and the input next state; that is, the next state = F(input, current state). Likewise, the output is also a function of the input and the current state output; that is, the output = F(input, current state).

Many security models are based on the secure state concept. According to the state machine model, a *state* is a snapshot of a system at a specific moment in time. If all aspects of a state meet the requirements of the security policy, that state is considered secure. A transition occurs when accepting input or producing output. A transition always results in a new state (also called a *state transition*). All state transitions must be evaluated. If each possible state transition results in another secure state, the system can be called a *secure state machine*. A secure state machine model system always boots into a secure state, maintains a secure state across all transitions, and allows subjects to access resources only in a secure manner compliant with the security policy. The secure state machine model is the basis for many other security models.

Information Flow Model

The *information flow model* focuses on the flow of information. Information flow models are based on a state machine model. The Bell-LaPadula and Biba models, which we will discuss in detail later in this chapter, are both information flow models. Bell-LaPadula is concerned with preventing information flow from a high security level to a low security level. Biba is concerned with preventing information flow from a low security level to a high security level. Information flow models don't necessarily deal with only the direction of information flow; they can also address the type of flow.

Information flow models are designed to prevent unauthorized, insecure, or restricted information flow, often between different levels of security (these are often referred to as multilevel models). Information flow can be between subjects and objects at the same classification level as well as between subjects and objects at different classification levels. An information flow model allows all authorized information flows, whether within the same classification level or between classification levels. It prevents all unauthorized information flows, whether within the same classification level or between classification levels.

Another interesting perspective on the information flow model is that it is used to establish a relationship between two versions or states of the same object when those two versions or states exist at different points in time. Thus, information flow dictates the transformation of an object from one state at one point in time to another state at another point in time. The information flow model also addresses covert channels by specifically excluding all nondefined flow pathways.

Noninterference Model

The *noninterference model* is loosely based on the information flow model. However, instead of being concerned about the flow of information, the noninterference model is concerned with how the actions of a subject at a higher security level affect the system state or the actions of a subject at a lower security level. Basically, the actions of subject A (high) should not affect the actions of subject B (low) or even be noticed by subject B. The real concern is to prevent the actions of subject A at a high level of security classification from affecting the system state at a lower level. If this occurs, subject B may be placed into an insecure state or be able to deduce or infer information about a higher level of classification. This is a type of information leakage and implicitly creates a covert channel. Thus, the noninterference model can be imposed to provide a form of protection against damage caused by malicious programs such as Trojan horses.

 Real World Scenario

Composition Theories

Some other models that fall into the information flow category build on the notion of how inputs and outputs between multiple systems relate to one another—which follows how information flows between systems rather than within an individual system. These are called *composition theories* because they explain how outputs from one system relate to inputs to another system. There are three recognized types of composition theories:

- *Cascading*: Input for one system comes from the output of another system.

- *Feedback*: One system provides input to another system, which reciprocates by reversing those roles (so that system A first provides input for system B and then system B provides input to system A).

- *Hookup*: One system sends input to another system but also sends input to external entities.

Take-Grant Model

The *Take-Grant model* employs a directed graph to dictate how rights can be passed from one subject to another or from a subject to an object. Simply put, a subject with the grant right can grant another subject or another object any other right they possess. Likewise, a subject with the take right can take a right from another subject. In addition to these two primary rules, the Take-Grant model may also adopt a create rule and a remove rule to generate or delete rights. The key to this model is that using these rules allows one to figure out when rights in the system can change and where leakage (i.e., unintentional distribution of permissions) can occur.

Take rule	Allows a subject to take rights over an object
Grant rule	Allows a subject to grant rights to an object
Create rule	Allows a subject to create new rights
Remove rule	Allows a subject to remove rights it has

Access Control Matrix

An *access control matrix* is a table of subjects and objects that indicates the actions or functions that each subject can perform on each object. Each column of the matrix is an access control list (ACL). Each row of the matrix is a *capabilities list*. An ACL is tied to the object; it lists valid actions each subject can perform. A capability list is tied to the subject; it lists valid actions that can be taken on each object. From an administration perspective, using only capability lists for access control is a management nightmare. A capability list method of access control can be accomplished by storing on each subject a list of rights the subject has for every object. This effectively gives each user a key ring of accesses and rights to objects within the security domain. To remove access to a particular object, every user (subject) that has access to it must be individually manipulated. Thus, managing access on each user account is much more difficult than managing access on each object (in other words, via ACLs).

Implementing an access control matrix model usually involves: 1. constructing an environment that can create and manage lists of subjects and objects, and 2. crafting a function that can return the type associated with whatever object is supplied to that function as input (this is important because an object's type determines what kind of operations may be applied to it).

The access control matrix shown in Table 11.1 is for a discretionary access control system. A mandatory or rule-based matrix can be constructed simply by replacing the subject names with classifications or roles. Access control matrixes are used by systems to quickly determine whether the requested action by a subject for an object is authorized.

TABLE 11.1 An access control matrix

Subjects	Document File	Printer	Network Folder Share
Bob	Read	No Access	No Access
Mary	No Access	No Access	Read
Amanda	Read, Write	Print	No Access
Mark	Read, Write	Print	Read, Write
Kathryn	Read, Write	Print, Manage Print Queue	Read, Write, Execute
Colin	Read, Write, Change Permissions	Print, Manage Print Queue, Change Permissions	Read, Write, Execute, Change Permissions

Bell-LaPadula Model

The US Department of Defense (DoD) developed the *Bell-LaPadula model* in the 1970s to address concerns about protecting classified information. The DoD manages multiple levels of classified resources, and the Bell-LaPadula multilevel model was derived from the DoD's multilevel security policies. The classifications the DoD uses are numerous; however, discussions of classifications within the CISSP CBK are usually limited to unclassified, sensitive but unclassified, confidential, secret, and top secret. The multilevel security policy states that a subject with any level of clearance can access resources at or below its clearance level. However, within the higher clearance levels, access is granted only on a need-to-know basis. In other words, access to a specific object is granted to the classified levels only if a specific work task requires such access. For example, any person with a secret security clearance can access secret, confidential, sensitive but unclassified, and unclassified documents but not top-secret documents. Also, to access a document within the secret level, the person seeking access must also have a need to know for that document.

By design, the Bell-LaPadula model prevents the leaking or transfer of classified information to less-secure clearance levels. This is accomplished by blocking lower-classified subjects from accessing higher-classified objects. With these restrictions, the Bell-LaPadula model is focused on maintaining the confidentiality of objects. Thus, the complexities involved in ensuring the confidentiality of documents are addressed in the Bell-LaPadula model. However, Bell-LaPadula does not address the aspects of integrity or availability for objects. Bell-LaPadula is also the first mathematical model of a multilevel security policy.

Real World Scenario

Lattice-Based Access Control

This general category for nondiscretionary access controls was introduced in Chapter 1, "Access Control." Here's a quick refresher on the subject (which drives the underpinnings for most access control security models): Subjects under lattice-based access controls are assigned positions in a lattice. These positions fall between defined security labels or classifications. Subjects can access only those objects that fall into the range between the least upper bound (the nearest security label or classification higher than their lattice position) and the highest lower bound (the nearest security label or classification lower than their lattice position) of the labels or classifications for their lattice position. Thus, a subject that falls between the private and sensitive labels in a commercial scheme that reads bottom up as public, sensitive, private, proprietary, and confidential can access only public and sensitive data but not private, proprietary, or confidential data. Lattice-based access controls also fit into the general category of information flow models and deal primarily with confidentiality (that's the reason for the connection to Bell-LaPadula).

This model is built on a state machine concept and the information flow model. It also employs mandatory access controls and the lattice concept. The lattice tiers are the *classification levels* used by the security policy of the organization. The state machine supports multiple states with explicit transitions between any two states; this concept is used because the correctness of the machine, and guarantees of document confidentiality, can be proven mathematically. There are three basic properties of this state machine:

- The *Simple Security Property* states that a subject may not read information at a higher sensitivity level (no read up).

- The ** (star) Security Property* states that a subject may not write information to an object at a lower sensitivity level (no write down). This is also known as the *Confinement Property*.

- The *Discretionary Security Property* states that the system uses an access matrix to enforce discretionary access control.

These first two properties define the states into which the system can transition. No other transitions are allowed. All states accessible through these two rules are secure states. Thus, Bell-LaPadula–modeled systems offer state machine model security (see Figure 11.1).

FIGURE 11.1   The Bell-LaPadula model

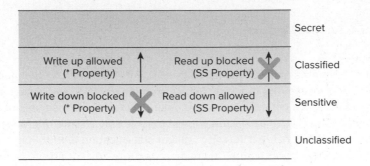

An exception in the Bell-LaPadula model states that a "trusted subject" is not constrained by the * Security Property. A trusted subject is defined as "a subject that is guaranteed not to consummate a security-breaching information transfer even if it is possible." This means that a trusted subject is allowed to violate the * Security Property and perform a write down, which is necessary when performing valid object declassification or reclassification.

The Bell-LaPadula properties are in place to protect data confidentiality. A subject cannot read an object that is classified at a higher level than the subject is cleared for. Because objects at one level have data that is more sensitive or secret than data in objects at a lower level, a subject (who is not a trusted subject) cannot write data from one level to an object at a lower level. That action would be similar to pasting a top-secret memo into an unclassified document file. The third property enforces a subject's need to know in order to access an object.

The Bell-LaPadula model addresses only the confidentiality of data. It does not address its integrity or availability. Because it was designed in the 1970s, it does not support many operations that are common today, such as file sharing and networking. It also assumes secure transitions between security layers and does not address covert channels (covered in Chapter 12, "Security Architecture Vulnerabilities, Threats, and Countermeasures"). Bell-LaPadula does handle confidentiality well, so it is often used in combination with other models that provide mechanisms to handle integrity and availability.

Biba Model

For many nonmilitary organizations, integrity is more important than confidentiality. Out of this need, several integrity-focused security models were developed, such those developed by Biba and by Clark-Wilson. The *Biba model* was designed after the Bell-LaPadula model. Where the Bell-LaPadula model addresses confidentiality, the Biba model addresses integrity. The Biba model is also built on a state machine concept, is based on information flow, and is a multilevel model. In fact, Biba appears to be pretty similar to the Bell-LaPadula model, except inverted. Both use states and transitions. Both have basic properties. The biggest difference is their primary focus: Biba primarily protects data integrity. Here are the basic properties of the Biba model state machine:

- The *Simple Integrity Property* states that a subject cannot read an object at a lower integrity level (no read down).

- The * *(star) Integrity Property* states that a subject cannot modify an object at a higher integrity level (no write up).

In both the Biba and Bell-LaPadula models, there are two properties that are inverses of each other: simple and * (star). However, they may also be labeled as axioms, principles, or rules. What you should focus on is the *simple* and *star* designations. Take note that *simple* is always about reading, and *star* is always about writing. Also, in both cases, simple and star are rules that define what cannot or should not be done. In most cases, what is not prevented or disallowed is supported or allowed.

Figure 11.2 illustrates these Biba model axioms.

FIGURE 11.2   The Biba model

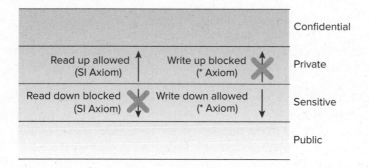

When you compare Biba to Bell-LaPadula, you will notice that they look like they are opposites. That's because they focus on different areas of security. Where the Bell-LaPadula model ensures data confidentiality, Biba ensures data integrity.

Biba was designed to address three integrity issues:

- Prevent modification of objects by unauthorized subjects.

- Prevent unauthorized modification of objects by authorized subjects.

- Protect internal and external object consistency.

As with Bell-LaPadula, Biba requires that all subjects and objects have a classification label. Thus, data integrity protection is dependent upon data classification.

Consider the Biba properties. The second property of the Biba model is pretty straightforward. A subject cannot write to an object at a higher integrity level. That makes sense. What about the first property? Why can't a subject read an object at a lower integrity level? The answer takes a little thought. Think of integrity levels as being like the purity level of air. You would not want to pump air from the smoking section into the clean room environment. The same applies to data. When integrity is important, you do not want unvalidated data read into validated documents. The potential for data contamination is too great to permit such access.

Critiques of the Biba model reveal a few drawbacks:

- It addresses only integrity, not confidentiality or availability.

- It focuses on protecting objects from external threats; it assumes that internal threats are handled programmatically.

- It does not address access control management, and it doesn't provide a way to assign or change an object's or subject's classification level.

- It does not prevent covert channels.

Because the Biba model focuses on data integrity, it is a more common choice for commercial security models than the Bell-LaPadula model. Most commercial organizations are more concerned with the integrity of their data than its confidentiality.

Clark-Wilson Model

Although the Biba model works in commercial applications, another model was designed in 1987 specifically for the commercial environment. The *Clark-Wilson model* uses a multi-faceted approach to enforcing data integrity. Instead of defining a formal state machine, the Clark-Wilson model defines each data item and allows modifications through only a small set of programs.

The Clark-Wilson model does not require the use of a lattice structure; rather, it uses a three-part relationship of subject/program/object (or subject/transaction/object) known as a *triple* or an *access control triple*. Subjects do not have direct access to objects. Objects can be accessed only through programs. Through the use of two principles—well-formed transactions and separation of duties—the Clark-Wilson model provides an effective means to protect integrity.

Well-formed transactions take the form of programs. A subject is able to access objects only by using a program. Each program has specific limitations on what it can and cannot do to an object. This effectively limits the subject's capabilities. If the programs are properly designed, then the triple relationship provides a means to protect the integrity of the object.

Clark-Wilson defines the following items and procedures:

- A constrained data item (CDI) is any data item whose integrity is protected by the security model.

- An unconstrained data item (UDI) is any data item that is not controlled by the security model. Any data that is to be input and hasn't been validated or any output would be considered an unconstrained data item.

- An integrity verification procedure (IVP) is a procedure that scans data items and confirms their integrity.

- Transformation procedures (TPs) are the only procedures that are allowed to modify a CDI. The limited access to CDIs through TPs forms the backbone of the Clark-Wilson integrity model. (We wonder whether this is where TPS reports come from . . . see the movie *Office Space*.)

The Clark-Wilson model uses security labels to grant access to objects, but only through transformation procedures and a *restricted interface model*. A restricted interface model uses classification-based restrictions to offer only subject-specific authorized information and functions. One subject at one classification level will see one set of data and have access to one set of functions, whereas another subject at a different classification level will see a different set of data and have access to a different set of functions. Through these mechanisms, the Clark-Wilson model ensures that data is protected from unauthorized changes from any user. In effect, the Clark-Wilson model enforces separation of duties. The Clark-Wilson design makes it a very good model for commercial applications.

Brewer and Nash Model (aka Chinese Wall)

This model was created to permit access controls to change dynamically based on a user's previous activity (making it a kind of state machine model as well). This model applies to a single integrated database; it seeks to create security domains that are sensitive to the notion of conflict of interest (for example, someone who works at Company C who has access to proprietary data for Company A should not also be allowed access to similar data for Company B if those two companies compete with one another). This model is known as the *Chinese Wall* because it creates a class of data that defines which security domains are potentially in conflict and prevents any subject with access to one domain that belongs to a specific conflict class from accessing any other domain that belongs to the same conflict class. Metaphorically, this puts a wall around all other information in any conflict class. Thus, this model also uses the principle of data isolation within each conflict class to keep users out of potential conflict-of-interest situations (for example, management of company datasets). Because company relationships change all the time, dynamic updates to members of and definitions for conflict classes is important.

Goguen-Meseguer Model

The Goguen-Meseguer model is an integrity model, although not as well known as Biba and the others. In fact, this model is said to be the foundation of noninterference conceptual theories. Often when someone refers to a noninterference model, they are actually referring to the Goguen-Meseguer model.

The Goguen-Meseguer model is based on predetermining the set or domain—a list of objects that a subject can access. This model is based on automation theory and domain separation. This means subjects are allowed only to perform predetermined actions against predetermined objects. When similar users are grouped into their own domain (i.e., collective), the members of one subject domain cannot interfere with the members of another subject domain. Thus, subjects are unable to interfere with each other's activities.

Sutherland Model

The Sutherland model is an integrity model. It focuses on preventing interference in support of integrity. It is formally based on the state machine model and the information flow model. However, it does not directly indicate specific mechanisms for protection of integrity. Instead, the model is based on the idea of defining a set of system states, initial states, and state transitions. Through the use of and limitations to only these predetermined secure states, integrity is maintained and interference is prohibited.

A common example of the Sutherland model is its use to prevent a covert channel from being used to influence the outcome of a process or activity. (For a discussion of covert channels, see Chapter 12.)

Graham-Denning Model

The Graham-Denning model is focused on the secure creation and deletion of both subjects and objects. Ultimately, Graham-Denning is a collection of eight primary protection rules or actions that define the boundaries of certain secure actions:

- Securely create an object.
- Securely create a subject.
- Securely delete an object.
- Securely delete a subject.
- Securely provide the read access right.
- Securely provide the grant access right.
- Securely provide the delete access right.
- Securely provide the transfer access right.

Usually the specific abilities or permissions of a subject over a set of objects was defined in an access matrix (aka access control matrix).

Objects and Subjects

Controlling access to any resource in a secure system involves two entities. The *subject* is the user or process that makes a request to access a resource. Access can mean reading from or writing to a resource. The *object* is the resource a user or process wants to access.

Keep in mind that the subject and object refer to some specific access request, so the same resource can serve as a subject and an object in different access requests.

For example, process A may ask for data from process B. To satisfy process A's request, process B must ask for data from process C. In this example, process B is the object of the first request and the subject of the second request:

| First request | process A (subject) | process B (object) |
| Second request | process B (subject) | process C (object) |

Closed and Open Systems

Systems are designed and built according to one of two differing philosophies: A *closed system* is designed to work well with a narrow range of other systems, generally all from the same manufacturer. The standards for closed systems are often proprietary and not normally disclosed. *Open systems*, on the other hand, are designed using agreed-upon industry standards. Open systems are much easier to integrate with systems from different manufacturers that support the same standards.

Closed systems are harder to integrate with unlike systems, but they can be more secure. A closed system often comprises proprietary hardware and software that does not incorporate industry standards. This lack of integration ease means that attacks on many generic system components either will not work or must be customized to be successful. In many cases, attacking a closed system is harder than launching an attack on an open system. Many software and hardware components with known vulnerabilities may not exist on a closed system. In addition to the lack of known vulnerable components on a closed system, it is often necessary to possess more in-depth knowledge of the specific target system to launch a successful attack.

Open systems are generally far easier to integrate with other open systems. It is easy, for example, to create a LAN with a Microsoft Windows 2008 machine, a Linux machine, and a Macintosh machine. Although all three computers use different operating systems and could represent up to three different hardware architectures, each supports industry standards and makes it easy for networked (or other) communications to occur. This ease comes at a price, however. Because standard communications components are incorporated into each of these three open systems, there are far more predictable entry points and methods for launching attacks. In general, their openness makes them more vulnerable to attack, and their widespread availability makes it possible for attackers to find (and even to practice on) plenty of potential targets. Also, open systems are more popular than closed systems and attract more attention. An attacker who develops basic attacking skills will find more targets on open systems than on closed ones. This larger "market" of potential targets usually means that there is more emphasis on targeting open systems. Inarguably, there's a greater body of shared experience and knowledge on how to attack open systems than there is for closed systems.

Another distinction to keep in mind is between open-source and closed-source systems. An open-source solution is one where the source code and other internal logic is exposed to the public. A closed-source solution is one where the source code and other internal logic is hidden from the public. Open-source solutions often depend upon public inspection and review to improve the product over time. Closed-source solutions are more dependent on the vendor/programmer to revise the product over time. Both open-source and closed-source solutions can be available for sale or at no charge, but the term *commercial* typically implies closed source.

Techniques for Ensuring Confidentiality, Integrity, and Availability

To guarantee the confidentiality, integrity, and availability of data, you must ensure that all components that have access to data are secure and well behaved. Software designers use different techniques to ensure that programs do only what is required and nothing more. Suppose a program writes to and reads from an area of memory that is being used by another program. The first program could potentially violate all three security tenets: confidentiality, integrity, and availability. If an affected program is processing sensitive or secret data, that data's confidentiality is no longer guaranteed. If that data is overwritten or altered in an unpredictable way (a common problem when multiple readers and writers inadvertently access the same shared data), there is no guarantee of integrity. And, if data modification results in corruption or outright loss, it could become unavailable for future use. Although the concepts we discuss in the following sections all relate to software programs, they are also commonly used in all areas of security. For example, physical confinement guarantees that all physical access to hardware is controlled.

Confinement

Software designers use process confinement to restrict the actions of a program. Simply put, process *confinement* allows a process to read from and write to only certain memory locations and resources. The operating system, or some other security component, disallows illegal read/write requests. If a process attempts to initiate an action beyond its granted authority, that action will be denied. In addition, further actions, such as logging the violation attempt, may be taken. Systems that must comply with higher security ratings usually record all violations and respond in some tangible way. Generally, the offending process is terminated.

Bounds

Each process that runs on a system is assigned an authority level. The authority level tells the operating system what the process can do. In simple systems, there may be only two authority levels: user and kernel. The authority level tells the operating system how to set the bounds for a process. The *bounds* of a process consist of limits set on the memory addresses and resources it can access. The bounds state the area within which a process is confined. In most systems, these bounds segment logical areas of memory for each process to use. It is the responsibility of the operating system to enforce these logical bounds and to disallow access to other processes. More secure systems may require physically bounded processes. Physical bounds require each bounded process to run in an area of memory that is physically separated from other bounded processes, not just logically bounded in the same memory space. Physically bounded memory can be very expensive, but it's also more secure than logical bounds.

Isolation

When a process is confined through enforcing access bounds, that process runs in *isolation*. Process isolation ensures that any behavior will affect only the memory and resources associated with the isolated process.

These three concepts (confinement, bounds, and isolation) make designing secure programs and operating systems more difficult, but they also make it possible to implement more secure systems.

Controls

We introduced the concept of security controls in Chapter 1. To ensure the security of a system, you need to allow subjects to access only authorized objects. A *control* uses access rules to limit the access of a subject to an object. Access rules state which objects are valid for each subject. Further, an object might be valid for one type of access and be invalid for another type of access. One common control is for file access. A file can be protected from modification by making it read-only for most users but read-write for a small set of users who have the authority to modify it.

Recall from Chapter 1 that there are both mandatory and discretionary access controls, often called MAC and DAC, respectively. With mandatory controls, static attributes of the subject and the object are considered to determine the permissibility of an access. Each subject possesses attributes that define its clearance, or authority, to access resources. Each object possesses attributes that define its classification. Different types of security methods classify resources in different ways. For example, subject A is granted access to object B if the security system can find a rule that allows a subject with subject A's clearance to access an object with object B's classification. This is called *rule-based access control*. The predefined rules state which subjects can access which objects.

Discretionary controls differ from mandatory controls in that the subject has some ability to define the objects to access. Within limits, discretionary access controls allow the subject to define a list of objects to access as needed. This access control list serves as a dynamic access rule set that the subject can modify. The constraints imposed on the modifications often relate to the subject's identity. Based on the identity, the subject may be allowed to add or modify the rules that define access to objects.

Both mandatory and discretionary access controls limit the access to objects by subjects. The primary goal of controls is to ensure the confidentiality and integrity of data by disallowing unauthorized access by authorized or unauthorized subjects.

Trust and Assurance

Proper security concepts, controls, and mechanisms must be integrated before and during the design and architectural period in order to produce a reliably secure product. Security issues should not be added on as an afterthought; this causes oversights, increased costs, and less reliability. Once security is integrated into the design, it must be engineered, implemented, tested, audited, evaluated, certified, and finally accredited.

A *trusted system* is one in which all protection mechanisms work together to process sensitive data for many types of users while maintaining a stable and secure computing environment. *Assurance* is simply defined as the degree of confidence in satisfaction of security needs. Assurance must be continually maintained, updated, and reverified. This is true if the trusted system experiences a known change or if a significant amount of time has passed. In either case, change has occurred at some level. Change is often the antithesis of security; it often diminishes security. So, whenever change occurs, the system needs to be reevaluated to verify that the level of security it provided previously is still intact. Assurance varies from one system to another and must be established on individual systems. However, there are grades or levels of assurance that can be placed across numerous systems of the same type, systems that support the same services, or systems that are deployed in the same geographic location.

Understand the Components of Information Systems Security Evaluation Models

Those who purchase information systems for certain kinds of applications—think, for example, about national security agencies where sensitive information may be extremely valuable (or dangerous in the wrong hands) or central banks or securities traders where certain data may be worth billions of dollars—often want to understand their security strengths and weaknesses. Such buyers are often willing to consider only systems that have been subjected to formal evaluation processes in advance and have received some kind of security rating. Buyers want to know what they're buying and, usually, what steps they must take to keep such systems as secure as possible.

When formal evaluations are undertaken, systems are usually subjected to a two-step process:

1. The system is tested and a technical evaluation is performed to make sure that the system's security capabilities meet criteria laid out for its intended use.

2. The system is subjected to a formal comparison of its design and security criteria and its actual capabilities and performance, and individuals responsible for the security and veracity of such systems must decide whether to adopt them, reject them, or make some changes to their criteria and try again.

Often trusted third parties (such as CyberTrust, well known for its security testing laboratories) are hired to perform such evaluations; the most important result from such testing is their "seal of approval" that the system meets all essential criteria.

Regardless of whether the evaluations are conducted inside an organization or out of house, the adopting organization must decide to accept or reject the proposed systems. An organization's management must take formal responsibility if and when a system is adopted and be willing to accept any risks associated with its deployment and use.

The three main product evaluation models or classification criteria models addressed here are TCSEC, ITSEC, and Common Criteria.

You should be aware that TCSEC was repealed and replaced by the Common Criteria (as well as many other DoD directives). It is still included here as a historical reference and as an example of static-based assessment criteria to offset the benefits of dynamic (although subjective) assessment criteria.

Rainbow Series

Since the 1980s, governments, agencies, institutions, and business organizations of all kinds have faced the risks involved in adopting and using information systems. This led to a historical series of information security standards that attempted to specify minimum acceptable security criteria for various categories of use. Such categories were important as purchasers attempted to obtain and deploy systems that would protect and preserve their contents or that would meet various mandated security requirements (such as those that contractors must routinely meet to conduct business with the government). The first such set of standards resulted in the creation of the Trusted Computer System Evaluation Criteria (TCSEC) in the 1980s, as the US Department of Defense (DoD) worked to develop and impose security standards for the systems it purchased and used. In turn, this led to a whole series of such publications through the mid-1990s. Since these publications were routinely identified by the color of their covers, they are known collectively as the *rainbow series*.

Following in the DoD's footsteps, other governments or standards bodies created computer security standards that built and improved on the rainbow series elements. Significant standards in this group include a European model called the Information Technology Security Evaluation Criteria (ITSEC), which was developed in 1990 and used through 1998.

Eventually TCSEC and ITSEC were replaced with the so-called Common Criteria, adopted by the United States, Canada, France, Germany, and the United Kingdom in 1998 but more formally known as the "Arrangement on the Recognition of Common Criteria Certificates in the Field of IT Security." Both ITSEC and the Common Criteria will be discussed in later sections.

When governments or other security-conscious agencies evaluate information systems, they make use of various standard evaluation criteria. In 1985, the National Computer Security Center (NCSC) developed the TCSEC, usually called the Orange Book because of the color of this publication's covers. The TCSEC established guidelines to be used when evaluating a stand-alone computer from the security perspective. These guidelines address basic security functionality and allow evaluators to measure and rate a system's functionality and trustworthiness. In the TSCEC, in fact, functionality and security assurance are combined and not separated as they are in security criteria developed later. TCSEC guidelines were designed to be used when evaluating vendor products or by vendors to ensure that they build all necessary functionality and security assurance into new products.

Next, we'll take a look at some of the details in the Orange Book itself and then talk about some of the other important elements in the rainbow series.

TCSEC Classes and Required Functionality

TCSEC combines the functionality and assurance rating of the confidentiality protection offered by a system into four major categories. These categories are then subdivided into additional subcategories identified with numbers, such as C1 and C2. Furthermore, TCSEC's categories are assigned through the evaluation of a target system. Applicable systems are stand-alone systems that are not networked. TCSEC defines the following major categories:

> **Category A:** Verified protection. The highest level of security.
>
> **Category B:** Mandatory protection.
>
> **Category C:** Discretionary protection.
>
> **Category D:** Minimal protection. Reserved for systems that have been evaluated but do not meet requirements to belong to any other category.

The list that follows includes brief discussions of categories A through C along with numeric suffixes that represent any applicable subcategories.

Discretionary protection (categories C1, C2)   Discretionary protection systems provide basic access control. Systems in this category do provide some security controls but are lacking in more sophisticated and stringent controls that address specific needs for secure systems. C1 and C2 systems provide basic controls and complete documentation for system installation and configuration.

> **Discretionary security protection (C1)**   A discretionary security protection system controls access by user IDs and/or groups. Although there are some controls in place that limit object access, systems in this category provide only weak protection.

Controlled access protection (C2)   Controlled access protection systems are stronger than C1 systems. Users must be identified individually to gain access to objects. C2 systems must also enforce media cleansing. With media cleansing, any media that are reused by another user must first be thoroughly cleansed so that no remnant of the previous data remains available for inspection or use. Additionally, strict logon procedures must be enforced that restrict access for invalid or unauthorized users.

Mandatory protection (categories B1, B2, B3)   Mandatory protection systems provide more security controls than category C or D systems. More granularity of control is mandated, so security administrators can apply specific controls that allow only very limited sets of subject/object access. This category of systems is based on the Bell-LaPadula model. Mandatory access is based on security labels.

Labeled security (B1)   In a labeled security system, each subject and each object has a security label. A B1 system grants access by matching up the subject and object labels and comparing their permission compatibility. B1 systems support sufficient security to house classified data.

Structured protection (B2)   In addition to the requirement for security labels (as in B1 systems), B2 systems must ensure that no covert channels exist. Operator and administrator functions are separated, and process isolation is maintained. B2 systems are sufficient for classified data that requires more security functionality than a B1 system can deliver.

Security domains (B3)   Security domain systems provide more secure functionality by further increasing the separation and isolation of unrelated processes. Administration functions are clearly defined and separate from functions available to other users. The focus of B3 systems shifts to simplicity to reduce any exposure to vulnerabilities in unused or extra code. The secure state of B3 systems must also be addressed during the initial boot process. B3 systems are difficult to attack successfully and provide sufficient secure controls for very sensitive or secret data.

Verified protection (category A1)   Verified protection systems are similar to B3 systems in the structure and controls they employ. The difference is in the development cycle. Each phase of the development cycle is controlled using formal methods. Each phase of the design is documented, evaluated, and verified before the next step is taken. This forces extreme security consciousness during all steps of development and deployment and is the only way to formally guarantee strong system security.

A verified design system starts with a design document that states how the resulting system will satisfy the security policy. From there, each development step is evaluated in the context of the security policy. Functionality is crucial, but assurance becomes more important than in lower security categories. A1 systems represent the top level of security and are designed to handle top-secret data. Every step is documented and verified, from the design all the way through to delivery and installation.

Other Colors in the Rainbow Series

Altogether, there are nearly 30 titles in the collection of DoD documents that either add to or further elaborate on the Orange Book. Although the colors don't necessarily mean anything, they're used to identify publications in this series.

 It is important to understand that most of the books in the rainbow series are now outdated and have been replaced by updated standards, guidelines, and directives. However, they are still included here for reference to address any exam items.

Other important elements in this collection of documents include the following:

Red Book   Because the Orange Book applies only to stand-alone computers not attached to a network, and so many systems were used on networks (even in the 1980s), the Red Book was developed to interpret the TCSEC in a networking context. In fact, the official title of the Red Book is *Trusted Network Interpretation of the TCSEC* so it could be considered an interpretation of the Orange Book with a bent on networking. Quickly the Red Book became more relevant and important to system buyers and builders than the Orange Book. The following list includes a few other functions of the Red Book:

- Rates confidentiality and integrity
- Addresses communications integrity
- Addresses denial of service protection
- Addresses compromise (in other words, intrusion) protection and prevention
- Is restricted to a limited class of networks that are labeled as "centralized networks with a single accreditation authority"
- Uses only four rating levels: None, C1 (Minimum), C2 (Fair), and B2 (Good)

Green Book   The Green Book, or the *Department of Defense Password Management Guidelines*, provides password creation and management guidelines; it's important for those who configure and manage trusted systems.

Table 11.2 has a more complete list of books in the rainbow series. For more information and to download the books, see the Rainbow Series web page at the following location:

    http://csrc.nist.gov/publications/secpubs/rainbow/

TABLE 11.2 Important rainbow series elements

Publication Number	Title	Book Name
5200.28-STD	*DoD Trusted Computer System Evaluation Criteria*	Orange Book
CSC-STD-002-85	*DoD Password Management Guidelines*	Green Book
CSC-STD-003-85	*Guidance for Applying TCSEC in Specific Environments*	Yellow Book
NCSC-TG-001	*A Guide to Understanding Audit in Trusted Systems*	Tan Book
NCSC-TG-002	*Trusted Product Evaluation: A Guide for Vendors*	Bright Blue Book
NCSC-TG-002-85	*PC Security Considerations*	Light Blue Book
NCSC-TG-003	*A Guide to Understanding Discretionary Access Controls in Trusted Systems*	Neon Orange Book
NCSC-TG-004	*Glossary of Computer Security Terms*	Aqua Book
NCSC-TG-005	*Trusted Network Interpretation*	Red Book
NCSC-TG-006	*A Guide to Understanding Configuration Management in Trusted Systems*	Amber Book
NCSC-TG-007	*A Guide to Understanding Design Documentation in Trusted Systems*	Burgundy Book
NCSC-TG-008	*A Guide to Understanding Trusted Distribution in Trusted Systems*	Lavender Book
NCSC-TG-009	*Computer Security Subsystem Interpretation of the TCSEC*	Venice Blue Book

Given all the time and effort that went into formulating the TCSEC, it's not unreasonable to wonder why evaluation criteria have evolved to newer, more advanced standards. The relentless march of time and technology aside, these are the major critiques of TCSEC; they help to explain why newer standards are now in use worldwide:

- Although the TCSEC puts considerable emphasis on controlling user access to information, it doesn't exercise control over what users do with information once access is granted. This can be a problem in military and commercial applications alike.

- Given the origins of evaluation standards at the US Department of Defense, it's understandable that the TCSEC focuses its concerns entirely on confidentiality, which assumes that controlling how users access data is of primary importance and that concerns about data accuracy or integrity are irrelevant. This doesn't work in commercial environments where concerns about data accuracy and integrity can be more important than concerns about confidentiality.

- Outside the evaluation standards' own emphasis on access controls, the TCSEC does not carefully address the kinds of personnel, physical, and procedural policy matters or safeguards that must be exercised to fully implement security policy. They don't deal much with how such matters can impact system security either.

- The Orange Book, per se, doesn't deal with networking issues (though the Red Book, developed later in 1987, does).

To some extent, these criticisms reflect the unique security concerns of the military, which developed the TCSEC. Then, too, the prevailing computing tools and technologies widely available at the time (networking was just getting started in 1985) had an impact as well. Certainly, an increasingly sophisticated and holistic view of security within organizations helps to explain why and where the TCSEC also fell short, procedurally and policy-wise. But because ITSEC has been largely superseded by the Common Criteria, coverage in the next section explains ITSEC as a step along the way toward the Common Criteria (covered in the section after that).

ITSEC Classes and Required Assurance and Functionality

The ITSEC represents an initial attempt to create security evaluation criteria in Europe. It was developed as an alternative to the TCSEC guidelines. The ITSEC guidelines evaluate the functionality and assurance of a system using separate ratings for each category. In this context, a system's functionality is a measurement of the system's utility value for users. The functionality rating of a system states how well the system performs all necessary functions based on its design and intended purpose. The assurance rating represents the degree of confidence that the system will work properly in a consistent manner.

ITSEC refers to any system being evaluated as a target of evaluation (TOE). All ratings are expressed as TOE ratings in two categories. ITSEC uses two scales to rate functionality and assurance.

The functionality of a system is rated from F-D through F-B3 (there is no F-A1). The assurance of a system is rated from E0 through E6. Most ITSEC ratings generally correspond with TCSEC ratings (for example, a TCSEC C1 system corresponds to an ITSEC F-C1, E1 system). See Table 11.4 (at the end of the section "Structure of the Common Criteria") for a comparison of TCSEC, ITSEC, and Common Criteria ratings.

There are some instances where the F ratings of ITSEC are defined using F1 through F5 rather than reusing the labels from TCSEC. These alternate labels are F1 = F–C1, F2 = F–C2, F3 = F–B1, F4 = F–B2, and F5 = F–B3. There is no numbered F rating for F-D, but there are a few cases where F0 is used. This is a fairly ridiculous label because if there are no functions to rate, there is no need for a rating label.

Differences between TCSEC and ITSEC are many and varied. Following are some of the most important differences between the two standards:

- Although the TCSEC concentrates almost exclusively on confidentiality, ITSEC addresses concerns about the loss of integrity and availability in addition to confidentiality, thereby covering all three elements so important to maintaining complete information security.

- ITSEC does not rely on the notion of a TCB, and it doesn't require that a system's security components be isolated within a TCB.

- Unlike TCSEC, which required any changed systems to be reevaluated anew—be it for operating system upgrades, patches, or fixes; application upgrades or changes; and so forth—ITSEC includes coverage for maintaining targets of evaluation after such changes occur without requiring a new formal evaluation.

For more information on ITSEC (now largely supplanted by the Common Criteria, covered in the next section), please visit the official ITSEC website at

`www.cesg.gov.uk/ServiceCatalogue/CCITSEC`

Or you can view the original ITSEC specification at

`www.ssi.gouv.fr/site_documents/ITSEC/ITSEC-uk.pdf`.

Common Criteria

The Common Criteria represents a more or less global effort that involves everybody who worked on TCSEC and ITSEC as well as other global players. Ultimately, it results in the ability to purchase CC-evaluated products (where CC, of course, stands for Common Criteria). The Common Criteria defines various levels of testing and confirmation of systems' security capabilities, and the number of the level indicates what kind of testing and confirmation has been performed. Nevertheless, it's wise to observe that even the highest CC ratings do not equate to a guarantee that such systems are completely secure or that they are entirely devoid of vulnerabilities or susceptibilities to exploit. The Common Criteria was designed as a product evaluation model.

Recognition of Common Criteria

Caveats and disclaimers aside, a document entitled "Arrangement on the Recognition of Common Criteria Certificates in the Field of IT Security" was signed by representatives from government organizations in Canada, France, Germany, the United Kingdom, and the

United States in 1998, making it an international standard. This document was converted by ISO into an official standard, namely, ISO 15408, Evaluation Criteria for Information Technology Security. The objectives of the CC guidelines are as follows:

- To add to buyer's confidence in the security of evaluated, rated IT products.

- To eliminate duplicate evaluations (among other things, this means that if one country, agency, or validation organizations follows the CC in rating specific systems and configurations, others elsewhere need not repeat this work).

- To keep making security evaluations and the certification process more cost effective and efficient.

- To make sure evaluations of IT products adhere to high and consistent standards.

- To promote evaluation and increase availability of evaluated, rated IT products.

- To evaluate the functionality (in other words, what the system does) and assurance (in other words, how much can you trust the system) of the TOE.

Common Criteria documentation is available online at www.niap-ccevs.org/cc-scheme/. Visit it to get information on the current version of the CC guidelines—3.1 Rev 3 updated in July 2009 was the latest revision as of this writing (March 2012)—and guidance on using the CC along with lots of other useful, relevant information.

The Common Criteria process is based on two key elements: protection profiles and security targets. *Protection profiles (PPs)* specify for a product that is to be evaluated (the TOE) the security requirements and protections, which are considered the security desires or the "I want" from a customer. *Security targets (STs)* specify the claims of security from the vendor that are built into a TOE. STs are considered the implemented security measures or the "I will provide" from the vendor. In addition to offering security targets, vendors may offer packages of additional security features. A *package* is an intermediate grouping of security requirement components that can be added or removed from a TOE (like the option packages when purchasing a new vehicle).

The PP is compared to various STs from the selected vendor's TOEs. The closest or best match is what the client purchases. The client initially selects a vendor based on published or marketed evaluation assurance levels, or EALs (see the next section for more details on EALs), for currently available systems. Using Common Criteria to choose a vendor allows clients to request exactly what they need for security rather than having to use static fixed security levels. It also allows vendors more flexibility on what they design and create. A well-defined set of Common Criteria supports subjectivity and versatility, and it automatically adapts to changing technology and threat conditions. Furthermore, the EALs provide a method for comparing vendor systems that is more standardized (like the old TCSEC).

Structure of the Common Criteria

The CC guidelines are divided into three topical areas, as follows:

Part 1   Introduction and General Model describes the general concepts and underlying model used to evaluate IT security and what's involved in specifying targets of evaluation.

It's useful introductory and explanatory material for those unfamiliar with the workings of the security evaluation process or who need help reading and interpreting evaluation results.

Part 2   Security Functional Requirements describes various functional requirements in terms of security audits, communications security, cryptographic support for security, user data protection, identification and authentication, security management, TOE security functions (TSFs), resource utilization, system access, and trusted paths. Covers the complete range of security functions as envisioned in the CC evaluation process, with additional appendices (called *annexes*) to explain each functional area.

Part 3   Security Assurance covers assurance requirements for TOEs in the areas of configuration management, delivery and operation, development, guidance documents, and life cycle support plus assurance tests and vulnerability assessments. Covers the complete range of security assurance checks and protects profiles as envisioned in the CC evaluation process, with information on evaluation assurance levels that describe how systems are designed, checked, and tested.

Most important of all the information that appears in these various CC documents (worth at least a cursory read-through) are the evaluation assurance levels commonly known as EALs. Table 11.3 summarizes EALs 1 through 7. For a complete description of EALs, consult the CC documents hosted at `http://www.niap-ccevs.org/cc_docs/` and view Part 3 of the latest revision.

TABLE 11.3   CC evaluation assurance levels

Level	Assurance Level	Description
EAL1	Functionally tested	Applies when some confidence in correct operation is required but where threats to security are not serious. This is of value when independent assurance that due care has been exercised in protecting personal information is necessary.
EAL2	Structurally tested	Applies when delivery of design information and test results are in keeping with good commercial practices. This is of value when developers or users require low to moderate levels of independently assured security. IT is especially relevant when evaluating legacy systems.
EAL3	Methodically tested and checked	Applies when security engineering begins at the design stage and is carried through without substantial subsequent alteration. This is of value when developers or users require a moderate level of independently assured security, including thorough investigation of TOE and its development.

TABLE 11.3 CC evaluation assurance levels *(continued)*

Level	Assurance Level	Description
EAL4	Methodically designed, tested, and reviewed	Applies when rigorous, positive security engineering and good commercial development practices are used. This does not require substantial specialist knowledge, skills, or resources. It involves independent testing of all TOE security functions.
EAL5	Semi-formally designed and tested	Uses rigorous security engineering and commercial development practices, including specialist security engineering techniques, for semi-formal testing. This applies when developers or users require a high level of independently assured security in a planned development approach, followed by rigorous development.
EAL6	Semi-formally verified, designed, and tested	Uses direct, rigorous security engineering techniques at all phases of design, development, and testing to produce a premium TOE. This applies when TOEs for high-risk situations are needed, where the value of protected assets justifies additional cost. Extensive testing reduces risks of penetration, probability of cover channels, and vulnerability to attack.
EAL7	Formally verified, designed, and tested	Used only for highest-risk situations or where high-value assets are involved. This is limited to TOEs where tightly focused security functionality is subject to extensive formal analysis and testing.

Though the CC guidelines are flexible and accommodating enough to capture most security needs and requirements, they are by no means perfect. As with other evaluation criteria, the CC guidelines do nothing to make sure that how users act on data is also secure. The CC guidelines also do not address administrative issues outside the specific purview of security. As with other evaluation criteria, the CC guidelines do not include evaluation of security *in situ*—that is, they do not address controls related to personnel, organizational practices and procedures, or physical security. Likewise, controls over electromagnetic emissions are not addressed, nor are the criteria for rating the strength of cryptographic algorithms explicitly laid out. Nevertheless, the CC guidelines represent some of the best techniques whereby systems may be rated for security. To conclude this discussion of security evaluation standards, Table 11.4 summarizes how various ratings from the TCSEC, ITSEC, and the CC can be compared.

TABLE 11.4 Comparing security evaluation standards

TCSEC	ITSEC	CC	Designation
D	F-D+E0	EAL0, EAL1	Minimal/no protection
C1	F-C1+E1	EAL2	Discretionary security mechanisms
C2	F-C2+E2	EAL3	Controlled access protection
B1	F-B1+E3	EAL4	Labeled security protection
B2	F-B2+E4	EAL5	Structured security protection
B3	F-B3+E5	EAL6	Security domains
A1	F-B3+E6	EAL7	Verified security design

Industry and International Security Implementation Guidelines

In addition to overall security access models, such as Common Criteria, there are many other more specific or focused security standards for various aspects of storage, communication, transactions, and the like. Two of these standards you should be familiar with are Payment Card Industry–Data Security Standard (PCI-DSS) and International Organization for Standardization (ISO).

PCI-DSS is a collection of requirements for improving the security of electronic payment transactions. These standards were defined by the PCI Security Standards Council members, who are primarily credit card banks and financial institutions. The PCI-DSS defines requirements for security management, policies, procedures, network architecture, software design, and other critical protective measures. For more information on PCI-DSS, please visit the website at www.pcisecuritystandards.org.

ISO is a worldwide standards-setting group of representatives from various national standards organizations. ISO defines standards for industrial and commercial equipment, software, protocols, and management, among others. It issues six main products: International Standards, Technical Reports, Technical Specifications, Publicly Available Specifications, Technical Corrigenda, and Guides. ISO standards are widely accepted across many industries and have even been adopted as requirements or laws by various governments. For more information in ISO, please visit the website at www.iso.org.

Certification and Accreditation

Organizations that require secure systems need one or more methods to evaluate how well a system meets their security requirements. The formal evaluation process is divided into two phases, called *certification* and *accreditation*. The actual steps required in each phase depend on the evaluation criteria an organization chooses. A CISSP candidate must understand the need for each phase and the criteria commonly used to evaluate systems. The two evaluation phases are discussed in the next two sections, and then we present various evaluation criteria and considerations you must address when assessing the security of a system. Certification and accreditation processes are used to assess the effectiveness of application security as well as operating system and hardware security.

The process of evaluation provides a way to assess how well a system measures up to a desired level of security. Because each system's security level depends on many factors, all of them must be taken into account during the evaluation. Even though a system is initially described as secure, the installation process, physical environment, and general configuration details all contribute to its true general security. Two identical systems could be assessed at different levels of security because of configuration or installation differences.

> The terms *certification*, *accreditation*, and *maintenance* as used in the following sections are official terms used by the defense establishment, and you should be familiar with them.

Certification and accreditation are additional steps in the software and IT systems development process normally required from defense contractors and others working in a military environment. The official definitions of these terms as used by the US government are from Department of Defense Instruction 5200.40, Enclosure 2.

Certification

The first phase in a total evaluation process is *certification*. Certification is the comprehensive evaluation of the technical and nontechnical security features of an IT system and other safeguards made in support of the accreditation process to establish the extent to which a particular design and implementation meets a set of specified security requirements.

System certification is the technical evaluation of each part of a computer system to assess its concordance with security standards. First, you must choose evaluation criteria (we will present criteria alternatives in later sections). Once you select criteria to use, you analyze each system component to determine whether it satisfies the desired security goals. The certification analysis includes testing the system's hardware, software, and configuration. All controls are evaluated during this phase, including administrative, technical, and physical controls.

After you assess the entire system, you can evaluate the results to determine the security level the system supports in its current environment. The environment of a system is a critical part of the certification analysis, so a system can be more or less secure depending on its surroundings. The manner in which you connect a secure system to a network can change its security standing. Likewise, the physical security surrounding a system can affect the overall security rating. You must consider all factors when certifying a system.

You complete the certification phase when you have evaluated all factors and determined the level of security for the system. Remember that the certification is valid only for a system in a specific environment and configuration. Any changes could invalidate the certification. Once you have certified a security rating for a specific configuration, you are ready to seek acceptance of the system. Management accepts the certified security configuration of a system through the accreditation process.

Accreditation

In the certification phase, you test and document the security capabilities of a system in a specific configuration. With this information in hand, the management of an organization compares the capabilities of a system to the needs of the organization. It is imperative that the security policy clearly states the requirements of a security system. Management reviews the certification information and decides whether the system satisfies the security needs of the organization. If management decides the certification of the system satisfies their needs, the system is *accredited*. Accreditation is the formal declaration by the designated approving authority (DAA) that an IT system is approved to operate in a particular security mode using a prescribed set of safeguards at an acceptable level of risk. Once accreditation is performed, management can formally accept the adequacy of the overall security performance of an evaluated system.

Certification and accreditation do seem similar, and thus it is often a challenge to really understand them. One perspective you might consider is that certification is often an internal verification of security and the results of that verification are trusted only by your organization. Accreditation is often performed by a third-party testing service, and the results are trusted by everyone in the world that trusts the specific testing group involved.

The process of certification and accreditation is often iterative. In the accreditation phase, it is not uncommon to request changes to the configuration or additional controls to address security concerns. Remember that whenever you change the configuration, you must recertify the new configuration. Likewise, you need to recertify the system when a specific time period elapses or when you make any configuration changes. Your security policy should specify what conditions require recertification. A sound policy would list the amount of time a certification is valid along with any changes that would require you to restart the certification and accreditation process.

Certification and Accreditation Systems

Two government standards are currently in place for the certification and accreditation of computing systems: the DoD standard is the Defense Information Technology Security Certification and Accreditation Process (DITSCAP), and the standard for all US government executive branch departments, agencies, and their contractors and consultants is the National Information Assurance Certification and Accreditation Process (NIACAP). Both of these processes are divided into four phases:

Phase 1: Definition   Involves the assignment of appropriate project personnel; documentation of the mission need; and registration, negotiation, and creation of a System Security Authorization Agreement (SSAA) that guides the entire certification and accreditation process

Phase 2: Verification   Includes refinement of the SSAA, systems development activities, and a certification analysis

Phase 3: Validation   Includes further refinement of the SSAA, certification evaluation of the integrated system, development of a recommendation to the DAA, and the DAA's accreditation decision

Phase 4: Post Accreditation   Includes maintenance of the SSAA, system operation, change management, and compliance validation

The phases of DITSCAP and NIACAP are adapted from Department of Defense Instruction 5200.40, Enclosure 3. DoDI 5200.40, which defines Department of Defense Information Technology Security Certification and Accreditation Process (DITSCAP) and was created on December 30, 1997, and replaced by the Interim DIACAP on July 6, 2006. The most recent version is Department of Defense Instruction 8510.01 from November 28, 2007. This latest update supersedes the Interim DIACAP. DoDI 8510.01 defines the DoD Information Assurance Certification and Accreditation Process (DIACAP). DIACAP is a five-step certification and accreditation process that covers the entire system life cycle from mission and information assurance requirements development to disposal.

The NIACAP process, administered by the Information Systems Security Organization of the National Security Agency, outlines three different types of accreditation that may be granted. The definitions of these types of accreditation (from National Security Telecommunications and Information Systems Security Instruction 1000) are as follows:

- For a system accreditation, a major application or general support system is evaluated.

- For a site accreditation, the applications and systems at a specific, self-contained location are evaluated.

- For a type accreditation, an application or system that is distributed to a number of different locations is evaluated.

Understand Security Capabilities Of Information Systems

The security capabilities of information systems include memory protection, virtualization, and trusted platform module. Memory protection is discussed throughout Chapter 12 in relation to the topics of isolation, virtual memory, segmentation, memory management, and protection rings.

Virtualization technology is used to host one or more operating systems within the memory of a single host computer. This mechanism allows virtually any OS to operate on any hardware. It also allows multiple OSes to work simultaneously on the same hardware. Common examples include VMware, Microsoft's Virtual PC, Microsoft Virtual Server 2005, Hyper-V with Windows Server 2008, and Parallels Desktop for Mac.

Virtualization has several benefits, such as being able to launch individual instances of servers or services as needed, real-time scalability, and being able to run the exact OS version needed for a specific application. Virtualized servers and services are indistinguishable from traditional servers and services from a user's perspective. Additionally, recovery from damaged, crashed, or corrupted virtual systems is often quick, simply consisting of replacing the virtual system's main hard drive file with a clean backup version and then relaunching it. (Additional coverage of virtualization and some of its associated risks are covered in Chapter 12 along with cloud computing.)

The Trusted Platform Module (TPM) is both a specification for a cryptoprocessor chip on a mainboard and the general name for implementation of the specification. A TPM chip is used to store and process cryptographic keys for the purposes of a hardware supported/implemented hard-drive encryption system. Generally, a hardware implementation, rather than a software-only implementation of hard-drive encryption, is considered to be more secure.

When TPM-based whole-disk encryption is in use, the user/operator must supply a password or physical USB token device to the computer to authenticate and allow the TPM chip to release the hard-drive encryption keys into memory. While this seems similar to a software implementation, the key difference is that if the hard drive is removed from its original system, it cannot be decrypted. Only with the original TPM chip can an encryption be decrypted and accessed. With software-only hard-drive encryption, the hard drive can be moved to a different computer without any access or use limitations.

A hardware security module (HSM) is a cryptoprocessor used to manage/store digital encryption keys, accelerate crypto operations, support faster digital signatures, and improve authentication. An HSM is often an add-on adapter or peripheral or can be a TCP/IP network device. HSMs include tamper protection to prevent their misuse even if physical access is gained by an attacker. A TPM is just one example of an HSM.

HSMs provide an accelerated solution for large (i.e., 2,048+ bit) asymmetric encryption calculations and a secure vault for key storage. Many certificate authority systems use HSMs to store certificates; ATM and POS bank terminals often employ proprietary HSMs; hardware SSL accelerators can include HSM support; and DNSSEC-compliant DNS servers use HSM for key and zone file storage.

Summary

Secure systems are not just assembled. They are designed to support security. Systems that must be secure are judged for their ability to support and enforce the security policy. This process of evaluating the effectiveness of a computer system is certification. The certification process is the technical evaluation of a system's ability to meet its design goals. Once a system has satisfactorily passed the technical evaluation, the management of an organization begins the formal acceptance of the system. The formal acceptance process is accreditation.

The entire certification and accreditation process depends on standard evaluation criteria. Several criteria exist for evaluating computer security systems. The earliest, TCSEC, was developed by the US Department of Defense. TCSEC, also called the Orange Book, provides criteria to evaluate the functionality and assurance of a system's security components. ITSEC is an alternative to the TCSEC guidelines and is used more often in European countries. Regardless of which criteria you use, the evaluation process includes reviewing each security control for compliance with the security policy. The better a system enforces the good behavior of subjects' access to objects, the higher the security rating.

When security systems are designed, it is often helpful to create a security model to represent the methods the system will use to implement the security policy. We discussed several security models in this chapter. The Bell-LaPadula model supports data confidentiality only. It was designed for the military and satisfies military concerns. The Biba model and the Clark-Wilson model address the integrity of data and do so in different ways. These two security models are appropriate for commercial applications.

All of this understanding must culminate into an effective system security implementation in terms of preventive, detective, and corrective controls. That's why you must also know the access control models and their functions. This includes the state machine model, Bell-LaPadula, Biba, Clark-Wilson, the information flow model, the noninterference model, the Take-Grant model, the access control matrix model, and the Brewer and Nash model.

Exam Essentials

Know details about each of the access control models. Know the access control models and their functions. The state machine model ensures that all instances of subjects accessing objects are secure. The information flow model is designed to prevent unauthorized, insecure, or restricted information flow. The noninterference model prevents the actions of one subject from affecting the system state or actions of another subject. The Take-Grant model dictates how rights can be passed from one subject to another or from a subject to an object. An access control matrix is a table of subjects and objects that indicates the actions or functions that each subject can perform on each object. Bell-LaPadula subjects have a clearance level that allows them to access only those objects with the corresponding classification levels. This enforces confidentiality. Biba prevents subjects with lower security levels from writing to objects at higher security levels. Clark-Wilson is an integrity model that relies on auditing to ensure that unauthorized subjects cannot access objects and that authorized users access objects properly. Biba and Clark-Wilson enforce integrity. Goguen-Meseguer and Sutherland focus on integrity. Graham-Denning focuses on the secure creation and deletion of both subjects and objects.

Know the definitions of certification and accreditation.   Certification is the technical evaluation of each part of a computer system to assess its concordance with security standards. Accreditation is the process of formal acceptance of a certified configuration from a designated authority.

Be able to describe open and closed systems.   Open systems are designed using industry standards and are usually easy to integrate with other open systems. Closed systems are generally proprietary hardware and/or software. Their specifications are not normally published, and they are usually harder to integrate with other systems.

Know what confinement, bounds, and isolation are.   Confinement restricts a process to reading from and writing to certain memory locations. Bounds are the limits of memory a process cannot exceed when reading or writing. Isolation is the mode a process runs in when it is confined through the use of memory bounds.

Be able to define *object* and *subject* in terms of access.   The subject is the user or process that makes a request to access a resource. The object is the resource a user or process wants to access.

Know how security controls work and what they do.   Security controls use access rules to limit the access by a subject to an object.

Be able to list the classes of TCSEC, ITSEC, and the Common Criteria.   The classes of TCSEC include verified protection, mandatory protection, discretionary protection, and minimal protection. Table 11.4 covers and compares equivalent and applicable rankings for TCSEC, ITSEC, and the CC (remember that functionality ratings from F7 to F10 in ITSEC have no corresponding ratings in TCSEC).

Define a trusted computing base (TCB).   A TCB is the combination of hardware, software, and controls that form a trusted base that enforces the security policy.

Be able to explain what a security perimeter is.   A security perimeter is the imaginary boundary that separates the TCB from the rest of the system. TCB components communicate with non-TCB components using trusted paths.

Know what the reference monitor and the security kernel are.   The reference monitor is the logical part of the TCB that confirms whether a subject has the right to use a resource prior to granting access. The security kernel is the collection of the TCB components that implement the functionality of the reference monitor.

Understand the security capabilities of information systems.   Common security capabilities include memory protection, virtualization, and trusted platform module (TPM).

Written Lab

1. Name at least seven security models.

2. Describe the primary components of TCB.

3. What are the two primary rules or principles of the Bell-LaPadula security model? Also, what are the two rules of Biba?

4. What is the difference between open and closed systems and open and closed source?

Review Questions

1. What is system certification?

   A. Formal acceptance of a stated system configuration

   B. A technical evaluation of each part of a computer system to assess its compliance with security standards

   C. A functional evaluation of the manufacturer's goals for each hardware and software component to meet integration standards

   D. A manufacturer's certificate stating that all components were installed and configured correctly

2. What is system accreditation?

   A. Formal acceptance of a stated system configuration

   B. A functional evaluation of the manufacturer's goals for each hardware and software component to meet integration standards

   C. Acceptance of test results that prove the computer system enforces the security policy

   D. The process to specify secure communication between machines

3. What is a closed system?

   A. A system designed around final, or closed, standards

   B. A system that includes industry standards

   C. A proprietary system that uses unpublished protocols

   D. Any machine that does not run Windows

4. Which best describes a confined or constrained process?

   A. A process that can run only for a limited time

   B. A process that can run only during certain times of the day

   C. A process that can access only certain memory locations

   D. A process that controls access to an object

5. What is an access object?

   A. A resource a user or process wants to access

   B. A user or process that wants to access a resource

   C. A list of valid access rules

   D. The sequence of valid access types

6. What is a security control?

   A. A security component that stores attributes that describe an object

   B. A document that lists all data classification types

   C. A list of valid access rules

   D. A mechanism that limits access to an object

7. For what type of information system security accreditation are the applications and systems at a specific, self-contained location evaluated?

   A. System accreditation

   B. Site accreditation

   C. Application accreditation

   D. Type accreditation

8. How many major categories do the TCSEC criteria define?

   A. Two

   B. Three

   C. Four

   D. Five

9. What is a trusted computing base (TCB)?

   A. Hosts on your network that support secure transmissions

   B. The operating system kernel and device drivers

   C. The combination of hardware, software, and controls that work together to enforce a security policy

   D. The software and controls that certify a security policy

10. What is a security perimeter? (Choose all that apply.)

   A. The boundary of the physically secure area surrounding your system

   B. The imaginary boundary that separates the TCB from the rest of the system

   C. The network where your firewall resides

   D. Any connections to your computer system

11. What part of the TCB concept validates access to every resource prior to granting the requested access?

   A. TCB partition

   B. Trusted library

   C. Reference monitor

   D. Security kernel

12. What is the best definition of a security model?

    A. A security model states policies an organization must follow.

    B. A security model provides a framework to implement a security policy.

    C. A security model is a technical evaluation of each part of a computer system to assess its concordance with security standards.

    D. A security model is the process of formal acceptance of a certified configuration.

13. Which security models are built on a state machine model?

    A. Bell-LaPadula and Take-Grant

    B. Biba and Clark-Wilson

    C. Clark-Wilson and Bell-LaPadula

    D. Bell-LaPadula and Biba

14. Which security model addresses data confidentiality?

    A. Bell-LaPadula

    B. Biba

    C. Clark-Wilson

    D. Brewer and Nash

15. Which Bell-LaPadula property keeps lower-level subjects from accessing objects with a higher security level?

    A. * (star) Security Property

    B. No write up property

    C. No read up property

    D. No read down property

16. What is the implied meaning of the simple property of Biba?

    A. Write down

    B. Read up

    C. No write up

    D. No read down

17. When a trusted subject violates the star property of Bell-LaPadula in order to write an object into a lower level, what valid operation could be taking place?

    A. Perturbation

    B. Polyinstantiation

    C. Aggregation

    D. Declassification

18. What security method, mechanism, or model reveals a capabilities list of a subject across multiple objects?

    A. Separation of duties

    B. Access control matrix

    C. Biba

    D. Clark-Wilson

19. What security model has a feature that in theory has one name or label, but when implemented into a solution, takes on the name or label of the security kernel?

    A. Graham-Denning model

    B. Deployment modes

    C. Trusted computing base

    D. Chinese Wall

20. Which of the following is not part of the access triple of the Clark-Wilson model?

    A. Object

    B. Interface

    C. Programming language

    D. Subject

Chapter

12

Security Architecture Vulnerabilities, Threats, and Countermeasures

THE CISSP EXAM TOPICS COVERED IN THIS CHAPTER INCLUDE:

6. Security Architecture and Design

- D. Understand the vulnerabilities of security architectures
    - D.1 System (e.g., covert channels, state attacks, emanations)
    - D.2 Technology and process integration (e.g., single point of failure, service oriented architecture)
- E. Understand software and system vulnerabilities and threats
    - E.1 Web-based (e.g., XML, SAML, OWASP)
    - E.2 Client-based (e.g., applets)
    - E.3 Server-based (e.g., data flow control)
    - E.5 Distributed systems (e.g., cloud computing, grid computing, peer to peer)
- F. Understand countermeasure principles (e.g., defense in depth)

In previous chapters of this book, we've covered basic security principles and the protective mechanisms put in place to prevent violation of them. We've also examined some of the specific types of attacks used by malicious individuals seeking to circumvent those protective mechanisms. Until this point, when discussing preventative measures, we have focused on policy measures and the software that runs on a system. However, security professionals must also pay careful attention to the system itself and ensure that their higher-level protective controls are not built upon a shaky foundation. After all, the most secure firewall configuration in the world won't do a bit of good if the computer it runs on has a fundamental security flaw that allows malicious individuals to simply bypass the firewall completely.

In this chapter, we'll cover those underlying security concerns by conducting a brief survey of a field known as *computer architecture*: the physical design of computers from various components. We'll examine each of the major physical components of a computing system—hardware and firmware—from a security perspective. Obviously, the detailed analysis of a system's hardware components is not always a luxury available to you because of resource and time constraints. However, all security professionals should have at least a basic understanding of these concepts in case they encounter a security incident that reaches down to the system design level.

The Security Architecture and Design domain addresses a wide range of concerns and issues, including secure design elements, security architecture, vulnerabilities, threats, and associated countermeasures.

Computer Architecture

Computer architecture is an engineering discipline concerned with the design and construction of computing systems at a logical level. Many college-level computer engineering and computer science programs find it difficult to cover all the basic principles of computer architecture in a single semester, so this material is often divided into two one-semester courses for undergraduates. Computer architecture courses delve into the design of central processing unit (CPU) components, memory devices, device communications, and similar topics at the bit level, defining processing paths for individual logic devices that make simple "0 or 1" decisions. Most security professionals do not need that level of knowledge, which is well beyond the scope of this book and the CISSP exam. However, if you will be involved in the security aspects of the design of computing systems at this level, you would be well advised to conduct a more thorough study of this field.

This initial discussion of computer architecture may seem at first to be irrelevant to CISSP, but most of the security architectures and design elements are based on a solid understanding and implementation of computer hardware.

The more complex a system, the less assurance it provides. More complexity means more areas for vulnerabilities exist and more areas must be secured against threats. More vulnerabilities and more threats mean that the subsequent security provided by the system is less trustworthy.

Hardware

Any computing professional is familiar with the concept of hardware. As in the construction industry, hardware is the physical "stuff" that makes up a computer. The term *hardware* encompasses any tangible part of a computer that you can actually reach out and touch, from the keyboard and monitor to its CPU(s), storage media, and memory chips. Take careful note that although the physical portion of a storage device (such as a hard disk or DIMM) may be considered hardware, the contents of those devices—the collections of 0s and 1s that make up the software and data stored within them—may not. After all, you can't reach inside the computer and pull out a handful of bits and bytes!

Processor

The central processing unit (CPU), generally called the *processor*, is the computer's nerve center—it is the chip (or chips in a multiprocessor system) that governs all major operations and either directly performs or coordinates the complex symphony of calculations that allows a computer to perform its intended tasks. Surprisingly, the CPU is actually capable of performing only a limited set of computational and logical operations, despite the complexity of the tasks it allows the computer to perform. It is the responsibility of the operating system and compilers to translate high-level programming languages used to design software into simple assembly language instructions that a CPU understands. This limited range of functionality is intentional—it allows a CPU to perform computational and logical operations at blazing speeds, often measured in units known as MIPS (which stands for "million instructions per second").

For an idea of the magnitude of the progress in computing technology over the years, view the Moore's Law article at *Wikipedia* at http:// en.wikipedia.org/wiki/Moore's_law.

Execution Types

As computer processing power increased, users demanded more advanced features to enable these systems to process information at greater rates and to manage multiple functions simultaneously. Computer engineers devised several methods to meet these demands.

At first blush, the terms *multitasking, multiprocessing, multiprogramming,* and *multithreading* may seem nearly identical. However, they describe very different ways of approaching the "doing two things at once" problem. We strongly advise that you take the time to review the distinctions between these terms until you feel comfortable with them.

Multitasking   In computing, *multitasking* means handling two or more tasks simultaneously. In reality, most systems do not truly multitask; they rely upon the operating system to simulate multitasking by carefully structuring the sequence of commands sent to the CPU for execution. After all, when your processor is humming along at 57,000 MIPS, it's hard to tell that it's switching between tasks rather than actually working on two tasks at once. However, you can assume that a multitasking system is able to juggle more than one task or process at any given time.

Multiprocessing   In a *multiprocessing* environment, a multiprocessor computing system (that is, one with more than one CPU) harnesses the power of more than one processor to complete the execution of a single application. For example, a database server might run on a system that contains three processors. If the database application receives a number of separate queries simultaneously, it might send each query to a separate processor for execution.

Two types of multiprocessing are most common in modern systems with multiple CPUs. The scenario just described, where a single computer contains more than one processor controlled by a single operating system, is called *symmetric multiprocessing (SMP)*. In SMP, processors share not only a common operating system but also a common data bus and memory resources. In this type of arrangement, systems may use a large number of processors. Fortunately, this type of computing power is more than sufficient to drive most systems.

Some computationally intensive operations, such as those that support the research of scientists and mathematicians, require more processing power than a single operating system can deliver. Such operations may be best served by a technology known as *massively parallel processing (MPP)*. MPP systems house hundreds or even thousands of processors, each of which has its own operating system and memory/bus resources. When the software that coordinates the entire system's activities and schedules them for processing encounters a computationally intensive task, it assigns responsibility for the task to a single processor. This processor in turn breaks the task up into manageable parts and distributes them to other processors for execution. Those processors return their results to the coordinating processor where they are assembled and returned to the requesting application. MPP systems are extremely powerful (not to mention extremely expensive!) and are used in a great deal of computing or computational based research.

Both types of multiprocessing provide unique advantages and are suitable for different types of situations. SMP systems are adept at processing simple operations at extremely high rates, whereas MPP systems are uniquely suited for processing very large, complex, computationally intensive tasks that lend themselves to decomposition and distribution into a number of subordinate parts.

Next-Generation Multiprocessing

Until the release of dual-core and quad-core processors, the only way to create a multiprocessing system was to place two or more CPUs onto the motherboard. However, today we have several options of multicore CPUs so that with a single CPU chip on the motherboard, there are two or four (or more!) execution paths. This truly allows single CPU multiprocessing because it allows two (or more) calculations to occur simultaneously. Do you have a multicore CPU in the desktop or notebook computer you use?

Multiprogramming   *Multiprogramming* is similar to multitasking. It involves the pseudosimultaneous execution of two tasks on a single processor coordinated by the operating system as a way to increase operational efficiency. For the most part, multiprogramming is a way to batch or serialize multiple processes so that when one process stops to wait on a peripheral, its state is saved and the next process in line begins to process. The first program does not return to processing until all other processes in the batch have had their chance to execute and they in turn stop for a peripheral. For any single program, this methodology causes significant delays in completing a task. However, across all processes in the batch, the total time to complete all tasks is reduced.

Multiprogramming is considered a relatively obsolete technology and is rarely found in use today except in legacy systems. There are two main differences between multiprogramming and multitasking:

- Multiprogramming usually takes place on large-scale systems, such as mainframes, whereas multitasking takes place on PC operating systems, such as Windows and Linux.
- Multitasking is normally coordinated by the operating system, whereas multiprogramming requires specially written software that coordinates its own activities and execution through the operating system.

Multithreading   *Multithreading* permits multiple concurrent tasks to be performed within a single process. Unlike multitasking, where multiple tasks occupy multiple processes, multithreading permits multiple tasks to operate within a single process. A thread is a self-contained sequence of instructions that can execute in parallel with other threads that are part of the same parent process. Multithreading is often used in applications where frequent context switching between multiple active processes consumes excessive overhead and reduces efficiency. In multithreading, switching between threads incurs far less overhead and is therefore more efficient. In modern Windows implementations, for example, the overhead involved in switching from one thread to another within a single process is on the order of 40 to 50 instructions, with no substantial memory transfers needed. By contrast, switching from one process to another involves 1,000 instructions or more and requires substantial memory transfers as well.

A good example of multithreading occurs when multiple documents are opened at the same time in a word processing program. In that situation, you do not actually run multiple instances of the word processor—this would place far too great a demand on the system. Instead, each document is treated as a single thread within a single word processor process, and the software chooses which thread it works on at any given moment.

Symmetric multiprocessing systems actually use threading at the operating system level. As in the word processing example just described, the operating system also contains a number of threads that control the tasks assigned to it. In a single-processor system, the OS sends one thread at a time to the processor for execution. SMP systems send one thread to each available processor for simultaneous execution.

Processing Types

Many high-security systems control the processing of information assigned to various security levels, such as the classification levels of unclassified, sensitive, confidential, secret, and top secret the US government assigns to information related to national defense. Computers must be designed so that they do not—ideally, so that they cannot—inadvertently disclose information to unauthorized recipients.

Computer architects and security policy administrators have attacked this problem at the processor level in two different ways. One is through a policy mechanism, whereas the other is through a hardware solution. The following list explores each of those options:

Single State   *Single state systems* require the use of policy mechanisms to manage information at different levels. In this type of arrangement, security administrators approve a processor and system to handle only one security level at a time. For example, a system might be labeled to handle only secret information. All users of that system must then be approved to handle information at the secret level. This shifts the burden of protecting the information being processed on a system away from the hardware and operating system and onto the administrators who control access to the system.

Multistate   *Multistate systems* are capable of implementing a much higher level of security. These systems are certified to handle multiple security levels simultaneously by using specialized security mechanisms such as those described in the next section, "Protection Mechanisms." These mechanisms are designed to prevent information from crossing between security levels. One user might be using a multistate system to process secret information, while another user is processing top-secret information at the same time. Technical mechanisms prevent information from crossing between the two users and thereby crossing between security levels.

In actual practice, multistate systems are relatively uncommon owing to the expense of implementing the necessary technical mechanisms. This expense is sometimes justified;

however, when you're dealing with a very expensive resource, such as a massively parallel system, the cost of obtaining multiple systems far exceeds the cost of implementing the additional security controls necessary to enable multistate operation on a single such system.

Protection Mechanisms

If a computer isn't running, it's an inert lump of plastic, silicon, and metal doing nothing. When a computer is running, it operates a runtime environment that represents the combination of the operating system and whatever applications may be active. When running, the computer also has the capability to access files and other data as the user's security permissions allow. Within that runtime environment it's necessary to integrate security information and controls to protect the integrity of the operating system itself, to manage which users are allowed to access specific data items, to authorize or deny operations requested against such data, and so forth. The ways in which running computers implement and handle security at runtime may be broadly described as a collection of protection mechanisms. What follows are descriptions of various protection mechanisms such as protection rings, operational states, and security modes.

Because the ways in which computers implement and use protection mechanisms are so important to maintaining and controlling security, you should understand how all three mechanisms covered here—rings, operational states, and security modes—are defined and how they behave. Don't be surprised to see exam questions about specifics in all three areas because this is such important stuff!

Protection rings   The ring protection scheme is an oldie but a goodie. It dates all the way back to work on the Multics operating system. This experimental operating system was designed and built between 1963 and 1969 through the collaboration of Bell Laboratories, MIT, and General Electric. It saw commercial use in implementations from Honeywell. Multics has left two enduring legacies in the computing world. First, it inspired the creation of a simpler, less intricate operating system called UNIX (a play on the word *multics*), and second, it introduced the idea of protection rings to operating system design.

From a security standpoint, *protection rings* organize code and components in an operating system (as well as applications, utilities, or other code that runs under the operating system's control) into concentric rings, as shown in Figure 12.1. The deeper inside the circle you go, the higher the privilege level associated with the code that occupies a specific ring. Though the original Multics implementation allowed up to seven rings (numbered 0 through 6), most modern operating systems use a four-ring model (numbered 0 through 3).

FIGURE 12.1 In the commonly used four-ring model, protection rings segregate the operating system into kernel, components, and drivers in rings 0 through 2 and applications and programs run at ring 3.

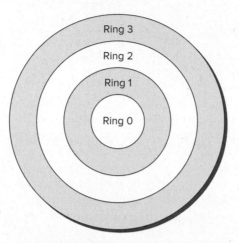

Ring 0: OS Kernel/Memory (Resident Components)
Ring 1: Other OS Components
Ring 2: Drivers, Protocols, etc.
Ring 3: User-Level Programs and Applications

Rings 0–2 run in supervisory or privileged mode.
Ring 3 runs in user mode.

As the innermost ring, 0 has the highest level of privilege and can basically access any resource, file, or memory location. The part of an operating system that always remains resident in memory (so that it can run on demand at any time) is called the *kernel*. It occupies ring 0 and can preempt code running at any other ring. The remaining parts of the operating system—those that come and go as various tasks are requested, operations performed, processes switched, and so forth—occupy ring 1. Ring 2 is also somewhat privileged in that it's where I/O drivers and system utilities reside; these are able to access peripheral devices, special files, and so forth that applications and other programs cannot themselves access directly. Those applications and programs occupy the outermost ring, ring 3.

The essence of the ring model lies in priority, privilege, and memory segmentation. Any process that wants to execute must get in line (a pending process queue). The process associated with the lowest ring number always runs before processes associated with higher-numbered rings. Processes in lower-numbered rings can access more resources and interact with the operating system more directly than those in higher-numbered rings. Those processes that run in higher-numbered rings must generally ask a handler or a driver in a lower-numbered ring for services they need; this is sometimes called a *mediated-access model*. In its strictest implementation, each ring has its own associated memory segment.

Thus, any request from a process in a higher-numbered ring for an address in a lower-numbered ring must call on a helper process in the ring associated with that address. In practice, many modern operating systems break memory into only two segments: one for system-level access (rings 0 through 2), often called *kernel mode* or *privileged mode*, and one for user-level programs and applications (ring 3), often called *user mode*.

From a security standpoint, the ring model enables an operating system to protect and insulate itself from users and applications. It also permits the enforcement of strict boundaries between highly privileged operating system components (such as the kernel) and less-privileged parts of the operating system (such as other parts of the operating system, plus drivers and utilities). Within this model, direct access to specific resources is possible only within certain rings; likewise, certain operations (such as process switching, termination, and scheduling) are allowed only within certain rings.

The ring that a process occupies determines its access level to system resources (and determines what kinds of resources it must request from processes in lower-numbered, more-privileged rings). Processes may access objects directly only if they reside within their own ring or within some ring outside its current boundaries (in numerical terms, for example, this means a process at ring 1 can access its own resources directly, plus any associated with rings 2 and 3, but it can't access any resources associated only with ring 0). The mechanism whereby mediated access occurs—that is, the driver or handler request mentioned previously—is usually known as a *system call* and usually involves invocation of a specific system or programming interface designed to pass the request to an inner ring for service. Before any such request can be honored, however, the called ring must check to make sure that the calling process has the right credentials and authorization to access the data and to perform the operation(s) involved in satisfying the request.

Process states   Also known as *operating states*, *process states* are various forms of execution in which a process may run. Where the operating system is concerned, it can be in one of two modes at any given moment: operating in a privileged, all-access mode known as *supervisor state* or operating in what's called the *problem state* associated with user mode, where privileges are low and all access requests must be checked against credentials for authorization before they are granted or denied. The latter is called the problem state not because problems are guaranteed to occur but because the unprivileged nature of user access means that problems can occur and the system must take appropriate measures to protect security, integrity, and confidentiality.

Processes line up for execution in an operating system in a processing queue, where they will be scheduled to run as a processor becomes available. Because many operating systems allow processes to consume processor time only in fixed increments or chunks, when a new process is created, it enters the processing queue for the first time; should a process consume its entire chunk of processing time (called a *time slice*) without completing, it returns to the processing queue for another time slice the next time its turn comes around. Also, the process scheduler usually selects the highest-priority process for execution, so reaching the front of the line doesn't always guarantee access to the CPU (because a process may be preempted at the last instant by another process with higher priority).

According to whether a process is running, it can operate in one of several states:

Ready   In the ready state, a process is ready to resume or begin processing as soon as it is scheduled for execution. If the CPU is available when the process reaches this state, it will transition directly into the running state; otherwise, it sits in the ready state until its turn comes up. This means the process has all the memory and other resources it needs to begin executing immediately.

Waiting   Waiting can also be understood as "waiting for a resource"—that is, the process is ready for continued execution but is waiting for a device or access request (an interrupt of some kind) to be serviced before it can continue processing (for example, a database application that asks to read records from a file must wait for that file to be located and opened and for the right set of records to be found). Some references label this state as a blocked state because the process could be said to be blocked from further execution until an external event occurs.

Running   The running process executes on the CPU and keeps going until it finishes, its time slice expires, or it is blocked for some reason (usually because it has generated an interrupt for access to a device or the network and is waiting for that interrupt to be serviced). If the time slice ends and the process isn't completed, it returns to the ready state (and queue); if the process blocks while waiting for a resource to become available, it goes into the waiting state (and queue).

The running state is also often called the *problem state*. However, don't associate the word *problem* with an error. Instead, think of the problem state as you would think of a math problem being solved to obtain the answer. But keep in mind that it is called the problem state because it is possible for problems or errors to occur, just as you could do a math problem incorrectly. The problem state is separated from the supervisory state so that any errors that might occur do not easily affect the stability of the overall system; they affect only the process that experienced the error.

Supervisory   The supervisory state is used when the process must perform an action that requires privileges that are greater than the problem state's set of privileges, including modifying system configuration, installing device drivers, or modifying security settings. Basically, any function not occurring in the user mode (ring 3) or problem state takes place in the supervisory mode.

Stopped   When a process finishes or must be terminated (because an error occurs, a required resource is not available, or a resource request can't be met), it goes into a stopped state. At this point, the operating system can recover all memory and other resources allocated to the process and reuse them for other processes as needed.

Figure 12.2 shows a diagram of how these various states relate to one another. New processes always transition into the ready state. From there, ready processes always transition into the running state. While running, a process can transition into the stopped state if it completes or is terminated, return to the ready state for another time slice, or transition to the waiting state until its pending resource request is met. When the operating system decides which process to run next, it checks the waiting queue and the ready queue and takes the highest-priority job that's ready to run (so that only waiting jobs whose pending requests have been serviced, or are ready to service, are eligible in this consideration). A special part of the kernel, called the *program executive* or the *process scheduler*, is always around (waiting in memory) so that when a process state transition must occur, it can step in and handle the mechanics involved.

In Figure 12.2, the process scheduler manages the processes awaiting execution in the ready and waiting states and decides what happens to running processes when they transition into another state (ready, waiting, or stopped).

FIGURE 12.2   The process scheduler

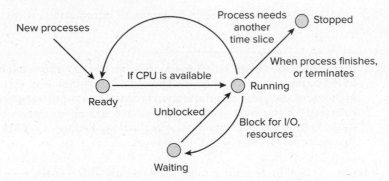

Security modes   The US government has designated four approved security modes for systems that process classified information. These are described next. In Chapter 5, "Security Governance Concepts, Principles, and Policies," we reviewed the classification system used by the federal government and the concepts of security clearances and access approval. The only new term in this context is *need to know*, which refers to an access authorization scheme in which a subject's right to access an object takes into consideration not just a privilege level but also the relevance of the data involved in the role the subject plays (or the job they perform). This indicates that the subject requires access to the object to perform their job properly or to fill some specific role. Those with no need to know may not access the object, no matter what level of privilege they hold. If you need a refresher on those concepts, please review them in Chapter 5 before proceeding.

Three specific elements must exist before the security modes themselves can be deployed:

- A hierarchical MAC environment
- Total physical control over which subjects can access the computer console
- Total physical control over which subjects can enter into the same room as the computer console

You will rarely, if ever, encounter the following modes outside of the world of government agencies and contractors. However, you may discover this terminology in other contexts, so you'd be well advised to commit the terms to memory.

Dedicated mode   Dedicated mode systems are essentially equivalent to the single state system described in the section "Processing Types" earlier in this chapter. Three requirements exist for users of dedicated systems:

- Each user must have a security clearance that permits access to all information processed by the system.

- Each user must have access approval for all information processed by the system.

- Each user must have a valid need to know for all information processed by the system.

In the definitions of each of these modes, we use "all information processed by the system" for brevity. The official definition is more comprehensive and uses "all information processed, stored, transferred, or accessed." If you want to explore the source, search for *Department of Defense 8510.1-M DoD Information Technology Security Certification and Accreditation Process (DITSCAP) Manual*.

System high mode   System high mode systems have slightly different requirements that must be met by users:

- Each user must have a valid security clearance that permits access to all information processed by the system.

- Each user must have access approval for all information processed by the system.

- Each user must have a valid need to know for some information processed by the system but not necessarily all information processed by the system.

Note that the major difference between the dedicated mode and the system high mode is that all users do not necessarily have a need to know for all information processed on a system high mode computing device. Thus, although the same user could access both a dedicated mode system and a system high mode system, that user could access all data on the former but be restricted from some of the data on the latter.

Compartmented mode   Compartmented mode systems weaken these requirements one step further:

- Each user must have a valid security clearance that permits access to all information processed by the system.

- Each user must have access approval for any information they will have access to on the system.

- Each user must have a valid need to know for all information they will have access to on the system.

Notice that the major difference between compartmented mode systems and system high mode systems is that users of a compartmented mode system do not necessarily have access approval for all the information on the system. However, as with system high and dedicated systems, all users of the system must still have appropriate security clearances. In a special implementation of this mode called *compartmented mode workstations (CMWs)*, users with the necessary clearances can process multiple compartments of data at the same time.

CMWs require that two forms of security labels be placed on objects: sensitivity levels and information labels. Sensitivity levels describe the levels at which objects must be protected. These are common among all four of the modes. Information labels prevent data overclassification and associate additional information with the objects, which assists in proper and accurate data labeling not related to access control.

Multilevel mode   The government's definition of multilevel mode systems pretty much parallels the technical definition given in the previous section. However, for consistency, we'll express it in terms of clearance, access approval, and need to know:

- Some users do not have a valid security clearance for all information processed by the system. Thus, access is controlled by whether the subject's clearance level dominates the object's sensitivity label.

- Each user must have access approval for all information they will have access to on the system.

- Each user must have a valid need to know for all information they will have access to on the system.

As you look through the requirements for the various modes of operation approved by the federal government, you'll notice that the administrative requirements for controlling the types of users that access a system decrease as you move from dedicated systems down to multilevel systems. However, this does not decrease the importance of limiting individual access so that users can obtain only the information they are legitimately entitled to access. As discussed in the previous section, it's simply a matter of shifting the burden of enforcing these requirements from administrative personnel—who physically limit access to a computer—to the hardware and software—which control what information can be accessed by each user of a multiuser system.

    Multilevel security mode can also be called the *controlled security mode.*

Table 12.1 summarizes and compares these four security modes according to security clearances required, need to know, and the ability to process data from multiple clearance levels (abbreviated PDMCL). When comparing all four security modes, it is generally understood that the multilevel mode is exposed to the highest level of risk.

TABLE 12.1: Comparing security modes

Mode	Clearance	Need to Know	PDMCL
Dedicated	Same	None	None
System high	Same	Yes	None
Compartmented	Same	Yes	Yes
Multilevel	Different	Yes	Yes

Clearance is **Same** if all users must have the same security clearances, **Different** if otherwise.
Need to Know is **None** if it does not apply and is not used or if it is used but all users have the need to know all data present on the system, **Yes** if access is limited by need-to-know restrictions.
PDMCL applies if and when CMW implementations are used (**Yes**); otherwise, PDMCL is **None**.

Operating Modes

Modern processors and operating systems are designed to support multiuser environments in which individual computer users might not be granted access to all components of a system or all the information stored on it. For that reason, the processor itself supports two modes of operation, user mode and privileged mode.

User   User mode is the basic mode used by the CPU when executing user applications. In this mode, the CPU allows the execution of only a portion of its full instruction set. This is designed to protect users from accidentally damaging the system through the execution of poorly designed code or the unintentional misuse of that code. It also protects the system and its data from a malicious user who might try to execute instructions designed to circumvent the security measures put in place by the operating system or who might mistakenly perform actions that could result in unauthorized access or damage to the system or valuable information assets.

Often processes within user mode are executed within a controlled environment called a *virtual machine (VM)* or a *virtual subsystem machine*. A virtual machine is a simulated environment created by the OS to provide a safe and efficient place for programs to execute. Each VM is isolated from all other VMs, and each VM has its own assigned memory address space that can be used by the hosted application. It is the responsibility of the elements in privileged mode (aka kernel mode) to create and support the VMs and prevent the processes in one VM from interfering with the processes in other VMs.

Privileged   CPUs also support privileged mode, which is designed to give the operating system access to the full range of instructions supported by the CPU. This mode goes by a number of names, and the exact terminology varies according to the CPU manufacturer. Some of the more common monikers are included in the following list:

- Privileged mode
- Supervisory mode
- System mode
- Kernel mode

No matter which term you use, the basic concept remains the same—this mode grants a wide range of permissions to the process executing on the CPU. For this reason, well-designed operating systems do not let any user applications execute in privileged mode. Only those processes that are components of the operating system itself are allowed to execute in this mode, for both security and system integrity purposes.

Don't confuse processor modes with any type of user access permissions. The fact that the high-level processor mode is sometimes called *privileged* or *supervisory* mode has no relationship to the role of a user. All user applications, including those of system administrators, run in user mode. When system administrators use system tools to make configuration changes to the system, those tools also run in user mode. When a user application needs to perform a privileged action, it passes that request to the operating system using a system call, which evaluates it and either rejects the request or approves it and executes it using a privileged mode process outside the user's control.

Memory

The second major hardware component of a system is *memory*, the storage bank for information that the computer needs to keep readily available. There are many different kinds of memory, each suitable for different purposes, and we'll take a look at each in the sections that follow.

Read-Only Memory

Read-only memory (ROM) works like the name implies—it's memory the PC can read but can't change (no writing allowed). The contents of a standard ROM chip are burned in at the factory, and the end user simply cannot alter it. ROM chips often contain "bootstrap" information that computers use to start up prior to loading an operating system from disk. This includes the familiar power-on self-test (POST) series of diagnostics that run each time you boot a PC.

ROM's primary advantage is that it can't be modified. There is no chance that user or administrator error will accidentally wipe out or modify the contents of such a chip. This attribute makes ROM extremely desirable for orchestrating a computer's innermost workings.

There is a type of ROM that may be altered by administrators to some extent. It is known as programmable read-only memory (PROM), and its several subtypes are described next:

Programmable read-only memory (PROM) A basic programmable read-only memory (PROM) chip is similar to a ROM chip in functionality, but with one exception. During the manufacturing process, a PROM chip's contents aren't "burned in" at the factory as with standard ROM chips. Instead, a PROM incorporates special functionality that allows an end user to burn in the chip's contents later. However, the burning process has a similar outcome—once data is written to a PROM chip, no further changes are possible. After it's burned in, a PROM chip essentially functions like a ROM chip.

PROM chips provide software developers with an opportunity to store information permanently on a high-speed, customized memory chip. PROMs are commonly used for hardware applications where some custom functionality is necessary but seldom changes once programmed.

Erasable programmable read-only memory (EPROM) Combine the relatively high cost of PROM chips and software developers' inevitable desires to tinker with their code once it's written and you have the rationale that led to the development of erasable PROM (EPROM). These chips have a small window that, when illuminated with a special ultraviolet light, causes the contents of the chip to be erased. After this process is complete, end users can burn new information into the EPROM as if it had never been programmed before.

Electronically erasable programmable read-only memory (EEPROM) Although it's better than no erase function at all, EPROM erasure is pretty cumbersome. It requires the physical removal of the chip from the computer and exposure to a special kind of ultraviolet light. A more flexible, friendly alternative is electronically erasable PROM (EEPROM), which uses electric voltages delivered to the pins of the chip to force erasure. EEPROM chips can be erased without removing them from the computer, which makes them much more attractive than standard PROM or EPROM chips. One well-known type of EEPROM is the flash memory chip. These are often used in modern computers, mobile phones, tablets, MP3 players, and digital cameras to store files, data, music, and images.

Random Access Memory

Random access memory (RAM) is readable and writable memory that contains information a computer uses during processing. RAM retains its contents only when power is continuously supplied to it. Unlike with ROM, when a computer is powered off, all data stored in RAM disappears. For this reason, RAM is useful only for temporary storage. Critical data should never be stored solely in RAM; a backup copy should always be kept on another storage device to prevent its disappearance in the event of a sudden loss of electrical power. The following are types of RAM:

Real memory Real memory (also known as *main memory* or *primary memory*) is typically the largest RAM storage resource available to a computer. It is normally composed of a number of dynamic RAM chips and, therefore, must be refreshed by the CPU on a periodic basis (see the sidebar "Dynamic vs. Static RAM" for more information on this subject).

Cache RAM   Computer systems contain a number of caches that improve performance by taking data from slower devices and temporarily storing it in faster devices when repeated use is likely; this is cache RAM. The processor normally contains an onboard cache of extremely fast memory used to hold data on which it will operate. This on-chip, or level 1, cache is often backed up by a static RAM cache on a separate chip, called a *level 2 cache*, which holds data from the computer's main bank of real memory. Likewise, real memory often contains a cache of information stored on magnetic media. This chain continues down through the memory/storage hierarchy to enable computers to improve performance by keeping data that's likely to be used next closer at hand (be it for CPU instructions, data fetches, file access, or what have you).

Many peripherals also include onboard caches to reduce the storage burden they place on the CPU and operating system. For example, many higher-end printers include large RAM caches so that the operating system can quickly spool an entire job to the printer. After that, the processor can forget about the print job; it won't be forced to wait for the printer to actually produce the requested output, spoon-feeding it chunks of data one at a time. The printer can preprocess information from its onboard cache, thereby freeing the CPU and operating system to work on other tasks.

 Real World Scenario

Dynamic vs. Static RAM

There are two main types of RAM: dynamic RAM and static RAM. Most computers contain a combination of both types and use them for different purposes.

To store data, dynamic RAM uses a series of capacitors, tiny electrical devices that hold a charge. These capacitors either hold a charge (representing a 1 bit in memory) or do not hold a charge (representing a 0 bit). However, because capacitors naturally lose their charges over time, the CPU must spend time refreshing the contents of dynamic RAM to ensure that 1 bits don't unintentionally change to 0 bits, thereby altering memory contents.

Static RAM uses more sophisticated technology—a logical device known as a *flip-flop*, which to all intents and purposes is simply an on/off switch that must be moved from one position to another to change a 0 to 1 or vice versa. More important, static memory maintains its contents unaltered so long as power is supplied and imposes no CPU overhead for periodic refresh operations.

Dynamic RAM is cheaper than static RAM because capacitors are cheaper than flip-flops. However, static RAM runs much faster than dynamic RAM. This creates a trade-off for system designers, who combine static and dynamic RAM modules to strike the right balance of cost vs. performance.

Registers

The CPU also includes a limited amount of onboard memory, known as *registers*, that provide it with directly accessible memory locations that the brain of the CPU, the arithmetic-logical unit (ALU), uses when performing calculations or processing instructions. In fact, any data that the ALU is to manipulate must be loaded into a register unless it is directly supplied as part of the instruction. The main advantage of this type of memory is that it is part of the ALU itself and, therefore, operates in lockstep with the CPU at typical CPU speeds.

Memory Addressing

When utilizing memory resources, the processor must have some means of referring to various locations in memory. The solution to this problem is known as *addressing*, and there are several different addressing schemes used in various circumstances. The following are five of the more common addressing schemes:

Register addressing   As you learned in the previous section, registers are small memory locations directly in the CPU. When the CPU needs information from one of its registers to complete an operation, it uses a register address (for example, "register 1") to access its contents.

Immediate addressing   Immediate addressing is not a memory addressing scheme per se but rather a way of referring to data that is supplied to the CPU as part of an instruction. For example, the CPU might process the command "Add 2 to the value in register 1." This command uses two addressing schemes. The first is immediate addressing—the CPU is being told to add the value 2 and does not need to retrieve that value from a memory location—it's supplied as part of the command. The second is register addressing; it's instructed to retrieve the value from register 1.

Direct addressing   In direct addressing, the CPU is provided with an actual address of the memory location to access. The address must be located on the same memory page as the instruction being executed. Direct addressing is more flexible than immediate addressing since the contents of the memory location can be changed more readily than reprogramming the immediate addressing's hard-coded data.

Indirect addressing   Indirect addressing uses a scheme similar to direct addressing. However, the memory address supplied to the CPU as part of the instruction doesn't contain the actual value that the CPU is to use as an operand. Instead, the memory address contains another memory address (perhaps located on a different page). The CPU reads the indirect address to learn the address where the desired data resides and then retrieves the actual operand from that address.

Base+offset addressing   Base+offset addressing uses a value stored in one of the CPU's registers as the base location from which to begin counting. The CPU then adds the offset supplied with the instruction to that base address and retrieves the operand from that computed memory location.

Secondary Memory

Secondary memory is a term commonly used to refer to magnetic/optical media or other storage devices that contain data not immediately available to the CPU. For the CPU to access data in secondary memory, the data must first be read by the operating system and stored in real memory. However, secondary memory is much more inexpensive than primary memory and can be used to store massive amounts of information. In this context, hard disks, floppy drives, and optical media such as CDs and DVDs can all function as secondary memory.

Virtual memory is a special type of secondary memory that the operating system manages to make look and act just like real memory. The most common type of virtual memory is the pagefile that most operating systems manage as part of their memory management functions. This specially formatted file contains data previously stored in memory but not recently used. When the operating system needs to access addresses stored in the pagefile, it checks to see whether the page is memory-resident (in which case it can access it immediately) or whether it has been swapped to disk, in which case it reads the data from disk back into real memory (this process is called *paging*).

Using virtual memory is an inexpensive way to make a computer operate as if it had more real memory than is physically installed. Its major drawback is that the paging operations that occur when data is exchanged between primary and secondary memory are relatively slow (memory functions in microseconds, disk systems in milliseconds; usually, this means four orders of magnitude difference!) and consume significant computer overhead, slowing down the entire system.

Memory Security Issues

Memory stores and processes your data—some of which may be extremely sensitive. It's essential that you understand the various types of memory and know how they store and retain data. Any memory devices that may retain sensitive data should be purged before they are allowed to leave your organization for any reason. This is especially true for secondary memory and ROM/PROM/EPROM/EEPROM devices designed to retain data even after the power is turned off.

However, memory data retention issues are not limited to those types of memory designed to retain data. Remember that static and dynamic RAM chips store data through the use of capacitors and flip-flops (see the sidebar "Dynamic vs. Static RAM"). It is technically possible that those electrical components could retain some of their charge for a limited period of time after power is turned off. A technically sophisticated individual could theoretically take electrical measurements of those components and retrieve portions of the data stored on such devices. However, this requires a good deal of technical expertise and is not a likely threat unless you have adversaries with mind-bogglingly deep pockets.

There is also an attack that freezes memory chips to delay the decay of resident data when the system is turned off or the RAM is pulled out of the motherboard. See http://en.wikipedia.org/wiki/Cold_boot_attack.

The greatest security threat posed by RAM chips is a simple one. They are highly pilferable and are quite often stolen. After all, who checks to see how much memory is in their computer at the start of each day? Someone could easily remove a single memory module from each of a large number of systems and walk out the door with a small bag containing valuable chips. Today, this threat is diminishing as the price of memory chips continues to fall ($20 for 4 GB DDR3 DIMM RAM as we write).

One of the most important security issues surrounding memory is controlling who may access data stored in memory while a computer is in use. This is primarily the responsibility of the operating system and is the main memory security issue underlying the various processing modes described in previous sections in this chapter. In the section "Security Protection Mechanisms" later in this chapter, you'll learn how the principle of process isolation can be used to ensure that processes don't have access to read or write to memory spaces not allocated to them. If you're operating in a multilevel security environment, it's especially important to ensure that adequate protections are in place to prevent the unwanted leakage of memory contents between security levels, through either direct memory access or covert channels (a full discussion of covert channels appears later in this chapter).

Storage

Data storage devices make up the third class of computer system components we'll discuss. These devices are used to store information that may be used by a computer anytime after it's written. We'll first examine a few common terms that relate to storage devices and then cover some of the security issues related to data storage.

Primary vs. Secondary

The concepts of primary and secondary storage can be somewhat confusing, especially when compared to primary and secondary memory. There's an easy way to keep it straight—they're the same thing! *Primary memory*, also known as *primary storage*, is the RAM that a computer uses to keep necessary information readily available to the CPU while the computer is running. *Secondary memory* (or *secondary storage*) includes all the familiar long-term storage devices that you use every day. Secondary storage consists of magnetic and optical media such as hard drives, solid state drives (SSDs), floppy disks, magnetic tapes, compact discs (CDs), digital video disks (DVDs), flash memory cards, and the like.

Volatile vs. Nonvolatile

You're already familiar with the concept of volatility from our discussion of memory, although you may not have heard it described using that term before. The volatility of a storage device is simply a measure of how likely it is to lose its data when power is turned off. Devices designed to retain their data (such as magnetic media) are classified as *nonvolatile*, whereas devices such as static or dynamic RAM modules, which are designed to lose their data, are classified as *volatile*. Recall from the discussion in the previous section that sophisticated technology may sometimes be able to extract data from volatile memory after power is removed, so the lines between the two may sometimes be blurry.

Random vs. Sequential

Storage devices may be accessed in one of two fashions. *Random access storage* devices allow an operating system to read (and sometimes write) immediately from any point within the device by using some type of addressing system. Almost all primary storage devices are random access devices. You can use a memory address to access information stored at any point within a RAM chip without reading the data that is physically stored before it. Most secondary storage devices are also random access. For example, hard drives use a movable head system that allows you to move directly to any point on the disk without spinning past all the data stored on previous tracks; likewise, CD and DVD devices use an optical scanner that can position itself anywhere on the platter surface.

Sequential storage devices, on the other hand, do not provide this flexibility. They require that you read (or speed past) all the data physically stored prior to the desired location. A common example of a sequential storage device is a magnetic tape drive. To provide access to data stored in the middle of a tape, the tape drive must physically scan through the entire tape (even if it's not necessarily processing the data that it passes in fast-forward mode) until it reaches the desired point.

Obviously, sequential storage devices operate much slower than random access storage devices. However, here again you're faced with a cost/benefit decision. Many sequential storage devices can hold massive amounts of data on relatively inexpensive media. This property makes tape drives uniquely suited for backup tasks associated with a disaster recovery/business continuity plan (see Chapter 15, "Business Continuity Planning," and Chapter 16, "Disaster Recovery Planning"). In a backup situation, you often have extremely large amounts of data that need to be stored, and you infrequently need to access that stored information. The situation just begs for a sequential storage device!

Storage Media Security

We discussed the security problems that surround primary storage devices in the previous section. There are three main concerns when it comes to the security of secondary storage devices; all of them mirror concerns raised for primary storage devices:

- Data may remain on secondary storage devices even after it has been erased. This condition is known as *data remanence*. Most technically savvy computer users know that utilities are available that can retrieve files from a disk even after they have been deleted. It's also technically possible to retrieve data from a disk that has been reformatted. If you truly want to remove data from a secondary storage device, you must use a specialized utility designed to destroy all traces of data on the device or damage or destroy it beyond possible repair (commonly called *sanitizing*).

- Secondary storage devices are also prone to theft. Economic loss is not the major factor (after all, how much does a CD-R disc or even a hard drive cost?), but the loss of confidential information poses great risks. If someone copies your trade secrets onto a removable media disc and walks out the door with it, it's worth a lot more than the cost of the disc itself.

- Access to data stored on secondary storage devices is one of the most critical issues facing computer security professionals. For hard disks, data can often be protected through a combination of operating system access controls. Removable media pose a greater challenge, so securing them often requires encryption technologies.

Input and Output Devices

Input and output devices are often seen as basic, primitive peripherals and usually don't receive much attention until they stop working properly. However, even these basic devices can present security risks to a system. Security professionals should be aware of these risks and ensure that appropriate controls are in place to mitigate them. The next four sections examine some of the risks posed by specific input and output devices.

Monitors

Monitors seem fairly innocuous. After all, they simply display the data presented by the operating system. When you turn them off, the data disappears from the screen and can't be recovered. However, technology from a program known as TEMPEST can compromise the security of data displayed on a monitor.

TEMPEST is a technology that allows the electronic emanations that every monitor produces (known as *Van Eck radiation*) to be read from a distance (this process is known as *Van Eck phreaking*) and even from another location. The technology is also used to protect against such activity. Various demonstrations have shown that you can easily read the screens of monitors inside an office building using gear housed in a van parked outside on the street. Unfortunately, the protective controls required to prevent Van Eck radiation (lots and lots of copper!) are expensive to implement and cumbersome to use. Generally, CRT monitors are more prone to radiate significantly, while LCD monitors leak much less (some claim not enough to reveal critical data). It is arguable that the biggest risk with any monitor is still shoulder surfing or telephoto lenses on cameras.

Printers

Printers also may represent a security risk, albeit a simpler one. Depending upon the physical security controls used at your organization, it may be much easier to walk out with sensitive information in printed form than to walk out with a floppy disk or other magnetic media. If printers are shared, users may forget to retrieve their sensitive printouts, leaving them vulnerable to prying eyes. Many modern printers also store data locally, often on a hard drive, and some retain copies of printouts indefinitely. These are all issues that are best addressed by an organization's security policy.

Keyboards/Mice

Keyboards, mice, and similar input devices are not immune to security vulnerabilities either. All of these devices are vulnerable to TEMPEST monitoring. Also, keyboards are vulnerable to less-sophisticated bugging. A simple device can be placed inside a keyboard or along its connection cable to intercept all the keystrokes that take place and transmit them to a remote receiver using a radio signal. This has the same effect as TEMPEST monitoring but can be done with much less expensive gear. Additionally, if your keyboard and mouse are wireless, including Bluetooth, their radio signals can be intercepted.

Modems

With the advent of ubiquitous broadband and wireless connectivity, modems are becoming a scarce legacy computer component. However, it is still common for a modem to be part of the hardware configuration in existing desktop and notebook systems. Whether common or not, the presence of a modem on a user system is often one of the greatest woes of a security administrator. Modems allow users to create uncontrolled access points into your network. In the worst case, if improperly configured, they can create extremely serious security vulnerabilities that allow an outsider to bypass all your perimeter protection mechanisms and directly access your network resources. At best, they create an alternate egress channel that insiders can use to funnel data outside your organization.

You should seriously consider an outright ban on modems in your organization's security policy unless you truly need them for business reasons. In those cases, security officials should know the physical and logical locations of all modems on the network, ensure that they are correctly configured, and make certain that appropriate protective measures are in place to prevent their illegitimate use.

Input/Output Structures

Certain computer activities related to general input/output (I/O) operations, rather than individual devices, also have security implications. Some familiarity with manual input/output device configuration is required to integrate legacy peripheral devices (those that do not autoconfigure or support Plug and Play, or PnP, setup) in modern PCs as well. Three types of operations that require manual configuration on legacy devices are involved here:

Memory-mapped I/O   For many kinds of devices, memory-mapped I/O is a technique used to manage input/output. That is, a part of the address space that the CPU manages functions to provide access to some kind of device through a series of mapped memory addresses or locations. Thus, by reading mapped memory locations, you're actually reading the input from the corresponding device (which is automatically copied to those memory locations at the system level when the device signals that input is available). Likewise, by writing to those mapped memory locations, you're actually sending output to that device (automatically handled by copying from those memory locations to the device at the system level when the CPU signals that the output is available).

From a configuration standpoint, it's important to make sure that only one device maps into a specific memory address range and that the address range is used for no other purpose than to handle device I/O. From a security standpoint, access to mapped memory locations should be mediated by the operating system and subject to proper authorization and access controls.

Interrupt (IRQ)   Interrupt (IRQ) is an abbreviation for *interrupt request*, a technique for assigning specific signal lines to specific devices through a special interrupt controller. When a device wants to supply input to the CPU, it sends a signal on its assigned IRQ (which usually falls in a range of 0 to 16 on older PCs for two cascaded 8-line interrupt controllers and 0 to 23 on newer ones with three cascaded 8-line interrupt controllers).

Where newer PnP-compatible devices may actually share a single interrupt (IRQ number), older legacy devices must generally have exclusive use of a unique IRQ number (a well-known pathology called *interrupt conflict* occurs when two or more devices are assigned the same IRQ number and is best recognized by an inability to access all affected devices). From a configuration standpoint, finding unused IRQ numbers that will work with legacy devices can be a sometimes trying exercise. From a security standpoint, only the operating system should be able to mediate access to IRQs at a sufficiently high level of privilege to prevent tampering or accidental misconfiguration.

Direct Memory Access (DMA)   Direct Memory Access (DMA) works as a channel with two signal lines, where one line is a DMA request (DMQ) line and the other is a DMA acknowledgment (DACK) line. Devices that can exchange data directly with real memory (RAM) without requiring assistance from the CPU use DMA to manage such access. Using its DRQ line, a device signals the CPU that it wants to make direct access (which may be read or write or some combination of the two) to another device, usually real memory. The CPU authorizes access and then allows the access to proceed independently while blocking other access to the memory locations involved. When the access is complete, the device uses the DACK line to signal that the CPU may once again permit access to previously blocked memory locations. This is faster than requiring the CPU to mediate such access and permits the CPU to move on to other tasks while the memory access is underway. DMA is used most commonly to permit disk drives, optical drives, display cards, and multimedia cards to manage large-scale data transfers to and from real memory. From a configuration standpoint, it's important to manage DMA addresses to keep device addresses unique and to make sure such addresses are used only for DMA signaling. From a security standpoint, only the operating system should be able to mediate DMA assignment and the use of DMA to access I/O devices.

If you understand common IRQ assignments, how memory-mapped I/O and DMA work, and related security concerns, you know enough to tackle the CISSP exam. If not, some additional reading may be warranted. In that case, PC Guide's excellent overview of system memory (`www.pcguide.com/ref/ram/`) should tell you everything you need to know.

Firmware

Firmware (also known as *microcode* in some circles) is a term used to describe software that is stored in a ROM chip. This type of software is changed infrequently (actually, never, if it's stored on a true ROM chip as opposed to an EPROM/EEPROM) and often drives the basic operation of a computing device. There are two types of firmware: BIOS on a motherboard and general internal and external device firmware.

BIOS

The Basic Input/Output System (BIOS) contains the operating-system-independent primitive instructions that a computer needs to start up and load the operating system from disk. The BIOS is contained in a firmware device that is accessed immediately by the computer at boot time. In most computers, the BIOS is stored on an EEPROM chip to facilitate version updates. The process of updating the BIOS is known as "flashing the BIOS."

There have been a few examples of malicious code embedding itself into BIOS/firmware. There is also an attack known as *phlashing*, in which a malicous variation of official BIOS or firmware is installed that introduces remote control or other malicious features into a device.

Device Firmware

Many hardware devices, such as printers and modems, also need some limited processing power to complete their tasks while minimizing the burden placed on the operating system itself. In many cases, these "mini" operating systems are entirely contained in firmware chips onboard the devices they serve. As with a computer's BIOS, device firmware is frequently stored on an EEPROM device so it can be updated as necessary.

Avoiding Single Points of Failure

Any element in your IT infrastructure, component in your physical environment, or person on your staff can be a single point of failure. A single point of failure is simply any element—such as a device, service, protocol, or communication link—that would cause total or significant downtime if compromised, violated, or destroyed, affecting the ability of members of your organization to perform essential work tasks. To avoid single points of failure, you must design your networks and your physical environment with redundancy and backups by doing such things as deploying dual network backbones. Avoiding single points of failure is a key element in security architecture and design, and is an important consideration in technology and process integration.

The use of systems, devices, and solutions with fault-tolerant capabilities is a means to improve resistance to single-point-of-failure vulnerabilities. Taking steps to establish a means to provide alternate processing, failover capabilities, and quick recovery will also aid in avoiding single points of failure.

Redundant Servers

Using redundant servers is one fault-tolerant deployment option. Redundant servers can take numerous forms:

Server mirroring is when you deploy a backup system along with the primary system. Every change made to the primary system is immediately duplicated to the secondary system.

Electronic vaulting is the collection of changes on a primary system into a transaction or change document. Periodically, the change document is sent to an offsite duplicate server where the changes are applied. This is also known as *batch processing* because changes are duplicated over intervals rather than in real time.

Remote journaling is the same as electronic vaulting except that changes are sent immediately to the offsite duplicate server rather than in batches. This provides a more real-time server backup.

Database shadowing is remote journaling to more than one destination duplicate server. There may be one or more local duplicates and one or more offsite duplicates.

Clusters are another type of redundant server. Clustering means deploying two or more duplicate servers in such a way as to share the workload of a mission-critical application. Users see the clustered systems as a single entity. A cluster controller manages traffic to and among the clustered systems to balance the workload across all clustered servers. As changes occur on one of the clustered systems, they are immediately duplicated to all other cluster partners.

Failover Solutions

When backup systems or redundant servers exist, there needs to be a means by which you can switch over to the backup in the event the primary system is compromised or fails. Rollover, or failover, is redirecting workload or traffic to a backup system when the primary system fails. Rollover can be automatic or manual:

- *Manual rollover*, also known as *cold rollover*, requires an administrator to perform some change in software or hardware configuration to switch the traffic load over the down primary to a secondary server.

- With *automatic rollover*, also known as *hot rollover*, the switch from primary to secondary system is performed automatically as soon as a problem is encountered.

Fail-secure, *fail-safe*, and *fail-soft* are terms related to these issues. A fail-secure system is able to resort to a secure state when an error or security violation is encountered. Fail-safe capability is a similar feature, but human safety is protected in the event of a system failure. However, these two terms are often used interchangeably to mean a system that is secure after a failure. Fail-soft describes a refinement of the fail-secure capability: Only the portion of a system that encountered or experienced the failure or security breach is disabled or secured, while the rest of the system continues to function normally.

A specific implementation of a fail-secure system would be the use of TFTP servers to store network device configurations. In the event of a system failure, configuration corruption, or power outage, most network devices (such as routers and switches) can be hard-coded to pull their configuration file from a TFTP server upon reboot. In this way, essential network devices can self-restore quickly.

Power failure is potentially a single point of failure. If electrical power is lost, all electronic devices will cease to function. Addressing this weakness is important if 24/7 uptime is essential to your organization. Ways to combat power failure or fluctuation issues include power conditioners (in other words, surge protectors), uninterruptible power supplies, and onsite electric generators.

RAID

Within individual systems, storage devices can be a single point of failure. Redundant Array of Independent Disks (RAID) is a storage device mechanism that uses multiple hard drives in unique combinations to produce a storage solution that provides better through-put as well as resistance to device failure. The two primary storage techniques employed by RAID are mirroring and striping. Striping can be further enhanced by storing parity information. Parity information enables on-the-fly recovery or reconstruction of data lost due to the failure of one or more drives. There are several levels or forms of RAID. Table 12.2 lists some of the more common ones.

TABLE 12.2 Common RAID levels

RAID Level	Description
0	Striping
1	Mirroring
2	Hamming code parity
3	Byte-level parity
4	Block-level parity
5	Interleave parity
6	Second parity data
10	RAID levels 1 + 0
15	RAID levels 1 + 5

RAID can be implemented in hardware or in software. Hardware-based RAID offers more reliable performance and fault tolerance protection. Hardware-based RAID performs all the processing necessary for multidrive access on the drive controllers. Software-based RAID performs the processing as part of the operating system. Thus, system resources are consumed in managing and using RAID when it is deployed through software. RAID 0 offers no fault tolerance, just performance improvements. RAID 1 and 5 are the most common implementations of RAID.

There are three forms of RAID drive swapping: hot, cold, and warm. *Hot-swappable* RAID allows for failed drives to be removed and replaced while the host server remains up and running. *Cold-swappable* RAID systems require the host server to be fully powered down before failed drives can be removed and replaced. *Warm-swappable* RAID allows for failed drives to be removed and replaced by disabling the RAID configuration via software, then replacing the drive, and then reenabling the RAID configuration. RAID is a specific technology example of fault-resistant disk systems (FRDSs).

No matter what fault-tolerant designs and mechanisms you employ to avoid single points of failure, no environment's security precautions are complete without a backup solution. Backups are the only means of providing reliable insurance against minor and catastrophic losses of your data. For a backup system to provide protection, it must be configured to store all data necessary to support your organization. It must perform the backup operation as quickly and efficiently as possible. The backups must be performed on a regular basis, such as daily, weekly, or in real time. And backups must be periodically tested to verify that they are functioning and that your restore processes are adequate. An untested backup cannot be assumed to work.

Distributed Architecture

As computing has evolved from a host/terminal model (where users could be physically distributed but all functions, activity, data, and resources resided on a single centralized system) to a client-server model (where users operate independent fully functional desktop computers but also access services and resources on networked servers), security controls and concepts have had to evolve to follow suit. This means that clients have computing and storage capabilities and, typically, that multiple servers do likewise. Thus, security must be addressed everywhere instead of at a single centralized host. From a security standpoint, this means that because processing and storage are distributed on multiple clients and servers, all those computers must be properly secured and protected. It also means that the network links between clients and servers (and in some cases, these links may not be purely local) must also be secured and protected. When evaluating security architecture, be sure to include an assessment of the needs and risks related to distributed architectures.

Vulnerabilities

Distributed architectures are prone to vulnerabilities unthinkable in monolithic host/terminal systems. Desktop systems can contain sensitive information that may be at some risk of being exposed and must therefore be protected. Individual users may lack general security savvy or awareness, and therefore the underlying architecture has to compensate for those deficiencies. Desktop PCs, workstations, and laptops can provide avenues of access into critical information systems elsewhere in a distributed environment because users require access to networked servers and services to do their jobs. By permitting user machines to access a network and its distributed resources, organizations must also recognize that those user machines can become threats if they are misused or compromised. Such software and system vulnerabilities and threats must be assessed and addressed properly.

Communications equipment can also provide unwanted points of entry into a distributed environment. For example, modems attached to a desktop machine that's also attached to an organization's network can make that network vulnerable to dial-in attacks. There is also a risk that wireless adapters on client systems can be used to create open networks. Likewise, users who download data from the Internet increase the risk of infecting their own and other systems with malicious code, Trojan horses, and so forth. Desktops, laptops, and workstations—and associated disks or other storage devices—may not be secure from physical intrusion or theft. Finally, when data resides only on client machines, it may not be secured with a proper backup (it's often the case that while servers are backed up routinely, the same is not true for client computers).

There is a wide variety of application and system vulnerabilities and threats, and the range is constantly expanding. Vulnerabilities occur in web-based attacks (such as XML exploitation, SAML abuses, and the OWASP top ten), client-based attacks (such as malicious applets), server-based attacks (such as data flow control), database infrastructures (such as inference/inferencing, aggregation, data mining, and warehousing; see Chapter 7, "Software Development Security"), and distributed systems (such as cloud computing, grid computing, and peer to peer).

XML exploitation is a form of programming attack that is used to either falsify information being sent to a visitor or cause their system to give up information without authorization. One area of growing concern in regard to XML attacks is Security Association Markup Language (SAML). SAML abuses are often focused on web-based authentication. SAML is an XML-based convention for the organization and exchange of communication authentication and authorization details between security domains, often over web protocols. SAML is often used to provide a web-based SSO (single sign-on) solution. If an attacker can falsify SAML communications or steal a visitor's access token, they may be able to bypass authentication and gain unauthorized access to a site.

Open Web Application Security Project (OWASP) is a nonprofit security project focusing on improving security for online or web-based applications. OWASP is not just an organization, it is also a large community that works together to freely share information, methodology, tools, and techniques related to better coding practices and more secure deployment architectures. For more information on OWASP and to participate in the community, visit the website at www.owasp.org.

Another important area of concern, often server based but which may include clients as well, is the issue of data flow control. Data flow is the movement of data between processes, between devices, across a network, or over communication channels. Management of data flow ensures not only efficient transmission with minimal delays or latency, but also reliable throughput using hashing and protection confidentiality with encryption. Data flow control also ensures that receiving systems are not overloaded with traffic, especially to the point of dropping connections or being subject to a malicious or even self-inflicted denial of service. When data overflow occurs, data may be lost or corrupted or may trigger a need for retransmission. These results are undesirable, and data flow control is often implemented to prevent these issues from occurring. Data flow control may be provided by networking devices, including routers and switches, as well as network applications and services.

Applets

Recall that agents are code objects sent from a user's system to query and process data stored on remote systems. *Applets* perform the opposite function; these code objects are sent from a server to a client to perform some action. In fact, applets are actually self-contained miniature programs that execute independently of the server that sent them.

Imagine a web server that offers a variety of financial tools to web users. One of these tools might be a mortgage calculator that processes a user's financial information and provides a monthly mortgage payment based upon the loan's principal and term and the borrower's credit information. Instead of processing this data and returning the results to the client system, the remote web server might send to the local system an applet that enables it to perform those calculations itself. This provides a number of benefits to both the remote server and the end user:

- The processing burden is shifted to the client, freeing up resources on the web server to process requests from more users.

- The client is able to produce data using local resources rather than waiting for a response from the remote server. In many cases, this results in a quicker response to changes in the input data.

- In a properly programmed applet, the web server does not receive any data provided to the applet as input, therefore maintaining the security and privacy of the user's financial data.

However, just as with agents, applets introduce a number of security concerns. They allow a remote system to send code to the local system for execution. Security administrators must take steps to ensure that code sent to systems on their network is safe and properly screened for malicious activity. Also, unless the code is analyzed line by line, the end user can never be certain that the applet doesn't contain a Trojan horse component. For example, the mortgage calculator might indeed transmit sensitive financial information to the web server without the end user's knowledge or consent.

Two common applet types are Java applets and ActiveX controls:

Java applets   Java is a platform-independent programming language developed by Sun Microsystems. Most programming languages use compilers that produce applications custom-tailored to run under a specific operating system. This requires the use of multiple compilers to produce different versions of a single application for each platform it must support. Java overcomes this limitation by inserting the Java Virtual Machine (JVM) into the picture. Each system that runs Java code downloads the version of the JVM supported by its operating system. The JVM then takes the Java code and translates it into a format executable by that specific system. The great benefit of this arrangement is that code can be shared between operating systems without modification. Java applets are simply short Java programs transmitted over the Internet to perform operations on a remote system.

Security was of paramount concern during the design of the Java platform, and Sun's development team created the "sandbox" concept to place privilege restrictions on Java code. The sandbox isolates Java code objects from the rest of the operating system and enforces strict rules about the resources those objects can access. For example, the sandbox would prohibit a Java applet from retrieving information from areas of memory not specifically allocated to it, preventing the applet from stealing that information. Unfortunately, while sandboxing reduces the forms of malicious events that can be launched via Java, there are still plenty of other vulnerabilities that have been widely exploited.

ActiveX controls   ActiveX controls are Microsoft's answer to Sun's Java applets. They operate in a similar fashion, but they are implemented using a variety of languages, including Visual Basic, C, C++, and Java. There are two key distinctions between Java applets and ActiveX controls. First, ActiveX controls use proprietary Microsoft technology and, therefore, can execute only on systems running Microsoft browsers. Second, ActiveX controls are not subject to the sandbox restrictions placed on Java applets. They have full access to the Windows operating environment and can perform a number of privileged actions. Therefore, you must take special precautions when deciding which ActiveX controls to download and execute. Some security administrators have taken the somewhat harsh position of prohibiting the download of any ActiveX content from all but a select handful of trusted sites.

Safeguards

You should see that the foregoing litany of potential vulnerabilities in distributed architectures means that such environments require numerous safeguards to implement appropriate security and to ensure that such vulnerabilities are eliminated, mitigated, or remedied. Clients must be subjected to policies that impose safeguards on their contents and their users' activities. These include the following:

- Email must be screened so that it cannot become a vector for infection by malicious software; email should also be subject to policies that govern appropriate use and limit potential liability.

- Download/upload policies must be created so that incoming and outgoing data is screened and suspect materials blocked.

- Systems must be subject to robust access controls, which may include multifactor authentication and/or biometrics to restrict access to desktops and to prevent unauthorized access to servers and services.

- Graphical user interface mechanisms and database management systems should be installed, and their use required, to restrict and manage access to critical information.

- File encryption may be appropriate for files and data stored on client machines (indeed, drive-level encryption is a good idea for laptops and other mobile computing gear that is subject to loss or theft outside an organization's premises).

- It's essential to separate and isolate processes that run in user and supervisory modes so that unauthorized and unwanted access to high-privilege processes and capabilities is prevented.

- Protection domains should be created so that compromise of a client won't automatically compromise an entire network.

- Disks and other sensitive materials should be clearly labeled as to their security classification or organizational sensitivity; procedural processes and system controls should combine to help protect sensitive materials from unwanted or unauthorized access.

- Files on desktop machines should be backed up, as well as files on servers—ideally, using some form of centralized backup utility that works with client agent software to identify and capture files from clients stored in a secure backup storage archive.

- Desktop users need regular security awareness training to maintain proper security awareness; they also need to be notified about potential threats and instructed on how to deal with them appropriately.

- Desktop computers and their storage media require protection against environmental hazards (temperature, humidity, power loss/fluctuation, and so forth).

- Desktop computers should be included in disaster recovery and business continuity planning because they're potentially as important (if not more important) to getting their users back to work as other systems and services within an organization.

- Developers of custom software built in and for distributed environments also need to take security into account, including using formal methods for development and deployment, such as code libraries, change control mechanisms, configuration management, and patch and update deployment.

In general, safeguarding distributed environments means understanding the vulnerabilities to which they're subject and applying appropriate safeguards. These can (and do) range from technology solutions and controls to policies and procedures that manage risk and seek to limit or avoid losses, damage, unwanted disclosure, and so on.

A reasonable understanding of countermeasure principles is always important when responding to vulnerabilities and threats. Some specific countermeasure principles are discussed in Chapter 6, "Risk and Personnel Management," in the section "Risk Management." But a common general principle is that of defense in depth. Defense in depth is a common security strategy used to provide a protective multilayer barrier against various forms of attack. It's reasonable to assume that there is greater difficulty in passing bad traffic or data through a network heavily fortified by a firewall, an IDS, and a diligent administration staff than one with a firewall alone. Why shouldn't you double up your defenses? Defense in depth is the use of multiple types of access controls in literal or theoretical concentric circles. This form of layered security helps an organization avoid a monolithic security stance. A monolithic or fortress mentality is the belief that a single security mechanism is all that is required to provide sufficient security. Unfortunately, every individual security mechanism has a flaw or a workaround just waiting to be discovered and abused by a hacker. Only through the intelligent combination of countermeasures is a defense constructed that will resist significant and persistent attempts of compromise.

Cloud Computing

Cloud computing is the popular term referring to a concept of computing where processing and storage are performed elsewhere over a network connection rather than locally. Cloud computing is often thought of as Internet-based computing. Ultimately, processing and storage still occurs on computers somewhere, but the distinction is that the local operator no longer needs to have that capacity or capability locally. This also allows a larger group of users to leverage cloud resources on demand. From the end-user perspective, all the work of computing is now performed "in the cloud" and thus the complexity is isolated from them.

Cloud computing is a natural extension and evolution of virtualization, the Internet, distributed architecture, and the need for ubiquitous access to data and resources. However, it does have some issues, including privacy concerns, regulation compliance difficulties, use of open/closed-source solutions, adoption of open standards, and whether or not cloud-based data is actually secured (or even securable).

Some of the concepts in cloud computing are listed here:

Platform as a service   Platform as a service is the concept of providing a computing platform and software solution stack as a virtual or cloud-based service. Essentially, this type of cloud solution provides all the aspects of a platform (i.e., operating system and complete solution package). The primary attraction of platform as a service is the avoidance of needing to purchase and maintain high-end hardware and software locally.

Software as a service   Software as a service is a derivative of platform as a service. Software as a service provides on-demand online access to specific software applications or suites without the need for local installation. In many cases, there are few local hardware and OS limitations. Software as a service can be implemented as a subscription service (for example, Microsoft Office 365), a pay-as-you-go service, or a free service (for example, Google Docs).

Infrastructure as a service   Infrastructure as a service takes the platform as a service model yet another step forward and provides not just on-demand operating solutions but complete outsourcing options. This can include utility or metered computing services, administrative task automation, dynamic scaling, virtualization services, policy implementation and management services, and managed/filtered Internet connectivity. Ultimately, infrastructure as a service allows an enterprise to scale up new software or data-based services/solutions through cloud systems quickly and without having to install massive hardware locally.

Grid Computing

Grid computing is a form of parallel distributed processing that loosely groups a significant number of processing nodes to work toward a specific processing goal. Members of the grid can enter and leave the grid at random intervals. Often, grid members join the grid only when their processing capacities are not being taxed for local workloads. When a system is otherwise in an idle state, it could join a grid group, download a small portion of work, and begin calculations. When a system leaves the grid, it saves its work and may upload completed or partial work elements back to the grid. Many interesting uses of grid computing have developed, ranging from projects seeking out intelligent aliens, performing protein folding, predicting weather, modeling earthquakes, planning financial decisions, and solving for primes.

The biggest security concern with grid computing is that the content of each work packet is potentially exposed to the world. Many grid computing projects are open to the world, so there is no restriction on who can run the local processing application and participate in the grid's project. This also means that grid members could keep copies of each work packet and examine the contents. Thus, grid projects will not likely be able to maintain secrecy and are not appropriate for private, confidential, or proprietary data.

Grid computing can also vary greatly in the computational capacity from moment to moment. Work packets are sometimes not returned, returned late, or returned corrupted. This requires significant reworking and causes instability in the speed, progress, responsiveness, and latency of the project as a whole and with individual grid members. Time-sensitive projects might not be given sufficient computational time to finish by a specific chronological deadline.

Grid computing often uses a central primary core of servers to manage the project, track work packets, and integrate returned work segments. If the central servers are overloaded or go offline, complete failure or crashing of the grid can occur. However, usually when central grid systems are inaccessible, grid members complete their current local tasks and then regularly poll to discover when the central servers come back online. There is also a potential risk that a compromise of the central grid servers could be leveraged to attack grid members or trick grid members into performing malicious actions instead of the intended purpose of the grid community.

Peer to Peer

Peer to peer (P2P) technologies are networking and distributed application solutions that share tasks and workloads among peers. This is similar to grid computing; the primary differences are that there is no central management system and the services provided are usually real time rather than as a collection of computational power. Common examples of P2P include many VoIP services, such as Skype, BitTorrent for data/file distribution, and Spotify for streaming audio/music distribution.

Security concerns with peer to peer solutions include a perceived inducement to pirate copyrighted materials, the ability to eavesdrop on distributed content, a lack of central control/oversight/management/filtering, and the potential for services to consume all available bandwidth.

Security Protection Mechanisms

The need for security mechanisms within an operating system comes down to one simple fact: Software should not be trusted. Third-party software is inherently untrustworthy, no matter who or where it comes from. This is not to say that all software is evil. Instead, this is a protection stance—because all third-party software is written by someone other than the OS creator, that software might cause problems. Thus, treating all non-OS software as potentially damaging allows the OS to prevent many disastrous occurrences through the use of software management protection mechanisms. The OS must employ protection mechanisms to keep the computing environment stable and to keep processes isolated from each other. Without these efforts, the security of data could never be reliable or even possible.

Computer system designers should adhere to a number of common protection mechanisms when designing secure systems. These principles are specific instances of the more general security rules that govern safe computing practices. Designing security into a system during the earliest stages of development will help ensure that the overall security architecture has the best chance for success and reliability. In the following sections, we'll divide the discussion into two areas: technical mechanisms and policy mechanisms.

Technical Mechanisms

Technical mechanisms are the controls that system designers can build right into their systems. We'll look at five: layering, abstraction, data hiding, process isolation, and hardware segmentation.

Layering

By *layering* processes, you implement a structure similar to the ring model used for operating modes (and discussed earlier in this chapter) and apply it to each operating system process. It puts the most-sensitive functions of a process at the core, surrounded by a series of increasingly larger concentric circles with correspondingly lower sensitivity levels (using a slightly different approach, this is also sometimes explained in terms of upper and lower layers, where security and privilege decrease when climbing up from lower to upper layers). In discussions of OS architectures, the protected ring concept is common, and it is not exclusive. There are other ways of representing the same basic ideas with levels rather than rings. In such a system, the highest level is the most privileged, while the lowest level is the least privileged.

Levels Compared to Rings

Many of the features and restrictions of the protecting ring concept apply also to a multilayer or multilevel system. Think about a high-rise apartment building. The low-rent apartments are often found in the lower floors. As you reach the middle floors, the apartments are often larger and offer better views. Finally, the top floor (or floors) is the most lavish and expensive (often deemed the penthouse). Usually, if you are living in a low-rent apartment in the building, you are unable to ride the elevators any higher than the highest floor of the low-rent apartments. If you are a middle-floor apartment resident, you can ride the elevators everywhere except to the penthouse floor(s). And if you are a penthouse resident, you can ride the elevators anywhere you want to go. You may also find this floor restriction system in office buildings and hotels.

The top of a layered or multilevel system is the same as the center ring of a protection ring scheme. Likewise, the bottom of a layered or multilevel system is the same as the outer ring of a protection ring scheme. In terms of protection and access concepts, *levels*, *layers*, and *rings* are similar. The term *domain* (that is, a collection of objects with a singular characteristic) might also be used.

Communication between layers takes place only through the use of well-defined, specific interfaces to provide necessary security. All inbound requests from outer (less-sensitive) layers are subject to stringent authentication and authorization checks before they're allowed to proceed (or denied, if they fail such checks). Using layering for security is similar to using security domains and lattice-based security models in that security and access controls over certain subjects and objects are associated with specific layers and privileges and that access increases as one moves from outer to inner layers.

In fact, separate layers can communicate only with one another through specific interfaces designed to maintain a system's security and integrity. Even though less-secure outer layers depend on services and data from more-secure inner layers, they know only how to interface with those layers and are not privy to those inner layers' internal structure, characteristics, or other details. So that layer integrity is maintained, inner layers neither know about nor depend on outer layers. No matter what kind of security relationship may exist between any pair of layers, neither can tamper with the other (so that each layer is protected from tampering by any other layer). Finally, outer layers cannot violate or override any security policy enforced by an inner layer.

Abstraction

Abstraction is one of the fundamental principles behind the field known as *object-oriented programming*. It is the "black-box" doctrine that says that users of an object (or operating system component) don't necessarily need to know the details of how the object works; they need to know just the proper syntax for using the object and the type of data that will be returned as a result (that is, how to send input and receive output). This is very much what's involved in mediated access to data or services, such as when user mode applications use system calls to request administrator mode services or data (and where such requests may be granted or denied depending on the requester's credentials and permissions) rather than obtaining direct, unmediated access.

Another way in which abstraction applies to security is in the introduction of object groups, sometimes called *classes*, where access controls and operation rights are assigned to groups of objects rather than on a per-object basis. This approach allows security administrators to define and name groups easily (the names are often related to job roles or responsibilities) and helps make the administration of rights and privileges easier (when you add an object to a class, you confer rights and privileges rather than having to manage rights and privileges for each object separately).

Data Hiding

Data hiding is an important characteristic in multilevel secure systems. It ensures that data existing at one level of security is not visible to processes running at different security levels. The key concept behind data hiding is a desire to make sure those who have no need to know the details involved in accessing and processing data at one level have no way to learn or observe those details covertly or illicitly. From a security perspective, data hiding relies on placing objects in security containers that are different from those that subjects occupy to hide object details from those with no need to know about them.

Process Isolation

Process isolation requires that the operating system provide separate memory spaces for each process's instructions and data. It also requires that the operating system enforce those boundaries, preventing one process from reading or writing data that belongs to another process. There are two major advantages to using this technique:

- It prevents unauthorized data access. Process isolation is one of the fundamental requirements in a multilevel security mode system.

- It protects the integrity of processes. Without such controls, a poorly designed process could go haywire and write data to memory spaces allocated to other processes, causing the entire system to become unstable rather than affecting only the execution of the errant process. In a more malicious vein, processes could attempt (and perhaps even succeed at) reading or writing to memory spaces outside their scope, intruding upon or attacking other processes.

Many modern operating systems address the need for process isolation by implementing so-called virtual machines on a per-user or per-process basis. A virtual machine presents a user or process with a processing environment—including memory, address space, and other key system resources and services—that allows that user or process to behave as though they have sole, exclusive access to the entire computer. This allows each user or process to operate independently without requiring it to take cognizance of other users or processes that might actually be active simultaneously on the same machine. As part of the mediated access to the system that the operating system provides, it maps virtual resources and access in user mode so that they use supervisory mode calls to access corresponding real resources. This not only makes things easier for programmers, it also protects individual users and processes from one another.

Hardware Segmentation

Hardware segmentation is similar to process isolation in purpose—it prevents the access of information that belongs to a different process/security level. The main difference is that hardware segmentation enforces these requirements through the use of physical hardware controls rather than the logical process isolation controls imposed by an operating system. Such implementations are rare, and they are generally restricted to national security implementations where the extra cost and complexity is offset by the sensitivity of the information involved and the risks inherent in unauthorized access or disclosure.

Security Policy and Computer Architecture

Just as security policy guides the day-to-day security operations, processes, and procedures in organizations, it has an important role to play when designing and implementing systems. This is equally true whether a system is entirely hardware based, entirely software based, or a combination of both. In this case, the role of a security policy is to inform and guide the design, development, implementation, testing, and maintenance of some particular system. Thus, this kind of security policy tightly targets a single implementation effort.

(Although it may be adapted from other, similar efforts, it should reflect the target as accurately and completely as possible.)

For system developers, a security policy is best encountered in the form of a document that defines a set of rules, practices, and procedures that describe how the system should manage, protect, and distribute sensitive information. Security policies that prevent information flow from higher security levels to lower security levels are called multilevel security policies. As a system is developed, the security policy should be designed, built, implemented, and tested as it relates to all applicable system components or elements, including any or all of the following: physical hardware components, firmware, software, and how the organization interacts with and uses the system. The overall point is that security needs be considered for the entire life of the project. When security is applied only at the end, it typically fails.

Policy Mechanisms

As with any security program, policy mechanisms should also be put into place. These mechanisms are extensions of basic computer security doctrine, but the applications described in this section are specific to the field of computer architecture and design.

Principle of Least Privilege

In Chapter 1, "Access Control," you learned about the general security *principle of least privilege* and how it applies to users of computing systems. This principle is also important to the design of computers and operating systems, especially when applied to system modes. When designing operating system processes, you should always ensure that they run in user mode whenever possible. The greater the number of processes that execute in privileged mode, the higher the number of potential vulnerabilities that a malicious individual could exploit to gain supervisory access to the system. In general, it's better to use APIs to ask for supervisory mode services or to pass control to trusted, well-protected supervisory mode processes as they're needed from within user mode applications than it is to elevate such programs or processes to supervisory mode altogether.

Separation of Privilege

The principle of *separation of privilege* builds upon the principle of least privilege. It requires the use of granular access permissions, that is, different permissions for each type of privileged operation. This allows designers to assign some processes rights to perform certain supervisory functions without granting them unrestricted access to the system. It also allows individual requests for services or access to resources to be inspected, checked against access controls, and granted or denied based on the identity of the user making the requests or on the basis of groups to which the user belongs or security roles that the user occupies.

Think of separation of duties as the application of the principle of least privilege to administrators. In most moderate to large organizations, there are many administrators, each with different assigned tasks. Thus, there are usually few or no individual administrators with complete and total need for access across the entire environment or infrastructure. For example, a user administrator has no need for privileges that enable reconfiguring network routing, formatting storage devices, or performing backup functions.

Separation of duties is also a tool used to prevent conflicts of interest in the assignment of access privileges and work tasks. For example, those persons responsible for programming code should not be tasked to test and implement that code. Likewise, those who work in accounts payable should not also have accounts receivable responsibilities. There are many such job or task conflicts that can be securely managed through the proper implementation of separation of duties.

Accountability

Accountability is an essential component in any security design. Many high-security systems contain physical devices (such as paper-and-pen visitor logs and nonmodifiable audit trails) that enforce individual accountability for privileged functionality. In general, however, such capabilities rely on a system's ability to monitor activity on and interactions with a system's resources and configuration data and to protect resulting logs from unwanted access or alteration so that they provide an accurate and reliable record of activity and interaction that documents every user's (including administrators or other trusted individuals with high levels of privilege) history on that system. In addition to the need for reliable auditing and monitoring systems to support accountability, there must be a resilient authorization system and an impeccable authentication system.

Common Flaws and Security Issues

No security architecture is complete and totally secure. Every computer system has weaknesses and vulnerabilities. The goal of security models and architectures is to address as many known weaknesses as possible. Due to this fact, corrective actions must be taken to resolve security issues. The following sections present some of the more common security issues that affect computer systems in relation to vulnerabilities of security architectures. You should understand each of the issues and how they can degrade the overall security of your system. Some issues and flaws overlap one another and are used in creative ways to attack systems. Although the following discussion covers the most common flaws, the list is not exhaustive. Attackers are very clever.

Covert Channels

A *covert channel* is a method that is used to pass information over a path that is not normally used for communication. Because the path is not normally used for communication, it may not be protected by the system's normal security controls. Using a covert channel provides a means to violate, bypass, or circumvent a security policy undetected. Covert channels are one of the important examples of vulnerabilities of security architectures.

As you might imagine, a covert channel is the opposite of an *overt channel*. An overt channel is a known, expected, authorized, designed, monitored, and controlled method of communication.

There are two basic types of covert channels:

Covert timing channel A covert timing channel conveys information by altering the performance of a system component or modifying a resource's timing in a predictable manner. Using a covert timing channel is generally a method to secretly transfer data and is very difficult to detect.

Covert storage channel A covert storage channel conveys information by writing data to a common storage area where another process can read it. When assessing the security of software, be diligent for any process that writes to any area of memory that another process can read.

Both types of covert channels rely on the use of communication techniques to exchange information with otherwise unauthorized subjects. Because the covert channel is outside the normal data transfer environment, detecting it can be difficult. The best defense is to implement auditing and analyze log files for any covert channel activity.

The lowest level of security that addresses covert channels is B2 (F-B2+E4 for ITSEC, EAL5 for CC). All levels at or above level B2 must contain controls that detect and prohibit covert channels.

Attacks Based on Design or Coding Flaws and Security Issues

Certain attacks may result from poor design techniques, questionable implementation practices and procedures, or poor or inadequate testing. Some attacks may result from deliberate design decisions when special points of entry built into code to circumvent access controls, login, or other security checks often added to code while under development are not removed when that code is put into production. For what we hope are obvious reasons, such points of egress are properly called *back doors* because they avoid security measures by design (they're covered later in this chapter in "Maintenance Hooks and Privileged Programs"). Extensive testing and code review are required to uncover such covert means of access, which are very easy to remove during final phases of development but can be incredibly difficult to detect during the testing and maintenance phases.

Although functionality testing is commonplace for commercial code and applications, separate testing for security issues has been gaining attention and credibility only in the past few years, courtesy of widely publicized virus and worm attacks, SQL injection attacks, cross-site scripting attacks, and occasional defacements of or disruptions to widely used public sites online. In the sections that follow, we cover common sources of attack or vulnerabilities of security architectures that can be attributed to failures in design, implementation, prerelease code cleanup, or out-and-out coding mistakes. Although they're avoidable, finding and fixing such flaws requires rigorous security-conscious design from the beginning of a development project and extra time and effort spent in testing and analysis. This helps to explain the often lamentable state of software security, but it does not excuse it!

Initialization and Failure States

When an unprepared system crashes and subsequently recovers, two opportunities to compromise its security controls may arise. Many systems unload security controls as part of their shutdown procedures. *Trusted recovery* ensures that all controls remain intact in the event of a crash. During a trusted recovery, the system ensures that there are no opportunities for access to occur when security controls are disabled. Even the recovery phase runs with all controls intact.

For example, suppose a system crashes while a database transaction is being written to disk for a database classified as top secret. An unprotected system might allow an unauthorized user to access that temporary data before it gets written to disk. A system that supports trusted recovery ensures that no data confidentiality violations occur, even during the crash. This process requires careful planning and detailed procedures for handling system failures. Although automated recovery procedures may make up a portion of the entire recovery, manual intervention may still be required. Obviously, if such manual action is needed, appropriate identification and authentication for personnel performing recovery is likewise essential.

Input and Parameter Checking

One of the most notorious security violations is a buffer overflow. This violation occurs when programmers fail to validate input data sufficiently, particularly when they do not impose a limit on the amount of data their software will accept as input. Because such data is usually stored in an input buffer, when the normal maximum size of the buffer is exceeded, the extra data is called *overflow*. Thus, the type of attack that results when someone attempts to supply malicious instructions or code as part of program input is called a *buffer overflow*. Unfortunately, in many systems such overflow data is often executed directly by the system under attack at a high level of privilege or at whatever level of privilege attaches to the process accepting such input. For nearly all types of operating systems, including Windows, UNIX, Linux, and others, buffer overflows expose some of the most glaring and profound opportunities for compromise and attack of any kind of known security vulnerability.

The party responsible for a buffer overflow vulnerability is always the programmer whose code allowed nonsanitized input. Due diligence from programmers can eradicate buffer overflows completely, but only if programmers check all input and parameters before storing them in any data structure (and limit how much data can be proffered as input). Proper data validation is the only way to do away with buffer overflows. Otherwise, discovery of buffer overflows leads to a familiar pattern of critical security updates that must be applied to affected systems to close the point of attack.

🌐 Real World Scenario

Checking Code for Buffer Overflows

In early 2002, Bill Gates acted in his traditional role as the archetypal Microsoft spokesperson when he announced something he called the "Trustworthy Computing Initiative," a series of design philosophy changes intended to beef up the often questionable standing of Microsoft's operating systems and applications when viewed from a security perspective. As discussion on this subject continued through 2002 and 2003, the topic of buffer overflows occurred repeatedly (more often, in fact, than Microsoft security bulletins reported security flaws related to this kind of problem, and is among the most serious yet most frequently reported types of programming errors with security implications). As is the case for many other development organizations and also for the builders of software development environments (the software tools that developers use to create other software), increased awareness of buffer overflow exploits has caused changes at many stages during the development process:

- Designers must specify bounds for input data or state acceptable input values and set hard limits on how much data will be accepted, parsed, and handled when input is solicited.

- Developers must follow such limitations when building code that solicits, accepts, and handles input.

- Testers must check to make sure that buffer overflows can't occur and attempt to circumvent or bypass security settings when testing input handling code.

In his book *Secrets & Lies: Digital Security in a Networked World (Wiley, 2004),* noted information security expert Bruce Schneier makes a great case that security testing is in fact quite different from standard testing activities like unit testing, module testing, acceptance testing, and quality assurance checks (see the glossary) that software companies have routinely performed as part of the development process for years and years. What's not yet clear at Microsoft (and at other development companies as well, to be as fair to the colossus of Redmond as possible) is whether this change in design and test philosophy equates to the right kind of rigor necessary to foil all buffer overflows (some of the most serious security holes that Microsoft Windows continues to be plagued by are still buffer overflows or "buffer overruns," or the cause is identified as an "unchecked buffer").

Maintenance Hooks and Privileged Programs

Maintenance hooks are entry points into a system that are known only by the developer of the system. Such entry points are also called *back doors*. Although the existence of maintenance hooks is a clear violation of security policy, they still pop up in many systems. The original purpose of back doors was to provide guaranteed access to the system for maintenance reasons or if regular access was inadvertently disabled. The problem is that this type of access bypasses all security controls and provides free access to anyone who knows that the back doors exist. It is imperative that you explicitly prohibit such entry points and monitor your audit logs to uncover any activity that may indicate unauthorized administrator access.

Another common system vulnerability is the practice of executing a program whose security level is elevated during execution. Such programs must be carefully written and tested so they do not allow any exit and/or entry points that would leave a subject with a higher security rating. Ensure that all programs that operate at a high security level are accessible only to appropriate users and that they are hardened against misuse.

Incremental Attacks

Some forms of attack occur in slow, gradual increments rather than through obvious or recognizable attempts to compromise system security or integrity. Two such forms of attack are data diddling and the salami attack.

Data diddling occurs when an attacker gains access to a system and makes small, random, or incremental changes to data during storage, processing, input, output, or transaction rather than obviously altering file contents or damaging or deleting entire files. Such changes can be difficult to detect unless files and data are protected by encryption or unless some kind of integrity check (such as a checksum or message digest) is routinely performed and applied each time a file is read or written. Encrypted file systems, file-level encryption techniques, or some form of file monitoring (which includes integrity checks like those performed by applications such as Tripwire) usually offer adequate guarantees that no data diddling is underway. Data diddling is often considered an attack performed more often by insiders rather than outsiders (in other words, external intruders). It should be obvious that since data diddling is an attack that alters data, it is considered an active attack.

The *salami attack* is more mythical by all published reports. The name of the attack refers to a systematic whittling at assets in accounts or other records with financial value, where very small amounts are deducted from balances regularly and routinely. Metaphorically, the attack may be explained as stealing a very thin slice from a salami each time it's put on the slicing machine when it's being accessed by a paying customer. In reality, though no documented examples of such an attack are available, most security experts concede that salami attacks are possible, especially when organizational insiders could be involved. Only by proper separation of duties and proper control over code can organizations completely prevent or eliminate such an attack. Setting financial transaction monitors to track very small transfers of funds or other items of value should help to detect such activity; regular employee notification of the practice should help to discourage attempts at such attacks.

 If you want an entertaining method of learning about the salami attack or the salami technique, view the movies *Office Space*, *Sneakers*, and *Superman III*.

Programming

We have already mentioned the biggest flaw in programming: the buffer overflow, which can occur if the programmer fails to check or sanitize the format and/or the size of input data. There are other potential flaws with programs. Any program that does not handle any exception gracefully is in danger of exiting in an unstable state. It is possible to cleverly crash a program after it has increased its security level to carry out a normal task. If an attacker is successful in crashing the program at the right time, they can attain the higher security level and cause damage to the confidentiality, integrity, and availability of your system.

All programs that are executed directly or indirectly must be fully tested to comply with your security model. Make sure you have the latest version of any software installed, and be aware of any known security vulnerabilities. Because each security model, and each security policy, is different, you must ensure that the software you execute does not exceed the authority you allow. Writing secure code is difficult, but it's certainly possible. Make sure all programs you use are designed to address security concerns.

Timing, State Changes, and Communication Disconnects

Computer systems perform tasks with rigid precision. Computers excel at repeatable tasks. Attackers can develop attacks based on the predictability of task execution. The common sequence of events for an algorithm is to check that a resource is available and then access it if you are permitted. The *time of check (TOC)* is the time at which the subject checks on the status of the object. There may be several decisions to make before returning to the object to access it. When the decision is made to access the object, the procedure accesses it at the *time of use (TOU)*. The difference between the TOC and the TOU is sometimes large enough for an attacker to replace the original object with another object that suits their own needs. *Time-of-check-to-time-of-use* (TOCTTOU) attacks are often called *race conditions* because the attacker is racing with the legitimate process to replace the object before it is used.

A classic example of a TOCTTOU attack is replacing a data file after its identity has been verified but before data is read. By replacing one authentic data file with another file of the attacker's choosing and design, an attacker can potentially direct the actions of a program in many ways. Of course, the attacker would have to have in-depth knowledge of the program and system under attack.

Likewise, attackers can attempt to take action between two known states when the state of a resource or the entire system changes. Communication disconnects also provide small windows that an attacker might seek to exploit. Anytime a status check of a resource precedes action on the resource, a window of opportunity exists for a potential attack in the brief interval between check and action. These attacks must be addressed in your security policy and in your security model. TOCTTOU attacks, race condition exploits, and communication disconnects are known as *state attacks* because they attack timing, data flow control, and transition between one system state to another.

Technology and Process Integration

It is important to evaluate and understand the vulnerabilities in system architectures, especially in regard to technology and process integration. As multiple technologies and complex processes are intertwined in the act of crafting new and unique business functions, new issues and security problems often surface. As systems are integrated, attention should be paid to potential single points of failure as well as to emergent weaknesses in service-oriented architecture (SOA). An SOA constructs new applications or functions out of existing but separate and distinct software services. The resulting application is often new; thus, its security issues are unknown, untested, and unprotected. All new deployments, especially new applications or functions, need to be thoroughly vetted before they are allowed to go live into a production network or the public Internet.

Electromagnetic Radiation

Simply because of the kinds of electronic components from which they're built, many computer hardware devices emit electromagnetic (EM) radiation during normal operation. The process of communicating with other machines or peripheral equipment creates emanations that can be intercepted. It's even possible to recreate keyboard input or monitor output by intercepting and processing electromagnetic radiation from the keyboard and computer monitor. You can also detect and read network packets passively (that is, without actually tapping into the cable) as they pass along a network segment. These emanation leaks can cause serious security issues but are generally easy to address.

The easiest way to eliminate electromagnetic radiation interception is to reduce emanation through cable shielding or conduit and block unauthorized personnel and devices from getting too close to equipment or cabling by applying physical security controls. By reducing the signal strength and increasing the physical buffer around sensitive equipment, you can dramatically reduce the risk of signal interception.

As discussed previously, several TEMPEST technologies could provide protection against EM radiation eavesdropping. These include Faraday cages, jamming or noise generators, and control zones. A *Faraday cage* is a special enclosure that acts as an EM capacitor. When a Faraday cage is in use, no EM signals can enter or leave the enclosed area. *Jamming* or *noise generators* use the idea that it is difficult or impossible to retrieve a signal when there is too much interference. Thus, by broadcasting your own interference, you can prevent unwanted EM interception. The only issue with this concept is that you have to ensure that the interference won't affect the normal operations of your devices. One way to ensure that is to use *control zones*, which are Faraday cages used to block purposely broadcast interference. For example, if you wanted to use wireless networking within a few rooms of your office but not allow it anywhere else, you could enclose those rooms in a single Faraday cage and then plant several noise generators outside the control zone. This would allow normal wireless networking within the designated rooms but completely prevent normal use and eavesdropping anywhere outside those designated areas.

Summary

Designing secure computing systems is a complex task, and many security engineers have dedicated their entire careers to understanding the innermost workings of information systems and ensuring that they support the core security functions required to safely operate in the current environment. Many security professionals don't necessarily require an in-depth knowledge of these principles, but they should have at least a broad understanding of the basic fundamentals that drive the process to enhance security within their own organizations.

Such understanding begins with an investigation of hardware, software, and firmware and how those pieces fit into the security puzzle. It's important to understand the principles of common computer and network organizations, architectures, and designs, including addressing (both physical and symbolic), the difference between address space and memory space, and machine types (real, virtual, multistate, multitasking, multiprogramming, multiprocessing, multiprocessor, and multiuser).

Additionally, a security professional must have a solid understanding of operating states (single state, multistate), operating modes (user, supervisor, privileged), storage types (primary, secondary, real, virtual, volatile, nonvolatile, random, sequential), and protection mechanisms (layering, abstraction, data hiding, process isolation, hardware segmentation, principle of least privilege, separation of privilege, accountability).

Avoiding single points of failure includes incorporating fault-tolerant systems and solutions into an environment's design. When designing a fault-tolerant system, you should make sure you include redundant or mirrored systems, use TFTP servers, address power issues, use RAID, and maintain a backup solution.

No matter how sophisticated a security model is, flaws exist that attackers can exploit. Some flaws, such as buffer overflows and maintenance hooks, are introduced by programmers, whereas others, such as covert channels, are architectural design issues. It is important to understand the impact of such issues and modify the security architecture when appropriate to compensate.

Exam Essentials

Be able to explain the differences between multitasking, multithreading, multiprocessing, and multiprogramming. Multitasking is the simultaneous execution of more than one application on a computer and is managed by the operating system. Multithreading permits multiple concurrent tasks to be performed within a single process. Multiprocessing is the use of more than one processor to increase computing power. Multiprogramming is similar to multitasking but takes place on mainframe systems and requires specific programming.

Understand the differences between single state processors and multistate processors.   Single state processors are capable of operating at only one security level at a time, whereas multistate processors can simultaneously operate at multiple security levels.

Describe the four security modes approved by the federal government for processing classified information.   Dedicated systems require that all users have appropriate clearance, access permissions, and need to know for all information stored on the system. System high mode removes the need-to-know requirement. Compartmented mode removes the need-to-know requirement and the access permission requirement. Multilevel mode removes all three requirements.

Explain the two layered operating modes used by most modern processors.   User applications operate in a limited instruction set environment known as user mode. The operating system performs controlled operations in privileged mode, also known as system mode, kernel mode, and supervisory mode.

Describe the different types of memory used by a computer.   ROM is nonvolatile and can't be written to by the end user. The end user can write data to PROM chips only once. EPROM chips may be erased through the use of ultraviolet light and then can have new data written to them. EEPROM chips may be erased with electrical current and then have new data written to them. RAM chips are volatile and lose their contents when the computer is powered off.

Know the security issues surrounding memory components.   Three main security issues surround memory components: the fact that data may remain on the chip after power is removed, the fact that memory chips are highly pilferable, and the control of access to memory in a multiuser system.

Describe the different characteristics of storage devices used by computers.   Primary storage is the same as memory. Secondary storage consists of magnetic and optical media that must be first read into primary memory before the CPU can use the data. Random access storage devices can be read at any point, whereas sequential access devices require scanning through all the data physically stored before the desired location.

Know the security issues surrounding secondary storage devices.   There are three main security issues surrounding secondary storage devices: Removable media can be used to steal data, access controls and encryption must be applied to protect data, and data can remain on the media even after file deletion or media formatting.

Understand security risks that input and output devices can pose.   Input/output devices can be subject to eavesdropping and tapping, used to smuggle data out of an organization, or used to create unauthorized, insecure points of entry into an organization's systems and networks. Be prepared to recognize and mitigate such vulnerabilities.

Understand I/O addresses, configuration, and setup.   Working with legacy PC devices requires some understanding of IRQs, DMA, and memory-mapped I/O. Be prepared to recognize and work around potential address conflicts and misconfigurations and to integrate legacy devices with Plug and Play (PnP) counterparts.

Know the purpose of firmware.   Firmware is software stored on a ROM chip. At the computer level, it contains the basic instructions needed to start a computer. Firmware is also used to provide operating instructions in peripheral devices such as printers.

Be able to describe process isolation, layering, abstraction, data hiding, and hardware segmentation.   Process isolation ensures that individual processes can access only their own data. Layering creates different realms of security within a process and limits communication between them. Abstraction creates "black-box" interfaces for programmers to use without requiring knowledge of an algorithm's or device's inner workings. Data hiding prevents information from being read from a different security level. Hardware segmentation enforces process isolation with physical controls.

Understand how a security policy drives system design, implementation, testing, and deployment.   The role of a security policy is to inform and guide the design, development, implementation, testing, and maintenance of some particular system.

Understand cloud computing.   Cloud computing is the popular term referring to a concept of computing where processing and storage are performed elsewhere over a network connection rather than locally. Cloud computing is often thought of as Internet-based computing.

Understand how the principle of least privilege, separation of privilege, and accountability apply to computer architecture.   The principle of least privilege ensures that only a minimum number of processes are authorized to run in supervisory mode. Separation of privilege increases the granularity of secure operations. Accountability ensures that an audit trail exists to trace operations back to their source.

Understand the issues around single points of failure.   Avoiding single points of failure includes incorporating fault-tolerant systems and solutions into an environment's design. Fault-tolerant systems include redundant or mirrored systems, TFTP servers, and RAID. You should also address power issues and maintain a backup solution.

Be able to explain what covert channels are.   A covert channel is any method that is used to pass information but that is not normally used for information.

Understand what buffer overflows and input checking are.   A buffer overflow occurs when the programmer fails to check the size of input data prior to writing the data into a specific memory location. In fact, any failure to validate input data could result in a security violation.

Describe common flaws to security architectures.   In addition to buffer overflows, programmers can leave back doors and privileged programs on a system after it is deployed. Even well-written systems can be susceptible to time-of-check-to-time-of-use (TOCTTOU) attacks. Any state change could be a potential window of opportunity for an attacker to compromise a system.

Written Lab

1. What are the terms used to describe the various computer mechanisms that allow multiple simultaneous activities?

2. What are the four security modes for systems processing classified information?

3. Name the three pairs of aspects or features used to describe storage.

4. Name some vulnerabilities found in distributed architectures.

Review Questions

1. Many PC operating systems provide functionality that enables them to support the simultaneous execution of multiple applications on single-processor systems. What term is used to describe this capability?

   A. Multiprogramming

   B. Multithreading

   C. Multitasking

   D. Multiprocessing

2. Which one of the following devices is most susceptible to TEMPEST monitoring of its emanations?

   A. Floppy drive

   B. CRT Monitor

   C. CD

   D. Keyboard

3. You have three applications running on a single-core single-processor system that supports multitasking. One of those applications is a word processing program that is managing two threads simultaneously. The other two applications are using only one thread of execution. How many application threads are running on the processor at any given time?

   A. One

   B. Two

   C. Three

   D. Four

4. What type of federal government computing system requires that all individuals accessing the system have a need to know all of the information processed by that system?

   A. Dedicated

   B. System high

   C. Compartmented

   D. Multilevel

5. What term describes the processor mode used to run the system tools used by administrators seeking to make configuration changes to a machine?

   A. User mode

   B. Supervisory mode

   C. Kernel mode

   D. Privileged mode

6. What type of memory chip allows the end user to write information to the memory only one time and then preserves that information indefinitely without the possibility of erasure?

   A. ROM

   B. PROM

   C. EPROM

   D. EEPROM

7. Which type of memory chip can be erased only when it is removed from the computer and exposed to a special type of ultraviolet light?

   A. ROM

   B. PROM

   C. EPROM

   D. EEPROM

8. Which one of the following types of memory might retain information after being removed from a computer and, therefore, represent a security risk?

   A. Static RAM

   B. Dynamic RAM

   C. Secondary memory

   D. Real memory

9. Why do operating systems need security mechanisms?

   A. Humans are perfect.

   B. Software is not trusted.

   C. Technology is always improving.

   D. Hardware is faulty.

10. What type of electrical component serves as the primary building block for dynamic RAM chips?

    A. Capacitor

    B. Resistor

    C. Flip-flop

    D. Transistor

11. Which one of the following storage devices is most likely to require encryption technology in order to maintain data security in a networked environment?

    A. Hard disk

    B. Backup tape

    C. Removable drives

    D. RAM

12. In which of the following security modes can you be assured that all users have access permissions for all information processed by the system but will not necessarily need to know of all that information?

    A. Dedicated

    B. System high

    C. Compartmented

    D. Multilevel

13. Which one of the following security modes does *not* require that all users have a security clearance for the highest level of information processed by the system?

    A. Dedicated

    B. System high

    C. Compartmented

    D. Multilevel

14. What type of memory device is usually used to contain a computer's motherboard BIOS?

    A. PROM

    B. EEPROM

    C. ROM

    D. EPROM

15. What type of memory is directly available to the CPU and is often part of the CPU?

    A. RAM

    B. ROM

    C. Register memory

    D. Virtual memory

16. In what type of addressing scheme is the data actually supplied to the CPU as an argument to the instruction?

    A. Direct addressing

    B. Immediate addressing

    C. Base+offset addressing

    D. Indirect addressing

17. What type of addressing scheme supplies the CPU with a location that contains the memory address of the actual operand?

    A. Direct addressing

    B. Immediate addressing

    C. Base+offset addressing

    D. Indirect addressing

18. What security principle helps prevent users from accessing memory spaces assigned to applications being run by other users?

    A. Separation of privilege

    B. Layering

    C. Process isolation

    D. Least privilege

19. Which security principle mandates that only a minimum number of operating system processes should run in supervisory mode?

    A. Abstraction

    B. Layering

    C. Data hiding

    D. Least privilege

20. Which security principle takes the concept of process isolation and implements it using physical controls?

    A. Hardware segmentation

    B. Data hiding

    C. Layering

    D. Abstraction

Chapter

13

Security Operations

THE CISSP EXAM TOPICS COVERED IN THIS CHAPTER INCLUDE:

7. Security Operations

  A. Understand security operations concepts

  A.1 Need-to-know/least privilege

  A.2 Separation of duties and responsibilities

  A.3 Monitor special privileges (e.g., operators, administrators)

  A.4 Job rotation

  A.5 Marking, handling, storing, and destroying of sensitive information

  A.6 Record retention

  B. Employ resource protection

  B.1 Media management

  B.2 Asset management (e.g., equipment life cycle, software licensing)

  E. Implement and support patch and vulnerability management

  F. Understand change and configuration management (e.g., versioning, baselining)

The Security Operations domain is focused on identifying and protecting critical information within an organization. There are several core security operations concepts that any organization needs to implement to provide basic security protection, and these concepts are covered in the first section of this chapter. Resource protection ensures that media and other assets that are valuable to an organization are protected throughout the lifetime of the resource.

Patch and vulnerability management controls ensure that systems are kept up-to-date and protected against known vulnerabilities. Configuration management helps ensure that systems are configured similarly, and change management protects against outages from unauthorized changes. Security audits of these controls provide assurances that the controls are in place and providing the desired protections.

The Security Operations domain is discussed in this chapter and further in the following chapter (Chapter 14, "Incident Management"). Be sure to read and study the materials from both chapters to ensure complete coverage of the essential material for this domain.

Security Operations Concepts

The primary purpose for security operations practices is to safeguard information assets that reside in a system on a day-to-day basis, to identify and safeguard any vulnerabilities that might be present in the system, and to prevent any exploitation of threats.

Chapter 5, "Security Governance Concepts, Principles, and Policies," introduced due care and due diligence. As a reminder, in the context of IT security, due care and due diligence refers to taking reasonable care to protect the assets of an organization on an ongoing basis. Senior management has a direct responsibility to exercise due care and due diligence. Implementing the common security operations concepts covered in the following sections, along with performing periodic security audits and reviews, demonstrates a level of due care and diligence that will reduce senior management's liability when a loss occurs.

Need to Know and Least Privilege

Need to know and least privilege are two standard principles followed in any secure IT environment. They help provide protection for valuable assets by limiting the access to the assets. Though they are related and the terms are often used interchangeably, there is a distinctive difference between the two. Need to know focuses on permissions and the ability to access information, while least privilege focuses on privileges, which include both rights and permissions.

Chapter 1, "Access Control," compared permissions, rights, and privileges. As a reminder, permissions are granted to allow access to objects such as files. Rights refer to the ability to take actions. Access rights are synonymous with permissions, but rights can also refer to the ability to take action on a system, such as the right to change the system time. Combined, rights and permissions are commonly referred to as privileges.

Need-to-Know Access

The *need to know principle* imposes the requirement that users are granted access only to data or resources they need to perform assigned work tasks. The primary purpose is to keep secret information secret. If you want to keep a secret, the best way is to tell no one. If you're the only person that knows it, you can ensure that it remains a secret. Tell a trusted friend, and it will likely remain secret. However, the risk of the secret's leaking out to others increases as more and more people learn it. Limit the people who know and you increase the chances of keeping it secret.

Need to know is commonly associated with security clearances. Access is not based on a user's clearance, but instead on the user's actual need. Even if users have an equal or greater security classification than the requested information, if they do not have a need to know, they are denied access. For example, Sally may have a secret clearance, indicating that she is cleared to access any secret data. However, she is granted access only to the secret data she actually needs.

The same concept is also used in civilian organizations. For example, database administrators may need access to a database server to perform maintenance, but they don't need access to all the data within the server's databases. Restricting access based on a need to know helps ensure that data is not inadvertently accessed.

The Principle of Least Privilege

The *principle of least privilege* states that subjects are granted only the privileges necessary to perform assigned work tasks and no more. Keep in mind that the idea of privilege often means the ability to write, create, alter, or delete data. Thus, limiting and controlling privilege based upon this concept can be a protection mechanism for data integrity. If users can change only those data files that their work tasks require them to change, then the integrity of all other files in the environment is protected.

The principle of least privilege relies on the assumption that all users have a definite and distinct job description that is well defined and understood. Without a specific job description, it is not possible to know what privileges a user does or does not need.

This principle extends beyond just accessing data though. It also applies to system access. For example, in many networks, regular users have the ability to log onto any computer in the network using a network account. However, organizations commonly restrict this privilege by preventing regular users from logging onto servers or restricting a user to a single system.

A common way the principle of least privilege is violated is by adding all users to the local Administrators group or granting root access to a computer. This gives the users full control over the computer, which is rarely needed by regular users.

Least privilege is usually focused on ensuring that user privileges are restricted, but it also applies to other subjects, such as applications or processes. Application developers often write an application with the assumption that it will have full access to an IT system. But when full access is granted, it results in increased risks. An implicit deny philosophy is often used in conjunction with a least privilege policy. In other words, all privileges are blocked unless they are specifically granted.

Separation of Duties and Responsibilities

Separation of duties and responsibilities ensures that no single person has total control over a critical function or system. This is necessary to ensure that no single person can compromise the system, or its security. Instead, two or more people must conspire or collude against the organization.

A separation of duties policy creates a checks-and-balances system where multiple users verify each other's actions and must work in concert to accomplish necessary work tasks. This makes it more difficult for individuals to engage in malicious, fraudulent, or unauthorized activities and broadens the scope of detection and reporting. Individuals may be more inclined to perform unauthorized acts if they think they can get away with them, but with two or more people involved, the risk of detection increases.

Here's a simple example: Movie theatres use separation of duties to prevent fraud. One person sells tickets, and another person collects the tickets and doesn't allow entry to individuals that don't have a ticket. If the same person collects the money and grants entry, this person can allow people in without a ticket or pocket the collected money without issuing a ticket. While it is still possible for these two people to scheme to steal from the theatre, it takes more effort and increases the risk to each of them.

Similarly, organizations often break down processes into multiple tasks or duties and assign these duties to different individuals to prevent fraud. For example, one person may be authorized to approve payment for a valid invoice, but someone else must actually make the payment. If one person controlled the entire process of approval and payment, it would be easy to approve bogus invoices and defraud the company.

Another way separation of duties is enforced is by dividing the security or administrative capabilities and functions among multiple trusted individuals. When administration and security responsibilities are divided among several users, no one person has sufficient access to circumvent or disable security mechanisms.

Separation of Privilege

Separation of privilege is similar in concept to separation of duties and responsibilities. It builds upon the principle of least privilege and applies it to applications and processes. A separation of privilege policy requires the use of granular access rights and permissions. Different rights and permissions are assigned for each type of privileged operation. Specific processes are granted only the privileges necessary to perform certain functions without granting them unrestricted access to the system.

Many server applications have underlying services that support the applications. These services must run in the context of an account, commonly called a service account. In the past, many application developers required these service accounts to have administrative privileges, which were often more than what was actually required. If the server is attacked and compromised, the attacker can assume the role of the service account. If this account has administrative privileges, the attacker has these same administrative privileges.

It is common today for server applications to have multiple service accounts. Each service account can be granted only the privileges needed to perform its functions to support a segregation of privilege policy.

Segregation of Duties

Segregation of duties is similar to a separation of duties and responsibilities policy, but it also combines the principle of least privilege. The goal is to ensure that individuals do not have excessive system access that may result in a conflict of interest. When duties are properly segregated, no single employee will have both the ability to commit fraud or make a mistake and the ability to cover it up. It's similar to separation of duties in that duties are separated, and it's also similar to a principle of least privilege in that privileges are limited.

A segregation of duties policy is highly relevant for any company that must abide by the Sarbanes-Oxley Act of 2002 (SOX) because SOX specifically requires it. However, segregation of duties policies also have applications in any IT environment.

 SOX applies to all public companies that have registered equity or debt securities with the Securities and Exchange Commission (SEC). It was passed in response to several high-profile financial scandals that resulted in the loss of billions of shareholder dollars.

One of the most common implementations of segregation of duties policies is ensuring that security duties are separate from other duties within an organization. In other words, anyone responsible for auditing, monitoring, and reviewing security should not have other operational duties. Whenever security duties are combined with other operational duties, an individual can use their security privileges to cover up activities related to their operational duties.

Figure 13.1 is a basic segregation of duties control matrix comparing different roles and tasks within an organization. The areas marked with an X indicate potential conflicts that should be avoided. For example, consider an application programmer and a security administrator. The programmer can make unauthorized modifications to an application, but auditing or reviews by a security administrator would detect the unauthorized modifications. However, if a single person had the duties (and the privileges) of both jobs, this person could modify the application and then cover up the modifications to prevent detection.

FIGURE 13.1   A segregation of duties control matrix

	Control Group	Systems Analyst	Application Programmer	Help Desk and Support Mgr.	End User	Data Entry	Computer Operator	DB Administrator	Network Administrator	System Administrator	Security Administrator	Tape Librarian	Systems Programmer	Quality Assurance
Control Group		X	X	X		X	X	X	X	X			X	
Systems Analyst	X			X	X		X				X	X		
Application Programmer	X			X	X	X	X	X	X	X	X	X	X	
Help Desk and Support Mgr.	X	X	X		X	X		X	X	X		X	X	
End User		X	X	X			X	X	X			X	X	X
Data Entry	X		X	X			X	X	X	X	X		X	
Computer Operator	X	X	X		X	X		X	X	X	X		X	
DB Administrator	X		X	X	X	X	X		X	X			X	
Network Administrator	X		X	X	X	X	X	X				X		
System Administrator	X		X	X		X	X	X				X		
Security Administrator		X	X			X	X					X	X	
Tape Librarian		X	X	X	X				X	X	X		X	
Systems Programmer	X		X	X	X	X	X	X			X	X		X
Quality Assurance				X								X	X	

X—Combination of these functions may create a potential control weakness.

A segregation of duties control matrix is not an industry standard but instead is tailored to fit an organization based on the roles and responsibilities of employees within the organization. The matrix shown in Figure 13.1 can be used as a guide to help identify potential conflicts. If necessary, compensating controls can be used to mitigate risks from these conflicts.

Two-Person Control

Two-person control (often called the two-man rule) is similar to segregation of duties. It requires the approval of two individuals for critical tasks. For example, safety deposit boxes in banks often require two keys. One key is controlled by a bank employee and the second key is held by the customer. The box can be opened only with both keys, and bank employees allow a customer access to the box only after verifying the customer's identification.

Using two-person controls within an organization ensures peer review and reduces the likelihood of collusion and fraud. For example, an organization can require key business decisions to be approved by two individuals within the company, such as the chief financial officer (CFO) and the chief executive officer (CEO). Additionally, some privileged activities can be configured so that they require two administrators to work together to complete a task.

Split knowledge combines the concepts of separation of duties and two-person control into a single solution. The basic idea is that the information or privilege required to perform an operation is divided among multiple users. This ensures that no single person has sufficient privileges to compromise the security of the environment.

Reducing Opportunities for Collusion

Collusion is an agreement among multiple people to perform an unauthorized or illegal action. It is hindered by implementing separation of duties, job rotation, and mandatory vacation policies. Together, these policies reduce the likelihood that a co-worker will agree to collaborate on an illegal or abusive scheme because of the higher risk of detection. The movie *Office Space* gives a great satirical example of collusion.

The movie depicts three disenfranchised workers—Peter, Michael, and Samir—plotting to embezzle money from an imaginary company (Initech). They work together to create and install a virus in the accounting system. Their goal is steal fractional portions of pennies in each transaction in a classic salami attack. The loss of fractions of pennies from a transaction will likely not be discovered, but it can add up with millions of transactions. Unfortunately, the virus has a misplaced decimal point, which results in their stealing over $300,000 in just a few days.

Although the movie is fictional, there are real-world accounts of such crimes, resulting in both success and failure. Implementing basic security controls helps prevent attacks in which employees decide to act in collusion against the organization.

Job Rotation

Further control and restriction of privileged capabilities can be implemented by using *job rotation*. Job rotation (sometimes called rotation of duties) means simply that employees are rotated through jobs, or at least some of the job responsibilities are rotated to different employees. Using job rotation as a security control provides peer review, reduces collusion and fraud, and enables cross-training. Cross-training helps make an environment less dependent on any single individual.

Job rotation can act as both a deterrent and a detection mechanism. If employees know that someone else will be taking over their job responsibilities at some point in the future, they are less likely to take part in fraudulent activities. If they choose to do so anyway, individuals taking over the job responsibilities later are likely to discover the fraud.

Mandatory Vacations

Many organizations require employees to take *mandatory vacations* in one-week or two-week increments. This provides a form of peer review and also helps detect fraud and collusion. This policy ensures that another employee takes over an individual's job responsibilities for at least a week. If an employee is involved in fraud, the person taking over the responsibilities is likely to discover it.

Financial organizations are at risk of significant losses from fraud and collusion by employees. They often use job rotation, separation of duties and responsibilities, and mandatory vacation policies to reduce these risks. Combined, these policies help prevent incidents and help detect them when they occur.

Monitor Special Privileges

Special privilege operations are activities that require special access or elevated rights and permissions to perform many administrative and sensitive job tasks. Examples of these tasks include creating new user accounts, adding new routes to a router table, altering the configuration of a firewall, and accessing system log and audit files. Using common security practices, such as the principle of least privilege, ensures that only a limited number of people have these special privileges. Monitoring ensures that users granted these privileges do not abuse them.

Accounts granted elevated privileges are often referred to as privileged entities that have access to special, higher-order capabilities inaccessible to normal users. If misused, these elevated rights and permissions can result in significant harm to the confidentiality, integrity, or availability of an organization's assets. Because of this, it's important to monitor privileged entities and their access.

In most cases, these elevated privileges are restricted to administrators and certain system operators. In this context, a system operator is a user that needs additional privileges to perform specific job functions. Regular users (or regular system operators) only need the most basic privileges to perform their jobs.

Employees filling these privileged roles are usually trusted employees. However, there are many reasons why an employee can change from a trusted employee to a disgruntled employee, or malicious insider. Reasons that can change a trusted employee's behavior can be as simple as a lower-than-expected bonus, a negative performance review, or just a personal grudge against another employee. However, by monitoring usage of special privileges, an organization can deter an employee from misusing the privileges, and detect the action if a trusted employee does misuse them.

In general, any type of administrator account has elevated privileges and should be monitored. However, privileges can also be granted without giving a user full administrative access. The following list includes some examples of privileged operations to monitor. Many automated tools are available that can monitor these activities and send alerts when the privileges are used:

- Accessing audit logs
- Changing system time
- Configuring interfaces
- Managing user accounts
- Controlling system reboots
- Controlling communication paths
- Backing up and restoring the system
- Running script/task automation tools
- Configuring security mechanism controls
- Using operating system control commands
- Using database recovery tools and log files

 The principle of monitoring special privileges is intended to be used in conjunction with other basic principles, such as least privilege and separation of duties and responsibilities. In other words, principles such as least privilege and separation of duties are implemented to prevent security policy violations, and monitoring is performed to deter and detect any violations that occur despite the use of preventive controls.

Managing Sensitive Information

Sensitive information is any information that isn't public or unclassified. It can include confidential, proprietary, or any other type of data that an organization needs to protect due to its value to the organization. Chapter 2, "Access Control Attacks and Monitoring" covered logging and audit trail data. It's common to define logs and audit trails as sensitive information and protect it as such.

Chapter 5 discussed the importance of classifying data. Data classifications used by governments are often labeled top secret, secret, confidential, sensitive but unclassified, and unclassified. Civilian classifications are often confidential, private, sensitive, and public. Both government and civilian classifications identify the relative value of the data to the organization, with top secret representing the highest classification for governments and confidential representing the highest classification for organizations. When these labels are used, sensitive information is any information that isn't unclassified (when using the government labels) or isn't public (when using the civilian classifications).

Civilian organizations aren't required to use any specific classification labels. However, no matter what labels an organization uses, it still has an obligation to protect sensitive information.

After classifying the data, an organization takes additional steps to manage it based on its classification. Unauthorized access to sensitive information can result in significant losses to an organization. However, these losses can be prevented by properly marking, handling, storing, and destroying it based on its classification.

Personally Identifiable Information

Personally identifiable information (PII) is also considered sensitive information. In general, PII is any information that can identify an individual. There are several legal definitions. For example, the US Government Accountability Office defines PII as "any information about an individual maintained by an agency, including (1) any information that can be used to distinguish or trace an individual's identity, such as name, social security number, date and place of birth, mother's maiden name, or biometric records; and (2) any other information that is linked or linkable to an individual, such as medical, educational, financial, and employment information."

Protection for personally identifiable information (PII) drives privacy and confidentiality requirements for rules, regulations, and legislation all over the world (especially in North America and the European Union). NIST publication 800-122, *Guide to Protecting the Confidentiality of Personally Identifiable Information (PII)*, provides more information on how to protect PII. It is available from the NIST Special Publications (800 Series) download page: http://csrc.nist.gov/publications/PubsSPs.html

Marking Sensitive Information

Marking (often called labeling) sensitive information ensures that users can easily identify the classification level of any data. The most important information that a mark or a label provides is the classification of the data. For example, a label of Top Secret makes it clear to anyone that sees the label that the information is classified top secret. When users know the value of the data, they are more likely to take appropriate steps to control and protect it based on the classification. Marking includes both physical and electronic marking and labels.

Physical labels are used to indicate the security classification for the data stored on media or processed on a system. For example, if a backup tape includes secret data, a physical label should be attached to the tape so that users know it holds secret data. Similarly, if a computer is used to process sensitive information, the computer would have a label indicating the highest classification of information that it processes. For example, if a computer is used to process confidential, secret, and top secret data, it should be marked with a label indicating that it processes top secret data.

In many secure environments, labels are also used for unclassified media and equipment. This prevents an error of omission where sensitive information isn't marked and is assumed to be unclassified.

Physical labels should be maintained over the entire lifetime of the system or media. Media used to store classified information should never be reused to store less-sensitive data unless a trusted method of purging and sanitization has been used to ensure that it no longer holds sensitive information. Similarly, systems are rarely downgraded. In other words, if a system has been processing secret data, it would be rare to downgrade it and relabel it as an unclassified system.

> If media or a system needs to be downgraded to a less-sensitive classification, it must be sanitized using appropriate procedures as described in the section "Destroying Sensitive Information" later in this chapter. However, it's often safer and easier to just purchase new media or equipment rather than follow through with the sanitization steps for reuse. Many organizations adopt a policy that media and systems are never downgraded.

Marking also includes using different types of digital marks or labels on systems and stored data. Instead of colorful pictures as a desktop background, an image can be used to clearly identify the classification of the system. Backup tapes often include header information, and the classification can be included in the header. Most files include the ability to include headers and footers, and these can be used to clearly mark the data. An added benefit of headers and footers is that they also appear on printouts. Even when headers and footers are used for printouts, most organizations require any printed sensitive information to be placed within a folder that includes a label clearly indicating the classification.

Handling Sensitive Information

Handling refers to the secure transportation of media through its lifetime. Information is handled differently depending on its value and classification, and as you'd expect, highly classified information needs much greater protection. Even though this is common sense, it isn't always followed. Many times people get accustomed to handling sensitive information and become lackadaisical with it.

For example, it was reported in April 2011 that the United Kingdom's Ministry of Defence mistakenly published classified information on nuclear submarines, in addition to other sensitive information, in response to Freedom of Information requests. They redacted the classified data by using image editing software to black it out when it was displayed. However, anyone who tried to copy the data was able to copy all the text, including the blacked-out data.

A common occurrence is the loss of control of backup tapes. Backup tapes should be protected with the same level of protection as the data that is backed up. In other words, if sensitive information is on a backup tape, the backup tape should be protected as sensitive information, but there are many examples where this just isn't followed. In 2011, Science Applications International Corporation (SAIC), a government contractor, lost control of backup tapes that included PII and personal health information (PHI) for 4.9 million patients. Because it is PHI, it falls under the Health Insurance Portability and Accountability Act (HIPAA) and required specific actions to protect it that apparently weren't implemented.

Policies and procedures need to be in place to ensure that people understand how to handle sensitive information. Additionally, as President Reagan famously said when discussing relations with the Soviet Union, "Trust, but verify." Chapter 2 discussed the importance of logging, monitoring, and auditing. These controls can be used to verify that sensitive information is handled appropriately before a significant loss occurs. If a loss does occur, audit trails can be used to help discover what went wrong. Any incidents that occur when data isn't handled appropriately should be quickly investigated and actions should be taken to prevent a reoccurrence.

Storing Sensitive Information

Sensitive information should be stored to ensure that it is protected against any type of loss. If sensitive information is stored on physical media, physical security practices should be followed to prevent losses due to theft. This includes storing sensitive data in locked safes or vaults and/or within a secure room that includes several additional physical controls, such as a server room within an organization. Additionally, environmental controls should be used to protect the media, as discussed in the section "Media Management" later in this chapter.

The value of any sensitive data is much greater than the value of the media it is stored on. In other words, it's cost effective to purchase high-quality media, especially if the data will be stored for a long time, such as on backup tapes.

Encryption of sensitive data provides an additional layer of protection and should be considered for any data at rest. Data at rest is any data stored on any type of media. If data is encrypted, it becomes much more difficult for an attacker to access it, even if it is stolen.

Destroying Sensitive Information

When data is no longer needed, it should be destroyed. Proper destruction ensures that it cannot fall into the wrong hands and result in unauthorized disclosure. Highly classified data requires different steps to destroy it than data classified at a lower level, and the requirements to destroy each should be spelled out in the organization's policies. For example, an organization may require the complete destruction of media holding highly classified data, but software tools may be used to overwrite data files classified at a lower level.

Data remanence is the data that remains after it has supposedly been removed. Using system tools to delete data generally leaves much of the data remaining on the media, and widely available tools can easily undelete it. Even when more sophisticated tools are used to overwrite the media, traces of the original data may still remain as less-perceptible magnetic fields. This is similar to a ghost image that can remain on some TV or computer monitors if the same data is displayed for long periods of time. Forensics experts and attackers have tools they can use to retrieve this data even after it has been supposedly overwritten.

Be careful when performing any type of clearing, purging, or sanitization process. The human operator or the tool involved in the activity may not properly perform the task of completely removing data from the media. Software can be flawed, magnets can be faulty, and either can be used improperly. Always verify that the desired result is achieved after performing any sanitization process.

The following list includes some of the common terms associated with destroying data:

Erasing   *Erasing* media is simply performing a delete operation against a file, a selection of files, or the entire media. In most cases, the deletion or removal process removes only the directory or catalog link to the data. The actual data remains on the drive and can be retrieved with widely available tools. As new files are written to the media, the erased data will be overwritten.

Clearing   *Clearing*, or *overwriting*, is a process of preparing media for reuse and assuring that the cleared data cannot be recovered using traditional recovery tools. When media is cleared, unclassified data is written over all addressable locations on the media. One method writes a single character, or a specific bit pattern, over the entire media. A more thorough method writes a single character over the entire media, writes the character's complement over the entire media, and then writes random bits over the entire media in three separate passes, as shown in Figure 13.2. While this sounds like the original data is lost forever, it is sometimes possible to retrieve some of the original data using sophisticated laboratory or forensics techniques. Additionally, some types of data storage don't respond well to clearing: spare sectors on hard drives, sectors labeled as "bad," and areas on many modern solid state drives (SSDs) are not cleared when this process is followed.

FIGURE 13.2 Clearing a hard drive

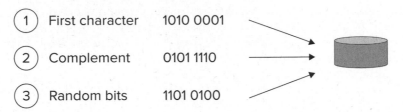

Purging *Purging* is a more intense form of clearing that prepares media for reuse in less-secure environments. It provides a level of assurance that the original data is not recoverable using any known methods. A purging process will repeat the clearing process multiple times and may combine it with another method such as degaussing to completely remove the data. Even though purging is intended to remove all data remanence, it isn't always trusted. For example, the US government doesn't consider any purging method acceptable to purge top secret data. Media labeled top secret will always remain top secret until it is destroyed.

Declassification *Declassification* involves any process that purges media or a system in preparation for reuse in an unclassified environment. Purging can be used to prepare media for declassification, but often the efforts required to securely declassify media are significantly greater than the cost of new media for a less-secure environment. Additionally, even though purged data is not recoverable using any known methods, there is a remote possibility that an unknown method is available. Instead of taking the risk, many organizations choose not to declassify any media.

Sanitization *Sanitization* is a combination of processes that removes data from a system or from media. It ensures that data cannot be recovered by any means. When a computer is disposed of, sanitization includes ensuring that all nonvolatile memory has been removed or destroyed, the system doesn't have CD/DVDs in any drive, and hard drives have been purged, removed, and/or destroyed. Sanitization can also refer to the destruction of media or using a trusted method to purge classified data from the media without destroying it.

Degaussing A degausser creates a strong magnetic field and can be used to erase data on some media in a process called *degaussing*. It is commonly used to remove data from magnetic tapes with the goal of returning the tape to its original state. While it is possible to degauss hard disks, it is not recommended. Degaussing a hard disk will normally destroy it, but there isn't any assurance that all of the data on the disk has actually been destroyed. Degaussing does not affect optical CDs or DVDs.

Destruction Destruction is the final stage in the life cycle of media. Destruction should occur after proper sanitization or as a means of sanitization. When media destruction takes place, you must ensure that the media cannot be reused or repaired and that data cannot be extracted from the destroyed media by any possible means. Methods of destruction can include incineration, crushing, shredding, and dissolving using caustic or acidic chemicals. Some organizations remove the platters in highly classified disk drives and destroy them separately.

When used computer equipment is donated or sold, it is usually recommended that you remove and destroy storage devices that held sensitive data rather than attempting to purge them. This eliminates the risk that the purging process wasn't complete, thus resulting in a loss of confidentiality.

Record Retention

Record retention involves retaining and maintaining important information as long as it is needed and also destroying it when it is no longer needed. An organization should have a policy that defines what information is maintained and for how long. Some laws and regulations dictate the length of time that data should be maintained, such as three years, seven years, or even indefinitely. However, even in the absence of external requirements, an organization should still identify how long to retain data.

 Many organizations have retention policies that require all logs used for audit trails to be maintained for three years or longer. This allows the organization to reconstruct the details of past security incidents.

When a retention policy is not identified, administrators may delete valuable data earlier than management expects them to or attempt to keep data indefinitely. The longer data is retained, the more it costs in terms of media and locations to store it and personnel to protect it.

 Real World Scenario

Retention Policies Can Reduce Liabilities

Saving data longer than necessary also presents unnecessary legal issues. Aircraft manufacturer Boeing was the target of a class action lawsuit in 1997. Attorneys for the claimants learned that Boeing had a warehouse filled with 14,000 email backup tapes and demanded the relevant tapes. Not all of the tapes were relevant to the lawsuit, but Boeing had to first restore the 14,000 tapes and examine the contents before they could turn them over. It ended up settling the lawsuit for $92.5 million, and analysts indicate that there would have been a different outcome if those 14,000 tapes hadn't existed.

The Boeing example is an extreme example, but it's not the only one. These events have prompted many companies to implement aggressive email retention policies. It is not uncommon for an email policy to require the deletion of all emails older than six months. These policies are often implemented using automated tools that search for old emails and delete them without any user or administrator intervention.

A company cannot legally delete data after a lawsuit is filed. However, if a retention policy dictates deleting data after a specific amount of time and the policy is followed, it is perfectly legal. Not only does this practice prevent wasting resources to store unneeded data, it also provides an added layer of legal protection against wasting resources by looking through old information.

Resource Protection

Resource protection refers to the protection of any type of resources valuable to an organization. In general, you can provide protection to resources using media management and asset management. The previous sections described how to mark, handle, store, and destroy sensitive information, and much of that topic applies to managing and protecting media. Asset management extends beyond just media to anything of value to an organization and is explained within the following sections.

The updated CISSP Candidate Information Bulletin (CIB) removed personnel privacy and protection from the Operations Security domain. This isn't to say that personnel privacy and protection isn't important. It is. However, the topics are covered in other domains. For example, the Information Security Governance and Risk Management domain includes "Privacy requirements compliance" and "Manage personnel security." These topics were directly covered in Chapter 5, and Chapter 6, "Risk and Personnel Management."

Media Management

Media management refers to the steps taken to protect media and the data it contains. In this context, media is anything that can hold data. It includes tapes, optical media such as CDs and DVDs, portable USB or FireWire drives, external SATA (eSATA) drives, internal hard drives, and USB flash drives. Many portable devices, such as smartphones, include memory cards that can hold data, so they fall into this category too. Media also includes any type of hard copy data. Chapter 16, "Disaster Recovery Planning," covers backups and the importance of offsite storage in depth. Backups are often contained on tapes, so media management directly relates to tapes. However, media management extends beyond just backup tapes to any type of media that can hold data.

When media includes sensitive information, it should be stored in a secure location with strict access controls to prevent losses due to unauthorized access. Additionally, any location used to store media should have temperature and humidity controls to prevent losses due to corruption.

Media management can also include technical controls to control what devices can be connected to a system or to control the media when it is connected. For example, due to the risks USB drives represent, technical controls can block their use and/or detect and record when they are being used. In some situations, a written security policy mandates that USB flash drives are not to be used, and automated detection methods are used to detect and report any violations.

The primary risks from USB flash drives are malware infections and data theft. A system infected with a virus can detect when a USB drive is inserted and infect the USB drive. When this drive is inserted into another system, it can infect the second system. Additionally, malicious users can easily copy and transfer large amounts of data and conceal the drive in their pocket.

Properly managing media directly addresses confidentiality, integrity and availability. When media is marked, handled, and stored properly, it helps prevent unauthorized disclosure (loss of confidentiality), unauthorized modification (loss of integrity), and unauthorized destruction (loss of availability).

Controlling USB Flash Drives

Many organizations restrict the use of USB flash drives to only specific brands purchased and provided by the organization. This allows the organization to protect data on the drives and also ensure that the drives are not being used to inadvertently transfer malicious software (malware) between systems. Users still have the benefit of the USB flash drives, but the risk to the organization is reduced.

For example, Imation sells IronKey flash drives that include multiple levels of built-in protection. Several authentication mechanisms are available to ensure that only authorized users can access data on the drive, and data is protected with built-in AES 256-bit hardware-based encryption. Active antimalware software on the flash drive helps prevent the drive from being infected with malware. The enterprise edition of IronKey also includes what is called the "Silver Bullet Service," used to protect data on lost or stolen devices; this service can remotely deny all access to the data, disable the device, or initiate a self-destruct sequence to destroy it. "Self-destruct" may evoke an image of a massive explosion from a science fiction movie. The IronKey self-destruct feature won't cause an explosion but instead destroys all the data and settings on the drive.

Tape Media

Tapes are commonly used for backup, and they are the most susceptible to loss due to corruption. As a best practice, at least two copies of backups are kept. One is kept onsite for immediate usage, and a second is kept at a secure location offsite. If a catastrophic disaster such as a fire destroys the primary location, the data is still available at the alternate location.

The cleanliness of the storage area will directly affect the life span and usefulness of tape media. Additionally, they should not be exposed to magnetic fields that can come from elevator motors, printers, and older CRT monitors. These magnetic fields can act as a degausser and erase or corrupt data on the tape. Here are some useful guidelines for managing tape media:

- Keep new media in its original sealed packaging until it's needed to protect it from dust and dirt.

- When opening a media package, take extra caution not to damage the media in any way. This includes avoiding sharp objects and not twisting or flexing the media.

- Avoid exposing the media to temperature extremes; it shouldn't be stored close to heaters, radiators, air conditioners, or other sources of extreme temperatures.

- Do not use media that has been damaged, exposed to abnormal levels of dust and dirt, or dropped.

- Media should be transported from one site to another in a temperature-controlled vehicle.

- Media should be protected from exposure to the outside environment; avoid sunlight, moisture, humidity, heat, and cold.

- Media should be acclimated for 24 hours before use.

- Appropriate security should be maintained over media from the point of departure from the backup device to the secured offsite storage facility. Media is vulnerable to damage and theft at any point during transportation.

- Appropriate security should be maintained over media throughout the lifetime of the media based on the classification level of data on the media.

Mobile Devices

Mobile devices include smartphones and tablets. These devices have internal memory or removable memory cards that can hold a significant amount of data. Data can include email with attachments, contacts, and scheduling information. Additionally, many devices include applications that allow users to read and manipulate different types of documents.

Organizations often purchase smartphones for users and maintain their data plans. This is certainly a great benefit for the employee, but it also gives the organization additional control over the user's phone and the data it contains. Some of the common controls organizations enable on user phones are encryption, screen lock, global positioning system (GPS), and remote wipe. Encryption protects the data if the phone is lost or stolen, the screen lock slows down someone that may have stolen a phone, and GPS provides information on the location of the phone if it is lost or stolen. A remote wipe signal can be sent to a lost device to delete all data on the device if it has been lost and includes valuable data. Many devices respond with a confirmation message when the remote wipe has succeeded.

Remote wipe doesn't provide guaranteed protection. Knowledgeable thieves who want data from a business smartphone often remove the subscriber identity module (SIM) card immediately. Additionally, they have used shielded rooms similar to Faraday cages when putting the SIM back into the phone to get the data. These techniques block the remote wipe signal. If a confirmation message is not received indicating that the remote wipe has succeeded, it's very possible that the data has been compromised.

Managing Media Life Cycle

All media has a useful, but finite, life cycle. Reusable media is subject to a *mean time to failure (MTTF)* that is sometimes represented in the number of times it can be reused or the number of years you can expect to keep it. For example, some tapes include specifications saying they can be reused as many as 250 times or last up to 30 years under ideal conditions. However, there are many variables affecting the lifetime of media that can in turn affect the manufacturer's specifications. It's important to monitor backups for errors and use these as a guide to gauge the lifetime in your environment. When a tape begins to generate errors it should be rotated out of use.

Once backup media has reached its MTTF, it should be destroyed. The classification of data held on the tape will dictate the method used to destroy the media. Some organizations degauss highly classified tapes when they've reached the end of their lifetime and then store them until they can be physically destroyed. Physical destruction is commonly done through incineration or bulk shredders.

> MTTF is different than mean time between failures (MTBF). MTTF is normally calculated for items that will not be repaired when they fail, such as a tape. In contrast, MTBF refers to the amount of time expected to elapse between failures of an item that will be repaired, such as a computer server.

Asset Management

Chapter 6 included a significant amount of information on assets. As a reminder, an asset is anything within the environment that should be protected based on its value to the organization. This includes physical assets such as computers and electronic assets such as files and purchased software. It also extends to intangible assets such as the reputation of the company or customer goodwill.

Physical assets are protected with physical security methods such as locked doors and entries manned by guards. Electronic assets are protected with technical access controls such as encryption and permissions. Of course files are stored on media, and by controlling the media using methods described earlier in this chapter, you also protect the files. An organization cannot directly manage intangible assets. However, by implementing effective security controls throughout the organization, it can indirectly protect these assets.

Equipment Life Cycle

Some organizations use databases to track hardware assets through the entire equipment life cycle. For example, bar code systems are available that can print bar codes to place on equipment. The bar code database includes relevant details on the hardware, such as the model, serial number, and location. On a regular basis, all of the hardware can be scanned with a bar code reader to verify that it is still controlled by the organization. A similar method uses radio frequency identification (RFID) tags. The RFID tags can be placed on the equipment and transmit information that can be read by RFID readers up to several meters away.

Many applications are available that can automate many of the asset management tasks such as routine inventories. These are often sold as full solutions with all the required hardware and software to manage hardware assets through the equipment's life cycle.

When equipment is disposed of, it needs to be sanitized to ensure that it doesn't hold any sensitive information, as discussed earlier in this chapter. When equipment is at the end of its lifetime, it's easy for individuals to lose sight of the data that it may contain, so using checklists to sanitize the system is often valuable. Checklists can include steps to sanitize hard drives, nonvolatile memory and removable media such as CDs, DVDs, and USB flash drives within the system.

Portable media holding sensitive data is also managed as an asset. For example, an organization can label portable media with bar codes and use a bar code inventory system to complete inventories on a regular basis. This allows them to easily inventory the media holding sensitive data on a regular basis.

Software Licensing

Organizations pay for software, and license keys are routinely used to activate the software. The activation process often requires contacting a licensing server over the Internet to prevent piracy. If the license keys are leaked outside the organization, it can invalidate the use of the key within the organization.

For example, an organization could purchase a license key for five installations of the software product but only install and activate one instance immediately. If the key is stolen and installed on four systems outside the organization, those activations will succeed. When the organization tries to install the application on internal systems, the activation will fail. Any type of license key is therefore highly valuable to an organization and should be protected.

Software licensing also refers to ensuring that systems do not have unauthorized software installed. Many tools are available that can inspect systems remotely to detect the system's details. For example, Microsoft's System Configuration Manager (SCCM) is a server product that can query each system on a network to identify the installed operating system and installed applications. The list of installed applications can be compared against the list of purchased licenses to ensure that the computers within the organization are using only authorized software.

Changes in Workstation and Location

Some organizations have employees use nonpermanent workstations or locations. In other words, users may be working on any computer on any day. For example, help desk employees working different shifts may have a bank of computers they share, but each employee could use a different computer on any shift.

Similar to job rotation, changing a user's workstation discourages the user from altering the system or installing unapproved software because the next person to use the system is likely to discover it. Additionally, having nonpermanent workstations encourages users to keep all materials stored on network servers where it can be easily protected, overseen, and audited.

Patch and Vulnerability Management

Patch management and vulnerability management work together to help protect an organization against emerging threats. Bugs and security vulnerabilities are routinely discovered in operating systems and applications. As they are discovered, vendors write and test patches to remove the vulnerability. Patch management ensures that appropriate patches are applied and vulnerability management helps verify that systems are not vulnerable to known threats.

Patch Management

Patch is a blanket term for any type of code written to correct a bug or vulnerability or improve the performance of existing software. The software can be either an operating system or an application. Patches are sometimes referred to as updates, quick fixes, and hot fixes. In the context of security, the patches that administrators are primarily concerned with are patches that affect the vulnerability of a system. These are often referred to as security patches. Service packs are collections of patches that bring a system up-to-date with current patches.

Even though vendors regularly write and release patches, these patches are useful only if they are applied. This may seem obvious, but many security incidents could have been completely avoided if systems were patched. An effective *patch management* program ensures that systems are kept up-to-date with current patches. These are the common steps within an effective patch management program:

Evaluate patches.   When patches are released, administrators evaluate the patch to determine if it applies to their systems. For example, a patch released to fix a vulnerability on a UNIX system configured as a Domain Name System (DNS) server is not relevant to a Windows DNS server. Similarly, a patch released to fix a problem with specific features in Windows systems is not needed if these features are not enabled.

Test patches.   Whenever possible, patches are tested on an isolated system to determine if they have any unwanted side effects. The worst case scenario is that a system will no longer start after a patch is applied. For example, a patch released in February 2010 for Windows XP and Windows Vista systems caused many systems to go into the Blue Screen of Death (BSOD). It turns out these systems were infected with malware and the update interfered with the malware, causing the BSOD. However, the result is the same. A system no longer works after an update is applied. If this occurs after a patch is applied to a single test system, only the test system is affected. However, if an organization has a thousand computers and they all crash after a patch is applied, it can have catastrophic results.

Smaller organizations often choose not to evaluate, test, and approve patches but instead use an automatic method to approve and deploy the patches. Windows systems include Windows Update, which makes this easy. However, larger organizations almost always take control of the process to prevent potential outages from an update.

Approve the patches. Once patches have been tested and are determined to be safe, they are approved for deployment. It's common to use a change management process (described later in this chapter) as part of the approval process.

Deploy the patches. After testing and approval, patches are deployed to systems. Many organizations use automated methods to deploy the patches. These can be third-party products or products provided by the software vendor.

Verify that patches are deployed. After patches are deployed, systems are regularly audited and tested to ensure that they are patched. Many deployment tools include the ability to routinely audit systems to ensure that they are patched. Additionally, many vulnerability assessment tools include the ability to check systems to ensure that they are patched.

Patch Tuesday and Exploit Wednesday

Microsoft regularly releases patches on the second Tuesday of every month, which is therefore called *patch Tuesday*. The regular schedule allows administrators to plan for the release of patches so that they have adequate time to test and deploy them. Many organizations that have support contracts with Microsoft have advance notification of the patches prior to patch Tuesday. Some vulnerabilities are considered to be significant enough that Microsoft releases them "out-of-band." In other words, instead of waiting for the next patch Tuesday to release a patch, it may choose to release a patch earlier.

Attackers realize that many organizations do not patch their systems right away. Some attackers have reverse-engineered patches to identify the vulnerability being fixed and then created methods to exploit the vulnerability. These attacks often start within a day after patch Tuesday, giving rise to the term *exploit Wednesday*.

However, many attacks occur on unpatched systems weeks, months, and even years after a patch has been released. In other words, many systems remain unpatched and are attacked much later than a day after a patch is released. For example, Microsoft released a fix in October 2008 to fix a vulnerability commonly referred to as conficker. Conficker includes many malicious capabilities and is considered a serious threat. However, in 2011, there were still more than 1.8 million computers worldwide infected with conficker, meaning at least this many computers haven't been updated to block it.

Vulnerability Management

Vulnerability management refers to regularly identifying vulnerabilities, evaluating them, and taking steps to mitigate risks associated with them. All risks cannot be eliminated. Similarly, all vulnerabilities cannot be eliminated. However, an effective vulnerability management program helps an organization ensure that they are regularly evaluating vulnerabilities and mitigating the vulnerabilities that represent the greatest risks. Two common elements of a vulnerability management program are routine vulnerability scans and periodic vulnerability assessments.

One of the most common vulnerabilities within an organization is an unpatched system, and so a vulnerability management program will often work in conjunction with a patch management program. In many cases, duties of the two programs are separated between different employees. One person or group would be responsible for keeping systems patched, and another person or group would be responsible for verifying that the systems are patched. As with other separation of duties implementations, this provides a measure of checks and balances within the organization.

Vulnerability Scans

Vulnerability scanners are software tools used to test systems and networks for known security issues. Chapter 8, "Malicious Code and Application Attacks," covered vulnerability scanners in the context of reconnaissance attacks. As a reminder, attackers use vulnerability scanners to detect weaknesses in systems and networks, such as missing patches or weak passwords. After they detect the weaknesses, they launch attacks to exploit them. Administrators in many organizations use the same types of vulnerability scanners to detect vulnerabilities on their network. Their goal is detect the vulnerabilities so that they can be mitigated before an attacker discovers them.

Just as antivirus software uses a signature file to detect known viruses, vulnerability scanners include a database of known security issues and they check systems against this database. Vendors regularly update this database and sell a subscription for the updates to customers. If a vulnerability scanner is not kept up-to-date, it won't be able to detect newer threats, just as antivirus software won't be able to detect newer viruses if it is not kept up-to-date.

Nessus is a popular vulnerability scanner managed by Tenable Network Security, and it combines multiple techniques to detect a wide range of vulnerabilities. It can discover systems on a network using IP probes and ping sweeps and it analyzes packets sent out from systems to determine the operating system running. It uses port scans to detect open ports and identify the services and protocols that are likely running on the target systems. Once Nessus discovers basic details about systems, it can then follow up with queries to test the systems for known vulnerabilities, such as if the system is not up-to-date with current patches.

It's important to realize that a vulnerability scanner does more than just check unpatched systems. For example, if a system is running a database server application, it can check the database for default passwords with default accounts. Similarly, if a system is hosting a website, it can check the website to determine if it is using input validation techniques to prevent different types of input attacks such as SQL injection or cross-site scripting (both described in Chapter 8).

In some large organizations, a dedicated security team will perform regular vulnerability scans using available tools. In smaller organizations, an IT or security administrator may perform the scans as part of their other responsibilities. Remember though, if the person responsible for deploying patches is also responsible for running scans to check for patches, it represents a potential conflict. If something prevents an administrator from deploying patches, the administrator can also skip the scan showing the patches haven't been deployed.

Scanners include the ability to generate reports identifying any vulnerabilities they discover. The reports may recommend applying patches or making specific configuration or security setting changes to improve or impose security. Obviously, the vulnerability is only mitigated if the recommended update or change is applied.

While it is recommended to implement the updates or changes to mitigate the vulnerability, there may be situations where it isn't feasible or desirable to do so. For example, if a patch fixing a minor security issue breaks an application on a system, management may decide not to implement the fix until the application can be modified. The vulnerability scanner will regularly report the vulnerability, but the risk has been addressed.

 Management can choose to accept a risk rather than mitigate it. Any risk that remains after applying a control is referred to as residual risk. Any losses that occur from residual risk are the responsibility of management.

In contrast, an organization that never performs vulnerability scans will likely have many vulnerabilities. In addition, these vulnerabilities will remain unknown and management will not have the opportunity to decide which vulnerabilities to mitigate and which vulnerabilities to accept.

Vulnerability Assessments

A vulnerability assessment will often include results from vulnerability scans, but the assessment will do more. For example, an annual vulnerability assessment may analyze all of the vulnerability scan reports from the past year to determine if vulnerabilities are being addressed. If the same vulnerability is repeated on every vulnerability scan report, a logical question to ask is, "Why hasn't this been mitigated?" There may be a valid reason that management chose to accept the risk, or it may be that the vulnerability scans are being performed but action is never taken to mitigate the discovered vulnerabilities.

Chapter 6 covered risk assessments within the context of risk management. A vulnerability assessment is often done as part of a risk analysis or risk assessment to identify the vulnerabilities at a point in time. Vulnerabilities are then matched to potential threats to identify the potential risk to the organization.

Additionally, vulnerability assessments can look at other areas to determine risks. For example, a vulnerability assessment can look at how sensitive information is marked, handled, stored, and destroyed throughout its lifetime to address potential vulnerabilities.

The term *vulnerability assessment* is sometimes used to indicate a risk assessment. In this context, a vulnerability assessment would include the same elements as a risk assessment, described in Chapter 6. This includes identifying the value of assets, identifying vulnerabilities and threats, and performing a risk analysis to determine the overall risk.

Chapter 14 covers penetration tests. Many penetration tests start with a vulnerability assessment. Additionally, many penetration testers include social engineering tactics as a part of their overall testing.

Common Vulnerabilities and Exposures

Vulnerabilities are commonly referred to using the Common Vulnerability and Exposures (CVE) database. The CVE database provides a standard convention used to identify vulnerabilities. MITRE maintains the CVE database and it can be viewed at www.cve.mitre.org.

MITRE looks like an acronym, but it isn't. The founders do have a history as research engineers at the Massachusetts's Institute of Technology (MIT) and the name reminds people of that history. However, MITRE is not a part of MIT. MITRE receives funding from the US government to maintain the CVE database.

Patch management and vulnerability management tools commonly use the CVE database as a standard when scanning for specific vulnerabilities. For example, conficker was mentioned earlier. Conficker takes advantage of a vulnerability in unpatched Windows systems, and Microsoft released Microsoft Security Bulletin MS08-067 with updates to address it. The same conficker vulnerability is identified as CVE-2008-4250 by MITRE and any CVE-compatible products.

The CVE database makes it easier for companies that create patch management and vulnerability management tools. They don't have to expend any resources to manage the naming and definition of vulnerabilities but can instead focus on methods used to check systems for the vulnerabilities.

Change and Configuration Management

Change and configuration management are closely related controls that help reduce outages resulting in a loss of availability. Change management helps reduce outages due to unauthorized changes, and configuration management helps ensure that systems are configured properly throughout their lifetime.

Many of the change management and configuration management concepts in use today are derived from the Information Technology Infrastructure Library (ITIL) documents published by the United Kingdom. The ITIL Core includes five publications addressing the overall life cycle of systems. ITIL as a whole identifies best practices that an organization can adopt to increase overall availability, and the Service Transition publication addresses configuration management and change management processes. Even though many of the concepts come from ITIL, organizations don't need to adopt ITIL to implement change and configuration management.

The updated CISSP CIB added change management with configuration management. Previously, it listed only configuration management, which implies change management. With configuration management specifically added to the CIB, we have some insight into how important (ISC)[2] considers change management. Many IT and security professionals who have witnessed outages as a direct result of unauthorized changes agree. An effective change management policy is a necessity.

Configuration Management

Configuration management is the process of ensuring that systems are configured properly throughout their lifetime. Baselining addresses the configuration of systems when they are first deployed, and documentation helps ensure that the proper configuration of any system is known. Change management processes help prevent unauthorized changes to these systems and are often intertwined with the configuration documentation to make sure changes are documented.

Baselining

A baseline is a starting point. Within the context of configuration management, it is the starting configuration for a system. Systems are commonly modified after they are deployed to meet specific needs, but when they are first deployed with a secure baseline, they are much more likely to stay secure. This is especially true if an organization has an effective change management program in place.

Baselines can be created with checklists that require someone to make sure a system is deployed a certain way or with a specific configuration. However, manual baselines are susceptible to human error. It's easy for a person to miss a step or accidentally misconfigure a system. Scripts and operating system tools are also used to implement baselines, and when automated methods are used, it reduces the potential for errors from manual baselines. For example, Microsoft operating systems include Group Policy. Administrators can configure a Group Policy setting one time and automatically have the setting apply to all of the computers in the domain.

Using Images for Baselining

Many organizations use images to create baselines. Figure 13.3 shows how baseline images are created and deployed to new systems as an overall three-step process. In practice, there are more details involved in this process, depending on what tools are being used for imaging. For example, the steps to capture and deploy images using Norton Ghost by Symantec are different than the steps to capture and deploy images using Microsoft's Windows Deployment Services (WDS).

FIGURE 13.3   Creating and deploying images

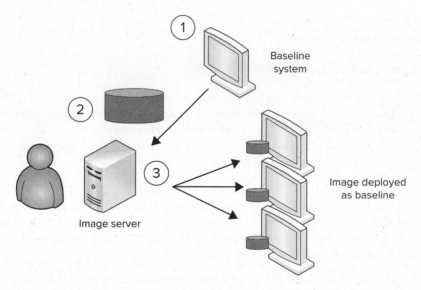

Here are the general steps to capture a baseline image:

1. An administrator starts by installing the operating system and all desired applications on a computer (labeled as the baseline system in the figure). The system is then configured with security and other settings to meet the needs of the organization. This system is thoroughly tested to ensure that it works as desired before proceeding.

2. Next, an image of the system is captured using imaging software. The captured image is often stored on a dedicated server that is also used to deploy images. However, it's often possible to capture and store images on external hard drives or DVDs.

3. The captured image can then be deployed to systems as needed. These systems often require additional configuration to finalize them, such as giving them unique names; however, the overall configuration of these systems are the same as the baseline system.

Baseline images improve the security of systems when they are first deployed by ensuring that desired security settings are always configured correctly. Additionally, they reduce the amount of time required to deploy and maintain systems, thus reducing the overall maintenance costs. Deployment of a prebuilt image can require only a few minutes of a technician's time. Additionally, when a user's system becomes corrupt, the image can be rebuilt in minutes instead of taking hours to troubleshoot the system or trying to rebuild it from scratch.

It's common to combine imaging with other automated methods for baselines. In other words, one image can be used for all desktop computers within an organization. Automated methods can then be used to add additional applications, features, or settings for specific groups of computers. For example, computers in one department may have additional security settings or applications applied through scripting or other automated tools.

 Real World Scenario

Baseline Images Use in the US Government

The US government recognized that many of the security problems it was having were due to misconfigured Windows systems. Many IT professionals knew about core security settings to protect systems, but often, systems were deployed by personnel that didn't have this knowledge. The result was that systems were routinely deployed with vulnerabilities, resulting in security incidents that could have been prevented.

In response, the US Air Force collaborated with Microsoft and created standardized images to use as baselines for their systems. Later, several government agencies again collaborated with Microsoft and created standardized images to use as baselines for all government agencies. These are currently known as United States Government Configuration Baseline (USGCB) images.

Currently, the Office of Management and Budget (OMB) mandates the use of these images for all general-purpose Windows-based systems such as desktops and laptops used in government agencies. The National Institute of Standards and Technology (NIST) maintains and updates the images as needed.

Configuration Documentation

Configuration documentation identifies the current configuration of systems and needs to be kept up-to-date. Basic documentation identifies who is responsible for the system, what the system does, how it is connected, and any modifications from the baseline. Years ago, many organizations used simple paper notebooks to record this information for servers, but it is much more common to store this information in files or databases today. Of course the challenge with storing the documentation in a data file is that it can be inaccessible during an outage.

Change Management

Once a system has been properly secured, it is important to keep that security intact. Of course the one thing that is constant is change, so the goal of change management isn't to prevent change. Instead, the goal is to ensure that changes are adequately reviewed, approved, and documented to reduce outages from changes. Changes often create unintended side effects that can cause outages. An administrator can make a change to one system to resolve a problem but unknowingly cause a problem in other systems.

Consider Figure 13.4. The web server is accessible from the Internet and accesses the database on the internal network. Appropriate ports are opened on Firewall 1 to allow Internet traffic to the web server and appropriate ports are opened on Firewall 2 to allow the web server to access the database server.

FIGURE 13.4 Web server and database server

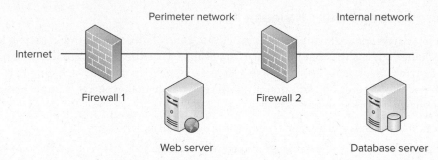

A well-meaning firewall administrator may see an unrecognized open port on Firewall 2 and decide to close it. Unfortunately, the web server needs this port open to communicate with the database server, so when the port is closed, the web server will begin having problems. The web server programmers (who may be working in another division) may be called in to fix the web server, and after some troubleshooting, they'd realize that the database server isn't answering queries. They could then bring in the database developers or database administrators (who may be working in another division) to check the database server. After a bunch of hooting, hollering, and finger pointing, they would eventually realize the port on Firewall 2 was closed. They would open the port and resolve the problem. Until of course, the well-meaning firewall administrator starts tinkering with Firewall 1.

Unauthorized changes directly affect the A in the CIA Triad, availability. However, change management processes give various IT experts an opportunity to review proposed changes for unintended side effects before they are implemented. And they give administrators time to check their work in controlled circumstances before implementing changes in production environments.

Additionally, some changes can weaken or reduce security. For example, if an organization isn't using an effective access control model to grant access to users, administrators may not be able to keep up with the requests for additional access. Frustrated administrators may decide to just add all users to an administrators group within the network. Users will now have all the access they need, improving their ability to use the network, and they will no longer bother the administrators with access requests. However, giving everyone administrator access directly violates the principle of least privilege and significantly weakens security.

 Organizations constantly seek the best balance between security and usability, and there are instances when an organization makes conscious decisions to improve performance or usability of a system by weakening security. However, change management helps ensure that an organization takes the time to evaluate the risk of weakening security and compare it to the benefits of increased usability.

Change Management Process

Change management controls provide a process to control, document, track, and audit all system changes. It ensures that all changes are evaluated before being deployed in a production environment. This includes changes to any aspect of a system, including hardware and software configuration. Additionally, effective change management is implemented throughout the life cycle of any system.

Common tasks within a change management process are as follows:

1. **Request the change.** Once the desired change is identified, it is requested. Some organizations use internal websites, allowing individuals to submit change requests via a web page. The website automatically logs the request in a database, which allows it to easily be tracked.

2. **Review the change.** IT professionals within the organization review the change. In some cases, the review may be quick. In other cases, the change may require approval at a formal change review board after extensive testing.

3. **Approve/disapprove the change.** Based on the review, the change is approved or disapproved. This approval/disapproval is also recorded in the change management documentation. In some cases, a rollback or back-out plan is required to ensure that the system can be returned to its original condition if the change results in a failure.

4. **Schedule and implement the change.** The change is scheduled so that it can be implemented with the least impact on the system. This may require scheduling the change during off-duty or non-peak hours.

5. **Document the change.** The last step is the documentation of the change to ensure that all interested parties are aware of it. This often requires a change in the configuration management documentation. If the system later needs to be rebuilt due to an unrelated disaster, the configuration management documentation ensures that the system can be returned to the state it was in after the change.

There may be instances when an emergency change is required. For example, if an attack or malware infection takes one or more systems down, an administrator may need to make changes to a system or network to contain the incident. These changes should be documented and carefully reviewed after the incident to ensure that they do not cause other problems. Additionally, documenting the emergency change ensures that the affected system will include the new configuration if it needs to be rebuilt.

When the change management process is enforced, it creates documentation for all changes to a system and provides a trail of information if the change needs to be reversed. It also provides a road map or procedure to follow if the same change is implemented on other systems.

Change management control is a mandatory element for some security assurance requirements (SARs) in the ISO Common Criteria (discussed in Chapter 11, "Principles of Security Models, Design, and Capabilities"). However, change management controls are implemented in many organizations that don't require it. It improves the security of an environment by protecting against unauthorized changes resulting in unintentional losses.

Versioning

Versioning refers to version control used in software configuration management. A labeling or numbering system is often used to differentiate between different software sets and configurations across multiple machines or at different points in time on a single machine. For example, the first version of an application may be labeled as 1.0. The first minor update would be labeled as 1.1, and the first major update would be 2.0. This helps keep track of changes over time to deployed software.

Chapter 7, "Software Development Security," includes a section on change control and configuration management with software applications. As a reminder, a software change process includes three primary components: request, change, and release. These components can be applied to any applications or documents that require versioning control.

While most software developers recognize the importance of versioning and revision control with applications, many new web developers don't recognize its importance. Many web developers have learned some excellent skills they use to create awesome websites but don't always recognize the importance of underlying principles such as versioning control. If changes and updates aren't controlled through some type of versioning control system, it's very possible to implement a change that effectively breaks the website.

Security Audits and Reviews

Security audits and reviews help ensure that management controls are being implemented properly. Chapter 2 discusses access review audits to assess the effectiveness of access controls. These reviews ensure that accounts are managed appropriately, don't have excessive privileges, and are disabled or deleted when required. In the context of the Security Operations domain, security audits help ensure that management controls are in place. The following list includes some common items to check:

Patch management   A patch management review ensures that patches are evaluated as soon as possible once they are available. It also ensures that the organization follows established procedures to evaluate, test, approve, deploy, and verify the patches. Vulnerability scan reports can be valuable in any patch management review or audit.

Vulnerability management   A vulnerability management review ensures that vulnerability scans and assessments are performed regularly in compliance with established guidelines. For example, an organization may have a policy document stating that vulnerability scans are performed at least weekly, and the review verifies that this is done. Additionally, the review will verify that the vulnerabilities discovered in the scans have been addressed and mitigated.

Configuration management   Systems can be audited periodically to ensure that the original configurations are not modified. It is often possible to use scripting tools to check specific configurations of systems and identify when a change has occurred. Additionally, logging can be enabled for many configuration settings to record configuration changes. A configuration management audit can check the logs for any changes and verify that they are authorized.

Change management   A change management review ensures that changes are implemented in accordance with the organization's change management policy. This often includes a review of outages to determine the cause. Outages that result from unauthorized changes are a clear indication that the change management program needs improvement.

Summary

Several basic security principles are at the core of security operations in any environment. These include need to know, least privilege, separation of duties and responsibilities, job rotation, and mandatory vacations. Combined, they help prevent security incidents from occurring, and limit the scope of incidents that do occur. Administrators and operators are often given special privileges to perform their jobs following these security principles. In addition to implementing the principles, it's important to monitor the granting and use of special privileges to make sure privileged entities do not abuse their access.

Sensitive information is any information that an organization keeps private and can include multiple levels of classifications. Organizations take specific steps to mark, handle, store, and destroy sensitive information, and these steps help prevent the loss of confidentiality due to unauthorized disclosure. Additionally, organizations commonly define specific rules for record retention to ensure that data is available when it is needed but also to reduce liabilities resulting from keeping data too long.

With resource protection, media and other assets are protected throughout their life cycle. Media includes anything that can hold data, such as tapes, internal drives, portable drives (USB, FireWire, and eSATA), CDs and DVDs, mobile devices, memory cards, and printouts. Media holding sensitive information should be marked, handled, stored, and destroyed using methods that are acceptable within the organization. Asset management extends beyond media to any asset considered valuable to an organization—physical assets such as computers and software assets such as purchased applications and software keys.

Patch and vulnerability management procedures work together to keep systems protected against known vulnerabilities. Patch management keeps systems up-to-date with relevant patches. Vulnerability management includes vulnerability scans to check for a wide variety of known vulnerabilities (including unpatched systems) and also includes vulnerability assessments done as part of a risk assessment.

Change and configuration management are two additional controls that help reduce outages. Configuration management ensures that systems are deployed in a consistent manner that is known to be secure. Imaging is a common configuration management technique that ensures that systems start with a known baseline. Change management helps reduce unintended outages from unauthorized changes and can also help prevent changes from weakening security.

Security audits and reviews are commonly done to guarantee that controls are implemented as directed and working as desired. It's common to include audits and reviews to check patch management, vulnerability management, change management, and configuration management programs.

Exam Essentials

Understand need to know and the principle of least privilege.   Need to know and the principle of least privilege are two standard IT security principles implemented in secure networks. They limit access to data and systems so that users and other subjects have access only to what they require. This limited access helps prevent security incidents and helps limit the scope of incidents when they occur. When these principles are not followed, security incidents result in far greater damage to an organization.

Understand the separation of duties and job rotation.   Separation of duties is a basic security principle that ensures that no single person can control all the elements of a critical function or system. With job rotation, employees are rotated into different jobs or tasks are assigned to different employees. Collusion is an agreement among multiple persons to perform some unauthorized or illegal actions, and implementing these policies helps prevent collusion and fraud.

Understand the importance of monitoring privileged operations.   Privileged entities are trusted, but they can abuse their privileges. Because of this, it's important to monitor all assignment of privileges and the use of privileged operations. The goal is to ensure that trusted employees do not abuse the special privileges they are granted.

Know how to manage sensitive information.   Sensitive information is any type of classified information, and proper management helps prevent unauthorized disclosure resulting in a loss of confidentiality. Proper management includes marking, handling, storing, and destroying sensitive information. The two areas where organizations often miss the mark are adequately protecting backup media holding sensitive information and sanitizing media or equipment when it is at the end of its life cycle.

Understand record retention.   Record retention policies ensure that data is kept in a usable state while it is needed and destroyed when it is no longer needed. Many laws and regulations mandate keeping data for a specific amount of time, but in the absence of formal regulations, organizations specify the retention period within a policy. Audit trail data needs to be kept long enough to reconstruct past incidents, but the organization must identify how far back they want to investigate. A current trend with many organizations is to reduce legal liabilities by implementing short retention policies with email.

Understand patch management.   Patch management ensures that systems are kept up-to-date with current patches. You should know that an effective patch management program will evaluate, test, approve, and deploy patches. Additionally, be aware that system audits verify the deployment of approved patches to systems. Patch management is often intertwined with change and configuration management to ensure that documentation reflects the changes. When an organization does not have a patch management program it will often experience outages and incidents from known issues that could have been prevented.

Explain vulnerability management.   Vulnerability management includes routine vulnerability scans and periodic vulnerability assessments. Vulnerability scanners are used to detect known security vulnerabilities and weaknesses such as the absence of patches or weak passwords. They are used to generate reports that indicate the technical vulnerabilities of a system and are an effective check for a patch management program. Vulnerability assessments extend beyond just technical scans and can include reviews and audits to detect vulnerabilities.

Be able to explain configuration and change control management.   Many outages and incidents can be prevented with effective configuration and change management programs. Configuration management ensures that systems are configured similarly and the configuration of systems are known and documented. Baselining ensures that systems are deployed with a common baseline or starting point, and imaging is a common baselining method. Change management helps reduce outages or weakened security from unauthorized changes. A change management process requires changes to be requested, approved, and documented. Versioning uses a labeling or numbering system to track changes in updated versions of software.

Understand the importance of security audits and reviews.   Security audits and reviews help ensure that management programs are effective and being followed. They are commonly associated with account management practices to prevent violations with least privilege or need to know principles. However, they can also be performed to oversee patch management, vulnerability management, change management, and configuration management programs.

Written Lab

1. Define the difference between need to know and principle of least privilege.

2. Name the common methods used to manage sensitive information.

3. What control prevents outages due to unauthorized modifications in system configuration?

Review Questions

1. A user is granted access to data needed to perform specific work tasks, but no more. What is being enforced?

   A. Principle of least permission

   B. Separation of duties

   C. Need to know

   D. Role-based access control

2. An organization has strictly implemented the principle of least privilege. Which of the following is not a likely outcome?

   A. Users can log onto any computer in the network.

   B. Users can log onto only a single system.

   C. Users have restricted access to files based on their jobs.

   D. Users do not have access to backup tapes.

3. Why is separation of duties important for security purposes?

   A. It ensures that multiple people can do the same job.

   B. It prevents an organization from losing important information when they lose important people.

   C. It prevents any single security subject (person) from being able to make major security changes without involving other subjects.

   D. It helps subjects concentrate their talents where they will be most useful.

4. A financial organization commonly has employees switch duty responsibilities every six months. What security principle are they employing?

   A. Job rotation

   B. Separation of duties

   C. Mandatory vacations

   D. Least privilege

5. Of the following choices, what is not a valid security practice related to special privileges?

   A. Monitor special privilege assignments.

   B. Grant access equally to administrators and operators.

   C. Monitor special privilege usage.

   D. Grant access to only trusted employees.

6. An organization wants to reduce vulnerabilities against collusion and fraud from malicious employees. Of the following choices, what would not help with this goal?

   A. Job rotation

   B. Separation of duties

   C. Mandatory vacations

   D. Baselining

7. What is the most important aspect of marking media?

   A. Date labeling

   B. Content description

   C. Electronic labeling

   D. Classification

8. Which operation is performed on media so it can be reused in a less-secure environment?

   A. Erasing

   B. Clearing

   C. Purging

   D. Overwriting

9. Sanitization can be unreliable because of which of the following?

   A. Methods are not available to remove data and ensure that it cannot be retrieved using any known methods.

   B. Even fully incinerated media can offer extractable data.

   C. The process can be performed improperly.

   D. Stored data is physically etched into the media.

10. Which of the following requires that archives of audit logs be kept for long periods of time?

   A. Data remanence

   B. Record retention

   C. Data diddling

   D. Data mining

11. What should be done with equipment that is at the end of its life cycle and is being donated to a charity?

   A. Ensure that CDs and DVDs are removed.

   B. Remove all software licenses.

   C. Sanitize it.

   D. Install the original software.

12. Backup tapes have reached the end of their life cycle and need to be disposed of. What should be done with the tapes?

    A. Throw them away. Because they are at the end of their life cycle, data cannot be obtained from them.

    B. Purge the tapes of all data before disposing of them.

    C. Erase data off the tapes before disposing of them.

    D. Store the tapes in a storage facility.

13. Which of the following is not a part of a patch management process?

    A. Evaluate patches.

    B. Test patches.

    C. Deploy all patches.

    D. Audit patches.

14. What would an administrator use to check systems for known issues that attackers may use to exploit the systems?

    A. Versioning tracker

    B. Vulnerability scanner

    C. Security audit

    D. Security review

15. Of the following choices, what is a primary goal of change management?

    A. Personnel safety

    B. Allowing rollback of changes

    C. Ensuring that changes do not reduce security

    D. Auditing privilege access

16. Which of the following steps would not be included in a change management process?

    A. Immediately implement the change if it will improve performance.

    B. Request the change.

    C. Create a rollback plan for the change.

    D. Document the change.

17. While troubleshooting a network problem, a technician realized it could be resolved by opening some ports on a firewall. After these ports were opened, the system worked, but later an attack was launched through these ports, causing other system outages. What could have prevented this problem?

    A. Patch management processes

    B. Vulnerability management processes

    C. Configuration management processes

    D. Change management processes

Refer the following scenario when answering questions 18 through 20.

An organization has a data center manned 24 hours a day that processes highly sensitive information. The data center includes email servers, and email older than six months is regularly purged. Access to the data center is controlled, and all systems that process sensitive information are marked. Administrators routinely back up data processed in the data center. They keep a copy of the backups on site and also keep a copy off site on unmarked media at one of their warehouses. The media is organized at the offsite location by date and includes backups from the last 20 years. Employees work at the warehouse during the day and it is locked at night and on weekends. Recently a theft at the warehouse resulted in the loss of all of the offsite backup tapes. Later, copies of their data, including sensitive emails from years ago, began appearing on Internet sites exposing the organization's internal sensitive data.

18. Of the following choices, what would have prevented this loss without sacrificing security?

    A. Mark the media kept off site.

    B. Don't store data off site.

    C. Destroy the backups off site.

    D. Use a secure offsite storage facility.

19. What should have been done with the backup tapes before they left the data center that may have prevented the incident?

    A. Mark the tapes.

    B. Purge the tapes before backing up data to them.

    C. Degauss the tapes before backing up data to them.

    D. Add the tapes to an asset management database.

20. Of the following choices, what policy was not applied to the backup media?

    A. Media destruction

    B. Record retention

    C. Configuration management

    D. Versioning

Chapter

14

Incident Management

**THE CISSP EXAM TOPICS COVERED
IN THIS CHAPTER INCLUDE:**

7. Security Operations

- A. Manage Incident Response

  - A.1 Detection

  - A.2 Response

  - A.3 Reporting

  - A.4 Recovery

  - A.5 Remediation and review (e.g., root cause analysis)

- D. Implement preventative measures against attacks
  (e.g. malicious code, zero-day exploit, denial of service)

- G. Understand system resilience and fault tolerance
  requirements

The Security Operations domain for the CISSP certification exam includes several objectives directly related to incident management. Effective incident management helps an organization respond appropriately when attacks occur to limit the scope of an attack. Incident management is an ongoing process and can help reduce future attacks by applying lessons learned to improve an organization's security posture. Security incidents are often the result of an attack, and there are preventive measures an organization can take to protect against and detect attacks. Many of these measures are discussed in this chapter.

We discussed several objectives of the Security Operations domain in Chapter 13, "Security Operations," and this chapter will cover the remaining objectives. Be sure to read and study the materials from both chapters to ensure complete coverage of the essential security operations material for the CISSP certification exam.

Managing Incident Response

One of the primary goals of any security program is to prevent security incidents. However, despite the best efforts of IT and security professionals, incidents do occur. When they happen, an organization must be able to quickly respond to limit or contain the incident and minimize the impact of the incident on the organization.

Defining an Incident

Before digging into incident response, it's important to understand the definition of an incident. While that may seem simple, you'll find that there are different definitions depending on the context.

An *incident* is any event that has a negative effect on the confidentiality, integrity, or availability of an organization's assets. Information Technology Infrastructure Library version 3 (ITILv3) defines an incident as "an unplanned interruption to an IT Service or a reduction in the quality of an IT service." Notice that these definitions encompass events as diverse as direct attacks, natural occurrences such as a hurricane or earthquake, and even accidents, such as someone accidentally cutting cables for a live network.

In contrast, a *computer security incident* (sometimes called just *security incident*) commonly refers to an incident that is the result of an attack, or the result of malicious or intentional actions on the part of users. For example, RFC 2350, "Expectations for

Computer Security Incident Response," defines both a security incident and a computer security incident as "any adverse event which compromises some aspect of computer or network security." National Institute of Standards and Technology (NIST) Special Publication (SP) 800-61 "Computer Security Incident Handling Guide" defines a computer security incident as "a violation or imminent threat of violation of computer security policies, acceptable use policies, or standard security practices." (NIST SP 800-61 is available from the NIST special publications download page: `http://csrc.nist.gov/publications/PubsSPs.html`.)

In the context of incident response, an incident is referring to a computer security incident. However, you'll often see it listed as just as incident. For example, in the CISSP Candidate Information Bulletin (CIB) within the Security Operations domain, the "Manage Incident Response" objective is clearly referring to computer security incidents.

 In this chapter, any reference to an incident refers to a computer security incident. Some incidents such as weather events or natural disasters are handled using other methods such as with a business continuity plan (covered in Chapter 15, "Business Continuity Planning") or with a disaster recovery plan (covered in Chapter 16, "Disaster Recovery Planning").

Organizations commonly define the meaning of a computer security incident within their security policy or incident response plans. The definition is usually one or two sentences long and includes examples of common events that are classified as security incidents, such as the following:

- Any attempted network intrusion
- Any attempted denial-of-service attack
- Any detection of malicious software
- Any unauthorized access of data
- Any violation of security policies

Incident Response Steps

Effective incident response management is handled in several steps or phases. Figure 14.1 shows the five steps involved in managing incident response as outlined in the CISSP CIB. It's important to realize that incident response is an ongoing activity and the results of the remediation and review stage are used to improve detection methods or help prevent a repeated incident. The following sections describe these steps in more depth.

FIGURE 14.1   Incident response

You may run across documentation that lists these steps differently. As an example, SP 800-61 is an excellent resource for learning more about incident handling, but it identifies the following four steps in the incident response life cycle: 1) preparation, 2) detection and analysis, 3) containment, eradication, and recovery, and 4) post-incident recovery. However, no matter how the steps are listed, they contain many of the same elements and have the same goal of managing incident response effectively.

Detection

IT environments include multiple methods of detecting potential incidents and they can be reported differently. The following list identifies many of the common ways that potential incidents are detected:

▪ Intrusion detection and prevention systems (described later in this chapter) can send alerts to administrators when an item of interest occurs.

▪ Antivirus software will often display a pop-up window to indicate malware has been detected.

▪ Many automated tools regularly scan audit logs and can send an alert or alarm when specific events occur.

▪ End users will report when they have problems such as the inability to access a resource on the network.

Notice that just because an IT professional receives an alert from an automated tool or a complaint from a user, this doesn't always mean an incident has occurred. Intrusion detection and prevention systems often give false alarms and end users are prone to simple user errors. These events must be investigated to determine if they are incidents.

Many IT professionals are classified as first responders for incidents. They are the first ones on the scene and have knowledge on how to differentiate typical IT problems from security incidents. They are similar to medical first responders who have outstanding skills and abilities to provide medical assistance at accident scenes, and help get the patients to medical facilities when necessary. The medical first responders have specific training to help them determine the difference between minor and major injuries, and what to do when they come across a major injury. Similarly, IT professionals need specific training so that they can determine the difference between a typical problem that needs troubleshooting and a security incident that needs to be escalated.

After an event has been investigated and determined to be a security incident, the next step is response. In many cases, the individual doing the initial investigation will escalate the incident to bring in other IT professionals to respond.

Response

After an incident has been detected and verified, the first response should be to contain the incident. One of the primary goals of an effective incident response is to limit the effect or scope of an incident. As a simple example, if an infected computer is sending data out the network interface card (NIC), the cable to the NIC can be disconnected to contain the problem. Sometimes containment involves disconnecting a network from other networks to contain the problem within a single network. When the problem is isolated, it can then be addressed without worrying about it spreading to the rest of the network.

 Real World Scenario

Delegating Incident Response to Users

In one organization, the responsibility to respond to computer infections was extended to users. Close to each computer was a checklist that identified common symptoms of malware infection. If users suspected their computers were infected, they were instructed to disconnect the NIC and contact the help desk to report the issue. By disconnecting the NIC, they quickly helped contain the malware to their system and stopped it from spreading any further.

This isn't possible in all organizations, but in this case, users were part of a very large network operations center and they were all involved in some form of computer support. In other words, they weren't typical end users but had a substantial amount of technical expertise.

Many organizations have a designated incident response team—sometimes called a computer incident response team (CIRT) or computer security incident response team (CSIRT). The team wouldn't necessarily be activated for minor incidents, but would be activated during a major incident. A formal incident response plan would document who would activate the team and under what conditions.

Team members would have training on incident response and the organization's incident response plan. Typically team members would assist with assessing the damage, collecting evidence, reporting the incident, and recovery procedures. They would also participate in the remediation and review stage, and help with the root cause analysis.

The quicker an organization can respond to an incident, the better chance they have at limiting the damage. On the other hand, if an incident continues for hours or days, the damage is likely to be greater. As an example, an attacker may be trying to access a customer database. A quick response can prevent the attacker from obtaining any meaningful data. However, if the attacker has continued unobstructed access to the database for several hours, he may be able to get a copy of the entire database.

After containing the incident, the next step in the response is investigation. This can take many paths depending on the organization's policies and procedures. After an investigation is over, the organization may decide to prosecute individuals who are responsible. Because of this, it's important to protect all data as evidence during the investigation. Chapter 18, "Incidents and Ethics," covers incident handling and response in the context of supporting investigations within the Legal, Regulations, Investigations, and Compliance domain. If there is any possibility of prosecution, extra steps should be taken to protect the evidence to support possible legal investigations and actions.

Computers should not be turned off when trying to contain an incident. Temporary files and data in volatile random access memory (RAM) will be lost if the computer is powered down. Forensics experts have tools they can use to retrieve data in temporary files and volatile RAM as long as the system is kept powered on, but all of this type of evidence is lost after power is removed.

It's important to stress that a response does not include a counterattack against the attacker. Launching attacks on others is counterproductive and often illegal. If a technician is able to identify the attacker and launch an attack, it will very likely result in an escalation of the attack by the attacker. In other words, the attacker may now consider it personal and regularly launch grudge attacks. In addition, it's likely that the attacker is hiding behind an innocent victim. Attackers often use spoofing or some other method to hide their identity. Counterattacks may be made against an innocent victim rather than the actual attacker.

Reporting

If an organization is governed by specific laws, they often have a requirement to report incidents to official entities as soon as possible. Most countries (and many smaller jurisdictions, including states and cities) have enacted significant regulatory compliance laws to govern security breaches, particularly as they apply to sensitive data retained within information systems. Laws differ from locale to locale, but all seek to protect the privacy of individual records and information, to protect consumer identities, and to establish standards for financial practice and corporate governance. Every organization has a responsibility to know what laws apply to it, and to abide by these laws.

For example, many jurisdictions have specific laws governing the protection of personally identifiable information (PII). If PII is compromised, the organization must report it. Different laws have different reporting requirements, but most include a requirement to notify individuals affected by the incident. In other words, if an attack on a system resulted in an attacker gaining PII about you, the owners of the system have a responsibility to inform you of the attack and what data the attackers accessed.

In any case where a critical security policy violation or personal information breach has occurred, an organization should seriously consider reporting the incident to official agencies. In the United States, this may mean notifying the Federal Bureau of Investigation (FBI), district attorney offices, and/or state and local law enforcement agencies. In Europe, organizations may report the incident to the International Criminal Police Organization (INTERPOL) or some other entity based on the incident and their location.

Many incidents are not reported because they aren't recognized as incidents. This is often the result of inadequate training, and the obvious solution is to ensure that personnel have relevant training. Training should teach individuals how to recognize incidents, what to do in the initial response, and how to report an incident.

Recovery

After all appropriate evidence has been collected from a system, the next step is to recover the system or return it to a fully functioning state. This can be very simple for minor incidents and may only require a reboot. However, a major incident may require completely rebuilding a system. Rebuilding the system includes restoring all data from the most recent backup.

When a compromised system is rebuilt from scratch, it's important to ensure it is configured properly and is at least as secure as it was before the incident. If an organization has effective configuration management and change management programs, these programs will provide necessary documentation to ensure the systems are configured properly. Some things to double-check include access control lists (ACLs) and ensuring that unneeded services and protocols are disabled or removed, all up-to-date patches are installed, and user accounts are modified from the defaults.

In some cases, an attacker may have installed malicious code on a system during an attack. This may not be apparent without a detailed inspection of the system. The most secure method of restoring a system after an incident is to completely rebuild the system from scratch. If it is suspected that the attacker may have modified code on the system, rebuilding a system may be a good option.

Remediation and Review

In the remediation and review stage, the incident is examined to determine whether there are any lessons to be learned from the incident and the subsequent response. The goal is to identify anything that can be modified to prevent a similar incident or to limit the severity of a similar incident. The incident response team will be involved in this stage, but other employees who are knowledgeable about the incident will also participate.

A root cause analysis examines the incident to determine what allowed it to happen. For example, if attackers successfully accessed a database through a website, all the elements of the system would be examined to determine what allowed the attackers to succeed. It could be that the web server wasn't kept up-to-date, allowing the attackers to gain remote control of the server. The website application may not be using adequate input validation techniques, allowing a successful SQL injection attack. The database may be located on the web server instead of in a back-end database accessed through an additional firewall. If the root cause analysis identifies a vulnerability that can be mitigated by making a change, reviewers will recommend a change.

Reviewers also examine the response to the incident. In some cases, the response may not have contained the incident, resulting in more damage than necessary. If employees are not adequately trained, they may not have the knowledge and expertise to respond effectively. They may not recognize the incident when they receive the first notification, allowing an attack to continue longer than necessary. First responders may not recognize the need to protect evidence and inadvertently corrupt it in an attempt to return a system to operation as quickly as possible.

Remember, the output of this stage can be fed back to the detection stage of incident management. As a result of an investigation, an organization may realize that attacks are getting through undetected and increase their detection capabilities. Of course, it's very possible that this step will discover a method that can prevent the same occurrence. For example, if an unpatched system is successfully attacked, this is a clear indication that an organization does not have an effective patch management program.

It is common for the incident response team to create a report when the review is over. Based on the findings, the team may recommend changes to procedures, the addition of security controls, or even changes to policies. Management will decide what recommendations to implement and is responsible for the remaining risk for any recommendations they reject.

Implement Preventive Measures Against Attacks

Security professionals need to be aware of common attack methods so that they can take proactive steps to prevent them, recognize them when they occur, and respond appropriately in response to an attack. This section provides an overview of basic protection steps and covers many common attacks. Additionally, it covers intrusion detection and prevention systems and penetration testing, which are additional methods used to prevent attacks.

We've attempted to avoid duplication of specific attacks but also provide a comprehensive coverage of different types of attacks throughout this book. In addition to this chapter, you'll see various types of attacks in other chapters. For example, Chapter 2, "Access Control Attacks and Monitoring," discussed some specific attacks related to access control; Chapter 4, "Secure Communications and Network Attacks," covered different types of network-based attacks; and Chapter 8, "Malicious Code and Application Attacks," covered several types of attacks related to malicious code and applications.

Basic Preventive Measures

While there is no single step you can take to protect against all attacks, there are some basic steps you can take that go a long way to protect against many types of attacks. Many of these steps are described in more depth in other areas of the book but are listed here as an introduction to this section.

Keep systems and applications up-to-date.   Vendors regularly release patches to correct bugs and security flaws, but they only help when they're applied. Patch management (covered in Chapter 13) ensures that systems and applications are kept up-to-date with relevant patches.

Remove or disable unneeded services and protocols.   If a service or protocol is not needed on a system, it should not be running. If it is not running, it can't be attacked. As an extreme contrast, imagine a web server is running every available service and protocol. If any one of these has a vulnerability, the web server can be attacked and exploited.

Use up-to-date antivirus software.   Chapter 8 covered the various types of malicious code, such as viruses and worms, as well as countermeasures. Additionally, this chapter includes a section on protection methods to prevent malicious code.

Use firewalls.   Firewalls (covered in Chapter 3, "Secure Network Architecture and Securing Network Components") can prevent many types of attacks. Network-based firewalls protect entire networks and host-based firewalls protect individual systems.

Use intrusion detection and prevention systems.   Intrusion detection and prevention systems observe activity, attempt to detect attacks, and provide alerts, and they can often respond to block or stop attacks. These systems are described in more depth later in this chapter.

Thwarting an attacker's attempts to breach your security requires vigilant effort to keep systems patched and properly configured. Firewalls and intrusion detection and prevention systems often provide the means to detect and gather evidence to prosecute attackers who have breached your security.

Malicious Code

Malicious code is any script or program that performs an unwanted, unauthorized, or unknown activity on a computer system. Malicious code can take many forms, including viruses, worms, Trojan horses, documents with destructive macros, and logic bombs. It is often called *malware*, short for malicious software, and less commonly *malcode*, short for malicious code. Malicious code exists for every type of computer or computing device and is the most common form of security breach. Chapter 8 covers malicious code in detail. This section is focused on preventive measures to stop or mitigate the various types of malicious code.

Distribution Methods

Methods of distributing viruses continue to evolve. Years ago, the most popular method was via floppy disks, hand carried from system to system. Later, the most popular method was via email either as an attachment or an embedded script. Today, many people consider drive-by downloads to be the most popular method.

A *drive-by download* is code downloaded and installed on a user's system without the user's knowledge. Attackers modify the code on a web page, and when the user visits, the code downloads and installs malware on the user's system without the user's knowledge or consent. Attackers sometimes modify code on legitimate websites to include drive-by downloads. They also host their own malicious websites and use phishing or redirection methods to get users to the malicious website. Most drive-by downloads take advantage of vulnerabilities in unpatched systems, so keeping your systems up-to-date protects them.

 Some recent drive-by downloads include Zeus and Gumblar. Zeus spread through drive-by downloads and phishing attempts, and once installed, it stole credentials for bank sites. A site infected with Gumblar redirected users to another site, which then downloaded and opened an infected Portable Document Format (PDF) file.

Another popular method uses a pay-per-install approach. Criminals pay website operators to host their malware, which is often a fake antivirus program (also called rogueware or ransomware). The website operators are paid for every installation initiated from their website. According to Symantec, payments can be anywhere between 13 cents per install to 30 dollars per install depending on what is installed and the location of the victim. Installations on computers in the United States pay more.

While the majority of malware is passed to systems from the Internet, some is passed to systems via USB flash drives. Many viruses can detect when a USB flash drive is inserted into a system and then infect the drive. When this USB drive is plugged into another system, it infects the other system.

Protection Methods

The most important protection against malicious code is the use of antivirus (AV) software with up-to-date signature files. Attackers regularly release new malware and often modify existing malware to prevent detection by AV software. AV software vendors look for these changes and develop new signature files to detect the new and modified malware. Years ago, AV vendors recommended updating signature files once a week. However, most AV software today includes the ability to automatically check for updates several times a day.

Many organizations use a multipronged approach to blocking malware and detecting any malware that gets in. Firewalls with content filter capabilities (or specialized content filter appliances) are commonly used at the boundary between the Internet and the internal network to filter out any type of malicious code. Specialized AV software is installed on email servers to detect and filter any type of malware passed via email. Additionally, AV software is installed on each individual system to detect and block malware. AV software must be updated regularly with new definitions, and it's common for an organization to automate these updates and control them through a central server.

The majority of antivirus software will protect against all types of malicious code, not just viruses. You can think of it as anti-malicious-code software or anti-malicious-software software, but you're unlikely to see it labeled or marketed that way.

A multipronged approach with antivirus software on each system in addition to filtering Internet content helps protect systems from infections from any source. As an example, using up-to-date AV software on each system will detect and block a virus on an employee's USB flash drive.

Antivirus vendors commonly recommend installing only one antivirus application on any system. When more than one antivirus application is installed, they often interfere with each other and can sometimes cause system problems. Additionally, having more than one scanner can consume excessive system resources.

Following the principle of least privilege also helps. Users will not have administrative permissions on systems and will not be able to install applications that may be malicious. If a virus does infect a system, it can often impersonate the logged-in user. When this user has limited privileges, the virus is limited in its capabilities. Additionally, vulnerabilities related to malware increase as additional applications are added. Each additional application provides another potential attack point for malicious code.

Another protection method is educating users about the dangers of malicious code, how it is transmitted, and activities they can take to limit their risks. Many times a user can avoid an infection simply by not clicking on a link or opening an attachment. Chapter 2 covered social engineering, including phishing, spear phishing, and whaling. When users are educated about these types of attacks, they are less likely to fall for them. Certainly many users are educated about these risks, but phishing emails continue to flood the Internet and land in users' inboxes. The only reason attackers continue to send them is that they continue to fool some users.

Education, Policy, and Tools

Malicious software is a constant challenge within any organization using IT resources. Consider Kim, who forwarded a seemingly harmless interoffice joke through email to Larry's account. Larry opened the document, which actually contained active code segments that performed harmful actions on his system. Larry then reported a host of "performance issues" and "stability problems" with his workstation, which he never complained about before.

In this scenario, Kim and Larry don't recognize the harm caused by their apparently innocuous activities. After all, sharing anecdotes and jokes through company email is a common way to bond and socialize. What's the harm in that, right? The real question is how can you educate Kim, Larry, and all your other users to be more discreet and discerning in handling shared documents and executables?

The key is a combination of education, policy, and tools. Education should inform Kim that forwarding nonwork materials on the company network is counter to policy and good behavior. Likewise, Larry should learn that opening attachments unrelated to specific work tasks can lead to all kinds of problems (including those he fell prey to here). Policies should clearly identify acceptable use of IT resources and the dangers of circulating unauthorized materials. Tools such as antivirus software should be employed to prevent and detect any type of malware within the environment.

Zero-Day-Exploit

A *zero-day exploit* refers to an attack on a system exploiting a vulnerability that is unknown to others. However, the term is used in different contexts and has some minor differences based on the context. As an example, imagine that a vulnerability exists on an operating system but currently no one knows about it. At some point, it will be discovered, the vendor will develop and release a patch, and administrators will apply the patch. However, if an attack is launched between the time that the vulnerability is discovered and the patch is applied, that may be referred to as a zero-day exploit. There are several ways this happens:

Attacker First Discovers a Vulnerability   When an attacker discovers a vulnerability, the attacker can easily exploit it because the attacker is the only one aware of the vulnerability. At this point, the vendor is unaware of the vulnerability and has not developed or released a patch. This is the common definition of a zero-day exploit.

Vendor Learns of Vulnerability   When the vendor learns of a vulnerability, they evaluate the seriousness of the threat and prioritize the development of a patch. Software patches can be complex and require extensive testing to ensure that the patch does not cause other problems. Vendors may develop and release patches within days for serious threats, or they may take months to develop and release a patch for a problem they do not consider serious. Attacks exploiting the vulnerability during this time are often called zero-day exploits because the vulnerability is not known by the public.

Vendor Releases Patch   Once a patch is developed and released, patched systems are no longer vulnerable to the exploit. However, organizations often take time to evaluate and test a patch before applying it, resulting in a gap between when the patch is released and when it is applied. Chapter 13 referred to "exploit Wednesday," the day after Microsoft patches are released on patch Tuesday. Some people refer to attacks the day after a patch is released as a zero-day attack, but this usage isn't as common.

If an organization doesn't have an effective patch management system, they can have systems that are vulnerable to known exploits. However, if an attack occurs weeks or months after a patch has been released, this is not known as a zero-day exploit.

Methods used to protect systems against zero-day exploits include many of the basic measures. Ensure systems are not running unneeded services and protocols to reduce a system's attack surface, enable both network-based and host-based firewalls to limit potentially malicious traffic, and use intrusion detection systems to help detect potential attacks. Additionally, when honeypots or padded cells (described later in this chapter) are used, it gives administrators an opportunity to observe attacks and may reveal an attack using a zero-day exploit.

Denial-of-Service Attacks

Denial-of-service (DoS) attacks are attacks that prevent a system from processing or responding to legitimate traffic or requests for resources and objects. A common form of DoS attack will transmit so many data packets to a server that it cannot process them all. Other forms of DoS attacks focus on the exploitation of a known fault or vulnerability in an operating system, service, or application. Exploiting the fault often results in a system crash or 100 percent CPU utilization. No matter what the actual attack consists of, any attack that renders its victim unable to perform normal activities can be considered a DoS attack. DoS attacks can result in system crashes, system reboots, data corruption, blockage of services, and more.

DoS attacks are common for any Internet-facing system. In other words, if a system can be accessed via the Internet, it is highly susceptible to a DoS attack. In contrast, DoS attacks are not common for internal systems that are not directly accessible via the Internet.

Another form of DoS attack is called a distributed denial of service (DDoS). A distributed denial of service occurs when multiple systems attack a single system at the same time. A DDoS could be launched by a group of attackers who launch coordinated attacks against a system. More often today, though, an attacker will compromise several systems and use them as launching platforms against the victims. Botnets (described later in this chapter) are commonly used to launch DDoS attacks.

A *distributed reflective denial-of-service (DRDoS) attack* is a variant of a DoS. It uses a reflected approach to an attack. In other words, it doesn't attack the victim directly, but instead manipulates traffic or a network service so that the attacks are reflected back to the victim from other sources. DNS poisoning attacks (covered in Chapter 4) and smurf attacks (covered later in this section) are examples.

SYN Flood Attack

The *SYN flood attack* is a common DoS attack. It disrupts the standard three-way handshake used by TCP to initiate communication sessions. Normally, a client sends a SYN (synchronize) packet to a server, the server responds with a SYN/ACK (synchronize/ acknowledge) packet to the client, and the client then responds with an ACK (acknowledge) packet back to the server. This three-way handshake establishes a communication session that is used for data transfer until the session is terminated with FIN (finish) or RST (reset) packets.

However, in a SYN flood attack, the attackers send multiple SYN packets but never complete the connection matching ACK packets. This is similar to a jokester sticking his hand out to shake hands, but when the other person sticks his hand out in response, the jokester pulls his hand back, leaving the other person hanging. Figure 14.2 shows an example. In this example, a single attacker has sent three SYN packets and the server has responded to each. For each of these requests, the server has reserved system resources to wait for the ACK. Servers often wait for the ACK for as long as three minutes before aborting the attempted session, though this time can be adjusted.

FIGURE 14.2 SYN flood attack

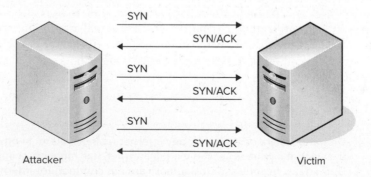

Attacker   Victim

Three incomplete sessions won't cause a problem. However, an attacker will send hundreds or thousands of SYN packets to the victim. Each incomplete session consumes resources, and at some point, the victim becomes overwhelmed and is not able to respond to legitimate requests. The attack can consume available memory and processing power, resulting in the victim slowing to a crawl or actually crashing.

It's common for the attacker to spoof the source address, making it difficult to simply block the attacker by the source IP address. Attackers have also been known to coordinate attacks, launching simultaneous attacks against a single victim as a DDoS attack. Limiting the number of allowable open sessions isn't effective as a defense because once this limit is reached, it blocks session requests from legitimate users. Increasing the number of allowable sessions on a server results in the attack consuming more system resources, and a server has a finite amount of RAM and processing power.

One method of blocking a SYN flood attack is with SYN cookies. These are small records that consume very few system resources until the ACK is received. When an ACK is received, the SYN cookies are checked and the session is established. Firewalls (covered in Chapter 4) often include mechanisms to check for SYN attacks, as do intrusion detection and intrusion prevention systems (covered later in this chapter).

TCP Reset Attack

Another type of attack that manipulates the TCP session is the TCP reset attack. Sessions are normally terminated with either the FIN (finish) or the RST (reset) packet. Attackers can spoof the source IP address in an RST packet and disconnect active sessions. The two systems then need to reestablish the session. This is primarily a threat for systems that need persistent sessions to maintain data with other systems. When the session is reestablished, they need to recreate the data so it's much more than just sending three packets back and forth to establish the session.

Smurf and Fraggle Attacks

Smurf and fraggle attacks are both DoS attacks. A *smurf attack* is another type of flood attack, but it floods the victim with Internet Control Message Protocol (ICMP) echo packets instead of with TCP SYN packets. More specifically, it is a spoofed broadcast ping request using the IP address of the victim as the source IP address.

ICMP is used by ping to check connectivity with remote systems. Normally, ping sends an echo request to a single system, and the system responds with an echo reply. However, in a smurf attack the attacker sends the echo request out as a broadcast to all systems on the network and spoofs the source IP address. All these systems respond with echo replies to the spoofed IP address, flooding the victim with traffic.

Smurf attacks take advantage of an amplifying network (also called a smurf amplifier), which receives the broadcast and then attacks the victim. However, RFC 2644 released in 1999 changed the standard default for routers so that they do not forward directed broadcast traffic. When routers are correctly configured in compliance with RFC 2644, a network cannot be an amplifying network. In other words, smurf attacks are limited to a single network. Additionally, it's becoming common to disable ICMP on firewalls, routers, and even many servers to prevent any type of attacks using ICMP. When standard security practices are used, smurf attacks are rarely a problem today.

Fraggle attacks are similar to smurf attacks. However, instead of using ICMP, a fraggle attack uses UDP packets over UDP ports 7 and 19. The fraggle attack will broadcast a UDP packet using the spoofed IP address of the victim. All systems on the network will then start sending traffic to the victim, just as with a smurf attack.

Ping-of-Death

A *ping-of-death attack* employs an oversized ping packet. Ping packets are normally 32 or 64 bytes, though some other sizes are used with different operating systems. The ping-of-death attack changed the size of ping packets to over 64 KB, which was bigger than many systems could handle. When a system received a ping packet larger than 64 KB, it resulted in a problem. In some cases the system crashed; in other cases it resulted in a buffer overflow error. Most systems have either been patched or updated so that the ping-of-death error does not cause problems today.

While the ping-of-death isn't a problem today, many other types of attacks cause buffer overflow errors (discussed in Chapter 8). When vendors discover bugs that can cause a buffer overflow, they release patches to fix them. One of the best protections against any buffer overflow attack is to keep a system up-to-date with current patches. Additionally, production systems should not include untested code or allow the use of system or root-level privileges.

Teardrop

In a *teardrop attack*, an attacker fragments traffic in such a way that data packets can't be put together. Large packets are normally divided into smaller fragments when they're sent over a network and the receiving system then puts the packet fragments back together into their original state. However, in a teardrop attack these packets are mangled in such a way that they cannot be put back together. Older systems couldn't handle this situation and crashed, but patches were able to resolve the problem. Although current systems aren't susceptible to teardrop attacks, this does emphasize the importance of keeping systems up-to-date. Additionally, intrusion detection systems can check for malformed packets.

Land Attacks

A *land attack* occurs when the attacker sends spoofed SYN packets to a victim using the victim's IP address as both source and destination IP address. This tricks the system into constantly replying to itself and can cause it to freeze, crash, or reboot. This attack was first discovered in 1997, and it has resurfaced several times, attacking different ports. Keeping a system up-to-date and filtering traffic to detect traffic with identical source and destination addresses helps to protect against land attacks.

Botnets

Botnets are quite common today. The computers in a botnet are like robots (often called zombies) and will do whatever they're instructed to do. A bot herder is typically a criminal who controls all the computers in the botnet via one (or more) command and control servers. The bot herder enters commands on the server and the zombies periodically check in with the command and control server to receive instructions. Bot herders commonly use computers within a botnet to launch a wide range of attacks, send spam and phishing emails, or rent the botnets out to other criminals.

Computers often join a botnet after being infected with some type of malicious code or malicious software. Once the computer is infected, it often gives the bot herder remote access to the system and additional malware is installed. In some cases, the zombies install malware that searches for files, including passwords or other information of interest to the attacker, or include keyloggers to capture user keystrokes.

Botnets of over 40,000 computers are relatively common and botnets controlling millions of systems have been active in the past. Most botnets are controlled by separate bot herders, but some bot herders may control more than one botnet.

The best protection against a computer's joining a botnet is to ensure antivirus software is running and the definitions are up-to-date. Additionally, since malware often takes advantage of unpatched flaws in operating systems and applications, keeping systems up-to-date with patches helps keep them protected.

 Real World Scenario

Some Recent Botnets

The Esthost botnet (also called DNS Changer) infected approximately 4 million computers. It manipulated DNS settings to use DNS servers controlled by the bot herders and manipulated advertising. It generated at least $14 million in illicit payments and also prevented users from updating antivirus software or updating their operating system. In this case, the inability to update the system was an important symptom, but one that was ignored by many users.

Rustock is a spamming botnet that controlled more than 815,000 zombies when it was taken down in 2011. It's estimated that Rustock was responsible for sending between one and two thousand spam emails per second. The Waledac botnet is another spamming botnet. It had infected hundreds of thousands of computers and was able to send over 1.5 billion spam emails a day before it was taken down in 2010.

These are a few of the well-known large botnets that have been taken down, but this list is certainly not complete. No one has released data on how many smaller botnets are currently running, but there are lists that identify many active botnets that are controlling tens of thousands of systems.

Ping Flood

A *ping flood attack* floods a victim with ping requests. This can be very effective when launched by zombies within a botnet as a DDoS attack. If tens of thousands of systems simultaneously send ping requests to a system, the system can be overwhelmed trying to answer the ping requests. The victim will not have time to respond to legitimate requests. A common way this is handled today is by blocking ICMP traffic. Active intrusion detection systems can detect a ping flood and modify the environment to block ICMP traffic during the attack.

Miscellaneous Attacks

The following sections cover some generic attacks that an organization needs to consider and protect against. These aren't necessarily denial-of-service attacks but are still important to recognize.

Man-in-the-Middle Attacks

A *man-in-the-middle* attack occurs when a malicious user is able to gain a position between the two endpoints of an ongoing communication. There are two types of man-in-the-middle attacks. One involves copying or sniffing the traffic between two parties; this is basically a sniffer attack, as described in Chapter 2. The other involves attackers positioning themselves in the line of communication where they act as a store-and-forward or proxy mechanism, as shown in Figure 14.3. The two systems think they are connected directly to the other system. However, the attacker captures and forwards all data between the two systems. Through this type of attack, the attacker can collect logon credentials or sensitive data as well as change the content of messages exchanged between the two systems.

FIGURE 14.3   A man-in-the-middle attack

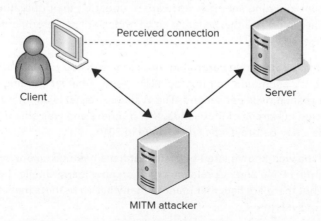

Man-in-the-middle attacks require more technical sophistication than many other attacks because the attacker needs to successfully impersonate a server from the perspective of the client and impersonate the client from the perspective of the server. A man-in-the-middle attack will often require a combination of multiple attacks. For example, the attacker may alter routing information and DNS values, steal IP addresses, or falsify address resolution protocol (ARP) lookups as a part of the attack.

Some man-in-the-middle attacks are thwarted by keeping systems up-to-date with patches. An intrusion detection system cannot usually detect man-in-the-middle or hijack attacks, but it can detect abnormal activities occurring over communication links and alert you to suspicious activity.

Sabotage

Employee *sabotage* is a criminal act of destruction or disruption committed against an organization by an employee. It can become a risk if an employee is knowledgeable enough about the assets of an organization, has sufficient access to manipulate critical aspects of the environment, and has become disgruntled. Employee sabotage occurs most often when an employee suspects they will be terminated without just cause, or if an employee retains access after being terminated.

This is another important reason employee terminations should be handled swiftly and account access should be disabled as soon as possible after the termination. Other safeguards against employee sabotage are intensive auditing, monitoring for abnormal or unauthorized activity, keeping lines of communication open between employees and managers, and properly compensating and recognizing employees for their contributions.

Espionage

Espionage is the malicious act of gathering proprietary, secret, private, sensitive, or confidential information about an organization for the express purpose of disclosing and often selling that data to a competitor or other interested organization (such as a foreign government). Espionage is sometimes committed by internal employees who have become dissatisfied with their jobs or who have become compromised in some way, such as through blackmail. It can also be committed by a mole or plant placed in your organization to steal information for a primary secret employer. Or it can occur far removed from the workplace, perhaps at a convention or an event, perpetrated by someone who specifically targets employees' mobile assets.

Countermeasures against espionage are to strictly control access to all nonpublic data, thoroughly screen new employee candidates, and efficiently track all employee activities.

War Dialing

War dialing means using a modem to search for a system that accepts inbound connection attempts. A war dialer might be a typical computer with a modem attached and running war dialer software, or it can be a stand-alone device. In either case, war dialers systematically dial phone numbers and listen for computer carrier tones. When a computer carrier tone is detected, the war dialer adds this number to a report generated at the end of the search process. A war dialer can search any range of numbers, such as all 10,000 numbers within a specific prefix or all 10,000,000 within a specific area code.

While the use of modems has dwindled significantly, they are still being used in some situations. They are an efficient way to provide remote access for employees who don't have direct access to the Internet while traveling. Also, employees have been known to install modems on their systems to access the Internet and bypass the organization's content monitoring tools.

A newer form of war dialing uses Voice over Internet Protocol (VoIP) to make calls without the use of modems. This allows an attacker to scan many more phone numbers, and also to detect devices other than modems, such as fax machines, voicemail boxes, dial tones, and voices. As an example, WarVOX is a war dialing tool that uses VoIP. WarVOX has been incorporated into Metasploit, a well-known penetration testing tool that can be used by both attackers and testers.

Countermeasures against malicious war dialing include imposing strong remote access security (including strong authentication), ensuring that no unauthorized modems are present, using callback security, restricting what protocols can be used, and using call logging.

Intrusion Detection and Prevention

An *intrusion* occurs when an attacker is able to bypass or thwart security mechanisms and gain access to an organization's resources. *Intrusion detection* is a specific form of monitoring that monitors recorded information and real-time events to detect abnormal activity indicating a potential incident or intrusion. An *intrusion detection system (IDS)* automates the inspection of logs and real-time system events to detect intrusion attempts and system failures.

IDSs are an effective method of detecting many of the DoS and DDoS attacks mentioned earlier in this section. They can recognize attacks that come from external connections, such as an attack from the Internet, as well as attacks that spread internally, such as a malicious worm. Once they detect a suspicious event, they respond by sending alerts or raising alarms, and in some cases, they can modify the environment to stop an attack. A primary goal of an IDS is to provide a means for a timely and accurate response to intrusions.

An IDS is intended as part of a defense-in-depth security plan. It will work with and complement other security mechanisms such as firewalls, but it should not replace them.

An intrusion prevention system (IPS) includes all the capabilities of an IDS but can also take additional steps to stop or prevent intrusions. If desired, administrators can disable the extra features of an IPS, essentially causing it to function as an IDS.

You'll often see the two terms combined as intrusion detection and prevention systems (IDPSs). As an example, NIST SP 800-94, "Guide to Intrusion Detection and Prevention

Systems" (available from the NIST special publications download page: `http://csrc`
`.nist.gov/publications/PubsSPs.html`) provides comprehensive coverage of both intrusion detection and intrusion prevention systems, but for brevity uses IDPS throughout the
document to refer to both. In this chapter we are describing methods used by IDSs to detect
attacks, how they can respond to attacks, the types of IDSs available, and then adding
information on IPSs where appropriate.

A Little History on CISSP Objectives

The CISSP certification was first established and launched in 1994, and it has gone
through several changes over the years. Similarly, IT security has also gone through
several changes as new threats emerge and controls are created or improved to protect
against them.

(ISC)² publishes the Candidate Information Bulletin (CIB), which identifies the 10 domains
and also outlines major topics and subtopics within the domains. The CIB provides a
limited exam blueprint, but it hasn't always been called a CIB. In 2002, (ISC)² called this
document *The CISSP Certification Common Body of Knowledge (CBK) Study Guide*. The
content in the CBK Study Guide was similar to the current CIB, though it often went into
more detail.

Intrusion detection is a topic that has been in the CISSP CBK and CIB for many years. In
the 2002 CBK Study Guide, intrusion detection topics were included in both the Access
Control Systems & Methodology domain and the Operations Security domain. (These
domains are currently named Access Control and Security Operations, respectively.)
However, if you look at either the 2009 or 2012 CIBs, you won't see "Intrusion Detection"
listed anywhere. This does not mean intrusion detection is not relevant or not tested. It
is. However, it does show how the objectives within the CIB are becoming much broader.

While analyzing the 2012 updated CIB, we decided that intrusion detection fits more in
the Security Operations domain than the Access Control domain. Specifically, we are
including it here as part of the "Implement preventive measures against attacks" objective. It could be included in both chapters, but a CISSP book is big enough on its own
without duplicating material. The important point isn't so much where it's included but
instead to ensure you understand the topic.

Knowledge- and Behavior-Based Detection

An IDS actively watches for suspicious activity by monitoring network traffic and inspecting logs. For example, an IDS can have sensors or agents monitoring key devices such as
routers and firewalls in a network. These devices have logs that can record activity and the
sensors can forward these log entries to the IDS for analysis. Some sensors send all the data

to the IDS whereas other sensors inspect the entries and only send specific log entries based on how it's configured.

The IDS evaluates the data and can detect malicious behavior using two common methods: knowledge-based detection and behavior-based detection. In short, knowledge-based detection uses signatures similar to the signature definitions used by antivirus software. Behavior-based detection doesn't use signatures but instead compares activity against a baseline of normal performance to detect abnormal behavior. Many IDSs use a combination of both methods.

Knowledge-Based Detection   The most common method of detection is *knowledge-based detection* (also called signature-based detection or pattern-matching detection). It uses a database of known attacks developed by the IDS vendor. For example, some automated tools are available to launch SYN flood attacks, and these tools have known patterns and characteristics that can be described in a signature database. Real-time traffic is matched against the database, and if the IDS finds a match, it raises an alert.

Knowledge-based detection on an IDS is similar to signature-based detection used by antivirus applications. The antivirus application has a database of known malware and checks files against the database looking for a match. The primary drawback for a knowledge-based IDS is that it is effective only against known attack methods. New attacks or slightly modified versions of known attacks often go unrecognized by the IDS. Just as antivirus software must be regularly updated with new signatures from the antivirus vendor, IDS databases must be regularly updated with new attack signatures. Most IDS vendors provide automated methods to update the signatures.

Behavior-Based Detection   The second detection type is *behavior-based detection* (also called statistical intrusion detection, anomaly detection, and heuristics-based detection). Behavior-based detection starts by creating a baseline of normal activities and events on the system. Once it has accumulated enough baseline data to determine normal activity, it can detect abnormal activity that may indicate a malicious intrusion or event.

This baseline is often created over a single finite period such as a week. If the network is modified, the baseline needs to be updated. Otherwise, the IDS may alert on normal behavior that it identifies as abnormal. In some cases, the IDS will continue to monitor the network to learn more about normal activity, and it will update the baseline based on the observations.

Behavior-based IDSs use the baseline, activity statistics, and heuristic evaluation techniques to compare current activity against previous activity to detect potentially malicious events. Many can perform stateful packet analysis similar to how stateful inspection firewalls (covered in Chapter 3) examine traffic based on the state or context of network traffic.

Anomaly analysis adds to an IDS's capabilities by allowing it to recognize and react to sudden increases in traffic volume or activity, multiple failed login attempts, logons or program activity outside normal working hours, or sudden increases in error or failure messages. All of these could indicate an attack that may not be recognized by knowledge-based detection.

A behavior-based IDS can be labeled an expert system or a pseudo-artificial intelligence system because it can learn and make assumptions about events. In other words, the IDS can act like a human expert by evaluating current events against known events. The more information provided to a behavior-based IDS about normal activities and events, the more accurately it can detect anomalies. A significant benefit of a behavior-based IDS is that it can detect newer attacks that have no signatures and are not detectable with the signature-based method.

The primary drawback for a behavior-based IDS is that it often raises a high number of false alarms, also called false alerts or false positives. Patterns of user and system activity can vary widely during normal operations, making it difficult to accurately define the boundaries of normal and abnormal activity.

 Real World Scenario

False Alarms

A challenge that many IDS administrators have is finding a balance between the number of false alarms or alerts an IDS sends, and ensuring that actual attacks are reported. In one organization we know about, an IDS sent a series of alerts over a couple of days that were aggressively investigated but turned out to be false alarms. Administrators began losing faith in the system and regretted wasting time chasing these false alarms.

Later, the IDS began sending alerts on an actual attack. However, administrators were actively troubleshooting another issue that they knew was real and they didn't have time to chase what they perceived as more false alarms. They simply dismissed the alarms on the IDS and didn't discover the attack until a few days later.

IDS Response

Although knowledge-based and behavior-based IDSs detect incidents differently, they both use an alert system. When the IDS detects an event, it triggers an alarm or alert. It can then respond using a passive or active method. A passive response logs the event and sends a notification. An active response changes the environment to block the activity in addition to logging and sending a notification.

 In some cases, you can measure a firewall's effectiveness by placing a passive IDS before the firewall and another passive IDS after the firewall. By examining the alerts in the two IDSs, you can determine what attacks the firewall is blocking in addition to determining what attacks are getting through.

Passive Response   Notifications can be sent to administrators via email, text or pager messages, or pop-up messages. In some cases, the alert can generate a report detailing the activity leading up to the event, and logs are available for administrators to get more information if needed. Many 24-hour network operations centers (NOCs) have central monitoring screens viewable by everyone in the main support center. For example, a single wall can have multiple large screen monitors providing data on different elements of the NOC. The IDS alerts can be displayed on one of these screens to ensure personnel are aware of the event. These instant notifications help administrators respond quickly and effectively to unwanted behavior.

Active Response   Active responses can modify the environment using several different methods. Typical responses include modifying access control lists (ACLs) to block traffic based on ports, protocols, and source addresses, and even disable all communications over specific cable segments. For example, if a SYN flood attack is detected from a single IP address, the IDS can change the ACL to block all traffic from this IP address. Similarly, if a ping flood attack is detected from multiple IP addresses, it can change the ACL to block all ICMP traffic. An IDS can also block access to resources for suspicious or ill-behaved users. Active responses are programmed in advance, and security administrators can tweak these responses to meet the needs of their own environment.

 An IDS that uses an active response is sometimes referred to as an IPS (intrusion prevention system). This is accurate in some situations. However, an IPS (described later in this section) is placed in line with the traffic. If an active IDS is placed in line with the traffic, it is an IPS. If is not placed in line with the traffic, it isn't a true IPS because it can only detect and respond to the attack after it has detected an attack in progress. NIST SP 800-94 recommends placing all active IDSs in line with the traffic so that they function as IPSs.

Host- and Network-Based IDSs

IDS types are commonly classified as host based and network based. A *host-based IDS (HIDS)* monitors a single computer or host. A *network-based IDS (NIDS)* monitors a network by observing network traffic patterns.

A less-used classification is an application-based IDS, which is a specific type of network-based IDS. It monitors specific application traffic between two or more servers. For example, an application-based IDS can monitor traffic between a web server and a database server looking for suspicious activity.

Host-Based IDS   An HIDS monitors activity on a single computer, including process calls and information recorded in system, application, security, and host-based firewall logs. It can often examine events in greater detail than an NIDS can, and it can pinpoint specific files compromised in an attack and processes employed by the attacker.

A benefit of HIDSs over NIDSs is that HIDSs can detect anomalies on the host system that cannot be detected by an NIDS. For example, an HIDS can detect infections where an intruder has infiltrated a system and is controlling it remotely. You may notice that this sounds similar to what antivirus software will do on a computer. It is. Many HIDSs include antivirus capabilities.

Although many vendors recommend installing host-based IDSs on all systems, this isn't common due to some of the disadvantages of HIDSs. Instead, many organizations choose to install HIDSs only on key servers as an added level of protection. Some of the disadvantages of HIDSs are related to the cost and usability. HIDSs are more costly to manage than NIDSs because they require administrative attention on each system, whereas NIDSs usually support centralized administration. An HIDS cannot detect network attacks on other systems. Additionally, it will often consume a significant amount of system resources, degrading the host system performance. While it's often possible to restrict the system resources used by the HIDS, this can result in it missing an active attack. Additionally, they are easier for an intruder to discover and disable, and their logs are maintained on the system, making the logs susceptible to modification during a successful attack.

Network-Based IDS   An NIDS monitors and evaluates network activity to detect attacks or event anomalies. It cannot monitor the content of encrypted traffic, but it can monitor other packet details. A single NIDS can monitor a large network by using remote sensors to collect data at key network locations, which send data to a central management console. These sensors can monitor traffic at routers, firewalls, network switches that support port mirroring, and other types of network taps.

Switches are often used as a preventive measure against rogue sniffers. If the IDS is connected to a normal port on the switch, it will capture only a small portion of the network traffic, which isn't very useful. Instead, the switch is configured to mirror all traffic to a specific port (commonly called port mirroring) used by the IDS. On Cisco switches, the port used for port mirroring is referred to as a Switched Port Analyzer (SPAN) port.

The central console is often installed on a single-purpose computer that is hardened against attacks. This reduces vulnerabilities in the NIDS and can allow it to operate almost invisibly, making it much harder for attackers to discover and disable it. An NIDS has very little negative effect on the overall network performance, and when it is deployed on a single-purpose system, it doesn't adversely affect performance on any other computer. On networks with large volumes of traffic, a single NIDS may be unable to keep up with the flow of data, but it is possible to add additional systems to balance the load.

Often, an NIDS can discover the source of an attack by performing Reverse Address Resolution Protocol (RARP) or reverse Domain Name System (DNS) lookups. However, because attackers often spoof IP addresses or launch attacks by zombies via a botnet, additional investigation is required to determine the actual source. This can be a laborious process and is beyond the scope of the IDS, but it is possible to discover the source of spoofed IPs.

It is considered unethical and risky to actively launch counterstrikes against an intruder or to actively attempt to reverse-hack an intruder's computer system. Instead, rely on your logging capabilities and sniffing collections to provide sufficient data to prosecute criminals or to simply improve the security of your environment in response.

An NIDS is usually able to detect the initiation of an attack or ongoing attacks, but they can't always provide information about the success of an attack. They won't know if specific systems, user accounts, files, or applications have been negatively affected. For example, an NIDS may discover a buffer overflow exploit was sent through the network, but it won't necessarily know if the exploit successfully infiltrated a system. However, after administrators receive the alert they can check relevant systems. Or, after an incident, the NIDS logs can be used as part of the audit trail to discover what occurred.

Intrusion Prevention Systems

An intrusion prevention system (IPS) is a special type of active IDS that attempts to detect and block attacks before they reach target systems. It's sometimes referred to as an intrusion detection and prevention system (IDPS). A distinguishing difference between an IDS and an IPS is that the IPS is placed in line with the traffic, as shown in Figure 14.4. In other words, all traffic must pass through the IPS and the IPS can choose what traffic to forward and what traffic to block after analyzing it. This allows the IPS to prevent an attack from reaching a target.

FIGURE 14.4 Intrusion prevention system

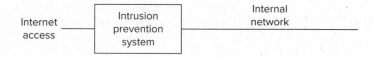

In contrast, an active IDS that is not placed in line can only check the activity after it has reached the target. The active IDS can take steps to block an attack after it starts but cannot prevent it.

An IPS can use knowledge-based detection, and/or behavior-based detection, just like any other IDS. Additionally, it can log activity and provide notification to administrators just as an IDS would.

IDS-Related Tools

Intrusion detection systems are often deployed in concert with other tools such as honeypots, pseudo flaws, padded cells, and darknets that work together to protect a network.

These IDS-related tools expand the usefulness and capabilities of IDSs and increase the overall security of a network.

Honeypots   *Honeypots* are individual computers created as a trap for intruders. They look and act like legitimate systems, but they do not host data of any real value for an attacker. Honeypots are often configured with vulnerabilities to tempt intruders into attacking them. They may be unpatched or have security vulnerabilities that are purposely not locked down. The goal is to grab the attention of intruders and keep them away from the legitimate network that has valuable resources. Legitimate users never access the honeypot, so any access to a honeypot is most likely an unauthorized intruder.

A honeynet is two or more networked honeypots used in tandem to simulate a network. Often, these honeynets are hosted on virtual systems.

In addition to keeping the attacker away from a production environment, the honeypot gives administrators an opportunity to observe an attacker's activity without compromising the live environment. In some cases, the honeypot is designed to delay an intruder long enough for the automated IDS to detect the intrusion and gather as much information about the intruder as possible. The longer the attacker spends with the honeypot, the more time an administrator has to investigate the attack and potentially identify the intruder. Many security professionals consider honeypots to be effective countermeasures against zero-day exploits.

The use of honeypots raises the issue of enticement versus entrapment. A honeypot can be legally used as an enticement device if the intruder discovers it through no outward efforts of the honeypot owner. Placing a system on the Internet with open security vulnerabilities and active services with known exploits is enticement. Enticement occurs when the opportunity for illegal or unauthorized actions is provided but perpetrators make their own decisions to perform such action. Entrapment, which is illegal, occurs when the honeypot owner actively solicits visitors to access the site and then charges them with unauthorized intrusion. In other words, it is entrapment when you trick or encourage someone into performing an illegal or unauthorized action.

Laws vary in different countries, so it's important to understand local laws related to enticement and entrapment.

Pseudo Flaws   *Pseudo flaws* are false vulnerabilities or apparent loopholes intentionally implanted in a system in an attempt to tempt attackers. They are often used on honeypot systems to emulate well-known operating system vulnerabilities. Attackers seeking to exploit a known flaw might stumble across a pseudo flaw and think that they have successfully penetrated a system. More sophisticated pseudo flaw mechanisms simulate the penetration and convince the attacker that they have gained additional access privileges to a system. However, while the attacker is exploring the system, monitoring and alerting mechanisms trigger in the background to alert administrators to the threat.

Padded Cells   A *padded cell* system is similar to a honeypot, but it performs intrusion isolation using a different approach. When an IDS detects an intruder, that intruder is automatically transferred to a padded cell. The padded cell has the look and feel of an actual network, but the attacker is unable to perform any malicious activities or access any confidential data from within the padded cell.

The padded cell is a simulated environment that offers fake data to retain an intruder's interest, similar to a honeypot. However, the IDS transfers the intruder into a padded cell without informing the intruder that the change has occurred. In contrast, the attacker chooses to attack the honeypot. A padded cell system is heavily monitored and used by administrators to gather evidence for tracing attacks and possible prosecution of attackers.

Darknets   Within the context of intrusion detection, a *darknet* is a portion of allocated IP addresses within a network that are not used. It includes one device configured to capture all the traffic into the darknet. Since the IP addresses are not used, the darknet does not have any other hosts and it should not have any traffic at all. Thus, if an attacker is probing a network, or malware is attempting to spread, the activity will be detected in the darknet and captured. A benefit to darknets is that there are few false positives. Legitimate traffic should not be in the darknet, so unless there is a misconfiguration on the network, traffic in the darknet is not legitimate.

Penetration Testing

Penetration testing is another preventive measure an organization can use to counter attacks. A penetration test (often shortened to *pen test*) mimics an actual attack in an attempt to identify what techniques attackers can use to circumvent security in an application, system, network, or organization. It may include vulnerability scans, port scans, packet sniffing, denial-of-service attacks, and social engineering techniques. However, penetration testing is performed by security professionals with prior approval and advance knowledge of senior management.

NIST SP 800-115, "Technical Guide to Information Security Testing and Assessment," includes a significant amount of information about testing including penetration testing. You can download it from the NIST special publications download page: http://csrc.nist.gov/publications/PubsSPs.html.

Regularly staged penetration tests are a good way to accurately evaluate the effectiveness of security controls used within an organization. Penetration testing may reveal areas where patches or security settings are insufficient, where new vulnerabilities have developed or become exposed, and where security policies are either ineffective or not being followed. Any of these vulnerabilities can be exploited by attackers.

A penetration test will commonly include a vulnerability scan or vulnerability assessment (as described in Chapter 13) to detect weaknesses. However, the penetration test goes a step further and attempts to exploit the weaknesses. For example, a vulnerability scanner may discover that a website with a back-end database is not using input validation techniques and is susceptible to a SQL injection attack. The penetration test may then use a SQL injection attack to access the entire database. Similarly, a vulnerability assessment may discover that employees aren't educated about social engineering attacks and a penetration test may use social engineering methods to gain access to a secure area or obtain sensitive information from employees.

Some of the goals of a penetration test are to:

- Determine how well a system can tolerate an attack
- Identify employees' ability to detect and respond to attacks in real time
- Identify additional controls that can be implemented to reduce risk

Penetration testing typically includes social engineering attacks, network and system configuration reviews, and environment vulnerability assessments. A penetration test takes vulnerability assessments and vulnerability scans a step further by verifying that vulnerabilities can be exploited.

Risks of Penetration Testing

A significant danger with penetration tests is that some methods can cause outages. For example, if a vulnerability scan discovers that an Internet-based server is susceptible to a buffer overflow attack, a penetration test can exploit that vulnerability, which may result in the server shutting down or rebooting.

Ideally, penetration tests should stop before they cause any actual damage. Unfortunately, the step that causes damage isn't known until it is taken. For example, fuzz testers send invalid or random data to applications or systems to check for the response. It is possible for the fuzz tester to send a stream of data that causes a buffer overflow and locks up an application, but the knowledge that this will occur isn't known until the penetration test reaches that point. Experienced penetration testers are able to minimize the risk of a test causing damage, but this risk cannot be eliminated.

Whenever possible, a penetration test should be performed on a test system instead of a live system. For example, if a penetration test is designed to test an application, it is often possible to run the application in an isolated environment. If the testing causes damage, it affects only the test system and does not impact the live network. The challenge is that test systems often don't provide a true view of a production environment. A simple application that doesn't interact with other components may be adequately tested in a test environment. However, most applications that need to be tested are not simple. When test systems are used, penetration testers will often qualify their analysis with a statement indicating that the test was done on a test system, so the results may not provide a valid analysis of the production environment.

Obtaining Permission for Penetration Testing

Penetration testing should only be performed after careful consideration and approval of senior management. Many penetration testers insist that approval be granted in writing with the risks spelled out. Performing unapproved security testing could cause productivity losses and trigger emergency response teams.

Malicious users intent on violating the security of an IT environment can be punished based on existing laws. Similarly, if internal users perform informal unauthorized tests against a security measure without authorization, their actions may be viewed as an illegal attack rather than as a penetration test. These users will very likely lose their jobs and may even face legal consequences.

Penetration Testing Techniques

It is common for organizations to hire external consultants to perform penetration testing. The organization can control what information they give to these testers, and the level of knowledge they are given identifies the type of tests they conduct.

Chapter 7, "Software Development Security," covered white-box testing, black-box testing, and gray-box testing in the context of software testing. These same terms are often associated with penetration testing and mean the same thing.

Black-Box Testing by Zero-Knowledge Team   A *zero-knowledge team* knows nothing about the target site except for publicly available information, such as domain name and company address. It's as if they are looking at the target as a black box and have no idea what is within the box until they start probing. An attack by a zero-knowledge team closely resembles a real external attack because all information about the environment must be obtained from scratch.

White-Box Testing by Full-Knowledge Team   A *full-knowledge team* has full access to all aspects of the target environment. They know what patches and upgrades are installed, and the exact configuration of all relevant devices. If the target is an application, they would have access to the source code. Full-knowledge teams perform white-box testing (sometimes called crystal-box testing). White-box testing is commonly recognized as being more efficient and cost effective in locating vulnerabilities because less time is needed for discovery.

Gray-Box Testing by Partial-Knowledge Team   Gray-box testing is performed by a *partial-knowledge team* that has some knowledge of the target but they are not provided access to all the information. They may be given information on the network design and configuration details so that they can focus on attacks and vulnerabilities for specific targets.

The regular security administration staff protecting the target of a penetration test can be considered a full-knowledge team. However, they aren't the best choice to perform a penetration test. They often have blind spots or gaps in their understanding, estimation, or capabilities with certain security subjects. If they knew about a vulnerability that could be exploited, they would likely already have recommended a control to minimize it. A full-knowledge team knows what has been secured, so it may fail to properly test every possibility by relying on false assumptions. Zero-knowledge or partial-knowledge testers are less likely to make these mistakes.

Penetration testing may employ automated attack tools or suites or be performed manually using common network utilities. Automated attack tools range from professional vulnerability scanners and penetration testers to wild, underground tools discovered on the Internet. Several open source and commercial tools (such as Metasploit and Core IMPACT) are available, and these tools may be used by both security professionals and attackers.

Social engineering techniques are often used during penetration tests. Depending on the goal of the test, the testers may use techniques to breach the physical perimeter of an organization or techniques to get users to reveal information. These tests help determine how vulnerable employees are to skilled social engineers and how familiar they are with security policies designed to thwart these types of attacks.

 Real World Scenario

Social Engineering in Pen Tests

The following example is from a penetration test conducted at a bank, but the same results are often repeated at many different organizations. The testers were specifically asked if they could get access to employee user accounts or employee user systems.

Penetration testers crafted a forged email that looked like it was coming from an executive within the bank. It indicated a problem with the network and said that all employees needed to respond with their username and password as soon as possible to ensure they didn't lose their access. Over 40 percent of the employees responded with their credentials.

Additionally, the testers installed malware on several USB drives and "dropped" them at different locations in the parking lot and within the bank. A well-meaning employee saw one, picked it up, and inserted it into a computer with the intent of identifying the owner. Instead, the USB drive infected the user's system, granting the testers remote access.

Similar methods are often used successfully by both testers and attackers. Education is often the most effective method at mitigating these types of attacks, and the pen test often reinforces the need for education.

Protect Reports

Penetration testers will provide a report documenting their results, and this report should be protected as sensitive information. The report will outline specific vulnerabilities, explain how these vulnerabilities can be exploited, and often provide recommendations on how to mitigate the vulnerability. If these results fall into the hands of an attacker before recommendations are implemented, the attacker can use them to easily launch an attack.

It's also important to realize that just because a penetration testing team makes a recommendation it doesn't mean the recommendation will be implemented. Management has the choice of implementing a recommendation to mitigate a risk or accept a risk if they decide the cost of the recommended control is not justified. In other words, a year-old report may outline a specific vulnerability that still remains and this year-old report should be protected just as closely as a report completed yesterday.

Ethical Hacking

Ethical hacking is often used as another name for penetration testing. An *ethical hacker* is someone who understands network security and methods to breach but does not use this knowledge for personal gain. Instead, an ethical hacker uses this knowledge to help organizations understand its vulnerabilities and take action to prevent malicious attacks. An ethical hacker will always stay within legal limits.

Chapter 2 mentioned the technical difference between crackers, hackers, and attackers. The original definition of a *hacker* is a technology enthusiast who does not have malicious intent whereas a cracker or attacker is malicious. The original meaning of the term *hacker* has become blurred because it is often used synonymously with *attacker*. In other words, a hacker is looked at as an attacker, giving the impression that ethical hacking is a contradiction in terms. However, the term *ethical hacking* uses the term *hacker* in its original sense.

Ethical hackers will learn about and often use the same tools and techniques used by attackers. However, they do not use them to attack systems. Instead, they use them to test systems for vulnerabilities and only after being granted explicit permission to test these systems.

Warning Banners

Warning banners serve to inform would-be intruders or those who attempt to violate security policy that their intended activities are restricted and that any further activities will be audited and monitored. A warning banner is basically an electronic equivalent of a "no trespassing" sign. In most situations, wording in banners is important from a legal standpoint because these banners can legally bind users to some permissible set of actions, behaviors, and processes.

Most intrusions and attacks can be prosecuted when warnings clearly state that unauthorized access is prohibited and that any activity will be monitored and recorded. Warning banners are used to inform both authorized and unauthorized users, though authorized users often know this through other means such as acceptable usage agreements.

Understand System Resilience and Fault Tolerance

Technical controls that add to system resilience and fault tolerance directly affect availability, one of the core goals of the CIA security triad (confidentiality, integrity, and availability). A primary goal of system resilience and fault tolerance is to eliminate single points of failure.

A *single point of failure* is any component that can cause an entire system to fail. If a computer has data on a single disk, failure of the disk can cause the computer to fail, so the disk is a single point of failure. If a database-dependent website includes multiple web servers all served by a single database server, the database server is a single point of failure.

Fault tolerance is the ability of a system to suffer a fault but continue to operate. Fault tolerance is achieved by adding redundant components such as additional disks within a redundant array of inexpensive disks (RAID) array, or additional servers within a failover clustered configuration.

System resilience refers to the ability of a system to maintain an acceptable level of service during an adverse event. This could be a hardware fault managed by fault-tolerant components, or it could be an attack managed by other controls such as effective intrusion detection and prevention systems. In some contexts, it refers to the ability of a system to return to a previous state after an adverse event. For example, if a primary server in a failover cluster fails, fault tolerance ensures that the system fails over to another server. System resilience implies that the cluster can fail back to the original server after the original server is repaired.

In previous versions of the CISSP CIB, fault tolerance was listed by itself. However, in the CIB effective in January 2012, (ISC)[2] added system resilience with fault tolerance. The term *system resilience* is being used more often to indicate high-availability solutions that go beyond fault tolerance and can handle adverse events from any source to keep a system operational.

It's also possible to provide fault tolerance for entire locations. Chapter 16 presents information on using alternate locations such as hot sites, cold sites, and warm sites in response to a disaster.

Protecting Hard Drives

A common way that fault tolerance and system resilience is added for computers is with a redundant array of disks (RAID) array. A RAID array includes two or more disks, and most RAID configurations will continue to operate even after one of the disks fails. Some of the common RAID configurations are:

RAID-0   This is also called striping. It uses two or more disks and improves the disk sub-system performance, but it does not provide fault tolerance.

RAID-1   This is also called mirroring. It uses two disks, which both hold the same data. If one disk fails, the other disk includes the data so a system can continue to operate after a single disk fails. Depending on the hardware used and which drive fails, the system may be able to continue to operate without intervention, or the system may need to be manually configured to use the drive that didn't fail.

RAID-5   This is also called striping with parity. It uses three or more disks with the equiv-alent of one disk holding parity information. If any single disk fails, the RAID array will continue to operate, though it will be slower.

RAID-10   This is also known as RAID 1 + 0 or a stripe of mirrors, and is configured as two or more mirrors (RAID-1) configured in a striped (RAID-0) configuration. It uses at least four disks but can support more as long as an even number of disks are added. It will continue to operate even if multiple disks fail, as long as at least one drive in each mirror continues to function. For example, if it had three mirrored sets (called M1, M2, and M3 for this example) it would have a total of six disks. If one drive in M1, one in M2, and one in M3 all failed, the array would continue to operate. However, if two drives in any of the mirrors failed, such as both drives in M1, the entire array would fail.

Fault tolerance is not the same as a backup. Occasionally, management may balk at the cost of backup tapes and point to the RAID, saying that the data is already backed up. However, if a catastrophic hardware failure destroys a RAID array, all the data is lost unless a backup exists. Similarly, if an acci-dental deletion or corruption destroys data, it cannot be restored if a backup doesn't exist. Chapter 16 covers backups in more depth.

Both software and hardware-based RAID solutions are available. Software-based sys-tems require the operating system to manage the disks in the array and can reduce overall system performance. They are relatively inexpensive since they don't require any additional hardware other than the additional disk(s). Hardware RAID systems are generally more efficient and reliable. While a hardware RAID is more expensive, the benefits outweigh the costs when used to increase availability of a critical component.

Hardware-based RAID arrays typically include spare drives that can be logically added to the array. For example, a hardware-based RAID-5 could include five disks, with three disks in a RAID-5 array and two spare disks. If one disk fails, the hardware senses the failure and logically swaps out the faulty drive with a good spare. Additionally, most hardware-based arrays support hot swapping, allowing technicians to replace failed disks without powering down the system. A cold swappable RAID requires the system to be powered down to replace a faulty drive.

Protecting Servers

Fault tolerance can be added for critical servers with failover clusters. A failover cluster includes two or more servers, and if one of the servers fails, another server in the cluster can take over its load in an automatic process called *failover*. Failover clusters can include multiple servers (not just two), and they can also provide fault tolerance for multiple services or applications.

As an example of a failover cluster, consider Figure 14.5. It shows multiple components put together to provide reliable web access for a heavily accessed website that uses a database. DB1 and DB2 are two database servers configured in a failover cluster. At any given time, only one server will function as the active database server, and the second server will be inactive. For example, if DB1 is the active server it will perform all the database services for the website. DB2 monitors DB1 to ensure it is operational, and if DB2 senses a failure in DB1, it will cause the cluster to automatically fail over to DB2.

FIGURE 14.5 Failover cluster with network load balancing

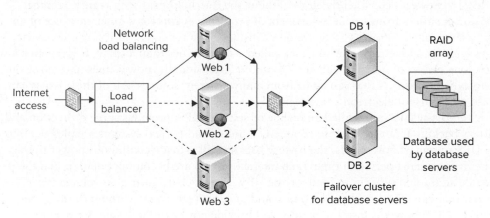

In Figure 14.5, you can see that both DB1 and DB2 have access to the data in the database. This data is stored on a RAID array providing fault tolerance for the disks.

Additionally, the three web servers are configured in a network load balancing cluster. The load balancer can be hardware or software based, and it balances the client load across the three servers. It makes it easy to add additional web servers to handle increased load while also balancing the load among all the servers. If any of the servers fail, the load balancer can sense the failure and stop sending traffic to that server. While network load balancing is primarily used to increase the scalability of a system so that it can handle more traffic, it also provides a measure of fault tolerance.

Failover clusters are not the only method of fault tolerance for servers. Some systems provide automatic fault tolerance for servers, allowing a server to fail without losing access to the provided service. For example, in a Microsoft domain with two or more domain controllers, each domain controller will regularly replicate data with the others so that all the domain controllers have the same data. If one fails, computers within the domain can still find the other domain controller(s) and the network can continue to operate. Similarly, many database server products include methods to replicate database content with other servers so that all servers have the same content. Chapter 16 discusses three of these methods: electronic vaulting, remote journaling, and remote mirroring.

Protecting Power Sources

Fault tolerance can be added for power sources with an *uninterruptible power supply (UPS)*, a generator, or both. In general, an UPS provides battery-supplied power for a short period of time between 5 and 30 minutes, and a generator provides long-term power. The goal of a UPS is to provide power long enough to complete a logical shutdown of a system, or until a generator is powered on and providing stable power.

Ideally, power is consistently clean without any fluctuations, but in reality, commercial power suffers from a wide assortment of problems. A *spike* is a quick instance of an increase in voltage whereas a *sag* is a quick instance of a reduction in voltage. If power stays high for a long period of time, it's called a *surge* rather than a spike. If it remains low for a long period of time, it's called a *brownout*. Occasionally, power lines have noise on them called *transients* that can come from many different sources. All of these issues can cause problems for electrical equipment.

A very basic UPS (also called an offline or standby UPS) provides surge protection and battery backup. It is plugged into commercial power and critical systems are plugged into the UPS system. If power fails, the battery backup will provide continuous power to the systems for a short period of time. Line-interactive UPS are becoming popular, and they provide additional services beyond a basic UPS. They include a variable-voltage transformer that can adjust to the overvoltage and undervoltage events without draining the battery. When power is lost, the battery will provide power to the system for a short period of time.

Generators provide power to systems during long-term power outages. The length of time that a generator will provide power is dependent on the fuel, and it's possible for a site to stay on generator power as long as they have fuel. Generators commonly use diesel fuel, natural gas, or propane.

Trusted Recovery

Trusted recovery provides assurances that after a failure or crash, the system is just as secure as it was before the failure or crash occurred. Depending on the failure, the recovery may be automated or require manual intervention by an administrator. However, in either case systems can be designed to ensure they support trusted recovery.

Systems can be designed so that they fail in a fail-secure state, or a fail-open state. A *fail-secure* system will default to a secure state in the event of a failure, blocking all access. A *fail-open* system will fail in an open state, granting all access. The choice is dependent on whether security or availability is more important after a failure.

As an example, firewalls provide a significant amount of security by controlling access in and out of a network. They are configured with an implicit deny philosophy and only allow traffic that is explicitly allowed based on a rule. Firewalls are typically designed to be fail secure, supporting the implicit deny philosophy. If a firewall fails, all traffic is blocked. Although this eliminates availability of communication through the firewall, it is secure. In contrast, if availability of traffic was more important than security, the firewall could be configured to fail into a fail-open state, allowing all traffic through. This wouldn't be secure, but the network would not lose availability of traffic.

In the context of physical security with electrical hardware locks, the terms *fail safe* and *fail secure* are used. Specifically, a fail-safe electrical lock will be unlocked when power is removed, but a fail-secure electrical lock will be locked when power is removed. For example, emergency exit doors will be configured to be fail safe so that personnel are not locked inside during a fire or other emergency. In this case, safety is a primary concern if a failure occurs. In contrast, a bank vault will likely be configured to be fail secure so that it remains locked if power is removed because security is the primary concern with a bank vault door.

Two elements of the recovery process are addressed to implement a trusted solution. The first element is failure preparation. This includes system resilience and fault-tolerant methods in addition to a reliable backup solution. The second element is the process of system recovery. The system should be forced to reboot into a single-user, nonprivileged state. This means that the system should reboot so that a normal user account can be used to log in and that the system does not grant unauthorized access to users. System recovery also includes the restoration of all affected files and services actively in use on the system at the time of the failure or crash. Any missing or damaged files are restored, any changes to classification labels corrected, and settings on all security critical files are then verified.

The Common Criteria (introduced in Chapter 11, "Principles of Security Models, Design, and Capabilities") includes a section on trusted recovery that is relevant to system resilience and fault tolerance. Specifically, it defines four types of trusted recovery:

Manual Recovery   If a system fails, it does not fail in a secure state. Instead, an administrator is required to manually perform the actions necessary to implement a secured or trusted recovery after a failure or system crash.

Automated Recovery   The system is able to perform trusted recovery activities to restore itself against at least one type of failure. For example, a hardware RAID provides automated recovery against the failure of a hard drive but not against the failure of the entire server. Some types of failures will require manual recovery.

Automated Recovery without Undue Loss   This is similar to automated recovery in that a system can restore itself against at least one type of failure. However, it includes mechanisms to ensure that specific objects are protected to prevent their loss. A method of automated recovery protective against undue loss would include steps to restore data or other objects. It may include additional protection mechanisms to restore corrupted files, rebuild data from transaction logs, and verify the integrity of key system and security components.

Function Recovery   Systems that support function recovery are able to automatically recover specific functions. This state ensures that the system is able to successfully complete the recovery for the functions, or the system will be able to roll back the changes to return to a secure state.

Summary

The CISSP CIB lists five specific incidence response steps. Detection is the first step and can come from automated tools or from employee observations. Alerts are investigated to determine whether an actual incident has occurred, and if so, the next step is response. Containment of the incident is important during the response stage, but it's also important to protect any evidence during this stage. Reporting may be required based on governing laws or an organization's security policy. In the recovery stage, the system is restored to full operation and it's important to ensure that it is restored to at least as secure a state as it was in before the attack. Last, the remediation and review stage includes a root cause analysis and will often include recommendations to prevent a reoccurrence.

Several basic steps can prevent many common attacks. These basic steps include keeping systems and applications up-to-date with current patches, removing or disabling unneeded services and protocols, using antivirus software with up-to-date signatures, enabling both host- and network-based firewalls, and using intrusion detection and prevention systems. Zero-day exploits are previously unknown vulnerabilities, and following these steps helps limit the risk from zero-day exploits.

Malicious code attacks are prevented with up-to-date antivirus (AV) software. AV software is commonly installed at the boundary between the Internet and the internal network, on email servers, and on each system. Limiting user privileges for software installations helps prevent accidental malware installation by users. Additionally, educating users about different types of malware and how criminals try to trick users helps them avoid risky behaviors.

Denial-of-service (DoS) attacks prevent a system from processing or responding to legitimate requests for service. They commonly attack systems that are accessible via the Internet, such as web servers. The SYN flood attack disrupts the TCP three-way handshake and is common today whereas other attacks are often variations on older attack methods. Botnets are often used to launch distributed DoS (DDoS) attacks.

Automated tools such as intrusion detection systems use logs to monitor the environment to detect attacks as they are occurring, and some can automatically block attacks. Two types of detection methods are employed by IDSs: knowledge based and behavior based. A knowledge-based IDS uses a database of attack signatures to detect intrusion attempts but cannot recognize new attack methods. A behavior-based system starts with a baseline of normal activity and then measures activity against the baseline to detect abnormal activity. A passive response will log the activity and possibly send an alert on items of interest. An active response will change the environment to block an attack in action. Host-based systems are installed on and monitor individual hosts, whereas network-based systems are installed on network devices and monitor overall network activity. Intrusion prevention systems are placed in line with the traffic and can block malicious traffic before it reaches the target system.

Honeypots, honeynets, and padded cells are useful tools to prevent malicious activity from occurring on a production network while enticing intruders to stick around long enough to gather evidence for prosecution. They often include pseudo flaws and fake data used to tempt attackers.

Penetration testing is a useful tool to check the strength and effectiveness of deployed security measures and an organization's security policies. It starts with vulnerability assessments or scans and then attempts to exploit vulnerabilities. Penetration testing should only be done with management approval and should be done on test systems instead of production systems whenever possible. Organizations often hire external consultants to perform penetration testing and can control the amount of knowledge these consultants have. Zero-knowledge testing is often called black-box testing, full-knowledge testing is often called white-box testing, and partial-knowledge testing is often called gray-box testing.

System resilience and fault tolerance refers to the ability of a system to suffer a fault but continue to operate. RAID arrays provide fault tolerance for disk subsystems, and failover clusters provide fault tolerance for servers. A UPS provides short-term power if commercial power is lost, and generators provide long-term power.

Exam Essentials

Know incident response steps.   Incident response steps are specifically listed in the CIB as detection, response, reporting, recovery, and remediation and review. After an incident is detected, the first response should be to limit or contain the scope of the incident while protecting evidence. Based on governing laws, the incident may need to be reported to official authorities, and if PII is affected, individuals need to be informed. The remediation and review stage includes root cause analysis to determine the cause and recommend a solution to prevent a reoccurrence.

Know basic preventive measures.   Basic preventive measures can prevent many incidents from occurring and they are repeated often. These include keeping systems up-to-date, removing or disabling unneeded protocols and services, using antivirus software with up-to-date signatures, enabling firewalls, and using intrusion detection systems.

Understand methods to block malicious code.   Malicious code is thwarted with a combination of tools. The obvious tool is antivirus software with up-to-date definitions installed on each system, at the boundary of the network, and on email servers. However, don't forget about policies enforcing basic security principles such as least privilege to prevent regular users from installing software that may be malicious. Additionally, educating users about the risks, and the methods attackers commonly use to spread viruses, helps users understand and avoid dangerous behaviors.

Understand zero-day exploit.   A zero-day exploit is an attack that uses a vulnerability that is either unknown to anyone but the attacker or known only to a limited group of people. On the surface, it sounds like you can't protect against an unknown vulnerability, but basic security practices go a long way to preventing zero-day exploits. Removing or disabling unneeded protocols and services reduces the attack surface, enabling firewalls blocks many access points, and using intrusion detection systems helps detect potential attacks. Additionally, using tools such as honeypots and padded cells helps protect live networks.

Know what denial-of-service (DoS) attacks are.   DoS attacks prevent a system from responding to legitimate requests for service. A common DoS attack still used is the SYN flood attack, which disrupts the TCP three-way handshake. Even though older attacks are not as common today because basic precautions block them, you may still be tested on them because many newer attacks are often variations on older methods. Smurf attacks employ an amplification network to send numerous response packets to a victim. Ping-of-death attacks send numerous oversized ping packets to the victim, causing the victim to freeze, crash, or reboot.

Understand botnets, botnet controllers, and botnet herders.   Botnets represent significant threats due to the massive number of computers that can launch attacks, so it's important to know what they are. A botnet is a collection of compromised PCs (often called zombies) organized in a network controlled by a criminal known as a bot herder. Bot herders use a command and control server to remotely control the zombies and often use the botnet to launch attacks on other systems or send spam or phishing emails. Bot herders also rent botnet access out to other criminals.

Understand man-in-the-middle attacks.   A man-in-the-middle attack occurs when a malicious user is able to gain a position between the two endpoints of a communications link. While it takes a significant amount of sophistication on the part of an attacker to complete a man-in-the middle attack, the amount of data obtained from the attack can be significant.

Understand sabotage and espionage.   Malicious insiders can perform sabotage against an organization if they become disgruntled for some reason. Espionage is when a competitor tries to steal information, and they may use an internal employee. Basic security principles (such as the principle of least privilege) and immediately disabling accounts for terminated employees limit the damage from these employees.

Understand intrusion detection and intrusion prevention.   IDSs and IPSs are important detective and preventive measures against attacks. Know the difference between knowledge-based detection (using a database similar to antivirus signatures) and behavior-based detection. Behavior-based detection starts with a baseline to recognize normal behavior and compares activity with the baseline to detect abnormal activity. The baseline can be outdated if the network is modified, so it must be updated when the environment changes.

Recognize IDS/IPS responses.   An IDS can respond passively by logging and sending notifications, or actively by changing the environment. Some people refer to an active IDS as an IPS. However, it's important to recognize that an IPS is placed in line with the traffic and includes the ability to block malicious traffic before it reaches the target.

Understand differences between HIDSs and NIDSs.   Host-based IDSs (HIDSs) can monitor activity on a single system only and can be discovered by attackers and disabled. Network-based IDSs (NIDSs) can monitor activity on a network and aren't as visible to attackers.

Understand honeypots, padded cells, and pseudo flaws.   A honeypot is a system that often uses pseudo flaws and fake data to lure intruders. Administrators can observe the activity of attackers while they are in the honeypot, and as long as attackers are in the honeypot, they are not in the live network. Some IDSs have the ability to transfer attackers into a padded cell after detection. While a honeypot and padded cell are similar, note that a honeypot lures the attacker but the attacker is transferred into the padded cell.

Understand penetration testing.   Penetration tests start by discovering vulnerabilities and then mimic an attack to identify what vulnerabilities can be exploited. It's important to remember pen tests should not be done without express consent and knowledge from management. Additionally, since pen tests can result in damage, they should be done on isolated systems whenever possible. You should also recognize the differences between black-box testing (zero knowledge), white-box testing (full knowledge), and gray-box testing (partial knowledge).

Understand basic fault tolerance methods.   Fault tolerance is a common method used to eliminate single points of failure and increase availability. RAID protects against disk failures, failover clusters protect against server failures, and UPS and generators protect against power failures. It's important to remember that fault tolerance does not negate the need for backups.

Written Lab

1. List the different phases of incident response identified in the CISSP CIB.
2. Describe the primary types of intrusion detection systems.
3. List the methods used to provide fault tolerance for disks, computers, and power.

Review Questions

1. What should be done as soon as an incident has been detected and verified?

   A. Contain it

   B. Report it

   C. Remediate it

   D. Gather evidence

2. Which of the following would be completed during the remediation and review stage of an incident response?

   A. Contain the incident

   B. Collect evidence

   C. Rebuild system

   D. Root cause analysis

3. Of the following choices, which is the most common method of distributing malware?

   A. Driving downloads

   B. Email

   C. Rogueware

   D. Unapproved software

4. Of the following choices, what is the best form of antivirus protection?

   A. Multiple solutions on each system

   B. A single solution throughout the organization

   C. Antivirus protection at several locations

   D. One hundred percent content filtering at all border gateways

5. A web server hosted on the Internet was recently attacked, exploiting a vulnerability in the operating system. The operating system vendor assisted in the incident investigation and verified the vulnerability was not previously known. What type of attack was this?

   A. Botnet

   B. Zero-day exploit

   C. Denial-of-service

   D. Distributed denial-of-service

6. Which of the following is *not* considered a denial-of-service attack?

   A. Teardrop

   B. Smurf

   C. Ping of death

   D. Spoofing

7. How does a SYN flood attack work?

   A. Exploits a packet processing glitch in Windows systems

   B. Uses an amplification network to flood a victim with packets

   C. Exploits a three-way handshake used by TCP

   D. Sends oversized ping packets to a victim

8. Which of the following attacks sends packets with the victim's IP address as both the source and the destination?

   A. Land

   B. Spamming

   C. Teardrop

   D. Ping flood

9. What type of attack includes fragmented packets that cannot be reassembled?

   A. Zero-day exploit

   B. Spamming

   C. Distributed denial-of-service

   D. Teardrop

10. Which of the following tools is most useful in sorting through large log files to search for intrusion-related events?

    A. Text editor

    B. Vulnerability scanner

    C. Password cracker

    D. IDS

11. Of the following choices, what indicates the primary purpose of an intrusion detection system (IDS)?

    A. Detect abnormal activity.

    B. Diagnose system failures.

    C. Rate system performance.

    D. Test a system for vulnerabilities.

12. Which of the following is true for a host-based intrusion detection system (HIDS)?

    A. It monitors an entire network.

    B. It monitors a single system.

    C. It's invisible to attackers and authorized users.

    D. It cannot detect malicious code.

13. Which of the following types of intrusion detection systems (IDSs) is effective only against known attack methods?

    A. Behavior-based

    B. Host-based

    C. Knowledge-based

    D. Network-based

14. Which of the following is a fake network designed to tempt intruders with unpatched and unprotected security vulnerabilities and false data?

    A. IDS

    B. Honeynet

    C. Padded cell

    D. Pseudo flaw

15. When using penetration testing to verify the strength of your security policy, which of the following is *not* recommended?

    A. Mimicking attacks previously perpetrated against your system

    B. Performing attacks without management knowledge

    C. Using manual and automated attack tools

    D. Reconfiguring the system to resolve any discovered vulnerabilities

16. Which of the following activities is *not* considered a valid form of penetration testing?

    A. Denial-of-service attacks

    B. Port scanning

    C. Distribution of malicious code

    D. Packet sniffing

17. You need to ensure a service provided by a server will continue even if the server fails. What should you use?

    A. Clustering

    B. A RAID array

    C. Hot site

    D. UPS

Refer to the following scenario when answering questions 18 through 20.

An organization has an incident response plan that requires reporting incidents when they are discovered. For security purposes, the plan is not published and the contents are only known to the members of the incident response team. Recently, a server administrator noticed that a web server he manages was running slower than normal. After a quick investigation, he realized an attack was coming from a specific IP address. He immediately rebooted the web server to reset the connection and stop the attack. He then used a utility he found on the Internet to launch a protracted attack against this IP address for several hours. Because attacks from this IP address stopped, he didn't report the incident.

18. What should have been done before the web server was rebooted?

   A. Review the incident

   B. Perform remediation steps

   C. Recovery

   D. Gather evidence

19. What is the most serious mistake made by the server administrator in this incident?

   A. Rebooting the server

   B. Not reporting the incident

   C. Attacking the IP address

   D. Resetting the connection

20. What was missed completely in this incident?

   A. Remediation and review

   B. Detection

   C. Response

   D. Recovery

Chapter 15

Business Continuity Planning

THE CISSP EXAM TOPICS COVERED IN THIS CHAPTER INCLUDE:

8. Business Continuity and Disaster Recovery Planning

- A. Understand business continuity requirements
    - A.1 Develop and document project scope and plan
- B. Conduct business impact analysis
    - B.1 Identify and prioritize critical business functions
    - B.2 Determine maximum tolerable downtime and other criteria
    - B.3 Assess exposure to outages (e.g., local, regional, global)
    - B.4 Define recovery objectives
- E. Exercise, assess and maintain the plan (e.g., version control, distribution)

Despite our best wishes, disasters of one form or another eventually strike every organization. Whether it's a natural disaster such as a hurricane or earthquake or a man-made calamity such as a building fire or burst water pipes, every organization will encounter events that threaten their operations or even their very existence. Resilient organizations have plans and procedures in place to help mitigate the effects a disaster has on their continuing operations and to speed the return to normal operations. Recognizing the importance of planning for business continuity and disaster recovery, the organization (ISC)² designated these two processes as one of the 10 domains of the Common Body of Knowledge for the CISSP program. Knowledge of these fundamental topics will help you prepare for the exam and help you prepare your organization for the unexpected.

In this chapter, we'll explore the concepts behind business continuity planning. Chapter 16, "Disaster Recovery Planning," will continue our discussion.

Planning for Business Continuity

Business continuity planning (BCP) involves assessing the risks to organizational processes and creating policies, plans, and procedures to minimize the impact those risks might have on the organization if they were to occur. BCP is used to maintain the continuous operation of a business in the event of an emergency situation. The goal of BCP planners is to implement a combination of policies, procedures, and processes such that a potentially disruptive event has as little impact on the business as possible.

BCP focuses on maintaining business operations with reduced or restricted infrastructure capabilities or resources. As long as the continuity of the organization's ability to perform its mission-critical work tasks is maintained, BCP can be used to manage and restore the environment. If the continuity is broken, then business processes have stopped and the organization is in disaster mode; thus, disaster recovery planning (DRP) takes over.

The top priority of BCP and DRP is always *people.* The primary concern is to get people out of harm's way; then you can address IT recovery and restoration issues.

> ### Business Continuity Planning vs. Disaster Recovery Planning
>
> You should understand the distinction between business continuity planning and disaster recovery planning. One easy way to remember the difference is that BCP comes first, and if the BCP efforts fail, DRP steps in to fill the gap. For example, consider the case of a data center located downstream from a dam. BCP efforts might involve verifying that municipal authorities perform appropriate preventive maintenance on the dam and reinforcing the data center to protect it from floodwaters.
>
> Despite your best efforts, it's possible that your business continuity efforts will fail. Pressure on the dam might increase to the point that the dam fails and the area beneath it floods. The level of those floodwaters might be too much for the data center reinforcements to handle, causing flooding of the data center and a disruption in business operations. At this point, your business continuity efforts have failed, and it's time to invoke your disaster recovery plan.
>
> We'll discuss disaster recovery planning in Chapter 16. The eventual goal of those efforts is to restore business operations in the primary data center as quickly as possible.

The overall goal of BCP is to provide a quick, calm, and efficient response in the event of an emergency and to enhance a company's ability to recover from a disruptive event promptly. The BCP process, as defined by (ISC)², has four main steps:

- Project scope and planning
- Business impact assessment
- Continuity planning
- Approval and implementation

The next three sections of this chapter cover each of these phases in detail. The last portion of this chapter will introduce some of the critical elements you should consider when compiling documentation of your organization's business continuity plan.

Project Scope and Planning

As with any formalized business process, the development of a strong business continuity plan requires the use of a proven methodology. This requires the following:

- Structured analysis of the business's organization from a crisis planning point of view
- The creation of a BCP team with the approval of senior management
- An assessment of the resources available to participate in business continuity activities
- An analysis of the legal and regulatory landscape that governs an organization's response to a catastrophic event

The exact process you use will depend on the size and nature of your organization and its business. There really isn't a "one-size-fits-all" guide to business continuity project planning. You should consult with project planning professionals within your organization and determine the approach that will work best within your organizational culture.

Business Organization Analysis

One of the first responsibilities of the individuals responsible for business continuity planning is to perform an analysis of the business organization to identify all departments and individuals who have a stake in the BCP process. Here are some areas to consider:

- Operational departments that are responsible for the core services the business provides to its clients

- Critical support services, such as the information technology (IT) department, plant maintenance department, and other groups responsible for the upkeep of systems that support the operational departments

- Senior executives and other key individuals essential for the ongoing viability of the organization

This identification process is critical for two reasons. First, it provides the groundwork necessary to help identify potential members of the BCP team (see the next section). Second, it provides the foundation for the remainder of the BCP process.

Normally, the business organization analysis is performed by the individuals spearheading the BCP effort. This is acceptable, given that they normally use the output of the analysis to assist with the selection of the remaining BCP team members. However, a thorough review of this analysis should be one of the first tasks assigned to the full BCP team when it is convened. This step is critical because the individuals performing the original analysis may have overlooked critical business functions known to BCP team members that represent other parts of the organization. If the team were to continue without revising the organizational analysis, the entire BCP process may be negatively affected, resulting in the development of a plan that does not fully address the emergency-response needs of the organization as a whole.

Each location of an organization should have its own distinct plan addressing the unique needs of that location. A single plan should not cover multiple geographic locations.

BCP Team Selection

In many organizations, the IT and/or security departments are given sole responsibility for BCP and no arrangements are made for input from other operational and support departments. In fact, those departments may not even know of the plan's existence until disaster strikes or is imminent. This is a critical flaw! The isolated development of a business continuity plan can spell disaster in two ways. First, the plan itself may not take into account knowledge possessed only by the individuals responsible for the day-to-day operation of the business. Second, it keeps operational elements "in the dark" about plan specifics until implementation becomes necessary. This reduces the possibility that operational elements will agree with the provisions of the plan and work effectively to implement it. It also denies organizations the benefits achieved by a structured training and testing program for the plan.

To prevent these situations from adversely impacting the BCP process, the individuals responsible for the effort should take special care when selecting the BCP team. The team should include, as a minimum, the following individuals:

- Representatives from each of the organization's departments responsible for the core services performed by the business
- Representatives from the key support departments identified by the organizational analysis
- IT representatives with technical expertise in areas covered by the BCP
- Security representatives with knowledge of the BCP process
- Legal representatives familiar with corporate legal, regulatory, and contractual responsibilities
- Representatives from senior management

Tips for Selecting an Effective BCP Team

Select your team carefully! You need to strike a balance between representing different points of view and creating a team with explosive personality differences. Your goal should be to create a group that is as diverse as possible and still operates in harmony.

Take some time to think about the BCP team membership and who would be appropriate for your organization's technical, financial, and political environment. Who would you include?

Each one of the individuals mentioned in the preceding list brings a unique perspective to the BCP process and will have individual biases. For example, the representatives from each of the operational departments will often consider their department the most critical to the organization's continued viability. Although these biases may at first seem divisive, the leader of the BCP effort should embrace them and harness them in a productive manner. If used effectively, the biases will help achieve a healthy balance in the final plan as each representative advocates the needs of their department. On the other hand, if proper leadership isn't provided, these biases may devolve into destructive turf battles that derail the BCP effort and harm the organization as a whole.

Senior Management and BCP

The role of senior management in the BCP process varies widely from organization to organization and depends on the internal culture of the business, interest in the plan from above, and the legal and regulatory environment in which the business operates. Important roles played by senior management usually include setting priorities, providing staff and financial resources, and arbitrating disputes about the criticality (i.e., relative importance) of services.

One of the authors recently completed a BCP consulting engagement with a large non-profit institution. At the beginning of the engagement, he had a chance to sit down with one of the organization's senior executives to discuss his goals and objectives for their work together. During that meeting, the senior executive asked him, "Is there anything you need from me to complete this engagement?"

He must have expected a perfunctory response because his eyes widened when the response began with, "Well, as a matter of fact..." He was then told that his active participation in the process was critical to its success.

When you work on a business continuity plan, you, as the BCP team leader, must seek and obtain as active a role as possible from a senior executive. This conveys the importance of the BCP process to the entire organization and fosters the active participation of individuals who might otherwise write BCP off as a waste of time better spent on operational activities. Furthermore, laws and regulations might require the active participation of those senior leaders in the planning process. If you work for a publicly traded company, you may want to remind executives that the officers and directors of the firm might be found personally liable if a disaster cripples the business and they are found not to have exercised due diligence in their contingency planning.

You may also have to convince management that BCP and DRP spending should not be viewed as a discretionary expense. Management's fiduciary responsibilities to the organization's shareholders require them to at least ensure that adequate BCP measures are in place.

In the case of this BCP engagement, the executive acknowledged the importance of his support and agreed to participate. He sent an email to all employees introducing the effort and stating that it had his full backing. He also attended several of the high-level planning sessions and mentioned the effort in an organization-wide "town hall" meeting.

Resource Requirements

After the team validates the business organization analysis, it should turn to an assessment of the resources required by the BCP effort. This involves the resources required by three distinct BCP phases:

BCP Development   The BCP team will require some resources to perform the four elements of the BCP process (project scope and planning, business impact assessment, continuity planning, and approval and implementation). It's more than likely that the major resource consumed by this BCP phase will be effort expended by members of the BCP team and the support staff they call upon to assist in the development of the plan.

BCP Testing, Training, and Maintenance   The testing, training, and maintenance phases of BCP will require some hardware and software commitments, but once again, the major commitment in this phase will be effort on the part of the employees involved in those activities.

BCP Implementation   When a disaster strikes and the BCP team deems it necessary to conduct a full-scale implementation of the business continuity plan, this implementation will require significant resources. This includes a large amount of effort (BCP will likely become the focus of a large part, if not all, of the organization) and the utilization of hard resources. For this reason, it's important that the team uses its BCP implementation powers judiciously yet decisively.

An effective business continuity plan requires the expenditure of a large amount of resources, ranging all the way from the purchase and deployment of redundant computing facilities to the pencils and paper used by team members scratching out the first drafts of the plan. However, as you saw earlier, personnel are one of the most significant resources consumed by the BCP process. Many security professionals overlook the importance of accounting for labor, but you can rest assured that senior management will not. Business leaders are keenly aware of the effect that time-consuming side activities have on the operational productivity of their organizations and the real cost of personnel in terms of salary, benefits, and lost opportunities. These concerns become especially paramount when you are requesting the time of senior executives. You should expect that leaders responsible for resource utilization management will put your BCP proposal under a microscope, and you should be prepared to defend the necessity of your plan with coherent, logical arguments that address the business case for BCP.

 Real World Scenario

Explaining the Benefits of BCP

At a recent conference, one of the authors discussed business continuity planning with the chief information security officer (CISO) of a health system from a medium-sized U.S. city. The CISO's attitude was shocking. His organization had not conducted a formal BCP process, and he was confident that a "seat-of-the-pants" approach would work fine in the unlikely event of a disaster.

This "seat-of-the-pants" attitude is one of the most common arguments against committing resources to BCP. In many organizations, the attitude that the business has always survived and the key leaders will figure something out in the event of a disaster pervades corporate thinking. If you encounter this objection, you might want to point out to management the costs that will be incurred by the business (both direct costs and the indirect cost of lost opportunities) for each day that the business is down. Then ask them to consider how long a "seat-of-the-pants" recovery might take when compared to an orderly, planned continuity of operations.

Legal and Regulatory Requirements

Many industries may find themselves bound by federal, state, and local laws or regulations that require them to implement various degrees of BCP. We've already discussed one example in this chapter—the officers and directors of publicly traded firms have a fiduciary responsibility to exercise due diligence in the execution of their business continuity duties. In other circumstances, the requirements (and consequences of failure) might be more severe. Emergency services, such as police, fire, and emergency medical operations, have a responsibility to the community to continue operations in the event of a disaster. Indeed, their services become even more critical in an emergency when public safety is threatened. Failure on their part to implement a solid BCP could result in the loss of life and/or property and the decreased confidence of the population in their government.

In many countries, financial institutions, such as banks, brokerages, and the firms that process their data, are subject to strict government and international banking and securities regulations designed to facilitate their continued operation to ensure the viability of the national economy. When pharmaceutical manufacturers must produce products in less-than-optimal circumstances following a disaster, they are required to certify the purity of their products to government regulators. There are countless other examples of industries that are required to continue operating in the event of an emergency by various laws and regulations.

Even if you're not bound by any of these considerations, you might have contractual obligations to your clients that require you to implement sound BCP practices. If your contracts include some type of *service-level agreement (SLA)*, you might find yourself in breach of those contracts if a disaster interrupts your ability to service your clients. Many clients may feel sorry for you and want to continue using your products/services, but their own business requirements might force them to sever the relationship and find new suppliers.

On the flip side of the coin, developing a strong, documented business continuity plan can help your organization win new clients and additional business from existing clients. If you can show your customers the sound procedures you have in place to continue serving them in the event of a disaster, they'll place greater confidence in your firm and might be more likely to choose you as their preferred vendor. Not a bad position to be in!

All of these concerns point to one conclusion—it's essential to include your organization's legal counsel in the BCP process. They are intimately familiar with the legal, regulatory, and contractual obligations that apply to your organization and can help your team implement a plan that meets those requirements while ensuring the continued viability of the organization to the benefit of all—employees, shareholders, suppliers, and customers alike.

Laws regarding computing systems, business practices, and disaster management change frequently and vary from jurisdiction to jurisdiction. Be sure to keep your attorneys involved throughout the lifetime of your BCP, including the testing and maintenance phases. If you restrict their involvement to a preimplementation review of the plan, you may not become aware of the impact that changing laws and regulations have on your corporate responsibilities.

Business Impact Assessment

Once your BCP team completes the four stages of preparing to create a business continuity plan, it's time to dive into the heart of the work—the *business impact assessment (BIA)*. The BIA identifies the resources that are critical to an organization's ongoing viability and the threats posed to those resources. It also assesses the likelihood that each threat will actually occur and the impact those occurrences will have on the business. The results of the BIA provide you with quantitative measures that can help you prioritize the commitment of business continuity resources to the various local, regional, and global risk exposures facing your organization.

It's important to realize that there are two different types of analyses that business planners use when facing a decision:

Quantitative Decision Making   Quantitative decision making involves the use of numbers and formulas to reach a decision. This type of data often expresses options in terms of the dollar value to the business.

Qualitative Decision Making   Qualitative decision making takes nonnumerical factors, such as emotions, investor/customer confidence, workforce stability, and other concerns, into account. This type of data often results in categories of prioritization (such as high, medium, and low).

Quantitative analysis and qualitative analysis both play an important role in the BCP process. However, most people tend to favor one type of analysis over the other. When selecting the individual members of the BCP team, try to achieve a balance between people who prefer each strategy. This will result in the development of a well-rounded BCP and benefit the organization in the long run.

The BIA process described in this chapter approaches the problem from both quantitative and qualitative points of view. However, it's tempting for a BCP team to "go with the numbers" and perform a quantitative assessment while neglecting the somewhat more difficult qualitative assessment. It's important that the BCP team performs a qualitative analysis of the factors affecting your BCP process. For example, if your business is highly dependent on a few very important clients, your management team is probably willing to suffer significant short-term financial loss in order to retain those clients in the long term. The BCP team must sit down and discuss (preferably with the involvement of senior management) qualitative concerns to develop a comprehensive approach that satisfies all stakeholders.

Identify Priorities

The first BIA task facing the BCP team is identifying business priorities. Depending on your line of business, there will be certain activities that are most essential to your day-to-day operations when disaster strikes. The priority identification task, or *criticality prioritization*, involves creating a comprehensive list of business processes and ranking them in order of importance. Although this task may seem somewhat daunting, it's not as hard as it seems. A great way to divide the workload of this process among the team members is to assign each participant responsibility for drawing up a prioritized list that covers the business functions for which their department is responsible. When the entire BCP team convenes, team members can use those prioritized lists to create a master prioritized list for the entire organization.

This process helps identify business priorities from a qualitative point of view. Recall that we're describing an attempt to simultaneously develop both qualitative and quantitative BIAs. To begin the quantitative assessment, the BCP team should sit down and draw up a list of organization assets and then assign an *asset value (AV)* in monetary terms to each asset. These numbers will be used in the remaining BIA steps to develop a financially based BIA. The second quantitative measure that the team must develop is the *maximum tolerable downtime (MTD)*, sometimes also known as maximum tolerable outage (MTO). The MTD is the maximum length of time a business function can be inoperable without causing irreparable harm to the business. The MTD provides valuable information when you're performing both BCP and DRP planning. This leads to another metric, the *recovery time objective (RTO)*, for each business function. This is the amount of time in which you think you can feasibly recover the function in the event of a disruption. Once you have defined your recovery objectives, you can design and plan the procedures necessary to accomplish the recovery tasks. The goal of the BCP process is to ensure that your RTOs are less than your MTDs, resulting in a situation in which a function should never be unavailable beyond the maximum tolerable downtime.

Risk Identification

The next phase of the BIA is the identification of risks posed to your organization. Some elements of this organization-specific list may come to mind immediately. The identification of other, more obscure risks might take a little creativity on the part of the BCP team.

Risks come in two forms: natural risks and man-made risks. The following list includes some events that pose natural threats:

- Violent storms/hurricanes/tornadoes/blizzards
- Earthquakes

- Mudslides/avalanches
- Volcanic eruptions

Man-made threats include the following events:

- Terrorist acts/wars/civil unrest
- Theft/vandalism
- Fires/explosions
- Prolonged power outages
- Building collapses
- Transportation failures

Remember, these are by no means all-inclusive lists. They merely identify some common risks that many organizations face. You may want to use them as a starting point, but a full listing of risks facing your organization will require input from all members of the BCP team.

The risk identification portion of the process is purely qualitative in nature. At this point in the process, the BCP team should not be concerned about the likelihood that each type of risk will actually materialize or the amount of damage such an occurrence would inflict upon the continued operation of the business. The results of this analysis will drive both the qualitative and quantitative portions of the remaining BIA tasks.

Likelihood Assessment

The preceding step consisted of the BCP team's drawing up a comprehensive list of the events that can be a threat to an organization. You probably recognized that some events are much more likely to happen than others. For example, a business in Southern California is much more likely to face the risk of an earthquake than to face the risk posed by a volcanic eruption. A business based in Hawaii might have the exact opposite likelihood that each risk would occur.

To account for these differences, the next phase of the business impact assessment identifies the likelihood that each risk will occur. To keep calculations consistent, this assessment is usually expressed in terms of an *annualized rate of occurrence (ARO)* that reflects the number of times a business expects to experience a given disaster each year.

The BCP team should sit down and determine an ARO for each risk identified in the previous section. These numbers should be based on corporate history, professional experience of team members, and advice from experts, such as meteorologists, seismologists, fire prevention professionals, and other consultants, as needed.

In many cases, you may be able to find likelihood assessments for some risks prepared by experts at no cost to you. For example, the U.S. Geological Survey (USGS) developed the earthquake hazard map shown in Figure 15.1. This map illustrates the ARO for earthquakes in various regions of the United States. Similarly, the Federal Emergency Management Agency (FEMA) coordinates the development of detailed flood maps of local communities throughout the United States. These resources are available online and offer a wealth of information to organizations performing a business impact assessment.

FIGURE 15.1   Earthquake hazard map of the United States

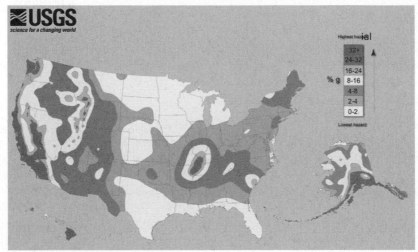

(Source: U.S. Geological Survey)

Impact Assessment

As you may have surmised based on its name, the impact assessment is one of the most critical portions of the business impact assessment. In this phase, you analyze the data gathered during risk identification and likelihood assessment and attempt to determine what impact each one of the identified risks would have on the business if it were to occur.

From a quantitative point of view, we will cover three specific metrics: the exposure factor, the single loss expectancy, and the annualized loss expectancy. Each one of these values is computed for each specific risk/asset combination evaluated during the previous phases.

The *exposure factor (EF)* is the amount of damage that the risk poses to the asset, expressed as a percentage of the asset's value. For example, if the BCP team consults with fire experts and determines that a building fire would cause 70 percent of the building to be destroyed, the exposure factor of the building to fire is 70 percent.

The *single loss expectancy (SLE)* is the monetary loss that is expected each time the risk materializes. You can compute the SLE using the following formula:

$$SLE = AV \times EF$$

Continuing with the preceding example, if the building is worth $500,000, the single loss expectancy would be 70 percent of $500,000, or $350,000. You can interpret this figure to mean that a single fire in the building would be expected to cause $350,000 worth of damage.

The *annualized loss expectancy (ALE)* is the monetary loss that the business expects to occur as a result of the risk harming the asset over the course of a year. You already have all the data necessary to perform this calculation. The SLE is the amount of damage you expect each time a disaster strikes, and the ARO (from the likelihood analysis) is the number of times you expect a disaster to occur each year. You compute the ALE by simply multiplying those two numbers:

$$ALE = SLE \times ARO$$

Returning once again to our building example, if fire experts predict that a fire will occur in the building once every 30 years, the ARO is ~1/30, or 0.03. The ALE is then 3 percent of the $350,000 SLE, or $11,667. You can interpret this figure to mean that the business should expect to lose $11,667 each year due to a fire in the building.

Obviously, a fire will not occur each year—this figure represents the average cost over the 30 years between fires. It's not especially useful for budgeting considerations but proves invaluable when attempting to prioritize the assignment of BCP resources to a given risk. These concepts were also covered in Chapter 6, "Risk and Personnel Management."

> Be certain you're familiar with the quantitative formulas contained in this chapter and the concepts of asset value, exposure factor, annualized rate of occurrence, single loss expectancy, and annualized loss expectancy. Know the formulas and be able to work through a scenario.

From a qualitative point of view, you must consider the nonmonetary impact that interruptions might have on your business. For example, you might want to consider the following:

- Loss of goodwill among your client base
- Loss of employees to other jobs after prolonged downtime
- Social/ethical responsibilities to the community
- Negative publicity

It's difficult to put dollar values on items like these in order to include them in the quantitative portion of the impact assessment, but they are equally important. After all, if you decimate your client base, you won't have a business to return to when you're ready to resume operations!

Resource Prioritization

The final step of the BIA is to prioritize the allocation of business continuity resources to the various risks that you identified and assessed in the preceding tasks of the BIA.

From a quantitative point of view, this process is relatively straightforward. You simply create a list of all the risks you analyzed during the BIA process and sort them in descending order according to the ALE computed during the impact assessment phase. This provides you with a prioritized list of the risks that you should address. Select as many items as you're willing and able to address simultaneously from the top of the list and work your way down. Eventually, you'll reach a point at which you've exhausted either the list of risks (unlikely!) or all your available resources (much more likely!).

Recall from the previous section that we also stressed the importance of addressing qualitatively important concerns. In previous sections about the BIA, we treated quantitative and qualitative analysis as mainly separate functions with some overlap in the analysis. Now it's time to merge the two prioritized lists, which is more of an art than a science. You must sit down with the BCP team and representatives from the senior management team and combine the two lists into a single prioritized list. Qualitative concerns may justify elevating or lowering the priority of risks that already exist on the ALE-sorted quantitative list. For example, if you run a fire suppression company, your number-one priority might be the prevention of a fire in your principal place of business despite the fact that an earthquake might cause more physical damage. The potential loss of reputation within the business community resulting from the destruction of a fire suppression company by fire might be too difficult to overcome and result in the eventual collapse of the business, justifying the increased priority.

Continuity Planning

The first two phases of the BCP process (project scope and planning and the business impact assessment) focus on determining how the BCP process will work and prioritizing the business assets that must be protected against interruption. The next phase of BCP development, continuity planning, focuses on developing and implementing a continuity strategy to minimize the impact realized risks might have on protected assets.

In this section, you'll learn about the subtasks involved in continuity planning:

- Strategy development
- Provisions and processes
- Plan approval
- Plan implementation
- Training and education

Strategy Development

The strategy development phase bridges the gap between the business impact assessment and the continuity planning phases of BCP development. The BCP team must now take the prioritized list of concerns raised by the quantitative and qualitative resource prioritization exercises and determine which risks will be addressed by the business continuity plan. Fully addressing all the contingencies would require the implementation of provisions and processes that maintain a zero-downtime posture in the face of every possible risk. For obvious reasons, implementing a policy this comprehensive is simply impossible.

The BCP team should look back to the MTD estimates created during the early stages of the BIA and determine which risks are deemed acceptable and which must be mitigated by BCP continuity provisions. Some of these decisions are obvious—the risk of a blizzard striking an operations facility in Egypt is negligible and would be deemed an acceptable risk. The risk of a monsoon in New Delhi is serious enough that it must be mitigated by BCP provisions.

 Keep in mind that there are four possible responses to a risk: reduce, assign, accept, and reject. Each may be an acceptable response based upon the circumstances.

Once the BCP team determines which risks require mitigation and the level of resources that will be committed to each mitigation task, they are ready to move on to the provisions and processes phase of continuity planning.

Provisions and Processes

The provisions and processes phase of continuity planning is the meat of the entire business continuity plan. In this task, the BCP team designs the specific procedures and mechanisms that will mitigate the risks deemed unacceptable during the strategy development stage. Three categories of assets must be protected through BCP provisions and processes: people, buildings/facilities, and infrastructure. In the next three sections, we'll explore some of the techniques you can use to safeguard these categories.

People

First and foremost, you must ensure that the people within your organization are safe before, during, and after an emergency. Once you've achieved that goal, you must make provisions to allow your employees to conduct both their BCP and operational tasks in as normal a manner as possible given the circumstances.

 Don't lose sight of the fact that people are your most valuable asset. The safety of people must always come before the organization's business goals. Make sure that your business continuity plan makes adequate provisions for the security of your employees, customers, suppliers, and any other individuals who may be affected!

People should be provided with all the resources they need to complete their assigned tasks. At the same time, if circumstances dictate that people be present in the workplace for extended periods of time, arrangements must be made for shelter and food. Any continuity plan that requires these provisions should include detailed instructions for the BCP team in the event of a disaster. The organization should maintain stockpiles of provisions sufficient to feed the operational and support teams for an extended period of time in an accessible location. Plans should specify the periodic rotation of those stockpiles to prevent spoilage.

Buildings and Facilities

Many businesses require specialized facilities in order to carry out their critical operations. These might include standard office facilities, manufacturing plants, operations centers, warehouses, distribution/logistics centers, and repair/maintenance depots, among others. When you perform your BIA, you will identify those facilities that play a critical role in your organization's continued viability. Your continuity plan should address two areas for each critical facility:

Hardening Provisions   Your BCP should outline mechanisms and procedures that can be put in place to protect your existing facilities against the risks defined in the strategy development phase. This might include steps as simple as patching a leaky roof or as complex as installing reinforced hurricane shutters and fireproof walls.

Alternate Sites   In the event that it's not feasible to harden a facility against a risk, your BCP should identify alternate sites where business activities can resume immediately (or at least in a period of time that's shorter than the maximum tolerable downtime for all affected critical business functions). Chapter 16 describes a few of the facility types that might be useful in this stage.

Infrastructure

Every business depends on some sort of infrastructure for its critical processes. For many businesses, a critical part of this infrastructure is an IT backbone of communications and computer systems that process orders, manage the supply chain, handle customer interaction, and perform other business functions. This backbone consists of a number of servers, workstations, and critical communications links between sites. The BCP must address how these systems will be protected against risks identified during the strategy development phase. As with buildings and facilities, there are two main methods of providing this protection:

Physically Hardening Systems   You can protect systems against the risks by introducing protective measures such as computer-safe fire suppression systems and uninterruptible power supplies.

Alternative Systems   You can also protect business functions by introducing redundancy (either redundant components or completely redundant systems/communications links that rely on different facilities).

These same principles apply to whatever infrastructure components serve your critical business processes—transportation systems, electrical power grids, banking and financial systems, water supplies, and so on.

Plan Approval

Once the BCP team completes the design phase of the BCP document, it's time to gain top-level management endorsement of the plan. If you were fortunate enough to have senior management involvement throughout the development phases of the plan, this should be a relatively straightforward process. On the other hand, if this is your first time approaching management with the BCP document, you should be prepared to provide a lengthy explanation of the plan's purpose and specific provisions.

 Senior management approval and buy-in is essential to the success of the overall BCP effort.

If possible, you should attempt to have the plan endorsed by the top executive in your business—the chief executive officer, chairman, president, or similar business leader. This move demonstrates the importance of the plan to the entire organization and showcases the business leader's commitment to business continuity. The signature of such an individual on the plan also gives it much greater weight and credibility in the eyes of other senior managers, who might otherwise brush it off as a necessary but trivial IT initiative.

Plan Implementation

Once you've received approval from senior management, it's time to dive in and start implementing your plan. The BCP team should get together and develop an implementation schedule that utilizes the resources dedicated to the program to achieve the stated process and provision goals in as prompt a manner as possible given the scope of the modifications and the organizational climate.

After all the resources are fully deployed, the BCP team should supervise the conduct of an appropriate BCP maintenance program to ensure that the plan remains responsive to evolving business needs.

Training and Education

Training and education are essential elements of the BCP implementation. All personnel who will be involved in the plan (either directly or indirectly) should receive some sort of training on the overall plan and their individual responsibilities. Everyone in the organization should receive at least a plan overview briefing to provide them with the confidence that business leaders have considered the possible risks posed to continued operation of the business and have put a plan in place to mitigate the impact on the organization should business be disrupted. People with direct BCP responsibilities should be trained and evaluated on their specific BCP tasks to ensure that they are able to complete them efficiently when disaster strikes. Furthermore, at least one backup person should be trained for every BCP task to ensure redundancy in the event personnel are injured or cannot reach the workplace during an emergency.

BCP Documentation

Documentation is a critical step in the business continuity planning process. Committing your BCP methodology to paper provides several important benefits:

- It ensures that BCP personnel have a written continuity document to reference in the event of an emergency, even if senior BCP team members are not present to guide the effort.

- It provides a historical record of the BCP process that will be useful to future personnel seeking to both understand the reasoning behind various procedures and implement necessary changes in the plan.

- It forces the team members to commit their thoughts to paper—a process that often facilitates the identification of flaws in the plan. Having the plan on paper also allows draft documents to be distributed to individuals not on the BCP team for a "sanity check."

In the following sections, we'll explore some of the important components of the written business continuity plan.

Continuity Planning Goals

First, the plan should describe the goals of continuity planning as set forth by the BCP team and senior management. These goals should be decided on at or before the first BCP team meeting and will most likely remain unchanged throughout the life of the BCP.

The most common goal of the BCP is quite simple: to ensure the continuous operation of the business in the face of an emergency situation. Other goals may also be inserted in this section of the document to meet organizational needs. For example, you might have goals that your customer call center experience no more than 15 consecutive minutes of downtime or that your backup servers be able to handle 75 percent of your processing load within 1 hour of activation.

Statement of Importance

The statement of importance reflects the criticality of the BCP to the organization's continued viability. This document commonly takes the form of a letter to the organization's employees stating the reason that the organization devoted significant resources to the BCP development process and requesting the cooperation of all personnel in the BCP implementation phase. Here's where the importance of senior executive buy-in comes into play. If you can put out this letter under the signature of the CEO or an officer at a similar level, the plan will carry tremendous weight as you attempt to implement changes throughout the organization. If you have the signature of a lower-level manager, you may encounter resistance as you attempt to work with portions of the organization outside of that individual's direct control.

Statement of Priorities

The statement of priorities flows directly from the identify priorities phase of the business impact assessment. It simply involves listing the functions considered critical to continued business operations in a prioritized order. When listing these priorities, you should also include a statement that they were developed as part of the BCP process and reflect the importance of the functions to continued business operations in the event of an emergency and nothing more. Otherwise, the list of priorities could be used for unintended purposes and result in a political turf battle between competing organizations to the detriment of the business continuity plan.

Statement of Organizational Responsibility

The statement of organizational responsibility also comes from a senior-level executive and can be incorporated into the same letter as the statement of importance. It basically echoes the sentiment that "business continuity is everyone's responsibility!" The statement of organizational responsibility restates the organization's commitment to business continuity planning and informs employees, vendors, and affiliates that they are individually expected to do everything they can to assist with the BCP process.

Statement of Urgency and Timing

The statement of urgency and timing expresses the criticality of implementing the BCP and outlines the implementation timetable decided on by the BCP team and agreed to by upper management. The wording of this statement will depend on the actual urgency assigned to the BCP process by the organization's leadership. If the statement itself is included in the same letter as the statement of priorities and statement of organizational responsibility, the timetable should be included as a separate document. Otherwise, the timetable and this statement can be put into the same document.

Risk Assessment

The risk assessment portion of the BCP documentation essentially recaps the decision-making process undertaken during the business impact assessment. It should include a discussion of all the risks considered during the BIA as well as the quantitative and qualitative analyses performed to assess these risks. For the quantitative analysis, the actual AV, EF, ARO, SLE, and ALE figures should be included. For the qualitative analysis, the thought process behind the risk analysis should be provided to the reader. It's important to note that the risk assessment must be updated on a regular basis because it reflects a point-in-time assessment.

Risk Acceptance/Mitigation

The risk acceptance/mitigation section of the BCP documentation contains the outcome of the strategy development portion of the BCP process. It should cover each risk identified in the risk analysis portion of the document and outline one of two thought processes:

- For risks that were deemed acceptable, it should outline the reasons the risk was considered acceptable as well as potential future events that might warrant reconsideration of this determination.

- For risks that were deemed unacceptable, it should outline the risk management provisions and processes put into place to reduce the risk to the organization's continued viability.

Vital Records Program

The BCP documentation should also outline a vital records program for the organization. This document states where critical business records will be stored and the procedures for making and storing backup copies of those records.

Emergency-Response Guidelines

The emergency-response guidelines outline the organizational and individual responsibilities for immediate response to an emergency situation. This document provides the first employees to detect an emergency with the steps they should take to activate provisions of the BCP that do not automatically activate. These guidelines should include the following:

- Immediate response procedures (security and safety procedures, fire suppression procedures, notification of appropriate emergency-response agencies, and so on)

- Whom to notify (executives, BCP team members, and so on)

- Secondary response procedures to take while waiting for the BCP team to assemble

Maintenance

The BCP documentation and the plan itself must be living documents. Every organization encounters nearly constant change, and this dynamic nature ensures that the business's continuity requirements will also evolve. The BCP team should not be disbanded after the plan is developed but should still meet periodically to discuss the plan and review the results of plan tests to ensure that it continues to meet organizational needs. Obviously, minor changes to the plan do not require conducting the full BCP development process from scratch; they can simply be made at an informal meeting of the BCP team by unanimous consent. However, keep in mind that drastic changes in an organization's mission or resources may require going back to the BCP drawing board and beginning again. Any time you make a change to the BCP, you must practice good version control. All older versions of the BCP should be physically destroyed and replaced by the most current version so that no confusion exists as to the correct implementation of the BCP. It is also a good practice to include BCP components in job descriptions to ensure that the BCP remains fresh and is performed correctly. Including BCP responsibilities in an employee's job description also makes them fair game for the performance review process.

Testing and Exercises

The BCP documentation should also outline a formalized exercise program to ensure that the plan remains current and that all personnel are adequately trained to perform their duties in the event of a disaster. The testing process is quite similar to that used for the disaster recovery plan, so we'll reserve the discussion of the specific test types for Chapter 16.

Summary

Every organization dependent on technological resources for its survival should have a comprehensive business continuity plan in place to ensure the sustained viability of the organization when unforeseen emergencies take place. There are a number of important concepts that underlie solid business continuity planning (BCP) practices, including project scope and planning, business impact assessment, continuity planning, and approval and implementation. Every organization must have plans and procedures in place to help mitigate the effects a disaster has on continuing operations and to speed the return to normal operations. To determine the risks that your business faces and that require mitigation, you must conduct a business impact assessment from both quantitative and qualitative points of view. You must take the appropriate steps in developing a continuity strategy for your organization and know what to do to weather future disasters.

Finally, you must create the documentation required to ensure that your plan is effectively communicated to present and future BCP team participants. Such documentation must include continuity planning guidelines. The business continuity plan must also contain statements of importance, priorities, organizational responsibility, and urgency and timing. In addition, the documentation should include plans for risk assessment, acceptance, and mitigation; a vital records program; emergency-response guidelines; and plans for maintenance and testing.

The next chapter will take this planning to the next step—developing and implementing a disaster recovery plan. The disaster recovery plan kicks in where the business continuity plan leaves off. When an emergency occurs that interrupts your business in spite of the BCP measures, the disaster recovery plan guides the recovery efforts necessary to restore your business to normal operations as quickly as possible.

Exam Essentials

Understand the four steps of the business continuity planning process.   Business continuity planning (BCP) involves four distinct phases: project scope and planning, business impact assessment, continuity planning, and approval and implementation. Each task contributes to the overall goal of ensuring that business operations continue uninterrupted in the face of an emergency situation.

Describe how to perform the business organization analysis. In the business organization analysis, the individuals responsible for leading the BCP process determine which departments and individuals have a stake in the business continuity plan. This analysis is used as the foundation for BCP team selection and, after validation by the BCP team, is used to guide the next stages of BCP development.

List the necessary members of the business continuity planning team. The BCP team should contain, at a minimum, representatives from each of the operational and support departments; technical experts from the IT department; security personnel with BCP skills; legal representatives familiar with corporate legal, regulatory, and contractual responsibilities; and representatives from senior management. Additional team members depend on the structure and nature of the organization.

Know the legal and regulatory requirements that face business continuity planners. Business leaders must exercise due diligence to ensure that shareholders' interests are protected in the event disaster strikes. Some industries are also subject to federal, state, and local regulations that mandate specific BCP procedures. Many businesses also have contractual obligations to their clients that must be met, before and after a disaster.

Explain the steps of the business impact assessment process. The five steps of the business impact assessment process are identification of priorities, risk identification, likelihood assessment, impact assessment, and resource prioritization.

Describe the process used to develop a continuity strategy. During the strategy development phase, the BCP team determines which risks will be mitigated. In the provisions and processes phase, mechanisms and procedures that will mitigate the risks are designed. The plan must then be approved by senior management and implemented. Personnel must also receive training on their roles in the BCP process.

Explain the importance of fully documenting an organization's business continuity plan. Committing the plan to writing provides the organization with a written record of the procedures to follow when disaster strikes. It prevents the "it's in my head" syndrome and ensures the orderly progress of events in an emergency.

Written Lab

1. Why is it important to include legal representatives on your BCP team?
2. What is wrong with the "seat-of-the-pants" approach to BCP?
3. What is the difference between quantitative and qualitative risk assessment?
4. What critical components should be included in your BCP training plan?
5. What are the four main steps of the BCP process?

Review Questions

1. What is the first step that individuals responsible for the development of a business continuity plan should perform?

   A. BCP team selection

   B. Business organization analysis

   C. Resource requirements analysis

   D. Legal and regulatory assessment

2. Once the BCP team is selected, what should be the first item placed on the team's agenda?

   A. Business impact assessment

   B. Business organization analysis

   C. Resource requirements analysis

   D. Legal and regulatory assessment

3. What is the term used to describe the responsibility of a firm's officers and directors to ensure that adequate measures are in place to minimize the effect of a disaster on the organization's continued viability?

   A. Corporate responsibility

   B. Disaster requirement

   C. Due diligence

   D. Going concern responsibility

4. What will be the major resource consumed by the BCP process during the BCP phase?

   A. Hardware

   B. Software

   C. Processing time

   D. Personnel

5. What unit of measurement should be used to assign quantitative values to assets in the priority identification phase of the business impact assessment?

   A. Monetary

   B. Utility

   C. Importance

   D. Time

6. Which one of the following BIA terms identifies the amount of money a business expects to lose to a given risk each year?

    A. ARO

    B. SLE

    C. ALE

    D. EF

7. What BIA metric can be used to express the longest time a business function can be unavailable without causing irreparable harm to the organization?

    A. SLE

    B. EF

    C. MTD

    D. ARO

8. You are concerned about the risk that an avalanche poses to your $3 million shipping facility. Based on expert opinion, you determine that there is a 5 percent chance that an avalanche will occur each year. Experts advise you that an avalanche would completely destroy your building and require you to rebuild on the same land. Ninety percent of the $3 million value of the facility is attributed to the building and 10 percent is attributed to the land itself. What is the single loss expectancy of your shipping facility to avalanches?

    A. $3,000,000

    B. $2,700,000

    C. $270,000

    D. $135,000

9. Referring to the scenario in question 8, what is the annualized loss expectancy?

    A. $3,000,000

    B. $2,700,000

    C. $270,000

    D. $135,000

10. You are concerned about the risk that a hurricane poses to your corporate headquarters in South Florida. The building itself is valued at $15 million. After consulting with the National Weather Service, you determine that there is a 10 percent likelihood that a hurricane will strike over the course of a year. You hired a team of architects and engineers who determined that the average hurricane would destroy approximately 50 percent of the building. What is the annualized loss expectancy (ALE)?

    A. $750,000

    B. $1.5 million

    C. $7.5 million

    D. $15 million

11. Which task of BCP bridges the gap between the business impact assessment and the continuity planning phases?

    A. Resource prioritization

    B. Likelihood assessment

    C. Strategy development

    D. Provisions and processes

12. Which resource should you protect first when designing continuity plan provisions and processes?

    A. Physical plant

    B. Infrastructure

    C. Financial

    D. People

13. Which one of the following concerns is not suitable for quantitative measurement during the business impact assessment?

    A. Loss of a plant

    B. Damage to a vehicle

    C. Negative publicity

    D. Power outage

14. Lighter Than Air Industries expects that it would lose $10 million if a tornado struck its aircraft operations facility. It expects that a tornado might strike the facility once every 100 years. What is the single loss expectancy for this scenario?

    A. 0.01

    B. $10,000,000

    C. $100,000

    D. 0.10

15. Referring to the scenario in question 14, what is the annualized loss expectancy?

    A. 0.01

    B. $10,000,000

    C. $100,000

    D. 0.10

16. In which business continuity planning task would you actually design procedures and mechanisms to mitigate risks deemed unacceptable by the BCP team?

    A. Strategy development

    B. Business impact assessment

    C. Provisions and processes

    D. Resource prioritization

17. What type of mitigation provision is utilized when redundant communications links are installed?

    A. Hardening systems

    B. Defining systems

    C. Reducing systems

    D. Alternative systems

18. What type of plan outlines the procedures to follow when a disaster interrupts the normal operations of a business?

    A. Business continuity plan

    B. Business impact assessment

    C. Disaster recovery plan

    D. Vulnerability assessment

19. What is the formula used to compute the single loss expectancy for a risk scenario?

    A. $SLE = AV \times EF$

    B. $SLE = RO \times EF$

    C. $SLE = AV \times ARO$

    D. $SLE = EF \times ARO$

20. Of the individuals listed, who would provide the best endorsement for a business continuity plan's statement of importance?

    A. Vice president of business operations

    B. Chief information officer

    C. Chief executive officer

    D. Business continuity manager

Chapter

16

Disaster Recovery Planning

THE CISSP EXAM TOPICS COVERED IN THIS CHAPTER INCLUDE:

8. Business Continuity and Disaster Recovery Planning

   C. Develop recovery strategy

      C.1 Implement a backup storage strategy (e.g., offsite storage, electronic vaulting, tape rotation)

      C.2 Recovery site strategies

   D. Understand disaster recovery process

      D.1 Response

      D.2 Personnel

      D.3 Communications

      D.4 Assessment

      D.5 Restoration

      D.6 Provide training

   E. Exercise, assess and maintain the plan (e.g., version control, distribution)

In Chapter 15, "Business Continuity Planning," you learned the essential elements of business continuity planning (BCP)—the art of helping your organization avoid business interruption as the result of an emergency or disaster. But business continuity plans do not seek to prevent every possible disaster.

Disaster recovery planning (DRP) steps in where BCP leaves off. When a disaster strikes and a business continuity plan fails to prevent interruption of business activities, the disaster recovery plan kicks in and guides the actions of emergency-response personnel until the end goal is reached, which is to see the business restored to full operating capacity in its primary operations facilities.

While reading this chapter, you may notice many areas of overlap between the BCP and DRP processes. Our discussion of specific disasters provides information on how to handle them from both BCP and DRP points of view. Although the (ISC)² CISSP curriculum draws a distinction between these two areas, most organizations simply have a single team and plan to address both business continuity and disaster recovery concerns. In many organizations, the single discipline known as business continuity management (BCM) encompasses BCP, DRP, and incident management under a single umbrella.

The Nature of Disaster

Disaster recovery planning brings order to the chaos that surrounds the interruption of an organization's normal activities. By its very nature, a *disaster recovery plan* is implemented only when tension is high and cooler heads may not naturally prevail. Picture the circumstances in which you might find it necessary to implement DRP measures—a hurricane destroys your main operations facility, a fire devastates your main processing center, terrorist activity closes off access to a major metropolitan area. Any event that stops, prevents, or interrupts an organization's ability to perform its work tasks is considered a disaster. The moment that IT becomes unable to support mission-critical processes is the moment DRP kicks in to manage the restoration and recovery procedures.

A disaster recovery plan should be set up so that it can almost run on autopilot. The DRP should also be designed to reduce decision-making activities during a disaster as much as possible. Essential personnel should be well trained in their duties and responsibilities in the wake of a disaster and also know the steps they need to take to get the organization up and running as soon as possible. We'll begin by analyzing some of the possible disasters that might strike your organization and the particular threats that they pose. Many of these are mentioned in Chapter 15, but we'll now explore them in further detail.

To plan for natural and unnatural disasters in the workplace, you must first understand their various forms, as explained in the following sections.

Natural Disasters

Natural disasters reflect the occasional fury of our habitat—violent occurrences that result from changes in the earth's surface or atmosphere that are beyond human control. In some cases, such as hurricanes, scientists have developed sophisticated predictive models that provide ample warning before a disaster strikes. Others, such as earthquakes, can cause devastation at a moment's notice. A disaster recovery plan should provide mechanisms for responding to both types of disasters, either with a gradual buildup of response forces or as an immediate reaction to a rapidly emerging crisis.

Earthquakes

Earthquakes are caused by the shifting of seismic plates and can occur almost anywhere in the world without warning. However, they are far more likely to occur along known fault lines that exist in many areas of the world. A well-known example is the San Andreas fault, which poses a significant risk to portions of the western United States. If you live in a region along a fault line where earthquakes are likely, your DRP should address the procedures your business will implement should a seismic event interrupt your normal activities.

You might be surprised by some of the regions of the world where earthquakes are considered possible. Table 16.1 shows parts of the United States (and U.S. territories) that the Federal Emergency Management Agency (FEMA) considers moderate, high, or very high seismic hazards. Note that the states listed in the table include 82 percent (41) of the 50 states, meaning that the majority of the country has at least a moderate risk of seismic activity.

TABLE 16.1   Seismic hazard level by U.S. state or territory

Moderate seismic hazard	High seismic hazard	Very high seismic hazard
Alabama	American Samoa	Alaska
Colorado	Arizona	California
Connecticut	Arkansas	Guam
Delaware	Illinois	Hawaii
Georgia	Indiana	Idaho
Maine	Kentucky	Montana
Maryland	Missouri	Nevada

TABLE 16.1 Seismic hazard level by U.S. state or territory *(continued)*

Moderate seismic hazard	High seismic hazard	Very high seismic hazard
Massachusetts	New Mexico	Oregon
Mississippi	South Carolina	Puerto Rico
New Hampshire	Tennessee	Virgin Islands
New Jersey	Utah	Washington
New York		Wyoming
North Carolina		
Ohio		
Oklahoma		
Pennsylvania		
Rhode Island		
Texas		
Vermont		
Virginia		
West Virginia		

Floods

Flooding can occur almost anywhere in the world at any time of the year. Some flooding results from the gradual accumulation of rainwater in rivers, lakes, and other bodies of water that then overflow their banks and flood the community. Other floods, known as *flash floods*, strike when a sudden severe storm dumps more rainwater on an area than the ground can absorb in a short period of time. Floods can also occur when dams are breached. Large waves caused by seismic activity, or *tsunamis*, combine the awesome power and weight of water with flooding, as we saw during the 2011 tsunami in Japan. This tsunami amply demonstrated the enormous destructive capabilities of water and the havoc it can wreak on various businesses and economies.

According to government statistics, flooding is responsible for more than $1 billion (that's billion with a *b*!) in damage to businesses and homes each year in the United States. It's important that your DRP make appropriate response plans for the eventuality that a flood may strike your facilities.

WARNING When you evaluate a firm's risk of damage from flooding to develop business continuity and disaster recovery plans, it's also a good idea to check with responsible individuals and ensure that your organization has sufficient insurance in place to protect it from the financial impact of a flood. In the United States, most general business policies do not cover flood damage, and you should investigate obtaining specialized government-backed flood insurance under FEMA's National Flood Insurance Program.

Although flooding is theoretically possible in almost any region of the world, it is much more likely to occur in certain areas. FEMA's National Flood Insurance Program is responsible for completing a flood risk assessment for the entire United States and providing this data to citizens in graphical form. You can view flood maps online at

`http://mapapps.esri.com/disasters/create-map/hazard/index.html`

This site also provides valuable information on recorded earthquakes, hurricanes, windstorms, hailstorms, and other natural disasters to help you prepare your organization's risk assessment.

When viewing flood maps, like the one shown in Figure 16.1, you'll find that the two risks often assigned to an area are the "100-year flood plain" and the "500-year flood plain." These evaluations mean that the government estimates chances of flooding in any given year at 1 in 100 or at 1 in 500, respectively. For a more detailed tutorial on reading flood maps, visit `www.fema.gov/media/fhm/firm/ot_firm.htm`.

FIGURE 16.1   Flood hazard map for Miami–Dade County, Florida

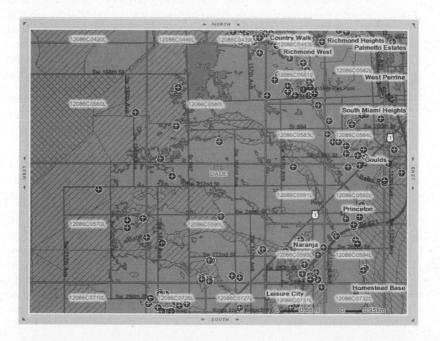

Storms

Storms come in many forms and pose diverse risks to a business. Prolonged periods of intense rainfall bring the risk of flash flooding described in the previous section. Hurricanes and tornadoes come with the threat of winds exceeding 100 miles per hour that undermine the structural integrity of buildings and turn everyday objects such as trees, lawn furniture, and even vehicles into deadly missiles. Hailstorms bring a rapid onslaught of destructive ice chunks falling from the sky. Many storms also bring the risk of lightning, which can cause severe damage to sensitive electronic components. For this reason, your business continuity plan should detail appropriate mechanisms to protect against lightning-induced damage, and your disaster recovery plan should provide adequate provisions for power outages and equipment damage that might result from a lightning strike. Never underestimate the damage that a single storm can do.

In 2005, the Category 5 Atlantic hurricane Katrina marked the costliest, deadliest, and strongest hurricane ever to make landfall in the continental United States. It bored a path of destruction from Louisiana to Alabama, destroying everything natural and man-made throughout those areas. The total economic impact stemming from the damage this storm caused is estimated at $81 billion, eliminating a major Gulf Coast highway and impeding commodities exports, not to mention inundating nearly 80 percent of the city of New Orleans.

If you live in an area susceptible to a certain type of severe storm, it's important to regularly monitor weather forecasts from responsible government agencies. For example, disaster recovery specialists in hurricane-prone areas should periodically check the website of the National Weather Service's Tropical Prediction Center (www.nhc.noaa.gov) during hurricane season. This website allows you to monitor Atlantic and Pacific storms that may pose a risk to your region before word about them hits the local news. This lets you begin a gradual response to the storm before time runs out.

Fires

Fires can start for a variety of reasons, both natural and man-made, but both forms can be equally devastating. During the BCP/DRP process, you should evaluate the risk of fire and implement at least basic measures to mitigate that risk and prepare the business for recovery from a catastrophic fire in a critical facility.

Some regions of the world are susceptible to wildfires during the warm season. These fires, once started, spread in somewhat predictable patterns, and fire experts working with meteorologists can produce relatively accurate forecasts of a wildfire's potential path.

As with many other types of large-scale natural disasters, you can obtain valuable information about impending threats on the Web. In the United States, the National Interagency Fire Center posts daily fire updates and forecasts on its website: http://www.nifc.gov/fireInfo/fireInfo_maps.html. Other countries have similar warning systems in place.

Other Regional Events

Some regions of the world are prone to localized types of natural disasters. During the BCP/DRP process, your assessment team should analyze all of your organization's operating locations and gauge the impact that such events might have on your business. For example, many parts of the world are subject to volcanic eruptions. If you conduct operations in an area in close proximity to an active or dormant volcano, your DRP should probably address this eventuality. Other localized natural occurrences include monsoons in Asia, tsunamis in the South Pacific, avalanches in mountainous regions, and mudslides in the western United States.

If your business is geographically diverse, it is prudent to include area natives on your planning team. At the very least, make use of local resources such as government emergency preparedness teams, civil defense organizations, and insurance claim offices to help guide your efforts. These organizations possess a wealth of knowledge and are usually more than happy to help you prepare your organization for the unexpected—after all, every organization that successfully weathers a natural disaster is one less organization that requires a portion of their valuable recovery resources after disaster strikes.

Man-Made Disasters

Our advanced civilization has become increasingly dependent on complex interactions between technological, logistical, and natural systems. The same complex interactions that make our sophisticated society possible also present a number of potential vulnerabilities from both intentional and unintentional *man-made disasters*. In the following sections, we'll examine a few of the more common disasters to help you analyze your organization's vulnerabilities when preparing a business continuity plan and disaster recovery plan.

Fires

Earlier in the chapter, we explained how some regions of the world are susceptible to wildfires during the warm season, and these types of fires can be described as natural disasters. Many smaller-scale fires result from human action—be it carelessness, faulty electrical wiring, improper fire protection practices, or other reasons. Studies from the Insurance Information Institute indicate that there are at least 1,000 building fires in the United States *every day*. If such a fire strikes your organization, do you have the proper preventative measures in place to quickly contain it? If the fire destroys your facilities, how quickly does your disaster recovery plan allow you to resume operations elsewhere?

Acts of Terrorism

Since the terrorist attacks on September 11, 2001, businesses are increasingly concerned about risks posed by terrorist threats. The attacks on September 11 caused many small businesses to fail because they did not have business continuity/disaster recovery plans in place that were adequate to ensure their continued viability. Many larger businesses experienced significant losses that caused severe long-term damage. The Insurance Information Institute issued a study one year after the attacks that estimated the total damage from the attacks in New York City at $40 billion (yes, that's with a *b* again!).

General business insurance may not properly cover an organization against acts of terrorism. Prior to the September 11, 2001, attacks, most policies either covered acts of terrorism or didn't mention them explicitly. After suffering such a catastrophic loss, many insurance companies responded by amending policies to exclude losses from terrorist activity. Policy riders and endorsements are sometimes available but often at extremely high cost. If your business continuity or disaster recovery plan includes insurance as a means of financial recovery (as it probably should!), you'd be well advised to check your policies and contact your insurance professionals to ensure that you're still covered.

Terrorist acts pose a unique challenge to DRP teams because of their unpredictable nature. Prior to the September 11, 2001, terrorist attacks in New York and Washington, DC, few DRP teams considered the threat of an airplane crashing into their corporate headquarters significant enough to merit mitigation. Many companies are now asking themselves a number of new "what if" questions regarding terrorist activity. In general, these questions are healthy because they promote dialogue between business elements regarding potential threats. On the other hand, disaster recovery planners must emphasize solid risk-management principles and ensure that resources aren't overallocated to terrorist threats to the detriment of other DRP/BCP activities that protect against more likely threats.

Bombings/Explosions

Explosions can result from a variety of man-made occurrences. Explosive gases from leaks might fill a room/building and later ignite and cause a damaging blast. In many areas, bombings are also cause for concern. From a disaster planning perspective, the effects of bombings and explosions are like those caused by a large-scale fire. However, planning to avoid the impact of a bombing is much more difficult and relies on physical security measures we cover in Chapter 19, "Physical Security Requirements."

Power Outages

Even the most basic disaster recovery plan contains provisions to deal with the threat of a short power outage. Critical business systems are often protected by uninterruptible power supply (UPS) devices to keep them running at least long enough to shut down or long enough to get emergency generators up and working. Even so, could your organization keep operating during a sustained power outage?

After Hurricane Katrina made landfall in 2005, a reported 2,400,000 people in Mississippi, Louisiana and Alabama lost power. Does your business continuity plan include provisions to keep your business viable during such a prolonged period without power? Does your disaster recovery plan make ample preparations for the timely restoration of power even if the commercial power grid remains unavailable?

Check your UPSs regularly! These critical devices are often overlooked until they become necessary. Many UPSs contain self-testing mechanisms that report problems automatically, but it's still a good idea to subject them to regular testing. Also, be sure to audit the number/type of devices plugged in to each UPS. It's amazing how many people think it's okay to add "just one more system" to a UPS, and you don't want to be surprised when the device can't handle the load during a real power outage!

Today's technology-driven organizations depend increasingly on electric power, so your BCP/DRP team should consider provisioning alternative power sources that can run business systems indefinitely. An adequate backup generator could make a huge difference when the survival of your business is at stake.

Other Utility and Infrastructure Failures

When planners consider the impact that utility outages may have on their organizations, they naturally think first about the impact of a power outage. However, keep other utilities in mind too. Do any of your critical business systems rely on water, sewers, natural gas, or other utilities? Also consider regional infrastructure such as highways, airports, and railroads. Any of these systems can suffer failures that might not be related to weather or other conditions described in this chapter. Many businesses depend on one or more of these infrastructure elements to move people or materials. Their failure can paralyze your business's ability to continue functioning.

If you quickly answered "no" to the question whether you have critical business systems that rely on water, sewers, natural gas, or other utilities, think again. Do you consider people a critical business system? If a major storm knocks out the water supply to your facilities and you need to keep those facilities up and running, can you supply your employees with enough drinking water to meet their needs?

What about your fire protection systems? If any of them are water based, is there a holding tank system in place that contains ample water to extinguish a serious building fire if the public water system is unavailable? Fires often cause serious damage in areas ravaged by storms, earthquakes, and other disasters that might also interrupt the delivery of water.

Hardware/Software Failures

Like it or not, computer systems fail. Hardware components simply wear out and refuse to continue performing, or they suffer physical damage. Software systems contain bugs or fall prey to improper or unexpected inputs. For this reason, BCP/DRP teams must provide adequate redundancy in their systems. If zero downtime is a mandatory requirement, the best solution is to use fully redundant failover servers in separate locations attached to separate communications links and infrastructures (also designed to operate in a failover mode). If one server is damaged or destroyed, the other will instantly take over the processing load. For more information on this concept, see the section "Remote Mirroring" later in this chapter.

Because of financial constraints, it isn't always feasible to maintain fully redundant systems. In those circumstances, the BCP/DRP team should address how replacement parts can be quickly obtained and installed. As many parts as possible should be kept in a local parts inventory for quick replacement; this is especially true for hard-to-find parts that must otherwise be shipped in. After all, how many organizations could do without telephones for three days while a critical PBX component is en route from an overseas location to be installed on site?

 Real World Scenario

NYC Blackout

On August 14, 2003, the lights went out in New York City and in large areas of the northeastern and midwestern United States when a series of cascading failures caused the collapse of a major power grid.

Fortunately, security professionals in the New York area were ready. Spurred to action by the September 11, 2001, terrorist attacks, many businesses updated their disaster recovery plans and took steps to ensure their continued operations in the wake of another disaster. This blackout served to test those plans, and many organizations were able to continue operating on alternate power sources or to transfer control seamlessly to offsite data-processing centers.

Lessons learned during this blackout offer insight for BCP/DRP teams around the world and include the following:

- Ensure that alternate processing sites are far enough away from your main site that they are unlikely to be affected by the same disaster.

- Remember that threats to your organization are both internal and external. Your next disaster may come from a terrorist attack, building fire, or malicious code running loose on your network. Take steps to ensure that your alternate sites are segregated from the main facility to protect against all of these threats.

- Disasters don't usually come with advance warning. If real-time operations are critical to your organization, be sure that your backup sites are ready to assume primary status at a moment's notice.

Strikes/Picketing

When designing your business continuity and disaster recovery plans, don't forget about the importance of the human factor in emergency planning. One form of man-made disaster that is often overlooked is the possibility of a strike or other labor crisis. If a large number of your employees walk out at the same time, what impact would that have on your business? How long would you be able to sustain operations without the regular full-time employees that staff a certain area? Your BCP and DRP teams should address these concerns, providing alternative plans should a labor crisis occur.

Theft/Vandalism

In a previous section, we talked about the threat that terrorist activities pose to an organization. Theft and vandalism represent the same kind of threat on a much smaller scale. In most cases, however, there's a far greater chance that your organization will be affected by theft or vandalism than by a terrorist attack. Insurance provides some financial protection against these events (subject to deductibles and limitations of coverage), but acts of this kind can cause serious damage to your business, on both a short-term and long-term basis. Your business continuity and disaster recovery plans should include adequate preventive measures to control the frequency of these occurrences as well as contingency plans to mitigate the effects theft and vandalism have on ongoing operations.

Theft of infrastructure is becoming increasingly common as scrappers target copper in air-conditioning systems, plumbing, and power subsystems. It's a common mistake to assume that fixed infrastructure is unlikely to be a theft target.

 Real World Scenario

Offsite Challenges to Security

The constant threat of theft and vandalism is the bane of information security professionals worldwide. Personal identity information, proprietary or trade secrets, and other forms of confidential data are just as interesting to those who create and possess them as they are to direct competitors and other unauthorized parties. Here's an example.

Aaron knows the threats to confidential data firsthand, working as a security officer for a very prominent and highly visible computing enterprise. His chief responsibility is to keep sensitive information from exposure to various elements and entities. Bethany is one of his more troublesome employees because she's constantly taking her notebook computer off site without properly securing its contents.

Even a casual smash-and-grab theft attempt could put thousands of client contacts and their confidential business dealings at risk of being leaked and possibly sold to malicious parties. Aaron knows the potential dangers, but Bethany just doesn't seem to care.

This poses the question: How might you better inform, train, or advise Bethany so that Aaron does not have to relieve her of her position should her notebook be stolen? Bethany must come to understand and appreciate the importance of keeping sensitive information secure. It may be necessary to emphasize the potential loss and exposure that comes with losing such data to wrongdoers, competitors, or other unauthorized third parties. It may suffice to point out to Bethany that the employee handbook clearly states that employees whose behavior leads to the unauthorized disclosure or loss of information assets are subject to loss of pay or termination. If such behavior recurs after a warning, Bethany should be rebuked and reassigned to a position where she can't expose sensitive or proprietary information—that is, if she's not fired on the spot.

Keep the impact that theft may have on your operations in mind when planning your parts inventory. It's a good idea to keep extra inventory of items with a high pilferage rate, such as RAM chips and laptops. It's also a good idea to keep such materials in secure storage and to require employees to sign such items out whenever they are used.

Recovery Strategy

When a disaster interrupts your business, your disaster recovery plan should kick in nearly automatically and begin providing support for recovery operations. The disaster recovery plan should be designed so that the first employees on the scene can immediately begin the recovery effort in an organized fashion, even if members of the official DRP team have not yet arrived on site. In the following sections, we'll cover critical subtasks involved in crafting an effective disaster recovery plan that can guide rapid restoration of regular business processes and resumption of activity at the primary business location.

In addition to improving your response capabilities, purchasing insurance can reduce the risk of financial losses. When selecting insurance, be sure to purchase sufficient coverage to enable you to recover from a disaster. Simple value coverage may be insufficient to encompass actual replacement costs. If your property insurance includes an actual cash value (ACV) clause, then your damaged property will be compensated based on the fair market value of the items on the date of loss less all accumulated depreciation since the time of their purchase. The important point here is that unless you have a replacement cost clause in your insurance coverage, your organization is likely to be out of pocket as a result of any losses it might sustain.

Valuable paper insurance coverage provides protection for inscribed, printed, and written documents and manuscripts and other printed business records. However, it does not cover damage to paper money and printed security certificates.

Business Unit and Functional Priorities

To recover your business operations with the greatest possible efficiency, you must engineer your disaster recovery plan so that those business units with the highest priority are recovered first. You must identify and prioritize critical business functions as well so you can define which functions to restore after a disaster or failure and in what order.

To achieve this goal, the DRP team must first identify those business units and agree on an order of prioritization, and they must do likewise with business functions. (And take note: Not all critical business functions will necessarily be carried out in critical business units, so the final results of this analysis will very probably comprise a superset of critical business units plus other select units.)

If this process sounds familiar, it should! This is very like the prioritization task the BCP team performs during the business impact assessment discussed in Chapter 15. In fact, most organizations will complete a business impact assessment (BIA) as part of their business continuity planning process. This analysis identifies vulnerabilities, develops strategies to minimize risk, and ultimately produces a BIA report that describes the potential risks that an organization faces and identifies critical business units and functions. A BIA also identifies costs related to failures that include loss of cash flow, equipment replacement, salaries paid to clear work backlogs, profit losses, opportunity costs from the inability to attract new business, and so forth. Such failures are assessed in terms of potential impacts on finances, personnel, safety, legal compliance, contract fulfillment, and quality assurance, preferably in monetary terms to make impacts comparable and to set budgetary expectations. With all this BIA information in hand, you should use the resulting documentation as the basis for this prioritization task.

At a minimum, the output from this task should be a simple listing of business units in priority order. However, a more detailed list, broken down into specific business processes listed in order of priority, would be a much more useful deliverable. This business process–oriented list is more reflective of real-world conditions, but it requires considerable additional effort. It will, however, greatly assist in the recovery effort—after all, not every task performed by the highest-priority business unit will be of the highest priority. You might find that it would be best to restore the highest-priority unit to 50 percent capacity and then move on to lower-priority units to achieve some minimum operating capacity across the organization before attempting a full recovery effort.

By the same token, the same exercise must be completed for critical business processes and functions. Not only can these things involve multiple business units and cross the lines between them, but they also define the operational elements that must be restored in the wake of a disaster or other business interruption. Here also, the final result should be a checklist of items in priority order, each with its own risk and cost assessment, and a corresponding set of mean time to recovery (MTR) and related recovery objectives and milestones.

Crisis Management

If a disaster strikes your organization, panic is likely to set in. The best way to combat this is with an organized disaster recovery plan. The individuals in your business who are most likely to first notice an emergency situation (that is, security guards, technical personnel, and so on) should be fully trained in disaster recovery procedures and know the proper notification procedures and immediate response mechanisms.

Many things that normally seem like common sense (such as calling 911 in the event of a fire) may slip the minds of panicked employees seeking to flee an emergency. The best way to combat this is with continuous training on disaster recovery responsibilities. Returning to the fire example, all employees should be trained to activate the fire alarm or contact emergency officials when they spot a fire (after, of course, taking appropriate measures to protect themselves). After all, it's better that the fire department receives 10 different phone calls reporting a fire at your organization than it is for everyone to assume that someone else already took care of it.

Crisis management is a science and an art form. If your training budget permits, investing in crisis training for your key employees is a good idea. This ensures that at least some of your employees know how to handle emergency situations properly and can provide all-important "on-the-scene" leadership to panic-stricken co-workers.

Emergency Communications

When a disaster strikes, it is important that the organization be able to communicate internally as well as with the outside world. A disaster of any significance is easily noticed, but if an organization is unable to keep the outside world informed of its recovery status, the public is apt to fear the worst and assume that the organization is unable to recover. It is also essential that the organization be able to communicate internally during a disaster so that employees know what is expected of them—whether they are to return to work or report to another location, for instance.

In some cases, the circumstances that brought about the disaster to begin with may have also damaged some or all normal means of communications. A violent storm or an earthquake may have also knocked out telecommunications systems; at that point it's too late to try to figure out other means of communicating both internally and externally.

Work Group Recovery

When designing a disaster recovery plan, it's important to keep your goal in mind—the restoration of work groups to the point that they can resume their activities in their usual work locations. It's easy to get sidetracked and think of disaster recovery as purely an IT effort focused on restoring systems and processes to working order.

To facilitate this effort, it's sometimes best to develop separate recovery facilities for different work groups. For example, if you have several subsidiary organizations that are in different locations and that perform tasks similar to the tasks that work groups at your office perform, you may want to consider temporarily relocating those work groups to the other facility and having them communicate electronically and via telephone with other business units until they're ready to return to the main operations facility.

Larger organizations may have difficulty finding recovery facilities capable of handling the entire business operation. This is another example of a circumstance in which independent recovery of different work groups is appropriate.

Alternate Processing Sites

One of the most important elements of the disaster recovery plan is the selection of alternate processing sites to be used when the primary sites are unavailable. Many options are available when considering recovery facilities, limited only by the creative minds of disaster recovery planners and service providers. In the following sections, we cover several types of sites commonly used in disaster recovery planning: cold sites, warm sites, hot sites, mobile sites, service bureaus, and multiple sites.

> When choosing any alternate processing site, be sure to situate it far away enough from your primary location that it won't be affected by the same disaster that disables your primary site. But it should be close enough that it takes less than a full day's drive to reach it.

Cold Sites

Cold sites are standby facilities large enough to handle the processing load of an organization and equipped with appropriate electrical and environmental support systems. They may be large warehouses, empty office buildings, or other similar structures. However, a cold site has no computing facilities (hardware or software) preinstalled and also has no active broadband communications links. Many cold sites do have at least a few copper telephone lines, and some sites may have standby links that can be activated with minimal notification.

 Real World Scenario

Cold Site Setup

A cold site setup is well depicted in the 2000 film *Boiler Room*, which involves a chop-shop investment firm telemarketing bogus pharmaceutical investment deals to prospective clients. In this fictional case, the "disaster" is man-made, but the concept is much the same, even if the timing is quite different.

Under threat of exposure and a pending law enforcement raid, the firm establishes a nearby building that is empty, save for a few banks of phones on dusty concrete floors in a mock-up of a cold recovery site. Granted, this work is both fictional and illegal, but it illustrates a very real and legitimate reason for maintaining a redundant failover recovery site for the purpose of business continuity.

> Research the various forms of recovery sites, and then consider which among them is best suited for your particular business needs and budget. A cold site is the least expensive option and perhaps the most practical. A warm site contains the data links and preconfigured equipment necessary to begin restoring operations but no usable data or information. The most expensive option is a hot site, which fully replicates your existing business infrastructure and is ready to take over for the primary site on short notice.

The major advantage of a cold site is its relatively low cost—there's no computing base to maintain and no monthly telecommunications bill when the site is idle. However, the drawbacks of such a site are obvious—there is a tremendous lag between the time the decision is made to activate the site and the time when that site is ready to support business operations. Servers and workstations must be brought in and configured. Data must be restored from backup tapes. Communications links must be activated or established. The time to activate a cold site is often measured in weeks, making timely recovery close to impossible and often yielding a false sense of security. It's also worth observing that the substantial time, effort, and expense required to activate and transfer operations to a cold site make this approach the most difficult to test.

Hot Sites

A *hot site* is the exact opposite of the cold site. In this configuration, a backup facility is maintained in constant working order, with a full complement of servers, workstations, and communications links ready to assume primary operations responsibilities. The servers and workstations are all preconfigured and loaded with appropriate operating system and application software.

The data on the primary site servers is periodically or continuously replicated to corresponding servers at the hot site, ensuring that the hot site has up-to-date data. Depending on the bandwidth available between the sites, hot site data may be replicated instantaneously. If that is the case, operators could move operations to the hot site at a moment's notice. If it's not the case, disaster recovery managers have three options to activate the hot site:

- If there is sufficient time before the primary site must be shut down, they can force replication between the two sites right before the transition of operational control.

- If replication is impossible, managers may carry backup tapes of the transaction logs from the primary site to the hot site and manually reapply any transactions that took place since the last replication.

- If there are no available backups and it isn't possible to force replication, the disaster recovery team may simply accept the loss of some portion of the data.

The advantages of a hot site are obvious—the level of disaster recovery protection provided by this type of site is unsurpassed. However, the cost is *extremely* high. Maintaining a hot site essentially doubles an organization's budget for hardware, software, and services and requires the use of additional employees to maintain the site.

If you use a hot site, never forget that it has copies of your production data. Be sure to provide that site with the same level of technical and physical security controls you provide at your primary site.

If an organization wants to maintain a hot site but wants to reduce the expense of equipment and maintenance, it might opt to use a shared hot site facility managed by an outside contractor. However, the inherent danger in these facilities is that they may be overtaxed in the event of a widespread disaster and be unable to service all clients simultaneously. If your organization considers such an arrangement, be sure to investigate these issues thoroughly, both before signing the contract and periodically during the contract term.

Warm Sites

Warm sites occupy the middle ground between hot and cold sites for disaster recovery specialists. They always contain the equipment and data circuits necessary to rapidly establish operations. As with hot sites, this equipment is usually preconfigured and ready to run appropriate applications to support an organization's operations. Unlike hot sites, however, warm sites do not typically contain copies of the client's data. The main requirement in bringing a warm site to full operational status is the transportation of appropriate backup media to the site and restoration of critical data on the standby servers.

Activation of a warm site typically takes at least 12 hours from the time a disaster is declared. This does not mean that any site that can be activated in less than 12 hours qualifies as a hot site, however; switchover times for most hot sites are often measured in seconds or minutes, and complete cutovers seldom take more than an hour or two.

Warm sites avoid significant telecommunications and personnel costs inherent in maintaining a near-real-time copy of the operational data environment. As with hot sites and cold sites, warm sites may also be obtained on a shared facility basis. If you choose this option, be sure that you have a "no lockout" policy written into your contract guaranteeing you the use of an appropriate facility even during a period of high demand. It's a good idea to take this concept one step further and physically inspect the facilities and the contractor's operational plan to reassure yourself that the facility will indeed be able to back up the "no lockout" guarantee should push ever come to shove.

Mobile Sites

Mobile sites are nonmainstream alternatives to traditional recovery sites. They typically consist of self-contained trailers or other easily relocated units. These sites include all the environmental control systems necessary to maintain a safe computing environment. Larger corporations sometimes maintain these sites on a "fly-away" basis, ready to deploy them to any operating location around the world via air, rail, sea, or surface transportation. Smaller firms might contract with a mobile site vendor in their local area to provide these services on an as-needed basis.

If your disaster recovery plan depends on a workgroup recovery strategy, mobile sites are an excellent way to implement that approach. They are often large enough to accommodate entire (small!) work groups.

Mobile sites are usually configured as cold sites or warm sites, depending on the disaster recovery plan they are designed to support. It is also possible to configure a mobile site as a hot site, but this is unusual because you seldom know in advance where a mobile site will need to be deployed.

Hardware Replacement Options

One thing to consider when determining mobile sites and recovery sites in general is hardware replacement supplies. There are basically two options for hardware replacement supplies. One option is to employ "in-house" replacement, whereby you store extra and duplicate equipment at a different but nearby location (that is, a warehouse on the other side of town). (*In-house* here means you own it already, not that it is necessarily housed under the same roof as your production environment.) If you have a hardware failure or a disaster, you can immediately pull the appropriate equipment from your stash. The other option is an SLA-type agreement with a vendor to provide quick response and delivery time in the event of a disaster. However, even a 4-, 12-, 24-, or 48-hour replacement hardware contract from a vendor does not provide a reliable guarantee that delivery will actually occur. There are too many uncontrollable variables to rely on this second option as your sole means of recovery.

Service Bureaus

A *service bureau* is a company that leases computer time. Service bureaus own large server farms and often fields of workstations. Any organization can purchase a contract from a service bureau to consume some portion of their processing capacity. Access can be on site or remote.

A service bureau can usually provide support for all your IT needs in the event of a disaster—even desktops for workers to use. Your contract with a service bureau will often include testing and backups as well as response time and availability. However, service bureaus regularly oversell their actual capacity by gambling that not all their contracts will be exercised at the same time. Therefore, there is potential for resource contention in the wake of a major disaster. If your company operates in an industry-dense locale, this could be an important issue. You may need to select both a local and a distant service bureau to be sure to gain access to processing facilities during a real disaster.

Multiple Sites

By splitting or dividing your organization into several divisions, branches, offices, and so on, you create multiple sites and reduce the impact of a major disaster. In fact, the more sites you employ, the less impact a major disaster will have. However, for multiple sites to be effective they must be far enough apart that a major disaster cannot affect too many of them simultaneously. One drawback of using multiple sites is that the difficulty of managing and administering the entire company increases when facilities are spread across a large geographic area in numerous locations.

Mutual Assistance Agreements

Mutual assistance agreements (MAAs), also called *reciprocal agreements*, are popular in disaster recovery literature but are rarely implemented in real-world practice. In theory, they provide an excellent alternate processing option. Under an MAA, two organizations pledge to assist each other in the event of a disaster by sharing computing facilities or other technological resources. They appear to be extremely cost effective at first glance— it's not necessary for either organization to maintain expensive alternate processing sites (such as the hot sites, warm sites, cold sites, and mobile processing sites described in the previous sections). Indeed, many MAAs are structured to provide one of the levels of service described. In the case of a cold site, each organization may simply maintain some open space in their processing facilities for the other organization to use in the event of a disaster. In the case of a hot site, the organizations may host fully redundant servers for each other.

However, many drawbacks inherent to MAAs prevent their widespread use:

- MAAs are difficult to enforce. The parties might trust each other to provide support in the event of a disaster. However, when push comes to shove, the nonvictim might renege on the agreement. A victim may have legal remedies available, but this doesn't help the immediate disaster recovery effort.

- Cooperating organizations should be located in relatively close proximity to each other to facilitate transportation of employees between sites. However, proximity means that both organizations may be vulnerable to the same threats. An MAA won't do you any good if an earthquake levels your city and destroys processing sites for *both* participating organizations.

- Confidentiality concerns often prevent businesses from placing their data in the hands of others. These may be legal concerns (such as in the handling of health-care or financial data) or business concerns (such as trade secrets or other intellectual property issues).

Despite these concerns, an MAA may be a good disaster recovery solution for an organization, especially if cost is an overriding factor. If you simply can't afford to implement any other type of alternate processing, an MAA might provide a degree of valuable protection in the event a localized disaster strikes your business.

Database Recovery

Many organizations rely on databases to process and track operations, sales, logistics, and other activities vital to their continued viability. For this reason, it's essential that you include database recovery techniques in your disaster recovery plans. It's a wise idea to have a database specialist on the DRP team who can provide input as to the technical feasibility of various ideas. After all, you shouldn't allocate several hours to restore a database backup when it's impossible to complete a restoration in less than half a day!

In the following sections, we'll cover the three main techniques used to create offsite copies of database content: electronic vaulting, remote journaling, and remote mirroring. Each one has specific benefits and drawbacks, so you'll need to analyze your organization's computing requirements and available resources to select the option best suited to your firm.

Electronic Vaulting

In an *electronic vaulting* scenario, database backups are moved to a remote site using bulk transfers. The remote location may be a dedicated alternative recovery site (such as a hot site) or simply an offsite location managed within the company or by a contractor for the purpose of maintaining backup data.

If you use electronic vaulting, remember that there may be a significant delay between the time you declare a disaster and the time your database is ready for operation with current data. If you decide to activate a recovery site, technicians will need to retrieve the appropriate backups from the electronic vault and apply them to the soon-to-be production servers at the recovery site.

Be careful when considering vendors for an electronic vaulting contract. Definitions of electronic vaulting vary widely within the industry. Don't settle for a vague promise of "electronic vaulting capability." Insist on a written definition of the service that will be provided, including the storage capacity, bandwidth of the communications link to the electronic vault, and the time necessary to retrieve vaulted data in the event of a disaster.

As with any type of backup scenario, be certain to periodically test your electronic vaulting setup. A great method for testing backup solutions is to give disaster recovery personnel a "surprise test," asking them to restore data from a certain day.

Remote Journaling

With *remote journaling*, data transfers are performed in a more expeditious manner. Data transfers still occur in a bulk transfer mode, but they occur on a more frequent basis, usually once every hour and sometimes more frequently. Unlike electronic vaulting scenarios, where entire database backup files are transferred, remote journaling setups transfer copies of the database transaction logs containing the transactions that occurred since the previous bulk transfer.

Remote journaling is similar to electronic vaulting in that transaction logs transferred to the remote site are not applied to a live database server but are maintained in a backup device. When a disaster is declared, technicians retrieve the appropriate transaction logs and apply them to the production database.

Remote Mirroring

Remote mirroring is the most advanced database backup solution. Not surprisingly, it's also the most expensive! Remote mirroring goes beyond the technology used by remote journaling and electronic vaulting; with remote mirroring, a live database server is maintained at the backup site. The remote server receives copies of the database modifications at the same time they are applied to the production server at the primary site. Therefore, the mirrored server is ready to take over an operational role at a moment's notice.

Remote mirroring is a popular database backup strategy for organizations seeking to implement a hot site. However, when weighing the feasibility of a remote mirroring solution, be sure to take into account the infrastructure and personnel costs required to support the mirrored server as well as the processing overhead that will be added to each database transaction on the mirrored server.

Recovery Plan Development

Once you've established your business unit priorities and have a good idea of the appropriate alternative recovery sites for your organization, it's time to put pen to paper and begin drafting a true disaster recovery plan. Don't expect to sit down and write the full plan in one sitting. It's likely that the DRP team will go through many draft documents before reaching a final written document that satisfies the operational needs of critical business units and falls within the resource, time, and expense constraints of the disaster recovery budget and available manpower.

In the following sections, we explore some important items to include in your disaster recovery plan. Depending on the size of your organization and the number of people involved in the DRP effort, it may be a good idea to maintain multiple types of plan documents, intended for different audiences. The following list includes various types of documents worth considering:

- Executive summary providing a high-level overview of the plan
- Department-specific plans
- Technical guides for IT personnel responsible for implementing and maintaining critical backup systems
- Checklists for individuals on the disaster recovery team
- Full copies of the plan for critical disaster recovery team members

Using custom-tailored documents becomes especially important when a disaster occurs or is imminent. Personnel who need to refresh themselves on the disaster recovery procedures that affect various parts of the organization will be able to refer to their department-specific plans. Critical disaster recovery team members will have checklists to help guide their actions amid the chaotic atmosphere of a disaster. IT personnel will have technical guides helping them get the alternate sites up and running. Finally, managers and public relations personnel will have a simple document that walks them through a high-level view of the coordinated symphony that is an active disaster recovery effort without requiring interpretation from team members busy with tasks directly related to that effort.

Visit the Professional Practices library at https://www.drii.org/certification/professionalprac.php to examine a collection of documents that explain how to work through and document your planning processes for BCP and disaster recovery. Other good standard documents in this area includes the BCI Good Practices Guideline (www.thebci.org/index.php?option=com_content&view=article&id=60&Itemid=98), ISO 27001 (www.27001-online.com), and NIST SP 800-34 (http://csrc.nist.gov/publications/PubsSPs.html).

Emergency Response

A disaster recovery plan should contain simple yet comprehensive instructions for essential personnel to follow immediately upon recognizing that a disaster is in progress or is imminent. These instructions will vary widely depending on the nature of the disaster, the type of personnel responding to the incident, and the time available before facilities need to be evacuated and/or equipment shut down. For example, instructions for a large-scale fire will be much more concise than the instructions for how to prepare for a hurricane that is still 48 hours away from a predicted landfall near an operational site. Emergency-response plans are often put together in the form of checklists provided to responders. When designing such checklists, keep one essential design principle in mind: Arrange the checklist tasks in order of priority, with the most important task first!

It's essential to remember that these checklists will be executed in the midst of a crisis. It is extremely likely that responders will not be able to complete the entire checklist, especially in the event of a short-notice disaster. For this reason, you should put the most essential tasks (that is, "Activate the building alarm") first on the checklist. The lower an item on the list, the lower the likelihood that it will be completed before an evacuation/shutdown takes place.

Personnel and Communications

A disaster recovery plan should also contain a list of personnel to contact in the event of a disaster. Usually, this includes key members of the DRP team as well as personnel who execute critical disaster recovery tasks throughout the organization. This response checklist should include alternate means of contact (that is, pager numbers, mobile phone numbers, and so on) as well as backup contacts for each role should the primary contact be incommunicado or unable to reach the recovery site for one reason or another.

The Power of Checklists

Checklists are invaluable tools in the face of disaster. They provide a sense of order amidst the chaotic events surrounding a disaster. Do what you must to ensure that response checklists provide first responders with a clear plan to protect life and property and ensure the continuity of operations.

A checklist for response to a building fire might include the following steps:

1. Activate the building alarm system.

2. Ensure that an orderly evacuation is in progress.

3. After leaving the building, use a mobile telephone to call 911 to ensure that emergency authorities received the alarm notification. Provide additional information on any required emergency response.

4. Ensure that any injured personnel receive appropriate medical treatment.

5. Activate the organization's disaster recovery plan to ensure continuity of operations.

Be sure to consult with the individuals in your organization responsible for privacy before assembling and disseminating a telephone notification checklist. You may need to comply with special policies regarding the use of home telephone numbers and other personal information in the checklist.

The notification checklist should be supplied to all personnel who might respond to a disaster. This enables prompt notification of key personnel. Many firms organize their notification checklists in a "telephone tree" style: Each member of the tree contacts the person below them, spreading the notification burden among members of the team instead of relying on one person to make lots of telephone calls.

If you choose to implement a telephone tree notification scheme, be sure to add a safety net. Have the last person in each chain contact the originator to confirm that their entire chain has been notified. This lets you rest assured that the disaster recovery team activation is smoothly underway.

Assessment

When the disaster recovery team arrives on site, one of their first tasks is to assess the situation. This normally occurs in a rolling fashion, with the first responders performing a very simple assessment to triage activity and get the disaster response underway. As the incident progresses, more detailed assessments will take place to gauge the effectiveness of disaster recovery efforts and prioritize the assignment of resources.

Backups and Offsite Storage

Your disaster recovery plan (especially the technical guide) should fully address the backup strategy pursued by your organization. Indeed, this is one of the most important elements of any business continuity plan and disaster recovery plan.

Many system administrators are already familiar with various types of backups, so you'll benefit by bringing one or more individuals with specific technical expertise in this area onto the BCP/DRP team to provide expert guidance. There are three main types of backups:

Full Backups   As the name implies, *full backups* store a complete copy of the data contained on the protected device. Full backups duplicate every file on the system regardless of the setting of the archive bit. Once a full backup is complete, the archive bit on every file is reset, turned off, or set to 0.

Incremental Backups   *Incremental backups* store only those files that have been modified since the time of the most recent full or incremental backup. Only files that have the archive bit turned on, enabled, or set to 1 are duplicated. Once an incremental backup is complete, the archive bit on all duplicated files is reset, turned off, or set to 0.

Differential Backups   *Differential backups* store all files that have been modified since the time of the most recent full backup. Only files that have the archive bit turned on, enabled, or set to 1 are duplicated. However, unlike full and incremental backups, the differential backup process does not change the archive bit.

The most important difference between incremental and differential backups is the time needed to restore data in the event of an emergency. If you use a combination of full and differential backups, you will need to restore only two backups—the most recent full backup and the most recent differential backup. On the other hand, if your strategy combines full backups with incremental backups, you will need to restore the most recent full backup as well as all incremental backups performed since that full backup. The trade-off is the time required to *create* the backups—differential backups don't take as long to restore, but they take longer to create than incremental ones.

The storage of the backup media is equally critical. It may be convenient to store backup media in or near the primary operations center to easily fulfill user requests for backup data, but you'll definitely need to keep copies of the media in at least one offsite location to provide redundancy should your primary operating location be suddenly destroyed.

Using Backups

In case of system failure, many companies use one of two common methods to restore data from backups. In the first situation, they run a full backup on Monday night and then run differential backups every other night of the week. If a failure occurs Saturday morning, they restore Monday's full backup and then restore only Friday's differential backup. In the second situation, they run a full backup on Monday night and run incremental backups every other night of the week. If a failure occurs Saturday morning, they restore Monday's full backup and then restore each incremental backup in original chronological order (that is, Wednesday's, then Friday's, and so on).

Most organizations adopt a backup strategy that utilizes more than one of the three backup types along with a media rotation scheme. Both allow backup administrators access to a sufficiently large range of backups to complete user requests and provide fault tolerance while minimizing the amount of money that must be spent on backup media. A common strategy is to perform full backups over the weekend and incremental or differential backups on a nightly basis. The specific method of backup and all of the particulars of the backup procedure are dependent on your organization's fault-tolerance requirements. If you are unable to survive minor amounts of data loss, then your ability to tolerate faults is low. However, if hours or days of data can be lost without serious consequence, then your tolerance of faults is high. You should design your backup solution accordingly.

 Real World Scenario

The Oft-Neglected Backup

Backups are probably the least practiced and most neglected preventive measure known to protect against computing disasters. A comprehensive backup of all operating system and personal data on workstations happens less frequently than for servers or mission-critical machines, but they all serve an equal and necessary purpose.

Damon, an information professional, learned this the hard way when he lost months of work following a natural disaster that wiped out the first floor at an information brokering firm. He never utilized the backup facilities built into his operating system or any of the shared provisions established by his administrator, Carol.

Carol has been there and done that, so she knows a thing or two about backup solutions. She has established incremental backups on her production servers and differential backups on her development servers, and she's never had an issue restoring lost data.

The toughest obstacle to a solid backup strategy is human nature, so a simple, transparent, and comprehensive strategy is the most practical. Differential backups require only two container files (the latest full backup and the latest differential) and can be scheduled for periodic updates at some specified interval. That's why Carol elects to implement this approach and feels ready to restore from her backups any time she's called on to do so.

Backup Tape Formats

The physical characteristics and the rotation cycle are two factors that a worthwhile backup solution should track and manage. The physical characteristics involve the type of tape drive in use. This defines the physical wear placed on the media. The rotation cycle is the frequency of backups and retention length of protected data. By overseeing these characteristics, you can be assured that valuable data will be retained on serviceable backup media. Backup media has a maximum use limit; perhaps 5, 10, or 20 rewrites may be made before the media begins to lose reliability (statistically speaking). A wide variety of backup tape formats exist:

- Digital Data Storage (DDS)/Digital Audio Tape (DAT)
- Digital Linear Tape (DLT) and Super DLT
- Linear Tape Open (LTO)

Disk to Disk Backup

Over the past decade, disk storage has become increasingly inexpensive. With drive capacities now measured in terabytes (TB), tape and optical media can't cope with data volume requirements anymore. Many enterprises now use disk-to-disk (D2D) backup solutions for some portion of their disaster recovery strategy.

One important note: organizations seeking to adopt an entirely disk-to-disk approach must remember to maintain geographical diversity. Some of those disks have to be located offsite. Many organizations solve this problem by hiring managed service providers to manage remote backup locations.

As transfer and storage costs come down, cloud-based backup solutions are becoming more cost effective. You may wish to consider using such a service as an alternative to physically transporting backup tapes to a remote location.

Backup Best Practices

No matter what the backup solution, media, or method, you must address several common issues with backups. For instance, backup and restoration activities can be bulky and slow. Such data movement can significantly affect the performance of a network, especially during regular production hours. Thus, backups should be scheduled during the low peak periods (for example, at night).

The amount of backup data increases over time. This causes the backup (and restoration) processes to take longer each time and to consume more space on the backup media. Thus, you need to build sufficient capacity to handle a reasonable amount of growth over a reasonable amount of time into your backup solution. What is reasonable all depends on your environment and budget.

With periodic backups (that is, backups that are run every 24 hours), there is always the potential for data loss up to the length of the period. Murphy's law dictates that a server never crashes immediately after a successful backup. Instead, it is always just before the next backup begins. To avoid the problem with periods, you need to deploy some form of real-time continuous backup, such as RAID, clustering, or server mirroring.

Finally, remember to test your organization's recovery processes. Organizations often rely on the fact that their backup software reports a successful backup and fail to attempt recovery until it's too late to detect a problem. This is one of the biggest causes of backup failures.

Tape Rotation

There are several commonly used tape rotation strategies for backups: the Grandfather-Father-Son (GFS) strategy, the Tower of Hanoi strategy, and the Six Cartridge Weekly Backup strategy. These strategies can be fairly complex, especially with large tape sets. They can be implemented manually using a pencil and a calendar or automatically by using either commercial backup software or a fully automated hierarchical storage management (HSM) system. An HSM system is an automated robotic backup jukebox consisting of 32 or 64 optical or tape backup devices. All the drive elements within an HSM system are configured as a single drive array (a bit like RAID).

Details about various tape rotations are beyond the scope of this book, but if you want to learn more about them, search by their names on the Internet.

Software Escrow Arrangements

A *software escrow arrangement* is a unique tool used to protect a company against the failure of a software developer to provide adequate support for its products or against the possibility that the developer will go out of business and no technical support will be available for the product.

Focus your efforts on negotiating software escrow agreements with those suppliers you fear may go out of business because of their size. It's not likely that you'll be able to negotiate such an agreement with a firm such as Microsoft, unless you are responsible for an extremely large corporate account with serious bargaining power. On the other hand, it's equally unlikely that a firm of Microsoft's magnitude will go out of business, leaving end users high and dry.

If your organization depends on custom-developed software or software products produced by a small firm, you may want to consider developing this type of arrangement as part of your disaster recovery plan. Under a software escrow agreement, the developer provides copies of the application source code to an independent third-party organization. This third party then maintains updated backup copies of the source code in a secure fashion. The agreement between the end user and the developer specifies "trigger events," such as the failure of the developer to meet terms of a service-level agreement (SLA) or the liquidation of the developer's firm. When a trigger event takes place, the third party releases copies of the application source code to the end user. The end user can then analyze the source code to resolve application issues or implement software updates.

External Communications

During the disaster recovery process, it will be necessary to communicate with various entities outside your organization. You will need to contact vendors to provide supplies as they are needed to support the disaster recovery effort. Your clients will want to contact you for reassurance that you are still in operation. Public relations officials may need to contact the media or investment firms, and managers may need to speak to governmental authorities. For these reasons, it is essential that your disaster recovery plan include appropriate channels of communication to the outside world in a quantity sufficient to meet your operational needs. Usually, it is not a sound business or recovery practice to use the CEO as your spokesperson during a disaster. A media liaison should be hired, trained, and prepared to take on this responsibility.

Utilities

As discussed in previous sections of this chapter, your organization is reliant on several utilities to provide critical elements of your infrastructure—electric power, water, natural gas, sewer service, and so on. Your disaster recovery plan should contain contact information and procedures to troubleshoot these services if problems arise during a disaster.

Logistics and Supplies

The logistical problems surrounding a disaster recovery operation are immense. You will suddenly face the problem of moving large numbers of people, equipment, and supplies to alternate recovery sites. It's also possible that the people will be living at those sites for an extended period of time and that the disaster recovery team will be responsible for providing them with food, water, shelter, and appropriate facilities. Your disaster recovery plan should contain provisions for this type of operation if it falls within the scope of your expected operational needs.

Recovery vs. Restoration

It is sometimes useful to separate disaster recovery tasks from disaster restoration tasks. This is especially true when a recovery effort is expected to take a significant amount of time. A disaster recovery team may be assigned to implement and maintain operations at the recovery site, and a salvage team is assigned to restore the primary site to operational capacity. Make these allocations according to the needs of your organization and the types of disasters you face.

Recovery and *restoration* are separate concepts. In this context, recovery involves bringing business *operations and processes* back to a working state. Restoration involves bringing a business *facility and environment* back to a workable state.

The recovery team members have a very short time frame in which to operate. They must put the DRP into action and restore IT capabilities as swiftly as possible. If the recovery team fails to restore business processes within the MTD/RTO, then the company fails.

Once the original site is deemed safe for people, the salvage team members begin their work. Their job is to restore the company to its full original capabilities and, if necessary, to the original location. If the original location is no longer in existence, then a new primary spot is selected. The salvage team must rebuild or repair the IT infrastructure. Since this activity is basically the same as building a new IT system, the return activity from the alternate/recovery site to the primary/original site is itself a risky activity. Fortunately, the salvage team has more time to work than the recovery team.

The salvage team must ensure the reliability of the new IT infrastructure. This is done by returning the least mission-critical processes to the restored original site to stress-test the rebuilt network. As the restored site shows resiliency, more important processes are transferred. A serious vulnerability exists when mission-critical processes are returned to the original site. The act of returning to the original site could cause a disaster of its own. Therefore, the state of emergency cannot be declared over until full normal operations have returned to the restored original site.

At the conclusion of any disaster recovery effort, the time will come to restore operations at the primary site and terminate any processing sites operating under the disaster recovery agreement. Your DRP should specify the criteria used to determine when it is appropriate to return to the primary site and guide the DRP recovery and salvage teams through an orderly transition.

Training and Documentation

As with a business continuity plan, it is essential that you provide training to all personnel who will be involved in the disaster recovery effort. The level of training required will vary according to an individual's role in the effort and their position within the company. When designing a training plan, consider including the following elements:

- Orientation training for all new employees
- Initial training for employees taking on a new disaster recovery role for the first time
- Detailed refresher training for disaster recovery team members
- Brief refresher training for all other employees (can be accomplished as part of other meetings and through a medium like email newsletters sent to all employees)

Loose-leaf binders are an excellent way to store disaster recovery plans. You can distribute single-page changes to the plan without destroying a national forest!

The disaster recovery plan should also be fully documented. Earlier in this chapter, we discussed several of the documentation options available to you. Be sure you implement the necessary documentation programs and modify the documentation as changes to the plan occur. Because of the rapidly changing nature of the disaster recovery and business continuity plans, you might consider publication on a secured portion of your organization's intranet.

Your DRP should be treated as an extremely sensitive document and provided to individuals on a compartmentalized, need-to-know basis only. Individuals who participate in the plan should understand their roles fully, but they do not need to know or have access to the entire plan. Of course, it is essential to ensure that key DRP team members and senior management have access to the entire plan and understand the high-level implementation details. You certainly don't want this knowledge to rest in the mind of only one individual.

Remember that a disaster may render your intranet unavailable. If you choose to distribute your disaster recovery and business continuity plans through an intranet, be sure you maintain an adequate number of printed copies of the plan at both the primary and alternate sites and maintain *only* the most current copy!

Testing and Maintenance

Every disaster recovery plan must be tested on a periodic basis to ensure that the plan's provisions are viable and that it meets an organization's changing needs. The types of tests that you conduct will depend on the types of recovery facilities available to you, the culture of your organization, and the availability of disaster recovery team members. The five main test types—checklist tests, structured walk-throughs, simulation tests, parallel tests, and full-interruption tests—are discussed in the remaining sections of this chapter.

Checklist Test

The *checklist test* is one of the simplest tests to conduct, but it's also one of the most critical. In this test, you distribute copies of disaster recovery checklists to the members of the disaster recovery team for review. This lets you accomplish three goals simultaneously:

- It ensures that key personnel are aware of their responsibilities and have that knowledge refreshed periodically.

- It provides individuals with an opportunity to review the checklists for obsolete information and update any items that require modification because of changes within the organization.

- In large organizations, it helps identify situations in which key personnel have left the company and nobody bothered to reassign their disaster recovery responsibilities. This is also a good reason why disaster recovery responsibilities should be included in job descriptions.

Structured Walk-Through

A *structured walk-through* takes testing one step further. In this type of test, often referred to as a *table-top exercise*, members of the disaster recovery team gather in a large conference room and role-play a disaster scenario. Usually, the exact scenario is known only to the test moderator, who presents the details to the team at the meeting. The team members then refer to their copies of the disaster recovery plan and discuss the appropriate responses to that particular type of disaster.

Simulation Test

Simulation tests are similar to the structured walk-throughs. In simulation tests, disaster recovery team members are presented with a scenario and asked to develop an appropriate response. Unlike with the tests previously discussed, some of these response measures are then tested. This may involve the interruption of noncritical business activities and the use of some operational personnel.

Parallel Test

Parallel tests represent the next level in testing and involve relocating personnel to the alternate recovery site and implementing site activation procedures. The employees relocated to the site perform their disaster recovery responsibilities just as they would for an actual disaster. The only difference is that operations at the main facility are not interrupted. That site retains full responsibility for conducting the day-to-day business of the organization.

Full-Interruption Test

Full-interruption tests operate like parallel tests, but they involve actually shutting down operations at the primary site and shifting them to the recovery site. For obvious reasons, full-interruption tests are extremely difficult to arrange, and you often encounter resistance from management.

Maintenance

Remember that a disaster recovery plan is a living document. As your organization's needs change, you must adapt the disaster recovery plan to meet those changed needs to follow suit. You will discover many necessary modifications by using a well-organized and coordinated testing plan. Minor changes may often be made through a series of telephone conversations or emails, whereas major changes may require one or more meetings of the full disaster recovery team.

A disaster recovery planner should refer to the organization's business continuity plan as a template for its recovery efforts. This and all the supportive material must comply with federal regulations and reflect current business needs. Business processes such as payroll and order generation should contain specified metrics mapped to related IT systems and infrastructure.

Most organizations apply formal change management processes so that whenever the IT infrastructure changes, all relevant documentation is updated and checked to reflect such changes. Regularly scheduled fire drills and dry runs to ensure that all elements of the DRP are used properly to keep staff trained present a perfect opportunity to integrate changes into regular maintenance and change management procedures. Design, implement, and document changes each time you go through these processes and exercises. Know where everything is, and keep each element of the DRP working properly. In case of emergency, use your recovery plan. Finally, make sure the staff stays trained to keep their skills sharp—for existing support personnel—and use simulated exercises to bring new people up to speed quickly.

Summary

Disaster recovery planning is critical to a comprehensive information security program. No matter how comprehensive your business continuity plan, the day may come when your business is interrupted by a disaster and you face the task of restoring operations to the primary site quickly and efficiently.

In this chapter, you learned about the different types of natural and man-made disasters that may impact your business. You also explored the types of recovery sites and backup strategies that bolster your recovery capabilities.

An organization's disaster recovery plan is one of the most important documents under the purview of security professionals. It should provide guidance to the personnel responsible for ensuring the continuity of operations in the face of disaster. The DRP provides an orderly sequence of events designed to activate alternate processing sites while simultaneously restoring the primary site to operational status. Once you've successfully developed your DRP, you must train personnel on its use, ensure that you maintain accurate documentation, and conduct periodic tests to keep the plan fresh in the minds of responders.

Exam Essentials

Know the common types of natural disasters that may threaten an organization.   Natural disasters that commonly threaten organizations include earthquakes, floods, storms, fires, tsunamis, and volcanic eruptions.

Know the common types of man-made disasters that may threaten an organization. Explosions, electrical fires, terrorist acts, power outages, other utility failures, infrastructure failures, hardware/software failures, labor difficulties, theft, and vandalism are all common man-made disasters.

Be familiar with the common types of recovery facilities.   The common types of recovery facilities are cold sites, warm sites, hot sites, mobile sites, service bureaus, and multiple sites. Be sure you understand the benefits and drawbacks for each such facility.

Explain the potential benefits behind mutual assistance agreements as well as the reasons they are not commonly implemented in businesses today.   Mutual assistance agreements (MAAs) provide an inexpensive alternative to disaster recovery sites, but they are not commonly used because they are difficult to enforce. Organizations participating in an MAA may also be shut down by the same disaster, and MAAs raise confidentiality concerns.

Understand the technologies that may assist with database backup.   Databases benefit from three backup technologies. Electronic vaulting is used to transfer database backups to a remote site as part of a bulk transfer. In remote journaling, data transfers occur on a more frequent basis. With remote mirroring technology, database transactions are mirrored at the backup site in real time.

Know the five types of disaster recovery plan tests and the impact each has on normal business operations.   The five types of disaster recovery plan tests are checklist tests, structured walk-throughs, simulation tests, parallel tests, and full-interruption tests. Checklist tests are purely paperwork exercises, whereas structured walk-throughs involve a project team meeting. Neither has an impact on business operations. Simulation tests may shut down noncritical business units. Parallel tests involve relocating personnel but do not affect day-to-day operations. Full-interruption tests involve shutting down primary systems and shifting responsibility to the recovery facility.

Written Lab

1. What are some of the main concerns businesses have when considering adopting a mutual assistance agreement?
2. List and explain the five types of disaster recovery tests.
3. Explain the differences between the three types of backup strategies discussed in this chapter.

Review Questions

1. What is the end goal of disaster recovery planning?

   A. Preventing business interruption

   B. Setting up temporary business operations

   C. Restoring normal business activity

   D. Minimizing the impact of a disaster

2. Which one of the following is an example of a man-made disaster?

   A. Tsunami

   B. Earthquake

   C. Power outage

   D. Lightning strike

3. According to the Federal Emergency Management Agency, approximately what percentage of U.S. states is rated with at least a moderate risk of seismic activity?

   A. 20 percent

   B. 40 percent

   C. 60 percent

   D. 80 percent

4. Which one of the following disaster types is not usually covered by standard business or homeowner's insurance?

   A. Earthquake

   B. Flood

   C. Fire

   D. Theft

5. In the wake of the September 11, 2001, terrorist attacks, what industry made drastic changes that directly impact DRP/BCP activities?

   A. Tourism

   B. Banking

   C. Insurance

   D. Airline

6. Which of the following statements about business continuity planning and disaster recovery planning is incorrect?

    A. Business continuity planning is focused on keeping business functions uninterrupted when a disaster strikes.

    B. Organizations can choose whether to develop business continuity planning or disaster recovery planning plans.

    C. Business continuity planning picks up where disaster recovery planning leaves off.

    D. Disaster recovery planning guides an organization through recovery of normal operations at the primary facility.

7. What does the term "100-year flood plain" mean to emergency preparedness officials?

    A. The last flood of any kind to hit the area was more than 100 years ago.

    B. The odds of a flood at this level are 1 in 100 in any given year.

    C. The area is expected to be safe from flooding for at least 100 years.

    D. The last significant flood to hit the area was more than 100 years ago.

8. In which one of the following database recovery techniques is an exact, up-to-date copy of the database maintained at an alternative location?

    A. Transaction logging

    B. Remote journaling

    C. Electronic vaulting

    D. Remote mirroring

9. What disaster recovery principle best protects your organization against hardware failure?

    A. Consistency

    B. Efficiency

    C. Redundancy

    D. Primacy

10. What business continuity planning technique can help you prepare the business unit prioritization task of disaster recovery planning?

    A. Vulnerability analysis

    B. Business impact assessment

    C. Risk management

    D. Continuity planning

11. Which one of the following alternative processing sites takes the longest time to activate?

    A. Hot site

    B. Mobile site

    C. Cold site

    D. Warm site

12. What is the typical time estimate to activate a warm site from the time a disaster is declared?

    A. 1 hour

    B. 6 hours

    C. 12 hours

    D. 24 hours

13. Which one of the following items is a characteristic of hot sites but not a characteristic of warm sites?

    A. Communications circuits

    B. Workstations

    C. Servers

    D. Current data

14. What type of database backup strategy involves maintenance of a live backup server at the remote site?

    A. Transaction logging

    B. Remote journaling

    C. Electronic vaulting

    D. Remote mirroring

15. What type of document will help public relations specialists and other individuals who need a high-level summary of disaster recovery efforts while they are underway?

    A. Executive summary

    B. Technical guides

    C. Department-specific plans

    D. Checklists

16. What disaster recovery planning tool can be used to protect an organization against the failure of a critical software firm to provide appropriate support for their products?

    A. Differential backups

    B. Business impact assessment

    C. Incremental backups

    D. Software escrow agreement

17. What type of backup involves always storing copies of all files modified since the most recent full backup?

    A. Differential backups

    B. Partial backup

    C. Incremental backups

    D. Database backup

18. What combination of backup strategies provides the fastest backup creation time?

    A. Full backups and differential backups

    B. Partial backups and incremental backups

    C. Full backups and incremental backups

    D. Incremental backups and differential backups

19. What combination of backup strategies provides the fastest backup restoration time?

    A. Full backups and differential backups

    B. Partial backups and incremental backups

    C. Full backups and incremental backups

    D. Incremental backups and differential backups

20. What type of disaster recovery plan test fully evaluates operations at the backup facility but does not shift primary operations responsibility from the main site?

    A. Structured walk-through

    B. Parallel test

    C. Full-interruption test

    D. Simulation test

Chapter

17

Laws, Regulations, and Compliance

THE CISSP EXAM TOPICS COVERED IN THIS CHAPTER INCLUDE:

9. **Legal, Regulations, Investigations, and Compliance**

   A. Understand legal issues that pertain to information security internationally

   A.1 Licensing and intellectual property (e.g., copyright, trademark)

   A.2 Import/export

   A.3 Trans-border data flow

   A.4 Privacy

   E. Understand compliance requirements and procedures

   E.1 Regulatory environment

   E.2 Audits

   E.3 Reporting

   F. Ensure security in contractual agreements and procurement processes (e.g., cloud computing, outsourcing, vendor governance)

In the early days of computer security, information security professionals were pretty much left on their own to defend their systems against attacks. They didn't have much help from the criminal and civil justice systems. When they did seek assistance from law enforcement, they were met with reluctance by overworked agents who didn't have a basic understanding of how something that involved a computer could actually be a crime. The legislative branch of government hadn't addressed the issue of computer crime, and the executive branch thought they simply didn't have statutory authority or obligation to pursue those matters.

Fortunately, both our legal system and the men and women of law enforcement have come a long way over the past two decades. The legislative branches of governments around the world have at least attempted to address issues of computer crime. Many law enforcement agencies have full-time, well-trained computer crime investigators with advanced security training. Those who don't usually know where to turn when they require this sort of experience.

In this chapter, we'll cover the various types of laws that deal with computer security issues. We'll examine the legal issues surrounding computer crime, privacy, intellectual property, and a number of other related topics. We'll also cover basic investigative techniques, including the pros and cons of calling in assistance from law enforcement.

Categories of Laws

Three main categories of laws play a role in our legal system. Each is used to cover a variety of circumstances, and the penalties for violating laws in the different categories vary widely. In the following sections, you'll learn how criminal law, civil law, and administrative law interact to form the complex web of our justice system.

Criminal Law

Criminal law forms the bedrock of the body of laws that preserve the peace and keep our society safe. Many high-profile court cases involve matters of criminal law; these are the laws that the police and other law enforcement agencies concern themselves with. Criminal law contains prohibitions against acts such as murder, assault, robbery, and arson. Penalties for violating criminal statutes fall in a range that includes mandatory hours of community service, monetary penalties in the form of fines (small and large), and deprivation of civil liberties in the form of prison sentences.

⊕ Real World Scenario

Cops Are Smart!

A good friend of one of the authors is a technology crime investigator for the local police department. He often receives cases of computer abuse involving threatening emails and website postings.

Recently, he shared a story about a bomb threat that had been emailed to a local high school. The perpetrator sent a threatening note to the school principal declaring that the bomb would explode at 1 P.M. and warning him to evacuate the school. The author's friend received the alert at 11 A.M., leaving him with only two hours to investigate the crime and advise the principal on the best course of action.

He quickly began issuing emergency subpoenas to Internet service providers and traced the email to a computer in the school library. At 12:15 P.M., he confronted the suspect with surveillance tapes showing him at the computer in the library as well as audit logs conclusively proving that he had sent the email. The student quickly admitted that the threat was nothing more than a ploy to get out of school a couple of hours early. His explanation? "I didn't think there was anyone around here who could trace stuff like that."

He was wrong.

A number of criminal laws serve to protect society against computer crime. In later sections of this chapter, you'll learn how some laws, such as the Computer Fraud and Abuse Act, the Electronic Communications Privacy Act, and the Identity Theft and Assumption Deterrence Act (among others), provide criminal penalties for serious cases of computer crime. Technically savvy prosecutors teamed with concerned law enforcement agencies have dealt serious blows to the "hacking underground" by using the court system to slap lengthy prison terms on offenders guilty of what used to be considered harmless pranks.

In the United States, legislative bodies at all levels of government establish criminal laws through elected representatives. At the federal level, both the House of Representatives and the Senate must pass criminal law bills by a majority vote (in most cases) in order for the bill to become law. Once passed, these laws then become federal law and apply in all cases where the federal government has jurisdiction (mainly cases that involve interstate commerce, cases that cross state boundaries, or cases that are offenses against the federal government itself). If federal jurisdiction does not apply, state authorities handle the case using laws passed in a similar manner by state legislators.

All federal and state laws must comply with the document that dictates how the U.S. system of government works—the U.S. Constitution. All laws are subject to judicial review by regional courts with the right of appeal all the way to the Supreme Court of the United States. If a court finds that a law is unconstitutional, it has the power to strike it down and render it invalid.

Keep in mind that criminal law is a serious matter. If you find yourself involved—as a witness, defendant, or victim—in a matter where criminal authorities become involved, you'd be well advised to seek advice from an attorney familiar with the criminal justice system and specifically with matters of computer crime. It's not wise to "go it alone" in such a complex system.

Civil Law

Civil laws form the bulk of our body of laws. They are designed to provide for an orderly society and govern matters that are not crimes but require an impartial arbiter to settle between individuals and organizations. Examples of the types of matters that may be judged under civil law include contract disputes, real estate transactions, employment matters, and estate/probate procedures. Civil laws also are used to create the framework of government that the executive branch uses to carry out its responsibilities. These laws provide budgets for governmental activities and lay out the authority granted to the executive branch to create administrative laws (see the next section).

Civil laws are enacted in the same manner as criminal laws. They must pass through the legislative process before enactment and are subject to the same constitutional parameters and judicial review procedures. At the federal level, both criminal and civil laws are embodied in the United States Code (USC).

The major difference between civil laws and criminal laws is the way in which they are enforced. Usually, law enforcement authorities do not become involved in matters of civil law beyond taking action necessary to restore order. In a criminal prosecution, the government, through law enforcement investigators and prosecutors, brings action against a person accused of a crime. In civil matters, it is incumbent upon the person who thinks they have been wronged to obtain legal counsel and file a civil lawsuit against the person they think is responsible for their grievance. The government (unless it is the plaintiff or defendant) does not take sides in the dispute or argue one position or the other. The only role of the government in civil matters is to provide the judges, juries, and court facilities used to hear civil cases and to play an administrative role in managing the judicial system in accordance with the law.

As with criminal law, it is best to obtain legal assistance if you think you need to file a civil lawsuit or if someone files a civil lawsuit against you. Although civil law does not impose the threat of imprisonment, the losing party may face severe financial penalties. You don't need to look any further than the nightly news for examples—multimillion-dollar cases against tobacco companies, major corporations, and wealthy individuals are filed every day.

Administrative Law

The executive branch of our government charges numerous agencies with wide-ranging responsibilities to ensure that government functions effectively. It is the duty of these agencies to abide by and enforce the criminal and civil laws enacted by the legislative branch. However, as can be easily imagined, criminal and civil law can't possibly lay out rules and procedures that should be followed in any possible situation. Therefore, executive branch agencies have some leeway to enact administrative law, in the form of policies, procedures, and regulations that govern the daily operations of the agency. Administrative law covers topics as mundane as the procedures to be used within a federal agency to obtain a desk telephone to more substantial issues such as the immigration policies that will be used to enforce the laws passed by Congress. Administrative law is published in the Code of Federal Regulations, often referred to as the CFR.

Although administrative law does not require an act of the legislative branch to gain the force of law, it must comply with all existing civil and criminal laws. Government agencies may not implement regulations that directly contradict existing laws passed by the legislature. Furthermore, administrative laws (and the actions of government agencies) must also comply with the U.S. Constitution and are subject to judicial review.

In order to understand compliance requirements and procedures, it is necessary to be fully versed in the complexities of the law. From administrative law to civil law to criminal law (and, in some countries, even religious law), navigating the regulatory environment is a daunting task. The CISSP exam focuses on the generalities of law, regulations, investigations, and compliance as they affect organizational security efforts. However, it is your responsibility to seek out professional help (i.e., an attorney) to guide and support you in your efforts to maintain legal and legally supportable security.

Laws

Throughout these sections, we'll examine a number of laws that relate to information technology. By necessity, this discussion is U.S.-centric, as is the material covered by the CISSP exam. We'll look briefly at several high-profile foreign laws, such as the European Union's data privacy act. However, if you operate in an environment that involves foreign jurisdictions, you should retain local legal counsel to guide you through the system.

WARNING
Every information security professional should have a basic understanding of the law as it relates to information technology. However, the most important lesson to be learned is knowing when it's necessary to call in an attorney: If you think you're in a legal "gray area," it's best to seek professional advice.

Computer Crime

The first computer security issues addressed by legislators were those involving computer crime. Early computer crime prosecutions were attempted under traditional criminal law, and many were dismissed because judges thought that applying traditional law to this modern type of crime was too far of a stretch. Legislators responded by passing specific statutes that defined computer crime and laid out specific penalties for various crimes. In the following sections, we'll cover several of those statutes.

> The U.S. laws discussed in this chapter are federal laws. But keep in mind that almost every state in the union has also enacted some form of legislation regarding computer security issues. Because of the global reach of the Internet, most computer crimes cross state lines and, therefore, fall under federal jurisdiction and are prosecuted in the federal court system. However, in some circumstances, state laws can be more restrictive than federal laws and impose harsher penalties.

Computer Fraud and Abuse Act of 1984

Congress first enacted the Computer Fraud and Abuse Act (CFAA) in 1984, and it remains in force today, with several amendments. This law was carefully written to exclusively cover computer crimes that crossed state boundaries to avoid infringing on states' rights and treading on thin constitutional ice. The major provisions of the act are that it is a crime to perform the following:

- Access classified information or financial information in a federal system without authorization or in excess of authorized privileges

- Access a computer used exclusively by the federal government without authorization

- Use a federal computer to perpetrate a fraud (unless the only object of the fraud was to gain use of the computer itself)

- Cause malicious damage to a federal computer system in excess of $1,000

- Modify medical records in a computer when doing so impairs or may impair the examination, diagnosis, treatment, or medical care of an individual

- Traffic in computer passwords if the trafficking affects interstate commerce or involves a federal computer system

The CFAA was amended in 1986 to change the scope of the act. Instead of merely covering federal computers that processed sensitive information, the act was changed to cover all "federal interest" computers. This widened the coverage of the act to include the following:

- Any computer used exclusively by the U.S. government

- Any computer used exclusively by a financial institution

- Any computer used by the government or a financial institution when the offense impedes the ability of the government or institution to use that system

- Any combination of computers used to commit an offense when they are not all located in the same state

When preparing for the CISSP exam, be sure you're able to briefly describe the purpose of each law discussed in this chapter.

1994 CFAA Amendments

In 1994, Congress recognized that the face of computer security had drastically changed since the CFAA was last amended in 1986 and made a number of sweeping changes to the act. Collectively, these changes are referred to as the Computer Abuse Amendments Act of 1994 and included the following provisions:

- Outlawed the creation of any type of malicious code that might cause damage to a computer system

- Modified the CFAA to cover any computer used in interstate commerce rather than just "federal interest" computer systems

- Allowed for the imprisonment of offenders, regardless of whether they actually intended to cause damage

- Provided legal authority for the victims of computer crime to pursue civil action to gain injunctive relief and compensation for damages

Computer Security Act of 1987

After amending the CFAA in 1986 to cover a wider variety of computer systems, Congress turned its view inward and examined the current state of computer security in federal government systems. Members of Congress were not satisfied with what they saw and they enacted the Computer Security Act (CSA) of 1987 to mandate baseline security requirements for all federal agencies. In the introduction to the CSA, Congress specified four main purposes of the act:

- To give the National Institute of Standards and Technology (NIST) responsibility for developing standards and guidelines for federal computer systems. For this purpose, NIST draws on the technical advice and assistance (including work products) of the National Security Agency where appropriate.

- To provide for the enactment of such standards and guidelines.

- To require the establishment of security plans by all operators of federal computer systems that contain sensitive information.

- To require mandatory periodic training for all people involved in management, use, or operation of federal computer systems that contain sensitive information.

This act clearly set out a number of requirements that formed the basis of federal computer security policy for many years. It also divided responsibility for computer security among two federal agencies. The National Security Agency (NSA), which formerly had authority over all computer security issues, retained authority over classified systems; but NIST gained responsibility for securing all other federal government systems. NIST produces the 800 series of Special Publications related to computer security in the federal government. These are useful for all security practitioners and are available for free online at the following address:

```
http://csrc.nist.gov/publications/PubsSPs.html
```

Federal Sentencing Guidelines

The Federal Sentencing Guidelines released in 1991 provided punishment guidelines to help federal judges interpret computer crime laws. Three major provisions of these guidelines have had a lasting impact on the information security community:

- The guidelines formalized the *prudent man rule*, which requires senior executives to take personal responsibility for ensuring the *due care* that ordinary, prudent individuals would exercise in the same situation. This rule, developed in the realm of fiscal responsibility, now applies to information security as well.

- The guidelines allowed organizations and executives to minimize punishment for infractions by demonstrating that they used due diligence in the conduct of their information security duties.

- The guidelines outlined three burdens of proof for *negligence*. First, the person accused of negligence must have a legally recognized obligation. Second, the person must have failed to comply with recognized standards. Finally, there must be a causal relationship between the act of negligence and subsequent damages.

National Information Infrastructure Protection Act of 1996

In 1996, Congress passed yet another set of amendments to the Computer Fraud and Abuse Act designed to further extend the protection it provides. The National Information Infrastructure Protection Act included the following main new areas of coverage:

- Broadens CFAA to cover computer systems used in international commerce in addition to systems used in interstate commerce

- Extends similar protections to portions of the national infrastructure other than computing systems, such as railroads, gas pipelines, electric power grids, and telecommunications circuits

- Treats any intentional or reckless act that causes damage to critical portions of the national infrastructure as a felony

Paperwork Reduction Act of 1995

The Paperwork Reduction Act of 1995 requires that agencies obtain Office of Management and Budget (OMB) approval before requesting most types of information from the public. Information collections include forms, interviews, record-keeping requirements, and a wide variety of other things. The Government Information Security Reform Act (GISRA) of 2000 amended this act, as described in the next section.

Government Information Security Reform Act of 2000

The Government Information Security Reform Act (GISRA) of 2000 amended the Paperwork Reduction Act to implement additional information security policies and procedures. In the text of the act, Congress laid out five basic purposes for establishing the GISRA:

- To provide a comprehensive framework for establishing and ensuring the effectiveness of controls over information resources that support federal operations and assets

- To recognize the highly networked nature of the federal computing environment, including the need for federal government interoperability, and in the implementation of improved security management measures, to assure that opportunities for interoperability are not adversely affected

- To provide effective government-wide management and oversight of the related information security risks, including coordination of information security efforts throughout the civilian, national security, and law enforcement communities

- To provide for development and maintenance of minimum controls required to protect federal information and information systems

- To provide a mechanism for improved oversight of federal agency information security programs

The provisions of the GISRA continue to charge the National Institute of Standards and Technology and the National Security Agency with security oversight responsibilities for unclassified and classified information processing systems, respectively. However, GISRA places the burden of maintaining the security and integrity of government information and information systems squarely on the shoulders of individual agency leaders.

GISRA also creates a new category of computer system. A mission-critical system meets one of the following criteria:

- It is defined as a national security system by other provisions of law.

- It is protected by procedures established for classified information.

- The loss, misuse, disclosure, or unauthorized access to or modification of any information it processes would have a debilitating impact on the mission of an agency.

GISRA provides specific evaluation and auditing authority for mission-critical systems to the secretary of defense and the director of central intelligence. This is an attempt to ensure that all government agencies, even those that do not routinely deal with classified national security information, implement adequate security controls on systems that are absolutely critical to the continued functioning of the agency.

Intellectual Property

America's role in the global economy is shifting away from a manufacturer of goods and toward a provider of services. This trend also shows itself in many of the world's large industrialized nations. With this shift toward providing services, intellectual property takes on an increasingly important role in many firms. Indeed, it is arguable that the most valuable assets of many large multinational companies are simply the brand names that we've all come to recognize. Company names such as Dell, Procter & Gamble, and Merck bring instant credibility to any product. Publishing companies, movie producers, and artists depend on their creative output to earn their livelihood. Many products depend on secret recipes or production techniques—take the legendary secret formula for Coca-Cola or Kentucky Fried Chicken's secret blend of herbs and spices, for example.

These intangible assets are collectively referred to as *intellectual property*, and a whole host of laws exist to protect the rights of their owners. After all, it simply wouldn't be fair if a music store bought only one copy of each artist's CD and burned copies for all of its customers—that would deprive the artist of the benefits of their labor. In the following sections, we'll explore the laws surrounding the four major types of intellectual property—copyrights, trademarks, patents, and trade secrets. We'll also discuss how these concepts specifically concern information security professionals. Many countries protect (or fail to protect) these rights in different ways, but the basic concepts ring true throughout the world.

Some countries are notorious for violating intellectual property rights. The most notable example is China. China is world renowned for its blatant disregard of copyright and patent law. If you're planning to do business in this region of the world, you should definitely consult with an attorney who specializes in this area.

Copyrights and the Digital Millennium Copyright Act

Copyright law guarantees the creators of "original works of authorship" protection against the unauthorized duplication of their work. Eight broad categories of works qualify for copyright protection:

- Literary works
- Musical works
- Dramatic works
- Pantomimes and choreographic works
- Pictorial, graphical, and sculptural works
- Motion pictures and other audiovisual works
- Sound recordings
- Architectural works

There is precedent for copyrighting computer software—it's done under the scope of literary works. However, it's important to note that copyright law protects only the expression inherent in computer software—that is, the actual source code. It does not protect the ideas or process behind the software. There has also been some question over whether copyrights can be extended to cover the "look and feel" of a software package's graphical user interface. Court decisions have gone in both directions on this matter; if you will be involved in this type of issue, you should consult a qualified intellectual property attorney to determine the current state of legislation and case law.

There is a formal procedure to obtain a copyright that involves sending copies of the protected work along with an appropriate registration fee to the U.S. Copyright Office. For more information on this process, visit the office's website at www.copyright.gov. However, it is important to note that officially registering a copyright is not a prerequisite for copyright enforcement. Indeed, the law states that the creator of a work has an automatic copyright from the instant the work is created. If you can prove in court that you were the creator of a work (perhaps by publishing it), you will be protected under copyright law. Official registration merely provides the government's acknowledgment that they received your work on a specific date.

Copyright ownership always defaults to the creator of a work. The exceptions to this policy are works for hire. A work is considered "for hire" when it is made for an employer during the normal course of an employee's workday. For example, when an employee in a company's public relations department writes a press release, the press release is considered a work for hire. A work may also be considered a work for hire when it is made as part of a written contract declaring it as such.

Current copyright law provides for a very lengthy period of protection. Works by one or more authors are protected until 70 years after the death of the last surviving author. Works for hire and anonymous works are provided protection for 95 years from the date of first publication or 120 years from the date of creation, whichever is shorter.

In 1998, Congress recognized the rapidly changing digital landscape that was stretching the reach of existing copyright law. To help meet this challenge, it enacted the hotly debated Digital Millennium Copyright Act (DMCA). The DMCA also serves to bring U.S. copyright law into compliance with terms of two World Intellectual Property Organization (WIPO) treaties.

The first major provision of the DMCA is the prohibition of attempts to circumvent copyright protection mechanisms placed on a protected work by the copyright holder. This clause was designed to protect copy-prevention mechanisms placed on digital media such as CDs and DVDs. The DMCA provides for penalties of up to $1,000,000 and 10 years in prison for repeat offenders. Nonprofit institutions such as libraries and schools are exempted from this provision.

The DMCA also limits the liability of Internet service providers when their circuits are used by criminals violating the copyright law. The DMCA recognizes that ISPs have a legal status similar to the "common carrier" status of telephone companies and does not hold them liable for the "transitory activities" of their users. To qualify for this exemption, the service provider's activities must meet the following requirements (quoted directly from the Digital Millennium Copyright Act of 1998, U.S. Copyright Office Summary, December 1998):

- The transmission must be initiated by a person other than the provider.

- The transmission, routing, provision of connections, or copying must be carried out by an automated technical process without selection of material by the service provider.

- The service provider must not determine the recipients of the material.

- Any intermediate copies must not ordinarily be accessible to anyone other than anticipated recipients, and must not be retained for longer than reasonably necessary.

- The material must be transmitted with no modification to its content.

The DMCA also exempts activities of service providers related to system caching, search engines, and the storage of information on a network by individual users. However, in those cases, the service provider must take prompt action to remove copyrighted materials upon notification of the infringement.

Congress also included provisions in the DMCA that allow the creation of backup copies of computer software and any maintenance, testing, or routine usage activities that require software duplication. These provisions apply only if the software is licensed for use on a particular computer, the usage is in compliance with the license agreement, and any such copies are immediately deleted when no longer required for a permitted activity.

Finally, the DMCA spells out the application of copyright law principles to the emerging field of *webcasting*, or broadcasting audio and/or video content to recipients over the Internet. This technology is often referred to as *streaming audio* or *streaming video*. The DMCA states that these uses are to be treated as "eligible nonsubscription transmissions." The law in this area is still under development, so if you plan to engage in this type of activity, you should contact an attorney to ensure that you are in compliance with current law.

Keep an eye on the development of the Anti-Counterfeiting Trade Agreement (ACTA), which proposes a framework for international enforcement of intellectual property protections. As of April 2012, the treaty awaited ratification by the European Union member states, the United States, and five other nations.

Trademarks

Copyright laws are used to protect creative works; there is also protection for *trademarks*, which are words, slogans, and logos used to identify a company and its products or services. For example, a business might obtain a copyright on its sales brochure to ensure that competitors can't duplicate its sales materials. That same business might also seek to obtain trademark protection for its company name and the names of specific products and services that it offers to its clients.

The main objective of trademark protection is to avoid confusion in the marketplace while protecting the intellectual property rights of people and organizations. As with copyright protection, trademarks do not need to be officially registered to gain protection under the law. If you use a trademark in the course of your public activities, you are automatically protected under any relevant trademark law and can use the ™ symbol to show that you intend to protect words or slogans as trademarks. If you want official recognition of your trademark, you can register it with the United States Patent and Trademark Office (USPTO). This process generally requires an attorney to perform a due diligence comprehensive search for existing trademarks that might preclude your registration. The entire registration process can take more than a year from start to finish. Once you've received your registration certificate from the USPTO, you can denote your mark as a registered trademark with the ® symbol.

One major advantage of trademark registration is that you may register a trademark that you intend to use but are not necessarily already using. This type of application is called an *intent to use* application and conveys trademark protection as of the date of filing provided that you actually use the trademark in commerce within a certain time period. If you opt not to register your trademark with the PTO, your protection begins only when you first use the trademark.

The acceptance of a trademark application in the United States depends on two main requirements:

- The trademark must not be confusingly similar to another trademark—you should determine this during your attorney's due diligence search. There will be an open opposition period during which other companies may dispute your trademark application.

- The trademark should not be descriptive of the goods and services that you will offer. For example, "Mike's Software Company" would not be a good trademark candidate because it describes the product produced by the company. The USPTO may reject an application if it considers the trademark descriptive.

In the United States, trademarks are granted for an initial period of 10 years and can be renewed for unlimited successive 10-year periods.

Patents

Patents protect the intellectual property rights of inventors. They provide a period of 20 years during which the inventor is granted exclusive rights to use the invention (whether directly or via licensing agreements). At the end of the patent exclusivity period, the invention is in the public domain available for anyone to use.

Patents have three main requirements:

- The invention must be new. Inventions are patentable only if they are original ideas.

- The invention must be useful. It must actually work and accomplish some sort of task.

- The invention must not be obvious. You could not, for example, obtain a patent for your idea to use a drinking cup to collect rainwater. This is an obvious solution. You might, however, be able to patent a specially designed cup that optimizes the amount of rainwater collected while minimizing evaporation.

In the technology field, patents have long been used to protect hardware devices and manufacturing processes. There is plenty of precedent on the side of inventors in those areas. Recent patents have also been issued covering software programs and similar mechanisms, but the jury is still out on whether these patents will hold up to the scrutiny of the courts.

Trade Secrets

Many companies have intellectual property that is absolutely critical to their business and significant damage would result if it were disclosed to competitors and/or the public—in other words, *trade secrets*. We previously mentioned two examples of this type of information from popular culture—the secret formula for Coca-Cola and KFC's "secret blend of herbs and spices." Other examples are plentiful—a manufacturing company may want to keep secret a certain manufacturing process that only a few key employees fully understand, or a statistical analysis company might want to safeguard an advanced model developed for in-house use.

Two of the previously discussed intellectual property tools—copyrights and patents—could be used to protect this type of information, but with two major disadvantages:

- Filing a copyright or patent application requires that you publicly disclose the details of your work or invention. This automatically removes the "secret" nature of your property and may harm your firm by removing the mystique surrounding a product or by allowing unscrupulous competitors to copy your property in violation of international intellectual property laws.

- Copyrights and patents both provide protection for a limited period of time. Once your legal protection expires, other firms are free to use your work at will (and they have all the details from the public disclosure you made during the application process!).

There actually is an official process regarding trade secrets—by their nature you don't register them with anyone; you keep them to yourself. To preserve trade secret status, you must implement adequate controls within your organization to ensure that only authorized personnel with a need to know the secrets have access to them. You must also ensure that anyone who does have this type of access is bound by a nondisclosure agreement (NDA) that prohibits them from sharing the information with others and provides penalties for violating the agreement. Consult an attorney to ensure that the agreement lasts for the maximum period permitted by law. In addition, you must take steps to demonstrate that you value and protect your intellectual property. Failure to do so may result in the loss of trade secret protection.

Trade secret protection is one of the best ways to protect computer software. As discussed in the previous section, patent law does not provide adequate protection for computer software products. Copyright law protects only the actual text of the source code and doesn't prohibit others from rewriting your code in a different form and accomplishing the same objective. If you treat your source code as a trade secret, it keeps it out of the hands of your competitors in the first place. This is the technique used by large software development companies such as Microsoft to protect its core base of intellectual property.

Economic Espionage Act of 1996

Trade secrets are very often the crown jewels of major corporations, and the U.S. government recognized the importance of protecting this type of intellectual property when Congress enacted the Economic Espionage Act of 1996. This law has two major provisions:

- Anyone found guilty of stealing trade secrets from a U.S. corporation with the intention of benefiting a foreign government or agent may be fined up to $500,000 and imprisoned for up to 15 years.

- Anyone found guilty of stealing trade secrets under other circumstances may be fined up to $250,000 and imprisoned for up to 10 years.

The terms of the Economic Espionage Act give true teeth to the intellectual property rights of trade secret owners. Enforcing this law requires that companies take adequate steps to ensure that their trade secrets are well protected and not accidentally placed into the public domain.

Licensing

Security professionals should also be familiar with the legal issues surrounding software licensing agreements. Three common types of license agreements are in use today:

Contractual license agreements utilize a written contract between the software vendor and the customer, outlining the responsibilities of each. These agreements are commonly found for high-priced and/or highly specialized software packages.

Shrink-wrap license agreements are written on the outside of the software packaging. They commonly include a clause stating that you acknowledge agreement to the terms of the contract simply by breaking the shrink-wrap seal on the package.

Click-wrap license agreements are becoming more commonplace than shrink-wrap agreements. In this type of agreement, the contract terms are either written on the software box or included in the software documentation. During the installation process, you are required to click a button indicating that you have read the terms of the agreement and agree to abide by them. This adds an active consent to the process, ensuring that the individual is aware of the agreement's existence prior to installation.

Uniform Computer Information Transactions Act

The Uniform Computer Information Transactions Act (UCITA) is a federal law designed for adoption by each of the 50 states to provide a common framework for the conduct of computer-related business transactions. UCITA contains provisions that address software licensing. The terms of the UCITA give legal backing to the previously question-able practices of shrink-wrap licensing and click-wrap licensing by giving them status as legally binding contracts. UCITA also requires that manufacturers provide software users with the option to reject the terms of the license agreement before completing the instal-lation process and receive a full refund of the software's purchase price.

 Industry groups provide guidance and enforcement activities regarding software licensing. You can get more information from their websites. One major group is the Business Software Alliance (BSA) at www.bsa.org.

Import/Export

The federal government recognizes that the very same computers and encryption technolo-gies that drive the Internet and e-commerce can be extremely powerful tools in the hands of a military force. For this reason, during the Cold War, the government developed a com-plex set of regulations governing the export of sensitive hardware and software products to other nations. The regulations include the management of trans-border data flow of new technologies, intellectual property, and personally identifying information.

Until recently, it was very difficult to export high-powered computers outside the United States, except to a select handful of allied nations. The controls on exporting encryption software were even more severe, rendering it virtually impossible to export any encryption technology outside the country. Recent changes in federal policy have relaxed these restric-tions and provided for more open commerce.

Computer Export Controls

Currently, U.S. firms can export high-performance computing systems to virtually any country without receiving prior approval from the government. There are exceptions to this rule for countries designated by the Department of Commerce as Tier 3 countries. They include countries such as India, Pakistan, Afghanistan, and many countries in the Middle East. The export of any computer that is capable of operating in excess of 0.75 weighted teraflops (a trillion floating-point operations per second) must be preapproved by the Department of Commerce.

You can find a list of countries and their corresponding computer export tiers on the Department of Commerce's website at `www.bis.doc.gov/hpcs`.

The export of high-performance computers to any country currently on the Tier 4 list is prohibited. These countries include Cuba, Iran, Libya, North Korea, and Syria.

Encryption Export Controls

The Department of Commerce's Bureau of Industry and Security sets forth regulations on the export of encryption products outside the United States. Under previous regulations, it was virtually impossible to export even relatively low-grade encryption technology outside the United States. This placed U.S. software manufacturers at a great competitive disadvantage to foreign firms that faced no similar regulations. After a lengthy lobbying campaign by the software industry, the president directed the Commerce Department to revise its regulations to foster the growth of the American security software industry.

Current regulations now designate the categories of retail and mass market security software. The rules now permit firms to submit these products for review by the Commerce Department, but the review will take no longer than 30 days. After successful completion of this review, companies may freely export these products.

Privacy

The right to privacy has for years been a hotly contested issue in the United States. The main source of this contention is that the Constitution's Bill of Rights does not explicitly provide for a right to privacy. However, this right has been upheld by numerous courts and is vigorously pursued by organizations such as the American Civil Liberties Union (ACLU).

Europeans have also long been concerned with their privacy. Indeed, countries such as Switzerland are world renowned for their ability to keep financial secrets. Later in this chapter, we'll examine how the new European Union data privacy laws impact companies and Internet users.

U.S. Privacy Law

Although there is no constitutional guarantee of privacy, a myriad of federal laws (many enacted in recent years) are designed to protect the private information the government maintains about citizens as well as key portions of the private sector such as financial, educational, and health-care institutions. In the following sections, we'll examine a number of these federal laws.

Fourth Amendment   The basis for privacy rights is in the Fourth Amendment to the U.S. Constitution. It reads as follows:

> The right of the people to be secure in their persons, houses, papers, and effects, against unreasonable searches and seizures, shall not be violated, and no warrants shall issue, but upon probable cause, supported by oath or affirmation, and particularly describing the place to be searched, and the persons or things to be seized.

The direct interpretation of this amendment prohibits government agents from searching private property without a warrant and probable cause. The courts have expanded their interpretation of the Fourth Amendment to include protections against wiretapping and other invasions of privacy.

Privacy Act of 1974   The Privacy Act of 1974 is perhaps the most significant piece of privacy legislation restricting the way the federal government may deal with private information about individual citizens. It severely limits the ability of federal government agencies to disclose private information to other persons or agencies without the prior written consent of the affected individual(s). It does provide for exceptions involving the census, law enforcement, the National Archives, health and safety, and court orders.

The Privacy Act mandates that agencies maintain only the records that are necessary for conducting their business and that they destroy those records when they are no longer needed for a legitimate function of government. It provides a formal procedure for individuals to gain access to records the government maintains about them and to request that incorrect records be amended.

Electronic Communications Privacy Act of 1986   The Electronic Communications Privacy Act (ECPA) makes it a crime to invade the electronic privacy of an individual. This act broadened the Federal Wiretap Act, which previously covered communications traveling via a physical wire, to apply to any illegal interception of electronic communications or to the intentional, unauthorized access of electronically stored data. It prohibits the interception or disclosure of electronic communication and defines those situations in which disclosure is legal. It protects against the monitoring of email and voicemail communications and prevents providers of those services from making unauthorized disclosures of their content.

One of the most notable provisions of the ECPA is that it makes it illegal to monitor mobile telephone conversations. In fact, such monitoring is punishable by a fine of up to $500 and a prison term of up to five years.

Communications Assistance for Law Enforcement Act (CALEA) of 1994   The Communications Assistance for Law Enforcement Act (CALEA) of 1994 amended the Electronic Communications Privacy Act of 1986. CALEA requires all communications carriers to make wiretaps possible for law enforcement with an appropriate court order, regardless of the technology in use.

Economic and Protection of Proprietary Information Act of 1996   The Economic and Protection of Proprietary Information Act of 1996 extends the definition of property to include proprietary economic information so that the theft of this information can be considered industrial or corporate espionage. This changed the legal definition of theft so that it was no longer restricted by physical constraints.

Health Insurance Portability and Accountability Act of 1996   In 1996, Congress passed the Health Insurance Portability and Accountability Act (HIPAA), which made numerous changes to the laws governing health insurance and health maintenance organizations (HMOs). Among the provisions of HIPAA are privacy and security regulations requiring strict security measures for hospitals, physicians, insurance companies, and other organizations that process or store private medical information about individuals.

The HIPAA privacy and security regulations are quite complex. You should be familiar with the broad intentions of the act, as described here. If you work in the health-care industry, consider devoting time to an in-depth study of this law's provisions.

HIPAA also clearly defines the rights of individuals who are the subject of medical records and requires organizations that maintain such records to disclose these rights in writing.

Children's Online Privacy Protection Act of 1998   In April 2000, provisions of the Children's Online Privacy Protection Act (COPPA) became the law of the land in the United States. COPPA makes a series of demands on websites that cater to children or knowingly collect information from children:

- Websites must have a privacy notice that clearly states the types of information they collect and what it's used for, including whether any information is disclosed to third parties. The privacy notice must also include contact information for the operators of the site.

- Parents must be provided with the opportunity to review any information collected from their children and permanently delete it from the site's records.

- Parents must give verifiable consent to the collection of information about children younger than the age of 13 prior to any such collection. Exceptions in the law allow websites to collect minimal information solely for the purpose of obtaining such parental consent.

Gramm-Leach-Bliley Act of 1999   Until the Gramm-Leach-Bliley Act (GLBA) became law in 1999, there were strict governmental barriers between financial institutions. Banks, insurance companies, and credit providers were severely limited in the services they could provide and the information they could share with each other. GLBA somewhat relaxed the regulations concerning the services each organization could provide. When Congress passed this law, it realized that this increased latitude could have far-reaching privacy implications. Because of this concern, it included a number of limitations on the types of information that could be exchanged even among subsidiaries of the same corporation and required financial institutions to provide written privacy policies to all their customers by July 1, 2001.

USA PATRIOT Act of 2001   Congress passed the Uniting and Strengthening America by Providing Appropriate Tools Required to Intercept and Obstruct Terrorism (USA PATRIOT) Act of 2001 in direct response to the September 11, 2001, terrorist attacks in New York City and Washington, DC. The PATRIOT Act greatly broadened the powers of law enforcement organizations and intelligence agencies across a number of areas, including when monitoring electronic communications.

One of the major changes prompted by the PATRIOT Act revolves around the way government agencies obtain wiretapping authorizations. Previously, police could obtain warrants for only one circuit at a time, after proving that the circuit was used by someone subject to monitoring. Provisions of the PATRIOT Act allow authorities to obtain a blanket authorization for a person and then monitor all communications to or from that person under the single warrant.

Another major change is in the way the government deals with Internet service providers (ISPs). Under the terms of the PATRIOT Act, ISPs may voluntarily provide the government with a large range of information. The PATRIOT Act also allows the government to obtain detailed information on user activity through the use of a subpoena (as opposed to a wiretap).

Finally, the USA PATRIOT Act amends the Computer Fraud and Abuse Act (yes, another set of amendments!) to provide more severe penalties for criminal acts. The PATRIOT Act provides for jail terms of up to 20 years and once again expands the coverage of the CFAA.

Family Educational Rights and Privacy Act   The Family Educational Rights and Privacy Act (FERPA) is another specialized privacy bill that affects any educational institution that accepts any form of funding from the federal government (the vast majority of schools). It grants certain privacy rights to students older than 18 and the parents of minor students. Specific FERPA protections include the following:

- Parents/students have the right to inspect any educational records maintained by the institution on the student.

- Parents/students have the right to request correction of records they think are erroneous and the right to include a statement in the records contesting anything that is not corrected.

- Schools may not release personal information from student records without written consent, except under certain circumstances.

Identity Theft and Assumption Deterrence Act   In 1998, the president signed the Identity Theft and Assumption Deterrence Act into law. In the past, the only legal victims of identity theft were the creditors who were defrauded. This act makes identity theft a crime against the person whose identity was stolen and provides severe criminal penalties (up to a 15-year prison term and/or a $250,000 fine) for anyone found guilty of violating this law.

Real World Scenario

Privacy in the Workplace

One of the authors of this book had an interesting conversation with a relative who works in an office environment. At a family Christmas party, the author's relative casually mentioned a story he had read online about a local company that had fired several employees for abusing their Internet privileges. He was shocked and couldn't believe that a company would violate their employees' right to privacy.

As you've read in this chapter, the U.S. court system has long upheld the traditional right to privacy as an extension of basic constitutional rights. However, the courts have maintained that a key element of this right is that privacy should be guaranteed only when there is a "reasonable expectation of privacy." For example, if you mail a letter to someone in a sealed envelope, you may reasonably expect that it will be delivered without being read along the way—you have a reasonable expectation of privacy. On the other hand, if you send your message on a postcard, you do so with the awareness that one or more people might read your note before it arrives at the other end—you do not have a reasonable expectation of privacy.

Recent court rulings have found that employees do not have a reasonable expectation of privacy while using employer-owned communications equipment in the workplace. If you send a message using an employer's computer, Internet connection, telephone, or other communications device, your employer can monitor it as a routine business procedure.

That said, if you're planning to monitor the communications of your employees, you should take reasonable precautions to ensure that there is no implied expectation of privacy. Here are some common measures to consider:

- Clauses in employment contracts that state the employee has no expectation of privacy while using corporate equipment

- Similar written statements in corporate acceptable use and privacy policies

- Logon banners warning that all communications are subject to monitoring

- Warning labels on computers and telephones warning of monitoring

As with many of the issues discussed in this chapter, it's a good idea to consult with your legal counsel before undertaking any communications-monitoring efforts.

European Union Privacy Law

On October 24, 1995, the European Union (EU) Parliament passed a sweeping directive outlining privacy measures that must be in place for protecting personal data processed by information systems. The directive went into effect three years later in October 1998. The directive requires that all processing of personal data meet one of the following criteria:

- Consent
- Contract
- Legal obligation
- Vital interest of the data subject
- Balance between the interests of the data holder and the interests of the data subject

The directive also outlines key rights of individuals about whom data is held and/or processed:

- Right to access the data
- Right to know the data's source
- Right to correct inaccurate data
- Right to withhold consent to process data in some situations
- Right of legal action should these rights be violated

Even organizations based outside of Europe must consider the applicability of these rules due to trans-border data flow requirements. In cases where personal information about European Union citizens leaves the EU, those sending the data must ensure that it remains protected. American companies doing business in Europe can obtain protection under a treaty between the EU and the United States that allows the Department of Commerce to certify businesses that comply with regulations and offer them "safe harbor" from prosecution.

To qualify for the safe harbor provision, U.S. companies conducting business in Europe must meet seven requirements for the processing of personal information:

Notice   They must inform individuals of what information they collect about them and how the information will be used.

Choice   They must allow individuals to opt out if the information will be used for any other purpose or shared with a third party. For information considered sensitive, an opt-in policy must be used.

Onward Transfer   Organizations can share data only with other organizations that comply with the safe harbor principles.

Access   Individuals must be granted access to any records kept containing their personal information.

Security   Proper mechanisms must be in place to protect data against loss, misuse, and unauthorized disclosure.

Data Integrity   Organizations must take steps to ensure the reliability of the information they maintain.

Enforcement   Organizations must make a dispute resolution process available to individuals and provide certifications to regulatory agencies that they comply with the safe harbor provisions.

 For more information on the safe harbor protections available to American companies, visit the Department of Commerce's Safe Harbor website at `export.gov/safeharbor`.

Compliance

Over the past decade, the regulatory environment governing information security has grown increasingly complex. Organizations may find themselves subject to a wide variety of laws (many of which were outlined earlier in this chapter) and regulations imposed by regulatory agencies or contractual obligations.

 Real World Scenario

Payment Card Industry Data Security Standard

The Payment Card Industry Data Security Standard (PCI DSS) is an excellent example of a compliance requirement that is not dictated by law but by contractual obligation. PCI DSS governs the security of credit card information and is enforced through the terms of a merchant agreement between a business that accepts credit cards and the bank that processes the business's transactions.

PCI DSS has 12 main requirements:

1. Install and maintain a firewall configuration to protect cardholder data.

2. Do not use vendor-supplied defaults for system passwords and other security parameters.

3. Protect stored cardholder data.

4. Encrypt transmission of cardholder data across open, public networks.

5. Use and regularly update anti-virus software.

6. Develop and maintain secure systems and applications.

7. Restrict access to cardholder data by business need-to-know.

8. Assign a unique ID to each person with computer access.

9. Restrict physical access to cardholder data.

10. Track and monitor all access to network resources and cardholder data.

11. Regularly test security systems and processes.

12. Maintain a policy that addresses information security.

Each of these requirements is spelled out in detail in the full PCI DSS standard, which may be found at www.pcisecuritystandards.org/.

Dealing with the many overlapping, and sometimes contradictory, compliance requirements facing an organization requires careful planning. Many organizations now employ full-time IT compliance staff responsible for tracking the regulatory environment, monitoring controls to ensure ongoing compliance, facilitating compliance audits, and meeting the organization's compliance reporting obligations.

Organizations may be subject to compliance audits, either by their standard internal and external auditors or by regulators or their agents. For example, an organization's financial auditors may conduct an IT controls audit designed to ensure that the information security controls for an organization's financial systems are sufficient to ensure compliance with the Sarbanes–Oxley Act. Some regulations, such as PCI DSS, may require the organization to retain approved independent auditors to verify controls and provide a report directly to regulators.

In addition to formal audits, organizations often must report regulatory compliance to a number of internal and external stakeholders. For example, an organization's Board of Directors (or, more commonly, that board's Audit Committee) may require periodic reporting on compliance obligations and status. Similarly, PCI DSS requires organizations that are not compelled to conduct a formal third-party audit to complete and submit a self-assessment report outlining their compliance status.

Contracting and Procurement

The increased use of cloud services and other external vendors to store, process, and transmit sensitive information leads organizations to a new focus on implementing security reviews and controls in their contracting and procurement processes. Security professionals should conduct reviews of the security controls put in place by vendors, both during the initial vendor selection and evaluation process, and as part of ongoing vendor governance reviews.

Some questions to cover during these vendor governance reviews include:

- What types of sensitive information are stored, processed, or transmitted by the vendor?
- What controls are in place to protect the organization's information?
- How is our organization's information segregated from that of other clients?
- If encryption is relied on as a security control, what encryption algorithms and key lengths are used? How is key management handled?
- What types of security audits does the vendor perform and what access does the client have to those audits?
- Does the vendor rely on any other third parties to store, process, or transmit data? How do the provisions of the contract related to security extend to those third parties?
- Where will data storage, processing, and transmission take place? If outside the home country of the client and/or vendor, what implications does that have?
- What is the vendor's incident response process and when will clients be notified of a potential security breach?
- What provisions are in place to ensure the ongoing integrity and availability of client data?

This is just a brief listing of some of the concerns that you may have. Tailor the scope of your security review to the specific concerns of your organization, the type of service provided by the vendor, and the information that will be shared with them.

Summary

Computer security necessarily entails a high degree of involvement from the legal community. In this chapter, you learned about the laws that govern security issues such as computer crime, intellectual property, data privacy, and software licensing.

There are three major categories of law that impact information security professionals. Criminal law outlines the rules and sanctions for major violations of the public trust. Civil law provides us with a framework for conducting business. Government agencies use administrative law to promulgate the day-to-day regulations that interpret existing law.

The laws governing information security activities are diverse and cover all three categories. Some, such as the Electronic Communications Privacy Act and the Digital Millennium Copyright Act, are criminal laws where violations may result in criminal fines and/or prison time. Others, such as trademark and patent law, are civil laws that govern business transactions. Finally, many government agencies promulgate administrative law, such as the HIPAA Security Rule, that affects specific industries and data types.

Information security professionals should be aware of the compliance requirements specific to their industry and business activities. Tracking these requirements is a complex task and should be assigned to one or more compliance specialists who monitor changes in the law, changes in the business environment, and the intersection of those two realms.

It's also not sufficient to simply worry about your own security and compliance. With increased adoption of cloud computing, many organizations now share sensitive and personal data with vendors who act as service providers. Security professionals must take steps to ensure that vendors treat data with as much care as the organization itself would and also meet any applicable compliance requirements.

Exam Essentials

Understand the differences between criminal law, civil law, and administrative law. Criminal law protects society against acts that violate the basic principles we believe in. Violations of criminal law are prosecuted by federal and state governments. Civil law provides the framework for the transaction of business between people and organizations. Violations of civil law are brought to the court and argued by the two affected parties. Administrative law is used by government agencies to effectively carry out their day-to-day business.

Be able to explain the basic provisions of the major laws designed to protect society against computer crime. The Computer Fraud and Abuse Act (as amended) protects computers used by the government or in interstate commerce from a variety of abuses. The Computer Security Act outlines steps the government must take to protect its own systems from attack. The Government Information Security Reform Act further develops the federal government information security program.

Know the differences among copyrights, trademarks, patents, and trade secrets. Copyrights protect original works of authorship, such as books, articles, poems, and songs. Trademarks are names, slogans, and logos that identify a company, product, or service. Patents provide protection to the creators of new inventions. Trade secret law protects the operating secrets of a firm.

Be able to explain the basic provisions of the Digital Millennium Copyright Act of 1998. The Digital Millennium Copyright Act prohibits the circumvention of copy protection mechanisms placed in digital media and limits the liability of Internet service providers for the activities of their users.

Know the basic provisions of the Economic Espionage Act of 1996. The Economic Espionage Act provides penalties for individuals found guilty of the theft of trade secrets. Harsher penalties apply when the individual knows that the information will benefit a foreign government.

Understand the various types of software license agreements. Contractual license agreements are written agreements between a software vendor and user. Shrink-wrap agreements are written on software packaging and take effect when a user opens the package.

Click-wrap agreements are included in a package but require the user to accept the terms during the software installation process.

Explain the impact of the Uniform Computer Information Transactions Act on software licensing.   The Uniform Computer Information Transactions Act provides a framework for the enforcement of shrink-wrap and click-wrap agreements by federal and state governments.

Understand the restrictions placed on export of high-performance hardware and encryption technology outside the United States.   No high-performance computers or encryption technology may be exported to Tier 4 countries. The export of hardware capable of operating in excess of 0.75 weighted teraflops to Tier 3 countries must be approved by the Department of Commerce. New rules permit the easy exporting of "mass market" encryption software.

Understand the major laws that govern privacy of personal information in both the United States and the European Union.   The United States has a number of privacy laws that affect the government's use of information as well as the use of information by specific industries, such as financial services companies and health-care organizations that handle sensitive information. The EU has a more comprehensive directive on data privacy that regulates the use and exchange of personal information.

Explain the importance of a well-rounded compliance program.   Most organizations are subject to a wide variety of legal and regulatory requirements related to information security. Building a compliance program ensures that you become and remain compliant with these often overlapping requirements.

Know how to incorporate security into the procurement and vendor governance process.   The expanded use of cloud services by many organizations requires added attention to conducting reviews of information security controls during the vendor selection process and as part of ongoing vendor governance.

Written Lab

1. What are the key rights guaranteed to individuals under the European Union's directive on data privacy?

2. What are some common questions that organizations should ask when considering outsourcing information storage, processing, or transmission?

3. What are some common steps that employers take to notify employees of system monitoring?

Review Questions

1. Which criminal law was the first to implement penalties for the creators of viruses, worms, and other types of malicious code that cause harm to computer system(s)?

    A. Computer Security Act

    B. National Infrastructure Protection Act

    C. Computer Fraud and Abuse Act

    D. Electronic Communications Privacy Act

2. Which law first required operators of federal interest computer systems to undergo periodic training in computer security issues?

    A. Computer Security Act

    B. National Infrastructure Protection Act

    C. Computer Fraud and Abuse Act

    D. Electronic Communications Privacy Act

3. What type of law does not require an act of Congress to implement at the federal level but rather is enacted by the executive branch in the form of regulations, policies, and procedures?

    A. Criminal law

    B. Common law

    C. Civil law

    D. Administrative law

4. Which federal government agency has responsibility for ensuring the security of government computer systems that are not used to process sensitive and/or classified information?

    A. National Security Agency

    B. Federal Bureau of Investigation

    C. National Institute of Standards and Technology

    D. Secret Service

5. What is the broadest category of computer systems protected by the Computer Fraud and Abuse Act, as amended?

    A. Government-owned systems

    B. Federal interest systems

    C. Systems used in interstate commerce

    D. Systems located in the United States

6. What law protects the right of citizens to privacy by placing restrictions on the authority granted to government agencies to search private residences and facilities?

    A. Privacy Act

    B. Fourth Amendment

    C. Second Amendment

    D. Gramm-Leach-Bliley Act

7. Matthew recently authored an innovative algorithm for solving a mathematical problem, and he wants to share it with the world. However, prior to publishing the software code in a technical journal, he wants to obtain some sort of intellectual property protection. Which type of protection is best suited to his needs?

    A. Copyright

    B. Trademark

    C. Patent

    D. Trade secret

8. Mary is the cofounder of Acme Widgets, a manufacturing firm. Together with her partner, Joe, she has developed a special oil that will dramatically improve the widget manufacturing process. To keep the formula secret, Mary and Joe plan to make large quantities of the oil by themselves in the plant after the other workers have left. They want to protect this formula for as long as possible. What type of intellectual property protection best suits their needs?

    A. Copyright

    B. Trademark

    C. Patent

    D. Trade secret

9. Richard recently developed a great name for a new product that he plans to begin using immediately. He spoke with his attorney and filed the appropriate application to protect his product name but has not yet received a response from the government regarding his application. He wants to begin using the name immediately. What symbol should he use next to the name to indicate its protected status?

    A. ©

    B. ®

    C. ™

    D. †

10. What law prevents government agencies from disclosing personal information that an individual supplies to the government under protected circumstances?

    A. Privacy Act

    B. Electronic Communications Privacy Act

    C. Health Insurance Portability and Accountability Act

    D. Gramm-Leach-Bliley Act

11. What law formalizes many licensing arrangements used by the software industry and attempts to standardize their use from state to state?

    A. Computer Security Act

    B. Uniform Computer Information Transactions Act

    C. Digital Millennium Copyright Act

    D. Gramm-Leach-Bliley Act

12. The Children's Online Privacy Protection Act was designed to protect the privacy of children using the Internet. What is the minimum age a child must be before companies can collect personal identifying information from them without parental consent?

    A. 13

    B. 14

    C. 15

    D. 16

13. Which one of the following is not a requirement that Internet service providers must satisfy in order to gain protection under the "transitory activities" clause of the Digital Millennium Copyright Act?

    A. The service provider and the originator of the message must be located in different states.

    B. The transmission, routing, provision of connections, or copying must be carried out by an automated technical process without selection of material by the service provider.

    C. Any intermediate copies must not ordinarily be accessible to anyone other than anticipated recipients and must not be retained for longer than reasonably necessary.

    D. The transmission must be originated by a person other than the provider.

14. Which one of the following laws is not designed to protect the privacy rights of consumers and Internet users?

    A. Health Insurance Portability and Accountability Act

    B. Identity Theft Assumption and Deterrence Act

    C. USA PATRIOT Act

    D. Gramm-Leach-Bliley Act

15. Which one of the following types of licensing agreements does not require that the user acknowledge that they have read the agreement prior to executing it?

    A. Standard license agreement

    B. Shrink-wrap agreement

    C. Click-wrap agreement

    D. Verbal agreement

16. What industry is most directly impacted by the provisions of the Gramm-Leach-Bliley Act?

    A. Health care

    B. Banking

    C. Law enforcement

    D. Defense contractors

17. What is the standard duration of patent protection in the United States?

    A. 14 years from the application date

    B. 14 years from the date the patent is granted

    C. 20 years from the application date

    D. 20 years from the date the patent is granted

18. Which one of the following is not a valid legal reason for processing information about an individual under the European Union's data privacy directive?

    A. Contract

    B. Legal obligation

    C. Marketing needs

    D. Consent

19. What compliance obligation relates to the processing of credit card information?

    A. SOX

    B. HIPAA

    C. PCI DSS

    D. FERPA

20. What provision of the European Union's privacy safe harbor requires that organizations only share information with other organizations that comply with the safe harbor provisions?

    A. Notice

    B. Choice

    C. Onward transfer

    D. Enforcement

Chapter

18

Incidents and Ethics

THE CISSP EXAM TOPICS COVERED IN THIS CHAPTER INCLUDE:

9. Legal, Regulations, Investigations, and Compliance

- A. Understand legal issues that pertain to information security internationally
- B. Understand professional ethics
    - B.1 (ISC)² code of professional ethics
    - B.2 Support organization's code of ethics
- C. Understand and support investigations
    - C.1 Policies, roles and responsibilities (e.g. rules of engagement, authorization, scope)
    - C.2 Incident handling and response
    - C.3 Evidence collection and handling (e.g., chain of custody, interviewing)
    - C.4 Reporting and documenting
- D. Understand forensic procedures
    - D.1 Media analysis
    - D.2 Network analysis
    - D.3 Software analysis
    - D.4 Hardware/embedded device analysis

In this chapter, we'll continue our discussion from Chapter 17, "Laws, Regulation, and Compliance," regarding the Legal Regulations, Investigations, and Compliance domain of the Common Body of Knowledge (CBK) for the CISSP certification exam. This domain deals with topics and issues related to computer crime laws and regulations, investigative techniques used to determine whether a computer crime has been committed and to collect evidence when appropriate, and ethics issues and code of conduct for the information security practitioner.

The first step in deciding how to respond to a computer attack is to know if and when an attack has taken place. You must know how to determine that an attack is occurring, or has occurred, before you can properly choose a course of action. Once you have determined that an incident has occurred, the next step is to conduct an investigation and collect evidence to find out what has happened and determine the extent of any damage that might have been done. You must be sure you conduct the investigation in accordance with local laws and regulations.

Investigations

Every information security professional will, at one time or another, encounter a security incident that requires an investigation. In many cases, this investigation will be a brief, informal determination that the matter is not serious enough to warrant further action or the involvement of law enforcement authorities. However, in some cases, the threat posed or damage done will be severe enough to require a more formal inquiry. When this occurs, investigators must be careful to ensure that proper procedures are followed. Failure to abide by the correct procedures may violate the civil rights of those individual(s) being investigated and could result in a failed prosecution or even legal action against the investigator.

Evidence

To successfully prosecute a crime, the prosecuting attorneys must provide sufficient evidence to prove an individual's guilt beyond a reasonable doubt. In the following sections, we'll explain the requirements that evidence must meet before it is allowed in court, the various types of evidence that may be introduced, and the requirements for handling and documenting evidence.

NIST's Guide to Integrating Forensic Techniques into Incident Response (SP 800-86) is a great reference and is available at www.csrc.nist .gov/publications/nistpubs/800-86/SP800-86.pdf.

Admissible Evidence

There are three basic requirements for evidence to be introduced into a court of law. To be considered *admissible evidence*, it must meet all three of these requirements, as determined by the judge, prior to being discussed in open court:

- The evidence must be *relevant* to determining a fact.

- The fact that the evidence seeks to determine must be *material* (that is, related) to the case.

- The evidence must be *competent*, meaning it must have been obtained legally. Evidence that results from an illegal search would be inadmissible because it is not competent.

Types of Evidence

Three types of evidence can be used in a court of law: real evidence, documentary evidence, and testimonial evidence. Each has slightly different additional requirements for admissibility.

Real Evidence   *Real evidence* (also known as *object evidence*) consists of things that may actually be brought into a court of law. In common criminal proceedings, this may include items such as a murder weapon, clothing, or other physical objects. In a computer crime case, real evidence might include seized computer equipment, such as a keyboard with fingerprints on it or a hard drive from a hacker's computer system. Depending on the circumstances, real evidence may also be *conclusive evidence*, such as DNA, that is incontrovertible.

Documentary Evidence   *Documentary evidence* includes any written items brought into court to prove a fact at hand. This type of evidence must also be authenticated. For example, if an attorney wants to introduce a computer log as evidence, they must bring a witness (for example, the system administrator) into court to testify that the log was collected as a routine business practice and is indeed the actual log that the system collected. Two additional evidence rules apply specifically to documentary evidence:

- The *best evidence rule* states that, when a document is used as evidence in a court proceeding, the original document must be introduced. Copies or descriptions of original evidence (known as *secondary evidence*) will not be accepted as evidence unless certain exceptions to the rule apply.

- The *parol evidence rule* states that, when an agreement between parties is put into written form, the written document is assumed to contain all the terms of the agreement and no verbal agreements may modify the written agreement.

If documentary evidence meets the materiality, competency, and relevancy requirements and also complies with the best evidence and parol evidence rules, it can be admitted into court.

Chain of Evidence

Real evidence, like any type of evidence, must meet the relevancy, materiality, and competency requirements before being admitted into court. Additionally, real evidence must be authenticated. This can be done by a witness who can actually identify an object as unique (for example, "That knife with my name on the handle is the one that the intruder took off the table in my house and stabbed me with").

In many cases, it is not possible for a witness to uniquely identify an object in court. In those cases, a *chain of evidence* (also known as a *chain of custody*) must be established. This documents everyone who handles evidence—including the police who originally collect it, the evidence technicians who process it, and the lawyers who use it in court. The location of the evidence must be fully documented from the moment it was collected to the moment it appears in court to ensure that it is indeed the same item. This requires thorough labeling of evidence and comprehensive logs noting who had access to the evidence at specific times and the reasons they required such access.

When evidence is labeled to preserve the chain of custody, the label should include the following types of information regarding the collection:

- General description of the evidence

- Time and date the evidence was collected

- Exact location the evidence was collected from

- Name of the person collecting the evidence

- Relevant circumstances surrounding the collection

Each person who handles the evidence must sign the chain of custody log indicating the time they took direct responsibility for the evidence and the time they handed it off to the next person in the chain of custody. The chain must provide an unbroken sequence of events accounting for the evidence from the time it was collected until the time of the trial.

Testimonial Evidence   *Testimonial evidence* is, quite simply, evidence consisting of the testimony of a witness, either verbal testimony in court or written testimony in a recorded deposition. Witnesses must take an oath agreeing to tell the truth, and they must have personal knowledge on which their testimony is based. Furthermore, witnesses must remember the basis for their testimony (they may consult written notes or records to aid their memory). Witnesses can offer *direct evidence*: oral testimony that proves or disproves a claim based upon their own direct observation. The testimonial evidence of most witnesses must be strictly limited to direct evidence based on the witness's factual observations. However, this does not apply if a witness has been accepted by the court as an expert in a certain field. In that case, the witness may offer an *expert opinion* based on the other facts presented and their personal knowledge of the field.

Testimonial evidence must not be *hearsay evidence*. That is, a witness cannot testify as to what someone else told them outside court. Computer log files that are not authenticated by a system administrator can also be considered hearsay evidence.

Evidence Collection and Forensic Procedures

Collecting digital evidence is a tricky process and should be attempted only by professional forensic technicians. The International Organization on Computer Evidence (IOCE) outlines six principles to guide digital evidence technicians as they perform media analysis, network analysis, and software analysis in the pursuit of forensically recovered evidence:

- When dealing with digital evidence, all of the general forensic and procedural principles must be applied.
- Upon seizing digital evidence, actions taken should not change that evidence.
- When it is necessary for a person to access original digital evidence, that person should be trained for the purpose.
- All activity relating to the seizure, access, storage, or transfer of digital evidence must be fully documented, preserved, and available for review.
- An individual is responsible for all actions taken with respect to digital evidence while the digital evidence is in their possession.
- Any agency that is responsible for seizing, accessing, storing, or transferring digital evidence is responsible for compliance with these principles.

As you conduct forensic evidence collection, it is important to preserve the original evidence. Remember that the very conduct of your investigation may alter the evidence you are evaluating. Therefore, when analyzing digital evidence, it's best to work with a copy of the actual evidence whenever possible. For example, when conducting an investigation into the contents of a hard drive, make an image of that drive, seal the original drive in an evidence bag, and then use the disk image for your investigation.

Media Analysis   Media analysis, a branch of computer forensic analysis, involves the identification and extraction of information from storage media. This may include the following:

- Magnetic media (e.g., hard disks, tapes)
- Optical media (e.g., CDs, DVDs)
- Memory (e.g., RAM, solid state storage)

Techniques used for media analysis may include the recovery of deleted files from unallocated sectors of the physical disk, the live analysis of storage media connected to a computer system (especially useful when examining encrypted media), and the static analysis of forensic images of storage media.

Network Analysis Forensic investigators are also often interested in the activity that took place over the network during a security incident. This is often difficult to reconstruct due to the volatility of network data—if it isn't deliberately recorded at the time it occurs, it generally is not preserved.

Network forensic analysis, therefore, often depends on either prior knowledge that an incident is underway or the use of preexisting security controls that log network activity. These include:

- Intrusion detection and prevention system logs
- Network flow data captured by a flow monitoring system
- Packet captures deliberately collected during an incident
- Logs from firewalls and other network security devices

The task of the network forensic analyst is to collect and correlate information from these disparate sources and produce as comprehensive a picture of network activity as possible.

Software Analysis Forensic analysts may also be called on to conduct forensic reviews of applications or the activity that takes place within a running application. In some cases, when malicious insiders are suspected, the forensic analyst may be asked to conduct a review of software code, looking for back doors, logic bombs, or other security vulnerabilities. For more on these topics, see Chapter 8, "Malicious Code and Application Attacks."

In other cases, forensic analysis may be asked to review and interpret the log files from application or database servers, seeking other signs of malicious activity, such as SQL injection attacks, privilege escalations, or other application attacks. These are also discussed in Chapter 8.

Hardware/Embedded Device Analysis Finally, forensic analysts often must review the contents of hardware and embedded devices. This may include a review of:

- Personal computers
- Smart phones
- Tablet computers
- Embedded computers in cars, security systems, and other devices

Analysts conducting these reviews must have specialized knowledge of the systems under review. This often requires calling in expert consultants who are familiar with the memory, storage systems, and operating systems of such devices. Because of the complex interactions between software, hardware, and storage, the discipline of hardware analysis requires skills in both media analysis and software analysis.

Investigation Process

When you initiate a computer security investigation, you should first assemble a team of competent analysts to assist with the investigation. This team should operate under the organization's existing incident response policy and be given a charter that clearly outlines the scope of the investigation; the authority, roles, and responsibilities of the investigators; and any rules of engagement that they must follow while conducting the investigation. These rules of engagement define and guide the actions that investigators are authorized to take at different phases of the investigation, such as calling in law enforcement, interrogating suspects, collecting evidence, and disrupting system access.

Calling in Law Enforcement

One of the first decisions that must be made in an investigation is whether law enforcement authorities should be called in. This is a relatively complicated decision that should involve senior management officials. There are many factors in favor of calling in the experts. For example, the FBI now maintains a National Computer Crime Squad that includes individuals with the following qualifications:

- Degrees in the computer sciences
- Prior work experience in industry and academic institutions
- Basic and advanced commercial training
- Knowledge of basic data and telecommunications networks
- Experience with UNIX and other computer operating systems

On the other hand, two major factors may cause a company to shy away from calling in the authorities. First, the investigation will more than likely become public and may embarrass the company. Second, law enforcement authorities are bound to conduct an investigation that complies with the Fourth Amendment and other legal requirements that may not apply if the organization conducted its own, private investigation.

Search Warrants

Even the most casual viewer of American crime television is familiar with the question, "Do you have a warrant?" The Fourth Amendment of the U.S. Constitution outlines the burden placed on investigators to have a valid search warrant before conducting certain searches and the legal hurdle they must overcome to obtain a warrant:

> The right of the people to be secure in their persons, houses, papers and effects, against unreasonable searches and seizures, shall not be violated, and no warrants shall issue, but upon probable cause, supported by oath or affirmation, and particularly describing the place to be searched, and the persons or things to be seized.

This amendment contains several important provisions that guide the activities of law enforcement personnel:

▪ Investigators must obtain a warrant before searching a person's private belongings, assuming that there is a reasonable expectation of privacy. There are a number of documented exceptions to this requirement, such as when an individual consents to a search, the evidence of a crime is in plain view, or there is a life-threatening emergency necessitating the search.

▪ Warrants can be issued only based on probable cause. There must be some type of evidence that a crime took place and that the search in question will yield evidence relating to that crime. The standard of "probable cause" required to get a warrant is much weaker than the standard of evidence required to secure a conviction. Most warrants are "sworn out" based solely on the testimony of investigators.

▪ Warrants must be specific in their scope. The warrant must contain a detailed description of the legal bounds of the search and seizure.

If investigators fail to comply with even the smallest detail of these provisions, they may find their warrant invalidated and the results of the search deemed inadmissible. This leads to another one of those American colloquialisms: "He got off on a technicality."

Conducting the Investigation

If you elect not to call in law enforcement, you should still attempt to abide by the principles of a sound investigation to ensure the accuracy and fairness of your inquiry. It is important to remember a few key principles:

▪ Never conduct your investigation on an actual system that was compromised. Take the system offline, make a backup, and use the backup to investigate the incident.

▪ Never attempt to "hack back" and avenge a crime. You may inadvertently attack an innocent third party and find yourself liable for computer crime charges.

▪ If in doubt, call in expert assistance. If you don't want to call in law enforcement, contact a private investigations firm with specific experience in the field of computer security investigations.

▪ Usually, it's best to begin the investigation process using informal interviewing techniques. These are used to gather facts and determine the substance of the case. When specific suspects are identified, they should be questioned using interrogation techniques. Interviewing typically involves open-ended questions to gather information. Interrogation often involves closed-ended questioning with a specific goal in mind and is more adversarial in nature. Again, this is an area best left untouched without specific legal advice.

Major Categories of Computer Crime

There are many ways to attack a computer system and many motivations to do so. Information system security practitioners generally put crimes against or involving computers into different categories. Simply put, a *computer crime* is a crime (or violation of a law or regulation) that involves a computer. The crime could be against the computer, or the computer could have been used in the actual commission of the crime. Each of the categories of computer crimes represents the purpose of an attack and its intended result.

Any individual who violates one or more of your security policies is considered to be an *attacker.* An attacker uses different techniques to achieve a specific goal. Understanding the goals helps to clarify the different types of attacks. Remember that crime is crime, and the motivations behind computer crime are no different from the motivations behind any other type of crime. The only real difference may be in the methods the attacker uses to strike.

Computer crimes are generally classified as one of the following types:

- Military and intelligence attacks
- Business attacks
- Financial attacks
- Terrorist attacks
- Grudge attacks
- Thrill attacks

It is important to understand the differences among the categories of computer crime to best understand how to protect a system and react when an attack occurs. The type and amount of evidence left by an attacker is often dependent on their expertise. In the following sections, we'll discuss the different categories of computer crimes and the types of evidence you might find after an attack. This evidence can help you determine the attacker's actions and intended target. You may find that your system was only a link in the chain of network hops used to reach the real victim, making the trail harder to follow back to the true attacker.

Military and Intelligence Attacks

Military and intelligence attacks are launched primarily to obtain secret and restricted information from law enforcement or military and technological research sources. The disclosure of such information could compromise investigations, disrupt military planning, and threaten national security. Attacks to gather military information or other sensitive intelligence often precede other, more damaging attacks.

An attacker may be looking for the following kinds of information:

- Military descriptive information of any type, including deployment information, readiness information, and order of battle plans
- Secret intelligence gathered for military or law enforcement purposes

- Descriptions and storage locations of evidence obtained in a criminal investigation
- Any secret information that could be used in a later attack

Because of the sensitive nature of information collected and used by the military and intelligence agencies, their computer systems are often attractive targets for experienced attackers. To protect from more numerous and more sophisticated attackers, you will generally find more formal security policies in place on systems that house such information. As you learned in Chapter 5, "Security Governance Concepts, Principles, and Policies," data can be classified according to sensitivity and stored on systems that support the required level of security. It is common to find stringent perimeter security as well as internal controls to limit access to classified documents on military and intelligence agency systems.

You can be sure that serious attacks to acquire military or intelligence information are carried out by professionals. Professional attackers are generally very thorough in covering their tracks. There is usually very little evidence to collect after such an attack. Attackers in this category are the most successful and the most satisfied when no one is aware that an attack occurred.

Business Attacks

Business attacks focus on illegally obtaining an organization's confidential information. This could be information that is critical to the operation of the organization, such as a secret recipe, or information that could damage the organization's reputation if disclosed, such as personal information about its employees. The gathering of a competitor's confidential information, also called *industrial espionage*, is not a new phenomenon. Businesses have used illegal means to acquire competitive information for many years. The temptation to steal a competitor's trade secrets and the ease with which a savvy attacker can compromise some computer systems makes this type of attack attractive.

The goal of business attacks is solely to extract confidential information. The use of the information gathered during the attack usually causes more damage than the attack itself. A business that has suffered an attack of this type can be put into a position from which it might not ever recover. It is up to you as the security professional to ensure that the systems that contain confidential data are secure. In addition, a policy must be developed that will handle such an intrusion should it occur. (For more information on security policies, see Chapter 6, "Risk and Personnel Management.")

Financial Attacks

Financial attacks are carried out to unlawfully obtain money or services. They are the type of computer crime you most commonly hear about in the news. The goal of a financial attack could be to steal credit card numbers, increase the balance in a bank account, or place "free" long-distance telephone calls. You have probably heard of individuals breaking into telephone company computers and placing free calls. This type of financial attack is called *phone phreaking*.

Shoplifting and burglary are both examples of financial attacks. You can usually tell the sophistication of the attacker by the dollar amount of the damages. Less sophisticated attackers seek easier targets, but although the damages are usually minimal, they can add up over time.

Financial attacks launched by sophisticated attackers can result in substantial damages. Although phone phreaking causes the telephone company to lose the revenue of calls placed, serious financial attacks can result in losses amounting to millions of dollars. As with the attacks previously described, the ease with which you can detect an attack and track an attacker is largely dependent on the attacker's skill level.

Terrorist Attacks

Terrorist attacks are a reality in modern society. Our increasing reliance on information systems makes them more and more attractive to terrorists. Such attacks differ from military and intelligence attacks. The purpose of a terrorist attack is to disrupt normal life and instill fear, whereas a military or intelligence attack is designed to extract secret information. Intelligence gathering generally precedes any type of terrorist attack. The very systems that are victims of a terrorist attack were probably compromised in an earlier attack to collect intelligence. The more diligent you are in detecting attacks of any type, the better prepared you will be to intervene before more serious attacks occur.

Possible targets of a computer terrorist attack could be systems that regulate power plants or control telecommunications or power distribution. Many such control and regulatory systems are computerized and vulnerable to terrorist action. In fact, the possibility exists of a simultaneous physical and computerized terrorist attack. Our ability to respond to such an attack would be greatly diminished if the physical attack were simultaneously launched with a computer attack designed to knock out power and communications.

Most large power and communications companies have dedicated a security staff to ensure the security of their systems, but many smaller businesses that have systems connected to the Internet are more vulnerable to attacks. You must diligently monitor your systems to identify any attacks and then respond swiftly when an attack is discovered.

Grudge Attacks

Grudge attacks are attacks that are carried out to damage an organization or a person. The damage could be in the loss of information or information processing capabilities or harm to the organization or a person's reputation. The motivation behind a grudge attack is usually a feeling of resentment, and the attacker could be a current or former employee or someone who wishes ill will upon an organization. The attacker is disgruntled with the victim and takes out their frustration in the form of a grudge attack.

An employee who has recently been fired is a prime example of a person who might carry out a grudge attack to "get back" at the organization. Another example is a person who has been rejected in a personal relationship with another employee. The person who has been rejected might launch an attack to destroy data on the victim's system.

Real World Scenario

The Insider Threat

It's common for security professionals to focus on the threat from outside an organization. Indeed, many of our security technologies are designed to keep unauthorized individuals out. We often don't pay enough (or much!) attention to protecting our organizations against the malicious insider, even though they often pose the greatest risk to our computing assets.

One of the authors of this book recently wrapped up a consulting engagement with a medium-sized subsidiary of a large, well-known corporation. The company had suffered a serious security breach, involving the theft of thousands of dollars and the deliberate destruction of sensitive corporate information. The IT leaders within the organization needed someone to work with them to diagnose the cause of the event and protect themselves against similar events in the future.

After only a very small amount of digging, it became apparent that they were dealing with an insider attack. The intruder's actions demonstrated knowledge of the company's IT infrastructure as well as an understanding of which data was most important to the company's ongoing operations.

Additional investigation revealed that the culprit was a former employee who ended his employment with the firm on less-than-favorable terms. He left the building with a chip on his shoulder and an ax to grind. Unfortunately, he was a system administrator with a wide range of access to corporate systems, and the company had an immature deprovisioning process that failed to remove all of his access upon his termination. He simply found several accounts that remained active and used them to access the corporate network through a VPN.

The moral of this story? Don't underestimate the insider threat. Take the time to evaluate your controls to mitigate the risk that malicious current and former employees pose to your organization.

Your security policy should address the potential of attacks by disgruntled employees. For example, as soon as an employee is terminated, all system access for that employee should be terminated. This action reduces the likelihood of a grudge attack and removes unused access accounts that could be used in future attacks.

Although most grudge attackers are just disgruntled people with limited hacking and cracking abilities, some possess the skills to cause substantial damage. An unhappy cracker can be a handful for security professionals. Take extreme care when a person with known cracking ability leaves your company. At the least, you should perform a vulnerability assessment of all systems the person could access. You may be surprised to find one or more "back doors" left in the system. (For more on back doors, see Chapter 8.) But even in the absence of any back doors, a former employee who is familiar with the technical architecture of the organization may know how to exploit its weaknesses.

Grudge attacks can be devastating if allowed to occur unchecked. Diligent monitoring and assessing systems for vulnerabilities is the best protection for most grudge attacks.

Thrill Attacks

Thrill attacks are the attacks launched only for the fun of it. Attackers who lack the ability to devise their own attacks will often download programs that do their work for them. These attackers are often called *script kiddies* because they run only other people's programs, or scripts, to launch an attack.

The main motivation behind these attacks is the "high" of successfully breaking into a system. If you are the victim of a thrill attack, the most common fate you will suffer is a service interruption. Although an attacker of this type may destroy data, the main motivation is to compromise a system and perhaps use it to launch an attack against another victim.

One common type of thrill attack involves website defacements, where the attacker compromises a web server and replaces an organization's legitimate web content with other pages, often boasting about the attacker's skills. For example, an attacker operating under the pseudonym iSKORPiTX conducted more than 20,000 website defacements in 2006, replacing legitimate websites with his own pages containing the text "Hacked by iSKORPiTX."

Recently, the world has seen a rise in the field of "hacktivism." These attackers, known as hacktivists (a combination of hacker and activist), often combine political motivations with the thrill of hacking. They organize themselves loosely into groups with names like Anonymous and Lolzsec and use tools like the Low Orbit Ion Cannon to create large-scale denial-of-service attacks with little knowledge required.

Incident Handling

When an incident occurs, you must handle it in a manner that is outlined in your security policy and consistent with local laws and regulations. The first step in handling an incident properly is recognizing when one occurs. You should understand the following two terms related to incident handling:

Event   Any occurrence that takes place during a certain period of time

Incident   An event that has a negative outcome affecting the confidentiality, integrity, or availability of an organization's data

The most common reason incidents are not reported is that they are never identified. You could have many security policy violations occurring each day, but if you don't have a way of identifying them, you will never know. Therefore, your security policy should identify and list all possible violations and ways to detect them. It's also important to update your security policy as new types of violations and attacks emerge.

What you do when you find that an incident has occurred depends on the type of incident and scope of damage. Law dictates that some incidents must be reported, such as those that impact government or federal interest computers (a federal interest computer is one that is used by financial institutions and by infrastructure systems such as water and power systems) or certain financial transactions, regardless of the amount of damage. Most U.S. states now have laws that require organizations that experience an incident involving certain types of personally identifying information (for example, credit card numbers, Social Security numbers, and driver's license numbers) to notify affected individuals of the breach.

In addition to laws, many companies have contractual obligations to report different types of security incidents to business partners. For example, the Payment Card Industry Data Security Standard (PCI DSS) requires any merchant that handles credit card information to report incidents involving that information to their acquiring bank as well as law enforcement.

Next, we'll cover some of the different types of incidents and typical responses.

Common Types of Incidents

We discussed the various types of attacks in Chapter 2, "Access Control Attacks and Monitoring." An incident occurs when an attack, or other violation of your security policy, is carried out against your system. There are many ways to classify incidents; here is a general list of categories:

- Scanning
- Compromises
- Malicious code
- Denial of service

These four areas are the basic entry points for attackers to impact a system. You must focus on each of these areas to create an effective monitoring strategy that detects system incidents. Each incident area has representative signatures that can tip off an alert security administrator that an incident has occurred. Make sure you know your operating system environment and where to look for the telltale signs of each type of incident.

Scanning

Scanning attacks are reconnaissance attacks that usually precede another, more serious attack. They're comparable to a burglar "casing" a neighborhood for targets, looking for homes with unlocked doors or where nobody is home on guard. Attackers will gather as much information about your system as possible before launching a directed attack. Look for any unusual activity on any port or from any single address. For example, a high volume of Secure Shell (SSH) packets on port 22 may point to a systematic scan of your network.

Remember that simply scanning your system may not be illegal, depending on your local laws. But it can indicate that illegal activity will follow, so it is a good idea to treat scans as incidents and to collect evidence of scanning activity. You may find that the evidence you collect at the time the system is scanned could be the link you need to find the party responsible for a later attack.

Because scanning is such a common occurrence, you definitely want to automate evidence collection. Set up your firewall to log rejected traffic and archive your log files. The logs may become large, but storage is cheap, and you should consider it a cost of doing business.

Compromise

A system *compromise* is any unauthorized access to the system or information the system stores. A compromise could originate inside or outside the organization. To make matters worse, a compromise could come from a valid user. An unauthorized use of a valid user ID is just as much of a compromise incident as an experienced cracker breaking in from the outside. Another example of a system compromise is when an attacker uses a normal user account to gain the elevated privileges of a system administrator without authorization.

System compromises can be difficult to detect. Most often, the data custodian notices something unusual about the data. It could be missing, altered, or moved; the time stamps could be different; or something else is just not right. The more you know about the normal operation of your system, the better prepared you will be to detect abnormal system behavior.

Malicious Code

When *malicious code* is mentioned, you probably think of viruses and spyware. Although a virus is a common type of malicious code, it is only one type of several. (In Chapter 8, we discussed different types of malicious code.) Detection of this type of a malicious code incident comes from either an end user reporting behavior caused by the malicious code or an automated alert reporting that scanned code containing a malicious component has been found.

The most effective way to protect your system from malicious code is to implement virus and spyware scanners and keep the signature database up-to-date. In addition, your security policy should address the introduction of outside code. Be specific as to what code you will allow end users to install.

Denial of Service

The final type of incident is a *denial of service (DoS)*. This type of incident is often the easiest to detect. A user or automated tool reports that one or more services (or the entire machine) is unavailable. Although they're simple to detect, avoidance is a far better course of action. It is theoretically possible to dynamically alter firewall rules to reject DoS network traffic, but in recent years the sophistication and complexity of DoS attacks make them extremely difficult to defend against. Because there are so many variations of the DoS attack, implementing this strategy is a nontrivial task.

A detailed discussion of DoS and distributed denial-of-service (DDoS) attacks appears in Chapter 8.

Response Teams

Many organizations now have a dedicated team responsible for investigating any computer security incidents that take place. These teams are commonly known as computer incident response teams (CIRTs) or computer security incident response teams (CSIRTs). When an incident occurs, the response team has four primary responsibilities:

- Determine the amount and scope of damage caused by the incident.

- Determine whether any confidential information was compromised during the incident.

- Implement any necessary recovery procedures to restore security and recover from incident-related damages.

- Supervise the implementation of any additional security measures necessary to improve security and prevent recurrence of the incident.

 Real World Scenario

The Gibson Research Denial-of-Service Attacks: Fun or Grudge?

Steve Gibson is a well-known software developer and personality in the IT industry whose high visibility derives not only from highly regarded products associated with his company, Gibson Research, but also from his many years as a vocal and outspoken columnist for *Computer World* magazine. In recent years, he has become quite active in the field of computer security, and his site offers free vulnerability-scanning services and a variety of patches and fixes for operating system vulnerabilities. He operates a website at http://grc.com that has been the subject of numerous well-documented denial-of-service attacks. It's interesting to speculate whether such attacks are motivated by grudges (that is, by those who seek to advance their reputations by breaking into an obvious and presumably well-defended point of attack) or by fun (that is, by those with excess time on their hands who might seek to prove themselves against a worthy adversary without necessarily expecting any gain other than notoriety from their actions).

Gibson's website has in fact been subject to two well-documented denial-of-service attacks that you can read about in detail on his site:

- "Distributed Reflection Denial of Service": http://www.cs.washington.edu/homes/arvind/cs425/doc/drdos.pdf

- "The Strange Tale of the Denial of Service Attacks against GRC.COM": http://www.crime-research.org/library/grcdos.pdf

Although his subsequent anonymous discussions with one of the perpetrators involved seem to indicate that the motive for some of these attacks was fun rather than business damage or acting on a grudge, these reports are fascinating because of the excellent model they provide for incident handling and reporting.

These documents contain a brief synopsis of the symptoms and chronology of the attacks that occurred, along with short- and long-term fixes and changes enacted to prevent recurrences. They also stress the critical importance of communication with service providers whose infrastructures may be involved in attacks as they're underway. What's extremely telling about Gibson's report on the denial-of-service attacks is that he experienced 17 hours of downtime because he was unable to establish contact with a knowledgeable, competent engineer at his service provider who could help define the right kinds of traffic filters to stymie the floods of traffic that characterize denial-of-service attacks.

Gibson's analysis also indicates his thoroughness in analyzing the sources of the distributed denial-of-service attacks and in documenting what he calls "an exact profile of the malicious traffic being generated during these attacks." This information permitted his Internet service provider (ISP) to define a set of filters that blocked further such traffic from transiting the final T1 links from Gibson's ISP to his servers. As his experience proves so conclusively, recognizing, analyzing, and characterizing attacks is absolutely essential to defining filters or other countermeasures that can block or defeat them.

As part of these duties, the team should facilitate a *postmortem review* of the incident within a week of the occurrence to ensure that key players in the incident share their knowledge and develop best practices to assist in future incident response efforts.

When putting together your incident response team, be sure to design a cross-functional group of individuals that represent the management, technical, and functional areas of responsibility most directly impacted by a security incident. Potential team members include the following:

- Representative(s) of senior management
- Information security professionals
- Legal representatives
- Public affairs/communications representatives
- Engineering representatives (system and network)

Incident Response Process

Many organizations use a three-step incident response process, consisting of the following phases:

1. Detection and identification
2. Response and reporting
3. Recovery and remediation

The next three sections outline each phase of the standard incident response process.

Step 1: Detection and Identification

The incident identification process has two main goals: detecting security incidents and notifying appropriate personnel. To successfully detect and identify incidents, a security team must monitor any relevant events that occur and notice when they meet the organization's defined threshold for a security incident. The key to identifying incidents is to detect abnormal or suspicious activity that may constitute evidence of an incident. Although you can detect many attacks by their characteristic signatures, experienced attackers know how to "fly under the radar." You must be aware of how your system operates normally and recognize *abnormal* or *suspicious* activity—that is, any system activity that does not normally occur on your system.

These are some of the tools you should monitor for events indicative of security incidents:

-   Intrusion detection/prevention systems
-   Antivirus software
-   Firewall logs
-   System logs
-   Physical security systems
-   File integrity monitoring software

Always use multiple sources of data when investigating an incident. Be suspicious of anything that does not make sense. Ensure that you can clearly explain any activity you see that is not normal for your system. Even if your sense is that "it just does not feel right," that could be the only clue you have to successfully intervene in an ongoing incident.

Once the initial evaluator identifies that an event or events met the organization's security incident criteria, the evaluator must notify the incident response team. This notification concludes the incident detection and identification phase and initiates the response and reporting phase.

Step 2: Response and Reporting

Once you determine that an incident has occurred, the next step is to choose an appropriate response. Your security policy should specify steps to take for various types of incidents. Always proceed with the assumption that an incident will end up in a court of law. Treat any evidence you collect as if it must pass admissibility standards. Once you taint evidence, there is no going back. You must ensure that the chain of evidence is maintained.

Isolation and Containment   The first actions you take should be dedicated to limiting the exposure of your organization and preventing further damage. In the case of a potentially compromised system, you should disconnect it from the network to prevent intruders from accessing the compromised system and also to prevent the compromised system from affecting other resources on the network.

In the isolation and containment phase of incident response, it is critical that you leave the system in a running state. Do not power down the system. Turning off the computer destroys the contents of volatile memory and may destroy evidence.

Gathering Evidence   It is common to confiscate equipment, software, or data to perform a proper investigation. The manner in which the evidence is confiscated is important. The confiscation of evidence must be carried out in a proper fashion. There are three basic alternatives.

First, the person who owns the evidence could *voluntarily surrender* it. This method is generally appropriate only when the attacker is not the owner. Few guilty parties willingly surrender evidence they know will incriminate them. Less experienced attackers may believe they have successfully covered their tracks and voluntarily surrender important evidence. A good forensic investigator can extract much "covered-up" information from a computer. In most cases, asking for evidence from a suspected attacker just alerts the suspect that you are close to taking legal action.

In the case of an internal investigation, you will gather the vast majority of your information through voluntary surrender. Most likely, you're conducting the investigation under the auspices of a senior member of management who will authorize you to access any organizational resources necessary to complete your investigation.

Second, you could get a court to issue a *subpoena*, or court order, that compels an individual or organization to surrender evidence and then have the subpoena served by law enforcement. Again, this course of action provides sufficient notice for someone to alter the evidence and render it useless in court.

The last option is a *search warrant*. This option should be used only when you must have access to evidence without tipping off the evidence's owner or other personnel. You must have a strong suspicion with credible reasoning to convince a judge to pursue this course of action.

The three alternatives apply to confiscating equipment both inside and outside an organization, but there is another step you can take to ensure that the confiscation of equipment that belongs to your organization is carried out properly. It is common to have all new employees sign an agreement that provides consent to search and seize any necessary evidence during an investigation. In this manner, consent is provided as a term of the employment agreement. This makes confiscation much easier and reduces the chances of a loss of evidence while waiting for legal permission to seize it. Make sure your security policy addresses this important topic.

You should consider the following sources of data when determining what evidence to gather:

- Computer systems involved in the incident (both servers and workstations)
- Logs from security systems (such as intrusion detection, file integrity monitoring, and firewalls)
- Logs from network devices
- Physical access logs
- Other relevant sources of information specific to the incident under investigation

Analysis and Reporting   Once you finish gathering evidence, you should analyze it to determine the most likely course of events leading up to your incident. Summarize those findings in a written report to management. In your report, you should be careful to distinguish fact from opinion. It is acceptable to theorize about possible causes, but you should be certain to state which of your conclusions are based entirely on fact and which involve a degree of estimation.

Step 3: Recovery and Remediation

After completing your investigation, you have two tasks remaining: restoring your environment to its normal operating state and completing a "lessons learned" process to improve how you handle future incidents.

Restoration   The goal of the restoration process is to remediate any damage that may have occurred to the organization and limit the damage incurred by similar incidents in the future. These are some of the key actions you should take during this phase:

- Rebuild compromised systems, taking care to remediate any security vulnerabilities that may have contributed to the incident.
- Restore backup data, if necessary, to replace data of questionable integrity.
- Supplement existing security controls, if necessary, to fill gaps identified during the incident analysis.

Once you have completed the restoration process, your business should be back up and running in the state it was in prior to the incident (although in a more secure manner!).

Lessons Learned   The final stage of the incident response process is to conduct a "lessons learned" session. During this important process, members of the incident response team review their actions during the incident and look for potential areas of improvement, both in their actions and in the incident response process. This hindsight review provides an important perspective on the success of your incident response process by analyzing its effectiveness during a real-world incident.

Interviewing Individuals

During your incident investigation, you may find it necessary to speak with individuals who might have information relevant to your investigation. If you seek only to gather information to assist with your investigation, this is called an *interview*. If you suspect the person of involvement in a crime and intend to use the information gathered in court, this is called an *interrogation*.

Interviewing and interrogating individuals are specialized skills and should be performed only by trained investigators. Improper techniques may jeopardize the ability of law enforcement to successfully prosecute an offender. Additionally, many laws govern holding or detaining individuals, and you must abide by them if you plan to conduct private interrogations. Always consult an attorney before conducting any interviews.

Incident Data Integrity and Retention

No matter how persuasive evidence may be, it can be thrown out of court if you somehow alter it during the evidence collection process. Make sure you can prove that you maintained the integrity of all evidence. But what about the integrity of data before it is collected?

You may not detect all incidents as they are happening. Sometimes an investigation reveals that there were previous incidents that went undetected. It is discouraging to follow a trail of evidence and find that a key log file that could point back to an attacker has been purged. Carefully consider the fate of log files or other possible evidence locations. A simple archiving policy can help ensure that key evidence is available upon demand no matter how long ago the incident occurred.

Because many log files can contain valuable evidence, attackers often attempt to sanitize them after a successful attack. Take steps to protect the integrity of log files and to deter their modification. One technique is to implement remote logging, where all systems on the network send their log records to a centralized log server that is locked down against attack and does not allow for the modification of data. This technique provides protection from post-incident log file cleansing. Administrators also often use digital signatures to prove that log files were not tampered with after initial capture. For more on digital signatures, see Chapter 10, "PKI and Cryptographic Applications."

As with every aspect of security planning, there is no single solution. Get familiar with your system, and take the steps that make the most sense for your organization to protect it.

Reporting Incidents

When should you report an incident? To whom should you report it? These questions are often difficult to answer. Your security policy should contain guidelines on both questions. There is a fundamental problem with reporting incidents. If you report every incident, you run the very real risk of being viewed as a noisemaker and being ignored if you subsequently report a serious incident. Also, reporting an unimportant incident could give the impression that your organization is more vulnerable than is the case. This can have a serious detrimental effect if your organization must maintain strict security. For example, if your bank reported daily security incidents, you might lose confidence in their security practices.

On the other hand, escalation and legal action become more difficult if you do not report an incident soon after discovery. If you delay notifying authorities of a serious incident, you will probably have to answer questions about your motivation for delaying. Even an innocent person could look as if they were trying to hide something by not reporting an incident in a timely manner.

As with most security topics, the answer is not an easy one. In fact, you are compelled by law or regulation to report some incidents. Make sure you know what incidents you must report. For example, any organization that stores credit card information must report any incident in which the disclosure of such information occurred.

Before you encounter an incident, it is wise to establish a relationship with your corporate legal personnel and the appropriate law enforcement agencies. Find out who the appropriate law enforcement contacts are for your organization and talk with them. When the time comes to report an incident, your efforts at establishing a prior working relationship will pay off. You will spend far less time in introductions and explanations if you already know the person with whom you are talking. It is a good idea to identify, in advance, a single point of contact in the organization that will act as your liaison with law enforcement. This provides two benefits. First, it ensures that law enforcement hears a single perspective from your organization and knows the "go-to" person for updates. Second, it allows the predesignated contact to develop working relationships with law enforcement personnel.

One great way to establish technical contacts with law enforcement is to participate in the FBI's InfraGard program. InfraGard exists in most major metropolitan areas in the United States and provides a forum for law enforcement and business security professionals to share information in a closed environment. For more information, visit www.infragard.net.

Once you determine that you should report an incident, make sure you have as much of the following information as possible:

- What is the nature of the incident, how was it initiated, and by whom?
- When did the incident occur? (Be as precise as possible with dates and times.)
- Where did the incident occur?

- If known, what tools did the attacker use?
- What was the damage resulting from the incident?

You may be asked to provide additional information. Be prepared to provide it in as timely a manner as possible. You may also be asked to quarantine your system.

As with any security action you take, keep a log of all communication, and make copies of any documents you provide as you report an incident.

> For more information on incident handling, read NIST SP 800-61, Computer Security Incident Handling Guide, available at http://csrc.nist.gov/publications/nistpubs/800-61-rev1/SP800-61rev1.pdf, and the Handbook for CSIRTs at www.cert.org/archive/pdf/csirt-handbook.pdf.

Ethics

Security professionals hold themselves and each other to a high standard of conduct because of the sensitive positions of trust they occupy. The rules that govern personal conduct are collectively known as rules of *ethics*. Several organizations have recognized the need for standard ethics rules, or codes, and have devised guidelines for ethical behavior.

We present two codes of ethics in the following sections. These rules are not laws. They are minimum standards for professional behavior. They should provide you with a basis for sound, ethical judgment. We expect all security professionals to abide by these guidelines regardless of their area of specialty or employer. Make sure you understand and agree with the codes of ethics outlined in the following sections. In addition to these codes, all information security professionals should also support their organization's code of ethics.

(ISC)² Code of Ethics

The governing body that administers the CISSP certification is the International Information Systems Security Certification Consortium, or (ISC)². The (ISC)² Code of Ethics was developed to provide the basis for CISSP behavior. It is a simple code with a preamble and four canons. The following is a short summary of the major concepts of the Code of Ethics.

> All CISSP candidates should be familiar with the entire (ISC)² Code of Ethics because they have to sign an agreement that they will adhere to this code. We won't cover the code in depth, but you can find further details about the (ISC)²'s Code of Ethics at www.isc2.org/ethics. You need to visit this site and read the entire code.

Code of Ethics Preamble

The Code of Ethics preamble is as follows:

- Safety of the commonwealth, duty to our principals, and to each other requires that we adhere, and be seen to adhere, to the highest ethical standards of behavior.

- Therefore, strict adherence to this code is a condition of certification.

Code of Ethics Canons

The Code of Ethics includes the following canons:

Protect society, the commonwealth, and the infrastructure.   Security professionals have great social responsibility. We are charged with the burden of ensuring that our actions benefit the common good.

Act honorably, honestly, justly, responsibly, and legally.   Integrity is essential to the conduct of our duties. We cannot carry out our duties effectively if others within our organization, the security community, or the general public have doubts about the accuracy of the guidance we provide or the motives behind our actions.

Provide diligent and competent service to principals.   Although we have responsibilities to society as a whole, we also have specific responsibilities to those who have hired us to protect their infrastructure. We must ensure that we are in a position to provide unbiased, competent service to our organization.

Advance and protect the profession.   Our chosen profession changes on a continuous basis. As security professionals, we must ensure that our knowledge remains current and that we contribute our own knowledge to the community's common body of knowledge.

Ethics and the Internet

In January 1989, the Internet Advisory Board (IAB) recognized that the Internet was rapidly expanding beyond the initial trusted community that created it. Understanding that misuse could occur as the Internet grew, IAB issued a statement of policy concerning the proper use of the Internet. The contents of this statement are valid even today. It is important that you know the basic contents of the document, titled "Ethics and the Internet," Request for Comments (RFC) 1087, because most codes of ethics can trace their roots back to this document.

The statement is a brief list of practices considered unethical. Where a code of ethics states what you should do, this document outlines what you should not do. RFC 1087 states that any activity with the following purposes is unacceptable and unethical:

- Seeks to gain unauthorized access to the resources of the Internet
- Disrupts the intended use of the Internet
- Wastes resources (people, capacity, computer) through such actions
- Destroys the integrity of computer-based information
- Compromises the privacy of users

Ten Commandments of Computer Ethics

The Computer Ethics Institute created its own code of ethics. The Ten Commandments of Computer Ethics are as follows:

1. Thou shalt not use a computer to harm other people.

2. Thou shalt not interfere with other people's computer work.

3. Thou shalt not snoop around in other people's computer files.

4. Thou shalt not use a computer to steal.

5. Thou shalt not use a computer to bear false witness.

6. Thou shalt not copy proprietary software for which you have not paid.

7. Thou shalt not use other people's computer resources without authorization or proper compensation.

8. Thou shalt not appropriate other people's intellectual output.

9. Thou shalt think about the social consequences of the program you are writing or the system you are designing.

10. Thou shalt always use a computer in ways that ensure consideration and respect for your fellow humans.

There are many ethical and moral codes of IT behavior to choose from. Another system you should consider is the Generally Accepted System Security Principles (GASSP). You can find the full text of the GASSP system at www.infosectoday.com/Articles/gassp.pdf.

Summary

Information security professionals must be familiar with the incident response process. This involves gathering and analyzing the evidence required to conduct an investigation. Security professionals should be familiar with the major categories of evidence, including real evidence, documentary evidence, and testimonial evidence. Electronic evidence is often gathered through the analysis of hardware, software, storage media, and networks. It is essential to gather evidence using appropriate procedures that do not alter the original evidence and preserve the chain of custody.

Computer crimes are grouped into several major categories, and the crimes in each category share common motivations and desired results. Understanding what an attacker is after can help in properly securing a system.

For example, military and intelligence attacks are launched to acquire secret information that could not be obtained legally. Business attacks are similar except that they target civilian systems. Other types of attacks include financial attacks (phone phreaking is an example of a financial attack) and terrorist attacks (which, in the context of computer crimes, are attacks designed to disrupt normal life). Finally, there are grudge attacks, the purpose of which is to cause damage by destroying data or using information to embarrass an organization or person, and thrill attacks, launched by inexperienced crackers to compromise or disable a system. Although generally not sophisticated, thrill attacks can be annoying and costly.

An incident is a violation or the threat of a violation of your security policy. When an incident is suspected, you should immediately begin an investigation and collect as much evidence as possible because, if you decide to report the incident, you must have enough admissible evidence to support your claims.

The set of rules that govern your personal behavior is a code of ethics. There are several codes of ethics, from general to specific in nature, that security professionals can use to guide them. The (ISC)^2 makes the acceptance of its code of ethics a requirement for certification.

Exam Essentials

Know the definition of computer crime.   Computer crime is a crime (or violation of a law or regulation) that is directed against, or directly involves, a computer.

Be able to list and explain the six categories of computer crimes.   Computer crimes are grouped into six categories: military and intelligence attack, business attack, financial attack, terrorist attack, grudge attack, and thrill attack. Be able to explain the motive of each type of attack.

Know the importance of collecting evidence.   As soon you discover an incident, you must begin to collect evidence and as much information about the incident as possible. The evidence can be used in a subsequent legal action or in finding the identity of the attacker. Evidence can also assist you in determining the extent of damage.

Understand that an incident is any violation, or threat of a violation, of your security policy.   Incidents should be defined in your security policy. Even though specific incidents may not be outlined, the existence of the policy sets the standard for the use of your system. An incident is any event that has a negative outcome affecting the confidentiality, integrity, or availability of an organization's data.

Be able to list the four common types of incidents, and know the telltale signs of each.   An incident occurs when an attack or other violation of your security policy is carried out against your system. Incidents can be grouped into four categories: scanning, compromises, malicious code, and denial of service. Be able to explain what each type of incident involves and what signs to look for.

Know the importance of identifying abnormal and suspicious activity.   Attacks will generate some activity that is not normal. Recognizing abnormal and suspicious activity is the first step toward detecting incidents.

Know how to investigate intrusions and how to gather sufficient information from the equipment, software, and data.   You must have possession of equipment, software, or data to analyze it and use it as evidence. You must acquire the evidence without modifying it or allowing anyone else to modify it.

Know the three basic alternatives for confiscating evidence and when each one is appropriate.   First, the person who owns the evidence could voluntarily surrender it. Second, a subpoena could be used to compel the subject to surrender the evidence. Third, a search warrant is most useful when you need to confiscate evidence without giving the subject an opportunity to alter it.

Know the importance of retaining incident data.   Because you will discover some incidents after they have occurred, you will lose valuable evidence unless you ensure that critical log files are retained for a reasonable period of time. You can retain log files and system status information either in place or in archives.

Be familiar with how to report an incident.   The first step is to establish a working relationship with the corporate and law enforcement personnel with whom you will work to resolve an incident. When you do have a need to report an incident, gather as much descriptive information as possible and make your report in a timely manner.

Know the basic requirements for evidence to be admissible in a court of law.   To be admissible, evidence must be relevant to a fact at issue in the case, the fact must be material to the case, and the evidence must be competent or legally collected.

Explain the various types of evidence that may be used in a criminal or civil trial.
Real evidence consists of actual objects that can be brought into the courtroom. Documentary evidence consists of written documents that provide insight into the facts. Testimonial evidence consists of verbal or written statements made by witnesses.

Understand the importance of ethics to security personnel.   Security practitioners are granted a very high level of authority and responsibility to execute their job functions. The potential for abuse exists, and without a strict code of personal behavior, security practitioners could be regarded as having unchecked power. Adherence to a code of ethics helps ensure that such power is not abused.

Know the (ISC)² Code of Ethics and RFC 1087, "Ethics and the Internet."   All CISSP candidates should be familiar with the entire (ISC)² Code of Ethics because they have to sign an agreement that they will adhere to it. In addition, be familiar with the basic statements of RFC 1087.

Written Lab

1. What are the major categories of computer crime?
2. What is the main motivation behind a thrill attack?
3. What is the difference between an interview and an interrogation?
4. What is the difference between an event and an incident?
5. Who are the common members of an incident response team?
6. What are the three phases of the incident response process?
7. What are the three basic requirements that evidence must meet in order to be admissible in court?

Review Questions

1. What is a computer crime?

   A. Any attack specifically listed in your security policy

   B. Any illegal attack that compromises a protected computer

   C. Any violation of a law or regulation that involves a computer

   D. Failure to practice due diligence in computer security

2. What is the main purpose of a military and intelligence attack?

   A. To attack the availability of military systems

   B. To obtain secret and restricted information from military or law enforcement sources

   C. To utilize military or intelligence agency systems to attack other nonmilitary sites

   D. To compromise military systems for use in attacks against other systems

3. What type of attack targets proprietary information stored on a civilian organization's system?

   A. Business attack

   B. Denial-of-service attack

   C. Financial attack

   D. Military and intelligence attack

4. What goal is not a purpose of a financial attack?

   A. Access services you have not purchased

   B. Disclose confidential personal employee information

   C. Transfer funds from an unapproved source into your account

   D. Steal money from another organization

5. Which one of the following attacks is most indicative of a terrorist attack?

   A. Altering sensitive trade secret documents

   B. Damaging the ability to communicate and respond to a physical attack

   C. Stealing unclassified information

   D. Transferring funds to other countries

6. Which of the following would not be a primary goal of a grudge attack?

   A. Disclosing embarrassing personal information

   B. Launching a virus on an organization's system

   C. Sending inappropriate email with a spoofed origination address of the victim organization

   D. Using automated tools to scan the organization's systems for vulnerable ports

7. What are the primary reasons attackers engage in thrill attacks? (Choose all that apply.)

   A. Bragging rights

   B. Money from the sale of stolen documents

   C. Pride of conquering a secure system

   D. Retaliation against a person or organization

8. What is the most important rule to follow when collecting evidence?

   A. Do not turn off a computer until you photograph the screen.

   B. List all people present while collecting evidence.

   C. Never modify evidence during the collection process.

   D. Transfer all equipment to a secure storage location.

9. What would be a valid argument for not immediately removing power from a machine when an incident is discovered?

   A. All of the damage has been done. Turning the machine off would not stop additional damage.

   B. There is no other system that can replace this one if it is turned off.

   C. Too many users are logged in and using the system.

   D. Valuable evidence in memory will be lost.

10. Hacktivists are motivated by which of the following factors? (Choose all that apply.)

   A. Financial gain

   B. Thrill

   C. Skill

   D. Political beliefs

11. What is an incident?

   A. Any active attack that causes damage to your system

   B. Any violation of a code of ethics

   C. Any crime (or violation of a law or regulation) that involves a computer

   D. Any event that adversely affects the confidentiality, integrity, or availability of your data

12. If port scanning does no damage to a system, why is it generally considered an incident?

   A. All port scans indicate adversarial behavior.

   B. Port scans can precede attacks that cause damage and can indicate a future attack.

   C. Scanning a port damages the port.

   D. Port scanning uses system resources that could be put to better uses.

13. What type of incident is characterized by obtaining an increased level of privilege?

    A. Compromise

    B. Denial of service

    C. Malicious code

    D. Scanning

14. What is the best way to recognize abnormal and suspicious behavior on your system?

    A. Be aware of the newest attacks.

    B. Configure your IDS to detect and report all abnormal traffic.

    C. Know what your normal system activity looks like.

    D. Study the activity signatures of the main types of attacks.

15. If you need to confiscate a PC from a suspected attacker who does not work for your organization, what legal avenue is most appropriate?

    A. Consent agreement signed by employees

    B. Search warrant

    C. No legal avenue is necessary.

    D. Voluntary consent

16. Why should you avoid deleting log files on a daily basis?

    A. An incident may not be discovered for several days and valuable evidence could be lost.

    B. Disk space is cheap, and log files are used frequently.

    C. Log files are protected and cannot be altered.

    D. Any information in a log file is useless after it is several hours old.

17. Which of the following conditions might require that you report an incident? (Choose all that apply.)

    A. Confidential information protected by government regulation was possibly disclosed.

    B. Damages exceeded $1,500.

    C. The incident has occurred before.

    D. The incident resulted in a violation of a law.

18. What are ethics?

    A. Mandatory actions required to fulfill job requirements

    B. Laws of professional conduct

    C. Regulations set forth by a professional organization

    D. Rules of personal behavior

19. According to the (ISC)^2 Code of Ethics, how are CISSPs expected to act?

    A. Honestly, diligently, responsibly, and legally

    B. Honorably, honestly, justly, responsibly, and legally

    C. Upholding the security policy and protecting the organization

    D. Trustworthy, loyally, friendly, courteously

20. Which of the following actions are considered unacceptable and unethical according to RFC 1087, "Ethics and the Internet"?

    A. Actions that compromise the privacy of classified information

    B. Actions that compromise the privacy of users

    C. Actions that disrupt organizational activities

    D. Actions in which a computer is used in a manner inconsistent with a stated security policy

Chapter 19

Physical Security Requirements

THE CISSP EXAM TOPICS COVERED IN THIS CHAPTER INCLUDE:

10. Physical (Environmental) Security

- A. Understand site and facility design considerations
- B. Support the implementation and operation of perimeter security (e.g., physical access control and monitoring, audit trails/access logs)
- C. Support the implementation and operation of internal security (e.g., escort requirements/visitor control, keys and locks)
- D. Support the implementation and operation of facilities security (e.g., technology convergence)
    - D.1 Communications and server rooms
    - D.2 Restricted and work area security
    - D.3 Data center security
    - D.4 Utilities and Heating, Ventilation, and Air Conditioning (HVAC) considerations
    - D.5 Water issues (e.g., leakage, flooding)
    - D.6 Fire prevention, detection, and suppression
- E. Support the protection and securing of equipment
- F. Understand personnel privacy and safety (e.g., duress, travel, monitoring)

The Physical (Environmental) Security domain of the Common Body of Knowledge (CBK) for the CISSP certification exam deals with topics and issues related to facility construction and location, the security features of a facility (i.e., facilities security), forms of physical access control, types of physical security technical controls, and the maintaining of security by properly sustaining the environment and protecting human life.

The purpose of physical security is to protect against physical threats. The following physical threats are among the most common: fire and smoke, water (rising/falling), earth movement (earthquakes, landslides, volcanoes), storms (wind, lightning, rain, snow, sleet, ice), sabotage/vandalism, explosion/destruction, building collapse, toxic materials, utility loss (power, heating, cooling, air, water), equipment failure, theft, and personnel loss (strikes, illness, access, transport).

This chapter explores each of these issues and discusses safeguards and countermeasures to protect against them. In many cases, you'll need a disaster recovery plan or a business continuity plan should a serious physical threat (such as an explosion, sabotage, or natural disaster) occur. Chapter 15, "Business Continuity Planning," and Chapter 16, "Disaster Recovery Planning," cover those topics in detail.

Site and Facility Design Considerations

It should be blatantly obvious if you've read the previous 18 chapters that without control over the physical environment, no collection of administrative, technical, or logical access controls can provide adequate security. If a malicious person can gain physical access to your facility or equipment, they can do just about anything they want, from destruction to disclosure or alteration. Physical controls are your first line of defense, and people are your last.

There are many aspects of and elements to implementing and maintaining physical security. A core or foundational element is selecting or designing the facility to house your IT infrastructure and your organization's operations. The process of selecting or designing facilities security always starts with a plan.

Secure Facility Plan

A secure facility plan outlines the security needs of your organization and emphasizes methods or mechanisms to employ to provide security. Such a plan is developed through a process known as *critical path analysis*. Critical path analysis is a systematic effort to identify relationships between mission-critical applications, processes, and operations and all the necessary supporting elements. For example, an e-commerce server used to sell products over the Web relies on Internet access, computer hardware, electricity, temperature control, storage facility, and so on.

When critical path analysis is performed properly, a complete picture of the interdependencies and interactions necessary to sustain the organization is produced. Once that analysis is complete, its results serve as a list of items to secure. The first step in designing a secure IT infrastructure is providing security for the basic requirements of the organization and its computers. These basic requirements include electricity, environmental controls (in other words, a building, air conditioning, heating, humidity control, and so on), and water/sewage.

While examining for critical paths, it is also important to evaluate completed or potential technology convergence. *Technology convergence* is the tendency for various technologies, solutions, utilities, and systems to evolve and merge over time. Often this results in multiple systems performing similar or redundant tasks or one system taking over the feature and abilities of another. While in some instances this can result in improved efficiency and cost savings, it can also represent a single point of failure and become a more valuable target for hackers and intruders. For example, if voice, video, fax, and data traffic all share a single connection path rather than individual paths, a single act of sabotage to the main connection is all that is required for intruders or thieves to sever external communications.

Security staff should participate in site and facility design considerations. Otherwise, many important aspects of physical security essential for the existence of logical security may be overlooked. With security staff involved in the physical facility design, you can be assured that your long-term security goals as an organization will be supported not just by your policies, personnel, and electronic equipment, but by the building itself.

Physical Security Controls

The security controls implemented to manage physical security can be divided into three groups: administrative, technical, and physical. Because these are the same categories used to describe access controls, it is vital to focus on the physical security aspects of these controls. *Administrative physical security controls* include facility construction and selection, site management, personnel controls, awareness training, and emergency response and procedures. *Technical physical security controls* include access controls, intrusion detection, alarms, closed-circuit television (CCTV), monitoring; heating, ventilating, and air conditioning (HVAC); power supplies; and fire detection and suppression. *Physical controls for physical security* include fencing, lighting, locks, construction materials, mantraps, dogs, and guards.

Corporate vs. Personal Property

Many business environments have both visible and invisible physical security controls. You see them at the post office, at the corner store, and in certain areas of your own computing environment. They are so pervasive that some people choose where they live based on their presence, as in gated access communities or secure apartment complexes.

Alison is a security analyst for a major technology corporation that specializes in data management. This company includes an in-house security staff (guards, administrators, and so on) that is capable of handling physical security breaches.

Brad experienced an intrusion—into his personal vehicle in the company parking lot. He asks Alison whether she observed or recorded anyone breaking into and entering his vehicle, but this is a personal item and not a company possession, and she has no control or regulation over damage to employee assets.

This is understandably unnerving for Brad, but he understands that she's protecting the business and not his belongings. When or where would you think it would be necessary to implement security measures for both? The usual answer is anywhere business assets are or might be involved. Had Brad been using a company vehicle parked in the company parking lot, then perhaps Alison could make allowances for an incidental break-in involving Brad's things, but even then she isn't responsible for their safekeeping. On the other hand, where key people are also important assets (executive staff at most enterprises, security analysts who work in sensitive positions, heads of state, and so forth), protection and safeguards usually extend to embrace them and their belongings as part of asset protection and risk mitigation. Of course, if danger to employees or what they carry with them becomes a problem, securing the parking garage with key cards and installing CCTV monitors on every floor begins to make sense. Simply put, if the costs of allowing break-ins to occur exceeds that of installing preventive measures, it's prudent to put them in place.

When designing physical security for an environment, focus on the functional order in which controls should be used. The order is as follows:

1. Deterrence
2. Denial
3. Detection
4. Delay

Security controls should be deployed so that initial attempts to access physical assets are *deterred* (boundary restrictions accomplish this). If deterrence fails, then direct access to physical assets should be *denied* (for example, locked vault doors). If denial fails, your system needs to *detect* intrusion (for example, using motion sensors), and the intruder should be *delayed* sufficiently in their access attempts to enable authorities to respond (for example, a cable lock on the asset). It's important to remember this order when deploying physical security controls: first deterrence, then denial, then detection, then delay.

Site Selection

Site selection should be based on the security needs of the organization. Cost, location, and size are important, but addressing the requirements of security should always take precedence. When choosing a site on which to build a facility or selecting a preexisting structure, be sure to examine every aspect of its location carefully.

Securing assets depends largely on site security, which involves numerous considerations and situational elements. Site location and construction play a crucial role in the overall site selection process. Susceptibility to riots, looting, break-ins, and vandalism or location within a high-crime area are obviously all poor choices but cannot always be dictated or controlled. Environmental threats such as fault lines, tornado/hurricane regions, and close proximity to other natural disasters present significant issues for the site selection process as well because you can't always avoid such threats.

Proximity to other buildings and businesses is another crucial consideration. What sorts of attention do they draw, and how does that affect your operation or facility? Proximity to emergency-response personnel is another consideration, along with other elements. Some companies can afford to buy or build their own campuses to keep neighboring elements out of play and to enable tighter access control and monitoring. However, not every company can exercise this option and must make do with what's available and affordable instead.

At a minimum, ensure that the building is designed to withstand fairly extreme weather conditions and that it can deter or fend off overt break-in attempts. Vulnerable entry points such as windows and doors tend to dominate such analysis, but you should also evaluate objects (trees, shrubs, or man-made items) that can obscure break-in attempts.

Visibility

Visibility is important. What is the surrounding terrain? Would it be easy to approach the facility by vehicle or on foot without being seen? The makeup of the surrounding area is also important. Is it in or near a residential, business, or industrial area? What is the local crime rate? Where are the closest emergency services located (fire, medical, police)? What unique hazards may be found in the vicinity (chemical plants, homeless shelters, universities, construction sites, and so on)?

Accessibility and Perimeter Security

The accessibility to the building or campus location is also important. Single entrances are great for providing security, but multiple entrances are better for evacuation during emergencies. What types of roads are nearby? What means of transportation are easily accessible (trains, highway, airport, shipping)? What about traffic levels throughout the day?

Keep in mind that accessibility is also constrained by the need for perimeter security. The needs of access and use should meld and support the implementation and operation of perimeter security. The use of physical access controls and monitoring personnel and equipment entering and leaving as well as auditing/logging all physical events are key elements in maintaining overall organizational security.

Natural Disasters

Another concern is the potential impact that natural disasters could make in the area. Is it prone to earthquakes, mudslides, sinkholes, fires, floods, hurricanes, tornadoes, falling rocks, snow, rainfall, ice, humidity, heat, extreme cold, and so on? You must prepare for natural disasters and equip your IT environment to either survive an event or be replaced easily.

Facility Design

When designing the construction of a facility, you must understand the level of security that your organization needs. A proper level of security must be planned and designed before construction begins.

Important issues to consider include combustibility, fire rating, construction materials, load rating, placement, and control of items such as walls, doors, ceilings, flooring, HVAC, power, water, sewage, gas, and so on. Forced intrusion, emergency access, resistance to entry, direction of entries and exits, use of alarms, and conductivity are other important aspects to evaluate. Every element within a facility should be evaluated in terms of how it could be used for and against the protection of the IT infrastructure and personnel (for example, positive flows for air and water from inside a facility to outside its boundaries).

There's also a well-established school of thought on "secure architecture" that's often called crime prevention through environmental design (CPTED). The guiding idea is to structure the physical environment and surroundings to influence individual decisions that potential offenders make before committing any criminal acts. The International CPTED Association is an excellent source for information on this subject (`www.cpted .net`), as is Oscar Newman's book *Creating Defensible Space,* published by HUD's Office of Policy Development and Research (free PDF download at `www.defensiblespace.com/ book.htm`).

Work Areas and Internal Security

The design and configuration of internal security, including work areas and visitor areas, should be considered carefully. There should not be equal access to all locations within a facility. Areas that contain assets of higher value or importance should have more restricted access. For example, anyone who enters the facility should be able to access the restrooms and the public telephone without going into sensitive areas, but only network administrators and security staff should have access to the server room. Valuable and confidential assets should be located in the heart or center of protection provided by a facility. In effect, you should focus on deploying concentric circles of physical protection. This type of configuration requires increased levels of authorization to gain access into more sensitive areas inside the facility.

Walls or partitions can be used to separate similar but distinct work areas. Such divisions deter casual shoulder surfing or eavesdropping (*shoulder surfing* is the act of gathering information from a system by observing the monitor or the use of the keyboard by the operator). Floor-to-ceiling walls should be used to separate areas with differing levels of sensitivity and confidentiality (where false or suspended ceilings are present, walls should cut these off as well to provide an unbroken physical barrier between more and less secure areas).

Each work area should be evaluated and assigned a classification just as IT assets are classified. Only people with clearance or classifications corresponding to the classification of the work area should be allowed access. Areas with different purposes or uses should be assigned different levels of access or restrictions. The more access to assets the equipment within an area offers, the more important become the restrictions that are used to control who enters those areas and what activities they are allowed to perform.

Your facility security design process should support the implementation and operation of internal security. In addition to the management of workers in proper work spaces, you should address visitors and visitor control. Should there be an escort requirement for visitors, and what other forms of visitor control should be implemented? In addition to basic physical security tools such as keys and locks, mechanisms such as mantraps, video cameras, written logs, security guards, and RFID ID tags should be implemented.

Server Rooms and Data Center Security

Server rooms, data centers, communications rooms, wiring closets, server vaults, and IT closets are enclosed, restricted, and protected rooms where your mission-critical servers and network devices are housed. Centralized server rooms need not be human compatible. In fact, the more human incompatible a server room is, the more protection it will offer against casual and determined attacks. Human incompatibility can be accomplished by including Halotron, PyroGen, or other halon-substitute oxygen-displacement fire detection and extinguishing systems, low temperatures, little or no lighting, and equipment stacked with little room to maneuver. Server rooms should be designed to support optimal operation of the IT infrastructure and to block unauthorized human access or intervention.

Server rooms should be located at the core of the building. Try to avoid locating these rooms on the ground floor, the top floor, and the basement whenever possible. Additionally, the server room should be located away from water, gas, and sewage lines. These pose too large a risk of leakage or flooding, which can cause serious damage and downtime.

  The walls of your server room should also have a one-hour minimum fire rating.

⊕ Real World Scenario

Making Servers Inaccessible

The running joke in the IT security realm is that the most secure computer is one that is disconnected from the network and sealed in a room with no doors or windows. No, seriously, that's the joke. But there's a massive grain of truth and irony in it as well.

Carlos operates security processes and platforms for a financial banking firm, and he knows all about one-way systems and unreachable devices. Sensitive business transactions occur in fractions of a second, and one wrong move could pose serious risks to data and involved parties.

In his experience, Carlos knows that the least accessible and least human-friendly places are his most valuable assets, so he stores many of his machines inside a separate bank vault. You'd have to be a talented burglar, a skilled safecracker, and a determined computer attacker to breach his security defenses.

Not all business applications and processes warrant this extreme sort of prevention. What security recommendations might you suggest to make a server more inconvenient or inaccessible, short of dedicating a vault? A basement with limited access or an interior room with no windows and only one entry/exit point makes an excellent substitute when an empty vault isn't available. The key is to select a space with limited access and then to establish serious hurdles to entry (especially unauthorized entry). CCTV monitoring on the door and motion detectors inside the space can also help maintain proper attention to who is coming and going.

Visitors

If a facility employs restricted areas to control physical security, a mechanism to handle visitors is required. Often an escort is assigned to visitors, and their access and activities are monitored closely. Failing to track the actions of outsiders when they are allowed into a protected area can result in malicious activity against the most protected assets.

In the real world, you will deploy multiple layers of physical access controls to manage the traffic of authorized and unauthorized individuals within your facility. The outermost layer will be lighting. The entire outer perimeter of your site should be clearly lit. This enables easy identification of personnel and makes it easier to notice intrusions and intimidate potential intruders. Just inside the lighted area, place a fence or wall designed to prevent intrusion. Specific controlled points along that fence or wall should be points for entry or exit. These should have gates, turnstiles, or mantraps all monitored by CCTV and security guards. Identification and authentication should be required at all entry points before entrance is granted.

Within the facility, areas of different sensitivity or confidentiality levels should be distinctly separated and compartmentalized. This is especially true for public areas and areas accessible to visitors. An additional identification/authentication process to validate the need to enter should be required when anyone moves from one area to another. The most sensitive resources and systems should be isolated from all but the most privileged personnel and located at the center or core of the facility.

Forms of Physical Access Controls

You can deploy many types of physical access control mechanisms in an environment to control, monitor, and manage access to a facility. These range from deterrents to detection mechanisms.

The various sections, divisions, or areas within a site or facility should be clearly designated as public, private, or restricted. Each of these areas requires unique and focused physical access controls, monitoring, and prevention mechanisms. The following sections discuss many such mechanisms that may be used to separate, isolate, and control access to various areas within a site.

Fences, Gates, Turnstiles, and Mantraps

A *fence* is a perimeter-defining device. Fences are used to clearly differentiate between areas that are under a specific level of security protection and those that aren't. Fencing can include a wide range of components, materials, and construction methods. It can consist of stripes painted on the ground, chain link fences, barbed wire, concrete walls, and even invisible perimeters using laser, motion, or heat detectors. Various types of fences are effective against different types of intruders:

- Fences 3 to 4 feet high deter casual trespassers.

- Fences 6 to 7 feet high are too hard to climb easily and deter most intruders, except determined ones.

- Fences 8 or more feet high with three strands of barbed wire deter even determined intruders.

A *gate* is a controlled exit and entry point in a fence. The deterrent level of a gate must be equivalent to the deterrent level of the fence to sustain the effectiveness of the fence as a whole. Hinges and locking/closing mechanisms should be hardened against tampering, destruction, or removal. When a gate is closed, it should not offer any additional access vulnerabilities. Keep the number of gates to a minimum. They can be manned by guards. When they're not protected by guards, use of dogs or CCTV is recommended.

A *turnstile* (see Figure 19.1) is a form of gate that prevents more than one person at a time from gaining entry and often restricts movement in one direction. It is used to gain entry but not to exit, or vice versa. A turnstile is basically the fencing equivalent of a secured revolving door.

A *mantrap* is a double set of doors that is often protected by a guard (also shown in Figure 19.1) or some other physical layout that prevents piggybacking and can trap individuals at the discretion of security personnel. The purpose of a mantrap is to immobilize a subject until their identity and authentication is verified. If a subject is authorized for entry, the inner door opens, allowing entry into the facility or onto the premises. If a subject is not authorized, both doors remain closed and locked until an escort (typically a guard or a police officer) arrives to escort the subject off the property or arrest the subject for trespassing (this is called a *delay feature*). Often a mantrap includes a scale to prevent piggybacking or tailgating.

FIGURE 19.1   A secure physical boundary with a mantrap and a turnstile

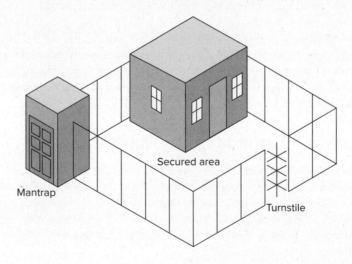

Lighting

Lighting is a commonly used form of perimeter security control. The primary purpose of lighting is to discourage casual intruders, trespassers, prowlers, or would-be thieves who would rather perform their misdeeds in the dark. However, lighting is not a strong deterrent. It should not be used as the primary or sole protection mechanism except in areas with a low threat level.

Lighting should not illuminate the positions of guards, dogs, patrol posts, or other similar security elements. It should be combined with guards, dogs, CCTV, or some other form of intrusion detection or surveillance mechanism. Lighting must not cause a nuisance or problem for nearby residents, roads, railways, airports, and so on. It should also never cause glare or reflective distraction to guards, dogs, and monitoring equipment, which could otherwise aid attackers during break-in attempts.

It is generally accepted as a de facto standard that lighting used for perimeter protection should illuminate critical areas with 2 candle feet of power. Another common issue for the use of lighting is the placement of the lights. Standards seem to indicate that light poles should be placed the same distance apart as the diameter of the illuminated area created by illumination elements. Thus, if a lighted area is 40 feet in diameter, poles should be 40 feet apart.

Security Guards and Dogs

All physical security controls, whether static deterrents or active detection and surveillance mechanisms, ultimately rely on personnel to intervene and stop actual intrusions and attacks. Security guards exist to fulfill this need. Guards can be posted around a perimeter or inside to monitor access points or watch detection and surveillance monitors. The real benefit of guards is that they are able to adapt and react to various conditions or situations. Guards can learn and recognize attack and intrusion activities and patterns, can adjust to a changing environment, and can make decisions and judgment calls. Security guards are often an appropriate security control when immediate situation handling and decision making onsite is necessary.

Unfortunately, using security guards is not a perfect solution. There are numerous disadvantages to deploying, maintaining, and relying on security guards. Not all environments and facilities support security guards. This may be because of actual human incompatibility or the layout, design, location, and construction of the facility. Not all security guards are themselves reliable. Prescreening, bonding, and training do not guarantee that you won't end up with an ineffective or unreliable security guard.

Even if a guard is initially reliable, guards are subject to physical injury and illness, take vacations, can become distracted, are vulnerable to social engineering, and may become unemployable because of substance abuse. In addition, security guards usually offer protection only up to the point at which their life is endangered. Additionally, security guards are usually unaware of the scope of the operations within a facility and are therefore not thoroughly equipped to know how to respond to every situation. Finally, security guards are expensive.

Guard dogs can be an alternative to security guards. They can often be deployed as a perimeter security control. As a detection and deterrent, dogs are extremely effective. However, dogs are costly, require a high level of maintenance, and impose serious insurance and liability requirements.

Keys and Combination Locks

Locks keep closed doors closed. They are designed and deployed to prevent access to everyone without proper authorization. A *lock* is a crude form of an identification and authorization mechanism. If you possess the correct key or combination, you are considered authorized and permitted entry. Key-based locks are the most common and inexpensive forms of physical access control devices. These are often known as *preset locks*. These types of locks are subject to picking, which is often categorized under a class of lock mechanism attacks called *shimming*.

 Real World Scenario

Using Locks

Keys or combination locks—which do you choose and for what purposes?

Ultimately, there will always be forgetful users. Elise constantly forgets her combination, and Francis can never remember to bring his security key card to work. Gino maintains a pessimistic outlook in his administrative style, so he's keen on putting combinations and key card accesses in all the right places.

Under what circumstances or conditions might you employ a combination lock, and where might you instead opt for a key or key card? What options put you at greater risk of loss if someone discovers the combination or finds the key? Can you be certain that these single points of failure do not significantly pose a risk to the protected assets?

Many organizations typically utilize separate forms of key or combination accesses throughout several areas of the facility. Key and key card access is granted at select shared entry points (exterior access into the building, access into interior rooms), and combination locks control access to individual entry points (storage lockers, file cabinets, and so on).

Programmable or combination locks offer a broader range of control than preset locks. Some programmable locks can be configured with multiple valid access combinations or may include digital or electronic controls employing keypads, smart cards, or cipher devices. For instance, an *electronic access control (EAC) lock* incorporates three elements: an electromagnet to keep the door closed, a credential reader to authenticate subjects and to disable the electromagnet, and a sensor to reengage the electromagnet when the door is closed.

Locks serve as an alternative to security guards as a perimeter entrance access control device. A gate or door can be opened and closed to allow access by a security guard who verifies your identity before granting access, or the lock itself can serve as the verification device that also grants or restricts entry.

Badges

Badges, *identification cards*, and *security IDs* are forms of physical identification and/ or electronic access control devices. A badge can be as simple as a name tag indicating whether you are a valid employee or a visitor. Or it can be as complex as a smart card or token device that employs multifactor authentication to verify and prove your identity and provide authentication and authorization to access a facility, specific rooms, or secured workstations. Badges often include pictures, magnetic strips with encoded data, and personal details to help a security guard verify identity.

Badges can be used in environments in which physical access is primarily controlled by security guards. In such conditions, the badge serves as a visual identification tool for the guards. They can verify your identity by comparing your picture to your person and consult a printed or electronic roster of authorized personnel to determine whether you have valid access.

Badges can also serve in environments guarded by scanning devices rather than security guards. In such conditions, a badge can be used either for identification or for authentication. When a badge is used for identification, it is swiped in a device, and then the badge owner must provide one or more authentication factors, such as a password, passphrase, or biological trait (if a biometric device is used). When a badge is used for authentication, the badge owner provides an ID, username, and so on and then swipes the badge to authenticate.

Motion Detectors

A *motion detector*, or *motion sensor*, is a device that senses movement or sound in a specific area. Many types of motion detectors exist, including infrared, heat, wave pattern, capacitance, photoelectric, and passive audio.

An **infrared motion detector** monitors for significant or meaningful changes in the infrared lighting pattern of a monitored area.

A **heat-based motion detector** monitors for significant or meaningful changes in the heat levels and patterns in a monitored area.

A **wave pattern motion detector** transmits a consistent low ultrasonic or high microwave frequency signal into a monitored area and monitors for significant or meaningful changes or disturbances in the reflected pattern.

A **capacitance motion detector** senses changes in the electrical or magnetic field surrounding a monitored object.

A **photoelectric motion detector** senses changes in visible light levels for the monitored area. Photoelectric motion detectors are usually deployed in internal rooms that have no windows and are kept dark.

A **passive audio motion detector** listens for abnormal sounds in the monitored area.

Intrusion Alarms

Whenever a motion detector registers a significant or meaningful change in the environment, it triggers an alarm. An *alarm* is a separate mechanism that triggers a deterrent, a repellent, and/or a notification.

Deterrent Alarms   Alarms that trigger deterrents may engage additional locks, shut doors, and so on. The goal of such an alarm is to make further intrusion or attack more difficult.

Repellant Alarms   Alarms that trigger repellants usually sound an audio siren or bell and turn on lights. These kinds of alarms are used to discourage intruders or attackers from continuing their malicious or trespassing activities and force them off the premises.

Notification Alarms   Alarms that trigger notification are often silent from the intruder/ attacker perspective but record data about the incident and notify administrators, security guards, and law enforcement. A recording of an incident can take the form of log files and/ or CCTV tapes. The purpose of a silent alarm is to bring authorized security personnel to the location of the intrusion or attack in hopes of catching the person(s) committing the unwanted or unauthorized acts.

Alarms are also categorized by where they are located: local, centralized or proprietary, or auxiliary.

Local Alarm System   *Local alarm systems* must broadcast an audible (up to 120 decibel, or db) alarm signal that can be easily heard up to 400 feet away. Additionally, they must be protected from tampering and disablement, usually by security guards. For a local alarm system to be effective, there must be a security team or guards positioned nearby who can respond when the alarm is triggered.

Central Station System   The alarm is usually silent locally, but offsite monitoring agents are notified so they can respond to the security breach. Most residential security systems are of this type. Most central station systems are well-known or national security companies, such as Brinks and ADT. A *proprietary system* is similar to a central station system, but the host organization has its own onsite security staff waiting to respond to security breaches.

Auxiliary Station   *Auxiliary alarm systems* can be added to either local or centralized alarm systems. When the security perimeter is breached, emergency services are notified to respond to the incident and arrive at the location. This could include fire, police, and medical services.

Two or more of these types of intrusion and alarm systems can be incorporated in a single solution.

Secondary Verification Mechanisms

When motion detectors, sensors, and alarms are used, secondary verification mechanisms should be in place. As the sensitivity of these devices increases, false triggers occur more often. Innocuous events such as the presence of animals, birds, bugs, or authorized personnel can trigger false alarms. Deploying two or more detection and sensor systems and requiring two or more triggers in quick succession to occur before an alarm is issued may significantly reduce false alarms and increase the likelihood that alarms indicate actual intrusions or attacks.

CCTV is a security mechanism related to motion detectors, sensors, and alarms. However, CCTV is not an automated detection-and-response system. CCTV requires personnel to watch the captured video to detect suspicious and malicious activities and to trigger alarms. Security cameras can expand the effective visible range of a security guard, therefore increasing the scope of the oversight. In many cases, CCTV is not used as a primary detection tool because of the high cost of paying a person to sit and watch the video screens. Instead, it is used as a secondary or follow-up mechanism that is reviewed after a trigger from an automated system occurs. In fact, the same logic used for auditing and audit trails is used for CCTV and recorded events. A CCTV is a preventive measure, whereas reviewing recorded events is a detective measure.

 Real World Scenario

Secondary Verification

As illustrated in the previous real-world scenario, Gino was at constant risk of security breaches because Elise is constantly forgetting (and therefore writes down) every password, whereas Francis is habitually forgetful about the location of his key card. What happens when someone else comes into possession of either of these items and has knowledge of how or where to use them?

Gino's biggest advantage will be any secondary verification mechanisms he has established in the workplace. This may include a CCTV system that identifies the face of the person who uses a key card for access or inputs a combination in some area designated under surveillance. Even videotape logs of ingress and egress through checkpoints can be helpful when it comes to chasing down accidental or deliberate access abuses.

With known "problem users" or "problem identities," many security systems can issue notifications or alerts when those identities are used. Depending on the systems that are available, and the risks that unauthorized access could pose, human follow-up may or may not be warranted. But any time Elise (or somebody who uses that identity) logs onto a system or anytime Francis's key card is used, a floating or roving security guard could be dispatched to ensure that everything is on the up and up. Of course, it's probably also a good idea to have Elise's and Francis's managers counsel them on the appropriate use (and storage) of passwords and key cards, just to make sure they understand the potential risks involved too.

Technical Controls

Technical controls most often employed as access control mechanisms to manage physical access include smart/dumb cards and biometrics. In addition to such controls, audit trails, access logs, and intrusion detection systems (IDSs) can serve as physical security mechanisms.

Smart Cards

Smart cards are credit-card-sized IDs, badges, or security passes with an embedded magnetic strip, bar code, or integrated circuit chip. They contain information about the authorized bearer that can be used for identification and/or authentication purposes. Some smart cards can even process information or store reasonable amounts of data in a memory chip. A smart card may be known by several phrases or terms:

- An identity token containing integrated circuits (ICs)
- A processor IC card
- An IC card with an ISO 7816 interface

Smart cards are often viewed as a complete security solution, but they should not be considered complete by themselves. As with any single security mechanism, smart cards are subject to weaknesses and vulnerabilities. Smart cards can fall prey to physical attacks, logical attacks, Trojan horse attacks, or social-engineering attacks.

Memory cards are machine-readable ID cards with a magnetic strip. Like a credit card, debit card, or ATM card, memory cards can retain a small amount of data but are unable to process data like a smart card. Memory cards often function as a type of two-factor control: The card is "something you have" and its PIN "something you know." However, memory cards are easy to copy or duplicate and are insufficient for authentication purposes in a secure environment.

Proximity Readers

In addition to smart and dumb cards, proximity readers can be used to control physical access. A *proximity reader* can be a passive device, a field-powered device, or a transponder. The proximity device is worn or held by the authorized bearer. When it passes a proximity reader, the reader is able to determine who the bearer is and whether they have authorized access. A passive device reflects or otherwise alters the electromagnetic field generated by the reader. This alteration is detected by the reader.

The passive device has no active electronics; it is just a small magnet with specific properties (like antitheft devices commonly found on DVDs). A field-powered device has electronics that activate when the device enters the electromagnetic field that the reader generates. Such devices actually generate electricity from an EM field to power themselves (such as card readers that require only that the access card be waved within inches of the reader to unlock doors). A transponder device is self-powered and transmits a signal received by the reader. This can occur consistently or only at the press of a button (like a garage door opener or car alarm keyfob).

In addition to smart/dumb cards and proximity readers, physical access can be managed with radio frequency identification (RFID) or biometric access control devices. See Chapter 1, "Access Control," for a description of biometric devices. These and other devices, such as cable locks, can support the protection and securing of equipment.

Access Abuses

No matter what form of physical access control is used, a security guard or other monitoring system must be deployed to prevent abuse, masquerading, and piggybacking. Examples of abuses of physical access controls are propping open secured doors and bypassing locks or access controls. *Masquerading* is using someone else's security ID to gain entry into a facility. *Piggybacking* is following someone through a secured gate or doorway without being identified or authorized personally.

Audit trails and access logs are useful tools even for physical access control. They may need to be created manually by security guards. Or they can be generated automatically if sufficient automated access control mechanisms (such as smart cards and certain proximity readers) are in use. The time a subject requests entry, the result of the authentication process, and the length of time the secured gate remains open are important elements to include in audit trails and access logs. In addition to using the electronic or paper trail, consider monitoring entry points with CCTV. CCTV enables you to compare the audit trails and access logs with a visual recording of the events. Such information is critical to reconstruct the events for an intrusion, breach, or attack.

Intrusion Detection Systems

Intrusion detection systems are systems—automated or manual—designed to detect an attempted intrusion, breach, or attack; the use of an unauthorized entry point; or the occurrence of some specific event at an unauthorized or abnormal time. Intrusion detection systems used to monitor physical activity may include security guards, automated access controls, and motion detectors as well as other specialty monitoring techniques. (These are discussed in more detail in the previous sections "Motion Detectors" and "Intrusion Alarms.")

Physical intrusion detection systems, also called *burglar alarms*, detect unauthorized activities and notify the authorities (internal security or external law enforcement). The most common type of system uses a simple circuit (aka dry contact switches) consisting of foil tape in entrance points to detect when a door or window has been opened.

An intrusion detection mechanism is useful only if it is connected to an intrusion alarm. (See "Intrusion Alarms," earlier in this chapter.) An intrusion alarm notifies authorities about a breach of physical security.

There are two aspects of any intrusion detection and alarm system that can cause it to fail: how it gets its power and how it communicates. If the system loses power, the alarm will not function. Thus, a reliable detection and alarm system has a battery backup with enough stored power for 24 hours of operation.

If communication lines are cut, an alarm may not function and security personnel and emergency services will not be notified. Thus, a reliable detection and alarm system incorporates a *heartbeat sensor* for line supervision. A heartbeat sensor is a mechanism by which the communication pathway is either constantly or periodically checked with a test signal. If the receiving station detects a failed heartbeat signal, the alarm triggers automatically. Both measures are designed to prevent intruders from circumventing the detection and alarm system.

Emanation Security

Many electrical devices emanate electrical signals or radiation that can be intercepted by unauthorized individuals. These signals may contain confidential, sensitive, or private data. Obvious examples of emanation devices are wireless networking equipment and mobile phones, but many other devices are vulnerable to interception. Other examples include monitors, modems, and internal or external media drives (hard drives, floppy drives, CDs, and so on). With the right equipment, unauthorized users can intercept electromagnetic or radio frequency signals (collectively known as *emanations*) from these devices and interpret them to extract confidential data.

TEMPEST

Clearly, if a device emits a signal that someone outside your organization can intercept, some security protection is needed. The types of countermeasures and safeguards used to protect against emanation attacks are known as TEMPEST countermeasures. TEMPEST was originally a government research study aimed at protecting electronic equipment from the electromagnetic pulse (EMP) emitted during nuclear explosions. It has since expanded to a general study of monitoring emanations and preventing their interception. Thus, TEMPEST is now a formal name for a broad category of activities.

Countermeasures

TEMPEST countermeasures include Faraday cages, white noise, and control zones.

Faraday Cage   A *Faraday cage* is a box, mobile room, or entire building designed with an external metal skin, often a wire mesh that fully surrounds an area on all sides (in other words, front, back, left, right, top, and bottom). This metal skin acts as an EMI absorbing capacitor (which is why it's named after Michael Faraday, a pioneer in the field of electromagnetism) that prevents electromagnetic signals (emanations) from exiting or entering the area that the cage encloses. Faraday cages are quite effective at blocking EM signals.

In fact, inside an active Faraday cage, mobile phones do not work, and you can't pick up broadcast radio or television stations.

White Noise   White noise simply means broadcasting false traffic at all times to mask and hide the presence of real emanations. White noise can consist of a real signal from another source that is not confidential, a constant signal at a specific frequency, a randomly variable signal (such as the white noise heard between radio stations or television stations), or even a jam signal that causes interception equipment to fail. White noise is most effective when created around the perimeter of an area so that it is broadcast outward to protect the internal area where emanations may be needed for normal operations.

 White noise describes any random sound, signal, or process that can drown out meaningful information. This can vary from audible frequencies to inaudible electronic transmissions, and it may even involve the deliberate act of creating line or traffic noise to disguise origins or disrupt listening devices.

Control Zone   A third type of TEMPEST countermeasure, a *control zone*, is simply the implementation of either a Faraday cage or white noise generation to protect a specific area in an environment; the rest of the environment is not affected. A control zone can be a room, a floor, or an entire building. Control zones are those areas where emanation signals are supported and used by necessary equipment, such as wireless networking, mobile phones, radios, and televisions. Outside the control zones, emanation interception is blocked or prevented through the use of various TEMPEST countermeasures.

Environment and Life Safety

An important aspect of physical access control and maintaining the security of a facility is protecting the basic elements of the environment and protecting human life. In all circumstances and under all conditions, the most important aspect of security is protecting people. Thus, preventing harm to people is the most important goal for all security solutions.

Personnel Privacy and Safety

Part of maintaining safety for personnel is maintaining the basic environment of a facility. For short periods of time, people can survive without water, food, air conditioning, and power. But in some cases, the loss of these elements can have disastrous results, or they can be symptoms of more immediate and dangerous problems. Flooding, fires, release of toxic materials, and natural disasters all threaten human life as well as the stability of a facility. Physical security procedures should focus on protecting human life and then on restoring the safety of the environment and restoring the utilities necessary for the IT infrastructure to function.

People should always be your top priority. Only after personnel are safe can you consider addressing business continuity. Many organizations adopt occupant emergency plans (OEPs) to guide and assist with sustaining personnel safety in the wake of a disaster. The OEP provides guidance on how to minimize threats to life, prevent injury, manage duress, handle travel, provide for safety monitoring, and protect property from damage in the event of a destructive physical event. The OEP does not address IT issues or business continuity, just personnel and general property. The BCP and DRP address IT and business continuity and recovery issues.

Power and Electricity

Power supplied by electric companies is not always consistent and clean. Most electronic equipment demands clean power to function properly. Equipment damage from power fluctuations is a common occurrence. Many organizations opt to manage their own power through various means. An *uninterruptible power supply (UPS)* is a type of self-charging battery that can be used to supply consistent clean power to sensitive equipment. A UPS functions by taking power in from the wall outlet, storing it in a battery, pulling power out of the battery, and then feeding that power to whatever devices are connected to it. By directing current through its battery, it is able to maintain a consistent clean power supply. A UPS has a second function, one that is often used as a selling point: it provides continuous power even after the primary power source fails. A UPS can continue to supply power for minutes or hours, depending on its capacity and how much power the equipment attached to it needs.

Another means to ensure that equipment is not harmed by power fluctuations requires use of power strips with surge protectors. A surge protector includes a fuse that will blow before power levels change enough to cause damage to equipment. However, once a surge protector's fuse or circuit is tripped, current flow is completely interrupted. Surge protectors should be used only when instant termination of electricity will not cause damage or loss to the equipment. Otherwise, a UPS should be employed instead.

If maintaining operations for considerable time in spite of a brownout or blackout is a necessity, onsite electric generators are required. Such generators turn on automatically when a power failure is detected. Most generators operate using a fuel tank of liquid or gaseous propellant that must be maintained to ensure reliability. Electric generators are considered alternate or backup power sources.

The problems with power are numerous. Here is a list of terms associated with power issues you should know:

Fault   A momentary loss of power

Blackout   A complete loss of power

Sag   Momentary low voltage

Brownout   Prolonged low voltage

Spike   Momentary high voltage

Surge   Prolonged high voltage

Inrush   An initial surge of power usually associated with connecting to a power source, whether primary or alternate/secondary

Noise   A steady interfering power disturbance or fluctuation

Transient   A short duration of line noise disturbance

Clean   Nonfluctuating pure power

Ground   The wire in an electrical circuit that is grounded

A brownout is an interesting power issue because its definition references ANSI standards for power. Those standards allow for an 8 percent drop in power between the power source and the facility meter and a drop of 3.5 percent between the facility meter and the wall outlet before any prolonged instance of low voltage is labeled as a brownout. The ANSI standard further distinguishes that low voltage outside your meter is to be repaired by the power company, whereas an internal brownout is your responsibility.

Noise

Noise can cause more than just problems with how equipment functions; it can also interfere with the quality of communications, transmissions, and playback. Noise generated by electric current can affect any means of data transmission that relies on electromagnetic transport mechanisms, such as telephone, cellular, television, audio, radio, and network mechanisms.

There are two types of *electromagnetic interference (EMI)*: common mode and traverse mode. *Common mode noise* is generated by a difference in power between the hot and ground wires of a power source or operating electrical equipment. *Traverse mode noise* is generated by a difference in power between the hot and neutral wires of a power source or operating electrical equipment.

Radio frequency interference (RFI) is another source of noise and interference that can affect many of the same systems as EMI. A wide range of common electrical appliances generate RFI, including fluorescent lights, electrical cables, electric space heaters, computers, elevators, motors, and electric magnets, so it's important to locate all such equipment when deploying IT systems and infrastructure elements.

Protecting your power supply and your equipment from noise is an important part of maintaining a productive and functioning environment for your IT infrastructure. Steps to take for this kind of protection include providing for sufficient power conditioning, establishing proper grounding, shielding all cables, and limiting exposure to EMI and RFI sources.

Temperature, Humidity, and Static

In addition to power considerations, maintaining the environment involves control over the HVAC mechanisms. Rooms intended primarily to house computers should be kept at 60 to 75 degrees Fahrenheit (15 to 23 degrees Celsius). Humidity in a computer room should be maintained between 40 and 60 percent. Too much humidity can cause corrosion. Too little humidity causes static electricity. Even on nonstatic carpeting, if the environment has low humidity, it is still possible to generate 20,000-volt static discharges. As you can see in Table 19.1, even minimal levels of static discharge can destroy electronic equipment.

TABLE 19.1   Static voltage and damage

Static voltage	Possible damage
40	Destruction of sensitive circuits and other electronic components
1,000	Scrambling of monitor displays
1,500	Destruction of data stored on hard drives
2,000	Abrupt system shutdown
4,000	Printer jam or component damage
17,000	Permanent circuit damage

Water

Water leakage and flooding should be addressed in your environmental safety policy and procedures. Plumbing leaks are not an everyday occurrence, but when they do happen, they can cause significant damage.

Water and electricity don't mix. If your computer systems come in contact with water, especially while they are operating, damage is sure to occur. Plus, water and electricity create a serious risk of electrocution for nearby personnel. Whenever possible, locate server rooms, data centers, and critical computer equipment away from any water source or transport pipes. You may also want to install water detection circuits on the floor around mission-critical systems. Water detection circuits will sound an alarm and alert you if water is encroaching upon the equipment.

To minimize emergencies, be familiar with shutoff valves and drainage locations. In addition to monitoring for plumbing leaks, you should evaluate your facility's ability to handle severe rain or flooding in its vicinity. Is the facility located on a hill or in a valley? Is there sufficient drainage? Is there a history of flooding or accumulation of standing water? Is a server room in the basement or on the first floor?

Fire Prevention, Detection, and Suppression

Fire prevention, detection, and suppression must not be overlooked. Protecting personnel from harm should always be the most important goal of any security or protection system. In addition to protecting people, fire detection and suppression is designed to keep damage caused by fire, smoke, heat, and suppression materials to a minimum, especially as regards the IT infrastructure.

Basic fire education involves knowledge of the fire triangle (see Figure 19.2). The three corners of the triangle represent fire, heat, and oxygen. The center of the triangle represents the chemical reaction among these three elements. The point of the fire triangle is to illustrate that if you can remove any one of the four items from the fire triangle, the fire can be extinguished. Different suppression mediums address different aspects of the fire:

FIGURE 19.2   The fire triangle

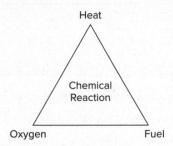

- Water suppresses the temperature.

- Soda acid and other dry powders suppress the fuel supply.

- CO_2 suppresses the oxygen supply.

- Halon substitutes and other nonflammable gases interfere with the chemistry of combustion and/or suppress the oxygen supply.

When selecting a suppression medium, consider what aspect of the fire triangle it addresses, what this really represents, how effective the suppression medium usually is, and what impact the suppression medium will exert on your environment.

In addition to understanding the fire triangle, you should understand the stages of fire. Fires go through numerous stages, and Figure 19.3 addresses the four most vital stages.

FIGURE 19.3   The four primary stages of fire

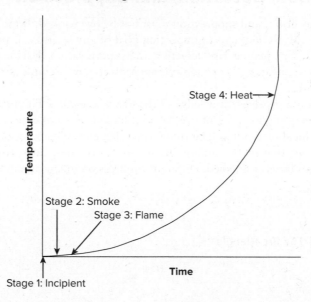

Stage 1: The incipient stage   At this stage, there is only air ionization but no smoke.

Stage 2: The smoke stage   In Stage 2, smoke is visible from the point of ignition.

Stage 3: The flame stage   This is when a flame can be seen with the naked eye.

Stage 4: The heat stage   At Stage 4, the fire is considerably further down the timescale to the point where there is an intense heat buildup and everything in the area burns.

The earlier a fire is detected, the easier it is to extinguish and the less damage it and its suppression medium(s) can cause.

One of the basics of fire management is proper personnel awareness training. Everyone should be thoroughly familiar with the fire suppression mechanisms in their facility. Everyone should also be familiar with at least two evacuation routes from their primary work area and know how to locate evacuation routes elsewhere in the facility. Personnel should be trained in the location and use of fire extinguishers. Other items to include in fire or general emergency-response training include cardiopulmonary resuscitation (CPR), emergency shutdown procedures, and a pre-established rendezvous location or safety verification mechanism (such as voicemail).

Most fires in a data center are caused by overloaded electrical distribution outlets.

Fire Extinguishers

There are several types of fire extinguishers. Understanding what type to use on various forms of fire is essential to effective fire suppression. If a fire extinguisher is used improperly or the wrong form of fire extinguisher is used, the fire could spread and intensify instead of being quenched. Fire extinguishers are to be used only when a fire is still in the incipient stage. Table 19.2 lists the three common types of fire extinguishers.

TABLE 19.2   Fire extinguisher classes

Class	Type	Suppression material
A	Common combustibles	Water, soda acid (a dry powder or liquid chemical)
B	Liquids	CO_2, halon*, soda acid
C	Electrical	CO_2, halon*
D	Metal	Dry powder

* Halon or an EPA-approved halon substitute

Water cannot be used on Class B fires because it splashes the burning liquids and such liquids usually float on water. Water cannot be used on Class C fires because of the potential for electrocution. Oxygen suppression cannot be used on metal fires because burning metal produces its own oxygen.

Fire Detection Systems

To properly protect a facility from fire requires installing an automated detection and suppression system. There are many types of fire detection systems. Fixed-temperature detection systems trigger suppression when a specific temperature is reached. The trigger is usually a metal or plastic component that is in the sprinkler head and melts at a specific temperature. Rate-of-rise detection systems trigger suppression when the speed at which the temperature changes reaches a specific level. Flame-actuated systems trigger suppression based on the infrared energy of flames. Smoke-actuated systems use photoelectric or radioactive ionization sensors as triggers.

Most fire detection systems can be linked to fire response service notification mechanisms. When suppression is triggered, such linked systems will contact the local fire response team and request aid using an automated message or alarm.

To be effective, fire detectors need to be placed strategically. Don't forget to place them inside dropped ceilings and raised floors, in server rooms, in private offices and public areas, in HVAC vents, in elevator shafts, in the basement, and so on.

As for suppression mechanisms used, they can be based on water or on a fire suppression gas system. Water is common in human-friendly environments, whereas gaseous systems are more appropriate for computer rooms where personnel typically do not reside.

Water Suppression Systems

There are four main types of water suppression systems:

- A *wet pipe system* (also known as a *closed head system*) is always full of water. Water discharges immediately when suppression is triggered.

- A *dry pipe system* contains compressed air. Once suppression is triggered, the air escapes, opening a water valve that in turn causes the pipes to fill and discharge water into the environment.

- A *deluge system* is another form of dry pipe system that uses larger pipes and therefore delivers a significantly larger volume of water. Deluge systems are inappropriate for environments that contain electronics and computers.

- A *preaction system* is a combination dry pipe/wet pipe system. The system exists as a dry pipe until the initial stages of a fire (smoke, heat, and so on) are detected, and then the pipes are filled with water. The water is released only after the sprinkler head activation triggers are melted by sufficient heat. If the fire is quenched before sprinklers are triggered, pipes can be manually emptied and reset. This also allows manual intervention to stop the release of water before sprinkler triggering occurs.

Preaction systems are the most appropriate water-based system for environments that house both computers and humans together.

The most common cause of failure for a water-based system is human error, such as turning off a water source when a fire occurs or triggering water release when there is no fire.

Gas Discharge Systems

Gas discharge systems are usually more effective than water discharge systems. However, gas discharge systems should not be used in environments in which people are located. Gas discharge systems usually remove the oxygen from the air, thus making them hazardous to personnel. They employ a pressurized gaseous suppression medium, such as CO_2, halon, or FM-200 (a halon replacement).

Halon is an effective fire suppression compound (it starves a fire of oxygen by disrupting the chemical reaction between oxygen and combustible materials), but it degrades into toxic gases at 900 degrees Fahrenheit. Also, it is not environmentally friendly (it is an ozone-depleting substance). In 1994, the EPA banned the manufacture of halon in the United States. It is also illegal to import halon manufactured after 1994. (Production of halon 1301, halon 1211, and halon 2403 ceased in developed countries on December 31, 2003.) However, according to the Montreal Protocol, you can obtain halon by contacting a halon recycling facility. The EPA seeks to exhaust existing stocks of halon to take this substance out of circulation.

Owing to issues with halon, it is often replaced by a more ecologically friendly and less toxic medium. The following list itemizes various EPA-approved substitutes for halon (see `http://www.berr.gov.uk/files/file29105.pdf` for more information):

- FM-200 (HFC-227ea)
- CEA-410 or CEA-308
- NAF-S-III (HCFC Blend A)
- FE-13 (HCFC-23)
- Argon (IG55) or Argonite (IG01)
- Inergen (IG541)

You can also replace halon substitutes with low-pressure water mists, but such systems are usually not employed in computer rooms or electrical equipment storage facilities. A low-pressure water mist is a vapor cloud used to quickly reduce the temperature in an area.

Damage

Addressing fire detection and suppression includes dealing with possible contamination and damage caused by a fire. The destructive elements of a fire include smoke and heat, but they also include the suppression media, such as water or soda acid. Smoke is damaging to most storage devices. Heat can damage any electronic or computer component. For example, temperatures of 100 degrees Fahrenheit can damage storage tapes, 175 degrees can damage computer hardware (that is, CPU and RAM), and 350 degrees can damage paper products (through warping and discoloration).

Suppression media can cause short circuits, initiate corrosion, or otherwise render equipment useless. All these issues must be addressed when designing a fire response system.

Don't forget that in the event of a fire, in addition to damage caused by the flames and your chosen suppression medium, members of the fire department may inflict damage using their hoses to spray water and their axes while searching for hot spots.

Equipment Failure

No matter the quality of the equipment your organization chooses to purchase and install, eventually it will fail. Understanding and preparing for this eventuality helps ensure the ongoing availability of your IT infrastructure and should help you to protect the integrity and availability of your resources.

Preparing for equipment failure can take many forms. In some non-mission-critical situations, simply knowing where you can purchase replacement parts for a 48-hour replacement timeline is sufficient. In other situations, maintaining onsite replacement parts is mandatory. Keep in mind that the response time in returning a system to a fully functioning state is directly proportional to the cost involved in maintaining such a solution. Costs include storage, transportation, prepurchasing, and maintaining onsite installation and restoration expertise. In some cases, maintaining onsite replacements is not feasible. For those cases, establishing a service-level agreement (SLA) with the hardware vendor is essential. An SLA clearly defines the response time a vendor will provide in the event of an equipment failure emergency.

Aging hardware should be scheduled for replacement and/or repair. The schedule for such operations should be based on the mean time to failure (MTTF) and mean time to repair (MTTR) estimates established for each device or upon prevailing best organizational practices for managing the hardware lifecycle. MTTF is the expected typical functional lifetime of the device given a specific operating environment. MTTR is the average length of time required to perform a repair on the device. A device can often undergo numerous repairs before a catastrophic failure is expected. Be sure to schedule all devices to be replaced before their MTTF expires.

When a device is sent out for repairs, you need to have an alternate solution or a backup device to fill in for the duration of the repair time. Often, waiting until a minor failure occurs before a repair is performed is satisfactory, but waiting until a complete failure occurs before replacement is an unacceptable security practice.

Privacy Responsibilities and Legal Requirements

The safety of personal information also needs to be addressed in any organization's security policy. In addition, the security policy must conform to the regulatory requirements of the industry and jurisdictions in which it is active. This section discusses these concerns.

Protection of Privacy

Privacy means protecting personal information from disclosure to any unauthorized individual or entity. In today's online world, the line between public and private information is often blurry. For example, is information about your web-surfing habits private or public? Can that information be gathered legally without your consent? And can the gathering organization sell that information for a profit that you don't share in? In addition, your personal information includes more than information about your online habits; it also includes who you are (name, address, phone, race, religion, age, and so on), your health and medical records, your financial records, and even your criminal or legal records. In general such information falls under the heading of personally identifiable information, aka PII, as described in the NIST publication *Guide to Protecting the Confidentiality of Personally Identifiable Information (PII)* available online at `http://csrc.nist.gov/publications/nistpubs/800-122/sp800-122.pdf`.

Dealing with privacy is a requirement for any organization that has employees. Thus, privacy is a central issue for all organizations. Protection of privacy should be a core mission or goal set forth in the security policy for any organization. Personnel privacy issues are discussed at greater length in Chapter 17, "Laws, Regulations, and Compliance."

Regulatory Requirements

Every organization operates within a certain industry and jurisdiction. Both of these entities (and possibly additional ones) impose legal requirements, restrictions, and regulations on the practices of organizations that fall within their realm. These *legal requirements* can apply to licensed use of software, hiring restrictions, handling of sensitive materials, and compliance with safety regulations.

Complying with all applicable legal requirements is a key part of sustaining security. The legal requirements for an industry and a country (and often also a state and city) must be considered a baseline or foundation on which the remainder of the security infrastructure is built.

Summary

If you don't have control over the physical environment, no amount of administrative or technical/logical access controls can provide adequate security. If a malicious person can gain physical access to your facility or equipment, they own it.

Several aspects and elements are involved in implementing and maintaining physical security. One core element is selecting or designing the facility to house your IT infrastructure and the operations of your organization. You must start with a plan that outlines the security needs for your organization and emphasizes methods or mechanisms to employ to provide such security. Such a plan is developed through a process known as *critical path analysis*.

The security controls implemented to manage physical security can be divided into three groups: administrative, technical, and physical. Administrative physical security controls include facility construction and selection, site management, personnel controls, awareness training, and emergency response and procedures. Technical physical security controls include access controls, intrusion detection, alarms, CCTV, monitoring, HVAC, power supplies, and fire detection and suppression. Examples of physical controls for physical security include fencing, lighting, locks, construction materials, mantraps, dogs, and guards.

There are many types of physical access control mechanisms that can be deployed in an environment to control, monitor, and manage access to a facility. These range from deterrents to detection mechanisms. They can be fences, gates, turnstiles, mantraps, lighting, security guards, security dogs, key locks, combination locks, badges, motion detectors, sensors, and alarms.

The technical controls most often employed as access control mechanisms to manage physical access include smart/dumb cards and biometrics. In addition to access control, physical security mechanisms can take the form of audit trails, access logs, and intrusion detection systems.

An important aspect of physical access control and maintaining the security of a facility is protecting the basic elements of the environment and protecting human life. In all circumstances and under all conditions, the most important goal of security is protecting people. Preventing harm is the utmost goal of all security solutions. Providing clean power sources and managing the environment are also important.

Fire detection and suppression must not be overlooked. In addition to protecting people, fire detection and suppression is designed to keep damage caused by fire, smoke, heat, and suppression materials to a minimum, especially in regard to the IT infrastructure.

People should always be your top priority. Only after personnel are safe can you consider addressing business continuity.

Exam Essentials

Understand why there is no security without physical security. Without control over the physical environment, no amount of administrative or technical/logical access controls can provide adequate security. If a malicious person can gain physical access to your facility or equipment, they can do just about anything they want, from destruction to disclosure and alteration.

Be able to list administrative physical security controls. Examples of administrative physical security controls are facility construction and selection, site management, personnel controls, awareness training, and emergency response and procedures.

Be able to list the technical physical security controls. Technical physical security controls can be access controls, intrusion detection, alarms, CCTV, monitoring, HVAC, power supplies, and fire detection and suppression.

Be able to name the physical controls for physical security. Physical controls for physical security are fencing, lighting, locks, construction materials, mantraps, dogs, and guards.

Know the functional order of controls. These are deterrence, then denial, then detection, and then delay.

Know the key elements in making a site selection and designing a facility for construction.   The key elements in making a site selection are visibility, composition of the surrounding area, area accessibility, and the effects of natural disasters. A key element in designing a facility for construction is understanding the level of security needed by your organization and planning for it before construction begins.

Know how to design and configure secure work areas.   There should not be equal access to all locations within a facility. Areas that contain assets of higher value or importance should have restricted access. Valuable and confidential assets should be located in the heart or center of protection provided by a facility. Also, centralized server or computer rooms need not be human compatible.

Understand how to handle visitors in a secure facility.   If a facility employs restricted areas to control physical security, then a mechanism to handle visitors is required. Often an escort is assigned to visitors, and their access and activities are monitored closely. Failing to track the actions of outsiders when they are granted access into a protected area can result in malicious activity against the most protected assets.

Know the three categories of security controls implemented to manage physical security and be able to name examples of each.   The security controls implemented to manage physical security can be divided into three groups: administrative, technical, and physical. Understand when and how to use each, and be able to list examples of each kind.

Know the common threats to physical access controls.   No matter what form of physical access control is used, a security guard or other monitoring system must be deployed to prevent abuse, masquerading, and piggybacking. Abuses of physical access control are propping open secured doors and bypassing locks or access controls. Masquerading is using someone else's security ID to gain entry into a facility. Piggybacking is following someone through a secured gate or doorway without being identified or authorized personally.

Understand the need for audit trails and access logs.   Audit trails and access logs are useful tools even for physical access control. They may need to be created manually by security guards. Or they can be generated automatically if sufficiently automated access control mechanisms are in place (in other words, smart cards and certain proximity readers). You should also consider monitoring entry points with CCTV. Through CCTV, you can compare the audit trails and access logs with a visually recorded history of the events. Such information is critical to reconstructing the events of an intrusion, breach, or attack.

Understand the need for clean power.   Power supplied by electric companies is not always consistent and clean. Most electronic equipment demands clean power in order to function properly. Equipment damage because of power fluctuations is a common occurrence. Many organizations opt to manage their own power through several means. A UPS is a type of self-charging battery that can be used to supply consistent clean power to sensitive equipment. UPSs also provide continuous power even after the primary power source fails. A UPS can continue to supply power for minutes or hours depending on its capacity and the draw by equipment.

Know the terms commonly associated with power issues.   Know the definitions of the following: fault, blackout, sag, brownout, spike, surge, inrush, noise, transient, clean, and ground.

Understand how to control the environment.   In addition to power considerations, maintaining the environment involves control over the HVAC mechanisms. Rooms containing primarily computers should be kept at 60 to 75 degrees Fahrenheit (15 to 23 degrees Celsius). Humidity in a computer room should be maintained between 40 and 60 percent. Too much humidity can cause corrosion. Too little humidity causes static electricity.

Know about static electricity.   Even on nonstatic carpeting, if the environment has low humidity, it is still possible to generate 20,000-volt static discharges. Even minimal levels of static discharge can destroy electronic equipment.

Understand the need to manage water leakage and flooding.   Water leakage and flooding should be addressed in your environmental safety policy and procedures. Plumbing leaks are not an everyday occurrence, but when they occur, they often cause significant damage. Water and electricity don't mix. If your computer systems come in contact with water, especially while they are operating, damage is sure to occur. Whenever possible, locate server rooms and critical computer equipment away from any water source or transport pipes.

Understand the importance of fire detection and suppression.   Fire detection and suppression must not be overlooked. Protecting personnel from harm should always be the most important goal of any security or protection system. In addition to protecting people, fire detection and suppression is designed to keep damage caused by fire, smoke, heat, and suppression materials to a minimum, especially in regard to the IT infrastructure.

Understand the possible contamination and damage caused by a fire and suppression.   The destructive elements of a fire include smoke and heat but also the suppression medium, such as water or soda acid. Smoke is damaging to most storage devices. Heat can damage any electronic or computer component. Suppression mediums can cause short circuits, initiate corrosion, or otherwise render equipment useless. All of these issues must be addressed when designing a fire response system.

Understand personnel privacy and safety.   In all circumstances and under all conditions, the most important aspect of security is protecting people. Thus, preventing harm to people is the most important goal for all security solutions.

Written Lab

1. What kind of device helps to define an organization's perimeter and also serves to deter casual trespassing?
2. What is the problem with halon-based fire suppression technology?
3. What kinds of potential issues can an emergency visit from the fire department leave in its wake?

Review Questions

1. Which of the following is the most important aspect of security?
   - **A.** Physical security
   - **B.** Intrusion detection
   - **C.** Logical security
   - **D.** Awareness training

2. What method can be used to map out the needs of an organization for a new facility?
   - **A.** Log file audit
   - **B.** Critical path analysis
   - **C.** Risk analysis
   - **D.** Inventory

3. What type of physical security controls focus on facility construction and selection, site management, personnel controls, awareness training, and emergency response and procedures?
   - **A.** Technical
   - **B.** Physical
   - **C.** Administrative
   - **D.** Logical

4. Which of the following is *not* a security-focused design element of a facility or site?
   - **A.** Separation of work and visitor areas
   - **B.** Restricted access to areas with higher value or importance
   - **C.** Confidential assets located in the heart or center of a facility
   - **D.** Equal access to all locations within a facility

5. Which of the following does *not* need to be true in order to maintain the most efficient and secure server room?
   - **A.** It must be human compatible.
   - **B.** It must include the use of nonwater fire suppressants.
   - **C.** The humidity must be kept between 40 and 60 percent.
   - **D.** The temperature must be kept between 60 and 75 degrees Fahrenheit.

6. What is a perimeter-defining device used to deter casual trespassing?

    A. Gates

    B. Fencing

    C. Security guards

    D. Motion detectors

7. Which of the following is a double set of doors that is often protected by a guard and is used to contain a subject until their identity and authentication is verified?

    A. Gate

    B. Turnstile

    C. Mantrap

    D. Proximity detector

8. What is the most common form of perimeter security devices or mechanisms?

    A. Security guards

    B. Fences

    C. CCTV

    D. Lighting

9. Which of the following is *not* a disadvantage of using security guards?

    A. Security guards are usually unaware of the scope of the operations within a facility.

    B. Not all environments and facilities support security guards.

    C. Not all security guards are themselves reliable.

    D. Prescreening, bonding, and training does not guarantee effective and reliable security guards.

10. What is the most common cause of failure for a water-based fire suppression system?

    A. Water shortage

    B. People

    C. Ionization detectors

    D. Placement of detectors in drop ceilings

11. What is the most common and inexpensive form of physical access control device?

    A. Lighting

    B. Security guard

    C. Key locks

    D. Fences

12. What type of motion detector senses changes in the electrical or magnetic field surrounding a monitored object?

    A. Wave

    B. Photoelectric

    C. Heat

    D. Capacitance

13. Which of the following is *not* a typical type of alarm that can be triggered for physical security?

    A. Preventive

    B. Deterrent

    C. Repellant

    D. Notification

14. No matter what form of physical access control is used, a security guard or other monitoring system must be deployed to prevent all but which of the following?

    A. Piggybacking

    B. Espionage

    C. Masquerading

    D. Abuse

15. What is the most important goal of all security solutions?

    A. Prevention of disclosure

    B. Maintaining integrity

    C. Human safety

    D. Sustaining availability

16. What is the ideal humidity range for a computer room?

    A. 20–40 percent

    B. 40–60 percent

    C. 60–75 percent

    D. 80–95 percent

17. At what voltage level can static electricity cause destruction of data stored on hard drives?

    A. 4,000

    B. 17,000

    C. 40

    D. 1,500

18. A Type B fire extinguisher may use all *except* which of the following suppression mediums?

    A. Water

    B. CO_2

    C. Halon or an acceptable halon substitute

    D. Soda acid

19. What is the best type of water-based fire suppression system for a computer facility?

    A. Wet pipe system

    B. Dry pipe system

    C. Preaction system

    D. Deluge system

20. Which of the following is typically *not* a culprit in causing damage to computer equipment in the event of a fire and a triggered suppression?

    A. Heat

    B. Suppression medium

    C. Smoke

    D. Light

Appendix A

Answers to Review Questions

Chapter 1: Access Control

1. C. The subject is active and is always the entity that receives information about or data from the object. A subject can be a user, a program, a process, a file, a computer, a database, and so on. The object is always the entity that provides or hosts information or data. The roles of subject and object can switch while two entities communicate to accomplish a task.

2. A. Access control mechanisms help to prevent losses, including any loss of confidentiality, loss of availability, or loss of integrity. Subjects authenticate on a system and objects are accessed. A first step in access control is the identification and authentication of subjects, but access control also includes authorization and accountability.

3. A. A preventive access control is deployed to stop an unwanted or unauthorized activity from occurring. Detective controls discover the activity after it has occurred, and corrective controls attempt to reverse any problems caused by the activity. Access controls are not categorized as authoritative.

4. B. Logical/technical access controls are the hardware or software mechanisms used to manage access to resources and systems and to provide protection for those resources and systems. Administrative controls are managerial controls and physical controls use physical items to control physical access. A preventive control attempts to prevent security incidents.

5. D. Authorization is not needed for accountability. However, users must be identified and authenticated and their actions logged using some type of auditing to provide accountability.

6. A. A Type 2 authentication factor is "something you have," including a smart card, token device, or memory card. Type 3 authentication is "something you are," and some behavioral biometrics include "something you do." Type 1 authentication is "something you know."

7. A. A synchronous token generates one-time passwords and displays them in an LCD, and this password is synchronized with an authentication server. An asynchronous token uses a challenge-response process to generate the token. Smart cards do not generate one-time passwords, and common access cards are a version of a smart card that includes a picture of the user.

8. B. A biometric factor is a behavioral or physiological characteristic that is unique to a subject, such as fingerprints and face scans, and is also known as a Type 3 authentication factor. An account ID provides identification. A token is a Type 2 authentication factor. A Personal Identity Verification (PIV) card is a smart card that includes a picture of the user.

9. C. The point at which biometric Type 1 errors (false rejection rate) and Type 2 errors (false acceptance rate) are equal is the crossover error rate (CER). The CER level is used as a standard assessment point to compare biometric authentication systems. It does not indicate that sensitivity is too high or too low or whether the device is configured properly.

10. A. A Type 1 error occurs when a valid subject is not authenticated and is also known as a false negative authentication. A Type 2 error occurs when an invalid subject

is authenticated. This is also known as a false positive authentication. The crossover error rate (also called equal error rate) compares the rate of Type 1 errors to Type 2 errors and provides a measurement of the accuracy of the biometric system.

11. B. An access control matrix includes multiple subjects and objects and lists subjects' access to various objects. A single list of subjects for any specific object within an access control matrix is an access control list. A federation refers to a group of companies that share a federated identity management system for single sign-on. Creeping privileges refers to excessive privileges a subject gathers over time.

12. A. An ACL is based on an object and includes a list of subjects that are granted access. A capability table is focused on a subject and includes a list of objects the subject can access. Roles and accounts are examples of subjects and may be included in an ACL, but they aren't the focus.

13. C. Mandatory access controls rely on use of labels for subjects and objects. Discretionary access control systems allow an owner of an object to control access to the object. Nondiscretionary access controls have centralized management such as a rule-based access control deployed on a firewall. Role-based access controls define a subject's access based on job-related roles.

14. D. A role-based access control policy grants specific privileges based on roles, and roles are frequently job based or task based. Discretionary access controls allow owners to control privileges, mandatory access controls use labels to control privileges, and rule-based access controls use rules.

15. C. TACACS+ is a centralized authentication service used for remote access clients but not for single sign-on. Kerberos and federated identity management systems are used to support single sign-on. Service Provisioning Markup Language (SPML) is a language used with some federated identity systems.

16. D. SPML is an XML-based framework used to exchange user information for single sign-on (SSO) between organizations within a federated identity management system. Kerberos supports SSO in a single organization, not a federation. HTML only describes how data is displayed. XML could be used, but it would require redefining tags already defined in SPML.

17. B. Diameter is based on RADIUS and it supports Mobile IP and Voice over IP. Distributed access control systems such as a federated identity management system are not a specific protocol, and they don't necessarily provide authentication, authorization, and accounting. TACACS and TACACS+ are AAA protocols, but they are alternatives to RADIUS, not based on RADIUS.

18. D. The principle of least privilege was violated because he retained privileges from all his previous administrator positions in different divisions. Implicit deny ensures that only access that is explicitly granted is allowed, but the administrator was explicitly granted privileges. While the administrator's actions could have caused loss of availability, loss of availability isn't a basic principle. Defense in depth is a principle that may not have been applied to accounts, but defensive privileges aren't a valid security principle.

19. C. The life cycle of accounts includes provisioning, review, and revocation, and his account should have been disabled as soon as his employment was terminated to ensure that his access was revoked. If his account was disabled, he could not have installed a malicious script. Provisioning creates the account and grants appropriate privileges. There is no indication whether separation of duties was addressed or not, but the scenario does not indicate that the administrator controlled any single process. Authentication wasn't addressed in the scenario.

20. D. Account review can discover when users have more privileges than they need and could have been used to discover that this employee had permissions from several positions. Strong authentication methods (including multifactor authentication) would not have prevented the problems in this scenario. Logging could have recorded activity, but a review is necessary to discover the problems.

Chapter 2: Access Control Attacks and Monitoring

1. A. An organization must first identify the value of assets when identifying risks so that they can focus on risks to their most valuable assets. They can then identify threats and vulnerabilities. Public attacks can be evaluated to determine if they present a risk to the organization, but this should not be the first step.

2. C. A vulnerability analysis identifies weaknesses and can include periodic vulnerability scans and penetration tests. Asset valuation determines the value of assets, not weaknesses. Threat modeling attempts to identify threats, and threats are often paired with vulnerabilities to identify risk, but threat modeling doesn't identify weaknesses. An access review audits account management and object access practices.

3. C. Requiring users to log in remotely does not protect against password attacks such as brute-force or dictionary attacks. Strong password policies, physical access control, and two-factor authentication all improve the protection against brute-force and dictionary password attacks.

4. C. A sniffing attack uses a sniffer (also called a packet analyzer or protocol analyzer) to capture data and can be used to read passwords sent across a network in cleartext. A spoofing attack attempts to hide the identity of the attacker. A spamming attack involves sending massive amounts of email. A side-channel attack is a passive, noninvasive attack used against smart cards.

5. B. An account lockout policy will prevent someone from logging into an account after they have entered an incorrect password too many times. A rainbow table is used by an attacker in offline password attacks, and password salts reduce the effectiveness of rainbow tables. Encrypting the password protects the password, but not against a brute-force attack.

6. B. A side-channel attack is a passive, noninvasive attack to observe the operation of a device. Methods include power monitoring, timing, and fault analysis attacks. Whaling is a type of phishing attack that targets high-level executives. A brute-force attack attempts to

discover passwords by using all possible character combinations. A rainbow table attack is used to crack passwords.

7. C. Whaling is a form of phishing that targets high-level executives. Spear phishing targets a specific group of people but not necessarily high-level executives. Vishing is a form of phishing that commonly uses Voice over IP (VoIP).

8. B. Log files provide an audit trail for recreating the history of an event, intrusion, or system failure. An audit trail includes log files and can reconstruct an event, extract information about an incident, and prove or disprove culpability. Security policies are documents that define security requirements for an organization. An audit report includes details gleaned from log files. Business continuity planning occurs before an event, in an attempt to reduce the impact.

9. A. Clipping is a form of nonstatistical sampling that reduces the amount of logged data based on a clipping-level threshold. Sampling is a statistical method that extracts meaningful data from audit logs. Log analysis reviews log information looking for trends, patterns, and abnormal or unauthorized events. An alarm trigger is a notification sent to administrators when specific events or thresholds occur.

10. B. Traffic analysis focuses more on the patterns and trends of data rather than the actual content. Keystroke monitoring records specific keystrokes to capture data. Event logging logs specific events to record data. Security auditing records security events and/or reviews logs to detect security incidents.

11. B. Accountability is maintained by monitoring the activities of subjects and objects as well as core system functions that maintain the operating environment and the security mechanisms. Authentication is required for effective monitoring, but it doesn't provide accountability by itself. Account lockout prevents login to an account if the wrong password is entered too many times. User entitlement reviews can identify excessive privileges.

12. B. Audit trails are a passive form of detective security control. Administrative controls are management practices. Corrective controls can correct problems related to an incident, and physical controls are controls that you can physically touch.

13. A. Failing to perform periodic security audits can result in the perception that due care is not being maintained. Such audits alert personnel that senior management is practicing due diligence in maintaining system security. An organization should not indiscriminately deploy all available controls but should choose the most effective ones based on risks. Performance reviews are useful managerial practices but not directly related to due care. Audit reports should not be shared with the public.

14. B. Auditing is a methodical examination or review of an environment to ensure compliance with regulations and to detect abnormalities, unauthorized occurrences, or outright crimes. Penetration testing attempts to exploit vulnerabilities. Risk analysis attempts to analyze risks based on identified threats and vulnerabilities. Entrapment is tricking someone into performing an illegal or unauthorized action.

15. D. Privileged accounts (such as administrator accounts) are granted the most access and should be a primary focus in an access review audit. Regular user and auditor accounts don't have as much access as privileged accounts and are not as important to audit.

16. B. A user entitlement audit can detect when users have more privileges than necessary. Account management practices attempt to ensure that privileges are assigned correctly. The audit detects whether the management practices are followed. Logging records activity, but the logs need to be reviewed to determine if practices are followed. Reporting is the result of an audit.

17. B. Audit reports should be secured because they contain information about the vulnerabilities of the system and disclosure of such vulnerabilities to the wrong person could lead to security breaches. They would not normally contain confidential data from the network. They are useful to both upper management and security professionals. They would not normally include details about security control configuration.

18. B. Threat modeling helps identify, understand, and categorize potential threats. Asset valuation identifies the value of assets, and vulnerability analysis identifies weaknesses that can be exploited by threats. An access review and audit ensure that account management practices support the security policy.

19. A. Asset valuation identifies the actual value of assets so that they can be prioritized. This will ensure that the consultant focuses on high-value assets. Threat modeling identifies threats, but asset valuation should be done first so that the focus is on threats to high-value assets. Vulnerability analysis identifies weaknesses but should be focused on high-value assets. Audit trails are useful to recreate events leading up to an incident, but if they aren't already created, creating them now won't help unless the organization is attacked again.

20. D. A user entitlement review can detect when employees have excessive privileges. Asset valuation identifies the value of assets. Threat modeling identifies threats to valuable assets. Vulnerability analysis detects vulnerabilities or weaknesses that can be exploited by threats.

Chapter 3: Secure Network Architecture and Securing Network Components

1. D. The Transport layer is layer 4. The Presentation layer is layer 6, the Data Link layer is layer 2, and the Network layer is layer 3.

2. B. Encapsulation is adding a header and footer to data as it moves down the OSI stack.

3. B. Layer 5, Session, manages simplex (one-direction), half-duplex (two-way, but only one direction can send data at a time), and full-duplex (two-way, in which data can be sent in both directions simultaneously) communications.

4. B. 10Base-T UTP is the least resistant to EMI because it is unshielded. Thinnet (10Base2) and thicknet (10Base5) are each a type of coaxial cable, which is shielded against EMI.

5. D. A VPN is a secure tunnel used to establish connections across a potentially insecure intermediary network. Intranet, extranet, and DMZ are examples of network segmentation.

6. B. UDP is a transport layer protocol that operates as the payload of an IP packet. While it is not IP itself, it depends upon IP. IPX, AppleTalk, and NetBEUI are all alternatives to IP and thus are labeled as non-IP protocols.

7. C. A bluejacking attack is a wireless attack on Bluetooth, and the most common device compromised in a bluejacking attack is a cell phone.

8. A. Ethernet is based on the IEEE 802.3 standard.

9. B. A TCP wrapper is an application that can serve as a basic firewall by restricting access based on user IDs or system IDs.

10. B. Encapsulation is both a benefit and a potentially harmful implication of multilayer protocols.

11. C. Stateful inspection firewalls are able to grant a broader range of access for authorized users and activities and actively watch for and block unauthorized users and activities.

12. B. Stateful inspection firewalls are known as third-generation firewalls.

13. B. Most firewalls offer extensive logging, auditing, and monitoring capabilities as well as alarms and even basic IDS functions. Firewalls are unable to block viruses or malicious code transmitted through otherwise authorized communication channels, prevent unauthorized but accidental or intended disclosure of information by users, prevent attacks by malicious users already behind the firewall, or protect data after it passed out of or into the private network.

14. C. There are numerous dynamic routing protocols, including RIP, OSPF, and BGP, but RPC is not a routing protocol.

15. B. A switch is an intelligent hub. It is considered to be intelligent because it knows the addresses of the systems connected on each outbound port.

16. A. Wireless Application Protocol (WAP) is a technology associated with cell phones accessing the Internet rather than 802.11 wireless networking.

17. C. Orthogonal Frequency-Division Multiplexing (OFDM) offers high throughput with the least interference. OSPF is a routing protocol, not a wireless frequency access method.

18. A. Endpoint security is the security concept that encourages administrators to install firewalls, malware scanners, and an IDS on every host.

19. C. Reverse Address Resolution Protocol (RARP) resolves physical addresses (MAC addresses) into logical addresses (IP addresses).

20. C. Enterprise extended infrastructure mode exists when a wireless network is designed to support a large physical environment through the use of a single SSID but numerous access points.

Chapter 4: Secure Communications and Network Attacks

1. B. Frame Relay is a layer 2 connection mechanism that uses packet-switching technology to establish virtual circuits between the communication endpoints. The Frame Relay network is a shared medium across which virtual circuits are created to provide point-to-point communications. All virtual circuits are independent of and invisible to each other.

2. D. A stand-alone system has no need for tunneling because no communications between systems are occurring and no intermediary network is present.

3. C. IPSec, or IP Security, is a standards-based mechanism for providing encryption for point-to-point TCP/IP traffic.

4. B. The 169.254.*x*.*x* subnet is in the APIPA range, which is not part of RFC 1918. The addresses in RFC 1918 are 10.0.0.0–10.255.255.255, 172.16.0.0–172.31.255.255, and 192.168.0.0–192.168.255.255.

5. D. An intermediary network connection is required for a VPN link to be established.

6. B. Static mode NAT is needed to allow an outside entity to initiate communications with an internal system behind a NAT proxy.

7. A, B, D. L2F, L2TP, and PPTP all lack native data encryption. Only IPSec includes native data encryption.

8. D. IPSec operates at the Network layer (layer 3).

9. A. The address range 169.172.0.0–169.191.255.255 is not listed in RFC 1918 as a private IP address range. It is in fact a public IP address range.

10. D. NAT does not protect against or prevent brute-force attacks.

11. B. When transparency is a characteristic of a service, security control, or access mechanism it is unseen by users.

12. B. Although availability is a key aspect of security in general, it is the least important aspect of security systems for Internet-delivered email.

13. D. The backup method is not an important factor to discuss with end users regarding email retention.

14. B. Mail-bombing is the use of email as an attack mechanism. Flooding a system with messages causes a denial of service.

15. B. It is often difficult to stop spam because the source of the messages is usually spoofed.

16. B. A permanent virtual circuit (PVC) can be described as a logical circuit that always exists and is waiting for the customer to send data.

17. B. Changing default passwords on PBX systems provides the most effective increase in security.

18. C. Social engineering can often be used to bypass even the most effective physical and logical controls. Whatever activity the attacker convinces the victim to perform, it is usually directed toward opening a back door that the attacker can use to gain access to the network.

19. C. A brute-force attack is not considered a DoS.

20. A. Password Authentication Protocol (PAP) is a standardized authentication protocol for PPP. PAP transmits usernames and passwords in the clear. It offers no form of encryption. It simply provides a means to transport the logon credentials from the client to the authentication server.

Chapter 5: Security Governance Concepts, Principles, and Policies

1. B. The primary goals and objectives of security are confidentiality, integrity, and availability, commonly referred to as the *CIA Triad*.

2. A. Vulnerabilities and risks are evaluated based on their threats against one or more of the CIA Triad principles.

3. B. Availability means that authorized subjects are granted timely and uninterrupted access to objects.

4. C. Hardware destruction is a violation of availability and possibly integrity. Violations of confidentiality include capturing network traffic, stealing password files, social engineering, port scanning, shoulder surfing, eavesdropping, and sniffing.

5. C. Violations of confidentiality are not limited to direct intentional attacks. Many instances of unauthorized disclosure of sensitive or confidential information are due to human error, oversight, or ineptitude.

6. D. Without integrity, confidentiality cannot be maintained.

7. C. Accessibility of data, objects, and resources is the goal of availability. If a security mechanism offers availability, then it is highly likely that the data, objects, and resources are accessible to authorized subjects.

8. B. One definition of privacy is freedom from being observed, monitored, or examined without consent or knowledge.

9. D. Users should be aware that email messages are retained, but the backup mechanism used to perform this operation does not need to be disclosed to them.

10. D. Ownership grants an entity full capabilities and privileges over the object they own. The ability to take ownership is often granted to the most powerful accounts in an operating system because it can be used to overstep any access control limitations otherwise implemented.

11. C. Nonrepudiation ensures that the subject of an activity or event cannot deny that the event occurred.

12. B. Layering is the deployment of multiple security mechanisms in a series. When security restrictions are performed in a series, they are performed one after the other in a linear fashion. Therefore, a single failure of a security control does not render the entire solution ineffective.

13. A. Preventing an authorized reader of an object from deleting that object is just an example of access control, not data hiding. If you can read an object, it is not hidden from you.

14. D. The prevention of security compromises is the primary goal of change management.

15. B. The primary objective of data classification schemes is to formalize and stratify the process of securing data based on assigned labels of importance and sensitivity.

16. B. Size is not a criterion for establishing data classification. When classifying an object, you should take value, lifetime, and security implications into consideration.

17. A. Military (or government) and private sector (or commercial business) are the two common data classification schemes.

18. B. Of the options listed, secret is the lowest classified military data classification. Keep in mind that items labeled as confidential, secret, and top secret are collectively known as classified, and confidential is below secret in the list.

19. B. The commercial business/private sector data classification of private is used to protect information about individuals.

20. C. Layering is a core aspect of security mechanisms, but it is not a focus of data classifications.

Chapter 6: Risk and Personnel Management

1. D. Regardless of the specifics of a security solution, humans are the weakest element.

2. A. The first step in hiring new employees is to create a job description. Without a job description, there is no consensus on what type of individual needs to be found and hired.

3. B. The primary purpose of an exit interview is to review the nondisclosure agreement (NDA) and other liabilities and restrictions placed on the former employee based on the employment agreement and any other security-related documentation.

4. B. You should remove or disable the employee's network user account immediately before or at the same time they are informed of their termination.

5. B. Third-party governance is the application of security oversight on third parties that your organization relies upon.

6. D. A portion of the documentation review is the logical and practical investigation of business processes and organizational policies.

7. C. Risks to an IT infrastructure are not all computer based. In fact, many risks come from noncomputer sources. It is important to consider all possible risks when performing risk evaluation for an organization. Failing to properly evaluate and respond to all forms of risk, a company remains vulnerable.

8. C. Risk analysis includes analyzing an environment for risks, evaluating each threat event as to its likelihood of occurring and the cost of the damage it would cause, assessing the cost of various countermeasures for each risk, and creating a cost/benefit report for safeguards to present to upper management. Selecting safeguards is a task of upper management based on the results of risk analysis. It is a task that falls under risk management, but it is not part of the risk analysis process.

9. D. The personal files of users are not usually considered assets of the organization and thus are not considered in a risk analysis.

10. A. Threat events are accidental or intentional exploitations of vulnerabilities.

11. A. A vulnerability is the absence or weakness of a safeguard or countermeasure.

12. B. Anything that removes a vulnerability or protects against one or more specific threats is considered a safeguard or a countermeasure, not a risk.

13. C. The annual costs of safeguards should not exceed the expected annual cost of asset loss.

14. B. SLE is calculated using the formula SLE = asset value ($) * exposure factor (SLE = AV * EF).

15. A. The value of a safeguard to an organization is calculated by ALE before safeguard – ALE after implementing the safeguard – annual cost of safeguard [(ALE1 – ALE2) – ACS].

16. C. The likelihood that a co-worker will be willing to collaborate on an illegal or abusive scheme is reduced because of the higher risk of detection created by the combination of separation of duties, restricted job responsibilities, and job rotation.

17. C. Training is teaching employees to perform their work tasks and to comply with the security policy. Training is typically hosted by an organization and is targeted to groups of employees with similar job functions.

18. A. Managing the security function often includes assessment of budget, metrics, resources, information security strategies, and assessing the completeness and effectiveness of the security program.

19. B. The threat of a fire and the vulnerability of a lack of fire extinguishers lead to the risk of damage to equipment.

20. D. A countermeasure directly affects the annualized rate of occurrence, primarily because the countermeasure is designed to prevent the occurrence of the risk, thus reducing its frequency per year.

Chapter 7: Software Development Security

1. D. Logic bombs are malicious code objects programmed to lie dormant until certain logical conditions, such as a certain date, time, system event, or other criteria, are met. At that time, they spring into action, triggering their payload.

2. A. Intelligent agents, also called *bots*, are code objects programmed to perform certain operations on behalf of a user in their absence.

3. C. The request control provides users with a framework to request changes and developers with the opportunity to prioritize those requests.

4. B. The major difference between viruses and worms is that worms are self-replicating, whereas viruses require user intervention to spread from system to system. Both viruses and worms are capable of carrying malicious payloads.

5. D. Microsoft's ActiveX technology supports a number of programming languages, including Visual Basic, C, C++, and Java. On the other hand, only the Java language can be used to write Java applets.

6. A. Content-dependent access control is focused on the internal data of each field.

7. C. Foreign keys are used to enforce referential integrity constraints between tables that participate in a relationship.

8. D. In this case, the process the database user is taking advantage of is aggregation. Aggregation attacks involve the use of specialized database functions to combine information from a large number of database records to reveal information that may be more sensitive than the information in individual records would reveal.

9. C. Polyinstantiation allows the insertion of multiple records that appear to have the same primary key values into a database at different classification levels.

10. B. Random access memory (RAM) allows for the direct addressing of any point within the resource. A sequential access storage medium, such as a magnetic tape, requires scanning through the entire media from the beginning to reach a specific address.

11. C. Expert systems utilize a knowledge base consisting of a series of "if/then" statements to form decisions based upon the previous experience of human experts.

12. D. The Next-Generation Intrusion Detection Expert System (NIDES) is an expert-system-based intrusion detection system. PIX is a firewall, and ID10T and AAFID are intrusion detection systems that do not utilize expert systems.

13. B. ODBC acts as a proxy between applications and the backend DBMS.

14. A. In order to conduct a static test, the tester must have access to the underlying source code.

15. A. The security kernel and reference monitor reside at Level 0 in the ring protection scheme, where they have unrestricted access to all system resources.

16. C. Contamination is the mixing of data from a higher classification level and/or need-to-know requirement with data from a lower classification level and/or need-to-know requirement.

17. A. Database developers use polyinstantiation, the creation of multiple records that seem to have the same primary key, to protect against inference attacks.

18. C. Configuration audit is part of the configuration management process rather than the change control process.

19. C. The isolation principle states that two transactions operating on the same data must be temporarily separated from each other such that one does not interfere with the other.

20. B. The cardinality of a table refers to the number of rows in the table while the degree of a table is the number of columns.

Chapter 8: Malicious Code and Application Attacks

1. A. Signature detection mechanisms use known descriptions of viruses to identify malicious code resident on a system.

2. B. The DMZ (demilitarized zone) is designed to house systems like web servers that must be accessible from both the internal and external networks.

3. B. The time-of-check-to-time-of-use (TOCTTOU) attack relies upon the timing of the execution of two events.

4. D. Application whitelisting requires that administrators specify approved applications and then the operating system uses this list to allow only known good applications to run.

5. A. In an attempt to avoid detection by signature-based antivirus software packages, polymorphic viruses modify their own code each time they infect a system.

6. A. LastPass is a tool that allows users to create unique, strong passwords for each service they use without the burden of memorizing them all.

7. D. Buffer overflow attacks allow an attacker to modify the contents of a system's memory by writing beyond the space allocated for a variable.

8. D. Except option D, the choices are forms of common words that might be found during a dictionary attack. *mike* is a name and would be easily detected. *elppa* is simply *apple* spelled backwards, and *dayorange* combines two dictionary words. Crack and other utilities can easily see through these "sneaky" techniques. Option D is simply a random string of characters that a dictionary attack would not uncover.

9. B. Shadow password files move encrypted password information from the publicly readable `/etc/passwd` file to the protected `/etc/shadow` file.

10. D. The single quote character (`'`) is used in SQL queries and must be handled carefully on web forms to protect against SQL injection attacks.

11. B. Developers of web applications should leverage database stored procedures to limit the application's ability to execute arbitrary code. With stored procedures, the SQL statement resides on the database server and may only be modified by database administrators.

12. B. Port scans reveal the ports associated with services running on a machine and available to the public.

13. A. Cross-site scripting attacks are successful only against web applications that include reflected input.

14. D. Multipartite viruses use two or more propagation techniques (for example, file infection and boot sector infection) to maximize their reach.

15. B. Input validation prevents cross-site scripting attacks by limiting user input to a predefined range. This prevents the attacker from including the HTML <SCRIPT> tag in the input.

16. A. Stuxnet was a highly sophisticated worm designed to destroy nuclear enrichment centrifuges attached to Siemens controllers.

17. B. Back doors are undocumented command sequences that allow individuals with knowledge of the back door to bypass normal access restrictions.

18. D. The Java sandbox isolates applets and allows them to run within a protected environment, limiting the effect they may have on the rest of the system.

19. D. The <SCRIPT> tag is used to indicate the beginning of an executable client-side script and is used in reflected input to create a cross-site scripting attack.

20. A. Packets with internal source IP addresses should not be allowed to enter the network from the outside because they are likely spoofed.

Chapter 9: Cryptography and Symmetric Key Algorithms

1. C. To determine the number of keys in a key space, raise 2 to the power of the number of bits in the key space. In this example, 24=16.

2. A. Nonrepudiation prevents the sender of a message from later denying that they sent it.

3. A. DES uses a 56-bit key. This is considered one of the major weaknesses of this cryptosystem.

4. B. Transposition ciphers use a variety of techniques to reorder the characters within a message.

5. A. The Rijndael cipher allows users to select a key length of 128, 192, or 256 bits, depending upon the specific security requirements of the application.

6. A. Nonrepudiation requires the use of a public key cryptosystem to prevent users from falsely denying that they originated a message.

7. D. Assuming that it is used properly, the one-time pad is the only known cryptosystem that is not vulnerable to attacks.

8. B. Option B is correct because 16 divided by 3 equals 5, with a remainder value of 1.

9. A. The cryptanalysts from the United States discovered a pattern in the method the Soviets used to generate their one-time pads. After this pattern was discovered, much of the code was eventually broken.

10. C. Block ciphers operate on message "chunks" rather than on individual characters or bits. The other ciphers mentioned are all types of stream ciphers that operate on individual bits or characters of a message.

11. A. Symmetric key cryptography uses a shared secret key. All communicating parties utilize the same key for communication in any direction.

12. B. M of N Control requires that a minimum number of agents (M) out of the total number of agents (N) work together to perform high-security tasks.

13. D. Output Feedback (OFB) mode prevents early errors from interfering with future encryption/decryption. Cipher Block Chaining and Cipher Feedback modes will carry errors throughout the entire encryption/decryption process. Electronic Codebook (ECB) operation is not suitable for large amounts of data.

14. C. A one-way function is a mathematical operation that easily produces output values for each possible combination of inputs but makes it impossible to retrieve the input values.

15. C. The number of keys required for a symmetric algorithm is dictated by the formula $(n*(n-1))/2$, which in this case, where n = 10, is 45.

16. C. The Advanced Encryption Standard uses a 128-bit block size, despite the fact that the Rijndael algorithm it is based on allows a variable block size.

17. C. The Caesar cipher (and other simple substitution ciphers) are vulnerable to frequency analysis attacks that analyze the rate at which specific letters appear in the ciphertext.

18. B. Running key (or "book") ciphers often use a passage from a commonly available book as the encryption key.

19. B. The Twofish algorithm, developed by Bruce Schneier, uses prewhitening and postwhitening.

20. B. In an asymmetric algorithm, each participant requires two keys: a public key and a private key.

Chapter 10: PKI and Cryptographic Applications

1. B. The number n is generated as the product of the two large prime numbers p and q. Therefore, n must always be greater than both p and q. Furthermore, it is an algorithm constraint that e must be chosen such that e is smaller than n. Therefore, in RSA cryptography, n is always the largest of the four variables shown in the options to this question.

2. B. The El Gamal cryptosystem extends the functionality of the Diffie-Hellman key exchange protocol to support the encryption and decryption of messages.

3. C. Richard must encrypt the message using Sue's public key so that Sue can decrypt it using her private key. If he encrypted the message with his own public key, the recipient would need to know Richard's private key to decrypt the message. If he encrypted it with his own private key, any user could decrypt the message using Richard's freely available public key. Richard could not encrypt the message using Sue's private key because he does not have access to it. If he did, any user could decrypt it using Sue's freely available public key.

4. C. The major disadvantage of the El Gamal cryptosystem is that it doubles the length of any message it encrypts. Therefore, a 2,048-bit plain-text message would yield a 4,096-bit ciphertext message when El Gamal is used for the encryption process.

5. A. The elliptic curve cryptosystem requires significantly shorter keys to achieve encryption that would be the same strength as encryption achieved with the RSA encryption algorithm. A 1,024-bit RSA key is cryptographically equivalent to a 160-bit elliptic curve cryptosystem key.

6. A. The SHA-1 hashing algorithm always produces a 160-bit message digest, regardless of the size of the input message. In fact, this fixed-length output is a requirement of any secure hashing algorithm.

7. C. The WEP algorithm has documented flaws that make it trivial to break. It should never be used to protect wireless networks.

8. A. WiFi Protected Access (WPA) uses the Temporal Key Integrity Protocol (TKIP) to protect wireless communications. WPA2 uses AES encryption.

9. B. Sue would have encrypted the message using Richard's public key. Therefore, Richard needs to use the complementary key in the key pair, his private key, to decrypt the message.

10. B. Richard should encrypt the message digest with his own private key. When Sue receives the message, she will decrypt the digest with Richard's public key and then compute the digest herself. If the two digests match, she can be assured that the message truly originated from Richard.

11. C. The Digital Signature Standard allows federal government use of the Digital Signature Algorithm, RSA, or the Elliptic Curve DSA in conjunction with the SHA-1 hashing function to produce secure digital signatures.

12. B. X.509 governs digital certificates and the public key infrastructure (PKI). It defines the appropriate content for a digital certificate and the processes used by certificate authorities to generate and revoke certificates.

13. B. Pretty Good Privacy uses a "web of trust" system of digital signature verification. The encryption technology is based upon the IDEA private key cryptosystem.

14. C. Secure Sockets Layer utilizes TCP port 443 for encrypted client-server communications.

15. C. The meet-in-the-middle attack demonstrated that it took relatively the same amount of computation power to defeat 2DES as it does to defeat standard DES. This led to the adoption of Triple DES (3DES) as a standard for government communication.

16. A. Rainbow tables contain precomputed hash values for commonly used passwords and may be used to increase the efficiency of password cracking attacks.

17. C. The WiFi Protected Access protocol encrypts traffic passing between a mobile client and the wireless access point. It does not provide end-to-end encryption.

18. B. Certificate revocation lists (CRLs) introduce an inherent latency to the certificate expiration process due to the time lag between CRL distributions.

19. D. The Merkle-Hellman Knapsack algorithm, which relies upon the difficulty of factoring super-increasing sets, has been broken by cryptanalysts.

20. B. IPSec is a security protocol that defines a framework for setting up a secure channel to exchange information between two entities.

Chapter 11: Principles of Security Models, Design, and Capabilities

1. B. A system certification is a technical evaluation. Option A describes system accreditation. Options C and D refer to manufacturer standards, not implementation standards.

2. A. Accreditation is the formal acceptance process. Option B is not an appropriate answer because it addresses manufacturer standards. Options C and D are incorrect because there is no way to prove that a configuration enforces a security policy and accreditation does not entail secure communication specification.

3.   C. A closed system is one that uses largely proprietary or unpublished protocols and standards. Options A and D do not describe any particular systems, and Option B describes an open system.

4.   C. A constrained process is one that can access only certain memory locations. Options A, B, and D do not describe a constrained process.

5.   A. An object is a resource a user or process want to access. Option A describes an access object.

6.   D. A control limits access to an object to protect it from misuse by unauthorized users.

7.   B. The applications and systems at a specific, self-contained location are evaluated for DITSCAP and NIACAP site accreditation.

8.   C. TCSEC defines four major categories: category A is verified protection, category B is mandatory protection, category C is discretionary protection, and category D is minimal protection.

9.   C. The TCB is the combination of hardware, software, and controls that work together to enforce a security policy.

10.   A, B. Although the most correct answer in the context of this chapter is option B, option A is also a correct answer in the context of physical security.

11.   C. The reference monitor validates access to every resource prior to granting the requested access. Option D, the security kernel, is the collection of TCB components that work together to implement the reference monitor functions. In other words, the security kernel is the implementation of the reference monitor concept. Options A and B are not valid TCB concept components.

12.   B. Option B is the only option that correctly defines a security model. Options A, C, and D define part of a security policy and the certification and accreditation process.

13.   D. The Bell-LaPadula and Biba models are built on the state machine model.

14.   A. Only the Bell-LaPadula model addresses data confidentiality. The Biba and Clark-Wilson models address data integrity. The Brewer and Nash model prevents conflicts of interest.

15.   C. The no read up property, also called the Simple Security Policy, prohibits subjects from reading a higher security level object.

16.   B. The simple property of Biba is no read down, but it implies that it is acceptable to read up.

17.   D. Declassification is the process of moving an object into a lower level of classification once it is determined that it no longer justifies being placed at a higher level. Only a trusted subject can perform declassification because this action is a violation of the verbiage of the star property of Bell-LaPadula, but not the spirit or intent, which is to prevent unauthorized disclosure.

18. B. An access control matrix assembles ACLs from multiple objects into a single table. The rows of that table are the ACEs of a subject across those objects, thus a capabilities list.

19. C. The trusted computing base (TCB) has a component known as the reference monitor in theory, which becomes the security kernel in implementation.

20. C. The three parts of the Clark-Wilson model access triple are subject, object, and program (or interface).

Chapter 12: Security Architecture Vulnerabilities, Threats, and Countermeasures

1. C. Multitasking is processing more than one task at the same time. In most cases, multitasking is actually simulated by the operating system even when not supported by the processor.

2. B. Although all electronic devices emit some unwanted emanations, CRT monitors are the devices most susceptible to this threat (at least from this list of options).

3. A. A single-processor system can operate on only one thread at a time. There would be a total of four application threads (ignoring any threads created by the operating system), but the operating system would be responsible for deciding which single thread is running on the processor at any given time.

4. A. In a dedicated system, all users must have a valid security clearance for the highest level of information processed by the system, they must have access approval for all information processed by the system, and they must have a valid need to know of all information processed by the system.

5. A. All user applications, regardless of the security permissions assigned to the user, execute in user mode. Supervisory mode, kernel mode, and privileged mode are all terms that describe the mode used by the processor to execute instructions that originate from the operating system.

6. B. Programmable read-only memory (PROM) chips may be written to once by the end user but may never be erased. The contents of ROM chips are burned in at the factory, and the end user is not allowed to write data. EPROM and EEPROM chips both make provisions for the end user to somehow erase the contents of the memory device and rewrite new data to the chip.

7. C. EPROMs may be erased through exposure to high-intensity ultraviolet light. ROM and PROM chips do not provide erasure functionality. EEPROM chips may be erased through the application of electrical currents to the chip pins and do not require removal from the computer prior to erasure.

8. C. *Secondary memory* is a term used to describe magnetic and optical media. These devices will retain their contents after being removed from the computer and may later be read by another user.

9. B. Security mechanisms are needed within an operating system because software is not trusted.

10. A. Dynamic RAM chips are built from a large number of capacitors, each of which holds a single electrical charge. These capacitors must be continually refreshed by the CPU in order to retain their contents. The data stored in the chip is lost when power is removed.

11. C. Removable drives are easily taken out of their authorized physical location, and it is often not possible to apply operating system access controls to them. Therefore, encryption is often the only security measure short of physical security that can be afforded to them. Backup tapes are most often well controlled through physical security measures. Hard disks and RAM chips are often secured through operating system access controls.

12. B. In system high mode, all users have appropriate clearances and access permissions for all information processed by the system but need to know only some of the information processed by that system.

13. D. In a multilevel security mode system, there is no requirement that all users have appropriate clearances to access all the information processed by the system.

14. B. BIOS and device firmware are often stored on EEPROM chips to facilitate future firmware updates.

15. C. Registers are small memory locations that are located directly on the CPU chip itself. The data stored within them is directly available to the CPU and can be accessed extremely quickly.

16. B. In immediate addressing, the CPU does not need to actually retrieve any data from memory. The data is contained in the instruction itself and can be immediately processed.

17. D. In indirect addressing, the location provided to the CPU contains a memory address. The CPU retrieves the operand by reading it from the memory address provided (which is why it's called *indirect*).

18. C. Process isolation provides separate memory spaces to each process running on a system. This prevents processes from overwriting each other's data and ensures that a process can't read data from another process.

19. D. The principle of least privilege states that only processes that absolutely need kernel-level access should run in supervisory mode. The remaining processes should run in user mode to reduce the number of potential security vulnerabilities.

20. A. Hardware segmentation achieves the same objectives as process isolation but takes them to a higher level by implementing them with physical controls in hardware.

Chapter 13: Security Operations

1. C. Need to know is the requirement to have access to, knowledge about, or possession of data to perform specific work tasks, but no more. The principle of least *privilege* includes both rights and permissions, but the term *principle of least permission* is not used within IT security. Separation of duties ensures that a single person doesn't control all the elements of a process. Role-based access control grants access to resources based on a role.

2. A. The principle of least privilege restricts user privileges to what they need and no more. Users do not have a need to log onto any computer in the network. A policy used to implement the principle of least privilege can restrict users to a single computer, restrict access to files, and restrict access to backups.

3. C. A separation of duties policy prevents a single person from controlling all elements of a process. When applied to security settings, it can prevent a person from making security changes without assistance. Job rotation helps ensure that multiple people can do the same job and can help prevent the organization from losing information when a single person leaves. Having subjects concentrate their talents is unrelated to separation of duties.

4. A. A job rotation policy has employees rotate jobs or job responsibilities and can help detect incidences of collusion and fraud. A separation of duties policy ensures that a single person doesn't control all elements of a specific function. Mandatory vacation policies ensure that employees take an extended time away from their job, requiring someone else to cover the responsibilities, which increases the ability to discover fraud. Least privilege ensures that users have only the permissions they need to perform the job and no more.

5. B. Special privileges should not be granted equally to administrators and operators. Special privileges are activities that require special access or elevated rights and permissions to perform many administrative and sensitive job tasks. Assignment and usage of these privileges should be monitored, and access should be granted only to trusted employees.

6. D. Baselining is used for configuration management and would not help reduce collusion or fraud. Job rotation, separation of duties, and mandatory vacation policies will all help reduce collusion and fraud.

7. D. Classification is the most important aspect of marking media because it clearly identifies the value of the media and users know how to protect it based on the classification. Including information such as the date and a description of the content isn't as important as marking the classification. Electronic labels or marks can be used, but when they are used, the most important information is still the classification of the data.

8. C. Purging media removes all data by writing over existing data multiple times to ensure that the data is not recoverable using any known methods. Purged media can then be used in less-secure environments. Erasing the media performs a delete, but the data remains and can easily be restored. Clearing, or overwriting, writes unclassified data over existing data but some sophisticated forensics techniques may be able to recover the original data, so this method should not be used to reduce the classification of media.

9. C. Sanitization can be unreliable because the purging, degaussing, or other processes can be performed improperly. When sanitation is done properly, purged data is not recoverable using any known methods. Data cannot be retrieved from incinerated, or burned, media. Data isn't physically etched into the media.

10. B. Record retention policies define the amount of time to keep any data, including logs. Data remanence is data that remains on media after it has supposedly been removed. Data diddling refers to the modification of data before or during data entry resulting in incorrect or corrupt data. Data mining refers to extracting meaningful knowledge from large amounts of data.

11. C. Systems should be sanitized when they reach the end of their life cycle to ensure that they do not include any sensitive data. Removing CDs and DVDs is part of the sanitation process, but other elements of the system, such as disk drives, should also be checked. Removing software licenses or installing the original software is not necessarily required unless the organization's sanitization process requires it.

12. B. The tapes should be purged, ensuring that data cannot be recovered using any known means. Even though tapes may be at the end of their life cycle, they can still hold data and should be purged before throwing them away. Erasing doesn't remove all usable data from media, but purging does. There is no need to store the tapes if they are at the end of their life cycle.

13. C. Only the patches that are needed should be deployed so an organization will not deploy *all* patches. Instead, an organization evaluates the patches to determine which patches are needed, tests them to ensure that they don't cause unintended problems, deploys the approved and tested patches, and audits systems to ensure that patches have been applied.

14. B. Vulnerability scanners are used to check systems for known issues and are part of an overall vulnerability management program. Versioning is used to track software versions and is unrelated to detecting vulnerabilities. Security audits and reviews help ensure that an organization is following its policies but wouldn't directly check systems for vulnerabilities.

15. C. The goal of change management is to ensure that any change does not lead to unintended outages or reduce security. Change management doesn't affect personnel safety. A change management plan will commonly include a rollback plan, but that isn't a specific goal of the program. Change management doesn't perform any type of auditing.

16. A. Change management processes may need to be temporarily bypassed to respond to an emergency situation, but they should not be bypassed simply because someone thinks it can improve performance. Even when a change is implemented in response to an emergency, it should still be documented and reviewed after the incident. Requesting changes, creating rollback plans, and documenting changes are all valid steps within a change management process.

17. D. Change management processes would ensure that changes are evaluated before being implemented to prevent unintended outages or needlessly weakening security. Patch management ensures systems are up-to-date, vulnerability management checks systems for known vulnerabilities, and configuration management ensures that systems are deployed similarly, but these other processes wouldn't prevent an unauthorized change.

18. D. Backup media should be protected with the same level of protection afforded the data it contains, and using a secure offsite storage facility would ensure this. The media should be marked, but that won't protect it if it is stored in an unmanned warehouse. A copy of backups should be stored off site to ensure availability if a catastrophe affects the primary location. If copies of data are not stored off site, or offsite backups are destroyed, security is sacrificed by risking availability.

19. A. If the tapes were marked before they left the data center, employees would recognize their value and it is more likely someone would challenge their storage in an unmanned warehouse. Purging or degaussing the tapes before using them will erase previously held data but won't help if sensitive information is backed up to the tapes after they are purged or degaussed. Adding the tapes to an asset management database will help track them but wouldn't prevent this incident.

20. B. The scenario states that onsite email older than six months is purged, but offsite back-ups included backups for the last 20 years, indicating record retention policies are applied on site but not to the backup media. Media destruction policies should be followed when the media is no longer needed, but some backups are needed. Configuration management ensures that systems are configured correctly using a baseline, but this does not apply to backup media. Versioning is applied to applications, not backup tapes.

Chapter 14: Incident Management

1. A. Containment should be the first step when an incident has been detected and verified to limit the effect or scope of an incident. It should be reported based on an organization's policies and governing laws, but this is not the first step. Remediation attempts to identify the cause of the incident and steps that can be taken to prevent a reoccurrence, but this is the last step, not the first. It is important to protect evidence while trying to contain an incident, but gathering the evidence will occur after containment.

2. D. An incident is examined during the remediation and review stage. A root cause analysis is generated in an attempt to discover the source of the problem. After the cause is discovered, the review will often identify a solution to help prevent a similar occurrence in the future. Containing the incident and collecting evidence is done early in the incident response process. Rebuilding a system may be needed during the recovery stage.

3. B. Of the choices offered, email is the most common distribution method for viruses of the choices given. *Driving downloads* isn't a term used in IT security, but drive-by downloads are thought by some professionals to be overtaking email as the most common method of distribution. Rogueware (fake antivirus software) is a common method of tricking users but not the most common method. If users are able to install unapproved software, they may inadvertently install malware, but this isn't the most common method either.

4. C. A multipronged approach provides the best solution. This involves having antivirus software at several locations, such as at the boundary between the Internet and the internal network, at email servers, and on each system. More than one antivirus application on a single system isn't recommended. A single solution for the whole organization is often

ineffective because malware can get into the network in more than one way. Content filtering at border gateways (the boundary between the Internet and the internal network) is a good partial solution, but it won't catch malware brought in through other methods.

5. B. A zero-day exploit takes advantage of a previously unknown vulnerability. A botnet is a group of computers controlled by a bot herder that can launch attacks, but they can exploit both known vulnerabilities and previously unknown vulnerabilities. Similarly, denial-of-service (DoS) and distributed DoS (DDoS) attacks could use zero-day exploits or use known methods.

6. D. Spoofing is used by attackers to hide their identity in a variety of attacks but is not an attack by itself. Teardrop, smurf, and ping of death are all types of denial-of-service attacks.

7. C. A SYN flood attack disrupts the TCP three-way handshake process by never sending the third packet. It is not unique to any specific operating system such as Windows. Smurf attacks use amplification networks to flood a victim with packets. A ping-of-death attack uses oversized ping packets.

8. A. In a land attack, the attacker sends a victim numerous SYN packets that have been spoofed to use the same source and destination IP address as the victim's IP address. Spamming attacks send unwanted email. A teardrop attack fragments traffic in such a way that data packets can't be put together. A ping flood attack floods the victim with ping requests.

9. D. In a teardrop attack, an attacker fragments traffic in such a way that data packets cannot be put together. A zero-day exploit refers to an attack using vulnerabilities that are unknown to others. Spamming refers to sending massive quantities of unsolicited email. A distributed denial-of-service (DDoS) attack is an attack on a single system from multiple sources.

10. D. An intrusion detection system (IDS) is the best tool to search through large log files looking for intrusion-related events. A text editor requires manually looking at logs. Vulnerability scanners and password crackers are not used to search through log files looking for intrusions.

11. A. An IDS automates the inspection of audit logs and real-time system events to detect abnormal activity indicating unauthorized system access. While IDSs can detect system failures and monitor system performance, they don't include the ability to diagnose system failures or rate system performance. Vulnerability scanners are used to test systems for vulnerabilities.

12. B. An HIDS monitors a single system looking for abnormal activity. A network-based IDS (NIDS) watches for abnormal activity on a network. An HIDS is normally visible as a running process on a system and provides alerts to authorized users. An HIDS can detect malicious code similar to how antivirus software can detect malicious code.

13. C. A knowledge-based (or signature-based) IDS is effective only against known attack methods. A behavior-based IDS starts by creating a baseline of activity to identify normal behavior and then measures system performance against the baseline to detect abnormal behavior, allowing it to detect previously unknown attack methods. Both host-based and network-based systems can be knowledge based, behavior based, or a combination of both.

14. B. Honeypots are individual computers, and honeynets are entire networks created to serve as a trap for intruders. They look like legitimate networks and tempt intruders with unpatched and unprotected security vulnerabilities as well as attractive and tantalizing but false data. An intrusion detection system (IDS) will detect attacks. In some cases an IDS can divert an attacker to a padded cell, which is a simulated environment with fake data intended to keep the attacker's interest. A pseudo flaw (used by many honeypots and honeynets) is a false vulnerability intentionally implanted in a system to tempt attackers.

15. B. Penetration testing should be performed only with the knowledge and consent of the management staff. Unapproved security testing could result in productivity loss, trigger emergency response teams, and legal action against the tester, including loss of employment. A penetration test can mimic previous attacks and use both manual and automated attack methods. After a penetration test, a system may be reconfigured to resolve discovered vulnerabilities.

16. C. Distribution of malicious code will almost always result in damage or loss of assets and is not used in a penetration test. However, denial-of-service attacks, port scanning, and packet sniffing may all be included in a penetration test.

17. A. Failover clustering uses two or more servers and will ensure that a service will continue even if a server fails. A redundant array of independent disks (RAID) allows a disk subsystem to continue to operate even if a disk fails. A hot site is an alternative location maintained in a ready state that can be used if the primary location suffers a serious outage. An uninterruptible power supply (UPS) provides short-term power for a system if the primary power source is lost.

18. D. Evidence should have been gathered that could be used against the attacker at a later time if necessary. The first response after an incident is detected and verified is to contain the incident, but it could have been contained without rebooting the server. Review and remediation are done as the last stage. Recovery is done after reporting the incident, but the administrator did not report the incident and instead rebooted the system, which may have been required for a full recovery.

19. C. Attacking the IP address was the most serious mistake because it is illegal in most locations. Additionally, because attackers often use spoofing techniques, it probably isn't the actual IP address of the attacker. Rebooting the server without gathering evidence and not reporting the incident were mistakes but won't have a potential lasting negative effect on the organization. Resetting the connection to isolate the incident would have been a good step if it was done without rebooting the server.

20. A. The administrator did not report the incident so there was no opportunity for remediation and review. It could be the incident occurred because of a vulnerability on the server, but without an examination the exact cause won't be known unless the attack is repeated. The administrator detected the event and responded (though inappropriately). Rebooting the server can be considered a recovery step. It's worth mentioning that the incident response plan was kept secret and the server administrator didn't have access to it and so likely does not know what the proper response should be.

Chapter 15: Business Continuity Planning

1. B. The business organization analysis helps the initial planners select appropriate BCP team members and then guides the overall BCP process.

2. B. The first task of the BCP team should be the review and validation of the business organization analysis initially performed by those individuals responsible for spearheading the BCP effort. This ensures that the initial effort, undertaken by a small group of individuals, reflects the beliefs of the entire BCP team.

3. C. A firm's officers and directors are legally bound to exercise due diligence in conducting their activities. This concept creates a fiduciary responsibility on their part to ensure that adequate business continuity plans are in place.

4. D. During the planning phase, the most significant resource utilization will be the time dedicated by members of the BCP team to the planning process itself. This represents a significant use of business resources and is another reason that buy-in from senior management is essential.

5. A. The quantitative portion of the priority identification should assign asset values in monetary units.

6. C. The annualized loss expectancy (ALE) represents the amount of money a business expects to lose to a given risk each year. This figure is quite useful when performing a quantitative prioritization of business continuity resource allocation.

7. C. The maximum tolerable downtime (MTD) represents the longest period a business function can be unavailable before causing irreparable harm to the business. This figure is useful when determining the level of business continuity resources to assign to a particular function.

8. B. The SLE is the product of the AV and the EF. From the scenario, you know that the AV is $3,000,000 and the EF is 90 percent, based on that the same land can be used to rebuild the facility. This yields an SLE of $2,700,000.

9. D. This problem requires you to compute the ALE, which is the product of the SLE and the ARO. From the scenario, you know that the ARO is 0.05 (or 5 percent). From question 8, you know that the SLE is $2,700,000. This yields an SLE of $135,000.

10. A. This problem requires you to compute the ALE, which is the product of the SLE and ARO. From the scenario, you know that the ARO is 0.10 (or 10 percent). From the scenario presented, you know that the SLE is $7.5 million. This yields an SLE of $750,000.

11. C. The strategy development task bridges the gap between business impact assessment and continuity planning by analyzing the prioritized list of risks developed during the BIA and determining which risks will be addressed by the BCP.

12. D. The safety of human life must always be the paramount concern in business continuity planning. Be sure that your plan reflects this priority, especially in the written documentation that is disseminated to your organization's employees!

13. C. It is very difficult to put a dollar figure on the business lost because of negative publicity. Therefore, this type of concern is better evaluated through a qualitative analysis.

14. B. The single loss expectancy (SLE) is the amount of damage that would be caused by a single occurrence of the risk. In this case, the SLE is $10 million, the expected damage from one tornado. The fact that a tornado occurs only once every 100 years is not reflected in the SLE but would be reflected in the annualized loss expectancy (ALE).

15. C. The annualized loss expectancy (ALE) is computed by taking the product of the single loss expectancy (SLE), which was $10 million in this scenario, and the annualized rate of occurrence (ARO), which was 0.01 in this example. These figures yield an ALE of $100,000.

16. C. In the provisions and processes phase, the BCP team actually designs the procedures and mechanisms to mitigate risks that were deemed unacceptable during the strategy development phase.

17. D. This is an example of alternative systems. Redundant communications circuits provide backup links that may be used when the primary circuits are unavailable.

18. C. Disaster recovery plans pick up where business continuity plans leave off. After a disaster strikes and the business is interrupted, the disaster recovery plan guides response teams in their efforts to quickly restore business operations to normal levels.

19. A. The single loss expectancy (SLE) is computed as the product of the asset value (AV) and the exposure factor (EF). The other formulas displayed here do not accurately reflect this calculation.

20. C. You should strive to have the highest-ranking person possible sign the BCP's statement of importance. Of the choices given, the chief executive officer is the highest ranking.

Chapter 16: Disaster Recovery Planning

1. C. Once a disaster interrupts the business operations, the goal of DRP is to restore regular business activity as quickly as possible. Thus, disaster recovery planning picks up where business continuity planning leaves off.

2. C. A power outage is an example of a man-made disaster. The other events listed—tsunamis, earthquakes, and lightning strikes—are all naturally occurring events.

3. D. As shown in Table 16.1, 41 of the 50 U.S. states are considered to have a moderate, high, or very high risk of seismic activity. This rounds to 80 percent to provide the value given in answer D.

4. B. Most general business insurance and homeowner's insurance policies do not provide any protection against the risk of flooding or flash floods. If floods pose a risk to your organization, you should consider purchasing supplemental flood insurance under FEMA's National Flood Insurance Program.

5. C. All the industries listed in the options made changes to their practices after September 11, 2001, but the insurance industry's change toward noncoverage of acts of terrorism most directly impacts the BCP/DRP process.

6. C. The opposite of this statement is true—disaster recovery planning picks up where business continuity planning leaves off. The other three statements are all accurate reflections of the role of business continuity planning and disaster recovery planning.

7. B. The term *100-year flood plain* is used to describe an area where flooding is expected once every 100 years. It is, however, more mathematically correct to say that this label indicates a 1 percent probability of flooding in any given year.

8. D. When you use remote mirroring, an exact copy of the database is maintained at an alternative location. You keep the remote copy up-to-date by executing all transactions on both the primary and remote site at the same time.

9. C. Redundant systems/components provide protection against the failure of one particular piece of hardware.

10. B. During the business impact assessment phase, you must identify the business priorities of your organization to assist with the allocation of BCP resources. You can use this same information to drive the DRP business unit prioritization.

11. C. The cold site contains none of the equipment necessary to restore operations. All of the equipment must be brought in and configured and data must be restored to it before operations can commence. This often takes weeks.

12. C. Warm sites typically take about 12 hours to activate from the time a disaster is declared. This is compared to the relatively instantaneous activation of a hot site and the lengthy time (at least a week) required to bring a cold site to operational status.

13. D. Warm sites and hot sites both contain workstations, servers, and the communications circuits necessary to achieve operational status. The main difference between the two alternatives is the fact that hot sites contain near-real-time copies of the operational data and warm sites require the restoration of data from backup.

14. D. Remote mirroring is the only backup option in which a live backup server at a remote site maintains a bit-for-bit copy of the contents of the primary server, synchronized as closely as the latency in the link between primary and remote systems will allow.

15. A. The executive summary provides a high-level view of the entire organization's disaster recovery efforts. This document is useful for the managers and leaders of the firm as well as public relations personnel who need a nontechnical perspective on this complex effort.

16. D. Software escrow agreements place the application source code in the hands of an independent third party, thus providing firms with a "safety net" in the event a developer goes out of business or fails to honor the terms of a service agreement.

17. A. Differential backups involve always storing copies of all files modified since the most recent full backup regardless of any incremental or differential backups created during the intervening time period.

18. C. Any backup strategy must include full backups at some point in the process. Incremental backups are created faster than differential backups because of the number of files it is necessary to back up each time.

19. A. Any backup strategy must include full backups at some point in the process. If a combination of full and differential backups is used, a maximum of two backups must be restored. If a combination of full and incremental backups is chosen, the number of required restorations may be unlimited.

20. B. Parallel tests involve moving personnel to the recovery site and gearing up operations, but responsibility for conducting day-to-day operations of the business remains at the primary operations center.

Chapter 17: Laws, Regulations, and Compliance

1. C. The Computer Fraud and Abuse Act, as amended, provides criminal and civil penalties for those individuals convicted of using viruses, worms, Trojan horses, and other types of malicious code to cause damage to computer system(s).

2. A. The Computer Security Act requires mandatory periodic training for all people involved in managing, using, or operating federal computer systems that contain sensitive information.

3. D. Administrative laws do not require an act of the legislative branch to implement at the federal level. Administrative laws consist of the policies, procedures, and regulations promulgated by agencies of the executive branch of government. Although they do not require an act of Congress, these laws are subject to judicial review and must comply with criminal and civil laws enacted by the legislative branch.

4. C. The National Institute of Standards and Technology (NIST) is charged with the security management of all federal government computer systems that are not used to process sensitive national security information. The National Security Agency (part of the Department of Defense) is responsible for managing those systems that do process classified and/or sensitive information.

5. C. The original Computer Fraud and Abuse Act of 1984 covered only systems used by the government and financial institutions. The act was broadened in 1986 to include all federal interest systems. The Computer Abuse Amendments Act of 1994 further amended the CFAA to cover all systems that are used in interstate commerce, covering a large portion (but not all) of the computer systems in the United States.

6. B. The Fourth Amendment to the U.S. Constitution sets the "probable cause" standard that law enforcement officers must follow when conducting searches and/or seizures of private property. It also states that those officers must obtain a warrant before gaining involuntary access to such property.

7. A. Copyright law is the only type of intellectual property protection available to Matthew. It covers only the specific software code that Matthew used. It does not cover the process or ideas behind the software. Trademark protection is not appropriate for this type of situation. Patent protection does not apply to mathematical algorithms. Matthew can't seek trade secret protection because he plans to publish the algorithm in a public technical journal.

8. D. Mary and Joe should treat their oil formula as a trade secret. As long as they do not publicly disclose the formula, they can keep it a company secret indefinitely.

9. C. Richard's product name should be protected under trademark law. Until his registration is granted, he can use the TM symbol next to it to inform others that it is protected under trademark law. Once his application is approved, the name becomes a registered trademark and Richard can begin using the ® symbol.

10. A. The Privacy Act of 1974 limits the ways government agencies may use information that private citizens disclose to them under certain circumstances.

11. B. The Uniform Computer Information Transactions Act (UCITA) attempts to implement a standard framework of laws regarding computer transactions to be adopted by all states. One of the issues addressed by UCITA is the legality of various types of software license agreements.

12. A. The Children's Online Privacy Protection Act (COPPA) provides severe penalties for companies that collect information from young children without parental consent. COPPA states that this consent must be obtained from the parents of children younger than the age of 13 before any information is collected (other than basic information required to obtain that consent).

13. A. The Digital Millennium Copyright Act does not include any geographical location requirements for protection under the "transitory activities" exemption. The other options are three of the five mandatory requirements. The other two requirements are that the service provider must not determine the recipients of the material and the material must be transmitted with no modification to its content.

14. C. The USA PATRIOT Act was adopted in the wake of the September 11, 2001, terrorist attacks. It broadens the powers of the government to monitor communications between private citizens and therefore actually weakens the privacy rights of consumers and Internet users. The other laws mentioned all contain provisions designed to enhance individual privacy rights.

15. B. Shrink-wrap license agreements become effective when the user opens a software package. Click-wrap agreements require the user to click a button during the installation process to accept the terms of the license agreement. Standard license agreements require that the user

sign a written agreement prior to using the software. Verbal agreements are not normally used for software licensing but also require some active degree of participation by the software user.

16. B. The Gramm-Leach-Bliley Act provides, among other things, regulations regarding the way financial institutions can handle private information belonging to their customers.

17. C. U.S. patent law provides for an exclusivity period of 20 years beginning at the time the patent application is submitted to the Patent and Trademark Office.

18. C. Marketing needs are not a valid reason for processing personal information, as defined by the European Union privacy directive.

19. C. The Payment Card Industry Data Security Standard (PCI DSS) applies to organizations involved in the storage, transmission, and processing of credit card information.

20. C. The onward transfer provisions of the safe harbor require that organizations share data only with other organizations that comply with the safe harbor principles.

Chapter 18: Incidents and Ethics

1. C. A crime is any violation of a law or regulation. The violation stipulation defines the action as a crime. It is a computer crime if the violation involves a computer either as the target or as a tool.

2. B. A military and intelligence attack is targeted at the classified data that resides on the system. To the attacker, the value of the information justifies the risk associated with such an attack. The information extracted from this type of attack is often used to plan subsequent attacks.

3. A. Confidential information that is not related to the military or intelligence agencies is the target of business attacks. The ultimate goal could be destruction, alteration, or disclosure of confidential information.

4. B. A financial attack focuses primarily on obtaining services and funds illegally.

5. B. A terrorist attack is launched to interfere with a way of life by creating an atmosphere of fear. A computer terrorist attack can reach this goal by reducing the ability to respond to a simultaneous physical attack.

6. D. Any action that can harm a person or organization, either directly or through embarrassment, would be a valid goal of a grudge attack. The purpose of such an attack is to "get back" at someone.

7. A, C. Thrill attacks have no reward other than providing a boost to pride and ego. The thrill of launching the attack comes from the act of participating in the attack (and not getting caught).

8. C. Although the other options have some merit in individual cases, the most important rule is to never modify, or taint, evidence. If you modify evidence, it becomes inadmissible in court.

9. D. The most compelling reason for not removing power from a machine is that you will lose the contents of memory. Carefully consider the pros and cons of removing power. After all is considered, it may be the best choice.

10. B, D. Hacktivists (the word is a combination of *hacker* and *activist*) often combine political motivations with the thrill of hacking. They organize themselves loosely into groups with names like Anonymous and Lolzsec and use tools like the Low Orbit Ion Cannon to create large-scale denial-of-service attacks with little knowledge required.

11. D. An incident is normally defined as any event that adversely affects the confidentiality, integrity, or availability of your data.

12. B. Some port scans are normal. An unusually high volume of port scan activity can be a reconnaissance activity preceding a more dangerous attack. When you see unusual port scanning, you should always investigate.

13. A. Any time an attacker exceeds their authority, the incident is classified as a system compromise. This includes valid users who exceed their authority as well as invalid users who gain access through the use of a valid user ID.

14. C. Although options A, B, and D are actions that can make you aware of what attacks look like and how to detect them, you will never successfully detect most attacks until you know your system. When you know what the activity on your system looks like on a normal day, you can immediately detect any abnormal activity.

15. B. In this case, you need a search warrant to confiscate equipment without giving the suspect time to destroy evidence. If the suspect worked for your organization and you had all employees sign consent agreements, you could simply confiscate the equipment.

16. A. Log files contain a large volume of generally useless information. However, when you are trying to track down a problem or an incident, they can be invaluable. Even if an incident is discovered as it is happening, it may have been preceded by other incidents. Log files provide valuable clues and should be protected and archived.

17. A, D. You must report an incident when the incident resulted in the violation of a law or regulation. This includes any damage (or potential damage) to or disclosure of protected information.

18. D. Ethics are simply rules of personal behavior. Many professional organizations establish formal codes of ethics to govern their members, but ethics are personal rules individuals use to guide their lives.

19. B. The second canon of the (ISC)^2 Code of Ethics states how a CISSP should act, which is honorably, honestly, justly, responsibly, and legally.

20. B. RFC 1087 does not specifically address the statements in A, C, or D. Although each type of activity listed is unacceptable, only "actions that compromise the privacy of users" are explicitly identified in RFC 1087.

Chapter 19: Physical Security Requirements

1. A. Physical security is the most important aspect of overall security. Without physical security, none of the other aspects of security are sufficient.

2. B. Critical path analysis can be used to map out the needs of an organization for a new facility. A critical path analysis is the process of identifying relationships between mission-critical applications, processes, and operations and all of the supporting elements.

3. C. Administrative physical security controls include facility construction and selection, site management, personnel controls, awareness training, and emergency response and procedures.

4. D. Equal access to all locations within a facility is not a security-focused design element. Each area containing assets or resources of different importance, value, and confidentiality should have a corresponding level of security restriction placed on it.

5. A. A computer room does not need to be human compatible to be efficient and secure. Having a human-incompatible server room provides a greater level of protection against attacks.

6. B. Fencing is a perimeter-defining device used to deter casual trespassing. Gates, security guards, and motion detectors do not define a facility's perimeter.

7. C. A mantrap is a double set of doors that is often protected by a guard and used to contain a subject until their identity and authentication is verified.

8. D. Lighting is the most common form of perimeter security devices or mechanisms. Your entire site should be clearly lit. This provides for easy identification of personnel and makes it easier to notice intrusions.

9. A. Security guards are usually unaware of the scope of the operations within a facility, which supports confidentiality of those operations and thus helps reduce the possibility that a security guard will be involved in the disclosure of confidential information.

10. B. The most common cause of failure for a water-based system is human error. If you turn off the water source after a fire and forget to turn it back on, you'll be in trouble for the future. Also, pulling an alarm when there is no fire will trigger damaging water release throughout the office.

11. C. Key locks are the most common and inexpensive form of physical access control device. Lighting, security guards, and fences are all much more costly.

12. D. A capacitance motion detector senses changes in the electrical or magnetic field surrounding a monitored object.

13. A. There is no such thing as a preventive alarm. Alarms are always triggered in response to a detected intrusion or attack.

14. B. No matter what form of physical access control is used, a security guard or other monitoring system must be deployed to prevent abuse, masquerading, and piggybacking. Espionage cannot be prevented by physical access controls.

15. C. Human safety is the most important goal of all security solutions.

16. B. The humidity in a computer room should ideally be from 40 to 60 percent.

17. D. Destruction of data stored on hard drives can be caused by 1,500 volts of static electricity.

18. A. Water is never the suppression medium in Type B fire extinguishers because they are used on liquid fires.

19. C. A preaction system is the best type of water-based fire suppression system for a computer facility.

20. D. Light is usually not damaging to most computer equipment, but fire, smoke, and the suppression medium (typically water) are very destructive.

Appendix

B

Answers to Written Labs

Chapter 1: Access Control

1. Access control types include preventive access control, deterrent access control, detective access control, corrective access control, recovery access control, compensation access control, directive access control, administrative access control, logical or technical access control, and physical control. They are implemented as administrative controls, logical/technical controls, and/or physical controls.

2. A Type 1 authentication factor is "something you know." A Type 2 authentication factor is "something you have." A Type 3 authentication factor is "something you are."

3. Federated identity management systems allow single sign-on to be extended beyond a single organization. Single sign-on allows users to authenticate once and access multiple resources without authenticating again.

4. The identity and access provisioning life cycle includes provisioning accounts, periodically reviewing and managing accounts, and revocation of accounts when they are no longer being used.

Chapter 2: Access Control Attacks and Monitoring

1. Assets, threats, and vulnerabilities should be identified through asset valuation, threat modeling, and vulnerability analysis.

2. Brute-force attacks, dictionary attacks, sniffer attacks, rainbow table attacks, and social engineering attacks are all methods used to discover passwords.

3. Auditing is a methodical examination or review of an environment and encompasses a wide variety of different activities to ensure compliance with regulations and to detect abnormalities, unauthorized occurrences, or outright crimes. Audit trails provide the data that supports such examination or review and essentially are what make auditing and subsequent detection of attacks and misbehavior possible.

4. Organizations should regularly perform access reviews and audits. These can detect when an organization is not following its own policies and procedures related to account management.

Chapter 3: Secure Network Architecture and Securing Network Components

1. Application (7), Presentation (6), Session (5), Transport (4), Network (3), Data Link (2), and Physical (1).

2. Problems with cabling and their countermeasures include attenuation (use repeaters or don't violate distance recommendations), using the wrong CAT cable (check the cable specifications against throughput requirements, and err on the side of caution), crosstalk (use shielded cables, place cables in separate conduits, or use cables of different twists per inch), cable breaks (avoid running cables in locations where movement occurs), interference (use cable shielding, use cables with higher twists per inch, or switch to fiber-optic cables), and eavesdropping (maintain physical security over all cable runs or switch to fiber-optic cables).

3. Some of the frequency spectrum-use technologies are spread spectrum, Frequency Hopping Spread Spectrum (FHSS), Direct Sequence Spread Spectrum (DSSS), and Orthogonal Frequency-Division Multiplexing (OFDM).

4. Methods to secure 802.11 wireless networking include disabling the SSID broadcast; changing the SSID to something unique; enabling MAC filtering; considering the use of static IPs or using DHCP with reservations; turning on the highest form of encryption offered (such as WEP, WPA, or WPA2/802.11i); treating wireless as remote access and employing 802.1X, RADIUS, or TACACS; separating wireless access points from the LAN with firewalls; monitoring all wireless client activity with an IDS; and considering requiring wireless clients to connect with a VPN to gain LAN access.

5. The LAN shared media access technologies are CSMA, CSMA/CA (used by 802.11 and AppleTalk), CSMA/CD (used by Ethernet), token passing (used by Token Ring and FDDI/CDDI), and polling (used by SDLC, HDLC, and some mainframe systems).

Chapter 4: Secure Communications and Network Attacks

1. IPSec's transport mode is used for host-to-host links and encrypts only the payload, not the header. IPSec's tunnel mode is used for host-to-LAN and LAN-to-LAN links and encrypts the entire original payload and header and then adds a link header.

2. Network Address Translation (NAT) allows for the identity of internal systems to be hidden from external entities. Often NAT is used to translate between RFC 1918 private IP addresses and leased public addresses. NAT serves as a one-way firewall because it allows only inbound traffic that is a response to a previous internal query. NAT also allows a few leased public addresses to be used to grant Internet connectivity to a larger number of internal systems.

3. Circuit switching is usually associated with physical connections. The link itself is physically established and then dismantled for the communication. Circuit switching offers known fixed delays, supports constant traffic, is connection oriented, is sensitive only to the loss of the connection rather than the communication, and was most often used for voice transmissions. Packet switching is usually associated with logical connections because the link is just a logically defined path among possible paths. Within a packet-switching system, each system or link can be employed simultaneously by other circuits. Packet switching divides the communication into segments, and each segment traverses the circuit to the destination. Packet switching has variable delays because each segment could take a unique path, is usually employed for bursty traffic, is not physically connection oriented but often uses virtual circuits, is sensitive to the loss of data, and is used for any form of communication.

4. Email is inherently insecure because it is primarily a plain-text communication medium and employs nonencrypted transmissions protocols. This allows for email to be easily spoofed, spammed, flooded, eavesdropped on, interfered with, and hijacked. Defenses against these issues primarily include having stronger authentication requirements and using encryption to protect the content while in transit.

Chapter 5: Security Governance Concepts, Principles, and Policies

1. The CIA Triad is the combination of confidentiality, integrity, and availability. This term is used to indicate the three key components of a security solution.

2. The requirements of accountability are identification, authentication, authorization, and auditing. Each of these components needs to be legally supportable to truly hold someone accountable for their actions.

3. The benefits of change control management include preventing unwanted security reduction because of uncontrolled change, documenting and tracking of all alterations in the environment, standardization, conforming with security policy, and the ability to roll back changes in the event of an unwanted or unexpected outcome.

4. (1) Identify the custodian, and define their responsibilities. (2) Specify the evaluation criteria of how the information will be classified and labeled. (3) Classify and label each resource. Although the owner conducts this step, a supervisor should review it. (4) Document any exceptions to the classification policy that are discovered, and integrate them into the evaluation criteria. (5) Select the security controls that will be applied to each classification level to provide the necessary level of protection. (6) Specify the procedures for declassifying resources and the procedures for transferring custody of a resource to an external entity. (7) Create an enterprise-wide awareness program to instruct all personnel about the classification system.

5. The six security roles are senior management, IT/security staff, owner, custodian, operator/ user, and auditor.

6. The four components of a security policy are policies, standards, guidelines, and procedures. Policies are broad security statements. Standards are definitions of hardware and software security compliance. Guidelines are used when there is not an appropriate procedure. Procedures are detailed step-by-step instructions for performing work tasks in a secure manner.

Chapter 6: Risk and Personnel Management

1. Possible answers include job descriptions, principle of least privilege, separation of duties, job responsibilities, job rotation/cross-training, performance reviews, background checks, job action warnings, awareness training, job training, exit interviews/terminations, nondisclosure agreements, noncompete agreements, employment agreements, privacy declaration, and acceptable use policies.

2. The formulas are as follows:

    SLE = AV * EF

    ARO = # / yr

    ALE = SLE * ARO

    Cost/benefit = (ALE1 − ALE2) − ACS

3. The Delphi technique is an anonymous feedback-and-response process used to enable a group to reach an anonymous consensus. Its primary purpose is to elicit honest and uninfluenced responses from all participants. The participants are usually gathered into a single meeting room. To each request for feedback, each participant writes down their response on paper anonymously. The results are compiled and presented to the group for evaluation. The process is repeated until a consensus is reached.

4. Risk assessment often involves a hybrid approach using both quantitative and qualitative methods. A purely quantitative analysis is not possible; not all elements and aspects of the analysis can be quantified because some are qualitative, some are subjective, and some are intangible. Since a purely quantitative risk assessment is not possible, balancing the results of a quantitative analysis is essential. The method of combining quantitative and qualitative analysis into a final assessment of organizational risk is known as hybrid assessment or hybrid analysis.

Chapter 7: Software Development Security

1. Worms travel from system to system under their own power by exploiting flaws in networking software.

2. The processing burden is shifted from the server to the client, allowing the web server to handle a greater number of simultaneous requests. The client uses local resources to process the data, usually resulting in a quicker response. The privacy of client data is protected because information does not need to be transmitted to the web server.

3. It must be tamperproof, it must always be invoked, and it must be small enough to be subject to analysis and tests, the completeness of which can be assured.

4. Microsoft Windows platforms only.

5. Primary key.

6. Polyinstantiation.

7. Static analysis performs assessment of the code itself, analyzing the sequence of instructions for security flaws. Dynamic analysis tests the code in a live production environment, searching for runtime flaws.

8. One phase.

Chapter 8: Malicious Code and Application Attacks

1. Viruses and worms both travel from system to system attempting to deliver their malicious payloads to as many machines as possible. However, viruses require some sort of human intervention, such as sharing a file, network resource, or email message, to propagate. Worms, on the other hand, seek out vulnerabilities and spread from system to system under their own power, thereby greatly magnifying their reproductive capability, especially in a well-connected network.

2. The Internet Worm used four propagation techniques. First, it exploited a bug in the sendmail utility that allowed it to spread itself by sending a specially crafted email message that contained its code to the sendmail program on a remote system. Second, it used a dictionary-based password attack to attempt to gain access to remote systems by utilizing the username and password of a valid system user. Third, it exploited a buffer overflow vulnerability in the finger program to infect systems. Fourth, it analyzed any existing trust relationships with other systems on the network and attempted to spread itself to those systems through the trusted path.

3. If possible, antivirus software may try to disinfect an infected file, removing the virus's malicious code. If that fails, it might either quarantine the file for manual review or automatically delete it to prevent further infection.

4. Data integrity assurance packages like Tripwire compute hash values for each file stored on a protected system. If a file infector virus strikes the system, this would result in a change in the affected file's hash value and would, therefore, trigger a file integrity alert.

Chapter 9: Cryptography and Symmetric Key Algorithms

1. The major obstacle to the widespread adoption of one-time pad cryptosystems is the difficulty in creating and distributing the very lengthy keys on which the algorithm depends.

2. The first step in encrypting this message requires the assignment of numeric column values to the letters of the secret keyword:

```
S E C U R E
5 2 1 6 4 3
```

Next, the letters of the message are written in order underneath the letters of the keyword:

```
S E C U R E
5 2 1 6 4 3
I W I L L P
A S S T H E
C I S S P E
X A M A N D
B E C O M E
C E R T I F
I E D N E X
T M O N T H
```

Finally, the sender enciphers the message by reading down each column; the order in which the columns are read corresponds to the numbers assigned in the first step. This produces the following ciphertext:

```
I S S M C R D O W S I A E E E M P E E D E F X H L H P N M I E T I A C X B
C I T L T S A O T N N
```

3. This message is decrypted by using the following function:

    P = (C – 3) mod 26
    C: F R Q J U D W X O D W L R Q V B R X J R W L W
    P: C O N G R A T U L A T I O N S Y O U G O T I T

    And the hidden message is "Congratulations You Got It." Congratulations, you got it!

Chapter 10: PKI and Cryptographic Applications

1. Bob should encrypt the message using Alice's public key and then transmit the encrypted message to Alice.

2. Alice should decrypt the message using her private key.

3. Bob should generate a message digest from the plain-text message using a hash function. He should then encrypt the message digest using his own private key to create the digital signature. Finally, he should append the digital signature to the message and transmit it to Alice.

4. Alice should decrypt the digital signature in Bob's message using Bob's public key. She should then create a message digest from the plain-text message using the same hashing algorithm Bob used to create the digital signature. Finally, she should compare the two message digests. If they are identical, the signature is authentic.

Chapter 11: Principles of Security Models, Design, and Capabilities

1. Security models include state machine, information flow, noninterference, Take-Grant, access control matrix, Bell-LaPadula, Biba, Clark-Wilson, Brewer and Nash (aka Chinese Wall), Goguen-Meseguer, Sutherland, and Graham-Denning.

2. The primary components of the trusted computing base (TCB) are the hardware and software elements used to enforce the security policy (these elements are called the TCB), the security perimeter distinguishing and separating TCB components from non-TCB components, and the reference monitor that serves as an access control device across the security perimeter.

3. The two primary rules of Bell-LaPadula are the simple rule of no read up and the star rule of no write down. The two rules of Biba are the simple rule of no read down and the star rule of no write up.

4. An open system is one with published APIs that allow third parties to develop products to interact with it. A closed system is one that is proprietary with no third-party product support. Open source is a coding stance that allows others to view the source code of a program. Closed source is an opposing coding stance that keeps source code confidential.

Chapter 12: Security Architecture Vulnerabilities, Threats, and Countermeasures

1. The terms used to describe the various computer mechanisms that allow multiple simultaneous activities are *multitasking*, *multiprocessing*, *multiprogramming*, *multithreading*, and *multistate processing*.

2. The four security modes are dedicated, system high, compartmented, and multilevel.

3. The three pairs of aspects or features used to describe storage are primary vs. secondary, volatile vs. nonvolatile, and random vs. sequential.

4. Some vulnerabilities found in distributed architecture include sensitive data found on desktops/terminals/notebooks, lack of security understanding among users, greater risk of physical component theft, compromise of a client leading to the compromise of the whole network, greater risk from malware because of user-installed software and removable media, and data on clients less likely to be included in backups.

Chapter 13: Security Operations

1. Need to know focuses on permissions and the ability to access information, while the principle of least privilege focuses on privileges. Privileges can include both rights and permissions. Both limit the access of users and subjects to only what they need. Following these principles prevents and limits the scope of security incidents.

2. Managing sensitive information includes properly marking, handling, storing, and destroying it based on its classification.

3. Change management helps prevent outages due to unauthorized changes in system configuration.

Chapter 14: Incident Management

1. Incident response steps listed in the CISSP CIB are detection, response, reporting, recovery, and remediation and review.

2. They can be described as host based or network based, determined by their detection methods (knowledge based or behavior based) and by their responses (passive and active).

    Host-based IDSs examine events on individual computers in great detail, including file activities, accesses, and processes. Network-based IDSs examine general network events and anomalies through traffic evaluation.

    A knowledge-based IDS uses a database of known attacks to detect intrusions. A behavior-based IDS starts with a baseline of normal activity and measures network activity against the baseline to identify abnormal activity.

    A passive response will log the activity and often provide a notification. An active response directly responds to the intrusion to stop or block the attack.

3. RAID arrays (such as RAID-1, RAID-5, and RAID-10) provide fault tolerance for disk subsystems. Failover clustering provides fault tolerance for servers. UPS and generators provide fault tolerance for power outages; a UPS provides short-term power and generators provide long-term power.

Chapter 15: Business Continuity Planning

1. Many federal, state, and local laws or regulations require businesses to implement BCP provisions. Including legal representation on your BCP team helps ensure that you remain compliant with laws, regulations, and contractual obligations.

2. The "seat-of-the-pants" approach is an excuse used by individuals who do not want to invest time and money in the proper creation of a BCP. This can lead to catastrophe when a firmly laid plan isn't in place to guide the response during a stressful emergency situation.

3. Quantitative risk assessment involves using numbers and formulas to make a decision. Qualitative risk assessment includes nonnumeric factors, such as emotions, investor/consumer confidence, and workforce stability.

4. The BCP training plan should include a plan overview briefing for all employees and specific training for individuals with direct or indirect involvement. In addition, backup personnel should be trained for each key BCP role.

5. The four steps of the BCP process are project scope and planning, business impact assessment, continuity planning, and approval/implementation.

Chapter 16: Disaster Recovery Planning

1.   Businesses have three main concerns when considering adopting a mutual assistance agreement. First, the nature of an MAA often necessitates that the businesses be located in close geographical proximity. However, this requirement also increases the risk that the two businesses will fall victim to the same threat. Second, MAAs are difficult to enforce in the middle of a crisis. If one of the organizations is affected by a disaster and the other isn't, the organization not affected could back out at the last minute, leaving the other organization out of luck. Finally, confidentiality concerns (both legal and business related) often prevent businesses from trusting others with their sensitive operational data.

2.   There are five main types of disaster recovery tests:

   ■   Checklist tests involve the distribution of recovery checklists to disaster recovery personnel for review.

   ■   Structured walk-throughs are "table-top" exercises that involve assembling the disaster recovery team to discuss a disaster scenario.

   ■   Simulation tests are more comprehensive and may impact one or more noncritical business units of the organization.

   ■   Parallel tests involve relocating personnel to the alternate site and commencing operations there.

   ■   Full-interruption tests involve relocating personnel to the alternate site and shutting down operations at the primary site.

3.   Full backups create a copy of all data stored on a server. Incremental backups create copies of all files modified since the last full or incremental backup. Differential backups create copies of all files modified since the last full backup without regard to any previous differential or incremental backups that may have taken place.

Chapter 17: Laws, Regulations, and Compliance

1.   Individuals have a right to access records kept about them and know the source of data included in those records. They also have the right to correct inaccurate records. Individuals have the right to withhold consent from data processors and have legal recourse if these rights are violated.

2.   Some common questions that organizations may ask about outsourced service providers include:

   ■   What type(s) of sensitive information are stored, processed, or transmitted by the vendor?

   ■   What controls are in place to protect the organization's information?

- How is our organization's information segregated from that of other clients?

- If encryption is relied on as a security control, what encryption algorithms and key lengths are used? How is key management handled?

- What types of security audits does the vendor perform and what access does the client have to those audits?

- Does the vendor rely on any other third parties to store, process, or transmit data? How do the provisions of the contract related to security extend to those third parties?

- Where will data storage, processing, and transmission take place? If outside the home country of the client and/or vendor, what implications does that have?

- What is the vendor's incident response process and when will clients be notified of a potential security breach?

- What provisions are in place to ensure the ongoing integrity and availability of client data?

3. Some common steps that employers take to notify employees of monitoring include clauses in employment contracts that state the employee should have no expectation of privacy while using corporate equipment, similar written statements in corporate acceptable use and privacy policies, logon banners warning that all communications are subject to monitoring, and labels on computers and telephones warning of monitoring.

Chapter 18: Incidents and Ethics

1. The major categories of computer crime are military/intelligence attacks, business attacks, financial attacks, terrorist attacks, grudge attacks, and thrill attacks.

2. Thrill attacks are motivated by individuals seeking to achieve the "high" associated with successfully breaking into a computer system.

3. Interviews are conducted with the intention of gathering information from individuals to assist with your investigation. Interrogations are conducted with the intent of gathering evidence from suspects to be used in a criminal prosecution.

4. An event is any occurrence that takes place during a certain period of time. Incidents are events that have negative outcomes affecting the confidentiality, integrity, or availability of your data.

5. Incident response teams normally include representatives from senior management, information security professionals, legal representatives, public affairs/communications representatives, and technical engineers.

6. The three phases of the incident response process are detection and identification, response and reporting, and recovery and remediation.

7. To be admissible, evidence must be reliable, competent, and material to the case.

Chapter 19: Physical Security Requirements

1. A fence is an excellent perimeter safeguard that can help to deter casual trespassing. Moderately secure installations work when the fence is 6 to 8 feet tall and will typically be cyclone (also known as chain link) fencing with the upper surface twisted or barbed to deter casual climbers. More secure installations usually opt for fence heights over 8 feet and often include multiple strands of barbed or razor wire strung above the chain link fabric to further deter climbers.

2. Halon degrades into toxic gases at 900 degrees Fahrenheit. Also, it is not environmentally friendly (it is an ozone-depleting substance). Recycled halon is available, but production of halon ceased in developed countries in 2003. Halon is often replaced by a more ecologically friendly and less toxic medium.

3. Anytime water is used to respond to fire, flame, or smoke, water damage becomes a serious concern, particularly when water is released in areas where electrical equipment is in use. Not only can computers and other electrical gear be damaged or destroyed by water, but also many forms of storage media can become damaged or unusable. Also, when seeking hot spots to put out, firefighters often use axes to break down doors or cut through walls to reach them as quickly as possible. This, too, poses the potential for physical damage to or destruction of devices and/or wiring that may also be in the vicinity.

Appendix C

About the Additional Study Tools

In this appendix:

- Additional study tools
- System requirements
- Using the study tools
- Troubleshooting

Additional Study Tools

The following sections are arranged by category and summarize the software and other goodies you'll find on the companion website. If you need help with installing the items, refer to the installation instructions in the section "Using the Study Tools" later in this appendix.

 The additional study tools can be found at www.sybex.com/go/cissp6e. Here, you will get instructions on how to download the files to your hard drive.

Sybex Test Engine

The files contain the Sybex test engine, which includes three full-length practice exams as well as the assessment test and the chapter review questions, which are also included in the book itself.

Electronic Flashcards

These handy electronic flashcards are just what they sound like. One side contains a question, and the other side shows the answer.

PDF of Glossary of Terms

We have included an electronic version of the glossary in PDF format. You can view the electronic version of the glossary with Adobe Reader.

Adobe Reader

We've also included a copy of Adobe Reader so you can view PDF files that accompany the book's content. For more information on Adobe Reader or to check for a newer version, visit Adobe's website at www.adobe.com/products/reader/.

System Requirements

Make sure your computer meets the minimum system requirements shown in the following list. If your computer doesn't match up to most of these requirements, you may have problems using the software and files. For the latest and greatest information, please refer to the ReadMe file included with the download files.

- A PC running Microsoft Windows 98, Windows 2000, Windows NT4 (with SP4 or later), Windows Me, Windows XP, Windows Vista, or Windows 7
- An Internet connection

Using the Study Tools

To install the items, follow these steps:

1. Download the ZIP file to your hard drive, and unzip to an appropriate location. Instructions on where to download this file can be found here: www.sybex.com/go/cissp6e.
2. Double-click the Start.exe file to open the study tools file.
3. Read the license agreement, and then click the Accept button if you want to use the study tools.

The main interface appears. The interface allows you to access the content with just one or two clicks.

Troubleshooting

Wiley has attempted to provide programs that work on most computers with the minimum system requirements. Alas, your computer may differ, and some programs may not work properly for some reason.

The likeliest problem is either you don't have enough memory (RAM) for the programs you want to use or you have other programs running that are affecting installation or how a program runs. If you get an error message such as "Not enough memory" or "Setup cannot continue," try one or more of the following suggestions and then try using the software again:

Turn off any antivirus software running on your computer.   Installation programs sometimes mimic virus activity and may make your computer incorrectly believe that it's being infected by a virus.

Close all running programs.   The more programs you have running, the less memory is available to other programs. Installation programs typically update files and programs, so if you keep other programs running, installation may not work properly.

Have your local computer store add more RAM to your computer.   This is, admittedly, a drastic and somewhat expensive step. However, adding more memory can really help the speed of your computer and allow more programs to run at the same time.

Customer Care

If you have trouble with the book's companion study tools, please call the Wiley Product Technical Support phone number at (800) 762-2974 Ext. 74, or contact them at `http://sybex .custhelp.com`.

Index

Note to the Reader: Throughout this index **boldfaced** page numbers indicate primary discussions of a topic. *Italicized* page numbers indicate illustrations.

A

AAA protocols, **31–32**
abstraction
  object-oriented programming, 512
  in security, **211**
  software development, **317–318**
abuse in voice communications, **187–188**
acceptable use policies, 182, 222
acceptance, risk, **255**
access aggregation attacks, **53**
access control, **1**
  AAA protocols, **31–32**
  attacks, **47**
    access aggregation, **53**
    asset valuation, **49–50**
    denial of service, **62**
    exam essentials, **80–82**
    overview, **48**
    password, **54–58**, *58*
    preventing, **62–64**
    review questions, **83–86**
    risk elements, **49**
    smart cards, **61–62**
    social engineering, **59–61**
    spoofing, **58–59**
    summary, **79**
    threat modeling, **50–52**
    vulnerability analysis, **53**
    written lab, **82**
  authentication. *See* authentication
  authorization, **33–34**
  centralized vs. decentralized, **26–27**
  CIA Triad, **3–4**
  content-dependent, **288–289**
  defense-in-depth strategy, **7–8**, *8*
  Diameter, **32–33**
  discretionary access controls, **22**
  elements, **8–11**
  email, 182
  exam essentials, **39–41**
  federated identity management, **30–31**
  identification. *See* identification
  identity and access provisioning life cycle, **35–38**
  Kerberos, **28–29**
  lattice-based, **23**, *23*, 445
  mandatory access controls, **24–25**
  monitoring. *See* monitoring
  nondiscretionary access controls, **22**
  overview, **2–3**
  permissions, rights, and privileges, **4–5**
  policies, **4**
  RADIUS, **32**
  review questions, **42–45**
  role-based, **25–26**
  rule-based, **22–23**
  security operations principles, **21–22**
  single sign-on, **27–28**, **30–31**
  summary, **38–39**
  TACACS+, **32**
  technical controls, **761**
  types, **5–7**
  users, owners, and custodians, **3**
  written lab, **41**
access control lists (ACLs)
  access control matrices, 443
  DACs, 22
  firewalls, 33, 115
access control matrices, 33, **443–444**
access control triples, **448**
access points in wireless networks, **132–137**
access review audits, **75**

accessibility security in site design, 750
accountability
    access control, **11**
    description, **515**
    monitoring, **71–72**
    security governance, **220**
accounts
    dual administrator, **76–77**
    lockout controls, 63
    managing, 64
    reviews, **36**
    revocation, **37–38**
accreditation in evaluation models,
    466–468
ACID model, **286–287**
acknowledge (ACK) packets, 102, 104–105
ACLs (access control lists)
    access control matrices, 443
    DACs, 22
    firewalls, 33, 115
ACTA (Anti-Counterfeiting Trade
    Agreement), 692
acting phase in IDEAL model, 311, *311*
active content in malicious code, **339**
active IDS responses, **594**
ActiveX controls
    signing, 340
    vulnerabilities, **281, 506–507**
actual cash value (ACV) clause, **654–655**
ad hoc networks, 133
Adams, Douglas, 122
Address Resolution Protocol (ARP)
    cache poisoning, 109
    description, **109**
    purpose, 94
    spoofing, **194**
addresses
    IP. *See* IP (Internet Protocol)
    MAC, 94, 112
addressing memory, **494**
Adleman, Leonard, 406
administrative access controls, 7, *8*
administrative law, **684–685**

administrative physical security
    controls, 747
Administrator group audits, 76
admissible evidence, 715
Advanced Encryption Standard (AES), 135,
    391–392
Advanced Persistent Threat (APT), **52**
advisory policies, 222
adware, **339**
AES (Advanced Encryption Standard), 135,
    391–392
agents
    DoS attacks, 191
    overview, **279–280**
    relay, 181
aggregation
    access aggregation attacks, **53**
    databases, **290–291**
agile software development, **308–309**
AHs (Authentication Headers), 159, 426
alarms, 758, 761
ALE (annualized loss expectancy)
    impact assessment, 629
    threat/risk calculations, **249–251**
algorithms, defined, 367
alternate processing sites, 657
    cold sites, **657–658**
    continuity planning, 632
    hot sites, **658–659**
    mobile sites, **659–660**
    multiple, **661**
    service bureaus, **660**
    warm sites, **659**
alternative systems, 632
ALUs (arithmetic-logical units), 494
American Civil War, cryptography in, **363**
amplifiers, 120
analog communications in LANs,
    141–142
analysis of incidents, 732
analytic attacks, 428
AND operation, **369**
annexes in Common Criteria, 463

annualized loss expectancy (ALE)
  impact assessment, 629
  threat/risk calculations, **249–251**
annualized rate of occurrence (ARO)
  likelihood assessment, 627, 629
  threat/risk calculations, **249–250**
anomaly detection, 592
Anti-Counterfeiting Trade Agreement
    (ACTA), 692
antivirus (AV) mechanisms, **332–333**, 581
APIPA (Automatic Private IP
    Addressing), **169**
applets
  hostile, 330
  vulnerabilities, **280–281**, **505–506**
application attacks, **344**
  back doors, **346**
  buffer overflows, **344–345**
  exam essentials, **354–355**
  masquerading, **352–353**
  privilege escalation attacks, **346**
  reconnaissance attacks, **350–352**
  review questions, **356–359**
  summary, **353–354**
  TOCTTOU issue, **345**
  Web applications, **346–350**, *348*
  written lab, **355**
application issues, **276**
  distributed computing, **278–281**
  local/nondistributed computing,
    276–277
  logs, 66
Application layer
  OSI model, **98–99**
  TCP/IP model, 99–100, *100–101*, **109–110**
application-level gateway firewalls, **116**
approval in continuity planning, **633**
APT (Advanced Persistent Threat), **52**
arc radius of cable, 124
arithmetic-logical units (ALUs), 494
ARO (annualized rate of occurrence)
  likelihood assessment, 627, 629
  threat/risk calculations, **249–250**

ARP (Address Resolution Protocol)
  cache poisoning, 109
  description, **109**
  purpose, 94
  spoofing, **194**
arpspoof tool, 194
"Arrangement on the Recognition of
    Common Criteria Certificates in the
    Field of IT Security", 461
ASs (authentication services), 28
assembly code, 300
assembly language, 300
assessments
  BIA. *See* business impact assessment
    (BIA)
  recovery plan development, **665**
  vulnerability, **554–555**
asset valuation
  attacks, **49–50**
  defined, **243**
  risk, **245–248**
asset value (AV) in BIA, 626, 628
assets
  defined, **242**
  managing, **549–550**
  in threat modeling, 51
assignment of risk, 255
assurance
  evaluation assurance levels, **463–464**
  overview, **454**
  software development security, **298**
asymmetric cryptography, 365, 405
  El Gamal, **408**
  elliptic curve, **408–409**
  hash functions, **409–412**
  keys
    algorithms, **383–386**, *384*
    managing, **419–420**
    public and private, **405–406**
  RSA, **406–407**
asynchronous communications
    in LANs, **142**
asynchronous dynamic password tokens, **16**

asynchronous tokens, **15–16**
asynchronous transfer mode (ATM), **177**
ATO (authorization to operate), 241
atomicity in ACID model, 286
attachments, email, 184–185
attackers
   defined, 48
   threat modeling, 51
attacks
   access control. *See* access control
   application. *See* application attacks
   cryptography, **428–430**
   defined, **244**
   incremental, **519**
   network. *See* networks
   password. *See* passwords
   preventive measures. *See* preventive
      measures for attacks
   wireless communications, **136**
attenuation, cable, 127
attributes in relational databases, 283
auction sniping, 280
audio streaming, 692
audit trails, 11
   physical access, 761
   purpose, **68–69**
auditors, 73, **210**
audits and auditing, 73–74
   access controls, 64
   access review, 75
   configuration, 314
   entitlement, 75
   external, 78
   inspection, **74–75**
   privileged groups, **75–77**
   report handling, **77–78**
   security, **561–562**
   security governance, **219**
authentication
   access control, **9–10**
   biometric factors, **17–20**, *19*
   configuration, 314
   cryptography for, **365–366**, *366*

   Diameter, **32–33**
   Kerberos, **28–29**
   multifactor, **20–21**, 63
   overview, **11–12**
   passwords, **12–14**
   protocols, **154**
   RADIUS, **32**
   remote access, **163**
   security governance, **218–219**
   smart cards, **14–15**
   tokens, **15–16**
Authentication Headers (AHs), 159, 426
authentication services (ASs), 28
authorization
   access control, **10–11**
   mechanisms, **33–34**
   security governance, **219**
authorization to operate (ATO), 241
automated provisioning systems, 35
automated recovery, 608
automated recovery without undue loss, 608
Automatic Private IP Addressing
   (APIPA), **169**
automatic rollover, 502
auxiliary alarm systems, **758**
AV (antivirus) mechanisms, **332–333**, 581
AV (asset value) in BIA, 626, 628
availability
   CIA Triad, 3–4, **217–218**
   techniques for, **452–453**
AVG function, 290
awareness training, **263–264**

B

back doors, **346**, 516, 518
back up keys, 420
background checks, **259**
backups, **666–667**
   best practices, **668–669**
   disk-to-disk, **668**
   neglecting, **667**

tapes
  formats, **667–668**
  protecting, **547–548**
  rotating, **669**
  sensitive information, 541–542
badges, **757**
bandwidth on demand, 176
base+offset addressing, **494**
baseband cable, **124–125**
baseband technology, **142**
baselines, **556**, *557*
  images, 557–558, *557*
  security governance, **222–223**
Basic Input/Output System (BIOS),
  500–501
basic preventive measures, **579**
Basic Rate Interface (BRI), **174**
basic service set identifiers (BSSIDs), 133
bastion hosts, 117
batch processing, 501
battery backup power, 606, 764
BCI Good Practices Guide, 664
BCP. *See* business continuity planning (BCP)
beacon frames, 134
behavior-based detection, **591–593**
behavioral biometric methods, 17
behaviors in object-oriented
  programming, 302
Bell-LaPadula model, 441, **444–446**, *446*
best-effort communications protocol, 106
best evidence rule, 715
BIA. *See* business impact assessment (BIA)
Biba models, **441–442**, **446–448**, *447*
binary code, 300
biometric factors
  error ratings, **19–20**, *19*
  types, **17–19**
biometric registration, **20**
BIOS (Basic Input/Output System),
  500–501
birthday attacks, **56**, **430**
bit size in cryptography, 367
BitLocker technology, 421

black-box approaches
  key management, 420
  object-oriented programming, 512
black-box testing, 315, **600–601**
black boxes in phreaking, 189
blackouts, **652**, 764
block ciphers, 380
blocking attachments, 184–185
Blowfish block cipher, **390**
blue boxes, 189
Blue Screen of Death (BSOD), 299
bluebugging, 132
bluejacking, 132
bluesnarfing, 132
Bluetooth standard, **132**
Boca Ciega High School, 18
Boehm, Barry, 306, 308
Boeing record retention case, 545
bombings, **650**
book ciphers, 379–380
Boolean mathematics, 368–371
boot sectors, 330
Bootstrap Protocol (BootP), 110
botmasters, 336
botnets, **336**, 587
bots, 191, **279–280**
bottom-up management approach, 206
boundaries, security, **190**
bounds, **452–453**
breaches
  defined, **244**
  Sony, 50
Brewer and Nash model, **449**
BRI (Basic Rate Interface), **174**
bridge mode infrastructure, 133
bridge routers (brouters), 96, **121**
bridges, **120–121**
broadband cable, **124–125**
broadband LAN technology, **142**
broadcast domains, 120, 140
broadcast messages, 140
broadcast technology, 140, 142
brouters (bridge routers), 96, **121**

brownouts, 606, 764–765
brute-force attacks
    cryptographic, **428**
    password, **55–56**
BSOD (Blue Screen of Death), 299
BSSIDs (basic service set identifiers), 133
buffer overflows
    application attacks, **344–345**
    coding issues, **517–518**
buildings in continuity planning, **632**
burglar alarms, 761
bus topologies, **138**
business attacks, **722**
business continuity planning (BCP), **617–618**
    benefits, **623**
    business impact assessment, **625–630**, 628
    business organization analysis, **620**
    continuity planning, **630–633**
    documentation, **634–637**
    exam essentials, **637–638**
    legal and regulatory requirements, **624**
    planning, **618–619**
    resource requirements, **622–623**
    review questions, **639–642**
    senior management, **622**
    summary, **637**
    team selection, **620–621**
    written lab, **638**
business impact assessment (BIA), **625–626**
    impact assessment, **628–629**
    likelihood assessment, **627–628**, 628
    priorities, **626**
    recovery strategy, 655
    resource prioritization, **629–630**
    risk identification, **626–627**
business organization analysis, **620**
business units in recovery strategy, 655

C

C++ language, 300
C3 cipher, 363
cable, **123**

baseband and broadband, **124–125**
    coaxial, **123–124**
    conductors, **126–127**
    shielding, 521
    twisted-pair, **125–126**
cache poisoning, 109
cache RAM, **493**
CACs (common access cards), 15
Caesar cipher, **362–363**, 375–376, 378
Cain & Abel tool, 56, 194
CALEA (Communications Assistance for
    Law Enforcement Act), **131**, **698**
callback mechanism, 164
Caller ID, 162, 164
cameras, 759
Candidate Information Bulletin (CIB), 591
candidate keys in relational databases, **284**
canons, 736
capabilities lists, 439, 443
Capability Maturity Model, 306
capacitance motion detectors, 757
cardinality in relational databases,
    283–284
carrier network communications, **173**
Carrier-Sense Multiple Access (CSMA), 143
Carrier-Sense Multiple Access with Collision
    Avoidance (CSMA/CA), 143
Carrier-Sense Multiple Access with Collision
    Detection (CSMA/CD), **143–144**
CAs (certificate authorities), **416–417**
cascading composition theory, 442
categories
    access control, 6
    computer crime, **721–725**
    data, **225–229**
CBC (Cipher Block Chaining)
    mode, **388**
CBK (Common Body of Knowledge), 206
CCMP (Counter Mode with Cipher Block
    Chaining Message Authentication Code
    Protocol), 135
CCTV, 759
CDDI (Copper Distributed Data Interface),
    141

CDIs (constrained data items), 449
cell phones, **129–131**
cell suppression, 289
central processing units (CPUs).
    See processors
central station systems, **758**
centralized access control, **26–27**
centralized remote authentication
    services, **165**
CER (crossover error rate), 19–20, *19*
certificate authorities (CAs), **416–417**
certificate path validation (CPV), 417
certificate practice statement (CPS), 419
certificate revocation lists (CRLs),
    418–419
certificates
    enrollment, **418**
    PKI, **415–416**
    revoking, **419**
    verifying, **418**
certification in evaluation models,
    466–468
CFAA (Computer Fraud and Abuse Act),
    686–687
CFB (Cipher Feedback) mode, **388**
CFR (Code of Federal Regulations),
    685
chain of evidence, **716**
Challenge Handshake Authentication
    Protocol (CHAP), 154
challenge-response authentication,
    365–366, *366*
change logs, 66
change management, **224–225**
    overview, **559–560**, *559*
    process, **560–561**
    software development, 306,
        313–314
    versioning, **561**
channel service unit/data service unit
    (CSU/DSU), 175
channels
    covert, **515–516**
    wireless networks, **133–134**

CHAP (Challenge Handshake
    Authentication Protocol), 154
Chapple, Mike, 292
Chauvaud, Pascal, 411
checklists, 665, **672–673**
checksums for hash totals, 180
Children's Online Privacy Protection Act
    (COPPA), **699**
Chinese Wall model, **449**
chipping codes, 129
chosen ciphertext attacks, 429
chosen plain-text attacks, 429
CIA Triad, **3–4**
    availability, **217–218**
    confidentiality, **214–215**
    integrity, **215–216**
    priorities, **216–217**
CIB (Candidate Information Bulletin), 591
CIDR (Classless Inter-Domain Routing)
    notation, 107
Cipher Block Chaining (CBC) mode, **388**
Cipher Feedback (CFB) mode, **388**
ciphers, 374
    block, 380
    vs. codes, 374–375
    one-time pads, **377–379**
    running key, **379–380**
    stream, 380
    substitution, **375–377**
    transposition, 375
ciphertext messages, 366
ciphertext only attacks, 429
CIR (Committed Information Rate), 176
circuit encryption in networks, **425**
circuit-level gateway firewalls, **116**
circuit proxies, 116
circuit switching, **170–171**
CIRTs (computer incident response teams),
    575, 728
*CISSP Certification Common Body
    of Knowledge (CBK) Study
    Guide*, 591
civil laws, **684**
Clark-Wilson model, **448–449**

classes
  IP, **107**
  ITSEC, **460–461**
  object, 301–302, 512
  TCSEC, **456–457**
classification levels in Bell-LaPadula
    model, 445
classification of data, **225–229**
classified data, 227
Classless Inter-Domain Routing (CIDR)
    notation, 107
clean power, 765
cleaning malicious code, 340
clearing sensitive information, **543**, *544*
click-wrap license agreements, **695**
client systems, malicious code
    countermeasures for, 340
Clipper chip, 391
clipping levels, **69**
closed head water suppression systems, 770
closed systems, **451–452**
cloud computing
  backups, 668
  concepts, **508–509**
clusters
  description, **502**
  failover, **605–606**, *605*
CMWs (compartmented mode workstations),
    489
coaxial cable, **123–124**
COBIT (Control Objectives for Information
    and Related Technology), 213
Code of Ethics, **735–736**
Code of Federal Regulations (CFR), 685
Code Red worm, **336–337**
code review walk-throughs, **305**
codes vs. ciphers, **374–375**
coding flaws, **516–520**
cognitive passwords, **14**
cold rollover, 502
cold sites, **657–658**
cold-swappable RAID systems, 503
collecting evidence, **717–718**

collision domains, **119–120**, 140
collisions
  attacks, 430
  LAN media access, **143–144**
collusion, **258**, **537**
columnar transposition, 375
combination locks, **756–757**
COMMIT command, 286
Committed Information Rate (CIR), **176**
common access cards (CACs), 15
Common Body of Knowledge (CBK), 206
Common Criteria, 456, **461**
  recognition, **461–462**
  structure, **462–465**
common mode noise, 765
common routers, 116
Common Vulnerability and Exposures
    (CVE) database, **555**
communications
  disconnects, **520**
  emergency, **656**
  network segmentation, 114
  recovery plan development, **664–665**
  switching technologies, 172
  voice, **186–189**
  wireless. *See* wireless communications
Communications Assistance for Law
    Enforcement Act (CALEA), **131**, **698**
companion viruses, **331**
comparative password analysis, *55*
compartmentalized environment, 25
compartmented mode systems, 318, **488–489**
compartmented mode workstations (CMWs),
    489
compensation access control, **6**
competent evidence, **715–717**
compiled languages, **300–301**
compilers, 300
complexity of passwords, 13
compliance
  issues, 208
  overview, **703–704**
  privacy requirements, **212–213**
composition passwords, 13

composition theories, 442
computer architecture, 478–479
    firmware, 500–501
    input and output devices, 498–499
    input/output structures, 499–500
    memory, 491–496
    processors. *See* processors
    storage, 496–498
computer crime, 721
    business attacks, 722
    financial attacks, 722–723
    incidents, 572
    laws, 685–689
    military and intelligence attacks, 721–722
    terrorist attacks, 723
    thrill attacks, 725
computer export controls, 696–697
Computer Fraud and Abuse Act (CFAA),
    686–687
computer incident response teams (CIRTs),
    575, 728
Computer Security Act (CSA), 687–688
concentrators, 120, 127
conceptual definition phase in systems
    development, 303–304
conclusive evidence, 715
concurrency of databases, 288
conductors, cable, 126–127
conficker vulnerability, 552
confidential data classification, 227–228
confidentiality
    CIA Triad, 3–4, 214–215
    cryptography for, 364–365
    techniques, 452–453
configuration management, 555–556
    baselining, 556–558, *557*
    documentation, 558
    software development security, 313–314
confinement, 452
Confinement Property, 445
confusion in cryptography, 380
connections in WANs, 174–177
consistency in ACID model, 286–287
constrained data items (CDIs), 449

constrained interfaces, 34
consultants
    controls, 261
    risk, 247
contamination, database, 287
content-dependent access controls, 34,
    288–289
content filters, 340
context-dependent access controls, 34
continuity planning, 630. *See also* business
    continuity planning (BCP)
    plan approval, 633
    plan implementation, 633
    provisions and processes, 631–632
    strategy development phase, 630–631
    training and education, 633
contractors
    controls, 261
    governance reviews, 704–705
contractual license agreements, 695
Control Objectives for Information and
    Related Technology (COBIT), 213
control zones, 521, 763
controlled access protection systems, 457
controlled security mode systems, 489
controls, 453–454
    access. *See* access control
    configuration, 314
    security governance, 213–214
    software development, 316–318, *316*
    specifications development,
        304–305
controls gap, 256
converting IP addresses, 169
COPPA (Children's Online Privacy
    Protection Act), 699
copper conductors, 126
Copper Distributed Data Interface
    (CDDI), 141
copyrights, 690–692
cordless phones, 132
corporate property, 748
corrective access control, 5–6
cost effective security, 265

cost functions in quantitative risk analysis, **248–249**

COUNT function, 290

Counter (CTR) mode, **388**

Counter Mode with Cipher Block Chaining Message Authentication Code Protocol (CCMP), 135

countermeasures
    defined, **244**
    malicious code, **339–341**
    password attacks, **344**
    TEMPEST, **762–763**

coupling in object-oriented programming, 303

covert channels, **515–516**

CPS (certificate practice statement), 419

CPTED (crime prevention through environmental design), 750

CPUs (central processing units).
    See processors

CPV (certificate path validation), 417

Crack program, 342

crackers, 48

Creating Defensible Space, 750

credentials, logon, 16

creeping privileges, **37**

crime prevention through environmental design (CPTED), 750

criminal law, **682–684**

crisis management, **656**

critical path analysis, **747**

criticality prioritization, 626

CRLs (certificate revocation lists), 418–419

cross-site scripting (XSS) attacks, **347**

cross-training, 538

crossover error rate (CER), 19–20, *19*

cryptanalysis, 367

cryptography, **361**
    asymmetric. *See* asymmetric cryptography
    attacks, **428–430**
    cipher systems, **374–380**
    concepts, 366–368
    digital signature systems, 413–415
    email, **421–424**, *424*
    exam essentials, **396–398**, **431–432**
    goals, **364–366**, *366*
    history, **362–364**
    keys, **381–382**
        asymmetric, **383–386**, *384*, **405–406**, **419–420**
        hashing algorithms, 386
        requirements, **384**
        static tokens, 16
        symmetric, **382–383**, *382*
    life cycle, **395–396**
    mathematics, 368
        Boolean, **368–371**
        modulo function, 371
        nonces, **372**
        one-way functions, **371–372**
        zero-knowledge proof, **372–373**, *373*
    networks, **425–428**
    PKI, **415–419**
    portable devices, **420–421**
    review questions, **399–402**, **433–436**
    split knowledge, **373**
    summary, **396**, **430–431**
    symmetric. *See* symmetric cryptography
    work function, **374**
    written lab, **398**, **432**

cryptology, 367

cryptosystems, 367

cryptovariables, 367

CSA (Computer Security Act), **687–688**

CSC-STD-003-85, 318

CSMA (Carrier-Sense Multiple Access), 143

CSMA/CA (Carrier-Sense Multiple Access with Collision Avoidance), 143

CSMA/CD (Carrier-Sense Multiple Access with Collision Detection), **143–144**

CSU/DSU (channel service unit/data service unit), 175

CTR (Counter) mode, 388

custodians, **3**

customer goodwill, 49
CVE (Common Vulnerability and Exposures) database, 555
CWR flag, 104–105
CyberTrust third party, 455

D

D2D (disk-to-disk) backup, **668**
DACs (discretionary access controls), **22**
damage from fire, **771**
darknets, **598**
DARPA model. *See* TCP/IP model
data at rest, cryptography for, 365
data breaches
    defined, **244**
    Sony, **50**
data center security, 751–752
data classification, 225–229
data custodian role, 209–210
Data Definition Language (DDL), 285
data diddling, **519**
Data Encryption Standard (DES), 382, 387–388
data extraction, **69**
data flow control, **505**
data hiding, 211, 318, **512**
data in motion, cryptography for, 365
data/information storage, 293–294
Data Link layer in OSI model, 93–95
Data Manipulation Language (DML), 285
data marts, 292
data mining, 291–292
data owners role, **209**
Data Protection Directive, 212
data remanence, 497, 543
data streams in OSI model, 91, *92*
data terminal equipment/data circuit-terminating equipment (DTE/DCE), 175–176
database contamination, 287

database management system (DBMS) architectures, **282–285**, *282, 284*
database recovery, **662**
    electronic vaulting, **662**
    remote journaling, **662–663**
    remote mirroring, **663**
databases and data warehousing, **282**
    aggregation, **290–291**
    data mining, **291–292**
    DBMS, **282–285**, *282, 284*
    multilevel, 287–289
    ODBC, **289**, *290*
    shadowing, 502
    transactions, **286–287**
datagrams in OSI model, 91, *92*
DBMS (database management system) architectures, **282–285**, *282, 284*
DDL (Data Definition Language), 285
DDoS (distributed denial of service) attacks, 62, **191–192**
decentralized access control, 26–27
decision making types, 625
decision support systems (DSSs), **297**
declassification of sensitive information, **544**
decryption routines, 334
dedicated mode systems, 318, **488**
dedicated WAN lines, 173
deencapsulation in OSI model, **90–91**, *90–92*
default subnet masks, 107
defense in depth, 7–8, *8*, 210–211
Defense Information Technology Security Certification and Accreditation Process (DITSCAP), **468**
definition phase in DITSCAP and NIACAP, 468
degaussing sensitive information, **544**
degrees in relational databases, 283–284
delay, security controls for, 749
delay feature, mantraps as, 754
delegation
    incident response, 575
    object-oriented programming, 302
Delphi technique, **254**

Delta rule, 296
deluge water suppression systems, 770
demilitarized zones (DMZs)
  firewalls, 117–118, *118*
  Web applications, 349
denial of service (DoS) attacks
  description, **62**
  incident handling, 727
  overview, **191–192**
  preventive measures, **583–584**
denial security controls, 749
Department of Defense, APT attacks, 52
*Department of Defense Password
  Management Guidelines*, **458**
deployment
  firewalls, **117–119**, *118*
  patches, 552
DES (Data Encryption Standard), 382,
  387–388
design
  site. *See* site and facility design
  vulnerabilities from, **516–520**
design review in software development, 305
desktops, virtual, 179
destroying sensitive information, 543, *544*
destruction
  sensitive information, **544**
  symmetric keys, **394**
  by viruses, 329
detection and identification, 730
  fire, **769–770**
  IDSs. *See* intrusion detection systems
    (IDSs)
  incidents, **574–575**
  security controls for, 749
detective access control, **5**
deterrent alarms, 758
deterrent control, **6**, 748
Devakumar, Vijay, 56
devices
  firmware, **501**
  Transport layer, 97
DHCP (Dynamic Host Configuration
  Protocol), 110

DIACAP (DoD Information Assurance
  Certification and Accreditation Process),
  468
diagnosing phase in IDEAL model,
  311, *311*
dial-up protocols
  encapsulation, **178**
  remote access security management,
    164–165
Diameter authentication, **32–33**
dictionaries
  data, 291
  password attacks, **54–55**, **342–343**
diddling, data, **519**
differential backups, 666
Diffie-Hellman key encryption, **393–394**
diffusion in cryptography, **380**
digital certificates
  enrollment, **418**
  PKI, **415–416**
  revoking, **419**
  verifying, **418**
digital communications in LANs, **141–142**
Digital Millennium Copyright Act (DMCA),
  690–692
Digital Signature Algorithm (DSA), 415
Digital Signature Standard (DSS), **415**
digital signatures, **413–414**
  DSS, **415**
  HMAC, **414–415**
  static tokens, 16
digital subscriber line (DSL), 174
direct addressing, **494**
direct evidence, 717
Direct Inward System Access (DISA),
  188–189
Direct Memory Access (DMA), **500**
Direct Sequence Spread Spectrum
  (DSSS), **129**
Directive 95/46/EC, 212
directive access control, **6**
Directory Service Markup Language
  (DSML), 31
directory services, 27

DISA (Direct Inward System Access), **188–189**

disaster recovery planning (DRP), 618–619, **643**

disasters

man-made, **649–654**

natural, **645–649**, *647*

nature of, **644–645**

exam essentials, **675**

maintenance, **674**

recovery plan development. *See* recovery plan development

recovery strategy. *See* recovery strategy

review questions, **676–679**

summary, **674**

testing, **672–673**

training and documentation, **671–672**

written lab, **675**

discretionary access controls (DACs), **22**

discretionary MAC models, 25

discretionary protection systems in TCSEC, **456–457**

Discretionary Security Property, 445

discretionary security protection systems in TCSEC, 456

disgruntled employees, 539

disk-to-disk (D2D) backup, **668**

distance vector routing protocols, 96

distributed access control, 27

distributed architecture, **504**

applets, **505–507**

cloud computing, **508–509**

grid computing, **509–510**

peer to peer technologies, **510**

safeguards, **507–508**

vulnerabilities, **504–505**

distributed computing, **278–281**

distributed databases, **282–283**, *282*

distributed denial of service (DDoS) attacks, 62, **191–192**

distributed reflective denial-of-service (DRDoS) attacks, 584

distributing audit reports, 78

distributing symmetric keys, **393**

distribution methods for malicious code, 580

DITSCAP (Defense Information Technology Security Certification and Accreditation Process), **468**

DMA (Direct Memory Access), 500

DMCA (Digital Millennium Copyright Act), **690–692**

DML (Data Manipulation Language), 285

DMZs (demilitarized zones)

firewalls, 117–118, *118*

Web applications, 349

DNS (Domain Name System)

poisoning, **194–195**

reverse lookups, 595

TCP/IP, **112–113**

DNS Changer botnet, 587

DNSSEC (Domain Name System Security Extensions), 195

Dobbertin, Hans, 412

documentary evidence, **715**

documentation

BCP, **634–637**

configuration, 558

disaster recovery planning, **671–672**

review process, 241

DoD Information Assurance Certification and Accreditation Process (DIACAP), 468

DOD model. *See* TCP/IP model

dogs, **755–756**

Domain Name System (DNS)

poisoning, **194–195**

reverse lookups, 595

TCP/IP, **112–113**

Domain Name System Security Extensions (DNSSEC), 195

domains

broadcast, 120, 140

collision, **119–120**, 140

layers, 511

mandatory access controls, 24

relational databases, 283

trusts, 27

DoS (denial of service) attacks
    description, **62**
    incident handling, 727
    overview, **191–192**
    preventive measures, **583–584**
Double DES (2DES), **429**
downloads, drive-by, 60, **580**
DRDoS (distributed reflective denial-of-service) attacks, 584
drive-by downloads, 60, **580**
DRP. *See* disaster recovery planning (DRP)
dry pipe water suppression systems, 770
DSA (Digital Signature Algorithm), 415
DSL (digital subscriber line), 174
DSML (Directory Service Markup Language), 31
DSS (Digital Signature Standard), **415**
DSSs (decision support systems), **297**
DSSS (Direct Sequence Spread Spectrum), **129**
DTE/DCE (data terminal equipment/data circuit-terminating equipment), 175–176
dual administrator accounts, **76–77**
dual-homed firewalls, **117**
due care, 214
due diligence, 214
dumpster diving, **352**
durability in ACID model, 287
duties
    rotating, 538
    separating from responsibilities, 534–537, *536*
dwell time in keystroke patterns, 18
Dynamic Host Configuration Protocol (DHCP), 110
dynamic NAT, **168–169**
dynamic packet filtering firewalls, 116
dynamic ports, 101
dynamic RAM, **493**
dynamic testing, **315**
dynamic tokens, 15
dynamic Web applications, **348–349**, *348*

E

EAC (electronic access control) locks, 756
EALs (evaluation assurance levels), **463–464**
EAP (Extensible Authentication Protocol), 154
earthquake hazard maps, 627, *628*
earthquakes, **645–646**
eavesdropping, 57, **192–193**, 751
ECB (Electronic Codebook) mode, **387**
ECDSA (Elliptic Curve DSA), 415
ECE flag, 104–105
Echoplex error control, 165
Economic and Protection of Proprietary Information Act, **698–699**
Economic Espionage Act, **695**
ECPA (Electronic Communications Privacy Act), **698**
eDirectory service, 27
edit control for databases, **288**
education
    continuity planning, **633**
    personnel, **263–264**
    users, 63
EEPROM (electronically erasable programmable read-only memory), **492**
EES (Escrowed Encryption Standard), 390
EF (exposure factor)
    cost functions, **248–249**
    impact assessment, 628
EFS (Encrypting File System) technology, 421
El Gamal algorithm, **408**
electricity, **764–765**. *See also* power
electrocution danger, 766
electromagnetic (EM) radiation, **521**
electromagnetic interference (EMI), 765
electronic access control (EAC) locks, 756
electronic access to password files, 62
Electronic Codebook (ECB) mode, **387**

Electronic Communications Privacy Act
    (ECPA), **698**
electronic mail. *See* email
electronic serial numbers (ESNs), 189
electronic vaulting, 501, **662**
electronically erasable programmable
    read-only memory (EEPROM), **492**
elevated privileges, **538–539**
elliptic curve cryptography theory,
    408–409
Elliptic Curve DSA (ECDSA), 415
elliptic curve groups, 409
EM (electromagnetic) radiation, **521**
EM (expectation maximization)
    clustering, 292
email
    cryptography, **421–423**
    phishing, 60
    security, **181**
        goals, **181–182**
        issues, **183**
        solutions, **183–185**
    spoofing, 59
emanation security, **762–763**
embedded device analysis, 718
emergency communications, **656**
emergency response
    BCP documentation, **636**
    recovery plan development, **664**
emergency-response personnel, proximity
    to, 749
EMI (electromagnetic interference), 765
employees. *See* personnel security
employment agreements, **259–260**
Encapsulating Security Payload (ESP),
    159, 426
encapsulation, 318
    dial-up protocols, **178**
    OSI model, **90–91**, *90–92*
    TCP/IP, 111
encrypted viruses, **334**
Encrypting File System (EFS)
    technology, 421

encryption. *See also* cryptography
    end-to-end, **425**
    export controls, **697**
    overview, **211–212**
    passwords, 12, 62
    sensitive information, 542
    TLS, 153
end-to-end encryption, **425**
end-to-end security, 122
end users
    access control, **2–3**
    education, 63
    remote assistance, **164**
    role, **210**
endpoint security in networks, **119**
Enigma code machine, **364**
enrollment
    biometric registration, 20
    certificates, **418**
    provisioning, 35
enterprise extended mode infrastructure, 133
entities in access control, 2
entitlement audits, **75**
environment and life safety, **763**
    fire, **767–772**, *767*
    noise, **765**
    personnel privacy and safety, **763–764**
    physical security. *See* physical security
    power and electricity, **764–765**
    temperature, humidity, and static, **766**
    water leakage and flooding, **766**
ephemeral ports, 101
EPROM (erasable programmable read-only
    memory), **492**
equal error rate (ERR), 19
equipment
    failures, **772**
    life cycle, **549–550**
erasable programmable read-only memory
    (EPROM), **492**
erasing sensitive information, 543
ERR (equal error rate), 19
error ratings in biometric factors, **19–20**, *19*

escalation of privileges, **346**

escrow

software, **669–670**

symmetric cryptography keys, **394**

Escrowed Encryption Standard (EES), 390

ESNs (electronic serial numbers), 189

ESP (Encapsulating Security Payload), 159, 426

espionage

Economic Espionage Act, **695**

industrial, 722

overview, **589**

ESSIDs (extended service set identifiers), 133–134

establishing phase in IDEAL model, 311, *311*

Esthost botnet, 587

Ethernet technologies, **140–141**

ethical hacking in penetration testing, **602**

ethics, **735–737**

Ettercap tool, 194

EUI-48 MAC addressing, 94

European Union privacy law, 701–703

evaluation assurance levels (EALs), **463–464**

Evaluation Criteria for Information Technology Security document, 462

evaluation models, **454–455**

certification and accreditation, **466–468**

Common Criteria, **461–465**

industry and international security implementation guidelines, **465**

ITSEC, **460–461**

rainbow series, **455–460**

Event Viewer logs, 64–65, *65*

events in incident handling, 725

evidence, **714**

admissible, **715**

chain of evidence, **716**

collection and forensic procedures, **717–718**

types, **715–717**

excessive privilege, 37

exclusive OR (XOR) function, **370–371**

execution types, **479–482**

exercises in BCP documentation, 637

expectation maximization (EM) clustering, 292

experienced exposure, 243

expert opinion, 717

expert systems, **295**

exploit Wednesday, 552

explosions, **650**

export laws, **696–697**

exposure, defined, **243**

exposure factor (EF)

cost functions, **248–249**

impact assessment, 628

extended LANs, 122

extended service set identifiers (ESSIDs), 133–134

extended TACACS (XTACACS), 32

Extensible Access Control Markup Language (XACML), 31

Extensible Authentication Protocol (EAP), 154

Extensible Markup Language (XML), 30

external audits, 78

external communications in recovery plan development, **670**

extinguishers, fire, **769**

extranets, 113

F

face scans, 17

facilities

continuity planning, **632**

design. *See* site and facility design

fail-open systems, 607

fail-secure and fail-open states, **298–299**

fail-secure systems, 502, 607

failover, **502**, **605–606**, *605*

failure states in initialization, **517**

fair cryptosystems approach, **395**

false acceptance rate (FAR) in biometric factors, 19, *19*

false alarms, 593

false rejection rate (FRR) in biometric
    factors, 19, *19*
false values, 368
Family Educational Rights and Privacy Act
    (FERPA), **700**
FAR (false acceptance rate) in biometric
    factors, 19, *19*
Faraday cages, *521*, **762–763**
fault-resistant disk systems (FRDSs), 503
fault tolerance, **603**
    carrier network communications, **173**
    hard drives, 502–504, **603–605**
    power sources, **606**
    servers, **605–606**, *605*
    trusted recovery, **606–608**
faults, defined, 764
fax encryptors, 185
faxes, **185**
FDDI (Fiber Distributed Data Interface), **141**
Federal Bureau of Investigation (FBI), 577, 719
Federal Information Processing Standard
    (FIPS) 140–2, 367
Federal Information Processing Standard
    (FIPS) 180, 410
Federal Information Processing Standard
    (FIPS) 185, 390
Federal Information Processing Standard
    (FIPS) 186–3, 415
Federal Information Processing Standard
    (FIPS) 197, 391
Federal Information Processing Standard
    (FIPS) 200, 67
Federal Sentencing Guidelines, **688**
federated identity management, **30–31**
feedback composition theory, 442
feedback loop characteristic of waterfall
    model, 306
fences, **753–754**
FERPA (Family Educational Rights and
    Privacy Act), **700**
FHSS (Frequency Hopping Spread
    Spectrum), **128**
Fiber Distributed Data Interface (FDDI), **141**
fiber-optic cable, 127

fields in relational databases, 283
fifth-generation languages (5GL), 301
file access control, 2
file infector viruses, 330–331
File Transfer Protocol (FTP), 109
FileVault encryption, 421
filters
    firewalls, 115
    malicious code countermeasures, 340
    screen, *59*
FIN (finish) packets, 102, 104–105
financial attacks, **722–723**
finger utility, **337–338**
fingerprints, 17
finish (FIN) packets, 102, 104–105
finite state machines (FSMs), 441
FIPS (Federal Information Processing
    Standard) 140-2, 367
FIPS (Federal Information Processing
    Standard) 180, 410
FIPS (Federal Information Processing
    Standard) 185, 390
FIPS (Federal Information Processing
    Standard) 186-3, 415
FIPS (Federal Information Processing
    Standard) 197, 391
FIPS (Federal Information Processing
    Standard) 200, 67
fire
    damage, **771**
    detection systems, **769–770**
    extinguishers, **769**
    gas discharge systems, **770–771**
    man-made, 649
    natural disasters, **648**
    overview, **767–768**, *767–768*
    water suppression systems, 770
fire triangle, 767, *767*
firewalls
    ACLs, 33
    deployment architectures, **117–119**, *118*
    logs, 66
    multihomed, **117**
    overview, **115–117**

firing employees, **261–263**, *589*

firmware, **500–501**

first-generation languages (1GL), 301

first normal form (1NF), 285

5-4-3 rule, **127**

fixed-temperature fire detection systems, 769

flame-actuated fire detection systems, 769

flame stage of fire, 768

flash drives, **546–547**

flash floods, 646

flashing BIOS, 500

flight time in keystroke patterns, 18

flip-flops, 493

flood attacks

    ping, **588**

    preventive measures, **584–585**, *584*

flood maps, 627, 647, *647*

floods

    disaster recovery plans, **646–647**, *647*

    plumbing leaks, 766

footers in OSI model, 90, *90*

foreign keys in relational databases, **285**

forensic procedures, **717–718**

FORTRAN language, 300

4G technology, 130

Fourth Amendment, **698**, 719

fourth-generation languages (4GL), 301

fraggle attacks, **585–586**

Frame Relay connections, **176–177**

frames

    beacon, 134

    Ethernet, 140

    OSI model messages, 91, *92*

fraud in voice communications, **187–188**

FRDSs (fault-resistant disk systems), 503

French government, APT attacks, 52

frequency, 128

frequency analysis cryptographic attacks, **429**

Frequency Hopping Spread Spectrum (FHSS), **128**

FRR (false rejection rate) in biometric factors, 19, *19*

FSMs (finite state machines), 441

FTP (File Transfer Protocol), 109

full backups, 666

full-duplex communication, 97

full-interruption tests, **673**

full-knowledge teams, **600–601**

full mesh topologies, 139

function recovery, 608

functional priorities in recovery strategy, **655**

functional requirements determination, 304

functions

    aggregate, **290–291**

    cost, **248–249**

    hash, **409–412**

    one-way, **371–372**

fuzzy logic, **296**

G

Gantt charts, **312**, *312*

gas discharge fire suppression systems, **770–771**

gates, **753–754**

Gates, Bill, 518

gateways, **121**

gathering evidence, 731

General Protection Faults (GPFs), 317

Generalized Markup Language (GML), 30

generators, 606

GFS (Grandfather-Father-Son) strategy, 669

Gibson, Steve, 728

GISRA (Government Information Security Reform Act), **689**

GLBA (Gramm-Leach-Bliley Act), 212, **699–700**

GML (Generalized Markup Language), 30

GnuPG PGP solution, 184

goals in documentation, **634**

Goguen-Meseguer model, **449–450**

Good Times virus warning, 334

Google, APT attacks, 52

governance. *See* security governance

Government Information Security Reform Act (GISRA), **689**

GPFs (General Protection Faults), 317

Graham-Denning model, **450**

Gramm-Leach-Bliley Act (GLBA), 212, **699–700**

Grandfather-Father-Son (GFS) strategy, 669

gray-box testing, 315, **600–601**

Green Book, **458**

grid computing, **509–510**

ground wires, 765

grudge attacks, **723–725**

guards, **755–756**

guessing passwords, **341–342**

Guide to Integrating Forensic into Incident Response, 715

"Guide to Intrusion Detection and Prevention Systems", 590–591

Guide to Protecting the Confidentiality of Personally Identifiable Information (PII), 540, 773

guidelines in security governance, **222–223**

Gumblar drive-by download, 580

H

hackers, 48

hacktivism, 725

hailstorms, 648

half-duplex communication, 97

halon, **770–771**

hand geometry, 18

hard drives, protecting, **502–504, 603–605**

hardening provisions, 632

hardware, **479**

    in evidence collection, 718

    failures, **651–652**

    firmware, **500–501**

    input and output devices, **498–499**

    input/output structures, **499–500**

    memory, **491–496**

    processors. *See* processors

    replacement options, **660**

    segmentation, 316, **513**

    storage, **496–498**

hardware-based RAID arrays, **604–605**

hardware security module (HSM), 469

Hash of Variable Length (HAVAL) algorithm, 410

hash totals, **180**

Hashed Message Authentication Code (HMAC) algorithm, **414–415**

hashes

    asymmetric cryptography, **409–412**

    cryptographic keys, **386**

    passwords, **55–56**

HAVAL (Hash of Variable Length) algorithm, 410

HDLC (High-Level Data Link Control), 177

headers

    authentication, 159, 426

    OSI model, 90, *90*

    TCP, 103–104

Health Insurance Portability and Accountability Act (HIPAA), 212, **699**

hearsay evidence, 717

heart patterns, 18

heartbeat sensors, 762

heat-based motion detectors, 757

heat damage, 771

heat stage of fire, 768

Hertz (Hz), 128

heuristics-based detection, 592

HIDS (host-based IDS), **594–596**

hierarchical databases, **282–283**, *282*

hierarchical environment, 25

hierarchical storage management (HSM) system, 669

high-level Administrator group audits, **76**

High-Level Data Link Control (HDLC), 177

High Speed Serial Interface (HSSI), 177

hijacking
    DNS, **194–195**
    session, **353**
HIPAA (Health Insurance Portability and
    Accountability Act), 212, **699**
hiring new staff, 36, **257**, **259**
history, password, 13
HMAC (Hashed Message Authentication
    Code) algorithm, **414–415**
hoaxes, **334–335**
honeypots, **597**
hookup composition theory, 442
host-based IDS (HIDS), **594–596**
host interfaces, 132
hostile applets, 330
hot rollover, 502
hot sites, **658–659**
hot-swappable RAID, 503
HSM (hardware security module), 469
HSM (hierarchical storage management)
    system, 669
HSSI (High Speed Serial Interface), 177
HTML (Hypertext Markup Language), 30
HTTP (Hypertext Transport Protocol), 110
HTTPS (Hypertext Transfer Protocol over
    Secure Sockets Layer), 422
hubs, **120**
humidity, **766**
hurricanes, 648
hybrid environments in MAC model, 25
hybrid password attacks, 55
hyperlink spoofing, **195**
Hypertext Markup Language (HTML), 30
Hypertext Transfer Protocol over Secure
    Sockets Layer (HTTPS), 422
Hypertext Transport Protocol (HTTP), 110
Hz (Hertz), 128

I

I Love You virus, 331
IAB (Internet Advisory Board), 736
IANA (International Assigned Numbers
    Authority), 101

ICMP (Internet Control Message Protocol),
    108, *585*
IDEA (International Data Encryption
    Algorithm) block cipher, 390
IDEAL model, **310–312**, *311*
identification, **11–12**
    access control, **9**
    biometric factors, **17–20**, *19*
    configuration, 314
    multifactor authentication, **20–21**
    passwords, **12–14**
    security governance, 218
    smart cards, **14–15**
    tokens, **15–16**
identification cards, 757
identity and access provisioning life cycle, 35
    account review, 36
    account revocation, **37–38**
    provisioning, **35–36**
identity-based access control, 22
Identity Theft and Assumption Deterrence
    Act, **700**
IDSs (intrusion detection systems), 590,
    761–762
    host- and network-based, **594–596**
    IDS response, **593–594**
    intrusion prevention systems, **596**, *596*
    knowledge- and behavior-based
        detection, **591–593**
    tools, **596–598**
IEEE 802.1x standard, 428
ighashgpu tool, 56
IGMP (Internet Group Management
    Protocol), **109**
IM (instant messaging), **163**
images in baselining, **557–558**, *557*
IMAP (Internet Message Access Protocol),
    110, 181
immediate addressing, **494**
impact assessment. *See* business impact
    assessment (BIA)
impersonation, 53, **193**
implementation
    continuity planning, **633**
    cryptographic attacks, 428

implementation phase in BCP, 623

implicit deny principle, **33**

import/export laws, 696–697

in-house hardware replacement, 660

incident handling, **713**

    computer crime categories,
        721–725

    data integrity and retention, 733

    defining, 572–573

    exam essentials, 738–739

    interviews, 733

    investigations, 714

        evidence, 714–718

        process, 719–720

    overview, 725–726

    reports, 734–735

    response process, 730–733

    response teams, 728–729

    review questions, 741–744

    summary, 737–738

    types, 726–728

    written lab, 740

incident management, **571**

    exam essentials, 609–611

    incidents defined, 572–573

    preventive measures. *See* preventive
        measures for attacks

    response steps, 573–578, *574*

    review questions, 612–615

    summary, 608–609

    system resilience and fault tolerance,
        603–608

    written lab, **611**

incipient stage in fire, 768

incremental attacks, **519**

incremental backups, 666

indirect addressing, **494**

industrial espionage, 722

industry guidelines, **465**

inference attacks, **291**

inference engines, 295

information flow model, **441–442**

information hiding, 318

information systems

    security capabilities, **469**

security evaluation models. *See* evaluation
    models

Information Systems Audit and Control
    Association (ISACA), 213

Information Technology Infrastructure
    Library (ITIL), 213, *556*

Information Technology Security Evaluation
    Criteria (ITSEC), 223–224

    classes and required assurance and
        functionality, **460–461**

    development, 455–456

informative policies, 222

InfraGard program, 734

infrared motion detectors, 757

infrastructure

    continuity planning, **632**

    failures, **651**

    wireless network nodes, 133

infrastructure as a service, *509*

inheritance in object-oriented programming,
    302

initialization failure states, 517

initiating phase in IDEAL model,
    311, *311*

injection attacks, **348–350**, *348*

input and output devices, **498–499**

input/output structures, **499–500**

input validation

    buffer overflow, 517

    cross-site scripting, 347

    SQL injection attacks, 350

inrush, 765

insider threats, **724**

inspection audits, 74–75

instances in object-oriented programming,
    302

instant messaging (IM), **163**

Integrated Services Digital Network
    (ISDN), **174**

integrity

    CIA Triad, 3–4, **215–216**

    cryptography for, **365**

    techniques for, 452–453

    verifying, **180**

integrity checking software, 340

integrity verification procedures
(IVPs), 449
intellectual property, **689–690**
intelligence attacks, **721–722**
intent to use applications, 693
interim reports, 78
internal security in site and facility
design, **751**
International Assigned Numbers Authority
(IANA), 101
International Criminal Police Organization
(INTERPOL), 577
International Data Encryption Algorithm
(IDEA) block cipher, **390**
International Information Systems
Security Certification Consortium
(ISC²), **735–736**
International Organization for
Standardization (ISO), 465
International Organization on Computer
Evidence (IOCE), 717
international security implementation
guidelines, **465**
Internet Advisory Board (IAB), 736
Internet Control Message Protocol (ICMP),
108, *585*
Internet Group Management Protocol
(IGMP), **109**
Internet layer in TCP/IP model, 99–100,
100–101
Internet Message Access Protocol (IMAP),
110, 181
Internet Protocol. *See* IP (Internet Protocol)
Internet Protocol Security (IPSec) standard,
33, **158–159**, **425–427**
Internet Security Association and Key
Management Protocol (ISAKMP), **427**
Internet Worm, 278, **337–338**
INTERPOL (International Criminal Police
Organization), 577
interpreted languages, 301
interrogation, 733
interrupt conflicts, 500

interrupt requests (IRQ), **499–500**
interviewing individuals, 733
intranets, 113
intrusion alarms, 758
intrusion detection systems (IDSs), 590,
761–762
host- and network-based, **594–596**
IDS response, **593–594**
intrusion prevention systems, 596, *596*
knowledge- and behavior-based
detection, **591–593**
tools, **596–598**
intrusion prevention systems (IPSs), 596, *596*
investigations, **714**
audit trails, **72–73**
evidence, **714–718**
process, **719–720**
IOCE (International Organization on
Computer Evidence), 717
IP (Internet Protocol), 106
classes, **107**
IP addresses, **106**
ARP spoofing, **194**
converting, **169**
DNS, 112
loopback, 170
NAT, **165–170**
private, **167–168**
spoofing, **352–353**
probes, **351**
IPSec (Internet Protocol Security),
33, **158–159**, **425–427**
IPSs (intrusion prevention systems),
596, *596*
IPv4 addresses, **106**
IPv6 addresses, **106**
iris scans, **17**
IronKey flash drives, 547
IRQ (interrupt requests), **499–500**
ISACA (Information Systems Audit and
Control Association), 213
ISAKMP (Internet Security Association and
Key Management Protocol), **427**

(ISC²) code of ethics, **735–736**
ISDN (Integrated Services Digital Network), **174**
iSKORPiTX, 725
ISO (International Organization for Standardization), 465
ISO/IEC 27002, 213
isolation
  in ACID model, **287**
  containment, 731
  process, **316**, **453**
iSteg tool, 424, *424*
ITIL (Information Technology Infrastructure Library), 213, 556
ITSEC (Information Technology Security Evaluation and Criteria), 223–224
  classes and required assurance and functionality, **460–461**
  development, **455–456**
IVPs (integrity verification procedures), 449

J

jamming generators, 521
Japanese Purple Machine, 364
Java language, 300
  applets, **281**, **506**
  sandbox, 340, 506
Java Virtual Machine (JVM), 281, 506
JavaScript language, 301
job descriptions, **257**
job responsibilities, **258–259**
job rotation, **258**, **538**
journaling, remote, 501
JVM (Java Virtual Machine), 281, 506

K

Kaminsky, Dan, 113, 194
Kaminsky vulnerability, 113, 194
KASs (Kerberos authentication servers), 28

Katrina hurricane, 648
KDCs (key distribution centers), 28
KDD (Knowledge Discovery in Databases), 292
Kerberos, **28–29**
Kerberos authentication servers (KASs), 28
Kerchoff principle, **367**
kernel mode, 485
kernels, **440–441**, 484, 487
key distribution centers (KDCs), 28
key escrows, 373
key space in cryptography, 367
keyboards, **498**
keys, 756–757
  cryptography, **365–367**, **381–382**
    asymmetric, **383–386**, *384*, **405–406**, **419–420**
    hashing algorithms, 386
    requirements, **384**
    symmetric, **382–383**, *382*, **393–394**
  relational databases, **284–285**
keystroke monitoring, **70**
keystroke patterns, **18**
knowledge-based detection, **591–592**
knowledge-based systems, **294–295**
  DSSs, **297**
  expert systems, **295**
  neural networks, **296**
  security applications, **297**
knowledge bases, 295
Knowledge Discovery in Databases (KDD), 292
known plain-text attacks, 429
Koblitz, Neal, 408
KryptoKnight authentication system, 31

L

L2F (Layer 2 Forwarding), **158**
L2TP (Layer 2 Tunneling Protocol), **158**, 426
L2TP/IPSec, 426

labels
  security, 439
  sensitive information, **541**
  TCSEC, 457
land attacks, **586**
LANs (local area networks), 123, **140**
  Ethernet, **140–141**
  extenders, **122**
  media access, **143–144**
  subtechnologies, **141–144**
  VPNs, **159–160**
last logon notification, 63
lattice-based access controls, **23**, *23*, **445**
law enforcement, calling in, **719**
laws, **681**
  administrative, **684–685**
  civil, **684**
  computer crime, **685–689**
  copyrights, **690–692**
  criminal, **682–684**
  exam essentials, **706–707**
  import/export, **696–697**
  intellectual property, **689–690**
  licensing, **695–696**
  patents, **693–694**
  privacy
    European Union, **701–703**
    U.S., **697–701**
  review questions, **708–711**
  summary, **705–706**
  trademarks, **692–693**
  written lab, **707**
Layer 2 Forwarding (L2F), **158**
Layer 2 Tunneling Protocol (L2TP),
  158, 426
layers
  defense in depth, **210–211**
  domains, 511
  OSI model. *See* Open Systems
    Interconnection (OSI)
    Reference Model
  security, **7–8**, *8*, **511–512**
  TCP/IP model. *See* TCP/IP model

LDAP (Lightweight Directory Access
  Protocol), 27
LEAP (Lightweight Extensible
  Authentication Protocol), 155
learning phase in IDEAL model, 311, *311*
learning rules, 296
leased WAN lines, 173
least privilege principle, 21, **514**,
  532–534, 581
legal requirements
  BCP, **624**
  regulations, **773**
legally defensible security, **220**
length, password, 13
Lenstra, Arjen, 412
lessons learned, 733
Level 0 protection ring, 317
Level 1 and 2 protection rings, 317
level 2 caches, 493
Level 3 protection ring, 317
levels vs. rings, **511**
licensing software, 550, **695–696**
life cycle assurance, 298
life cycles
  cryptographic, **395–396**
  media, **549**
  models, **306**
    agile software development, **308–309**
    Gantt charts, 312, *312*
    IDEAL, **310–312**, *311*
    PERT, **313**
    Software Capability Maturity
      Model, **310**
    spiral, 308, *308*
    waterfall, **306–307**, *307*
  systems development, **303**
    code review walk-throughs, 305
    conceptual definition phase, **303–304**
    control specifications development,
      304–305
    design review, 305
    functional requirements
      determination, **304**

maintenance and change
   management, **306**
   system test review, **305**
life safety. *See* environment and life safety
light yellow book, 318
lighting, 755
Lightweight Directory Access Protocol
   (LDAP), 27
Lightweight Extensible Authentication
   Protocol (LEAP), 155
likelihood assessment in BIA, **627–628**, *628*
limit checks in software development, **298**
line-interactive UPSs, 606
Line Print Daemon (LPD), 110
linear bus topology, 138
link encryption, **425**
Link layer in TCP/IP model, 99–100,
   100–101
Link-Local address assignment, **169**
link state routing protocols, 96
LLC (Logical Link Control) sublayer, 94
local alarm systems, **758**
local area networks (LANs), 123, **140**
   Ethernet, **140–141**
   extenders, **122**
   media access, **143–144**
   subtechnologies, **141–144**
   VPNs, **159–160**
local/nondistributed computing, **276–277**
locations, employee, 550
locking databases, 288
lockout controls, 63
locks, **756–757**
logging, **64–65**, *65*
logic bombs, 278, **335**
logical access controls, 7, *8*
Logical Link Control (LLC) sublayer, 94
logical operations, 368
   AND, **369**
   exclusive OR, **370–371**
   NOT, **370**
   OR, **369–370**
logical topologies, 137, 139

logistics in recovery plan development, **670**
logs
   credentials, 16
   Kerberos, **29**
   protecting, **66–67**
   SSO scripts, 31
   types, **65–66**
loopback addresses, 107, **170**
loose-leaf binders, 672
loss potential, 248
LPD (Line Print Daemon), 110

M

M of N Control, 373
MAAs (mutual assistance agreements), **661**
MAC (mandatory access control) systems,
   24–25
MAC (Media Access Control) address,
   94, 112
MAC sublayer in OSI model, 94
machine language, 300
macro viruses, 277, **331**
mail-bombing, 183
main memory, 492
maintenance
   BCP documentation, **636–637**
   disaster recovery planning, **674**
   software development, 306
maintenance hooks, **518–519**
maintenance phase in BCP, 623
malicious code, 327, 580, 727
   active content, 339
   countermeasures, **339–341**
   exam essentials, **354–355**
   logic bombs, 335
   password attacks, **341–344**
   preventive measures, 580
   review questions, **356–359**
   sources, **328–329**
   spyware and adware, 339
   summary, **353–354**

malicious code (*continued*)
  Trojan horses, 335–336
  viruses. *See* viruses
  worms, **336–339**
  written lab, 355
man-in-the-middle (MitM) attacks
  description, **429–430**
  overview, **588–589**, *588*
  VoIP, 162
man-made disasters, **649**
  bombings and explosions, **650**
  fires, **649**
  hardware and software failures, **651–652**
  power outages, **650–651**
  strikes and picketing, **653**
  terrorism, **649–650**
  theft and vandalism, **653–654**
  utility and infrastructure failures, **651**
mandatory access control (MAC)
    systems, 24
mandatory protection systems in
    TCSEC, **457**
mandatory vacations, **538**
Manifesto for Agile Software Development,
    308–309
MANs (metropolitan area networks), 177
mantraps, **753–754**, *754*
manual recovery, 607
manual rollover, 502
marking sensitive information, **541**
masking, password, 63
masks, subnet, 107
masquerading, 58, **193**, 352–353, 761
massively parallel processing (MPP), 480
master boot record (MBR) viruses, **330**
master boot records, 330
material evidence, 715
mathematics in cryptography, **368**
  Boolean, **368–371**
  modulo function, **371**
  nonces, **372**
  one-way functions, **371–372**
  zero-knowledge proof, **372–373**, *373*

matrices, access control, 33, **443–444**
MAUs (multistation access units), 139, 141
MAX function, 290
maximum tolerable downtime (MTD), 626
maximum tolerable outage (MTO), 626
MBR (master boot record) viruses, **330**
MD2 (Message Digest 2) algorithm, **411**
MD4 (Message Digest 4) algorithm,
    411–412
MD5 (Message Digest 5), 55–56, **412**
mean time between failures (MTBF), 549
mean time to failure (MTTF), 549, 772
mean time to repair (MTTR), 772
measurable security, 265
Media Access Control (MAC) address,
    94, 112
media access in LANs, **143–144**
media analysis, **717–718**
media life cycle, **549**
media management, **546–549**
mediated-access model, 484
meet-in-the-middle attacks, **429**
memory, 293–294, 491
  addressing, **494**
  RAM, **492–493**
  registers, **494**
  ROM, **491–492**
  secondary, **495**
  security issues, **495–496**
memory cards, 760
memory-mapped I/O, **499**
Merkle-Hellman Knapsack algorithm, 407
mesh topologies, 139, *140*
Message Digest 2 (MD2) algorithm, **411**
Message Digest 4 (MD4) algorithm,
    411–412
Message Digest 5 (MD5), 55–56, **412**
message digests, 180, 409–410
messages
  object-oriented programming, 302
  OSI model, 90–91, *90–91*
metadata in data mining, 292
metamodels, 308

Metasploit tool, 590
methods in object-oriented
    programming, 302
metropolitan area networks (MANs), 177
mice, **498**
Michelangelo virus, 335
microcode, 500
Microcom Networking Protocol
    (MNP), 165
Microsoft Point-to-Point Encryption
    (MPPE), 158
military attacks, **721–722**
Miller, Victor, 408
MIME Object Security Services
    (MOSS), 184
MIN function, 290
*Minimum Security Requirements for
    Federal Information and Information
    Systems*, 67
mining, data, **291–292**
MINs (mobile identification numbers), 189
mirroring
    RAID, **604**
    remote, **663**
    server, 501
mitigation of risk, **255**
MitM (man-in-the-middle) attacks
    description, **429–430**
    overview, **588–589**, *588*
    VoIP, 162
Mitnick, Kevin, 352
MITRE, 555
MNP (Microcom Networking Protocol), 165
Mobile Broadband standard, 137
mobile devices, **548**
mobile identification numbers (MINs), 189
mobile sites, **659–660**
mod function, 371
modems, **120**, **499**
modes in software development security, 318
modification attacks, **193**
modulo function, **371**
monitoring

access control effectiveness, **73–74**
accountability, **71–72**
audits. *See* audits and auditing
clipping levels, **69**
exam essentials, **80–82**
investigations, **72–73**
keystroke, **70**
logging, **64–67**, *65*
problem identification, **73**
review questions, **83–86**
special privileges, **538–539**
summary, **79**
techniques, **67–71**
written lab, **82**
monitors, **498**
Moore's law, 407
Morris, Robert Tappan, 278, 337
MOSS (MIME Object Security Services),
    184
motion detectors, **757–758**
MPP (massively parallel processing), 480
MPPE (Microsoft Point-to-Point
    Encryption), 158
MTBF (mean time between failures), 549
MTD (maximum tolerable downtime), 626
MTO (maximum tolerable outage), 626
MTTF (mean time to failure), 549, 772
MTTR (mean time to repair), 772
Mueller, Frederic, 411
Multic operating system, 483
multicast technology, 142
multifactor authentication, **20–21**, 63
multihomed firewalls, **117**
multilayer protocols, **110–111**
multilayer switches, 159
multilevel databases, **287–289**
multilevel mode systems, 318, **489**
multimedia collaboration, **162–163**
multipartite viruses, **334**
multiple sites, 661
multiprocessing, **480–481**
multiprogramming, **481**
multistate systems, 482

multistation access units (MAUs), 139, 141
multitasking, 480–481
multithreading, 481–482
mutual assistance agreements (MAAs), 661
Myer, Albert, 363

N

NAC (Network Access Control), 114–115
NAT (Network Address Translation), 122
    description, 165–167
    stateful, 168
    static and dynamic, 168–169
National Computer Crime Squad, 719
National Computer Security Center
    (NCSC), 456
National Flood Insurance Program, 647
National Information Assurance
    Certification and Accreditation Process
    (NIACAP), 468
National Information Infrastructure
    Protection Act, 688
National Intraagency Fire Center, 648
National Security Agency (NSA), 687
natural disasters, 645
    earthquakes, 645–646
    fires, 648
    floods, 646–647, 647
    regional events, 649
    site design, 750
    storms, 648
NCAs (noncompete agreements), 260
NCSC (National Computer Security Center),
    456
NDAs (nondisclosure agreements), 259–260
NDS (NetWare Directory Services), 27
need to know principle, 21, 24, 487, 532–533
Nessus tool, 351, 553
NetSP product, 31
NetWare Directory Services (NDS), 27
NetWitness sniffer, 192
Network Access Control (NAC), 114–115
Network Address Translation (NAT), 122

description, 165–167
stateful, 168
static and dynamic, 168–169
network analysis in evidence collection, 718
network-based IDS (NIDS), 594–596
Network File System (NFS), 110
Network layer
    OSI model, 95–96
    TCP/IP model, 106–109
networks, 87
    attacks, 151
        ARP spoofing, 194
        DNS poisoning, spoofing, and
            hijacking, 194–195
        DoS and DDoS, 191–192
        eavesdropping, 192–193
        email, 181–185
        exam essentials, 197–199
        hyperlink spoofing, 195
        impersonation and masquerading, 193
        modification, 193
        NAT, 165–170
        protocol security mechanisms,
            152–154
        remote access security management,
            160–165
        replay, 193
        review questions, 201–204
        security boundaries, 190
        summary, 196–197
        switching technologies, 170–172
        transmission mechanisms, 181
        transparency, 179–180
        verifying integrity, 180
        virtualization technology, 178–179
        voice communications, 186–189
        VPNs, 155–160
        WANs, 172–178
        written lab, 200
    cabling, 123–127
    cryptography, 425–428
    data loss prevention, 71
    devices, 119–122
    endpoint security, 119

exam essentials, **145–146**
firewalls, **115–119**, *118*
LANs, **140–144**
NAC, **114–115**
neural, **296**
OSI Reference Model. *See* Open Systems
    Interconnection (OSI) Reference
    Model
review questions, **147–150**
secure components overview, **113–114**
summary, **144–145**
TCP/IP model. *See* TCP/IP model
topologies, **137–139**, *138–140*
wireless communications. *See* wireless
    communications
written lab, **146**
neural networks, **296**
Newman, Oscar, 750
Next-Generation Intrusion Detection Expert
    System (NIDES), 297
NFS (Network File System), 110
NIACAP (National Information Assurance
    Certification and Accreditation Process),
    468
NIDES (Next-Generation Intrusion
    Detection Expert System), 297
NIDS (network-based IDS), **594–596**
noise
    electrical, **765**
    white, **763**
noise generators, 521
nonces, **372**
noncompete agreements (NCAs), **260**
nondedicated WAN lines, 173
nondisclosure agreements (NDAs),
    259–260
nondiscretionary access controls, **22**
nondistributed computing, **276–277**
noninterference model, **442**
nonrepudiation
    cryptography for, **366**
    security governance, **220–221**
    symmetric key algorithms, 383
nonstatistical sampling, 69

nonvolatile storage, 294, **496**
normalization of databases, **285**
NOT operation, 370
notification alarms, 758
NSA (National Security Agency), 687
Nyberg-Rueppel signature algorithm, 415

O

object evidence, **715**
object-oriented databases (OODBs), 283
object-oriented programming (OOP),
    301–303, 512
objects
    access control, 2
    classes, 301
    security models, **450–454**
    trusted paths, 440
occupant emergency plans (OEPs), 764
OCSP (Online Certificate Status
    Protocol), 419
ODBC (Open Database Connectivity),
    289, *290*
OEPs (occupant emergency plans), 764
OFB (Output Feedback) mode, **388**
OFDM (Orthogonal Frequency-Division
    Multiplexing), 129
offline distribution of symmetric keys, 393
offline UPSs, 606
offsite security challenges, **653–654**
offsite storage, **666**
one-time pads, **377–379**
one-time passwords, **16**
one-to-many data models, 283
one-upped-constructed passwords, 54
one-way functions, **371–372**
Online Certificate Status Protocol
    (OCSP), 419
OODBs (object-oriented databases), 283
OOP (object-oriented programming),
    301–303, 512
Open Database Connectivity (ODBC),
    289, *290*

open relays, 181
Open Source Security Testing Methodology
    Manual (OSSTMM), 213
open system authentication (OSA), **134**
open systems, **451–452**
Open Systems Interconnection (OSI)
    Reference Model, **88**
    encapsulation/deencapsulation, **90–91**,
        90–92
    functionality, **89–90**, *89*
    history, **89**
    layers, 92
        Application, **98–99**
        Data Link, **93–95**
        Network, **95–96**
        Physical, **93**
        Presentation, **98**
        Session, **97**
        Transport, **97**
    vs. TCP/IP model, 100, *100*
Open Web Application Security Project
    (OWASP), 505
OpenPGP product, 184
operating modes in processors, **490–491**
operating states, **485–487**, *487*
operational plans, 207
operations management software, 67
operators role, **210**
OR operation, **369–370**
Orange Book, 456, 460
Orthogonal Frequency-Division
    Multiplexing (OFDM), 129
OSA (open system authentication), **134**
OSI model. *See* Open Systems
    Interconnection (OSI) Reference Model
OSSTMM (Open Source Security Testing
    Methodology Manual), 213
output devices, **498–499**
Output Feedback (OFB) mode, **388**
overflows, buffer
    application attacks, **344–345**
    coding issues, **517–518**
overt channels, 516
overwriting sensitive information, **543**, *544*

OWASP (Open Web Application Security
    Project), *505*
owners of access control, **3**

P

P2P (peer to peer) technologies, 133, **510**
packages in Common Criteria, 462
packet sniffing, 112
packet switching, **171–172**
padded cell systems, **598**
paging process, 495
pairing Bluetooth standard, 132
Palin, Sarah, 14
palm scans, **18**
PANs (personal area networks), 132
PAP (Password Authentication Protocol),
    154
Paperwork Reduction Act, **688**
parallel layers, **210–211**
parallel tests in disaster recovery planning, **673**
parameter checking, **517**
parity information, 503
parol evidence rule, 715
Paros tool, 192
partial-knowledge teams, **600–601**
partial mesh topologies, 139
partitions in work areas, 751
passive audio motion detectors, 758
passive IDS response, **594**
passive proximity readers, 760
Password Authentication Protocol (PAP), 154
passwords
    administrator, 77
    attacks, **54**, 341
        brute-force, **55–56**
        countermeasures, **344**
        dictionary, **54–55**, **342–343**
        guessing, **341–342**
        sniffer, **57–58**, *58*
        social engineering, **343**
    cognitive, **14**
    encrypting, 12

one-time, **16**
overview, **12**
phrases, **13**
selection, **12–13**
PAT (Port Address Translation), 166, 168
patch Tuesday, 552
patches
　managing, 551–552
　zero-day exploits, 583
patents, **693–694**
PATRIOT Act, **700**
pattern-matching detection, 592
pay-per-install approach, 580
Payment Card Industry Data Security
　Standard (PCI DSS), 212, 465, **703–704**
PBX (private branch exchange) systems,
　186–188
PDMCL (process data from multiple
　clearance levels), 490
PDUs (Protocol Data Units), 97
PEAP (Protected Extensible Authentication
　Protocol), 155
peer to peer (P2P) technologies, 133, **510**
PEM (Privacy Enhanced Mail), 184
penetration testing, **598–599**
　ethical hacking, **602**
　permissions, **600**
　reports, **602**
　risks, **599**
　social engineering, **601**
　techniques, **600–601**
　warning banners, **602**
people in continuity planning, **631–632**
percent sign (%) operator for modulo
　function, 371
performance in network segmentation, 114
perimeter security, **440**, 750
permanent physical connections, 170
permanent virtual circuits (PVCs), 172
permissions
　access control, **4**
　penetration testing, **600**
personal area networks (PANs), 132
Personal Identity Verification (PIV) cards, 15

personal property, 748
personally identifiable information (PII),
　212, 540
personnel in recovery plan development,
　664–665
personnel privacy and safety, 763–764
personnel security, **257–259**
　awareness training, 263–264
　employee agreements, 259–260
　exam essentials, 266–269
　review questions, 270–273
　sabotage, 589
　screening and background checks, 259
　security function, 264–265
　summary, 265–266
　terminations, 261–263, 589
　training, 36
　vendor, consultant, and contractor
　　controls, **261**
　written lab, **269**
PERT (Program Evaluation Review
　Technique) tool, **313**
PGP (Pretty Good Privacy), 390
　description, 184
　email systems, **421–422**
phishing, **60–61**, 162, **195**
phlashing, 501
phone number spoofing, 59
phone phreaking, 189, 722
phones, cordless, **132**
photoelectric motion detectors, 758
phrases, password, **13**
phreakers, 188
phreaking, **189**, 722
physical access controls, 7, 8, 62, 753
　badges, 757
　fences, gates, turnstiles, and mantraps,
　　753–754, 754
　intrusion alarms, 758
　keys and combination locks, 756–757
　lighting, 755
　motion detectors, 757–758
　secondary verification mechanisms, 759
　security guards and dogs, 755–756

physical controls for physical security, 747

physical labels for sensitive information, 541

Physical layer, **93**

physical security, 745

   environment and life safety. *See* environment and life safety

   equipment failure, 772

   exam essentials, 774–776

   physical access controls. *See* physical access controls

   privacy, 772–773

   regulatory requirements, 773

   review questions, 777–780

   site and facility design. *See* site and facility design

   summary, 773–774

   technical controls, 760–763

   written lab, 776

physically hardening systems, 632

physiological biometric methods, 17

picketing, **653**

picking locks, 756

piggybacking, 761

PII (personally identifiable information), 212, **540**

ping flood attacks, **588**

ping-of-death attacks, **586**

ping sweeps, **351**

PINs in Bluetooth standard, 132

PIV (Personal Identity Verification) cards, 15

PKCS (Public Key Cryptography Standard) encryption, 183

PKI (public key infrastructure), **415**

   certificate authorities, 416–417

   certificates, **415–416**

      enrollment, **418**

      revoking, **419**

      verifying, **418**

plain old telephone service (POTS), **161**

plain-text attacks, **429**

plaintext messages, 366

planning

   BCP. *See* business continuity planning (BCP)

   to plan, **213–214**

   remote access security management, **163–164**

   security management, **206–207**

platform as a service, 509

platforms in virus vulnerabilities, **332**

PlayStation breach, **50**

plenum cable, 127

plumbing leaks, 766

Point-to-Point Protocol (PPP), 157, **164**, 178

Point-to-Point Tunneling Protocol (PPTP), **157–158**

point-to-point WAN links, 173

poisoning

   ARP cache, 109

   DNS, **194–195**

policies

   access control, **4**

   passwords, 12, 63

   security, **221–222, 513–515**

polling in LAN technologies, **144**

polyalphabetic substitution ciphers, 376

polyinstantiation, 289

polymorphic viruses, **334**

polymorphism in object-oriented programming, 302

POP3 (Post Office Protocol), 109, 181

Porras, Phillip, 297

Port Address Translation (PAT), 166, 168

port numbers in Transport layer, 101

port scans, **351**

portable devices, **420–421**

post accreditation phase in DITSCAP and NIACAP, 468

Post Office Protocol (POP3), 109, 181

postadmission philosophy, 115

postmortem reviews, 729

postwhitening in Twofish algorithm, 392

POTS (plain old telephone service), **161**

power

   intrusion detection systems, 762

   issues, **764–765**

   outages, **650–651**

   protecting, **606**

PPP (Point-to-Point Protocol), 157, **164**, 178

PPs (protection profiles), 462

PPTP (Point-to-Point Tunneling Protocol), 157–158

preaction water suppression systems, 770

preadmission philosophy, 114

Presentation layer, **98**

preset locks, 756

pretexting, 195

Pretty Good Privacy (PGP), 390
  description, 184
  email systems, **421–422**

preventive access control, 5, **62–64**

preventive measures for attacks, **578–579**
  basic measures, **579**
  botnets, **587**
  denial-of-service attacks, **583–584**
  intrusion detection. *See* intrusion
    detection systems (IDSs)
  land attacks, **586**
  malicious code, **580–582**
  miscellaneous attacks, **588–590**
  penetration testing, **598–602**
  ping flood attacks, **588**
  ping-of-death attacks, **586**
  smurf and fraggle attacks, **585–586**
  SYN flood attacks, **584–585**, *584*
  teardrop attacks, **586**
  zero-day exploits, **582–583**

prewhitening in Twofish algorithm, 392

PRI (Primary Rate Interface), **174**

primary keys in relational databases, 284

primary memory, 293, 492, **496**

Primary Rate Interface (PRI), **174**

principle of least privilege, 21, **514**, **532–534**, 581

printers, **498**

priorities
  BIA, **626**
  CIA, **216–217**
  recovery strategy, **655**
  resources, **629–630**
  statements of priorities, **635**

privacy
  laws
    European Union, **701–703**
    U.S., **697–701**
  personnel, **763–764**
  protecting, **772–773**
  requirements compliance, **212–213**
  workplace, **701**

Privacy Act, 698

Privacy Enhanced Mail (PEM), 184

private branch exchange (PBX) systems, **186–188**

private data classification, 228

private IP addresses, **167–168**

private keys
  asymmetric cryptography, **405–406**
  static tokens, 16
  symmetric cryptography, 382

privileged group audits, **75–77**

privileged mode, 317, 485, **490–491**

privileged programs, **518–519**

privileges
  access control, 5
  escalation, 346
  excessive, 37
  monitoring, **538–539**
  separation of, 535
  SQL injection attacks, 350

probability determinations, 249

probable cause, 720

problem identification, **73**

problem state, 485–486

procedures, security, **223–224**

process data from multiple clearance levels (PDMCL), 490

process scheduler, 487

process states, **485–487**, *487*

processes
  continuity planning, **631–632**
  integrating, 521
  isolating, 316, 513

processors, **479**
  execution types, **479–482**
  operating modes, **490–491**
  processing types, **482–483**
  protection mechanisms, **483–490**, *484, 487*
procurement, **704–705**
Professional Practice Library, 664
Program Evaluation Review Technique
    (PERT) tool, **313**
program executive, 487
programmable read-only memory
    (PROM), **492**
programming
  languages, **300–301**
  vulnerabilities from, **520**
projects, Gantt charts for, 312
PROM (programmable read-only memory),
    492
propagation techniques for viruses, **329–332**
property, corporate vs. personal, **748**
proprietary alarm systems, 758
proprietary data, 228
Protected Extensible Authentication Protocol
    (PEAP), 155
protected mode, 317
protection
  audit results, 77
  backup tapes, **547–548**
  hard drives, **502–504, 603–605**
  log data, **66–67**
  processors, **483–490**, *484, 487*
  resources, **546–549**
  security governance, **210–212**
  servers, **605–606**, *605*
protection profiles (PPs), 462
protection rings, **316–317**, *316*, **483–485**, *484*
Protocol Data Units (PDUs), 97
protocol security mechanisms, networks,
    152–154
protocol translators, 121
protocols
  authentication, **154**
  defined, 88

dial-up, **164–165, 178**
discovery, 105
  multilayer, **110–111**
  VPNs, **157–159**
provisioning, 35
provisions phase in continuity
    planning, **631–632**
proxies, 116, **121–122**
proximity readers, 61, **760–761**
proxy firewalls, 116
proxy logs, 66
pseudo flaws, **597–598**
PSH flag, **104–105**
PSTN (public switched telephone network),
    161
public data classification, 228
Public Key Cryptography Standard (PKCS)
    encryption, 183
public key infrastructure (PKI), **415**
  certificate authorities, **416–417**
  certificates, **415–416**
    enrollment, **418**
    revoking, **419**
    verifying, **418**
public keys
  algorithms, **383–386**, *384*
  asymmetric cryptography, **405–406**
  encryption, 393
public switched telephone network
    (PSTN), **161**
pulse patterns, 18
purging sensitive information, **544**
PVCs (permanent virtual circuits), 172

Q

qualitative decision making, 625
qualitative risk analysis, 248, **253–254**
quantitative decision making, 625
quantitative risk analysis, **248**
  cost functions, **248–249**
  threat/risk calculations, **249–253**

R

race conditions, 520
radiation
    EM, **521**
    van Eck, 498
radio frequency identification (RFID)
    tags, 549
radio frequency interference (RFI), 765
RADIUS (Remote Authentication Dial-In
    User Service), **32**, 165
RAID (Redundant Array of Independent
    Disks), 502–504, 603–605
rainbow series, 455–456
    elements, 458–460
    TCSEC, 456–457
rainbow table attacks, 57, 428
random access memory (RAM), **492–493**
random access storage, 293, **497**
random ports, 101
ransomware, 580
RARP (Reverse Address Resolution
    Protocol), 94, **109**, 595
RAs (registration authorities), 417
rate-of-rise fire detection systems, 769
RBAC (role-based access control), 23, **25–26**
RBAC (rule-based access control) systems,
    22–23, 453
RC5 (Rivest Cipher 5), 391
RDBMSs (relational database management
    systems), 282
read-only memory (ROM), **491–492**
ready state, **486**
real evidence, **715**
real memory, 293, 492
realms of security in mandatory access
    controls, 24
reasonable expectation of privacy, 701
reasonableness checks in software
    development, 314
reciprocal agreements, 661
reconnaissance attacks, 53, 350–352
record retention, **545**

recovery and remediation, 732
    access control, **6**
    vs. restoration, **670–671**
    symmetric cryptography keys, **394**
    trusted, **606–608**
recovery plan development, **663–664**
    assessment, **665**
    backups and offsite storage, **666–669**
    emergency response, **664**
    external communications, **670**
    logistics and supplies, **670**
    personnel and communications, **664–665**
    recovery vs. restoration, **670–671**
    software escrow arrangements, **669–670**
    utilities, **670**
recovery response step for incidents, 577
recovery strategy, 654
    alternate processing sites, **657–661**
    business unit and functional
        priorities, **655**
    crisis management, **656**
    database recovery, **662–663**
    emergency communications, **656**
    mutual assistance agreements, **661**
    work groups, **656–657**
recovery time objective (RTO), 626
Red Book, **458**, 460
red boxes, 189
Redundant Array of Independent Disks
    (RAID), 502–504, 603–605
redundant servers, **501–502**
reference monitors, **440–441**
reference profiles, 20
referential integrity in relational databases,
    285
reflected input in cross-site scripting, 347
regional natural disasters, **649**
register addressing, **494**
registered software ports, 101
registers, **494**
registration, biometric, **20**
registration authorities (RAs), 417
regulatory policies, 222

regulatory requirements
  BCP, **624**
  complying with, **773**
rejection of risk, 256
relational database management systems
    (RDBMSs), 282
relational databases, **283–285**, *284*
relations in relational databases, 283
relay agents, 181
release control process, **314**
relevant evidence, 715
remediation response step for incidents,
    577–578
remote access security management, **160–163**
  centralized services, **165**
  dial-up protocols, **164–165**
  planning, **163–164**
Remote Authentication Dial-In User Service
    (RADIUS), **32**, 165
remote control, 175
remote journaling, 501, **662–663**
remote mirroring, **663**
remote wipe, 548
removal of viruses, 340
repeaters, 120, 127
repellant alarms, 758
replay attacks, **193**, 430
reports
  incidents, **576–577**, 734
  penetration testing, **602**
repudiating messages, **366**
request control process in change
    management, 313
reset attacks in TCP, **585**
reset (RST) packets, 102, **104–105**
residual risk, 256
resolution attacks, **194–195**
resources
  managing, **549–550**
  prioritization in BIA, **629–630**
  protecting, **546–549**
  requirements in BCP, **622–623**
  security, 265

response steps for incidents, **573–574,**
    574, 730
  detection, **574–575**
  recovery, 577
  remediation and review, **577–578**
  reporting, **576–577**
  response, **575–576**
response teams, **728–729**
responsibilities
  duties separated from, **534–537,** *536*
  security governance, **209–210**
restoration
  process, 732
  vs. recovery, **670–671**
restricted interfaces, **34**, 449
restrictions, passwords, 12
retina scans, **17**
Reverse Address Resolution Protocol
    (RARP), 94, **109,** *595*
reverse DNS lookups, 595
reverse hash matching attacks, 430
review response step for incidents,
    577–578
reviews, security, **561–562**
revoking
  accounts, **37–38**
  certificates, **418–419**
RFI (radio frequency interference), 765
RFID (radio frequency identification)
    tags, 549
rights in access control, **4**
ring topologies, 137, *138*
rings
  vs. levels, **511**
  protection, **483–485,** *484*
risk and risk management
  analysis, 242, 245
  asset valuation, **245–248**
  attacks, **49**
  BCP documentation, **635–636**
  BIA, **626–627**
  defined, **243**
  exam essentials, **266–269**

handling, 255–257
overview, **241**
personnel management, **239**
qualitative risk analysis, 253–254
quantitative risk analysis,
      248–253
review questions, 270–273
summary, 265–266
terminology, 242–244, *244*
third-party governance, 240–241
written lab, **269**
Rivest, Ronald, 406, 411–412
Rivest, Shamir, Adleman (RSA) algorithm,
      52, **406–407**, 415
Rivest Cipher 5 (RC5), 391
Rogier, Nathalie, 411
rogueware, 60, 580
role-based access control (RBAC),
      23, **25–26**
roles in security governance,
      209–210
ROLLBACK command, 286
rollover, **502**
ROM (read-only memory), **491–492**
rootkits, 346
Rosenberger, Rob, 335
ROT3 cipher, 363, 376
rotation
      job, **258**, 538
      tape backups, **669**
rounds of encryption, 387
routers, 96, 116, **121**
routing protocols, **96**
Royce, Winston, 306
RSA (Rivest, Shamir, Adleman) algorithm,
      52, **406–407**, 415
RST (reset) packets, 102, 104–105
RTO (recovery time objective), 626
rule-based access controls (RBACs),
      22–23, 453
running key ciphers, **379–380**
running state, **486**
Rustock botnet, 587

S

S/MIME (Secure Multipurpose Internet Mail
      Extensions) protocol, **183–184, 422**
S-RPC (Secure Remote Procedure Call),
      153, 393
sabotage by employees, 589
safeguards
      cost/benefits, **250–252**
      defined, **244**
      distributed architecture, 507–508
sags, 606, 764
SAIC (Science Applications International
      Corporation), 542
Saint scanner, 351
salami attacks, 519
SAML (Security Assertion Markup
      Language), 30, 505
sampling in monitoring, 69
sandboxes in Java, 340, 506
sanitizing data, 497, **544**
Sarbanes-Oxley Act (SOX), 212, 535
SAs (security associations)
      IPSec, 426
      ISAKMP, 427
satellite connections, 174
scalability of symmetric key algorithms, 383
scanners, vulnerability, 64, **553–554**
scanning attacks, **726–727**
scenarios for risk analysis, **253–254**
schedules
      changes, 560
      Gantt charts, 312
schema for relational databases, 285
Schneier, Bruce, 390, 392, 518
Schnorr signature algorithm, 415
Science Applications International
      Corporation (SAIC), 542
screen filters, 59
screen scrapers, **175–176**
screened hosts, 117
screening checks in personnel security, **259**
screening routers, 116

script kiddies, 328–329, 725

scripted access in SSO, 31

SCTP (Stream Control Transmission Protocol) port, 33

SDLC (Synchronous Data Link Control), 177

Search for Extraterrestrial Intelligence (SETI) project, 279

search warrants, **719–720**, 731

second-generation languages (2GL), 301

second normal form (2NF), 285

secondary evidence, 715

secondary memory, **495–496**

secondary storage, 293

secondary verification mechanisms, **759**

secret data classification, 227

secret key cryptography, 382

secure communication protocols, **153–154**

Secure Electronic Transaction (SET), **154**

Secure European System for Applications in a Multivendor Environment (SESAME), 31

secure facility plans, **746–747**

Secure Hash Algorithm (SHA), **410–411**

Secure Hash Algorithm version 2 (SHA-2), 56

Secure Hash Standard (SHS), 410

Secure Multipurpose Internet Mail Extensions (S/MIME) protocol, **183–184, 422**

Secure Remote Procedure Call (S-RPC), 153, 393

Secure Shell (SSH), 425

Secure Sockets Layer (SSL), 110, 153, **422–423**

secure state machines, 441

secured enveloped messages, 183

security applications in knowledge-based systems, **297**

Security Assertion Markup Language (SAML), 30, 505

security associations (SAs)
  IPSec, 426
  ISAKMP, 427

Security Assurance section in Common Criteria, 463

security boundaries, **190**

security cameras, 759

security domain systems, **457**

Security Event Management (SEM), 68

Security Functional Requirements section in Common Criteria, 463

security governance, **205–206**
  accountability, **220**
  auditing, **219**
  authentication, **218–219**
  authorization, **219**
  availability, **217–218**
  change control/management, **224–225**
  compliance issues, 208
  confidentiality, **214–215**
  control frameworks, **213–214**
  data classification, **225–229**
  exam essentials, **230–232**
  identification, **218**
  integrity, **215–216**
  legally defensible, **220**
  nonrepudiation, **220–221**
  overview, **208**
  planning, **206–207**
  policies, **221–222**
  privacy requirements, **212–213**
  procedures, **223–224**
  protection mechanisms, **210–212**
  review questions, **234–237**
  roles and responsibilities, **209–210**
  standards, baselines, and guidelines, **222–223**
  summary, **229–230**
  written lab, **233**

security guards and dogs, **755–756**

security IDs, 757

Security Information and Event Management (SIEM), 68

Security Information Management (SIM), 68

security kernels, **440–441**

security labels, 439
security logs, 65–66
security models, 437
    access control matrices, **443–444**
    Bell-LaPadula, **444–446**, *446*
    Biba, **446–448**, *447*
    Brewer and Nash, **449**
    Clark-Wilson, **448–449**
    concepts, **438–439**
    evaluation. *See* evaluation models
    exam essentials, **470–471**
    Goguen-Meseguer, **449–450**
    Graham-Denning, **450**
    information flow, **441–442**
    noninterference, **442**
    objects and subjects, **450–454**
    review questions, **473–476**
    security capabilities of information
        systems, **469**
    state machine, **441**
    summary, **470**
    Sutherland, **450**
    Take-Grant, **443**
    TCB, **440–441**
    written lab, **472**
security modes, **487–490**
Security Operations, **531**
    audits and reviews, **561–562**
    change management, **559–561**, *559*
    configuration management, **555–558**, *557*
    exam essentials, **563–564**
    job rotation, **538**
    mandatory vacations, **538**
    need to know and least privilege, **532–534**
    patch management, **551–552**
    principles, **21–22**
    resource protection, **546–550**
    review questions, **566–569**
    sensitive information. *See* sensitive
        information
    separating duties and responsibilities,
        534–537, *536*
    special privileges, **538–539**

    summary, **562–563**
    vulnerability management, **552–555**
    written lab, **565**
security perimeters, **440**
security policies, 4, **513–515**
security professionals roles, **209**
security protection mechanisms, **510–511**
    security policy and computer
        architecture, **513–515**
    technical, **511–513**
security targets (STs) in Common
    Criteria, 462
security through obscurity, 367, 381
segmentation
    hardware, 316, **513**
    network, **113–114**
segments in OSI model, 91, *92*
segregation of duties, **535–537**, *536*
seismic hazard level, **645–646**
SEM (Security Event Management), 68
sendmail program, 181, 337
senior management
    BCP process, **622**
    roles, **209**
    security plans, 207
sensitive but unclassified data, 227
sensitive data, 228
sensitive information
    destroying, **543**, *544*
    handling, **542**
    managing, **539–540**
    marking, **541**
    PII, **540**
    record retention, **545**
    storing, **542**
separation of duties, **258**
separation of duties and responsibilities
    principle, 21, **534–537**, *536*
separation of privilege, **514–515**, 535
sequential storage, 294, **497**
Serial Line Internet Protocol (SLIP),
    165, 178
series layers, **210–211**

servers
  malicious code countermeasures, 340
  protecting, **605–606**, *605*
  redundant, **501–502**
  security, **751–752**
service bureaus, **660**
service injection viruses, **331–332**
service-level agreements (SLAs)
  BCPs, 624
  equipment failures, 772
  issues, 261
  overview, **318–319**
service-oriented architecture (SOA), 521
service ports in Transport layer, 101
Service Provisioning Markup Language
  (SPML), 30–31
service set identifiers (SSIDs), 133–134
service-specific remote access, 175
service tickets (STs), 28
SESAME (Secure European System
  for Applications in a Multivendor
  Environment), 31
session hijacking, **353**
Session Initiation Protocol (SIP), 153
Session layer in OSI model, **97**
SET (Secure Electronic Transaction), **154**
SETI (Search for Extraterrestrial
  Intelligence) project, 279
SGML (Standard Generalized Markup
  Language), 30
SHA (Secure Hash Algorithm), **410–411**
SHA-2 (Secure Hash Algorithm
  version 2), 56
Shamir, Adi, 406
shared key authentication (SKA), 135
shared private keys, 382
shielded twisted-pair (STP) cable, 125
shielding, cable, 521
shimming locks, 756
shoulder surfing, 59, 751
shrink-wrap license agreements, *695*
SHS (Secure Hash Standard), 410
side-channel attacks, 61

SIEM (Security Information and Event
  Management), 68
signature-based filters, 340
signature-based virus detection,
  332–333, 592
signature dynamics, 18
signatures, **413–414**
  DSS, **415**
  HMAC, **414–415**
  static tokens, 16
signed messages, 183
Silver Bullet Service, 547
SIM (Security Information Management), 68
SIM (subscriber identity module) cards, 548
Simple Integrity Property, 447
Simple Key Management for Internet
  Protocol (SKIP), 153
Simple Mail Transfer Protocol (SMTP),
  109, 181
Simple Network Management Protocol
  (SNMP), 110
Simple Security Property, 445
simplex communication, 97
simulation tests in disaster recovery
  planning, **673**
single loss expectancy (SLE)
  impact assessment, 628–629
  threat/risk calculations, **249**
single points of failure, **501**, 603
  failover solutions, **502**
  RAID, 502–504
  redundant servers, **501–502**
single sign-on (SSO) access control
  description, **27–28**
  examples, **31**
  federated identity management, **30–31**
single state systems, **482**
single-tier firewall deployment, 117, *118*
SIP (Session Initiation Protocol), 153
site and facility design, **746**
  accessibility and perimeter security, 750
  facility design, 750
  natural disasters, 750

physical security controls, **747–749**
secure facility plans, **746–747**
server rooms and data center security, **751–752**
site selection, **749**
visibility, **749**
visitors, **752**
work areas and internal security, **751**
Site Digger product, 176
Six Cartridge Weekly Backup strategy, 669
SKA (shared key authentication), 135
SKIP (Simple Key Management for Internet Protocol), 153
Skipjack algorithm, **390–391**
SLAs (service-level agreements)
    BCPs, 624
    equipment failures, 772
    issues, 261
    overview, **318–319**
SLE (single loss expectancy)
    impact assessment, 628–629
    threat/risk calculations, 249
sliding windows, 103
SLIP (Serial Line Internet Protocol), 165, 178
smart cards
    attacks, **61–62**
    overview, **14–15**, **760**
smartphones
    cryptology, 421
    protecting, 548
SMDS (Switched Multimegabit Data Service), **177**
smoke-actuated fire detection systems, 769
smoke damage, 771
smoke stage in fire, 768
SMP (symmetric multiprocessing), 480
SMTP (Simple Mail Transfer Protocol), 109, 181
smurf attacks, **585–586**
sniffers, **57–58**, *58*, 192
sniping, auction, 280
SNMP (Simple Network Management Protocol), 110

snooping attacks, 57
SOA (service-oriented architecture), 521
social engineering
    overview, **59–61**
    password attacks, **343**
    penetration tests, **601**
    voice communications, **186–187**
software
    escrow arrangements, **669–670**
    in evidence collection, **718**
    failures, **651–652**
    licensing, 550, **695–696**
    threat modeling, 51
software as a service, 509
Software Capability Maturity Model, 310
software development security, 275
    application issues, **276–281**
    assurance procedures, **298**
    change and configuration management, **313–314**
    control architecture, **316–318**, *316*
    data/information storage, **293–294**
    databases. *See* databases and data warehousing
    exam essentials, **319–321**
    knowledge-based systems, **294–297**
    life cycle. *See* life cycles
    modes, **318**
    object-oriented programming, **301–303**
    programming languages, **300–301**
    review questions, **322–325**
    SLAs, **318–319**
    software development process, **297–298**
    software testing, **314–316**
    summary, **319**
    system failures, **298–300**, *300*
    written lab, **321**
Software IP Encryption (swIPe), 153
"something you have" authentication factor, 9
"something you know" authentication factor, 9
"somewhere you are" authentication factor, 10

Sony data breaches, **50**
Soviet cryptosystem, 378
SOX (Sarbanes-Oxley Act), 212, 535
Spam over Internet Telephony (SPIT)
    attacks, 162
spamming, 183
SPAN (Switched Port Analyzer) ports, 595
spear phishing, **61**
special privileges, **538–539**
speed of symmetric key algorithms, 383
spikes, 606, 765
spiral model, **308**, *308*
SPIT (Spam over Internet Telephony) attacks,
    162
split knowledge principle, **373**, **394**, **537**
SPML (Service Provisioning Markup
    Language), 30–31
spoofing attacks, **58–59**
    ARP, **194**
    DNS, **194–195**
    email, 59, 183
    hyperlink, **195**
    IP, **352–353**
spread spectrum communication, 128
spyware, **339**
SQL (Structured Query Language)
    features, 285
    injection attacks, **348–350**, *348*
SSAAs (System Security Authorization
    Agreements), 468
SSH (Secure Shell), 425
SSIDs (service set identifiers), 133–134
SSL (Secure Sockets Layer), 110, 153,
    422–423
SSO (single sign-on) access control
    description, **27–28**
    examples, **31**
    federated identity management, **30–31**
stand-alone mode infrastructure, 133
Standard Generalized Markup Language
    (SGML), 30
standards in security governance, **222–223**
standby UPSs, 606, 650–651, 764

*(star) Integrity Property, 447
*(star) Security Property, 445–446
star topologies, **138–139**, *139*
state attacks, 520
state changes, **520**
state laws, 685
state machine model, **441**
state transitions, 441
stateful inspection firewalls, **116–117**
stateful NAT, **168**
statements of importance, **634–635**
statements of organizational
    responsibility, **635**
statements of priorities, **635**
statements of urgency and timing, **635**
static electricity, **766**
static NAT, **168–169**
static packet-filtering firewalls, **116**
static RAM, **493**
static testing, **315**
static tokens, 15–16
static Web pages, 348
statistical cryptographic attacks, 428
statistical intrusion detection, 592
statistical sampling, **69**
status accounting configuration, 314
stealth viruses, **334**
steganography, **423–424**, *424*
stolen storage devices, 496
STOP errors, 299
stop orders, **279–280**
stopped state, 486
storage
    backups. *See* backups
    covert channels, 516
    overview, **496–498**
    sensitive information, **542**
    symmetric keys, **394**
    threats, **294**
    types, **293–294**
store-and-forward devices, 121
stored procedures, 350
storms, **648**

STP (shielded twisted-pair) cable, 125
strategic plans, **207**
strategy development phase in continuity
    planning, **630–631**
stream ciphers, **380**
Stream Control Transmission Protocol
    (SCTP) port, 33
streaming media, 692
strikes, **653**
stripe of mirrors, **604**
striping, 604
striping with parity, 604
strong passwords, **54**, 63
structured protection systems in
    TCSEC, 457
Structured Query Language (SQL)
    features, 285
    injection attacks, **348–350**, *348*
structured walk-throughs, **673**
STs (security targets) in Common
    Criteria, 462
STs (service tickets) in Kerberos, 28
Stuxnet worm, *52*, **338–339**
subjects
    access control, 2
    security models, **450–454**
    trusted paths, 440
subnet masks, 107
subpoenas, 731
subscriber identity module (SIM)
    cards, 548
substitution ciphers, **375–377**
SUM function, 290
summation in neural networks, 296
super-increasing sets theory, 407
supervisor state, 485
supervisory mode, 491
supervisory state, **486**
supplicants in IEEE 802.1x standard, 428
supplies in recovery plan development, **670**
surges, 765
Sutherland model, **450**
SVCs (switched virtual circuits), 172

swIPe (Software IP Encryption), 153
Switched Multimegabit Data Service
    (SMDS), **177**
Switched Port Analyzer (SPAN)
    ports, 595
switched virtual circuits (SVCs), 172
switches, **121**, *595*
switching technologies, **170**
    circuit switching, **170–171**
    packet switching, **171–172**
    virtual circuits, **172**
symmetric cryptography, 365, **386–387**
    AES, **391–392**
    Blowfish, 390
    DES, **387–388**
    IDEA, **390**
    key management, 393
        algorithms, **382–383**, *382*
        creating and distributing, **393**
        escrow and recovery, **394**
        storage and destruction, **394**
    Skipjack algorithm, **390–391**
    Triple DES, **389–390**
symmetric multiprocessing (SMP), 480
SYN (synchronize) packets, 102, 104–105
SYN/ACK (synchronize and acknowledge)
    packets, 102
SYN flood attacks, **584–585**, *584*
synchronization, time, 73
Synchronous Data Link Control
    (SDLC), 177
synchronous LAN communications, **142**
synchronous tokens, **15–16**
system calls, 485
system compromise, 727
system failures, avoiding, **298–300**, *300*
system high mode systems, 318, **488**
system logs, 66
system resilience, 603
    hard drives, **603–605**
    power sources, 606
    servers, **605–606**, *605*
    trusted recovery, **606–608**

System Security Authorization Agreements
      (SSAAs), 468
system test review, 305

T

T-sight tool, 192
table-top exercises in disaster recovery
      planning, 673
tablets, 548
TACACS (Terminal Access Controller
      Access-Control System), 32, 165
TACACS Plus (TACACS+), 32
tactical plans, 207
Take-Grant model, 443
tape backups
      formats, 667–668
      protecting, 547–548
      rotating, 669
      sensitive information, 541–542
targets of evaluation (TOEs), 460
task-based access control (TBAC), 26
TATO (temporary authorization to
      operate), 241
TBAC (task-based access control), 26
TCB (trusted computing base), 440–441
TCP (Transmission Control Protocol)
      overview, 101–104
      reset attacks, 585
TCP/IP model, 99–100, 100
      Application layer protocols, 109–110
      DNR, 112–113
      multilayer protocols, 110–111
      Network layer protocols, 106–109
      Transport layer protocols, 101–106
      vulnerabilities, 112
TCP wrappers, 101
TCSEC (Trusted Computer System
      Evaluation Criteria), 223, 455–456
      classes and required functionality,
            456–457
      limitations, 459–460

teams
      BCP, 620–621
      CIRT, 575
      response, 728–729
      testing, 600–601
teardrop attacks, 586
technical controls, 7, 8, 760
      access abuses, 761
      emanation security, 762–763
      intrusion detection systems, 761–762
      physical security, 747
      proximity readers, 760–761
      smart cards, 760
technical security mechanisms, 511
      abstraction, 512
      data hiding, 512
      hardware segmentation, 513
      layering processes, 511–512
      process isolation, 513
technology and process integration
      vulnerabilities, 521
technology convergence, 747
telcos, 131
telecommuting, 160–165, 175–176
Telnet protocol, 109
temperature, 766
TEMPEST technologies
      countermeasures, 762–763
      screen eavesdropping, 498, 521
Temporal Key Integrity Protocol (TKIP), 427
temporary authorization to operate
      (TATO), 241
Ten Commandments of Computer
      Ethics, 737
Terminal Access Controller Access-Control
      System (TACACS), 32, 165
termination of employees, 261–263, 589
terrorism, 649–650, 723
testimonial evidence, 716–717
testing
      BCP documentation, 637
      disaster recovery planning, 672–673
      patches, 551

penetration. *See* penetration testing
  software, 314–316
testing phase in BCP, 623
TFTP (Trivial File Transfer Protocol), 109
TGTs (ticket-granting tickets), 28
theft, 653–654
thicknet, 124
thinnet, 124
third-generation languages (3GL), 301
third normal form (3NF), 285
third-party governance, **240–241**
threats
  attacks. *See* attacks
  defined, **243**
  insider, **724**
  modeling, 50–52
  storage, 294
  threat/risk calculations, 249–253
three-tier firewall deployment, 118–119
thrill attacks, **725**
throughput rate in biometric registration, 20
ticket-granting tickets (TGTs), 28
tickets in Kerberos, 28–29
time, synchronization, 73
time of check (TOC), 520
time-of-check-to-time-of-use (TOCTTOU)
  attacks, 345, **520**
time of use (TOU), 520
time slices, 485
timing covert channels, 516
timing issues, **520**
TJX security breach, 427
TKIP (Temporal Key Integrity Protocol), 427
TLS (Transport Layer Security), 33, **153,**
  422–423
TOC (time of check), 520
TOCTTOU (time-of-check-to-time-of-use)
  attacks, 345, **520**
TOEs (targets of evaluation), 460
Token Ring technologies, **141**
tokens
  identification and authentication,
    15–16

LAN technologies, **144**
  security, 439
top-down management approach, 206
top secret data classification, 227
topologies, network, **137–139,** *138–140*
tornadoes, 648
total risk, 256
TOU (time of use), 520
Tower of Hanoi backup strategy, 669
TPMs (Trusted Platform Modules),
  421, 469
TPs (transformation procedures), 449
trade secrets, **694–695**
trademarks, **692–693**
traffic analysis, 71
training
  continuity planning, **633**
  cross-training, 538
  disaster recovery planning, **671–672**
  hiring process, 36
  personnel, **263–264**
  users, 63
training phase in BCP, 623
transactions, database, **286–287**
transformation procedures (TPs), 449
transients, 606, 765
transitions, state, 441
Transmission Control Protocol (TCP)
  overview, **101–104**
  reset attacks, 585
transmission mechanisms, **181**
transmission protection for remote
  access, **163**
transmission windows, 103
transparency, **179–180**
transponder proximity readers, 761
Transport layer
  OSI model, **97**
  TCP/IP model, 99–106, *100–101*
Transport Layer Security (TLS), 33,
  153, 422–423
transport mode in IPSec, 426
transposition ciphers, 375

traverse mode noise, 765

tree bus topology, 138

trend analysis, **71**

Triple DES (3DES), **389–390**

triples in Clark-Wilson model, 448

Tripwire tool, 313, 333

Trivial File Transfer Protocol (TFTP), 109

Trojan horses, **277–278**, **335–336**

Tropical Prediction Center, 648

true values, 368

TrueCrypt package, 421

trust relationships and worms, **338**

Trusted Computer System Evaluation Criteria (TCSEC), 223, **455–456**

    classes and required functionality, **456–457**

    limitations, **459–460**

trusted computing base (TCB), **440–441**

Trusted Network Interpretation of the TCSEC, 458

trusted paths, 440

Trusted Platform Modules (TPMs), 421, 469

trusted recovery, 517, **606–608**

trusted systems, **454**

trusts in domains, 27

Trustworthy Computing Initiative, 518

tsunamis, 646

tunnel mode in IPSec, 426

tunneling in VPNs, **155–157**

tuples in relational databases, 283

turnstiles, **753–754**, *754*

twisted-pair cabling, **125–126**

two-factor authentication, 20

two-person control, **537**

two-tier firewall deployment, 118

Twofish algorithm, **392**

Type 1 authentication factor, 9

Type 1 biometric factor errors, 19

Type 2 authentication factor, 9

Type 2 biometric factor errors, 19

Type 3 authentication factor, 10

U

UCITA (Uniform Computer Information Transactions Act), 696

UDIs (unconstrained data items), 449

UDP (User Datagram Protocol), 101, 106

    fraggle attacks, 586

    RADIUS, 32

Ultra effort, **364**

unchecked buffers, 518

unclassified data, 227

unconstrained data items (UDIs), 449

unicast technology, 142

Uniform Computer Information Transactions Act (UCITA), 696

uninterruptible power supplies (UPSs), 606, 650–651, 764

United States Code (USC), 684

United States Government Configuration Baseline (USGCB) images, 558

United States Patent and Trademark Office (USPTO), 693

UNIX operating system, 332

unlocking databases, 288

unshielded twisted-pair (UTP) cable, **125–126**

UPSs (uninterruptible power supplies), 606, 650–651, 764

URG flag, 104–105

U.S. Geological Survey (USGS), 627, *628*

USA PATRIOT Act, 700

USB flash drives, **546–547**

User Datagram Protocol (UDP), 101, 106

    fraggle attacks, 586

    RADIUS, 32

user-friendliness, 300, *300*

user mode, 317, 485, **490**

users

    access control, **2–3**

    education, 63

    remote assistance, **164**

    role, **210**

USGCB (United States Government Configuration Baseline) images, *558*

USGS (U.S. Geological Survey), 627, *628*
USPTO (United States Patent and Trademark
    Office), 693
utilities
    failures, **651**
    recovery plan development, **670**
UTP (unshielded twisted-pair) cable,
    125–126

V

vacations, mandatory, **538**
validation and verification steps in waterfall
    model, 307
validation phase in DITSCAP
    and NIACAP, 468
valuation of assets, **245–248**
Van Eck phreaking, 498
Van Eck radiation, 498
vandalism, **653–654**
vaulting, electronic, 501, **662**
VBScript language, 301
vendor controls in personnel security, **261**
VENONA project, 378–379
verification
    certificates, **418**
    integrity, **180, 449**
    patches, **552**
    secondary, **759**
verification phase in DITSCAP and
    NIACAP, 468
verified protection systems in TCSEC, **457**
Vernam, Gilbert Sandford, 378
Vernam ciphers, 378
versioning in change management, **561**
video streaming, 692
views, databases, **287–288**
Vigenere cipher, 376–377
virtual circuits, **172**
virtual desktops, 179
virtual LANs (VLANs), **159–160**
virtual machines (VMs), 490

virtual memory, 293, **495**
virtual private networks (VPNs), **155**
    IPSec, 426
    operation, **157**
    protocols, **157–159**
    TCP/IP model links, 101
    tunneling, **155–157**
    virtual LANs, **159–160**
virtual storage, 293
virtualization technology, **178–179**, 469
viruses, **277**
    antivirus mechanisms, **332–333**, 581
    countermeasures, **339–341**
    decryption routines, 334
    hoaxes, **334–335**
    overview, 329
    platforms vulnerable to, 332
    propagation techniques, 329–332
    technologies, **333–334**
vishing (VoIP phishing), **61**, 162
visibility in site design, **749**
visitors, tracking, **752**
vital records program in BCP
    documentation, 636
VLANs (virtual LANs), **159–160**
VMs (virtual machines), 490
voice communications, **186**
    fraud and abuse, **187–188**
    phreaking, **189**
    social engineering, **186–187**
voice pattern recognition, 18
VoIP (Voice over Internet Protocol),
    162, 590
VoIP phishing (vishing), **61**, 162
volatile storage, 294, **496**
voluntarily surrender of information, 731
VPNs. *See* virtual private networks (VPNs)
vulnerabilities
    analysis, **53**
    assessments, **554–555**
    covert channels, **515–516**
    CVE database, 555
    defined, **243**

vulnerabilities (*continued*)
  design and coding flaws, **516–520**
  distributed architecture. *See* distributed
    architecture
  electromagnetic radiation, **521**
  exam essentials, **522–524**
  managing, **552–553**
  review questions, **526–529**
  risk, 49
  scanners, 64, **553–554**
  security protection mechanisms, **510–515**
  single-point-of-failure, **501–504**
  summary, **522**
  TCP/IP, **112**
  technology and process integration, **521**
  timing issues, **520**
  written lab, **525**
  zero-day exploits, **582–583**
vulnerability scans, **351–352**

W

waiting state, **486**
Waledac botnet, 587
walk-throughs
  code review, **305**
  disaster recovery planning, **673**
walls in work areas, 751
WANs (wide area networks), 123
  connection technologies, **174–177**
  overview, **172–174**
WAP (Wireless Application Protocol), 131
war dialing, **589–590**
wardriving, **136**
warm sites, **659**
warm-swappable RAID, 503
warning banners for penetration testing, **602**
warrants, search, **719–720**, 731
WarVOX tool, 590
water fire suppression systems, 770
water leakage and flooding, 766
waterfall model, **306–307**, *307*

watermarking, **423–424**
wave pattern motion detectors, 757
WDS (Windows Deployment Services), 557
Web application security, **346–347**, **422–423**
  dynamic applications, **348–349**, *348*
  SQL injection attacks, **348–350**, *348*
  XSS attacks, **347**
webcasting, 692
well-known ports, 101
WEP (Wired Equivalent Privacy), **135**, **427**
wet pipe water suppression systems, 770
whaling, **61**
white-box testing, 315, **600–601**
white boxes, 189
white noise, **763**
whitelisting, 340
wide area networks (WANs), 123
  connection technologies, **174–177**
  overview, **172–174**
WiFi Protected Access (WPA), **135**, **427–428**
WiMax standard, 137
Windows Deployment Services (WDS), 557
Windows Update, 551
WIPO (World Intellectual Property
    Organization) treaties, 691
Wired Equivalent Privacy (WEP), **135**, **427**
wired extension infrastructure mode, 133
Wireless Application Protocol (WAP), 131
wireless communications, **128**
  attacks, **136**
  Bluetooth, **132**
  cell phones, **129–131**
  concepts, **128–129**
  cordless phones, **132**
  networks, **132–137**, **427–428**
Wireless Transport Layer Security
    (WTLS), 131
Wireshark protocol analyzer, **57–58**, *58*, 192
wiretapping, 70
work areas, **751**
work function in cryptography, 374
work group recovery, **656–657**
workers. *See* personnel security

workplace privacy, **701**
workstation changes, 550
World Intellectual Property Organization
    (WIPO) treaties, 691
worms, **278, 336**
    Code Red, 336–337
    Internet, 337–338
    Stuxnet, 338–339
WPA (WiFi Protected Access), **135, 427–428**
wrappers in TCP, 101
WTLS (Wireless Transport Layer Security),
    131

X

X.25 WAN connections, **176**
X.509 certificates, 416
X Window, 110

XACML (Extensible Access Control Markup
    Language), 31
XML (Extensible Markup Language), 30
XOR (exclusive OR) function, **370–371**
XSS (cross-site scripting) attacks, **347**
XTACACS (extended TACACS), 32

Z

zero-day exploits, **582–583**
zero-knowledge proof, **372–373**, *373*
zero-knowledge teams, **600–601**
Zeus Trojan horse, 329, 580
Zimmerman, Phil, 390, 421
zombies
    botnets, 587
    DoS attacks, 191
    ping floods, 588

Free Online Study Tools

Register on Sybex.com to gain access to a complete set of study tools to help you prepare for your CISSP exam

Comprehensive Study Tool Package Includes:

- **Assessment test** to help you focus your study to specific objectives

- **Chapter review questions** for each chapter of the book

- **Three full-length practice exams** to test your knowledge of the material

- **Electronic flashcards** to reinforce your learning and give you that last-minute test prep before the exam

- **Searchable glossary** to give you instant access to the key terms you'll need to know for the exam

Go to www.sybex.com/go/cissp6e to register and gain access to this comprehensive study tool package.

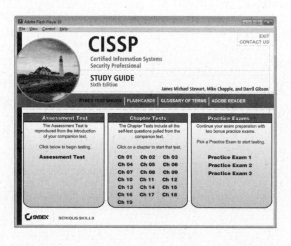